macquarie
little
dictionary

MACQUARIE

macquarie
little
dictionary

Published by Macquarie Dictionary Publishers, an imprint of
Pan Macmillan Australia Pty Ltd
1 Market Street, Sydney, New South Wales, Australia 2000

Copyright © Macquarie Dictionary Publishers, 2024

First published 1983
This edition published 2024

ISBN: 9781761562730

Cover design: Natalie Bowra
Typeset by Macmillan Publishing Solutions, Bangalore-25

Printed in China

A Cataloguing-in-Publication entry is available from the
National Library of Australia

http://catalogue.nla.gov.au

All rights reserved. No part of this publication may be reproduced
or transmitted by any person or entity (including Google, Amazon
or similar organisation), in any form or by any means, electronic or
mechanical, including photocopying, recording, scanning or by any
information storage and retrieval system, without prior permission in
writing from the publisher.
A number of words entered in this dictionary are derived from
trademarks. However, the presence or absence of indication of this
derivation should not be regarded in any way as affecting the legal
status of any trademark.

contents

explanatory notes

The entry

All information within one complete entry has been arranged for the convenience of the user. In general, information about spelling and pronunciation comes first, meanings next, then run-on headwords, and usage notes last.

Headword

The headword is the word or words which are being defined in a particular entry; it appears in large bold-face type at the left, slightly farther into the left margin than the usual line of text.

Separate entries are made for all words which, although spelt identically, are of quite distinct derivation; in such cases, each headword is followed by a small superscript number, as in, for example, **gum**[1] and **gum**[2]. Entries are arranged under headwords in strict alphabetical order. A particular headword can be located by taking each successive letter of the headword in alphabetical order, ignoring hyphens, apostrophes and word spaces.

Variant spellings

Definitions always appear under the most common spelling of a word. Less common variants cross-refer to the main headword. For example, the word **cipher** has a variant **cypher** which appears as a headword followed by **→ cipher** to show that the entry is at the main spelling **cipher**.

Pronunciation

The pronunciation, where given, follows the headword within slant brackets. It is given in the International Phonetic Alphabet, for which a guide may be found on pages x and xi.

Parts of speech

The pronunciation is usually followed by an abbreviation in italics which indicates the part of speech of the headword, such as *n.* (noun) and *adj.* (adjective).

If the headword is used in more than one grammatical form, the part-of-speech label precedes each set of definitions to which it applies.

Inflected forms

If a headword has irregularly inflected forms (any form not made by the simple addition of the suffix to the main entry), the summary of these forms is given immediately after the relevant part of speech. Regularly inflected forms, not generally shown, include:

1. Nouns forming a plural merely by the addition of *-s* or *-es*, such as **dog** (**dogs**) or **class** (**classes**);

2. Verbs forming the past tense by adding *-ed*, such as **halt** (**halted**);

3. Verbs forming the present tense by adding *-s* or *-es*, such as **talk** (**talks**) or **smash** (**smashes**);

4. Verbs forming the present participle by adding *-ing*, such as **walk** (**walking**);

5. Verbs which drop -*e* before an inflection is added, such as **save** (**saved**, **saving**);
6. Adjectives forming the comparative and superlative by adding -*er*, -*est*, such as **black** (**blacker**, **blackest**).

Regular forms are given, however, when necessary for clarity or the avoidance of confusion.

The past tense, past participle and present participle are given as the inflected forms of verbs; where, as commonly happens, the past tense and past participle are the same in form, this form is shown once. For example, the inflected forms indicated for **put** are **put**, **putting**, where **put** is both the past tense and past participle.

Restrictive labels

Entries that are limited in usage as to the level of style, region, time or subject, are marked with such labels as *Informal*, *US*, *Law*, etc.

If the restrictive label applies to the entire entry, it appears before the definition(s) at the beginning of the entry. If however the restrictive label applies to only one grammatical form, it appears after that part-of-speech label to which it applies and before the definition(s). If the restrictive label applies to only one definition, it appears before that definition, after the definition number.

Some headwords are marked with the restrictive label *taboo*. This indicates that the word itself may give offence essentially because of its taboo nature. This label is also used if there is a particularly crass and offensive meaning given to a usually neutral word. Taboo words are to be differentiated from words which are intended to denigrate another person, which are labelled *derog.* (for *derogatory*). Some words can attract a combination of these restrictive labels.

Definitions

Definitions are individually numbered; numbers appear in a single sequence which does not begin afresh with each grammatical form. In some cases in which two definitions are very closely related, usually within the same field of information, they are marked with letters of the alphabet under the same definition number.

Secondary headwords

Idiomatic phrases, prepositional phrases, etc., are placed at the entry for the key word, and are listed, in bold-face type, alphabetically at the end of the entry following the label *phr.* (for *phrase*).

Cross-referencing

There are several forms of cross-referencing in this dictionary. The arrow → indicates that the headword which precedes it is not defined in thi s place but that a suitable definition is to be found under the headword which follows the arrow.

The word 'See' directs the reader to information relevant to the current definition but to be found within a different part of the dictionary.

The word 'Compare' is similar in function but limited to those cases where the information is in some way complementary or matching.

Run-on headwords

Words which are derivatives of the headword and which are simple extensions of the meaning are run on after the last definition in the entry. Such headwords appear in bold-face type followed by an indication of their part of speech.

pronunciation guide

Vowels

i	as in 'peat'	/pit/
ɪ	as in 'pit'	/pɪt/
ɛ	as in 'pet'	/pɛt/
æ	as in 'pat'	/pæt/
a	as in 'part'	/pat/
ɒ	as in 'pot'	/pɒt/
ʌ	as in 'putt'	/pʌt/
ɔ	as in 'port'	/pɔt/
ʊ	as in 'put'	/pʊt/
u	as in 'pool'	/pul/
ɜ	as in 'pert'	/pɜt/
ə	as in 'apart'	/ə'pat/
ɒ̃	as in 'bon voyage'	/bɒ̃ vwa'jaʒ/

Diphthongs

aɪ	as in 'buy'	/baɪ/
eɪ	as in 'bay'	/beɪ/
ɔɪ	as in 'boy'	/bɔɪ/
aʊ	as in 'how'	/haʊ/
oʊ	as in 'hoe'	/hoʊ/
ɪə	as in 'here'	/hɪə/
ɛə	as in 'hair'	/hɛə/
ʊə	as in 'tour'	/tʊə/

Stress

Primary stress: ' as in 'clatter' /'klætə/
Secondary stress: ‚ as in 'encyclopedia' /ɛn‚saɪklə'pidɪə/

x

Consonants

Plosives

p	as in 'pet'	/pɛt/
b	as in 'bet'	/bɛt/
t	as in 'tale'	/teɪl/
d	as in 'dale'	/deɪl/
k	as in 'came'	/keɪm/
g	as in 'game'	/geɪm/

Fricatives

f	as in 'fine'	/faɪn/
v	as in 'vine'	/vaɪn/
θ	as in 'thin'	/θɪn/
ð	as in 'then'	/ðen/
s	as in 'seal'	/sil/
z	as in 'zeal'	/zil/
ʃ	as in 'show'	/ʃoʊ/
ʒ	as in 'pleasure'	/ˈplɛʒə/
h	as in 'heal'	/hil/
r	as in 'real'	/ril/

Affricates

tʃ	as in 'choke'	/tʃoʊk/
dʒ	as in 'joke'	/dʒoʊk/

Nasals

m	as in 'mail'	/meɪl/
n	as in 'nail'	/neɪl/
ŋ	as in 'sing'	/sɪŋ/

Semi-vowels

j	as in 'you'	/ju/
w	as in 'woo'	/wu/

Laterals

l	as in 'love'	/lʌv/

abbreviations used in the dictionary

abbrev.	abbreviation	*Elect.*	Electricity	*Obs.*	Obsolete
ACT	Australian Capital Territory	*Eng.*	Engineering	*Ornith.*	Ornithology
		Geog.	Geography		
adj.	adjective	*Geol.*	Geology	*Pathol.*	Pathology
adv.	adverb	*Geom.*	Geometry	*Pharm.*	Pharmacy
Agric.	Agriculture	*Govt*	Government	*Philos.*	Philosophy
Anat.	Anatomy	*Gram.*	Grammar	*phr.*	phrase
Archit.	Architecture			*Physiol.*	Physiology
Astron.	Astronomy	*Hist.*	History	*pl.*	plural
Aust.	Australia, Australian	*interj.*	interjection	*prep.*	preposition
		Ling.	Linguistics	*Psychol.*	Psychology
Biochem.	Biochemistry	*Lit.*	Literature		
Biol.	Biology			*Qld*	Queensland
Bot.	Botany	*Maths*	Mathematics		
Brit.	British	*Meteorol.*	Meteorology	*SA*	South Australia
		Mil.	Military	*Scot.*	Scottish
Chem.	Chemistry	*Mineral.*	Mineralogy	*sing.*	singular
Colloq.	Colloquial	*Myth.*	Mythology	*sth*	south
conj.	conjunction			*sthn*	southern
		n.	noun	*Surg.*	Surgery
def.	definition	*Naut.*	Nautical		
derog.	derogatory	*Navig.*	Navigation	*US*	United States of America
det.	determiner	*NSW*	New South Wales		
				v.	verb
eastn	eastern	*NT*	Northern Territory	*Vet.*	Veterinary
Eccles.	Ecclesiastical			*WA*	Western Australia
Ecol.	Ecology	*nth*	north		
Econ.	Economics	*nthn*	northern	*westn*	Western
Educ.	Education	*NZ*	New Zealand	*Zool.*	Zoology

A, a

A, a *n.* **1.** the first letter of the English alphabet. **2.** the first in any series.

a[1] *indefinite article* a word used especially before nouns beginning with a consonant to mean: **1.** some (referring to one individual of a class but not a particular or specific one): *a child; a dog.* **2.** (used before proper nouns) another: *He is quite a Romeo.* **3.** one: *a kilo of grapes.* **4.** indefinite plural number or amount: *a few books; a bit of paper.* Also, (*before a vowel*), **an**.

Pronunciation rather than spelling is how you decide whether to use **a** or **an**: for example, words like **hour** and **honour** have *an* before them because the *h* is not pronounced, while words like **union** and **user** take *a* because they are pronounced as if beginning with a *y* consonant.
Articles are sometimes called **determiners**.

a[2] *adj. or indefinite article* each; every: *twice a day.*

aardvark /ˈadvak/ *n.* a large, nocturnal, burrowing mammal of Africa.

aback *phr.* **taken aback**, suddenly disconcerted.

The more usual word is **surprised**.

abacus /ˈæbəkəs/ *n.* (pl. **-ci** /-si/ or **-cuses**) a device for calculating, consisting of beads strung on wires set in a frame.

abalone /æbəˈloʊni/ *n.* (pl. **-lone** or **-lones**) a type of shellfish, the flesh of which is used for food and the shell for ornaments.

For information about the different plural forms, see the note at **fish**.

abandon[1] *v.* **1.** to leave completely and finally; desert. **2.** to give up (something begun) without finishing.

abandon[2] *n.* freedom from constraint or conventionality: *to dance with abandon.*

abase *v.* to reduce or lower, as in rank or reputation; humble; degrade.

abashed *adj.* embarrassed; mortified.

abate *v.* to reduce or become less in amount, intensity, etc.; lessen.

The more usual expression is **ease off**.

abattoir /ˈæbətwa, -tə/ *n.* a place where animals are slaughtered for food. Also, **abattoirs**.

Note that the form **abattoirs** may be thought of as either singular or plural: *A new abattoirs is being built; New abattoirs are being built.*

abbess *n.* the female head of a convent.

abbey *n.* a monastery or convent.

abbot *n.* the male head of a monastery.

abbreviate *v.* to make shorter by contraction or omission. **–abbreviation**, *n.*

abdicate *v.* to renounce a throne, claim, right, power, or trust. **–abdication**, *n.*

abdomen /ˈæbdəmən, əbˈdoʊmən/ *n.* that part of the body of a mammal between the thorax and the pelvis; the belly. **–abdominal**, *adj.*

abduct *v.* to carry off by force. **–abduction**, *n.*

The more usual word is **kidnap**.

aberrant *adj.* deviating from the right or usual course or the normal type.

aberration *n.* a change or departure from what is right, normal, or true.

abet *v.* (**abetted**, **abetting**) to encourage or allow (usually something wrong) by aid or approval.

The more usual word is **help**.

abeyance *phr.* **in abeyance**, in a state of temporary inactivity or suspension.

The more usual expression is **on hold**.

abhor v. to regard with repugnance; loathe.
–**abhorrent**, adj.

The more usual word is **hate**.

abide v. (**abided** or, Archaic, **abode** /ə'boʊd/, **abiding**) **1.** to put up with; tolerate. **2.** Old-fashioned to remain; continue; stay. –phr. **3. abide by, a.** to accept and continue to observe (an undertaking, promise, agreement, rule, law, etc.) **b.** to stand by: to abide by a friend. **c.** to await or accept the consequences of: to abide by the decision.

For def. 1, the more usual word is **bear**.

ability n. (pl. **-ties**) power or capacity to do or act.

abiotic adj. of or relating to the non-living parts of an ecosystem.

abject adj. **1.** utterly humiliating or disheartening. **2.** humble; servile.

abjure v. to renounce; retract, especially with solemnity.

ablation n. **1.** Med. removal of organs, growths, etc. **2.** the melting or wearing away of a solid body.

ablaze adj. **1.** on fire. **2.** excited.

able adj. **1.** having sufficient power, strength, or qualifications. **2.** showing talent or knowledge. –**ably**, adv.

abled adj. **1.** having the usual range of human physical and mental abilities: a sport for abled and disabled people. –phr. **2. differently abled**, having a variation from the usual range of abilities.

Note that **differently abled** is the term that some people prefer to use instead of **disabled**, because it is more positive, stressing the possession of different abilities, rather than a lack of ability.

ablution n. **1.** ceremonial purification with water or other liquid. **2.** (pl.) the act of washing oneself.

Note that def. 2 is rather formal and is not used very often. When people do use this expression, they are usually being humorous.

abnegate v. to refuse or deny to oneself; renounce.

abnormal adj. deviating from the usual type.

aboard adv., prep. on board; on or in a ship, train, etc.

abode n. **1.** a dwelling place. **2.** continuance in a place; sojourn. –v. **3.** past tense and past participle of **abide**.

abolish v. to put an end to; annul. –**abolition**, n.

abominable adj. detestable; loathsome.

abomination n. **1.** an object greatly disliked. **2.** intense aversion; detestation.

Aboriginal /æbə'rɪdʒənəl/ adj. **1.** of or relating to Australian Aboriginal peoples. **2.** (lower case) of or relating to an aborigine (def. 3). –n. **3.** an Australian Aborigine.

See the note at **Aborigine**.

Aborigine /æbə'rɪdʒəni/ n. **1.** a member of a tribal people, the earliest known habitants of Aust. **2.** a descendant of this people. **3.** (lower case) one of the people living in a country at the earliest known period.

You can use **Aborigine** or **Aboriginal** for def. 1, although there is a community preference for **Aboriginal people**. Other terms in general use for Aboriginal people come from Aboriginal languages and usually depend on where the people are from. For example, **Koori** usually refers to people from southern NSW and Victoria, **Murri** to people from parts of Qld and NSW, **Nunga** to those from southern SA, **Nyungar** to people from south-western WA, **Anangu** to those from central Australia, and **Yolngu** to people from north-eastern Arnhem Land.

Aboriginal is widely used to refer to Aboriginal and Torres Strait Islander people. This is regarded as offensive by some people, so it is best to say 'Aboriginal and Torres Strait Islander people' if you want to refer to the complete group. Another term which is commonly used is 'Indigenous Australians'.

abort v. **1.** to (cause to) miscarry before the fetus is capable of living. **2.** to come to nothing; fail. –**abortive**, adj.

abortion n. **1. a.** the removal of a fetus from the mother's womb before it is viable. **b.** Also, **spontaneous abortion.** the involuntary expulsion of a fetus before it is matured. **2.** anything which fails before it is matured.

abound v. **1.** to be in great plenty. **2.** to be rich (*in*). **3.** to be filled; teem (*with*). –**abounding**, adj.

about prep. **1.** of; concerning; in regard to. **2.** near; close to. **3.** on every side of. **4.** on the point of (followed by an infinitive). **5.** concerned with; engaged in doing. –adv. **6.** near in time, number, degree, etc.; approximately. **7.** on every side. **8.** half round; in the reverse direction. **9.** to and fro; here and there. **10.** in rotation or succession. –phr. **11. up and about**, astir; active (after sleep).

above adv. **1.** in or to a higher place. **2.** higher in rank or power. **3.** before in order, especially in a book or writing. –prep. **4.** in or to a higher place than. **5.** more in quantity or number than. **6.** superior to, in rank or authority. **7.** not capable of (an undesirable thought, action, etc.). –adj. **8.** said, mentioned, or written above.

abrade v. to scrape off, wear down, or injure by rubbing. –**abrasive**, adj., n.

abrasion n. the act, process, or result of rubbing or abrading.

abreast adv. **1.** side by side. **2.** alongside, in progress or attainment (*of* or *with*).

abridge v. to shorten by condensation or omission; rewrite on a smaller scale.

abroad adv. **1.** in or to a foreign country or countries. **2.** at large; in circulation.

abrogate v. to abolish by an authoritative act; repeal.

abrupt adj. **1.** ending or changing suddenly. **2.** sudden or rude.

abscess /'æbses, 'æbsəs/ n. Med. a localised collection of pus in a cavity.

abscond v. to depart in a sudden and secret manner, especially to avoid facing legal action.

The more usual expression is **run away**.

abseil /'æbseɪl/ v. to go down a cliff or wall using a rope attached to a harness and a device to control downward movement. –**abseiling**, n. –**abseiler**, n.

absent adj. /'æbsənt/ **1.** not in a certain place at a given time. **2.** lacking. **3.** forgetful. –v. /əb'sent/ **4.** to take or keep (oneself) away. –**absence**, n.

absentee n. someone who is absent.

absolute adj. **1.** complete; perfect. **2.** free from restriction or limitation. **3.** arbitrary or despotic. **4.** not comparative or relative. **5.** positive.

absolve v. **1.** to free (*from*) the consequences of actions. **2.** to set free, as (*from*) some duty, obligation, or responsibility. –**absolution**, n.

absorb v. **1.** to swallow up the identity or individuality of. **2.** to engross wholly. **3.** to suck up or drink in (liquids). **4.** to assimilate (ideas, knowledge, etc.). –**absorption**, n. –**absorbent**, adj.

abstain v. **1.** to refrain voluntarily, especially (*from*) doing or enjoying something. **2.** to choose not to cast one's vote.

abstemious adj. moderate in the use of food and drink.

abstention n. an act of abstaining, especially from voting.

abstinence n. an act or the practice of abstaining, especially from drinking alcohol.

abstract adj. /'æbstrækt/ **1.** thought of separately from matter, practice and particular examples. **2.** theoretical; not applied. **3.** difficult to understand. –n. /'æbstrækt/ **4.** a summary of a statement, document, etc. **5.** an idea or term considered apart from some material basis or object. *–v.* /əbˈstrækt/ **6.** to draw or take away; remove. **7.** to consider as a general object apart from special circumstances.

abstracted *adj.* lost in thought.

abstraction *n.* **1.** an abstract or general idea or term. **2.** the act of taking away or separating; withdrawal. **3.** absentmindedness; reverie.

abstract noun *n. Gram.* a noun referring to something that our 5 senses (touch, sight, hearing, smell and taste) cannot pick up, such as *fear*, *love* and *beauty*.

Compare this with **concrete noun**, which refers to something which our senses can pick up.

abstruse *adj.* difficult to understand; esoteric.

absurd *adj.* contrary to reason or common sense; ridiculous. **–absurdity,** *n.*

abundant *adj.* **1.** present in great or sufficient quantity. **2.** possessing in great quantity; abounding (*in*). **–abundance,** *n.*

abuse *v.* /əˈbjuz/ **1.** to use wrongly or improperly. **2.** to revile; malign. **3.** to inflict a sexual act on (a person). *–n.* /əˈbjus/ **4.** wrong or improper use. **5.** insulting language. **6.** sexual violation as rape or sexual assault, especially of a child. **–abusive,** *adj.*

abut *v.* (**abutted, abutting**) to be adjacent to (*on, upon,* or *against*). **–abuttal,** *n.*

abysmal /əˈbɪzməl/ *adj.* **1.** immeasurable. **2.** immeasurably bad.

abyss /əˈbɪs/ *n.* any deep, immeasurable space. **–abyssal,** *adj.*

acacia *n.* a tree or shrub native to warm regions; usually known as wattle in Aust.

academic *adj.* **1.** relating to an advanced institution of learning; relating to higher education and the subjects studied. **2.** theoretical; not practical. *–n.* **3.** a teacher or researcher in a university or college.

academy *n.* (*pl.* **-mies**) **1.** an association or institution for the promotion of literature, science, or art. **2.** a school for instruction in a particular art or science.

accede *v.* **1.** to give consent; yield. **2.** to come, as (*to*) a high office: *to accede to the throne.*

Don't confuse this with **exceed**, which means to go beyond something: *to exceed the speed limit.*
For def. 1, the more usual expression is **give in.**

accelerate *v.* **1.** to (cause to) move or advance faster. **2.** *Physics* to change the magnitude and/or direction of the velocity of (a body). **–acceleration,** *n.*

accelerator *n. Motor Vehicles* a device which increases the speed of a vehicle by opening the throttle, especially one operated by the foot.

accent *n.* /ˈæksənt/ **1.** the distinctive character of a vowel or syllable determined by its degree or pattern of stress or musical tone. **2.** a mark indicating stress, musical tone, or vowel quality. **3.** characteristic style of pronunciation as of a dialect. **4.** *Music* stress or emphasis given to certain notes. *–v.* /ækˈsɛnt/ **5.** to pronounce or mark (a vowel, syllable, etc.) with an accent.

Accents (def. 2) are found on some words taken into English from other languages. They may be helpful in telling some words apart (such as *lamé* and *lame*), but are often left out where no confusion is likely, as in *fete* (from French *fête*) and *naive* (from French *naïve*).

accentuate *v.* to emphasise.

accept *v.* **1.** to take or receive (something offered). **2.** to admit and agree to. **3.** to accommodate oneself to. **4.** to understand. **–acceptable,** *adj.* **–acceptance,** *n.*

Don't confuse **accept** with **except**, which means excluding or leaving out, as in *They all went except me.*

accepted *adj.* customary; established; approved.

access *n.* **1.** the act or privilege of coming (*to*). **2.** way, means, or opportunity of approach. **3.** a parent's right to see a child.

–*v.* **4.** to gain entry or admittance. **5.** *Computers* to locate and be able to work with (data). –**accessible**, *adj.*

> Don't confuse **access** with **assess**, which means to work out the value of, or with **excess**, which means an amount more than is necessary.

accession *n.* **1.** the act of coming into the possession of a right, office, etc. **2.** an increase by something added. **3.** consent.

accessory *n.* (*pl.* **-ries**) **1.** something added or attached for convenience, attractiveness, etc. **2.** *Law* someone who is not the chief actor at a crime, nor present when it is committed, but yet is in some way involved in it. **3.** an item such as a bag, belt, piece of jewellery, etc., chosen to go with a particular outfit.

accident *n.* **1.** an undesirable or unfortunate happening; mishap. **2.** anything that happens unexpectedly by chance. –**accidental**, *adj.*

acclaim *v.* **1.** to salute with words or sounds of joy or approval. **2.** to announce or proclaim by shouts or other demonstrations of welcome, etc. –*n.* **3.** strong approval. –**acclamation**, *n.* –**acclamatory**, *adj.*

> For def. 1, the more usual word is **applaud**; for def. 3, **applause**.

acclimatise *v.* to accustom or become accustomed to a new climate or environment. Also, **acclimatize**.

> The more usual word is **adjust**.

accolade *n.* **1.** a ceremony used in conferring knighthood. **2.** any award; honour.

accommodate *v.* **1.** to do a favour to. **2.** to provide suitably. **3.** to make suitable or consistent. **4.** to adjust; reconcile. **5.** to find or provide space for (something).

accommodation *n.* **1.** the act or result of accommodating. **2.** lodging, or food and lodging.

accompaniment *n.* **1.** something added for ornament, symmetry, etc. **2.** *Music* that

part of a composition which provides the harmonic and rhythmic backing to a melody.

accompany *v.* (**-nied, -nying**) **1.** to go or be in company with. **2.** *Music* to play or sing an accompaniment to.

accomplice *n.* a partner in a crime or wrongdoing.

accomplish *v.* to carry out; finish. –**accomplishment**, *n.*

accomplished *adj.* **1.** completed. **2.** perfected; expert. **3.** perfected in the ways of polite society.

accord *v.* **1.** to be in harmony; agree. **2.** to grant; concede. –*n.* **3.** harmony of relation. **4.** consent or concurrence of opinions or wills; agreement. –*phr.* **5. of one's own accord**, voluntarily. **6. with one accord**, with spontaneous agreement.

according *phr.* **according to**, **1.** in accordance with. **2.** proportionately. **3.** on the authority of; as stated by.

accordion *n.* **1.** a portable wind instrument with bellows and button-like keys. –*adj.* **2.** having folds like the bellows of an accordion.

accost *v.* to approach, especially with a greeting or remark.

account *v.* **1.** to give an explanation (*for*). **2.** to cause death, capture, etc. (*for*). **3.** to count; consider as. –*n.* **4.** a verbal or written recital of particular transactions and events; narrative. **5.** a statement of pecuniary transactions. **6.** *Bookkeeping* a formal record of debits and credits. –*phr.* **7. bring** (or **call**) **to account**, demand explanation or justification of actions. **8. on** (or **to**) **account**, as an interim payment. **9. on account of**. **a.** because of; by reason of. **b.** for the sake of.

accountable *adj.* answerable: *to be accountable for one's actions.*

> Note that this is used only after a verb, not before a noun. You cannot talk about 'an accountable person'.

accountant n. a person who inspects and audits business accounts. –**accountancy**, n.

accounting n. the art of analysing the financial position and operating results of a business firm from a study of its sales, purchases, overheads, etc.

accoutrements /ə'kuːtrəmənts/ pl. n. equipment or trappings.

accredit v. 1. to attribute: *He was accredited with the discovery. The discovery is accredited to him.* 2. to supply (a recognised agent) with credentials. 3. to certify as meeting official requirements.

accretion n. 1. an increase by natural growth. 2. an extraneous addition. 3. the growing together of separate parts into a single whole.

accrue v. to accumulate in the course of time. –**accrual**, n.

The more usual expression is **build up**.

accumulate v. 1. to heap up; gather as into a mass. 2. to grow into a heap or mass or an increasing quantity. –**accumulation**, n. –**accumulative**, adj.

accurate adj. 1. in exact conformity to truth, etc.; free from error or defect. 2. showing precision; meticulous. –**accuracy**, n. –**accurately**, adv.

accursed /ə'kɜːsəd, ə'kɜːst/ adj. 1. subject to a curse; ruined. 2. detestable.

accuse v. 1. to charge with the fault or crime (*of*). 2. to blame. –**accusation**, n. –**accusatory**, adj.

accustom v. to familiarise by custom or use; habituate. –**accustomed**, adj.

ace n. 1. a single spot or mark on a card or die. 2. (in tennis, badminton, etc.) a serve which the opponent fails to touch. 3. a highly skilled person. –adj. 4. *Informal* excellent.

acerbity n. 1. sourness. 2. harshness or severity, as of temper or expression. –**acerbic**, adj.

acetate n. a salt or ester of acetic acid.

acetic /ə'siːtɪk/ adj. of vinegar.

acetone n. a colourless, flammable liquid, used as a solvent and in varnishes, etc.

ache v. (**ached**, **aching**) 1. to have or be in continuous pain. –n. 2. pain of some duration, as opposed to sudden twinges.

achieve v. to bring to a successful end.

achievement n. 1. something accomplished; a great deed. 2. the act of achieving.

acid[1] n. 1. a substance with a sour taste. –adj. 2. sharp or sour. –**acidic**, adj. –**acidity**, n.

acid[2] n. *Informal* LSD.

acidophilus /æsə'dɒfələs/ n. See **lactobacillus**.

acidophilus milk n. a fermented milk which alters the bacterial content of the intestines. See **lactobacillus**.

acknowledge v. 1. to grant to be real or true; recognise the existence, etc., of. 2. to express recognition or awareness of. 3. to recognise the claims of. 4. to indicate appreciation for. 5. to certify the receipt of. –**acknowledgement**, **acknowledgment**, n. –**acknowledgeable**, **acknowledgable**, adj.

acknowledgement of country n. the official recognition of the Indigenous traditional custodians of a locality, given in the preamble to a public event, meeting, etc.

acme /'ækmi/ n. the highest point; culmination.

acne /'ækni/ n. an inflammatory disease of the skin, especially of the face, characterised by eruptions (often pustular).

acolyte /'ækəlaɪt/ n. an attendant; an assistant.

acorn n. a nut, the fruit of the oak.

acoustic adj. 1. Also, **acoustical**. relating to the sense of hearing, or the science of sound. 2. *Music* of instruments whose sound is not electronically amplified.

acquaint v. to make more or less familiar (*with*).

acquaintance *n.* **1.** person(s) known to one, but not intimately. **2.** the state of being acquainted; personal knowledge.

acquiesce /ˌækwiˈɛs/ *v.* to assent tacitly; agree; consent.

acquire *v.* to come into possession of. –**acquisition**, *n.*

acquisitive *adj.* fond of acquiring possessions.

acquit *v.* to release or discharge (a person) from a charge of a crime, or an obligation. –**acquittal**, *n.*

acre *n.* a unit of land measurement in the imperial system, equal to almost half a hectare. –**acreage**, *n.*

acrid *adj.* sharp or biting to the taste.

acrimony *n.* sharpness or severity of temper; bitterness of expression. –**acrimonious**, *adj.*

acrobat *n.* a performer who can walk on a tightrope, perform on a trapeze, etc. –**acrobatic**, *adj.*

acronym *n.* a word formed from the initial letters of a sequence of words, as *radar* (from *radio detection and ranging*) or *ANZAC* (from *Australian and New Zealand Army Corps*).

across *prep.* **1.** from side to side of. **2.** on the other side of. **3.** so as to meet with. –*adv.* **4.** from one side to another. **5.** on the other side.

acrostic *n.* a series of lines or verses in which the first, last, or other letters form a word or phrase, etc.

acrylic *adj.* **1.** of synthetic fibres or fabrics woven from synthetic fibres. –*n.* **2.** a particular synthetic fibre or fabric.

act *n.* **1.** anything done or performed. **2.** the process of doing. **3.** (*oft. upper case*) a decree, law, statute, etc., especially one passed by a legislature. **4.** one of the main divisions of a play or opera. **5.** an individual performance forming part of a variety show, etc. **6.** behaviour which is contrived and artificial. –*v.* **7.** to do something; exert force; be employed or

operative. **8.** to behave (as): *to act badly; to act the fool.* **9.** to pretend. **10.** to perform as an actor. **11.** to substitute (*for*). –*phr.* **12. act up**, *Informal* to misbehave.

actinium *n.* a radioactive chemical element occurring in pitchblende. *Symbol:* Ac

action *n.* **1.** the process or state of being active. **2.** something done; deed. **3.** way of moving. **4.** military or naval combat. **5.** the main subject of a story, play, etc. **6.** *Law* a proceeding instituted by one party against another.

action verb *n. Gram.* → **dynamic verb**.

activate *v.* **1.** to make active. **2.** *Physics* to render radioactive. –**activation**, *n.*

active *adj.* **1.** in a state of action; in actual progress or motion. **2.** constantly engaged in action; busy. **3.** nimble. **4.** capable of exerting influence. **5.** *Gram.* denoting a voice of verb inflection, in which the subject performs the action expressed by the verb, as in *I hit him.* **6.** (of a volcano) erupting. **7.** *Chem.* capable of acting or reacting, especially in some specific manner: *active carbon.* **8.** (of a communications satellite) able to retransmit signals. Compare def. 5 with **passive** (def. 3).

activist *n.* a zealous worker for a cause, especially political.

activity *n.* (*pl.* **-ties**) **1.** the state of action. **2.** a specific deed or sphere of action. **3.** liveliness.

actor *n.* someone who plays the part of a character in a play, etc. –**actress**, *fem. n.*

An actor can be either male or female. The word 'actress' for a female actor is not used as much now as in the past.

actual *adj.* **1.** existing in fact; real. **2.** now existing.

actuality *n.* (*pl.* **-ties**) **1.** reality. **2.** (*pl.*) actual conditions or circumstances.

actually *adv.* as an actual or existing fact.

actuary /ˈæktʃuəri/, *Orig. US* /ˈæktʃuɛri/ *n.* someone who computes risks, rates, etc., according to probabilities shown by statistics. –**actuarial**, *adj.*

actuate *v.* to incite or to put into action.

The more usual word is **motivate**.

acuity /ə'kjuəti/ *n.* sharpness of the senses, etc.; acuteness.

acumen /'ækjəmən/ *n.* quickness of perception; mental acuteness.

acupuncture *n.* a Chinese medical practice, diagnostic and therapeutic, involving puncturing specific areas of skin with long sharp needles. **–acupuncturist**, *n.*

acute *adj.* **1.** sharp at the end; ending in a point. **2.** sharp in effect; intense. **3.** severe. **4.** (of an illness, pain, etc.) sudden and severe. **5.** sharp or penetrating in intellect, etc. **6.** *Geom.* (of an angle) less than 90° (opposed to **obtuse**).

Compare def. 4 with **chronic**, which describes an illness that has continued for a long time, as in *a chronic heart condition*.

ad *n. Informal* an advertisement.

adage /'ædɪdʒ/ *n.* a proverb.

The more usual word is **saying**.

adamant /'ædəmənt/ *adj.* firm in purpose or opinion.

The more usual word is **determined**.

Adam's apple *n.* a projection of cartilage at the front of the throat, usually more prominent in men than in women.

adapt *v.* **1.** to make suitable to requirements. **2.** to adjust oneself. **–adaptable**, *adj.* **–adaptive**, *adj.* **–adaptation**, *n.* **–adaptor**, *n.*

Don't confuse **adapt** with **adept**, which means skilful.

add *v.* **1.** to unite so as to increase the number, quantity, size, or importance. **2.** to total (*up*). **3.** to say or write further. **4.** to include (*in*). **5.** to perform the arithmetical operation of addition. **6.** to be or serve as an addition (*to*). **–phr. 7. add up**, **a.** to accumulate. **b.** *Informal* to make sense, to be logically consistent.

addendum *n.* (*pl.* **-da**) a thing to be added.

adder *n.* small poisonous snake of Europe.

addict *n.* someone who is addicted to something.

addicted *adj.* devoted or given up (to a practice, habit, or substance).

addiction *n.* the state of being addicted to some habit, practice, or substance, especially to narcotics. **–addictive**, *adj.*

addition *n.* **1.** the act or process of adding. **2.** the process of uniting 2 or more numbers into one sum. **3.** anything added. **–additional**, *adj.*

additive *n.* something added, especially as an ingredient.

address *n.* /ə'drɛs, 'ædrɛs/ **1.** a formal speech. **2.** a direction as to name and residence inscribed on a letter, etc. **3.** a place where a person lives or may be reached. **4.** manner of speaking to persons. **–v.** /ə'drɛs/ **5.** to direct for delivery; put a direction on: *to address a letter.* **6.** to speak to a person in an official position, using their formal title. **7.** to direct to the ear or attention. **8.** to deal with. **9.** to direct the energy or force of: *She addressed herself to her work.* **–addresser**, **addressor**, *n.* **–addressee**, *n.*

adduce *v.* to bring forward in argument; cite as conclusive.

adenoids *pl. n.* the mass of lymphoid tissue in the upper pharynx; enlargement can prevent nasal breathing, especially in young children.

adept *adj.* highly skilled; proficient.

Don't confuse **adept** with **adapt**, which means to change or adjust.

adequate *adj.* fully sufficient or suitable (*to* or *for*). **–adequacy**, *n.*

adhere *v.* **1.** to stick fast; cling (*to*). **2.** to be attached as a follower (*to*). **–adhesion**, *n.*

adherent *n.* **1.** someone who follows a leader, cause, etc.; supporter (*of*). **–adj.** **2.** sticking.

adhesive *adj.* **1.** sticking fast. **–n.** **2.** a substance for sticking things together.

ad hoc *adj.* **1.** for this (special purpose); an **ad hoc committee** is one set up to deal with one subject only. **2.** impromptu; an **ad hoc decision** is one made with regard to the needs of the moment. *–adv.* **3.** with respect to this (subject or thing).

ad infinitum /ˌæd ɪnfəˈnaɪtəm/ *adv.* to infinity; endlessly.

> This is often used humorously to mean for a very long time, as in *The speech went on ad infinitum.*

adipose /ˈædəpous/ *adj.* fatty.

adjacent *adj.* lying near or close; adjoining.

adjective *n. Gram.* one of the major parts of speech comprising words used to modify or limit a noun. *–adjectival, adj.*

adjoin *v.* **1.** to be in contact with; abut on. **2.** to lie or be next to. *–adjoining, adj.*

adjourn *v.* **1.** to suspend the meeting of (a public or private body) to a future time or to another place. **2.** to postpone or transfer proceedings. *–adjournment, n.*

> Note that def. 1 is usually used in relation to meetings, court proceedings, etc.

adjudge *v.* **1.** to pronounce formally. **2.** to award judicially.

adjudicate *v.* **1.** to pass judgement on; to determine (an issue or dispute). **2.** to sit in judgement (*upon*). *–adjudication, n. –adjudicator, n.*

adjunct *n.* **1.** something added to another thing but not essentially a part of it. **2.** a person joined to another in some duty or service.

adjure *v.* **1.** to bind or command, earnestly and solemnly, often under oath. **2.** to entreat earnestly.

adjust *v.* **1.** to make conformable; adapt. **2.** to put in working order; bring to a proper state. **3.** to settle or bring to a state of agreement between parties. **4.** *Insurance* to fix or settle (the sum to be paid on a claim). **5.** to adapt oneself. *–adjustable, adj. –adjustment, n.*

adjutant /ˈædʒətənt/ *n. Mil.* a staff officer who assists the commanding officer. *–adjutancy, n.*

ad lib *adv.* **1.** in an impromptu manner. *–adj.* **2.** of an improvised performance.

administer *v.* **1.** to manage (affairs, government, etc.). **2.** to bring into use or operation. **3.** to impose. **4.** to perform the duties of an administrator. Also, **administrate.**

administration *n.* **1.** the management or direction of any office, etc. **2.** the function of exercising governmental duties. **3.** any body of people with administrative powers. *–administrator, n. –administrative, adj.*

admirable /ˈædmərəbəl/ *adj.* worthy of admiration. *–admirably, adv.*

admiral *n.* a naval officer of high rank. *–admiralty, n.*

admire *v.* to regard with wonder and approbation. *–admiration, n. –admirer, n.*

admissible *adj.* **1.** that may be allowed or conceded. **2.** *Law* allowable as evidence.

admission *n.* **1.** the act of allowing to enter. **2.** the price paid for entrance, as to a theatre, etc. **3.** the act or condition of being accepted in a position or office. **4.** a point or statement admitted.

admit *v.* **1.** to allow to enter. **2.** to permit. **3.** to permit to exercise a certain function or privilege. **4.** to allow as valid. **5.** to acknowledge; confess. *–admittedly, adv.*

admonish *v.* **1.** to caution or advise against something. **2.** to reprove for a fault, especially mildly. **3.** to incite to duty. *–admonition, n.*

> For def. 1, the more usual word is **warn**; for def. 2, **scold.**

ad nauseam /æd ˈnɔziəm, -si-/ *adv.* to a sickening extent.

ado *n.* activity; fuss.

adolescence *n.* the period between puberty and adult stages of development. *–adolescent, adj., n.*

adopt v. **1.** to choose for or take to oneself. **2.** to take as one's own child, by a formal legal act. **3.** to vote to accept. –**adoptive**, adj. –**adopter**, n. –**adoption**, n.

Note that when people adopt a child, they become that child's **adoptive** parents. The child can be described as either their **adopted** child or their **adoptive** child. Compare def. 2 with **foster** (def. 3.), which means to care for someone else's child within your family without adopting the child.

adoration n. **1.** worship. **2.** devoted love.

adore v. **1.** to regard with the utmost love and respect. **2.** to honour as divine. –**adorable**, adj.

adorn v. **1.** to make more attractive. **2.** to lend beauty to, as ornaments; decorate.

adrenal adj. **1.** situated near or on the kidneys. **2.** of or produced by the adrenal glands.

adrenaline n. a hormone produced in the body especially in response to stress, increasing heart rate, etc. Also, **adrenalin**.

adrift adj. not fastened by any kind of moorings.

adroit adj. expert in the use of the hand or mind.

The more usual word is **skilful**.

adulation n. pretended or undiscriminating devotion.

adult adj. **1.** having attained full size and strength; mature. **2.** relating to or designed for adults. –n. **3.** a person who has reached the age at which an individual is considered legally responsible and able to perform certain civic duties, such as voting. **4.** a full-grown person, animal or plant.

adulterate v. to make impure by mixing. –**adulterator**, n. –**adulteration**, n. –**adulterant**, adj., n.

adultery n. voluntary sexual intercourse between a married person and another, not the lawful spouse. –**adulterous**, adj.

advance n. **1.** a moving forwards. **2.** (usu. pl.) an effort to bring about acquaintance, understanding, etc. **3.** addition to price. **4.** Commerce **a.** a giving beforehand. **b.** a loan against securities, or in advance of payment due.

advantage n. **1.** any favourable state, circumstance, opportunity, or means to a desired end. **2.** benefit; gain. **3.** Tennis the first point scored after deuce. –v. (**-taged**, **-taging**) **4.** to be of service to; benefit. –phr. **5. take advantage of,** to make use of. –**advantageous**, adj.

advent n. a coming into place, view, or being; arrival.

adventitious adj. accidentally or casually acquired or added.

adventure n. **1.** an undertaking (often hazardous) of uncertain outcome. **2.** an exciting experience. **3.** participation in exciting undertakings. **4.** a venture. –**adventurous**, adj.

adverb n. Gram. a part of speech comprising words used to limit a verb, adjective, or another adverb, by expressing time, manner, place, cause, degree, etc. –**adverbial**, adj.

adversary /ˈædvəsri, -səri/ n. someone against whom one is competing or fighting. –**adversarial**, adj.

The more usual word is **opponent**.

adverse /ˈædvɜs, ədˈvɜs/ adj. antagonistic in purpose or effect. –**adversity**, n.

advert /ədˈvɜt/ v. to make a remark about; refer (to).

advertise v. **1.** to give information to the public about (something). **2.** to praise by advertisement in order to sell. **3.** to ask (for) by placing an advertisement in a newspaper, etc. –**advertisement**, n.

advertorial n. a media piece that looks like a news or feature article but which is written and paid for by an advertiser.

advice n. **1.** an opinion recommended, or offered, as worthy to be followed. **2.** a communication, especially from a distance, containing information.

> Don't confuse this with the verb **advise**, which means to tell what you think should be done.
> Note that you should not say 'an advice'. You can say 'advice', 'some advice' or 'a piece of advice'.

advisable *adj.* proper to be advised or to be recommended.

advise *v.* **1.** to give counsel to. **2.** to recommend as wise, prudent, etc. **3.** to give (a person, etc.) information or notice (*of*). **4.** to give advice. –**adviser**, *n.*

> For def. 3, the more usual word is **tell**.
> Don't confuse **advise** with the noun **advice**, which is an opinion someone gives you to help you decide what to do.

advisory *adj.* **1.** of, or giving, advice; having power to advise. –*n.* (*pl.* **-sories**) **2.** a statement of advice.

advocate *v.* /ˈædvəkeɪt/ **1.** to plead in favour of; urge by argument; recommend publicly. –*n.* /ˈædvəkət, -keɪt/ **2.** someone who defends, vindicates, or supports a cause by argument (*of*). –**advocacy**, *n.* –**advocator**, *n.* –**advocatory**, *adj.*

> For def. 1, the more usual word is **support**; for def. 2, **supporter**.

aegis /ˈiːdʒəs/ *n.* protection; sponsorship.

aeon /ˈiːən/ *n.* an indefinitely long period of time. Also, **eon**.

aerate *v.* to charge or treat with air or a gas, especially with carbon dioxide.

aerial *n.* **1.** that part of a radio or television system which radiates or receives electromagnetic waves into or from free space. –*adj.* **2.** of, in, or produced by the air. **3.** inhabiting or frequenting the air. **4.** unsubstantial. **5.** relating to aircraft. –**aerially**, *adv.*

aerobic *adj.* (of organisms or tissues) living or active only in the presence of free oxygen (opposed to *anaerobic*).

aerodrome *n.* a landing field (usually small) for aeroplanes, especially private aeroplanes.

aerodynamics *n.* the study of air in motion and of the action of solids moving through the air. –**aerodynamic**, *adj.*

aerogenerator *n.* → **wind turbine**.

aeronautics *n.* the science of flight. –**aeronautic**, *adj.*

aeroplane *n.* an aircraft, heavier than air, driven by propellers, jet propulsion, etc.

aerosol *n.* a metal container for storing a substance under pressure and subsequently dispensing it as a spray; spray can.

aesthetic /əsˈθetɪk/ *adj.* relating to the sense of the beautiful. Also, **esthetic**. –**aesthetics**, *n.*

aetiology /itiˈɒlədʒi/ *n.* the study of the causes of anything, especially diseases. Also, **etiology**.

afar *adv.* (usu. preceded by *from*) from a distance.

affable *adj.* easy to talk to or to approach; polite.

> The more usual word is **friendly**.

affair *n.* **1.** anything done or to be done; business; concern. **2.** (*pl.*) matters of interest or concern. **3.** an event or a performance. **4.** Also, **love affair**. a sexual relationship, especially one outside marriage; liaison.

affect¹ *v.* **1.** to act on; produce a change in. **2.** to impress; move (in feelings).

> Don't confuse **affect** with the verb **effect**, which means to produce, or to bring about, or with the noun **effect**, which is something which is produced by some cause, as in *Wrinkles are an effect of age.*

affect² *v.* **1.** to make a show of. **2.** to use or adopt by preference.

affectation *n.* **1.** pretence. **2.** artificiality of manner or conduct.

affected¹ *adj.* **1.** acted upon; influenced. **2.** influenced injuriously; impaired. **3.** moved; touched.

affected² *adj.* **1.** artificial (in manner). **2.** pretending to have characteristics which are not natural.

affection *n.* a settled goodwill, love, or attachment. –**affectionate**, *adj.*

affidavit *n.* a written statement on oath, often used as evidence in court proceedings.

affiliate *v.* /ə'filiert/ **1.** to attach as a branch or part (*with*). **2.** to bring into close connection. **3.** to associate oneself in action or interest. –*n.* /ə'filiət/ **4.** someone or something that is affiliated. –**affiliation**, *n.*

affinity *n.* (*pl.* **-ties**) **1.** a natural liking for, or attraction to, a person or thing. **2.** close resemblance. **3.** relationship by marriage.

For def. 2, the more usual word is **similarity**.

affirm *v.* **1.** to state or assert positively. **2.** to establish or confirm. –**affirmation**, *n.*

affirmative *adj.* **1.** giving affirmation or assent. –*n.* **2.** an affirmative word or phrase, as *yes* or *I do*.

affirmative action *n.* action designed to provide increased employment opportunities for groups who have previously suffered discrimination.

affix *v.* /ə'fiks/ **1.** to fix; fasten or attach (*to*). –*n.* /'æfiks/ **2.** *Gram.* a meaningful part added to the stem or base of a word, for example *-ed* added to *want* to form the past tense *wanted*, or *un-* added to *kind* to form the word *unkind*. Look up **prefix** and **suffix**.

afflict *v.* to distress greatly with mental or bodily pain. –**affliction**, *n.*

affluent *adj.* rich. –**affluence**, *n.*

afford *v.* **1.** to be able to meet the expense of: *I can afford it.* **2.** to be able to give or spare: *I can't afford the time to go to the beach.* **3.** to give or confer upon. –**affordable**, *adj.* –**affordability**, *n.*

affront *n.* **1.** a personally offensive act or word often intentional. –*v.* **2.** to offend by open disrespect.

The more usual word is **insult**.

afield *adv.* **1.** abroad; away from home. **2.** far and wide.

afloat *adj.* **1.** borne on the water. **2.** flooded.

afoot *adj.* in progress.

A4 *n.* a size of paper, 297 × 210 mm, which has replaced the older foolscap and quarto sizes.

afraid *adj.* **1.** feeling fear. **2.** regretfully of the opinion (*that*).

Note that **afraid** is often followed by *of* or *to* when used in the sense of def. 1 but is never followed by *by*. You cannot say 'He is afraid by the dark' but you can say 'He is frightened by the dark.'

afresh *adv.* anew; again.

aft *adv. Naut.* at, in, or towards the stern.

after *prep.* **1.** behind in place or time. **2.** in pursuit of; in search of; with or in desire for. **3.** concerning: *I asked after him.* **4.** subsequent to and in consequence of. **5.** below in rank or excellence; next to. **6.** in imitation of (the style of): *poetry after Milton.* **7.** with name of. **8.** in proportion to. **9.** according to the nature of; in agreement or unison with. –*adv.* **10.** behind. –*adj.* **11.** later in time; next. **12.** *Naut.* farther aft. –*conj.* **13.** subsequent to the time that.

afterbirth *n.* the placenta, etc., expelled from the uterus after parturition.

aftermath *n.* resultant conditions, especially of a catastrophe.

afternoon *n.* the time from noon until evening.

afternoon tea *n.* a short break from work, etc., taken in the afternoon, usually with food and drink.

afterwards *adv.* in later or subsequent time. Also, **afterward**.

again *adv.* **1.** once more; in addition. **2.** moreover; besides; furthermore. **3.** on the other hand. **4.** to the same place or person.

against *prep.* **1.** in an opposite direction to, so as to meet; upon. **2.** in contact with, or pressing on. **3.** in opposition to. **4.** in resistance to or defence from. **5.** in preparation for. **6.** in contrast with; having as background. **7.** in exchange for; as a balance to. **8.** (sometimes preceded by *as*) instead of, in contrast with,.

agape *adv.* **1.** in an attitude of wonder or eagerness; with the mouth wide open. –*adj.* **2.** wide open.

agate /'ægət/ *n.* a variety of quartz showing coloured bands or other markings.

age *n.* **1.** the length of time of something's existence. **2.** the lifetime of an individual; an average lifetime. **3.** one of the periods or stages of human life. **4.** old age. **5.** a particular period of history; a historical epoch. **6.** a generation. **7.** *Informal* a great length of time. **8.** *Geol.* a part of the world's history distinguished by special features. –*v.* (**aged**, **ageing** *or* **aging**) **9.** to make or become old or mature. –*phr.* **10. of age**, having full adult rights and responsibilities.

ageism /'eɪdʒɪzəm/ *n.* an attitude which stereotypes a person, especially an elderly person, according to age.

agency *n.* (*pl.* **-cies**) **1.** a commercial or other organisation furnishing some form of service. **2.** the office of agent; the business of an agent. **3.** the state of being in action or of exerting power; operation. **4.** a mode of exerting power; instrumentality.

agenda *n.* **1.** a list of things to be done, discussed, etc.: *What's on the agenda for today?* **2.** a set of motivating factors: *to be acting on a personal agenda.*

Note that this word was originally a plural, meaning things to be done, but it is now regularly used as a singular (as in *The agenda is quite short*), with the plural

agendas (as in *We can't have two agendas for one meeting*).

agent *n.* **1.** a person acting on behalf of another. **2.** someone or something that acts or has the power to act. **3.** a representative of a business firm, especially a commercial traveller.

age spot → **liver spot.**

agglomerate *v.* /ə'glɒməreɪt/ **1.** to collect into a mass. –*n.* /ə'glɒmərət/ **2.** a rock formation of large angular volcanic fragments. –**agglomeration**, *n.*

agglutinate *v.* to unite or cause to adhere, as with glue. –**agglutination**, *n.*

aggrandise *v.* **1.** to make great or greater in power, wealth, etc. **2.** to make (something) appear greater. Also, **aggrandize**. –**aggrandisement**, *n.*

aggravate *v.* **1.** to make worse or more severe. **2.** *Informal* to provoke; irritate.

Note that some people think that def. 2 is not a correct use.

aggregate *adj.* /'ægrəgət/ **1.** formed by the conjunction or collection of particulars into a whole mass or sum; combined. –*n.* /'ægrəgət/ **2.** a sum, or assemblage of particulars; a total. **3.** any hard material added to cement to make concrete. –*v.* /'ægrəgeɪt/ **4.** to collect into one sum, mass, or body. **5.** to amount to (the number of).

aggression *n.* **1.** any offensive action; an inroad or encroachment. **2.** *Psychol.* the emotional drive to attack. –**aggressive**, *adj.* –**aggressor**, *n.*

aggrieved *adj.* oppressed or grievously wronged.

aggro *adj.* *Aust. Informal* aggressive; dominating.

aghast *adj.* struck with amazement; stupefied with fright or horror.

agile *adj.* **1.** quick and light in movement. **2.** active. –**agility**, *n.*

agist *v.* to take in and feed or pasture (livestock) for payment. –**agistment**, *n.*

agitate v. **1.** to move or force into violent irregular action. **2.** to disturb, or excite into tumult. **3.** to arouse or attempt to arouse public feeling as in some political or social question. –**agitation**, n.

agnostic n. someone who holds that the existence of any god cannot be known for sure, or that human knowledge is limited to experience.

Compare this with **atheist**, which means someone who does not believe in the existence of any god.

ago adv. in past time.

agog adj. highly excited by eagerness or curiosity.

agony n. extreme, and generally prolonged, pain. –**agonise**, **agonize**, v.

agoraphobia /ægərə'foubiə/ n. a morbid fear of being in open or public spaces. –**agoraphobic**, adj., n.

agrarian adj. **1.** relating to land or land tenure. **2.** rural; agricultural.

agree v. **1.** to consent; say yes (to). **2.** to be of one mind (with). **3.** to come to one opinion or mind; come to an understanding (upon). **4.** to be health-giving, or compatible (with): this food does not agree with me. **5.** to concede (followed by noun clause). **6.** to determine (usually followed by noun clause). –**agreed**, adj.

agreeable adj. **1.** pleasing. **2.** ready to agree or consent.

agreement n. **1.** (the act of coming to) a mutual arrangement. **2.** the state of being in accord; conformity.

agriculture n. the cultivation of land, including crop-raising, forestry, stock-raising, etc. –**agricultural**, adj.

ahead adv. **1.** in or to the front. **2.** forward.

ahoy interj. a call used in hailing, especially on ships.

AI n. artificial intelligence.

aid v. **1.** to help. **2.** help; support.

aide-de-camp /eɪd-də-'kɒm/ n. (pl. **aides-de-camp**) a military or naval officer assisting a superior, especially a general, governor, etc.

AIDS /eɪdz/ n. acquired immunity deficiency syndrome; a disease which destroys the body's white cells, resulting in reduced immunity, and ultimately death.

aikido /aɪ'kidoʊ, 'aɪkədoʊ/ n. a Japanese martial art in which the attacker's energy or force is deflected and used against them.

ail v. **1.** to affect with pain; trouble. **2.** to feel pain; be unwell. –**ailing**, adj. –**ailment**, n.

aileron /'eɪlərɒn/ n. a hinged, movable flap of an aeroplane wing, used primarily to maintain balance.

aim v. **1.** to direct or point (something) at something. **2.** to point (a gun); give direction to (a blow, missile, etc.). **3.** to direct efforts towards an object. –n. **4.** the act of aiming. **5.** something intended or desired to be attained; purpose. –**aimless**, adj.

air n. **1.** a mixture of oxygen, nitrogen and other gases, which forms the earth's atmosphere. **2.** the general character of anything. **3.** (pl.) Also, **airs and graces**. an affected manner; haughtiness. **4.** Music a tune; a melody. –v. **5.** to expose to the air. **6.** to expose ostentatiously; bring into public notice. **7.** Communications to broadcast or telecast. –phr. **8.** off (the) **air**, no longer being broadcast. **9.** on (the) **air**, in the act of broadcasting.

airbag n. a bag which inflates instantly in front of someone in a motor vehicle on collision.

aircon n. Informal air conditioning.

air conditioning n. a system of treating air in buildings or vehicles to assure temperature, humidity, etc., remain at a level conducive to personal comfort, etc. Also, **air-conditioning**. –**air-conditioned**, adj. –**air conditioner**, n.

aircraft n. (pl. **-craft**) any machine supported for flight in the air such as balloons, etc., or aeroplanes, helicopters, gliders, etc.

air crane *n.* (*from trademark*) a powerful helicopter designed to lift and transport heavy objects, as construction materials, water to be dumped on bushfires, etc.

airfare *n.* the price of a flight in a commercial aircraft.

air force *n.* the branch of armed forces concerned with military aircraft.

airhead *n. Informal* an absent-minded or forgetful person.

airline *n.* (a company that owns or operates) a system of scheduled air transport between specified points.

airlock *n.* **1.** an obstruction to a flow of liquid in a pipe caused by an air bubble. **2.** airtight compartment.

airmail *n.* the system of transmitting mail by aircraft.

airplay *n.* the amount of public exposure a recording receives on radio or television.

air pollution *n.* the contamination of the air by substances such as chemical fumes, particulate matter, gases, etc.

airport *n.* a large airfield usually equipped with a control tower, hangars, and areas for passengers and cargo in transit.

airtight *adj.* so tight or close as to be impermeable to air.

airtime *n.* **1.** the amount of television or radio broadcasting time dedicated to a particular subject, person, recording, etc. **2.** the amount of time a mobile phone is able to be used, especially as that allocated under a mobile phone service provision contract: *unlimited airtime.*

airy *adj.* (**-rier, -riest**) **1.** open to a free current of air. **2.** light in appearance. **3.** light in manner; lively. **4.** casual; flippant.

aisle /aıl/ *n.* a passageway between seats in a church, hall, etc.

ajar *adv.* **1.** partly opened. *–adj.* **2.** partly open.

akimbo *adv.* with hands on hips and elbows bent outwards.

akin *adj.* **1.** related by blood. **2.** allied by nature.

alabaster *n.* a finely granular variety of gypsum, often white and translucent, used for ornamental objects, such as lamp bases, figurines, etc.

alacrity /ə'lækrəti/ *n.* **1.** liveliness; briskness. **2.** cheerful willingness.

alarm *n.* **1.** a sudden fear or painful suspense caused by apprehension of danger; fright. **2.** any sound or information giving notice of approaching danger. **3.** a sound from a device used to call attention, wake from sleep, warn of danger, etc. *–v.* **4.** to surprise with sudden fear. **–alarmist**, *n.*, *adj.*

alas *interj.* (an exclamation expressing sorrow, grief, pity, concern, or apprehension of evil.)

albatross *n.* a large seabird related to the petrels.

albeit /ɔl'biət, æl-/ *conj.* although.

albino /æl'binoʊ, -'banoʊ/ *n.* (*pl.* **-nos**) a person with a pale skin, light hair, and pink eyes, born lacking pigmentation.

album *n.* **1.** a book consisting of blank leaves for the insertion of photographs, stamps, etc. **2.** a long-playing CD or record containing a collection of songs or pieces.

alchemy *n.* medieval chemistry, especially seeking to change metals into gold.

alcohol *n.* **1.** a colourless, flammable liquid the intoxicating principle of fermented liquors. **2.** any intoxicating liquor containing this spirit. **3.** *Chem.* any of a class of compounds derived from the hydrocarbon by replacement of a hydrogen atom by the hydroxyl radical, OH.

alcoholic *adj.* **1.** relating to alcohol. *–n.* **2.** someone addicted to intoxicating drinks.

alcoholism *n.* an addiction to alcohol which is detrimental to one's health or social functioning.

alcove *n.* a recess opening out of a room.

alderman *n.* (*pl.* **-men**) an elected local government representative having powers varying according to locality.

Nowadays, the non-sexist term **councillor** is used more than **alderman**.

ale *n.* beer not flavoured with hops.

Note that in Australian English this distinction is not usually made and the word **beer** is used in general.

aleatory *adj.* dependent on chance.

alert *adj.* **1.** vigilantly attentive. *–n.* an attitude of vigilance or caution. *–v.* **3.** to prepare (troops, etc.) for action.

alfalfa *n.* **1.** → **lucerne**. **2.** → **alfalfa sprouts**.

alfalfa sprouts *pl. n.* the sprouts of alfalfa seeds, used in salads.

alfresco *adv.* **1.** in the open air; out-of-doors: *to dine alfresco. –adj.* **2.** open-air: *an alfresco cafe.* Also, **al fresco**.

algae /ˈældʒi, -gi/ *pl. n.* any of various chlorophyll-containing plants such as seaweed, etc.

The singular is **alga** but this is not often used.

algebra *n.* a branch of mathematics involving reasoning by the use of symbols. *–algebraic, adj.*

algorithm /ˈælgəˈnðəm/ *n.* a procedure for solving a particular mathematical problem. Also, **algorism**.

alias /ˈeɪliəs/ *adv.* **1.** known sometimes as: *Simpson alias Smith. –n.* (*pl.* **aliases**) **2.** an assumed name; another name: *living under an alias.*

alibi /ˈæləbaɪ/ *n.* (*pl.* **-bis**) *Law* a provable claim not to have been in a place suggested, especially by investigating police.

alien *n.* **1.** someone who is not a citizen of the country in which they are living.

2. *Science Fiction* a being from outer space.

alienate *v.* **1.** to make indifferent or averse; estrange. **2.** to send or turn away. *–alienation, n.*

alight *v.* (**alighted** *or* **alit** (**alighting**)) to get down from a horse or out of a vehicle.

align *v.* **1.** to adjust to a line. **2.** to adjust (mechanical items such as car wheels) so that as a group they are in positions favouring optimum performance. **3.** to come into line; be in line.

alike *adv.* **1.** in the same manner or form; equally. *–adj.* **2.** having resemblance or similarity.

Note that, for def. 2, you would say 'The boys are alike', not 'The boys are both alike'.

alimentary canal *n.* the digestive passage in any animal from mouth to anus.

alimony *n. US* → **maintenance** (def. 2).

A-list *n. Informal* a list of the most desirable celebrities or other public figures sought for prestigious or spectacular social events, etc. Also, **A list**. *–A-lister, n.*

alive *adj.* **1.** in existence; living. **2.** in force or operation; unextinguished. **3.** full of life.

alkali /ˈælkəlaɪ/ *n. Chem.* any of various bases which neutralise acids to form salts. *–alkaline, adj. –alkalinity, n.*

all *adj.* **1.** the whole of (with reference to quantity, extent, duration, or degree). **2.** the whole number of (with reference to individuals or particulars). *–pron.* **3.** the whole quantity or amount. *–n.* **4.** a whole; a totality of things or qualities. **5.** one's whole interest, concern, or property. *–adv.* **6.** wholly; quite. **7.** only; exclusively. **8.** each; apiece. **9.** so much; to that extent: *all the better to see you with.*

allay *v.* **1.** to put at rest; quiet (fear, suspicion, etc.); appease (wrath). **2.** to mitigate.

The more usual word is **relieve**.

allege v. **1.** to assert without proof. **2.** to declare as if upon oath. **3.** to declare with positiveness. –**allegation**, n.

allegiance n. **1.** a citizen's duty owed to a sovereign or state. **2.** faithfulness to any person or thing.

allegory n. figurative treatment of a subject presenting an abstract or spiritual meaning under concrete or material forms. –**allegorical**, adj.

allergen /'ælədʒən/ n. any substance which might induce an allergy.

allergy n. (pl. **-gies**) a physical hypersensitivity to certain things, as pollens, food, fruits, etc., which are harmless to others. –**allergic**, adj.

alleviate v. to make more endurable; lessen.

> The more usual word is **relieve**.

alley n. (pl. **-leys**) a narrow backstreet or lane.

alliance n. **1.** the state of being allied or connected; the resultant relationship. **2.** any joining together by persons, families, states, or organisations.

alligator n. the broad-snouted representative of the crocodile group.

alliteration n. the repeated use of the same letter or sound to start 2 or more words in a group, as in 'Round the rugged rocks we ran.'

> Compare this with **assonance**.

allocate v. to set apart for a particular purpose. –**allocation**, n.

allot v. to divide or distribute as by lot; apportion. –**allotment**, n.

allotrope n. one of 2 or more existing forms of a chemical element.

allow v. **1.** to grant permission to or for; permit. **2.** to admit; acknowledge; concede. –phr. **3.** allow for, to make concession, allowance, or provision for.

allowance n. **1.** a definite amount or share allotted; a ration. **2.** an addition, as to a wage, etc., for some extra expense or

circumstance: *travel allowance; isolation allowance*. **3.** sanction; tolerance.

alloy n. a substance composed of 2 or more metals (or, sometimes, a metal and a nonmetal).

all right adj. **1.** safe and sound: *Are you all right?* **2.** satisfactory; acceptable: *His work is sometimes all right.* –adv. **3.** satisfactorily; acceptably; correctly: *He did his job all right.* Also, **alright**.

allude v. to refer casually or indirectly (to).

> The more usual word is **mention**.
> Don't confuse **allude** with **elude**, which means to avoid or escape.

all-up adj. in total; inclusive: *That will be $45 all-up; It took us six hours all-up.*

allure v. **1.** to attract by the offer of some real or apparent good. –n. **2.** fascination; charm.

allusion n. a passing or casual reference or mention either directly or by implication.

> Don't confuse this with **illusion**, which is something that seems to be true but isn't.

alluvium n. (pl. **-viums** or **-via** /-viə/) a deposit of sand, mud, etc., formed by flowing water. –**alluvial**, adj.

all-wheel drive n. **1.** a motor vehicle drive system which gives a constant connection of all four wheels to the source of power. **2.** a motor vehicle which has such a system. *Abbrev.:* AWD

ally v. /ə'laɪ/ (**-lied**, **-lying**) **1.** to unite by marriage, treaty, league, or confederacy (to or with). –n. /'ælaɪ/ (pl. **-lies**) **2.** an allied person, nation, sovereign, etc. **3.** someone who cooperates with another; associate.

almanac /'ɔlmənæk, 'æl-/ n. a calendar with information regarding events, tides, etc.

> Note that an old spelling of this is **almanack**.

almighty adj. possessing all power.

almond n. a nut grown in warm temperate regions.

almost adv. very nearly.

alms /amz/ *n.* (*sing. or pl.*) that which is given to the poor or needy.

aloe vera /ˈæləʊ ˈvɪərə/ *n.* a plant with fleshy leaves whose sap is used in skin lotions, etc.

aloft *adv., adj.* high up; in or into the air.

alone *adj.* (*used in the predicate or placed after the noun*) **1.** apart from another or others: *she is alone in her room.* **2.** to the exclusion of all others or all else: *He alone knows the truth.* –*adv.* **3.** solitarily. **4.** only; merely.

Note that when this word is used as an adjective, it never comes before the noun it is describing. For example, you cannot say 'an alone person'.

along *prep.* **1.** by the length of; parallel to. –*adv.* **2.** in a line, or with a progressive motion. **3.** by the length. **4.** in company (with).

aloof *adv.* **1.** at a distance, but within view; withdrawn. –*adj.* **2.** reserved; unsympathetic.

aloud *adv.* **1.** with the natural tone of the voice. **2.** with a loud voice; loudly.

alp *n.* **1.** a high mountain. **2.** (*pl.*) a high mountain system, usually with snowy peaks. –**alpine**, *adj.*

alpaca /ælˈpækə/ *n.* a domesticated camel-like South American ruminant allied to the llama, having long, soft, silky hair or wool.

alpha *n.* **1.** the first letter in the Greek alphabet, often used to designate the first in a series, especially in scientific classifications. –*adj.* **2.** *Zool.* holding the dominant position in a group of social animals: *alpha male.*

alphabet *n.* the letters of a language in their customary order. –**alphabetical**, *adj.*

already *adv.* by this (or that) time.

alright *adj.* **1.** safe and sound: *Are you alright?* **2.** satisfactory; acceptable: *His work is sometimes alright.* –*adv.* **3.** satisfactorily; acceptably; correctly: *He did his job alright.* Also, **all right**.

Alsatian *n.* → **German shepherd**.

also *adv.* in addition; too.

You usually put **also** before the verb in a sentence, as in *I also ride horses.* However, if there is an auxiliary verb, **also** comes between the auxiliary and the main verb, as in *I have also seen the film,* and if there are more than one auxiliary verbs, **also** follows the first, as in *I have also been looking at the paintings.*

altar *n.* an elevated place or structure at which religious rites are performed.

Don't confuse this with **alter**.

alter *v.* to make different in some particular; modify.

Don't confuse this with **altar**.

altercation *n.* a heated or angry dispute.

The more usual word is **argument**.

alternate *v.* /ˈɔːltəneɪt, ˈɒl-/ **1.** to follow one another in time or place reciprocally. **2.** to perform by turns, or one after another. –*adj.* /ɔːlˈtɜːnət, ɒl-/ **3.** following each after the other, in succession. **4.** every other one of a series.

Don't confuse def. 3 or 4 with **alternative**.

alternative *n.* **1.** a possibility of one out of 2 (or, less strictly, more) things. –*adj.* **2.** affording a choice between 2 things.

Don't confuse def. 2 with **alternate**. Note that **alternative** used to be limited to a choice between just two options. Nowadays it can apply to two or more.

alternative energy *n.* energy which is not derived from fossil fuels, such as wind energy, solar energy, etc.; usually not including nuclear power.

alternative medicine *n.* any of a number of practices and treatments, often based on traditional remedies, which fall outside the scope of mainstream medicine.

although *conj.* even though (practically equivalent to *though,* but often preferred to it in stating fact).

altimeter /'æltəmitə/ n. an instrument for measuring height.

altitude n. 1. the height above sea level of any point on the earth's surface or in the atmosphere. 2. distance upwards.

alto n. (pl. **-tos**) Music 1. the lowest female voice or voice part; contralto. 2. the highest male voice or voice part.

altogether adv. 1. wholly; entirely; completely; quite. 2. in all. 3. on the whole.

Don't confuse this with **all together**, which you use when a lot of things are grouped close to each other, as in The workers were all together in the canteen.

altruism /'æltru,ɪzəm/ n. the seeking of the welfare of others. **–altruistic**, adj.

aluminium n. a silver-white, ductile, malleable, rust-resistant, metallic element. Symbol: Al

always adv. 1. all the time; uninterruptedly: There is always dirt on your shoes. 2. every time: He always rings before he visits.

Alzheimer's disease /'æltshaɪməz/ n. a brain disease usually affecting elderly people and involving memory loss, confusion, etc.

am v. the form of the verb **be** used for the first person singular (**I**) in the present tense: I am very tired.

Note that this word is often shortened to '**m**: I'm tired.

amalgam n. 1. a mixture or combination. 2. an alloy of mercury with another metal or metals.

amalgamate v. to mix so as to make a combination; unite. **–amalgamation**, n.

The more usual word is **combine**. Note that you usually use **amalgamate** in relation to organisations.

amanuensis /əmænju'ensəs/ n. (pl. **-enses** /-'ensiz/) a person employed to write or type what another dictates or has written.

amass v. to collect into a mass or pile.

amateur /'æmətə, 'æmətʃə/ n. 1. someone involved in a study, art or activity for personal pleasure rather than for gain. 2. a sportsperson who does not earn money from playing sport: The Olympic Games used to be open to amateurs only.

Someone who earns a living by a skill or by playing a sport is called a **professional**.

amatory /'æmətri/ adj. relating to lovers or lovemaking.

amaze v. to overwhelm with surprise.

amazon /'æməzən, 'æməzɒn/ n. a tall, physically strong woman.

ambassador n. a diplomat of the highest rank representing his or her country in a foreign country.

amber n. 1. a pale yellow, sometimes reddish or brownish, fossil resin of vegetable origin. **–adj**. 2. resembling amber.

ambidextrous adj. able to use both hands equally well. **–ambidexter**, n.

ambience n. environment; surrounding atmosphere.

ambient adj. 1. completely surrounding. 2. circulating.

ambiguous adj. open to various interpretations. **–ambiguity**, n.

ambit n. 1. boundary; limits; sphere. 2. scope; extent.

ambition n. 1. an eager desire for distinction, power, etc. 2. the object desired. **–ambitious**, adj.

ambivalence /æm'bɪvələns/ n. 1. the coexistence in one person of conflicting feelings on one subject. 2. uncertainty, especially due to inability to make up one's mind. Also, **ambivalency**. **–ambivalent**, adj.

amble v. (**-bled, -bling**) 1. to go at an easy pace. **–n**. 2. an ambling gait.

ambulance n. a vehicle for carrying sick or wounded persons.

ambush n. 1. the act of attacking unexpectedly from a concealed position. **–v**. 2. to attack from ambush.

ameliorate v. to make or become better.

amen /ɑɪˈmɛn, ɑ-/ interj. so be it (used after a prayer, creed, or other formal statement).

amenable /əˈmɛnəbəl, əˈmiːn-/ adj. 1. disposed or ready to answer, yield, or submit. 2. legally responsible.

For def. 1, the more usual word is **agreeable**.

amend v. 1. to alter (a motion, bill, constitution, etc.) by formal procedure. 2. to change for the better. 3. to remove or correct faults in. –**amendment**, n.

amends phr. **make amends**, to compensate or make up for some offence, damage, loss, etc., caused: He made amends for his rude behaviour by ringing to apologise.

amenities /əˈmɛnətiz, əˈmiːn-/ pl. n. 1. agreeable features, circumstances, etc. 2. Aust. public toilets.

amethyst n. Mineral. a purple or violet quartz used in jewellery.

amiable adj. having agreeable qualities, as good temper, kindness, etc.

amicable adj. characterised by or exhibiting friendliness.

amid prep. in the midst of or surrounded by. Also, **amidst**.

amino acid /əˈmiːnoʊ ˈæsəd, ˈæmənoʊ-/ n. a protein-forming organic compound.

amiss adj. wrong; faulty; out of order; improper: She could tell that something was amiss.

Note that you only use this word after the noun or pronoun it is describing, usually a pronoun such as *something*, *nothing* or *anything*. You cannot say 'an amiss machine', for example.

amity n. friendship; harmony.

ammeter n. an instrument for measuring electric currents in amperes.

ammonia n. a colourless, pungent, suffocating gas, a compound of nitrogen and hydrogen, soluble in water.

ammunition n. 1. projectiles that can be discharged from firearms, etc., as bullets, etc. 2. evidence used to support an argument.

amnesia n. loss of memory.

amnesty n. (pl. **-ties**) a general pardon for offences against a government.

amoeba /əˈmiːbə/ n. (pl. **-bae** /-biː/ or **-bas**) an extremely small, irregularly shaped, single-celled organism which changes shape as it moves and absorbs food. Also, **ameba**. –**amoebic**, adj.

amok phr. **run amok**, to rush about wildly. Also, **amuck**.

among prep. 1. in or into the midst of. 2. included in a group of. 3. to each of. 4. each with the other. Also, **amongst**.

Note that **among** is only used when you are talking about more than two people or things. You would use **between** when there are only two.

amoral adj. neither moral nor immoral.

Don't confuse this with **immoral**, which means wrong or wicked.

amorous adj. 1. disposed to love. 2. enamoured.

amorphous adj. lacking definite form.

amortise /əˈmɔːtaɪz, ˈæmətaːz/ v. to liquidate (an indebtedness or charge) usually by periodic payments to a creditor or to an account. Also, **amortize**.

amount n. 1. quantity or extent. –v. 2. to reach, extend, or be equal in number, quantity, effect, etc. (to).

ampere n. the base unit of electric current. Symbol: A

ampersand n. the character &, meaning and.

amphetamine /æmˈfɛtəmɪn, -mən/ n. a type of stimulant drug.

amphibian n. 1. an animal that lives on land but breeds in water, as a frog, etc. 2. a vehicle suited for both land and water, as a tank. –**amphibious**, adj.

amphitheatre n. **1.** a level area, usually oval or circular, surrounded by rising ground. **2.** an arena. **3.** a semicircular sloping gallery in a modern theatre.

ample adj. **1.** in full or abundant measure. **2.** bulky in form or figure.

amplify v. (**-fied, -fying**) **1.** to make larger or greater. **2.** to expand in stating or describing, as by adding details, illustration, etc. **3.** to make louder. **–amplifier,** n. **–amplification,** n.

Note that def. 2 is only used in relation to statements, stories, feelings, etc.

amplitude n. **1.** extension in space, especially breadth or width; largeness. **2.** large or full measure; abundance.

amputate v. to cut off (a limb, arm, etc.) by surgery. **–amputation,** n.

amuse v. **1.** to hold the attention of agreeably. **2.** to excite mirth in. **–amusement,** n.

an adj. or indefinite article the form of **a** before an initial vowel sound.

See the notes at **a¹**.

anachronism /əˈnækrənɪzəm/ n. something out of its proper time. **–anachronistic,** adj.

anaemia /əˈniːmiə/ n. a deficiency in red blood cells. Also, **anemia. –anaemic,** adj.

anaerobic adj. (of organisms or tissues) needing the absence of free oxygen or not needing its presence (opposed to aerobic).

anaesthesia /ænəsˈθiːʒə, -ziə/ n. Med. general or local insensibility, as to pain, etc., induced by certain drugs. Also, **anesthesia.**

anaesthetic n. a substance such as ether, chloroform, cocaine, etc., that produces anaesthesia. Also, **anesthetic. –anaesthetise, anaesthetize,** v. **–anaesthetist,** n.

A **general anaesthetic** is one which makes you lose consciousness so that you cannot feel pain in any part of the body.

A **local anaesthetic** makes you unable to feel pain in a particular part of the body and does not make you unconscious.

anagram n. a word or sentence formed from letters of another word or sentence, as caned is an anagram of dance.

anal adj. of, relating to, or near the anus.

analgesic /ænəlˈdʒiːzɪk, -sɪk/ n. a remedy that relieves or removes pain.

analog adj. Electronics **1.** of or relating to a device which shows measurement as a moving display, such as a dial or face with pointers or a needle: an analog watch. **2.** of or relating to a device which represents physical quantities as continuously variable physical quantities (as voltages, etc.). Also, **analogue.**

Compare this with **digital**.

analogue n. **1.** something having analogy to something else. –adj. **2. → analog.**

analogy /əˈnælədʒi/ n. (pl. **-gies**) a partial similarity in particular circumstances on which a comparison may be based. **–analogous,** adj.

analyse v. **1.** to resolve into constituent parts; determine the essential features of. **2.** to examine critically.

analysis n. (pl. **-lyses** /-lɪsɪz/) **1.** separation of a whole into its constituent elements (opposed to synthesis). **2.** an outline or summary, as of a book. **–analyst,** n. **–analytic,** adj.

anaphylactic shock /ænəfəˈlæktɪk/ n. an acute systemic reaction produced by an allergen to which the victim has become sensitised.

anarchy /ˈænəki/ n. **1.** a state of society without government or law. **2.** total disorder. **–anarchic,** adj. **–anarchist,** n.

anathema /əˈnæθəmə/ n. (pl. **-mas**) a detested person or thing.

anatomy n. (the science of) the structure of an animal or plant, or of any of its parts. **–anatomical,** adj.

ancestor *n.* someone from whom a person is descended, usually distantly. –**ancestral**, *adj.*

The study of who your ancestors were is called **genealogy**.

ancestry *n.* (*pl.* **-ries**) ancestral descent.

anchor *n.* **1.** a device for holding boats, floating bridges, etc., in place. **2.** a means of stability. **3.** the host or main presenter of a radio or TV broadcast. –*v.* **4.** to hold fast by an anchor. **5.** to affix firmly. **6.** to drop anchor. **7.** to be firmly fixed. **8.** to act as the anchor (def. 3) of a radio or TV broadcast. –*phr.* **9. weigh anchor**, to take up the anchor. –**anchorage**, *n.*

anchorite *n.* someone living in a solitary place for a life of religious seclusion; a hermit.

anchovy *n.* (*pl.* **-vies**) a small, herring-like fish.

ancient *adj.* **1.** of or in time long past. **2.** of great age.

ancillary /æn'sɪləri/ *adj.* accessory; auxiliary.

and *conj.* **1.** (along) with; together with; besides; also; moreover (used to connect grammatically coordinate words, phrases, or clauses). **2.** as well as. **3.** (used between verbs): *Go and see if he will help.*

You use **and** to connect words (*black and white*), phrases (*around the corner and up the hill*) or clauses (*Come around tonight and we will have dinner*).
Some writers don't like sentences beginning with **and** because it is a conjunction which should link clauses or phrases within a sentence and should not appear to link two sentences. In fact many writers *do* use **and** at the beginning of a sentence and there is no reason not to do it, provided that it is not done too often in one piece of writing.

androgynous /æn'drɒdʒənəs/ *adj.* **1.** being both male and female. **2.** not conforming to a male or a female stereotype in appearance or behaviour. –**androgyny**, *n.*

android *n.* (especially in science fiction) a robot made to resemble a human being.

anecdote /'ænəkdoʊt/ *n.* a short narrative of a particular incident or occurrence. –**anecdotal**, *adj.*

anemone /ə'nɛməni/ *n.* **1.** a plant with mostly red and blue flowers. **2.** → **sea anemone**.

aneroid *adj.* using no fluid.

aneurysm /'ænjərɪzəm/ *n.* abnormal widening of the wall of a weakened blood vessel. Also, **aneurism**.

anew *adv.* **1.** once more. **2.** in a new form.

The more usual word is **again**.

angel *n.* **1.** in some religions, **a.** a spiritual being, an attendant of God. **b.** a messenger, especially of God. **2.** a person like an angel in beauty, kindliness, etc. –**angelic**, *adj.*

Don't confuse this with **angle**, which is the pointed shape made when two lines meet.

anger *n.* **1.** strong displeasure aroused by real or supposed wrongs; wrath; ire. –*v.* **2.** to excite to anger.

angina /æn'dʒaɪnə/ *n.* a pain in the chest caused by lack of blood to the heart, usually due to coronary artery disease.

angle¹ *n.* **1.** *Maths* the space within 2 lines or 3 planes diverging from a common point, or within 2 planes diverging from a common line. **2.** a corner. **3.** a point of view. **4.** *Informal* a devious, cunning scheme, etc. –*v.* **5.** to move, direct, etc., at an angle or in an angular course.

Don't confuse this with **angel**, which is a spiritual being.

angle² *v.* to fish with hook and line. –**angler**, *n.*

Angora *n.* (yarn or fabric made from) the long, silky hair of certain goats and rabbits. Also, **angora**.

angry *adj.* **(-grier, -griest)** **1.** feeling or showing anger or resentment. **2.** inflamed, as a sore. **–angrily,** *adv.*

Note that you are **angry with** or **at** a person, but you are **angry about** or **at** a thing or something that has happened. You can also use **angry** without a preposition, as in *Are you still angry?*

angst /æŋst/ *n.* a feeling or outlook of dread, fear, etc.

anguish *n.* agonising pain of either body or mind.

angular *adj.* **1.** having an angle or angles. **2.** situated at or forming an angle. **3.** gaunt. **–angularity,** *n.*

animal *n.* **1.** any living thing that is not a plant. **2.** any animal other than a human. **3.** a brutish person. **–adj.** **4.** of or derived from animals. **5.** relating to the physical or carnal nature of humans.

animate *v.* /ˈænəmeɪt/ **1.** to give life to. **2.** to make lively. **3.** to cause to appear as if alive, as in an animated film. **–adj.** /ˈænəmət/ **4.** alive. **–animation,** *n.*

animated *adj.* **1.** full of life, action, or spirit; lively. **2.** of or relating to a film which consists of a series of drawings, each slightly different from the ones before and after it, run through a projector to create the illusion of movement. **–animatedly,** *adv.*

anime /ˈænəmeɪ/ *n.* **1.** → **manga movie.** **2.** the genre of Japanese animation.

animosity *n.* an active feeling of ill will or enmity (*between* or *towards*).

The more usual word is **dislike**.

aniseed *n.* the seed of the anise, used in medicine, cookery, etc.

ankle *n.* the joint connecting the foot with the leg.

annals *pl. n.* history of events recorded year by year.

anneal *v.* to heat (glass, earthenware, metals, etc.) to strengthen.

annex *v.* **1.** to attach, join, or add, especially to something larger or more important. **2.** to take possession of. **–n.** **3.** something annexed or added, especially a supplement to a document. **–annexation,** *n.*

annexe *n.* a subsidiary building.

annihilate /əˈnaɪəleɪt/ *v.* **1.** to reduce to nothing. **2.** to defeat utterly in argument, competition, etc. **–annihilation,** *n.*

For def. 1, the more usual word is **destroy**.

anniversary *n.* (*pl.* **-ries**) the yearly recurrence of the date of a past event.

annotate *v.* to remark upon in notes. **–annotator,** *n.* **–annotation,** *n.*

announce *v.* **1.** to make known publicly. **2.** to state the approach or presence of. **–announcement,** *n.*

annoy *v.* to disturb (a person) in a way that displeases or irritates. **–annoyed,** *adj.* **–annoyance,** *n.* **–annoying,** *adj.*

Note that you are **annoyed with** or **at** a person, but you are **annoyed about** or **at** a thing or something that has happened. You can also use **annoyed** without a preposition, as in *Don't be annoyed.*

annual *adj.* **1.** yearly. **–n.** **2.** a plant living only one year or season.

annuity /əˈnjuəti/ *n.* (*pl.* **-ties**) a specified income payable often for the recipient's life, in consideration of a premium paid. **–annuitant,** *n.*

annul *v.* **(-nulled, -nulling)** to make void or null; abolish.

Note that **annul** is used only in relation to laws and other formal contracts.

annunciate *v.* to announce.

anode *n.* the positive pole of a battery or other source of current. Compare **cathode.**

anoint *v.* to apply an unguent or oily liquid to, especially to consecrate.

anomaly *n.* (*pl.* **-lies**) deviation from the common rule. **–anomalous,** *adj.*

anonymous *adj.* **1.** without any name acknowledged, as that of author, contributor, etc. **2.** lacking individuality. —**anonymity**, *n.*

The short form of this is **anon**.

anorak /ˈænəræk/ *n.* → **parka**.

anorexia /ˌænəˈrɛksiə/ *n.* a mental disorder, most common in adolescent girls, causing an aversion to food, which may lead to serious malnutrition. Also, **anorexia nervosa**. —**anorexic**, *adj.*

another *adj.* **1.** a second; an additional: *Give me another one.* **2.** a different; a distinct: *That is another breed of dog.* —*pron.* **3.** one more: *Give me another.*

answer *n.* **1.** a reply to a question, letter, etc., or to an accusation. **2.** a solution to a problem, especially in mathematics. —*v.* **3.** to reply. **4.** to respond to (a stimulus, direction, command, etc.). **5.** to declare oneself responsible (*for*). **6.** to act or suffer in consequence of (*for*). **7.** to correspond (*to*). **8.** to make a defence against (a charge or argument).

answerable *adj.* **1.** responsible (*for* a person, act, etc.). **2.** liable to be asked to defend one's actions.

ant *n.* any of certain small, usually wingless, insects, very widely distributed in thousands of species, and having some social organisation.

antagonise *v.* to make hostile. Also, **antagonize**.

antagonism *n.* **1.** active opposition. **2.** an opposing force, principle, or tendency. —**antagonist**, *n.*

antarctic *adj.* very cold: *antarctic conditions.*

This comes from **the Antarctic** which is the area around the South Pole.

anteater *n.* any of various mammals which eat ants.

Two varieties of Australian anteaters are **echidnas** and **numbats**.

antedate *v.* **1.** to precede in time. **2.** to affix an earlier date to (a document, etc.).

antelope *n.* (*pl.* **-lopes** *or, especially collectively,* **-lope**) a slenderly built, hollow-horned ruminant allied to cattle, etc., found chiefly in Africa and Asia.

antenatal *adj.* → **prenatal**.

antenna /ænˈtɛnə/ *n.* (*pl.* **-tennae** /-ˈtɛni/ *for def.* 1, **-tennas** *for def.* 2) **1.** one of the pair of long, thin growths on the heads of insects, crustaceans, etc.; feeler. **2. a.** an electrical device that receives, and sometimes sends, signals. **b.** such a device designed to be attached to a vehicle, phone, television, etc., for the reception of information conveyed in this way.

anterior *adj.* **1.** situated more to the front (opposed to *posterior*). **2.** going before in time.

anthem *n.* a hymn, as of praise, devotion, or patriotism.

anthology *n.* (*pl.* **-gies**) a collection of literary pieces, especially poems, of varied authorship.

anthropogenic /ˌænθrəpəˈdʒɛnɪk/ *adj.* caused by human beings: *anthropogenic climate change.*

anthropoid *adj.* resembling a human.

anthropology *n.* the systematic study that deals with the origin, development and varieties of humanity. —**anthropologist**, *n.* —**anthropological**, *adj.*

antibacterial *adj.* **1.** of or relating to a substance that kills or inhibits the growth of bacteria. —*n.* **2.** such a substance.

antibiotic *n.* a chemical substance used in the treatment of bacterial infections.

antibody *n.* (*pl.* **-dies**) a substance in the blood which counteracts bacterial or viral poisons in the system.

anticipate *v.* **1.** to expect, or realise beforehand. **2.** to consider, do, or mention before the proper time. —**anticipation**, *n.*

anticlimax *n.* an abrupt descent in dignity of thought or expression; disappointing conclusion.

anticlockwise *adv.*, *adj.* in a direction opposite to that of the rotating hands of a clock.

antics *pl. n.* odd, amusing or ridiculous behaviour.

antidepressant *n.* **1.** any of a class of drugs used in treating mental depression. –*adj.* **2.** of or relating to this class of drugs.

antidote *n.* a remedy for counteracting the effects of poison, disease, etc.

antihistamine *n.* any of certain drugs which decrease the effect of the histamine released in allergic conditions of the body, as in hay fever, etc.

antipathy /æn'tɪpəθi/ *n.* a strong, fixed dislike: *an antipathy to dogs.*

> The more usual word is **dislike**, but note that **antipathy** is followed by *to* or *towards*, while **dislike** is followed by *of*: *a dislike of dogs.*

antipodes /æn'tɪpədiz/ *pl. n.* points diametrically opposite to each other on the earth or any globe. –**antipodean**, *adj.*, *n.*

antiquary /'æntəkwəri/ *n.* (*pl.* **-ries**) an expert on or collector of ancient things.

antiquated *adj.* out-of-date because replaced by something newer and better.

antique *adj.* **1.** belonging to former times. –*n.* **2.** an object of art or a furniture piece of a former period.

antiquity *n.* (*pl.* **-ties**) **1.** the quality of being ancient. **2.** (*usu. pl.*) something belonging to ancient times.

antiseptic *n.* an agent which destroys the micro-organisms that produce septic disease.

antisocial *adj.* **1.** unwilling or unable to be sociable. **2.** opposing or damaging to social order.

antithesis /æn'tɪθəsəs/ *n.* (*pl.* **-theses** /-θəsiz/) **1.** opposition; contrast. **2.** the direct opposite (*of* or *to*).

antitoxin *n.* a substance which counteracts a specific toxin. –**antitoxic**, *adj.*

antivenene *n.* an antitoxic serum which counteracts venom of snakes, etc. Also, **antivenin**, **antivenom**.

antler *n.* one of the solid deciduous horns, usually branched, of a deer, etc.

antonym *n.* a word opposed in meaning to another: *'Hot' is an antonym of 'cold'.*

antsy *adj. Informal* **1.** agitated; irritable. **2.** restless; impatient.

anus *n.* the opening at the lower end of the alimentary canal.

anvil *n.* a heavy iron block on which hot metals are hammered into desired shapes.

anxiety /æŋ'zaɪəti/ *n.* (*pl.* **-ties**) distress or uneasiness of mind caused by fear.

anxious /'æŋʃəs, 'æŋk-/ *adj.* **1.** full of anxiety or solicitude. **2.** (fol. by infinitive or *for*) earnestly desirous.

any *adj.* **1.** one or some: *Do you have any pets?* **2.** in whatever quantity: *Are you in any pain?* **3.** (*with a negative*) even the smallest amount: *This won't be of any use.* **4.** every: *Any schoolchild would know that.* –*pron.* **5.** any person; anybody: *Does any of them object?* **6.** any persons: *Are any of your friends here?* **7.** any quantity or number. –*adv.* **8.** in any degree; at all: *Are you feeling any better?*

> Note that, because **any** can refer to a group or a single member of a group, it can be used with plural or singular verbs, nouns and pronouns, as in *If any of the plants die, they can be replaced* or *If any of the plants dies, it can be replaced.*

anybody *pron.* any person.

> **Anybody** is singular, so takes a singular verb (as in *If anybody needs a lift, let me know*), but sometimes, when you need to use a personal pronoun after **anybody**, there can be a problem if you are not sure of the sex of the person you are talking about, or if there is a mixture of males and females. It is awkward to have to say *Anybody who knows the answer should put his or her hand up*, so the plural

pronoun **their** is often used, as in *Anybody who knows the answer should put their hand up.* Some people say that this is not correct, but it is extremely common and neatly solves a difficult problem.

anyhow *adv.* **1.** in any case. **2.** in a careless manner.

anymore *adv.* any longer; from now on: *I can't stand this noise anymore.*

This word is usually used in a negative sentence with words like *can't*, *doesn't*, etc.

anyone *pron.* any person; anybody.

Don't confuse **anyone** with **any one**, which means any individual (person or thing) out of a group, as in *Any one of the drivers could have made that mistake.* For information about what pronouns to use with **anyone**, see the note at **anybody**.

anything *pron.* **1.** any thing whatever; something. **2.** a thing of any kind.

anyway *adv.* in any case; anyhow.

anywhere *adv.* in, at, or to any place.

Anzac biscuit *n.* a biscuit made from wheat flour, rolled oats, desiccated coconut, and golden syrup. Also, **anzac biscuit**.

aorta /eɪˈɔtə/ *n.* the main artery, conveying blood from the left ventricle of the heart to all the body except the lungs.

apart *adv.* **1.** in or to pieces. **2.** separately or aside. **3.** to or at one side. **4.** individually in consideration. **5.** aside (used with a noun or gerund). –*adj.* **6.** separate; independent.

apartheid /əˈpatad, -eɪt/ *n.* (especially as applied to the former policy in Sth Africa) racial segregation.

apartment *n.* a flat or unit.

apathy /ˈæpəθi/ *n.* lack of emotion or excitement. –**apathetic**, *adj.*

ape *n.* **1.** a tailless monkey or one with a very short tail. –*v.* (**aped**, **aping**) **2.** to mimic.

aperture *n.* a hole, slit, or other opening.

apex *n.* (*pl.* **apexes** *or* **apices** /ˈeɪpəsiz/) the tip or highest point of anything.

aphid *n.* a plant-sucking insect.

aphorism /ˈæfərɪzəm/ *n.* a terse saying embodying a general truth.

aphrodisiac /æfrəˈdɪziæk/ *n.* a drug or food that arouses sexual desire.

apiary *n.* (*pl.* **-ries**) a place in which bees are kept. –**apiarist**, *n.*

apiece *adv.* for each one; each.

aplomb *n.* imperturbable self-possession or poise.

apnoea /ˈæpniə/ *n.* suspension of respiration. Also, **apnea**.

apocalypse /əˈpɒkəlɪps/ *n.* revelation; discovery. –**apocalyptic**, *adj.*

apocryphal /əˈpɒkrəfəl/ *adj.* **1.** of doubtful authorship. **2.** false. **3.** mythical.

apologise *v.* to offer excuses or regrets. Also, **apologize**. –**apologetic**, *adj.*

apology *n.* (*pl.* **-gies**) **1.** an expression of regret. **2.** a poor specimen or substitute. **3.** a formal defence.

apoplexy /ˈæpəplɛksi/ *n.* **1.** loss of bodily function due to haemorrhage in the brain. **2.** extreme anger; rage. –**apoplectic**, *adj.*

apostasy /əˈpɒstəsi/ *n.* rejection of one's religion, party, cause, etc.

apostle *n.* a zealous supporter (of a principle, cause, etc.). –**apostolic**, *adj.*

apostrophe /əˈpɒstrəfi/ *n.* the sign (') used to indicate: **1.** the omission of one or more letters in a word, as in *o'er* for *over*. **2.** the possessive case, as in *lion's, lions'.* –**apostrophic**, *adj.*

apothecary /əˈpɒθəkri, -kəri/ *n.* (*pl.* **-ries**) *Old-fashioned* a pharmacist.

app *n. Computers* **1.** a digital product which can be downloaded onto a smartphone, tablet, etc. **2.** an application (def. 6).

appal *v.* (**-palled**, **-palling**) **1.** to overcome with fear and horror. **2.** to shock; dismay.

apparatus /æpəˈrɑːtəs, -ˈreɪtəs/ *n.* (*pl.* **-tus** *or* **-tuses**) equipment etc., for a particular use.

apparel *n.* a person's outer clothing.

The more usual word is **clothes**.

apparent *adj.* **1.** plain or clear to the eye or mind. **2.** ostensible. **3.** open to view.

For def. 1, the more usual word is **obvious**.

apparition *n.* **1.** a ghost. **2.** anything that appears, especially something remarkable.

appeal *n.* **1.** a call for aid, mercy, etc. **2.** a request to some authority for confirmation, decision, etc. **3.** power to move the feelings. –*v.* **4.** to make an appeal (*to*). **5.** to be attractive (*to*).

appear *v.* **1.** to come into sight. **2.** to seem. **3.** to be obvious. **4.** to come before the public. **5.** *Law* to come before a court, etc. –**appearance**, *n.*

appease *v.* **1.** to bring to a state of peace or ease. **2.** to satisfy. –**appeasement**, *n.* –**appeasing**, *adj.*

appellation *n.* a name or title.

append *v.* to add, as an accessory. –**appendage**, *n.* –**appendant**, *adj.*

appendicitis *n.* inflammation of the appendix.

appendix *n.* (*pl.* **-dixes** *or* **-dices** /-dəsiz/) **1.** matter which supplements the main text of a book. **2.** Also, **vermiform appendix**. *Anat.* a small outgrowth at the beginning of the large intestine.

appetising *adj.* appealing to the appetite. Also, **appetizing**.

appetite *n.* a desire for food or drink or any bodily wants.

applaud *v.* **1.** to express approval by clapping hands, etc. **2.** to praise. –**applause**, *n.*

apple *n.* an edible fruit, usually round, crisp, and with red, yellow or green skin.

applet *n.* a small computer program which can be transferred over the internet and which runs on the client machine rather than the server.

appliance *n.* a device, usually operated by electricity and designed for household use.

applicable /əˈplɪkəbəl, ˈæp-/ *adj.* capable of being applied; relevant.

applicant *n.* someone who applies.

application *n.* **1.** the act of putting to a special use. **2.** the quality of being usable for a particular purpose. **3.** something applied. **4.** (a written) request or appeal, as for a job, loan, etc. **5.** close, persistent attention. **6.** Also, **application program**. *Computers* a program which is written specifically to perform a specialised task.

apply *v.* (**-plied, -plying**) **1.** to lay on; bring into contact. **2.** to put into operation, as a rule. **3.** to employ. **4.** to give earnestly. **5.** to be pertinent. **6.** to make (an) application.

appoint *v.* **1.** to assign to a position or to a function: *to appoint a secretary.* **2.** to fix; settle. **3.** to equip.

appointment *n.* **1.** the act of appointing or placing in office. **2.** an office held by a person appointed. **3.** an engagement to meet.

apportion *v.* to distribute proportionally.

The more usual word is **share**.

apposite *adj.* suitable; pertinent.

appraise *v.* **1.** to estimate generally, as to quality, weight, etc. **2.** to value in current money. –**appraisal**, *n.*

For def. 1, the more usual word is **assess**.

appreciable *adj.* **1.** capable of being perceived. **2.** fairly large.

appreciate *v.* **1.** to place a sufficiently high estimate on. **2.** to be aware of. **3.** to be pleased with. **4.** to increase in value. –**appreciation**, *n.* –**appreciative**, *adj.*

apprehend *v.* **1.** to take into custody. **2.** to grasp the meaning of. –**apprehension**, *n.*

For def. 1, the more usual word is **catch**; for def. 2, **understand**.

apprehensive *adj.* fearful.

apprentice *n.* **1.** someone who works for another whilst learning a trade. **2.** a learner.

apprise *v.* to inform; advise (*of*).

approach *v.* **1.** to come near or nearer (to). **2.** to make a proposal or. –*n.* **3.** the act of drawing near. **4.** any means of access. **5.** the method used in setting about a task. **–approachable,** *adj.*

approbation *n.* approval. **–approbatory,** *adj.*

appropriate *adj.* /ə'proupriət/ **1.** suitable for a particular purpose, occasion, etc. –*v.* /ə'prouprieɪt/ **2.** to set apart for a specific use. **3.** to take for oneself. **–appropriation,** *n.* **–appropriateness,** *n.*

approval *n.* **1.** the act of approving. **2.** sanction. –*phr.* **3. on approval,** for examination, without obligation to buy.

approve *v.* **1.** to agree to officially. **2.** to be in favour (*of*).

approximate *adj.* /ə'prɒksəmət/ **1.** nearly exact. **2.** inaccurate; rough. –*v.* /ə'prɒksəmeɪt/ **3.** to come or make near to. **–approximately,** *adv.*

apricot *n.* **1.** a downy yellow fruit resembling a small peach. **2.** a pinkish yellow.

apron *n.* a protective garment covering the front of a worker in a kitchen, factory, etc.

apse *n.* a vaulted recess especially in a church.

apt *adj.* **1.** inclined; likely. **2.** quick to learn. **3.** suited to the purpose or occasion.

aptitude *n.* **1.** a tendency or inclination. **2.** readiness in learning; talent. **3.** special fitness or suitability.

aqua *n.* light blue-green or greenish blue.

aqualung *n.* (*from trademark*) a diver's underwater breathing apparatus.

aquamarine *n.*, *adj.* light blue-green.

aquarium *n.* (*pl.* **-riums** *or* **-ria**) a pond, tank, etc., for keeping live aquatic animals or plants.

aquatic /ə'kwɒtɪk/ *adj.* **1.** of or relating to water. **2.** living or growing in water.

aqueduct *n.* an artificial channel for conducting water.

aquifer *n.* a geological formation which holds water and allows water to percolate through it.

aquiline /'ækwəlaɪn/ *adj.* **1.** of or like the eagle. **2.** (of the nose) curved like an eagle's beak.

arable /'ærəbəl/ *adj.* able to be tilled to produce crops.

arachnid /ə'ræknɪd/ *n.* any arthropod of the class which includes the spiders, scorpions, mites, etc.

arbiter /'ɑbətə/ *n.* a person empowered to decide points at issue.

The more usual word is **judge**.

arbitrary /'ɑbətrəri, 'ɑbətri/ *adj.* **1.** subject to individual will or judgement. **2.** not attributable to any rule or law. **3.** unreasonable. **4.** selected at random.

arbitrate *v.* **1.** to decide as arbiter; determine. **2.** to settle by arbitration. **–arbitrator,** *n.*

arbitration *n.* the hearing and resolving of disputes, especially industrial, by an appointed third party.

arboreal /ɑ'bɔriəl/ *adj.* **1.** of or relating to trees. **2.** *Zool.* living in trees.

arbour *n.* a bower formed by trees, shrubs, or vines, etc. Also, **arbor.**

arc *n.* **1.** any part of a circle or other curve. **2.** *Elect.* the luminous bridge formed by the passage of a current across a gap between 2 conductors or terminals.

arcade *n.* a pedestrian way with shops usually on both sides.

arcane *adj.* mysterious; secret.

arch¹ *n.* **1.** a curved structure supported at both ends. –*v.* **2.** to span with an arch. **3.** to curve.

arch² *adj.* cunning; sly.

archaeology *n.* the study of any culture, especially a prehistoric one, by excavation of its remains. Also, **archeology**.

archaic /a'kenk/ *adj.* **1.** characteristic of an earlier period. **2.** no longer used in ordinary speech or writing. **–archaism,** *n.*

archangel /'akeındʒəl/ *n.* a chief angel.

archbishop *n.* a bishop of the highest rank.

archer *n.* someone who shoots with a bow and arrow. **–archery,** *n.*

archetype /'akətaɪp/ *n.* the original pattern or model. **–archetypal,** *adj.*

archipelago /akə'pɛləgoʊ/ *n.* (*pl.* **-gos** or **-goes**) (sea with) group of many islands.

architect *n.* professional designer of buildings.

architecture *n.* **1.** the art or science of designing and constructing buildings. **2.** the style of building.

architrave *n.* a band of mouldings, etc., about a door or other opening.

archive *n.* (*oft. pl.*) (a place for keeping) historical documents or non-current records of a family, organisation, etc.

arctic *adj.* very cold: *arctic conditions.*

This comes from **the Arctic** which is the area around the North Pole.

ardent *adj.* **1.** glowing with feeling or zeal; passionate. **2.** burning.

ardour *n.* warmth of feeling; fervour. Also, **ardor.**

arduous *adj.* laborious; strenuous.

are[1] /a/ *v.* the form of the verb **be** used with the first person plural (**we**), the second person singular and plural (**you**), and the third person plural (**they**) in the present tense.

Note that this word is often shortened to **'re**: *We're coming soon.*

are[2] /ɛə/ *n.* one hundredth of a hectare.

area *n.* **1.** any particular extent of surface; region. **2.** an open space. **3.** extent or scope. **4.** a field of study or knowledge. **5.** *Maths* two-dimensional extent.

arena *n.* **1.** an enclosure for sports contests, etc. **2.** a field of conflict or endeavour.

argon *n.* a colourless, odourless, chemically inactive, gaseous element. *Symbol:* Ar

argot /'agoʊ/ *n.* the jargon of any class or group.

arguable *adj.* **1.** plausible. **2.** open to argument. **3.** able to be argued. **–arguably,** *adv.*

argue *v.* **1.** to present reasons for or against (a thing). **2.** to dispute.

argument *n.* **1.** a debate. **2.** a matter of contention. **3.** a statement supporting a point. **–argumentative,** *adj.*

aria /'ariə/ *n.* a melody for a single voice in an opera, oratorio, etc.

arid *adj.* dry; parched.

arise *v.* (**arose, arisen, arising**) **1.** to come into being; originate. **2.** to rise; get up from sitting, etc.

aristocracy *n.* (*pl.* **-cies**) a class of hereditary nobility.

aristocrat /'ærəstəkræt, ə'nstəkræt/ *n.* **1.** someone belonging to a superior group or class. **2.** (one of) the best of its kind. **–aristocratic,** *adj.*

arithmetic *n.* the art of computation with figures. **–arithmetical,** *adj.*

ark *n.* **1.** a wooden chest. **2.** a large, floating vessel, as Noah's Ark.

arm[1] *n.* **1.** the human limb from the shoulder to the hand. **2.** the forelimb of any four-legged vertebrate. **3.** any arm-like part. **4.** the sleeve of a garment. **5.** side part of a chair to support the arm.

arm[2] *n.* **1.** (*usu. pl.*) a weapon. **–v. 2.** to equip with arms. **3.** to fit (a thing) for any specific purpose.

armada /a'madə/ *n.* a fleet of warships.

armadillo *n.* (*pl.* **-los**) an armoured, burrowing mammal of Central and Sth America.

armament *n.* the weapons with which a military unit is equipped.

armature *n.* protective covering.

armchair n. a chair with arms to support the forearms or elbows.

armistice n. a truce.

armour n. **1.** defensive equipment or covering. **2.** that which serves as a protection. Also, **armor**.

armoury n. (pl. **-ries**) a storage place for weapons and other war equipment. Also, **armory**.

armpit n. the hollow under the arm at the shoulder.

arms pl. n. weapons.

army n. (pl. **-mies**) a large body of people trained and armed for war.

army reserve n. the part of a country's fighting force not in active service, but used as a further means of defence in case of necessity.

aroma n. a smell, especially an agreeable smell; fragrance. –**aromatic**, adj.

arose v. past tense of **arise**.

around adv. **1.** in a circle; on every side. **2.** here and there; about. –prep. **3.** about; on all sides; encircling. **4.** approximately.

arouse v. **1.** to excite into action; call into being. **2.** to wake from sleep. –**arousal**, n. For def. 2, the more usual expression is **wake up**.

arpeggio /aˈpedʒioʊ/ n. (pl. **-gios**) Music the sounding of the notes of a chord one after the other instead of together.

arraign /əˈreɪn/ v. Law to call or bring before a court to answer to a charge or accusation.

arrange v. **1.** to place in order; adjust properly. **2.** to come to an agreement regarding. **3.** to prepare or plan. –**arrangement**, n.

arrant adj. downright; thorough.

array v. **1.** to place in proper order, as troops for battle. **2.** to clothe, especially with ornamental garments. –n. **3.** regular arrangement. **4.** attire.

arrear n. **1.** (usu. pl.) that which is behind in payment. –phr. **2. in arrear** or **in arrears**, behind in payments.

arrest v. **1.** to seize (a person) by legal warrant. **2.** to bring to a standstill; stop. –n. **3.** the lawful taking of a person into custody.

arrive v. **1.** to reach one's destination. **2.** to reach in any process (at). –**arrival**, n.

arrogant adj. pretending to superior importance or rights. –**arrogance**, n.

arrow n. **1.** a slender, long, pointed, missile shot from a bow. **2.** a figure of an arrow used to indicate direction.

arrowroot n. a tropical American plant whose rhizomes yield a nutritious starch.

arse n. Informal (taboo) the buttocks; rump. Note that this word is taboo and may give offence. Other words you could use that are not taboo are **buttocks** (Formal), **bottom** (Informal) and **behind** (Informal).

arsenal n. a repository of arms and military stores.

arsenic n. a greyish-white element having a metallic lustre, and forming poisonous compounds. Symbol: As

arson n. the act of unlawfully burning any property.

art n. **1.** the production or expression of what is beautiful (especially visually) or appealing. **2.** (pl.) a branch of learning or university study. **3.** skilled workmanship. **4.** a skill or knack. **5.** cunning.

artefact n. any object made by a human. Also, **artifact**.

arteriosclerosis /aˌtɪərioʊskləˈroʊsəs/ n. a disease causing thickening of the artery walls, with lessened blood flow.

artery n. (pl. **-ries**) **1.** a blood vessel carrying blood from the heart to any part of the body. **2.** a main channel, as in systems of communication and transport. –**arterial**, adj.

artesian bore n. a bore in which the water level, under pressure, rises above ground. Also, **artesian well**.

arthritis n. inflammation of a joint, as in gout or rheumatism. –**arthritic**, adj., n.

arthropod n. any of the phylum of segmented invertebrates, having jointed legs, as the insects, arachnids, crustaceans, and myriapods.

artichoke n. a herbaceous, thistle-like plant with an edible flower head.

article n. **1.** a piece of writing on a specific topic. **2.** an individual piece or thing; an item. **3.** *Gram.* in English, one of the words *a*, *an* (**indefinite article**) or *the* (**definite article**), used before a noun to indicate it relates to a particular person or thing. **4.** a clause, item or point in a contract, treaty, statute, etc.

Articles (def. 3) are sometimes called **determiners**.

articulate v. /aˈtɪkjəleɪt/ **1.** to utter clearly. –adj. /aˈtɪkjələt/ **2.** uttered clearly. **3.** capable of speech or self-expression. –**articulation**, n.

articulated adj. **1.** connected by a joint or joints. **2.** (of a road vehicle) consisting of sections connected by a flexible joint.

artifice n. **1.** a clever trick or stratagem. **2.** trickery.

artificial adj. **1.** made by human skill and labour. **2.** made in imitation of; not genuine. **3.** feigned.

artificial intelligence n. the ability of a computer or other machine to function as if possessing human intelligence.

artillery n. mounted guns, movable or stationary, as distinguished from small arms.

artisan /ˈɑːtəzan/ n. **1.** a skilled worker, especially in a craft. –adj. **2.** made by traditional methods: *artisan food*.

artist n. **1.** a person who practises one of the fine arts, especially a painter or sculptor. **2.** an actor or singer, etc. –**artistic**, adj.

artistry n. artistic workmanship, effect, or quality.

art union n. Aust., NZ a lottery.

as adv. **1.** to such a degree or extent. –conj. **2.** used in the correlations *as* (or *so*) … *as*, *same … as*, etc., denoting degree, extent, manner, etc. (*as good as gold, in the same way as before*), or in the correlations *so as*, *such as*, denoting purpose or result. **3.** in the degree, manner, etc., of or that: *Speak as he does*. **4.** though: *Bad as it is, it could be worse*. **5.** as if; as though. **6.** when or while. **7.** since; because. **8.** for instance. –*relative pron.* **9.** (esp. after *such* and *the same*) that; who; which. **10.** (of) which fact, contingency, etc. (referring to a statement). –prep. **11.** in the role, or manner of. –phr. **12. as for** or **as to**, with regard or respect to. **13. as if** or **as though**, as it would be if. **14. as it were**, so to speak. **15. as well**, **a.** equally; also; too. **b.** equally well; better; advisable. **16. as well as**, as much as; just as; equally as; in addition to. **17. as yet**, **a.** up to now. **b.** for the moment.

asbestos /asˈbɛstəs, æs-, -tɒs/ n. (fireproof article made from) a fibrous mineral.

ascend v. **1.** to climb upwards; rise. **2.** to climb; mount. –**ascension**, n.

ascendant n. **1.** a position of controlling influence. –adj. **2.** superior. –**ascendancy**, n.

ascent n. **1.** the act of ascending; upward movement. **2.** gradient.

Don't confuse this word with **assent**, which is a rather formal word meaning to agree.

ascertain /æsəˈteɪn/ v. to determine by trial, examination, or experiment.

ascetic /əˈsɛtɪk/ n. **1.** someone who leads an austere life. –adj. **2.** austere.

ascorbic acid /əskɔbɪk ˈæsəd/ n. vitamin C, found in citrus fruits, tomatoes, etc.

ascribe v. to attribute or impute.

asexual adj. **1.** not sexual. **2.** having no sex or no sexual organs. –**asexuality**, n.

ash[1] n. **1.** the powdery residue that remains after burning. –v. **2.** to cause the ash collected on the tip of (a cigar or cigarette) to fall, usually by giving a light tap: *Don't ash your cigarette on the carpet!*

Note that this word may be used in either singular or plural form, with the same meaning: *There was only ash left where the fire had been*; *There were only ashes left where the fire had been*.

ash² *n.* **1.** a tree of the Nthn Hemisphere producing hard, valuable timber. **2.** any of many Sthn Hemisphere trees with timber or foliage like that of the ash.

ashamed *adj.* **1.** feeling shame or guilt. **2.** unwilling through fear of shame. **3.** loath to acknowledge (*of*).

ashore *adv.* **1.** to shore; on or to the land. –*adj.* **2.** on land: *The crew is ashore.*

aside *adv.* **1.** on or to one side; away from some position or direction. **2.** away from one's thoughts. –*n.* **3.** words spoken so as not to be heard by everyone. **4.** a remark incidental to the main subject.

asinine /ˈæsənaɪn/ *adj.* stupid or obstinate.

ask *v.* **1.** to put a question to. **2.** to seek information. **3.** to request. **4.** to make a request (*for*). **5.** to call for. **6.** to invite.

askance /əsˈkæns/ *adv.* with suspicion or disapproval.

askew *adv.* to one side; awry.

asleep *adv.* **1.** in a state of sleep. –*adj.* **2.** sleeping. **3.** (of the foot, hand, leg, etc.) numb.

asp *n.* any of several poisonous snakes.

asparagus *n.* a plant cultivated for its edible shoots.

aspect *n.* **1.** appearance to the eye or mind. **2.** a view or direction: *a southerly aspect.* **3.** the side facing a particular direction. **4.** *Gram.* the form of a verb which indicates whether the action it refers to is complete. Verbs with **perfect aspect** usually refer to actions that are complete, as in *I have done my work*, and those with **continuous aspect** refer to actions that are still in progress, as in *I am doing my work*.

asperity /æsˈpɛrəti, əs-/ *n.* **1.** sharpness of temper. **2.** hardship. **3.** roughness of surface.

aspersion *n.* a damaging or derogatory remark.

asphalt /ˈæʃfɛlt, ˈæsfɛlt/ *n.* any of various solid bituminous substances occurring naturally in various parts of the earth.

asphyxiate /əsˈfɪksieɪt/ *v.* **1.** to be unable to breathe, usually resulting in death. **2.** to kill someone by making them unable to breathe. –**asphyxiation**, *adj.*, *n.* –**asphyxia**, *n.*

The more usual word is **suffocate**.

aspic *n.* a jellied mould of meat, fish, etc.

aspirate *v. Med.* **1.** to remove (fluids) from body cavities by use of an aspirator. **2.** to inhale (foreign matter) into the lungs. –**aspiration**, *n.*

aspirator *n.* **1.** an apparatus or device using suction. **2.** *Med.* an instrument for removing fluids from the body by suction.

aspire *v.* to aim or seek ambitiously, especially something great or lofty. –**aspiration**, *n.*

aspirin *n.* (*from trademark*) (a tablet of) a white crystalline substance, used to relieve pain.

ass *n.* **1.** a long-eared mammal related to the horse; the donkey. **2.** a fool.

assail *v.* **1.** to assault. **2.** to set upon vigorously with arguments, abuse, etc. –**assailant**, *n.*, *adj.*

assassin *n.* someone who murders from fanaticism or for a reward.

assassinate *v.* to kill for political or religious motives. –**assassination**, *n.*

assault *n.* **1.** an attack; onslaught. **2.** *Law* an attempt to attack another, as by threatening with a weapon. –*v.* **3.** to make an assault upon.

assay /əˈseɪ/ *v.* **1.** to examine by test or trial. **2.** to judge the quality of.

assemblage *n.* a number of persons or things assembled.

assemble *v.* **1.** to bring or come together. **2.** to put or fit (parts) together.

assembly n. (pl. **-lies**) **1.** a company of persons gathered together. **2.** the putting together of complex machinery.

Def. 1 is a collective noun and can be used with a singular or plural verb. Look up **collective noun**.

assent v. **1.** to express agreement or concurrence. –n. **2.** agreement, as to a proposal.

Don't confuse **assent** with **ascent**, which is a journey or movement upwards.

assert v. **1.** to state as true. **2.** to put (oneself) forward insistently. –**assertion**, n. –**assertive**, adj. –**assertable**, adj.

assess v. **1.** to estimate officially the value of. **2.** to determine the amount of. –**assessor**, n.

Don't confuse **assess** with **access**, which means a way of getting to a place, or with **excess**, which means more than necessary.

asset n. **1.** a useful thing or quality. **2.** an item of property. **3.** (pl.) financial resources, including property.

assiduous adj. **1.** constant; unremitting. **2.** constant in application. –**assiduity**, n.

assign v. **1.** to give, as in distribution; allot. **2.** to appoint, as to a duty: *assigned to stand guard.* **3.** to ascribe; attribute. –**assigner**, n.

assignation n. **1.** an appointment for a meeting. **2.** the act of assigning.

assignment n. something assigned, as a particular task or duty.

assimilate v. **1.** to absorb or become absorbed into the body, mind, society, etc. **2.** to make or become like (*to* or *with*). –**assimilation**, n.

assist v. **1.** to give support or aid (to). **2.** to be an assistant. –**assistance**, n.

assistance dog n. a dog trained to perform a number of functions for their disabled owner, such as opening and closing doors, turning light switches on and off, pressing pedestrian crossing buttons, retrieving objects, etc.

assistant n. **1.** someone who assists a superior. –adj. **2.** helpful. **3.** associated with a superior.

associate v. /ə'souʃieɪt, ə'sousieɪt/ **1.** to connect by some relation, as in thought. **2.** to join as a companion or ally. **3.** to unite. **4.** to enter into a union. **5.** to keep company, as a friend. –n. /ə'souʃiət, -siət/ **6.** a partner, as in business. –adj. /ə'souʃiət, -siət/ **7.** having subordinate membership.

association n. **1.** an organisation of people with a common purpose and having a formal structure. **2.** companionship. **3.** connection or combination. **4.** the connection of ideas in thought.

assonance n. the repetition of the same vowel sound in words close together, as in 'fly high'.

Compare this with **alliteration**.

assorted adj. consisting of various kinds; miscellaneous.

assortment n. **1.** distribution according to kind; classification. **2.** a miscellaneous collection.

assuage /ə'sweɪdʒ/ v. **1.** to make milder or less severe. **2.** to satisfy.

assume v. **1.** to suppose as a fact. **2.** to undertake. **3.** to pretend to have or be. **4.** to appropriate. –**assumption**, n.

assurance n. **1.** a positive declaration. **2.** pledge; guarantee. **3.** full confidence or trust. **4.** freedom from timidity; self-reliance. **5.** insurance (now usually restricted to life insurance).

assure v. **1.** to inform or tell positively. **2.** to convince, as by a promise or declaration. **3.** to make (a future event) sure. **4.** to secure or confirm. **5.** to give confidence to.

Don't confuse this with **ensure**, which means to make certain, or with **insure**, which means to pay money so that your property will replaced if it is stolen or damaged.

asterisk *n.* the figure of a star (*), used in writing and printing as a reference mark.

asteroid *n.* one of several hundred small celestial bodies with orbits mostly between those of Mars and Jupiter.

asthma /ˈæsmə/ *n.* a paroxysmal disorder of respiration with laboured breathing. –**asthmatic**, *adj.*, *n.*

astonish *v.* to surprise greatly; amaze.

astound *v.* to overwhelm with amazement; astonish greatly.

astral *adj.* relating to the stars.

astray *adv.* out of the right way; straying.

astride *adv.* 1. in the posture of straddling. –*prep.* 2. with a leg on each side of.

astringent *adj.* 1. (as affecting the skin) refreshing, tightening. 2. severe, sharp. –*n.* 3. an astringent agent (especially cosmetic).

astrology *n.* the study of the possible effects of the celestial bodies on human affairs. –**astrologer**, *n.* –**astrological**, *adj.*

Don't confuse this with **astronomy**. which is the scientific study of the sun, moon, stars and planets.

An astrological forecast or chart is called a **horoscope**.

astronaut *n.* someone trained as a pilot, navigator, etc., of a spacecraft.

astronomical *adj.* 1. of, relating to, or connected with astronomy. 2. very large. Also, **astronomic**.

astronomy *n.* the science or study of the celestial bodies. –**astronomer**, *n.*

Don't confuse this with **astrology**, which is the study of the possible effects of the sun, moon, stars and planets on human affairs.

astute *adj.* of keen discernment; shrewd.

asunder *adv.* into separate parts.

asylum /əˈsaɪləm/ *n.* 1. *Old-fashioned* an institution for the care of the insane, the blind, orphans, etc. 2. an inviolable

refuge; a sanctuary. 3. *International Law* protection granted to foreign political or other refugees.

asymmetric *adj.* lacking symmetry. Also, **asymmetrical**. –**asymmetry**, *n.*

at *prep.* a particle specifying a point occupied, attained, sought, etc., and used in many phrases expressing position, degree or rate, action, manner: *at noon, at home, at length.*

atavism *n.* reversion to an earlier type. –**atavistic**, *adj.*

ate *v.* past tense of **eat**.

atheist *n.* someone who does not believe in the existence of any god. –**atheism**, *n.*

Compare this with **agnostic**, which means someone who believes that we cannot know for sure whether any god exists.

atherosclerosis /ˌæθərouskləˈrousəs/ *n.* a form of the disease arteriosclerosis in which fatty substances deposit in the arteries and harden to form plaque, thus immobilising the artery.

athlete *n.* 1. anyone trained in physical agility and strength. 2. someone trained for running, hurdling, throwing, etc. –**athletic**, *adj.*

athletics *n.* athletic sports, as running, hurdling, etc.

Note that this word is usually used as a plural: *Athletics are good for improving fitness.*

atlas *n.* a bound collection of maps.

ATM *n.* automatic teller machine; a computerised outlet outside a bank, etc.

atmosphere *n.* 1. the gaseous fluid surrounding the earth; the air. 2. a feeling or mood. –**atmospheric**, *adj.*

atoll *n.* a ringlike coral island enclosing a lagoon.

atom *n.* the smallest unitary constituent of a chemical element.

atomic *adj.* 1. relating to atoms. 2. driven by atomic energy. 3. using or having developed atomic weapons.

atomic bomb *n.* a bomb whose explosion is extremely violent and attended by great heat, brilliant light and strong radiation. Also, **atom bomb, A-bomb**.

atomic number *n.* the number of protons in the nucleus of an atom of a given element. *Abbrev.*: at. no.

atomiser *n.* an apparatus for reducing liquids to a fine spray. Also, **atomizer**.

atone *v.* to make amends or reparation. –**atonement**, *n.*

The more usual expression is **make up for**.

atrium *n.* (*pl.* **atria**) **1.** an open area which is central to the design of a building. **2.** one of the two chambers of the heart through which blood from the veins passes into the ventricles.

atrocious *adj.* **1.** shockingly wicked or cruel. **2.** shockingly bad or lacking in taste.

atrocity /ə'trɒsəti/ *n.* (*pl.* **-ties**) an atrocious deed or thing.

atrophy /'ætrəfi/ *n.* **1.** wasting away of the body or of an organ or part, as from defective nutrition or other cause. **2.** degeneration; reduction in size and functional power through lack of use. –*v.* (**-phied, -phying**) **3.** to affect with or undergo atrophy.

attach *v.* **1.** to fasten to; connect. **2.** to join in action or function. **3.** to associate. **4.** to attribute. **5.** to bind by ties of affection. –**attachment**, *n.*

attaché /ə'tæʃeɪ/ *n.* someone attached to an official staff, especially that of an embassy or legation.

attaché case *n.* a small rectangular case with a hinged lid, for documents, etc.

attack *v.* **1.** to set upon with force or weapons. **2.** to blame or abuse violently. **3.** to set about (a task) vigorously. **4.** (of disease, destructive agencies, etc.) to begin to affect. –*n.* **5.** onslaught; assault. **6.** criticism; abuse.

attain *v.* **1.** to reach or accomplish by continued effort: *to attain one's goals.* **2.** to come to or arrive at. –*phr.* **3. attain to**, to arrive at; succeed in reaching or obtaining.

For def. 1, the more usual word is **achieve**.

attempt *v.* **1.** to make an effort at; try. **2.** to attack. –*n.* **3.** effort to accomplish something. **4.** an attack.

attend *v.* **1.** to be present at. **2.** to go with as a result. **3.** to minister to. **4.** to pay heed. **5.** to apply oneself.

For def. 4, the more usual expression is **pay attention**.

attendance *n.* **1.** the act of attending. **2.** (the number of) persons present.

attendant *n.* **1.** someone who attends another. **2.** someone employed to direct or assist people in a public place. –*adj.* **3.** concomitant.

attention *n.* **1.** observant care; consideration. **2.** courtesy. **3.** (*pl.*) acts of courtesy, as in courtship.

attentive *adj.* **1.** giving attention; observant. **2.** assiduous in service. –**attentiveness**, *n.*

attenuate *v.* **1.** to make thin or fine. **2.** to weaken.

attest *v.* **1.** to certify, especially affirm in an official capacity. **2.** to give proof or evidence of. –**attestation**, *n.*

attic *n.* that part of a building, especially a house, directly under a roof; garret.

attire *v.* **1.** to dress, especially for special occasions, ceremonials, etc. –*n.* **2.** (rich or splendid) outer clothing.

attitude *n.* **1.** manner with regard to a person or thing. **2.** position of the body.

attorney /ə'tɜni/ *n.* (*pl.* **-neys**) **1.** a person empowered to act for another; to transact any business on their behalf. **2.** *US* lawyer.

attract *v.* **1.** to pull or draw by a physical force. **2.** to draw by having appealing qualities. –**attraction**, *n.*

attractive *adj.* appealing to one's liking or admiration; engaging; alluring; pleasing.

attribute *v.* /ə'trɪbjuːt/ **1.** to consider as belonging (*to*). –*n.* /ˈætrəbjuːt/ **2.** something attributed as belonging; a quality or property. –**attributive**, *adj.*

attrition *n.* a wearing down or away.

atypical /eɪˈtɪpɪkəl/ *adj.* not typical; not conforming to the type. Also, **atypic**. –**atypically**, *adv.*

> The more usual expression is **not typical**.

aubergine /ˈoʊbəʒiːn, -dʒiːn/ *n.* → eggplant.

auburn *n.* a reddish-brown or golden-brown colour.

auction *n.* a public sale at which buyers make bids. –**auctioneer**, *n.*

audacious *adj.* **1.** bold or daring. **2.** reckless or bold in wrongdoing. –**audacity**, *n.*

audible *adj.* able to be heard.

audience *n.* **1.** an assembly of hearers or spectators. **2.** formal interview.

> **Audience** (def. 1) is a collective noun and can be used with a singular or plural verb. Look up **collective noun**.

audiology *n.* the study of hearing and especially its impairment.

audit *n.* **1.** an official examination and verification of financial accounts and records. –*v.* **2.** to make audit of. –**auditor**, *n.*

audition *n.* **1.** a hearing given to an actor, musician, etc., to test performance, voice quality, etc. –*v.* **2.** to perform or test in an audition.

> An audition for a part in a film is called a **screen test**.

auditorium *n.* (*pl.* **-riums** *or* **-ria**) **1.** the space for the audience in a concert hall, etc. **2.** a large building or room for meetings, assemblies, theatrical performances, etc.

auditory *adj.* relating to hearing, or to the sense or organs of hearing. –**auditorily**, *adv.*

auger /ˈɔːgə/ *n.* a tool for boring holes in wood.

augment *v.* to make larger; increase.

augur /ˈɔːgə/ *v.* to be a sign or omen (of).

august /ɔːˈgʌst/ *adj.* **1.** inspiring reverence or admiration; majestic. **2.** venerable.

aunt *n.* **1.** the sister of one's father or mother. **2.** the wife of one's uncle or aunt.

aunty *n.* (*pl.* **-ties**) **1.** *Informal* an aunt. **2.** (*upper case*) a title of respect for a female elder of an Aboriginal community. Also, **auntie**.

aura *n.* a distinctive air, atmosphere, character, etc.

aural /ˈɔːrəl/ *adj.* of, or perceived by, the organs of hearing. –**aurally**, *adv.*

auriferous *adj.* yielding or containing gold.

aurora /əˈrɔːrə/ *n.* moving bands of light in the skies, visible at high latitudes.

auspice *n.* (*usu. pl.*) favouring influence; patronage.

auspicious *adj.* of good omen; favourable.

austere *adj.* **1.** harsh in manner; stern in appearance. **2.** severe in disciplining oneself. **3.** severely simple. –**austerity**, *n.*

Australian crawl *n.* → freestyle.

Australian Rules *pl. n.* a code of football requiring 2 teams of 18 players, which originated in Aust. Also, **Aussie Rules**, **Australian National Football**, **Australian Football**.

Australian salute *n.* *Informal* (*humorous*) the movement of hand and arm to brush away flies from one's face.

authentic *adj.* **1.** entitled to acceptance or belief. **2.** of genuine origin. –**authenticity**, *n.* –**authenticate**, *v.*

author *n.* a person who writes a novel, poem, essay, etc.

authorise *v.* **1.** to give legal power to. **2.** to formally approve. **3.** to justify. Also, **authorize**. –**authorisation**, *n.*

authoritarian *adj.* favouring the principle of subjection to authority.

authority n. (pl. **-ties**) **1.** the right to determine issues or disputes; the right to control or command. **2.** a person or body with such rights. **3.** an accepted source of information, etc. **4.** a statute, court rule, or judicial decision. **5.** a warrant for action. –**authoritative,** adj.

autism n. Psychiatry a syndrome of unknown cause characterised by the sufferer's inability to understand or relate to his or her environment. –**autistic,** adj.

autobiography n. (pl. **-phies**) an account of a person's life written by himself or herself.

Compare this with **biography**, which is someone's life story written by someone else.

autocracy n. unlimited authority over others invested in a single person; the government or power of an absolute monarch. –**autocrat,** n. –**autocratic,** adj.

autograph n. **1.** a person's signature. –v. **2.** to write one's name on or in.

autoimmune system n. Med. the system within the body which produces antibodies.

automated adj. of machinery, procedures, etc., running by automatic operation. –**automate,** v.

automatic adj. **1.** self-moving or self-acting; mechanical. **2.** done unconsciously or from force of habit. –n. **3.** a machine which operates automatically, as a motor car with automatic gear shift. –**automatically,** adv.

automation n. **1.** the use of automatic machinery in industrial processes. **2.** the act of automating a mechanical process.

automaton /ɔ'tɒmətən/ n. (pl. **-tons** or **-ta**) **1.** a robot. **2.** a person acting mechanically or repetitively.

automobile n. Chiefly US a car.

automotive adj. **1.** propelled by a self-contained power plant. **2.** relating to motor vehicles.

autonomous /ɔ'tɒnəməs/ adj. self-governing; independent. –**autonomy,** n.

autopilot n. a device in an aircraft that can be engaged to keep it flying on a preset course. Also, **automatic pilot.**

autopsy n. (pl. **-sies**) medical examination of a body to determine the cause of death.

autumn n. the season between summer and winter.

auxiliary adj. **1.** giving support; helping. **2.** subsidiary. –n. (pl. **-ries**) **3.** person or thing that gives aid of any kind. **4.** an organisation which assists a larger one.

auxiliary verb n. Gram. a verb that goes with main verbs to show person, tense, etc. The most common auxiliary verbs are those that come from be and have, as in 'I am eating', 'they were eating' and 'I had eaten'.

avail v. **1.** to have force; be of use. **2.** to be of value. **3.** to advantage. –n. **4.** efficacy or advantage for a purpose. –phr. **5.** **avail oneself of,** to make use of.

available adj. suitable or ready for use. –**availability,** n.

avalanche n. a large mass of snow, ice, etc., sliding suddenly down a mountain slope.

avarice /'ævərəs/ n. insatiable greed for riches. –**avaricious,** adj.

avatar n. Internet the representation of a person in virtual reality.

avenge v. to take vengeance.

avenue n. **1.** a street or road, especially one lined with a double row of trees. **2.** a means of access or attainment.

When def. 1 is used in an address, it is often shortened to **Ave,** as in 27 Macquarie Ave.

aver /ə'vɜ/ v. (**averred, averring**) to affirm with confidence.

average n. **1.** an arithmetical mean. **2.** the ordinary, normal, or typical amount, quality, etc. –adj. **3.** estimated by average; forming an average. –v. (**-raged, -raging**) **4.** to find an average value for.

averse adj. having antipathy; opposed.

aversion n. 1. repugnance or rooted dislike (to). 2. an object of repugnance.

avert v. 1. to turn away or aside. 2. to ward off.

avian flu /'eɪvɪən/ n. → **avian influenza**.

avian influenza n. any of a wide range of influenza viruses affecting birds, some strains of which, such as the H5N1 virus, are transmittable from birds to humans. Also, **avian flu, bird flu**.

aviary n. (pl. **-ries**) a large cage or enclosure in which birds are kept.

aviation n. the act or science of flying by mechanical means.

aviator n. a pilot of an aeroplane.

avid /'ævɪd/ adj. keenly desirous; eager.

avocado n. (pl. **-dos**) 1. a tropical pear-shaped fruit, green to black in colour used often as a salad fruit. 2. the tree. Also, **avocado pear**.

avoid v. to keep away from; evade. –**avoidance**, n.

avowed adj. openly stated or admitted: one's avowed beliefs.

The more usual word is **declared**. Note that **avowed** can only be used before the noun.

avuncular /ə'vʌŋkjələ/ adj. like or characteristic of an uncle.

await v. 1. to wait for. 2. to be in store for; be ready for. 3. to wait, as in expectation.

awake v. (**awoke, awoken, awaking**) 1. to rouse from sleep. 2. to stir the interest of. 3. to stir, disturb (the memories, fears, etc.). 4. to come to realise the truth; to rouse to action, etc. –adj. 5. not sleeping. 6. alert.

awakening adj. 1. rousing. –n. 2. the act of awaking from sleep. 3. an arousal or revival of interest or attention.

award v. 1. to adjudge to be merited; bestow. 2. to bestow by judicial decree, as in arbitration. –n. 3. something awarded, as a medal, rate of pay, particular working conditions, etc.

aware adj. 1. conscious or having knowledge (of). 2. informed or up-to-date. –**awareness**, n.

away adv. 1. from this or that place. 2. apart; at a distance. 3. aside. 4. continuously: The fire blazed away. –adj. 5. absent. 6. distant. 7. Informal on the move.

awe n. 1. respectful or reverential fear. –v. (**awed, awing**) 2. to inspire with awe.

awesome adj. inspiring awe.

awful adj. 1. extremely bad; unpleasant. 2. Informal very great. 3. inspiring fear; dreadful. –**awfulness**, n.

awfully adv. 1. extremely badly. 2. Informal very.

awkward adj. 1. clumsy. 2. ungraceful. 3. ill-adapted for use or handling. 4. requiring caution. 5. difficult to handle. 6. embarrassing or trying. 7. deliberately obstructive or difficult.

awl n. a pointed instrument for piercing small holes in leather, wood, etc.

awning n. a roof-like shelter of canvas, etc., over a window, door, deck, etc. 2. a shelter.

awoke v. past tense of **awake**.

awry /ə'raɪ/ adv. 1. with a turn or twist to one side. 2. amiss; wrong.

axe n. (pl. **axes**) 1. an instrument with a bladed head on a handle used for hewing, cleaving, etc. –v. (**axed, axing**) 2. to shape or trim with an axe. 3. Informal to dismiss from a position. –phr. 4. **the axe**, Informal a. a drastic cutting down (of expenses). b. dismissal from a job, etc.

axes /'æksiz/ n. plural of **axis**.

The plural of **axe**, a tool, is also spelt **axes**, but is pronounced /'æksəz/.

axiom n. 1. a recognised truth. 2. an established principle. –**axiomatic**, adj.

axis n. (pl. **axes** /'æksiz/) 1. the line about which a rotating body, such as the earth, turns. 2. a fixed line of reference for plotting a curve on a graph, in crystal-lography, etc. –**axial**, *adj.*

axle *n.* the pin, shaft, etc., on which or with which a wheel or pair of wheels rotate.

axolotl /ˈæksəˈlɒtl, ˈæksəlɒtl/ *n.* any of several Mexican salamanders that breed in the larval stage.

ayatollah /aɪəˈtɒlə/ *n.* a Muslim religious leader in Iran.

aye *adv.* **1.** yes. –*n.* (*pl.* **ayes**) **2.** an affirmative vote or voter. Also, **ay**.

azalea *n.* a shrub with handsome, variously coloured flowers.

azure /ˈeɪʒə, æˈzjʊə/ *adj.* of a sky blue colour.

B, b

B, b *n.* the 2nd letter of the English alphabet.

babble *v.* (**-led, -ling**) **1.** to utter words imperfectly or indistinctly. **2.** to make a continuous murmuring sound. –*n.* **3.** inarticulate speech. **4.** a murmuring sound.

babe *n.* **1.** a baby. **2.** *Informal* a very attractive person.

baboon *n.* a large, terrestrial monkey.

baby *n.* (*pl.* **-bies**) **1.** very young child of either sex. **2.** *Informal* an invention or creation of which one is particularly proud.

bachelor *n.* **1.** an unmarried man. **2.** a person who has taken the first degree at a university (used only in titles and certain other expressions referring to such a degree).

bacillus /bəˈsiləs/ *n.* (*pl.* **-cilli** /-ˈsɪli/) any of the group of rod-shaped bacteria which produce spores in the presence of free oxygen.

back¹ *n.* **1.** the hinder part of the human body, extending from the neck to the end of the spine. **2.** the part of the body of animals corresponding to the human back. **3.** the part opposite to or farthest from the face or front. **4.** *Football, etc.* one of the defending players behind the forwards. –*v.* **5.** to support, as with authority, influence, or money (*up*). **6.** to (cause to) move backwards. **7.** to bet in favour of. –*adj.* **8.** lying or being behind. **9.** away from the front position or rank; remote. –*phr.* **10. back up,** *Computers* to copy data on to a tape, disk, etc., as a safety measure.

back² *adv.* **1.** at, to, or towards the rear. **2.** towards the past. **3.** towards the original starting point, place, or condition. **4.** in reply, in return.

backbench *n.* the non-office-holding parliamentary membership of a political party. –**backbencher,** *n.*

backbone *n.* **1.** the spinal or vertebral column. **2.** strength of character; resolution.

backdate *v.* to date (something) earlier; apply retrospectively.

backdrop *n.* the painted curtain or hanging at the back of a theatrical set.

backfire *v.* **1.** (of an internal-combustion engine) to have a premature explosion in the cylinder or in the admission or exhaust passages. **2.** to bring results opposite to those planned.

back foot *phr.* **on the back foot,** at a disadvantage.

backgammon *n.* a game played by 2 persons at a board with pieces moved in accordance with throws of dice.

background *n.* **1.** the portions of a picture represented as in the distance. **2.** the social, historical and other earlier circumstances which explain an event or condition. –*adj.* **3.** of or relating to the background.

backhand *n.* a stroke, as in tennis, by a right-handed player from the left of the body (or the reverse for a left-handed player).

backlash *n.* any sudden, violent, or unexpected reaction.

backlog *n.* **1.** an accumulation of business resources, stock, etc., acting as a reserve. **2.** an accumulation of work, correspondence, etc., awaiting attention.

backpack *n.* a light, strong bag designed to be carried on the back, especially by travellers, walkers, etc.

backpacker *n.* a traveller who carries their personal belongings in a backpack, and usually stays in low-priced accommodation.

backside *n.* *Informal* the buttocks.

backslash *n.* a short diagonal line (\), either printed or on a computer screen.

backspace v. (in keyboarding) to move back in the text one space at a time, by depressing a particular key.

backstage adv. in the wings or dressing rooms of a theatre.

backstop n. 1. *Sport* a person, screen, or fence placed to prevent a ball going too far. 2. a person or a thing relied on for assistance when all else fails.

backstroke n. a swimming stroke in which the swimmer is on their back.

backtrack v. 1. to return over the same course or route. 2. to pursue a reverse policy.

backup n. 1. a pent-up accumulation, especially of a liquid. 2. a reserve supply or resource; a second means of support. 3. *Computers* a. the process of copying data to a tape, CD-ROM, etc., so that a version is available if the original data is lost, corrupted, etc. b. the data so copied.

backward adj. 1. turned or moving towards the back. 2. behind in growth, progress or development. –adv. 3. → **backwards**.

Note that you can use **backward** for both the adjective (*a backward glance, a backward student*) and the adverb (*to step backward*), but **backwards** can only be used for the adverb (*to step backwards*).

backwards adv. 1. towards the back or rear. 2. with the back foremost. 3. towards the past. 4. towards a worse condition. Also, **backward**.

backwater n. 1. a body of stagnant water connected to a river. 2. an unprogressive place or state.

backwoods pl. n. any unfamiliar or unfrequented area.

backyard n. 1. an area, with gardens and lawn, at the back of a house. 2. *Informal* one's own neighbourhood, community, or society. –adj. 3. illegal, illicit, improper or unqualified.

bacon n. cured meat from the back and sides of the pig.

bacteria pl. n. (sing. **-rium**) microscopic organisms, various species of which produce disease. –**bacterial**, adj.

Note that this is a plural word, with the singular form **bacterium**. However, there is some evidence to show that **bacteria** is being used in the singular (as in *This bacteria is dangerous*), and so is following the path that *data* and *media* have already travelled.

bad adj. 1. not good. 2. unsatisfactory; poor; inadequate. 3. regretful; sorry; upset. 4. severe. 5. rotten. –phr. 6. **not bad**, quite good; fair. 7. **too bad**, *Informal* a. (an expression indicating a lack of sympathy or an unwillingness to compromise). b. (an expression of sympathy at some misfortune). –**badly**, adv.

Def. 6 is a form of understatement because you don't just mean that something is not bad – you actually mean that it is quite good.

bade /bæd/ v. past tense of **bid**.

badge n. a mark, token or device worn as a sign of allegiance, membership, authority, achievement. –**badging**, n.

badger n. 1. a burrowing carnivorous mammal of Europe and America. –v. 2. to harass.

badminton n. a tennis-like game played with a high net and shuttlecock.

baffle v. 1. to thwart or frustrate disconcertingly. 2. to puzzle.

bag n. 1. a receptacle of leather, cloth, paper, etc. 2. (pl.) *Informal* a lot; an abundance: *bags of energy*. 3. a sac, as in the body of an animal or insect. –v. (**bagged**, **bagging**) 4. to hang loosely like an empty bag. 5. to put into a bag. 6. to kill or catch, as in hunting.

bagel /'beɪɡəl/ n. a small ring-shaped, hard roll, made of dough.

baggage n. luggage.

baggy adj. (**-gier**, **-giest**) bag-like; hanging loosely.

bagpipes *n.* a musical instrument consisting of reeded pipes protruding from a windbag into which the air is blown.

bail¹ *n.* **1.** (in criminal proceedings) the release of a prisoner from legal custody into the custody of someone who undertakes to produce the prisoner to the court at a later date or forfeit the security deposited as a condition of the release. **2.** property given as security that a person released on bail will appear in court at the appointed time. *–v.* Also, **bail out**. **3. a.** to help someone get their freedom by giving bail. **b.** to help someone out of trouble. *–phr.* **4. jump bail**, to fail to appear in court at the appointed time and lose one's bail as a result.

Note that **bail** and **bale** sound the same but have different meanings. **Bail** has several meanings (see also **bail**² and **bail**³), and **bale** refers to a large bundle of something such as *a bale of wool*. The spelling **bale** can also sometimes be used for the meanings of **bail**².

bail² *v.* **1.** to remove (water) especially from a boat, as with a bucket or a can. *–phr.* **2. bail out**, to make a parachute-jump from a plane (especially in emergency). Also, **bale**.

bail³ *n.* *Cricket* either of the 2 small bars or sticks laid across the tops of the stumps. **2.** Also, **bails**. a framework for securing a cow's head during milking. *–phr.* **3. bail up**, *Aust.*, *NZ* to delay (someone) as in conversation.

bailiff /ˈbeɪləf/ *n.* officer employed to deliver court orders, collect debts, etc.

bails *pl. n.* **1. →** **bail**³ (def. 2). **2. the bails**, the milking shed.

bait *n.* **1.** food, etc., used as a lure in fishing, trapping, etc. **2.** food containing a harmful additive used to lure and kill animals considered pests. *–v.* **3.** to prepare (a hook or trap) with bait. **4.** to add substances to (food) to kill or drug animals.

5. to goad to anger; torment (someone) for amusement.

bake *v.* **1.** to cook by dry heat in an oven, etc. **2.** to harden by heat.

baker *n.* someone who makes and sells bread, cake, etc. **–bakery**, *n.*

balaclava /bæləˈklavə/ *n.* knitted woollen hood covering the whole head except for the face.

balance *n.* **1.** an instrument for weighing, typically a bar poised or swaying on a central support according to the weights borne in scales (pans) suspended at the ends. **2.** a state of equilibrium. **3.** mental steadiness or calmness. **4.** harmonious arrangement or adjustment, especially in design. **5.** something used to produce equilibrium. **6.** the act of balancing; comparison as to weight, amount, importance, etc. **7.** the remainder. **8.** *Commerce* **a.** equality between the totals of the 2 sides of an account. **b.** the difference between the debit and credit totals of an account. **c.** amount still owing. **9.** an adjustment of accounts. *–v.* **(-anced, -ancing) 10.** to weigh in a balance. **11.** to estimate the relative weight or importance of. **12.** to arrange or adjust the parts of symmetrically. **13.** to be equal or proportionate to. **14.** *Commerce* **a.** to add up the 2 sides of (an account) and determine the difference. **b.** to make the necessary entries in (an account) so that the sums of the 2 sides will be equal. **c.** to pay what remains due on an account.

balanced *adj.* **1.** having a balance; having weight evenly distributed or being in good proportion. **2.** (of a discussion, opinion, etc.) taking everything into account in a fair, well-judged way; not biased. **3.** (of a diet) having different kinds of food in the correct proportion to maintain health.

balcony *n.* (*pl.* **-nies**) a raised and railed platform projecting from an upper storey of a building.

bald *adj.* **1.** lacking hair on some part of the scalp. **2.** (of tyres) having the rubber tread worn off. **3.** bare; plain.

bale¹ *n.* a large bundle or package prepared for storage or transportation, especially one closely compressed and secured by cords, wires, etc.

Bale and **bail** sound the same but have different meanings. Both words mean several things. **Bail** refers to the money left with a court to ensure that an accused person will come back for trial. If you **bail** someone out you help them out of a difficult situation. A **bail** is also part of a wicket in cricket. To **bale** is to scoop water out of a boat, or to jump out of an aeroplane. When it has this meaning, you can also spell it **bail** (*We had to bale / bail out the water; He baled / bailed out of the plane when it caught on fire*).

bale² *v.* (**baled, baling**) → **bail**².

baleful *adj.* full of menacing or malign influences.

ball¹ *n.* **1.** a spherical or approximately spherical body. **2.** a round or roundish body, hollow or solid, etc., as used in various games, as cricket, football, tennis, or golf. **3.** *Informal* (*taboo*) a testicle. –*phr.* **4. on the ball**, alert.

Note that def. 3 is a taboo use and may give offence.

ball² *n.* **1.** a social gathering (usually formal) at which people dance. **2.** *Informal* an enjoyable occasion.

ballad *n.* **1.** a simple narrative poem, in short stanzas, often adapted for singing. **2.** a romantic or sentimental pop song.

ballast /'bæləst/ *n.* **1.** any heavy material carried by a ship or boat to ensure proper stability. **2.** something heavy, as bags of sand, placed in the car of a balloon for control of altitude, etc. **3.** anything that gives material, moral, or political stability.

ball bearing *n.* **1.** (one of the balls from) a bearing in which moving parts turn on rolling steel balls.

ballerina *n.* female ballet-dancer.

ballet /'bæleɪ/ *n.* (performance of) theatrical style of dance using a formal technique, usually narrative structure, and choreography.

ballistic *adj.* **1.** relating to projectiles. –*phr.* **2. go ballistic**, *Informal* become extremely angry.

balloon *n.* a usually spherical bag filled with some gas lighter than air.

ballot *n.* **1.** Also, **ballot-paper**. a ticket or paper used in voting. **2.** Also, **secret ballot**. the system of secret voting by means of printed or written ballots or voting machines.

ballpark *phr.* **in the ballpark**, *Informal* within acceptable limits; relatively close to a desired target.

ballpoint *n.* a pen with a fine ball bearing as the point, depositing a thin film of ink as it turns.

balm /bam/ *n.* **1.** any fragrant ointment. **2.** anything which heals or soothes.

balmy *adj.* (**-mier, -miest**) mild and refreshing; soft; soothing.

balsa /'bɒlsə/ *n.* an extremely light wood, now much used in crafts.

balsam /'bɒlsəm, 'bɔl-/ *n.* **1.** any of various fragrant resins from certain trees. **2.** a common garden plant often with red, pink or white flowers. **3.** a balm.

balustrade *n.* a railing with a row of short pillars holding it up, usually part of a balcony or staircase. –**balustraded**, *adj.*

bamboo *n.* **1.** any of various treelike tropical and semitropical grasses. **2.** the hollow woody stem of such a plant, used for building, furniture making, etc.

bamboozle *v.* **1.** to deceive by trickery. **2.** to perplex.

ban *v.* (**banned, banning**) **1.** to prohibit; interdict –*n.* **2.** a prohibition.

banal /bə'nal, 'beɪnəl/ *adj.* hackneyed; trite. –**banality**, *n.*

banana *n.* (a tropical plant, cultivated for) a nutritious yellow fruit.

band[1] n. **1.** a group of people or animals. **2.** a company of musicians usually playing for performance or as an accompaniment to dancing. –v. **3.** to unite; form a group (*together*).

band[2] n. **1.** any strip that contrasts with its surroundings in colour, texture or material. **2.** *Radio* a well-defined range of frequencies.

bandage n. a strip of cloth used to bind up a wound, hold a dressing in place, etc.

bandaid n. (*from trademark*) a light adhesive dressing for covering a wound.

bandicoot n. any of various small, omnivorous, somewhat rat-like Aust. marsupials.

bandit n. **1.** an armed robber. **2.** an outlaw.

bandwidth n. **1.** the difference between the upper and lower frequencies of a band (**band**[2] def. 2). **2.** *Telecommunications* the volume of information per unit of time that a transmission medium such as a cable is capable of carrying, usually measured in bits per second.

bandy v. (**-died, -dying**) **1.** to pass from one to another, or back and forth. –adj. **2.** (of legs) having a bend outward.

bane n. a destructive person or thing.

bang n. **1.** a loud, sudden explosive noise. **2.** a knock; a bump. –v. **3.** to strike or beat resoundingly. **4.** to slam. **5.** to knock or bump. **6.** to strike violently or noisily.

bangle n. a ring-shaped bracelet without a clasp.

banish v. to condemn to exile; relegate to a country or place by decree.

banister n. (one of the supports of) a stair rail. Also, **bannister**.

banjo n. (*pl.* **-jos**) a musical instrument of the guitar family, having a circular body.

bank[1] n. **1.** a long pile or mass. **2.** a slope or incline. **3.** the land bordering the course of a river. **4.** a lateral inclination during a curve. –v. **5.** to rise in or form banks, as clouds or snow. **6.** to tip or incline laterally, as an aircraft, road, cycle racing track, etc.

bank[2] n. **1.** an institution for receiving and lending money and transacting other financial business. **2.** any store or reserve. –v. **3.** to function as a bank or banker. **4.** to keep money in, or have an account with, or deposit in a bank. **5.** *Informal* to rely or count (*on* or *upon*). –phr. **6. bank up,** to accumulate. –**banker,** n.

bank[3] n. **1.** an arrangement of objects in line. **2.** a row or tier of oars.

banknote n. paper money issued by a bank.

bankroll n. **1.** a roll of money notes. –v. **2.** to provide funds for.

bankrupt n. **1.** *Law* a person adjudged insolvent by a court, and whose property is therefore to be administered by a trustee for the benefit of the creditors in accordance with bankruptcy legislation. **2.** any insolvent debtor; one unable to satisfy any just claims made upon him or her. **3.** a person completely depleted of some human quality or resource: *a moral bankrupt.* –adj. **4.** *Law* subject to having (one's) property administered by a trustee in accordance with bankruptcy legislation. **5.** completely depleted of some human quality or resource. **6.** relating to bankrupts. –v. **7.** to make bankrupt. –**bankruptcy,** n.

banksia n. any of various shrubs and trees with leathery leaves and dense cylindrical heads of flowers, sometimes called a bottlebrush.

banner n. the flag of a country, army, troop, etc.

banns *pl. n.* public announcement in church of intended marriage.

banquet /ˈbæŋkwət/ n. a formal and ceremonious meal, often given for a special occasion.

bantam n. any of certain very small varieties of domestic fowl.

banter n. **1.** good-humoured teasing. –v. **2.** to use banter.

baptism n. **1.** a ceremonial immersion in or sprinkling of water, as a sacrament of the Christian church. **2.** any similar ceremony or action of initiation, dedication, etc.: *a soldier's baptism of fire.* –**baptise**, **baptize**, v.

bar¹ n. **1.** a relatively long and evenly shaped piece of some solid substance. **2.** a band or stripe. **3.** a ridge of sand or gravel in coastal waters. **4.** anything which obstructs, hinders, or impedes. **5.** Also, **barline**. Music the vertical line drawn across the stave to mark the metrical accent. **6.** a counter or a room where alcoholic drinks, etc., are served to customers. **7.** practising barristers collectively. **8.** any tribunal. –v. (**barred**, **barring**) **9.** to fasten with a bar or bars. **10.** to block (a way, etc.) as with a barrier. **11.** to forbid; preclude. –prep. **12.** except; omitting; but.

bar² n. a unit for measuring pressure in the metric system.

barb n. **1.** a pointed part projecting backwards from a main point, as of a fishhook or a fence wire. **2.** a sharp or unkind implication in a remark.

barbarian n. an ignorant, uncouth and cruel person. –**barbaric**, **barbarous**, adj.

barbecue n. **1.** a metal frame for cooking meat, etc., above an open fire. **2.** a social occasion, usually outdoors, where barbecued food is served –v. **3.** to cook on a barbecue. Also, **barbeque**, **bar-b-q**.

barber n. someone whose occupation it is to cut and style men's hair and to shave or trim beards.

barbie n. Aust., NZ Informal a barbecue. Also, **barby**.

barbiturate /baˈbɪtʃərət/ n. a drug used as an anaesthetic or a sedative.

barcode n. Also, **bar code**. **1.** a product code containing information about prices, etc., in the form of a series of bars of varying thickness, designed to be read by an optical scanner. –v. (**-coded**, **-coding**) **2.** to identify by means of a barcode.

bard n. Old-fashioned a poet.

bare adj. (**barer**, **barest**) **1.** without covering; naked. **2.** without the usual furnishings, contents, etc. **3.** open to view; undisguised. **4.** unadorned; bald. **5.** just sufficient. –v. (**bared**, **baring**) **6.** to make bare.

> Don't confuse **bare** with **bear**, which is an animal. **Bear** can also mean to hold or carry.

barely adv. only just; no more than: *She is barely 13; I can barely hear you.*

> Note that you can say **barely any**, as in *There's barely any butter in the fridge,* but you cannot say **barely no**, as in *There's barely no butter in the fridge.*

bargain n. **1.** an agreement between parties in a transaction. **2.** an advantageous purchase. –v. **3.** to discuss the terms of a bargain; haggle over terms.

barge n. **1.** a large flat-bottomed vessel, used for transporting freight. –v. (**barged**, **barging**) **2.** to move aggressively or with undue energy.

bariatrics n. the branch of medical science concerned with the causes and treatment of obesity. –**bariatric**, adj.

barista n. (pl. **-ristas** or **-risti**) a person skilled in making espresso coffee in a cafe or restaurant.

baritone Music –n. **1.** a male voice or voice part between tenor and bass. –adj. **2.** relating to or having the range of a baritone: *a baritone saxophone.*

barium /ˈbeəriəm/ n. a whitish, active, metallic element. Symbol: Ba

bark¹ n. **1.** the abrupt, explosive cry of a dog. –v. **2.** to utter such a cry or cries, as a dog. **3.** to speak or cry out sharply or gruffly.

bark² n. the external covering of the woody stems, branches, and roots of plants, as distinct from the wood itself.

barley *n.* a cereal plant whose grain is used as food and in the making of whisky.

barn *n.* a building for storing hay, grain, etc., and often for stabling livestock.

barnacle *n.* any of certain crustaceans which attach themselves to marine rocks, etc.

barometer /bəˈrɒmətə/ *n.* **1.** an instrument for measuring atmospheric pressure, thus determining height, weather changes, etc. **2.** anything that indicates changes.

baron *n.* **1.** a peer of the lowest titular rank. **2.** a rich and powerful man.

baronet *n.* a British hereditary titled man, ranking below the barons.

baroque /bəˈrɒk, bəˈroʊk/ *adj.* **1.** of or relating to the ornate style of musical or literary composition, art and architecture of the 17th and early 18th centuries. **2.** extravagantly ornamented.

barrack¹ *n.* (*usu. pl.*) a building or buildings for lodging soldiers, especially in garrison.

barrack² *v.* to support; shout encouragement and approval (*for*).

barracouta /bærəˈkutə/ *n.* (*pl.* **-couta** or **-coutas**) an elongated, cold water, sport and food fish.

For information about the different plural forms, see the note at **fish**.

barracuda /bærəˈkudə/ *n.* (*pl.* **-cuda** or **-cudas**) an elongated, predatory, tropical and subtropical marine fish.

For information about the different plural forms, see the note at **fish**.

barrage *n.* **1.** *Mil.* a barrier of artillery fire. **2.** a sustained attack.

barramundi /bærəˈmʌndi/ *n.* (*pl.* **-di** or **-dis**) a large, silver-grey food fish.

For information about the different plural forms, see the note at **fish**.

barrel *n.* **1.** a wooden cylindrical vessel having slightly bulging sides and flat ends. **2.** the tube of a gun.

barren *adj.* **1.** incapable of producing, or not producing, offspring. **2.** unproductive.

barricade *n.* **1.** a defensive barrier hastily constructed, as in a street. *–v.* **2.** to obstruct with a barricade. **3.** to shut in and defend with or as with a barricade.

barrier *n.* anything that bars passage or access.

barrister *n.* a lawyer whose main work is to present cases in court.

Compare this with **solicitor**.

barrow *n.* **1.** a small hand-drawn or horse-drawn cart used by street vendors. **2.** a wheelbarrow.

barter *v.* to trade by exchange of commodities instead of using money.

BAS /bæz, bæs/ *n.* → **business activity statement**.

basalt /ˈbæsɒlt, ˈbæsɒlt/ *n.* a dark, dense igneous rock.

base¹ *n.* **1.** the bottom of anything, considered as its support. **2.** the principal or fundamental element or ingredient of anything. **3.** a fortified or protected area or place used by any of the armed services. **4.** *Maths* the number which serves as a starting point for a logarithmic or other numerical system. **5.** *Chem.* any of numerous compounds which react with an acid to form a salt. *–v.* (**based**, **basing**) **6.** to form a base or foundation for. **7.** to establish, as a fact or conclusion (*on* or *upon*). **8.** to place or establish on a base or basis.

Don't confuse **base** with **bass**, which refers to the deepest range of musical notes, or to a man who sings in this range.

base² *adj.* **1.** morally low; mean-spirited; cowardly. **2.** debased or counterfeit.

baseball *n.* **1.** a game played with a wooden bat and a hard ball by 2 teams of 9 players. **2.** the ball used in this game. **–baseballer**, *n.*

baseline adj. a basic standard or level, usually regarded as a reference point for comparison.

basement n. a storey of a building partly or wholly underground.

bash v. to strike with a crushing or smashing blow.

bashful adj. uncomfortably shy; timid and easily embarrassed.

basic adj. **1.** of, relating to, or forming a base; fundamental. –n. **2.** something that is basic or essential. –**basically,** adv.

basil /'bæzəl/ n. a herb used in cookery.

basilica /bə'sɪlɪkə, -'zɪl-/ n. **1.** oblong building, especially a church with nave higher than its aisles. **2.** Roman Catholic church with special ceremonial rights.

basin n. **1.** a circular container of greater width than depth, with sloping sides, used chiefly for washing. **2.** a small circular container used chiefly for mixing, cooking, etc. **3.** a hollow or depression in the earth's surface.

basis /'beɪsəs/ n. (pl. **bases** /'beɪsiz/) **1.** a starting point or base. **2.** a groundwork or fundamental principle. **3.** the principal constituent.

bask v. to lie in or be exposed to a pleasant warmth.

basket n. a receptacle made of firm, flexible material, woven together.

basketball n. a ball game, the object of which is to throw the ball through an elevated basket.

bass¹ /beɪs/ Music –n. **1.** the range of musical notes which can be sung by a male singer with a deep voice. **2.** a man with a deep singing voice. –adj. **3.** deep sounding; having a range of notes of low pitch: a bass guitar.

Don't confuse this with **base**, which is the bottom of something. **Base** can also mean morally low. Note that there is another word **bass** (pronounced /bæs/). See **bass²**.

bass² /bæs/ n. (pl. **bass** or **basses**) an Aust. freshwater fish.

For information about the different plural forms, see the note at **fish**.

basset n. a long-bodied, short-legged dog resembling a dachshund but larger and heavier. Also, **basset hound**.

bassinet n. a basket in which a baby sleeps. Also, **bassinette**.

bassoon n. a double-reed woodwind instrument.

bastard /'bastəd/ n. **1.** an illegitimate child. **2.** Informal an unpleasant or despicable person or thing. **3.** Aust., NZ Informal any person.

Note that this word as in defs 2 and 3 may give offence. When **bastard** is used to address someone or to talk about them, it can indicate dislike and be offensive (as in def. 2), or it can be used in quite a fond manner (as in def. 3). What the speaker intends is usually clear from their tone of voice, what else has been said, etc. Note, however, that you should be careful about calling someone 'a bastard', even if you mean it affectionately, unless you know them very well.

baste /beɪst/ v. to moisten (meat, etc.) while cooking, with dripping, butter, etc.

bastion n. **1.** a fortified place. **2.** any person or object which supports or defends.

bat¹ n. **1. a.** the club used in cricket, baseball, etc., used to strike the ball. **b.** a racquet, especially one used in table tennis. **2.** Informal rate of motion. –v. (**batted, batting**) **3.** to strike or hit with or as with a bat or club.

bat² n. a small, nocturnal flying mammal.

bat³ v. (**batted, batting**) to wink or flutter (one's eyelids).

batch n. **1.** a quantity or a number taken together. **2.** the quantity of material prepared or required for, or produced by one operation.

bath n. **1.** a washing of the body in water or other liquid. **2.** (a vessel for containing) water or other liquid, etc., used for a bath. **3.** (pl.) a public swimming pool. –v. **4.** to put or wash in a bath.

Don't confuse def. 4 with **bathe**.

bathe /beɪð/ v. **1.** to immerse in water or other liquid for cleansing, refreshment, etc. **2.** to apply water or other liquid to, with a sponge, cloth, etc.

Don't confuse **bathe** with **bath**.

bathers pl. n. Aust. → **swimming costume.**

bathos /'beɪθɒs/ n. **1.** Lit. a comical drop from an elevated to a commonplace level. **2.** insincere emotion.

bathroom n. **1.** a room fitted with a bath or a shower (or both), and sometimes with a toilet and washbasin. **2.** a room fitted with a toilet.

batik /'batɪk, 'bætɪk/ n. (fabric with pattern made by) method of applying wax before dyeing.

baton /'bætn/ n. **1.** a staff or truncheon, especially as a mark of office or authority. **2.** Music the wand used by a conductor. **3.** (in relay racing) a metal or wooden tube, handed on by one relay runner to the next.

battalion /bə'tæljən/ n. Mil. a ground-force unit composed of 3 or more companies or similar units.

batten n. **1.** a light strip of wood used to fasten main members of a structure together. –v. **2.** to fasten (down) with battens or tarpaulins.

batter¹ v. **1.** to beat persistently or hard. **2.** to damage by beating or hard usage.

batter² n. a mixture of flour, milk or water, eggs, etc., beaten together.

battery n. (pl. **-ries**) **1.** Elect. chemical cells or groups of cells which produce or store electrical energy. **2.** a group of similar items or people used together: a battery of machine guns, experts. **3.** a

large number of cages in which chickens, etc., are reared for intensive productivity. **4.** Law unlawful and intentional interference with the person of another.

battle n. **1.** a hostile engagement between opposing forces. **2.** any extended or intense fight, struggle or contest. –v. **3.** to fight.

bauble /'bɔbl/ n. a cheap piece of ornament; trinket.

baulk /bɔk/ v. **1.** to stop, as at an obstacle. **2.** Sport to make an incomplete or misleading move, especially an illegal one.

bauxite /'bɔksaɪt/ n. a rock, the principal ore of aluminium.

bawdy adj. rollickingly vulgar; lewd.

bawl v. to cry loudly and vigorously.

bay¹ n. an inlet in the shore of a sea or lake.

bay² n. **1.** a space projecting outwards from the line of a wall, as to contain a window. **2.** the aisle between parallel rows of shelves as in a library.

bay³ n. a deep, prolonged bark, as of a hound or hounds in hunting.

bay⁴ n. a reddish-brown colour.

bayonet n. a stabbing or slashing instrument of steel, made to be attached to the muzzle of a rifle.

bazaar /bə'za/ n. a marketplace.

Don't confuse this with **bizarre**, which means very strange or unusual.

be v. **1.** a word connecting a subject either with a predicate or with adjectives, in statements, questions, and commands: You are late; Tomorrow is Thursday; Is he here?; Be sensible and take an umbrella. **2.** a word serving to form certain phrases, as in **a.** infinitive phrases: (I wanted) to be a dancer. **b.** participial phrases: (the art of) being agreeable. **3.** a word used as an auxiliary verb with a present participle of another verb, to form the continuous aspect: I am waiting. **4.** a word used as an auxiliary verb with a past participle, in passive forms of transitive verbs: The date was fixed. **5.** (a rather formal or literary use) to exist or have reality: *He is no more.* **6.** to happen or happen: *The wedding was last week.* **7.** (*used in the perfect and pluperfect*) to pay a visit; go: *I have been to Spain; Have you been to the shops today?* **8.** to be suitable for or characteristic of: *That dress is really you; Insulting his mother-in-law was him all over.*

The different forms of the verb **to be** are as follows:
Present tense: I **am**, you **are**, he / she / it **is**, we **are**, they **are**
Past tense: I **was**, you **were**, he / she / it **was**, we **were**, they **were**
Past participle: **been**
Present participle: **being**

beach n. **1.** that part of the sandy shore of the sea, or of a large river or lake, washed by the tide or waves. **2.** the seaside as a place of recreation. –v. **3.** to run or haul up (a ship or boat) on the beach.

Don't confuse **beach** with **beech**, which is a type of tree.

beacon n. a guiding or warning signal, such as a lighthouse, fire, etc.

bead n. **1.** a small ball of glass, pearl, wood, etc., with a hole through it, for stringing and use as an ornament or in a rosary. **2.** a drop of liquid.

beagle n. a small hound with short legs and drooping ears.

beak n. the horny bill of a bird.

beaker n. a large drinking vessel with a wide mouth.

beam n. **1.** a thick, long piece of timber, for structural use. **2.** the side of a vessel, or the direction at right angles to the keel, with reference to the wind, sea, etc. **3.** the widest point. **4.** the transverse bar of a balance from which the pans are suspended. **5.** a ray, or bundle of parallel rays, of light or other radiation. **6.** *Radio, Aeronautics* a signal transmitted to guide pilots through darkness, bad weather, etc.

–v. **7.** to emit beams, as of light. **8.** to look or smile radiantly.

bean n. **1.** the edible fruit or seed of various plants. **2.** any of various other bean-like seeds, as the coffee bean.

Don't confuse this with **been**, which is the past participle of the verb **be**, as in *Have you been well lately?*

beanie n. a small close-fitting knitted cap, often having a pompom or other decoration on top.

bean sprout n. the very young shoot of any of certain beans, used in Chinese and some other Asian cookery and as a salad vegetable. Also, **beansprout**, **bean shoot**.

bear[1] v. (**bore**, **borne** or **born**, **bearing**) **1.** to hold up. **2.** to carry. **3.** to give: *to bear witness.* **4.** to undergo. **5.** to be fit for or worthy of. **6.** to give birth (to); bring forth young. **7.** to produce by natural growth. **8.** to be patient (*with*). **9.** to press (*on*, *against*, etc.). **10.** to have an effect, reference, or bearing (*on*). **11.** to have relevance to. **12.** to tend in course or direction. –*phr.* **13. bear out**, to confirm; prove right. **14. bear up**, to hold, or remain firm, as under pressure.

Note that **born**, an old form of this verb, is now only used to mean 'brought into life', as in *She was born in Hobart.*
Don't confuse **bear** with **bare**, which describes something or someone without any covering.

bear[2] n. a large carnivorous or omnivorous mammal, with coarse, heavy fur, short limbs, and a very short tail.

beard n. the growth of hair on the face of an adult male, sometimes exclusive of the moustache.

bearing n. **1.** the manner in which one bears or carries oneself, including posture, gestures, etc. **2.** reference, relation, or relevance (*on*). **3.** *Machinery* a part in which a pivot, etc., turns or moves. **4.** (*oft. pl.*) direction or relative position.

beast n. 1. any animal except a human, but especially a large four-footed one. 2. a coarse, filthy, or rude person.

beastly adj. (-lier, -liest) 1. of or like a beast; bestial. 2. nasty; disagreeable.

beat (**beat, beaten** or **beat, beating**) 1. to strike repeatedly and usually violently, especially as a punishment; pound. 2. to whisk. 3. to flutter or flap. 4. to sound as (on) a drum. 5. to hammer (metal) thin; flatten (out). 6. to make (a path) by repeated treading. 7. Music to mark (time) by strokes, as with the hand or a metronome. 8. to overcome in a contest. 9. to be superior to. 10. to throb. 11. to radiate light or heat. –n. 12. a stroke or blow. 13. a throb. 14. a beaten path or habitual round. 15. the marking of the metrical divisions of music. –adj. 16. Informal exhausted.

Don't confuse **beat** with **beet**, which is a type of vegetable.

beatific /biə'tɪfɪk/ adj. 1. bestowing blessedness. 2. blissful.

beatify /bi'ætɪfaɪ/ v. (-fied, -fying) 1. to make blissfully happy. 2. Roman Catholic Church to declare (a deceased person) to be entitled to specific religious honour.

beaut Aust., NZ Informal –adj. 1. fine; good. –interj. Also, **you beaut!**. 2. (an exclamation of approval, delight, enthusiasm, etc.)

beauteous adj. beautiful.

beautician n. a person skilled in cosmetic treatment and beauty aids.

beautiful adj. 1. having or exhibiting beauty. 2. very pleasant.

Note that when you are describing someone's appearance, you would normally only use **beautiful** if you were talking about a female, or a baby of either sex. You could use **handsome** if you were describing a man, or **attractive** or **good-looking**, both of which can refer to either males or females.

beauty n. (pl. **-ties**) 1. that quality which excites an admiring pleasure, or delights the eye. 2. something or someone beautiful. 3. a particular advantage. –interj. 4. Aust., NZ (an exclamation of approval, delight, etc.) –**beautify**, v.

beaver n. an amphibious rodent which dams streams with branches, mud, etc.

because conj. 1. for the reason that. –adv. 2. by reason; on account (of).

beckon v. 1. to summon or direct by a gesture. 2. to lure; entice.

become v. (**-came, -come, -coming**) 1. to come into being; grow to be (as stated). 2. to be the fate (of). 3. to befit; suit.

becoming adj. 1. attractive. 2. suitable; proper.

bed n. 1. a piece of furniture upon which a person sleeps. 2. a piece of ground (in a garden) in which plants are grown. 3. a part forming a foundation or base.

bedlam n. a scene of wild uproar and confusion.

bedraggled adj. limp, wet and dirty.

bedridden adj. confined to bed.

bedroom n. a room set aside to sleep in.

bee¹ n. a four-winged insect which gathers pollen.

Note that the place where bees live is called a **beehive** or **hive**.

bee² n. a local gathering for work, contests, etc.

beech n. a type of tree growing in temperate regions.

Don't confuse this with **beach**, which is the sandy or pebbly land at the edge of a sea, lake or river.

beef n. 1. the edible flesh of a bull or cow. –v. 2. Informal to complain.

beefy adj. (-fier, -fiest) fleshy; brawny; solid; heavy.

been v. past participle of **be**.

Don't confuse this with **bean**, which is a type of vegetable.

beer *n.* an alcoholic beverage brewed and fermented from malted barley and flavoured with hops, etc.

beet *n.* any of various biennial plants including the red beet and the sugar beet.

Don't confuse this with **beat**, which means to hit over and over again or to defeat. It can also refer to a regular rhythm, such as your heart makes or that you hear in music.

beetle *n.* any insect with forewings modified as hard, horny structures, not vibrated in flight.

beetroot *n.* the edible root of the red beet.

befall *v.* (-**fell**, -**fallen**, -**falling**) to happen (to) or occur.

The more usual expression is **happen to**.

befit *v.* (-**fitted**, -**fitting**) to be fitting or appropriate for; be suited to.

before *adv.* **1.** in front; in advance. **2.** earlier or sooner. –*prep.* **3.** in front of; in advance of. **4.** previously to; earlier than. **5.** in preference to. **6.** in precedence of. **7.** in the presence or sight of. **8.** under the jurisdiction or consideration of. –*conj.* **9.** previously to the time when. **10.** rather than.

beforehand *adv.* in anticipation; ahead of time.

befriend *v.* to act as a friend to; aid.

befuddle *v.* **1.** to make stupidly drunk. **2.** to confuse, as with glib argument.

beg *v.* (**begged**, **begging**) **1.** to ask for in charity. **2.** to ask (for, or of) with humility or earnestness; or as a favour. **3.** to ask alms or charity; live by asking alms.

beget *v.* (-**got**, -**gotten** *or* -**got**, -**getting**) to procreate (used chiefly of the male parent).

beggar *n.* **1.** someone who begs alms, or lives by begging. **2.** a penniless person.

begin *v.* (**began**, **begun**, **beginning**) **1.** to enter upon an action; start. **2.** to come into existence; arise. **3.** to take the first step in; set about. **4.** to be the originator of. –**beginning**, *n.* –**beginner**, *n.*

begrudge *v.* to be discontented at seeing (a person) have (something).

beguile /bə'gail, bi-/ *v.* **1.** to influence by guile; mislead. **2.** to charm. –**beguiling**, *adj.* –**beguilingly**, *adv.*

behalf *n.* (preceded by *on*) the side or interest.

behave *v.* **1.** to conduct oneself or itself. **2.** Also, **behave oneself**. to act in a socially acceptable manner. –**behaviour**, **behavior**, *n.*

behead *v.* to cut off the head of; execute.

behest *n.* bidding; command: *It was done at the behest of the Queen.*

behind *prep.* **1.** at the back of. **2.** after. **3.** less advanced than; inferior to. **4.** on the farther side of. **5.** supporting; promoting. **6.** hidden by. –*adv.* **7.** at or towards the back. **8.** in arrears. –*n.* **9.** *Informal* the buttocks.

behold *v.* (-**held**, -**holding**) to observe; look at.

behove *v.* to be needful or proper for (now only in impersonal use).

beige /berʒ/ *n.*, *adj.* very light brown.

being *n.* **1.** (conscious) existence; life. **2.** substance or nature. **3.** a living thing.

belated *adj.* coming or being late: *a belated birthday card.*

Note that this word is never used to describe people, only to describe things or actions.

belch *v.* **1.** to eject wind spasmodically and noisily from the stomach through the mouth. **2.** to emit contents violently, as a gun, geyser, or volcano. **3.** to eject spasmodically or violently. –*n.* **4.** a belching.

beleaguer /bə'ligə/ *v.* **1.** to surround: *to beleaguer the city.* **2.** to beset with troubles. –**beleaguered**, *adj.*

belfry /ˈbelfri/ n. (pl. **-ries**) a tower for a bell, either attached to a church or other building or standing apart.

belie /bəˈlaɪ/ v. (**-lied**, **-lying**) 1. to misrepresent. 2. to show to be false.

belief n. 1. that which is believed. 2. acceptance of the truth or reality of a thing without absolute proof. 3. confidence; trust.

believe v. 1. to have confidence (*in*); rely through faith (*on*). 2. to accept a doctrine, principle, system, etc. (*in*). 3. to have belief in. 4. to think. **–believable**, adj. **–believer**, n.

belittle v. to make little or less important; disparage.

bell n. 1. a cup-shaped sounding instrument, usually of metal, rung by the strokes of a clapper suspended within it. 2. any instrument emitting a ringing signal, as a doorbell. 3. *Naut.* the half-hourly subdivisions of a watch of 4 hours. *–phr.* 4. **ring a bell**, to remind one; jog the memory.

bellbird n. a yellowish-green honeyeater with a tinkling, bell-like call.

bellicose adj. warlike; pugnacious.

belligerent /bəˈlɪdʒərənt/ adj. 1. warlike. 2. relating to war. *–n.* 3. a state or nation at war.

bellow v. 1. to make a hollow, loud cry, as a bull or cow. 2. to roar; bawl.

bellows n. an instrument which is pumped to produce a strong current of air.

Note that this word may be used as either a singular or a plural noun: *The bellows is over there by the fire*; *The bellows are over there by the fire.*

belly n. (pl. **-lies**) the front or underpart of a vertebrate body from the chest to the thighs, containing the stomach, etc.; abdomen.

belong v. 1. to have one's rightful place. 2. to be proper or due. *–phr.* 3. **belong to**, **a.** to be the property of. **b.** to be connected with as a member, etc.

belongings pl. n. possessions.

beloved /bəˈlʌvd, -ˈlʌvɪd, bɪ-/ adj. 1. greatly loved. *–n.* 2. someone who is greatly loved.

below adv. 1. in or to a lower place. 2. at a later point on a page or in writing. 3. in a lower rank or grade. *–prep.* 4. lower down than. 5. not worthy of.

belt n. 1. a band of leather, etc., worn around the waist to support clothing, for decoration, etc. 2. any encircling or transverse band or strip. 3. a flexible band connecting 2 or more wheels, etc., to transmit motion. *–v.* 4. to gird or furnish with a belt. 5. *Informal* to hit. 6. to sing very loudly and often raucously (*out*). 7. *Informal* to move quickly. *–phr.* 8. **belt up**, *Informal* to be quiet.

bemused adj. 1. confused; stupefied. 2. lost in thought.

bench n. 1. a long seat with or without a back for several people. 2. a seat for members in a house of parliament. 3. the strong work-table of a carpenter or other mechanic. *–phr.* 4. **the bench**, **a.** the position or office of a judge. **b.** the body of person sitting as judges.

benchmark n. a point of reference from which quality or excellence is measured.

bend v. (**bent**, **bending**) 1. to make or become curved, crooked, or bent. 2. to turn or incline in a particular direction. 3. to (force to) bow in submission or reverence. *–n.* 4. the act of bending. 5. the state of being bent. 6. a bent thing or part; curve.

beneath adv. 1. below; in a lower place, position, state, etc. *–prep.* 2. below; under. 3. unworthy of.

Beneath in the senses of defs 1 and 2 is slightly more formal or literary than underneath or below.

benediction n. (the act of uttering) a blessing.

benefactor n. 1. kindly helper. 2. someone who makes a bequest or endowment.

beneficial *adj.* conferring benefit; advantageous; helpful.

beneficiary *n.* someone who receives assistance, especially money left in a will.

benefit *n.* **1.** an act of kindness. **2.** anything that is for the good of a person or thing. **3.** a payment made by an insurance company, public agency, etc. *–v.* (**-fited**, **-fiting**) **4.** to do good to; be of service to. **5.** to gain advantage; make improvement.

You may see the forms of the verb spelt **benefitted** and **benefitting**, although this is not very common. Usually, verbs ending in *t* do not double the *t* if the last part of the word is not said with a strong stress.

benevolent /bə'nevələnt/ *adj.* **1.** desiring to do good for others. **2.** intended for benefits rather than profit.

benighted *adj.* intellectually or morally ignorant; unenlightened.

benign *adj.* **1.** of a kind disposition; kind. **2.** (of a tumour, etc.) not malignant; not causing death or serious harm to the body.

bent *adj.* **1.** curved; crooked. *–n.* **2.** direction taken; inclination; leaning. *–phr.* **3.** bent on (or upon), set on: *bent on having fun.*

bequeath *v.* to hand down or pass on to someone in one's will (personal property, especially money). *–***bequest**, *n.*

The more usual expression is **leave**.

berate *v.* to scold.

bereave *v.* (**-reaved** *or* **-reft**, **-reaving**) to make desolate through loss (*of*), especially by death.

bereft *adj.* suffering loss; deprived of possession.

beret /'berei, bə'rei/ *n.* a soft, round, peakless cap that fits closely.

berry *n.* (*pl.* **-ries**) any small, (usually) stoneless and juicy fruit, as the gooseberry, strawberry, etc.

Don't confuse this with **bury**, which is to put something in the ground and cover it with earth.

berserk /bə'zɜk/ *adj.* violently and destructively frenzied.

berth *n.* a shelf-like space, bunk, or whole room allotted to a traveller on a vessel or a train.

Don't confuse this with **birth**, which is the act of being born, as in *the birth of the baby.*

beryl /'berəl/ *n.* a mineral group which includes the emerald.

beseech *v.* (**-sought** *or* **-seeched**, **-seeching**) **1.** to implore urgently. **2.** to beg eagerly for.

beset *v.* (**-set**, **-setting**) to attack on all sides; assail; harass.

beside *prep.* **1.** by or at the side of; near. **2.** compared with.

Don't confuse this with **besides**.

besides *adv.* **1.** moreover. **2.** in addition. **3.** otherwise; else. *–prep.* **4.** over and above; in addition to. **5.** other than; except.

Don't confuse this with **beside**.

besiege *v.* **1.** to lay siege to. **2.** to ply, as with requests, etc.

besotted *adj.* very much in love; infatuated.

bespoke *adj.* made to order.

best *adj.* (*superlative of* **good**) **1.** of the highest quality or standing. **2.** most advantageous or suitable. **3.** favourite. *–adv.* (*superlative of* **well**) **4.** most excellently or suitably; with most advantage or success. **5.** in or to the highest degree; most fully. *–n.* **6.** the best thing, state, or part. **7.** best quality. *–v.* **8.** to defeat. **9.** to outdo.

Best is the *superlative* form of the adjective **good** and the adverb **well**. The *comparative* form of both **good** and **well** is **better**.

bestial *adj.* **1.** of or belonging to a beast. **2.** brutal; inhuman; irrational.

best man *n.* the chief attendant of a bridegroom.

bestow *v.* to present as a gift or reward; confer.

The more usual word is **give**. However, note that you **bestow** an award *on* someone for something they have done. You **give** an award *to* someone for something they have done.

bet *v.* (**bet** or **betted**, **betting**) **1.** to agree to pay a forfeit to another if one's opinion is proved wrong; wager. **2.** to lay a wager. **3.** to make a practice of betting. **4.** to predict a certain outcome: *I bet it rains on the weekend.* –*n.* **5.** a pledge to be forfeited in a wager.

betide *v.* Old-fashioned to happen; befall; come to.

betray *v.* **1.** to expose to an enemy by treachery. **2.** to be unfaithful in keeping or upholding. **3.** to disclose in violation of confidence. **4.** to show: *His face betrayed his emotions.* **5.** to deceive. –**betrayal**, *n.*

betrothed /bə'trouðd, bi-/ *adj.* **1.** engaged to be married. –*n.* **2.** an engaged person.

better *adj.* (*comparative* of **good**) **1.** of superior value, use, etc. **3.** larger. –*adv.* (*comparative* of **well**) **4.** in a superior way. **5.** to a superior degree. –*v.* **6.** to make better; improve. –*n.* **7.** that which is superior. **8.** (*usu. pl.*) one's superior(s) in wisdom, wealth, etc. –*phr.* **9. better off**, in better circumstances. **10. had better**, would be wiser, safer, etc., to.

Better is the *comparative* form of the adjective **good** and the adverb **well**. The *superlative* form of both **good** and **well** is **best**. Note that, because **better** is already the comparative, you should not say *more better.*

bettong *n.* any of various small nocturnal marsupials which resemble a small wallaby, with brown-grey fur above and white below.

between *prep.* **1.** in the space separating (2 or more points, objects, etc.). **2.** intermediate to, in time, quantity, or degree: *between 12 and 1 o'clock, between pink and red.* **3.** distinguishing one thing from another. –*adv.* **4.** in the intervening space or time; in an intermediate position or relation.

Some people think that **between** should be used only with two things or people (*between the two of us*) and that you should use **among** for more than two (*among the three of us*). But not many people follow this rule strictly when they use **between**, and it actually sounds more natural to say *Between us all we'll find a solution* rather than *Among us all we'll find a solution.* However, you should not use **among** for only two.
Note that *between you and I* is not considered correct. You should say *between you and me.*

bevel *n.* a sloping edge or surface.

beverage *n.* a drink of any kind.

bevy /'bevi/ *n.* (*pl.* **-vies**) a flock.

beware *v.* (usu. fol. by *of* or a clause) to be wary or careful.

Note that this word is now only used as a command, as in *Beware of the dog!*, following the word **to**, as in *Swimmers are advised to beware of the slippery rocks*, or following a modal verb, as in *Tourists should beware of dangerous snakes in the area.*

bewilder *v.* to confuse or puzzle completely; perplex.

bewitch *v.* to affect by witchcraft or magic.

beyond *prep.* **1.** on or to the farther side of. **2.** farther on than. **3.** past. **4.** more than; over and above. –*adv.* **5.** farther on or away: *as far as the house and beyond.*

biannual *adj.* occurring twice a year.

Compare this with **biennial**, which refers to something happening every two years.

bias *n.* **1.** an oblique or diagonal line of direction, especially across a woven fabric. **2.** a particular tendency often indicating prejudice. –*v.* (**biased, biasing**) **3.** to influence, usually unfairly; prejudice.

biased *adj.* having or showing an opinion based on personal prejudice.

bib *n.* a protective cloth worn under the chin by a child while eating.

bible *n.* any book accepted as an authority or essential text on a subject: *the home renovator's bible.* –**biblical,** *adj.*

This general use of the word comes from **the Bible**, the sacred writings of the Jewish and Christian religions.

bibliography *n.* (*pl.* **-phies**) **1.** a list of literature on a particular subject. **2.** a list of source materials used in the preparation of a work.

bicameral *adj.* having 2 branches, chambers, or houses, as a legislative body. Compare **unicameral**.

bicentenary *n.* a 200th anniversary. –**bicentennial,** *adj.*

biceps /ˈbaɪsɛps/ *n.* the muscle on the front of the upper arm.

Note that the singular and plural forms of this word are the same. Occasionally the form **bicep** is used, either as the singular or in adjectival use: *bicep machine.*

bicker *v.* to engage in petulant argument; wrangle.

bicycle *n.* a vehicle with 2 wheels driven by pedals and having a saddle-like seat for the rider. Also, **bike.**

bid *v.* (**bade** /bæd/ *or* **bad** /bæd/ *or* **bidden** *or* **bid, bidding**) **1.** to command; direct. **2.** to say as a greeting or benediction. **3.** to offer, as a price at an auction or to secure a contract. –*n.* **4.** an offer, as at an auction. **5.** an attempt to attain some goal.

biddy *n.* (*pl.* **-dies**) *Informal* an old woman.

bide *phr.* (**bided, biding**) **bide one's time,** to wait for a favourable opportunity.

bidet /ˈbiːdeɪ/ *n.* a small low bath for washing the genitals.

biennial /baɪˈɛniəl/ *adj.* happening every 2 years.

Compare this with **biannual**, which refers to something taking place twice a year.

bier /bɪə/ *n.* a stand on which a corpse, or the coffin, is laid before burial.

bifocal *adj.* (of spectacle lenses) having 2 portions, one for near and the other for far vision.

big *adj.* (**bigger, biggest**) **1.** large in size, amount, etc. **2.** large in compass or conception; magnanimous.

bigamy *n.* the crime of marrying while still legally married to another. –**bigamist,** *n.* –**bigamous,** *adj.*

Compare this with **monogamy** and **polygamy.**

bight *n.* **1.** the loop or bent part of a rope. **2.** a bend or curve in the shore of a sea or a river.

Don't confuse **bight** with **bite** or **byte.** A **bite** is a wound made with the teeth, or a mouthful of food. A **byte** is a unit of information stored by a computer.

bigot /ˈbɪgət/ *n.* a person convinced of the rightness of a particular creed, culture, etc., and intolerant of all others.

This word is used in a disapproving way.

bike *n.* a bicycle, tricycle, or motorcycle.

bikini *n.* a very brief, two-piece swimming costume.

bilateral *adj.* relating to or involving 2 sides or parties.

bilby *n.* (*pl.* **-bies**) a small bandicoot with big rabbit-like ears

bile *n.* **1.** a bitter yellow or greenish liquid secreted by the liver and aiding in digestion of fats; gall. **2.** ill nature; peevishness.

bilge /bɪldʒ/ n. **1.** the lowest portion of a ship's interior. **2.** Also, **bilge water**. foul water that collects there.

bilingual adj. able to speak 2 languages.

bilious adj. **1.** relating to bile or to an excess secretion of bile. **2.** peevish; cross. **3.** sick; nauseated. **4.** nauseating.

bill¹ n. **1.** an account of money owed for goods or services. **2.** a draft of a proposed statute presented to a legislature, but not yet made law. **3.** a printed public notice or advertisement. **4.** a bill of exchange. **5.** program; entertainment. –v. **6.** to announce by bill or public notice. **7.** to schedule as part of a program. **8.** to render an account of money owed.

bill² n. the horny sheath covering the jaws of a bird.

billabong n. Aust. a waterhole, originally part of a river, formed when the channel connecting to it the river dries up.

billboard n. → **hoarding** (def. 2).

billet n. **1.** lodging for a soldier, especially in private or non-military buildings. **2.** private, usually unpaid, temporary lodgings arranged for members of a group or team.

billiards n. a game played on a rectangular table, with balls driven by means of cues.

billion n. (pl. **-lions**, as after a numeral, **-lion**) **1.** a thousand times a million, or 10^9. **2.** (becoming obsolete) a million times a million, or 10^{12}. –adj. **3.** amounting to one billion in number. –**billionth**, adj., n.

Note that def. 2 is becoming rare throughout the world, with people everywhere tending to use **billion** in the sense of 'a thousand times a million'. However, it is usually safer to write the number out in figures or as a power of ten.

Numbers used before a noun are sometimes called **determiners**.

billionaire n. the owner of a billion dollars, pounds, euros, etc.

billow n. **1.** a great wave or surge of the sea. –v. **2.** to rise or roll in or like billows.

billy n. (pl. **-lies**) Aust., NZ a cylindrical container for liquids, usually having a close-fitting lid.

billycart n. Aust., NZ a small four-wheeled cart.

billy goat n. a male goat.

bin n. **1.** a box or enclosed space used for storing grain, wool, coal, rubbish, etc. **2.** a winemaker's stand for storing wine in bottles.

binary adj. **1.** consisting of, indicating, or involving 2. **2.** using, involving, or expressed in binary code. **3.** Maths having 2 variables.

binary code n. any means of representing information by a sequence of the digits 1 and 0.

bind v. (**bound**, **binding**) **1.** to make fast with a band or bond. **2.** to swathe or bandage (up). **3.** to unite by any legal or moral tie. **4.** to hold to a particular state, place, employment, etc. **5.** (usu. passive) to place under obligation or compulsion. **6.** to secure within a cover, as a book. **7.** to become compact or solid; cohere. **8.** to have power to oblige. –n. **9.** something that binds, especially a situation with few or no choices available.

Also look up **bound**¹.

bindi-eye n. any of a number of plants with small, burr-like fruits. Also, **bindi**, **bindy-eye**, **bindy**.

binge n. Informal a spree; a period of excessive indulgence, as in eating or drinking.

bingo n. a gambling game in which players put markers on a card of numbered squares according to the numbers drawn and announced by a caller.

binocular adj. **1.** involving (the use of) 2 eyes. –n. **2.** (pl.) a double telescope held by both eyes at once; field-glasses.

binomial n. Maths an expression which is a sum or difference of 2 terms, as $3x + 2y$ and $x^2 - 4x$.

bio- a word element meaning 'life', 'living things'.

biodegradable *adj.* capable of being decomposed.

biodiesel *n.* a biodegradable fuel, produced from field crop oils, especially from recycled cooking oil.

biodiversity *n.* variety in the types of organisms living within an area. **–biodiverse**, *adj.*

biodynamic *adj.* of or relating to agricultural or horticultural techniques and management which aim to improve the soil and vegetation without chemical fertilisers and in a way that is environmentally sound and sustainable.

bioethanol *n.* ethanol produced from the starch or sugar in various crops, such as corn, for use as a biofuel.

biofuel *n.* a fuel derived from renewable sources such as biological matter.

biography *n.* (*pl.* **-phies**) an account of a person's life written by someone else. **–biographer**, *n.* **–biographical**, *adj.*

Compare this with **autobiography**.

biohazard *n.* a biological agent considered likely to cause human disease or environmental contamination. **–biohazardous**, *adj.*

biology *n.* the science of life or living matter in all its forms and phenomena. **–biologist**, *n.* **–biological**, *adj.*

biomarker *n. Med.* a molecule which, if detected, can provide early indication of the onset and status a disease.

biomass *n.* organic matter used as a source of energy.

biome *n.* a large community of plants and animals adapted to a particular climate or environment, as coral reef, tropical rainforest, etc.

bionic /baɪ'nɪk/ *adj.* of or relating to body parts or functions replaced or improved by electronic equipment.

biopsy *n.* (*pl.* **-sies**) the excision and diagnostic study of a piece of tissue from a living body.

bioremediation *n.* a process that uses microorganisms, enzymes, fungi, green plants, etc., to decontaminate the environment.

biorhythms *pl. n.* the 3 supposed cycles of human energy, the physiological, emotional, and intellectual.

biosecurity *n.* **1.** security measures against the transmission of disease to the plants or animals of a particular region. **2.** security measures taken against bioterrorism.

biotechnology *n.* the use of micro-organisms to produce desirable products (as drugs) and services (as waste recycling). **–biotechnological**, *adj.* **–biotechnologist**, *n.*

bioterrorism *n.* terrorism involving the use of biological agents such as bacteria, viruses, etc., that affect humans, domestic animals or food crops. **–bioterrorist**, *n.*

biotic *adj.* relating to life, especially to the animal and plant life of a region or period. Also, **biotical**.

bioweapon *n.* a weapon which uses a living organism or a toxin produced by it to cause the death of humans or the destruction of crops.

bipartite *adj.* being in 2 corresponding parts.

bipolar disorder *n.* a mental disorder marked by alternating periods of excitation and depression; manic depression. Also, **bipolar affective disorder**, **bipolar mood disorder**.

birch *n.* a tree or shrub with a smooth bark and close-grained wood.

bird *n.* **1.** any of the class of warm-blooded, feathered vertebrates with wings by means of which most species fly. **2.** *Informal* a woman.

bird flu *n.* → **avian influenza**.

birdie n. Golf a score of one stroke under par on a hole.

bird of prey n. any flesh-eating bird such as the eagle, hawk, vulture, owl, etc., usually with a strong beak and claws for catching, killing or eating animals or other birds.

biro n. (from trademark) a type of pen whose point is a very small ball which spreads a thin film of ink, stored in an inner tube, onto the writing surface.

birth n. 1. the fact of being born. 2. the act of bearing or bringing forth. 3. lineage; extraction. 4. supposedly natural heritage. 5. any coming into existence; origin.

Don't confuse this with **berth**, which is a place to sleep on a boat or train or a place where a ship can tie up.

birthday n. (the anniversary of) the day of one's birth, or the origin of something.

birthmark n. a congenital mark on the body.

birthplace n. place of birth or origin.

birthright n. any right or privilege to which a person is entitled by birth.

biscuit n. a mixture of flour, liquid, shortening, etc., baked in small pieces.

bisect v. to cut or divide into 2 parts.

bisexual adj. 1. of both sexes. –n. 2. a person sexually attracted to both sexes.

bishop n. 1. a member of the clergy in charge of a diocese. 2. a chess piece.

bison n. (pl. **bison**) a large Nth American bovine ruminant.

bistro n. (pl. **-tros**) 1. a wine bar. 2. a small casual restaurant.

bit n. 1. a small piece or quantity of anything. 2. share or part of a duty, task, etc.

bit² n. 1. the metal mouthpiece of a bridle attached to the reins. 2. anything that curbs or restrains. 3. the cutting or penetrating part of various tools.

bit³ n. a single, basic unit of information stored by a computer, having one of only two possible values, 0 or 1.

bit⁴ v. past tense of **bite**.

bitch n. 1. a female dog. 2. Informal a disagreeable or malicious woman. 3. Informal a complaint. 4. Informal something which causes difficulties or dissatisfaction. –**bitchy**, adj.

Note that, for def. 1, the male animal is called a **dog**.
The use of this word as in def. 2 may offend people. If you call someone 'a bitch', you are intending to insult them.

bite v. (**bit**, **bitten** or **bit**, **biting**) 1. to cut into or wound, or cut (off, out, etc.) with the teeth. 2. to press the teeth (into, on, etc.); snap. 3. to sting, as an insect. 4. to cheat; deceive. 5. (of fish) to take the bait. 6. to accept a deceptive offer or suggestion. –n. 7. the act of biting. 8. a wound made by biting. 9. pungency; sharpness.

Don't confuse this with **bight** or **byte**. A **bight** is the looped part of a rope, or a curve in a shore forming a large bay. A **byte** is a unit of information stored by a computer.

bitmap n. a computer graphics image consisting of rows and columns of dots stored as bits. –**bitmapped**, adj. –**bit-mapping**, n.

bitter adj. 1. having a harsh, disagreeable taste. 2. hard to bear; grievous 3. characterised by intense animosity.

bittersweet adj. 1. both bitter and sweet to the taste. 2. both pleasant and painful.

bitumen /ˈbɪtʃəmən/ n. any of various natural substances, as asphalt, etc., used for sealing roads.

bivalve n. a mollusc having 2 shells hinged together.

bivouac /ˈbɪvuːæk/ n. a temporary camp made out in the open.

bizarre /bəˈzaː/ adj. strange or unusual in appearance, style, or general character; odd

Don't confuse **bizarre** with **bazaar**, which is a type of market.

blab v. (**blabbed, blabbing**) to reveal indiscreetly and thoughtlessly.

black adj. **1.** without brightness or colour; absorbing all or nearly all the rays emitted by a light source. **2.** relating to an ethnic group characterised by dark skin pigmentation. **3.** soiled with dirt. **4.** gloomy; dismal. **5.** indicating censure, disgrace, etc. **6.** illicit. **7.** banned by a trade union. **8.** a colour without hue, opposite to white. **9.** (*sometimes upper case*) a person belonging to an ethnic group characterised by dark skin pigmentation. –v. **10.** to make or become black. **11.** (of a trade union) to declare (a factory, etc.) black. –*phr.* **12. black out**, to lose consciousness. **13. in the black**, financially solvent.

Def. 9 is often written with a capital letter. The term **Black** was once considered an offensive way to refer to people with dark skin. However, many people of African or Indigenous Australian origin now consider the term as one to be used with pride and dignity.

blackball v. **1.** to ostracise. **2.** to vote against.

blackberry n. (*pl.* **-ries**) a black or very dark purple fruit.

blackbird n. a European songbird.

blackboard n. a smooth dark board for writing or drawing on with chalk.

blackcurrant n. a small, black edible fruit.

black eye n. bruising round the eye.

blackguard /ˈblæɡad/ n. a coarse, despicable person; a scoundrel.

blackhead n. a small black-tipped pimple, especially on the face.

black hole n. a region postulated as arising from the collapse of a star under its own gravitational forces and from which no radiation or matter can escape.

black ice n. a thin, barely visible coating of newly formed ice, as on a road, etc.

blackjack n. **1.** black flag of a pirate ship. **2.** → **pontoon²**.

blackleg n. **1.** → **scab** (def. 2). **2.** a swindler especially in racing or gambling.

blacklist n. **1.** a list of persons under suspicion, disfavour, censure, etc., or a list of fraudulent or unreliable customers or firms. –v. **2.** to put on a blacklist. –**blacklisted**, adj.

black magic n. magic used for evil purposes.

blackmail n. **1.** act of demanding payment usually by threats of damaging revelations. **2.** the payment itself. –v. **3.** to demand such payment from.

black market n. an illegal market violating price controls, rationing, etc.

blackout n. **1.** the extinguishing or covering of all visible lights in a city, etc., as a wartime protection. **2.** the loss of lighting as in a power failure. **3.** temporary loss of consciousness or vision.

black sheep n. a person regarded as a disappointment or failure in comparison to the other members of their family or group.

blacksmith n. someone who works in or with iron or, in the modern era, steel.

black spot n. any of various fungal infections causing black spots on plant foliage.

blackspot n. any dangerous or difficult place where accidents frequently occur, esp. on a road.

bladder n. **1.** *Anat., Zool.* a membranous and muscular sac for storage and expulsion of urine. **2.** the inflatable inner bag of a football, or the like.

blade n. **1.** the flat cutting part of a sword, knife, etc. **2.** a sword. **3.** the leaf of a plant, especially of a grass or cereal. **4.** a thin, flat part of something, as of a bone, an oar, etc. **5.** a dashing or rakish young fellow.

blame v. (**blamed, blaming**) **1.** to lay the responsibility of (a fault, error, etc.) (*on*) (a person): *I blame the mistakes on him; I blame you for the delay.* –n. **2.** imputation of fault; censure. **3.** responsibility for a fault, error, etc. –*phr.* **4. to blame**, responsible for a fault or error; blamable; culpable.

blanch v. **1.** to make or become white; turn pale. **2.** to dip briefly in boiling water.

blancmange /blə'mɒnʒ/ n. a sweet dessert made of thickened and flavoured milk.

bland adj. **1.** (of a person's manner) suave; deliberately agreeable but often without real feeling. **2.** soothing or balmy, as air. **3.** mild, as food or medicines.

blandish v. to treat flatteringly; coax; cajole. **–blandishment,** n.

blank adj. **1.** (of paper, etc.) free from marks, writing or printing. **2.** not filled in. **3.** unrelieved by ornament or opening. **4.** lacking some usual or completing feature. **5.** complete or utter. –n. **6.** a void; emptiness. **7.** a space left (to be filled in) in written or printed matter. **8.** Machinery a piece of metal prepared to be stamped or cut into a finished object, such as a coin or key.

blanket n. **1.** a large piece of soft fabric, used especially as a bed covering. **2.** any heavy concealing layer or covering. –adj. **3.** covering a group or class of things, conditions, etc.

blare v. to emit a loud raucous sound.

blasé /blɑː'zeɪ, 'blɑːzeɪ/ adj. bored by pleasures of life.

blaspheme /blæs'fim/ v. **1.** to speak irreverently of (God or sacred things). **2.** to utter irreverent words. **–blasphemy,** n. **–blasphemous,** adj.

blast n. **1.** a sudden gust of wind. **2.** the blowing of a trumpet, whistle, etc. **3.** a forcible stream of air from the mouth, from bellows, or the like. **4.** explosion. **5.** severe criticism. –v. **6.** to blow (a trumpet, etc.). **7.** to tear (rock, etc.) to pieces with an explosive. **8.** to criticise (someone) abusively. –interj. **9.** an exclamation of anger or irritation.

blast furnace n. a furnace using a forced blast to produce molten iron.

blatant adj. (of actions, etc.) flagrantly obvious or undisguised.

blaze[1] n. **1.** a bright flame or fire. **2.** a sudden, intense outburst, as of fire, passion, fury. –v. (**blazed**, **blazing**) **3.** to burn brightly.

blaze[2] n. **1.** a spot or mark made on a tree as an indicator. **2.** a white spot on the face of a horse, cow, etc.

blazer n. a jacket.

bleach v. **1.** to make white or pale. –n. **2.** a bleaching agent.

bleak adj. **1.** bare, desolate. **2.** cold and piercing.

bleary adj. (**-rier, -riest**) (of the eyes) dim and watery.

bleat v. **1.** to cry as a sheep, goat, or calf. **2.** to complain.

bleed v. (**bled, bleeding**) **1.** to lose blood. **2.** to cause to lose blood, especially surgically. **3.** to exude sap, juice, etc. **4.** Informal to extort money from.

blemish v. **1.** to mar the beauty or perfection of. –n. **2.** a defect; a disfigurement.

blend v. **1.** to mix smoothly and inseparably together. **2.** to mix (various sorts or grades). –n. **3.** a mixture or kind produced by blending.

bless v. **1.** to consecrate by a religious rite; pronounce holy. **2.** to request the bestowal of divine favour on. **3.** to bestow good of any kind upon. **–blessing,** n.

blight n. **1.** a destructive plant disease. **2.** any cause of destruction or frustration. –v. **3.** to destroy; frustrate.

For def. 3, the more usual word is **ruin**.

blind adj. **1.** lacking the sense of sight. **2.** unwilling or unable to understand. **3.** having no outlets: a blind alley. **4.** made without knowledge in advance. –v. **5.** to make blind. –n. **6.** something that obstructs vision or keeps out light. **7.** a shade for a window. –adv. **8.** without being able to see one's way. **9.** without prior consideration.

blindfold v. **1.** to cover the eyes of. –n. **2.** a cover over the eyes.

blindsided adj. caught off guard.

bling n. Informal showy jewellery, especially when worn in large quantity, as by American rappers. Also, **bling-bling**.

blink v. **1.** to wink, especially rapidly and repeatedly. –n. **2.** a glance or glimpse. –phr. **3. on the blink**, Informal not working properly.

blinker n. **1.** a flashing indicator light on a car. **2.** either of 2 flaps on a bridle, to prevent a horse from seeing sideways.

bliss n. **1.** blitheness; gladness. **2.** supreme happiness.

blister n. **1.** a watery swelling on the skin as from a burn or other injury. **2.** any similar swelling, as an air bubble in a casting or a paint blister. –v. **3.** to rise in blisters; become blistered.

blithe /blaɪð/ adj. joyous, merry, or happy in disposition; glad.

blitz n. **1.** war waged by surprise, swiftly and violently. **2.** any swift, vigorous attack.

blizzard n. a violent windstorm with dry, driving snow and intense cold.

bloat v. **1.** to make or become distended, as with air, water, etc.; cause to swell. **2.** to puff up.

bloated adj. swollen: bloated features.

bloc n. a group of states or territories united by some common factor.

block n. **1.** a solid mass of wood, stone, etc. **2.** a piece of wood prepared for wood engraving. **3.** a letter-press printing plate. **4. a.** a device consisting of pulleys mounted in a casing or shell, to which a hook is attached, used for transmitting power, etc. **b.** the casing holding the pulley. **5.** a blocking or obstructing, or obstructed state or condition. **6.** Also, NZ, **section**. Aust. a section of land, often in a suburb, for building a house on, etc.: a block of land; a vacant block. **7.** one large building, divided into offices, apartments, etc.: an office block; a block of flats. **8.** a portion of a city, etc., enclosed by (usually 4) streets. **9.** a writing or sketching pad. –v. **10.** to fit with blocks; mount on a block. **11.** to sketch or outline roughly (out or in). **12.** to obstruct (a space, progress, etc.); check or hinder (a person, etc.).

blockade n. any obstruction of passage or progress.

blockage n. an obstruction.

blockbuster n. anything large and spectacular.

blockout n. Aust. (from trademark) → **sunscreen** (def. 1).

blog n. **1.** a record of items of interest found on the internet, edited and published as a website with comments and links. **2.** a personal diary published on the internet. –v. (**blogged**, **blogging**) **3.** to post entries on a blog. –**blogger**, n.

bloke n. Informal man; fellow; guy.

blond adj. **1.** (of a person or a people) having light-coloured hair and skin. **2.** light-coloured. –n. **3.** a blond person.

Note that you will sometimes see the spelling **blonde** used to refer to fair-headed women and girls.

blood n. **1.** the fluid that circulates in the arteries and veins. **2.** physical and cultural extraction. **3.** descent from a common ancestor. –phr. **4. in cold blood**, calmly, coolly, and deliberately.

bloodbath n. a massacre.

bloodhound n. a large, powerful dog used for tracking game, human fugitives, etc.

blood-poisoning n. → **septicaemia**.

bloodshed n. destruction of life; slaughter.

bloodshot adj. (of the eyes) red from dilated blood vessels.

bloodstream n. the blood flowing through a circulatory system.

blood sugar n. glucose in the blood. Also, **blood glucose**.

bloodthirsty *adj.* eager to shed blood; murderous.

bloody *adj.* (**-dier**, **-diest**) **1.** stained with blood. **2.** attended with bloodshed. **3.** *Informal* an intensifier: *bloody idiot.* –*v.* (**-died**, **-dying**) **4.** to stain with blood. –*adv.* **5.** *Informal* very; extremely: *bloody good; bloody awful.*

Note that the use of this word as in defs 3 and 5 might offend people.

bloom *n.* **1.** the flower of a plant. **2.** a flourishing, healthy condition. **3.** a whitish, powdery surface coating. –*v.* **4.** to produce blossoms. **5.** to flourish.

bloomers *n.* loose trousers gathered at the knee, formerly worn by women.

blossom *n.* **1.** *Bot.* the flower of a plant, especially of one producing an edible fruit. –*v.* **2.** to flourish; develop: *Her talents blossomed with a new teacher.*

blot *n.* **1.** a spot or stain, especially of ink on paper. –*v.* (**blotted**, **blotting**) **2.** to spot or stain. **3.** to make indistinguishable (*out*). **4.** to dry with absorbent material. **5.** (of ink, etc.) to spread in a stain. **6.** to become blotted or stained.

blotch *n.* a large irregular spot or blot.

blouse /blaʊz/ *n.* **1.** a loosely fitting bodice or shirt usually held in at the waist. –*v.* **2.** to hang loose and full.

blow¹ *n.* **1.** a sudden stroke with hand, fist, or weapon. **2.** a sudden shock, or a calamity.

blow² *v.* (**blew**, **blown**, **blowing**) **1.** (of the wind or air) to be in motion. **2.** to emit a current of air, as with the mouth, etc. **3.** to (cause to) give out sound, as of a trumpet, whistle, etc. **4.** (of a fuse, tyre, etc.) to burn (*out*) or perish. **5.** to extinguish or be extinguished, as by the wind or a puff of air (*out*). **6.** to drive by means of a current of air. **7.** to waste; squander. –*phr.* **8. blow up**, **a.** to develop, especially to a crisis. **b.** to explode. **c.** *Photography* to reproduce by enlargement. **d.** *Informal* to lose one's temper.

blowfly *n.* (*pl.* **-flies**) a fly which deposits its eggs or larvae on carcasses or meat, etc.

blowout *n.* a rupture of a tyre.

blowtorch *n.* a portable apparatus which gives an extremely hot flame.

blow-up *n.* **1.** an explosion. **2.** a violent outburst of temper. **3.** *Photography* an enlargement.

blubber *n.* **1.** the fat of whales and other cetaceans, from which oil is made. –*v.* **2.** to weep, usually noisily.

bludge *Aust., NZ Informal* –*v.* (**bludged**, **bludging**) **1.** to evade responsibilities. **2.** to cadge. –*n.* **3.** a job which entails next to no work. –*phr.* **4. bludge on**, to impose on (others). –**bludger**, *n.*

bludgeon *n.* **1.** a short, heavy club. –*v.* **2.** to strike with a bludgeon. **3.** to force (someone) into something.

blue *n.* **1.** the pure hue of clear sky. **2.** *Aust., NZ Informal* a fight. **3.** *Aust., NZ Informal* a mistake. **4.** *Aust., NZ Informal* (a nickname for a red-headed person). –*adj.* (**bluer**, **bluest**) **5.** of the colour blue. **6.** *Informal* depressed in spirits. **7.** *Informal* obscene. –*phr.* **8. true blue**, loyal; genuine.

blueberry *n.* (*pl.* **-ries**) a small bluish berry.

bluebottle *n.* a small sea animal found in warm seas with a deep blue body from which trail stinging tentacles.

blue-collar *adj.* relating to factory or production line workers, etc.

This term comes from the blue shirt traditionally worn as part of a uniform by people in such positions. Compare this with **white-collar**, which refers to workers in professional or business positions.

blueprint *n.* a photographic print, white on a blue ground, especially of building plans, etc.

blue-ribbon *adj.* **1.** (of an electorate) sure to be held by a particular party or candidate. **2.** of or relating to a prize-winner.

blues *pl. n.* **1.** despondency; melancholy. **2.** a melancholy style of music, of African American origin, usually in slow tempo.

blue-tongue *n.* any of several large, harmless, stout-bodied Aust. skinks which display their broad blue tongues when disturbed. Also, **blue-tongue lizard**.

bluetooth *adj.* of or relating to a wireless technology that provides connectivity between mobile phones, mobile computers, portable handheld devices and the internet.

bluff[1] *adj.* **1.** somewhat abrupt and unconventional in manner. −*n.* **2.** a cliff or hill with a broad, steep face.

bluff[2] *v.* to mislead by presenting a bold front.

blunder *n.* **1.** a stupid mistake. −*v.* **2.** to move or act blindly, stupidly, or without direction.

blunt *adj.* **1.** having a thick or dull edge or tip; rounded. **2.** abrupt in address or manner; plain-spoken.

blur *v.* (**blurred, blurring**) **1.** to obscure by making confused in form or outline. **2.** to make or become indistinct. −*n.* **3.** a blurred condition; indistinctness.

blurb *n.* an announcement or advertisement, usually laudatory, especially on the jacket flap or back of a book.

blurt *v.* to utter suddenly or inadvertently (*out*).

blush *v.* **1.** to redden as from embarrassment, shame, or modesty. −*n.* **2.** a rosy or pinkish tinge.

bluster *v.* **1.** to roar and be tumultuous, as wind. −*n.* **2.** noisy, empty menaces or protests; inflated talk.

boa *n.* **1.** any of various non-venomous snakes which coil around and crush their prey. **2.** a long, snake-shaped wrap of silk, feathers, or other material.

boar *n.* an uncastrated male pig.

Don't confuse this with **boor** or **bore**. A **boor** is a rude person, and a **bore** is a hole made by drilling, or a dull person.

board *n.* **1.** a long, narrow, thin piece of sawn timber. **2.** daily meals, especially as provided for pay: *bed and board*. **3.** an official body of persons who direct a business, etc. **4.** the border or edge of anything, as in *seaboard*. **5.** to cover or close with boards (*up* or *in*). **6.** to go on board of or enter (a ship, train, etc.). **7.** to be supplied with food and lodging at a fixed price. −*phr.* **8. on board**, on or in a ship, aeroplane, etc.

Don't confuse this with **bored**, which describes someone who is tired of something.

boarder *n.* **1.** someone who pays for meals and a room to sleep in. **2.** a pupil who resides at a boarding school during term.

Don't confuse this with **border**, which is the edge of something.

board shorts *pl. n.* shorts with an extended leg, often made of quick-drying fabric, originally designed to protect surfers against waxed surfboards.

boast *v.* **1.** to speak exaggeratedly, especially about oneself. **2.** to speak with pride (*of*). **3.** to be proud in the possession of.

boat *n.* a vessel for transport by water.

Note that some people do not think **boat** should be used to refer to a ship. They say that boats are small and ships are big.

boater *n.* a straw hat with a flat hard brim.

boatswain /ˈbəʊsən/ *n.* officer on a ship in charge of deck equipment and crew. Also, **bosun**.

bob *n.* **1.** a short jerky motion up and down. **2.** a quick curtsy. −*v.* (**bobbed, bobbing**) **3.** to move up and down with a bouncing motion.

bobbin *n.* a reel or spool upon which yarn or thread is wound.

bobby pin *n.* tightly closing metal pin for holding the hair.

bobsleigh *n.* a racing sledge with two sets of runners, one behind the other.

bodice *n.* the fitted upper part of a woman's dress.

body *n.* (*pl.* **-dies**) **1.** the physical structure of an animal. **2.** a corpse; carcass. **3.** the main mass of a thing. **4.** a number of things or people. **5.** consistency or density; substance. **6.** matter or physical substance (as opposed to *spirit* or *soul*).

bodyguard *n.* a personal guard.

body mass index *n.* a measure of body mass that is calculated as weight divided by height squared, used to define nutritional status in relation to health risk. *Abbrev.*: BMI

bog[1] *n.* **1.** wet, spongy ground, full of decayed vegetable matter. *–v.* (**bogged**, **bogging**) **2.** to sink in or as in a bog (*down*). *–***boggy**, *adj.*

bog[2] *n. Informal* a toilet.

bogan *n. Aust. Informal* (*mildly derog.*) a person, generally from an outer suburb of a city or town and from a lower socio-economic background, viewed as uncultured.

bogey[1] /ˈboʊɡi/ *Golf* *–n.* (*pl.* **-geys**) **1.** a score of one over par. *–v.* (**-geyed**, **-geying**) **2.** to score a bogey.

bogey[2] *n. Aust. Informal* **1.** a swim or bath. **2.** a swimming hole. Also, **bogie**.

bogeyman /ˈboʊɡimæn, ˈbuɡimæn, ˈbuɡimæn/ *n.* (*pl.* **-men**) **1.** an evil spirit in the guise of a man. **2.** anything that is persistently frightening. Also, **bogyman**, **boogieman**.

boggle *v.* **1.** to take alarm; start with fright. **2.** to be overwhelmed.

bogie[1] *n.* a low truck or trolley.

bogie[2] *n.* → **bogey**[2].

bogus *adj.* counterfeit; spurious.

bogy *n.* (*pl.* **-gies**) **1.** a hobgoblin; evil spirit. **2.** anything that haunts or annoys.

bohemian /boʊˈhimiən/ *n.* **1.** a person, usually artistic or intellectual, who lives and acts unconventionally. *–adj.* **2.** relating to bohemians.

boil[1] *v.* **1.** (to cause) to change from liquid to gas with bubbles rising through, and agitating, the liquid. **2.** to cook by bubbling. **3.** to be agitated by angry feeling. **4.** *Informal* to feel very hot.

boil[2] *n.* a suppurating, inflammatory sore forming a central core.

boiler *n.* **1.** a closed vessel in which steam is generated for heating or for driving engines. **2.** a vessel for boiling or heating.

boisterous *adj.* rough and noisy.

bok choy /bɒk ˈtʃɔɪ/ *n.* a vegetable with white stalks and dark green leaves. Also, **buk choy**.

bold *adj.* **1.** not hesitating in the face of danger or rebuff. **2.** disrespectful or forward. **3.** (of type, etc.) with heavy lines.

bolster *n.* **1.** a long ornamental pillow for a bed, sofa, etc. **2.** a support. *–v.* Also, **bolster up**. **3.** to prop, support, or uphold (something weak, unworthy, etc.).

bolt *n.* **1.** a movable bar which fastens a door, gate, etc. **2.** a strong metal pin, with a screw thread to receive a nut. **3.** a woven length of cloth. **4.** any sudden dash, flight, etc. **5.** Also, **thunderbolt**. a shaft of lightning. *–v.* **6.** to fasten with bolts. **7.** to swallow (one's food) hurriedly. **8.** to run away in alarm and uncontrollably. *–phr.* **9. bolt upright**, stiffly upright.

bomb *n.* **1.** a hollow projectile filled with an explosive charge. **2.** *Aust., NZ Informal* an old car. **3.** *Informal* a failure. *–v.* **4.** to hurl bombs (at); drop bombs (upon). **5.** *Informal* to fail; perform badly (at).

bombard *v.* to assail vigorously.

bombardier /bɒmbəˈdɪə/ *n. Mil.* the member of a plane crew who releases the bombs.

bombastic /bɒmˈbæstɪk/ *n.* using words or remarks that sound important but are often not sincere. *–***bombast**, *n.*

The more usual word is **pompous**.

bombora n. Aust. **1.** a submerged reef of rocks. **2.** a dangerous current over a reef.

bombshell n. **1.** a bomb. **2.** a sudden or devastating action or effect. **3.** Informal a sexually attractive woman.

bona fide /ˌboʊnə ˈfaɪdi/ adj. **1.** Also, **bona-fide**. performed, etc., in good faith; without fraud. **2.** genuine; real.

bond n. **1.** something that binds, fastens, confines, or holds together. **2.** something that unites individuals. **3.** a document guaranteeing payment of a stated sum of money on or before a specified day. **4.** any binding written obligation. **5.** Law a written acknowledgement of a debt. **6.** a document certifying the amount of a loan to a government or other corporation, and usually bearing a fixed rate of interest. **7.** → **bond money**. **8.** a substance that causes particles to adhere. **9.** Chem. any linkage between atoms in a compound. –v. **10.** to put (goods, an employee, official, etc.) in or under bond. **11.** to cause (bricks, etc.) to hold together firmly by laying them in some overlapping pattern. **12.** to unite members of a group, etc. **13.** to establish a close interpersonal relationship with another or others. –phr. **14. in bond**, (of goods) held until customs or excise duty is paid.

Def. 1 is usually in the plural: *He broke his bonds and ran to freedom.*

bondage n. the state of being bound by or subjected to external control.

bond money n. an initial payment made by a tenant to guarantee against damage or failure to pay rent. Also, **bond**.

bone n. **1.** any of the separate pieces of which the skeleton of a vertebrate is composed. **2.** any bone-like substance, such as ivory, whalebone, etc. **3.** an off-white colour. –v. (**boned**, **boning**) **4.** to remove the bones from.

bonfire n. a large fire in an open place, for entertainment, celebration, or as a signal.

bongo n. (pl. **-gos** or **-goes**) one of a pair of small drums, played by beating with the fingers.

bonnet n. **1.** a woman's or child's closely fitting hat, usually tied under the chin. **2.** any of various covers or protective devices, such as the metal cover over the engine of a car.

bonny adj. (**-nier**, **-niest**) radiant with health; handsome; pretty.

bonsai /ˈbɒnsaɪ/ n. **1.** the art of keeping trees and shrubs very small and shaping them in particular ways. **2.** a tree or shrub so grown.

bonus n. something given or paid over and above what is due.

bonzer adj. Aust., NZ Informal excellent, attractive, pleasing. Also, **bonza**.

boob[1] n. Informal a fool; a dunce.

boob[2] n. Informal a woman's breast.

Note that this word is mildly taboo and may give offence.

booby prize n. a prize given to the worst player in a game or contest.

booby trap n. an object so placed as to fall on or trip up an unsuspecting person.

book n. **1.** a written or printed work of some length, especially on consecutive sheets fastened or bound together. **2.** a number of sheets of writing paper bound and used to record commercial transactions. **3.** a set of tickets, cheques, stamps, etc., bound together like a book. **4.** anything that serves for the recording of facts or events. –v. **5.** to enter in a book or list; record; register. **6.** to reserve or engage (a place, ticket, performer, etc.) beforehand. **7.** to record the name of, for possible prosecution for a minor offence. **8.** to register one's name (in). –phr. **9. the books**, a record of commercial transactions.

bookcase n. a set of shelves for books.

bookkeeping n. the work or skill of keeping account books. –**bookkeeper**, n.

bookmaker *n.* a professional betting person, who accepts the bets of others, as on horses in racing.

bookmark *n.* **1.** a strip of cardboard, ribbon, or the like placed between the pages of a book to mark a place. *–v. Internet* a URL reference stored in a file by a browser for future reference. *–v. Internet* to store (a URL) in a file for future reference by a browser.

bookworm *n.* a person very fond of reading or studying.

boom¹ *v.* **1.** to make a deep, prolonged, resonant sound. **2.** to progress or flourish vigorously, as a business, a city, etc. *–n.* **3.** a deep, hollow, continued sound. **4.** a rapid increase in prices, business activity, etc.

boom² *n.* **1.** *Naut.* a long pole or spar used to extend the foot of certain sails. Also, **boom gate**, a barrier to traffic comprising a long horizontal pole hinged at one end and raised and lowered as required.

boomerang *n.* **1.** a bent or curved piece of hard wood used as a missile by Aboriginal people, one form of which can be thrown so as to return to the thrower. **2.** *Informal* that which is expected to be returned by a borrower. *–v.* **3.** to return to, or recoil upon, the originator.

boon *n.* a benefit enjoyed; a thing to be thankful for.

boor *n.* a rude or unmannerly person.

Don't confuse this with **boar** or **bore**. A **boar** is a male pig, and a **bore** is a hole made by drilling, or a dull person.

boost *v.* **1.** to lift or raise by pushing from behind or below. **2.** to increase. *–n.* **3.** an upward shove or push. **4.** an aid or encouragement to success. **–booster**, *n.*

boot¹ *n.* **1.** a heavy shoe, especially one reaching above the ankle. **2.** a place for baggage, usually at the rear of a vehicle. **3.** a kick.

boot² *phrase* **boot up**, **1.** to start (a computer) and bring it into an operational

state. **2.** (of a computer) to become operational.

booth *n.* a small compartment for a telephone, film projector, etc.

bootleg *v.* **(-legged, -legging)** to deal in (spirits or other goods) illicitly.

bootscoot *v.* to dance in a linedance. **–bootscooting**, *n.*

booty *n.* spoil taken from an enemy in war.

booze *n. Informal* alcoholic drink.

border *n.* **1.** a side, edge, or margin. **2.** the line that separates one country, state, etc., from another. *–phr.* **3. border on** (or **upon**), **a.** to touch or abut at the border. **b.** to approach closely in character.

Don't confuse **border** with **boarder**, which is someone who pays for meals and somewhere to sleep.

borderline *adj.* **1.** on or near a border or boundary. **2.** (in examinations, etc.) qualifying or failing to qualify by a narrow margin.

bore¹ *v.* **(bored, boring)** **1.** to pierce (a solid substance) or make (a round hole, etc.) with an auger, drill, etc. **2.** to force by persistent forward thrusting. *–n.* **3.** a deep hole through which water is obtained from beneath the ground. **4.** the inside diameter of a hollow cylindrical object or device, such as the barrel of a gun.

Don't confuse this with **boar** or **boor**. A **boar** is a male pig, and a **boor** is a rude person.

bore² *v.* **1.** to weary by tedious repetition, dullness, unwelcome attentions, etc. *–n.* **2.** a dull or tiresome person. **–boredom**, *n.* **–bored**, *adj.* **–boring**, *adj.*

Don't confuse this with **boar** or **boor**. A **boar** is a male pig, and a **boor** is a rude person.

Also, don't confuse **bored** with **board**, which is a long, flat piece of wood.

bore³ *v.* past tense of **bear**¹.

borer *n.* any insect that burrows in trees, fruits, etc.

born adj. **1.** brought forth into independent being or life. **2.** possessing from birth the quality or character stated: a born liar.

> This is an old form of the verb **bear¹**. Don't confuse it with **borne**, which also comes from **bear¹**. See below.

borne v. a past participle of **bear¹**: She was borne along by the current.

> Don't confuse this with **born**, an old form of **bear¹** which means brought into life.

boron n. a non-metallic element. Symbol: B

boronia n. any of a number of Aust. shrubs.

borough /'bʌrə/ n. in Victoria, an area of land corresponding to a municipality in the other states of Aust.

borrow v. **1.** to take or obtain (a thing) on the promise to return it or its equivalent. **2.** to get from another or from a foreign source.

> Compare def. 1 with **lend**, which is to give someone the use of something for a short time.

bosom /'buzəm/ n. **1.** the breast of a human being, especially a woman. **2.** the breast, conceived of as the seat of thought or emotion. –adj. **3.** intimate; close.

boss n. Informal **1.** someone who employs or superintends workers. **2.** anyone who asserts mastery, especially someone who controls a political or other body. –v. **3.** to domineer.

> **Boss** can be rather informal, especially if you refer to someone in a high position in a large organisation as 'the boss'.

bosun n. → **boatswain**.

botany n. the science of plants and plant life. –**botanist**, n. –**botanical**, adj.

botch v. to spoil by poor work; bungle.

both adj., pron. **1.** the one and the other; the 2 together. –adv. **2.** alike; equally: I both like and respect her.

> Note that you should use a plural verb when you use **both** as a pronoun (as in

Both are welcome) or as an adjective (as in Both students are doing well).
> Note also that you can use **both** in various positions in a sentence and with different combinations of words. The following four sentences all mean the same thing: Both girls have been swimming; Both the girls have been swimming; Both of the girls have been swimming; The girls have both been swimming. However, it would be incorrect to say 'Both of girls have been swimming'.

bother v. **1.** to give trouble to; annoy. **2.** to trouble oneself. –n. **3.** an annoying disturbance. **4.** worried or perplexed state. –**bothersome**, adj.

botox /'boutɒks/ n. (from trademark) a preparation which causes muscle relaxation and paralysis, used for medical and cosmetic purposes.

bottle n. **1.** a portable vessel with a neck or mouth, usually made of glass or plastic, used for holding liquids. –v. **2.** to put into or seal in a bottle; to preserve (fruit or vegetables) in bottles.

bottlebrush n. an Aust. plant whose flower spikes resemble a cylindrical brush.

bottleneck n. **1.** a place, or stage in a process, where progress is retarded. **2. a.** a narrow part of a road between 2 wide stretches. **b.** a congested junction, road, town, etc.

bottom n. **1.** the lowest or deepest part of anything. **2.** the underside. **3.** the ground under any body of water. **4.** the buttocks. **5.** the basic aspect. –v. **6.** to be based; rest. **7.** to strike against or reach the bottom or end. –adj. **8.** lowest.

bougainvillea /bougən'vɪliə/ n. a shrub or spiny climber with brightly coloured bracts.

bough /bau/ n. a large branch of a tree.

> Don't confuse this with **bow**, which is pronounced in the same way. The **bow** of a boat is its front end, and to **bow** is to bend towards someone as a sign of respect. When **bow** is pronounced /bou/,

it refers to a type of knot, or to the bent piece of wood you use when shooting an arrow, or to an implement used to play certain musical instruments, such as the violin.

bought v. past tense and past participle of **buy**.

boulder n. a detached and rounded rock.

boulevard /'buːləvɑːd/ n. **1.** a broad avenue of a city, often having trees. **2.** a street. Also, **boulevarde**.

bounce v. (**bounced, bouncing**) **1.** to (cause to) move with a bound, and re-bound, as a ball. **2.** Informal (of cheques) to be returned unpaid. **3.** Informal to eject or discharge summarily. –n. **4.** a rebound or bound. **5.** ability to bounce; resilience.

bound[1] v. **1.** past tense of **bind**. –adj. **2.** tied; in bonds. **3.** made fast as by a band or bond. **4.** secured within a cover, as a book. **5.** under obligation, legally or morally. **6.** destined or sure.

bound[2] v. **1.** to move by leaps; spring. –n. **2.** a leap onwards or upwards.

bound[3] n. **1.** (usu. pl.) a limiting line, or boundary. –v. **2.** to form the boundary of. –phr. **3. out of bounds**, forbidden or access to certain persons.

Def. 2 is almost always used in the passive.

bound[4] adj. going or intending to go; on the way to; destined (for).

boundary n. (pl. **-ries**) something that indicates bounds or limits.

bounteous adj. **1.** giving or disposed to give freely. **2.** freely bestowed; plentiful.

bountiful adj. **1.** liberal in bestowing gifts or favours; generous. **2.** abundant; ample.

bounty n. (pl. **-ties**) **1.** generosity in giving. **2.** a benevolent, generous gift. **3.** a reward, especially one offered by a government.

bouquet /buˈkeɪ, booˈkeɪ/ n. **1.** a bunch of flowers. **2.** the characteristic aroma of wine, liqueurs, etc.

bourbon /'bɜːbən/ n. a kind of whisky distilled from maize. Also, **bourbon whisky**.

bourgeois /'bʊəʒwɑː, 'bu-/ n. (pl. **-geois**) **1.** a member of the middle class. **2.** a capitalist, as opposed to a member of the wage-earning class. –adj. **3.** of the middle class; conventional. –**bourgeoisie**, n.

bout n. **1.** a contest, especially a boxing or wrestling match. **2.** period; spell.

boutique /buˈtik/ n. a small shop selling fashionable or luxury articles.

bovine adj. **1.** of the ox family. **2.** stolid; dull.

bow[1] /baʊ/ v. **1.** to bend or curve downwards; stoop. **2.** to yield; submit. **3.** to bend (the body or head) in worship, salutation, respect, or submission. –n. **4.** a bowing movement of head or body.

Don't confuse this or **bow**[3] with **bough**, which is a branch of a tree. Note that there is another word **bow** (pronounced /boʊ/). See **bow**[2].

bow[2] /boʊ/ n. **1.** a strip of flexible material bent by a string stretched between its ends, used for shooting arrows. **2.** something curved or arc-shaped. **3.** a looped knot, as of ribbon, composed of one or 2 loops and 2 ends. **4.** Music an implement designed for playing a violin, etc. –adj. **5.** curved; bent like a bow. –v. **6.** to bend into the form of a bow; curve.

bow[3] /baʊ/ n. (sometimes pl.) the forward part of a ship, boat, airship, etc.

bowdlerise /'baʊdləraɪz/ v. to expurgate prudishly. Also, **bowdlerize**.

bowel /'baʊəl/ n. **a.** an intestine. **b.** (usu. pl.) (usu. pl.) the intestines or entrails. **2.** (usu. pl.) (usu. pl.) the inward or interior parts: the bowels of the building.

bower /'baʊə/ n. a leafy shelter or recess; an arbour.

bowerbird n. any of various birds which build bowerlike structures to attract the females.

bowl¹ *n.* **1.** a deep, round dish used to hold liquids, etc. **2.** any bowl-shaped depression.

bowl² *n.* **1.** one of the biased or weighted balls used in the game of lawn bowls. **2.** a delivery of the ball in bowling. –*v.* **3.** to play with bowls, or at bowling. **4.** to roll or trundle (a ball, hoop, etc.). **5.** to knock or strike (*over* or *down*), as by the ball in bowling. **6.** *Cricket* to deliver a ball with a straight arm down the pitch to the person batting. **7.** *Cricket* to dismiss (the person batting) by delivering a ball which breaks their wicket.

bowler *n.* a hard felt hat with a rounded crown and narrow brim.

bowls *n.* → **lawn bowls**.

bowser /'bauzə/ *n.* *Aust., NZ* (*from trademark*) a fuel pump at a service station.

box¹ *n.* **1.** a receptacle with a lid or removable cover. **2.** a compartment for the accommodation of a small number of people in a public place, especially in theatres, etc. **3.** (in a court of law) a stand or pew reserved for witnesses, the accused or the jury. –*v.* **4.** to put into a box. –*phr.* **5. box up** (or **in**), to enclose or confine as in a box.

box² *n.* **1.** a blow as with the hand or fist. –*v.* **2.** to strike with the hand or fist, especially on the ear. **3.** to fight in a boxing match.

boxer *n.* **1.** someone who boxes. **2.** a smooth-coated dog related to the bulldog and terrier.

box jellyfish *n.* (*pl.* **-fish** or **-fishes**) a highly venomous tropical jellyfish.

For information about the different plural forms, see the note at **fish**.

box office *n.* the office in which tickets are sold at a theatre, etc.

boy *n.* **1.** a male child or young person. –*interj.* **2.** (an exclamation of surprise, delight, etc.)

boycott *v.* **1.** to combine in abstaining from, or preventing dealings with, as a means of intimidation or coercion. **2.** to abstain from buying or using. –*n.* **3.** the practice or an instance of boycotting.

boyfriend *n.* a man with whom one has a steady romantic relationship.

boysenberry /'bɔɪzənberi/ *n.* (*pl.* **-ries**) blackberry-like fruit with a flavour similar to raspberries.

bra *n.* a woman's undergarment which supports the breasts.

This is short for **brassiere**.

brace *n.* **1.** something that holds parts together or in place. **2.** anything that imparts rigidity or steadiness. **3.** a device for holding and turning tools for boring or drilling. **4.** a piece of timber, metal, etc., used to support or strengthen a framework. **5.** (*oft. pl.*) metal wire used to straighten irregular teeth. **6.** *Med.* an appliance for supporting a weak joint or joints. **7.** (*pl.*) straps worn over the shoulders to hold up trousers. **8.** a pair. –*v.* (**braced, bracing**) **9.** to furnish, fasten, or strengthen with or as with a brace. **10.** to fix firmly; make steady.

bracelet *n.* **1.** an ornamental band or circlet for the wrist or arm. **2.** *Informal* a handcuff.

bracken *n.* a large, coarse fern.

bracket *n.* **1.** a triangular support for a shelf or the like. **2.** either of 2 sets of signs ( ) or [ ] used to group words or figures together. **3.** (*pl.*) *Maths* parentheses of various forms indicating that the enclosed quantity is to be treated as a unit. **4.** a grouping of persons, especially based on the amount of their taxable income: *low income bracket.* **5.** a small group of musical items in a performance. –*v.* **6.** to furnish with or support by a bracket or brackets (def. 1). **7.** to place brackets (def. 2) around: *Just bracket the bits you think I should delete.* **8.** to associate or mention together.

brackish *adj.* slightly salt; having a salty or briny flavour.

bract *n.* a specialised leaf or leaf-like part, usually at the base of a flower.

brag *v.* (**bragged, bragging**) to use boastful language. –**braggart**, *n.*

braid *v.* to weave together strips or strands of; plait.

braille *n.* a system of printing for the blind, in which combinations of raised points represent letters, etc.

brain *n.* **1.** (*sometimes pl.*) the nerve substance which fills the cranium of humans and other vertebrates; centre of sensation, body coordination, thought, emotion, etc. **2.** (*usu. pl.*) understanding; intellectual power: *Use your brains!*

brainstorm *n.* **1.** a sudden inspiration, idea, etc. –*v.* **2.** to use brainstorming as a means to address or solve a problem, etc.

brainstorming *n.* a technique in which a group meets in order to stimulate creative thinking, develop new ideas, devise a solution to a problem, etc.

brainteaser *n. Informal* a mental puzzle.

brainwashing *n.* systematic indoctrination to change someone's convictions, especially political.

brainy *adj.* (**-nier, -niest**) having brains; intelligent; clever.

braise *v.* to cook (meat or vegetables) slowly in very little moisture.

brake *n.* **1.** any mechanical device for arresting the motion of a wheel, a motor, or a vehicle, chiefly by means of friction. –*v.* **2.** to use or apply a brake.

> Don't confuse this with **break**, which has many meanings. For example, if you **break** a plate, it smashes. If you have a **break** from work, you have a rest.

bramble *n.* **1.** the common blackberry. **2.** any rough prickly shrub.

bran *n.* the ground husk of wheat or other grain.

branch *n.* **1.** a division or subdivision of the stem of a tree, shrub, or other plant (as opposed to twigs, shoots, etc.). **2.** a limb, offshoot, or ramification. **3.** a section or subdivision of a body or system. **4.** a tributary stream. –*v.* **5.** to put forth branches; spread in branches. **6.** to divide into separate parts or subdivisions; diverge.

brand *n.* **1.** a trademark or trade name to identify a product. **2.** a mark made by burning or otherwise, to indicate kind, grade, make, ownership, etc. **3.** any mark of infamy.

brandish *v.* **1.** to shake or wave, as a weapon; flourish. –*n.* **2.** a wave or flourish, as of a weapon.

brandy *n.* (*pl.* **-dies**) the spirit distilled from the fermented juice of grapes or, sometimes, of apples, peaches, plums, etc.

brash *adj.* impertinent; impudent. –**brashly**, *adv.* –**brashness**, *n.*

brass *n.* **1.** a durable, malleable, and ductile yellow alloy, consisting essentially of copper and zinc. **2.** musical instruments of the trumpet and horn families collectively (brass instruments). **3.** *Informal* excessive assurance; impudence. **4.** *Informal* money. –*phr.* **5. top brass**, *Informal* high-ranking people.

brasserie /ˈbrasəri/ *n.* a restaurant, especially one for informal dining.

brassiere /ˈbræziə, -siə/ *n.* → **bra**.

brat *n.* a badly behaved child.

bravado /brəˈvadoʊ/ *n.* boasting; swaggering pretence.

brave *adj.* **1.** possessing or exhibiting courage or courageous endurance. –*v.* **2.** to meet or face courageously. **3.** to defy; challenge. –**bravery**, *n.*

brawl *n.* a noisy quarrel; a squabble.

brawn *n.* **1.** well-developed muscles. **2.** meat, especially pork, boiled, pickled, and pressed.

bray *n.* a harsh, breathy cry, as of the donkey.

brazen *adj.* **1.** made of brass. **2.** like brass. **3.** shameless or impudent.

brazier *n.* a metal receptacle for holding burning charcoal or other fuel.

brazil nut *n.* a triangular edible nut.

breach *n.* **1.** the act or result of breaking. **2.** a gap made in a wall, dyke, fortification, etc. **3.** an infraction or violation, as of law, trust, etc. **4.** a severance of friendly relations.

bread *n.* **1.** a food made of flour or meal, milk or water, etc., mixed with or without yeast or the like, and baked. **2.** food or sustenance. **3.** *Informal* money; earnings.

breadline *phr.* **on the breadline**, living at subsistence level.

breadth *n.* **1.** *Maths* the measure of the 2nd principal dimension of a surface or solid, the first being length, and the 3rd (in the case of a solid) thickness; width. **2.** freedom from narrowness or restraint. **3.** extent.

breadwinner *n.* someone who earns a livelihood for a family.

break *v.* (**broke**, **broken**, **breaking**) **1.** to divide or separate into parts, especially violently; reduce to pieces or fragments. **2.** to separate into parts or pieces: *to break bread.* **3.** to detach from a larger object: *to break a leaf from a plant.* **4.** to separate into components: *to break a difficult job into manageable steps.* **5.** to violate: *to break one's word.* **6.** to fracture a bone of. **7.** to destroy the regularity of. **8.** to put an end to; overcome. **9.** to exchange for a smaller amount or smaller units. **10.** to make or force one's way through; penetrate. **11.** to force a way (*in, through, out,* etc.). **12.** to burst (*in, forth, from,* etc.). **13.** to disable or destroy. **14.** to ruin financially, or make bankrupt. **15.** to impair or weaken in strength, spirit, force, or effect. **16.** to defeat the purpose of (a strike). **17.** to train to obedience; tame. **18.** *Elect.* to detach (a circuit) incomplete. **19.** to sever relations (*up* or *with*). **20.** (of a wave) to topple forward after developing a crest. **21.** to free oneself or escape suddenly, as from restraint (*away*). **22.** to change state or activity (*into*). **23.** to dawn, as the day. **24.** (of the heart) to be overwhelmed, especially by grief. **25.** (of the voice) to vary between 2 registers, especially in emotion or during adolescence. **26.** (in a race) to start before the signal. –*n.* **27.** a forcible disruption or separation of parts; a breaking. **28.** a gap. **29.** an attempt to escape. **30.** an interruption of continuity. **31.** an abrupt or marked change, as in sound or direction. **32.** an opportunity; chance. **33.** a brief rest, as from work. **34.** a premature start in racing. –*phr.* **35. break down**, **a.** to take down or destroy by breaking. **b.** to overcome. **c.** to analyse. **d.** to collapse. **e.** to cease to function. **36. break in**, **a.** to interrupt. **b.** to adapt to one's convenience by use. **c.** to accustom (a horse) to harness and use. **d.** to enter (a house or the like) forcibly, as a burglar. **37. break off**, **a.** to end or finish. **b.** to stop or interrupt. **38. break out**, **a.** to issue forth; arise. **b.** (of certain diseases) to appear in eruptions. **39. break up**, **a.** to separate; disband. **b.** (of a relationship) to cease. **c.** to put an end to; discontinue. **d.** to cut up or separate into pieces. **e.** *Informal* to collapse with laughter.

Don't confuse **break** with **brake**, which is a device used to slow down or stop a vehicle or machine.

breakage *n.* **1.** an act of breaking; a break. **2.** the amount or quantity of things broken.

breakaway *n.* **1.** the formation of a splinter group in a political party, etc. **2.** a panic rush of or among a mob of cattle, horses, etc.

breakdancing *n.* a style of energetic dancing performed to rap music. –**breakdance**, *v.*

breakfast *n.* the first meal of the day.

breakneck *adj.* dangerous; hazardous.

breakthrough n. any development which removes a barrier to progress.

breakwater n. a structure built to break the force of waves, especially near a harbour.

bream /briːm/ n. (pl. **bream** or **breams**) an edible fish.

> For information about the different plural forms, see the note at **fish**.

breast n. 1. the front part of the body from neck to belly; the chest. 2. a mammary or milk gland, especially of a woman. 3. the bosom regarded as the seat of thoughts and feelings.

breastbone n. the long bone extending vertically down the centre of the chest.

breastfeed v. (-**fed**, -**feeding**) 1. to feed (a child) from the breast (opposed to *bottle-feed*). 2. (of a baby) to feed from the breast.

breaststroke n. a swimming stroke in the prone position, in which the swimmer's arms move outwards and back from their chest and their legs kick in a frog-like manner.

breath /brɛθ/ n. 1. the air inhaled and exhaled in respiration. 2. ability to breathe, especially freely. 3. a light current of air.

> Don't confuse the noun **breath** with the verb **breathe**.

breathalyser n. a device which analyses the amount of alcohol in the breath.

breathe /briːð/ v. (**breathed** /briːðd/, **breathing**) 1. to inhale and exhale (air, fumes, etc.). 2. to blow lightly, as air. 3. to live; exist. 4. to give utterance to; whisper.

> Don't confuse the verb **breathe** with the noun **breath**.

breathtaking adj. causing amazement. –**breathtakingly**, adv.

breathy adj. (of the voice) characterised by excessive emission of breath.

breech n. 1. the posterior or buttocks. 2. the hinder or lower part of anything. 3. the part of a gun behind the barrel.

breeches /ˈbrɪtʃəz/ pl. n. trousers, especially designed for horse-riding, or those reaching just to the knee.

breed v. (**bred**, **breeding**) 1. to produce (offspring). 2. to procure by the mating of parents. 3. to cause to reproduce by controlled pollination or fertilisation. 4. to cause; occasion. –n. 5. a genetically similar group of animals within a species, developed and maintained by humans.

breeze n. 1. a light or moderate wind. 2. *Informal* an easy task. –v. (**breezed**, **breezing**) 3. *Informal* to move or proceed light-heartedly (along, in). –phr. 4. **breeze through**, *Informal* to perform without effort.

brethren n. 1. *Old-fashioned* plural of **brother**. 2. fellow members.

> Nowadays this is used mainly to refer to people who belong to a particular organisation or religious group. It is not used in everyday language.

breve /briːv/ n. *Music* a note equal in length to two semibreves.

brevity n. shortness of time or duration; briefness.

> This comes from the adjective **brief**, meaning short.

brew v. 1. to make (beer, ale, etc.). 2. to make (tea). 3. to concoct or contrive. 4. to be in preparation; be forming or gathering. –n. 5. a quantity brewed in a single process. –**brewery**, n.

briar n. a prickly shrub or plant.

bribe n. 1. anything of value offered to influence corrupt behaviour in the performance of duty. –v. 2. to influence or corrupt by a bribe. –**bribery**, n.

brick n. 1. a baked block of clay used for building, paving, etc. 2. *Informal* a person who has gained one's special admiration. –phr. 3. **like a ton of bricks**, heavily.

bridal shower n. a party for a bride-to-be at which she receives household gifts; shower tea.

bride *n.* a woman newly married, or about to be married. –**bridal**, *adj.*

bridegroom *n.* a man newly married, or about to be married.

> The short form of this is **groom**.

bridesmaid *n.* a woman who attends the bride at a wedding.

bridge¹ *n.* **1.** a structure spanning a river, road, etc., and affording passage. **2.** the ridge or upper line of the nose. –*v.* (**bridged**, **bridging**) **3.** to make a bridge over; span.

bridge² *n.* a card game for 4 players, derived from whist.

bridle *n.* **1.** the part of the harness of a horse, etc., around the head. –*v.* **2.** to draw up the head and draw in the chin, as in disdain or resentment (*at*).

brie /bri/ *n.* a kind of salted, white, soft cheese, ripened through bacterial action, waxy to semiliquid, as made in Brie, a district in nthn France.

brief *adj.* **1.** of little duration. **2.** using few words. **3.** abrupt or curt. –*n.* **4.** an outline of all the possible arguments and information on one side of a controversy. **5.** instructions or notes for a particular task. –*v.* **6.** to give instructions to for a particular task.

briefcase *n.* a flat, rectangular case used for carrying documents, etc.

briefing *n.* a short, accurate summary of a plan or operation given to a military unit, etc., before it undertakes the operation.

brig *n.* two-masted vessel with square sails.

brigade *n.* **1.** a large body of troops. **2.** a group organised for a special purpose.

brigadier /brɪgə'dɪə/ *n.* an army rank above colonel.

brigand /'brɪgənd/ *n.* a bandit.

bright *adj.* **1.** radiating or reflecting light; luminous. **2.** vivid or brilliant, as colour. **3.** quick-witted or intelligent. **4.** animated; lively. –*adv.* **5.** in a bright manner; brightly.

brighten *v.* to become or make bright or brighter. Also, **brighten up**.

brilliant *adj.* **1.** shining brightly; sparkling. **2.** distinguished; illustrious. **3.** having or showing great intelligence. –**brilliance**, *n.*

brim *n.* **1.** the upper edge of anything hollow. **2.** a projecting edge. –*v.* (**brimmed**, **brimming**) **3.** to be full to the brim or overflowing.

brindled *adj.* grey or tawny with darker streaks or spots.

brine *n.* water strongly impregnated with salt. –**briny**, *adj.*

bring *v.* (**brought**, **bringing**) **1.** to cause to come with oneself; convey. **2.** to lead or induce. –*phr.* **3. bring about**, to cause; accomplish. **4. bring down**, **a.** to shoot down or cause to fall (a plane, animal, etc.). **b.** to reduce (a price); lower in price. **c.** to humble or subdue. **d.** to introduce (proposed legislation). **5. bring forward**, **a.** to produce to view. **b.** to move to an earlier date or hour. **6. bring in**, **a.** to introduce. **b.** to pronounce (a verdict). **7. bring off**, to bring to a successful conclusion. **8. bring out**, **a.** to expose. **b.** to encourage (a shy person). **c.** to induce to go on strike. **9. bring up**, **a.** to care for during childhood. **b.** to introduce for consideration. **c.** to vomit.

> Note that you use both **bring** and **take** when you are talking about carrying something or going somewhere with someone. The difference between the two is that **bring** involves movement towards the speaker and **take** movement away from the speaker. For example, *Please bring the car to the shops* suggests that the person speaking is at the shops, and *Take the plate to the sink, Michael* suggests that Michael needs to go away from the speaker. **Take** is also used when the speaker is not a part of the situation they are describing, as in *She took the car to the shops* or *Michael took the plate to the sink.*

brink n. any extreme edge; verge.

brinkmanship n. the practice of courting disaster to gain one's ends.

brisk adj. quick and active; lively.

brisket n. (meat from) the breast of an animal.

bristle n. **1.** one of the short, stiff, coarse hairs of certain animals, especially pigs, used in making brushes, etc. −v. **2.** to erect the bristles, as an irritated animal. **3.** to be visibly roused to anger or resistance.

brittle adj. breaking readily.

broach v. to mention or suggest for the first time.

broad adj. **1.** of great breadth. **2.** of great extent. **3.** widely diffused. **4.** not limited or narrow; liberal. **5.** main or general. **6.** (of pronunciation) strongly dialectal.

broadband n. **1.** high-speed internet access having a bandwidth sufficient to carry multiple voice, video and data channels simultaneously. −v. **2.** to link to a broadband network: *to broadband the office.*

broadcast v. (**-cast** or **-casted, -casting**) **1.** to send (sound and images) by radio or television. **2.** to spread widely. −n. **3.** that which is broadcast.

broadleaf n. any of various trees or shrubs having broad leaves. −adj. **2.** having broad leaves.

broadsheet n. **1.** a sheet of paper, especially of large size, printed on one side only, as for distribution or posting. **2.** a newspaper printed on the standard sheet size of paper.

broadside n. the whole side of a ship above the waterline.

brocade n. fabric woven with an elaborate, raised design from any yarn.

broccoli /ˈbrɒkəli, -lɪ/ n. a plant resembling the cauliflower.

brochure /ˈbrəʊʃə, brəˈʃʊə/ n. a small book with a paper cover, containing information or advertisements.

brogue¹ /brəʊɡ/ n. a broad accent, especially Irish, in the pronunciation of English.

brogue² /brəʊɡ/ n. a strongly made, comfortable shoe.

broil v. to cook by direct radiant heat; grill; pan fry.

broke v. **1.** past tense of **break**. −phr. **2.** (**flat**) **broke**, Informal completely out of money.

broken v. **1.** past participle of **break**. −adj. **2.** having undergone breaking. **3.** (of a machine, etc.) not working properly. **4.** (of a surface) rough or uneven. **5.** imperfectly spoken.

broker n. **1.** an agent who buys or sells for another, on commission. **2.** a middleman or agent. −v. **3.** to negotiate (a deal, etc.). −**brokerage**, n.

brolga n. a large, silvery-grey crane.

brolly n. Informal an umbrella.

bromance n. Informal a non-sexual but intense friendship between two males.

bromide n. Chem. a compound of bromine with one other element.

bromine n. an element, a dark-reddish fuming liquid, resembling chlorine and iodine in chemical properties. Symbol: Br

bronchial adj. of or relating to branches of the trachea.

bronchitis /brɒŋˈkaɪtəs/ n. an inflammation of the bronchial membranes.

bronze n. a durable brown alloy of copper and tin.

brooch /brəʊtʃ/ n. an ornament with a pin made to be fastened to clothing.

brood n. **1.** a number of young produced or hatched at one time; a family of offspring. −v. **2.** to meditate moodily. **3.** to incubate (eggs).

broody adj. (**-dier, -diest**) inclined to brood or sit on eggs.

brook¹ n. a small, natural stream of fresh water; creek.

brook² v. to bear; suffer (usually in a negative sentence).

broom n. a sweeping implement on a long handle.

broth n. thin soup of concentrated meat or fish stock.

brothel n. a house of prostitution.

brother n. **1.** a male child of the same parents as one's own. **2.** a male child of only one of one's parents (**half-brother**). **3.** a male member of the same kinship group, nationality, profession, etc.; an associate; a fellow countryman, fellow man, etc. **4.** a male lay member of a religious organisation which has a priesthood.

If you want to use one word to refer to a brother and a sister, or to talk about brothers and sisters in general, you can use the word **sibling**. This is more formal than **brother** or **sister**.

brother-in-law n. (pl. **brothers-in-law**) **1.** the brother of one's spouse. **2.** the husband of one's sibling. **3.** the husband of one's spouse's sibling.

brought v. past tense and past participle of **bring**.

brow n. **1.** the ridge over the eye. **2.** Also, **eyebrow**. the hair growing on that ridge. **3.** the edge or top of a hill, etc.

browbeat v. (**-beat, -beaten, -beating**) to intimidate by overbearing looks or words; bully.

brown n. a dark shade with yellowish or reddish hue. –adj. **1.** of the colour brown. **2.** having skin of that colour. **3.** sunburned or tanned. –v. **5.** to make brown.

brownout n. a partial blackout, resulting in a dimming of lights, sometimes imposed deliberately to conserve electricity.

browse v. **1.** to glance though merchandise in a shop. **2.** to glance at random through a book or books.

browser n. Internet computer software designed to facilitate searches on the World Wide Web by viewing the contents of web pages. Also, **web browser**.

bruise v. (**bruised, bruising**) **1.** to injure by striking or pressing, without breaking the skin or drawing blood. **2.** to develop a discoloured spot on the skin as the result of a blow, fall, etc. **3.** to damage fruit, etc., by applying pressure, without breaking the skin. –n. **4.** an injury due to bruising. **5.** a damaged area on a piece of fruit, etc., due to bruising.

brumby n. Aust., NZ a wild horse, especially one descended from runaway stock.

brunch n. a midmorning meal that serves as both breakfast and lunch.

brunette n. a person with dark or brown hair.

brunt n. the shock or force of an attack, etc.

brush¹ n. **1.** an instrument consisting of bristles, hair, or the like, set in or attached to a handle. **2.** an act of brushing; application of a brush. **3.** the bushy tail of an animal. **4.** a slight skimming touch. **5.** a brief hostile encounter; argument. –v. **6.** to sweep, rub, clean, polish, etc., with a brush. **7.** to touch lightly in passing. **8.** to remove by brushing.

brush² n. a dense growth of bushes, shrubs, etc.

brusque /brʌsk, brʊsk/ adj. blunt or abrupt in manner; rough.

brussels sprout n. a plant with small, edible, cabbage-like heads or sprouts along the stalk.

brutal adj. **1.** savage; inhuman. **2.** crude; coarse; harsh. –**brutality**, n.

brute n. **1.** a non-human animal; beast. **2.** a brutal person.

bubble n. **1.** a small globule of gas in a liquid or solid. –v. (**-bled, -bling**) **2.** to send up bubbles.

bubblegum n. a type of chewing gum which can be blown into bubbles.

bubbler n. Aust. a small fountain which ejects water for drinking.

bubble wrap n. a plastic wrapping material consisting of small, sealed air pockets, used for protecting delicate items during transport or storage.

buccaneer n. a pirate.

buck[1] *n.* the male of certain animals, as the deer, rabbit, etc.

Note that the female animal is called a **doe**.

buck[2] *v.* **1.** (of a saddle or pack animal) to leap with arched back in order to dislodge rider or pack. **2.** *Informal* to resist obstinately; object strongly: *to buck at improvements.* −*phr.* **3. buck up**, *Informal* to become more cheerful, vigorous, etc.

buck[3] *phr.* **pass the buck**, *Informal* to shift the responsibility or blame to another person.

buck[4] *n. Informal* a dollar.

bucket *n.* **1.** a vessel, with a semicircular handle, for carrying water, sand, etc. −*phr.* **2. kick the bucket**, *Informal* to die.

buckle *n.* **1.** a clasp used for fastening together 2 loose ends, as of a belt. **2.** a bend or kink, as in a saw blade. −*v.* **3.** to fasten with a buckle. **4.** to bend and shrivel, by applying heat or pressure; warp. **5.** to bend, warp, or give way suddenly. −*phr.* **6. buckle down**, to set to work with vigour.

bucolic /bjuːˈkɒlɪk/ *adj.* rustic; rural.

bud *n.* a small protuberance on a plant, containing the first stages of a leaf, or flower or both.

buddy *n.* (pl. **-dies**) *Informal* **1.** comrade; mate. **2.** someone who acts as either a mentor or partner to another, to provide emotional, physical or practical support with a particular task or experience.

This word was originally used mainly in American English but is now commonly used in Australia.

budge *v.* to (cause to) move slightly or give way: *This door is so stuck, it just won't budge; She refused to budge.*

Note that **budge** is usually used with a negative word as in the examples above. You do not say 'Let's budge this table.'

budgerigar *n.* a small endemic Aust. parrot of arid and semi-arid grasslands and woodlands; green and yellow with a blue tail in the wild, it has been widely domesticated and bred in many coloured varieties. Also, **budgie**.

budget *n.* an estimate, often itemised, of expected income and expenditure, etc. −**budgetary**, *adj.*

buff *n.* **1.** a kind of thick leather. **2.** yellowish brown; medium or light tan. **3.** *Informal* the bare skin. **4.** *Informal* an enthusiast; an expert (sometimes self-proclaimed). −*v.* **5.** to polish (metal).

buffalo *n.* (pl. **-loes** or **-los** or, *especially collectively,* **-lo**) a kind of cattle, of which various kinds are found in parts of Asia and Africa, especially those valued as draught animals.

Also look up **water buffalo**.

buffer *n.* **1.** anything serving to neutralise the shock of opposing forces. **2.** *Computers* an area of temporary storage where data is held during computer operations.

buffet[1] /ˈbʌfət/ *n.* **1.** a blow, as with the hand. −*v.* (**-feted, -feting**) **2.** to strike, as with the hand.

buffet[2] /ˈbʌfeɪ, ˈbʊfeɪ/ *n.* **1.** a counter, bar, or the like, for lunch or refreshments. **2.** a sideboard for holding china, plate, etc. −*adj.* **3.** (of a meal) spread on tables or buffets from which the guests serve themselves.

buffoon *n.* someone who amuses others by tricks, odd gestures and postures, jokes, etc.

bug *n.* **1.** any insect. **2.** *Informal* an illness caused by bacteria or a virus. **3.** *Informal* an idea or belief with which one is obsessed. **4.** *Informal* a microphone hidden in a room. −*v.* (**bugged, bugging**) *Informal* **5.** to install a bug in (a room, etc.). **6.** to cause annoyance or distress to (a person).

bugbear *n.* any source of needless fright or fear.

bugger *n.* **1.** (*taboo*) someone who practises bestiality or sodomy. **2.** *Informal* a contemptible person. **3.** *Informal* any person. –*interj*. **4.** (a strong exclamation of annoyance, disgust, etc.). –*phr.* **5. bugger all**, *Informal* nothing. –**buggery**, *n.*

Note that this word is taboo and may give offence. When **bugger** is used to address someone or to talk about them, it can indicate dislike and be offensive (as in def. 2), or it can be used in quite a fond manner (as in def. 3). What the speaker intends is usually clear from their tone of voice, what else has been said, etc. Note, however, that you should be careful about calling someone 'a bugger,' even if you mean it affectionately, unless you know them very well.

buggy *n.* (*pl.* **-gies**) a two-wheeled horse-drawn carriage.

bugle *n.* a cornet-like military wind instrument.

build *v.* (**built**, **building**) **1.** to construct by assembling and combining parts. **2.** to establish, increase, and strengthen (*up*). **3.** to base; form. **4.** to form a plan, system of thought, etc. (*on* or *upon*). –*n.* **5.** manner or style of construction or formation. –**building**, *n.*

building society *n.* an organisation which uses money subscribed by its members as a fund for lending money to members, as for the purchase of homes.

buk choy /bʌk ˈtʃɔɪ/ *n.* → **bok choy**.

bulb *n.* **1.** an underground storage organ with a flat, disc-shaped stem from which roots grow, as in the onion, lily, etc. **2.** the glass housing holding the filament of an incandescent electric light globe. –**bulbous**, *adj.*

bulge *n.* **1.** a rounded projecting or protruding part. –*v.* (**bulged**, **bulging**) **2.** to swell out; be protuberant.

bulimia /bəˈlimiə/ *n.* a compulsive eating disorder marked by bouts of overeating followed by induced vomiting. Also, **bulimia nervosa**. –**bulimic**, *adj.*, *n.*

bulk *n.* **1.** size in 3 dimensions. **2.** the greater part. –*phr.* **3. in bulk**,

a. unpackaged. **b.** in large quantities. –**bulky**, *adj.*

bull¹ *n.* **1.** the uncastrated male of a bovine animal. **2.** the male of various other animals, as the elephant, whale, etc.

bull² *n. Informal* nonsense.

bulldog *n.* a large-headed, short-haired, heavily built and muscular dog of comparatively small size.

bulldozer *n.* a powerful tractor on continuous tracks with a front vertical blade for moving earth, tree stumps, rocks, etc.

bullet *n.* **1.** a small metal projectile fired from a gun. **2.** a heavy dot used in a document to make a particular passage of text more prominent.

bulletin *n.* **1.** a brief account or statement, as of news or events. **2.** a periodical publication, as of a learned society.

bulletin board *n.* **1.** *US* → **noticeboard**. **2.** an electronic message directory accessible on a computer.

bull-headed *adj.* obstinate; blunderingly stubborn; stupid.

bullion *n.* gold or silver in mass, bars or ingots.

bullock *n.* a castrated male bovine animal; ox; steer.

bullseye *n.* the central spot of a target.

bullshit *n. Informal* (*taboo*) nonsense.

Note that **bullshit** is taboo and may give offence. However, it is often shortened to **bull** which is not as taboo. Other informal words you could use that are not taboo are **garbage** or **rubbish**.

bull-terrier *n.* a breed of dog produced by crossing the bulldog and the terrier.

bully *n.* (*pl.* **-lies**) **1.** an overbearing person who browbeats weaker people. –*v.* (**-lied**, **-lying**) **2.** to be loudly arrogant and overbearing.

bulrush /ˈbʊlrʌʃ/ *n.* a tall, rush-like plant from which mats, chair seats, etc., are made.

bulwark /ˈbʊlwək/ n. **1.** earthen wall used for defence. **2.** anything serving as a protection. **3.** (*usu. pl.*) solid part of ship's side above deck level.

bum n. *Informal* **1.** the rump; buttocks. **2.** a shiftless or dissolute person.

bumble v. to proceed clumsily or inefficiently.

bumblebee n. any of various large, hairy social bees. Also, **humblebee**.

bump v. **1.** to come more or less heavily in contact with; strike; collide with. –n. **2.** the act of bumping; a blow. **3.** a dull thud; the noise of collision. **4.** a small area raised above the level of the surrounding surface. –phr. **5. bump into**, **a.** to collide with. **b.** to meet by chance. **6. bump up**, *Informal* to increase (in extent, etc.).

bumper bar n. a horizontal bar affixed to the front or rear of a vehicle for protection in collisions.

bumptious adj. offensively self-assertive.

bun n. **1.** a round-shaped bread roll, usually sweet, and often containing dried currants, etc. **2.** hair arranged at the back of the head in a bun shape.

bunch n. **1.** a connected group; cluster. –v. **2.** to group together; make a bunch of.

bundle n. **1.** a group loosely held or tied together. –v. **2.** to put together loosely: *to bundle books into a bag*. –phr. **3. bundle off** (or **out**), to send away hurriedly or unceremoniously. **4. drop one's bundle**, *Aust.*, *NZ* to give up or not be able to cope with something any more.

Compare this with **package**, which is something wrapped up rather than tied together.

bundy n. *Aust. Informal (from trademark)* a clock which records the arrival and departure times of employees on a card inserted into it.

bung¹ n. **1.** a stopper, as for the hole of a cask. –v. **2.** *Informal* to put. –phr. **3. bung it on**, **a.** to behave temperamentally. **b.** to act in a pretentious or ostentatious manner.

bung² adj. *Aust.*, *NZ Informal* not in good working order.

bungalow /ˈbʌŋɡəloʊ/ n. a house or cottage of one storey.

bungee jumping /ˈbʌndʒi dʒʌmpɪŋ/ n. a sport in which one throws oneself from a high place such as a bridge to which one is attached by an elastic cord (**bungee**). –bungee jumper, n.

bungle v. to do clumsily and awkwardly; botch.

bunion n. a swelling on the foot.

bunk n. a built-in platform bed.

bunker n. **1.** a chest or box; a large bin or receptacle. **2.** a fortified shelter, often underground. **3.** *Golf* a shallow excavation, usually at the side of a green, partly filled with sand.

bunkum n. insincere talk; humbug.

bunny n. (*pl.* **-nies**) *Informal* **1.** a rabbit. **2.** someone who accepts the responsibility for a situation.

Children often use the expression **bunny rabbit** for def. 1.

bunting n. **1.** a coarse open fabric used for flags, signals. **2.** decorations made from bunting, paper, etc., usually in the form of wide streamers.

bunyip n. an imaginary creature of Aboriginal legend, said to haunt rushy swamps and billabongs.

buoy /bɔɪ/ n. *Naut.* **1.** an anchored float, sometimes carrying a light, whistle, or bell, marking a channel or obstruction. **2.** Also, **lifebuoy**. a floating ring used to rescue people from deep water. –v. **3.** to support by or as by a buoy; keep afloat in a fluid. **4.** to bear up or sustain: *Hope buoyed their courage*.

buoyant adj. **1.** tending to float. **2.** not easily depressed.

burble v. to make a bubbling sound; bubble.

burden *n.* **1.** that which is carried. **2.** that which is borne with difficulty. *–v.* **3.** to load heavily. **–burdensome,** *adj.*

bureau /ˈbjuːrou, bjuˈrou/ *n.* (*pl.* **-eaus** *or* **-eaux** /-ouz/) **1.** a desk or writing table with drawers. **2.** a division of a government department.

bureaucracy /bjuˈrɒkrəsi/ *n.* (*pl.* **-cies**) **1.** government by officials organised into departments, bureaus, etc. **2.** the body of such officials. **3.** excessive governmental red tape and routine. **–bureaucrat,** *n.* **–bureaucratic,** *adj.*

burgeon /ˈbɜdʒən/ *v.* to grow rapidly.

The more usual word is **increase**.

burger *n.* **1.** → **hamburger**. **2.** any of various adaptations of the hamburger which have different main contents in the bun: *fish burger*.

burglary *n.* (*pl.* **-ries**) the crime of breaking into and entering a house with intent to steal, etc. **–burglar,** *n.*

burgundy /ˈbɜɡəndi/ *n.* (*pl.* **-dies**) **1.** wine of many varieties, red and white, usually still and dry. **2.** a purplish red.

burial /ˈberiəl/ *n.* the act of burying.

burka *n.* → **burqa**.

burkini /bɜˈkɪni/ *n.* (*from trademark*) a swimsuit designed for Muslim women, comprising leggings and a top with a hood. Also, **burqini**.

burl *n.* *Aust., NZ Informal* an attempt.

burlesque /bɜˈlɛsk/ *n.* **1.** comic work which vulgarises lofty material or treats ordinary material with mock dignity. **2.** a theatrical entertainment featuring coarse, often vulgar comedy.

burly *adj.* (**-lier, -liest**) **1.** great in bodily size; sturdy. **2.** bluff; brusque.

burn *v.* (**burnt** *or* **burned, burning**) **1.** to be on fire. **2.** to feel heat. **3.** to give light. **4.** to feel strong passion. **5.** to become discoloured or charred through heat. **6.** to consume with fire. **7.** to injure, discolour, char, or treat with heat. *–n.* **8.** an injury produced by heat or by abnormal cold,

chemicals, etc. *–phr.* **9. burn off,** to clear (land) by burning the cover.

burnish *v.* to polish (a surface) by friction.

burp *v., n.* → **belch** (defs 1 and 4).

burqa /ˈbɜkə/ *n.* a traditional garment for Muslim women, giving full body covering with a mesh-covered opening for the eyes. Compare **chador, hijab.** Also, **burka.**

burr¹ *n.* the rough, prickly case around the seeds of certain plants.

burr² *n.* **1.** a tool or appliance for cutting or drilling. *–v.* **2.** to form a rough point or edge on.

burrow *n.* **1.** a hole in the ground made by a rabbit, fox, or similar small animal. *–v.* **2.** to make a hole or passage (*in, into,* or *under* something).

bursar *n.* **1.** a treasurer or business officer, especially of a college or university. **2.** a student holding a bursary.

bursary *n.* (*pl.* **-ries**) a scholarship.

burst *v.* (**burst, bursting**) **1.** to fly apart or break open with sudden violence; explode. **2.** to issue forth suddenly, as from confinement. **3.** to give way from violent pain or emotion. **4.** to be extremely full, as if ready to break open. *–n.* **5.** the act of bursting. **6.** a sudden display or manifestation: *a burst of energy or anger.*

bury *v.* (**-ried, -rying**) **1.** to put in the ground and cover with earth. **2.** to cover in order to conceal. **3.** to occupy (oneself) completely.

Don't confuse this with **berry**, which is a small fruit.

bus *n.* (*pl.* **buses** *or* **busses**) **1.** a passenger vehicle with a long body usually operating as part of a scheduled service. **2.** *Computers* → **bus** (def. 2).

This is short for **omnibus**.

busbar *n.* **1.** an electrical conductor having low resistance connecting several like points in an electrical system, frequently used to supply power to various points.

2. *Computers* a group of such electrical conductors providing a communication path within a computer or between two or more computerised devices.

bush *n.* **1.** a woody plant with many branches which usually arise from or near the ground. **2.** something resembling or suggesting this, as a thick, shaggy head of hair. **3.** a stretch of land covered with bushy vegetation or trees. *–adj.* **4.** found in or typical of the bush: *a bush nurse; a bush pub; bush hospitality.* **5.** uncivilised; rough; makeshift: *a bush bed; bush carpentry. –phr.* **6. the bush,** *Aust.* the countryside in general, as opposed to towns.

bushcare *n.* the maintenance of remnant bush or the revegetation of land with native trees, as by landowners and community groups. *–***bushcarer** *n.*

bushed *adj. Informal* **1.** lost. **2.** exhausted. **3.** confused.

bushel *n.* a unit of dry measure in the imperial system equal to $36.368\,72 \times 10^{-3}$ m^3 (8 gal).

bushfire *n. Aust., NZ* a fire in forest or scrub country.

bushman *n. Aust., NZ* **1.** a dweller in the bush. **2.** someone skilled in survival in the bush.

bushranger *n. Aust., NZ Hist.* a bandit who hid in the bush and robbed travellers, etc.

bush regeneration *n.* the regeneration of areas of bush in which the native flora has been supplanted by exotic species, or destroyed.

bushwalk *v.* **1.** to hike through the bush for pleasure. *–n.* **2.** such a hike. *–***bush-walker** *n. –***bushwalking** *n.*

bushwhacker *n. Aust., NZ Informal* an unsophisticated person who lives in the bush.

business /ˈbɪznəs/ *n.* **1.** one's occupation, profession, or trade. **2.** the purchase and sale of goods in an attempt to make a

profit. **3.** a person, partnership, or corporation engaged in this. **4.** volume of trade. **5.** that with which one is principally and seriously concerned. **6.** affair; matter.

Don't confuse **business** with **busyness** (pronounced /ˈbɪznəs/), which refers to the state of being busy.

business activity statement *n.* a statement which a business is required to submit to the government agency on a regular basis, containing an account of transactions and allowing the calculation of tax, especially GST, payable. Also, **BAS.**

businesslike *adj.* conforming to the methods of business or trade.

businessperson *n.* a person engaged in business or commerce. *–***businessman** *–***businesswoman**

busker *n.* an entertainer who gives performances in streets, etc., usually collecting donations.

bust[1] *n.* **1.** the head and shoulders of a person done in sculpture. **2.** the chest or breast; the bosom.

bust[2] *Informal –v.* **1.** to burst. **2.** to (cause to) go bankrupt. **3.** to reduce in rank or grade. *–n.* **4.** a complete failure; bankruptcy. **5.** a police raid, often in search of an illegal substance. *–adj.* **6. busted** broken; ruined. **7.** bankrupt. *–phr.* **8. bust up, a.** to part finally; quarrel and part. **b.** to smash. **c.** to interrupt violently (a meeting, etc.).

bustard *n.* a large, heavy bird inhabiting plains and open scrub of Aust. and New Guinea.

bustle[1] *v.* to move (*about*) with a great show of energy.

bustle[2] *n.* (formerly) a pad worn by women on the back below the waist, to expand and support the skirt.

busy /ˈbɪzi/ *adj.* (**busier, busiest**) **1.** actively and attentively engaged. **2.** full of activity. **3.** → **engaged** (def. 1). *–v.* (**busied, busying**) **4.** to keep occupied;

make or keep busy. **–busily**, *adv.* **–busyness**, *n.*

Don't confuse **busyness** with **business** (pronounced /'bɪznəs/), which is the work someone does to earn a living.

busybody *n.* (*pl.* **-dies**) a person who meddles in the affairs of others.

but *conj.* **1.** on the contrary; yet. **2.** except, rather than, or save. **3.** (fol. by a clause, oft. with *that* expressed) except that. **4.** without the circumstance that, or that not. **5.** otherwise than. **6.** who or which not. **–prep. 7.** with the exception of; except; save. **–adv. 8.** only; just. **–n. 9.** a restriction or objection.

Some writers don't like sentences beginning with **but**, as in *But this isn't the end of the story.* They argue that **but** is a conjunction which should link clauses within a sentence and should not link two separate sentences. In fact many writers *do* use **but** at the beginning of a sentence and there is no reason not to do it, occasionally.

Some speakers put **but** at the end of a sentence rather than at the beginning, as in *I've broken by arm. I can still write, but.* Many people regard this as incorrect.

Don't confuse **but** with **butt**, which has several meanings. It can refer to the end of something like a cigarette, or to someone who is a target of unkindness. It can also mean to push something with the head or horns.

butane /'bjutem/ *n.* a hydrocarbon used as a fuel.

butch *adj. Informal* (of a man or woman) exhibiting strong masculine characteristics.

butcher *n.* **1.** a retail dealer in meat. **2.** a person guilty of cruel or indiscriminate slaughter. **–v. 3.** to murder indiscriminately or brutally. **–butchery**, *n.*

butcherbird *n.* any of several birds which impale their prey on spikes or thorns or wedge it in the forks of trees.

butler *n.* the head male servant of a household.

butt¹ *n.* **1.** the thicker, larger, or blunt end of anything, especially of a rifle, fishing rod, etc. **2.** a hind leg of beef on the bone. **3.** an end which is not used up. **4.** *Informal* the buttocks; bottom: *shift your butt.*

Don't confuse this with **but**, a common word usually used as a conjunction, as in *I'd like to come, but I have to work.*

butt² *n.* **1.** a person or thing that is an object of ridicule, contempt, etc. **2.** the target for archery practice. **–v. 3.** to have an end or projection; be adjacent (*onto*).

butt³ *v.* **1.** to strike with the head or horns. **2.** to project. **–phr. butt in 3.** to interrupt; interfere; intrude. **4. butt out,** to mind one's own business and not interfere in something which is not one's proper concern.

butter *n.* **1.** the yellowish, fatty solid made from churned cream. **–v. 2.** to put butter on or in. **–phr. 3. butter up,** to flatter grossly.

butterfly *n.* (*pl.* **-flies**) **1.** an insect with large, broad wings often conspicuously coloured and marked. **2.** (*pl.*) *Informal* nervousness. **3.** Also, **butterfly stroke.** a swimming stroke in prone position, with both arms flung forward simultaneously.

buttermilk *n.* the liquid remaining after the butter has been separated from milk or cream.

butterscotch *n.* a kind of toffee made with butter.

buttock *n.* either of the 2 protuberances which form the rump.

button *n.* **1.** a disc or knob on a garment which passes through a slit or loop to serve as a fastening. **2.** anything resembling a button. **3.** a disc pressed to close an electric circuit, as in ringing a bell; push-button. **4.** *Computers* a small outlined area on a screen which, when selected, performs some function. –v. **5.** to fasten with a button or buttons.

buttonhole n. **1.** the hole, slit, or loop through which a button is passed. **2.** a small flower or posy worn on the lapel of a jacket.

buttress n. **1.** a stabilising structure built against a wall or building. **2.** any prop or support.

buxom adj. (of a woman) full-bosomed, plump, and attractive.

buy v. (**bought, buying**) **1.** to acquire the possession of by payment. **2.** *Informal* to accept. **3.** to be or become a purchaser. –n. **4.** *Informal* a purchase, especially a good purchase. –phr. **5. buy into**, to choose to become involved in. **6. buy off**, to get rid of (a claim, opposition, etc.) by payment; bribe. **7. buy out**, to secure (an owner's or partner's) share in an enterprise. **8. buy up**, to buy as much as one can of.

> Don't confuse **buy** with **by** or **bye**. If something is **by** something else, it is near it. A **bye** is when your sporting team does not have to play in a certain round. **Bye** can also mean 'goodbye'.

buyer n. **1.** someone who buys; a purchaser. **2.** a purchasing agent, as for a department store.

buzz n. **1.** a low, vibrating, humming sound, as of bees. **2.** *Informal* a telephone call. **3.** *Informal* **a.** a feeling of exhilaration, especially as induced by drugs. **b.** a similar experience of pleasure, delight, etc.: *I get a real buzz out of going sailing.* –v. **4.** to make a low, vibrating, humming sound (*with*). **5.** to move (*about*) busily from place to place . **6.** *Informal* to leave or go (*off.* or *along*). **7.** *Informal* to fly an aeroplane very low over.

buzzard n. any of various birds of prey related to but smaller than eagles.

by prep. **1.** near to. **2.** using as a route. **3.** through or on as a means of conveyance. **4.** not later than. **5.** to the extent of. **6.** through evidence or authority of. **7.** in conformity with. **8.** before; in the presence of. **9.** through the agency or efficacy of. **10.** after; in serial order. **11.** combined with in multiplication or relative dimension. –adv. **12.** near to something. **13.** to and past a point near something. **14.** aside. **15.** over; past. –phr. **16. by and by**, at some time in the future; before long. **17. by and large**, in general.

> Don't confuse this with **buy** or **bye**. If you **buy** something, you pay money for it. A **bye** is when your sporting team does not have to play in a certain round. **Bye** can also mean 'goodbye'.

bye[1] n. the state of having no competitor in a contest where competitors are paired, giving the right to compete in the next round. Also, **by**.

> Don't confuse this with **by** or **buy**. If something is **by** something else, it is near it. If you **buy** something you pay money for it.

bye[2] interj. goodbye.

by-election n. a parliamentary election held between general elections, to fill a vacancy caused by the death or resignation of a member of parliament. Also, **bye-election**.

bygone adj. **1.** past; out of date. –n. **2.** that which is past.

by-law n. **1.** a regulation made by a local government and enforceable only within its area. **2.** subordinate legislation, generally at the level of local government. Also, **bye-law**.

by-line n. a line under the heading of a newspaper or magazine article giving the writer's name.

byname n. **1.** a secondary name. **2.** a nickname.

bypass n. **1.** a road enabling motorists to avoid towns and other heavy traffic points on a main road. **2.** *Med.* a tube-like device inserted by surgery to circumvent a diseased area, such as the blood vessels of the heart. *—adj.* **3.** relating to surgery that inserts a bypass. *—v.* **4.** to avoid (obstructions, etc.). **5.** to go over the head of (one's immediate supervisor, etc.).

by-product *n.* a secondary or incidental product, as in a process of manufacture.

byre *n.* a cowhouse or shed.

bystander *n.* a person present but not involved.

byte /bait/ *n.* a unit of information, usually 8 bits, stored by a computer. See **bit³**.

Don't confuse this with **bight** or **bite**. A **bight** is the looped part of a rope, or a curve in a shore forming a large bay. A **bite** is a wound made with the teeth, or a mouthful of food.

byway *n.* **1.** a secluded, or obscure road. **2.** a subsidiary field of research, endeavour, etc.

byword *n.* **1.** the name of a quality or concept which characterises some person or group; the epitome (of). **2.** a word or phrase used proverbially.

84

C, c

C, c *n.* a consonant, the third letter of the English alphabet.

cab *n.* **1.** → taxi. **2.** the covered part of a truck etc., for the driver.

cabaret /ˈkæbəreɪ/ *n.* musical entertainment at a restaurant, nightclub, etc.

cabbage *n.* a vegetable with a compact head of edible leaves.

caber *n.* a pole thrown as a trial of strength in a Scottish game.

cabin *n.* **1.** a small temporary house. **2.** a room in a ship, aircraft, etc.

cabinet *n.* **1.** a piece of furniture with shelves, drawers, etc. **2.** (*also upper case*) the group of ministers responsible for the government of a nation.

cable *n.* **1.** a thick, strong rope. **2.** (formerly) a message sent by electric signals, especially along submarine cable. **3.** → cable TV.

cable TV *n.* a system of broadcasting television programs by sending them directly from the distribution centre to the receiving set by means of a linking cable. Also, **cable television, cable.**

cabriolet /ˈkæbriəʊˌleɪ/ *n.* a type of car resembling a coupé, with a folding top.

cacao /kəˈkeɪəʊ/ *n.* a small evergreen tropical American tree, from the seeds of which cocoa and chocolate are made.

cache /kæʃ/ *n.* a hiding place.

Don't confuse this with **cash**, which is money in notes and coin.

cache memory /keɪʃ/ *n.* a section of computer memory which can be accessed at high speed and in which information is stored for fast retrieval.

cackle *v.* to utter the shrill, broken sound of a hen.

cacophony /kəˈkɒfəni/ *n.* (*pl.* **-nies**) a harsh sound.

cactus *n.* (*pl.* **-tuses** *or* **-ti**) any of various fleshy-stemmed plants of the American deserts.

cad *n.* a contemptible person.

cadaver /kəˈdævə, -ˈdɑːvə/ *n.* a corpse.

caddie *n.* *Golf* an attendant hired to carry the player's clubs, etc.

caddy *n.* (*pl.* **-dies**) a small box, tin, or chest, especially one for holding tea.

cadence /ˈkeɪdns/ *n.* **1.** rhythmic flow of poetry, etc. **2.** the general modulation of the voice.

cadet *n.* a person undergoing training, especially in the armed services.

cadge *v.* (**cadged, cadging**) to borrow without intent to repay.

cadmium *n.* a white metallic element like tin in appearance. Symbol: Cd

cadre /ˈkɑːdə, ˈkeɪdə/ *n.* a personnel unit within an organisational framework.

caesarean section /səˈzeəriən/ *n.* the operation by which a baby is born by cutting through the walls of the abdomen and womb.

The short form of this is **caesarean**. Another spelling is **caesarian**.

caesar salad /ˈsiːzə/ *n.* a salad containing lettuce, bread croutons, parmesan cheese and sometimes anchovies, seasoned and dressed with egg, oil and vinegar.

caesium /ˈsiːziəm/ *n.* a rare, extremely active, soft, monovalent metallic element. Symbol: Cs

cafe *n.* a shop where coffee and light refreshments are served. Also, **café.**

cafe latte /ˈlateɪ/ *n.* a style of coffee in which espresso coffee is poured into a large glass of hot milk. Also, **caffe latte, latte.**

cafeteria *n.* an inexpensive restaurant or snack-bar, usually self-service.

caffeine /ˈkæfin/ n. a bitter substance obtained from coffee, tea, etc.

caftan n. a long, loose garment. Also, **kaftan**.

cage n. **1.** a box-shaped receptacle or enclosure with bars or wires for confining birds or other animals. –v. **(caged, caging) 2.** to confine in a cage.

cagey adj. **(cagier, cagiest)** Informal cautious; secretive. Also, **cagy**.

cahoots phr. **in cahoots**, in partnership; in league.

caiman /ˈkeimən/ n. a tropical American reptile resembling and related to the alligators, but with overlapping abdominal plates. Also, **cayman**.

cajole v. to persuade by flattery or promises. –**cajolery**, n.

cake n. **1.** a sweet baked food in loaf or layer form, usually made from flour, butter, sugar, eggs, etc. **2.** a small mass of something with a definite shape: *a fish cake; a cake of soap.* –v. **3.** to cover with a thick crust of something: *She caked her face with make-up.*

calamari n. squid used as food.

calamine n. a liquid soothing to the skin. Also, **calamine lotion**.

calamity n. **(pl. -ties)** a disaster. –**calamitous**, adj.

calcify v. **(-fied, -fying)** to become chalky or bony.

calcium n. a silver-white divalent metal. *Symbol:* Ca

calculate v. to ascertain by mathematical methods. –**calculation**, n. –**calculable**, adj.

calculating adj. shrewd.

calculator n. a machine that performs mathematical operations.

calculus /ˈkælkjələs/ n. **(pl. -luses** for def. **1, -li** /-laɪ/ for def. **2) 1.** a method of calculation. **2.** a hard stone-like mass which has formed in the body.

calendar n. a system of reckoning time, especially with reference to the divisions of the year.

calf¹ n. **(pl. calves)** the young of the cow or certain other animals.

calf² n. **(pl. calves)** the fleshy part of the back of the human leg below the knee.

calibrate v. to determine or check the graduation or accuracy of. –**calibration**, n.

calibre /ˈkælɪbə/ n. **1.** the diameter of something circular, especially of the inside of the bore of a gun. **2.** personal character.

calico n. a coarse, white cotton cloth.

caliper n. **1.** **(usu. pl.)** a tool for measuring diameters. **2.** Med. a limb brace. Also, **calliper**.

caliph /ˈkeɪlæf/ n. the head of a Muslim state. –**caliphate**, n.

call v. **1.** to cry out or speak in a loud voice as to attract attention (of). **2.** (of a bird or other animal) to utter (its characteristic cry). **3.** to command or request to come. **4.** to give a name to. **5.** to make a short visit. **6.** to telephone. –n. **7.** a cry or shout. **8.** the cry of a bird or other animal. **9.** a short visit. **10.** a telephone conversation. **11.** a summons; invitation. **12.** a demand or claim. –adj. **13.** repayable on demand. –phr. **14. call in**, **a.** to collect. **b.** to withdraw from circulation. **15. on call**, **a.** Also, **at call**. payable without advance notice. **b.** (of doctors, etc.) available for duty at short notice.

call centre n. a location at which operators make phone calls for client organisations, as for marketing, information services, etc.

callgirl n. a prostitute who makes appointments by telephone.

calligraphy /kəˈlɪɡrəfi/ n. the art of doing beautiful handwriting.

calling n. a vocation, profession, or trade.

callisthenics /kæləsˈθɛnɪks/ pl. n. light gymnastic exercises.

callous adj. not caring about the feelings of others; hardened.

Don't confuse **callous** with **callus**, which is a part of your skin which has grown thick and hard.

callow *adj.* immature or inexperienced.

callus *n.* a hardened or thickened part of the skin.

Don't confuse this with **callous**, which describes someone who shows no concern for another's feelings.

calm *adj.* **1.** without rough motion; still. **2.** free from excitement or passion. –*n.* **3.** freedom from movement, excitement, etc. –*v.* **4.** to make calm.

calorie *n.* a non-SI unit, approx. equal to 4 kilojoules, used to express the heat energy value of a food.

Nowadays **kilojoule** is used instead of **calorie**. It is the metric unit.

calumny /'kæləmnɪ/ *n.* slander. –**calumniate**, *v.*

calve *v.* to give birth to a calf.

calyx /'keɪlɪks, 'kæl-/ *n.* (*pl.* **calyces** /'kæləsiz, 'keɪ-/ or **calyxes**) the outermost parts of a flower, usually green.

cam *n.* a webcam.

camaraderie /kæmə'radərɪ/ *n.* comradeship; close friendship.

came *v.* past tense of **come**.

camel *n.* **1.** a large humped ruminant quadruped. **2.** a light fawn colour.

camellia *n.* a glossy leaved shrub with white, pink, or red, waxy, roselike flowers.

camembert /'kæməmbeə/ *n.* a rich, cream-coloured variety of soft, ripened cheese, usually made in small, flat, round loaves, covered with a thin greyish-white rind.

cameo *n.* (*pl.* **-meos**) **1.** an engraving in relief upon a gem, stone, etc. **2.** a short performance or appearance in a play or film by a celebrity.

camera[1] *n.* an apparatus for taking photographs or moving pictures.

camera[2] *phr.* **in camera**, *Law* in a judge's private room.

camisole *n.* a woman's simple top with narrow shoulder straps, now usually worn as an undergarment.

camomile *n.* → **chamomile**.

camouflage /'kæməflaʒ, -fladʒ/ *n.* the means by which any object disguises itself against its background.

camp[1] *n.* **1.** a group of tents, caravans, or other temporary shelters. **2.** a group of people with the same ideals, doctrines, etc. –*v.* **3.** to establish or pitch a camp. –*phr.* **4.** **camp out**, to live temporarily in a tent or similar shelter.

camp[2] *adj.* **1.** exaggeratedly theatrical and flashy in style. **2.** of a male, homosexual.

campaign *n.* any course of aggressive activities for some special purpose.

camphor /'kæmfə/ *n.* **1.** a crystalline substance used in medicine, etc. **2.** any of various similar substances, for household use as an insect deterrent.

campus *n.* the grounds of a university or other such institute.

can[1] *v.* a verb used **1.** to indicate ability to do something: *I don't think I can lift that box.* **2.** to indicate permission: *Can I speak to you a moment?*; *You can come too, if you like.*

Some people say you should always use **may**, not **can**, for def. 2, but in modern English **can** is much more common than **may**.
This is a modal verb and is always used with another verb. Its past tense is **could**. Look up **modal verb**.

can[2] *n.* **1.** a metal container usually coated with tin. **2.** *Informal* the blame for something. –*v.* (**canned**, **canning**) **3.** to put in a container, usually sealed for preservation.

canal *n.* an artificial waterway.

canary *n.* (*pl.* **-ries**) a small, yellow bird. Also, **canary bird**.

cancel *v.* (**-celled**, **-celling**) **1.** to decide not to proceed with. **2.** to cross out by drawing a line or lines over. **3.** to make void.

cancer n. a malignant growth or tumour. –**cancerous**, adj.

candela /kæn'deilə, -'delə/ n. the SI base unit of luminous intensity. *Symbol:* cd

candelabrum n. (pl. **-bra**) an ornamental branched candlestick.

candid adj. frank; outspoken; open and sincere.

candidate n. someone who seeks an office, an honour, etc.

candle n. a long, slender piece of wax, etc., with an embedded wick, burnt to give light.

candour n. frankness; sincerity. Also, **candor**.

candy n. (pl. **-dies**) **1.** a sweet made of sugar crystallised by boiling. –v. (**-died**, **-dying**) **2.** to cook in heavy syrup until transparent, as fruit, fruit peel, or ginger.

cane n. **1.** a long, hollow or pithy, jointed woody stem, as that of bamboo, rattan, sugar cane, certain palms, etc. **2.** the stem of a bamboo, etc., used as a rod for punishing school children. **3.** a walking stick.

canine adj. relating to dogs.

canister n. a small container for holding tea, flour, etc.

cannabis /'kænəbəs/ n. hashish.

cannibal n. any animal that eats its own kind.

cannon n. **1.** a large ancient gun mounted on a carriage. **2.** any strike and rebound, as a ball striking a wall and glancing off.

Don't confuse this with **canon**, which can mean either a church official or a set of rules.

cannula /'kænjələ/ n. a metal tube for insertion into the body, used to keep a passage open, to draw off fluid, or to introduce medication.

canny adj. (**-nier**, **-niest**) careful; cautious; wary. –**cannily**, adv.

canoe n. any light and narrow boat propelled by paddles.

canola n. a variety of rapeseed from which is produced an oil extract for human consumption, and a meal for livestock feed.

canon[1] n. **1.** a church rule or law. **2.** the body of such laws. **3.** a fundamental principle. –**canonical**, adj.

Don't confuse this with **cannon**, which is a type of large gun.

canon[2] n. one of a body of clergy attached to a cathedral.

canonise /'kænənaiz/ v. to acknowledge as a saint. Also, **canonize**. –**canonisation**, n.

canoodle /kə'nudl/ v. *Informal* to indulge in fondling and petting.

canopy n. (pl. **-pies**) a covering suspended over a throne, bed, etc.

cant[1] n. **1.** insincere statements. **2.** the words, phrases, etc., peculiar to a particular class, party, profession, etc.

cant[2] n. **1.** a slope. **2.** a sudden movement that tilts or overturns a thing.

can't v. contraction of *cannot*.

cantaloupe /'kæntəloup, 'kæntəlup/ n. a type of melon with orange-coloured flesh; rockmelon.

cantankerous adj. ill-natured; quarrelsome.

canteen n. **1.** a restaurant or cafeteria attached to a workplace. **2.** Also, **tuckshop**, **kiosk**. a similar food outlet in a school, sportsground, etc., usually staffed by volunteer parents. **3.** a box containing a set of cutlery. **4.** a small container for carrying water.

canter n. **1.** a horse's gait, slower than a gallop. –v. **2.** to ride at a canter.

cantilever /'kæntaliva/ n. **1.** *Machinery* a free part of any horizontal member projecting beyond a support. **2.** *Civil Eng.* either of two bracket-like arms projecting towards each other from opposite banks or piers, serving to form the span of a bridge (**cantilever bridge**) when united.

canton n. a small district, especially in Switzerland.

canvas n. 1. a closely woven, heavy cloth used for tents, sails, etc. 2. a piece of this used for an oil painting.

Don't confuse this with **canvass**.

canvass v. to solicit votes, subscriptions, opinions, etc., from (a district, group of people, etc.).

Don't confuse this with **canvas**.

canyon n. a deep valley with steep sides.

canyoning n. the sport of following a river down a canyon, usually involving whitewater rafting, rock climbing, abseiling, etc.

cap n. 1. a close-fitting head covering of soft material, with a peak. 2. the detachable protective top of a fountain pen, jar, etc. 3. a noisemaking device for toy pistols. –v. (**capped, capping**) 4. to provide or cover with or as with a cap. 5. to surpass.

capable adj. 1. having much intelligence or ability; efficient. –phr. 2. **capable of, a.** having the ability to: *capable of running a kilometre.* **b.** likely to: *capable of murder.* –**capability**, n.

capacious adj. capable of holding much.

capacity n. (pl. -**ties**) 1. cubic contents; volume. 2. power or ability, to do something. 3. position; function: *in the capacity of legal adviser.*

cap-and-trade adj. of or relating to an emissions trading scheme in which a cap is set for allowable emissions in a particular area, and individual emitters are given their allocation of emission permits which they can use or sell provided the overall cap is not breached.

cape¹ n. a sleeveless garment fastened round the neck and falling over the shoulders.

cape² n. a piece of land jutting into the sea.

caper¹ v. 1. to leap about in a sprightly manner. –n. 2. a prank.

caper² n. the pickled flower bud of a bramble-shrub used in cookery.

capillary n. (pl. -**ries**) 1. a minute blood vessel. –adj. 2. relating to or occurring in or as in a tube of fine bore. 3. *Physics* or relating to the property of surface tension

capillary action n. the raising or lowering of liquids in thin tubes, etc., due to forces between molecules, such as surface tension, and between molecules of the liquid and the tube, etc.

capital n. 1. Also, **capital city**. the city where the government of a country etc. sits. 2. wealth capable of producing more wealth. 3. the ownership interest in a business. 4. → **capital letter**. –adj. 5. relating to capital. 6. principal; highly important. 7. punishable by death.

capitalise v. 1. to write or print in capital letters, or with an initial capital. 2. to supply with capital. –phr. 3. **capitalise on,** to take advantage of; turn to one's advantage. Also, **capitalize**. –**capitalisation,** n.

capitalism n. a political and economic system under which property and industry are mainly owned privately, rather than by the government or by the people as a whole, and in which private organisations compete against each other to make profits. –**capitalist,** n.

Compare this with **communism** and **socialism**.

capital letter n. one of the set of larger letters of the alphabet which are used at the start of sentences, and at the start of the names of particular people, places, etc. Also, **capital, upper-case letter.**

capitation n. 1. a numbering or assessing by the head. 2. a fee or payment of a uniform amount for each person.

capitulate v. to surrender unconditionally or on stipulated terms. –**capitulation,** n.

The more usual expression is **give in**.

cappuccino /kæpə'tʃinou/ n. coffee made on an espresso machine, topped with hot frothy milk.

capricious adj. characterised by or subject to whim; unpredictable. –**caprice**, n.

capsicum n. the common pepper with mild to hot, pungent seeds.

capsicum spray n. → **pepper spray**.

capsize v. 1. to overturn. 2. to upset.

capsule n. 1. a gelatinous case enclosing a dose of medicine. 2. the compartment of a spacecraft containing the crew and or instruments.

captain n. 1. someone who is in authority over others; leader; chief. 2. an officer in the army. 3. the commander or master of a merchant ship or other vessel.

caption n. 1. a legend for a picture or illustration. 2. *Film* the title of a scene, the text of a speech, etc., shown on the screen.

captivate v. to enthral by beauty or excellence.

captive n. 1. a prisoner. –adj. 2. made or held prisoner, especially in war. –**captivity**, n.

captor n. a person who captures.

capture v. 1. to take prisoner; seize. –n. 2. the act of capturing. 3. the thing or person captured.

car n. 1. a motor car. 2. a vehicle running on rails, as a tramcar, etc.

carafe /kəˈraf, -ˈræf/ n. a glass bottle for water, wine, etc.

caramel n. burnt sugar, used for colouring and flavouring food, etc.

carat /ˈkærət/ n. 1. Also, **metric carat**. a unit of weight used for gem stones. 2. a measurement for the purity of gold.

> Don't confuse this with **caret** or **carrot**.
> A **caret** is a mark you make in writing to show where something has to be added.
> A **carrot** is a vegetable.

caravan n. 1. a vehicle in which people may live, designed to be drawn by a motor car. 2. a group of merchants or others travelling together, especially over deserts, etc.

carbide n. a compound of carbon.

carbine n. (formerly) a short rifle for cavalry use.

carbohydrate n. a class of organic compounds including sugars, starch, etc., which are important food for animals.

carbon n. a widely distributed element which forms organic compounds in combination with hydrogen, oxygen, etc., and which occurs in a pure state as charcoal. *Symbol*: C

carbonate v. to treat (soft drinks, etc.) with carbon dioxide so as to make them bubbly.

carbon cap n. an upper limit, set by a government or international body, of permissible production of carbon dioxide as part of a strategy to limit global production and reduce the risk of climate change.

carbon capture n. the process of removing carbon dioxide from a point where it is normally released in large quantities, as from a power plant, so that it can then be prevented from entering the atmosphere. See **carbon sequestration**.

carbon credit n. a credit earned within the carbon tax system for decreasing carbon dioxide in the atmosphere, as by planting forests, etc.

carbon dioxide n. a colourless, odourless, incombustible gas, CO_2, used extensively in industry.

carbon footprint n. the carbon dioxide emissions for which an individual or organisation can be held responsible, as by their travel, fuel consumption, diet, energy requirements, etc.

carbon monoxide n. a colourless, odourless, poisonous gas.

carbon-neutral adj. having achieved carbon neutrality.

carbon paper n. paper faced with a preparation of carbon or other material, used to make copies as one writes or types.

carbon sequestration n. the process by which carbon dioxide is removed from the atmosphere, naturally by plants in their growth but artificially by various means, and then prevented from returning to the atmosphere by the creation of products with long-term use, as timber from forests, or by storing it in sealed reservoirs, as by injecting it into underground geological formations.

carbon sink *n.* a large vegetated area which absorbs carbon dioxide from the atmosphere, thus reducing the level of greenhouse gases.

carbon tax *n.* a tax on the consumption of fossil fuels.

carbuncle *n.* a painful circumscribed mass of boils.

carburettor *n.* a device in an internal-combustion engine for mixing a volatile fuel with the correct proportion of air.

carcass /ˈkakəs/ *n.* the dead body of an animal or (now only in contempt) of a human being.

carcinogen /kɑˈsɪnədʒən/ *n.* any substance which tends to cause a cancer in a body. –**carcinogenic**, *adj.*

carcinoma /kasəˈnoumə/ *n.* (*pl.* **-mas** or **-mata** /-mətə/) a malignant and invasive tumour that spreads and often recurs after excision; a cancer.

card[1] *n.* **1.** a piece of stiff paper or thin pasteboard. **2.** one of a set of small pieces of cardboard with spots or figures, used in playing various games. **3.** *Computers* a circuit board: *a video card; a sound card*.

card[2] *n.* a toothed implement or wire brush used in combing out fibres of wool, flax, etc., preparatory to spinning.

cardamom *n.* the aromatic seed of various Asian plants, used as a spice.

cardboard *n.* thick, stiff type of paper.

cardiac *adj.* relating to the heart.

cardigan *n.* a knitted jacket.

cardinal *adj.* **1.** of prime importance; chief; fundamental. –*n.* **2.** a member of the Sacred College of the Roman Catholic Church, which elects the pope.

cardinal number *n.* a number used in counting or indicating how many, as *one*, *two*, *three*, etc.

Compare this with **ordinal number**, which is a number which tells you the order of a thing in a series.

cardiology *n.* the branch of medical science that deals with the heart and its functions. –**cardiologist**, *n.*

cardiovascular /ˌkadiouˈvæskjələ/ *adj.* relating to the heart and blood vessels.

card skimming *n.* the practice of copying the magnetic stripe details of a plastic card with a card reader for use in counterfeiting.

care *n.* **1.** worry; concern. **2.** serious attention; caution. **3.** protection. –*v.* (**cared**, **caring**) **4.** to be affected emotionally. **5.** to be concerned or solicitous. **6.** to have a fondness or affection (*for*). **7.** to look after; make provision (*for*). –*phr.* Also, **c/o. 8. care of**, at the address of.

careen *v.* to lean or sway, as a ship.

career *n.* **1.** general progress of a person through life. **2.** an occupation, profession, etc., followed as one's lifework. –*v.* **3.** to move at high speed.

careful *adj.* **1.** taking care to avoid risks. **2.** paying close attention to detail, or carried out with close attention to detail. –**carefully**, *adv.*

careless *adj.* **1.** done without paying enough attention. **2.** done or said without thinking. –**carelessly**, *adv.* –**carelessness**, *n.*

caress *n.* **1.** a gesture expressing affection. –*v.* **2.** to touch affectionately.

caret *n.* a mark (^) in written or printed matter to show where something is to be inserted.

Don't confuse this with **carat** or **carrot**. A **carat** is a measure of the weight of a gem or the purity of gold. A **carrot** is a vegetable.

caretaker *n.* **1.** a person who maintains and protects a building or group of buildings.

–*adj.* **2.** holding office temporarily until a new appointment can be made.

cargo *n.* (*pl.* **-goes**) **1.** the goods carried on a ship, aircraft, truck, etc. **2.** any load.

caribou /ˈkærɪbuː/ *n.* (*pl.* **-bou** or **-bous**) a Nth American species of reindeer.

caricature /ˈkærəkətʃʊə/ *n.* a picture, description, etc., ludicrously exaggerating the peculiarities of persons or things.

caries /ˈkɛəriːz/ *n.* decay of bone or teeth.

carillon /kəˈrɪljən/ *n.* a set of bells hung in a tower and sounded manually, or by machinery.

carjack *v.* to steal (a car) by forcing the driver to vacate it, or by forcing the driver to drive to a chosen destination. Also, **carjack**. **–carjacker**, *n.* **–carjacking**, *n.*

car kit *n.* a hands-free mobile phone system installed in a vehicle.

carmine *n.* crimson.

carnage *n.* the slaughter of a great number.

carnal *adj.* **1.** relating to the flesh or the body; sensual. **2.** sexual.

carnation *n.* a garden plant with fragrant flowers of various colours.

carnival *n.* **1.** a festive procession. **2.** a fair or amusement show, especially one erected temporarily. **3.** a series of sporting events as a racing carnival, etc.

carnivorous *adj.* feeding on flesh. **–carnivore**, *n.*

Compare this with **herbivorous**, **omnivorous**, and **insectivorous**.

carol *n.* a song, especially of joy.

carotid /kəˈrɒtɪd/ *n.* either of the 2 great arteries, one on each side of the neck.

carouse /kəˈrauz/ *v.* **1.** a noisy or drunken feast; jovial revelry. –*v.* (**-roused**, **-rousing**) **2.** to engage in a carouse. **–carousal**, *n.*

carousel /kærəˈsɛl/ *n.* **1.** → **merry-go-round**. **2.** a revolving device by which luggage is returned to travellers after a journey by plane, ship, bus, etc. **3.** a revolving tray in a microwave oven, on which the food is placed to ensure even cooking.

carp[1] *v.* to find fault.

carp[2] *n.* (*pl.* **carp** or **carps**) a large, coarse freshwater food fish.

For information about the different plural forms, see the note at **fish**.

carpenter *n.* a person who erects the wooden parts of houses etc. **–carpentry**, *n.*

carpet *n.* a heavy fabric for covering floors.

car pool *n.* an arrangement whereby a group of people travel together in one car on a regular basis, taking turns to drive their own car.

carpool *v.* to take part in a car pool. **–carpooling**, *n.*

carriage *n.* **1.** a wheeled vehicle for passengers. **2.** manner of carrying the head and body.

carriage return *n.* **1.** (on a typewriter) a key or lever which causes the next character typed to be positioned at the left margin and down a line. **2.** (on a computer) a key or character which performs a similar function.

carrier pigeon *n.* a pigeon trained to fly home from great distances and thus transport written messages.

carrion *n.* dead and putrefying flesh.

carrot *n.* an orange-coloured root vegetable.

Don't confuse this with **caret** or **carat**. A **caret** is a mark you make in writing to show where something has to be added. A **carat** is a measure of the weight of a gem or the purity of gold.

carry *v.* (**-ried**, **-rying**) **1.** to cause to be moved or brought from one place to another. **2.** to bear the weight, burden, etc., of. **3.** to hold (the body, head, etc.) in a certain manner. **4.** to secure the election of (a candidate) or the adoption of (a motion or bill). **5.** to support or give validity to (a related claim, etc.). **6.** *Commerce* **a.** to keep on hand or in stock. **b.** to keep on one's account books, etc. **7.** to be transmitted, propelled, or sustained. *–phr.* **8. carry away,** to influence greatly or beyond reason. **9. carry off,** to face consequences boldly. **10. carry on, a.** to manage; conduct. **b.** to behave in an excited, foolish, or improper manner; flirt. **11. carry out,** to complete or complete. **12. carry over,** to postpone; hold off until later.

cart *n.* a small vehicle, sometimes pulled by a horse, used for carrying a load.

carte blanche /kat ˈblɒntʃ/ *n.* unconditional authority; full power.

cartel /kaˈtɛl/ *n.* an international syndicate formed to regulate prices, etc.

cartilage /ˈkatəlɪdʒ, ˈkatlɪdʒ/ *n.* a firm, elastic, flexible connective tissue; gristle.

cartography *n.* the production of maps.

carton *n.* a cardboard box, especially one in which food is packaged.

cartoon *n.* **1.** a humorous or satirical sketch of some subject or person of current interest, as in a newspaper, etc. **2.** a film consisting of a series of drawings, each slightly different from the ones before and after it, run through a projector.

cartridge *n.* **1.** a cylindrical case for holding the bullet or the shot, for a rifle, etc. **2.** anything resembling a cartridge, as the disposable container of ink for some types of fountain pen. **3.** (in a tape recorder) a plastic container enclosing recording tape.

carve *v.* **1.** to fashion by cutting wood, etc. **2.** to cut into slices or pieces, as meat.

cascade *n.* **1.** a waterfall over steep rocks. *–v.* **2.** to fall in or like a cascade.

case[1] *n.* **1.** an instance of something. **2.** the actual state of things. **3.** a statement of facts, reasons, etc. **4.** a suit or action at law. **5.** *Gram.* a category in the inflection of nouns, pronouns, and adjectives, denoting the syntactic relation of these words to other words in the sentence. *–phr.* **6. (just) in case, a.** if; if it should

happen that: *just in case there is an emergency; insurance in case civil action is brought.* **b.** as a precaution: *I'll take an umbrella, just in case.*

The three cases (def. 5) in English are **subjective**, **objective** and **possessive**.

case[2] *n.* **1.** a receptacle. **2.** a sheath or outer covering. **3.** a suitcase. *–v.* **4.** to put or enclose in a case.

casement *n.* a window sash opening on hinges.

cash *n.* **1.** money, especially money on hand. **2.** money paid at the time of buying something, as opposed to credit. *–v.* **3.** to give or obtain cash for (a cheque, etc.).

Don't confuse this with **cache**, which is a hiding place for storing things.
Compare def. 2 with buying something **on credit**, which means that you agree to pay for what you've bought at a later time, often with several payments.

cashew *n.* a small, edible, kidney-shaped nut.

cashier *n.* someone who has charge of cash and who superintends monetary transactions.

cashmere *n.* the fine downy wool of Kashmir goats.

casino *n.* (*pl.* **-nos**) a building or large room for gambling, etc.

cask *n.* **1.** a barrel-like container for holding liquids, etc. **2.** a lightweight container, with a small tap, used for holding wine for domestic use.

casket *n.* **1.** a small chest or box, as for jewels. **2.** a coffin.

casserole *n.* **1.** a baking dish of glass, pottery, etc., usually with a cover. **2.** any food, usually a mixture, baked in such a dish.

cassette *n.* a plastic container enclosing a recording tape.

cassock *n.* a long, close-fitting garment worn by ecclesiastics.

cassowary /ˈkæsəwəri/ n. (pl. **-ries**) a large, flightless bird of Aust., New Guinea and nearby islands.

cast v. (**cast**, **casting**) 1. to throw; fling; hurl (*away*, *off*, *out*, etc.) 2. to direct the eye, a glance, etc. 3. to shed or drop (hair, fruit, etc.), especially prematurely. 4. to deposit (a vote, etc.) –n. 5. the act of casting. 6. the form in which something is made or written. 7. the actors in a play. 8. something shaped in a mould while in a fluid or plastic state; a casting. 9. any impression or mould made from an object. 10. a rigid surgical dressing usually made of plaster-of-Paris bandage. 11. a permanent twist or turn, especially a squint. –phr. 12. **cast about**, to consider; plan or scheme. 13. **cast off**, **a.** to let (a vessel) loose from a mooring. **b.** to discard or reject. **c.** *Knitting* to make the final row of stitches. 14. **cast on**, *Knitting* to make the initial row of stitches. 15. **cast out**, to throw a fishing line or the like.

Don't confuse **cast** with **caste**, which is a social group or class.

castanet n. a pair or one of a pair of shells held in the palm of the hand and struck together as an accompaniment to music and dancing.

castaway n. a shipwrecked person.

caste n. 1. one of the social groups or divisions into which Hindus are born. 2. a social group.

Don't confuse this with **cast**, which means all the actors in a play or film. **Cast** also means to throw something.

castigate v. to punish in order to correct.

The more usual word is **scold**.

cast iron n. an alloy of iron, carbon, and other elements.

castle n. 1. a fortified residence. 2. → **rook²**.

castor n. a small wheel on a swivel, set under a piece of furniture, etc. Also, **caster**.

castor oil n. a viscous oil used as a purgative, lubricant, paint.

castrate v. to remove the testicles of. –**castration**, n.

casual adj. 1. happening by chance. 2. offhand. 3. careless; negligent. 4. occasional. 5. informal. 6. employed only irregularly.

casualty n. (pl. **-ties**) 1. a soldier missing, killed, wounded, or captured in action. 2. someone who is injured or killed in an accident. 3. the section of a hospital to which accident or emergency cases are taken.

casuarina n. any member of a group of Aust. trees and shrubs with jointed stems and no real leaves; she-oak.

cat n. any of the carnivorous feline mammals, as the domesticated cat, or the lion, tiger, etc.

cataclysm /ˈkætəklɪzəm/ n. any violent upheaval. –**cataclysmic**, adj.

catacomb /ˈkætəkoom, -kum/ n. a series of underground tunnels and caves, especially for burial.

catalogue n. 1. a list, usually in alphabetical or thematic order, with brief notes on names, articles, prices, etc., listed. –v. (**-logued**, **-loguing**) 2. to enter in a catalogue.

catalyst n. 1. a substance which causes or accelerates a chemical change. 2. the manipulating agent of any event.

catamaran /ˈkætəməræn/ n. any craft with twin parallel hulls.

catapult n. 1. an ancient military engine for hurling darts, stones, etc. 2. a Y-shaped stick with an elastic strip for propelling stones, etc.

cataract n. 1. a large waterfall. 2. an opacity of the lens of the eye.

catarrh /kəˈtɑː/ n. excessive secretions from the mucous membrane, especially of the nasal passages.

catastrophe /kəˈtæstrəfi/ n. 1. a sudden and widespread disaster. 2. a disastrous conclusion. **–catastrophic** /kætəs'trɒfɪk/, *adj.* **–catastrophically** /kætəs'trɒfɪkli/, *adv.*

catch *v.* **(caught, catching) 1.** to capture, especially after pursuit. **2.** to entrap or deceive. **3.** to be in time to reach (a train, boat, etc.). **4.** to surprise or detect, as in some action. **5.** to strike. **6.** to intercept and seize (a ball, etc.). **7.** to incur or contract (often used figuratively): *to catch the blame; to catch a cold.* **8.** to become fastened or entangled. **9.** to take hold. **10.** to become lit, take fire. **11.** to spread or be communicated, as a disease. *–n.* **12.** the act of catching. **13.** a device for checking motion. **14.** that which is caught, as a quantity of fish. **15.** anything worth getting.

catchcry *n.* a memorable expression voicing a popular sentiment.

catchment area *n.* a drainage area, especially of a reservoir or river. Also, **catchment basin.**

catechism /'kætəkɪzəm/ *n.* a book of questions and answers containing a summary of the principles of the Christian religion.

categorical *adj.* not involving a condition, qualification, etc.

category *n.* (*pl.* **-ries) 1.** a classificatory division in any field of knowledge. **2.** any general or comprehensive division; a class.

cater *v.* **1.** to provide food and service, etc., (*for*) at functions. **2.** to pander or give in (*to*).

caterpillar *n.* the wormlike larva of a butterfly or a moth.

caterwaul /'kætəwɔl/ *v.* to cry as cats on heat.

catharsis /kə'θasəs/ *n.* the purifying or cleansing of strong, especially negative emotions. **–cathartic,** *adj.*

cathedral *n.* the principal church of a diocese.

catheter /'kæθətə/ *n.* a tube employed to drain fluids from body cavities.

cathode *n.* the negative pole of a battery or other source of current. Compare **anode.**

catholic *adj.* wide-ranging or universal in extent.

> If this word is spelt with a capital letter (**Catholic**), it usually refers to the Roman Catholic Church, one of the divisions of Christianity, or to a member of that church.

CAT scan /kæt/ *n. Med.* an examination of part of the body using a **CAT scanner,** which produces a series of X-rays.

cattle *n.* ruminants of the bovine kind.

cattle dog *n.* one of several breeds of dog bred and trained to watch and tend cattle.

catwalk *n.* **1.** any narrow walking space. **2.** a platform on which fashion models parade clothes.

caucus *n.* the parliamentary members of a political party or faction of a political party.

caught *v.* past tense and past participle of **catch.**

cauldron *n.* a large kettle or boiler.

cauliflower *n.* a vegetable with a compact, fleshy head.

caulk /kɔk/ *v.* to fill or close (a seam, joint, etc.), as in a boat.

causal *adj.* of, constituting, or implying a cause.

causality *n.* (*pl.* **-ties) 1.** the relation of cause and effect. **2.** causal quality.

causation *n.* **1.** the action of causing or producing. **2.** the relation of cause to effect. **3.** anything that produces an effect.

cause *n.* **1.** that which produces an effect or result. **2.** the ground of any action or result; reason; motive. **3.** that side of a question which a person or party supports; the aim, purpose, etc., of a group. *–v.* **4.** to be the cause of.

causeway *n.* a raised road or path.

caustic /'kɒstɪk, 'kɔstɪk/ *adj.* **1.** capable of burning, corroding, or destroying living tissue. **2.** severely critical or sarcastic.

cauterise *v.* to burn, especially for curative purposes. Also, **cauterize.**

caution n. **1.** prudence; carefulness. **2.** a warning. –v. **3.** to give warning to. –**cautionary**, adj.

cautious adj. taking great care to avoid danger or risk.

cavalcade n. any procession.

cavalier n. **1.** a courtly gentleman. –adj. **2.** haughty, disdainful. **3.** reckless. **4.** off-hand; casual.

cavalry n. (pl. -**ries**) part of an army, formerly on horseback, but now equipped with armoured vehicles.

cave n. **1.** a hollow opening into the side of a hill, etc. –v. **2.** to fall or sink (in).

caveat /ˈkeɪviæt/ n. **1.** Law a notice to suspend a proceeding until the notifier is given a hearing. **2.** any warning or caution.

cavern n. a cave, especially a large, deep cave. –**cavernous**, adj.

caviar n. the salted roe of sturgeon or other large fish, considered a great delicacy.

cavil v. (-**illed**, -**illing**) to raise trivial objections.

cavity n. (pl. -**ties**) any hollow place.

cavort v. Informal to prance or caper about.

CD n. → compact disc.

CD-ROM /si di ˈrɒm/ n. a laser disc designed for storing digitised text and graphics which can be displayed on a visual display unit.

cease v. **1.** to stop. **2.** to put a stop or end to. –**ceaseless**, adj.

cedar n. any of several coniferous trees having fine-grained wood.

cede v. (**ceded**, **ceding**) to yield or for-mally surrender to another.

The more usual expression is **hand over**.

ceiling n. **1.** the overhead interior lining of a room. **2.** top limit.

celebrant n. **1.** the priest or minister who officiates at the performance of a religious rite. **2.** an official who is not a priest or minister but who has the authority to conduct a marriage ceremony, funeral, etc. –**celebrancy**, n.

celebrate v. **1.** to observe (a day) or commemorate (an event) with cere-monies or festivities. **2.** to make known publicly. **3.** to sound the praises of. –**cele-bration**, n.

celebrated adj. famous; well known.

celebrity n. (pl. -**ties**) **1.** a famous or well-known person. **2.** fame; renown.

celerity n. swiftness; speed.

celery n. a plant whose leafstalks are used raw for salad, and cooked as a vegetable.

celestial adj. **1.** relating to heaven; divine. **2.** relating to the sky.

celibate adj. **1.** abstaining from sexual relations: He has been celibate for ten years. **2.** unmarried. –n. **3.** someone who remains unmarried and abstains from sexual relations, especially for religious reasons. –**celibacy**, n.

cell n. **1.** a small room in a convent, prison, etc. **2.** a unit within a larger organisation. **3.** the structural unit of plant and animal life. **4.** a device which generates electrici-ty. –**cellular**, adj.

cellar n. an underground room or store.

cello /ˈtʃɛloʊ/ n. (pl. -**los** or -**li**) a four-stringed instrument of the violin family. Also, '**cello**, **violoncello**. –**cellist**, n.

cellophane n. (from trademark) a trans-parent, paper-like product used to wrap sweets, gifts, etc.

cell phone n. → cellular telephone.

cellular telephone n. a type of tele-phone, usually portable or for use in a car.

cellulite n. deposits of fat and fibrous tis-sue, resulting in a dimply appearance of the overlying skin.

celluloid (from trademark) n. **1.** a type of plastic. **2.** films; the cinema.

cellulose n. the chief constituent of the cell walls of plants.

Celsius adj. denoting or relating to a scale of temperature on which the boiling point of water is approximately 100°C. *Symbol:* C

cement *n.* **1.** a mixture of clay and limestone, used for making concrete. **2.** a type of glue. –*v.* **3.** to fix firmly: *to cement a friendship.*

Note that **cement** is only a component of **concrete**, so, strictly speaking, it is incorrect to talk about a *cement path.* However, many people do use **cement** in this way, and in normal contexts there is no confusion as to what is meant.

cemetery *n.* (*pl.* **-ries**) a burial ground.

cenotaph *n.* a memorial to those killed in war.

censor *n.* **1.** an official who examines books, plays, films, etc., to determine, and ban, what is thought objectionable on moral, political, military, or other grounds. –*v.* **2.** to examine and act upon as a censor does.

censorious *adj.* fault-finding; carping.

The more usual word is **critical**.

censure *n.* **1.** an expression of disapproval. –*v.* **2.** to criticise adversely in a formal way.

census *n.* an official enumeration of inhabitants, with details as to age, sex, pursuits, etc.

cent *n.* (a coin equal to) one hundredth part of the dollar.

Don't confuse this with **sent** or **scent**. **Sent** is the past form of the verb **send** (*I sent the letter yesterday*). A **scent** is a particular smell.

centenary /sɛnˈtinəri, -ˈtɛn-/ *adj.* **1.** of or relating to a 100th anniversary. –*n.* (*pl.* **-ries**) **2.** a 100th anniversary. **3.** a period of 100 years.

centennial *adj.* marking the completion of 100 years.

centimetre *n.* a unit of length in the metric system, equal to 0.01 metre. *Symbol:* cm

centipede *n.* small segmented arthropod with a pair of legs attached to each segment.

central *adj.* **1.** of or forming the centre. **2.** in, at, or near the centre. **3.** principal; chief; dominant.

centralise *v.* **1.** to draw or come towards a centre. **2.** to bring under one control, especially in government. Also, **centralize.**

centre *n.* **1.** *Geom.* the middle point. **2.** a point, pivot, axis, etc., round which anything rotates or revolves. **3.** the middle or most important part of something, around which things are grouped or to which things are attracted: *the centre of activity; the centre of attention.* **4.** a building or building complex which houses a number of related specified services: *shopping centre; sports centre; medical centre.* –*v.* (**-tred, -tring**) **5.** to place in or on a centre.

centrifugal force /sɛnˈtrɪfəgəl, sɛntrəˈfjugəl/ *n.* an effect of inertia, in that the natural tendency of a moving object is to travel in a straight line, which is mistakenly perceived to be a force pulling an object outwards when it is travelling around a central point.

centripetal force /sɛnˈtrɪpətl/ *n.* a force, directed towards the centre of a circle or curve, which causes a body to move in a circular or curved path.

century *n.* (*pl.* **-ries**) **1.** a period of 100 years. **2.** any group or collection of 100.

cephalic /səˈfælɪk/ *adj.* of or relating to the head.

ceramic *adj.* **1.** relating to products made from clay and similar materials, such as pottery, brick, etc. or to their manufacture. –*n.* **2.** such a product. –**ceramics,** *n.*

cereal *n.* **1.** a plant yielding an edible grain, as wheat, rye, oats, rice, maize, etc. **2.** a breakfast food made from grain.

Don't confuse this with **serial**, which is a story that is published or broadcast in parts.

cerebral /'sɛrəbrəl, sə'riːbrəl/ *adj.* **1.** of or relating to the brain. **2.** intellectual.

cerebral palsy *n.* a form of paralysis caused by brain damage.

People who suffer from this condition are sometimes called **spastics**. However, because some people use **spastic** to refer informally to someone they think is foolish, the term has taken on negative and offensive overtones. For that reason, it is avoided by many people when referring to sufferers of cerebral palsy.

ceremony *n.* (*pl.* **-nies**) **1.** the formalities observed on some important public occasion. **2.** a solemn rite. **3.** any formal act or observance, often used of a meaningless one. –**ceremonious**, *adj.* –**ceremonial**, *adj.*,

cerise /sə'riːs, -riːz/ *adj.*, *n.* mauve-tinged cherry red.

certain *adj.* **1.** having no doubt; confident. **2.** sure; inevitable. **3.** unquestionable. **4.** definite or particular, but not named. –**certainty**, *n.*

certificate *n.* a document certifying to the truth of something or to status, qualifications, privileges, etc.

certify *v.* (**-fied, -fying**) **1.** to guarantee as certain; give reliable information of. **2.** to declare insane.

cervical /'sɜːvɪkəl, sɜː'vaɪkəl/ *adj.* **1.** relating to the neck. **2.** relating to the cervix of the uterus.

cervix *n.* (*pl.* **cervixes** *or* **cervices** /sə-'vaɪsɪz/) **1.** the neck. **2.** the neck of the uterus.

cessation *n.* a ceasing; discontinuance; pause.

cession /'sɛʃən/ *n.* a ceding or giving up of rights, territory, etc., to another, as by treaty or agreement.

This word is related to the verb **cede**. Don't confuse this with **session**, which is a period of time during which an activity is performed.

cesspool *n.* **1.** a cistern or pit for retaining the sediment of a drain or for sewage. **2.** any filthy receptacle or place.

cetacean /sə'teɪʃən/ *n.* an aquatic mammal as the whale, dolphin, etc. –**cetaceous**, *adj.*

chador /'tʃɑːdə/ *n.* an outer piece of clothing worn by some Muslim women, consisting of a loose, dark cloak which covers the whole body but leaves the face uncovered.

chafe *v.* **1.** to warm by rubbing. **2.** to wear or abrade by rubbing. **3.** to irritate; annoy.

chaff¹ *n.* the husks of grains and grasses separated from the seed.

chaff² *v.* to ridicule or tease good-naturedly.

chagrin /'ʃægrən, ʃə'grɪn/ *n.* a feeling of vexation and disappointment or humiliation.

chai /tʃaɪ/ *n.* a sweet milky tea beverage flavoured with spices such as cardamom, cinnamon, cloves, vanilla, etc.

chain *n.* **1.** a connected series of metal or other links. **2.** something that binds or restrains. **3.** any connected series: *a chain of events.* **4.** a number of shops, hotels, theatres, etc. that belong to one owner. –*v.* **5.** to fasten or secure with or as with a chain.

chain reaction *n.* a series of reactions provoked by one event.

chair *n.* **1.** a seat with a back usually for one person. **2.** a seat of office or authority. **3.** the person occupying a seat of office, especially the chairperson of a meeting. –*v.* **4.** to preside over. –*phr.* **5. take the chair**, to assume the role of chair (def. 3) of a meeting.

chairman *n.* (*pl.* **-men**) **1.** → **chairperson**. **2.** a male chairperson.

Because this term includes the word *man*, many people think that it excludes women. Unless you want to refer specifically to a man, you should use **chairperson**, or another term such as **the chair**, **convener, coordinator, moderator,** leader, presiding officer or president. These all have similar meanings.

chairperson *n.* the presiding officer of a meeting, committee, board, etc.

This is often used instead of **chairman**, especially when the person is a woman or if the sex of the person is unknown. It is best to use **chairman** only if you are referring to a man, just as you would only use **chairwoman** if you were referring to a woman.

chalet /ˈʃæleɪ/ *n.* a kind of cottage built for alpine regions.

chalice *n.* a cup for the wine of the eucharist.

chalk *n.* **1.** a soft, white, pure limestone. **2.** a prepared piece of chalk or chalk-like substance for marking. –*v.* **3.** to mark or write with chalk. –*phr.* **4. chalk up**, to score. **5. chalk up to, a.** to ascribe to. **b.** to regard as having contributed towards the gain of.

challenge *n.* **1.** a call to a contest of skill, strength, etc. **2.** something that makes demands upon one's abilities, etc. **3.** a calling to account or into question. –*v.* **(-lenged, -lenging) 4.** to summon to a contest. **5.** to make stimulating demands upon. **6.** to call in question.

chamber *n.* **1.** a private room, especially a bedroom. **2.** the meeting hall, especially of a legislature. **3.** (*pl.*) a place where a judge hears matters not requiring action in court. **4.** (*pl.*) a suite of rooms of barristers. **5.** a compartment or enclosed space.

chamber-pot *n.* a portable vessel used chiefly in bedrooms as a toilet.

chameleon /kəˈmiliən, ʃə-/ *n.* a slow-moving lizard noted for its power to change colour.

chamois /ˈʃæmwɑ/ *for def. 1*, /ˈʃæmi/ *for defs 2 and 3* –*n.* (*pl.* -**ois** /ˈʃæmwɑ/ *for def. 1*, /ˈʃæmiz/ *for defs 2 and 3*) *n.* **1.** an agile goatlike antelope. **2.** a soft, pliable leather. **3. a.** a piece of chamois used

for drying glass, motor vehicles, etc., after washing. **b.** an absorbent cloth made of synthetic material, similarly used. Also (for defs 2 and 3), **shammy**.

chamomile /ˈkæməmaɪl/ *n.* a herb used medicinally. Also, **camomile**.

champ[1] *v.* to bite upon, especially impatiently.

champ[2] *n. Informal* a champion.

champagne *n.* a sparkling white wine.

champignon /ˈʃæmpɪnjɒ/ *n.* a very small mushroom.

champion *n.* **1.** someone who has defeated all opponents. **2.** someone who fights for or defends any person or cause. –*v.* **3.** to act as champion of.

chance *n.* **1.** the absence of any known reason why an event should turn out one way rather than another. **2.** fortune; fate; luck. **3.** a possibility or probability of anything happening. **4.** an opportunity. **5.** a risk or hazard. –*v.* (**chanced, chancing**) **6.** to come by chance (*on* or *upon*). **7.** *Informal* to take the chances of; risk. –*adj.* **8.** due to chance.

chancellor *n.* the honorary head of a university.

chandelier /ʃændəˈlɪə/ *n.* a branched support for a number of lights, suspended from a ceiling.

change *v.* (**changed, changing**) **1.** to make or become different in condition, appearance, etc. **2.** to substitute another or others for; exchange. **3.** to change trains, etc.: *Change at the next station.* **4.** to change one's clothes: *I'll wait while you change.* –*n.* **5.** variation; alteration. **6.** a substitution. **7.** variety or novelty. **8.** the passing from one place, or phase, etc., to another. **9.** money returned when the sum offered is larger than the sum due. **10.** coins of low denomination.

channel *n.* **1.** the bed of a stream or waterway. **2.** the deeper part of a waterway. **3.** a route through which anything passes, such as a means of communication. **4.** a frequency band for one-way communication (as telephone, radio, television, etc.) **5.** a television station. –v. (**-nelled, -nelling**) **6.** to convey through a channel. **7.** to direct towards or into some particular course.

chant n. **1.** a short, simple melody, especially with multiple syllables sung to each note. –v. **2.** to sing to, or in the manner of, a chant.

chaos n. utter confusion or disorder. –**chaotic**, adj.

chap¹ v. (**chapped, chapping**) **1.** (of cold weather) to crack, roughen, and redden (the skin). **2.** to become chapped.

chap² n. Informal a man.

chapel n. a separate part of a church, or a small church, devoted to special services.

chaperone /ˈʃæpəroʊn/ n. **1.** an older person who accompanies a younger person on an outing to ensure they behave respectably. –v. **2.** to accompany someone in this way. Also, **chaperon**.

chaplain n. a member of the clergy attached to a royal court, military unit, college, etc.

chapter n. a main division, usually numbered, of a book, etc.

char v. (**charred, charring**) **1.** to burn or reduce to charcoal. **2.** to burn slightly; scorch.

character n. **1.** the aggregate of qualities that distinguishes one person or thing from others. **2.** good moral constitution or reputation. **3.** a person. **4.** Informal an odd or interesting person. **5.** a person represented in a drama, story, etc. **6.** a symbol used in a writing system.

characterise v. **1.** to be a characteristic of. **2.** to describe the characteristic or peculiar quality of. Also, **characterize**.

characteristic adj. **1.** typical; distinctive. –n. **2.** a distinguishing feature or quality.

charade /ʃəˈrɑːd/ n. **1.** a game in which a player or players mime a word or phrase which the others try to guess. **2.** a pointless act.

charcoal n. the carbon-containing material obtained by the imperfect combustion of wood etc.

chardonnay n. (sometimes upper case) a dry white wine.

charge v. (**charged, charging**) **1.** to put a load on or in. **2.** to fill or furnish (a thing) with the appropriate quantity. **3.** to supply with a quantity of electricity. **4.** to lay a command or injunction upon. **5.** to lay blame upon; accuse (with). **6.** to hold liable for payment. **7.** to postpone payment on (a service or purchase) by having it recorded on one's account. **8.** to ask as a price. **9.** to attack by rushing against. **10.** to rush, as to an attack. –n. **11.** a load or burden. **12.** the quantity an apparatus can hold. **13.** a quantity of electricity. **14.** (anything or anybody committed to one's) care, custody or superintendence. **15.** an injunction. **16.** an accusation. **17.** a price charged. **18.** an onset or attack, as of soldiers. **19.** the quantity of electrical energy in a battery, etc. –phr. **20. in charge**, having supervisory powers.

chariot n. a two-wheeled, horse-drawn vehicle.

charisma /kəˈrɪzmə/ n. personal qualities that give an individual influence or authority over large numbers of people. –**charismatic**, adj., n.

charity n. (pl. **-ties**) **1.** private or public aid to needy people. **2.** a charitable fund, etc. **3.** benevolent feeling, especially towards those in need. –**charitable**, adj.

charlatan /ˈʃɑːlətən/ n. someone who pretends to have more knowledge or skill than they actually possess.

A charlatan in the medical field is sometimes called a **quack**.

charm n. **1.** a power to please and attract. **2.** a trinket worn on a chain, bracelet, etc. **3.** a verse or formula. –v. **4.** to attract

chart 100 **cheddar**

powerfully by beauty, etc. **5.** to act upon with or as with a charm.

chart n. **1.** a sheet of information in tabulated form. **2.** a map, especially a marine map. –v. **3.** to make a chart of. **4.** to plan.

charter n. **1.** a document or contract, especially relating to land transfers. **2.** an official document giving privileges, rights, the benefit of a new invention, a peerage, etc. –v. **3.** to establish by charter. **4.** to hire a vehicle, etc. –adj. **5.** founded, granted, or protected by a charter. **6.** hired for a particular purpose or journey.

chary adj. (**-rier, -riest**) **1.** careful; wary. **2.** shy.

chase[1] v. **1.** to pursue in order to seize, overtake, etc. **2.** to follow in pursuit. –n. **3.** the act of chasing. **4.** a flora and fauna reserve.

chase[2] v. to ornament (metal) by engraving or embossing.

chasm /'kæzəm/ n. a deep cleft in the earth's surface.

chassis /'ʃæzi/ n. (pl. **chassis** /'ʃæziz/) the frame, wheels, etc., of a motor vehicle, on which the body is supported.

chaste adj. **1.** virgin; virtuous; undefiled. **2.** pure in style; simple. –**chastity**, n.

chasten /'tʃeɪsən/ v. to chastise.

chastise v. to punish or scold.

chat v. (**chatted, chatting**) **1.** to converse in a familiar or informal manner. **2.** Internet to take part in real-time communication using internet relay chat. –n. **3.** informal conversation. **4.** Internet a session of real-time communication using internet relay chat.

chat line n. Internet a real-time connection to a chat room.

chat room n. Internet a virtual venue on the internet for conversation, discussion, etc., using internet relay chat.

chattels pl. n. movable articles of property.

chatter v. to talk rapidly and to little purpose.

chatterbox n. a very talkative person.

chauffeur /'ʃoʊfə, ʃoʊ'fɜ/ n. a person employed to drive a private motor car. –**chauffeuse**, fem. n.

chauvinism /'ʃoʊvənɪzəm/ n. narrow-minded belief in the superiority of one's own gender, group, ideology, etc.

cheap adj. **1.** of a relatively low price. **2.** of poor quality. **3.** Informal (of a person) not willing to spend money unless absolutely necessary; mean; stingy.

Don't confuse **cheap** with **cheep**, which is to make a high weak sound like a baby bird does.

cheat v. **1.** to defraud; swindle. **2.** to practise fraud or deception. –n. **3.** a person who cheats. **4.** a fraud; swindle. –**cheating**, n.

check v. **1.** to stop the motion of, forcibly. **2.** to restrain. **3.** to investigate or verify as to correctness. **4.** to mark in a pattern of checks or squares. **5.** Chess to place (an opponent's king) under direct attack. **6.** to prove to be right; to correspond accurately. –n. **7.** a person or thing that checks or restrains. **8.** a sudden arrest or stoppage. **9.** control with a view to ascertaining performance or preventing error. **10.** a pattern formed of squares, as on a draughtboard. –phr. **11.** check in, a. to register one's arrival. b. to leave in temporary custody: to check in one's coat. **12.** check out, to register one's departure. **13.** check up (or on), to investigate for verification.

Don't confuse **check** with **cheque**, which is a written order to a bank to pay money to someone. However, note that in America, this bank order is actually spelt **check**.

checkmate n. Chess the act of putting the opponent's king into an inextricable check.

check-up n. **1.** an examination to verify accuracy, make a comparison, etc. **2.** a complete physical examination.

cheddar n. a smooth white or yellow cheese.

cheek n. **1.** either side of the face below eye level. **2.** the side wall of the mouth. **3.** a buttock. **4.** *Informal* impudence or effrontery.

cheeky adj. (**-kier, -kiest**) impudent; insolent.

cheep v. to make a high, weak sound as a baby bird does; chirp; peep.

Don't confuse this with **cheap**, which describes something which does not cost very much, or something of poor quality.

cheer n. **1.** a shout of encouragement, approval, congratulation, etc. **2.** gladness, gaiety, or animation. –v. **3.** to salute with shouts of approval, etc. –*phr.* **4. cheer on,** to encourage or incite. **5. cheer up,** to inspire with cheer. –**cheerful,** adj.

cheese n. a food made from the curd of milk separated from the whey.

cheetah n. an animal of the cat family, having a pale yellow coat covered with small black spots; reputed to be the fastest four-legged animal.

chef /ʃef/ n. a cook, especially a head cook.

chemical adj. **1.** of or concerned with the science of chemistry. –n. **2.** a substance produced by or used in a chemical process.

chemist n. **1.** someone who studies or is professionally qualified in the science of chemistry. **2.** a retailer of medicinal drugs and toilet preparations.

chemistry n. **1.** the science concerned with the composition of substances, the various elementary forms of matter, and the interactions between them. **2.** chemical properties, reactions, etc.

chemotherapy /kimou'θerəpi/ n. treatment of disease with chemicals which have a specific toxic effect on the disease-producing microorganism.

chenille /ʃə'nil/ n. **1.** (a fabric with a weft of) velvety yarn. **2.** cotton fabric with a pattern of lines of tufts of cotton.

cheque n. a written order, usually on a standard printed form, directing a bank to pay a specified sum of money to a payee named or to the person presenting it.

Don't confuse **cheque** with **check**, which means to find out whether something is correct or not. It also means to stop the progress of something. However, note that Americans spell the bank order **check**.

chequered adj. marked with (squares of) different or contrasting colours. –**chequer,** v.

chequered flag n. *Car Racing* a black and white chequered flag which is waved to signal the end of a race.

cherish v. to hold or treat as dear.

cheroot /ʃə'rut/ n. a cigar having open, unpointed ends.

cherry n. (pl. **-ries**) (a tree bearing) small, round, bright red stone fruit.

cherub n. (pl. **cherubim** for def. 1, **cherubs** for def. 2) **1.** a kind of celestial being. **2.** a beautiful or innocent person, especially a child.

chess n. a game of battle strategy, played by 2 persons on a chequered board.

chest n. **1.** the part of the body from the neck to the waist. **2.** a storage box, usually a large, strong one.

chestnut n. **1.** (a type of beech tree bearing) an edible nut. –adj. **2.** a reddish brown.

chew v. **1.** to crush or grind with the teeth; masticate. –*phr.* **2. chew over,** to meditate on; consider deliberately. **3. chew up,** to damage to or as if by chewing.

chewing gum n. a sweetened and flavoured gum, prepared for chewing. Also, **chewie.**

chewy adj. requiring chewing; tough.

chia /'tʃiə/ n. a plant of the mint family with seeds high in antioxidants and dietary fibre.

chic /ʃik/ adj. stylish.

chicanery /ʃə'keinəri/ n. legal trickery, quibbling, or sophistry.

chick n. **1.** a young chicken or other bird. **2.** *Informal* a young woman.

Note that if you refer to a woman as a **chick** you may offend her.

chicken *n.* **1.** a common domesticated bird having a prominent comb and wattles and farmed for its eggs and flesh; bred into numerous breeds and varieties. **2.** the young of the domestic fowl; chick. **3.** a slaughtered and dressed chicken, either raw or cooked. **4.** the flesh of this bird used as food. **5.** *Informal* a coward. –*phr.* **6. chicken out**, *Informal* to withdraw because of cowardice, tiredness, etc.

chickenpox *n.* a mild, contagious eruptive disease, usually of children.

chickpea *n.* a small, round, yellow vegetable.

chide *v.* (**chided**, **chiding**) **1.** to scold; find fault. **2.** to drive, impel, etc., by chiding.

chief *n.* **1.** the head or ruler of a clan, tribe, etc. **2.** *Informal* boss. –*adj.* **3.** highest in rank or authority. **4.** most important.

chieftain *n.* the chief of a clan or a tribe.

chiffon /ʃəˈfɒn, ˈʃɪfɒn/ *n.* sheer fabric of silk, nylon, or rayon in plain weave.

chihuahua /tʃəˈwawə/ *n.* a very small Mexican breed of dog.

chilblain *n.* (*usu. pl.*) an inflammation on the hands and feet caused by exposure to cold.

child *n.* (*pl.* **children**) **1.** a baby or infant. **2.** a boy or girl. **3.** any descendant. –**childhood**, *n.* –**childish**, *adj.*

child care *n.* professional supervision of children.

chill *n.* **1.** a moderate but penetrating coldness. **2.** a sensation of cold, usually with shivering, often the first stage of a cold: *Come inside before you catch a chill.* **3.** a depressing influence or sensation. **4.** a coldness of manner. **5.** cold; tending to cause shivering: *a chill wind.* **6.** depressing or discouraging. –*v.* **7.** to make or become cold. **8.** to make cool, but not freeze. –**chilly**, *adj.*

Note that the usual adjective form of this word is **chilly**, as in *a chilly day*. **Chill** used as an adjective is more literary.

chilli *n.* (*pl.* **-lies**) the small, hot, pungent fruit of some species of capsicum.

chime *n.* **1.** (sound produced by striking) a set of tuned bells or tubes. –*v.* **2.** to sound harmoniously or in chimes. **3.** to harmonise; agree.

chimney *n.* (*pl.* **-neys**) a structure containing a flue for the passage of the smoke, gases, etc., of a fire or furnace.

chimpanzee *n.* an anthropoid ape, smaller than the gorilla.

chin *n.* the lower extremity of the face, below the mouth.

china *n.* **1.** a vitreous, translucent earthenware, originally produced in China. **2.** plates, cups, etc., collectively.

Chinese gooseberry *n.* → kiwifruit.

chink¹ *n.* a crack, cleft, or fissure.

chink² *v.* to make a short, sharp sound, as of coins striking together.

chintz *n.* a printed cotton (curtain) fabric, often shiny.

chip *n.* **1.** a small piece, as of wood, separated by chopping, cutting, or breaking. **2. a.** a deep-fried finger of potato. **b.** a wafer of potato, fried, dried, and usually served cold; crisp. **3.** *Electronics* a small square of semiconducting material, processed in various ways to have certain electrical characteristics. –*v.* (**chipped**, **chipping**) **4.** to hew or cut with an axe, chisel, etc. **5.** to become chipped. –*phr.* **6.** *Informal* **chip in**, to contribute money, help, etc. **7. chip on the shoulder**, a grudge.

chipboard *n.* a resin-bonded artificial wood made from wood chips, sawdust, etc.

chipmunk *n.* any of various small striped terrestrial squirrels.

chiropody /kəˈrɒpədi, ʃəˈrɒpədi/ *n.* the treatment of minor foot ailments. –**chiropodist**, *n.*

chiropractic /ˌkaɪrəˈpræktɪk/ n. a therapeutic system based upon restoring normal nerve function by adjusting the segments of the spinal column. –**chiropractor**, n.

chirp v. to make a short, sharp sound, as small birds and certain insects.

chirpy adj. Informal cheerful.

chirrup v. (**-ruped, -ruping**) to chirp.

chisel n. 1. a steel tool with a cutting edge for shaping wood, stone, etc. –v. (**-elled, -elling**) 2. to work with a chisel.

chit n. a voucher.

chivalry /ˈʃɪvəlri/ n. 1. the rules and customs of medieval knighthood. 2. good manners. –**chivalrous**, adj.

chives pl. n. a small bulbous plant related to the onion.

chloride /ˈklɔːraɪd/ n. 1. a compound usually of 2 elements only, one of which is chlorine. 2. a salt of hydrochloric acid.

chlorine n. a greenish-yellow gaseous element used as a powerful bleaching agent and in industry. Symbol: Cl

chlorofluorocarbon /ˌklɔːrəʊˌflʊərəʊ-ˈkabən/ n. any of a class of generally unreactive compounds of carbon, fluorine, chlorine and hydrogen, the use of which in refrigeration and aerosols is being gradually phased out because of the damage they cause to the ozone layer. Abbrev.: CFC

chloroform n. a colourless volatile liquid used as an anaesthetic and solvent.

chlorophyll n. the green colouring substances of leaves and plants necessary for photosynthesis.

chock n. 1. a block or wedge of wood, etc., used to prevent movement, as of a wheel or a cask. –adv. 2. as close or tight as possible: chock full.

chocolate n. a preparation made from cocoa beans.

choice n. 1. the act of choosing; selection. 2. power of choosing; option. 3. the person or thing chosen. 4. an abundance and variety from which to choose. –adj.

(**choicer, choicest**) 5. excellent; superior. 6. carefully selected.

choir /ˈkwaɪə/ n. an organised group of singers.

> **Choir** is a collective noun and can be used with a singular or plural verb. Look up **collective noun**.

choke v. 1. to stop the breath of, by obstructing the windpipe; strangle; suffocate. 2. to suffer strangling or suffocation. 3. to make or become obstructed or clogged. 4. to be temporarily overcome, as with emotion. –n. 5. the act or sound of choking. 6. (in internal-combustion engines) the mechanism regulating the air supply to a carburettor.

choko n. (pl. **-kos** or **-koes**) a pear-shaped green fruit used as a vegetable.

cholera /ˈkɒlərə/ n. an acute, infectious disease marked by diarrhoea, vomiting, cramp, etc.

cholesterol /kəˈlestərɒl/ n. an organic compound present in the liver, the blood and brain, the yolk of eggs, etc.

chook n. Aust., NZ Informal a domestic chicken.

choose v. (**chose, chosen, choosing**) 1. to select from a number, or in preference to another. 2. to prefer and decide (to do something).

choosy adj. Informal hard to please. Also, **choosey**.

chop¹ v. (**chopped, chopping**) 1. to cut with a quick, heavy blow or series of blows, using an axe, etc. 2. to make a quick heavy stroke or a series of strokes. –n. 3. the act of chopping. 4. a cutting blow. 5. a slice of lamb, veal, pork, etc., containing some bone.

chop² v. (**chopped, chopping**) to turn, shift, or change suddenly, as the wind.

chopper n. Informal 1. a helicopter. 2. a motorcycle with wide, high handle bars.

choppy adj. (**-pier, -piest**) (of the sea, etc.) forming short, irregular, broken waves.

chopstick *n.* one of a pair of thin sticks used to raise food to the mouth.

chord[1] *n.* **1.** a string of a musical instrument. **2.** a feeling or emotion.

Don't confuse this with **cord**, which is a rope, or a kind of fabric.

chord[2] *n. Music* a combination of 3 or more tones, usually in harmonic relation.

Don't confuse this with **cord**, which is a rope, or a kind of fabric.

chore *n.* a small or odd job; a piece of minor domestic work.

choreography /kɒri'ɒgrəfi/ *n.* the art of composing ballets, dances, etc. –**choreographer**, *n.* –**choreographic**, *adj.* –**choreograph**, *v.*

chortle *v.* to chuckle with glee.

chorus *n.* **1. a.** a group of persons singing together. **b.** a part of a song in which others join the principal singer(s). **c.** any recurring refrain. **2.** simultaneous utterance in singing, speaking, etc. **3.** (in musical shows) the company of dancers and singers. –**choral**, *adj.*

Don't confuse **choral** with **coral**, which is the hard colourful shapes formed from the skeletons of small sea animals.

chose *v.* past tense of **choose**.

chowder *n.* a kind of soup or stew made of clams, fish, or vegetables.

choy sum *n.* a cabbage with flat green leaves and small heads of yellow flowers. Also, **choi sum**.

christen *v.* to give a name to at baptism.

chromatic *adj.* **1.** relating to colour or colours. **2.** *Music* (of a scale) moving by semitones.

chrome *n.* chromium, especially as a source of various pigments.

chromium *n.* a metallic element used for making pigments in photography, etc.; also used in corrosion-resisting chromium plating. *Symbol:* Cr

chromosome *n.* any of several bodies in the cell nucleus which carry the genes.

chronic *adj.* constant or continuing for a long time: *chronic pain.*

Compare **chronic** with **acute** (def. 4), which describes an illness which is brief and severe, as *an acute attack of bronchitis.* Many people use **chronic** to describe an illness which is very severe, as in *a chronic case of indigestion,* but this is generally regarded as incorrect.

chronicle *n.* **1.** a record of events in the order of time. –*v.* (**-cled, -cling**) **2.** to record as in a chronicle.

chronology *n.* (*pl.* **-gies**) a statement of the accepted order of past events. –**chronological**, *adj.*

chronometer *n.* a very accurate clock.

chrysalis /'krɪsəlɪs/ *n.* (*pl.* **chrysalises** or **chrysalids** or **chrysalides** /krə'sælədiːz/) the form which a butterfly or moth takes when changing from a grub to an adult insect, inside a cocoon.

chrysanthemum *n.* a garden plant with large, colourful flowers.

chubby *adj.* (**-bier, -biest**) round and plump.

chuck *v.* **1.** to pat or tap lightly, as under the chin. **2.** to throw with a quick motion, usually a short distance. **3.** *Informal* to vomit.

chuckle *v.* **1.** to laugh in a soft, amused manner. –*n.* **2.** a soft, amused laugh.

chum *n.* **1.** an intimate friend. –*phr.* **2. chum up with,** to become friendly with.

chump *n.* **1.** *Informal* a blockhead or dolt. **2.** the thick blunt end of anything.

chunder *v. Aust., NZ Informal* to vomit.

chunk *n.* a thick mass or lump of anything.

church *n.* **1.** an edifice for public Christian worship. **2.** (*upper case*) a Christian denomination.

churl *n.* a rude, boorish, or surly person. –**churlish**, *adj.*

churn n. 1. a vessel or machine in which butter is made. –v. 2. to shake or agitate with violence or continued motion.

chute n. a channel, trough, etc., for conveying water, grain, etc., to a lower level.

chutney n. a fruit or vegetable relish.

cicada n. a large insect which makes a shrill sound by vibrating membranes on the underside of the abdomen. Also, *Informal*, **locust**.

cider n. the expressed juice of apples.

cigar n. a small, shaped roll of tobacco leaves prepared for smoking.

cigarette n. finely cut tobacco rolled in paper for smoking.

cinch n. 1. a strong girth for a saddle or pack. 2. *Informal* something certain or easy.

cinder n. 1. a burnt-out piece of coal, wood, etc. 2. (*pl.*) ashes.

cinema n. 1. a film theatre. 2. films in general or the art of making films. –**cinematic**, *adj.*

cinematography /sɪnəmə'tɒɡrəfɪ/ n. the art or practice of film photography. –**cinematographer**, n.

cinnamon n. a spice from the inner bark of certain trees.

cipher n. 1. an arithmetical symbol (0) which denotes no quantity or magnitude. 2. any Arabic numeral. 3. something of no value or importance. 4. (the key to) a secret method of writing. Also, **cypher**.

circa /'sɜːkə/ prep., adv. about; approximately (used especially with dates).

The short form of this is **c.**, **c** or **ca**.

circle n. 1. a closed plane curve which is at all points equidistant from it's centre. 2. any circular object or arrangement. 3. an upper section of seats in a theatre. 4. an area of activity, influence, etc. 5. a complete series forming a connected whole. 6. a number of persons bound by a common tie. –v. (**-cled, -cling**) 7. to enclose in a circle. 8. to move in a circle or circuit (*round*).

circuit n. 1. the act of going or moving round. 2. any circular or roundabout journey. 3. a number of venues or events at which an entertainer, etc., performs in turn. 4. a course regularly travelled. 5. the complete path of an electric current.

circuit board n. *Electronics* 1. an insulated board on which circuits are mounted or printed, which can be inserted into a piece of electronic equipment such as a computer. 2. → **power board**

circuitous /sə'kjuːtəs/ adj. not direct.

circular adj. 1. having the form of a circle. –n. 2. a letter, notice, etc., for general circulation or within an organisation. –**circularise**, v.

circulate v. 1. to move in a circle or circuit. 2. to move amongst the guests at a social function.

circulation n. 1. the act of circulating. 2. *Physiol.* the recurrent movement of the blood throughout the body. 3. the distribution of copies of a publication among readers.

circumcise /'sɜːkəmsaɪz/ v. to remove the foreskin of (males). –**circumcision**, n.

circumference n. the distance around a circle or circular object.

circumlocution n. a roundabout way of speaking.

circumnavigate v. to sail round.

circumscribe v. 1. to draw a line round. 2. to enclose within bounds; limit, especially narrowly.

circumspect adj. taking careful consideration before acting; prudent.

More usual words are **careful** and **cautious**.

circumstance n. 1. a condition which accompanies, determines, or modifies a fact or event. 2. ceremonious accompaniment or display. –**circumstantial**, adj.

circumvent /sɜːkəm'vɛnt, 'sɜːkəmvɛnt/ v. 1. to avoid or get around. 2. to gain advantage over by artfulness or deception.

For def. 1, the more usual expression is **go around**; for def. 2, **get around**.

circus n. a company of performers, animals, etc., especially a travelling company.

cirrhosis /sɪ'rousəs, sə-/ n. a disease of the liver.

cirrus /'sɪrəs/ n. a high, thin cloud.

cistern /'sɪstən/ n. a reservoir, tank, etc., for holding water, etc.

citadel /'sɪtədɛl/ n. any strongly fortified place.

cite v. 1. to quote (a passage, book, author, etc.), especially as an authority. 2. to refer to as an example. –**citation**, n.

Don't confuse this with **sight**, which is the ability to see, or with **site**, which is a piece of land where something is built.

citizen n. 1. a member of a state or nation. 2. an inhabitant of a city or town. –**citizenry**, n.

Compare def. 1 with **alien** (def. 1).

citrus n. any tree or shrub of the lemon, lime, orange, grapefruit, etc., genus.

city n. (pl. **-ties**) 1. a large or important town. 2. the central business area of a city.

civic adj. 1. of or relating to a city. 2. of or relating to citizenship.

civil adj. 1. of, consisting of, or relating to citizens. 2. of or relating to the state or state authorities, as opposed to religious or other authorities. 3. polite; courteous.

civilian n. someone engaged in civil pursuits, distinguished from a soldier, etc.

civilisation n. 1. state of human society with a high level of art, science, religion, and government. 2. the type of culture, society, etc., of a specific group. 3. the act or process of civilising. Also, **civilization**.

civilise v. to bring out of a savage state. Also, **civilize**.

civilised adj. 1. having an advanced culture, society, etc. 2. polite; well-bred. Also, **civilized**.

civility n. courtesy; politeness.

civil war n. a war between parties, regions, etc., within their own country.

civvies pl. n. Informal civilian clothes.

clack v. to make a quick, sharp sound as by striking or cracking.

clad v. a past tense and past participle of **clothe**: clad only in a towel.

This word can also be used with other words to form compound adjectives: a pyjama-clad figure; ivy-clad walls.

claim v. 1. to demand as a right. 2. to assert as a fact. –n. 3. a demand for something as due. 4. a just title to something. 5. that which is claimed. 6. a payment demanded in accordance with an insurance policy, etc.

claimant n. someone who makes a claim.

clairvoyant adj. 1. having supernatural powers of prediction. –n. 2. a clairvoyant person.

clam n. 1. a type of mollusc. –phr. 2. **clam up**, Informal to be silent.

clamber v. to climb, using both feet and hands.

clammy adj. (**-mier, -miest**) covered with a cold, sticky moisture.

clamour n. 1. a loud outcry. 2. popular outcry. –v. 3. to make a clamour. Also, **clamor**.

clamp n. 1. a device for strengthening, supporting or fastening objects together. –v. 2. to fasten with or fix in a clamp. –phr. 3. **clamp down**, to become more strict.

clan n. a group of related families who share a common ancestor. –**clannish**, adj.

This originally referred to family groups in Scotland, and it is still commonly used there as well as in other parts of the world.

clandestine /klæn'dɛstən/ adj. private or secret, and sometimes illicit: a clandestine affair.

clang v. 1. to give out a loud, resonant, metallic sound. 2. such a sound.

clangour n. a loud, resonant, metallic sound, as of a trumpet. Also, **clangor**.

clap *v.* (**clapped**, **clapping**) **1.** to strike with a quick, smart blow, producing an abrupt, sharp sound. **2.** to strike the hands, etc.) together resoundingly, as to express applause. **3.** to make an abrupt, sharp sound, as of bodies in collision. –*n.* **4.** the act or sound of clapping. **5.** a resounding blow. **6.** a loud and abrupt noise, as of thunder.

claret *n.* a red table wine.

clarify *v.* (**-fied**, **-fying**) **1.** to make or become clear, pure, or intelligible. **2.** to make (a liquid) clear by removing sediment. –**clarification**, *n.* –**clarifier**, *n.*

clarinet *n.* a wind instrument in the form of a cylindrical tube with a single reed attached to its mouthpiece.

clarion *adj.* **1.** clear and shrill. **2.** inspiring.

clarity *n.* clearness.

clash *v.* **1.** to make a loud, harsh noise. **2.** to collide, especially noisily. **3.** to conflict; disagree, as of temperaments, colours, etc. **4.** to coincide unfortunately (especially of events). –*n.* **5.** the noise of, or as of, a collision. **6.** an unfortunate coinciding, as of events.

clasp *n.* **1.** a fastening device, usually of metal. **2.** a grasp. –*v.* **3.** to take hold of with an enfolding grasp.

class *n.* **1.** a number of persons, things, animals, etc., regarded as forming one group through the possession of similar qualities. **2.** any division according to rank or grade. **3. a.** a group of pupils taught together. **b.** a period during which they are taught. **4.** a social stratum sharing similar economic and cultural characteristics. **5.** *Informal* high quality in style of dress or manner. **6.** a grade of accommodation in railway carriages, ships, aeroplanes, etc. –*v.* **7.** to arrange, place, or rate as to class.

> **Class** (defs 1, 3a and 4) is a collective noun and can be used with a singular or plural verb. Look up **collective noun**.

classic *adj.* **1.** serving as a standard, model, or guide. **2.** of literary or historical renown. –*n.* **3.** an author or a literary work of the first rank. **4.** (*pl.*) the literature or language of ancient Greece and Rome. **5.** something considered to be a perfect example of its type. –**classical**, *adj.*

classical *adj.* **1.** of or relating to the culture, language and literature of the ancient world. **2.** conforming to established taste or critical standards; adhering to traditional forms. **3.** (of music) often taking traditional forms, as a sonata, symphony, etc., and distinguished from more popular music, as jazz, pop, folk, rock, etc.

classified ad *n.* a short advertisement in a newspaper, advertising something for sale, a job, etc.

> You can also use the short form **classified**, particularly in the plural form to refer to the section of a newspaper where such advertisements appear: *We advertised our car for sale in the classifieds.*

classify *v.* (**-fied**, **-fying**) **1.** to arrange or distribute in classes. **2.** to mark and limit access to (a secret document, information, etc.). –**classification**, *n.*

classmate *n.* a member of the same class, as at school.

classroom *n.* a room in a school, etc., in which classes meet.

clatter *v.* **1.** to make a loud rattling sound. –*n.* **2.** a clattering noise.

clause *n.* **1.** *Gram.* a group of words containing a subject and a predicate. **2.** part of a legal document dealing with a section of the matter concerned, as in a contract, will, etc.

claustrophobia *n.* a dread of confined places. –**claustrophobic**, *adj.*

claves *pl. n.* a musical instrument consisting of two wooden sticks which are struck together.

clavicle *n.* → **collarbone**.

claw *n.* **1.** a sharp, usually curved, nail on the foot of an animal or bird. **2.** any part or thing resembling a claw. –*v.* **3.** to tear, scratch, seize, etc., with or as with claws.

clay n. **1.** a natural earthy material used for making bricks, pottery, etc. **2.** earth.

claymation n. (from trademark) an animation technique using clay figures as the basis for the film rather than drawn figures.

clean adj. **1.** free from dirt or filth; unstained. **2.** free from defect. **3.** free from disease, bacteria or infection. **4.** shapely; trim: the clean lines of a ship. –adv. **5.** in a clean manner. **6.** wholly; completely. –v. **7.** to make clean. –phr. **8. come clean,** to make a full confession.

clean coal n. coal which has been processed to make it environmentally less damaging. See **clean-coal technology.**

clean-coal technology n. any of various processes which aim to reduce the amount of carbon dioxide or other pollutants produced in the burning of coal as a fuel.

clean-cut adj. **1.** distinctly outlined. **2.** definite. **3.** neatly dressed; wholesome.

> Def. 3 is most frequently used of men, because it was originally used to describe a man with a short, tidy haircut and a clean-shaven face.

clean fuel n. a fuel which produces minimal greenhouse gas emissions.

cleanliness n. the condition or quality of being clean or being kept clean.

cleanse /klenz/ v. (**cleansed, cleansing**) to make clean.

clear adj. **1.** free from darkness, obscurity, or cloudiness. **2.** bright. **3.** transparent. **4.** distinct to the eye, ear, or mind. **5.** free from guilt or blame. **6.** free from obstructions. **7.** unentangled or disengaged (of). **8.** without limitation or qualification. **9.** free from debt. **10.** without deduction. –v. **11.** to make or become clear. **12.** to pass over without entanglement or collision. **13.** to gain as profit. **14.** to approve or authorise, or to obtain approval or authorisation for (a thing or person). **15.** to remove trees, undergrowth, etc., from (an area of land).

clearance n. **1.** the act of clearing. **2.** a clear space. **3.** amount of room available or required to clear an obstacle.

clearway n. a stretch of road on which, between stated times, motorists may not stop.

cleat n. a small wedge-shaped block.

cleavage n. **1.** the state of being cleft or split. **2.** Informal the cleft between a woman's breasts.

cleave[1] v. (**cleaved, cleaving**) to stick or adhere; cling or hold fast (to).

cleave[2] v. (**cleft** or **cleaved** or **clove,** **cleft** or **cleaved** or **cloven, cleaving**) to part or split, especially along a natural line of division.

> Note that the words **cloven** and **cleft,** both meaning split, come from **cleave.**

cleaver n. a heavy knife used by butchers.

clef n. Music a symbol placed upon a stave to indicate the name and pitch of the notes.

cleft[1] n. a space or opening made by cleavage; a split.

cleft[2] adj. split into 2 parts or sections: a cleft chin; a cleft palate.

> This word comes from the verb **cleave**[2].

clement adj. **1.** lenient; compassionate. **2.** (of the weather, etc.) mild or pleasant. –**clemency,** n.

clench v. to close (the hands, teeth, etc.) tightly.

clergy n. the body of ordained people in the Christian church. –**clergyman,** n.

> **Clergy** is a collective noun and can be used with a singular or plural verb. Look up **collective noun.**

cleric n. a member of the clergy.

clerical adj. **1.** relating to a clerk or to clerks. **2.** of or relating to the clergy.

clerk /klak/ n. someone employed in an office, shop, etc., to keep records, etc.

> Note that in Australia this word is pronounced /klak/. In America it is pronounced /kl3k/.

clever *adj.* **1.** having quick intelligence. **2.** dexterous or nimble with the hands.

cliché /ˈkliːʃeɪ/ *n.* (*pl.* **clichés** /-ʃeɪz/) a trite, stereotyped expression, idea, practice, etc.

click *n.* **1.** a slight, sharp sound. –*v.* **2.** to make a click or clicks. **3.** *Informal* to fall into place or be understood. **4.** *Informal* to understand. **5.** *Computers* to operate the mouse button.

clickbait *n.* an attention-grabbing link on a website which turns out to be of spurious value or interest.

client *n.* **1.** someone who consults a professional adviser. **2.** a customer.

clientele /klaɪənˈtel/ *n.* the customers, clients, etc. (of a solicitor, businessperson, etc.) as a whole.

cliff *n.* the high, steep face of a rocky mass.

climate *n.* the composite weather conditions of a region.

climate change *n.* a significant change in the usual climatic conditions, especially that thought to be caused by global warming.

climax *n.* **1.** the crisis point of anything; the culmination. –*v.* **2.** to reach the climax. –**climactic**, *adj.*

climb *v.* **1.** to move up something, especially by using both hands and feet; ascend. **2.** to move upwards slowly by, or as by, continued effort. **3.** to slope upward.

clinch *v.* **1.** to secure (a driven nail, etc.) by beating down the point. **2.** to settle (a matter) decisively. –*n.* **3.** *Boxing, etc.* a close hold which hinders the opponent's punches.

cling *v.* (**clung**, **clinging**) to adhere closely.

cling wrap *n.* thin, clear plastic wrapping, usually for packaging food. Also, **cling film**.

clinic *n.* **1.** any medical centre offering a variety of services. **2.** an organised session of instruction in a particular activity or subject: *a maths clinic; a basketball clinic.*

clinical *adj.* **1.** relating to a clinic. **2.** scientific; not affected by the emotions.

clinical pathology *n.* → **pathology** (def. 2).

clink *v.* to make a light, sharp, ringing sound.

clip¹ *v.* (**clipped**, **clipping**) **1.** to cut, or cut off or out, as with shears. **2.** to punch a hole in (a ticket). **3.** to omit sounds of (a word) in pronouncing. **4.** *Informal* to hit with a quick, sharp blow. **5.** to move swiftly. –*n.* **6.** the act of clipping. **7.** anything clipped off.

clip² *n.* a device for gripping and holding tightly.

clip art *n.* *Computers* a collection of images designed to be copied and used in other applications.

clipper *n.* **1.** (*oft. pl.*) a cutting tool, especially shears. **2.** a sailing vessel built for speed.

clique /kliːk/ *n.* a small set or coterie, especially one that is snobbishly exclusive.

clitoris /ˈklɪtərəs/ *n.* the sensitive organ of the vulva.

cloak *n.* a loose outer garment.

clobber *v.* *Informal* to batter severely; maul.

clock *n.* **1.** an instrument for measuring and indicating time. –*v.* **2.** to time or ascertain by the clock.

clockwise *adj.*, *adv.* in the direction of rotation of the hands of a clock.

clockwork *n.* **1.** the mechanism of a clock. –*phr.* **2. like clockwork**, with perfect regularity or precision.

clod *n.* **1.** a lump or mass, especially of earth or clay. **2.** a stupid person.

clodhoppers *pl. n.* strong, heavy shoes.

clog *v.* (**clogged**, **clogging**) **1.** to hinder or obstruct, especially by sticky matter. –*n.* **2.** a kind of shoe with a thick sole usually of wood.

cloister *n.* **1.** a covered walk. **2.** any quiet, secluded place. –*v.* **3.** to confine in retirement.

clone *n.* **1.** an asexually produced descendant, identical to the original. *–v.* (**cloned**, **cloning**) **2.** to develop such descendant(s).

close /klouz/ *v.*, /klous/ *adj.*, /klouz/ for def 17, /klous/ for def. 18, *n. –v.* (**closed**, **closing**) **1.** to stop or obstruct (a gap, entrance, aperture, etc.). **2.** to stop or obstruct the entrances or holes in (a container, etc.). **3.** to refuse access to or passage across. **4.** to bring together the parts of. **5.** to bring or come to an end; to shut down, temporarily or permanently. **6.** to become closed. **7.** to come together; unite. *–adj.* (**closer**, **closest**) **8.** shut tight. **9.** confined; narrow. **10.** lacking fresh air. **11.** practising secrecy. **12.** stingy. **13.** near in space, time, or relation. **14.** intimate; confidential. **15.** not deviating from a model or original. **16.** nearly even or equal. *–n.* **17.** the end or conclusion. **18.** a cul-de-sac.

For def. 10, the more usual word is **stuffy**.

closed-circuit television *n.* a television system in which cameras and receivers are linked by wire, used to watch what is happening in another part of a building for security, monitoring production operations, etc. *Abbrev.*: CCTV

closet *n.* **1.** a small room or cabinet for clothing, food, utensils, etc. *–adj.* **2.** secret.

closure *n.* **1.** the act of closing or shutting. **2.** the end of an episode, as in a play or a book, or in one's life.

clot *n.* **1.** a semisolid mass, as of coagulated blood. **2.** *Informal* a stupid person.

cloth *n.* (*pl.* **cloths**) a fabric formed by weaving, etc., used for garments, upholstery, etc.

Don't confuse the noun **cloth** with the verb **clothe**.

clothe *v.* (**clothed** *or* **clad**, **clothing**) to dress; attire.

Don't confuse the verb **clothe** with the noun **cloth**.

clothes *pl. n.* fitted articles, usually of cloth, worn on the body for warmth, protection, etc.; garments.

cloud *n.* **1.** a visible collection of particles of water or ice suspended in the air. **2.** any similar mass, especially of smoke or dust. **3.** anything that darkens, or causes gloom, etc. *–v.* **4.** to cover with, or as with, a cloud. **–cloudy**, *adj.*

cloud computing *n.* the provision of computer applications over the internet as a service to users of a particular site.

cloud server *n.* a server which handles the applications provided and managed by cloud computing.

clout *n.* **1.** a blow, especially with the hand. **2.** effectiveness; force.

clove[1] *n.* the dried flower bud of a tropical tree used as a spice.

clove[2] *n.* one of the small bulbs forming a mother bulb, as in garlic.

clove[3] *v.* past tense of **cleave**[2].

cloven *adj.* divided.

This comes from the verb **cleave**[2].

clover *n.* any of various three-leafed herbs.

clown *n.* **1.** a jester or buffoon in a circus, etc. *–v.* **2.** to act like a clown.

cloy *v.* to weary by an excess of food, sweetness, pleasure, etc.

cloying *adj.* **1.** sickeningly sweet. **2.** excessively emotional; sentimental. **–cloyingly**, *adv.* **–cloyingness**, *n.*

club *n.* **1.** a heavy stick, usually thicker at one end, used as a weapon. **2.** a stick or bat used in various ball games. **3.** a group of persons organised for various social purposes and regulated by rules agreed by its members. **4.** the building or rooms used by such a group. **5.** a black, three-leafed figure on a playing card. *–v.* (**clubbed**, **clubbing**) **6.** to beat with a club. **7.** to unite; join together.

Club (def. 3) is a collective noun and can be used with a singular or plural verb. Look up **collective noun**.

cluck v. to utter the cry of a hen.

clucky adj. Aust., NZ (of a hen) broody.

clue n. a guide or aid in the solution of a problem, mystery, etc.

cluey adj. Informal 1. well-informed. 2. showing good sense and keen awareness.

clump n. 1. a cluster, especially of trees, or other plants. –v. 2. to walk heavily and clumsily.

clumsy adj. (-sier, -siest) lacking dexterity or skill in movement or action.

clung v. past tense and past participle of cling.

cluster n. a number of things of the same kind, growing or held together.

clutch[1] v. 1. to seize with the hands or claws. 2. to grip tightly or firmly. –n. 3. (usu. pl.) power of disposal or control. 4. a device for gripping something. 5. (especially in a motor vehicle) the device which engages and disengages the engine from the transmission.

clutch[2] n. a hatch of eggs.

clutter v. 1. to heap or strew in a disorderly manner. –n. 2. a disorderly heap; litter.

CMS n. Internet content management system; a software application which assists in the creation, control, and management of content on a website.

coach n. 1. a large, enclosed, four-wheeled carriage. 2. a bus used for long distances or for sightseeing. 3. a person who trains athletes. 4. a private tutor. –v. 5. to act in the capacity of a coach.

coagulate /koʊ'ægjəleɪt/ v. to change from a fluid into a thickened mass.

coal n. a black or brown coloured compact and earthy organic rock used as a fuel.

coalesce /koʊə'lɛs/ v. (-lesced, -lescing) to unite so as to form one mass, community, etc.

The more usual expression is **join together**.

coalition /koʊə'lɪʃən/ n. an alliance, especially one between political parties, states, etc.

coarse adj. 1. of inferior or faulty quality. 2. composed of relatively large particles. 3. lacking in fineness or delicacy.

Don't confuse **coarse** with **course**, which has several meanings. It can be a part of a meal, a series of classes, or the way along which something progresses.

coast n. 1. the land next to the sea. –v. 2. to move along after effort has ceased. –**coastal**, adj.

coastguard n. a coastal police force responsible for preventing smuggling, watching for and aiding ships in distress or danger, etc.

coat n. 1. an outer garment with sleeves. 2. a natural covering, as the hair of an animal, etc. 3. anything that covers or conceals. –v. 4. to cover with a layer or coating.

coathanger n. a curved piece of wood, plastic, etc., with a hook attached, on which clothes are hung.

coating n. a thin covering of a substance spread over a surface.

coat of arms n. a design, usually in the form of a shield, used as a symbol of a family, organisation, city, etc.

coax v. 1. to influence by, or use gentle persuasion, etc. 2. to get by coaxing.

cob n. 1. the long, woody core in which the grains of corn or maize are embedded. 2. a short-legged, thickset horse.

cobalt n. a silver-white metallic element used in alloys, ceramics, etc., and (as an isotope) in the treatment of cancer. Symbol: Co

cobber n. Aust., NZ Informal mate; friend.

cobbler n. 1. someone who mends shoes. 2. a clumsy worker.

cobra /'kɒbrə, 'koʊbrə/ n. any of several extremely venomous snakes able to dilate the neck to a hood-like form.

cobweb n. a web or net spun by a spider to catch its prey.

cocaine *n.* a bitter substance, used illegally as a recreational drug and formerly in medicine as a local anaesthetic.

coccyx /'kɒksɪks, 'kɒkɪks/ *n. Anat.* a small triangular bone forming the lower extremity of the spinal column in humans.

cochineal /kɒtʃə'niːl/ *n.* a red dye.

cochlea /'kɒklɪə/ *n.* (*pl.* **-leae** /-liːi/) *Anat.* a division, spiral in form, of the internal ear, in humans and most other mammals. –**cochlear**, *adj.*

cock[1] *n.* **1.** the male of any bird, especially the domestic chicken. **2.** a device for controlling the flow of a liquid or gas. –*v.* **3.** to pull back and set the hammer of (a firearm).

For the male of the domestic chicken, the more common word is **rooster**.

cock[2] *v.* to set or turn up or to one side, often in an assertive, jaunty, or significant manner.

cockatoo *n.* any of several crested parrots.

cockerel *n.* a young domestic cock.

cocker spaniel *n.* a breed of small spaniels used in hunting or kept as pets.

cockeyed *adj.* having a squinting eye.

cockle *n.* a type of mollusc.

cockpit *n.* **1.** (in some aeroplanes) an enclosed space containing seats for the pilot and copilot. **2.** the driver's seat in a racing car.

cockroach *n.* any of various insects, usually nocturnal, and having a flattened body.

cockscomb *n.* the comb of a cock.

cocksure *adj.* overconfident.

cocktail *n.* any of various short mixed drinks.

cocky[1] *adj.* (**-kier, -kiest**) *Informal* arrogantly smart; full of conceit.

cocky[2] *n. Informal* **1.** *Aust.* a cockatoo, or other parrot. **2.** *Aust., NZ* a farmer, especially one who farms in a small way.

cocoa *n.* **1.** the roasted, ground seeds of the cacao. **2.** a beverage made from this.

coconut *n.* the seed of the coconut palm, large, hard-shelled, lined with a white edible meat, and containing a milky liquid.

cocoon *n.* the silky envelope spun by the larvae of many insects to protect them in the pupal state.

cod *n.* (*pl.* **cod** or **cods**) any of a number of freshwater or marine fishes.

For information about the different plural forms, see the note at **fish**.

coda *n.* a passage at the end of a musical composition.

coddle *v.* **1.** to cook (eggs, fruit, etc.) slowly in water just below boiling point. **2.** to treat indulgently.

code *n.* **1.** any system of rules and regulations. **2.** a system of symbols for use in communication by telegraph, etc. **3.** a system of symbols, words etc., used for secrecy.

codeine *n.* a drug obtained from opium, used in medicine as an analgesic.

codger *n. Informal* a man, especially elderly.

codicil /'kɒdəsɪl/ *n.* a supplement to a will, containing an addition, explanation, modification, etc.

codify *v.* (**-fied, -fying**) to reduce (laws, etc.) to a code.

co-education *n.* joint education of both sexes in the same institution.

coefficient *n.* a number or quantity placed (generally) before and multiplying another quantity.

coelenterate /sə'lɛntəreɪt, -tərət/ *n.* one of the group of invertebrate animals that includes the jellyfishes, corals, polyps, etc.

coeliac /'siːliæk/ *adj.* **1.** of or relating to the cavity of the abdomen. **2.** of or relating to coeliac disease. –*n.* **3.** a person suffering from coeliac disease. Also, **celiac**.

coeliac disease *n.* a congenital disorder characterised by diarrhoea due to intolerance of the bowels to gluten. Also, **celiac disease**.

coerce /koʊˈɜs/ v. to compel by force. –**coercion**, n. –**coercive**, adj.

coffee n. a beverage made from the roasted and ground beans or seeds of various tropical trees and shrubs.

coffer n. **1.** a box or chest for valuables. **2.** (pl.) a treasury; funds.

Def. 2 usually refers to the funds of a government or some other kind of organisation. However, it can also be used informally to refer to your own fund of money: *I don't think we can afford to go on a holiday this year – there's not much in the coffers.*

coffin n. the box in which a corpse is placed for burial.

cog n. a tooth or projection on a wheel, etc., for transmitting motion to, or receiving motion from, a corresponding part with which it engages.

cogent /ˈkoʊdʒənt/ adj. compelling assent or belief; convincing: *a cogent argument.* –**cogency**, n.

The more usual word is **powerful**.

cogitate v. to think hard; ponder.

cognac /ˈkɒnjæk/ n. French brandy.

cognate adj. related by birth or origin.

cognisance /ˈkɒgnɪzəns/ n. knowledge; notice. Also, **cognizance**. –**cognisant**, adj.

cognition n. the act or process of knowing; perception. –**cognitive**, adj.

cohabit v. to live together in a sexual relationship.

cohere v. (**-hered, -hering**) **1.** to hold fast, as parts of the same mass. **2.** to be congruous.

coherent adj. **1.** able to express oneself in a clear and logical way. **2.** clear and logical. –**coherence**, n. –**coherently**, adv.

cohesion n. the state of cohering, uniting, or sticking together. –**cohesive**, adj.

cohort n. **1.** any group or company. **2.** an ally; supporter. **3.** a group of people at the same level, as in education, skill development, etc.

coiffure /kwʌˈfjʊə/ n. a style of arranging the hair.

The more usual word is **hairstyle**.

coil v. **1.** to wind into rings one above another. –n. **2.** a connected series of spirals or rings. **3.** a single such ring.

coin n. **1.** a piece of metal stamped and issued officially as money. **2.** such pieces collectively. –v. **3.** to make; invent.

coincide v. to be or happen at the same point in space or time.

coincidence n. **1.** the condition or fact of coinciding. **2.** a striking chance occurrence of 2 or more events at one time. –**coincidental**, adj.

coitus /ˈkoʊətəs, ˈkɔɪtəs/ n. sexual intercourse. Also, **coition** /koʊˈɪʃən/. –**coital**, adj.

coke n. a solid fuel remaining after the removal of gas from coal.

cola n. a carbonated soft drink containing an extract made from the tropical cola nut.

colander /ˈkʌləndə, ˈkɒl-/ n. a strainer used in cookery. Also, **cullender**.

cold adj. **1.** having a relatively low temperature. **2.** producing or feeling a marked lack of warmth. **3.** *Informal* unconscious because of a severe blow, shock, etc. **4.** not affectionate or friendly. –n. **5.** the relative absence of heat. **6.** the sensation produced by loss of heat from the body. **7.** Also, **the common cold**. an indisposition caused by a virus, characterised by catarrh, etc.

cold-blooded adj. **1.** unsympathetic; cruel. **2.** designating animals, as fishes and reptiles, whose body temperature approximates to that of the surrounding medium.

cold-call v. to attempt to sell a product or service by making an unsolicited call to a prospective customer, usually by telephone. –**cold-calling**, n.

cold-shoulder v. to ignore; show indifference to.

cold sore n. a watery eruption on the face often accompanying a cold (def. 7).

coleslaw n. a salad of finely sliced white cabbage, etc. Also, **slaw**.

colic n. paroxysmal pain in the abdomen. –**colicky**, adj.

coliform n. 1. one of a group of bacteria of the intestine, such as E. coli, whose presence in water, for instance, is an indication of faecal contamination. –adj. 2. of or relating to such bacteria.

collaborate v. 1. to work, one with another. 2. to cooperate treacherously. –**collaboration**, n. –**collaborator**, n. –**collaborative**, adj.

collage /kə'laʒ, 'kɒlaʒ, 'kɒlaʒ/ n. a picture composed of various materials.

collapse v. (-lapsed, -lapsing) 1. to fall or cave in; crumble suddenly. 2. to break down; come to nothing. –n. 3. a sudden, complete failure.

collapsible adj. designed to fold into a compact size.

collar n. 1. anything worn or placed round the neck. 2. the part of a shirt, etc., round the neck. –v. 3. to put a collar on. 4. to seize by the collar or neck.

collarbone n. a slender bone connecting the breastbone with the shoulderblade, and forming the front part of the shoulder.

The scientific name for this is **clavicle**.

collate v. to put together (a document) by sorting its pages into the correct order. –**collator**, n.

collateral adj. 1. situated at the side. 2. accompanying; auxiliary.

colleague n. an associate in business, etc.

collect v. 1. to gather together. 2. to accumulate; make a collection of. 3. to regain control of (one's thoughts, etc.). 4. to call for and remove. 5. Informal to run into or collide with. –adj., adv. 6. to be paid for by the receiver. –**collection**, n.

collective adj. 1. forming a collection or aggregate; combined. 2. relating to a group of individuals taken together. –n. 3. a collective body. 4. a communal enterprise.

collective noun n. Gram. a noun which is singular in form but which expresses a grouping of individual objects or people, as family, jury, and army.

Collective nouns can be treated as singular or plural depending on whether you want to emphasise the fact that you are talking about a single group acting together, or about a collection of individuals. For example, you might say The jury was called into the court, but The jury were undecided about the verdict.

college n. 1. a (usually) post-secondary, diploma-awarding, technical or professional school. 2. an institution for special or professional instruction often part of a university. 3. a self-governing association of scholars incorporated within a university. 4. a large private school. 5. an association of persons having certain powers and engaged in a particular pursuit. –**collegian**, n. –**collegiate**, adj.

collide v. to come together with force; come into violent contact (with). –**collision**, n.

collie n. a dog used for tending sheep.

colliery n. (pl. -ries) a coal mine, including all buildings and equipment.

collocate v. to set or place together. –**collocation**, n.

colloquial adj. appropriate to conversational or informal speech or writing.

collusion n. secret agreement for a fraudulent purpose.

cologne /kə'loun/ n. a perfumed toilet water. Also, **eau de Cologne**.

colon[1] n. a punctuation mark (:) used especially to separate the main part of a sentence from a list of examples, as in I want you to bring the following things: a pencil, a rubber, and a piece of paper.

colon² *n.* the large intestine excluding the rectum.

colonel /'kɜːnəl/ *n.* a senior officer in the army.

colonnade *n.* **1.** a series of columns set at regular intervals. **2.** a long row of trees.

colony *n.* (*pl.* **-nies**) **1.** a group of people who settle a new land and are subject to the parent state. **2.** the country or district so settled. **3.** any people or territory separated from but subject to a ruling power. **4.** a group of animals or plants of the same kind, living together. –**colonial**, *adj.* –**colonise**, **colonize**, *v.* –**colonist**, *n.*

colossal *adj.* gigantic; vast.

colostomy *n.* (*pl.* **-tomies**) the surgical formation of an artificial anus.

colour *n.* **1.** that quality of light (reflected or transmitted by a substance) which is basically determined by its spectral composition and is perceived as (a mixture of) red, blue, yellow, etc. **2.** skin pigmentation as an indication of ethnicity or race. **3.** vivid or distinctive quality, as of literary work. **4.** that which is used for colouring; pigment. **5.** (*pl.*) a flag, ensign, etc., as of a military body or ship. –*v.* **6.** to give or apply colour to; tinge. **7.** to cause to appear different from the reality. **8.** to take on or change colour. **9.** to flush. Also, **color**.

colour blindness *n.* defective colour perception. Also, **color blindness**. –**colourblind**, *adj.*

colourfast *adj.* of fabric dyes, lasting. Also, **colorfast**.

colourful *adj.* **1.** brightly coloured or having many colours. **2.** interesting and exciting: *a colourful story*. Also, **colorful**. –**colourfully**, *adv.*

colt *n.* a male horse not past its fourth birthday.

column *n.* **1.** an upright shaft usually serving as a support; a pillar. **2.** any column-like object, mass, or formation. **3.** one of the 2 or more vertical rows of lines of type

or printed matter on a page. **4.** a regular contribution to a newspaper, usually signed, and consisting of comment, news, etc.

coma *n.* a state of prolonged unconsciousness. –**comatose**, *adj.*

comb *n.* **1.** a toothed piece of bone, metal, etc., for arranging or holding the hair. **2.** any comb-like instrument. **3.** the fleshy growth on the head of the domestic fowl. –*v.* **4.** to dress (the hair, etc.) with a comb. **5.** to search with great thoroughness.

combat *v.* /'kɒmbæt, kəm'bæt/ (**-bated**, **-bating**) **1.** to fight or contend against. –*n.* /'kɒmbæt/ **2.** a fight between 2 people, armies, etc.

combine *v.* to bring or join into a close union or whole. –**combination**, *n.*

combustion *n.* the process of burning. –**combustible**, *adj.*

come *v.* (**came**, **come**, **coming**) **1.** to move towards or arrive at a particular place. **2.** to issue; be derived. **3.** to arrive or appear as a result. **4.** to turn out to be. –*phr.* **5. come about**, to come to pass. **6. come across**, to meet with, especially by chance. **7. come (a)round**, **a.** to relent. **b.** to recover consciousness. **c.** to change (an opinion, direction, etc.). **8. come down with**, to contract (a disease). **9. come from**, **a.** to have been born in; to live in. **b.** to derive or be obtained from. **10. come in**, to become useful, fashionable, etc. **11. come into**, **a.** to get. **b.** to inherit. **12. come out**, **a.** to appear; be published. **b.** to be revealed. **c.** to declare one's homosexuality. **13. come to**, **a.** to extend to; reach. **b.** to recover consciousness. **c.** to amount to.

comedian *n.* an actor or writer of comedy.

comedy *n.* (*pl.* **-dies**) **1.** a play, film, etc., of light and humorous character. **2.** the comic element of drama, literature, or life.

comely /'kʌmli/ *adj.* (**-lier**, **-liest**) pleasing in appearance.

comet n. a celestial body moving about the sun in an elongated orbit.

comfort v. 1. to soothe when in grief. –n. 2. relief in affliction; consolation. 3. a person or thing that consoles. 4. a state of ease.

comfortable adj. 1. producing or attended with comfort or ease of mind or body. 2. being in a state of comfort or ease; easy and undisturbed. 3. having adequate income or wealth. 4. easily achieved, as a victory.

comic adj. 1. relating to comedy. 2. provoking laughter. –n. 3. a comic actor. 4. a magazine containing one or more stories in comic strip form. 5. (pl.) comic strips.

comical adj. provoking laughter, or amusing.

comic strip n. a series of cartoon drawings relating a comic incident, an adventure story, etc.

comma n. a mark of punctuation (,) used to indicate the places in a sentence where one would pause in speaking.

command v. 1. to order with authority. 2. to require with authority. 3. to have authority over. –n. 4. the act of commanding or ordering. 5. control; disposal: *to have influential friends at one's command.* –**commanding**, adj.

commandant n. the commanding officer of a place, group, etc.

commandeer v. to seize (private property) for military or other public use.

commander n. someone who exercises authority; a chief officer.

commandment n. a command or edict.

commando n. (pl. **-dos** or **-does**) (a member of) a small specially trained fighting force.

commemorate v. 1. to serve as a memento of. 2. to honour the memory of by some act.

commence v. to begin; start.

commend v. 1. to praise or congratulate. 2. to mention as worthy of confidence, notice, etc. 3. to entrust. –**commendation**, n.

For def. 2, the more usual word is **recommend**.

commensurate adj. 1. of equal extent or duration. 2. proportionate.

comment n. 1. a short note or statement. –v. 2. to make such a note or statement.

commentary n. (pl. **-ries**) 1. a series of comments or annotations. 2. a description of a public event broadcast or televised as it happens.

commentate v. to act as a commentator.

commentator n. a writer or broadcaster who makes critical or explanatory remarks about news, events, or describes sporting events etc.

commerce n. interchange of goods or commodities, especially on a large scale; trade; business.

commercial adj. 1. of, or of the nature of, or engaged in commerce. 2. capable of being sold in great numbers. 3. setting possible commercial return above artistic considerations. 4. *Radio, TV* financially dependent on advertising. –n. 5. *Radio, TV* an advertisement.

commercial artist n. an artist who makes a living from creating artwork for commercial use, as for advertising, publishing, etc.

commiserate v. to sympathise (with). –**commiseration**, n.

commission n. 1. the act of giving in charge. 2. an authoritative order or charge. 3. an official body charged with particular functions. 4. the condition of anything in active service or use. 5. a task or matter committed to one's charge. 6. authority to act as agent for another. 7. a sum or percentage allowed to an agent, salesperson, etc. 8. the position or rank of an officer in the army or navy. –v. 9. to give a commission to. 10. to send on a mission.

commissioner *n.* **1.** a member of a commission. **2.** a government official in charge of a department.

commit *v.* (**-mitted, -mitting**) **1.** to give in trust or charge. **2.** to consign to custody in a jail, mental hospital, etc. **3.** to hand over for treatment, disposal, etc. **4.** to do; perpetrate. **5.** to bind by pledge. **–commitment,** *n.*

committee *n.* a group of persons appointed to investigate, report, or act in special cases.

Committee is a collective noun and can be used with a singular or plural verb. Look up **collective noun**.

commode *n.* **1.** a piece of furniture containing drawers or shelves. **2.** a stand or cupboard containing a chamber-pot or washbasin.

commodious *adj.* convenient and roomy.

The more usual word is **spacious**.

commodity *v.* (*pl.* **-ties**) an article of trade.

commodore *n.* the senior captain of a line of merchant vessels.

common *adj.* **1.** belonging equally to, or shared alike by, 2 or more. **2.** of frequent occurrence; familiar; usual. **3.** of mediocre or inferior quality. *–n.* **4.** Also, **town common**. (*also pl.*) an area of public land. **5.** *Internet* (*pl.*) a website where material is freely available: *information commons*; *software commons*.

commoner *n.* one of the common people.

common law *n.* **1.** the system of law based on custom and court decision, as distinct from statute or ecclesiastical law. **2.** the law administered through the system of writs.

common noun *n. Gram.* a noun applicable to any one or all the members of a class, as *man, men, city, cities*, in contrast to *Shakespeare, Hobart*.

Note that common nouns are spelt with a lower-case letter rather than a capital.

Compare this with **proper noun**, which is the name of a particular place, person or thing, such as *Robert*, as opposed to the common noun *boy*.

commonplace *adj.* ordinary; without individuality.

common sense *n.* sound, practical understanding.

commonwealth *n.* **1.** the whole body of people of a nation. **2.** a group of people or countries united by a common interest. **3.** (*upper case*) a federation of states and territories with powers and responsibilities divided between a central government and a number of smaller governments, as *the Commonwealth of Australia*.

The **Commonwealth of Australia** is the name that was chosen for the whole of the nation in 1901 when the states joined together to form a federation. Therefore the **Commonwealth Government** refers to the federal government of Australia as compared with the state governments. The **Commonwealth of Nations** is a group of countries which used to be part of the British Empire, and the **Commonwealth of Independent States (CIS)** is a federation formed in 1991 of countries which had been part of the former Soviet Union.

commotion *n.* violent or tumultuous motion or disturbance.

communal /kə'mjunəl, 'kɒmjənəl/ *adj.* relating to a commune or a community.

commune[1] /kə'mjun/ *v.* to interchange thoughts or feelings; converse.

The more usual word is **communicate**.

commune[2] /'kɒmjun/ *n.* any community of like-minded people choosing to live independently.

communicate *v.* **1.** to give to another as a partaker; impart; transmit. **2.** to make known. **3.** to have interchange of thoughts. **–communication,** *n.* **–communicable,** *adj.*

communion *n.* **1.** the act of sharing, or holding in common. **2.** interchange of thoughts or interests; intimate talk. **3.** (*oft. upper case*) Also, **Holy Communion.** a Christian religious ceremony held in commemoration of the Last Supper.

This is the noun from **commune¹**.

communiqué /kə'mjunəkeɪ/ *n.* an official bulletin or communication usually to the press or public.

communism *n.* a political and economic system in which the government runs all trade, business and industry, and property is meant to be owned equally by all the people. –**communist**, *n.* –**communistic**, *adj.*

Compare this with **capitalism** and **socialism**.

community *n.* (*pl.* **-ties**) all the people of a specific locality or country.

commute *v.* **1.** to change (a penalty, etc.) for one less burdensome or severe. **2.** to serve as a substitute. **3.** to travel regularly between home and work. –**commuter**, *n.*

compact¹ *adj.* /kəm'pækt, 'kɒmpækt/ **1.** joined or packed together; closely and firmly united. **2.** arranged within a relatively small space. **3.** expressed concisely. –*v.* /kəm'pækt/ **4.** to join or pack closely together. –*n.* /'kɒmpækt/ **5.** a small case containing a mirror, face powder, etc.

compact² /'kɒmpækt/ *n.* an agreement between parties.

compact disc *n.* a digitally-encoded disc, used for the reproduction of high-fidelity sound and low-resolution video information, and decoded by a laser beam. Also, **CD.**

companion *n.* **1.** someone who accompanies or associates with another. **2.** a handbook.

companionable *adj.* fitted to be a companion; sociable.

company *n.* **1.** a group of people. **2.** a guest or guests. **3.** a number of persons united or incorporated for joint action, especially for business. **4.** *Mil.* a subdivision of a regiment or battalion.

Company (defs 1, 3 and 4) is a collective noun and can be used with a singular or plural verb. Look up **collective noun**.

comparative *adj.* **1.** relating to comparison. **2.** estimated by comparison; not positive or absolute. **3.** *Gram.* relating to the form of an adjective or adverb which expresses the intermediate degree of the comparison: '*Smoother*' *is the comparative form of* '*smooth*' *and* '*more easily*' *is the comparative form of* '*easily*'.

Compare def. 3 with **superlative** (def. 2), which describes an adjective or adverb which expresses the greatest degree. For example, *smoothest* is the superlative form of *smooth*, and *most easily* is the superlative form of *easily*.

compare *v.* **1.** to represent as similar (*to*). **2.** to note the similarities and differences of: *to compare apples with pears.* **3.** to bear comparison. –**comparable**, *adj.*

Don't confuse **compare** with **compere**, which is someone who introduces the different acts in a show.
Compare def. 2 with **contrast**, which is to show only the differences between things, rather than both the similarities and the differences.

comparison *n.* **1.** the state of being compared. **2.** a likening; a comparative estimate or statement.

compartment *n.* **1.** a space marked or partitioned off. **2.** a separate room, section, etc.

compass *n.* **1.** an instrument for determining directions. **2.** space within limits; scope. **3.** Also, **pair of compasses.** an instrument for drawing circles, measuring distances, etc. –*v.* **4.** to extend or stretch around.

compassion *n.* pity for the sufferings or misfortunes of another. –**compassionate**, *adj.*

compatible *adj.* **1.** capable of existing together in harmony. **2.** (of a computer device) able to work in conjunction with another specified device.

compatriot *n.* a fellow citizen.

compel *v.* (**-pelled**, **-pelling**) to force, especially to a course of action.

compelling *adj.* (of a person, writer, actor, etc.) demanding attention, respect.

compensate *v.* **1.** to offset; make up (*for*). **2.** to provide or be an equivalent. **3.** make amends (*for*). **–compensation**, *n.*

compere *n.* **1.** someone who introduces the acts in an entertainment. **–v. 2.** to act as compere.

Don't confuse this with **compare**, which is to point out the similarities and differences between things.

compete *v.* to contend with another for a prize, profit, etc. **–competitive**, *adj.*

competent *adj.* properly qualified, capable. **–competence**, *n.*

competition *n.* **1.** a contest for some prize or advantage. **2.** rivalry between competing people, teams, businesses, etc. **3.** a competitor or competitors.

competitor *n.* someone who competes; a rival.

compile *v.* to put together (literary materials) in one book or work. **–compilation**, *n.*

complacent *adj.* pleased, especially with oneself or one's own merits, etc. **–complacency**, *n.*

complain *v.* to express grief, pain, uneasiness, censure, resentment, etc. **–complaint**, *n.*

complement *n.* /ˈkɒmpləmənt/ **1.** that which completes or makes perfect, or which emphasises the best qualities of: *This wine is the perfect complement to the meal.* **2.** full quantity or amount: *the full complement of players.* **–v.** /ˈkɒmpləˌment/ **3.** to serve as a complement to: *These shoes will complement the outfit.* **–complementary**, *adj.*

Don't confuse this with **compliment**, which is something you say or do to praise someone. Take care also with **complementary** and **complimentary**. **Complementary** describes something which completes or brings the best out of something else (*complementary accessories*), and **complimentary** means free (*complimentary tickets*) or relating to a compliment (*complimentary remarks*).

complementary medicine *n.* the range of treatments and procedures of an alternative nature which are considered, on scientific evidence, to assist mainstream medical treatments and procedures.

complete *adj.* **1.** having all its parts or elements. **2.** finished. **–v. 3.** to make complete. **–completion**, *n.*

complex *adj.* **1.** composed of interconnected parts. **2.** difficult to understand. **–n. 3.** a complex whole or system. **4.** the buildings and ancillary equipment required for a specified purpose: *a shopping complex*; *a launch complex.* **–complexity**, *n.*

complexion *n.* **1.** the natural colour and appearance of the skin, especially the face. **2.** appearance; aspect.

compliance /kəmˈplaɪəns/ *n.* the act of complying; an acquiescing.

complicate *v.* to make complex or involved. **–complicated**, *adj.* **–complication**, *n.*

complicit *adj.* involved with a degree of guilt.

complicity *n.* the state of being an accomplice: *complicity in a crime.*

The more usual word is **involvement**.

compliment *n.* /ˈkɒmpləmənt/ **1.** an expression of praise or admiration. **2.** a formal expression of civility or respect. **–v.** /ˈkɒmpləˌment/ **3.** to pay a compliment to.

Don't confuse **compliment** with **complement**, which is something that completes or perfects something else.

complimentary *adj.* **1.** praising, or expressing a compliment. **2.** free or without cost.

Don't confuse this with **complementary**, which describes something which completes something else.

comply *v.* (**-plied**, **-plying**) to act in accordance with wishes, commands, requirements, etc.: *She complied with his request.*

component *adj.* **1.** constituent. *–n.* **2.** a constituent part.

comport *v.* **1.** to bear or conduct (oneself). **2.** to agree or accord (*with*): *to comport with the facts.*

compose *v.* **1.** to make by uniting parts or elements. **2.** to make up or form: *Smog is composed of smoke and fog.* **3.** to write (a literary or musical production). **4.** to bring (the body or mind) to a condition of repose, calmness, etc. **–composer,** *n.*

Don't confuse def. 2, which is often used in the phrase **composed of**, with **comprise**. *Composed of* always follows a form of the verb *to be*: *The class is composed of four women and three men.* You can use **comprise** with the same sense, but it is not used with the verb *to be* nor followed by *of*: *The class comprises four women and three men.*

Note that you can also use **consist of**: *The class consists of four women and three men.*

composite *adj.* made up of various parts or elements.

composite class *n.* a class, especially in primary school, in which 2 or more different grade levels are taught by one teacher in the same classroom.

composition *n.* **1.** the act of combining parts or elements. **2.** the resulting state or product. **3.** a short essay.

compositor *n.* a person who assembles the type for a printed page.

compost *n.* a mixture of organic matter used for fertilising land.

composure *n.* serene state of mind; calmness.

compound¹ *adj.* /ˈkɒmpaʊnd/ **1.** composed of 2 or more parts, elements, or ingredients. *–n.* /ˈkɒmpaʊnd/ **2.** something formed by compounding or combining parts, etc. *–v.* /kəmˈpaʊnd/ **3.** to put together into a whole. **4.** to pay (interest) on the accrued interest as well as the principal. **5.** to increase or make worse: *The rain compounded their problems.*

compound² /ˈkɒmpaʊnd/ *n.* an enclosure in which people live, sometimes against their will.

compound interest *n.* interest paid on a debt plus its interest as it falls due.

comprehend *v.* **1.** to understand the meaning or nature of. **2.** to take in; include. **–comprehension,** *n.*

comprehensive *adj.* inclusive; comprehending much; of large scope.

compress *v.* /kəmˈprɛs/ **1.** to press together; force into less space. **2.** Computers to convert (data) into a form that uses less storage space; zip. *–n.* /ˈkɒmprɛs/ **3.** a soft pad held in place by a bandage, to supply pressure, moisture, cold, etc. **–compression,** *n.*

comprise *v.* **1.** to include; contain: *Our class comprises both boys and girls.* **2.** to be composed of: *Australia comprises six states and two territories.* **3.** to combine to make up: *Smokers and people with high blood pressure comprise the group most at risk.*

Note that many people regard the use of **comprise** followed by *of* as incorrect. In standard English you might say 'The house comprises seven rooms', or 'The house consists of seven rooms', or 'The house is made up of seven rooms', but not 'The house is comprised of seven rooms'.
You can also use **consist of** and be **composed of**. See the note at **compose**.

compromise /ˈkɒmprəmaɪz/ *n.* **1.** a settlement of differences by mutual concessions. **2.** something intermediate between different things. **3.** an endangering, especially of reputation. –*v.* **4.** to settle by a compromise. **5.** to make liable to danger, suspicion, scandal, etc.

compulsion *n.* **1.** the act of compelling; constraint. **2.** a strong irrational impulse to carry out a given act. –**compulsive**, *adj.*

compulsory *adj.* **1.** using compulsion. **2.** compelled; obligatory.

compunction *n.* regret or guilt for some wrongdoing: *She felt no compunction about what she had done.*

Compunction is usually used in a negative sentence, with words like *not*, *without*, etc.

compute *v.* to determine by calculation. –**computation**, *n.*

computer *n.* an apparatus for performing mathematical computations electronically according to a series of stored instructions.

computer geek *n. Informal* a person whose lifestyle revolves around computers.

This expression is usually used in a mildly disapproving way.

computerise *v.* **1.** to process or store (data) in a computer. **2.** to provide with a computer system. Also, **computerize**. –**computerisation**, *n.*

computer language *n.* any artificial language coded in text or graphics that can be interpreted by a machine, particularly a computer. Also, **programming language**.

computer program *n.* → program (def. 5). –**computer programming**, *n.* –**computer programmer**, *n.*

computer terminal *n.* an input or output device connected to a computer but at a distance from it.

computing *n.* **1.** the science or study of the principles and uses of computers. **2.** the field of computer technology. –*adj.* **3.** relating to computers: *computing skills.*

comrade *n.* an associate in occupation or friendship.

con[1] *adv.* **1.** against a proposition, opinion, etc. (opposed to *pro*). –*n.* **2.** the argument, arguer, or voter against (something) (opposed to *pro*).

con[2] *n.* a confidence trick. –*v.* (**conned**, **conning**) **2.** to swindle.

con artist *n.* a person who swindles a victim out of their money or property, or persuades them to do something they would not otherwise have done, by initially gaining their trust.

concave *adj.* curved like the interior of a circle.

conceal *v.* to hide.

concede *v.* **1.** to admit as true, just, or proper. **2.** to grant as a right or privilege.

conceit *n.* an exaggerated estimate of one's own ability, etc. a fanciful thought or expression, especially far-fetched. –**conceited**, *adj.*

conceivable *adj.* imaginable.

conceive *v.* **1.** to form (a notion, purpose, etc.). **2.** to apprehend in the mind. **3.** to become pregnant (with). **4.** to form an idea (*of*).

concentrate *v.* **1.** to converge or draw to a common centre. **2.** make more intense, stronger, or purer by removing or reducing what is inessential. **3.** to become more intense, etc. **4.** to direct one's thoughts or actions towards one subject. –*n.* **5.** a concentrated form of something. –**concentration**, *n.*

concentrated *adj.* **1.** applied with great energy and intensity; focused: *concentrated attention.* **2.** reduced to the essential ingredient, as by removing water: *concentrated juice.* **3.** clustered densely together: *concentrated population.*

concentric *adj.* having a common centre, as circles or spheres.

concept *n.* **1.** a generalised thought, idea, or notion. **2.** an idea that includes all that is associated with a word or other symbol. –**conceptual**, *adj.*

conception *n.* **1.** the act or state of conceiving or being conceived. **2.** fertilisation; the beginning of pregnancy. **3.** a notion, idea or thought. **4.** beginning.

This is the noun from **conceive**.

concern *v.* **1.** to relate to; be of interest or importance to. **2.** to interest or involve. **3.** to disquiet. –*n.* **4.** a matter that engages one's attention, interest, or care, or that affects one's welfare. **5.** solicitude. **6.** a commercial or manufacturing firm.

concert *n.* **1.** a public performance, usually by 2 or more musicians. **2.** agreement of 2 or more in a design or plan.

concerted *adj.* done by agreement.

concerto /kən'fɜtou, kən'tʃtou/ *n.* (*pl.* **-tos** *or* **-ti**) a musical composition for one or more solo instruments with an orchestral accompaniment.

concession *n.* **1.** the act of conceding or yielding, as a right, or as a point in an argument. **2.** a thing or point yielded. **3.** an outlet, especially a food outlet, at a sporting or entertainment venue, etc.

This is the noun from **concede**.

conch /kɒntʃ, kɒŋk/ *n.* (*pl.* **conches** /'kɒntʃəz/ *or* **conchs** /kɒŋks/) the spiral shell of a gastropod.

concierge /kɒnsi'ɛəʒ, -'ɜʒ/ *n.* a hotel employee whose job is to assist guests with their travel arrangements, theatre and restaurant reservations, etc.

conciliate *v.* **1.** to overcome the distrust or hostility of. **2.** to render compatible.

conciliation *n.* **1.** the act of conciliating. **2.** a procedure for the resolution of a dispute.

concise *adj.* expressing much in few words.

conclave *n.* any private meeting.

conclude *v.* **1.** to bring or come to an end. **2.** to determine by reasoning. **3.** to arrive at an opinion or judgement; come to a decision. –**conclusion**, *n.*

conclusive *adj.* serving to settle or decide a question.

concoct *v.* to prepare; make up. –**concoction**, *n.*

concomitant /kən'kɒmətənt/ *adj.* accompanying; concurrent.

concord *n.* agreement.

concourse *n.* **1.** an assembly. **2.** an open space in a public building, especially a railway station.

concrete *n.* **1.** a mixture of cement, sand, water, and gravel, which hardens as it dries and is used in building. –*adj.* **2.** constituting an actual thing. **3.** representing or applied to an actual substance or thing as opposed to an abstract quality. **4.** made of concrete: *a concrete path.* –*v.* **5.** to treat or lay with concrete. –**concretion**, *n.*

See the note at **cement**.

concrete noun *n. Gram.* a noun referring to something that our 5 senses (touch, sight, hearing, smell and taste) can pick up, such as *boat*, *sun* and *dog*.

Compare this with **abstract noun**, which refers to something which our senses cannot pick up.

concubine *n.* (among polygamous peoples) a secondary wife.

concur *v.* (**-curred, -curring**) **1.** to agree in opinion. **2.** to cooperate; combine. **3.** to coincide. –**concurrent**, *adj.*, *n.*

concussion *n.* the act of shaking or shocking, as by a blow. **2.** shock occasioned by a blow or collision.

condemn *v.* **1.** to express strong disapproval of. **2.** to pronounce to be guilty. **3.** to pronounce to be unfit for use. –**condemnation**, *n.* –**condemnatory**, *adj.*

condense *v.* **1.** to make more dense or compact. **2.** to reduce (a gas or vapour) to a liquid or solid state. **3.** to compress into fewer words. –**condensation**, *n.*

condescend v. **1.** to stoop or deign (to do something). **2.** to behave as if one is descending from a superior rank, etc.

condiment n. a sauce or seasoning, etc., used to give a special flavour to food.

condition n. **1.** particular mode of being of a person or thing; existing state or case. **2.** fit or requisite state. **3.** a circumstance indispensable to some result. **4.** something demanded as an essential part of an agreement. –v. **5.** to put in fit or proper state. **6.** to subject to particular conditions or circumstances.

conditional adj. imposing or depending on a condition or conditions.

condole v. to express sympathy with one in affliction. –**condolence**, n.

condom n. a contraceptive device worn over the penis.

condominium n. Chiefly US **1.** an apartment. **2.** a block of apartments. Also, **condo**.

condone v. to pardon or overlook (an offence).

conducive adj. leading or contributing to a result: conducive to good health.

conduct n. /ˈkɒndʌkt/ **1.** personal behaviour. **2.** direction or management. –v. /kən-ˈdʌkt/ **3.** to behave (oneself). **4.** to direct in action or course; manage. **5.** to lead or guide. **6.** to serve as a channel or medium for (heat, electricity, sound, etc.).

conductivity n. the property of conducting heat, electricity, or sound.

conductor n. **1.** someone who conducts. **2.** the director of an orchestra, etc. **3.** the person on a public transport vehicle, who collects fares, issues tickets, etc. **4.** something that readily conducts heat, electricity, sound.

conduit /ˈkɒndʒuət, ˈkɒndjuət, ˈkɒndɪt/ n. a pipe for conveying water or other fluid.

cone n. **1.** a solid which tapers to a point from a circular base. **2.** the multiple fruit of the pine, fir, etc. **3.** anything cone-shaped.

confection n. a piece of confectionery.

confectionery n. lollies, candies or sweets.

confederacy n. (pl. **-cies**) an alliance of persons, parties, or states.

confederate adj. /kənˈfedərət/ **1.** united in a league or alliance. –n. /kənˈfedərət/ **2.** an accomplice. –v. /kənˈfedərət/ **3.** to unite in a league or alliance, or a conspiracy. –**confederation**, n.

confer v. (**-ferred, -ferring**) to bestow as a gift, favour, honour, etc. (on or upon).

conference n. a meeting for consultation or discussion.

confess v. **1.** to acknowledge or avow. **2.** to own or agree to being responsible for. **3.** to acknowledge one's belief in. –**confession**, n.

confessor n. a priest authorised to hear confessions of sins.

confetti pl. n. small bits of coloured paper, thrown at weddings, etc.

confidant /ˈkɒnfəˌdænt, ˈkɒnfədənt/ n. someone to whom secrets are confided. –**confidante**, fem. n.

confide v. **1.** to trust by imparting secrets (in): He confided in her about his fears. **2.** to tell in confidence: She confided her plans to him.

Note that you **confide in** someone, but **confide** secrets **to** someone.

confidence n. **1.** full trust; belief in the reliability of a person or thing. **2.** self-reliance, self-assurance. **3.** a confidential communication. –phr. **4. in confidence**, as a secret or private matter.

confidence trick n. a swindle in which the victim's confidence is first gained.

confident adj. **1.** having strong belief or full assurance. **2.** sure of oneself.

confidential adj. **1.** spoken or written in confidence. **2.** enjoying another's confidence.

configuration n. the relative disposition of the parts of a thing.

confine v. /kən'faɪn/ 1. to enclose within bounds. –n. /'kɒnfaɪn/ 2. (usu. pl.) a boundary or bound. **–confiner,** n. **–confinement,** n.

confirm v. 1. to make certain or sure; verify. 2. to make valid by some formal act. 3. to reaffirm (a booking, appointment, etc.). 4. to strengthen (a person) in habit, resolution, etc. **–confirmation,** n.

confiscate v. 1. to seize as forfeited. 2. to seize as if by authority.

conflict v. /kən'flɪkt/ 1. to clash, or be in opposition or at variance. –n. /'kɒnflɪkt/ 2. a battle or struggle, especially prolonged.

conflicting adj. 1. in disagreement: *conflicting opinions.* 2. generating conflict: *a conflicting issue.*

conform v. to act according to rules, laws or someone's wishes. **–conformist,** n. **–conformity,** n.

confound v. 1. to throw into confusion. 2. to refute in argument.

confront v. 1. to meet face to face. 2. to oppose boldly. **–confrontation,** n.

confronting adj. intimidating; challenging.

confuse v. 1. to combine without order or clearness. 2. to throw into disorder. 3. to fail to distinguish between; associate by mistake. 4. to perplex. **–confusion,** n.

congeal v. to change from a fluid to a solid state.

congenial adj. agreeing or suited in nature or character.

congenital adj. existing at or from one's birth.

congest v. to fill to excess. **–congestion,** n.

conglomerate n. /kən'glɒmərət, kən-/ 1. anything composed of various elements. 2. a company engaged in a wide range of activities. –adj. /kən'glɒmərət, kən-/ 3. gathered into a rounded mass. –v. /kən'glɒmərət, kən-/ 4. to collect or cluster together.

congratulate v. to express sympathetic joy to (a person), as on a happy occasion. **–congratulation,** n. **–congratulatory,** adj.

congregate v. to assemble, especially in large numbers. **–congregation,** n.

congress n. a formal meeting or assembly of representatives for discussion, etc. **–congressional,** adj.

When this is spelt with a capital letter, it refers to a particular congress. It is also the name of the parliament of the United States of America.

congruent adj. agreeing; corresponding; congruous.

congruous adj. harmonious in character. **–congruity,** n.

conifer n. any of the cone-bearing (mostly evergreen) trees and shrubs. **–coniferous,** adj.

conjecture n. 1. the forming of an opinion without sufficient evidence for proof. 2. an opinion thus formed. –v. 3. to conclude or suppose from weak or unsure evidence.

For def. 1, the more usual word is **guessing**; for defs 2 and 3, **guess**.

conjoined twins pl. n. any twins who are born joined together in any manner.

conjugal adj. marital.

conjugate v. /'kɒndʒəgeɪt/ 1. *Gram.* to recite or display all, or some subset of, the inflected forms of (a verb), in a fixed order. –adj. /'kɒndʒəgət/ 2. joined together, especially in a pair or pairs; coupled. **–conjugation,** n.

conjunction n. 1. the act or result of joining together; combination. 2. *Gram.* a word, such as 'and' or 'because', used for joining parts of a sentence.

conjunctiva n. (pl. **-vas** or **-vae** /-tarvi/) the mucous membrane lining the eyelids.

conjunctivitis /kəndʒʌŋktɪ'vaɪtəs/ n. a painful disease of the conjunctiva.

conjure v. /'kʌndʒə, 'kɒndʒə/ v. 1. to effect, produce, etc., by, or as by, magic. 2. to practise sleight of hand or magic. –**conjuration**, *n.*

conk *v. Informal* **1.** to hit, especially on the head. **2.** to faint; collapse.

connect *v.* **1.** to bind or fasten together. **2.** to establish communication between. **3.** to think of as related. **4.** to become connected; join or unite. –**connection**, *n.* –**connective**, *adj.*

connive *v.* **1.** to help wrongdoing, especially by not opposing it. **2.** to cooperate secretly (*with*).

connoisseur /kɒnə'sɜ/ *n.* an expert judge of one of the fine arts, or in matters of taste.

connote *v.* **1.** to signify in addition to the primary meaning: *The smell of strong coffee connotes lazy Sunday breakfasts.* –**connotation**, *n.*

The more usual word is **suggest**. Compare **connote** with **denote**, which means to be a straightforward indication or sign of something, as in *The smell of strong coffee denotes that there is a cafe nearby.*

conquer *v.* **1.** to overcome by force. **2.** to gain the victory over. –**conqueror**, *n.* –**conquest**, *n.*

For def. 1, the more usual word is **defeat**.

conscience /'kɒnʃəns/ *n.* one's sense of right and wrong as regards one's actions and motives.

conscientious /kɒnʃi'enʃəs/ *adj.* **1.** hardworking and diligent: *a conscientious student.* **2.** controlled by or done according to conscience: *a conscientious objector to war.*

conscious /'kɒnʃəs/ *adj.* **1.** aware of one's own existence, sensations, cognitions, etc. **2.** having the mental faculties awake. –**consciousness**, *n.*

conscript *n.* /'kɒnskrɪpt/ **1.** a recruit obtained by compulsory enrolment. –*v.* /kɒn-'skrɪpt/ **2.** to enrol compulsorily for service in the armed forces. –**conscription**, *n.*

consecrate *v.* to make or declare sacred. –**consecration**, *n.*

consecutive *adj.* following one another without interruption.

consensus *n.* general agreement or concord.

Note that this word is commonly misspelt *concensus*, probably because of the unrelated word *census* (a counting of the population). A **consensus** has more to do with *consent* (agreement) than with a *census*.

consent *v.* **1.** (fol. by *to* or infinitive) to give assent. –*n.* **2.** assent; permission.

consequence *n.* **1.** (the act or fact of following as) an effect or result. **2.** importance or significance. –**consequent**, *n., adj.* –**consequential**, *adj.* –**consequently**, *adv.*

conservation *n.* the act of conserving; preservation, especially of natural resources.

Don't confuse this with **conversation**, which is a talk between people.

conservative *adj.* **1.** disposed to preserve existing conditions, etc. **2.** having the power or tendency to conserve. –*n.* **3.** a person of conservative principles. –**conservatism**, *n.*

conservatorium *n.* a school of music. Also, **con**, **conservatoire**.

conservatory *n.* (*pl.* **-ries**) a glass-covered house or room for plants in bloom.

conserve *v.* /kən'sɜv/ **1.** to keep safe or sound. –*n.* /'kɒnsɜv, kən'sɜv/ **2.** (*oft. pl.*) fruits cooked with sugar to a jam-like consistency. –**conserver**, *n.*

consider *v.* **1.** to contemplate mentally. **2.** to regard as. **3.** to make allowance for. **4.** to regard with consideration or respect.

Note that **consider** (def. 2) is sometimes, but not always, followed by *to be.*

considerable *adj.* **1.** worthy of consideration. **2.** fairly large.

considerate *adj.* showing regard for another's feelings, etc.

consideration n. 1. the act of considering. 2. regard or account; something taken into account. 3. a recompense for service rendered, etc. 4. thoughtfulness for others. 5. estimation; esteem.

consign v. 1. to hand over or deliver formally (to). 2. to transfer to another's custody (to). –**consignment**, n. –**consignor**, n. –**consignee**, n.

consist v. 1. to be made up or composed (of): *The book consists of two parts.* 2. to have as a basis; exist (in): *The appeal of this film consists in its sensitive treatment of a controversial issue.*

> Compare def. 1 with **comprise**, which is a more formal word meaning the same as **consist of**. Note that you do not use of after **comprise**: *The book comprises two parts.*
>
> Note that you can also use **be composed of**: *The book is composed of two parts.*

consistency n. 1. agreement between the parts of a complex thing. 2. degree of density. 3. adherence to the same principles, course, etc. –**consistent**, adj.

console[1] /ˈkɒnsoʊl/ v. to alleviate the grief or sorrow of; comfort. –**consolation**, n.

console[2] /ˈkɒnsoʊl/ n. a desk on which are mounted the controls of an electrical or electronic system.

consolidate v. to bring together compactly in one mass or connected whole. –**consolidation**, n.

consommé /ˈkɒnsɒmeɪ, kənˈsɒmeɪ/ n. a clear soup made from a concentrated clarified meat or vegetable stock. Also, **consomme**.

consonant n. 1. *Phonetics* a sound made when exhaled air is obstructed or partly obstructed by the tongue or lips, as the *l*, *s*, and *t* of *list*. 2. any letter of the alphabet other than *a*, *e*, *i*, *o* or *u* –adj. 3. in agreement; consistent (to or with).

> Compare def. 1 with **vowel**, which is a speech sound made by allowing air to pass through the middle of your mouth without being blocked by your tongue or lips, or one of the letters of the alphabet standing for these sounds (*a*, *e*, *i*, *o*, *u*).

consort n. /ˈkɒnsɔːt/ 1. a spouse, especially of a reigning monarch. 2. a ship accompanying another. –v. /kənˈsɔːt/ 3. to associate; keep company.

consortium n. (pl. **-tiums** or **-tia**) a combination of financial institutions, capitalists, etc., formed to provide capital for a costly undertaking.

conspicuous adj. 1. easy to be seen. 2. readily attracting the attention.

conspiracy n. (pl. **-cies**) 1. the act of conspiring. 2. a combination of persons for an evil or unlawful purpose; a plot.

conspirator n. someone who is part of a conspiracy. –**conspiratorial**, adj. –**conspiratorially**, adv.

conspire v. to agree together, especially secretly, to do something wrong or illegal.

constable /ˈkʌnstəbəl, ˈkɒn-/ n. an officer of the lowest rank in a police force.

constant adj. 1. invariable; always present. 2. continuing without intermission. 3. standing firm in mind or purpose. –n. 4. something constant or unchanging.

constellation n. a group of stars to which a name has been given.

consternation n. amazement or dismay.

constipation n. a condition of the bowels marked by defective or difficult evacuation.

constituency n. (pl. **-cies**) → **electorate**.

constituent adj. 1. serving to make up a thing. 2. having power to frame or alter a political constitution or fundamental law. –n. 3. a constituent element, material, etc. 4. a voter, or (loosely) a resident, in an electorate.

constitute v. 1. (of elements, etc.) to compose; form. 2. to appoint to an office or function. 3. to give legal form to (an assembly, etc.).

constitution n. 1. the way in which anything is constituted. 2. the physical

constrain v. **1.** to force, compel, or oblige. **2.** to confine forcibly. **3.** to repress or restrain. **–constraint**, n.

constrict v. **1.** to draw together; compress. **2.** to restrict. **–constriction**, n. **–constrictive**, adj.

construct v. /kən'strʌkt/ **1.** to form by putting together parts; build. –n. /'kɒnstrʌkt/ **2.** a complex image or idea.

construction n. **1.** the act of constructing. **2.** the way in which a thing is constructed. **3.** that which is constructed. **4.** explanation or interpretation.

constructive adj. constructing; helpful: *constructive advice*.

construe v. (-strued, -struing) to understand (an utterance, action, etc.) in a particular way.

> The more usual word is **interpret**.

consul n. a government agent residing in a foreign state and discharging certain administrative duties. **–consular**, adj. **–consulate**, n.

consult v. **1.** to refer to for information or advice. **2.** to consider or deliberate. **–consultation**, n.

consultant n. someone who gives professional or expert advice.

consumable adj. **1.** able to be consumed. **2.** (of an item of equipment or supply) normally consumed in use: *consumable fuel; consumable paper products.* –n. **3.** a consumable product or supply. **–consumability**, n.

consume v. **1.** to use up. **2.** to eat or drink up. **3.** to absorb.

consumer n. someone who uses a commodity or service.

consumerism n. **1.** a movement which aims at educating consumers to protect themselves from dishonest trading practices. **2.** a theory that the economy of a capitalist society requires an ever increasing consumption of goods.

consummate v. /'kɒnsəmeɪt, 'kɒnsjumeɪt/ **1.** to bring to completion or perfection. **2.** to fulfil (a marriage) by having sexual intercourse. –adj. /'kɒnsjumət, 'kɒnsəmət/ **3.** complete or perfect.

consumption n. **1.** the act of consuming. **2.** the amount consumed. **3.** the using up of goods and services. **4.** a wasting disease, especially tuberculosis of the lungs. **–consumptive**, adj., n.

contact n. /'kɒntækt/ **1.** the state or fact of touching. **2.** immediate proximity or association. **3.** a person through whom an association is established. –v. /'kɒntækt, kən'tækt/ **4.** to put or bring into contact. **5.** to get in touch with (a person). **–contactable**, adj.

contact lens n. a small lens to aid defective vision, usually of plastic, which covers the iris and is held in place by eye fluid.

contagious adj. **1.** (of a disease) transmitted by physical contact with an affected person or with something an affected person has touched. **2.** spreading rapidly from one person to another: *happiness is contagious.*

> Compare def. 1 with **infectious**, which is similar, except that an infectious disease is spread by germs being transmitted through the air or in a liquid: *The flu is infectious.* Note that you can use either **contagious** or **infectious** for def. 2 (*contagious laughter, infectious laughter*).

contain v. **1.** to have within itself; hold within fixed limits. **2.** to have as contents or constituent parts. **3.** to restrain.

container n. **1.** anything that can contain, as a carton, tin, etc. **2.** a box-shaped unit for transporting goods.

contaminate v. to render impure by contact or mixture. **–contamination**, n.

contemplate v. 1. to observe thoughtfully. 2. to have as a purpose. 3. to think studiously; consider deliberately. **—contemplation**, n. **—contemplative**, adj.

contemporaneous adj. contemporary.

contemporary adj. 1. belonging to, existing, or occurring at the same time. 2. of the present time; modern. —n. (pl. **-ries**) 3. someone belonging to the same time or period with another or others.

Note that confusion can occur with the first two meanings of this word. For example, if you talk about a 19th-century house with contemporary furniture, you might mean that the furniture is of the same period as the house itself, or that it is modern. You may need to explain further.

contempt n. 1. the feeling one has for anything mean, vile, or worthless. 2. the state of being despised. 3. Law disobedience to, or open disrespect of, the rules or orders of a court or legislature.

contemptible adj. deserving of or held in contempt; despicable.

contemptuous adj. manifesting or expressing contempt.

contend v. 1. to struggle in opposition. 2. to assert earnestly.

content¹ /ˈkɒntɛnt/ n. 1. (usu. pl.) that which is contained. 2. (usu. pl.) (a list of) the chapters or chief topics of a book or document. 3. substance or purport, as of a document. 4. the information which is in a communication, as opposed to the format, design, etc.: the content of a web page.

content² /kənˈtɛnt/ adj. 1. being satisfied with what one has. 2. willing or resigned.

contention n. 1. a struggling together in opposition; strife in debate; a dispute. **—contentious**, adj.

This is the noun from **contend**.

contest n. /ˈkɒntɛst/ 1. struggle for victory. —v. /kənˈtɛst/ 2. to struggle or fight for. 3. to argue against.

contestant n. someone who takes part in a contest or competition.

context n. 1. the parts of a discourse or writing which precede or follow a given passage or word. 2. the circumstances surrounding a particular situation, event, etc. **—contextual**, adj. **—contextualise**, **contextualize**, v.

contiguous /kənˈtɪɡjuəs/ adj. 1. touching. 2. in close proximity.

continence n. ability to exercise control over natural functions, especially urination and defecation. Also, **continency**. **—continent**, adj.

continent n. one of the main land masses of the globe.

continental drift n. the movement of continents away from the original single landmass to their present position.

continental quilt n. → doona.

contingent adj. 1. dependent for existence, occurrence, character, etc., on something not yet certain. 2. accidental or unpredictable. —n. 3. a share to be contributed or furnished. 4. any one of the representative groups composing an assemblage. **—contingency**, n.

Note that def. 1 is often followed by on or upon.

continual adj. 1. of regular or frequent recurrence: His continual lateness is becoming a problem. 2. proceeding without interruption or cessation: a continual noise.

Note that some people say that def. 1 is the only correct meaning of this word, and that if you want to describe something that keeps going without stopping, as in def. 2, you should use the word **continuous**, as in The continuous drone of the engine made me drowsy.

continue v. 1. to go forwards or onwards in any course or action. 2. to go on after interruption. 3. to remain in a particular state. 4. to go on with. 5. to extend from one point to another in space. **—continuation**, n.

continuous *adj.* **1.** having successive parts connected: *a continuous chain.* **2.** uninterrupted in time: *a continuous noise.* **3.** *Gram.* relating to the form of a verb (its *aspect*) which shows that something is continuing, such as 'am running' in *I am running.* **–continuity,** *n.*

See the note at **continual.**

continuum /kən'tınjuəm/ *n.* (*pl.* **-tinuums** or **-tinua** /-'tınjuə/) a continuous extent, series, or whole.

contort *v.* to twist; bend or draw out of shape. **–contortion,** *n.*

contour *n.* the outline of a figure or body.

contraband *n.* any prohibited imports or exports.

contraception *n.* the prevention of conception by deliberate measures; birth control. **–contraceptive,** *adj.*, *n.*

contract *n.* /'kɒntrækt/ **1.** an agreement between 2 or more parties for the doing or not doing of some definite thing. **2.** an agreement enforceable by law. *–v.* /'kɒntrækt, kən'trækt/ **3.** to draw together or into smaller limits or area. **4.** to shorten (a word, etc.) by combining or omitting some of its elements. **5.** to acquire, as by habit or contagion; incur, as a liability or obligation. **6.** to settle by agreement. **–contraction,** *n.* **–contractor,** *n.* **–contractual,** *adj.*

contra deal *n.* an agreement involving an exchange of goods or services, rather than money.

contradict *v.* to assert the contrary of. **–contradiction,** *n.* **–contradictory,** *adj.*

contralto *n.* (*pl.* **-tos** or **-ti**) the lowest female voice.

contraption *n.* a complicated device or mechanism.

contrary /'kɒntrəri/ *for defs 1, 2 and 4;* /kən'trεəri/ *for def. 3,* *–adj.* **1.** opposite in nature. **2.** opposite in direction or position. **3.** perverse; self-willed. *–n.* **4.** that which is contrary or opposite. **–contrariety,** *n.*

contrast *v.* /kən'trast/ **1.** to compare by observing differences. **2.** to afford or form a contrast to. **3.** to exhibit unlikeness on comparison. *–n.* /'kɒntrast/ **4.** the state of being contrasted or unlike. **5.** something strikingly unlike. **6.** variation in tones and forms in a work of art, photograph, etc. **–contrasting,** *adj.*

Note that **contrast** and **compare** are related words but that **compare** means to show the differences and similarities between things, rather than just the differences.

contravene *v.* to violate or infringe: *to contravene an agreement.* **–contravention,** *n.*

The more usual word is **break.**

contribute *v.* to give to a common stock. **–contribution,** *n.* **–contributor,** *n.* **–contributory,** *adj.*

contrite *adj.* feeling a strong sense of guilt; penitent. **–contrition,** *n.*

The more usual word is **sorry.**

contrive *v.* **1.** to plan with ingenuity. **2.** to bring about or effect by a device, stratagem, etc.; manage (to do something). **–contrivance,** *n.*

control *v.* (**-trolled, -trolling**) **1.** to exercise restraint or direction over. *–n.* **2.** the act or power of controlling. **3.** check or restraint. **4.** a standard of comparison in scientific experimentation. **5.** (*pl.*) an arrangement of devices for regulating a machine.

controversy /'kɒntrəvəsi, kən'trɒvəsi/ *n.* (*pl.* **-sies**) dispute, debate, or contention. **–controversial,** *adj.*

contumely /'kɒntʃuməli, kən'tjuməli/ *n.* contemptuous or humiliating treatment.

contuse *v.* to bruise. **–contusion,** *n.* **–contusive,** *adj.*

conundrum *n.* a riddle.

convalesce /kɒnvə'lεs/ *v.* to grow stronger after illness. **–convalescence,** *n.* **–convalescent,** *adj.*, *n.*

convection *n.* the transference of heat by the circulation of the heated parts of a liquid or gas.

convene *v.* to (cause to) assemble, usually for a public purpose. **–convener**, *n.*

convenient *adj.* **1.** suited to the needs or purpose. **2.** easily accessible. **–convenience**, *n.*

convent *n.* **1.** a community of nuns devoted to religious life. **2.** a Roman Catholic or other school where children are taught by nuns.

convention *n.* **1.** a meeting or assembly, especially a formal one. **2.** general agreement or consent; accepted usage, or procedure. **–conventional**, *adj.*

converge *v.* **1.** to tend to meet in a point or line. **2.** to tend to a common result, conclusion, etc. **–convergence**, *n.* **–convergent**, *adj.*

conversant *adj.* familiar by use or study (*with*).

conversation *n.* informal interchange of thoughts by spoken words.

Don't confuse this with **conservation**, which is the protection of nature and historic objects.

converse[1] /kən'vɜs/ *v.* to talk informally with another.

converse[2] /'kɒnvɜs/ *adj.* **1.** turned about. *–n.* **2.** a thing which is the opposite of another.

convert *v.* /kən'vɜt/ **1.** to change into something of different form or properties. **2.** to cause to adopt a different religion, party, opinion, etc. *–n.* /'kɒnvɜt/ **3.** someone who has been converted. **–conversion**, *n.*

convertible *adj.* **1.** capable of being converted. **2.** (of a motor car) having a removable top.

convex *adj.* bulging and curved.

convey *v.* **1.** to carry or transport. **2.** to communicate.

conveyance *n.* **1.** the act of conveying; transmission. **2.** a means of transport;

especially a vehicle. **3.** *Law* the transfer of property from one person to another.

conveyancing *n.* that branch of legal practice concerned with the transfer of property.

conveyor belt *n.* a flexible band used to transport objects, especially in a factory. Also, **conveyer belt**.

convict *v.* /kən'vɪkt/ **1.** to prove or declare guilty of an illegal act. *–n.* /'kɒnvɪkt/ **2.** a person proved or declared guilty of an offence. **3.** a person serving a prison sentence.

conviction *n.* **1.** the fact or state of being convicted. **2.** the state of being convinced. **3.** a firm belief.

convince *v.* **(-vinced, -vincing)** to persuade by argument or proof.

convivial *adj.* agreeable; sociable; merry.

convolution *n.* a rolled up or coiled condition.

convoy *n.* any group of vehicles travelling together.

convulse *v.* **1.** to shake violently. **2.** to cause to laugh violently. **3.** to cause to suffer violent muscular spasms. **–convulsion**, *n.* **–convulsive**, *adj.*

coo *v.* to utter the soft, murmuring sound characteristic of pigeons or doves.

cooee *n. Aust., NZ* a prolonged clear call, rising in pitch, used in the bush as a signal.

cook *v.* **1.** to prepare (food) by the action of heat. **2.** (of food) to undergo cooking. *–n.* **3.** someone who cooks. **–cookery**, *n.*

cookie *n.* **1.** *Chiefly US* a biscuit. **2.** *Informal* a person: *a smart cookie; a tough cookie.* **3.** *Internet* a small data file sent by a web server to a browser for use by the web server when being accessed in the future. Also, **cooky**.

cooktop *n.* an assemblage of electric hotplates or gas burners for cooking, designed to be fitted into a benchtop.

cool *adj.* **1.** moderately cold. **2.** not excited; deliberate; aloof. **3.** deficient in ardour or enthusiasm. **4.** *Informal* in fashion or stylish. **5.** *Informal* all right; okay: *Don't worry, it's cool.* −*n.* **6.** the cool part, place, time, etc. −*v.* **7.** to make cool.

coolibah *n.* a species of eucalypt. Also, **coolabah.**

co-op *n.* a cooperative shop, store, or society.

coop *n.* **1.** an enclosure, usually with bars or wires, in which fowls, etc., are confined. −*v.* **2.** to place in, or as in, a coop; confine narrowly (*up* or *in*).

cooperate *v.* to work or act together or jointly. Also, **co-operate.** −**cooperation,** *n.*

cooperative *adj.* **1.** cooperating. **2.** helpful. −*n.* Also, **cooperative society, co-op. 3.** a business owned and controlled by its members, formed to provide them with work or with goods at reasonable prices. Also, **co-operative.**

coordinate *v.* /kou'ɔdəneɪt/ **1.** to make or become coordinate. **2.** to arrange or act in harmonious combination. −*adj.* /kou-'ɔdənət/ **3.** of the same order or degree. −*n.* /kou'ɔdənət/ **4.** an equal in rank or importance. **5.** any of the magnitudes which define the position of a point, line, or the like. −**coordinated,** *adj.* −**coordination,** *n.* −**coordinator,** *n.*

cop *Informal* −*n.* **1.** a police officer. −*v.* (**copped, copping**) **2.** to accept resignedly.

cope *v.* to struggle or contend (*with*), especially with a degree of success.

copha /ˈkoʊfə/ *n.* Aust. (*from trademark*) a white waxy solid derived from coconut flesh used as shortening. Also, **copha butter.**

copious *adj.* large in quantity or number.
The more usual word is **plentiful.**

cop-out *n.* *Informal* an easy way out of a difficult situation.

copper[1] *n.* **1.** a metallic element of a reddish-brown colour. Symbol: Cu **2.** a large vessel for boiling clothes.

copper[2] *n.* *Informal* a police officer.

copperplate *n.* style of handwriting, formerly much used in engravings.

coppice *n.* a wood or thicket, of small trees or bushes. Also, **copse.**

copra *n.* the dried kernel or meat of the coconut.

copula *n.* (*pl.* **-lae** *or* **-las**) **1.** something that connects or links together. **2.** a word, as the verb *be*, which acts as a connecting link between subject and predicate.

copulate *v.* to unite in sexual intercourse.

copy *n.* (*pl.* **copies**) **1.** a transcript, reproduction, or imitation of an original. **2.** matter intended to be reproduced in print. −*v.* (**copied, copying**) **3.** to make a copy of; transcribe. **4.** to follow as a pattern or model.

copyright *n.* the exclusive right granted by law to control a literary, musical, dramatic, or artistic work. Symbol: ©

coral *n.* **1.** the chalky skeleton of any of various marine animals. **2.** such skeletons collectively, as forming reefs, islands, etc.
Don't confuse this with **choral**, which describes music sung by a choir. (See **chorus**.)

cord *n.* **1.** a thick string or thin rope. **2.** a wire or wires, protected by cloth or plastic, used to connect electrical appliances to a power point. **3.** a ribbed fabric.
Don't confuse this with **chord**, which is a string on a musical instrument, a feeling or emotion, or a group of musical notes played together.

cordial *adj.* **1.** hearty; warmly friendly. −*n.* **2.** a flavoured concentrated syrup to be mixed with water as a drink.

corduroy *n.* a cotton pile fabric with lengthwise ridges.

core *n.* **1.** the central part of a fleshy fruit, containing the seeds. **2.** the most essential part of anything. −*v.* **3.** to remove the core of (fruit).

corella *n.* any of three Aust. cockatoos having predominantly white plumage tinged with pink or red.

corgi *n.* a short-legged Welsh dog with erect ears.

cork *n.* **1.** the outer bark of a certain type of oak tree. **2.** a piece of cork, or other material (as rubber), used as a stopper for a bottle, etc.

corkage *n.* a charge made by a restaurant, etc., for serving liquor brought in by the customers.

cormorant *n.* a large waterbird with webbed toes, a long neck and a pouch under the bill in which captured fish are held; shag.

corn¹ *n.* **1.** a cereal plant bearing grain in large ears. *–v.* **2.** to preserve in brine, as meat.

corn² *n.* a horny callus, usually with a central core, especially on the toes.

cornea *n.* (*pl.* **-neas** or **-neae**) the transparent outer membrane of the eye, covering the iris and the pupil.

corner *n.* **1.** (the space at) the meeting place of 2 converging lines or surfaces. **2.** the place where 2 streets meet. **3.** any situation from which escape is impossible. **4.** a monopoly of the available supply of a stock or commodity. **5.** a region; quarter. *–v.* **6.** to place in or drive into a corner. **7.** to form a corner in (a stock, etc.). **8.** in a motor vehicle, to turn a corner, especially at speed. *–adj.* **9.** situated at a junction of 2 roads. **10.** made to be fitted or used in a corner. *–phr.* **11. cut corners, a.** to take short cuts habitually. **b.** to bypass an official procedure, or the like.

cornet *n.* a brass wind instrument of the trumpet class.

cornflour *n.* a starchy flour made from maize, rice, or other grain.

cornice *n.* the moulding between the walls and ceiling.

corny *adj.* (**-nier**, **-niest**) *Informal* **1.** lacking subtlety: *a corny joke.* **2.** sentimental; mawkish.

corollary *n.* (*pl.* **-ries**) a natural consequence or result.

corona *n.* (*pl.* **-nas** or **-nae** /-ni/) a circle of light seen round a luminous body. *–coronal, adj.*

coronary /ˈkɒrənri/ *adj.* **1.** relating to the arteries which supply the heart tissues. *–n.* **2.** a heart attack.

coronation *n.* the ceremony of crowning a sovereign.

coronavirus *n.* **1.** a virus affecting mammals, the cause of a variety of illnesses in humans, including the common cold. **2.** → **COVID-19**.

coroner *n.* an officer, as of a county or municipality, who investigates by inquest any death not clearly due to natural causes. *–coronial, adj.*

coronet *n.* a small or inferior crown.

corporal¹ *adj.* of the human body; physical.

corporal² *n.* a junior officer in the army or air force.

corporate *adj.* forming, or of a corporation.

corporation *n.* an association of individuals, created by law and having powers and liabilities distinct from those of its members.

corporeal /kɔːˈpɔːriəl/ *adj.* of the nature of the physical body.

corps /kɔː/ *n.* (*pl.* **corps** /kɔːz/) **1.** a unit of soldiers. **2.** a group of persons associated or acting together.

Don't confuse this with **corpse**.

corpse /kɔːps/ *n.* a dead body, usually of a human being.

Don't confuse this with **corps**.

corpulent *adj.* stout; fat.

corpus *n.* (*pl.* **-puses** or **-pora**) a large or complete collection of writings, laws, etc.

corpuscle *n.* one of the minute bodies which form a constituent of the blood.

correct *v.* **1.** to set right; remove the errors or faults of. **2.** to mark the errors in. *–adj.* **3.** conforming to fact or truth. **4.** in accordance with an acknowledged or accepted standard. **–correction**, *n.* **–corrective**, *adj.*

Note that the noun **correction** is the act of correcting something (*We need to work on the correction of your posture*), or a mark made when correcting something (*Her essay came back covered with corrections*). The other noun from **correct** is **correctness** and this refers to how correct something is (*How can we be sure of the correctness of this information?*)

correlation *n.* mutual relation of 2 or more things, parts, etc. **–correlate**, *v.* **–correlative**, *adj.*

correspond *v.* **1.** to be in agreement or conformity (*with* or *to*). **2.** to be similar or analogous. **3.** to communicate by letters.

correspondence *n.* **1.** the act or fact of corresponding. **2.** letters between correspondents.

correspondent *n.* **1.** someone who communicates by letters. **2.** someone employed to contribute news, etc., regularly from a distant place. **3.** a thing that corresponds to something else. **–adj.** **4.** corresponding.

corridor *n.* a passage connecting parts of a building.

corroborate /kəˈrɒbəreɪt/ *v.* to confirm: *The evidence corroborated her story.* **–corroboration**, *n.* **–corroborative**, *adj.*

The more usual expression is **back up**.

corroboree *n.* an Aboriginal assembly of sacred, festive, or warlike character.

corrode *v.* to eat away gradually as by chemical action. **–corrosion**, *n.* **–corrosive**, *n.*, *adj.*

corrugate *v.* to draw or bend into alternate furrows and ridges. **–corrugation**, *n.*

corrupt *adj.* **1.** guilty of dishonesty, especially involving bribery. **2.** made bad by errors, as text or computer data. **–v.** **3.** to destroy the integrity of. **4.** to lower morally; pervert. **–corruption**, *n.*

corsage /kɔːˈsɑː/ *n.* a small bouquet worn on the clothes.

corset *n.* (*oft. pl.*) an undergarment worn to support the body.

cortege /kɔːˈteɪʒ, -ˈteɪʒ/ *n.* a train of attendants.

cortex *n.* (*pl.* **cortices** /ˈkɔːtəsiːz/) the layer of grey matter around the brain. **–cortical**, *adj.*

corvette *n.* a small, lightly armed, fast ship.

cosh *n.* any instrument, usually flexible, used as a bludgeon.

cosmetic *n.* **1.** a preparation for beautifying the skin, etc. **–adj.** **2.** serving to beautify. **3.** designed to effect a superficial alteration while keeping the basis unchanged.

cosmopolitan *adj.* **1.** belonging to all parts of the world. **2.** free from provincial or national ideas, prejudices, etc.

cosmos *n.* the physical universe. **–cosmic**, *adj.*

cosset *v.* to pamper.

cossie *n. Informal* → **swimming costume**. Also, **cozzie**.

cost *n.* **1.** the price paid for anything. **2.** outlay or expenditure of money, time, labour, trouble, etc. **3.** (*pl.*) *Law* expenses incurred in litigation, often awarded to the successful party. **–v.** (**costing**) **4.** to require the expenditure of (money, time, labour, etc.). **5.** to estimate or determine the cost of.

costly *adj.* (**-lier, -liest**) of great price or value.

costume *n.* the style of dress, especially that of a nation or period.

cosy *adj.* (**-sier, -siest**) snug; comfortable. Also, *US*, **cozy**.

cot *n.* a child's bed with enclosed sides.

coterie *n.* a group of people, usually friends, with a common interest.

cottage *n.* a small bungalow.

cottage cheese *n.* a kind of soft, unripened, white cheese.

cotton n. **1.** the soft, white, downy fibres used in making fabrics, thread, etc. **2.** a plant yielding cotton. **3.** cloth, thread, etc., made of cotton. *–phr.* **4.** **cotton on (to).** *Informal* to understand.

cottonwool n. raw cotton for surgical dressings, etc.

couch¹ /kautʃ/ n. **1.** a seat for 2 or more people, with a back and sometimes armrests. **2.** a single piece of upholstered furniture, without a back but with a headrest at one end. *–v.* **3.** to arrange or frame (words, a sentence, etc.); put into words.

couch² /kutʃ/ n. any of various grasses popular as lawn grass.

cougar /ˈkuɡə/ n. → **puma**.

cough /kɒf/ v. **1.** to expel the air from the lungs suddenly and with a characteristic noise. *–n.* **2.** the act or sound of coughing.

could v. **1.** past tense of **can¹**: *I could have picked you up on my way home.* **2.** a verb used **a.** to indicate possibility: *I could come tomorrow if you like.* **b.** in polite requests: *Could you close the door, please?* **c.** to request permission: *Could I go to the park?*

This is a modal verb and is always used with another verb. Look up **modal verb**.

coulomb /ˈkuːlɒm/ n. the derived SI unit of electric charge. *Symbol:* C

council n. **1.** an assembly of persons convened or appointed for consultation, deliberation, or advice. **2.** the local administrative body of a city, municipality, or shire. *–councillor, n.*

Don't confuse **council** with **counsel**. Council is a collective noun and can be used with a singular or plural verb. Look up **collective noun**.

counsel n. **1.** advice. **2.** interchange of opinions as to future procedure; consultation. **3.** the barrister(s) engaged in the direction of a cause in court. *–v.* **(-selled, -selling) 4.** to give counsel to. *–counsellor, n.*

For def. 4, the more usual word is **advise**. Don't confuse **counsel** with **council**.

count¹ v. **1.** to check over one by one (the individuals of a collection) in order to ascertain their total number. **2.** to include in a reckoning. **3.** to esteem; consider. **4.** to depend or rely (*on* or *upon*). **5.** to be accounted or worth. **6.** to enter into consideration. *–n.* **7.** the act of counting. **8.** the total number. **9.** *Law* a distinct charge or cause of action in a declaration or indictment.

count² n. (in some European countries) the equivalent of an English earl. *–countess, fem. n.*

countenance n. **1.** appearance, especially the look of the face. **2.** encouragement; moral support. *–v.* **(-anced, -ancing) 3.** to show favour to; encourage. **4.** to tolerate.

counter¹ n. **1.** a table or board in a shop, bank, etc., over which business is transacted. **2.** (in a cafe, restaurant or hotel) a long, narrow table, shelf, bar, etc., at which customers eat. **3.** anything used in keeping count or account.

counter² adv. **1.** in the wrong way; in the reverse direction. *–adj.* **2.** opposite. *–n.* **3.** that which is opposite or contrary to something else. *–v.* **4.** to go counter to. **5.** to meet or answer (a move, blow, etc.) by another in return. **6.** to make an opposing move.

counteract v. to act in opposition to.

counterfeit /ˈkaʊntəfət, -fit/ adj. **1.** not genuine. *–n.* **2.** an imitation designed to pass as an original.

counterintuitive adj. contrary to what one would normally think or expect. Also, **counter-intuitive.** *–counterintuitively, adv. –counterintuitiveness, n.*

countermand v. to revoke (a command, order, etc.).

counterpart n. **1.** a copy; duplicate. **2.** one of 2 things or people which matches or has the same role as the other.

countersign v. to sign (a document) in addition to another's signature, especially in confirmation.

countless adj. too many to count.

count noun n. Gram. a noun referring to something which is being presented as an individual entity, so that a group of such entities can be counted, as *apple*, *jug*.

Compare this with **mass noun**, which refers to something which is thought of as existing as a mass, rather than one of a series that can be counted.

country n. (pl. **-tries**) **1. a.** a relatively large area of land occupied by a group of people organised under a single, usually independent, government; nation; state; land: *the countries of Asia; to visit a foreign country.* **b.** the people forming such a group: *the whole country rebelled.* **2.** the rural districts (as opposed to towns or cities). **3.** (*usually upper case*) Aboriginal English traditional land with its embedded cultural values relating to the Dreaming.

county n. (pl. **-ties**) an area of land delineated for local government purposes.

coup /ku/ n. (pl. **coups** /kuz/) **1.** an unexpected and successfully executed stratagem. **2.** → coup d'état.

coup d'état /ku deɪˈta/ n. (pl. **coups d'état** /ku deɪˈta/) a sudden and decisive measure in politics, especially one effecting a change of government illegally or by force.

coupé /ˈkupeɪ/ n. an enclosed two-door motor car. Also, *Chiefly US,* **coupe**.

couple n. **1.** two things, especially of the same sort. **2.** two people, especially when married or in a romantic relationship. **3.** a small number; a few: *a couple of minutes; a couple of things to do.* –v. (**-pled, -pling**) **4.** to join or link together.

Compare def. 1 with **pair**. Both words refer to two things, but a **pair** is two things of the same kind that usually go together (*a pair of shoes*), and a **couple** is two of anything (*a couple of children*).

coupon n. **1.** a separable part of a certificate, ticket, advertisement, etc., entitling the holder to something. **2.** a printed entry form for lotteries, newspaper competitions, etc.

courage n. ability to meet danger without fear. –**courageous**, adj.

courgette /kɔˈʒɛt/ n. → zucchini.

courier n. a messenger.

course n. **1.** onward movement. **2.** the path along which anything moves. **3.** a particular manner of proceeding. **4.** a systematised or prescribed series. **5.** a part of a meal. –v. **6.** to run; move swiftly. –phr. **7.** of course, certainly; obviously.

court n. **1.** an open space, usually enclosed by a wall, buildings, etc. **2.** an area on which to play tennis, netball, etc. **3.** the residence of a sovereign or other high dignitary. **4.** the body of persons forming a sovereign's retinue. **5.** assiduous attention directed to gain favour, affection, etc. **6.** Law **a.** a place where justice is administered. **b.** the judge(s) who sit in a court. –v. **7.** to endeavour to win the favour of.

courteous adj. having or showing good manners.

courtesan /ˈkɔtəzæn/ n. **1.** a court mistress. **2.** any female prostitute.

courtesy n. (pl. **-sies**) **1.** excellence of manners or behaviour. **2.** a courteous act or expression.

court martial n. (pl. **courts martial** or **court martials**) a court consisting of military officers which tries offenders against military law.

courtroom n. a room in which the sessions of a law court are held.

courtship n. the seeking of a person's affections, especially with a view to marriage.

courtyard n. a space enclosed by walls.

couscous /ˈkʊskʊs/ n. small grains comprising largely of semolina but with some flour and salt added.

cousin n. the son or daughter of an uncle or aunt.

couturier /kuˈtuːriə/ n. a designer and seller of fashionable clothes for women.

cove[1] n. a small indentation or recess in a shoreline.

cove[2] n. Informal a man.

coven n. a gathering of witches.

covenant n. 1. an agreement; a contract. −v. 2. to enter into a covenant.

cover v. 1. to put something over or upon. 2. to extend over; occupy the surface of. 3. to shelter; serve as a defence for. 4. to hide from view. 5. to spread thickly the surface of. 6. to include; take in. 7. to suffice to meet (a charge, expense, etc.). 8. to act as reporter of (occurrences, performances, etc.). 9. to travel over. 10. to serve as substitute for someone who is absent. −n. 11. that which covers. 12. protection; concealment.

cover note n. a document given to provide temporary insurance protection until a policy is issued.

covert adj. 1. covered. 2. concealed; disguised.

covet v. to desire (another's possessions) greedily.

COVID-19 n. a highly contagious respiratory disease caused by the coronavirus, SARS-CoV-2. Also, **COVID**, **Covid**, **Covid-19**, **covid**, **covid-19**, **coronavirus**.

cow[1] n. 1. a large domesticated bovine kept for dairy and beef farming. 2. the female of a bovine animal. 3. the female of various other large animals, as the elephant, whale, etc. 4. Informal an ugly or bad-tempered woman.

cow[2] v. to intimidate.

coward n. someone who lacks courage to meet danger or difficulty. −**cowardice**, n. −**cowardly**, adj., adv.

cower v. to crouch in fear or shame.

cowry n. (pl. **-ries**) a glossy, tropical shell. Also, **cowrie**.

coxswain /ˈkɒksən, -swem/ n. the person at the helm who steers a boat. Also, **cox**.

coy adj. affectedly shy.

coyote /kɔɪˈoʊti, kaɪˈoʊti/ n. a wild dog of North and Central America.

CPR n. cardiopulmonary resuscitation; an emergency procedure to restore breathing and heart function.

CPU n. central processing unit; that section of a computer which controls arithmetic, logical and control functions.

crab n. a crustacean having a short, broad, more or less flattened body.

crack v. 1. to make a sudden, sharp sound in, or as in, breaking. 2. to break with a sudden, sharp sound. 3. to break without complete separation of parts. 4. Informal to break into (a safe, vault, etc.). 5. to utter, as a joke. −n. 6. a sudden, sharp noise, as of something breaking. 7. a break without complete separation of parts. 8. a slight opening, as one between door and doorpost. 9. Informal a try. −phr. 10. **crack up**, Informal to suffer a physical, mental or moral breakdown.

cracker n. 1. a thin, crisp biscuit. 2. a kind of firework which explodes with a loud report.

crackle v. 1. to (cause to) make slight, sudden, sharp noises, rapidly repeated. −n. 2. a crackling noise.

crackling n. 1. slight cracking sounds rapidly repeated. 2. the crisp browned skin or rind of roast pork.

cradle n. 1. a cot for an infant, usually built on rockers. 2. the place where anything is nurtured during its early existence. −v. 3. to place or rock in or as in a cradle.

craft n. 1. skill; ingenuity. 2. cunning. 3. an art, trade, or occupation requiring special skill, especially manual skill. 4. (pl. **craft**) a boat, ship, aeroplane, etc. −**craftsman**, n. −**craftsmanship**, n.

Because **craftsman** and **craftsmanship** include the word *man*, they are seen by many to exclude women. If you are not referring specifically to a man, it is best to use other terms such as **craftsperson** for **craftsman**, and **skill** or **expertise** for **craftsmanship**.

crafty *adj.* (**-tier, -tiest**) skilful in underhand or evil schemes; cunning, deceitful.

crag *n.* a steep, rugged rock.

craggy *adj.* (**-gier, -giest**) rugged.

cram *v.* (**crammed, cramming**) **1.** to fill (something) by force. **2.** to prepare for an examination by hastily learning facts.

cramp[1] *n.* **1.** a sudden, involuntary, persistent contraction of a muscle. *–v.* **2.** to affect with, or as with, a cramp.

cramp[2] *n.* **1.** a small metal bar with bent ends, for holding together planks, masonry, etc. *–v.* **2.** to confine narrowly; hamper.

crane *n.* **1.** any of a group of large wading birds. **2.** a device with a hoisting tackle, for lifting and moving heavy weights. *–v.* **3.** to stretch (the neck) as a crane does.

cranium *n.* (*pl.* **-nia** *or* **-niums**) the skull of a vertebrate.

crank[1] *n.* **1.** *Machinery* a device for communicating motion. *–v.* **2.** to cause (a shaft) to revolve by applying force to a crank.

crank[2] *Informal –n.* **1.** an eccentric person. *–adj.* **2.** odd, false, or phoney.

crankshaft *n.* a shaft driving or driven by a crank.

cranky *adj.* (**-kier, -kiest**) ill-tempered.

cranny *n.* (*pl.* **-nies**) a small, narrow opening (in a wall, rock, etc.).

crap *Informal* (*taboo*) *–n.* **1.** excrement. **2.** nonsense; rubbish. *–adj.* **3.** of poor quality: *a crap movie.* **4.** unpleasant: *a crap day.*

Note that **crap** is a taboo word and may give offence.

crash *v.* **1.** to force or impel with violence and noise. **2.** to damage (a car, aircraft, etc.) in a collision. **3.** to break (something) into pieces violently and noisily. **4.** to make a loud, clattering noise as of something dashed to pieces. **5.** to collapse or fail suddenly, as a financial enterprise. **6.** (of an aircraft) to fall to the ground. **7.** (of a computer system) to shut down because of a software or hardware malfunction. **8.** *Informal* to attend uninvited (a party, etc.). **9.** *Informal* to fall asleep, especially when exhausted. *–n.* **10.** a breaking or falling to pieces with loud noise. **11.** an accident or collision. **12.** a sudden loud noise. **13.** a sudden collapse of a financial enterprise or the like. **14.** a computer shutdown caused by a software or hardware malfunction.

crass *adj.* gross; stupid.

crate *n.* a box or framework, usually of wooden slats, for packing and transporting fruit, furniture, etc.

crater *n.* the cup-shaped cavity at the top of a volcano.

cravat /krəˈvæt/ *n.* a scarf worn round the neck as a tie.

crave *v.* **1.** to long for or desire eagerly. **2.** to need greatly. **3.** to ask earnestly for (something).

craven *adj.* cowardly.

craw *n.* **1.** the crop of a bird or insect. **2.** the stomach of an animal.

crawl *v.* **1.** to move by dragging the body along the ground, as a worm, or on the hands and knees, as a baby. **2.** to progress slowly. **3.** to behave abjectly and obsequiously. **4.** to have a sensation as of something crawling over the skin: *The thought of it makes my skin crawl. –n.* **5.** a slow, crawling motion. **6.** → **freestyle**.

crayfish *n.* (*pl.* **-fish** *or* **-fishes**) any of various freshwater crustaceans.

For information about the different plural forms, see the note at **fish**.

crayon *n*. **1.** a pencil of coloured wax, chalk, etc., used for drawing. **2.** a drawing in crayons.

craze *v*. **1.** to make small cracks on the surface of (pottery, etc.). *-n*. **2.** a popular fashion, etc., usually short-lived.

crazy *adj*. (**-zier**, **-ziest**) **1.** demented; mad. **2.** eccentric. **3.** unrealistic.

creak *v*. **1.** to make a sharp, harsh, grating, or squeaking sound. **2.** to move with creaking. *-n*. **3.** a creaking sound.

Don't confuse **creak** with **creek**, which is a small stream.

cream *n*. **1.** the fatty part of milk, which rises to the surface. **2.** any creamlike substance. **3.** the best part of anything. **4.** yellowish white. *-v*. **5.** to work (butter and sugar, etc.) to a smooth, creamy mass.

crease *n*. **1.** a line or mark produced in anything by folding. *-v*. **2.** to make a crease or creases in or on.

create *v*. **1.** to bring into being. **2.** to evolve from one's own thought or imagination. **3.** to make by investing with new character or functions. **–creator**, *n*.

creation *n*. **1.** the act of creating. **2.** that which is created. **3.** the world; universe. **4.** an original work, especially of the imaginative faculty.

creative *adj*. **1.** having the power of creating. **2.** resulting from originality of thought or expression.

creature *n*. an animate being.

creche /kreʃ, kreɪʃ/ *n*. an establishment for the minding of babies or young children.

credence *n*. (cause for) belief or confidence.

credential *n*. **1.** anything which is the basis for the belief or trust of others in a person's abilities, authority, etc. **2.** (*usu. pl.*) a letter, etc., confirming the bearer's right to confidence or authority.

credible *adj*. **1.** capable of being believed. **2.** worthy of belief or confidence.

Don't confuse **credible** with **creditable** or **credulous**. Something is **creditable** if it is done well and is worthy of credit, and a **credulous** person is one who believes things a little too easily.

credit *n*. **1.** commendation or honour given for some action, quality, etc. **2.** influence or authority resulting from the confidence of others. **3.** trustworthiness. **4.** (*pl.*) a list, appearing at the beginning or end of a film or television program, which shows the names of those associated with its production. **5.** an amount of money one may spend or borrow. **6. a.** an entry in an account showing payment received. **b.** the balance in one's favour in an account. *-v*. **7.** to believe. **8.** to give reputation or honour to. **9.** to ascribe (something) to a person, etc. **10.** to enter upon the credit side of an account. *–phr*. **11. on credit**, by deferred payment.

Compare def. 5 with **debit**, which refers to debts rather than amounts of money received, and compare def. 11 with **cash**. If you pay cash for something you pay the full amount for it immediately.

creditable *adj*. bringing credit, honour, reputation, or esteem.

Don't confuse **creditable** with **credible** or **credulous**. **Credible** describes something which you can believe (*a credible story*), and someone who is **credulous** believes things a little too easily.

credit card *n*. a card which the holder uses to charge purchases to an account.

creditor *n*. someone to whom money is owed.

credit union *n*. a lending organisation usually formed by workers in some industry or at some place of employment.

credulous *adj*. ready to believe, especially on weak or insufficient evidence. **–credulity**, *n*.

Don't confuse **credulous** with **credible** or **creditable**. **Credible** describes something which you can believe (*a credible story*), and something is **creditable** if it is done well and is worthy of credit.

creed *n.* **1.** any system of belief or of opinion. **2.** any formula of religious belief.

creek *n.* a small stream.

> Don't confuse **creek** with **creak**, which is to make a squeaking noise.

creep *v.* (**crept, creeping**) **1.** to move with the body close to the ground, as a reptile or an insect. **2.** to move slowly, imperceptibly, or stealthily. **3.** to have a sensation as of something creeping over the skin: *My skin crept as I watched the horror movie.* –*n.* **4.** the act of creeping. **5.** *Informal* an unpleasant or obnoxious person. –*phr.* **6. the creeps**, *Informal* a sensation as of something creeping over the skin, usually as a result of feelings of fear or horror.

creeper *n.* a plant which grows upon the surface of the ground, or other surface.

cremate *v.* to reduce (a corpse) to ashes by fire. –**cremation**, *n.*

crematorium *n.* an establishment for cremating dead bodies.

creole *n.* a language which has changed from a pidgin to a community's native language.

crepe *n.* **1.** a thin, light fabric with a finely crinkled surface. **2.** Also, **crepe paper**. thin paper wrinkled to resemble crepe. **3.** a thin pancake.

crept *v.* past tense and past participle of **creep**.

crescendo /krə'ʃendou/ *n.* (*pl.* **-dos** /'douz/) a gradual increase in force or loudness.

crescent *n.* the shape of the moon in its first or last quarter.

cress *n.* a plant used for salad or as a garnish.

crest *n.* **1.** a tuft or other natural growth of the top of an animal's head. **2.** anything resembling such a tuft. **3.** the head or top

of anything. **4.** a figure or design used as a family emblem.

crestfallen *adj.* dejected; dispirited.

cretin *n.* a stupid person; fool. –**cretinous**, *adj.*

crevasse *n.* a deep cleft in the ice of a glacier.

crevice *n.* a crack forming an opening.

crew[1] *n.* a group of persons engaged upon a particular work, especially the staff of a boat or aircraft.

> **Crew** is a collective noun and can be used with a singular or plural verb. Look up **collective noun**.

crew[2] *v.* a past tense of **crow**[2].

crew cut *n.* a very closely cropped haircut.

crib *n.* **1.** a child's bed. **2.** a book which gives a summary of information, sometimes used as a study aid. –*v.* (**cribbed, cribbing**) **3.** to pilfer or steal, as a passage from an author.

cribbage *n.* a game at cards.

crick *n.* a sharp, painful spasm of the muscles, as of the neck or back.

cricket[1] *n.* any of the insects noted for the ability of the males to produce shrill sounds by friction of their leathery forewings.

cricket[2] *n.* **1.** an outdoor game played with ball, bats, and wickets, by 2 sides of 11 players each. **2.** *Informal* fair play.

crime *n.* an act committed or an omission of duty, injurious to the public welfare, and punishable by law.

criminal *adj.* **1.** of or relating to crime or its punishment. **2.** of the nature of or involving crime. –*n.* **3.** a person convicted of a crime.

criminology *n.* the science dealing with the causes and treatment of crimes and criminals.

crimp *v.* to press into small regular folds.

crimson *adj.* deep purplish red.

cringe *v.* (**cringed, cringing**) **1.** to shrink, bend, or crouch, especially from fear or servility. **2.** to feel embarrassment or discomfort, as when confronted by inappropriate or distasteful social behaviour.

crinkle v. to wrinkle.

crinoline /'krɪnəlɪn/ n. a petticoat made of stiff material, formerly worn by women under a full skirt.

cripple n. **1.** someone who is partially or wholly deprived of the use of one or more limbs. –v. **2.** to disable. –**crippled**, adj. –**crippling**, adj.

Some people might find the use of this word as in def. 1 offensive. See the note at **disabled**.

crisis n. (pl. **crises** /'kraɪsiːz/) a decisive or vitally important time or occasion.

crisp adj. **1.** hard but easily breakable. **2.** firm and fresh. –n. **3.** → **chip** (def. 2b).

criteria n. the plural of **criterion**.

criterion n. (pl. **-teria**) an established rule or principle for testing anything.

Note that **criterion** is the singular form and **criteria** is the plural. Some people use **criteria** as a singular noun, but this is not generally regarded as correct.

critic n. **1.** a person skilled in judging the qualities or merits of some class of things. **2.** someone who censures or finds fault.

critical adj. **1.** of or relating to critics or criticism. **2.** relating to, or of the nature of, a crisis.

For def. 2, the more usual word is **crucial**.

criticise v. **1.** to make judgements as to merits and faults. **2.** to find fault. Also, **criticize**. –**criticism**, n.

critique n. **1.** an article or essay criticising a literary or other work. –v. **(-tiqued, -tiquing)** **2.** to review critically; evaluate.

croak v. **1.** to utter a low, hoarse, dismal cry, as a frog or a raven. **2.** to speak with a low, hollow voice. **3.** Informal to die.

crochet /'krəʊʃə, 'krəʊʃeɪ/ n. **1.** a kind of needlework done with a small hook for drawing the thread or yarn into intertwined loops. –v. **(-cheted** /-ʃəd, -ʃeɪd/, **-cheting** /-ʃərɪŋ, -ʃeɪɪŋ/) **2.** to form by crochet.

crock n. an earthen pot, jar, etc.

crockery n. china in general, especially for domestic use.

crocodile n. a large, thick-skinned, lizard-like reptile.

croissant /'krwæsɪ̃/ n. a crescent-shaped roll of bread or puff pastry.

crone n. an old woman, especially one who is withered in appearance and disagreeable in manner.

crony n. (pl. **-nies**) an intimate friend or companion.

cronyism n. unfair partiality shown for one's friends, especially in political or business appointments.

crook n. **1.** a bent or curved implement, piece, appendage, etc. **2.** any bend, turn, or curve. **3.** Informal a dishonest person, especially a swindler, or thief. –adj. Aust., NZ Informal **4.** sick; disabled. **5.** bad; inferior.

crooked /'krʊkəd/ adj. **1.** bent; not straight. **2.** not honest.

croon v. to sing softly, especially with exaggerated feeling.

crop n. **1.** the cultivated produce of the ground, as grain or fruit, etc. **2.** the handle of a whip. **3.** a style of wearing the hair cut short. **4.** a special pouch-like enlargement of the gullet of many birds. –v. **(cropped, cropping)** **5.** to cut off the ends or a part of. **6.** to cut short. **7.** to bear or yield a crop or crops. –phr. **8.** **crop up**, to appear unexpectedly.

cropper phr. **come a cropper**, Informal to fall heavily.

croquet /'krəʊkeɪ/ n. an outdoor game played by knocking wooden balls through a series of iron arches.

cross n. **1.** a structure consisting essentially of an upright and a transverse piece, upon which persons were formerly put to death. **2.** the cross as the symbol of Christianity. **3.** any burden, etc., that one has to bear. **4.** any object, figure, or mark resembling a cross, as 2 intersecting lines. **5.** a mixing of breeds. **6.** something intermediate in character between 2 things. *−v.* **7.** to make the sign of the cross upon or over. **8.** to mark with a cross. **9.** to put or draw (a line, etc.) across. **10.** to lie, pass or be across. **11.** to move, pass, or extend from one side to the other side of (a street, river, etc.). **12.** to meet and cross. **13.** to oppose; thwart. **14.** to interbreed. *−adj.* **15.** lying or passing crosswise or across each other. **16.** involving interchange. **17.** contrary. **18.** adverse. **19.** ill-humoured. *−phr.* **20. cross the floor,** *Parliament* to vote with an opposing party.

cross-country *adj.* **1.** directed across open or forested country; not following roads. *−n.* **2.** a running race which is routed across the country, often on difficult terrain, as opposed to one held on a prepared track. *−adv.* **3.** across open country.

cross-dress *v.* to adopt a manner of dress typical of the opposite sex. **−cross-dressing,** *n.,* *adj.* **−cross-dresser.** *n.*

cross-examine *v.* to examine by questions intended to check a previous examination. **−cross-examination,** *n.*

cross-eye *n.* a disorder in which both eyes turn towards the nose. **−cross-eyed,** *adj.*

crossing *n.* **1.** the act of someone or something that crosses. **2.** a place where lines, tracks, etc., cross each other. **3.** a place at which a road, river, etc., may be crossed.

cross-reference *n.* a reference from one part of a book, etc., to a word, item, etc., in another part.

cross-section *n.* **1.** a section made by cutting anything transversely, especially at right angles. **2.** a typical selection.

crossword *n.* a puzzle in which words are to be worked out from clues and fitted, running across or down, into an arrangement of numbered squares. Also, **crossword puzzle.**

crotch *n.* **1.** a forked piece, part, support, etc. **2.** a place of forking, as of the human body between the legs.

crotchet *n. Music* a note having half the value of a minim.

crotchety *adj. Informal* irritable, difficult, or cross.

crouch *v.* **1.** (of people) to lower the body with one or both knees bent, and incline the trunk forward. **2.** (of animals) to lie close to or on the ground with legs bent ready to spring.

croup /krup/ *n.* inflammation of the larynx, especially in children, marked by a hoarse cough and difficulty in breathing.

croupier *n.* an attendant who collects and pays the money at a gaming table.

crouton *n.* a small piece of fried or toasted bread served in soup, etc.

crow[1] *n.* **1.** any of several large lustrous black birds having a harsh call. *−phr.* **2. as the crow flies,** in a straight line.

crow[2] *v.* (**crowed** *or,* for *def 1,* **crew,** **crowed,** **crowing**) **1.** (of a rooster) to utter its characteristic cry. **2.** to utter an inarticulate cry of pleasure, as an infant does. **3.** to exult loudly.

crowbar *n.* a bar of iron, for use as a lever, etc.

crowd *n.* **1.** a large number of persons gathered closely together. **2.** a large number of things gathered or considered together. *−v.* **3.** to gather in large numbers. **4.** to press forward. **5.** to press closely together; force into a confined space. **6.** to fill to excess.

Crowd (defs 1 and 2) is a collective noun and can be used with a singular or plural verb. Look up **collective noun.**

crowd-surfing *n.* an activity at a rock concert or party in which someone is held up by the main group and moved about over their heads.

crown *n.* **1.** a decorative covering for the head, worn as a symbol of sovereignty. **2.** the power of a sovereign. **3.** the highest part of anything. *−v.* **4.** to invest with a regal crown. **5.** to honour as with a crown. **6.** to surmount as with a crown.

crucial *adj.* involving a final and supreme decision.

crucible /ˈkruːsəbəl/ *n.* a vessel for heating substances to high temperatures.

crucifix *n.* a cross, especially one with the figure of Jesus crucified upon it.

crucify *v.* (**-fied, -fying**) to put to death by nailing or binding the body to a cross. –**crucifixion**, *n.*

crude *adj.* 1. in a raw or unprepared state. 2. lacking culture, refinement, tact, etc. –**crudity**, *n.*

crude oil *n.* oil as it is found in nature.

cruel *adj.* 1. (of a person) liking or likely to cause pain. 2. causing great pain or distress. –**cruelty**, *n.*

cruet /ˈkruːət/ *n.* a set, on a stand, of containers for salt, pepper, etc.

cruise *v.* (**cruised, cruising**) 1. to sail to and fro, or from place to place. 2. (of a car, aeroplane, etc.) to move along at a moderate speed. 3. to cruise over. –*n.* 4. a voyage made by cruising.

crumb *n.* 1. a small particle of bread, cake, etc. 2. a small particle or portion of anything. –*v.* 3. to dress or prepare with breadcrumbs. 4. to break into crumbs.

crumble *v.* to break into small fragments or crumbs.

crummy *adj.* (**-mier, -miest**) *Informal* very inferior, mean, or shabby.

crumpet *n.* a kind of flat round bread with small holes, usually served toasted and buttered.

crumple *v.* 1. to draw or press into irregular folds. 2. to collapse.

crunch *v.* 1. to crush with the teeth; chew with a crushing noise. –*n.* 2. *Informal* a moment of crisis.

crusade *n.* any vigorous, aggressive movement for the defence or advancement of an idea, cause, etc.

crush *v.* 1. to press and bruise between 2 hard bodies. 2. to break into small fragments or particles. 3. to force out by pressing or squeezing. 4. to put down,

overpower, or subdue completely. 5. to oppress harshly. 6. to become crushed. 7. to press or crowd forcibly. –*n.* 8. the act of crushing. 9. the state of being crushed. 10. a great crowd. 11. *Informal* an infatuation.

crust *n.* 1. the hard outer part of a loaf of bread, a pie, etc. 2. any more or less hard coating.

crustacean *n.* any of a class of (chiefly marine) animals with a hard shell, as the lobsters, crabs, barnacles, etc.

crusty *adj.* (**-tier, -tiest**) 1. of the nature of or resembling a crust; having a crust. 2. harsh; surly.

crutch *n.* 1. a support to assist a lame or infirm person in walking. 2. the crotch of the human body. 3. anything relied on as a comfort or support in adversity.

crux *n.* (*pl.* **cruxes** or **cruces** /ˈkrusiz/) a vital, basic, or decisive point.

cry *v.* (**cried, crying**) 1. to utter inarticulate sounds, especially of grief or suffering, usually with tears. 2. to shed tears. 3. to call loudly. 4. to utter or pronounce loudly. –*n.* (*pl.* **cries**) 5. the act or sound of crying. 6. a political or party slogan. 7. the call of an animal. –*phr.* 8. **cry down**, to disparage. 9. **cry off**, to break an appointment. 10. **cry up**, to praise.

cryogenics *n.* that branch of physics concerned with the properties of materials at very low temperatures.

crypt *n.* an underground vault used as a burial place, etc.

cryptic *adj.* hidden; secret.

crystal *n.* 1. a clear, transparent mineral or glass resembling ice. 2. *Chem., Mineral.* a solid body having a characteristic internal structure. –**crystalline**, *adj.*

crystallise *v.* 1. to form into crystals. 2. to (cause to) assume definite form: *a plan crystallised in his mind.* Also, **crystallize**.

cub n. 1. the young of certain animals, as the fox, bear, etc. 2. a novice or apprentice, especially a reporter.

cubbyhouse n. Aust. a children's playhouse.

cube n. 1. a solid bounded by 6 equal squares. 2. the third power of a quantity. –v. (**cubed**, **cubing**) 3. to make into a cube or cubes. 4. to raise to the third power; find the cube of. –**cubic**, adj.

cubicle n. any small space or compartment partitioned off.

cuckold n. the husband of an unfaithful wife.

cuckoo n. 1. any of a number of widespread birds noted for their habit of laying eggs in the nests of other birds. 2. Informal a fool.

cucumber n. a long fleshy fruit used in salads or for pickling.

cud n. food which a ruminating animal returns from the first stomach to the mouth to chew a second time.

cuddle v. 1. to hold close in an affectionate manner. –n. 2. the act of cuddling; a hug.

cudgel n. a short, thick stick used as a weapon.

cue¹ n. 1. anything said or done on or behind the stage that is followed by a specific line or action. 2. a hint; a guiding suggestion.

cue² n. a long tapering rod used in billiards, etc.

cuff¹ n. 1. a fold or band serving as a trimming for the bottom of a sleeve or trouser leg. –phr. 2. **off the cuff**, impromptu.

cuff² v. to strike with the open hand.

cufflink n. a link which fastens a shirt cuff.

cul-de-sac n. a street, lane, etc., closed at one end.

culinary adj. relating to the kitchen or to cookery.

cull v. 1. to pick out the best from: to cull the main points from the long report. 2. to

remove animals of inferior quality from (a herd or flock). 3. to kill (animals, such as deer, kangaroos, etc.), with a view to controlling numbers. 4. the killing of animals in order to reduce their numbers: a kangaroo cull.

culminate v. to reach the highest point. –**culmination**, n.

culpable adj. deserving blame or censure.

culprit n. someone guilty of a specified offence or fault.

cult n. 1. a particular system of religious worship, especially with reference to its rites and ceremonies. 2. (derog.) a religious or pseudo-religious movement, characterised by the extreme devotion of its members, who usually form a relatively small, tightly controlled group under an authoritarian and charismatic leader. 3. an almost religious veneration for a person or thing.

cultivate v. 1. to work (land) in raising crops. 2. to develop or improve by education or training. 3. to seek the acquaintance or friendship of (a person). –**cultivation**, n.

culture n. 1. skills, arts, customs, etc., of a people passed from generation to generation. 2. development or improvement by education or training. 3. the action or practice of cultivating land. –**cultural**, adj.

cumbersome adj. 1. burdensome. 2. clumsy.

cumquat /ˈkʌmkwɒt/ n. a small, round, citrus fruit. Also, **kumquat**.

cumulative adj. increasing or growing by successive additions.

cumulus /ˈkjuːmjələs/ n. (pl. **-li** /-liˈ/) a cloud made up of rounded heaps, and with a flat base.

cuneiform /ˈkjuːnəfɔːm/ adj. 1. wedge-shaped. 2. relating to the writing of ancient Persia, etc.

cunning adj. 1. exhibiting or done with ingenuity or craftiness. –n. 2. skill employed in a crafty manner.

cup n. **1.** a small, open container used mainly to drink from. **2.** (*oft. upper case*) an ornamental cup or other article, especially of precious metal, offered as a prize for a contest: *Melbourne Cup, Davis Cup.* **3.** a unit of volume, measuring 250 ml. **4.** any cuplike utensil, organ, part, cavity, etc. –v. (**cupped, cupping**) **5.** to take or place in or as in a cup.

cupboard n. a place or article of furniture used for storage.

cur n. **1.** a snarling, worthless dog. **2.** a despicable person.

curate[1] /'kjuːrət/ n. a member of the clergy employed as assistant or deputy of a rector or vicar.

curate[2] /kjuˈreɪt/ v. to act as a curator. –**curation**, n.

curator n. the person in charge of a museum, art collection, etc.

curb n. **1.** anything that restrains or controls. –v. **2.** to control as with a curb.

curd n. (*oft. pl.*) a substance obtained from milk by coagulation, used for making into cheese or eaten as food.

curdle v. to change into curd.

cure n. **1.** a method or course of remedial medical treatment. **2.** restoration to health. –v. **3.** to relieve or rid of something troublesome or detrimental, as an illness, a bad habit, etc. **4.** to prepare (meat, fish, etc.) for preservation, by salting, drying, etc. –**curable**, adj. –**curative**, n., adj.

curfew n. a regulation which establishes strict controls on movement after nightfall.

curious adj. **1.** desirous of learning or knowing. **2.** exciting attention or interest because of strangeness or novelty. **3.** odd. –**curiosity**, n.

curl v. **1.** to form into ringlets, as the hair. **2.** to form into a spiral or curved shape. –n. **3.** a ringlet of hair. **4.** anything of a spiral or curved shape.

currant n. a small seedless raisin.

Don't confuse this with **current**, which describes something happening in the present. A **current** is also a flow.

currawong[1] n. any of several large black and white or greyish Aust. birds.

currawong[2] n. a small tree found in inland eastn Aust.

currency n. (pl. **-cies**) **1.** the money in actual, current use in a country. **2.** the fact or quality of being passed on, as from person to person. **3.** general acceptance.

current adj. **1.** belonging to the time actually passing. **2.** circulating, as coin. **3.** prevalent. –n. **4.** a flowing; flow, as of a river. **5.** a movement or flow of electric charges.

Don't confuse this with **currant**, which is a small seedless raisin.

curriculum n. (pl. **-lums** or **-la**) the aggregate of courses of study given in a school, etc. –**curricular**, adj.

curry[1] n. (pl. **-ries**) any of several hot sauces or dishes originating in India.

curry[2] v. (**-ried, -rying**) to rub and clean (a horse, etc.) with a comb.

curse n. **1.** the expression of a wish that evil, etc., befall another. **2.** a profane oath. –v. **3.** to wish or invoke evil, calamity, etc. **4.** to utter curses.

cursive adj. (of writing or printing type) in flowing strokes, with the letters joined together.

cursor n. **1.** an indicator on a computer screen, usually a small rectangle of light, which shows where the next character will form. **2.** the sliding part of a measuring tool.

cursory adj. going rapidly over something, without noticing details.

curt adj. rudely brief in speech, manner, etc.

curtail v. to cut short; abridge; reduce.

curtain n. **1.** a piece of fabric hung at a window to shut out light. **2.** anything that shuts off, covers, or conceals.

curtsy n. (pl. **-sies**) **1.** a bow by women in recognition or respect. -v. (**-sied, -sying**) **2.** to make a curtsy. Also, **curtsey.**

curvature n. curved condition, often abnormal.

curve n. **1.** a continuously bending line without angles. **2.** a line on a graph, diagram, etc. -v. **3.** to bend in a curve.

cushion n. **1.** a soft bag filled with feathers, air, etc., used to sit, kneel, or lie on. **2.** anything similar in appearance or use. **3.** something to absorb a shock or jar, as a body of air or steam. -v. **4.** to lessen the effects of.

cusp n. **1.** a point; pointed end. **2.** Astrology the period of change from one sign to the next.

custard n. a sauce made from milk, eggs and sugar.

custard apple n. a tropical fruit with a soft pulp.

custody n. **1.** keeping; guardianship. **2.** arrest or imprisonment by officers of the law. **-custodian**, n. **-custodial**, adj.

custom n. **1.** a habitual practice; the usual way of acting in given circumstances. **2.** habits or usages collectively. **3.** (pl.) customs duties. **4.** business patronage. **-customary**, adj.

customer n. someone who purchases goods from another; a patron.

custom-made adj. made to individual order.

cut v. (**cut, cutting**) **1.** to penetrate, with or as with a sharp-edged instrument. **2.** to divide, with or as with a sharp-edged instrument. **3.** to reap; mow. **4.** to halt the running of: *He cut the engine.* **5.** to reduce. **6.** Informal to make or fashion by cutting. **7.** Informal to absent oneself from. **8.** to make an incision. **9.** to allow incision or severing: *The metal will not cut easily.* **10.** to pass, go, or come, especially in the most direct way. **11.** to stop filming or recording. -n. **12.** the act or result of cutting. **13.** Informal share. **14.** manner

or fashion in which anything is cut: *the cut of his clothes.* **15.** a passage or course straight across: *a short cut.* **16.** a reduction in price, salary, etc. -phr. **17. cut one's losses**, to abandon a project so as not to incur more losses.

cutaneous /kju'temiəs/ adj. of, relating to, or affecting the skin. **-cutaneously**, adv.

cute adj. Informal appealing in manner or appearance.

cuticle n. the skin around the edges of the fingernail or toenail.

cutlass n. a short, heavy, slightly curved sword.

cutlery n. knives, forks, and spoons collectively, as used for eating.

cutlet n. a cut of meat, usually lamb or veal.

cuttlefish n. (pl. **-fish** or **-fishes**) any of various marine animals which eject a black, ink-like fluid.

For information about the different plural forms, see the note at **fish**.

CV n. → **résumé.**

This is short for **curriculum vitae**, Latin words meaning 'the course of one's life'.

cyanide n. a highly poisonous chemical.

cyberbully n. (pl. **-bullies**) **1.** a person who bullies another using email, social network sites, online forums, etc. -v. (**-bullied, -bullying**) **2.** to bully (another) in this way. Also, **cyber-bully, cyber bully. -cyberbullying**, n.

cybernetics n. the scientific study of methods of control and communication common to animals and machines, especially computers.

cyber safety n. safety in an online environment achieved by taking precautions in one's dealings online, as by not providing personal information, online.

cybersecurity n. protection provided for an information system, such as computer and telecommunications networks, against attacks over the internet.

cyberspace *n.* a communication network, conceived of as a separate world, access to which is gained through the use of computers, such as the internet.

cyberthreat *n.* an attack on a computer network, as a worm (def. 6), virus (def. 3), hacker intrusion, etc.

cyclamate *n.* artificial sweetener.

cyclamen *n.* any of various plants with white, purple, pink or red flowers whose petals fold backwards.

cycle *n.* 1. a recurring period of time, especially one in which certain events or phenomena are repeated in the same order and at the same intervals. 2. any round of operations or events. 3. a bicycle, tricycle, etc. *–v.* (**-cled, -cling**) 4. to ride or travel by a bicycle, etc. 5. to move or revolve in cycles. **–cyclic**, *adj.*

cyclone *n.* a tropical hurricane. **–cyclonic**, *adj.*

cygnet /ˈsɪgnət/ *n.* a young swan.

cylinder *n. Geom.* a tube-like figure. **–cylindrical**, *adj.*

cymbal *n.* a brass or bronze concave plate giving a metallic sound when struck.

cynic /ˈsɪnɪk/ *n.* someone who doubts or denies the goodness of human motives. **–cynical**, *adj.*

cypher *n.* → **cipher**.

cypress *n.* any of several coniferous evergreen trees.

cyst /sɪst/ *n.* a closed bladder-like sac formed in animal tissues, containing fluid or semifluid matter.

cystitis /sɪsˈtaɪtəs/ *n.* inflammation of the urinary bladder.

czar /zɑ/ *n.* → **tsar**. **–czardom**, *n.*

D, d

D, d *n.* the 4th letter of the English alphabet.

'd contraction of: **1.** had. **2.** would.

dab *v.* (**dabbed, dabbing**) to tap lightly, as with the hand.

dabble *v.* **1.** to play in water, as with the hands or feet. **2.** to do anything in a slight or superficial manner.

dachshund /'dæksənd, 'dækshʊnd/ *n.* one of a German breed of small dogs with a long body and very short legs.

dad *n. Informal* father.

daddy *n.* (*pl.* **-dies**) *Informal* (*with children*) dad; father.

daddy-long-legs *n.* (*pl.* **daddy-long-legs**) *Aust., NZ* a small web-spinning spider with long, thin legs, frequently found indoors.

daffodil *n.* a plant with single or double yellow nodding flowers.

daft *adj.* simple or foolish.

dag[1] *n. Aust., NZ Informal* someone who dresses or behaves in an unfashionable or unstylish manner.

dag[2] *n. Aust., NZ* wool on a sheep's rear quarters which is dirty with mud and excreta.

dagger *n.* a short-edged and pointed weapon, like a small sword, used for thrusting and stabbing.

dahlia /'deɪljə/ *n.* a plant widely cultivated for its showy, variously coloured flowers.

daily *adj.* **1.** of, done, occurring, or issued each day or each weekday. *–adv.* **2.** every day.

dainty *adj.* (**-tier, -tiest**) of delicate beauty or charm; exquisite.

dairy *n.* (*pl.* **-ries**) **1.** the place on a farm where cows are milked. **2.** a cool place where milk and cream are stored and made into butter, cheese, etc. *–adj.* **3.** of or relating to milk, milk products or milk production: *dairy foods; the dairy industry.*

Don't confuse **dairy** with **diary**, which is a book in which you write down what happens each day.

dais /'deɪəs/ *n.* a raised platform, as at the end of a room, for a throne, a lecturer's desk, etc.

daisy *n.* (*pl.* **-sies**) a plant whose flower heads have a yellow disc and white rays.

dak /dæk/ *v.* (**dakked, dakking**) *Informal* to forcibly pull down the trousers of someone. Also, **dack**.

dale *n.* a vale; valley.

dally *v.* (**-lied, -lying**) to waste time; loiter; delay.

Dalmatian *n.* one of a breed of dogs of a white colour profusely marked with small black or liver-coloured spots.

dam[1] *n.* **1.** a barrier to obstruct the flow of water, especially one of earth, masonry, etc., built across a river. **2.** a body of water confined by such a barrier. *–v.* (**dammed, damming**) **3.** to stop up; block up.

Don't confuse this with **damn**, which is a mildly taboo expression of anger or annoyance.

dam[2] *n.* a female parent (used especially of horses, etc.).

Don't confuse this with **damn**, which is a mildly taboo expression of anger or annoyance.

damage *n.* **1.** injury or harm that impairs value or usefulness. **2.** (*pl.*) *Law* the estimated money equivalent for detriment or injury sustained. *–v.* (**-aged, -aging**) **3.** to cause damage to; injure or harm.

damask *n.* a reversible fabric of linen, silk, cotton, or wool, woven with patterns.

dame *n.* **1.** (*upper case*) the title of a woman who holds a particular honour, as a Dame of the Order of Australia. **2.** *Informal* a woman.

Def. 2 is mostly used by men in America and may offend some women.

damn v. **1.** to declare (something) to be bad, unfit, invalid, or illegal: *The minister damned the report.* **2.** to bring condemnation upon. –*interj.* **3.** (an expression of anger, annoyance, etc.) –*phr.* **4. not give a damn,** to not care at all. –**damnation,** n. –**damnable,** adj.

Note that this word is mildly taboo and may give offence.

Don't confuse **damn** with **dam,** which is a wall built across a river to hold back water. A **dam** is also a name for the mother of an animal such as a horse.

damned *Informal* –*adj.* **1.** very great: *a damned nuisance.* –*adv.* **2.** very or extremely: *It's damned annoying.*

Note that this word is mildly taboo and may give offence.

damp adj. **1.** moderately wet; moist. –v. Also, **dampen. 2.** to make moist. **3.** to stifle or suffocate; extinguish.

damper n. bread made from a simple flour and water dough, traditionally cooked in the coals of an open fire.

dance v. **1.** to move with the feet or body rhythmically, especially to music. **2.** to bob up and down. –n. **3.** a successive group of rhythmical steps, generally performed to music. **4.** an act or round of dancing. **5.** a social gathering for dancing; ball. –**dancer,** n.

dandelion n. a common weed, with golden yellow flowers.

dandruff n. dry skin which forms on the scalp and comes off in small scales.

dandy n. (pl. **-dies**) **1.** a man who is excessively concerned about clothes and appearance. **2.** *Informal* something very fine or first rate.

danger n. liability or exposure to harm or injury. –**dangerous,** adj.

dangle v. to hang loosely with a swaying motion.

dank adj. unpleasantly moist or humid.

dapper adj. neat; trim; smart.

dapple n. mottled marking, as of an animal's skin or coat.

dare v. **1.** to have the necessary courage or boldness for something. **2.** to meet defiantly. **3.** to challenge or provoke to action, especially by doubting one's courage; defy. –*phr.* **4. dare say,** to assume as probable; have no doubt.

daredevil n. **1.** a recklessly daring person. –*adj.* **2.** recklessly daring.

dark adj. **1.** without light; with very little light. **2.** not pale or fair. **3.** gloomy; cheerless. **4.** evil; wicked. –n. **5.** absence of light. **6.** ignorance.

darling n. (a term of address for a beloved person).

darn[1] v. to mend (clothes, etc., or a tear or hole) with rows of stitches, sometimes crossing and interwoven.

darn[2] v. *Informal* to confound; curse.

dart n. **1.** a long, slender, pointed, missile weapon propelled by the hand or otherwise. –v. **2.** to move swiftly.

dash v. **1.** to strike violently, especially so as to break in pieces. **2.** to throw or thrust violently or suddenly. **3.** to ruin or frustrate (hopes, plans, etc.). **4.** to confound. **5.** to write, make, sketch, etc., hastily: *to dash off a note; to dash down an address.* **6.** to move with violence; rush. –n. **7.** a violent and rapid blow or stroke. **8.** a small quantity of anything thrown into or mixed with something else. **9.** a hasty stroke, especially of a pen. **10.** a horizontal line of varying length (– or —) used in writing and printing as a mark of punctuation to indicate an abrupt break or pause in a sentence, to begin and end a parenthetic clause, as an indication of omission of letters, words, etc., as a dividing line between distinct portions of matter, and for other purposes. **11.** an impetuous movement; a rush. **12.** *Athletics* a short race or sprint. –*interj.* **13.** a mild expletive. –*phr.* **14. do one's dash**, *Aust.* exhaust one's energies or opportunities.

dashboard *n.* the instrument board of a motor vehicle, aeroplane or boat. Also, **dash**.

dashing *adj.* **1.** spirited; lively. **2.** brilliant; showy; stylish.

dastardly /ˈdastədli, ˈdæstədli/ *adj.* cowardly; meanly base; sneaking.

data /ˈdeɪtə, ˈdatə/ *pl. n.* **1.** plural of **datum**. **2.** figures, statistics, etc., known or available; information collected for analysis or reference. **3.** *Computers* digital information.

Although **data** is plural in form, you can use a singular or plural verb with it: *When the computer crashed all the data was lost* (singular). *The data have been collected from all over Australia* (plural).

database *n.* any large collection of information, especially computerised. Also, **data bank**.

date[1] *n.* **1.** a particular day, as denoted by some system for marking the passage of time. **2.** *Informal* an appointment made for a particular time. **3.** *Informal* a person with whom one has a social appointment. –*v.* **4.** to belong to a particular period. **5.** to ascertain or fix the date or time of. **6.** to have a romantic relationship or date(s) with: *Are you dating anyone at the moment?* **7.** to show to be of a certain age, or old-fashioned. –*phr.* **8. to date**, to the present time.

More usual expressions for def. 6 include **go out with** and **see**: *Are you seeing anyone at the moment?*

date[2] *n.* the oblong, fleshy fruit of the date palm.

datum /ˈdeɪtəm, ˈdatəm/ *n.* (*pl.* **-ta** /-tə/) **1.** any proposition assumed or given, from which conclusions may be drawn. **2.** (*oft. pl.*) any fact assumed to be a matter of direct observation.

daub *v.* to cover or coat with soft, adhesive matter, such as plaster, mud, etc.

daughter *n.* **1.** a female child or person in relation to her parents. **2.** any female descendant. **3.** someone related as if by the ties binding daughter to parent. –**daughterly**, *adj.*

daughter-in-law *n.* (*pl.* **daughters-in-law**) the wife of one's son or daughter.

daunt *v.* **1.** to overcome with fear. **2.** to lessen the courage of; dishearten. –**daunting**, *adj.* –**dauntingly**, *adv.*

dauntless *adj.* not to be daunted; fearless; intrepid; bold.

dawdle *v.* **1.** to waste time. **2.** to walk slowly or lag behind others.

dawn *n.* **1.** the first appearance of daylight in the morning. **2.** the beginning or rise of anything. –*v.* **3.** to begin to open or develop. **4.** to begin to be perceived: *The truth dawned on him.*

day *n.* **1.** the interval of light between 2 successive nights; the time between sunrise and sunset. **2.** a period of 24 hours, especially from midnight to succeeding midnight. **3.** the light of day; daylight. **4.** a day as a point or unit of time, or on which something occurs. **5.** a day of contest, or the contest itself: *He won the day.* **6.** a particular time or period: *in my grandmother's day.* **7.** period of power or influence.

Def. 6 can also be used in the plural: *the olden days.*

daydream *n.* **1.** a visionary fancy indulged in while awake; reverie. –*v.* (**-dreamed** *or* **-dreamt**, **-dreaming**) **2.** to indulge in daydreams.

daylight saving *n.* a system of reckoning time as being one or more hours later than the standard time, usually used during summer months to give more hours of daylight after the working day.

daze *v.* **1.** to stun or stupefy with a blow, a shock, etc. **2.** to confuse; bewilder; dazzle.

dazzle v. 1. to overpower or dim the vision by intense light. 2. to bewilder by brilliance or display of any kind.

deacon n. 1. a low-ranking member of the clergy. 2. a church official with variously defined duties. **–deaconess**, *fem. n.*

dead adj. 1. no longer living. 2. not endowed with life; inanimate. 3. without sensation; insensible; numb: *my foot is dead.* 4. no longer in existence or use. 5. *Informal* very tired; exhausted. 6. a. without resonance. b. without resilience or bounce. 7. not glossy, bright, or brilliant. 8. complete; absolute. *–adv.* 9. absolutely; completely. 10. with abrupt and complete stoppage of motion, etc.

deaden v. 1. to make less sensitive, active, energetic, or forcible. 2. to make impervious to sound.

deadline n. the latest time for finishing something.

deadlock¹ n. a state of affairs in which progress is impossible.

deadlock² n. a type of lock which can only be opened from inside and outside with a key.

deadly adj. (**-lier, -liest**) causing or tending to cause death.

deadpan adj. (of a person or their face) completely lacking expression or reaction.

deaf adj. unable to hear. **–deafen** v. **–deafness**, n.

deal v. (**dealt, dealing**) 1. to trade or do business: *She deals in rare books.* 2. to distribute, especially the cards required in a game. 3. to give to someone as their share; apportion (*out*). 4. *Informal* to sell illegal drugs. 5. to deliver (blows, etc.). *–n.* 6. a business transaction. 7. an indefinite but large amount or extent. 8. any undertaking, organisation, etc.; affair. *–phr.* 9. **deal with, a.** to be concerned with: *This book deals with French history.* **b.** to treat; behave towards. **–dealer**, n.

dealt /dɛlt/ v. past tense and past participle of **deal**.

dean n. 1. the head of a medical school, university faculty, or the like. 2. any of various ecclesiastical dignitaries, as the head of a division of a diocese.

dear adj. 1. beloved or loved. 2. (in the salutation of a letter) highly esteemed. 3. precious in one's regard. 4. high-priced; expensive. *–n.* 5. (a term of address for a beloved person).

Don't confuse **dear** with **deer**, which is a type of animal.

dearth /dɜːθ/ n. scarcity or scanty supply.

The more usual word is **lack**.

death n. 1. the act of dying; the end of life; the total and permanent cessation of the vital functions of an animal or plant. 2. the state of being dead. 3. extinction; destruction.

death adder n. a venomous snake of Aust. and New Guinea with thick body and broad head.

debacle /deɪˈbɑːkəl, də-/ n. a general breakup, overthrow or collapse; an overwhelming disaster.

debar v. (**-barred, -barring**) to exclude or prohibit.

debase v. 1. to reduce in quality or value. 2. to lower in rank or dignity.

debate n. 1. a discussion, especially of a public question in an assembly. 2. deliberation; consideration. 3. a systematic contest of speakers in which 2 opposing points of view of a proposition are advanced. *–v.* 4. to engage in discussion, especially in a legislative or public assembly. 5. to dispute about. **–debater**, n. **–debatable**, adj.

debauch /dəˈbɔːtʃ/ v. to corrupt by sensuality, intemperance, etc.; seduce. **–debauchery**, n.

debenture n. a note or certificate acknowledging a debt.

debilitate v. to make weak: *The illness debilitated him.* **–debility**, n.

debit n. 1. the recording of an entry of debt in an account. 2. the balance shown to be owing in an account. –v. **3.** to charge with a debt. **4.** to enter upon the debit side of an account.

Compare this with **credit** (def. 5), which refers to amounts received rather than debts.

debonair adj. **1.** suave; stylish. **2.** of pleasant manners; courteous.

debrief v. to question (someone) after any kind of undertaking in order to assess performance, etc. –**debriefing**, n.

debris /'debri, 'deɪbri, də'bri/ n. the remains of anything broken down or destroyed; ruins; fragments; rubbish.

debt n. **1.** that which is owed. **2.** the condition of being under such an obligation. –phr. **3. bad debt**, a debt of which there is no prospect of payment.

debtor n. someone who has a debt.

debunk v. Informal to challenge or destroy the good standing of.

debut /'deɪbju, -bu, də'bu/ n. **1.** a first public appearance. –v. (**debuted** /'deɪbjud/, **debuting** /'deɪbjuŋ/) **2.** to make a first appearance.

debutant /'debjətənt, -tɒnt/ n. Sport a young player making their first appearance at a particular level.

debutante /'debjətɒnt/ n. **1.** a young woman making a debut, especially into society. **2.** Sport a young player making her first appearance at a particular level.

decade /'dɛkeɪd, də'keɪd/ n. **1.** a period of 10 years. **2.** a group, set, or series of 10.

decadence n. **1.** the act or process of falling into an inferior condition or state, especially moral; decay. **2.** luxurious self-indulgence. –**decadent**, adj.

decaffeinated /di'kæfəneɪtəd/ adj. with the drug caffeine removed: decaffeinated coffee.

decant v. **1.** to pour off gently, as liquor, without disturbing the sediment. **2.** to pour from one container to another.

decanter n. a vessel from which wine, water, etc., are served.

decapitate v. to cut off the head of; behead.

decathlon n. an athletic contest comprising 10 different events, and won by the contestant having the highest total score. –**decathlete**, n.

decay v. **1.** to fall away from a state of excellence, prosperity, health, etc.; deteriorate. **2.** to become decomposed; rot. –n. **3.** a gradual falling into an inferior condition. **4.** decomposition; rotting.

decease n. departure from life; death.

deceased adj. dead.

Don't confuse **deceased** with **diseased**, which means affected with a disease: diseased kidneys.

deceive v. to mislead by a false appearance or statement. –**deceit**, n. –**deceitful**, adj.

decent adj. **1.** conforming to recognised standards of propriety, good taste, modesty, etc. **2.** Informal kind; obliging. –**decency**, n.

decentralise v. **1.** to disperse (industry, population, etc.), especially from large cities to relatively undeveloped rural areas. **2.** to undo the centralisation of administrative powers (of an organisation, government, etc.). Also, **decentralize**. –**decentralisation**, n.

deception n. **1.** the act or result of deceiving. **2.** something that deceives or is intended to deceive. –**deceptive**, adj.

decibel /'dɛsɪbel/ n. a unit expressing difference in power, usually between electric or acoustic signals, or between some particular signal and a reference level understood. Symbol: dB

decide v. **1.** to bring (a person) to a decision. **2.** to settle (something in dispute or doubt). **3.** to pronounce a judgement; come to a conclusion.

decided adj. resolute; determined.

deciduous /də'sɪdʒuəs/ adj. **1.** shedding the leaves annually, as trees, shrubs, etc. **2.** falling off at a particular season, stage of growth, etc., as leaves, teeth, horns, etc.

Compare this with **evergreen**, which describes trees which keep their leaves all year.

decimal *adj.* **1.** relating to tenths, or to the number 10. **2.** proceeding by tens. –*n.* **3.** a decimal fraction. **4.** a decimal number.

decimal fraction *n.* a fraction whose denominator is some power of 10, usually indicated by the decimal point written before the numerator, as $0.4 = \frac{4}{10}$.

decimal number *n. Maths* any finite or infinite string of digits containing a decimal point: *1.0, 5.23, 3.14159… are decimal numbers.*

decimal point *n.* (in the decimal system) a dot preceding the fractional part of a number.

decimate *v.* to destroy a great number or proportion of.

This word originally meant to kill or destroy one tenth of a total number of people or things, but nowadays it is most often used to refer to almost total destruction. A small number of people don't accept this change in meaning and think that only the original meaning is correct.

decipher *v.* **1.** to make out or discover the meaning of. **2.** to interpret, as something written in code.

This comes from the noun **cipher**, which is a secret language or code.

decision *n.* **1.** the act of deciding; determination (of a question or doubt). **2.** a judgement, as one formally pronounced by a court.

decisive /dəˈsaɪsɪv/ *adj.* **1.** having the power or quality of determining; putting an end to controversy. **2.** decided; determined.

deck *n.* **1.** a horizontal platform extending from side to side of a ship or of part of a ship, forming a covering for the space below and itself serving as a floor. **2.** a floor, platform or tier. **3.** a pack of playing cards. –*v.* **4.** to clothe in something ornamental.

declaim *v.* **1.** to speak aloud rhetorically; make a formal speech. **2.** to inveigh (against). –**declamatory**, *adj.*

declare *v.* **1.** to make known, especially in explicit or formal terms. **2.** to state emphatically. **3.** to make your statement of (dutiable goods, etc.). –**declaration**, *n* –**declaratory**, *adj.*

declension *n.* **1.** *Gram.* the inflection of nouns, etc., for categories such as case and number. **2.** a bending, sloping, or moving downward.

decline *v.* **1.** to withhold consent to do enter upon, or accept. **2.** to cause to slope or incline downward. **3.** *Gram.* to inflec (a noun, pronoun, or adjective). **4.** to express courteous refusal. **5.** to bend or slant down; slope or trend downward. **6.** to fail in strength, vigour, character, value, etc. –*n.* **7.** a downward incline or slope. **8.** failing or gradual loss, as in strength character, value, etc.

decode *v.* to translate from code into the original language or form.

decommission *v.* **1.** to remove from service, as a naval vessel, army officer, etc **2.** to close down (a facility, as a powe station, sewerage plant, etc.).

decompose *v.* **1.** to separate or resolv into constituent parts or elements. **2.** to ro putrefy. –**decomposition**, *n.*

For def. 2, the more usual words are **rot** o **decay**.

decompress *v.* **1.** to undergo or caus to undergo decompression. **2.** *Computer* to decode (data) from a compressed stor age format into its original format; unzip

decompression *n.* **1.** the act or proces of relieving pressure. **2.** the gradual retur of persons, as divers or constructio workers, to normal atmospheric pressure

decongestant *n.* a substance used to re lieve congestion especially in the uppe respiratory tract.

decor /ˈdeɪkɔ, ˈdɛkɔ/ *n.* **1.** decoration general. **2.** a style of decoration.

decorate v. **1.** to furnish or deck with something becoming or ornamental. **2.** to confer distinction upon by a badge, a medal of honour, etc. **–decoration**, n. **–decorator**, n. **–decorative**, adj.

decorum n. propriety of behaviour, speech, dress, etc. **–decorous**, adj.

decoy n. someone who entices or allures, as into a trap, danger, etc.

decrease v. /də'kris/ **1.** to diminish gradually in extent, quantity, strength, power, etc. –n. /'dikris, də'kris/ **2.** a process of growing less, or the resulting condition. **3.** the amount by which a thing is lessened.

decree n. **1.** a decision or edict promulgated by civil or other authority. **–v.** (**-creed, -creeing**) **2.** to ordain or decide by decree.

The more usual word is **order**.

decrepit adj. broken down or weakened by old age; feeble; infirm. **–decrepitude**, n.

decriminalise v. to remove legal restrictions against (an activity, such as smoking marijuana), and thus eliminate the legal penalties previously associated with it. Also, **decriminalize**.

decry v. (**-cried, -crying**) to speak badly of.

The more usual word is **ridicule**.

dedicate v. **1.** to set apart and consecrate to a deity or to a sacred purpose. **2.** to give up wholly or earnestly, as to some person or end; set apart. **–dedication**, n. **–dedicated**, adj. **–dedicatory**, adj.

deduce v. (**-duced, -ducing**) to derive as a conclusion from something known or assumed; infer.

The more usual expression is **work out**. Don't confuse **deduce** with **deduct**.

deduct v. to take away, as from a sum or amount.

Don't confuse this with **deduce**.

deduction n. **1.** an act of deducting; subtraction. **2.** an amount deducted. **3.** (the

process of drawing) a conclusion from something known or assumed.

deed n. **1.** that which is done, performed, or accomplished; an act. **2.** Law a signed agreement, usually about ownership of land.

deejay n. → DJ.

deem v. to form or have an opinion; judge; think.

The more usual word is **consider**.

deep adj. **1.** extending far downwards, inwards, or backwards. **2.** having a specified dimension downwards, inwards, or backwards. **3.** situated far or at a certain distance down, in, or back. **4.** difficult to penetrate or understand. **5.** not superficial; profound. **6.** intense: *deep sleep.* **7.** dark and vivid: *deep red.* **8.** low in pitch, as sound. **9.** absorbed. –n. **10.** the deep part of the sea, etc. –adv. **11.** to or at a considerable or specified depth.

deepfake n. a video of a computer-generated likeness of an individual, created without their knowledge, often out of malice or to spread misleading information. Also, **deep fake**.

deep-fry v. (**-fried, -frying**) to fry in a sufficient quantity of fat or oil to cover the food being cooked.

deep vein thrombosis n. Med. a thrombosis occurring in a non-superficial vein, usually in the thigh or calf, which can dislodge from the vein wall and travel to the lungs, causing a life-threatening pulmonary embolism. Also, **deep venous thrombosis**, **DVT**.

deer n. (pl. **deer**) a large, grass-eating ruminant with hoofs, the male of which has branching horns or antlers.

deface v. (**-faced, -facing**) **1.** to mar the face or appearance of. **2.** to blot out.

de facto /di 'fæktou, də, deı/ adj. **1.** in fact; in reality. **2.** actually existing, whether with or without right. **3.** Aust., NZ living with, but not married to, one's partner. –n. **4.** Aust., NZ a person who lives with someone as their husband or wife without actually being married to them.

defame *v.* to attack the good name or reputation of, as by uttering or publishing maliciously anything injurious; slander; libel. –**defamation**, *n.* –**defamatory**, *adj.*

default *n.* **1.** failure to act, perform or participate. **2.** a procedure which has preset parameters which operate unless changed by the user. –*v.* **3.** to fail to perform or pay.

defeat *v.* **1.** to overcome in a contest, battle, etc.; vanquish. **2.** to frustrate; thwart. –*n.* **3.** the act or result of defeating.

defecate /ˈdefəkeɪt/ *v.* to void excrement. –**defecation**, *n.*

defect *n.* /ˈdiːfekt, dəˈfekt/ **1.** a falling short; a fault or imperfection. –*v.* /dəˈfekt/ **2.** to desert a country, cause, etc. –**defection**, *n.* –**defector**, *n.* –**defective**, *adj.*

defence *n.* **1.** resistance against attack; protection. **2.** the defending of a cause or the like by speech, argument, etc. **3.** *Law* the denial or pleading of the defendant in answer to the claim or charge against them.

defend *v.* **1.** to ward off attack; guard against assault or injury (*from* or *against*). **2.** to maintain by argument, evidence, etc. **3.** to contest (a legal charge, claim, etc.). **4.** to act as counsel for (an accused person). –**defendable**, *adj.* –**defender**, *n.*

defendant *n.* *Law* the party against whom a claim or charge is brought in a proceeding.

defensive *adj.* **1.** serving to defend; protective. **2.** made or carried on for the purpose of resisting attack.

defer[1] *v.* (**-ferred**, **-ferring**) to put off (action, etc.) to a future time. –**deferment**, *n.* **deferral**, *n.*

Don't confuse **defer** with **differ**, which is to be unlike or something: *This style differs from that one.*

defer[2] *v.* (**-ferred**, **-ferring**) to yield in judgement or opinion (*to*).

defiance *n.* **1.** a daring or bold resistance to authority or to any opposing force. **2.** open disregard. –**defiant**, *adj.*

This comes from the verb **defy**.

deficient *adj.* lacking some element or characteristic; inadequate. –**deficiency**, *n.*

deficit /ˈdefəsət/ *n.* the amount by which a sum of money falls short of the required amount.

defile *v.* (**-filed**, **-filing**) **1.** to make foul, dirty, or unclean. **2.** to violate the chastity of.

define *v.* **1.** to explain the nature or essential qualities of; describe. **2.** to fix or lay down definitely. –**definition**, *n.*

definite *adj.* **1.** clearly defined or determined; not vague or general. **2.** certain, sure.

definite article *n.* *Gram.* the article *the*, used when the noun has already been referred to, or is about to be identified, as in *the dog next door*, or when the noun is referring to a whole category, as in *The tiger likes to hunt at night.*

definitive /dəˈfɪnətɪv/ *adj.* **1.** having the function of deciding or settling; determining; conclusive; final. **2.** having its fixed and final form.

deflate *v.* **1.** to release the air or gas from (something inflated, as a tyre). **2.** to reduce (currency, prices, etc.) from an inflated condition. **3.** to reduce in esteem, especially self-esteem (a person or a person's ego). –**deflation**, *n.*

deflect *v.* **1.** to bend or turn aside. **2.** to cause to turn from a true course or right line. –**deflection**, *n.*

defoliate *v.* to strip or deprive (a tree, etc.) of leaves. –**defoliant**, *n.*

deforestation *n.* the permanent removal of forests or trees from a large area, usually for commercial purposes.

deform *v.* to mar the natural form, shape, or beauty of; disfigure; spoil. –**deformity**, *n.* –**deformed**, *adj.*

defrag Computers Informal –v. **1.** → defragment. –n. **2.** the process of defragmenting a disk.

defragment v. Computers to reorganise the data stored on (a disk) so that whole files are stored in the same place. Also, Informal, **defrag**. –**defragmentation**, n.

defraud v. to deprive of a right or property by fraud; cheat.

defray v. to bear or pay (the costs, expenses, etc.).

de-friend v. → unfriend.

defrost v. to remove ice from; cause (food, ice, etc.) to thaw.

deft adj. dexterous; nimble; skilful; clever.

defunct adj. **1.** deceased; dead; extinct. **2.** no longer operative; not in use.

Note that this word can be used in a formal or a humorous way: *a defunct company*; *This heater is completely defunct.*

defuse v. **1.** to remove the fuse from (a bomb). **2.** to calm (a situation or action).

defy v. (-fied, -fying) **1.** to challenge the power of; resist boldly or openly. **2.** to challenge (one) to do something deemed impossible.

degenerate v. /də'dʒɛnəreɪt/ **1.** to decline in physical, mental, or moral qualities or powers. –adj. /də'dʒɛnərət/ **2.** having declined in physical or moral qualities; degraded. –n. /də'dʒɛnərət/ **3.** someone who has retrogressed from a normal type or standard, as in morals, or character. –**degenerative**, adj. –**degeneracy**, n. –**degeneration**, n.

degrade v. **1.** to reduce from a higher to a lower rank, degree, etc., especially as punishment. **2.** to lower in character or quality. **3.** to lower in dignity or reputation. –**degradation**, n.

degree n. **1.** a step or stage in an ascending or descending scale, or in a course or process. **2.** a level or amount: *a degree of satisfaction.* **3.** Geom. a unit of measurement of angles, one degree equalling $^1/_{360}$ of the circumference of a circle. **4.** a unit in the measurement of temperature. **5.** Geog. the unit of measurement of latitude or longitude. **6.** a qualification conferred by a university, etc., for successful work.

The symbol for defs 3, 4 and 5 is ° as in *a 90° angle, 20°C* and *40° south.*

dehydrate v. **1.** to deprive of water. **2.** to free (vegetables, etc.) of moisture, for preservation. **3.** to lose water or moisture. –**dehydration**, n.

deify /'diəfaɪ, 'deɪə-/ v. (-fied, -fying) **1.** to make a god of; exalt to the rank of a deity. **2.** to adore or regard as a deity.

deign /deɪn/ v. to think fit or in accordance with one's dignity; condescend.

deity /'diəti, 'deɪ-/ n. (pl. -ties) **1.** a god or goddess. **2.** divine character or nature.

dejected adj. depressed in spirits; disheartened.

delay v. **1.** to put off to a later time; defer. **2.** to impede the progress of. –n. **3.** the act of delaying; procrastination. **4.** an instance of being delayed.

delectable adj. delightful; highly pleasing.

delegate n. /'dɛləgət/ **1.** someone representing a person or group, as at a conference, etc.; deputy; representative. –v. /'dɛləgeɪt/ **2.** to send or appoint (a person) as deputy or representative. **3.** to commit (powers, functions, etc.) to another as agent or deputy.

delegation n. a group of delegates.

delete v. to strike out or take out (anything written or printed). –**deletion**, n.

deleterious /dɛlə'tɪəriəs/ adj. **1.** injurious to health. **2.** hurtful; injurious.

deliberate adj. /də'lɪbərət/ **1.** carefully weighed or considered; intentional. **2.** careful or slow in deciding. –v. /də'lɪbəreɪt/ **3.** to think carefully or attentively; reflect. –**deliberation**, n. –**deliberative**, adj.

delicacy n. (pl. **-cies**) **1.** quality of being delicate. **2.** something delightful or pleasing, especially to the palate.

delicate adj. **1.** fine in texture, quality, construction, etc. **2.** so fine or slight as to be scarcely perceptible. **3.** easily damaged; fragile. **4.** requiring great care, caution, or tact. **5.** distinguishing subtle differences. **6.** fastidious.

delicatessen n. a shop selling smallgoods, cheeses, and other cooked or tinned foods. Also, **deli**.

delicious adj. highly pleasing to the senses, especially to taste or smell.

delight n. a high degree of pleasure or enjoyment; joy. –**delightful**, adj.

delineate /dɪˈlɪniˌeɪt/ v. **1.** to trace the outline of; represent pictorially. **2.** to portray or describe in words.

For def. 1, the more usual word is **draw**.

delinquent adj. **1.** guilty of a misdeed or offence. –n. **2.** someone who is delinquent, especially a young person. –**delinquency**, n.

delirium n. (pl. **-riums** or **-ria**) a temporary mental disorder marked by excitement, hallucinations, etc. –**delirious**, adj.

deliver v. **1.** to give into another's possession or keeping. **2.** to strike (a blow). **3.** to assist at the birth of. **4.** to give or declare (a verdict, etc.). **5.** to rescue or set free. –**delivery**, n. –**deliverance**, n.

For def. 5, the more usual word is **save**.

delta n. a nearly flat plain of alluvial deposit between diverging branches of the mouth of a river.

delude v. to mislead the mind or judgement of. –**delusion**, n.

The more usual word is **trick**.

deluge /ˈdɛljudʒ/ n. a flood.

deluxe /dəˈlʌks/ adj. of special elegance, sumptuousness, or fineness. Also, **de luxe**.

delve v. to carry on intensive research for information, etc.

demagogue /ˈdɛməgɒg/ n. an unprincipled popular orator or agitator.

demand v. **1.** to ask for with authority; claim as a right. –n. **2.** the act of demanding. **3.** an urgent or pressing requirement. **4.** the state of being in request for purchase or use. –phr. **5. on demand, a.** subject to payment upon presentation and demand. **b.** as required.

demarcation n. **1.** the marking off of the boundaries of something. **2.** a division between things, especially the division between types of work carried out by members of different trade unions.

demean v. to lower in dignity or standing; debase.

demeanour n. conduct; behaviour; bearing. Also, **demeanor**.

demented adj. out of one's mind; insane.

dementia /dəˈmɛnʃə, -ʃiə/ n. a state of mental disorder characterised by impairment or loss of mental powers.

demerit n. **1.** censurable or punishable quality; fault. **2.** a mark against a person for misconduct or deficiency.

demilitarise v. to withdraw military forces from (a zone, area, etc.). Also, **demilitarize**.

demise n. death or decease.

demist v. to direct air, usually heated, onto a car windscreen, to clear it of mist. –**demister**, n.

democracy n. (pl. **-cies**) **1.** a form of government in which the supreme power is vested in the people. **2.** a nation, etc. having such a form of government. –**democrat**, n. –**democratic**, adj.

demolish v. to throw or pull down (a building, etc.); reduce to ruins. –**demolition**, n.

demon n. an evil spirit; a devil. –**demonic, demoniac**, adj.

demonstrate v. **1.** to make evident by arguments or reasoning; prove. **2.** to describe and explain with the help or specimens or by experiment. **3.** to manifest or exhibit. –**demonstration,** n.

demonstrative /dəˈmɒnstrətɪv/ adj. **1.** characterised by showing feelings openly. **2.** serving to demonstrate. **3.** Gram. relating to a word which indicates or specifies the thing referred to.

Demonstrative words, as in def. 3, can be adjectives (this book, that pen) or pronouns (This is pretty, That is interesting).

demoralise v. to deprive of spirit, courage, etc. Also, **demoralize.**

demote v. to reduce to a lower grade or class. –**demotion,** n.

demur /dəˈmɜ/ v. (-**murred, -murring**) **1.** to make objection; take exception. –n. **2.** an objection raised. –**demurral,** n. –**demurrer,** n.

demure adj. (-**murer, -murest**) affectedly or unnaturally modest, decorous, or prim.

den n. **1.** a cave, etc., serving as the habitation of a wild beast. **2.** a cosy or secluded room for personal use. **3.** a place devoted to an illicit activity: a gambling den.

denial n. **1.** a contradiction of a statement, etc. **2.** refusal. –phr. **3. in denial,** closing one's mind to an unpleasant fact or experience.

denigrate v. to defame or speak disparagingly of.

The more usual word is **belittle.**

denim n. a heavy cotton for overalls, trousers, etc.

denizen /ˈdɛnəzən/ n. an inhabitant.

denomination n. **1.** a class or kind of persons or things distinguished by a specific name. **2.** a religious group.

denominator n. Maths the term of a fraction (usually written under the line) which shows the number of equal parts into which the unit is divided.

Compare this with **numerator,** which is the number above the line in a fraction.

denote v. to be a mark or sign of; indicate: The smell of strong coffee denotes that there is a cafe nearby. –**denotation,** n.

The more usual word is **mean.**
Compare **denote** with **connote,** which is to suggest a meaning other than the main meaning, as in The smell of strong coffee connotes lazy Sunday breakfasts.

denounce v. to condemn openly; assail with censure.

dense adj. **1.** having the component parts closely compacted together; compact. **2.** obtuse; stupid. –**density,** n.

dent n. a hollow or depression in a surface, as from a blow.

dental adj. **1.** of or relating to the teeth. **2.** of or relating to dentistry.

dentistry n. the science or art dealing with the prevention and treatment of oral disease. –**dentist,** n.

denture n. an artificial restoration of teeth.

denude v. to make naked or bare; strip.

denunciation n. a denouncing.

deny v. (-**nied, -nying**) **1.** to assert the negative of; declare not to be true. **2.** to refuse to grant (a claim, request, etc.). **3.** to refuse to recognise or acknowledge; repudiate.

deodorant n. an agent for destroying odours.

depart v. **1.** to go away. **2.** to turn aside (from). –**departure,** n.

department n. a distinct part or division of a complex whole or organised system.

department store n. a large shop selling a wide range of goods in different departments.

depend v. **1.** to rely; trust. **2.** to be conditioned or contingent. –**dependable,** adj.

dependant n. someone who depends on or looks to another for support, favour, etc.

Don't confuse this with **dependent,** which is the adjective related to this word: a dependent child. Note that there is a difference here between Australian

English and American English – in America both the adjective and the noun are generally spelt **dependent**.

dependent *adj.* depending on something or someone else: *A child is dependent upon its parents.* **–dependence,** *n.*

Don't confuse **dependent** with **dependant,** which is the noun related to this word.

depict *v.* to represent by or as by painting; portray; delineate.

depilatory /dəˈpɪlətri/ *adj.* 1. capable of removing hair. *–n.* (*pl.* **-ries**) 2. a depilatory agent.

deplete *v.* to decrease the fullness of; lessen the stock or amount of: *to deplete our natural resources.* **–depletion,** *n.*

The more usual word is **reduce**.

deplorable *adj.* 1. causing grief; lamentable. 2. causing censure; bad; wretched. **–deplore,** *v.*

deploy *v.* 1. to spread out or place efficiently. 2. to make careful or effective use of.

For def. 2, the more usual word is **use**.

deport *v.* to expel (an illegal immigrant, etc.) from a country.

deportment *n.* manner of bearing; carriage.

depose *v.* 1. to remove from office or position. 2. to declare or testify. **–deposal,** *n.*

deposit *v.* 1. to put or lay down. 2. to place for safekeeping or in trust. *–n.* 3. anything laid or thrown down, as matter precipitated from a fluid; sediment. 4. an accumulation. 5. money placed in a financial institution. 6. anything given as security or in part payment.

depot /ˈdepoʊ/ *n.* 1. a storehouse. 2. a place where buses, trams, trucks, etc., are kept when they are not in service.

depraved *adj.* corrupt or perverted, especially morally; wicked. **–depravity,** *n.*

deprecate *v.* to express earnest disapproval of. **–deprecatory,** *adj.*

depreciation *n.* 1. a decrease in value due to wear and tear, decay, decline in price, etc. 2. a decrease in the purchasing or exchange value of money. **–depreciate,** *v.*

depredation *n.* 1. robbery. 2. destruction.

depress *v.* 1. to lower in spirits. 2. to press down.

depressed *adj.* 1. feeling sad and as if there is no hope. 2. in a situation where prices and values are held down.

depression *n.* 1. unhappiness and a feeling that there is no resources. 2. a mental illness where one feels in a low mood for a long time without there being an apparent cause of unhappiness. 3. a period when there is a lot of unemployment and businesses are not making profits. 4. a part of a surface which is lower than the rest, forming a slight hole.

deprive *v.* to divest of something; dispossess. **–deprivation,** *n.*

depth *n.* 1. measure or distance downwards, inwards, or backwards. 2. intensity, as of silence, colour, etc. 3. lowness of pitch. 4. extent of intellectual penetration or sagacity.

deputation *n.* 1. appointment to represent or act for another or others. 2. the person(s) so appointed.

deputy *n.* (*pl.* **-ties**) 1. a person appointed or authorised to act for another or others. 2. a person appointed or elected as assistant to a public official.

derail *v.* 1. to cause (a train, etc.) to run off the rails. 2. (of a train, etc.) to run off the rails of a track. **–derailment,** *n.*

deranged *adj.* insane.

derelict *adj.* 1. left or abandoned, as by the owner or guardian. *–n.* 2. a person forsaken or abandoned, especially by society.

dereliction *n.* culpable neglect, as of duty; delinquency; fault.

deride v. to scoff or jeer at in contempt; mock. **–derision,** n. **–derisive,** adj.

The more usual expression is **laugh at.**

derive v. **1.** to receive or obtain from a source or origin: *to derive knowledge from books.* **2.** to trace, as from a source or origin. **3.** to obtain by reasoning. **4.** to come from a source; originate. **–derivation,** n. **–derivative,** n., adj.

For def. 1, the more usual word is **get.**

dermatitis n. inflammation of the skin.

dermatology n. the science of the skin and its diseases. **–dermatologist,** n.

derogatory /dəˈrɒgətri, -ətəri/ adj. disparaging.

derrick n. a tower-like structure, especially for lifting weights, etc.

desalination n. the process of removing the dissolved salts from sea water so that it becomes suitable for drinking water or for agricultural irrigation. Also, **desalinisation.**

descant /ˈdɛskænt/ n. Music an additional, usually higher melody accompanying a simple theme.

descend v. **1.** to move or pass from a higher to a lower place; fall; sink. **2.** to be derived by birth or extraction. **3.** to approach in a hostile or intimidating manner, especially as a large group (*on*): *The gang descended on him after school; The relatives all descended on us at Christmas time.* **–descendent,** adj.

descendant n. someone descended from an ancestor.

descent n. **1.** the act of descending. **2.** a downward slope. **3.** derivation from an ancestor.

describe v. **1.** to give a spoken or written account of. **2.** to draw or trace, as an arc: *He took a stick and described a circle in the sand.* **–description,** n. **–descriptive,** adj.

desecrate /ˈdɛsəkreɪt/ v. to divest of sacred or hallowed character.

desert¹ /ˈdɛzət/ n. **1.** an area so deficient in moisture as to support little or no vegetation. **–adj. 2.** of, relating to, or like a desert. **3.** uninhabited: *a desert island.*

Don't confuse this with **dessert,** which is a sweet course eaten at the end of a meal.

desert² /dəˈzɜt/ v. **1.** to abandon. **2.** (especially of a soldier or sailor) to forsake one's duty, etc. **–desertion,** n.

Don't confuse this with **dessert,** which is a sweet course eaten at the end of a meal.

desert³ /dəˈzɜt/ n. that which is deserved; a due reward or punishment: *to receive one's just deserts.*

Don't confuse this with **dessert,** which is a sweet course eaten at the end of a meal.

deserve v. to merit (reward, punishment, esteem, etc.) in return for actions, qualities, etc.

desiccate v. to dry thoroughly; dry up.

desiccated /ˈdɛsəkeɪtəd/ adj. **1.** dehydrated or powdered: *desiccated coconut.* **2.** completely dried out.

design v. **1.** to plan or fashion artistically or skilfully. **2.** to intend for a definite purpose. **3.** to form or conceive in the mind. **–n. 4.** an outline, sketch, or plan. **5.** the combination of details or features of a picture, building, etc. **6.** the end in view; intention. **–designer,** n.

designate v. /ˈdɛzɪgneɪt/ **1.** to mark or point out; indicate; show; specify. **2.** to nominate or select for a duty, office, purpose, etc.; appoint. **–adj.** /ˈdɛzɪgnət, -neɪt/ **3.** appointed to an office but not yet in possession of it.

For def. 2, the more usual words are **select** or **choose.**

designer gene n. a gene created or modified by genetic engineering.

desire v. **1.** to wish or long for; crave. **–n. 2.** a longing or craving. **3.** an expressed wish. **–desirable,** adj.

desirous *phr.* **desirous of**, having or experiencing a wish or hope for.

desist *v.* to cease, as from some action or proceeding.

The more usual word is **stop**.

desk *n.* a table specially adapted for convenience in writing or reading.

desolate *adj.* /'desələt, 'dez-/ **1.** devastated. **2.** deserted. **3.** left alone; lonely. –*v.* /'desəleit, 'dez-/ **4.** to devastate. **5.** to depopulate. –**desolation**, *n.*

despair *n.* total loss of hope.

desperate *adj.* **1.** reckless from despair. **2.** very serious or dangerous. –**desperation**, *n.*

despicable *adj.* that is to be despised; contemptible.

despise *v.* to look down upon, as in contempt. –**despicable**, *adj.*

despite *prep.* in spite of.

despondent *adj.* depressed or dejected. –**despondency**, *n.*

despot *n.* a ruler who has unlimited powers. –**despotic**, *adj.*

dessert /də'zɜt/ *n.* the final, sweet course of a meal.

Don't confuse this with **desert** (pronounced /'dezət/), a dry sandy place, or with **desert** (pronounced /də'zɜt/), which means to abandon. Your **deserts** (pronounced /də'zɜts/) are what you deserve – a reward or a punishment.

destabilise *v.* **1.** to make unstable. **2.** *Politics* to deliberately create uncertainty about: *to destabilise the leadership.* Also, **destabilize**. –**destabilising**, *adj.* –**destabilisation**, *n.*

destination *n.* the predetermined end of a journey or voyage.

destine *v.* to appoint or ordain beforehand; predetermine.

destined *adj.* **1.** bound for a certain destination. **2.** predetermined.

destiny *n.* (*pl.* **-nies**) **1.** a predetermined course of events. **2.** the power or agency which determines the course of events.

destitute *adj.* bereft of means or resources.

destroy *v.* **1.** to ruin; spoil; demolish. **2.** to put an end to. –**destruction**, *n.* –**destructive**, *adj.*

desultory /'desəltri, -tari, 'dez-/ *adj.* lacking purpose, method, or enthusiasm.

The more usual word is **aimless**.

detach *v.* to unfasten and separate; disengage.

detail *n.* **1.** an individual or minute part; an item or particular. **2.** fine, intricate decoration.

detain *v.* **1.** to keep from proceeding; keep waiting. **2.** to keep under restraint or in custody. –**detention**, *n.*

detect *v.* to discover or notice a fact, a process, or an action. –**detection**, *n.*

detective *n.* a person, usually a member of the police force, who investigates crimes.

détente /dei'tɒnt/ *n.* a relaxing of international tension.

detention centre *n.* an institution for holding people in custody, as one used to confine illegal immigrants, or certain categories of criminal offenders.

deter *v.* (**-terred**, **-terring**) to discourage or restrain (one) from acting or proceeding. –**deterrent**, *adj.*, *n.*

detergent *n.* any cleaning agent, including soap.

deteriorate *v.* to become worse. –**deterioration**, *n.*

determination *n.* **1.** the quality of being determined or resolute. **2.** the act or result of determining.

determine *v.* **1.** to settle or decide (a dispute, question, etc.) by an authoritative decision. **2.** to conclude or ascertain, as after reasoning, observation, etc. **3.** to fix or condition (an outcome).

determined *adj.* resolute; firm.

determiner *n. Gram.* a word such as an article or a number, which comes before a noun to give more specific information about what is being referred to, as *that* in *that dog*, and *seven* in *seven dwarfs*.

detest v. to feel abhorrence of; hate. –**detestable**, *adj.*

detonate v. to cause to explode. –**detonator**, n. –**detonation**, n.

detour n. a roundabout or circuitous way or course, especially one used temporarily instead of the main route.

detox n. **1.** the process of detoxification. –v. **2.** to go through the process of detoxification.

detoxification n. the process of withdrawing from physical or psychological dependency on a substance of abuse, such as drugs, alcohol, etc.

detract v. to take away a part, as from quality, value, or reputation.

detriment n. loss, damage, or injury. –**detrimental**, *adj.*

detritus /dəˈtraɪtəs/ n. any disintegrated material; debris.

deuce n. **1.** a card, or the side of a dice, having 2 pips. **2.** *Tennis, etc.* a juncture in a game at which the scores are level at 40 all.

devastate v. to lay waste; ravage; render desolate. –**devastation**, n.

develop v. **1.** to bring out the capabilities or possibilities of. **2.** to (cause to) grow into a more mature or advanced state. **3.** to bring or come gradually into being or activity; evolve. **4.** to build on (land). **5.** to treat (a photographic plate, etc.) with chemical agents so as to bring out the latent image. –**development**, n.

deviant *adj.* **1.** deviating from an accepted norm, especially in sexual behaviour. –n. **2.** someone or something that is deviant.

deviate v. **1.** to turn aside (from a way or course). **2.** to depart or swerve, as from a procedure, course of action, or acceptable standard. –**deviation**, n.

device n. **1.** a mechanism designed for a particular purpose. **2.** a plan or scheme for effecting a purpose. **3.** a design used as an emblem, badge, etc. **4.** *Computers* → **peripheral device**.

Don't confuse this with **devise**, which is to think out, invent or plan.

device driver n. *Computers* a program that enables the operating system of a computer to recognise peripheral devices, such as modems, printers, mouses, etc. Also, **driver**.

devil n. **1.** (*sometimes upper case*) *Theology* the supreme spirit of evil; Satan. **2.** (in many religions) an evil spirit; demon. **3.** an atrociously wicked, cruel, or ill-tempered person.

devious *adj.* **1.** departing from the accepted way; roundabout. **2.** not straightforward; deceptive.

devise v. to order or arrange the plan of; contrive; invent.

The more usual expression is **work out**. Don't confuse **devise** with **device**, which is something which has been invented for a particular purpose: *a clever device for opening the door.*

devoid *adj.* empty, not possessing, or destitute (*of*).

The more usual expression is **lacking in**.

devolve v. **1.** to transfer or delegate (a duty, responsibility, etc.) to or upon another. **2.** to fall as a duty or responsibility on a person.

devote v. to give up to or concentrate on a particular pursuit, occupation, purpose, cause, person, etc. –**devotion**, n. –**devotee**, n.

devour v. to swallow or eat up voraciously or ravenously.

devout *adj.* devoted to divine worship or service; pious.

dew n. moisture condensed from the atmosphere, especially at night, and deposited in the form of small drops upon any cool surface.

Don't confuse this with **due**, which means expected: *The train is due at 10 o'clock.*

dexterity *n.* adroitness or skill in using the hands or the mind. –**dexterous**, *adj.*

diabetes /daɪə'biːtiːz/ *n.* a disease in which the ability of the body to use sugar is impaired. –**diabetic**, *n.*, *adj.*

diabolical *adj.* having the qualities of a devil; fiendish. Also, **diabolic**.

diagnosis *n.* (*pl.* **-noses** /-'nəʊsiːz/) *Med.* the process of determining by examination the nature and circumstances of a diseased condition. –**diagnose**, *v.* –**diagnostic**, *adj.*

diagonal *adj.* **1.** *Maths* slanted or sloping, as a straight line joining opposite corners of a square or rectangle. –*n.* **2.** a diagonal line, plane, or the like.

Compare this with **vertical** and **horizontal**.

diagram *n.* a drawing or plan that outlines and explains, the parts, operation, etc., of something.

dial *n.* **1.** a face upon which time is indicated by hands, pointers, or shadows. **2.** a plate or disc with graduations or figures, as for measuring, or on a telephone, etc.

dialect *n.* the language of a particular district or group.

dialogue *n.* **1.** conversation between 2 or more persons. **2.** an exchange of ideas or opinions on a particular issue.

dialysis /daɪ'æləsəs/ *n. Med.* (in cases of defective kidney function) the removal of waste products from the blood by causing them to diffuse through a semipermeable membrane. –**dialyse**, *v.*

diameter *n. Geom.* a straight line passing through the centre of a circle or sphere and terminated at each end by the circumference or surface.

diametric *adj.* **1.** relating to or along a diameter. **2.** direct; complete. Also, **diametrical**.

diamond *n.* **1.** an extremely hard, pure or nearly pure form of carbon, which, when used as a precious stone, has great brilliance. **2.** an equilateral quadrilateral, especially as placed with its diagonals vertical and horizontal.

diaphanous /daɪ'æfənəs/ *adj.* transparent; translucent.

diaphragm /'daɪəfræm/ *n.* **1.** *Anat.* the partition separating the thoracic cavity from the abdominal cavity in mammals. **2.** a contraceptive membrane covering the cervix.

diarrhoea /daɪə'rɪə/ *n.* an intestinal disorder characterised by high frequency and fluidity of faecal evacuations. Also, **diarrhea**.

diary *n.* a daily record, especially of the writer's own experiences or observations. –**diarist**, *n.*

Don't confuse **diary** with **dairy** which is a place where cows are milked.

diatribe *n.* a bitter and violent denunciation, attack, or criticism.

dice *pl. n.* (*sing.* **die**) **1.** small cubes marked on each side with a different number of spots (1 to 6), or with symbols, usually used in pairs in games of chance or in gambling. –*v.* (**diced**, **dicing**) **2.** to cut into small cubes.

Note that the singular of def. 1 is **die**. However, many people use **dice** as the singular, and this is considered quite acceptable: *Please bring me that dice from the box.*

dicey *adj. Informal* dangerous; risky; tricky.

dichotomy /daɪ'kɒtəmi/ *n.* (*pl.* **-mies**) division into 2 parts or into twos.

dick *n. Informal* (taboo) the penis.

Note that this word is taboo and may give offence.

dictate *v.* **1.** to say or read aloud (something) to be taken down in writing or recorded mechanically. **2.** to prescribe positively; command with authority. –**dictation**, *n.*

dictator n. a person exercising absolute power. –**dictatorial**, adj.

diction n. style of speaking or writing as dependent upon choice of words.

dictionary n. (pl. **-ries**) a reference work containing a selection of the words of a language, usually arranged alphabetically, with explanations of their meanings, pronunciations, and other information concerning them.

did v. past tense of **do**.

didactic adj. **1.** intended for instruction. **2.** inclined to teach or lecture others too much.

diddle v. Informal to cheat; swindle; victimise. –**diddler**, n.

didjeridu n. an Aboriginal wind instrument. Also, **didgeridoo**.

die¹ v. (**died**, **dying**) **1.** to cease to live; undergo the complete and permanent cessation of all vital functions. **2.** to pass gradually; fade or subside gradually (away, out, or down). –phr. Informal **3. be dying for**, to desire or want keenly or greatly: I'm dying for a drink. **4. be dying to**, to desire or want keenly to: I'm dying to see Venice.

Don't confuse **die** with **dye**, which is a substance you use to colour things.

die² n. **1.** (pl. **dies**) any of various devices for cutting or forming material in a press or a stamping or forging machine. **2.** singular of **dice**.

Note that, although def. 2 is the singular of **dice**, many people use the form **dice** as a singular, and this is considered quite acceptable.

diesel /'dizəl/ n. the oil left after petrol and kerosene have been taken from crude petroleum; used in diesel engines.

diesel engine n. a type of internal-combustion engine in which an oil is used as fuel.

diet n. **1.** a particular selection of food, especially as prescribed to improve health or regulate weight. **2.** the usual or regular food(s) a person eats most frequently. –v. (**-eted**, **-eting**) **3.** to follow a diet (def. 1). –**dietitian**, n. –**dietary**, adj.

differ v. **1.** to be unlike or dissimilar; to be distinct in nature or qualities (from). **2.** to disagree in opinion, belief, etc. (with or from).

Don't confuse this with **defer**, which means to put something off until a later time or to give way in judgement.

difference n. **1.** the state or relation of being different; dissimilarity. **2.** a significant change in or effect upon a situation. **3.** a disagreement in opinion; dispute; quarrel. **4.** Maths the amount by which one quantity is greater or less than another.

different adj. **1.** differing in character; having unlike qualities. **2.** separate or distinct: a different country. **3.** various; several. **4.** unusual; not ordinary.

You will hear **different** followed by from, to and than. **Different from** is traditionally considered the most correct (These two plates are different from the others), but **different to** is also perfectly acceptable (Your bag is different to mine). **Different than** is used quite a lot in speech, but many people still regard it as incorrect (He is different than the rest of his family).

differential adj. **1.** constituting a difference; distinctive. –n. **2.** Machinery a set of gears in a motor car which permit the driving wheels to revolve at different speeds when the car is turning.

differentiate v. **1.** to mark off by differences; distinguish. **2.** Maths to obtain the derivative of. **3.** to make a distinction; discriminate.

For def. 1, the more usual expression is **tell the difference**.

difficult adj. **1.** hard to do, perform, or accomplish; requiring much effort. **2.** hard to deal with or get on with. –**difficulty**, n.

diffident adj. lacking confidence; timid. –**diffidence**, n.

The more usual word is **shy**.

diffraction *n.* the breaking up of light. –**diffract**, *v.*

diffuse *v.* /dəˈfjuːz/ **1.** to spread or scatter widely or thinly. –*adj.* /dəˈfjuːs/ **2.** widely spread or scattered. –**diffusion**, *n.*

The more usual expression is **spread out**.

dig *v.* (**dug**, **digging**) **1.** to break up and turn over, or penetrate and loosen (the ground). **2.** to make (a hole, tunnel, etc.) by removing material. **3.** to obtain or remove by digging (*up* or *out*). –*n.* **4.** thrust; poke. **5.** a cutting, sarcastic remark. **6.** an archaeological site undergoing excavation. **7.** (*pl.*) lodgings.

digest *v.* /dəˈdʒɛst, daɪ-/ **1.** to prepare (food) in the alimentary canal for assimilation into the system. **2.** to assimilate mentally. –*n.* /ˈdaɪdʒɛst/ **3.** a collection or summary, especially of literary, historical, legal, or scientific matter. –**digestion**, *n.*

digger *n.* **1.** a miner, especially a gold-miner. **2.** *Informal* an Aust. soldier.

diggings *pl. n.* a mining operation or locality.

digit *n.* **1.** a finger or toe. **2.** any of the figures 0, 1, … 9.

digital *adj.* **1.** *Electronics* of or relating to units of information that exist in two states only, on and off; binary. **2.** of or relating to a device which displays information in the form of digits, as a digital watch or a digital tuner. **3.** of or relating to an electronic device, such as a smartphone, tablet, etc., which processes digital data. –**digitally**, *adv.*

Compare this with **analog**.

digitise *v.* *Computers* to convert (information) into digital form, so that it can be processed by a computer. Also, **digitize**.

dignitary *n.* (*pl.* **-ries**) someone who holds a high rank or office, especially in the church.

dignity *n.* **1.** nobility of manner or style; stateliness; gravity. **2.** nobleness or elevation of mind; worthiness. –**dignify**, *v.*

digress /daɪˈɡrɛs/ *v.* to deviate or wander away from the main purpose. –**digression**, *n.*

dike[1] *n.* → **dyke**[1].

dike[2] *n.* → **dyke**[2].

dilapidated *adj.* reduced to, or fallen into, ruin or decay.

dilate *v.* to make wider or larger. –**dilation**, *n.*

dilatory /ˈdɪlətri, -təri/ *adj.* inclined to delay or procrastinate; slow.

dilemma *n.* a situation requiring a choice between equally undesirable alternatives.

diligent /ˈdɪlədʒənt/ *adj.* careful and persistent in one's work or efforts: *a diligent student.* –**diligence**, *n.*

The more usual word is **hardworking**.

dill[1] *n.* a herb of the parsley family, with aromatic seeds and finely divided leaves used as a flavouring in cooking.

dill[2] *n.* *Informal* a fool.

dillybag *n.* *Aust.* a small bag.

dilute *v.* **1.** to make thinner or weaker by the addition of water or the like. –*adj.* **2.** reduced in strength. –**dilution**, *n.*

dim *adj.* (**dimmer**, **dimmest**) **1.** not bright or strong. –*v.* (**dimmed**, **dimming**) **2.** to make or become dim.

dimension *n.* **1.** magnitude measured in a particular direction. **2.** an aspect; appearance.

diminish *v.* to make, or cause to seem, smaller; lessen; reduce. –**diminution**, *n.*

diminutive *adj.* **1.** small; little; tiny. –*n.* **2.** *Gram.* a word which tells you something is small: '*Booklet*' is the diminutive of '*book*'.

dimple *n.* a small natural hollow, especially in the cheek.

din *n.* a loud, confused noise.

dine *v.* to eat the principal meal of the day; have dinner.

ding v. 1. to sound, as a bell; ring, especially with wearisome continuance. -n. 2. a blow or stroke. 3. the sound of a bell or the like. 4. *Aust., NZ Informal* a minor accident involving a car, etc.

dinghy /'dɪŋgi, 'dɪŋi/ n. (pl. **-ghies**) a small rowing or sailing boat.

dingo n. (pl. **-goes** or **-gos**) a wild dog, often tawny-yellow in colour, with erect ears, a bushy tail, and with a call resembling a howl or yelp rather than a bark, found throughout mainland Aust.

dingy /'dɪndʒi/ adj. (**-gier, -giest**) of a dark, dull, or dirty colour or aspect.

dinkum *Aust., NZ Informal* -adj. Also, **dinky-di** 1. true; honest; genuine. -adv. 2. truly. See **fair dinkum**.

dinner n. the main meal, taken either before noon or in the evening.

dinosaur n. an extinct reptile of gigantic size.

dint phr. **by dint of**, by means of: *by dint of argument*.

diocese /'daɪəsəs/ n. (pl. **dioceses** /'daɪəsiːz/) the district, with its population, falling under the care of a bishop.

dip v. (**dipped, dipping**) 1. to plunge temporarily or quickly into a liquid. 2. to lower and raise. 3. to sink or drop down, as if plunging into water. 4. to incline or slope downwards. -n. 5. the act of dipping; a plunge into water, etc. 6. a liquid in which something is dipped. 7. a lowering momentarily; a sinking down. 8. downward extension, inclination, or slope. 9. a hollow or depression in the land. 10. a soft savoury mixture into which biscuits, etc., are dipped before being eaten.

diphtheria /dɪf'θɪəriə/ n. an infectious disease marked by the growth of a false membrane in the air passages.

diphthong /'dɪfθɒŋ/ n. *Phonetics* a speech sound made by the tongue gliding from one vowel to another in the same syllable, as *ei* in *vein*.

diploma n. a document stating one's success in an examination, etc.

diplomacy n. 1. the conduct by government officials of negotiations and other relations between states. 2. skill in managing any negotiations. -**diplomat**, n. -**diplomatic**, adj.

dipsomaniac n. someone who suffers from an irresistible craving for intoxicants.

dire v. (**direr, direst**) causing or attended with great fear or suffering; dreadful; awful.

direct v. 1. to guide. 2. to give authoritative instructions to; command. 3. to organise and supervise the artistic production of a play or film. -adj. 4. proceeding in a straight line or by the shortest course. 5. without intervening agency; personal. 6. going straight to the point; straightforward; downright. -adv. 7. in a direct manner; straight. -**director**, n.

direction n. 1. the act of directing, pointing, aiming, etc. 2. the line along which anything lies, faces, moves, etc., with reference to the point or region towards which it is directed. 3. management.

directive n. an authoritative instruction or direction.

The more usual word is **order**.

directly adv. 1. in a direct line, way, or manner; straight. 2. without delay; immediately. 3. presently; soon.

directorate n. 1. the office of a director. 2. a body of directors.

directory v. (pl. **-ries**) 1. a book or the like containing names, addresses, telephone numbers, etc. 2. Also, (*in some operating systems*), **folder**. *Computers* a defined area on a computer disk used to store files.

dirge n. a funeral song or tune.

dirt n. 1. earth or soil, especially when loose. 2. any foul or filthy substance, as excrement, mud, etc. 3. unsavoury or malicious gossip.

dirt bike n. a motorbike designed for cross-country conditions, often of especially light construction. Also, **dirtbike**, **trail bike**.

dirty adj. (**-tier**, **-tiest**) **1.** soiled with dirt; foul. **2.** morally unclean; indecent. **3.** stormy or squally, as the weather. **4.** Aust. Informal angry. –v. (**-tied**, **-tying**) **5.** to make or become dirty.

disability n. (pl. **-ties**) lack of some physical or mental ability.

> Don't confuse this with **inability**, which is the lack of ability to do something: an inability to swim.

disable v. **1.** to weaken or destroy the capability of; incapacitate. **2.** to make legally incapable; disqualify.

disabled adj. lacking a physical or mental ability, especially because of an illness or injury.

> Note that, although **disabled** is very commonly used, there are some people who don't like the negative nature of the word (dis- means not).

disadvantage n. **1.** an unfavourable circumstance or condition. –v. **2.** to subject to disadvantage.

disagree v. **1.** to fail to agree; differ (with). **2.** to differ in opinion; dissent. –**disagreement**, n.

disagreeable adj. unpleasant.

disallow v. to refuse to admit the truth or validity of.

disappear v. **1.** to cease to appear or be seen; vanish from sight. **2.** to cease to exist or be known; end gradually. –**disappearance**, n.

disappoint v. **1.** to fail to fulfil the expectations or wishes of (a person). **2.** to defeat the fulfilment of (hopes, plans, etc.); thwart. –**disappointment**, n.

disapprove v. to have an unfavourable opinion (of). –**disapproval**, n.

disarm v. **1.** to deprive of weapons. **2.** to divest of hostility, suspicion, etc.; make friendly. **3.** to take out of a state of readiness for any specific purpose or effective

use: to disarm the cabin doors. –**disarming**, adj. –**disarmingly**, adv.

disarray n. disorder; confusion.

disassociate v. → **dissociate**. –**disassociation**, n. –**disassociative**, adj.

disaster n. any unfortunate event, especially a sudden or great misfortune. –**disastrous**, adj.

disavow v. to disclaim knowledge of connection with, or responsibility for; disown.

disband v. to break up or disorganise (a band or company).

disburse v. to pay out (money); expend.

disc n. **1.** any thin, flat, circular plate or object. **2.** a round, flat area. **3.** a compact disc. **4.** Computers: a disk.

> Note that this word is spelt **disk** when you are talking about computers, so you would write floppy disk and hard disk. However compact discs are spelt with c, even though there is some overlap with computers.

discard v. /dɪsˈkad/ **1.** to cast aside; reject; dismiss, especially from use. **2.** Cards: to throw out (a card or cards) from one's hand. –n. /ˈdɪskad/ **3.** someone or something that is cast out or rejected.

discern v. **1.** to perceive by the sight or some other sense or by the intellect. **2.** to distinguish: to discern good from bad. –**discernment**, n.

> For def. 1, the more usual word is **see**; for def. 2, **tell**.

discharge v. /dɪsˈtʃadʒ/ (**-charged**, **-charging**) **1.** to relieve of a charge or load. **2.** to fulfil or perform. **3.** to dismiss from service. –n. /ˈdɪstʃadʒ/ **4.** the act of discharging a ship, load, etc. **5.** a sending or coming forth; ejection; emission. **6.** a relieving or a getting rid, of something or the nature of a charge.

disciple n. an adherent of the doctrines of another.

discipline n. **1.** training to act in accordance with rules. **2.** punishment inflicted by way of correction and training. **3.** the training effect of experience, adversity, etc. **4.** a branch of instruction or learning. *–v.* (**-plined, -plining**) **5.** to bring to a state of order and obedience by training and control.

disc jockey *n.* → **DJ**.

disclaim *v.* to repudiate or deny interest in or connection with; disavow.

disclose *v.* **1.** to cause to appear; allow to be seen; make known. **2.** to uncover.

The more usual word is **reveal**.

disco *n.* (*pl.* **-cos**) a place of public entertainment or a club in which patrons may dance, especially to recorded music.

discolour *v.* to change or spoil the colour of. Also, **discolor**.

discomfiture *n.* **1.** frustration of hopes or plans. **2.** confusion.

discomfort *n.* absence of comfort or pleasure; uneasiness; pain.

disconcert /dɪskən'sɜt/ *v.* to make (someone) feel embarrassed, uncertain or anxious.

disconnect *v.* to separate or to break the connection of or between: *to disconnect a hose; to disconnect the telephone.* –**disconnected**, *adj.* –**disconnection**, *n.*

disconsolate *adj.* without consolation or solace; unhappy.

discontinue *v.* to cause to finish or to come to an end. –**discontinuation**, *n.*

discord *n.* lack of harmony. –**discordant**, *adj.*

discotheque /'dɪskətɛk/ *n.* → **disco**.

discount /'dɪskaʊnt/ *for def. 1,* /dɪs'kaʊnt/ *for def. 2, v.,* /'dɪskaʊnt/ *for defs 3 and 4, n.* *–v.* **1.** to deduct. **2.** to leave out of account; disregard. *–n.* **3.** the act of discounting. **4.** amount deducted. *–phr.* **5. at a discount,** below usual retail price.

discourage *v.* **1.** to cause to lose spirit or courage; dishearten. **2.** to dissuade.

discourse *n.* communication of thought by words; conversation.

discover *v.* to learn of, or find out; gain sight or knowledge of (something previously unseen or unknown). –**discovery**, *n.*

discredit *v.* to injure the credit or reputation of.

discreet *adj.* **1.** wise or judicious in avoiding mistakes or faults. **2.** not given to careless talk.

Don't confuse this with **discrete**, which describes something which is separate from other things.

discrepancy *n.* (*pl.* **-cies**) an instance of difference or inconsistency.

discrete *adj.* detached from others; distinct.

The more usual word is **separate**.
Don't confuse **discrete** with **discreet**, which describes someone who is careful in their behaviour and about what they say.

discretion *n.* **1.** freedom of judgement or choice. **2.** the quality of being discreet. –**discretionary**, *adj.*

discriminate *v.* **1.** to make a distinction, as in favour of or against a person or thing. **2.** to note or observe a difference; distinguish accurately. –**discrimination**, *n.*

discursive *adj.* passing irregularly from one subject to another; rambling.

discus *n.* (*pl.* **-ses** *or* **disci** /'dɪskaɪ/) a disc, usually made of wood rimmed with metal, thrown by athletes.

discuss *v.* to talk over or examine by argument, often in order to reach a decision; debate.

discussion *n.* **1.** the act of discussing; critical examination by argument; debate. **2.** a written or spoken text type or form which offers a balanced presentation of different points of view on an issue.

disdain *n.* a feeling of contempt for anything regarded as unworthy; haughty contempt.

disease *n.* a sickness which can affect a part or all of any living thing. –**diseased**, *adj.*

Don't confuse **diseased** with **deceased**, which means dead.

disembark v. to leave a ship, plane, etc., as after a journey; land.

disembowel v. (**-elled** or, Chiefly US, **-eled**, **-elling** or, Chiefly US, **-eling**) to remove the bowels or entrails from.

disfigure v. to mar the figure, appearance, or beauty of.

disgorge v. (**-gorged**, **-gorging**) to throw up (as) from the throat; vomit.

disgrace n. **1.** the state of being in dishonour. **2.** the state of being out of favour. –v. **3.** to bring or reflect shame or reproach upon. –**disgraceful**, adj.

disgruntled adj. mildly upset; discontented.

disguise v. **1.** to conceal the identity of –n. **2.** that which disguises.

disgust v. **1.** to cause nausea or loathing in. –n. **2.** strong distaste; loathing.

dish n. **1.** an open, more or less shallow container of pottery, glass, metal, wood, etc., used for various purposes, especially for holding or serving food. **2.** a particular article or preparation of food.

dishevelled /dɪˈʃɛvəld/ adj. untidy.

dishonest adj. not honest; disposed to lie, cheat, or steal. –**dishonesty**, n.

dishonour n. **1.** lack of honour; dishonourable character or conduct. **2.** disgrace; ignominy. –v. **3.** to bring reproach or shame on. **4.** to refuse or fail to pay (a cheque, etc.). Also, **dishonor**. –**dishonourable**, adj.

disillusion v. to free from illusion; disenchant.

disinfectant n. any chemical agent that destroys bacteria. –**disinfect**, v.

disinherit v. to deprive of the right to inherit. –**disinheritance**, n.

disintegrate v. to fall apart; break up. –**disintegration**, n.

disinterested adj. **1.** unbiased by personal involvement or advantage. **2.** not interested; indifferent.

Note that some people think that def. 2 is wrong and that only the word **uninterested** can have this meaning. However, it is becoming quite common to use **disinterested** in this way.

disjointed adj. disconnected; incoherent.

disk n. a storage unit for computers consisting of a rapidly spinning magnetic disc on which information is recorded by magnetising the surface. Also, **disc**.

Note that if you were talking about a thin, flat, circular object not connected with computers, you would spell it **disc**: *Our dog wears a metal disc on her collar with her name engraved on it.*

dislike **1.** to regard with displeasure or aversion. –n. **2.** displeasure or aversion felt towards someone or something.

dislocate v. **1.** to displace. **2.** to put out of joint. –**dislocation**, n.

dislodge v. (**-lodged**, **-lodging**) to remove or drive from a place of rest or lodgement.

disloyal adj. not loyal.

dismal adj. **1.** gloomy; dreary. **2.** terrible; dreadful.

dismantle v. to pull down; take apart; take to pieces.

dismay v. **1.** to dishearten utterly; daunt. –n. **2.** consternation.

dismember v. **1.** to deprive of limbs. **2.** to separate into parts.

dismiss v. **1.** to bid or allow (a person) to go; give permission to depart. **2.** to discharge or remove, as from office or service. **3.** to put off or away; to put aside from consideration. **4.** Law to put out of court, as a complaint or appeal. –**dismissal**, n.

disobey v. to neglect or refuse to obey (an order, person, etc.). –**disobedient**, adj.

disorder n. **1.** lack of order or regular arrangement; confusion. **2.** a derangement of physical or mental health or functions. **–disorderly,** *adj.*

disorganise *v.* to destroy the organisation of. Also, **disorganize.**

disorganised *adj.* **1.** in a state of confusion or disorder. **2.** prone to disorder: *a disorganised person.* Also, **disorganized.**

disorientate *v.* **1.** to confuse as to direction. **2.** to perplex; to confuse. Also, **disorient. –disorientation,** *n.*

disown *v.* to deny the ownership of or responsibility for; renounce.

disparage *v.* to speak of or treat in a critical way.

> The more usual word is **belittle.**

disparate /ˈdɪspərət/ *adj.* essentially different; dissimilar. **–disparity,** *n.*

dispassionate *adj.* free from or unaffected by passion; devoid of personal feeling or bias.

dispatch *v.* **1.** to send off; put under way. **–***n.* **2.** the sending off of a messenger, letter, etc., to a destination. **3.** prompt or speedy transaction, as of business. **4.** a written message sent in haste.

dispel *v.* **(-pelled, -pelling)** to drive off or scatter.

> The more usual expression is **get rid of.**

dispensable *adj.* that may be dispensed with or done without.

dispensary *n.* *(pl.* **-ries)** a place where something is dispensed, especially medicines.

dispensation *n.* **1.** the act of dispensing. **2.** *Roman Catholic Church* the relaxation of a law in a specific case.

dispense *v.* **1.** to deal out; distribute. **2.** to administer (laws, etc.). **–***phr.* **3. dispense with, a.** to do without; forgo. **b.** to grant exemption from (a law, promise, etc.).

disperse *v.* to scatter.

displace *v.* to put out of the usual or proper place.

display *v.* **1.** to show; exhibit. **2.** to reveal; betray. **3.** to show ostentatiously. **–***n.* **4.** the act of displaying; exhibition. **5.** the thing(s) displayed.

displease *v.* to annoy.

dispose *v.* **1.** to put in a particular or the proper order or arrangement. **2.** to incline. **–***phr.* **3. dispose of,** to deal with definitely; get rid of.

disposition *n.* **1.** mental or moral constitution; character. **2.** arrangement.

dispossess *v.* to put (a person) out of possession, especially of real property; oust.

disprove *v.* to prove to be false or wrong. **–disproval,** *n.*

dispute *v.* **1.** to engage in argument or discussion. **2.** to argue or debate about. **–***n.* **3.** argumentation; strong difference of opinion or desires; a quarrel.

disqualify *v.* **(-fied, -fying)** to render unfit or ineligible.

disquiet *v.* **1.** to disturb; make uneasy. **–***n.* **2.** unrest; uneasiness.

disregard *v.* **1.** to pay no attention to; leave out of consideration. **–***n.* **2.** lack of regard or attention.

disrepair *n.* the state of being out of repair; impaired condition.

disrepute *n.* ill repute; loss of good reputation. **–disreputable,** *adj.*

> Note that you usually use this word in the phrases **in disrepute** or **into disrepute.**

disrespect *n.* lack of respect.

disrupt *v.* to break or rend asunder. **–disruption,** *n.* **–disruptive,** *adj.*

dissect *v.* **1.** to cut apart (an animal body, plant, etc.) to examine it. **2.** to examine minutely part by part.

dissemble *v.* **1.** to conceal the real nature of. **2.** to speak or act hypocritically.

disseminate *v.* to scatter, or spread.

dissent *v.* **1.** to disagree. **–***n.* **2.** difference in sentiment or opinion. **–dissension,** *n.*

dissertation *n.* a written essay, treatise, or thesis.

disservice *n.* harm; injury; an ill turn.

dissident *n.* someone who differs; a dissenter, especially against a particular political system.

dissimulation *n.* a false appearance; the disguising of one's real feelings or motives.

dissipate *v.* 1. to scatter in various directions; disperse. 2. to scatter wastefully; squander.

dissociate *v.* to sever the association of; separate. Also, **disassociate**. **–dissociation**, *n.*

dissolute *adj.* given to immoral behaviour.

dissolution *n.* the undoing or breaking up of a tie, bond, union, etc.

dissolve *v.* 1. to make a solution of in a solvent. 2. to break up (an assembly or organisation); dismiss. 3. to bring to an end; destroy; dispel. 4. *Law* to deprive of force; annul. 5. to become dissolved, as in a solvent. 6. to disappear gradually.

dissonance *n.* 1. discord, harsh sound. 2. disagreement.

dissuade *v.* to persuade (someone) not to do something.

distance *n.* 1. the extent of space intervening between things or points. 2. remoteness. 3. reserve or aloofness.

distant *adj.* 1. far off or apart in space; not near; remote. 2. far apart in any respect. 3. reserved; not familiar or cordial.

distaste *n.* dislike; disinclination.

distemper¹ *n.* an infectious disease of animals, especially young dogs.

distemper² *n.* a water paint used for the decoration of interior walls and ceilings.

distend *v.* to swell.

distil *v.* (-tilled, -tilling) 1. to subject to a process of vaporisation and subsequent condensation, as for purification or concentration. 2. to fall in drops; trickle; exude. Also, **distill**. **–distillery**, *n.* **–distillation**, *n.*

distinct *adj.* 1. (fol. by *from* or used absolutely) distinguished as not being the same; separate. 2. clear to the senses or intellect; definite.

distinction *n.* 1. a marking off or distinguishing as different. 2. a discrimination made between things as different. 3. a distinguishing characteristic. 4. a mark of special favour. 5. marked superiority; eminence. **–distinctive**, *adj.*

distinguish *v.* 1. to mark off as different (*from*). 2. to recognise as distinct or different; discriminate. 3. to perceive clearly by sight or other sense; discern. 4. to be a distinctive characteristic of; characterise. 5. to make prominent, conspicuous, or eminent. 6. to indicate or show a difference (*between*). 7. to recognise or note differences.

distinguished *adj.* important and famous.

distort *v.* 1. to twist awry or out of shape; make crooked or deformed. 2. to pervert; misrepresent. **–distortion**, *n.*

distract *v.* 1. to draw away or divert, as the mind or attention. 2. to entertain; amuse; divert. **–distraction**, *n.*

distraught *adj.* 1. distracted; deeply agitated. 2. crazed.

distress *n.* great pain, anxiety, or sorrow; acute suffering; trouble.

distressed *adj.* 1. in a troubled emotional state; upset. 2. (of wood) artificially weathered so as to create an aged appearance. 3. (of furniture) built using distressed wood.

distribute *v.* 1. to give out: *to distribute pamphlets.* 2. to divide and give out in shares: *to distribute the profits among the staff.* 3. to scatter or spread: *to distribute manure evenly over the garden.* **–distribution**, *n.* **–distributor**, *n.*

district *n.* a region or locality.

disturb *v.* 1. to interfere with; interrupt. 2. to throw into commotion or disorder; agitate. 3. to perplex; trouble. **–disturbance**, *n.*

disuse *n.* discontinuance of use.

ditch *n.* **1.** a long, narrow hollow in the earth, especially made by digging, for draining or irrigating land. –*v.* **2.** *Informal* to get rid of; get away from.

dither *v.* to be vacillating or uncertain.

ditto *n.* the same (used in lists, etc., to avoid repetition). *Symbol:* "

ditty *n.* (*pl.* **-ties**) a simple song.

ditzy *adj. Informal* flighty; empty-headed; scatterbrained. Also, **ditsy**.

diurnal /daɪ'ɜnəl/ *adj.* **1.** daily. **2.** of or belonging to the daytime.

divan /dɑ'væn/ *n.* a low bed.

dive *v.* (**dived** *or, Chiefly US,* **dove, diving**) **1.** to plunge, especially head first, as into water. **2.** to go below the surface of the water, as a submarine, scuba diver, etc. **3.** to dart. –*n.* **4.** the act of diving. **5.** an instance of diving. **6.** *Informal* a disreputable place, as for gambling, etc. –**diver,** *n.* –**diving,** *v.*

diverge *v.* to move or lie in different directions from a common point; branch off. –**divergence,** *n.* –**divergent,** *adj.*

diverse *adj.* different; varied. –**diversity,** *n.* –**diversify,** *v.*

divert *v.* **1.** to turn aside or from a path or course. **2.** to draw off to a different object, purpose, etc. **3.** to distract from serious occupation; entertain or amuse. –**diversion,** *n.*

divest *phr.* **1. divest oneself of,** to take off (clothing): *She divested herself of the thick jumper.* **2. divest someone of,** to take away from someone: *The new laws divested the police of much of their power.*

divide *v.* **1.** to separate. **2.** to deal out in parts; apportion; share. **3.** *Maths* to separate into equal parts by the process of division. **4.** to become divided or separated. **5.** to share something with others. –**divisible,** *adj.*

dividend *n.* **1.** *Maths* a number to be divided by another number: *In the sum 15 ÷ 3, the dividend is 15.* **2.** *Finance* **a.** a sum of money paid to shareholders of a company or trading concern out of earnings. **b.** interest payable on public funds. **3.** a payment to creditors and shareholders in a liquidated company. **4.** a share of anything divided.

> Compare def. 1 with **divisor**, which is the number by which you divide another number, and with **quotient**, which is the number you get as the result of the division.

divine *adj.* **1.** of or relating to a god. –*v.* **2.** to discover (water, metal, etc.), by magical means. **3.** to prophesy, know the future.

divinity *n.* **1.** the quality of being divine; divine nature. **2.** the science of divine things; theology.

division *n.* **1.** the act of dividing; partition. **2.** the state of being divided. **3.** *Maths* the operation inverse to multiplication; the finding of a quantity (the quotient) which, when multiplied by a given quantity (the divisor), gives another number (the dividend). *Symbol:* ÷. **4.** one of the parts into which a thing is divided.

divisive /dɑ'vaɪsɪv, -'vɪzɪv/ *adj.* creating division or discord.

divisor *n. Maths* a number by which another number is divided: *In the sum 15 ÷ 3, the divisor is 3.*

> Compare this with **dividend,** which is the number to be divided by another number, and with **quotient,** which is the number you get as the result of the division.

divorce *n.* the dissolution of the marriage contract.

divulge *v.* (**-vulged, -vulging**) to disclose or reveal: *to divulge information.*

dizzy *adj.* (**-zier, -ziest**) **1.** affected with a sensation of whirling, with tendency to fall; giddy. **2.** *Informal* foolish or stupid.

DJ *n.* someone who plays and announces recorded music, as on a radio program, at a dance, etc. Also, **deejay.**

This is short for **disc jockey**.

DNA n. deoxyribonucleic acid; a molecule found in cells and responsible for passing on genetic characteristics.

DNA fingerprinting n. → **genetic fingerprinting**.

do v. **1.** to perform (acts, duty, penance, a part, etc.). **2.** to be the cause of (good, harm, credit, etc.); bring about. **3.** to render (homage, justice, etc.). **4.** to serve (a period of time) in a prison. **5.** to make. **6.** to study. **7.** to get along or fare (*well* or *badly*); manage (*with, without,* etc.). **8.** to serve or be satisfactory, as for the purpose; suffice; be enough. –v. (*aux.*) **9.** (used without special meaning in interrogative, negative, and inverted constructions): *Do you swim every day?* **10.** (used to lend emphasis to a principal verb): *I do mean what I say.* –n. **11.** *Informal* a festivity or treat.

Usage: The different forms of the verb **to do** are as follows:
Present tense: I **do**, you **do**, he/she/it **does**, we **do**, they **do**
Past tense: I, you, he/she/it, we, they **did**
Past participle: **done**
Present participle: **doing**

dob *Aust., NZ Informal* –v. (**dobbed, dobbing**) **1.** to report another's misdemeanour: *Please don't dob.* –phr. **2. dob in,** to betray or report (someone), as for a misdemeanour: *He dobbed me in when I broke the window.*

docile adj. easily managed or handled.

dock¹ n. **1.** a wharf. **2.** the space or waterway between 2 wharves, as for receiving a ship while in port. **3.** a semi-enclosed structure which a plane, truck, etc., can enter for loading, repair, etc.

dock² n. **1.** the solid or fleshy part of an animal's tail. **2.** the part of a tail left after cutting or clipping. –v. **3.** to cut off the end of (a tail, etc.). **4.** to deduct a part from (wages, etc.).

dock³ n. an enclosed place in a courtroom where the accused is placed during trial.

docket n. a receipt.

doctor n. **1.** a person licensed to practise medicine. **2.** a person who has received a doctorate.

doctorate n. the highest academic degree awarded in any branch of knowledge. –**doctoral,** adj.

doctrine n. a body or system of teachings relating to a particular subject.

document n. /ˈdɒkjəmənt/ **1.** a written or printed paper, or a file on a computer, containing information. **2.** *Computers* a file produced by an application, especially a text-based file produced by word processing software. –v. /ˈdɒkjuˌment/ **3.** to furnish with documents, evidence, or the like. **4.** to record, give an account of: *an attempt to document the period.* –**documentation,** n.

documentary adj. **1.** relating to, consisting of, or derived from documents. –n. (pl. **-ries**) **2.** a factual television or radio program, film, etc.

dodge v. (**dodged, dodging**) **1.** to move aside or change position suddenly, as to avoid a blow or to get behind something. **2.** to use evasive methods. **3.** to elude by a sudden shift of position or by strategy.

dodo n. (pl. **-does** or **-dos**) **1.** an extinct, large, ground-dwelling bird. –phr. **2. dead as a dodo,** *Colloq.* completely lifeless or inactive.

doe n. the female of the deer, antelope, and certain other animals.

The male of these animals is usually called a **buck**.

does v. 3rd person singular present indicative of **do**.

doff v. to remove (the hat) in salutation.

dog n. **1.** a domesticated four-legged carnivorous mammal, bred in a great many varieties. **2.** the male of this type of animal. **3.** any animal belonging to the same family, including the dingo, wolf, jackal, fox, etc. –v. (**dogged**, **dogging**) **4.** to follow or track constantly like a dog; hound; worry; plague. –*phr.* **5. the black dog**, (in figurative use) clinical depression.

Note that a female dog is sometimes called a **bitch**.

dogged /ˈdɒɡəd/ *adj.* not giving in easily; determined; obstinate. –**doggedly**, *adv.*

doggerel *n.* comic verse, usually poor in quality.

dogma *n.* (*pl.* **-mas** or **-mata** /-məta/) **1.** a system of principles or tenets, as of a church. **2.** prescribed doctrine.

dogmatic *adj.* **1.** of, relating to, or of the nature of a dogma or dogmas. **2.** asserting opinions in an authoritative, positive, or arrogant manner.

doily *n.* (*pl.* **-lies**) a small ornamental mat, as of embroidery or lace.

doldrums *pl. n.* **the**, **1.** the region of relatively calm winds near the equator. **2. a.** a period of dullness, gloominess, etc. **b.** a period of stagnation or inactivity.

dole *n.* **1.** a payment by a government to an unemployed person. –*v.* (**doled**, **doling**) **2.** to give (*out*) sparingly or in small quantities.

doleful *adj.* full of grief; sorrowful; gloomy.

doll *n.* Also, **dolly**. **1.** a toy representing a child or other human being. –*phr.* **2. doll up**, to dress (oneself) rather too smartly or too much.

dollar *n.* **1.** the monetary unit of Aust., equal to 100 cents. *Symbol:* **$ 2.** any of various units elsewhere, as in the US, Canada, etc.

dolly *n.* (*pl.* **-lies**) **1.** (*with children*) a doll. **2.** a low truck or platform with small wheels for moving loads.

dolphin *n.* any of various cetaceans, some of which are commonly called porpoises.

domain *n.* **1.** an estate; any land held in possession. **2.** a field of action, thought, etc. **3.** a region with specific characteristics, types of growth, animal life, etc.

domain name *n. Computers* the name of a server connected to the internet.

dome *n. Archit.* a large, hemispherical roof.

domestic *adj.* **1.** of or relating to the home, the household, or household affairs. **2.** living with humans; tame. **3.** belonging, produced, or existing within a country; not foreign. –**domesticate**, *v.* –**domesticity**, *n.*

domicile *n.* a place of residence; a house or home.

dominate *v.* **1.** to rule (over); govern; control. **2.** to tower above; overshadow. –**dominant**, *adj.* –**domination**, *n.*

domineer *v.* to govern arbitrarily; tyrannise.

dominion *n.* **1.** the power or right of governing and controlling. **2.** a territory, usually of considerable size, in which a single rulership holds sway.

domino *n.* (*pl.* **-noes**) **1.** (*pl.*) various games played with flat, oblong pieces, the face of which is divided into 2 parts, each either left blank or marked with pips, usually from 1 to 6. **2.** one of these pieces.

Note that def. 1 is used as a singular noun: *Dominoes is my favourite game.*

domino effect *n.* an effect whereby one event or action triggers a chain reaction of consequential or similar events or actions.

don *v.* (**donned**, **donning**) to put on (clothing, etc.).

donate *v.* to present as a gift, especially to a fund or cause. –**donation**, *n.* –**donor**, *n.*

done *v.* past participle of **do**.

doner kebab *n.* a dish of cooked meat and salad rolled up in a piece of flat bread.

donkey *n.* (*pl.* **-keys**) a domesticated ass used as a beast of burden.

donut *n.* → **doughnut**.

doodle *v.* to scribble idly.

doof *n.* a type of popular electronic dance music characterised by a heavy beat.

doom *n.* **1.** fate or destiny, especially adverse fate. –*v.* **2.** to destine, especially to an adverse fate. **3.** to pronounce judgement against.

doona *n. Aust. (from trademark)* a quilted bedcover, filled with down, or synthetic padding, and often used instead of top sheets and blankets; continental quilt.

door *n.* **1.** a movable barrier of wood, etc., commonly turning on hinges or sliding in a groove, for closing and opening a passage or opening, etc. **2.** Also, **doorway.** the entrance to a room or building. **3.** the house or building to which a door belongs: *She lives two doors down the street.*

dopamine /'doʊpəmɪn/ *n.* a hormone-like substance, present in the brain where it functions as a neurotransmitter; an imbalance in dopamine activity can cause central nervous system disorders such as Parkinson's disease and schizophrenia.

dope *n.* **1.** any drug, especially marijuana. **2.** information or data. **3.** a stupid person. *–v.* **4.** *Informal* to affect with dope or drugs. **5.** to take performance-enhancing drugs.

dormant *adj.* lying asleep; inactive as in sleep.

dormitory *n. (pl.* **-ries)** a (large) room for sleeping, for the residents of a school or other institution.

Dorothy Dixer /ˌdɒrəθi 'dɪksə/ *n. Informal* a question asked in parliament specifically to allow a minister to reply with political propaganda.

dorsal *adj. Zool.* of, relating to, or situated on the back.

dosage *n.* **1.** the administration of medicine in doses. **2.** the amount of medicine to be given.

dose *n.* a quantity of medicine prescribed to be taken at one time.

doss *v. Informal* to make a temporary sleeping place for oneself.

dossier *n.* a bundle of documents on the same subject, especially information about a particular person.

dot *n.* **1.** a small spot on a surface. **2.** a small, roundish mark made with or as with a pen. **3.** anything relatively small or speck-like. **4. a.** a full stop. **b.** a decimal point. **c.** the keyboard symbol (.), especially as used in domain names. *–v.* **(dotted, dotting) 5.** to mark with or as with a dot or dots.

dot art *n.* a style of Aboriginal art in which ochre or other pigment is applied as a series of dots to build up a composite picture.

dotcom *n.* **1.** a company trading over the internet. **2.** a company involved in the information technology industry. *–adj.* **3.** of or relating to a dotcom. **4.** (of a company) trading over the internet. Also, **dot com, dot‑com, dot.com.**

dote *v.* **1.** to bestow excessive love or fondness (*on* or *upon*). **2.** to be weak-minded, especially from old age. **–dotage,** *n.*

dotty *adj.* **(-tier, -tiest)** *Informal* crazy; eccentric.

double *adj.* **1.** twice as great, heavy, strong, etc. **2.** twofold in form, size, amount, extent, etc. **3.** composed of 2 like parts or members; paired. **4.** a twofold size or amount. **5.** a duplicate; a counterpart. **6.** *Film, etc.* a substitute actor who takes another's place, as in dangerous scenes. **7.** (*pl.*) a game in which there are 2 players on each side. *–v.* **8.** to make or become double or twice as great. **9.** to bend or fold with one part upon another (*over, up, back,* etc.). **10.** *Aust., NZ* to convey a second person on a horse, bicycle or motorcycle. **11.** to turn (*back*) on a course. **12.** to serve in 2 capacities. *–adv.* **13.** twofold; doubly.

double bass *n.* the largest instrument of the violin family.

doublecross *Informal –v.* **1.** to prove treacherous to; betray. *–n.* **2.** such a betrayal.

double take *n.* a second look, given to a person, event, etc., whose significance is suddenly understood.

doubt v. **1.** to be uncertain in opinion about. **2.** to distrust. **3.** to feel uncertainty as to something. –n. **4.** undecidedness of opinion or belief; a feeling of uncertainty. **5.** distrust; suspicion.

Note that the verb **doubt** can be followed by various words: *I doubt that you will get there on time; I doubt if you will get there on time; I doubt whether you will get there on time; I doubt you will get there on time.*

doubtful adj. **1.** admitting of or causing doubt; uncertain. **2.** undecided in opinion or belief; hesitating.

douche /duʃ/ n. a jet or current of water applied to a body part, organ, or cavity for medicinal, hygienic, or contraceptive purposes.

dough n. **1.** flour or meal combined with water, milk, etc., in a mass for baking into bread, cake, etc. **2.** *Informal* money.

doughnut n. a small, usually ring-shaped cake of dough. Also, **donut**.

doula /ˈduːlə/ n. a woman experienced in childbirth, who provides physical, emotional and informational support to a new mother, before, during and following childbirth.

dour /ˈdaʊə, dʊə/ adj. hard or severe.

The more usual word is **stern**.

douse v. **1.** to plunge into water or the like; drench. **2.** *Informal* to put out or extinguish (a light).

dove n. a bird of the pigeon family.

dowager n. a woman who holds some title or property from her deceased husband, especially the widow of a king, duke, or the like.

dowdy adj. (**-dier, -diest**) ill-dressed; not smart, or stylish.

dowel n. *Carpentry* a pin, usually round, fitting into corresponding holes in 2 adjacent pieces.

down¹ adv. **1.** into or in a lower position or condition: *to jump down.* **2.** on or to the ground. **3.** to a point of submission, inactivity, etc. **4.** to or in a position spoken of as lower, as the south, etc. **5.** from a greater to a less bulk, strength, etc. **6.** in due position or state. **7.** on paper or in a book: *Take this letter down.* **8.** in cash; at once. –prep. **9.** to, towards, or at a lower place on or in: *We climbed down the mountain.* **10.** to, towards, near, or at a lower station, condition, or rank in. –adj. **11.** downwards; going or directed downwards. **12.** (of a computer or a computerised system) not operational, usually because of a malfunction. **13.** *Games* losing or behind an opponent by a specified number of points, holes, etc. **14.** depressed; unhappy. –n. **15.** a downward movement; a descent. **16.** *Informal* a grudge. –v. **17.** to put or throw down; subdue. **18.** to drink down. –phr. **19.** down to earth, practical; realistic.

down² n. **1.** the first feathering of young birds. **2.** a soft hairy growth.

down³ n. (usu. pl.) open, rolling, upland country with fairly smooth slopes.

downfall n. **1.** descent to a lower position or standing; overthrow; ruin. **2.** a fall, as of rain or snow.

download v. *Computers* to transfer or copy data from one computer to another, or from a computer to a disk or peripheral device.

down-market adj. of or relating to commercial services and goods of inferior status, quality and price.

downpour n. a heavy, continuous fall of water, rain, etc.

downsize v. to reduce the number of employees in an organisation. –**downsizing**, n.

Down syndrome n. a genetic condition resulting from a chromosomal abnormality, characterised by varying degrees of intellectual and physical impairment. Also, **Down's syndrome**.

downward adj. **1.** moving or going towards a lower place or condition. –adv. **2.** → **downwards**.

Note that you can use **downward** for both the adjective (*a downward trend*) and the adverb (*to slide downward*), but **downwards** can only be used for the adverb (*to slide downwards*).

downwards *adv.* from a higher to a lower place or condition. Also, **downward**.

dowry *n.* (*pl.* **-ries**) the money, goods, or estate which a woman in some cultures brings to her husband at marriage.

doyen *n.* the senior member of a body, class, profession, etc.

doze *v.* to sleep lightly or fitfully.

dozen *n.* (*pl.* **-zen** or **-zens**) **1.** a group of 12 units or things. *–determiner* **2.** amounting to a dozen in number: *a dozen eggs*.

drab *adj.* (**drabber**, **drabbest**) dull or uninteresting.

draft *n.* **1.** a drawing, sketch, or design. **2.** a first or preliminary form of any writing. **3.** compulsory enrolment in the armed forces. **4.** a written order for payment of money. **5.** an animal or animals selected and separated from the herd or flock. *–v.* **6.** to draw the outlines or plan of, or sketch. **7.** to draw up in written form, as a first draft. **8.** to enrol compulsorily for service in the armed forced: *to be drafted into the army*.

Note that there is another word **draught**, which is sometimes spelt **draft**. See the note at **draught**.

draftsman *n.* (*pl.* **-men**) someone who makes drawings of the plans or designs of things such as bridges, roads, and buildings. Also, **draughtsman**.

Because this term includes the word *man*, it is seen by some to exclude women. Unless you are specifically talking about a man, it is best to use another term such as **drafting officer** or **drafter**.

drag *v.* (**dragged**, **dragging**) **1.** to draw with force, effort, or difficulty; pull heavily or slowly along. **2.** *Computers* to move text, a file, etc., across a computer screen by selecting with the mouse and moving the cursor to another part of the screen. **3.** to introduce, as an irrelevant matter (*in*). **4.** to protract or pass tediously (*out* or *on*). **5.** to be drawn or hauled along. **6.** to trail on the ground. **7.** to proceed or pass with tedious slowness. *–n.* **8.** something used by or for dragging. **9.** the force due to the relative airflow exerted on an aeroplane or other body tending to reduce its forward motion. **10.** *Informal* somebody or something that is extremely boring. **11.** *Informal* the clothes and accessories typically worn by one sex, when worn by the other.

dragnet *n.* a net to be drawn along the bottom of a river, pond, etc., or along the ground, to catch something.

dragon *n.* **1.** a mythical monster variously represented, generally as a huge winged reptile with crested head and terrible claws, and often spouting fire, but in the Eastern tradition as powerful but generous. **2.** a fierce, violent person. **3.** any of various lizards, as the frillneck lizard of Aust.

dragonfly *n.* (*pl.* **-flies**) a large, harmless insect which feeds on mosquitoes and other insects.

dragon's teeth *pl. n.* *NSW* a road marking indicating a school zone where vehicles must slow to 40 km/h at specified times.

drain *v.* **1.** to draw off gradually, as a liquid. **2.** to draw off or take away completely. *–n.* **3.** that by which anything is drained, as a pipe or conduit. **4.** gradual or continuous outflow, withdrawal, or expenditure.

drainage *n.* **1.** the act or process of draining. **2.** a system of drains, artificial or natural.

drake *n.* a male duck.

dram *n.* **1.** a unit of measurement in the imperial system. **2.** a small quantity of anything.

drama *n.* **1.** a composition in prose or verse presenting in dialogue a story involving conflict, especially one intended to be acted; a play. **2.** any series of events having dramatic interest or results.

dramatic adj. 1. of or relating to the drama. 2. characteristic of or appropriate to the drama; involving conflict or contrast.

drank v. past tense and former past participle of **drink**.

drape v. to cover or hang with cloth or some fabric.

draper n. a dealer in textiles and cloth goods, etc. –**drapery**, n.

drastic adj. acting with force or violence; violent.

draught /draft/ n. 1. a current of air, especially in a room or other enclosed space. 2. an act of drawing or pulling, or that which is drawn. 3. the drawing of a liquid from its receptacle, as of beer from a cask. 4. an amount drunk as a continuous act: *a long draught of water.* 5. *Naut.* the depth of water needed by a ship to float: *a draught of 30 metres.* 6. (pl.) a game played by 2 people each with 12 pieces on a chequered board. –adj. 7. being on draught; drawn as required: *draught beer.* 8. used or suited for pulling loads: *a draught horse.*

Note that def. 6 is used as a singular noun: *Draughts is my favourite game.* Another term you can use for this game is **chequers**.

Note that there is another word **draft**, with different meanings to those of **draught**. It is slightly confusing because American English uses the spelling **draft** for both words. Australian English is starting to follow this trend, so you will sometimes see the meanings above spelt **draft**.

draughtsman n. (pl. -men) → **draftsman**.

See the note at **draftsman**.

draw v. (**drew**, **drawn**, **drawing**) 1. to cause to come in a particular direction by a pulling force; pull; drag; lead (*along, away, in, out, off,* etc.). 2. to bring towards oneself or itself, as by inherent force or influence; attract. 3. to pick or choose at random. 4. to sketch in lines or words.

5. to frame or formulate, as a distinction. 6. to pull out to full or greater length; stretch. 7. to write or sign a draft, cheque, etc. 8. to use or practise the art of tracing figures; practise drawing. 9. *Games* to leave a contest undecided. –n. 10. the act of drawing. 11. that which is drawn, as a lot. 12. *Sport* a drawn or undecided contest.

Don't confuse **draw** with **drawer**, which is pronounced the same way. A **drawer** is the part of a cupboard or desk that slides in and out.

drawback n. a hindrance or disadvantage.

drawbridge n. a bridge of which the whole or a part may be drawn up or aside to prevent access or to leave a passage open for boats, etc.

drawer n. 1. a sliding compartment, as in a piece of furniture, that may be drawn out. 2. (pl.) → **underpants**. 3. *Finance* someone who draws an order, cheque, etc.

Don't confuse this with **draw**, which is pronounced the same but means to sketch a picture.

drawing n. 1. the act of a person or thing that draws. 2. representation by lines; delineation of form without reference to colour. 3. a sketch, plan, or design, especially one made with pen, pencil, or crayon. 4. the art of making these.

drawing-pin n. a short broad-headed tack designed to be pushed in by the thumb. Also, **thumbtack**.

drawl v. 1. to say or speak with slow, lingering utterance. –n. 2. the act or utterance of someone who drawls.

drawn v. 1. past participle of **draw**. –adj. 2. haggard; tired; tense.

dray n. a low, strong cart.

dread v. 1. to fear greatly. –n. 2. terror or apprehension. 3. deep awe. –adj. 4. greatly feared.

dreadful adj. 1. extremely bad, unpleasant, ugly, etc. 2. causing great dread, fear, or terror.

dream n. **1.** a succession of images or ideas present in the mind during sleep. **2.** a vision voluntarily indulged in while awake; daydream. **3.** something or somebody of an unreal beauty or charm. **4.** a hope that gives one inspiration; an aim. –v. (**dreamed** or **dreamt, dreaming**) **5.** to have a dream or dreams (of).

dreary adj. (**-rier, -riest**) dull or depressing.

dredge n. **1.** a machine for gathering material or objects from the bed of a river, etc. –v. (**dredged, dredging**) **2.** to clear out with a dredge. –phr. **3. dredge up**, to find, usually with some difficulty.

dregs pl. n. **1.** sediment of wine or other drink; lees; grounds. **2.** any waste or worthless residue. –phr. **3. the dregs (of society)**, a person or a class of people considered to be worthless, especially irretrievably immoral.

drench v. **1.** to wet thoroughly; steep; soak. **2.** Vet. Science to administer medicine to (an animal), especially by force.

dress n. **1.** a one-piece outer garment worn by women and girls, comprising a skirt and bodice, with or without sleeves. **2.** clothing; apparel; garb. –adj. **3.** of or for a dress or dresses. **4.** of or for a formal occasion. –v. **5.** to put clothes on; attire. **6.** to arrange a display in; ornament or adorn. **7.** to prepare (fowl, skins, timber, stone, ore, etc.) by special processes. **8.** to treat (wounds or sores). **9.** to clothe oneself, especially in formal or evening clothes. –phr. **10. dress down**, to scold severely.

dress circle n. the first gallery above the floor in a theatre, etc.

dresser n. a kitchen sideboard.

dressing-gown n. a loose gown or robe generally worn over night attire.

dressing table n. a table or stand, usually surmounted by a mirror.

drew v. past tense of **draw**.

dribble v. **1.** to (let) fall or flow in drops or small quantities. **2.** to drivel; slaver. **3.** Soccer, Hockey, etc. to advance (a ball) by a series of short kicks or pushes.

dried v. past tense and past participle of **dry**.

drift n. **1.** a driving movement or force; impulse; impetus. **2.** Navig. movement or course under the impulse of water currents, wind, etc. **3.** the course of anything; tendency; aim. **4.** something driven, or formed by driving. –v. **5.** to be carried along by currents of water or air, or by the force of circumstances. **6.** to wander aimlessly.

drill[1] n. **1.** a tool or machine for making cylindrical holes, especially by rotation. **2.** Mil. training in formal marching or other precise military or naval movements. **3.** any strict, methodical training, instrument, or exercise. –v. **4.** to pierce or bore a hole in (anything). **5.** to impart (knowledge) by strict training or discipline.

drill[2] n. strong cotton fabric.

drink v. (**drank, drunk, drinking**) **1.** to swallow water or other liquid. **2.** to take in alcoholic beverages, especially habitually or to excess. **3.** to take in (a liquid) in any manner; absorb. **4.** to take in through the senses, especially with eagerness and pleasure. –n. **5.** any liquid which is swallowed to quench thirst, for nourishment, etc. **6.** an alcoholic drink.

drip v. (**dripped, dripping**) **1.** to fall in drops, as a liquid. –n. **2.** the liquid that drips. **3.** Med. the continuous slow infusion of fluid containing nutrients or drugs to a patient. **4.** Informal a dull or boring person.

Note that if you call someone 'a drip', as in def. 4, you usually intend to insult them.

dripping n. fat exuded from meat in cooking.

drive v. (**drove, driven, driving**) **1.** to send away, off, in, out, back, etc., by compulsion; force along. **2.** to overwork. **3.** to cause and guide the movement of (an animal, vehicle, etc.). **4.** to convey or travel in a vehicle. **5.** to go along before an impelling force; be impelled. **6.** to rush or dash violently. **7.** to make an effort to reach or obtain; aim (*at*). —*n.* **8.** the act of driving. **9.** *Psychol.* a source of motivation. **10.** a vigorous onset or onward course. **11.** a united effort to accomplish some purpose, especially to raise money. **12.** energy and initiative. **13.** a trip in a driven vehicle. **14.** *Computers* a controlling mechanism for moving magnetic tapes, floppy disks, etc., thus enabling data to be accessed.

drive-in *n.* **1.** a cinema so designed that patrons park in front of an outdoor screen and view the film while seated in their cars. —*adj.* **2.** (of any shop, etc.) catering for customers in cars.

drivel *v.* (**-elled, -elling**) **1.** to let saliva flow from the mouth; slaver; drool. —*n.* **2.** idiotic or silly talk.

driven *adj.* pursuing a goal with relentless determination.

driver *n.* **1.** someone who drives a vehicle. **2.** *Machinery* a part that transmits force or motion. **3.** *Computers* → **device driver**. **4.** a golf club with a long shaft, used for making long shots, as from the tee.

drizzle *v.* **1.** to rain gently and steadily in fine drops. —*n.* **2.** very light rain; mist.

droll *adj.* amusingly odd.

drone[1] *n.* the male of the honey bee and other bees, stingless and making no honey.

drone[2] *v.* **1.** to make a dull, continued, monotonous sound; hum; buzz. **2.** to speak in a monotonous tone.

drool *v.* **1.** to let saliva spill from the mouth. —*phr.* **2. drool over**, to have a greedy interest in: *She drooled over her friend's new car.*

droop *v.* to sink, bend, or hang down, as from weakness or exhaustion.

drop *n.* **1.** a small quantity of liquid which falls in a more or less spherical mass. **2.** a minute quantity of anything. **3.** something like or likened to a drop. **4.** the distance or depth to which anything drops or falls. **5.** a steep slope. **6.** a fall in degree, amount, value, etc. —*v.* (**dropped, dropping**) **7.** to (let) fall in globules or small portions, as water or other liquid. **8.** to (let) fall vertically like a drop. **9.** to withdraw; disappear (*out*). **10.** to fall lower in condition, degree, etc.; sink. **11.** to fall or move (back, behind, to the rear, etc.). **12.** to make a visit, come or go casually or unexpectedly (*in, by, across,* etc.). **13.** to utter or express casually or incidentally, as a hint. **14.** to send or post (a note, etc.). **15.** to set down, as from a ship, car, etc. **16.** to omit (a letter or syllable) in pronunciation or writing. **17.** to cease to keep up or have to do with.

drop-down menu *n.* → **pull-down menu.**

dropout *n.* someone who decides to opt out of conventional society, or an educational institution.

droppings *pl. n.* animal dung.

dross *n.* waste matter, especially that taken off molten metal during refining.

drought /draʊt/ *n.* **1.** dry weather; lack of rain. **2.** scarcity.

droughtproof *v.* **1.** to ensure a supply of drinking water for. —*adj.* **2.** designed so as to be unaffected by drought. —**drought-proofing,** *n.*

drove[1] *v.* past tense of **drive.**

drove[2] *n.* **1.** a number of oxen, sheep, or swine driven in a group; herd; flock. **2.** (*usu. pl.*) a large crowd of people, especially in motion. —*v.* **3.** to drive cattle or sheep over long distances, to market or to better pasture, etc. —**drover,** *n.* —**droving,** *n.*

drown *v.* **1.** to suffocate by immersion in water or other liquid. **2.** to make inaudible; muffle; obscure.

drowse to be sleepy; be half asleep.
–**drowsy**, adj.

drudge n. someone who labours at servile or uninteresting tasks; a hard toiler.
–**drudgery**, n.

drug n. **1.** a chemical substance given to prevent or treat disease. **2.** a chemical substance taken to bring about a change in behaviour, mood or perception. –v. (**drugged, drugging**) **3.** to stupefy or poison with a drug.

drug mule n. → **mule** (def. 3).

drum n. **1.** a musical instrument consisting of a hollow body, often covered at one or both ends with a tightly stretched membrane, which is struck with the hand, or stick(s). **2.** something resembling a drum in shape or structure, or in the noise it produces. –v. (**drummed, drumming**) **3.** to beat or play a drum. **4.** to beat rhythmically; perform (a tune) by drumming. **5.** to drive or force by persistent repetition. –phr. **6. drum up**, to seek or obtain (trade, customers, etc.).

drunk v. **1.** past participle of **drink**. –adj. **2.** intoxicated or affected with, or as with, alcoholic drink. –n. **3.** Informal a person intoxicated with alcoholic drink. –**drunkard**, n.

dry adj. (**drier, driest**) **1.** free from moisture; not moist; not wet. **2.** having little or no rain. **3.** not under, in, or on water. **4.** not yielding water or other liquid. **5.** desiring drink; thirsty. **6.** dull; uninteresting. **7.** humorous or sarcastic in an unemotional or impersonal way. **8.** (of wines) not sweet. –v. (**dried, drying**) **9.** to make or become dry; to free from or lose moisture. –n. (pl. **dries**) **10.** a dry state, condition, or place. **11.** Informal dry ginger ale: brandy and dry. –**dryly, drily,** adv. –**dryer**, n.

dry-clean v. to clean (garments, etc.) with chemical solvents, etc., rather than water.

dryland salinity n. the presence of high levels of salt in soil, resulting in the death of plants and soil organisms, and caused by the rise in the watertable that follows land clearing.

dry season n. the period of an annual cycle in the tropics when there is little rainfall and the days are hot and sunny, usually as a result of prevailing winds. Compare **wet season**.

dual adj. **1.** of or relating to 2. **2.** composed or consisting of 2 parts; twofold.

Don't confuse **dual** with **duel**, which is a kind of fight.

dub[1] v. (**dubbed, dubbing**) to strike lightly with a sword in the ceremony of conferring knighthood; make, or designate as, a knight.

dub[2] v. (**dubbed, dubbing**) to change the soundtrack (of a film or videotape), as in substituting a dialogue in another language.

dubious adj. **1.** doubtful; marked by or occasioning doubt. **2.** wavering or hesitating in opinion; inclined to doubt.

duchess n. the wife or widow of a duke.

duck[1] n. any of numerous wild or domesticated web-footed swimming birds.

Note that a **duck** can be either male or female. The word **drake** means specifically a male duck.

duck[2] v. **1.** to plunge the whole body or the head momentarily under water. **2.** to avoid a blow, unpleasant task, etc.

duck[3] n. Cricket an individual score of nought made when batting.

duckling n. a young duck.

duct n. **1.** any tube, canal, or conduit by which fluid or other substances are conducted or conveyed. –v. **2.** to convey by means of a duct or ducts.

ductile adj. **1.** capable of being hammered out thin, as certain metals; malleable. **2.** capable of being moulded or shaped; plastic.

dud Informal –n. **1.** any thing or person that proves a failure. –adj. **2.** useless; defective.

dudgeon *phr.* **in high dudgeon,** in a state of anger or indignation.

due *adj.* **1.** immediately payable. **2.** owing, irrespective of whether the time of payment has arrived. **3.** rightful; proper; fitting. **4.** attributable, as to a cause. **5.** expected to be ready, be present, or arrive. –*n.* **6.** (*usu. pl.*) a payment due, as a charge, a fee, a membership subscription, etc.

Don't confuse this with **dew**, which is the moisture that forms on outdoor surfaces overnight.

duel *n.* a prearranged combat between 2 persons, fought with deadly weapons according to an accepted code of procedure.

Don't confuse **duel** with **dual**, which describes something with two parts.

duet *n.* a musical composition for 2 voices or performers.

duffer *n.* a foolish person: *you're a silly duffer!*

Note that this word is almost always used in an affectionate, humorous way.

dug *v.* past tense and past participle of **dig**.

dugong /'djuːɡɒŋ/ *n.* a tropical plant-eating water mammal with flipper-like forelimbs.

duke *n.* **1.** a sovereign prince, the ruler of a small state. **2.** (in Britain) a nobleman of the highest rank after that of a prince. –**ducal**, *adj.*

dulcet *adj.* agreeable to the feelings, the eye, or, especially the ear; soothing.

dull *adj.* **1.** slow of understanding; obtuse; stupid. **2.** not intense or acute. **3.** listless; spiritless. **4.** tedious; uninteresting. **5.** not bright, intense, or clear. –*v.* **6.** to make or become dull.

duly *adv.* **1.** in a due manner; properly. **2.** in due season; punctually. **3.** adequately.

dumb *adj.* **1.** without the power of speech. **2.** made, done, etc., without speech. **3.** *Informal* stupid; dull-witted.

dumbbell *n.* a weight used for exercises, consisting of two balls joined by a bar-like handle.

dumbfound *v.* to strike dumb with amazement.

dummy *n.* (*pl.* **-mies**) **1.** an imitation or copy of something, as for display, to indicate appearance, exhibit clothing, etc. **2.** *Informal* a stupid person. **3.** (especially in buying land) someone secretly acting for another. **4.** *Cards* **a.** (in bridge) the dealer's partner whose hand is exposed and played by the dealer. **b.** the cards so exposed. **5.** a rubber teat given to a baby to suck. –*adj.* **6.** counterfeit; sham; imitation.

dummy spit *n.* *Informal* a display of exasperation or bad temper, similar to a child's tantrum.

dump *v.* **1.** to throw down in a mass; fling down or drop heavily. **2.** to get rid of; hand over to somebody else. –*n.* **3.** Also, **rubbish dump.** → **tip²** (def. 2). **4.** *Mil.* a collection of ammunition, stores, etc., to be distributed for use. **5.** *Informal* a place, house, or town that is poorly kept up, and generally of wretched appearance.

dumpling *n.* a rounded mass of steamed dough.

dumps *phr.* **down in the dumps,** *Informal* in an unhappy state of mind.

dumpy *adj.* (**-pier, -piest**) short and stout; squat.

dun *adj.* **1.** dull or greyish brown. **2.** dark; gloomy.

dunce *n.* a dull-witted or stupid person.

dune *n.* a sand hill or sand ridge formed by the wind, usually in desert regions or near lakes and oceans.

dung *n.* manure; excrement, especially of animals.

dungeon *n.* any strong, close cell, especially underground.

dunk *v.* **1.** to immerse in water. **2.** to dip (biscuits, etc.) into coffee, milk, etc.

dunnart *n.* a type of narrow-footed marsupial mouse.

dunny *n. Aust., NZ Informal* a toilet.

duo *n.* a pair of singers, entertainers, etc.

duodenum *n.* the first portion of the small intestine. –**duodenal**, *adj.*

dupe *v.* (**duped, duping**) **1.** to trick or deceive. –*n.* **2.** a person who is imposed upon or deceived.

duplex *adj.* **1.** twofold; double. –*n.* **2.** *Aust., US* a building consisting of 2 separate dwellings, arranged either on each storey of a two-storey building, or as a pair of semidetached cottages.

duplicate *adj.* /'djuːplǝkǝt/ **1.** exactly like or corresponding to something else. **2.** double; consisting of or existing in 2 corresponding parts. –*n.* /'djuːplǝkǝt/ **3.** a copy exactly like an original. –*v.* /'djuːplǝkeɪt/ **4.** to make an exact copy of; repeat. –**duplication**, *n.* –**duplicator**, *n.*

duplicity *n.* deceitfulness in speech or conduct.

> The more usual word is **deception**.

durable *adj.* having the quality of lasting or enduring. –**durability**, *n.*

duration *n.* **1.** continuance in time. **2.** the length of time anything continues.

duress /djuˈrɛs/ *n.* **1.** constraint; compulsion. **2.** forcible restraint of liberty; imprisonment.

during *prep.* **1.** throughout the continuance of. **2.** in the course of.

dusk *n.* a state between light and darkness; twilight.

dusky *adj.* (**-kier, -kiest**) somewhat dark; dark-coloured.

dust *n.* **1.** earth or other matter in fine, dry particles. **2.** any finely powdered substance, as sawdust. –*v.* **3.** to free from dust; wipe the dust from. **4.** to sprinkle with dust or powder. –**dusty**, *adj.*

duty *n.* (*pl.* **-ties**) **1.** that which one is bound to do by moral or legal obligation. **2.** action required by one's position or occupation. **3.** a levy imposed by law on the import, export, sale, or manufacture of goods, the legal recognition of deeds and documents, etc. –**dutiful**, *adj.* –**dutiable**, *adj.*

dux *n. Aust., NZ* the top pupil academically.

DVD *n.* a high-capacity disk with enough capacity to store the video and audio data for a full-length movie.

DVT *n.* → **deep vein thrombosis**.

dwarf *n.* (*pl.* **dwarfs** or **dwarves**) **1.** a person suffering from a genetic condition resulting in short stature. **2.** an unusually small person or thing. –*adj.* **3.** of unusually small stature or size. –*v.* **4.** to cause to appear or seem small in size, extent, character, etc.

dwell *v.* (**dwelt** or **dwelled, dwelling**) **1.** to abide as a permanent resident. **2.** to continue for a time. –*phr.* **3. dwell on** (or **upon**), to linger over in thought, speech, or writing; to emphasise.

dwelling *n.* a place to live; home.

dwindle *v.* to become smaller and smaller.

dye *n.* **1.** a colouring material or matter. –*v.* (**dyed, dyeing**) **2.** to colour or stain.

> Don't confuse this with **die**, which is to stop living.

dying *adj.* **1.** ceasing to live; approaching death. **2.** given, uttered, or manifested just before death. **3.** drawing to a close.

dyke[1] *n. Informal* a lesbian. Also, **dike**.

> Note that this used to be an offensive term, but is now often used by lesbians themselves.

dyke[2] *n.* **1.** an embankment for restraining the waters of the sea or a river. **2.** *Aust., NZ Informal* a toilet. Also, **dike**.

dynamic *adj.* **1.** of or relating to dynamics. **2.** relating to or characterised by energy or effective action.

dynamics *n.* **1.** the science or principles of the forces that cause or affect motion. **2.** the forces at work in any situation.

> Note that def. 2 is thought of as plural: *The dynamics of government are often very complex.*

dynamic verb *n. Gram.* a verb which indicates an action or process, as *The child jumps*, or *The light fades*. Compare **stative verb**. Also, **action verb**.

dynamite *n.* **1.** a high explosive. **2.** *Informal* anything or anyone potentially dangerous and liable to cause trouble. **3.** *Informal* anything or anyone exceptional.

dynamo *n.* (*pl.* **-mos**) **1.** any rotating machine in which mechanical energy is converted into electrical energy. **2.** *Informal* a forceful, energetic person.

dynasty /'dɪnəsti/ *n.* (*pl.* **-ties**) a sequence of rulers from the same family or stock. –**dynastic**, *adj.*

dysentery /'dɪsəntri/ *n.* an infectious disease marked by inflammation and ulceration of the lower part of the bowels, with diarrhoea and bleeding.

dysfunctional *adj.* **1.** not functioning properly or normally: *a dysfunctional engine.* **2.** not functioning in a way that conforms behaviourally, socially, etc., to accepted norms: *a dysfunctional family*; *a dysfunctional relationship.* –**dysfunctionality**, *n.*

dyslexia *n.* impairment in reading ability, often associated with other disorders especially in writing and co-ordination. –**dyslectic**, **dyslexic**, *n., adj.*

dyspepsia *n.* upset digestion; indigestion.

E, e

E, e *n.* the 5th letter of the English alphabet.

each *adj.* **1.** every, of 2 or more things considered individually: *each hair on my head.* –*adv.* **2.** for every piece or person; apiece: *The tickets are five dollars each.* –*pron.* **3.** each one: *Each had different interests, but they were all good friends.*

Each takes a singular verb (as in *Each person in the room is standing*), but sometimes, when you need to use a personal pronoun after **each**, there can be a problem if you are not sure of the sex of the person you are talking about, or if there is a mixture of males and females. It is awkward to have to say *Each person gave his or her answer quickly*, so the plural pronoun **their** is often used, as in *Each person gave their answer quickly*. Some people say that this is not correct, but it is extremely common and neatly solves a difficult problem.

eager *adj.* keen or ardent in desire or feeling.

eagle *n.* **1.** a large bird of prey. **2.** *Golf* a score two below par on any but par-three holes.

ear[1] *n.* **1.** the organ of hearing. **2.** attention, especially favourable.

ear[2] *n.* that part of a cereal plant which contains the grains or kernels.

earl *n.* a British nobleman.

earlobe *n.* the soft pendulous lower part of the external ear.

early *adv.* (**-lier, -liest**) **1.** in or during the first part of some division of time, or of some course or series. **2.** before the usual or appointed time. –*adj.* (**-lier, -liest**) **3.** occurring in the first part of some division of time, or of some course or series.

4. occurring before the usual or appointed time. **5.** belonging to a period far back in time.

earn *v.* (**earnt** *or* **earned, earning**) **1.** to gain by labour or service. **2.** to gain (interest or profit). **3.** to merit or deserve. –**earnings,** *pl. n.*

earnest *adj.* serious in intention, or effort.

earphone *n.* a small device for converting electric signals into soundwaves, fitted into the ear or held close to it.

earring *n.* a ring or other ornament worn in or on the lobe of the ear.

earshot *n.* range of hearing: *within earshot.*

earth *n.* **1.** (*oft. upper case*) the planet which we inhabit. **2.** the softer part of the land, as distinguished from rock; soil. **3.** *Elect.* a conducting connection between an electric circuit or equipment and the ground. –**earthen,** *adj.*

earthquake *n.* tremors or earth movements in the earth's crust.

earthworm *n.* any one of many segmented worms that burrow in soil and feed on soil and decaying organic matter.

earthy *adj.* (**-thier, -thiest**) **1.** of the nature of soil. **2.** coarse or unrefined. **3.** direct; unaffected.

ease *n.* **1.** freedom from pain or annoyance of any kind. **2.** freedom from stiffness or constraint. –*v.* **3.** to give rest or relief to. **4.** to make or become less in severity, pressure, etc. **5.** to facilitate. **6.** to move slowly and with great care.

easel *n.* a frame for supporting an artist's canvas, etc.

easement *n. Law* a right held by one person to make use of the land of another.

east *n.* **1.** a cardinal point of the compass corresponding to the point where the sun is seen to rise. –*adj.* **2.** directed or proceeding towards the east. **3.** (of wind) coming from the east. –*adv.* **4.** in the direction of the sunrise; towards or in the east. –**eastern,** *adj.* –**easterly,** *adj.*, *n.*

easy adj. (**-sier, -siest**) **1.** not difficult; requiring no great effort. **2.** free from pain, worry, or care. **3.** *Informal* having no firm preferences in a particular matter. **4.** free from constraint or embarrassment. –adv. **5.** *Informal* in an easy manner. –phr. **6. take it easy,** *Informal* **a.** to proceed at a comfortable pace. **b.** to relax and rest. –**easily,** adv.

easygoing adj. taking matters in an easy way.

eat v. (**ate, eaten, eating**) **1.** to take (food) into the mouth and swallow for nourishment. **2.** to consume by or as by devouring. **3.** to make a way as by gnawing or corrosion.

eating disorder n. a pattern of eating which involves compulsive over-eating or abstinence to such an extent that it affects one's physical and mental health.

eaves pl. n. the overhanging lower edge of a roof.

eavesdrop v. (**-dropped, -dropping**) to listen secretly.

ebb n. **1.** the falling of the tide. –v. **2.** to flow back or away. **3.** to decline or decay.

Ebola /ə'boʊlə/ n. a virus causing high fever and internal haemorrhaging, often fatal.

ebony n. a hard, durable wood, usually black.

ebook n. a book in an electronic format. Also, **e-book**.

ebullient /ə'bʊljənt, ə'bʌl-, ə'bjul-/ adj. bubbling like a boiling liquid.

eccentric /ək'sɛntrɪk/ adj. **1.** not conventional; odd. **2.** not concentric, as 2 circles or spheres. –n. **3.** an eccentric person. –**eccentricity,** n.

ecclesiastical /əklizi'æstɪkəl/ adj. of or relating to the church or the clergy.

echelon /'ɛʃəlɒn/ n. a level of command.

echidna /ə'kɪdnə/ n. a spine-covered insectivorous egg-laying monotreme; spiny anteater.

echinacea /ɛkə'neɪʃə/ n. a North American plant, extracts of which are used in herbal medicine as a cold remedy, antibiotic, and immune system stimulant.

echo n. (pl. **echoes**) **1.** a repetition of sound, produced by the reflection of soundwaves from an obstructing surface. –v. (**echoed, echoing**) **2.** to emit an echo; resound with an echo. **3.** to repeat by or as by an echo.

eclair n. a light, finger-shaped pastry, filled with cream or custard, and coated with icing.

eclectic adj. selecting; choosing from various sources.

eclipse n. **1.** *Astron.* the obscuring of the light of a satellite by the intervention of its primary planet between it and the sun. –v. (**eclipsed, eclipsing**) **2.** to make dim by comparison.

eco /'ikoʊ/ adj. of, relating to, or employing environmentally friendly practices, materials, technology, etc.

ecological footprint n. a measure of the demands put on the environment by humans, as in growing food, providing fuel, etc., taking into account the emissions produced in the production of food and in goods and services, as well as those produced in fuel consumption and household requirements such as heating, cooling, etc. Also, **footprint**.

ecological sustainability n. the capacity for development that can be sustained into the future without destroying the environment in the process.

ecology n. the branch of biology that deals with the relations between organisms and their environment.

economical adj. avoiding waste or extravagance; thrifty.

Note that although **economical** and **economic** are similar words, you cannot use **economical** to mean having to do with the management of money, etc., in a country. You cannot say 'a period of slow economical growth'.

economics *n.* the science that deals with the production, distribution, and consumption of goods and services. —**economist**, *n.* —**economic**, *adj.*

economise *v.* to be thrifty; avoid waste. Also, **economize**.

economy *n.* (*pl.* **-mies**) **1.** thrifty management; frugality. **2.** *Econ.* the interrelationship between the factors of production and the means of production, distribution, and exchange. **3.** the management of the resources of a community.

ecosystem *n.* a community of organisms, interacting with one another, plus the environment in which they live and with which they also interact.

ecstasy /ˈɛkstəsi/ *n.* **1.** overpowering emotion, especially delight. **2.** a synthetic drug used as a stimulant. —**ecstatic**, *adj.*

ecumenical /ɛkjəˈmɛnɪkəl, ik-/ *adj.* tending to work towards unity among all Christian Churches.

eczema /ˈɛksəmə/ *n.* an inflammatory disease of the skin.

eddy *n.* (*pl.* **eddies**) a current at variance with the main current in a stream of liquid or gas.

edge *n.* **1.** a brim or margin. **2.** a brink or verge. **3.** one of the narrow surfaces of a thin, flat object. **4.** the line in which 2 surfaces of a solid object meet. **5.** sharpness or keenness. —*v.* (**edged**, **edging**) **6.** to put an edge on. **7.** to move, advance or force gradually.

edgy *adj.* (**edgier**, **edgiest**) **1.** impatient; irritable. **2.** *Informal* at the forefront or cutting edge: *edgy fashion designers.*

edible *adj.* fit to be eaten.

edict /ˈidɪkt/ *n.* an authoritative proclamation or command.

edifice *n.* a building, especially large.

edify *v.* (**-fied, -fying**) to instruct or benefit, especially morally. —**edification**, *n.*

This is often used humorously, as in *Spending the afternoon at the soccer match was not the most edifying experience of my life.*

edit *v.* **1.** to direct the preparation of (a newspaper, magazine, etc.). **2.** to make (a film, sound recording, etc.) by cutting and arranging, etc. **3.** to revise and correct (written material). —**editor**, *n.*

edition *n.* one of a number of printings of the same book, newspaper, etc.

editorial *n.* **1.** an article, in a newspaper or the like, presenting the opinion or comment of an editor; leader. —*adj.* **2.** of or relating to an editor.

educate *v.* to develop the faculties and powers of by teaching. —**education**, *n.*

eel *n.* a snake-like fish.

eerie /ˈɪəri/ *adj.* (**eerier, eeriest**) weird or uncanny.

efface *v.* to wipe out; destroy.

effect *n.* **1.** a result; consequence. **2.** power to produce results. **3.** the state of being operative. **4.** a mental impression produced, as by a painting, speech, etc. **5.** (of stage properties) a sight, sound, etc., giving a particular impression. **6.** a scientific phenomenon: *the greenhouse effect.* **7.** (*pl.*) personal property. —*v.* **8.** to bring about, accomplish or execute; to produce as an effect: *The scheme will effect a reduction in the unemployment figures.*

Don't confuse this with the verb *affect*, which means to cause a change in.

effective *adj.* **1.** producing the intended result. **2.** actually in effect. **3.** producing a striking impression.

effectual *adj.* producing, or capable of producing, an intended effect.

effeminate *adj.* (of a man) soft or delicate in a way considered more typical of a woman than of a man.

effervesce /ɛfəˈvɛs/ *v.* to give off bubbles of gas, as fermenting liquors. —**effervescence**, *n.* —**effervescent**, *adj.*

effete /əˈfit/ *adj.* **1.** weak and ineffectual as a result of over-refinement: *an effete* *intellectual.* **2.** that has lost its vigour or energy.

efficacy /'ɛfɪkəsi/ *n.* capacity to produce effects. –**efficacious,** *adj.*

The more usual word is **effectiveness.**

efficient *adj.* **1.** effective in the use of energy and resources. **2.** avoiding waste. –**efficiency,** *n.*

effigy *n.* (*pl.* **-gies**) a representation or image, as of a person.

effluent /'ɛfluənt/ *adj.* **1.** flowing out. –*n.* **2.** that which flows out. –**effluence,** *n.*

effort *n.* exertion of power, physical or mental.

effrontery *n.* shameless or impudent boldness.

The more usual word is **cheek.**

effusive *adj.* unduly demonstrative.

EFTPOS /'ɛftpɒs/ *n.* electronic funds transfer at point of sale; a system of electronic funds transfer from a customer's account to a merchant's account.

egalitarian *adj.* asserting the equality of all people.

egg[1] *n.* **1.** the female reproductive cell. **2.** the egg, with a hard shell, produced by birds, especially the domestic hen. **3.** the contents of an egg, especially that of a domestic hen, used as food.

egg[2] *v.* to incite or urge; encourage.

eggplant *n.* a plant with purple egg-shaped fruit; aubergine.

ego *n.* the 'I' or self of any person.

egotism *n.* **1.** self-conceit. **2.** selfishness. Also, **egoism.**

egress *n.* a means or place of going out.

egret *n.* any of various herons.

eiderdown *n.* (a quilt filled with) down or soft feathers, especially from a type of duck.

eight *n.* **1.** a cardinal number, 7 plus 1. –*adj.* **2.** amounting to 8 in number. –**eighth,** *adj.*, *n.*

Numbers used before a noun are sometimes called **determiners.**

eighteen *n.* **1.** a cardinal number, 10 plus 8. –*adj.* **2.** amounting to 18 in number. –**eighteenth,** *adj.*, *n.*

Numbers used before a noun are sometimes called **determiners.**

eighty *n.* **1.** a cardinal number, 10 times 8. –*adj.* **2.** amounting to 80 in number. –**eightieth,** *adj.*, *n.*

Numbers used before a noun are sometimes called **determiners.**

eisteddfod /ə'stɛdfəd/ *n.* (*pl.* **-fods** or **-fodau** /-fədaɪ/) *Aust.* a competitive music festival.

either *adj.* **1.** one or the other of 2: *Sit at either end of the table.* **2.** both one and the other of 2; each of the 2: *There were trees on either side of the river.* –*pron.* **3.** one or the other but not both: *Take either.* –*conj.* **4.** used with *or* to present 2 alternatives: *You can either phone or write.* –*adv.* **5.** (*used in negative sentences*) also: *If you don't go, I won't go either; I helped her look, but I couldn't find it either.*

Note that **either** is used when two things or people are involved. When there are more than two, you use **any:** *You can use any of these colours.*
Either takes a singular verb (as in *Either hat is fine with me*), but sometimes, when you need to use a pronoun after **either,** there can be a problem if you are not sure of the sex of the person you are talking about, or if there is a mixture of males and females. It is awkward to have to say *Either competitor may use his or her notes during the contest,* so the plural pronoun **their** is often used, as in *Either competitor may use their notes during the contest.* Some people say that this is not correct, but it is extremely common and neatly solves a difficult problem.

ejaculate *v.* **1.** to discharge semen. **2.** to utter suddenly and briefly. —**ejaculation**, *n.*

For def. 2, the more usual word is **exclaim**.

eject *v.* **1.** to drive or force out. **2.** to propel oneself out of an aeroplane, etc., by means of a mechanical device. —**ejection**, *n.*

eke *phr.* **eke out. 1.** to use (resources) frugally. **2.** to contrive to make (a living).

elaborate *adj.* /ɒˈlæbərət/ **1.** worked out with great care and nicety of detail. —*v.* /ɒˈlæbəreɪt, -i-/ **2.** to give additional or fuller treatment (*on* or *upon*). —**elaboration**, *n.*

elapse *v.* (**elapsed, elapsing**) (of time) to slip by or pass away.

elastic *adj.* **1.** rebounding or returning to the original shape. —*n.* **2.** elastic material. —**elasticity**, *n.*

elate *v.* to put in high spirits. —**elated**, *adj.* —**elation**, *n.*

elbow *n.* **1.** the bend or joint of the arm between upper arm and forearm. —*v.* **2.** to push with or as with the elbow; jostle.

elder *adj.* **1.** older; senior. **2.** a person who is older than oneself. **3.** one of the older and more influential members of a tribe or community.

Def. 1 is mainly used for people in the same family (*my elder brother, her elder daughter*).

elderly *adj.* in one's old age.

Elderly is a polite way of describing an old person. It can also be sometimes used for a person who is quite old but not extremely old.

eldest *adj.* oldest.

This is used when there are three or more people. You would use **elder** if there were only two. Like **elder**, **eldest** is mainly used for members of the same family: *her eldest son.*

elect *v.* **1.** to select by vote, as for an office. **2.** to determine in favour of (a course of action, etc.). —*adj.* **3.** selected for an office, but not yet inducted: *the president elect.* —**elector**, *n.*

Unlike most adjectives, def. 3 is always placed after the noun, often with a hyphen: *premier-elect.*

election *n.* the selection by vote of a person or persons for office.

elective *adj.* **1.** (of an office) filled by election. —*n.* **2.** an optional course of study.

electoral *adj.* relating to electors or election.

electorate *n.* the body of voters and geographical subdivision represented by an elected member; constituency.

electric *adj.* relating to, derived from, produced by, or involving electricity. —**electrical**, *adj.*

There is a difference in the way you use **electric** and **electrical**. Both relate to electricity, but **electric** is used to describe a device, appliance, etc., that runs on electricity (*electric toaster, electric toothbrush*), and **electrical** describes something other than an appliance (*electrical contractor, electrical fault*). Don't confuse **electric** with **electronic**, which describes a piece of equipment which uses a device, such as a microchip, that controls and changes an electric current: *an electronic calculator.*

electrician *n.* someone who installs, operates, maintains, or repairs electrical devices.

electricity *n.* an agency producing various physical phenomena, due to the presence and movements of electrons, protons, and other electrically charged particles.

electrify *v.* (**-fied, -fying**) **1.** to charge with or subject to electricity. **2.** to excite.

electrocute *v.* to kill by electricity. —**electrocution**, *n.*

electrode *n.* a conductor of electricity through which a current enters or leaves an electrolytic cell, etc.

electrolysis /əlɛk'trɒləsəs, i-, ˌɛlək-'trɒləsəs/ *n.* **1.** the decomposition of a chemical compound by an electric current. **2.** *Surg.* the destruction of tumours, hair roots, etc., by an electric current. –**electrolytic**, *adj.*

electromagnetic *adj.* relating to the interaction of electricity and magnetism. –**electromagnetism**, *n.*

electron *n.* a tiny particle which moves around the nucleus in every atom, and which has a negative electric charge that balances the positive charge of the proton.

Compare this with **proton** and **neutron**.

electronic *adj.* relating to or using any of various devices, such as microchips, that control and change an electric current: *an electronic calculator.* –**electronically**, *adv.*

Don't confuse **electronic** with **electric**, which describes something which is run by electricity (*an electric stove*) or produced by it (*an electric shock*).

electronics *n.* the investigation and application of phenomena involving the movement of electrons in valves and semiconductors.

electronic tag *n.* → e-tag.

electronic whiteboard *n.* a whiteboard that has digital capability and can be connected to the internet, a printer, etc.

elegant *adj.* tastefully fine or luxurious in dress, manner, etc. –**elegance**, *n.*

elegy *n.* (*pl.* **-gies**) a mournful or plaintive poem, expressing a lament for the dead. –**elegiac**, *adj.*

element *n.* **1.** a component or constituent part of a whole. **2.** (*pl.*) the rudimentary principles of an art, science, etc. **3.** (*pl.*) atmospheric agencies or forces. **4.** *Chem.* one of a class of substances which consist entirely of atoms having the same number of protons in the nucleus. **5.** *Elect.* the heating unit of an electric domestic appliance. –**elemental**, *adj.*

elementary *adj.* relating to or dealing with elements, rudiments, or first principles.

elephant *n.* **1.** a very large, herbivorous mammal, having a long, prehensile trunk and curved tusks. –*phr.* **2. the elephant in the room**, a topic that everyone knows about but no-one wants to discuss openly. –**elephantine**, *adj.*

elevate *v.* to move or raise to a higher place or position; lift up.

elevation *n.* **1.** height above sea or ground level. **2.** the act of elevating. **3.** the state of being elevated. **4.** *Archit.* a drawing or design of a face of a building.

elevator *n. Chiefly US* → **lift** (def. 6).

eleven *n.* **1.** a cardinal number, 10 plus 1. –*adj.* **2.** amounting to 11 in number. –**eleventh**, *adj.*, *n.*

Numbers used before a noun are sometimes called **determiners**.

elf *n.* (*pl.* **elves**) one of a class of imaginary beings, usually a diminutive human. –**elfish**, **elvish**, *adj.*

elfin *adj.* small and sprightly or delicate.

elicit /ə'lɪsət/ *v.* to draw or bring out or forth; evoke.

eligible /'ɛlɪdʒəbəl/ *adj.* fit or proper to be chosen.

eliminate *v.* to get rid of; expel; remove. –**elimination**, *n.*

elite *n.* **1.** persons of the highest class. **2.** the most privileged or socially advantaged groups in a society, organisation, etc.

Note that this word is used as a plural: *Only the elite are able to afford such luxuries.*

elixir *n.* a preparation formerly believed to prolong life.

elk *n.* (*pl.* **elks** *or, especially collectively,* **elk**) the largest existing European and Asiatic deer.

ellipse *n.* a plane figure, oval in shape or outline. –**elliptical**, *adj.*

ellipsis n. (pl. **-lipses** /-ˈlɪpsiːz/) Gram. the omission from a sentence of something which would complete or clarify the construction. –**elliptical**, adj.

elm n. a large, deciduous tree.

elocution n. manner of speaking or reading in public.

elongate v. to draw out to greater length. –**elongation**, n.

elope v. to run away with a lover, usually in order to marry without parental consent.

eloquent adj. characterised by fluent, persuasive expression. –**eloquence**, n.

else adv. other than the person or the thing mentioned.

elsewhere adv. somewhere else.

elucidate v. to make lucid or clear; explain.

The more usual word is **clarify**.

elude v. 1. to avoid or escape by dexterity or artifice. 2. to temporarily escape one's memory: Her name eludes me at the moment.

For def. 1, the more usual word is **evade**. Don't confuse **elude** with **allude to**, which means to mention or refer to casually.

emaciated adj. lean; wasted, as by disease.

email n. 1. Also, **electronic mail**. messages sent on a telecommunications system linking computers or terminals. 2. such a message. –v. 3. to send (a message) by email. Also, **e-mail**.

emanate v. to flow out, issue, or proceed as from a source or origin: There was a strange smell emanating from the kitchen. –**emanation**, n.

The more usual expression is **come from**.

emancipate v. to free from restraint. –**emancipation**, n.

The more usual terms are **free** or **set free**.

emasculate v. 1. to castrate. 2. to deprive of strength or vigour.

embalm v. to treat (a corpse) in order to preserve from decay.

embankment n. a bank, mound, dyke, or the like, raised to hold back water, carry a road, etc.

embargo n. (pl. **-goes**) 1. an order of a government prohibiting the movement of merchant vessels from or into its ports. 2. any restriction imposed upon commerce by law, as when a government suspends trade with another country.

embark v. 1. to board a ship, plane, etc., as for a voyage. 2. to begin (on) a journey, project, etc.

embarrass v. to disconcert; make uncomfortable, self-conscious, etc.

embassy n. (pl. **-sies**) the official headquarters of an ambassador.

embellish v. 1. to beautify by or as by ornamentation; enhance. 2. to make (a story, etc.) more interesting by adding details which may be untrue.

For def. 1, the more usual word is **decorate**.

ember n. a small, still glowing coal.

embezzle v. to appropriate (money, etc.) fraudulently to one's own use.

emblem n. an object or representation which identifies persons, things, qualities, etc.; symbol.

embody v. (**-bodied**, **-bodying**) to give bodily or concrete form to. –**embodiment**, n.

embolism n. the obstruction of a blood vessel by any material such as tissue fragments, bacteria, etc., carried by the bloodstream.

emboss v. to raise designs on the surface of (leather, etc.).

embrace v. (**-braced**, **-bracing**) 1. to hug. 2. to accept (an idea, etc.) willingly. 3. to include or contain. –n. 4. a hug.

embroider v. 1. to decorate with ornamental needlework. 2. to adorn or embellish rhetorically, especially with fictitious additions. –**embroidery**, n.

embroil v. **1.** to involve in contention or strife. **2.** to throw into confusion; complicate.

embryo /ˈɛmbriou/ n. (pl. **-bryos**) the young of an animal in the very early stages of growing in an egg or in its mother's uterus.

> Compare **embryo** with **fetus**, which is the developing young in its later stages.

emeer n. → **emir**.

emend v. to free from faults or errors. **–emendation,** n.

> The more usual word is **correct**.

emerald n. a green gemstone.

emerge v. (**emerged, emerging**) to rise or come forth, as from concealment or obscurity.

emergency n. (pl. **-cies**) a sudden and urgent occasion for action.

emergent adj. **1.** (of a nation) recently independent or newly formed as a political entity. **2.** emerging. **–emergence,** n.

emery n. a granular mineral substance used for grinding and polishing.

emetic adj. inducing vomiting, as a medicinal substance.

emigrate v. to leave one country or region to settle in another. **–emigration,** n. **–emigrant,** n.

> Don't confuse **emigrate** with **immigrate**, which is to come into a different country to live. To **migrate** can mean to **emigrate** or **immigrate**.

eminent adj. high-ranking, distinguished or important. **–eminence,** n.

> Don't confuse **eminent** with **imminent**, which describes something which is likely to happen at any moment.

emir n. a Muslim or Arabian chieftain or prince. Also, **emeer**. **–emirate,** n.

emissary /ˈɛməsəri, -əsri/ n. (pl. **-ries**) an agent sent on a mission.

emission n. **1.** the act of emitting. **2.** something that is emitted; a discharge; an emanation. **3.** such a discharge, especially of pollutants such as greenhouse gases, into the environment.

emission permit n. a permit to release a certain quota of emissions of a pollutant such as carbon dioxide into the atmosphere.

emissions market n. a market in which emission permits are bought and sold.

emissions trading n. trading in emission permits under a system by which countries or organisations not using their quotas are able to sell their excess permits to others exceeding their quota. See **carbon cap**.

emit v. (**emitted, emitting**) to give out or forth; discharge. **–emitter,** n.

emoji n. (pl. **emoji**) a small image used in digital communication to express an emotion, concept, etc.

emollient adj. soothing.

emoticon n. Computers an image, created with keyboard characters, used in texts to indicate an emotion, such as :-) to denote happiness and :-(unhappiness.

emotion n. **1.** any of the feelings of joy, sorrow, fear, hate, love, etc. **2.** a state of agitation of the feelings.

emotional adj. **1.** easily affected by emotion. **2.** appealing to the emotions.

emotive adj. exciting emotion.

empathy n. an entering into the feeling or spirit of another; appreciative perception or understanding. **–empathetic,** adj. **–empathise, empathize,** v.

emperor n. the sovereign or supreme ruler of an empire. **–empress,** fem. n.

emphasis n. (pl. **-phases** /-fəsiz/) **1.** stress laid upon, or importance or significance attached to anything. **2.** intensity or force of expression, action, etc. **3.** prominence, as of outline. **–emphasise, emphasize,** v. **–emphatic,** adj.

empire n. an aggregate of nations or peoples ruled over by an emperor or other powerful sovereign or government.

empirical adj. derived from or guided by experience or experiment.

employ v. **1.** to use the services of (a person). **2.** to make use of (an instrument, means, etc.). **3.** to occupy or devote (time, energies, etc.). –n. **4.** employment; service. –**employment,** n. –**employer,** n. –**employee,** n.

empower v. **1.** to give power or authority to; authorise. **2.** to cause (a person or group of people) to feel confident and in control of their own life.

empty adj. **(-tier, -tiest) 1.** containing nothing. **2.** vacant; unoccupied. –v. **(-tied, -tying) 3.** to make empty.

emu n. (pl. **emu** or **emus**) a large, flightless, Aust. bird.

emulate v. to imitate with intent to equal or excel.

emulsion n. a suspension of a liquid in another liquid. –**emulsify,** v.

enable v. to make able; give power, means, or ability to.

enact v. **1.** to make into an act or statute. **2.** to act the part of.

enamel n. **1.** a glassy substance, usually opaque, applied by fusion to the surface of metal, pottery, etc. **2.** a paint, varnish, etc. **3.** Anat., Zool. the hard outer structure of the crowns of the teeth.

encapsulate v. **1.** to enclose in or as in a capsule. **2.** to put in shortened form; condense; abridge. –**encapsulation,** n.

For def. 2, the more usual word is **summarise.**

enchant v. **1.** to cast a spell over; bewitch. **2.** to delight; charm.

enclave /ˈɛnkleɪv, ˈɒnkleɪv/ n. a portion of a country surrounded by the territory of another country.

enclose v. **1.** to shut in; close in on all sides. **2.** to insert in the same envelope, etc., with the main letter, etc. –**enclosure,** n.

encompass v. **1.** to encircle; surround. **2.** to enclose; contain.

encore n. an extra piece of music performed in answer to continued clapping by the audience.

encounter v. **1.** to come upon; meet with, especially unexpectedly. **2.** to meet (a person, military force, etc.) in conflict. –n. **3.** a meeting with a person or thing, especially casually or unexpectedly. **4.** a meeting in conflict or opposition; battle; combat.

encourage v. **1.** to inspire with courage, spirit, or confidence. **2.** to stimulate by assistance, approval, etc. –**encouragement,** n.

encroach v. to trespass (on or upon) the property or rights of another.

encumber v. to impede or hamper. –**encumbrance,** n.

encyclopedia n. a work treating separately various topics from one or all branches of knowledge, usually in alphabetical arrangement. Also, **encyclopaedia.**

end n. **1.** an extreme or farthermost part of anything extended in space. **2.** anything that bounds an object at one of its extremities. **3.** the act of coming to an end; termination. **4.** a purpose or aim. **5.** a remnant or fragment. –v. **6.** to bring to an end or natural conclusion. **7.** to form the end of. **8.** to come to an end; terminate; cease. **9.** to issue or result.

endear v. to make dear, esteemed, or beloved. –**endearment,** n.

endeavour v. **1.** to make an effort; try; strive. –n. Also, **endeavor. 2.** an attempt.

endemic adj. peculiar to a particular people or locality, as a disease.

endive n. a herb, used in salads and as a cooked vegetable.

endocrine gland n. a gland (as the thyroid gland) which secretes hormones directly to the blood or lymph.

endorse v. **1.** to write (something) on the back of a document, etc. **2.** to sign one's name on (a commercial document or other instrument), especially to acknowledge payment. **3.** (of a branch of a political party) to select as a candidate for an election. Also, **indorse**. **–endorsement**, n.

endoscope n. a slender tubular medical instrument used to examine the interior of a body cavity or hollow organ. **–endoscopic**, adj.

endoscopy n. a medical examination by means of an endoscope. **–endoscopist**, n.

endow v. **1.** to provide with a permanent fund or source of income. **2.** to furnish as with some gift, faculty, or quality; equip. **–endowment**, n.

endure v. **1.** to sustain without impairment or yielding; undergo. **2.** to bear without resistance or with patience; tolerate. **–endurance**, n.

enema /ˈɛnəmə/ n. (pl. **-mas** or **-mata** /əˈnɛmətə, i-/) a fluid injected into the rectum, to evacuate the bowels.

enemy n. (pl. **-mies**) **1.** someone who cherishes hatred or harmful designs against another; an adversary or opponent. **2.** a (subject of a) hostile nation or state. **3.** something harmful or prejudicial.

energy n. **1.** (the capacity or habit of) vigorous activity: *She always has a lot of energy.* **2.** electrical or other power: *Our energy bill was very high this month.* **3.** *Physics* the capacity for doing work, which exists in various forms: *kinetic energy; nuclear energy.* **–energetic**, adj.

> The unit we use for measuring energy in physics is the **joule**.

enervate v. to deprive of nerve, force, or strength.

> The more usual word is **weaken**.

enforce v. (**-forced**, **-forcing**) **1.** to put or keep in force; compel obedience to. **2.** to obtain (payment, obedience, etc.) by force or compulsion.

engage v. **1.** to occupy the attention or efforts of (a person, etc.). **2.** to secure for aid, employment, use, etc.; hire. **3.** to reserve or secure. **4.** to attract or please. **5.** to

bring (troops) into conflict. **6.** *Mechanics* to cause to become interlocked; interlock with. **–engagement**, n.

engaged adj. **1.** (of a telephone) already in use. **2.** busy: *I will be engaged all morning.* **3.** having agreed to get married.

engender v. to produce or cause.

> The more usual expression is **give rise to**.

engine n. any mechanism or machine designed to convert energy into mechanical work.

engineer n. **1.** a person professionally qualified in the design, construction, and use of engines or machines. –v. **2.** to plan, construct, or manage as an engineer. **3.** to arrange, manage or carry through by skilful or cunning methods.

English muffin n. a thick, flat yeast cake, made from a soft, risen dough, baked without browning, served cut open and usually toasted, with butter, etc.

English spinach n. → **spinach** (def. 1).

engrain v. → **ingrain**.

engrave v. to cut (letters, designs, etc.) on a hard surface.

engross v. to occupy wholly, as the mind or attention.

engulf v. to swallow up in or as in a chasm.

enhance v. (**-hanced**, **-hancing**) to raise to a higher degree.

enigma /əˈnɪgmə/ n. somebody or something puzzling or inexplicable. **–enigmatic**, adj.

enjoy v. **1.** to experience with joy; take pleasure in. **2.** to have the benefit of. **3.** to find or experience pleasure for (oneself). **–enjoyment**, n.

enlarge v. **1.** to make larger. **2.** to speak or write at large. **–enlargement**, n.

enlighten v. to give knowledge; instruct.

enlist v. to (secure someone to) enter into some cause or activity.

enmity n. a feeling or condition of hostility.

enormity n. **1.** enormousness; hugeness of size, scope, extent, etc. **2.** outrageous or heinous character; atrociousness: *the enormity of his offences.*

Note that some people think that the use of **enormity** as in def. 1 is incorrect, and that **enormousness** should be used for this sense.

enormous *adj.* **1.** greatly exceeding the common size, extent, etc.; huge; immense. **2.** outrageous or atrocious.

enough *adj.* **1.** as much as is wanted or needed; adequate; sufficient: *We have enough food. –n.* **2.** an adequate quantity or number: *Have you had enough? –adv.* **3.** sufficiently: *It is clean enough.*

Note that the adverb **enough** comes *after* an adjective (*good enough*), another adverb (*well enough*) or a verb (*to heat the water enough*).

enquire *v.* → inquire.

enrage *v.* (**-raged, -raging**) to put into a rage; infuriate.

enrich *v.* **1.** to supply with riches. **2.** to enhance; make finer.

enrol *v.* (**-rolled, -rolling**) to insert the name of a person or oneself in a roll or register. **–enrolment,** *n.*

enrolled nurse *n.* a nurse with a non-degree qualification, as from a nursing college, TAFE college, etc. *Abbrev.:* EN Compare **registered nurse.**

ensconce *v.* (**-sconced, -sconcing**) to settle securely or snugly.

ensemble /ɒnˈsɒmbəl/ *n.* **1.** all the parts of a thing taken together. **2.** a harmonious set of clothes and accessories.

ensign /ˈɛnsən, ˈɛnsaɪn/ *n.* **1.** a flag or banner, as of a nation. **2.** any sign, token, or emblem.

enslave *v.* to make a slave of.

ensnare *v.* to trap.

ensue *v.* (**-sued, -suing**) to follow, especially in immediate succession.

ensuite /ɒnˈswit, ˈɒnswit/ *n. Aust., NZ* a small bathroom attached to a bedroom. Also, **en suite.**

ensure *v.* (**-sured, -suring**) to make sure or certain to come, occur, etc.

Don't confuse this with **assure**, which means to tell with certainty, or with **insure**, which means to pay money so that your property will be replaced if it is stolen or damaged.

entail *v.* to bring on by necessity or as a logical result.

The more usual word is **involve**.

entangle *v.* to involve in difficulties, etc.

entente /ɒnˈtɒnt/ *n.* an understanding or agreement between parties.

enter *v.* **1.** to come or go in. **2.** to make a beginning (*on* or *upon*). **3.** to become a member of, or join. **4.** to make a record of, as on a computer or in a register. **5.** to type data, text, etc., into a computer file.

enterprise *n.* **1.** a project, especially one that requires boldness or energy. **2.** boldness or readiness in undertaking. **3.** a company organised for commercial purposes.

enterprise bargaining *n.* bargaining on wages and conditions conducted between the employer and employees of an enterprise, the results of which are drawn up in a contract.

entertain *v.* **1.** to hold the attention of agreeably; divert; amuse. **2.** to receive as a guest. **3.** to admit into the mind; consider. **–entertainment,** *n.*

enthral /ɛnˈθrɔl, ən-/ *v.* (**-thralled, -thralling**) to captivate; charm.

enthusiasm *n.* absorbing or controlling possession of the mind by any interest or pursuit; lively interest. **–enthusiast,** *n.* **–enthusiastic,** *adj.* **–enthuse,** *v.*

entice *v.* (**-ticed, -ticing**) to draw on by exciting hope or desire.

entire *adj.* **1.** whole; complete. **2.** full or thorough. **–entirety,** *n.*

entitle *v.* to give (a person or thing) a title, right, or claim to something.

entity n. (pl. **-ties**) something that has a real existence; a thing, especially when considered as independent of other things.

entomology n. the branch of zoology that deals with insects.

entourage /'ɒnturaʒ/ n. any group of people accompanying or assisting someone.

entrails pl. n. the inner organs of the body, especially the intestines.

entrance[1] /'entrəns/ n. **1.** the act of entering. **2.** a point or place of entering.

entrance[2] /en'træns, -'trans, ən-/ v. (**-tranced, -trancing**) to fill with delight.

entrant n. a competitor in a contest.

entreat v. to make supplication to (a person); beseech; implore. **–entreaty**, n.

entree /'ɒntreɪ/ n. a dish served before the main course. Also, **entrée**.

entrenched adj. firmly established: en-trenched beliefs.

Note that this is used mainly in relation to ideas, traditions, etc.

entrepreneur /ɒntrəprə'nɜ/ n. (originally in theatrical use) someone who organises and manages any enterprise.

entrust v. **1.** to invest with a trust or responsibility. **2.** to give (something) in trust (to).

entry n. (pl. **-tries**) **1.** an act of entering. **2.** a place of entrance.

entwine v. to twine with, about, or around.

enumerate v. to name one by one.

enunciate v. to utter or pronounce (words, etc.), especially in a particular manner. **–enunciation**, n.

envelop /en'vɛləp, ən-/ v. to wrap up in or as in a covering.

envelope /'ɛnvəloʊp, 'ɒn-/ n. a cover for a letter, etc., usually sealable.

enviable adj. that is to be envied; highly desirable.

envious adj. full of envy.

environment n. **1.** the aggregate of surrounding things, conditions, or influences. **2.** the totality of the surrounding conditions, physical and social, of a particular area. –phr. **3. the environment**, the broad natural surrounding conditions, such as the bush, the rivers, the air, the sea, in which human beings live: The burning of fossil fuels harms the environment. **–environmental**, adj. **–environmentally**, adv. **–environmentalism**, n.

environs /ɛn'vaɪrənz, ən-/ pl. n. surrounding parts or districts.

envisage /ɛn'vɪzədʒ, -zɪdʒ, ən-/ v. (**-aged, -aging**) to form a mental image of.

envoy n. a diplomatic agent.

envy n. **1.** a feeling of discontent at another's good fortune, etc. **2.** desire for some advantage possessed by another. –v. (**-vied, -vying**) **3.** to regard with envy.

enzyme n. any protein capable of catalysing a chemical reaction necessary to the cell.

eon n. → **aeon**.

epaulet /'ɛpəlɛt, -'lɛt/ n. an ornamental shoulder piece worn on uniforms. Also, **epaulette**.

ephemeral /ə'fɛmərəl/ adj. short-lived; transitory.

The more usual word is **passing**.

epic adj. **1.** of or relating to poetry dealing with a series of heroic achievements or events, in a long narrative with elevated style. –n. **2.** an epic poem. **3.** any novel or film depicting great events.

epicentre n. a point from which earthquake waves go out. Also, US, **epicenter**.

epicure n. someone who cultivates a refined taste, especially in food. **–epicurean**, adj., n.

epidemic adj. **1.** affecting at the same time a large number of people in a locality. –n. **2.** a temporary prevalence of a disease.

epidermis n. Anat. the outer layer of the skin. **–epidermal**, adj.

epidural /ɛpi'djurəl/ adj. situated on or over the membrane forming the outermost covering of the brain and spinal cord: an epidural anaesthetic.

epigram n. any witty or pointed saying tersely expressed.

epilepsy n. a nervous disease usually characterised by convulsions. —**epileptic**, adj., n.

epilogue /ˈɛpilog, ˈɛpə-/ n. 1. a speech by one of the actors after the conclusion of the action of a play. 2. a concluding part added to a literary work.

epiphany n. (pl. **-nies**) 1. an appearance, revelation, or manifestation of a divine being. 2. a revelation of the basic nature of something.

episcopal adj. relating to a bishop.

episode n. 1. an incident in the course of a series of events. 2. (in radio, television, etc.) any of the separate programs constituting a serial. —**episodic**, adj.

epistle n. a letter, especially one of formal or didactic character.

epitaph n. a commemorative inscription on a tomb, etc.

epithet n. a term applied to a person or thing to express an attribute.

epitome /əˈpɪtəmi/ n. something typically representing or characteristic of something else. —**epitomise**, **epitomize**, v.

epoch n. a period of time of distinct character.

equable adj. 1. uniform, as motion or temperature. 2. tranquil, as the mind.

equal adj. 1. like or alike in quantity, degree, value, etc. 2. evenly proportioned or balanced. 3. having adequate powers, ability, or means. —n. 4. someone or something that is equal. —v. (**equalled**, **equalling**) 5. to make, be, or become equal to. —**equalise**, **equalize**, v. —**equality**, n.

Note that the opposite of **equal** is **unequal**, but the opposite of **equality** is **inequality**.

equanimity n. calmness of mind or temper; composure.

equate v. 1. to state the equality of or between. 2. to regard, treat, or represent as equivalent.

equation n. Maths an expression of, or a proposition asserting, the equality of 2 quantities, employing the sign = between them.

equator n. the great circle of the earth, midway between the Nth and Sth Poles. —**equatorial**, adj.

equestrian adj. of or relating to horses and horseriding.

equilateral adj. having all the sides equal.

equilibrium n. a state of rest due to the action of forces that counteract each other.

equine adj. of or resembling a horse.

equine influenza n. a viral respiratory disease which causes flu-like symptoms in horses; horse flu. Abbrev.: EI Also, **equine flu**.

equinox n. the time when the sun crosses the plane of the earth's equator, making night and day all over the earth of equal length. —**equinoctial**, adj.

equip v. (**equipped**, **equipping**) to furnish or provide with whatever is needed for any task or services.

equipment n. tools, machines, resources, etc., needed for a job.

equity n. 1. fairness; impartiality. 2. the interest of a shareholder of common stock in a company. 3. the value of an owner's share (in an asset subject to a mortgage). —**equitable**, adj.

equivalent adj. 1. equal in value, measure, force, effect, significance, etc. 2. corresponding in position, function, etc. —n. 3. that which is equivalent.

equivocal /əˈkwɪvəkəl, i-/ adj. questionable; dubious; suspicious.

equivocate v. to use equivocal or ambiguous expressions, especially in order to mislead.

era n. 1. an epoch. 2. a system of chronological notation reckoned from a given date.

eradicate v. to remove or destroy utterly.

erase v. to rub or scrape out, as written letters, etc.

ereader n. a handheld electronic device for reading publications in electronic form. Also, **e-reader**.

erect adj. **1.** upright in position or posture. –v. **2.** to build; construct; raise. **3.** to raise and set in an upright or perpendicular position.

erection n. **1.** the act or process of erecting something. **2.** something erected, as a building or other structure. **3. a.** a distended and rigid condition of an organ or other part of the body. **b.** an erect penis.

ergonomics n. the study of the relationship between workers and their working environment. –**ergonomic**, adj.

ermine /'ɜmən/ n. (pl. **-mines** or, especially collectively, **-mine**) a weasel of nthn regions, which turns white in winter. See **stoat**.

erode v. to wear away, especially by action of wind and water. –**erosion**, n. –**erosive**, adj.

erogenous /ə'rɒdʒənəs, ɛ-, i-/ adj. arousing or tending to arouse sexual desire. –**erogenity**, n.

erotic adj. **1.** of or relating to sexual love. **2.** arousing or satisfying sexual desire. –**erotically**, adv.

err v. **1.** to be mistaken or incorrect. **2.** to do wrong; sin.

For def. 1, the more usual expression is **make a mistake**.

errand n. a short journey for a specific purpose.

errant adj. wandering or travelling. –**errantry**, n.

erratic adj. **1.** irregular in conduct or opinion. **2.** having no certain course; wandering.

erroneous adj. containing error; mistaken; incorrect.

error n. **1.** deviation from accuracy or correctness. **2.** a mistake.

erudition n. learning or scholarship, especially in literature, history, etc. –**erudite**, adj.

erupt v. **1.** (of a volcano, geyser, etc.) to eject matter. **2.** to break out suddenly or violently, as if from restraint. –**eruption**, n.

erythrocyte /ə'rɪθrəsaɪt, ə'nθroʊ-/ n. one of the red corpuscles of the blood; red blood cell.

escalate v. to intensify. –**escalation**, n.

escalator n. (from trademark) a continuously moving staircase.

escapade n. a reckless proceeding; a wild prank.

escape v. **1.** to slip or get away, as from confinement or restraint. **2.** to slip away from or elude (pursuers, captors, etc.). **3.** to fail to be noticed or recollected by (a person). –n. **4.** an act or instance of escaping.

Someone who has escaped, especially from prison, is called an **escapee** or an **escaper**.

escarpment n. a long, cliff-like ridge of rock, or the like.

eschew /ə'ʃu, ɛ'ʃu, əs'tʃu, ɛs-/ v. to abstain from.

The more usual word is **avoid**.

escort n. /'ɛskɔt/ **1.** one or more people or things accompanying another or others for protection, guidance, or courtesy. –v. /əs'kɔt, ɛs-/ **2.** to attend or accompany as an escort.

escutcheon /əs'kʌtʃən/ n. the shield or shield-shaped surface on which a coat of arms is depicted.

esky n. (pl. **-kies**) Aust. (from trademark) a container for keeping things cold.

esophagus /ə'sɒfəgəs/ n. (pl. **-gi**) → **oesophagus**.

esoteric /ɛsə'tɛrɪk, isə-/ adj. understood by or meant for a select few; profound; recondite.

The more usual word is **unusual**.

ESP /ɪ es 'pi/ *n.* extrasensory perception; perception or communication outside of normal sensory activity, as in telepathy and clairvoyance. Also, **e.s.p.**

especially *adv.* **1.** particularly; unusually: *Be especially watchful.* **2.** principally: *especially on Sundays.*

espionage *n.* the practice of spying on others.

esplanade *n.* any open level space serving for public walks, etc.

espouse *v.* to make one's own, adopt, or embrace, as a cause. –**espousal,** *n.*

espresso *n.* coffee made by forcing steam under pressure or boiling water through ground coffee beans.

esquire *n.* (*upper case*) a polite title, usually abbreviated to *Esq.*, after a man's family name.

essay /ˈeseɪ *for def. 1,* ˈeseɪ, eˈseɪ/ *for def. 2 n.,* /eˈseɪ/ *v. –n.* **1.** a short literary composition on a particular subject. **2.** an attempt. –*v.* **3.** to try; attempt. **4.** to put to the test; make trial of.

essence *n.* **1.** intrinsic nature; important elements or features of a thing. **2.** a concentrated extract.

essential *adj.* **1.** absolutely necessary. **2.** relating to or constituting the essence of a thing. –*n.* **3.** an indispensable element.

establish *v.* **1.** to set up on a firm or permanent basis; institute; found. **2.** to settle or install in a position, business, etc. **3.** to show to be valid or well grounded; prove.

establishment *n.* **1.** a place of business or residence. **2.** an institution.

estate *n.* **1.** a piece of landed property, especially a large one. **2.** *Law* **a.** property or possessions. **b.** the property of a deceased person, a bankrupt, etc., viewed as an aggregate. **3.** a housing development. **4.** social status or rank.

estate agent *n.* → **real estate agent**.

esteem *v.* **1.** to regard highly or favourably. **2.** to set a value on; value. –*n.*

3. favourable opinion or judgement; respect or regard.

ester *n.* a compound formed by the reaction between an organic acid and an alcohol.

esthetic *adj.* → **aesthetic**.

estimable /ˈestəməbəl/ *adj.* **1.** worthy of esteem. **2.** capable of being estimated.

estimate *v.* /ˈestəmeɪt/ **1.** to form an approximate judgement or opinion regarding the value, amount, size, weight, etc., of; calculate approximately. –*n.* /ˈestəmət/ **2.** an approximate judgement or calculation. –**estimation,** *n.*

estrange *v.* (**estranged, estranging**) to alienate the affections of.

estrogen *n.* → **oestrogen**.

estuary /ˈestʃuri, ˈestʃuəri/ *n.* (*pl.* **-ries**) **1.** that part of the mouth of a river in which its current meets the sea's tides. **2.** an arm or inlet of the sea.

e-tag *n.* an electronic device attached to a vehicle which, when it comes within range, activates an electronic reader, causing a toll to be debited from the customer's account. Also, **etag, electronic tag**.

et cetera and others; and so forth; and so on.

The short form is **etc.**

etch *v.* **1.** to engrave (metals, etc.) with an acid or the like. **2.** to fix in the memory.

eternity *n.* infinite time; duration without beginning or end. –**eternal,** *adj.*

ethanol /ˈeθənɒl, ˈiθ-/ *n.* an alcohol produced from crops and used as a biofuel.

ether *n.* **1.** *Chem.* a volatile, flammable, colourless liquid used as an anaesthetic. **2.** the upper regions of space; the heavens.

ethereal /əˈθɪəriəl/ *adj.* **1.** light, airy or tenuous. **2.** heavenly or celestial.

ethernet *n.* (*from trademark*) a system used to connect computers in a network, allowing them to communicate with each other in a regulated way. Also, **Ethernet**.

ethical *adj.* relating to or dealing with moral principles.

ethics pl. n. a system of moral principles, by which human actions and proposals may be judged good or bad or right or wrong.

ethnic adj. **1.** relating to or peculiar to a human population or group, especially one with a common ancestry, language, etc. **2.** of or relating to members of the community whose first language is not English.

ethos /'iːθɒs/ n. Sociology the fundamental spiritual characteristics of a culture.

etiology /iːtɪ'ɒlədʒi/ n. → aetiology.

etiquette n. conventional requirements as to social behaviour.

etymology /etə'mɒlədʒi/ n. (pl. -gies) **1.** the study of historical linguistic change, especially as applied to individual words. **2.** the derivation of a word.

eucalyptus n. (pl. -tuses or -ti) → gum tree. Also, eucalypt.

eulogy /'juːlədʒi/ n. (pl. -gies) a speech or writing in praise of a person or thing. –eulogise, eulogize, v. –eulogistic, adj.

eunuch /'juːnək/ n. a castrated man.

euphemism /'juːfəmɪzəm/ n. **1.** the substitution of a mild, indirect, or vague expression for a harsh or blunt one. **2.** the expression so substituted. –euphemistic, adj.

euphoria /juː'fɔːriə/ n. a feeling or state of wellbeing or elation. –euphoric, adj. –euphorically, adv.

euro¹ /'juːroʊ/ n. (pl. euros) → wallaroo.

euro² /'juːroʊ/ n. (pl. euros) the monetary unit of the European Union, introduced as legal tender in most of the member nations in 2002.

euthanase /'juːθəneɪz/ v. to subject to euthanasia. Also, euthanise.

euthanasia /juːθə'neɪʒə/ n. the deliberate bringing about of the death of a person suffering from an incurable disease or condition.

evacuate v. **1.** to leave empty; vacate. **2.** to move (persons or things) from a threatened place, disaster area, etc. –evacuation, n.

evade v. **1.** to escape from by trickery or cleverness. **2.** to avoid answering directly.

evaluate v. to ascertain the value of.

evangelist n. someone who spreads the gospel. –evangelical, adj. –evangelism, n.

evaporate v. to turn to vapour; pass off in vapour. –evaporation, n.

evasion n. the act or an instance of evading. –evasive, adj.

eve n. the evening, or often the day, before a particular date or event.

even adj. **1.** level; flat; without irregularities; smooth. **2.** on the same level; parallel. **3.** uniform in action, character, or quality. **4.** equal in measure or quantity. **5.** divisible by 2 (opposed to odd). **6.** leaving no balance of debt on either side. **7.** equitable, impartial, or fair. –adv. **8.** evenly. **9.** still; yet (used to emphasise a comparative). **10.** indeed (used for stressing identity or truth of something). –v. **11.** to make even; level; smooth.

evening n. the latter part of the day and the early part of the night.

event n. anything that happens; an occurrence, especially one of some importance. –eventful, adj.

eventual adj. consequent; ultimate.

eventuality n. (pl. -ties) a possible occurrence or circumstance.

eventuate v. to come about.

ever adv. **1.** at all times. **2.** continuously. **3.** at any time.

evergreen adj. **1.** (of a tree, bush, etc.) having green leaves all year round. **2.** maintaining strength or popularity from an earlier period: an evergreen song. –n. **3.** an evergreen plant.

Compare this with **deciduous**, which describes trees which lose their leaves each year.

every adj. **1.** each (referring one by one to all the members of an aggregate). **2.** all possible.

everybody pron. every person.

Everybody takes a singular verb (as in *Everybody in the room is standing*), but sometimes, when you need to use a pronoun after **everybody**, there can be a problem if you are not sure of the sex of the people you are talking about, or if there is a mixture of males and females. It is awkward to have to say *Everybody gave his or her answer quickly*, so the plural pronoun **their** is often used, as in *Everybody gave their answer quickly*. Some people say that this is not correct, but is extremely common and neatly solves a difficult problem.

everyday adj. relating to ordinary or informal situations; ordinary; commonplace.

Note that when you write this as two words (**every day**), it means each day: *We go for a walk every day.*

everyone pron. every person.

Everyone takes a singular verb (as in *Everyone in the room is standing*), but sometimes, when you need to use a pronoun after **everyone**, there can be a problem if you are not sure of the sex of the people you are talking about, or if there is a mixture of males and females. It is awkward to have to say *Everyone put his or her hand up*, so the plural pronoun **their** is often used, as in *Everyone put their hand up*. Some people say that this is not correct, but it is extremely common and neatly solves a difficult problem. Don't confuse **everyone** with the expression **every one**. Everyone is only ever used to talk about people, but **every one** means 'each singular one of a set of people of other things'.

everything pron. every thing or particular of an aggregate or total; all.

everywhere adv. in every place.

evict v. to expel (a person, especially a tenant) from land, a building, etc., by legal process. **–eviction**, n.

evidence n. **1.** that which tends to prove or disprove something. **2.** something that makes evident; an indication or sign.

evident adj. plain or clear to the sight or understanding.

evil adj. **1.** violating or inconsistent with the moral law; wicked. **2.** harmful; injurious. **3.** characterised by anger, irascibility, etc. –n. **4.** that which is evil.

evince v. (**evinced**, **evincing**) to show clearly; make evident.

evoke v. to call up or forth, or produce (memories, feelings, etc.). **–evocation**, n. **–evocative**, adj.

evolution n. **1.** any process of formation or growth; development. **2.** *Biol.* the continuous genetic adaptation of organisms or species to the environment.

evolve v. to develop gradually.

ewe n. a female sheep.

ewer n. a pitcher with a wide spout.

exacerbate /ɑg'zæsəbeɪt/ v. to increase the strength or violence of (disease, ill feeling, etc.)

The more usual expression is **make worse**.

exact adj. **1.** strictly accurate or correct. **2.** strict or rigorous. –v. **3.** to call for, demand, or require. **4.** to force or compel the payment, yielding, or performance of. **–exactitude, exactness**, n.

exaggerate v. to magnify beyond the limits of truth. **–exaggeration**, n.

exalt v. **1.** to elevate in rank, honour, power, character, etc. **2.** to praise; extol. **–exaltation**, n.

exam n. an examination. See **examine** (def. 2).

examine v. **1.** to inspect or scrutinise carefully; inquire into or investigate. **2.** to test the knowledge of, as by questions. **3.** to interrogate. **–examination**, n.

example n. **1.** one of a number of things, or a part of something, taken to show the character of the whole. **2.** something to be imitated; a pattern or model. **3.** an instance serving for illustration; specimen. –*phr.* **4. for example**, as a case to show a general point: *Many animals may be kept as pets, for example, dogs.*

Def. 4 is often shortened to **e.g.**, which stands for the Latin words *exempli gratia* with the same meaning.

exasperate v. to irritate to a high degree. –**exasperation**, *n.*

excavate v. to make a hole or cavity in, as by digging. –**excavation**, *n.*

exceed v. to go beyond in quantity, degree, rate, etc.

excel v. (**-celled**, **-celling**) to surpass others.

excellence n. the fact or state of excelling; superiority; eminence.

excellent adj. very good, or of a very high quality. –**excellently**, *adv.*

except prep. **1.** with the exclusion of; excluding. –*conj.* **2.** with the exception (that).

Don't confuse this with **accept**, which means to take or receive something willingly.

exception n. **1.** something excepted; an instance or case not conforming to the general rule. **2.** opposition of opinion; objection; demurral.

exceptional adj. **1.** unusual; extraordinary. **2.** extraordinarily good or clever.

excerpt n. a passage taken out of a book or the like.

excess n. /ək'sɛs, 'ɛk-/ **1.** the amount or degree by which one thing exceeds another. **2.** an extreme amount or degree. **3.** immoderate indulgence. –*adj.* /'ɛksɛs/ **4.** more than necessary, usual or proper: *excess baggage.* –**excessive**, *adj.*

Don't confuse **excess** with **access**, which means a way of getting to a place,

or with **assess**, which means to work out the value of.

exchange v. (**-changed**, **-changing**) **1.** to replace by something else; change for another. –*n.* **2.** the act or process of exchanging. **3.** a place for buying and selling commodities, securities, etc.: *the stock exchange.* **4.** a central office or station: *a telephone exchange.* **5.** the reciprocal transference of equivalent sums of money, as in the currencies of 2 different countries.

excise[1] /'ɛksaɪz, 'ɛksaɪs/ n. **1.** a tax or duty on certain commodities, as spirits, tobacco, etc. **2.** a tax levied for a licence to carry on certain types of employment, pursue certain sports, etc. –**excisable**, *adj.*

excise[2] /ɛk'saɪz/ v. to cut out or off. –**excision**, *n.*

excite v. **1.** to arouse or stir up the feelings of. **2.** to stir to action; stir up. **3.** *Physiol.* to stimulate. –**exciting**, adj. –**excitement**, n. –**excitation**, n.

exclaim v. to cry out or speak suddenly and vehemently. –**exclamation**, *n.*

exclamation mark n. a punctuation mark (!) used after an exclamation.

exclude v. to shut or keep out; prevent the entrance of. –**exclusion**, *n.*

exclusive adj. **1.** excluding from consideration or account. **2.** shutting out all other activities, means, etc. **3.** single or sole. **4.** disposed to shut out outsiders from association, intimacy, etc. **5.** fashionable.

excommunicate v. to cut off from communion or membership, especially from the church.

excrement /'ɛkskrəmənt/ n. waste matter discharged from the body, especially the faeces.

excrescence /ɛks'krɛsəns/ n. abnormal growth or increase.

excrete v. to separate and eliminate from the blood or tissues, as waste matter. –**excreta**, pl. n. –**excretion**, n. –**excretory**, adj.

excruciating adj. very painful.

excursion n. **1.** a short journey or trip for a special purpose. **2.** deviation or digression.

excuse v. /ək'skjuz, ɛk-/ (-**cused**, -**cusing**) **1.** to pardon or forgive. **2.** to apologise for. **3.** to justify. **4.** to release from an obligation or duty. –n. /ək'skjus/ **5.** that which is offered as a reason for being excused. **6.** an inferior or inadequate example of something expected.

execrable /'ɛksəkrəbəl/ adj. abominable.

execute v. **1.** to carry out; accomplish. **2.** to put to death according to law. –**execution**, n.

executive adj. **1.** of the kind requisite for practical performance or direction. **2.** charged with or relating to execution of laws, or administration of affairs. –n. **3.** a person or body having administrative authority.

executor /əg'zɛkjətə/ n. Law a person named by a testator in his or her will to carry out the provisions of the will. –**executrix**, fem. n.

exemplary adj. **1.** worthy of imitation; commendable. **2.** serving as a model, pattern or example.

exemplify v. (-**fied**, -**fying**) **1.** to show or illustrate by example. **2.** to furnish, or serve as, an example of.

exempt v. to free from an obligation or liability to which others are subject; release. –**exemptible**, adj. –**exemption**, n.

exercise n. **1.** bodily or mental exertion. **2.** something done or performed as a means of practice or training. **3.** a putting into action, use, operation, or effect. –v. (-**cised**, -**cising**) **4.** to put through forms of practice or exertion, designed to train, develop, etc. **5.** to put (faculties, rights, etc.) into action, practice, or use. **6.** to discharge (a function); perform.

Don't confuse this with **exorcise**, which means to drive evil spirits away.

exert v. to put forth, as power, ability or influence. –**exertion**, n.

exhale v. to breathe out.

exhaust v. **1.** to empty by drawing out the contents. **2.** to use up or consume completely. **3.** to drain of strength or energy. –n. **4.** Machinery the escape of gases from the cylinder of an engine. –**exhaustion**, n. –**exhaustive**, adj.

exhibit v. **1.** to present for inspection. **2.** to manifest or display. **3.** to place on show. –n. **4.** that which is exhibited. –**exhibition**, n.

exhilarate /əg'zɪləreɪt/ v. to enliven; stimulate; invigorate. –**exhilaration**, n.

exhort /əg'zɔt/ v. to urge, advise, or caution earnestly; admonish urgently. –**exhortation**, n.

exhume v. to dig (something buried, especially a corpse) out of the earth; disinter.

exigent /'ɛksədʒənt/ adj. requiring immediate action or aid; urgent; pressing. –**exigency**, **exigence**, n.

exile n. **1.** prolonged forced separation from one's country or home. –v. (-**iled**, -**iling**) **2.** to separate from country, home, etc.

exist v. **1.** to have actual being; be. **2.** to have life or animation; live.

existence n. **1.** the continuous state of being or life: a struggle for existence. **2.** all that exists.

exit n. **1.** a way or passage out. **2.** a going out or away; departure. –v. **3.** to depart; go away. **4.** to depart from: she exited the stage to great applause.

exodus n. a departure or emigration, usually of a large number of people.

exonerate v. to clear, as of a charge; free from blame.

exorbitant adj. exceeding the bounds of custom, propriety, or reason, especially in amount or extent.

exorcise v. to seek to expel (an evil spirit) by religious or solemn ceremonies. Also, **exorcize**. –**exorcism**, n. –**exorcist**, n.

Don't confuse this with **exercise**, which is to train or improve the body or mind with some kind of activity.

exotic adj. 1. of foreign origin or character. 2. strikingly unusual or colourful in appearance or effect. 3. rare: *an exotic item impossible to buy.* –**exotically**, adv.

expand v. 1. to increase in extent, size, volume, scope, etc. 2. to express in fuller form or greater detail; develop. –**expansion**, n.

expanse n. an uninterrupted space or area; a wide extent of anything.

expatriate v. /eks'pætrient/ 1. to banish (a person) from their native country. 2. to withdraw (oneself) from residence in and/or allegiance to one's native country. –adj. /eks'pætriət, -rieɪt/ 3. expatriated; exiled. –n. /eks'pætriət, -rieɪt/ 4. an expatriated person.

expect v. 1. to regard as likely to happen. 2. to look for with reason or justification. –**expectation**, n. –**expectancy**, n. –**expectant**, adj.

expectorate v. to eject or expel (phlegm, etc.) from the mouth; spit. –**expectorant**, n.

expedient adj. 1. fit or suitable for a particular purpose. 2. conducive to advantage or interest, as opposed to right. 3. acting in accordance with what is thought to be expedient. –n. 4. a means to an end. –**expediency**, n.

expedite /'ekspədaɪt/ v. to speed up the progress of; hasten.

expedition n. 1. an excursion, journey, or voyage made for some specific purpose. 2. promptness or speed in accomplishing something.

expel v. (-pelled, -pelling) 1. to drive or force out or away. 2. to cut off from membership or relations.

expend v. 1. to use up (energy, etc.). 2. to pay out or spend (money). –**expendable**, adj.

expenditure n. 1. the act of expending. 2. that which is expended; expense.

expense n. 1. cost or charge. 2. a cause or occasion of spending.

expensive adj. costly.

experience n. 1. a particular instance of personally encountering or undergoing something. 2. the process or fact of personally observing, encountering, or undergoing something. 3. knowledge or practical wisdom gained from what one has observed, encountered, or undergone. –v. 4. to have experience of; meet with; undergo; feel. –**experienced**, adj. –**experiential**, adj.

experiment n. 1. an act or operation for the purpose of discovering something unknown or testing a principle, supposition, etc. –v. 2. to try or test in order to find something out. –**experimental**, adj. –**experimentation**, n.

expert n., adj. (a person) having special skill or knowledge in some particular field.

expertise /ekspə'tiz/ n. expert skill or knowledge.

expiate v. to make amends or reparation for.

expire v. 1. to come to an end; terminate. 2. to die. 3. (of food products) to be beyond the use-by date: *this milk has expired.* –**expiration**, **expiry**, n.

explain v. 1. to make plain or clear; render intelligible. 2. to make known in detail. 3. to give a meaning to; interpret. –**explanatory**, adj.

explanation n. 1. the act or process of explaining. 2. something that explains; a statement made to clarify something and make it understandable; an exposition. 3. a meaning or interpretation: *to find an explanation of a mystery.* 4. a written or spoken text type or form which describes how something operates or why something happens.

expletive /ək'splitɪv, εk-/ n. an exclamatory oath.

explicate v. to make plain or clear; interpret. –**explication**, n.

The more usual word is **explain**.

explicit adj. leaving nothing merely implied; clearly expressed; unequivocal.

explode v. to expand with force and noise because of rapid chemical change or decomposition, as gunpowder, nitroglycerine, etc. –**explosion**, n. –**explosive**, adj., n.

exploit[1] /'εksplɔɪt/ n. a striking or notable deed.

exploit[2] /ək'splɔɪt, εk-/ v. 1. to turn to practical account; use for profit. 2. to use selfishly for one's own ends. –**exploitation**, n.

explore v. 1. to traverse or range over (a region, etc.) for the purpose of discovery. 2. to look into closely; scrutinise; examine. –**exploration**, n. –**exploratory**, adj.

exponent n. someone or something that expounds, explains, or interprets. 2. Maths a symbol placed above and at the right of another symbol (the base), to denote to what power the latter is to be raised, as in x^3. –**exponential**, adj.

export v. /ək'spɔt, εk-, 'εkspɔt/ 1. to send (commodities) to other countries or places for sale, exchange, etc. –n. /'εkspɔt/ 2. the act of exporting; exportation. 3. an article exported. –**exportation**, n.

Compare this with **import**, which means to bring into a country to sell.

expose v. 1. to lay open. 2. to uncover. 3. to display. 4. to hold up to public censure or ridicule. 5. Photography to subject (a plate, film or paper) to the action of light. –**exposure**, n.

exposé /εkspou'zeɪ/ n. 1. a formal explanation. 2. public exposure of something discreditable.

exposition n. 1. Also, **expo**. an exhibition or show. 2. an act of expounding,

setting forth, or explaining. 3. a written or spoken text type or form which represents a detailed statement or explanation; an explanatory treatise. 4. Lit. the opening section of a text in which characters are introduced and the background of their situation presented.

expostulate v. to reason earnestly.

expound v. 1. to set forth or state in detail. 2. to explain or interpret.

express v. 1. to put (thought) into words. 2. to show, manifest, or reveal. 3. to press or squeeze out. –adj. 4. clearly indicated; distinctly stated. 5. special; particular; definite. 6. specially direct or fast, as a train, etc. –n. 7. an express train or bus. –**expressive**, adj.

expression n. 1. the act of expressing or setting forth in words. 2. a particular word, phrase, or form of words. 3. indication of feeling, spirit, character, etc. –**expressionless**, adj.

expressway n. a freeway.

expropriate v. to take, especially for public use.

expulsion n. the act of driving out or expelling.

expunge v. to erase; obliterate. –**expunction**, n.

expurgate /'εkspзgeɪt, -pəgeɪt/ v. to amend by removing offensive or objectionable matter.

exquisite /ək'skwɪzət, εk-, 'εkskwəzət/ adj. 1. of peculiar beauty or charm, or rare and appealing excellence. 2. intense or keen, as pleasure, pain, etc.

extant /εk'stænt, 'εkstænt/ adj. in existence; still existing.

extempore /ək'stεmpəri, εk-/ adv. without premeditation or preparation.

extend v. 1. to stretch out. 2. to increase the length or duration of. 3. to stretch out in various or all directions; expand. 4. to hold forth as an offer or grant. –**extension**, n.

extensive adj. of great extent.

extent *n.* the space or degree to which something extends; length, area or volume.

extenuate *v.* to represent (a fault, offence, etc.) as less serious.

exterior *adj.* **1.** outer; being on the outer side. –*n.* **2.** the outer surface or part; the outside; outward form or appearance.

exterminate *v.* to get rid of by destroying; extirpate. –**extermination**, *n.*

external *adj.* **1.** of or relating to the outside or outer part; outer. **2.** relating to the outward or visible appearance or show.

extinct *adj.* **1.** extinguished; quenched, as a volcano. **2.** having come to an end; without a living representative, as a species. –**extinction**, *n.*

extinguish *v.* **1.** to put out (a fire, light, etc.). **2.** to put an end to or bring to an end.

extirpate /ˈekstəpeɪt, -stə-/ *v.* to remove utterly; destroy totally.

extol *v.* (**-tolled**, **-tolling**) to praise highly.

extort *v.* to obtain (money, information, etc.) by force, torture, threat, or the like. –**extortion**, *n.* –**extortionate**, *adj.* –**extortionist**, *n.*

extra *adj.* **1.** beyond or more than what is usual, expected, or necessary; additional. –*n.* **2.** something extra or additional. –*adv.* **3.** over the usual or specified amount.

extract *v.* /əkˈstrækt, ɛk-/ **1.** to draw forth or get out by force, as a tooth. **2.** to derive or obtain from a particular source. **3.** to take or copy out (matter from a book, etc.). **4.** to separate or obtain (a juice, ingredient, principle, etc.) from a mixture. –*n.* /ˈekstrækt/ **5.** something extracted. –**extraction**, *n.*

extradite *v.* to give up (a fugitive or prisoner) to another nation, state, or authority. –**extradition**, *n.*

extraneous *adj.* not belonging or proper to a thing; foreign; not essential.

extraordinary *adj.* **1.** beyond what is ordinary. **2.** exceptional; unusual; remarkable. **3.** (of a meeting) in addition to the usual scheduled meetings, usually to

discuss an urgent item of business that has arisen: *an extraordinary general meeting.*

extrapolate *v.* to infer (what is not known) from that which is known; conjecture.

extrasensory *adj.* outside the normal sense perception.

extrasensory perception *n.* → ESP.

extravagant *adj.* **1.** wasteful. **2.** exceeding the bounds of reason. –**extravagance**, *n.*

extravaganza *n.* a lavish, elaborate opera or other entertainment.

extreme *adj.* **1.** of a character or kind farthest removed from the ordinary or average. **2.** utmost or exceedingly great in degree. **3.** last or final. –*n.* **4.** the utmost or highest degree, or a very high degree. **5.** one of 2 things as remote or different from each other as possible. –**extremity**, *n.*

extreme sport *n.* a sport, such as bungee jumping, etc., in which a person contends with the forces of nature, and in so doing incurs a high degree of physical risk.

extricate *v.* to disentangle; disengage; free.

extrinsic *adj.* extraneous.

extrovert *n.* a person with a lively and outgoing nature. –**extroversion**, *n.* –**extroverted**, *adj.*

extrude *v.* to force or press out.

exuberant *adj.* **1.** lavish; effusive. **2.** full of vigour and high spirits.

exude *v.* to come out gradually in drops like sweat through pores; ooze out. –**exudation**, *n.*

exult *v.* to show or feel a lively or triumphant joy (*in*, *at* or *over*).

eye *n.* (*pl.* **eyes**) **1.** the organ of sight. **2.** the region surrounding the eye: *a black eye.* **3.** sight; vision. **4.** appreciative or discriminating visual perception: *an eye for colour.* **5.** (*oft. pl.*) look, glance, or gaze. **6.** (*oft. pl.*) estimation or opinion. **7.** something resembling or suggesting the eye. **8.** *Meteorol.* the central region of low pressure in a tropical hurricane, where calm conditions prevail. −*v.* (**eyed**, **eye-ing** *or* **eying**) **9.** to fix the eyes upon; view. **10.** to observe or watch narrowly. −*phr.* **11. keep an eye on**, to watch attentively; mind. **12. see eye to eye**, to have the same opinion; agree.

eyeball *n.* the ball or globe of the eye.

eyebrow *n.* **1.** the arch or ridge above the eye. **2.** the fringe of hair growing upon it.

eye candy *n. Informal* **1.** something that is visually appealing but not of intrinsic value. **2.** a person considered as such.

eyelash *n.* one of the short, thick, curved hairs growing as a fringe on the edge of an eyelid. Also, **lash**.

eyelid *n.* the movable lid of skin which serves to cover and uncover the eyeball. Also, **lid**.

eyesore *n.* something unpleasant to look at.

eyrie *n.* **1.** the nest of a bird of prey. **2.** an elevated habitation or situation. Also, **aerie**, **aery**, **eyry**.

ezine *n.* a magazine published on the internet. Also, **e-zine**.

F, f

F, f n. the 6th letter of the English alphabet.

fable n. a short tale to teach a moral.

fabric n. **1.** cloth, especially woven. **2.** framework.

fabricate v. **1.** to construct. **2.** to assemble. **3.** to invent (a legend, lie, etc.). **–fabrication,** n.

fabulous adj. **1.** Informal wonderful. **2.** told about in fables; not true or real.

facade /fə'sɑd, fæ-/ n. **1.** Archit. a face or front of a building. **2.** appearance, especially a misleading one.

face n. **1.** the front part of the head. **2.** a person, especially with regard to familiarity or some other quality. **3.** a look or expression on the face, especially showing ridicule, disgust, etc. **4.** Informal impudence. **5.** a surface. **6.** any one of the surfaces of a solid figure. **7.** Printing the style or appearance of type; typeface. –v. (**faced, facing**) **8.** to have the front towards. **9.** to confront. **10.** to be turned (to, towards). –phr. **11. in one's face,** Informal demanding attention.

face lift n. plastic surgery to eliminate wrinkles, etc. Also, **facelift.**

facet n. **1.** one of the polished surfaces of a cut gem. **2.** aspect.

facetious /fə'siʃəs/ adj. intended or trying to be amusing.

face washer n. a small piece of towelling used for washing the face or body; flannel. Also, **face cloth, washer.**

facia n. → **fascia.**

facial adj. **1.** of the face. –n. **2.** a massage or treatment for the face.

facile /'fæsaɪl/ adj. **1.** proceeding, etc., with ease. **2.** glib.

facilitate v. to make easier.

The more usual word is **help.**

facility n. (pl. **-ties**) **1.** freedom from difficulty. **2.** skill or cleverness: her facility with words impressed us. **3.** a service provided: The taxation office has a translation facility. **4.** (usu. pl.) **a.** the equipment necessary to perform some particular activity: sporting facilities; banking facilities. **b.** bathroom and toilet: a hotel room with facilities.

Don't confuse this with **faculty,** which is one of your mental or physical abilities. A **faculty** is also a department at a university.

facsimile /fæk'sɪməli/ n. **1.** an exact copy. **2.** → **fax.**

fact n. **1.** truth; reality. **2.** something known to have happened. **–factual,** adj.

faction n. a smaller group of people within a larger group, especially comprising those who hold a different opinion to the main group.

Don't confuse **faction** with **fraction,** which is a part of a whole number.

factor n. **1.** one of the elements that contribute to bringing about any given result. **2.** Maths one of 2 or more numbers, algebraic expressions, or the like, which when multiplied together produce a given product.

factorial n. Maths the product of an integer multiplied by all the lower integers.

factory n. (pl. **-ries**) building(s), usually with equipment, where goods are manufactured.

faculty n. (pl. **-ties**) **1.** one of the powers of the mind, as memory, reason, speech, etc. **2.** one of the senses or abilities of the body: the faculty of sight. **3.** Educ. one of the branches of learning in a university: the science faculty.

Don't confuse this with **facility,** which is a service or equipment provided, or a particular skill.

fad *n.* a temporary pursuit, fashion, etc.

fade *v.* **1.** to lose freshness or strength. **2.** to disappear or die gradually (*away*, *out*).

faeces /'fisiz/ *pl. n.* waste matter from the intestines; excrement. Also, **feces**. –**faecal**, *adj.*

fag *Informal* –*v.* (**fagged, fagging**) **1.** to tire (*out*). –*n.* **2.** a cigarette.

faggot *n.* a bundle of sticks.

Fahrenheit /'færənhaɪt/ *adj.* of or relating to a scale of temperature in which the boiling point of water is 212°F.

fail *v.* **1.** to be unsuccessful. **2.** to become smaller or less. **3.** to neglect to perform or observe. **4.** to take (an examination, etc.) without passing. **5.** to declare (a person) unsuccessful in a test, course of study, etc.

failure *n.* **1.** an act of failing or being unsuccessful. **2.** something or someone that does not succeed.

faint *adj.* **1.** lacking brightness, loudness, strength, etc. **2.** feeling weak. –*v.* **3.** to lose consciousness temporarily.

fair[1] *adj.* **1.** free from bias, dishonesty, or injustice. **2.** proper according to the rules. **3.** moderately good, large, or satisfactory. **4.** (of the weather) fine. **5.** of a light hue. **6.** beautiful. –*adv.* **7.** in a fair manner.

fair[2] *n.* **1.** an event at which things are displayed or sold and entertainment is provided. **2.** an exhibition or display, especially industrial.

fair dinkum *adj. Aust., NZ Informal* true or genuine: *Are you fair dinkum?* Also, **fair dink, dinkum.**

fairly *adv.* **1.** in a fair manner; justly; impartially. **2.** moderately; tolerably. **3.** actually; completely: *the wheels fairly spun.* **4.** properly; legitimately.

fairway *n.* **1.** an unobstructed passage or way. **2.** *Golf* that part of the course between tees and greens where the grass is kept short.

fairy *n.* (*pl.* **-ries**) a small magical being.

fairytale *n.* Also, **fairy story**. **1.** a tale, usually involving magical happenings, as told to children. **2.** a lie; fabrication. –*adj.* **3.** unreal.

faith *n.* **1.** confidence or trust in a person or thing. **2.** belief which is not based on proof. **3.** belief in the teachings of religion. **4.** a system of religious belief.

faithful *adj.* **1.** strict or thorough in the performance of duty. **2.** that may be relied upon, or believed. **3.** true to fact or an original.

fake *Informal* –*v.* (**faked, faking**) **1.** to pretend. –*n.* **2.** something faked. **3.** someone who fakes. –*adj.* **4.** designed to deceive or cheat.

falcon /'fælkən, 'fɔlkən/ *n.* any of various birds of prey.

fall *v.* (**fell, fallen, falling**) **1.** to drop or come down suddenly. **2.** to become less or lower. **3.** to extend downwards. **4.** to succumb to temptation. **5.** to succumb to attack. **6.** to happen. **7.** to be naturally divisible (*into*). **8.** to lose animation, as the face. **9.** to slope, as land. –*n.* **10.** the act of falling. **11.** (*usu. pl.*) a waterfall. **12.** *Chiefly US* autumn. –*phr.* **13.** fall apart, to cease to operate or function effectively. **14.** fall away, **a.** to withdraw support. **b.** to decline; decay; perish. **15.** fall back, to give way; retreat. **16.** fall back on, **a.** *Mil.* to retreat to. **b.** to have recourse to. **17.** fall down, *Informal* to fail. **18.** fall flat, to fail to have a desired effect. **19.** fall for, *Informal* to be deceived by. **20.** fall for someone (like a ton of bricks), to fall in love with. **21.** fall foul, **a.** to come into collision, as ships. **b.** to come into conflict. **22.** fall in, **a.** to sink inwards. **b.** to take one's proper place in line, as a soldier. **c.** to agree. **23.** fall in with, **a.** to meet and become acquainted with. **b.** to agree to. **24.** fall into place, to eventuate in a satisfactory way. **25.** fall off, **a.** to drop off. **b.** to separate or withdraw. **c.** to decrease in number, amount, intensity, etc. **26.** fall on (or upon), **a.** to assault; attack. **b.** to chance upon. **27. fall short, a.** to fail to reach a particular amount, degree, standard, etc. **b.** to prove insufficient. **28. fall through,** to come to naught; fail; miscarry. **29. fall to, a.** to apply oneself; begin: *to fall to work, argument, etc.* **b.** to begin to eat. **30. fall under,** to be classed as; be included in.

allacy *n.* (pl. **-cies**) a misleading, or false notion, belief, etc. **–fallacious,** *adj.*

allible *adj.* liable to be deceived or mistaken; liable to err.

allout *n.* the falling of airborne particles of radioactive materials resulting from a nuclear explosion.

allow *adj.* ploughed and left unseeded for a season or more; uncultivated.

alse *adj.* **1.** not true or correct. **2.** used to deceive or mislead. **3.** not genuine. **–falsify,** *v.*

alsehood *n.* a lie.

alsetto *n.* (pl. **-tos**) an unnaturally or artificially high-pitched voice, especially in a man.

alter *v.* to hesitate or waver.

ame *n.* widespread reputation. **–famed,** *adj.*

amiliar *adj.* **1.** commonly or generally known or seen. **2.** well-acquainted (*with*). **3.** easy or informal, sometimes excessively so. **–familiarity,** *n.* **–familiarise, familiarize,** *v.*

Note the difference in meaning between defs 1 and 2: *The actor's face was familiar to thousands of people*; *Thousands of people are familiar with the actor's face.*

amily *n.* (pl. **-lies**) **1.** parents and their children (and sometimes other relatives such as grandparents, aunts and uncles), whether dwelling together or not. **2.** all those persons descended from a common ancestor. **3.** any group of related things. **–familial,** *adj.*

A family consisting of parents and children is sometimes called a **nuclear family**. The wider group of related people is

sometimes called an **extended family**. **Family** is a collective noun and can be used with a singular or plural verb. Look up **collective noun**.

family name *n.* the name shared with the rest of one's family: *His family name is Ivanov and his given name is Peter.* Also, **surname.**

family room *n.* *Aust., NZ* a room in a house which is devoted to the leisure pursuits of the members of a family, rather than entertaining visitors.

famine *n.* extreme and general scarcity of food.

famished *adj.* very hungry.

famous *adj.* very well-known.

fan[1] *n.* **1.** any device for causing a current of air. **–v.** (**fanned, fanning**) **2.** to move or agitate (the air) with, or as with, a fan. **3.** to spread (something) (*out*) like a fan.

fan[2] *n.* an enthusiastic devotee or follower.

fanatic *n.* **1.** a person who is extremely enthusiastic about or devoted to an activity, practice, etc. **2.** a person with an extreme and unreasoning enthusiasm or zeal, especially in religious matters. **–fanatical,** *adj.* **–fanaticism,** *n.*

fancy *n.* (pl. **-cies**) **1.** imagination. **2.** a mental image; whim; vagary. **–adj.** (**-cier, -ciest**) **4.** adapted to please the taste or fancy; of delicate or refined quality. **–v.** (**-cied, -cying**) **5.** to picture to oneself. **6.** to have a desire or appetite for: *I fancy a cold drink just now.* **7.** to be sexually attracted to: *I think she fancies you, mate!*

fanfare *n.* a flourish or short air played on trumpets or the like.

fang *n.* **1.** one of the teeth of a snake, by which venom is injected. **2.** a canine tooth.

fanlight *n.* a fan-shaped or grotesque window above a door.

fantastic *adj.* **1.** odd or grotesque. **2.** extravagantly fanciful; irrational. **3.** *Informal* very good. Also, (for defs 1 and 2), **fantastical.**

fantasy n. (pl. **-sies**) **1.** imagination, especially when unrestrained. **2.** an imaginative mental image. **3.** an imagined event that one hopes will happen in reality. **4.** *Informal* → **GHB**. **-fantasise, fantasize,** v.

FAQ n. a frequently asked question.

far adv. (**further, farther, furthest** or **farthest**) **1.** at or to a great distance; a long way off; to a remote point. **2.** to or at a remote distance, etc. **3.** to a great degree; very much: *I far prefer the blue hat.* **-adj.** (**further** or **farther, furthest** or **farthest**) **4.** distant. **5.** more distant of the 2.

farad n. the derived SI unit of electric capacitance. *Symbol:* F

faraway adj. **1.** distant; remote. **2.** abstracted or dreamy, as look.

farce n. **1.** a light, humorous play. **2.** a ridiculous sham. **-farcical,** adj.

fare n. **1.** the price of travelling on a bus, train, plane, etc. **2.** the person or persons who pay to be conveyed in a vehicle. **3.** food. **-v.** (**fared, faring**) **4.** to experience good or bad fortune, treatment, etc.; get on. **5.** to happen (used impersonally).

farewell interj. goodbye.

farm n. **1.** a tract of land devoted to agriculture or some other industry. **-v.** **2.** to cultivate (land). **3.** to raise (livestock, fish, etc.) on a farm. **4.** to distribute (responsibilities, duties, etc.) (*out*). **-farmer,** n. **-farming,** n.

fart *Informal* **-n.** **1.** an emission of intestinal gas from the anus, especially an audible one. **-v.** **2.** to emit intestinal gas from the anus.

Note that this word is mildly taboo and may give offence.

farther adj., adv. comparative of **far**. **-farthest,** adj., adv.

You can also use **further**.
This word is part of the set **far, farther, farthest**.

farthing n. a former British coin.

fascia /'feɪʃə, 'feɪʃiə, *for def. 3* /'fæʃi/ **-n.** (pl. **fasciae** /'fæʃii/) **1.** a band or fillet. **2.** *Archit.* a long, flat member or band. **b.** a long flat board covering the ends of rafters. **3.** *Anat., Zool.* a band or sheath of connective tissue surrounding, supporting, or binding together internal organs or parts of the body. **4.** the plastic covering for the face of a mobile phone, often coloured, decorated or branded. Also, **facia**.

fascinate v. to attract and hold irresistibly the attention of. **-fascination,** n.

fascism /'fæʃɪzəm, 'fæsɪzəm/ n. (*oft. upper case*) a governmental system with strong centralised power, permitting no opposition or criticism, and emphasising an aggressive nationalism.

fashion n. **1.** a prevailing custom or style of dress or behaviour. **2.** styles of dress in general: *Are you interested in fashion?* **3.** manner; way; mode. **4.** the make or form of anything. **-v.** **5.** to give a particular shape or form to; make. **-fashionable,** adj.

fast[1] adj. **1.** moving or able to move quickly. **2.** finished in comparatively little time. **3.** (of a clock) indicating a time in advance of the correct one. **4.** securely attached. **5.** deep or sound, as sleep. **6.** deceptive or unreliable. **-adv.** **7.** tightly attached. **8.** soundly. **9.** rapidly.

fast[2] v. **1.** to abstain from all food. **2.** to eat only sparingly or of certain kinds of food, especially as a religious observance. **-n.** **3.** a fasting.

fasten v. to fix securely.

fastidious adj. **1.** hard to please; excessively critical. **2.** particular or thorough: *fastidious attention to detail.*

The more usual word is **fussy**.

fast-track v. **1.** to move (people, etc.) into or through a system with unusual speed. **2.** to bring (something) about with unusual speed.

fat adj. (**fatter, fattest**) **1.** having much flesh other than muscle; stout; obese. **-n.**

2. the yellowish, greasy substance forming the storage material of animals, also found in plants. **3.** the richest or best part of anything. –*adj*, **fatty**, *adj*.

fatal *adj*. **1.** causing death. **2.** causing destruction or ruin. **3.** decisively important: *that fatal day; a fatal decision*.

Def. 3 is similar in meaning to **fateful**, but note that **fateful** can never mean the same as defs 1 or 2 of **fatal**. You can say 'a fateful decision' but not 'a fateful disease'.

fatalism *n*. **1.** the doctrine that all events are influenced by fate. **2.** the acceptance of all things and events as inevitable. –**fatalist**, *n*. –**fatalistic**, *adj*.

fatality *n*. (*pl*. **-ties**) **1.** a disaster, often one resulting in death. **2.** someone who is killed in an accident or disaster.

fate *n*. **1.** that which is to happen to a particular person or thing, or the power which predetermines this; fortune; destiny. –*v*. (**fated**, **fating**) **2.** (*usu. in the passive*) to predetermine: *It felt like I was fated to win*.

Don't confuse **fate** with **fete**, which is a small fair or carnival.

fateful *adj*. decisively important.

This can mean the same as def. 3 of **fatal**, but don't confuse it with defs 1 or 2 of **fatal**, which mean causing death or destruction (*a fatal crash*).

father *n*. **1.** a male parent. **2.** any male ancestor. **3.** (*oft. upper case*) a title of reverence. –*v*. **4.** to beget. –**fatherly**, *adj*. –**fatherhood**, *n*.

father-in-law *n*. (*pl*. **fathers-in-law**) the father of one's spouse.

fathom *n*. (*pl*. **-thoms** *or, especially collectively*, **-thom**) **1.** a measure of the depth of water in the imperial system, equal to 6 feet, or nearly 2 metres in the metric system. *Symbol*: **fm** –*v*. **2.** to penetrate to or find the bottom or extent of.

fatigue *n*. **1.** weariness from bodily or mental exertion. **2.** a weakening as of

metal subjected to stress. –*v*. (**-tigued**, **-tiguing**) **3.** to weary with bodily or mental exertion.

For def. 1, the more usual word is **tiredness**; for def. 3, **tire**.

fatuous *adj*. foolish, especially in an unconscious, complacent manner.

The more usual word is **silly**.

fatwa *n*. a religious decree issued by a Muslim scholar qualified to issue such decrees. Also, **fatwah**.

fault *n*. **1.** a defect or failing. **2.** an error. **3.** culpability. **4.** a break in the continuity of a body of rock. **5.** *Sport* an infringement of the rules which results in a warning or a penalty. –*v*. **6.** to find fault with. –*phr*. **7. to a fault**, excessively. –**faulty**, *adj*.

fault line *n*. *Geol.* the line along which the movement in an earthquake is liable to occur. Also, **faultline**.

fauna *n*. (*pl*. **-nas** *or* **-nae**) the animals of a given region or period.

Compare this with **flora**, which is the plant life of a particular area or time.

favour *n*. **1.** a kind act; something done or granted out of goodwill. **2.** a state of being approved. –*v*. **3.** to regard with favour. **4.** to have a preference for. –*phr*. **5. in favour of**, **a.** in support of. **b.** to the advantage of. **c.** (of a cheque, etc.) payable to. Also, **favor**.

favourable *adj*. promising well; helpful. Also, **favorable**.

favourite *n*. **1.** a person or thing regarded with special favour or preference. **2.** *Sport* a competitor considered likely to win. –*adj*. **3.** regarded with particular favour or preference. Also, **favorite**.

favouritism *n*. the favouring of one person or group over others having equal claims. Also, **favoritism**.

fawn[1] *n*. **1.** a young deer. –*adj*. **2.** light yellowish brown.

fawn[2] *v*. to seek notice or favour by servile demeanour.

fax n. Also, **facsimile**. **1.** a method of transmission of documents, pictures, etc., by wire or radio. **2.** a document, picture, etc., so transmitted. **3.** a machine which transmits and receives such data. –v. **4.** to send (a document, picture, etc.) by fax.

fear n. **1.** a painful feeling of impending danger, trouble, etc. **2.** reverential awe, especially towards God. –v. **3.** to regard with fear; be afraid of.

fearsome adj. causing fear.

feasible adj. **1.** capable of being done. **2.** likely; probable. –**feasibility**, **feasibleness**, n. –**feasibly**, adv.

feast n. **1.** a commemorative celebration of religious or other character. **2.** a sumptuous entertainment or meal, especially one for many guests. –v. **3.** to have, or partake of, a feast; eat sumptuously.

feat n. an act or achievement requiring great skill, courage or strength.

Don't confuse this with **feet**, which is the plural of **foot**.

feather n. **1.** one of the quills which constitute the plumage of birds. **2.** something like a feather. –v. **3.** to provide with feathers, as an arrow. –phr. **4.** feather one's nest, to provide for oneself.

feature n. **1.** any part of the face, as the nose, chin, etc. **2.** a prominent or conspicuous part or characteristic. **3.** the main film in a cinema program. **4.** a special article, column, cartoon, etc., in a newspaper or magazine. –v. **5.** to make or be a feature of. **6.** (sometimes fol. by in) to be a feature or distinctive mark: *Fine details feature in her paintings.*

feces /'fisiz/ pl. n. → **faeces**.

feckless adj. **1.** ineffective; feeble. **2.** worthless.

fed v. past tense and past participle of **feed**.

federal adj. of or relating to a league, especially a league between nations or states.

federate v. to unite in a federation.

federation n. **1.** a forming of a political unity, with a central government, out of a number of separate states, etc., each of which retains control of its own internal affairs. **2.** the unity so formed.

fee n. a payment for services.

feeble adj. **1.** physically weak, as from age, sickness, etc. **2.** weak intellectually or morally.

feed v. (**fed**, **feeding**) **1.** to give food to supply with nourishment. **2.** to satisfy **3.** to eat. –n. **4.** food, especially for cattle etc.

feedback n. **1.** an indication of reaction as of an audience. **2.** the input of a signal into a microphone from the output of the same system, usually causing a high pitched screech.

feel v. (**felt**, **feeling**) **1.** to perceive or examine by touch. **2.** to perceive by intuition, emotion, etc. **3.** to be emotionally affected by. **4.** to experience the effects of **5.** to have sympathy or compassion (with or for). –n. **6.** a quality of an object that is perceived by feeling or touching. –phr. **7.** feel like, to have a desire for.

feeler n. Zool. an organ of touch, as an antenna or a tentacle.

feeling n. **1.** the function or the power of perceiving by touch. **2.** a consciousness or impression. **3.** an intuition or premonition. **4.** capacity for emotion; pity. **5.** (pl.) sensibilities.

feet n. plural of **foot**.

Don't confuse this with **feat**, which is something done with great courage or skill.

feign v. **1.** to invent (an excuse, etc.). **2.** to pretend. **3.** to imitate deceptively.

feint n. a movement made with the object of deceiving an adversary.

feisty /'faisti/ adj. (**-tier**, **-tiest**) **1.** excitable; quarrelsome. **2.** showing courage and independence; high-spirited. –**feistily** adv. –**feistiness**, n.

felicitate v. to compliment upon a happy event; congratulate. –**felicitation**, n.

felicity n. 1. the state of being happy. 2. excellence, as of expression or taste. **–felicitous**, adj.

feline adj. belonging or relating to the cat family.

fell¹ v. past tense of **fall**.

fell² v. to cause to fall; cut down.

fellow n. 1. Informal a man or boy. 2. one of a pair; a mate or match. 3. (usu. upper case) a member of any of certain learned or professional societies. –adj. 4. belonging to the same class or group. **–fellowship**, n.

felony n. (pl. **-nies**) Law any of various indictable offences, as murder, burglary, etc., of graver character than those called misdemeanours. **–felon**, n. **felonious**, adj.

The more usual word is **crime**.

felt¹ v. past tense and past participle of **feel**.

felt² n. a non-woven fabric.

felt pen n. a pen with a thick nib made of felt, usually in a bright colour, used for colouring in, etc. Also, **texta**.

female n. 1. a human being of the sex which conceives and brings forth young; a woman or girl. 2. any animal of corresponding sex. –adj. 3. relating to or characteristic of this sex.

feminine adj. 1. relating to the female sex. 2. having qualities thought to be typical of women. **–femininity**, n.

feminism n. advocacy of equal rights and opportunities for women. **–feminist**, n.

femur /ˈfimə/ n. (pl. **femurs** or **femora** /ˈfɛmərə/) Anat. the thighbone.

fence n. 1. an enclosure or barrier. 2. Informal a person who receives and disposes of stolen goods. –v. (**fenced**, **fencing**) 3. to enclose by some barrier.

fencing n. the art of using a sword, foil, etc., for defence and attack.

fend v. 1. to ward (off). 2. to provide (for).

fender n. a metal guard as before an open fire.

feng shui /fɛŋ ˈʃweɪ, fʌŋ, ˈʃwiː/ n. the balancing of Yin and Yang in one's physical surroundings in accordance with Chinese tradition, achieved by following rules in relation to the architecture and location of buildings, the position of objects and furniture in a room, etc. Also, **fung shui**.

fennel n. a plant bearing aromatic fruits used in cookery and medicine.

feral adj. wild, or existing in a state of nature.

ferment n. /ˈfɜmɛnt/ 1. any of various agents or substances which cause fermentation. –v. /fəˈmɛnt, fɜ-/ 2. to act upon as a ferment. 3. to seethe with agitation or excitement.

fermentation n. Biochem. the breakdown of complex molecules brought about by a ferment, as in the changing of grape sugar into ethyl alcohol by yeast enzymes. **–fermentative**, adj.

fern n. a leafy plant bearing spores.

ferocious adj. savagely fierce or cruel. **–ferocity**, n.

ferret n. a small animal used for hunting rabbits and rats in their burrows.

ferrous adj. of or containing iron.

ferry n. (pl. **-ries**) 1. (a vessel used in) a service for transport across a body of water. –v. (**-ried**, **-rying**) 2. to carry or convey over water in a boat or plane.

fertile adj. 1. (capable of) bearing abundantly, as land or soil. 2. abundantly productive or inventive. 3. able to produce offspring.

fertilise v. 1. Biol. to render (an egg, ovum, or female cell) capable of development by union with the male cell or sperm. 2. to enrich (soil, etc.) for crops, etc. Also, **fertilize**. **–fertility**, n. **–fertilisation**, n.

fervour n. great warmth and earnestness of feeling. Also, **fervor**. **–fervid**, adj.

fester v. 1. to generate pus; suppurate. 2. to rankle, as a feeling of resentment.

festival n. a public festivity, with performances of music, processions, exhibitions, etc.

festive adj. joyful; merry. **–festivity**, n.

festoon n. a string or chain of flowers, foliage, ribbon, etc.

fetch v. **1.** to go and return with, or bring to or from a particular place. **2.** to bring in (a price, etc.).

fetching adj. charming; captivating.

fete /feɪt/ n. **1.** a small fair held to raise money for a charity, church, school, etc. –v. **(feted, feting) 2.** to give a hospitable public reception to.

Don't confuse **fete** with **fate**, which is someone's destiny.

fetid /ˈfɛtəd, ˈfiːtəd/ adj. having a strong, offensive smell. Also, **foetid**.

fetish /ˈfɛtɪʃ/ n. an obsession or fixation.

fetlock n. lower part of a horse's leg.

fetta n. a soft, ripened white cheese, originally from Greece, made originally from goats' or ewes' milk and now also from cows' milk, and cured in brine. Also, **feta**.

fetter n. **1.** a chain or shackle tied around the ankles. **2.** (usu. pl.) anything that confines or restrains: to shake off the fetters of convention. –v. **3.** to restrict: Our actions were fettered by government regulations.

fettle phr. **in fine fettle, 1.** in good condition. **2.** in good health or spirits.

fettuccine /fɛtəˈtʃiːni/ n. pasta cut into long narrow strips. Also, **fettucine, fettucini**.

fetus /ˈfiːtəs/ n. the young of an animal during its development in an egg or in its mother's womb, especially in the later stages. Also, **foetus**. **–fetal, fetal**, adj.

Compare **fetus** with **embryo**, which is the developing young in its early stages.

feud n. **1.** a bitter, continuous hostility, especially between 2 families, clans, etc. –v. **2.** to conduct a feud.

feudal adj. relating to a way of life in which ordinary people lived on and used the land of a noble person, giving military and other service in return: a feudal lord.

We usually talk about the **feudal system** which was in force in Europe in medieval times.

fever n. an unusually high body temperature caused by illness.

few adj. **1.** not many; a small number of. –phr. **2. a few**, a small number.

Note that **few** is used with things you can count (count nouns), as in few people, a few books. You use **little** for things you can't count (uncount nouns), as in little cash, a little butter. So, strictly speaking, you should use **fewer** for count nouns and **less** for uncount nouns: You should eat less sugar and fewer biscuits. However, many people do use **less** with count nouns and it is generally regarded as acceptable: The new system means less problems.

fey adj. **1.** as if enchanted. **2.** slightly crazy.

fiancée /fiˈɒnseɪ/ n. a woman engaged to be married. Also, **fiancee**. **–fiancé, fiance**, masc. n.

fiasco n. (pl. **-cos**) a complete and usually ignominious failure.

fib Informal –n. **1.** a trivial falsehood. –v. **(fibbed, fibbing) 2.** to tell a fib.

fibre n. a fine threadlike piece, as of cotton, jute, or asbestos. **–fibrous**, adj.

fibreglass n. (from trademark) a material made from extremely fine filaments of glass, and used to insulate buildings, make surfboards and boats, etc.

fibro n. Aust., NZ (from trademark) compressed asbestos and cement used for building materials.

fibula /ˈfɪbjələ/ n. (pl. **-las** or **-lae** /-liː/) Anat. one of the 2 bones of the lower leg. **–fibular**, adj.

fickle adj. likely to change.

fiction n. **1.** the branch of literature comprising prose works of imaginative narration. **2.** a story or idea which is not true.

fictitious adj. false; not genuine.

fiddle v. **1.** to make aimless movements, as with the hands. **2.** to play on the fiddle. —n. **3.** a violin. **4.** *Informal* a manipulation of laws, rules etc., to execute an underhand transaction.

fiddly adj. *Informal* difficult or exacting, as something small done with the hands.

fidelity n. **1.** loyalty; faithfulness. **2.** quality of sound reproduction.

fidget v. to move about restlessly or impatiently.

fiefdom /'fiːfdəm/ n. **1.** a feudal lord's estate. **2.** a powerful person's area of control.

field n. **1.** a piece of open or cleared ground. **2.** a piece of ground devoted to sports or contests. **3.** a sphere, or range of activity. **4.** *Computers* a specified area of a record, considered as a unit of information. —v. **5.** *Cricket, etc.* to stop, or catch, and throw (the ball).

fiend n. **1.** any evil spirit. **2.** a diabolically cruel or wicked person.

fierce adj. **1.** wild or vehement in temper, appearance, or action. **2.** violent in force, intensity, etc.

fiery /'faɪəri/ adj. (**-rier**, **-riest**) **1.** characterised by or containing fire. **2.** flashing or glowing, as the eye. **3.** easily angered.

fiesta /fi'estə/ n. a festival.

fife n. a high-pitched flute.

fifteen n. **1.** a cardinal number, 10 plus 5. —adj. **2.** amounting to 15 in number. —**fifteenth**, n., adj.

Numbers used before a noun are sometimes called **determiners**.

fifty n. **1.** a cardinal number, 10 times 5. —adj. **2.** amounting to 50 in number. —**fiftieth**, adj., v.

Numbers used before a noun are sometimes called **determiners**.

fig n. (a tree bearing) a small, pear-shaped fruit.

fight n. **1.** a battle or combat. **2.** any quarrel, contest, or struggle. **3.** ability or inclination to fight. —v. (**fought**, **fighting**)

4. to engage in battle or in single combat. **5.** to contend (with) in any manner.

figment n. a mere product of the imagination.

figurative adj. (of a word or phrase) not used with its ordinary, straightforward meaning, but used to create an image; metaphorical; for example, *He cried his eyes out* is a figurative expression because it means *He cried a lot*, not *He cried until his eyes came out*.

Compare **figurative** with **literal**, which describes words, phrases, etc., which are used with their usual meaning.

figure n. **1.** a written symbol other than a letter. **2.** an amount or value expressed in numbers. **3.** shape or appearance. **4.** a representation, especially of the human form. **5.** a series of movements in skating. —v. **6.** to conclude, judge, or reason. **7.** to compute or work with numerical figures. **8.** to be conspicuous. —phr. **9. figure out**, to solve; understand. **10. go figure**, *Chiefly US Informal* an expression used after a statement to indicate that the listener should try to make sense of it because the speaker cannot.

figurehead n. a person who is nominally the head of a society, community, etc., but has no real authority or responsibility.

figure of speech n. a word or phrase that is not used in its basic sense, but gives a special effect instead, especially by making a comparison or creating an image: *Calling someone 'brainless' doesn't mean they literally don't have a brain – it is just a figure of speech.*

Look up **metaphor** and **simile**. These are types of figures of speech.

figurine /'fɪgjuriːn/ n. a small ornamental figure of pottery, metalwork, etc.

filament n. a very fine thread or threadlike structure.

filch v. to steal (especially something of small value).

file¹ *n.* **1.** any device, as a cabinet or folder, in which papers, etc., are arranged or classified for convenient reference. **2.** *Computers* a collection of data with a unique name. **3.** a line of persons or things arranged one behind another. –*v.* (**filed, filing**) **4.** to place in a file. **5.** *Law* to bring (a suit) before a court of law.

file² *n.* **1.** a tool for smoothing or cutting. –*v.* (**filed, filing**) **2.** to reduce or smooth, as with a file.

filial *adj.* relating to or befitting a son or daughter.

filibuster /ˈfiləbʌstə/ *n.* the use of obstructive tactics, especially long speeches to delay legislative action.

filigree *n.* ornamental work of fine wires.

fill *v.* **1.** to make (or become) full. **2.** to supply to fullness or plentifully. **3.** to extend throughout. **4.** to occupy and perform the duties of (a position, post, etc.). **5.** to execute (a business order). –*n.* **6.** a full supply; enough to satisfy want or desire: *He has eaten his fill.* –*phr.* **7. fill in**, **a.** to complete (a document, design, etc.) by filling blank spaces. **b.** to act as a substitute; replace. **8. fill out**, to complete the details of (a plan, form, etc.).

fillet *n. Cookery* **1.** a boneless piece of fish or chicken. **2.** a cut of beef or pork.

filly *n.* (*pl.* **-lies**) a young mare.

film *n.* **1.** a thin layer or coating. **2.** a strip or roll of cellulose used in photography. **3.** a moving picture which is shown on a screen; movie; picture. –*v.* **4.** to reproduce in the form of a film or films.

film clip *n.* a short extract from a film, usually shown as part of promotional material.

filo pastry /ˈfiːloʊ, ˈfaɪloʊ/ *n.* a paper-thin pastry made from flour and water, often used in Greek cooking. Also, **fillo pastry**.

filter *n.* **1.** any device through which liquid is passed to remove suspended impurities or recover solids. –*v.* **2.** to remove by the action of a filter.

filthy *adj.* **1.** foul. **2.** obscene. **3.** disgustingly dirty. –**filth**, *n.*

fin *n.* **1.** an organ of fishes used for propulsion, steering, or balancing. **2.** anything resembling a fin.

final *adj.* **1.** coming at the end; last in place, order, or time. **2.** conclusive or decisive. –*n.* **3.** that which is last, especially of a series. –**finalise, finalize**, *v.* –**finality**, *n.*

finale /fəˈnɑːli, -ˈnɑːleɪ/ *n.* the concluding part of any performance, course of proceedings, etc.

finance *n.* **1.** the conduct or transaction of money matters. **2.** (*pl.*) pecuniary resources. –*v.* **3.** to supply with means of payment. –**financial**, *adj.* –**financier**, *n.*

finch *n.* a type of small bird with a large beak for eating seeds.

find *v.* (**found, finding**) **1.** to come upon by chance; meet. **2.** to discover. **3.** to recover (something lost). **4.** *Law* to pronounce (a verdict or judgement). –*n.* **5.** a discovery.

fine¹ *adj.* **1.** of very high grade or quality. **2.** consisting of minute particles. **3.** very thin or slender.

fine² *n.* **1.** a sum of money exacted as a penalty for an offence. –*v.* (**fined, fining**) **2.** to punish by a fine.

finery *n.* fine or showy dress, ornaments, etc.

finesse *n.* fine skill; delicacy of execution.

finger *n.* **1.** any of the terminal members of the hand, especially one other than the thumb. **2.** something like a finger. –*v.* **3.** to handle; toy or meddle with.

fingerprint *n.* an impression of the markings of the end of the thumb or a finger.

finicky *adj.* fussy about details.

finish *v.* **1.** to bring or come to an end or to completion. **2.** to use completely (*up* or *off*). **3.** to put the final touches on. –*n.* **4.** the end or last stage. **5.** the quality of being completed with smoothness, elegance, etc. **6.** the surface coating or texture of wood, metal, etc.

finite *adj.* having bounds or limits.

fink *n. Informal* a contemptible or undesirable person.

fiord /ˈfiɒd/ *n.* → **fjord**.

fir *n.* a pyramidal coniferous tree.

fire *n.* **1.** the active principle of burning as seen in the production of light and heat. **2.** a burning mass of material, as on a hearth or in a furnace. **3.** the destructive burning of a building, town, forest, etc. **4.** burning passion; enthusiasm. **5.** the discharge of firearms. –*v.* (**fired, firing**) **6.** to (be) set on fire. **7.** to apply heat to in a kiln. **8.** to discharge (a gun). **9.** to dismiss from a job. **10.** (of an internal-combustion engine) to cause the air-fuel mixture in the cylinders to burn.

firearm *n.* a gun that fires bullets.

firebreak *n.* a strip of ploughed or cleared land made to check the spread of fire.

firefighter *n.* a person employed to extinguish or prevent fires. Also, **fire officer**.

If the person is a man, you can also use **fireman**.

firefly *n.* (*pl.* **-flies**) a beetle with abdominal light-producing organs.

fire front *n.* the part of a fire within which continuous flaming combustion is taking place.

fireplace *n.* that part of a chimney which opens into a room and in which fuel is burnt.

firewall *n.* **1.** a wall made of fireproof material, designed to prevent the spread of a fire, as in buildings, aircraft, motor vehicles, etc. **2.** *Computers* a system designed for the protection of a network from unauthorised users.

fireworks *pl. n.* combustible or explosive devices for producing a striking display of light, etc.

firm[1] *adj.* **1.** fairly solid or stiff. **2.** securely fixed in place. **3.** steady; not shaking or trembling.

firm[2] *n.* **1.** a business organisation or partnership. **2.** the name or title under which associated parties transact business.

firmament *n.* the vault of heaven; the sky.

first *adj.* **1.** being before all others: *the first person to arrive.* –*adv.* **2.** before all others: *She arrived first.* **3.** before doing anything else: *First, eat your dinner.* **4.** for the first time: *when I first saw you.* –*n.* **5.** that which is first in time, order, rank, etc.: *the first to arrive.*

first aid *n.* emergency aid or treatment given to persons suffering from accident, etc.

first-class *adj.* **1.** of the highest or best class or quality. **2.** by first-class conveyance: *to travel first-class.*

firsthand *adj.* direct from the original source: *a firsthand account of events.*

first name *n.* the name that comes before the family name or surname: *My first name is Mario and my family name is Rossi.*

You can also use **given name**, which is more appropriate when the family name comes first, as with some Asian names.

First Nation *n.* (in Australia) any of various Aboriginal or Torres Strait Islander peoples. Also, **First People**.

first person *n.* See **person** (def. 3).

fiscal *adj.* **1.** of or relating to the public treasury or revenues. **2.** relating to financial matters in general.

fish *n.* (*pl.* **fish** *or* **fishes**) **1.** any of various cold-blooded, completely aquatic vertebrates, having gills, fins, and typically an elongated body usually covered with scales. –*v.* **2.** to catch or attempt to catch fish. **3.** to draw as by fishing (*up, out,* etc.). **4.** to seek to obtain something indirectly (*for*).

Note that this word has two acceptable plurals. You can use either, but **fish** is the more usual. Zoologists use *fish* when they are talking about a group consisting of a single species, and *fishes* when it is a group consisting of two or more different species. In most cases, this also applies to the plural of the names of particular fish (for example, *salmon* or *salmons*, *bream* or *breams*). However, there are some fish which usually do take the -*s* form of the plural. For example, *ten sardines* is more commonly used than *ten sardine*.

fisherman *n.* (*pl.* **-men**) a man engaged in fishing.

You can also use **angler** for someone who fishes for pleasure.
Because **fisherman** refers to a man engaged in fishing, it is best to use another term such as **fisher** or **fisherperson** if you are not referring specifically to a man.

fishy *adj.* (**fishier**, **fishiest**) **1.** fishlike. **2.** *Informal* odd or questionable.

fission *n.* the act of cleaving or splitting into parts.

fissure *n.* a narrow opening produced by cleavage or separation of parts; a cleft.

The more usual word is **crack**.

fist *n.* the hand closed tightly, with the fingers doubled into the palm.

fisticuffs *pl. n.* combat with the fists.

fit[1] *adj.* (**fitter**, **fittest**) **1.** well adapted or suited. **2.** proper or becoming. **3.** in good health. -*v.* (**fitted**, **fitting**) **4.** to be suitable (for a purpose, etc.). **5.** to conform or adjust to something. **6.** to furnish; equip. **7.** to be or the right size or shape. -*n.* **8.** the manner in which a thing fits: *The shirt is a good fit.* -**fitness**, *n.*

fit[2] *n.* **1.** a sudden, acute attack, as of a disease. **2.** a burst or period of emotion, activity, etc. **3.** a convulsion.

fitful *adj.* happening irregularly.

five *n.* **1.** a cardinal number, plus 1. -*adj.* **2.** amounting to 5 in number. -**fifth**, *n.*, *adj.*

Numbers used before a noun are sometimes called **determiners**.

fix *v.* **1.** to make fast, firm, or stable. **2.** to settle definitely; determine. **3.** to direct (the eyes, the attention, etc.) steadily. **4.** to

put or place (responsibility, blame, etc.) on a person. **5.** to repair. -*n.* **6.** *Informal* a predicament.

fixation *n.* *Psychol.* the state of being fixed in one idea, stage of development, etc.; an obsession.

fixture *n.* **1.** something or someone securely fixed in position. **2.** a sporting event.

fizz *v.* **1.** to make a hissing or sputtering sound. -*n.* **2.** a hissing sound; effervescence.

fizzle *v.* **1.** to make a hissing or sputtering sound, especially one that dies out weakly. -*phr.* **2. fizzle out**, *Informal* to fail ignominiously after a good start.

fjord /'fiɔd/ *n.* a long, relatively narrow arm of the sea, bordered by steep cliffs, as on the coast of Norway. Also, **fiord**.

flab *n.* *Informal* bodily fat.

flabbergast *v.* to overcome with surprise and bewilderment; astound.

flaccid /'flæsəd/ *adj.* soft and drooping.

The more usual word is **limp**.

flag[1] *n.* **1.** a piece of cloth, bearing a design, used as a symbol, signal, decoration, etc., especially one used as the emblem of a country. -*v.* (**flagged**, **flagging**) **2.** to signal or warn as with a flag.

flag[2] *v.* (**flagged**, **flagging**) to fall off in vigour, interest, etc.

flagellate /'flædʒəleɪt/ *v.* to whip; lash.

flagon *n.* a large bottle.

flagrant /'fleɪgrənt/ *adj.* obvious or open in a shameless or shocking way; blatant; scandalous: *a flagrant lie*; *flagrant disobedience*.

flagship *n.* **1.** a ship which carries the admiral of a fleet, etc. **2.** the best example of a commercial item or enterprise. -*adj.* **3.** relating to the finest example of some commercial item or enterprise.

flail *v.* to strike out wildly (at).

flair *n.* talent; aptitude.

Don't confuse this with **flare**, which is a bright light used as a signal.

flak *n.* anti-aircraft fire.

flake[1] *n.* **1.** a small, flat, thin piece of anything. **2.** to peel off or separate in flakes. **3.** Also, **flake out**. *Informal* to collapse, faint, or fall asleep.

flake[2] *n.* the flesh of various sharks.

flamboyant *adj.* **1.** consciously theatrical in personality. **2.** flaming; gorgeous. **3.** florid; ornate; showy.

flame *n.* **1.** burning gas or vapour, as from wood, etc., undergoing combustion. **2.** heat or ardour. **3.** *Informal* a sweetheart. –*v.* **4.** to burn with a flame; blaze. **5.** *Internet* to express in emails, chat rooms, etc., one's strongly felt opinions, especially one's hostile reactions to others' opinions, with great intensity and frequency. **6.** *Internet* to attack by flaming.

flamingo *n.* (*pl.* **-gos** *or* **-goes**) an aquatic bird with very long neck and legs and pinkish plumage.

flammable *adj.* easily set on fire. –**flammability,** *n.*

Another word for this is **inflammable**, but it is not used very much nowadays. Many people took it to mean *not* easily set on fire because *in-* at the beginning of a word often does mean 'not', as in *inactive* and *insensitive*. This misunderstanding could have placed people in danger, so it was decided to use **flammable** to mean easily set on fire and **nonflammable** as its opposite, to mean not likely to burn easily.

flan *n.* an open tart.

flange *n.* a projecting rim.

flank *n.* **1.** the side of an animal or a human being between the ribs and hip. **2.** the side of anything, as of a building. –*v.* **3.** to stand or be placed or posted at the flank or side of.

flannel *n.* **1.** a warm, soft fabric. **2.** → **face washer**.

flannelette *n.* a cotton fabric made to imitate flannel.

flap *v.* (**flapped, flapping**) **1.** to swing or sway about loosely, especially with noise. **2.** to move (wings) up and down. –*n.* **3.** a flapping motion. **4.** something that hangs loosely, attached at one side only. **5.** *Informal* a state of panic or nervous excitement.

flare *v.* (**flared, flaring**) **1.** to burn with an unsteady flame. **2.** to blaze (*up*) with a sudden burst of flame. **3.** (of anger, violence, etc.) to burst (*up*) into sudden fierce activity. **4.** to spread outwards, as the end of a trumpet. –*n.* **5.** a sudden blaze of fire or light used as a signal, etc. **6.** a sudden burst, as of zeal or of temper.

Don't confuse **flare** with **flair**, which is a natural talent: *a flair for maths.*

flash *n.* **1.** a sudden burst of flame or light. **2.** a sudden, brief outburst or display of joy, wit, etc. **3.** an instant. **4.** ostentatious display. –*v.* **5.** to gleam. **6.** to move like a flash. **7.** to emit or send forth (fire or light) in sudden flashes. –*adj.* **8.** *Informal* showy or ostentatious.

flashback *n.* a representation, during the course of a novel, film, etc., of some event or scene which occurred at a previous time.

flashforward *n.* a representation, during the course of a novel, film, etc., of an event or scene from some future time.

flask *n.* a bottle-shaped container.

flat[1] *adj.* (**flatter, flattest**) **1.** level, even, as of land, etc. **2.** lying at full length, as a person. **3.** (of feet) having little or no arch. **4.** spread out. **5.** collapsed; deflated. **6.** unqualified, downright, or positive: *a flat refusal.* **7.** uninteresting, dull, or tedious. **8.** (of beer, etc.) having lost its effervescence. –*adv.* **9.** in a flat position; horizontally; levelly. **10.** *Music* below the true pitch. –*n.* **11.** *Music* **a.** a note that is one semitone below a given note. **b.** the music sign 'b' which lowers a note by a semitone when it is placed before it. –*phr.*

12. flat out, *Informal* **a.** as fast as possible. **b.** very busy. –**flatness**, *n.* –**flatly**, *adv.*

flat² *n.* **1.** a group of rooms for living in, usually part of a larger building and often rented. –*v.* (**flatted**, **flatting**) **2.** *Aust.*, *NZ* to live in a flat.

flatbread *n.* any of various unleavened breads, baked in thin sheets.

flatfish *n.* (*pl.* **-fish** *or* **-fishes**) any of a group of flat-bodied fishes which swim on one side, having both eyes on the upper side.

For information about the different plural forms, see the note at **fish**.

flathead *n.* (*pl.* **-head** *or* **-heads**) a food fish with a depressed, ridged head.

For information about the different plural forms, see the note at **fish**.

flatline *v. Informal* to die.

flatter *v.* **1.** to compliment or praise, especially insincerely. **2.** to show to advantage. –**flattery**, *n.*

flatulent *adj.* **1.** generating gas in the alimentary canal. **2.** pretentious; empty. –**flatulence**, *n.*

flaunt *v.* to parade or display conspicuously or boldly: *to flaunt one's wealth.*

The more usual expression is **show off**. Don't confuse **flaunt** with **flout**, which is to deliberately disobey.

flautist *n.* a flute player.

flavour *n.* **1.** (a noticeable element in) the taste of a thing. **2.** the characteristic quality of a thing. Also, **flavor**.

flaw *n.* a defect.

The more usual word is **fault**. Don't confuse **flaw** with **floor**, which is the flat surface that you walk on in a building.

flax *n.* **1.** a plant cultivated for its fibre and seeds. **2.** the fibre of this plant, manufactured into linen yarn.

flaxen *adj.* **1.** made of flax. **2.** of a pale yellowish colour.

flay *v.* **1.** to strip off the skin or outer covering of. **2.** to criticise severely.

flea *n.* any of numerous small, wingless, bloodsucking insects.

Don't confuse this with **flee**, which is to run away.

fleck *n.* **1.** any spot or patch of colour, light, etc. –*v.* **2.** to mark with a fleck or flecks; spot; dapple.

fled *v.* past tense and past participle of **flee**.

fledgling *n.* **1.** a young bird. **2.** an inexperienced person. –*adj.* **3.** new or inexperienced. Also, **fledgeling**.

flee *v.* (**fled**, **fleeing**) to run away (from).

Don't confuse this with **flea**, which is a tiny bloodsucking insect.

fleece *n.* **1.** the coat of wool that covers a sheep or some similar animal. –*v.* (**fleeced**, **fleecing**) **2.** to plunder; swindle.

fleet¹ *n.* **1.** the largest organised unit of naval ships. **2.** the vessels, aeroplanes or vehicles collectively of a single transport company or undertaking.

Compare def. 1 with **flotilla**.

fleet² *adj.* swift; rapid.

fleeting *adj.* passing swiftly; transient.

flesh *n.* **1.** the soft substance of an animal body, consisting of muscle and fat. **2.** the soft pulpy portion of a fruit, vegetable, etc.

flew *v.* past tense of **fly¹**.

flex *v.* **1.** to bend (something pliant or jointed). –*n.* **2.** an insulated electric cable or wire.

flexible *adj.* **1.** easily bent. **2.** adaptable. –**flexibility**, *n.*

flexiday *n.* a day taken off from work under a scheme that allows employees to vary their working hours while maintaining the total time worked.

flexitime *n.* an arrangement by which employees may vary their commencing, ceasing, and meal-break times while still working the total number of hours required.

flick n. **1.** a sudden light blow or stroke, as with a whip or the finger. −v. **2.** to remove with a flick.

flicker v. **1.** to burn or shine unsteadily. −n. **2.** an unsteady flame or light. **3.** a brief spark.

flick-knife n. a knife whose blade springs out at the press of a button on the handle; switchblade.

flight[1] n. **1.** the act, manner, or power of flying. **2.** the distance covered or the course pursued by a flying object. **3.** a journey by air, especially by aeroplane. **4.** a series of steps or stairs. −**flightless**, adj.

flight[2] n. the act of fleeing.

flighty adj. (**-tier, -tiest**) given to flights of fancy, caprice, etc.

flimsy adj. (**-sier, -siest**) without material strength or solidity.

flinch v. to draw back from what is dangerous, painful, etc.

fling v. (**flung, flinging**) **1.** to throw, especially with violence. **2.** to put suddenly or violently. −n. **3.** a spell of unrestrained indulgence of one's impulses.

flint n. a hard kind of stone.

flip v. (**flipped, flipping**) **1.** to toss with a snap of a finger and thumb; flick. −n. **2.** a smart tap or strike. **3.** a somersault.

flip-flop n. → **thong** (def. 2).

flippant adj. **1.** clever or pert in speech. **2.** characterised by a shallow or disrespectful levity.

flipper n. **1.** a broad, flat limb, as of a seal, whale, etc. **2.** a swimming aid resembling in form an animal's flipper.

flirt v. **1.** to trifle in love. −n. **2.** a person given to flirting.

flit v. (**flitted, flitting**) to move lightly and swiftly.

float v. **1.** to rest on the surface of a liquid; be buoyant. **2.** to move or drift about free from attachment. **3.** to launch (a company, scheme, etc.). **4.** to allow the rate of exchange of (a currency) to find its own level in a foreign exchange market. −n. **5.** something that floats, as a raft, a life jacket, etc. **6.** a decorated platform on wheels drawn along in a procession.

flock[1] n. **1.** a number of animals or of birds of one kind. −v. **2.** to gather or go in a flock.

flock[2] n. a tuft of wool, hair, etc.

floe n. a field of floating ice formed on the surface of the sea, etc.

flog v. (**flogged, flogging**) **1.** to beat hard with a whip. **2.** Informal to sell or attempt to sell. **3.** Informal to steal.

flood n. **1.** an overflowing of water, especially over land not usually submerged. **2.** any great outpouring or stream. −v. **3.** to flow or pour in or as in a flood. **4.** to overwhelm with an abundance of something.

floor n. **1.** that part of a room or the like upon which one walks. **2.** a storey of a building. **3.** any more or less flat extent or surface. **4.** the part of a legislative chamber, etc., where the members sit. −v. **5.** to cover or furnish with a floor. **6.** Informal to confound or puzzle completely: *She floored me with her ideas.*

Don't confuse **floor** with **flaw**, which is a defect or fault.

flop v. (**flopped, flopping**) **1.** to drop or turn with a sudden bump or thud. **2.** Informal to yield or break down suddenly; fail. −n. **3.** Informal a failure.

floppy disk n. a computer disk that can be put in and removed from a slot in the front of a computer.

Although the square plastic case surrounding such a disk is hard, the disk inside is bendable or 'floppy'. Compare this with **hard disk**.

flora n. the plants of a particular region or period.

Compare this with **fauna**, which is the animal life of a particular area or time.

floral *adj.* relating to or consisting of flowers.

florid *adj.* **1.** highly coloured or ruddy, as complexion, cheeks, etc. **2.** flowery.

florin *n.* a former silver coin worth 2 shillings.

florist *n.* a retailer of flowers. –**floristry**, *n.*

floss *n.* **1.** silky thread-like matter. **2.** Also, **dental floss** soft, waxed thread used for cleaning between the teeth.

flotation *n.* **1.** the act or state of floating. **2.** the launching of a commercial venture, a loan, etc.

flotilla *n.* a number of small naval vessels.

Compare this with **fleet¹** (def. 1).

flotsam and jetsam *n.* the wreckage of a ship and its cargo found either floating upon the sea or washed ashore.

flounce¹ *v.* (**flounced, flouncing**) to go with an impatient or angry fling of the body.

flounce² *n.* a gathered strip of material on a skirt, etc.

flounder¹ *v.* **1.** to struggle with stumbling or plunging movements: *to flounder through the bush.* **2.** to struggle helplessly because of embarrassment or confusion: *The actor forgot his lines and began to flounder.*

Don't confuse this with **founder**, which is to fill with water and sink.

flounder² *n.* (*pl.* **-der** or **-ders**) any of numerous species of flatfishes.

For information about the different plural forms, see the note at **fish**.

flour *n.* the finely ground meal of wheat or other grain.

Don't confuse **flour** with **flower**, which is the blossom of a plant.

flourish *v.* **1.** to be in a vigorous state; be successful. **2.** to brandish or wave (a sword, etc.) about in the air. –*n.* **3.** a parade or ostentatious display. **4.** *Music* a trumpet call or fanfare.

flout /flaʊt/ *v.* to show no respect for; treat with disdain or contempt; scoff at: *to flout the rules; to flout tradition.*

Don't confuse **flout** with **flaunt**, which is to show off boldly: *Don't flaunt your wealth.*

flow *v.* **1.** to move along smoothly and continuously as in a stream; circulate. –*n.* **2.** the act of flowing. **3.** any continuous movement, as of thought, speech, trade, etc.

flower *n.* **1.** the blossom of a plant. –*v.* **2.** to blossom, as a plant. **3.** to reach the stage of full development.

Don't confuse **flower** with **flour**, which is the fine powder from wheat or other grains that you cook with.

flowery *adj.* (**-rier, -riest**) **1.** full of or covered with flowers. **2.** containing highly ornate language.

flown *v.* past participle of **fly¹**.

flu *n.* → **influenza**.

fluctuate *v.* to change continually, as from one course to another. –**fluctuation**, *n.*

The more usual word is **vary**.

flue *n.* any duct or passage for air, gases, or the like.

fluent *adj.* **1.** flowing smoothly and easily. **2.** able to speak or write readily.

fluff *n.* **1.** light, downy particles, as of cotton. **2.** *Informal* a blunder or error.

fluid *n.* a substance which is capable of flowing ; a liquid or a gas.

fluke¹ *n.* any accidental advantage; a lucky chance.

fluke² *n.* **1.** one of the the flat triangular pieces at the end of an anchor. **2.** either half of the triangular tail of a whale.

flummox *v.* *Informal* to bewilder; confuse.

flung *v.* past tense and past participle of **fling**.

flunk *v.* *Informal* to fail, as a student in an examination.

flunkey *n.* (*pl.* **-keys**) **1.** a male servant in uniform. **2.** a servile follower.

fluorescence n. a light emitted by certain substances. –**fluorescent**, adj.

fluoride n. an organic compound used to prevent tooth decay.

fluorine n. a pale yellow corrosive gas. Symbol: F

flurry n. 1. a sudden gust of wind. 2. commotion.

flush¹ n. 1. a blush; a rosy glow. 2. a rushing or overspreading flow, as of water. 3. waves of heat, as during fever, menopause.

flush² adj. 1. even or level, as with a surface; in one plane. 2. well-supplied, as with money.

flush³ phr. **flush out**, to cause (others) to reveal themselves.

flush⁴ n. a hand of cards all of one suit.

fluster v. to confuse; make nervous.

flute n. 1. a musical wind instrument consisting of a tube with a series of finger holes or keys. 2. a channel or furrow.

flutter v. 1. to flap or wave lightly in air, as a flag. 2. to beat fast and irregularly, as the heart. –n. 3. a fluttering movement. 4. Informal a small wager or bet.

flux n. a flowing or flow; a continuous movement or change.

fly¹ v. (**flew**, **flown**, **flying**) 1. to move through the air on wings, as a bird. 2. to (cause to) be carried through the air. 3. to move or pass swiftly. 4. to flee. –n. (pl. **flies**) 5. a strip sewn along one edge of a garment, to aid in concealing the buttons or other fasteners. 6. (pl.) Theatre the space and apparatus above the stage. –**flyer**, n.

fly² n. (pl. **flies**) 1. any of various two-winged insects, especially the common housefly. 2. Angling a fishhook designed to resemble an insect.

flying saucer n. any of various disc-shaped objects allegedly seen flying at high speeds and altitudes; UFO.

flyleaf n. (pl. **-leaves**) a blank leaf in the front or at the back of a book.

foal n. 1. the young of a horse. –v. 2. to bring forth a foal.

foam n. 1. minute bubbles formed on the surface of a liquid. 2. the froth of perspiration or saliva. 3. a light material, in either spongy or rigid form, used for packing, etc.

fob¹ n. Also, **fob pocket**. a small pocket just below the waistline in trousers. a short chain for a watch.

fob² phr. (**fobbed**, **fobbing**) **fob off**, 1. to rid oneself of something dishonestly: She fobbed the stolen watch off on him; I fobbed the job off onto Bill. 2. to put off or appease someone dishonestly: She asked where you were but I managed to fob her off.

focaccia /fə'katʃia/ n. flat Italian bread which can be eaten with various fillings or toppings.

focus n. (pl. **-cuses** or **-ci** /-kaɪ, -saɪ/) 1. clear and sharply defined condition of an image. 2. a central point, as of attention. –v. (**-cused** or **-cussed**, **-cusing** or **-cussing**) 3. to bring to a focus or into focus. 4. to concentrate. –**focal**, adj.

fodder n. food for livestock.

foe n. an enemy or opponent.

foetus /'fiːtəs/ n. → fetus. –**foetal**, adj.

fog n. 1. a thick mist. 2. a state of mental confusion or obscurity.

fogey n. (pl. **-gies** or **-geys**) an old-fashioned or excessively conservative person. Also, **fogy**.

foible n. a weakness or failing of character.

foil¹ v. to frustrate (a person, an attempt, a purpose).

The more usual word is **block**.

foil² n. 1. a metallic substance formed into very thin sheets. 2. anything that serves to set off another thing by contrast.

foil³ n. a flexible, thin sword for use in fencing.

foist v. to impose dishonestly or unjustifiably (on or upon).

fold[1] v. **1.** to bend (cloth, paper, etc.) over upon itself. **2.** to cover or enclose (a person or thing) with something bent around them. **3.** to shut by bending and laying parts together (up). **4.** Cookery to mix (in) gently. **5.** to be closed or brought to an end, usually with financial loss. −n. **6.** a part that is folded; pleat; layer. **7.** a hollow place in undulating ground.

fold[2] n. **1.** an enclosure for domestic animals, especially sheep. **2.** a church or congregation.

folder n. **1.** an outer cover, usually a folded sheet of light cardboard, for papers. **2.** Also, (in some operating systems), **directory**. Computers a defined area on a computer disk used to store files.

foliage n. the leaves of a plant, collectively.

folio n. **1.** a sheet of paper folded once to make 2 leaves (4 pages) of a book. **2.** a paper size. **3.** Printing the page number of a book.

folk n. (pl. **folk** or **folks**) people in general, especially the common people.

folklore n. the traditional beliefs, legends, customs, etc., of a people.

follicle n. **1.** Bot. a seed vessel. **2.** Anat. a small cavity, sac, or gland.

follow v. **1.** to come after in natural sequence, order of time, etc. **2.** to move behind in the same direction. **3.** to accept as a guide or leader. **4.** to move forward along (a path, etc.). **5.** to watch the movements, progress, or course of. **6.** to occur as a consequence: It follows that you are penalised for the error. −phr. **7. follow suit**, to follow the example of another. **8. follow through**, to carry out completely. **9. follow up**, **a.** to follow closely, or to a conclusion. **b.** to take further action.

folly n. (pl. **-lies**) **1.** the state or quality of being foolish. **2.** a foolish action, practice, idea, etc.

foment v. to cause or help the growth or development of (discord, rebellion, etc.); to foster.

The more usual expression is **stir up**.

fond adj. **1.** loving. **2.** foolishly tender; doting. −phr. **3. fond of**, liking.

fondle v. to show fondness, as by manner, words, or caresses.

fondue n. a dish of melted cheese or other sauce into which pieces of bread, meat, etc., are dipped.

font[1] n. a receptacle for the water used in baptism.

font[2] n. a complete assortment of printing type of one style and size.

food n. **1.** what is eaten, or taken into the body, for nourishment. **2.** more or less solid nourishment (as opposed to drink).

food chain n. a series of organisms dependent on each other in their feeding habits.

fool n. **1.** a silly or stupid person. **2.** a professional jester. −v. **3.** to make a fool of. **4.** to act like a fool. −**foolish**, adj.

foolhardy adj. (**-dier, -diest**) bold without judgement.

The more usual word is **reckless**.

foolscap n. a size of paper.

This is an old paper size. A4 is mainly used nowadays.

foot n. (pl. **feet**) **1.** the part of the leg below the ankle joint on which the body stands and moves. **2.** a unit of length in the imperial system, equal to about 30 centimetres. **3.** any thing or part resembling a foot, as in function. **4.** the part of a stocking, etc., covering the foot. **5.** the part of anything opposite the top or head. −v. **6.** Informal to pay or settle (a bill).

footage n. **1.** length or extent in feet. **2. a.** material recorded on a film or video camera. **b.** a length of cinematographic film.

football n. 1. any game in which the kicking of a ball has a large part. 2. the ball used in such a game.

footing n. 1. a secure position; foothold. 2. the basis on which anything, especially some kind of relationship, is established: *to be on friendly footing; to be on an equal footing.*

Note that for def. 2 you cannot use **footing** by itself. It must have an adjective before it describing the nature of the basis or relationship.

footlights pl. n. Theatre a row of lights at the front of the stage.

footloose adj. free to go or travel about.

footman n. (pl. **-men**) a male servant in livery.

footnote n. a note or comment at the foot of a page.

footpath n. a path for pedestrians only, especially one at the side of a road or street.

footprint n. 1. a mark left by the foot. 2. the area of the earth's surface covered by a satellite transmission. 3. the amount of space taken up on a desk, etc., by a computer or other appliance. 4. the area of land which is overshadowed by something else, as a building. 5. → **ecological footprint**.

footstep n. a step or tread of the foot, or the sound produced by it.

fop n. a man who is excessively concerned about his manners and appearance.

for prep. 1. with the object or purpose of: *The meat was bought for dinner.* 2. intended to belong to or be used in connection with: *Those shoes are for dancing.* 3. in order to obtain: *He sang for his supper.* 4. in consideration of, or in return for: *You can have it for nothing.* 5. during the continuance of: *for the rest of the performance.* 6. in favour of, or on the side of: *to stand for open government.* 7. in place of, or instead of: *to act for the governor.* 8. by reason of, or because of: *famed for its beauty.*

forage /ˈfɒrɪdʒ/ n. 1. food for horses and cattle. −v. (**-raged, -raging**) 2. to hunt or search about.

foray n. 1. a raid for the purpose of taking plunder. 2. a first attempt.

For def. 1, the more usual word is **attack**.

forbear¹ v. (**-bore, -borne, -bearing**) to hold back from; refrain.

The more usual expression is **keep yourself from**.

forbear² n. → **forebear**.

forbearance n. patience.

forbid v. (**-bade** or **-bad, -bidden** or **-bid, -bidding**) 1. to command (a person, etc.) not to do, have, use, etc., something. 2. to prohibit (something).

force n. 1. strength; power. 2. Law violence offered to persons or things. 3. (oft. pl.) a large body of armed soldiers; an army. 4. any body of persons combined for joint action. 5. Physics an influence which tends to produce motion. 6. value; meaning. −v. (**forced, forcing**) 7. to compel or make (someone) to do something. 8. to break open (a door, lock, etc.).

forceps /ˈfɔːsəps/ n. (pl. **-ceps** or **-cipes** /-səpiz/) an instrument, as pincers or tongs, for seizing and holding objects, used especially in surgical operations.

Note that this word is a singular noun: *The doctor used a forceps during the operation.* It is sometimes thought of as a plural noun, like **scissors**, and used in phrases such as 'a pair of forceps', but some people do not regarded this as correct.

forcible adj. 1. effected by force: *forcible entry.* 2. having force; effective.

ford n. 1. a place where a river or other body of water may be crossed by wading. −v. 2. to cross (a river, etc.) by a ford.

fore adj. 1. situated at or towards the front, as compared with something else. −n. 2. the forepart of anything; the front.

forearm n. the part of the arm between the elbow and the wrist.

forebear n. (usu. pl.) an ancestor. Also, **forbear**.

Note that although **forbear** can be another spelling for **forebear**, it is usually a verb meaning to hold yourself back from doing something (look up **forbear¹**). Also note that you cannot use the spelling **forebear** to mean to hold yourself back from doing something.

forebode v. to foretell or predict (especially something bad); portend. –**foreboding**, n.

forecast v. (-**cast** or -**casted**, -**casting**) **1.** to predict. –n. **2.** a prediction, especially as to the weather.

foreclose v. Law to deprive (a mortgagor or pledgor) of the right to redeem his or her property.

forefinger n. the finger next to the thumb. Also, **index finger**.

forego v. (-**went**, -**gone**, -**going**) to go before.

foreground n. the area represented as situated in the front.

forehand adj. Sport (of a stroke, etc.) made to the right side of the body (when the player is right-handed).

forehead /'fɒrəd, 'fɔhed/ n. the part of the face above the eyes; the brow.

foreign adj. **1.** relating to another country or nation. **2.** not related to the thing under consideration. –**foreigner**, n.

forelock n. the lock of hair that grows from the front part of the head.

foreman (pl. -**men**) **1.** the supervisor of a group of workers. **2.** the spokesperson of a jury. Also, **foreperson**, –**forewoman**, f.

The attempt to find a gender-neutral form of **foreman** seems to have not had any effect. **Foreman** remains the term generally used in courts and applies to both men and women.

foremost adj., adv. first in place, order, rank, etc.

forensic /fə'renzɪk, -sɪk/ adj. **1.** relating to courts of law or legal proceedings. **2.** applied to the process of collecting evidence for a legal case: forensic linguistics.

foresee v. (-**saw**, -**seen**, -**seeing**) to know beforehand.

foreshore n. **1.** the part of the shore between the ordinary high-water mark and low-water mark. **2.** the ground between the water's edge and the land cultivated or built upon.

foresight n. care or provision for the future.

foreskin n. → prepuce.

forest n. a large tract of land covered with trees. –**forestry**, n.

forestall v. to take measures to prevent or thwart (a thing) in advance.

forever adv. **1.** without ever ending. **2.** continually.

foreword n. a preface or introductory statement in a book, etc.

forfeit /'fɔfət/ n. **1.** a fine; a penalty. –v. **2.** to lose, or become liable to lose, in consequence of fault, broken agreement, etc.

forge¹ n. **1.** the special furnace in which metal is heated before shaping. –v. **2.** to form by heating and hammering. **3.** to imitate (a signature, etc.) fraudulently. –**forgery**, n.

forge² v. (**forged**, **forging**) to move ahead slowly.

forget v. (-**got**, -**gotten** or -**got**, -**getting**) **1.** to cease or fail to remember. **2.** to overlook. –**forgetful**, adj.

forgive v. (-**gave**, -**given**, -**giving**) **1.** to pardon an offence or an offender. **2.** to cease to feel resentment against.

forgo v. (-**went**, -**gone**, -**going**) to do without.

fork n. **1.** (anything resembling) an instrument having 2 or more prongs for holding, lifting, etc. **2.** a branch of a river, road, etc. –v. **3.** to lift, dig, etc., with a fork. **4.** to divide into 2 branches.

forlorn *adj.* **1.** unhappy or miserable, as in appearance. **2.** desperate or hopeless, as in outlook.

form *n.* **1.** external shape or appearance considered apart from colour or material. **2.** a document with blank spaces to be filled in. **3.** procedure or conduct, as judged by social standards: *good form*; *bad form.* **4.** condition, especially good condition, with reference to fitness. **5.** type or kind: *surfing as a form of sport.* **6.** a single division of a school containing pupils of about the same age or of the same level of scholastic progress. **7.** a bench or long seat. *–v.* **8.** to construct or frame. **9.** to make or produce; serve to make up, or constitute. **10.** to develop (habits, friendships, etc.). **11.** to give shape to; fashion. **12.** to take or assume form. *–phr.* **13. have form,** *Informal* to have a criminal record. **14. in good form, a.** in good health. **b.** performing at one's peak: *a batsman in good form.* **c.** entertaining by being lively and amusing: *in good form at the party.*

formal *adj.* **1.** following official procedure or ceremony: *a formal complaint*; *a formal welcome.* **2.** not relaxed or casual; not suitable for everyday life: *formal language*; *formal clothes.* *–n.* **3.** *Aust., NZ* a dance at which formal evening dress is worn: *a school formal.* *–formalise, formalize, v. –formality, n. –formally, adv.*

Don't confuse **formally** with **formerly**, which means previously or in the past.

formaldehyde /fə'mældəhaɪd/ *n.* a disinfectant and preservative gas.

format *n.* **1.** the general physical appearance of a book, newspaper, or magazine, etc. **2.** the plan or style of something. **3.** *Computers* the arrangement of data for storage, display, etc.

formation *n.* **1.** the manner in which a thing is formed. **2.** a group of things arranged according to a fixed plan.

formative *adj.* giving form or shape.

former *adj.* **1.** preceding in time; prior or earlier: *the former Prime Minister.* **2.** being the first of 2 (opposed to *latter*). *–phr.* **3. the former,** the item or person (out of 2) previously mentioned. *–formerly, adv.*

Don't confuse **formerly** with **formally**, which means in a formal manner: *They dressed formally for the ball.*

formidable /'fɔmədəbəl, fɔ'mɪdəbəl/ *adj.* that is to be feared or dreaded.

The more usual word is **frightening**.

formula *n.* (*pl.* **-las** *or* **-lae** /-li/) **1.** a set form of words. **2.** *Maths* a rule or principle, frequently expressed in algebraic symbols. **3.** a recipe or prescription.

Note that this word has two acceptable plurals, but **formulae** is used mainly for defs 2 and 3.

formulate *v.* to state precisely, definitely or systematically. *–formulation, n.*

fornication *n.* voluntary sexual intercourse between unmarried persons. *–fornicate, v.*

forsake *v.* (**-sook, -saken, -saking**) **1.** to desert or abandon. **2.** to give up or renounce (a habit, way of life, etc.).

fort *n.* a strong or fortified place.

forte /'fɔteɪ/ *n.* a strong point, as of a person; that in which one excels.

forth *adv.* **1.** forwards; onwards or outwards: *from that day forth*; *to go forth into the world.* **2.** out into view or consideration: *to bring forth new ideas.*

Don't confuse this with **fourth**, which numbers something next in order after third.

forthcoming *adj.* **1.** about to appear. **2.** ready or available when required. **3.** ready to provide information; open.

For def. 1, the more usual word is **approaching**.

forthright *adj.* going straight to the point.

forthwith *adv.* without delay.

The more usual word is **immediately**.

fortify v. (**-fied**, **-fying**) **1.** to strengthen against attack. **2.** to reinforce against strain, wear, etc. **3.** to add alcohol to wines, etc. to increase the strength. –**fortification**, n.

fortitude n. moral strength or endurance.

The more usual word is **courage**.

fortnight n. 2 weeks.

fortress n. a large fortified place.

fortuitous /fɔ'tjuːətəs/ adj. happening or produced by chance: *a fortuitous meeting*.

fortunate adj. **1.** having good fortune. **2.** bringing or presaging good fortune.

fortune n. **1.** position in life as determined by wealth. **2.** great wealth. **3.** chance; luck.

forty n. **1.** a cardinal number, 10 times 4. –adj. **2.** amounting to 40 in number. –**fortieth**, adj., n.

Numbers used before a noun are sometimes called **determiners**.

forum n. (*pl.* **forums** or **fora**) **1.** an assembly for the discussion of questions of public interest. **2.** a vehicle for public discussion, as a publication, radio program, etc. **3.** *Internet* an online discussion website, usually devoted to a particular topic.

forward adj. **1.** moving ahead; onward. **2.** well-advanced. **3.** presumptuous, pert, or bold. **4.** situated in the front. –n. **5.** *Sport* a player placed in front of the rest of the team. –adv. **6.** → **forwards**. –v. **7.** to send forward, especially to a new address. **8.** to advance or help onwards.

Note that although **forward** and **forwards** are very similar words, **forwards** is only an adverb (*to step forwards*) while **forward** can be an adjective, adverb, verb or noun.

forwards adv. **1.** towards or at a place, point, or time in advance; onwards; ahead. **2.** towards the front. **3.** into view or consideration. Also, **forward**.

forward slash n. a solidus.

fossick v. *Aust., NZ* to search unsystematically or in a small way, especially for gold.

fossil n. any remains or trace of an animal or plant of a former geological age.

fossil fuel n. fuel formed underground from ancient plant and animal matter, as coal, oil and gases.

foster v. **1.** to encourage. **2.** to care for (a child) for a period of time within one's family.

Compare def. 2 with **adopt** (def. 2), which is to take a child into your family permanently.

foster-child n. (*pl.* **foster-children**) a child brought up by someone who is not their natural or adoptive mother or father.

fought v. past tense and past participle of **fight**.

foul adj. **1.** grossly offensive to the senses. **2.** filthy or dirty. **3.** unfavourable or stormy, as weather. **4.** wicked or vile. **5.** contrary to the rules. –adv. **6.** in a foul manner. –n. **7.** a violation of the rules of a sport or game. –v. **8.** to make foul. **9.** to defile; disgrace.

Don't confuse this with **fowl**, which is a chicken or similar bird.

found[1] v. past tense and past participle of **find**.

found[2] v. **1.** to set up or establish. **2.** to lay the lowest part of (a structure) on a firm base. **3.** to base or ground (*on* or *upon*).

foundation n. **1.** that on which something is founded. **2.** (*oft. pl.*) the natural or prepared ground or base on which some structure rests. **3.** the act of establishing, etc. **4.** an endowed institution. **5.** a cosmetic preparation, usually in the form of a cream or liquid, which is spread over the face to hide or minimise blemishes and to improve the colour and texture of the skin; make-up.

founder[1] n. someone who begins or establishes something.

founder² v. **1.** to fill with water and sink, as a ship. **2.** to fail completely: *The project foundered for lack of funds.*

Don't confuse this with **flounder**, which is to struggle along clumsily.

foundling n. an infant found abandoned.

foundry n. (*pl.* **-ries**) a factory for producing metal casts.

fount n. **1.** a spring of water; fountain. **2.** a source or origin.

This is the short form of **fountain**.

fountain n. **1.** a spring, source or mechanical jet of water. **2.** the source or origin of anything.

fountain pen n. a pen holding ink which is supplied to the point of the nib.

four n. **1.** a cardinal number, 3 plus 1. *–adj.* **2.** amounting to 4 in number. **–fourth**, *n.*, *adj.*

Don't confuse **fourth** with **forth**, which is a literary word meaning onward: *from that day forth.*

Numbers used before a noun are sometimes called **determiners**.

fourteen n. **1.** a cardinal number, 10 plus 4. *–adj.* **2.** amounting to 14 in number. **–fourteenth**, *n.*, *adj.*

Numbers used before a noun are sometimes called **determiners**.

four-wheel drive n. **1.** the system which connects all four wheels of a motor vehicle to the source of power. **2.** a motor vehicle which has such a system. *Abbrev.:* 4WD **–four-wheel driving**, *n.*

fowl n. (*pl.* **fowls** or, *especially collectively*, **fowl**) **1.** → **chicken** (def. 1). **2.** any bird used as food, as a duck, goose, etc. **3.** any bird (now chiefly in combination): *waterfowl.*

Don't confuse this with **foul**, which means dirty or unpleasant.

fox n. **1.** any of certain carnivores of the dog family. **2.** a cunning or crafty person. *–v.* **3.** *Informal* to deceive or trick.

foyer n. **1.** (in theatres and cinemas) the area between the outer lobby and the auditorium. **2.** a hall or anteroom, especially in a hotel.

fracas /ˈfrækɑː, -kəs/ n. (*pl.* **fracas** /ˈfrækɑː, ˈfrækɑːz/ or **fracases** /ˈfrækəsəz/) an uproar.

fractal n. an irregular geometric structure forming a pattern.

fraction n. **1.** *Maths* one or more parts of a unit or whole number. **2.** a part as distinct from the whole of anything. **3.** a very small amount or part: *a fraction of the normal price.* **–fractional**, *adj.*

Compare def. 1 with **integer**, which is a whole number.
Don't confuse **fraction** with **faction**, which is a small group of people within a larger group, who hold a different opinion to the larger group.

fractious adj. **1.** cross, fretful, or peevish: *a fractious child.* **2.** unmanageable or stubborn.

For def. 1, the more usual word is **bad-tempered**.

fracture n. **1.** a break or split, especially in a bone. *–v.* (**-tured, -turing**) **2.** to break or crack, as a bone, etc.

fragile adj. easily broken or damaged. **–fragility**, *n.*

fragment n. **1.** a part broken off or detached. **2.** an odd piece, bit, or scrap. **–fragmentary**, *adj.*

fragrant adj. having a pleasant odour. **–fragrance**, *n.*

frail adj. **1.** having delicate health. **2.** easily broken; weak. **–frailty**, *n.*

frame n. **1.** an enclosing border as for a picture. **2.** a structure. **3.** the body with reference to its build. **4.** a particular state, as of the mind. **5.** one of the successive small pictures on a strip of film. *–v.* (**framed, framing**) **6.** to construct as by fitting and uniting parts. **7.** *Informal* to incriminate unjustly by a plot.

framework *n.* **1.** a structure composed of parts fitted together. **2.** a structure designed to support or enclose something.

franchise *n.* **1.** the rights of a citizen, especially the right to vote. **2.** permission granted by a manufacturer to a distributor or retailer to sell the manufacturer's products. **–franchisor**, *v.* **–franchising**, *n.*

frangipani *n.* (*pl.* **-nis**) a shrub or tree with yellow and white, occasionally pink, flowers.

frank *adj.* **1.** open or unreserved in speech. **2.** undisguised. **–v. 3.** to mark (a letter, parcel, etc.) to indicate that postage has been paid or that it does not need to be paid.

frankfurt *n.* a reddish pre-cooked sausage made of beef or pork, commonly re-heated by steaming or boiling; saveloy. Also, **frankfurter**, **frank**.

When a frankfurt is served in a bread roll, it is often called a **hot dog**.

frantic *adj.* wild with excitement, pain, etc.

fraternal *adj.* brotherly.

fraternise /ˈfrætənaɪz/ *v.* to associate in a fraternal or friendly way. Also, **fraternize**.

fraternity *n.* (*pl.* **-ties**) a body of persons associated as by ties of brotherhood.

fraud *n.* **1.** deceit by which it is sought to gain some unfair or dishonest advantage. **2.** someone who makes deceitful pretences. **–fraudulent**, *adj.*

fraught *phr.* **fraught with**, involving; full of: *fraught with danger.*

fray[1] *n.* a fight, skirmish, or battle.

fray[2] *v.* **1.** to exasperate; upset. **2.** to be worn to threads, as cloth, etc.

frazzled *adj.* weary; tired out.

freak *n.* **1.** any curiously unusual object. **–adj. 2.** unusual; odd.

freckle *n.* a small brownish spot on the skin.

free *adj.* (**freer**, **freest**) **1.** enjoying personal rights or liberty. **2.** not literal, as a translation. **3.** clear of obstructions. **4.** available; unoccupied. **5.** exempt or released from something specified: *free from obligations.* **6.** able to be used by or open to all. **7.** easy, firm, or swift in movement. **8.** not held fast or attached. **9.** ready in giving. **10.** provided without charge. **–v. (freed, freeing) 11.** to set at liberty. **12.** to disengage (*from* or *of*).

Note that the forms of the adjective are **freer** and **freest**, but if you find the *ee* spelling confusing, you can either write *free-er* and *free-est*, or change the wording to *more free* and *most free.*

freecycle *v.* (**-cled, -cling**) to give away (items) so that they can be used again by others, by placing them in a public area so that people can take them away as they wish.

freedom *n.* **1.** exemption from external control. **2.** absence of obligations, etc. **3.** ease of movement or action.

freehand *adj.* done by the hand without aids.

freehold *n.* unconditional ownership of property for unlimited time.

freelance *n.* a journalist, commercial artist, editor, etc., who does not work on a regular salaried basis for any one employer.

freeload *v.* to contrive to take food, benefits, etc., without paying or contributing; cadge.

free market *n. Econ.* an economic system that allows unrestricted supply and demand, thus intended to be self-regulating in terms of prices, wages, etc., rather than government controlled. **–free marketeer**, *n.*

freesia /ˈfriːʒə/ *n.* a fragrant flowering plant.

freestyle *n.* **1.** Also, **crawl**, **Australian crawl**. a swimming stroke in prone position characterised by alternate overarm movements and a continuous up and down kick. **2.** a style of BMX or skateboard riding consisting of complicated tricks and manoeuvres. **3.** (in sports such as skiing, skating, gymnastics, etc.) a style which allows the performer scope to demonstrate skill, as by featuring unrestricted movement, aerobatics, etc.

freeway *n.* a road designed for high-speed traffic. Also, **expressway**, **motorway**.

freeze *v.* (**froze**, **frozen**, **freezing**) **1.** to (cause something) change from the liquid to the solid state by loss of heat. **2.** to be extremely cold. **3.** to (cause something) suffer the effects of intense cold. **4.** to stop suddenly, as through fear, shock, etc. **5.** (of a computer) to stop producing or accepting data due to some fault. **6.** to fix (wages, prices, etc.) at a specific level. *–n.* **7.** the act of freezing. **8.** legislative action by a government to fix wages, prices, etc., at a specific level. *–phr.* **9. freeze out**, to exclude from society, business, etc., as by chilling behaviour, severe competition, etc. **–freezer**, *n.*

Don't confuse this with **frieze**, which is a decorative band around the top of a wall.

freeze-dry *v.* (**-dried**, **-drying**) to dry (food, blood, serum, etc.) while frozen and under high vacuum, as for prolonged storage. **–freeze-drying**, *n.*

freight *n.* **1.** cargo carried for pay. **2.** the charge made for transporting goods. *–v.* **3.** to transport as freight; send by freight.

French horn *n.* a mellow-toned brass wind instrument.

frenetic *adj.* frantic.

frenzy *n.* (*pl.* **-zies**) **1.** wild excitement or enthusiasm. **2.** mental derangement. **–frenzied**, *adj.*

frequency *n.* (*pl.* **-cies**) **1.** frequent occurrence. **2.** rate of recurrence. **3.** *Physics* the number of cycles or vibrations of a wave motion in unit time.

frequent *adj.* /ˈfrikwənt/ **1.** occurring at short intervals. **2.** constant, or regular. *–v.* /frəˈkwent/ **3.** to visit often.

fresco *n.* (*pl.* **-coes** or **-cos**) **1.** the art of painting on fresh lime plaster. **2.** a picture or design so painted.

fresh *adj.* **1.** newly made or obtained, etc. **2.** newly arrived. **3.** not previously known.

4. (of water) not salt. **5.** not deteriorated. **6.** pure, cool, or refreshing, as air. **7.** cheeky.

fret¹ *v.* (**fretted**, **fretting**) to give oneself up to feelings of resentful discontent, worry, etc. **–fretful**, *adj.*

fret² *n.* an interlaced, angular design; fretwork.

fretwork *n.* ornamental work consisting of interlacing parts.

friable *adj.* easily crumbled.

friar *n.* a brother or member of one of certain Christian religious orders.

friction *n.* **1.** clashing or conflict, as of opinions, etc. **2.** *Mechanics*, *Physics* the resistance to the relative motion (sliding or rolling) of surfaces of bodies in contact. **3.** the rubbing of the surface of one body against that of another.

fridge *n.* *Informal* → **refrigerator**.

fried *v.* past tense and past participle of **fry¹**.

friend *n.* someone with whom one is on good terms and likes well. **–friendly**, *adj.* **–friendship**, *n.*

frieze /friz/ *n.* any decorative band or feature, as on a wall.

Don't confuse this with **freeze**, which is to turn to ice.

frigate /ˈfrɪgət/ *n.* a general-purpose warship.

fright *n.* **1.** sudden and extreme fear. **2.** a person or thing of shocking or ridiculous appearance. **–frighten**, *v.* **–frightened**, *adj.*

frightful *adj.* terrible or alarming.

frigid *adj.* **1.** very cold in temperature. **2.** without warmth of feeling; unfriendly.

For def. 2, the more usual word is **cold**.

frill *n.* a strip of material or lace gathered at one edge; a ruffle.

fringe *n.* **1.** an ornamental bordering of lengths of thread, cord, etc. **2.** hair falling over the brow. **3.** a border or extremity. *–adj.* **4.** accessory; supplementary: *fringe benefits*. **5.** of or relating to persons living on the outskirts of social acceptability.

frisbee n. (from trademark) a flat plastic disc with a rim, designed to stay aloft for some time when thrown with horizontal spin.

frisk v. 1. to dance, leap, or skip. 2. Informal to search (a person) for concealed weapons, etc. —**frisky**, adj.

fritter[1] phr. **fritter away**, to waste (money, etc.) little by little.

fritter[2] n. a small fried cake of batter, sometimes containing fruit, etc.

frivolous adj. 1. not worthy of serious notice. 2. not serious, as persons.

frizz v. (**frizzed**, **frizzing**) 1. to make into small, crisp curls. —n. (pl. **frizzes**) 2. something frizzed, as hair. Also, **friz**. —**frizzy**, adj.

frizzle v. 1. to frizz. —n. 2. a short, crisp curl.

fro phr. **to and fro**, back and forth.

frock n. a dress.

frog n. 1. a tailless amphibian. —phr. 2. **a frog in one's throat**, a slight hoarseness of voice.

frolic n. 1. merry play; fun. —v. (**-icked**, **-icking**) 2. to play merrily; have fun.

from prep. a particle specifying a starting point, and hence used to express removal or separation in space, time, order, etc., distinction, source and cause.

frond n. a finely divided leaf, often large.

front n. 1. the foremost part or surface of anything. 2. someone or something that serves as a cover for another activity, especially an illegal or disreputable one. 3. Mil. (during a war) the position held by the enemy. 4. → **fire front**. 5. Meteorol. a surface separating 2 dissimilar air masses. —adj. 6. of or relating to the front. —v. 7. to have or turn the front towards; face. 8. Also, **front up**. Aust., NZ Informal to arrive; turn up. —**frontal**, adj., n.

frontier n. that part of a country which borders another country.

frontispiece n. an illustrated leaf preceding the title page of a book.

frost n. 1. a covering of minute ice needles, formed from the atmosphere at night on cold surfaces. —v. 2. to cover with frost. 3. to give a frost-like surface to (glass, etc.)

frostbite n. an inflammation on a part of the body due to excessive exposure to extreme cold.

frosting n. a kind of cake icing.

froth n. a mass of bubbles; foam.

frown v. to contract the brow as in displeasure.

frozen v. past participle of **freeze**.

fructose /ˈfruktouz, -tous, ˈfrʌk-/ n. a white, crystalline, very sweet sugar found in honey and fruit.

frugal adj. economical in use or expenditure.

fruit n. 1. Bot. the developed ovary of a seed plant, with its contents and related parts. 2. any product of vegetable growth useful to humans or animals. 3. anything produced; effect; profit.

Because **fruit** (def. 1) is an uncount noun, it does not usually appear in the plural: *Do you like fruit?*; *The fruit in season over summer is delicious.* However, you can use the plural if you are talking about different kinds of fruit: *Mangoes and pawpaws are tropical fruits.* You usually talk about an individual item of fruit as a **piece of fruit**.

fruitful adj. producing pleasing, useful results: *a fruitful discussion.*

The more usual word is **productive**.

fruition /fruˈɪʃən/ n. attainment of some desired goal; realisation of results.

fruitless adj. useless; not achieving anything: *a fruitless search.*

fruity adj. (**-tier**, **-tiest**) **1.** having the taste or flavour of fruit. **2.** (of wine) having body and fullness of flavour.

frump n. a dowdy, drably dressed woman.

frustrate v. **1.** to make (plans, efforts, etc.) ineffective. **2.** to disappoint or thwart (a person). –**frustration**, n.

fry¹ v. (**fried**, **frying**) to cook in fat, oil, etc., usually over direct heat.

fry² n. (pl. **fry**) **1.** the young of fishes. –phr. **2.** **small fry**, **a.** unimportant or insignificant people. **b.** young children.

fuchsia /ˈfjuːʃə/ n. any of several plants with handsome drooping flowers.

fuddy-duddy n. (pl. **-duddies**) a fussy, stuffy, or old-fashioned person.

fudge¹ n. a soft sweet made of sugar, butter, etc.

fudge² v. (**fudged**, **fudging**) **1.** to put together in a makeshift, clumsy, or dishonest way; fake. **2.** (in games and contests) to cheat.

fuel n. combustible matter used to maintain a fire or feed an engine, as wood, petrol, etc.

fugitive /ˈfjuːdʒətɪv, -əv/ n. a runaway.

The more usual word is **escapee**.

fugue /fjuːg/ n. Music a composition based upon one, 2, or even more interwoven themes.

fulcrum /ˈfʊlkrəm/ n. (pl. **-crums** or **-cra** /-krə/) the support on which a lever turns in moving a body.

fulfil v. (**-filled**, **-filling**) **1.** to carry out, as a prophecy, promise, etc. **2.** to satisfy (requirements, etc.).

full adj. **1.** containing all that can be held. **2.** complete; entire; maximum. **3.** Also, **full up**, having eaten much. **4.** (of garments, etc.) wide, ample. **5.** *Aust., NZ Informal* intoxicated.

fullback n. (in football, hockey, etc.) a defender in a team.

full stop n. the point or character (.) used to mark the end of a sentence, indicate an abbreviation, etc.; period. Also, **stop**, **full point**.

full-time adj. **1.** done during the whole length of normal working hours: *full-time work*. –adv. **2.** during the whole of normal working hours: *to work full-time*.

Compare this with **part-time**.

fulminate v. to issue denunciations or the like (*against*).

fulsome adj. **1.** immoderate, excessive or insincere, as flattery, praise, etc. **2.** given in full; lavish; unrestrained.

Some people think that def. 1 is the correct meaning for this word, and that def. 2 is incorrect. However, the use of **fulsome** as in def. 2 is very common and many people find it acceptable.

fumble v. to feel or grope about clumsily.

fume n. **1.** (*oft. pl.*) any smoke-like or vaporous exhalation. –v. (**fumed**, **fuming**) **2.** to show irritation or anger.

fumigate v. to expose to smoke or fumes, as in disinfecting.

fun n. enjoyment or amusement. –phr. **2.** **make fun of** or **poke fun at**, to ridicule.

function n. **1.** an activity proper to a person, thing, or institution. **2.** any ceremonious public or social gathering or occasion. –v. **3.** to act; serve; operate. **4.** to carry out normal work or processes. –**functional**, adj. –**functionally**, adv.

functional grammar n. a grammar in which the analysis begins with the functions of language and words rather than their forms.

functionality n. **1.** the purpose designed to be fulfilled by a device, tool, machine, etc. **2.** *Computers* the range of functions which an application has.

fund n. **1.** a stock of money. **2.** a store or stock of something: *She is a fund of knowledge*. –v. **3.** to provide funds for.

fundamental adj. **1.** serving as a foundation and affecting all other parts;

underlying; essential: *the fundamental problem*. *–n.* **2.** a basic or underlying rule or principle: *to learn the fundamentals of computer programming*.

The more usual word is **basic**.

funeral *n.* a ceremony connected with the disposal of the body of a dead person. *–funereal, adj.*

fung shui /fʊŋ ˈʃweɪ, fʌŋ, ˈʃwi/ *n.* → **feng shui**.

fungus /ˈfʌŋɡəs/ *n.* (*pl.* **fungi** /ˈfʌŋɡi/ *or* **funguses**) a plant without chlorophyll, as mushrooms, moulds, or mildews.

funicular railway /fəˈnɪkjələ/ *n.* a railway system of cable-linked cars operating up steep gradients.

funk¹ *n. Informal* a state of abject terror.

funk² *n.* a style of soul music with a fast rhythm, originating on the west coast of America.

funky *adj. Informal* exciting, satisfying, or pleasurable.

funnel *n.* **1.** a cone-shaped utensil for pouring liquid, etc., through a small opening. **2.** a metal chimney, especially of a ship or a steam-engine.

funnel-web *n.* either of 2 species of large, aggressive, venomous, eastn Aust. spiders.

funny *adj.* (**-nier, -niest**) **1.** amusing; comical. **2.** strange; queer; odd.

fur *n.* **1.** the skin of certain animals, covered with a thick, hairy coating. **2.** the cured and treated skin of animals used in garments, etc.

furious *adj.* **1.** full of rage. **2.** intensely violent, as wind, storms, etc.

furl *v.* to draw into a compact roll, as a sail, etc.

furlong *n.* a unit of distance in the imperial system, just over 200 metres long. *Symbol:* fur

furlough *n.* leave of absence from official duty, usually for a longish period.

furnace *n.* a structure or apparatus in which to generate heat.

furnish *v.* **1.** to provide or supply. **2.** to fit up (a house, room, etc.) with necessary appliances, especially furniture.

furniture *n.* the movable articles required for use or ornament in a house, office, or the like.

furore /ˈfjurə/ *n.* a public reaction of anger, disapproval, etc. Also, **furor**.

furphy *n.* (*pl.* **-phies**) *Aust.* a rumour; a false story.

furrow *n.* a narrow trench or groove.

further *adv.* (*comparative of* **far**) **1.** at or to a greater distance. **2.** at or to a more advanced point; to a greater extent. **3.** in addition; moreover. *–adj.* (*comparative of* **far**) **4.** more distant or remote: *the further horizon*. **5.** additional; more: *further assistance*. *–v.* **6.** to help forward (a cause, etc.).

You can also use **farther** for defs 1, 2 and 4.

This word is part of the set **far**, **further**, **furthest**.

furtive *adj.* **1.** taken, done, used, etc., by stealth. **2.** sly; shifty.

fury *n.* unrestrained violent passion, especially anger.

fuse¹ *n.* **1.** *Elect.* a device for preventing an excessive current from passing through a circuit. **2.** a tube, ribbon, or the like, filled or saturated with combustible matter, for igniting an explosive.

fuse² *v.* to combine or blend by melting together.

fuselage /ˈfjuzəlɑːʒ, -lɪdʒ/ *n.* the body of an aircraft.

fusion *n.* **1.** the act or process of fusing. **2.** that which is fused.

fuss *n.* **1.** an excessive display of useless activity. **2.** a commotion or dispute. *–v.* **3.** to make a fuss; move fussily about. *–fussy, adj.*

futile *adj.* incapable of producing any result; ineffective: *a futile effort*. *–futility, n.*

The more usual word is **useless**.

futon *n.* a Japanese-style bed consisting of a mattress on a support of wooden slats.

future *n.* **1.** the time that is to be or come. **2.** what will exist or happen in future time. *–adj.* **3.** relating to or connected with time to come.

future tense *n. Gram.* a tense which indicates that the action will take place at some time in the future.

In English, the form of the verb itself does not change to indicate future action. Instead, auxiliary verbs (usually *will*) are used with the infinitive of the main verb, as in *I will see you tomorrow*.

futuristic *adj.* (of design) anticipating the age of space travel and living; ultra-modern.

fuzz *n.* **1.** loose, light, fibrous, or fluffy matter. **2.** *Informal* a blur. **3.** *Informal* the police force. *–***fuzzy**, *adj.*

G, g

G, g *n.* the 7th letter of the English alphabet.

gaberdine *n.* a closely woven fabric of cotton or rayon. Also, **gabardine**.

gable *n.* the triangular wall formed by the 2 slopes of a roof.

gadget *n.* a mechanical device.

gaffe *n.* a social blunder.

gaffer tape *n.* a strong adhesive cloth tape for electrical and other purposes.

gag¹ *v.* (**gagged, gagging**) **1.** to stop up the mouth so as to prevent speech. **2.** to restrain by force or authority from freedom of speech or expression. **3.** to retch, as with nausea. –*n.* **4.** something thrust into or bound around the mouth to prevent speech.

gag² *v.* (**gagged, gagging**) **1.** to make jokes. –*n.* **2.** a joke.

gage *n., v.* → **gauge**.

gaggle *n.* a flock of geese.

gaiety *n.* the state of being happy or cheerful.

gain *v.* **1.** to obtain (something desired). **2.** to acquire as an increase or addition. **3.** to reach by effort; arrive at. **4.** to improve; make progress. –*n.* **5.** profit; advantage. **6.** an increase or advance.

gainsay *v.* (**-said, -saying**) **1.** to deny. **2.** to speak or act against.

gait *n.* **1.** a particular manner of walking. **2.** the pace of a horse.

Don't confuse **gait** with **gate**, which is a type of door in a fence.

gaiter *n.* a covering for the ankle and instep.

gala *n.* a festive occasion.

galah *n.* **1.** a common pink and grey cockatoo. **2.** *Aust. Informal* a fool.

galaxy *n.* (*pl.* **-xies**) a large system of stars. –**galactic**, *adj.*

The galaxy which includes our solar system, containing several billion stars, is called **the Milky Way**.

gale *n.* a strong wind.

gall *n.* **1.** → **bile** (def. 1). **2.** something very bitter or severe. **3.** bitterness of spirit. **4.** impudence; effrontery.

For def. 4, the more usual word is **nerve**.

gallant /'gælənt, gə'lænt/ *adj.* **1.** brave and dashing. **2.** (of a man) polite and attentive to women. **3.** generous or sporting.

gall bladder *n.* a small sac attached to the liver containing bile.

galleon /'gæliən, 'gæljən/ *n.* a kind of large sailing vessel.

gallery *n.* (*pl.* **-ries**) **1.** a place for exhibiting works of art. **2.** a long covered walk or corridor. **3.** a platform above the body of a church, theatre, etc., which provides extra seating.

Don't confuse this with **galley**.

galley *n.* (*pl.* **-leys**) **1.** an early ship propelled by oars. **2.** the kitchen of a ship or aeroplane.

Don't confuse this with **gallery**.

gallivant *v.* to go from place to place in a light-hearted manner.

gallon *n.* a measure of liquid in the imperial system, equal to about 4.5 litres.

gallop *v.* **1.** to ride a horse at full speed. **2.** to race, or hurry. –*n.* **3.** fastest gait of a horse.

gallows *n.* (*pl.* **-lows** *or* **-lowses**) a wooden frame used for the hanging of criminals.

gallstone *n.* a stone formed in the bile ducts or gall bladder.

gallup poll *n.* the questioning of a cross-section of the population in order to assess voting intentions.

galore *adj.* in great abundance: *kids galore; food galore*.

Note that this adjective always follows the noun it describes.

galoshes *pl. n.* a pair of rubber coverings for the shoes, for use in wet weather.

galvanise *v.* **1.** to startle into sudden activity. **2.** to coat (iron or steel) with zinc. Also, **galvanize**.

gambit *n.* **1.** an opening move in chess, in which the player sacrifices a pawn or other piece so as to obtain some advantage. **2.** any course of action designed to obtain some advantage.

For def. 2, the more usual word is **ploy**.

gamble *v.* **1.** to play at any game of chance for stakes. **2.** to act on favourable hopes or assessment. –*n.* **3.** anything risky or uncertain.

Don't confuse **gamble** with **gambol**.

gambol *v.* (**-bolled** *or, Chiefly US,* **-boled, -bolling** *or, Chiefly US,* **-boling**) to frolic and run or skip about.

Don't confuse this with **gamble**.

game *n.* **1.** an amusement or pastime. **2.** a contest; match. **3.** sport of any kind; joke. **4.** wild animals hunted for sport, food, or profit. –*adj.* (**gamer, gamest**) **5.** relating to animals hunted as game. **6.** with fighting spirit; plucky.

gamete /'gæmiːt, gə'miːt/ *n.* either of the 2 germ cells which unite to form a new organism.

gamin *adj.* (of a person's appearance, or hairstyle) elfin.

gammon *n.* a smoked or cured ham.

gamut /'gæmət/ *n.* the whole scale or range.

gander *n.* **1.** a male goose. –*phr.* **2. take** (**or have**) **a gander at**, *Informal* to take a look at.

The female of def. 1 is called a **goose**.

gang *n.* a band or group, especially of persons associated for some disreputable purpose. –**gangster**, *n.*

gangly /'gæŋgli/ *adj.* awkwardly tall and spindly. Also, **gangling**.

gangplank *n.* a plank used as a bridge into a ship, etc. Also, **gangway**.

gangrene /'gæŋgrin/ *n.* the dying of tissue, as from interruption of circulation. –**gangrenous**, *adj.*

gangway *n.* **1.** a passageway, especially on a ship. **2.** → **gangplank**.

gannet *n.* a large seabird.

gantry *n.* (*pl.* **-tries**) a spanning framework.

gaol /dʒeɪl/ *n.* → **jail**.

Don't confuse this with **goal**, which is something you aim for.
Nowadays **jail** is the main spelling of this word in Australian English, although it used to be **gaol**. This is why you will still sometimes see **gaol** in the names of some older prisons, such as *Parramatta Gaol*.

gap *n.* **1.** a break or opening. **2.** a vacant space or interval.

gape *v.* **1.** to stare with open mouth, as in wonder. **2.** to split or become wide open.

garage *n.* **1.** a building for housing cars, etc. **2.** → **service station**.

garb *n.* fashion or mode of dress.

garbage *n.* rubbish.

garble *v.* to distort, corrupt or confuse (statements, etc.).

garden *n.* **1.** a plot of ground for the cultivation of plants. –*v.* **2.** to lay out or cultivate a garden. –**gardener**, *n.*

gardenia *n.* a plant cultivated for its fragrant, waxlike, white flowers.

garfish *n.* (*pl.* **-fish** *or* **-fishes**) a fish having a slender body and a needle-like lower jaw.

For information about the different plural forms, see the note at **fish**.

gargantuan /gɑ'gæntʃuən/ *adj.* gigantic; prodigious.

gargle *v.* to wash or rinse (the throat or mouth) with a liquid held in the throat.

gargoyle *n.* a spout, often terminating in a grotesque head.

garish /'geərɪʃ, gar-/ adj. glaring, or excessively bright.

garland n. a wreath or string of flowers, etc.

garlic n. a hardy plant, with a strong-scented bulb used in cookery and medicine.

garment n. any article of clothing.

garnet n. a deep red gemstone.

garnish v. 1. to fit out with something that adorns or decorates. –n. 2. something that decorates, especially food.

garret n. → attic.

garrison n. a body of troops stationed in a fortified place.

garrotte n. a Spanish mode of capital punishment, originally by strangulation.

garrulous adj. given to much talking, especially about trivial matters.

garter n. a fastening to keep up stockings or long socks.

gas¹ n. (pl. **gases**) **1.** Physics a substance whose molecules are sufficiently mobile for it to occupy the whole of the space in which it is contained. –v. (**gassed, gassing**) **2.** to overcome, or asphyxiate with gas or fumes.

gas² n. **1.** Chiefly US petrol. –phr. **2. step on the gas,** to hurry.

gash n. a long, deep wound or cut.

gasket n. anything used as a packing or jointing material for making joints fluid-tight.

gasp n. **1.** a sudden, short breath. **2.** a short, convulsive utterance. –v. **3.** to catch the breath or struggle for breath with open mouth.

gastric adj. relating to the stomach.

gastroenteritis /ˌgæstroʊentəˈraɪtəs/ n. Pathol. inflammation of the stomach and intestines.

gastronomy n. the art or science of good eating. –**gastronomic,** adj.

gastropod n. a mollusc of the snail class.

gate n. **1.** a movable barrier in a fence or wall, or across a passageway. **2.** a device

for regulating the passage of water, etc., as in a dam, pipe, etc.; valve.

Don't confuse **gate** with **gait,** which is a way of walking or moving: *a leisurely gait.*

gatecrash v. to attend (a party, etc.) uninvited.

gateway n. **1.** a passage or entrance which is closed by a gate. **2.** a location through which one has access to an area: *this harbour is the gateway to the city.* **3.** Computers **a.** a piece of software or hardware which acts as a translator between dissimilar networks or protocols. **b.** → router.

gather v. **1.** to bring or come together into one company or aggregate. **2.** to learn or infer from observation. **3.** to draw (someone or something) close. **4.** to draw up (cloth) on a thread in fine folds. **5.** to increase (speed, etc.).

gauche /goʊʃ/ adj. awkward; clumsy. –**gaucheness,** n.

gaudy adj. (**-dier, -diest**) excessively showy without taste; vulgar; flashy.

gauge /geɪdʒ/ v. (**gauged, gauging**) **1.** to appraise, estimate, or judge. **2.** to determine the dimensions, capacity, quantity, or force of. –n. **3.** a standard of measure. **4.** a means of estimating or judging; criterion; test. **5.** any instrument for measuring pressure, volume, or dimensions. Also, **gage.**

gaunt adj. abnormally thin; emaciated; haggard.

gauntlet n. **1.** a medieval glove. –phr. **2. throw down the gauntlet,** to extend a challenge, originally to a duel.

gauze n. any thin transparent fabric.

gave v. past tense of **give.**

gavel n. a small mallet used by a presiding officer to signal for attention or order.

gawk v. Informal to stare stupidly. Also, **gawp.**

gawky adj. (**-kier, -kiest**) awkward; ungainly; clumsy.

gay *adj.* **1.** homosexual. **2.** having or showing a joyous mood. **3.** bright or showy. *–n.* **4.** a homosexual person.

Note that nowadays the most common sense of **gay** is homosexual, and its use in defs 2 and 3 is becoming quite rare. **Gay** can be used to refer to both men and women, but it is more commonly used of men, with **lesbian** being the usual term for a homosexual woman.

gaze *v.* **1.** to look steadily or intently. *–n.* **2.** a steady or intent look.

gazebo *n.* (*pl.* **-bos** or **-boes**) a structure, especially in garden, etc., commanding an extensive view.

gazelle *n.* (*pl.* **-zelles** *or, especially collectively,* **-zelle**) a small antelope.

gazette *n.* **1.** a newspaper. **2.** an official government journal, containing lists of government appointments, etc. *–v.* (**-zetted, -zetting**) **3.** to publish, announce or make official by listing in a gazette.

This is an old-fashioned word for a newspaper which you will still see in the name of some newspapers: *The Western Gazette*.

gazump *v.* to bypass a buyer of real estate with whom a price has been agreed, by selling at a higher price to another.

gear *n.* **1.** *Machinery* **a.** a mechanism for transmitting or changing motion, as by toothed wheels. **b.** a toothed wheel which engages with another wheel or part. **2.** tools or apparatus; harness; tackle.

gearstick *n.* a device for connecting gears for passing on power, especially in a motor vehicle. Also, **gearlever, gearshift, shift**.

gecko *n.* a small nocturnal lizard.

geek *n.* *Informal* person who has an awkward personality and dresses in a conservative way; a person who is not cool (def. 4).

Note that if you call someone 'a geek' you usually intend to insult them.

geese *n.* plural of **goose**.

Geiger counter /ˈgaɪgə/ *n.* an instrument for detecting radioactivity.

gel *n.* a jelly-like substance.

gelatine *n.* an organic substance, obtained by boiling in water the ligaments, bones, skin, etc., of animals, and forming the basis of jellies, glues, etc. *–***gelatinous**, *adj.*

gelato *n.* (*pl.* **-latos** or **-lati**) an iced confection made from cream, milk, or water, with fruit or nut flavouring.

geld *v.* to castrate (an animal).

gelding *n.* a castrated animal, especially a horse.

gelignite *n.* an explosive.

gem *n.* **1.** Also, **gemstone**. a stone used in jewellery. **2.** something likened to, or prized as, a gem, especially something small.

gender *n.* **1.** the condition of being either male or female. **2.** sexual identity, such as male, female, genderqueer, etc., distinguished from physiological determination as to one's sex. **3.** (in many languages) a set of classes, such as masculine, feminine and neuter, which together include all nouns.

genderqueer *adj.* not identifying as either male or female, but identifying as both, neither, or a combination.

gene *n.* the unit of inheritance, situated on the chromosome, which passes on hereditary characteristics.

genealogy /dʒiniˈælədʒi/ *n.* (*pl.* **-gies**) an account of the descent of a person or family through an ancestral line.

genera *n.* plural of **genus**.

general *adj.* **1.** relating to the whole, or to all members of a class or group; not partial or particular. **2.** not specific or special. *–n.* **3.** an army officer of very high rank.

generalise *v.* **1.** to give a general (rather than specific or special) character to. **2.** to infer (a general principle, etc.) from facts, etc. **3.** to form general notions. Also, **generalize**.

generality n. (pl. **-ties**) **1.** a general or vague statement. **2.** general principle; general rule or law.

general practitioner n. a doctor who does not specialise in any particular branch of medicine.

The short form of this is **GP**.

generate v. to bring into existence; give rise to.

The more usual word is **produce**.

generation n. **1.** the whole body of individuals born about the same time. **2.** production by natural or artificial processes; evolution, as of heat or sound.

generator n. a machine which converts mechanical energy into electrical energy.

generic adj. **1.** relating to a genus. **2.** referring to all the members of a genus or class.

generous adj. **1.** bountiful; unselfish. **2.** free from meanness or smallness of mind or character. **–generosity,** n.

genesis /'dʒɛnəsəs/ n. (pl. **-neses** /-nəsiz/) origin; creation.

The more usual word is **beginning**.

genetically-modified adj. (of a food or organism) having had its genetic make-up altered by technological means.

genetic engineering n. the modification of an organism's genes through the transference of DNA material from one organism to another. **–genetically engineered,** adj.

genetic fingerprinting n. a process by which the genetic code of the DNA in human organic material such as skin, hair, blood, semen, etc., found at the scene of a crime is matched against the DNA of a suspect, thus, because of the uniqueness of each person's genetic code, establishing whether the suspect was or was not present. Also, **DNA fingerprinting.**

genetics n. the science of heredity, dealing with resemblances and differences of related organisms. **–geneticist,** n. **–genetic,** adj.

genial adj. pleasantly warm and friendly.

genie n. a spirit of Arabian mythology.

genitals pl. n. the reproductive organs, especially the external organs. Also, **genitalia. –genital,** adj.

genius n. **1.** the highest natural capacity for creative and original ideas. **2.** a person having such capacity.

Don't confuse this with **genus**, which is a biological division of living things.

genocide n. planned extermination of a national or racial group. **–genocidal,** adj.

genome /'dʒinoʊm/ n. the complete genetic material for any cell. **–genomic** /dʒə'noʊmɪk/, adj. **–genomically** /dʒə-'noʊmikli/, adv.

genre /'ʒɒnrə/ n. **1.** genus; kind; sort; style. **2.** a conventional literary form, such as the novel, etc. **3.** a type of text, such as exposition, report, narrative, recount, procedure, etc.

genteel adj. belonging or suited to polite society. **–gentility,** n.

gentile n. any person who is not Jewish, especially a Christian.

gentle adj. **1.** mild, kindly, or amiable. **2.** not severe, rough, or violent. **3.** moderate; gradual. **4.** of good birth or family.

gentleman n. (pl. **-men**) **1.** a man of good breeding, education, and manners. **2.** (as a polite form of speech) any man.

You would use def. 2 if you were referring politely to a man: *There is a gentleman here to see you.*

gentry n. Brit. the class below the nobility.

genuflect v. to bend the knee in reverence.

genuine adj. **1.** being truly such; real; authentic. **2.** sincere; free from pretence or affectation.

genus n. (pl. **genera**) **1.** a kind; sort; class. **2.** Biol. the usual major subdivision of a family or subfamily.

Don't confuse this with **genius**, which is an extremely clever person.

geography *n.* the study of the earth's surface, climate, vegetation, population, etc. –**geographer,** *n.* –**geographical,** *adj.*

geology *n.* the science that deals with the composition and changes in structure of the earth. –**geological,** *adj.* –**geologist,** *n.*

geometry *n.* that branch of mathematics which deduces the properties of figures in space. –**geometric,** *adj.*

geophysics *n.* the physics of the earth, dealing especially with the study of inaccessible portions of the earth.

geranium *n.* a plant cultivated for its showy flowers.

geriatric *adj.* **1.** of or relating to the medical field of geriatrics or to aged persons. –*n.* **2.** an aged person, especially an incapacitated one.

geriatrics *n.* the science of the medical and hygienic care of, or the diseases of, aged persons. –**geriatrician,** *n.*

germ *n.* **1.** a microorganism, especially when disease-producing. **2.** that from which anything springs as if from a seed.

german *adj.* **1.** having the same father and mother (always placed after the noun): *a brother-german; a sister-german.* **2.** being the child of the brother or sister of one's father or mother, or from brothers or sisters.

germane *adj.* closely related; pertinent.

The more usual word is **relevant**.

German measles *n.* a contagious disease, usually mild, accompanied by fever, often some sore throat, and a rash, causing birth defects in the first 3 months of pregnancy; rubella.

German shepherd *n.* a highly intelligent wolf-like breed of dog; Alsatian.

germinate *v.* to begin to grow or develop.

gerrymander *n. Politics* an arbitrary arrangement of electoral boundaries made so as to give one party an unfair advantage in elections.

gerund /ˈdʒerənd/ *n. Gram.* a noun formed from a verb, as *skiing* in *Skiing is fun.*

gestate /ˈdʒesteɪt/ *v.* to carry in the womb from conception to delivery. –**gestation,** *n.*

gesticulate *v.* to make or use gestures, especially in an animated or excited manner, with or instead of speech.

gesture /ˈdʒestʃə/ *n.* **1.** movement of the body that expresses an idea or an emotion. **2.** any action or proceeding intended for effect or as a formality; demonstration. –*v.* **3.** to make or use gestures.

get *v.* (**got, getting**) **1.** to obtain, gain, or acquire by any means. **2.** to fetch or bring. **3.** to hear or understand. **4.** to be afflicted with (an illness, etc.). **5.** *Informal* to hit. **6.** to come to or arrive. **7.** to become; grow. **8.** to succeed in coming or going (*away, in, into, out, over, through,* etc.). –*phr.* **9. get across,** to make understood. **10. get at, a.** to reach; make contact with. **b.** *Informal* to hint at or imply. **c.** *Informal* to influence, as by bribery. **11. get away with,** to avoid punishment or blame for. **12. get by,** to manage in spite of difficulties. **13. get down,** to depress; discourage. **14. get even with,** to square accounts with; be revenged against. **15. get his** (or **hers,** etc.), to receive a just reward. **16. get on, a.** to age. **b.** to make progress; proceed; advance. **c.** to agree or be friendly (*with*). **17. get one's own back,** to be revenged. **18. get round, a.** to outwit. **b.** to cajole or ingratiate oneself with (someone). **c.** to overcome (difficulties, etc.). **19. get (stuck) into,** *Informal* **a.** to attack (someone) physically or verbally. **b.** to set about (a task) vigorously. **20. get to, a.** to arouse deep feeling in. **b.** to annoy or irritate. **21. get up, a.** to arise. **b.** to dress elaborately. **c.** to prepare, arrange, or organise. **22. get up to,** to be involved in (mischief, etc.).

The verb form *gotten* is sometimes used as a past participle: *Things had gotten very difficult.* This is the normal form in America, but is not regarded as correct by some people in Australia.

geyser /'gizə, 'gaɪzə/ *n.* a hot spring which intermittently sends up jets of water and steam into the air.

ghastly *adj.* (**-lier, -liest**) frightful; dreadful; horrible.

GHB *n.* gamma hydroxybutyric acid; an anaesthetic drug used recreationally as a stimulant; fantasy.

gherkin /'gɜkən/ *n.* a small immature cucumber used in pickling.

ghetto *n.* (*pl.* **-tos** *or* **-toes**) an area in a city in which any minority group lives.

ghost *n.* **1.** the disembodied spirit of a dead person imagined as haunting living persons. *–v.* **2.** to write for someone else who is publicly known as the author.

ghoul *n.* **1.** an evil demon. **2.** a grave robber. **3.** someone who revels in what is revolting. **–ghoulish**, *adj.*

giant *n.* **1.** a huge imaginary human being. **2.** a person or thing of unusually great size, endowments, importance, etc. *–adj.* **3.** gigantic; huge.

giardia /dʒi'adiə, gi'adiə/ *n.* any flagellate, parasitic to the intestines of vertebrates.

gibber¹ /'dʒɪbə/ *v.* to speak inarticulately; chatter. **–gibberish**, *n.*

gibber² /'gɪbə/ *n. Aust.* a rounded stone, especially one found in the arid Aust. inland.

gibbon *n.* a kind of small ape.

gibe *v.* (**gibed, gibing**) **1.** to utter mocking words; scoff; jeer. *–n.* **2.** a taunting or sarcastic remark. Also, **jibe**.

giblet /'dʒɪblət/ *n.* (*usu. pl.*) the heart, liver, or gizzard from a fowl.

giddy *adj.* (**-dier, -diest**) **1.** frivolously light; flighty. **2.** affected with vertigo; dizzy.

gift *n.* **1.** something given; a present. **2.** a special ability; natural endowment; talent.

gig¹ *n.* a light horse carriage.

gig² *n. Informal* (a booking for a band, etc., to perform at) a jazz or pop concert.

gig³ *n. Computers Informal* → **gigabyte**.

gigabyte *n. Computers* a measure of computer memory equal to 2^{30} (approximately 10^9) bytes. *Symbol:* G, GB

gigajoule *n.* a metric unit of energy equal to 10^9 joules.

gigantic *adj.* **1.** huge. **2.** of, like, or of a giant.

giggle *v.* **1.** to laugh in a silly, childish way; titter. *–n.* **2.** a silly, childish laugh; a titter. **3.** *Informal* an amusing occasion.

gigolo /'ʒɪgəloʊ/ *n.* (*pl.* **-los**) a man supported by a woman, especially a young man supported by an older woman in return for companionship.

gild *v.* (**gilded** *or* **gilt**, **gilding**) to coat with gold, gold leaf, etc.

gill /gɪl/ *n.* an aquatic respiratory organ.

gimlet /'gɪmlət/ *n.* a small tool for boring holes.

gimmick *n. Informal* a pronounced eccentricity, especially one exploited to gain publicity.

gin¹ *n.* an alcoholic beverage obtained by redistilling spirits with juniper berries, orange peel, angelica root, etc.

gin² *n.* **1.** a machine for separating cotton from its seeds. **2.** a trap or snare for game, etc.

gin³ *n.* a card game similar to rummy. Also, **gin rummy**.

ginger /'dʒɪndʒə/ *n.* **1.** a pungent, spicy rhizome used in cookery and medicine. **2.** (of hair) red. *–v.* **3.** *Informal* to impart spiciness or piquancy to; make lively.

gingerly *adv.* with extreme care or caution; warily. **–gingerliness**, *n.*

The more usual word is **carefully**.

gingham /'gɪŋəm/ *n.* yarn-dyed, plain-weave cotton fabric.

gipsy *n.* (*pl.* **-sies**) → **gypsy**.

giraffe *n.* a tall, long-necked, spotted ruminant of Africa.

gird *v.* (**girt** or **girded, girding**) **1.** to encircle, as with a belt or girdle. *–phr.* **2. gird oneself (up) for,** to prepare oneself mentally for.

girder *n.* a main horizontal supporting beam.

girdle *n.* **1.** a belt, etc., worn about the waist. **2.** a lightweight undergarment which supports the abdominal region of the body. *–v.* **3.** to encompass; enclose; encircle.

girl *n.* a female child or young person.

Note that many adult women find it offensive to be called girls, particularly by men. However, some women, particularly those of older generations, use it about themselves: *I'm going to play cards with the girls this afternoon.*

girlfriend *n.* **1.** a woman with whom one has a steady romantic relationship. **2.** any female friend.

girth *n.* **1.** the measure around anything; circumference. **2.** a band passed under the belly of a horse, etc., to secure a saddle.

gist /dʒɪst/ *n.* the substance or pith of a matter; essential part.

give *v.* (**gave, given, giving**) **1.** to deliver freely; hand over: *to give a present.* **2.** to deliver to another in exchange for something; pay: *She gave $5 for it.* **3.** to grant permission or opportunity to. **4.** to present (as to an audience): *I give you the Mayor.* **5.** to suppose; assume: *given these facts.* **6.** to assign to someone as their right, lot, etc.: *to give him the benefit of the doubt.* **7.** *Informal* tell; offer as explanation: *Don't give me that.* **8.** to furnish or provide. **9.** to produce; present: *to give a play.* **10.** to yield under pressure or strain. *–n.* **11.** the act or fact of yielding to pressure; elasticity. *–phr.* **12. give in, a.** to yield; acknowledge defeat. **b.** to hand in. **13. give up, a.** to lose all hope. **b.** to abandon as hopeless. **c.** to desist

from; forsake: *give up a task.* **d.** to surrender. **e.** to devote entirely. **f.** Also, **give away.** to inform against.

given name *n.* the name one is given at birth, which is different from the names of other members of one's family: *Her given name is Irena and her family name is Popov.*

You can also often use **first name**, but note that this is not appropriate when the family name comes first rather than the given name, as with some Asian names.

gizzard *n.* the grinding or muscular stomach of birds.

glacier /ˈgleɪsiə, ˈglæsiə/ *n.* an extended mass of ice formed from falling snow and moving very slowly. *–glacial, adj.*

glad *adj.* delighted or pleased.

glade *n.* an open space in a forest.

gladiator *n. Roman Hist.* a person, often a slave or captive, who fought in public to entertain the people.

gladiolus /glædiˈoʊləs/ *n.* (*pl.* **-lus** or **-li** /-laɪ/ or **-luses**) a plant with spikes of variously coloured flowers.

glamour *n.* alluring and often illusory charm; fascination. Also, **glamor.** *–glamorous, adj.*

glance *v.* (**glanced, glancing**) **1.** to look quickly or briefly. **2.** to gleam or flash. **3.** to go off in an oblique direction from an object struck. *–n.* **4.** a quick or brief look.

gland *n. Anat.* an organ or tissue which secretes a substance which is used elsewhere in the body or is eliminated. *–glandular, adj.*

glare *n.* **1.** a strong, dazzling light. *–v.* **2.** to shine with a strong, dazzling light. **3.** to be conspicuous. **4.** to stare fiercely.

glass *n.* **1.** a hard, brittle, usually transparent substance produced from silica. **2.** (*pl.*) glass or plastic lenses set in a frame worn to defect defective eyesight; spectacles. **3.** a glass container for drinking.

glaucoma /glɔ'koumə/ n. a disease of the eye, causing gradual loss of vision.

glaze v. **1.** to furnish, fit or cover with glass. **2.** to produce a vitreous or glossy surface on (pottery, pastry, etc.). –n. **3.** a smooth, glossy surface or coating.

gleam n. **1.** a flash or beam of light. **2.** dim or subdued light. –v. **3.** to send forth a gleam or gleams. **4.** to appear suddenly and clearly.

Don't confuse this with **glean**.

glean v. **1.** to gather slowly and laboriously in bits. **2.** to discover or find out.

The more usual word is **obtain**.
Don't confuse **glean** with **gleam**.

glee n. demonstrative joy.

glen n. a small, narrow, secluded valley.

glib adj. (**glibber**, **glibbest**) spoken or speaking fluently, often thoughtlessly or insincerely so.

glide v. **1.** to move smoothly and effortlessly along. **2.** Aeronautics to move in the air, especially gradually downwards, by gravity or momentum already acquired. –n. **3.** a gliding movement, as in dancing.

glider n. Aeronautics a motorless aeroplane for gliding from a higher to a lower level by gravity, or from a lower to a higher level by air currents.

glimmer n. a faint or unsteady light; gleam.

glimpse n. **1.** a momentary sight or view. –v. **2.** to catch a glimpse of.

glint n. **1.** a gleam or glimmer; flash. **2.** gleaming brightness; lustre. –v. **3.** to gleam or flash.

glisten v. **1.** to shine with a sparkling light, especially as a result of being wet. –n. **2.** a glistening; sparkle.

glitch n. a hitch; snag; malfunction.

glitter v. to shine with a brilliant, sparkling light.

gloat v. to smile smugly or scornfully.

global adj. **1.** relating to or covering the whole world. **2.** all-embracing; comprehensive. **3.** (of a computer command)

operating over an entire database, set o records, etc. –**globally**, adv.

globalisation n. **1.** the process of becoming international in scope, application or influence, as of an industry, etc. **2.** the perceived development of a single world wide economy and culture, brought abou by the removal of restrictions to interna tional trade, travel and mass communica tion. Also, **globalization**. –**globalise globalize**, v.

globalism n. **1.** the pursuit of globali sation. **2.** the worldwide integration of economies. –**globalist**, n., adj.

global warming n. the significant rise in temperature of the whole of the earth's atmosphere.

globe n. **1.** the earth. **2.** a sphere with a map of the earth. **3.** anything spherical.

globule n. a small spherical body. –**globu lar**, adj.

glockenspiel /'glɒkənspil, -kənʃpil/ n. a musical instrument comprising a set of steel bars mounted in a frame and struck with hammers.

gloom n. **1.** darkness or dimness. **2.** a state of melancholy or depression; low spirits. –**gloomy**, adj.

glorious adj. **1.** giving, having, or full of glory: a glorious victory. **2.** brilliantly beautiful, wonderful, etc.: a glorious day.

For def. 1, the more usual word is **great**.

glory n. (pl. **-ries**) **1.** exalted praise, honour, or distinction, accorded by common consent. **2.** resplendent beauty or magnificence. **3.** the splendour and bliss of heaven; heaven. –v. (**-ried**, **-rying**) **4.** to be boastful; exult arrogantly (in).

gloss¹ n. a superficial lustre. –**glossy**, adj.

gloss² n. **1.** an explanation by means of a note in a manuscript text. –phr. **2.** **gloss over**, to give a specious interpretation of; explain away.

glossary n. (pl. **-ries**) a list of technical and difficult terms in a subject or field, with definitions.

glove n. a covering for the hand.

glove box n. a small space in a car, set into the dashboard, for storing small objects, such as maps, etc. Also, **glove compartment**.

glow n. **1.** light emitted by a substance heated to luminosity; incandescence. **2.** warmth of emotion or passion; ardour. –v. **3.** to emit bright light and heat without flame. **4.** to be animated with emotion.

glower /'glouǝ, 'glauǝ/ v. to stare with sullen dislike or discontent.

glucosamine /glu'kousǝmin/ n. a compound used in the treatment of osteoarthritis.

glucose n. Chem. a sugar occurring in many fruits, animal tissues and fluids, etc.

glue n. **1.** any adhesive substance made from any natural or synthetic resin, etc. –v. (**glued**, **gluing**) **2.** to join or fasten with glue.

gluggy adj. Informal sticky.

glum adj. (**glummer**, **glummest**) gloomily sullen or silent; dejected.

glut v. (**glutted**, **glutting**) **1.** to feed or satisfy to the full. **2.** to overstock. –n. **3.** a full supply. **4.** a surfeit.

gluten n. the tough, viscous nitrogenous substance remaining when the flour of wheat or other grain is washed to remove the starch.

glutinous adj. gluey; viscous; sticky.

glutton n. **1.** someone who eats to excess. **2.** someone who accepts an inordinate amount of unpleasantness, etc.: *a glutton for punishment.* **–gluttonous**, adj. **–gluttony**, n.

glycerol n. a colourless, odourless, liquid alcohol, of syrupy consistency and sweet taste, used as a solvent, in plastics, or as a sweetener. Also, **glycerine**.

gnarled /nald/ adj. **1.** (of trees) having many knots. **2.** (of persons) having a rugged, weather-beaten appearance.

gnash /næʃ/ v. to grind (the teeth).

gnat /næt/ n. a small winged insect.

gnaw /nɔ/ v. (**gnawed**, **gnawed** or **gnawn**, **gnawing**) **1.** to bite persistently. **2.** to consume with passion; torment. **–gnawer**, n.

gnocchi /'njɒki, 'nɒki/ pl. n. small dumplings made from potato and flour or semolina.

gnome /noum/ n. (in fairy stories) a shrivelled little old man.

gnomic /'noumik, 'nɒm-/ adj. like or containing aphorisms.

gnu /nu/ n. (pl. **gnus** or, especially collectively, **gnu**) → **wildebeest**.

go v. (**went**, **gone**, **going**) **1.** to move or pass (along); proceed. **2.** to move away or out; depart. **3.** to keep or be in motion; act, work, or run. **4.** to become: *to go mad.* **5.** to reach or extend: *This road goes to the city.* **6.** to belong; have a place: *That book goes on the top shelf.* **7.** (of colours, etc.) to harmonise; be compatible. **8.** to develop, especially with reference to success, or failure: *How did the exam go?* **9.** to fail; give way. **10.** to carry final authority: *What I say goes.* **11.** to be about, intending, or destined (used in the present participle followed by an infinitive): *I am going to drive to town.* –n. (pl. **goes**) **12.** the act of going. **13.** *Informal* energy, spirit, or animation. **14.** *Informal* one's turn to play or to make an attempt at something. **15.** *Informal* a success: *to make a go of something.* –phr. **16. fair go**, *Aust., NZ Informal* adequate opportunity. **17. go at**, **a.** to undertake with vigour. **b.** to attack; assail. **18. go down**, **a.** to descend; slope down. **b.** to be defeated. **c.** to be remembered by posterity. **19. go into**, to investigate thoroughly. **20. go off**, **a.** to discharge; explode. **b.** (of food, etc.) to deteriorate. **c.** to take place (in a specified manner): *The party went off well.*

d. *Informal* to come to dislike. **21. go over, a.** to read or re-read. **b.** to repeat. **c.** to examine. **d.** to have an effect (as specified): *Our suggestion went over badly.* **22. have a go.** *Informal* to make attempt; try. **23. on the go.** *Informal* very active.

goad *n.* **1.** a stick with a pointed end, for driving cattle, etc. –*v.* **2.** to prick or drive with or as with a goad; incite.

goal *n.* **1.** an area, basket or structure into which players in a game try to send the ball. **2.** the point gained by doing this: *We got three goals.* **3.** that towards which effort is directed; aim or end: *My goal is to finish this tonight.*

> Don't confuse this with **gaol**, which is another spelling of **jail**.

goanna *n.* a large Aust. monitor lizard.

goat *n.* **1.** an agile hollow-horned ruminant closely related to the sheep. **2.** *Informal* a fool.

goatee *n.* a man's beard trimmed to a tuft or a point on the chin.

gob *n.* a mass or lump.

gobble[1] *v.* to swallow hastily in large pieces; gulp.

gobble[2] *v.* to make the characteristic throaty cry of a turkey cock.

gobbledegook /'gobəldi,gʊk, -,guk/ *n.* *Informal* language characterised by circumlocution and jargon.

goblet *n.* a drinking glass with a foot and stem.

goblin *n.* a mischievous sprite or elf.

gobsmacked *adj. Informal* astonished.

go-cart *n.* → **go-kart**.

god *n.* **1.** a supernatural being believed to have power over humans or nature and worshipped according to different religious beliefs. **2. God**, in religions that believe in only one god, the highest being who is the maker and ruler of the universe. –*interj.* **3.** (an exclamation of surprise, fear, etc.): *Oh, God! I've left the oven on!*

Note that the use of this word as an exclamation (as in def. 3) may give offence.

godchild *n.* (*pl.* **-children**) someone for whom a person (godparent) takes responsibility at baptism.

goddaughter *n.* a female godchild.

goddess *n.* a female god or deity.

godfather *n.* a man who sponsors a child at baptism.

godly *adj.* (**-lier, -liest**) pious.

godmother *n.* a woman who sponsors a child at baptism.

godparent *n.* someone who takes responsibility for a child (their godchild) at baptism.

> A female godparent is a **godmother** and a male is a **godfather**.

godson *n.* a male godchild.

goggle *n.* **1.** (*pl.*) special spectacles designed to protect the eyes from wind, dust, water, or glare. –*v.* **2.** to stare with bulging eyes. **3.** to roll the eyes.

goitre /'gɔɪtə/ *n.* an enlargement of the thyroid gland, on the front and sides of the neck.

go-kart *n.* a small light vehicle with low-powered engine, used for relatively safe racing. Also, **go-cart, kart**.

gold *n.* **1.** a precious yellow metal, highly malleable and ductile, and free from liability to rust. *Symbol*: Au **2.** something like gold in brightness, preciousness, etc. **3.** bright yellow-brown. –**golden**, *adj.*

golden syrup *n.* a sweet viscous substance derived from sugar processing; used in cookery and as a sauce for porridge, desserts, etc.

goldfish *n.* (*pl.* **-fish** *or* **-fishes**) a small fish of the carp family.

> For information about the different plural forms, see the note at **fish**.

golf *n.* an outdoor game, in which a small ball is driven with special clubs into a series of holes. –**golfer**, *n.*

golf course *n.* the ground or course over which golf is played. Also, **golf links**, **links**.

gonad *n.* the sex gland, male or female, in which gametes develop and appropriate sex hormones are produced.

gondola /'gɒndələ/ *n.* a long, narrow boat used on the Venetian canals.

gone *adj.* departed; left.

gong *n. Music* a bronze disc to be struck with a soft-headed stick.

gonorrhoea /gɒnə'riə/ *n.* a contagious disease causing inflammation of the urethra and cervix. Also, **gonorrhea**.

good *adj.* (**better**, **best**) 1. morally excellent; righteous; pious. 2. satisfactory in quality, quantity, or degree; excellent. 3. right; proper. 4. (of food) fresh and palatable. 5. reliable; safe. 6. pleasant. 7. (of clothes) best or newest. 8. competent or skilful; clever. *–n.* 9. profit; worth; advantage; benefit. 10. excellence or merit; righteousness; kindness; virtue. 11. (*pl.*) possessions. 12. (*pl.*) articles of trade; wares; merchandise. *–interj.* 13. an expression of approval or satisfaction. *–phr.* 14. be up to no good, *Informal* to do wrong; behave in a suspicious manner. 15. for good (and all), for ever; permanently; for ever. 16. good for, a. valid for. b. giving rights or entitlement to provide: *This coupon is good for 2 free tickets.* c. (of a person) willing to provide: *He is good for a loan.* 17. good for you, *Informal* (*often patronising or ironic*) an expression of approval, encouragement, etc. 18. good luck, an expression wishing a person well. 19. good on you, *Informal* an expression of approval, encouragement, etc. 20. make good, a. to make recompense; pay for. b. to keep to an agreement. c. to be successful. d. to prove the truth of; substantiate.

Note that the other forms of **good** are **better** and **best**. **Better** is the *comparative* form and **best** is the *superlative*.

Compare **good** with **well**[1], which is an adverb meaning 'in a good way'. Because it is an adverb, **well** rather than **good** is the word to use with verbs, so you would say 'She sings well', not 'She sings good'.

goodbye *interj.* (a conventional expression used at parting).

goods and services tax *n.* a tax, usually imposed on the consumption of goods and services and most often calculated on the value that is added at each stage of the manufacturing and distribution process. Also, **GST**.

goodwill *n.* friendly disposition; benevolence; favour.

google *v.* (*from trademark*) to search for information on the internet, in particular using the Google search engine.

goose *n.* 1. a web-footed bird, larger and with a longer neck than a duck. 2. the female of this bird, as distinguished from the male. 3. a foolish person; simpleton.

The male of this bird is a **gander**, and a young goose is called a **gosling**. Note that **goose**, as in def. 3, can be insulting but is often used in an affectionate way.

gooseberry /'gʊzbəri, -brɪ/ *n.* (*pl.* **-ries**) the small fruit or berry of certain prickly shrubs.

goose pimples *pl. n.* a rough condition of the skin induced by cold or fear. Also, **goosebumps**, **goose flesh**.

gopher *n.* a rodent of North America.

gore[1] *n.* blood that is shed, especially when clotted. *–gory*, *adj.*

gore[2] *v.* (of an animal) to pierce with the horns or tusks.

gorge *n.* 1. a narrow cleft with steep, rocky walls, especially one through which a stream runs. 2. the throat; gullet. *–v.* (**gorged**, **gorging**) 3. to stuff (oneself, etc.) with food.

gorgeous *adj.* sumptuous; magnificent in appearance or colouring.

gorilla *n.* the largest of the anthropoid apes.

gormless adj. Informal (of a person) dull; stupid.

gosling n. a young goose.

gospel n. 1. (oft. upper case) (the writings containing) the body of doctrine taught by Christ and the apostles. 2. something regarded as true and implicitly believed.

gossamer n. 1. a fine filmy cobweb. 2. a very fine fabric.

gossip n. 1. idle talk, especially about the affairs of others. 2. a person given to tattling or idle talk. –v. (**-siped** or **-sipped**, **-siping** or **-sipping**) 3. to talk idly, especially about the affairs of others; go about tattling.

got v. past tense and past participle of **get**.

goth n. (sometimes upper case) 1. a type of pop music which typically features bleak imagery, and which is associated with a style of dress featuring black clothes, hair, make-up, etc. 2. a person who adopts this style of dress. –**gothic**, adj.

gotten v. a past participle of **get**.

gouge /gaʊdʒ/ n. 1. a chisel whose blade is curved. –v. (**gouged**, **gouging**) 2. to dig or force out with or as with a gouge.

gourd n. the fruit of various melon or pumpkin plants, whose dried shell is used for bottles, bowls, etc.

gourmet /ˈɡʊəmeɪ, ˈɡɔː-/ n. a connoisseur of food; an epicure.

gout n. a disease characterised by painful inflammation of the joints.

govern v. 1. to rule by right of authority. 2. to exercise a directing or restraining influence over; guide.

governess n. a woman who directs the education of children, generally in their own homes.

government n. 1. the authoritative direction and restraint exercised over societies and states. 2. the governing body of persons in a state.

Government (def. 2) is a collective noun and can be used with a singular or plural verb. Look up **collective noun**.

governor n. 1. a person charged with the direction or control of an institution, society, etc. 2. the principal representative of the sovereign in a state of the Commonwealth of Australia.

In Australia, **governor** is the title given to the person who represents the sovereign in one of the states. The actual head of government in a state is called the **premier**.

governor-general n. (pl. **governor-generals** or **governors-general**) the principal representative of the sovereign in certain independent Commonwealth countries.

In Australia, **governor-general** is the title given to the person who represents the sovereign at the federal level of government. The actual head of the federal government is called the **prime minister**.

gown n. 1. a dress worn by women on formal occasions. 2. a loose, flowing, outer garment.

GPS n. 1. global positioning system; a navigational system which relies on information received from a network of satellites to provide the latitude and longitude of an object, as a ship at sea, etc. 2. a device which uses this system to determine location.

grab v. (**grabbed**, **grabbing**) 1. to take suddenly and eagerly; snatch. 2. Informal to affect; impress: The film was OK but it didn't really grab me.

grace n. 1. elegance or beauty of form, motion, etc. 2. mercy; clemency; pardon. 3. (pl.) affected manner. 4. a short prayer before or after a meal. –v. 5. to lend or add grace to; adorn. –**graceful**, adj.

Don't confuse **graceful**, which means elegant, with **gracious**.

gracious adj. kind; benevolent; courteous.

Don't confuse this with **graceful**, which means elegant.

gradation *n.* any process or change taking place through a series of stages, by degrees, or gradually.

grade *n.* **1.** a degree in a scale, as of rank, advancement, quality, value, intensity, etc. **2.** a step or stage in a course or process. **3.** → **gradient** (def. 2). –*v.* **4.** to arrange in a series of grades; class; sort. **5.** to determine the grade of.

gradient *n.* **1.** the degree of inclination, or the rate of ascent or descent, in a railway, etc. **2.** an inclined surface; grade; ramp.

gradual *adj.* **1.** taking place, changing, moving, etc., by degrees or little by little. **2.** rising or descending at an even, moderate inclination.

graduate *n.* /ˈɡrædʒuət/ **1.** someone who has received a degree from a university or college. –*v.* /ˈɡrædʒueɪt/ **2.** to receive a degree or diploma on completing a course of study. **3.** to divide into or mark with degrees or other divisions, as the scale of a thermometer. –**graduation**, *n.*

graffiti *pl. n.* (*sing.* **graffito** /ɡrəˈfitoʊ/) drawings or words written without permission on public walls.

This word comes from Italian where it is a plural noun. However, in English it is usually considered singular: *Graffiti is a problem in the city.*

graft[1] *n.* **1.** *Hort.* part of a plant inserted in a groove in another plant so as to become united with it. **2.** a portion of living tissue surgically transplanted. –*v.* **3.** to cause (a plant) to reproduce through grafting. **4.** to transplant (a portion of living tissue) as a graft.

graft[2] *n.* **1.** work, especially hard work. **2.** gain or advantage achieved by dishonest or unfair means.

grain *n.* **1.** a small hard seed. **2.** any small, hard particle, as of sand, gold, pepper, etc. **3.** the arrangement or direction of fibres in wood. **4.** temper or natural character.

gram *n.* a measure of weight in the metric system, one thousandth of a kilogram. *Symbol:* g

gramma *n.* a type of pumpkin.

grammar *n.* the features of a language (sounds, words, formation and arrangement of words, etc.) considered systematically as a whole, especially with reference to their mutual contrasts and relations. –**grammarian**, *n.* –**grammatical**, *adj.*

gramophone *n.* a record-player.

grampus *n.* **1.** a marine mammal of the dolphin family. **2.** the killer whale.

granary *n.* (*pl.* **-ries**) a storehouse or repository for grain.

grand *adj.* **1.** imposing in size or appearance or general effect. **2.** magnificent or splendid. **3.** of great importance, distinction, or pretension. –**grandeur**, *n.*

grandchild *n.* (*pl.* **-children**) a child of one's son or daughter.

granddaughter *n.* **1.** a daughter of one's son or daughter. Also, **grand-daughter**.

grandfather *n.* the father of one's father or mother.

grandiloquent /ɡrænˈdɪləkwənt/ *adj.* speaking or expressed in a lofty or pompous style; bombastic.

grandiose *adj.* grand in an imposing or pompous way.

grandmother *n.* the mother of one's father or mother.

grandparent *n.* a parent of a parent.

grandson *n.* a son of one's son or daughter.

grandstand *n.* **1.** the principal stand for spectators at a racecourse, athletic field, etc. –*v.* **2.** to behave ostentatiously in order to impress or win approval.

granite *n.* a granular igneous rock.

grant *v.* **1.** to bestow or confer, especially by a formal act. **2.** to give or accord. **3.** to admit or concede; accept for the sake of argument. –*n.* **4.** something given, as a privilege or right, a sum of money, or a tract of land. –*phr.* **5. take for granted**, to accept without appreciation.

granular *adj.* **1.** of the nature of granules. **2.** composed of or bearing granules.

granulate *v.* to form into granules or grains. –**granulator**, *n.* –**granulation**, *n.*

granule *n.* a little grain, pellet, or particle.

grape *n.* the edible, pulpy, smooth-skinned fruit which grows in clusters on certain vines.

grapefruit *n.* a large roundish, yellow-skinned citrus fruit.

graph *n.* **1.** a diagram representing a system of connections or inter-relations among 2 or more things by a number of distinctive dots, lines, bars, etc. –*v.* **2.** to draw a graph of.

graphic *adj.* **1.** life-like; vivid. **2.** relating to the use of diagrams, graphs, etc.; diagrammatic. **3.** relating to writing. –*n.* **4.** a graphic image or icon: *computer graphics.*

graphic designer *n.* a designer, as of advertisements, books, etc., who uses print styles, images, page layout, etc., as design elements. –**graphic design**, *n.*

graphite *n.* a very common mineral, soft native carbon.

grapnel *n.* a device consisting of one or more hooks or clamps, for grasping or holding something; grapple.

grapple *n.* **1.** → **grapnel**. –*v.* **2.** to hold or make fast to something. **3.** to seize another, or each other, in a firm grip, as in wrestling; clinch. **4.** to try to overcome or deal (*with*).

grasp *v.* **1.** to seize and hold; grip. **2.** understand; comprehend. –*n.* **3.** a grasping or gripping. **4.** hold, possession, or mastery. **5.** broad or thorough comprehension.

grass *n.* **1.** a low-growing green plant with thin leaves growing close together. **2.** *Informal* marijuana.

grasshopper *n.* a terrestrial, herbivorous insect with long hind legs for leaping.

grassland *n.* an area in which the natural vegetation consists largely of perennial grasses, characteristic of subhumid and semi-arid climates.

grate[1] *n.* **1.** a frame of metal bars for holding burning fuel in a fireplace or furnace. **2.** a framework of parallel or crossed bars used as a partition, guard, cover, etc.

Don't confuse **grate** with **great**, which means large, notable or extremely good.

grate[2] *v.* **1.** to reduce to small particles by rubbing against a rough surface. **2.** to rub together with a harsh, jarring sound. **3.** to have an irritating or unpleasant effect on the feelings. **4.** to make a sound as of rough scraping. –**grater**, *n.*

Don't confuse **grate** with **great**, which means large, notable or extremely good.

grateful *adj.* warmly or deeply appreciative of kindness or benefits received; thankful. –**gratitude**, *n.*

gratify *v.* (**-fied**, **-fying**) to give pleasure to (someone) by satisfying desires or humouring inclinations or feelings. –**gratifier**, *n.* –**gratification**, *n.*

gratuitous /grə'tjuətəs/ *adj.* **1.** freely bestowed or obtained; free. **2.** being without reason, cause, or justification.

gratuity /grə'tjuəti/ *n.* (*pl.* **-ties**) a gift, usually of money, over and above payment due for service.

The more usual word is **tip**.

grave[1] *n.* an excavation made in the earth to receive a dead body in burial.

grave[2] *adj.* **1.** dignified; sedate; earnest; solemn. **2.** important or critical; involving serious issues.

The more usual word is **serious**.

gravel *n.* small stones and pebbles, or a mixture of these with sand.

gravitate *v.* **1.** to move or tend to move under the influence of gravitational force. **2.** to have a natural tendency to be strongly attracted (*to* or *towards*).

gravitation *n. Physics* that force of attraction between all particles or bodies, or that acceleration of one towards another, of which the fall of bodies to the earth is an instance. –**gravitational**, *adj.* –**gravitationally**, *adv.*

gravity *n.* **1.** *Physics* the force of attraction by which terrestrial bodies tend to fall towards the centre of the earth. **2.** seriousness; dignity; solemnity. **3.** serious or critical character.

gravy *n.* a sauce made with meat drippings as its basic ingredient.

graze¹ *v.* to feed on growing grass, etc., as cattle, sheep, etc.

graze² *v.* **1.** to touch or rub lightly in passing. **2.** to scrape the skin from (the leg, arm, etc.); abrade. –*n.* **3.** a slight scratch in passing; abrasion.

grazier *n.* *Aust., NZ* the owner of a rural property on which sheep or cattle are grazed.

grease *n.* /gris/ **1.** soft melted or rendered fat of animals. **2.** fatty or oily matter in general; lubricant. –*v.* /griz, gris/ **3.** to smear with grease.

great *adj.* **1.** large. **2.** notable or remarkable. **3.** important. **4.** being such in an extreme degree. **5.** *Informal* first-rate; very good; fine.

> Don't confuse **great** with **grate**, which is a frame of metal bars. It can also mean to rub something, making a rough sound.

greed *n.* inordinate or rapacious desire, especially for food or wealth. –**greedy**, *adj.*

green *adj.* **1.** of the colour of growing foliage, between yellow and blue in the spectrum. **2.** covered with grass or foliage; verdant. **3.** characterised by, or relating to, a concern for environmental issues. **4.** not fully developed; unripe. **5.** immature; inexperienced. **6.** (of certain foods, such as prawns) uncooked; raw. –*n.* **7.** green colour. **8.** a grassed playing area for golf or bowls.

greenfield *adj.* **1.** of or relating to a location for a business where there has not previously been any building. **2.** of or

relating to any enterprise which is becoming active in a market where there has been little or no previous activity. Also, **greenfields**.

greenfields *pl. n.* **1.** parkland or agricultural land on the outskirts of a city. –*adj.* **2.** → **greenfield**.

greengrocer *n.* a retailer of fresh vegetables and fruit.

greenhouse *n.* **1.** a building, chiefly of glass, for the cultivation or protection of plants by the trapping of heat within the glass. –*adj.* **2.** relating to a greenhouse. **3.** relating to the increase in the temperature of the earth caused by the atmosphere acting as the glass of a greenhouse does.

greenhouse effect *n.* the increase in the temperature of the earth caused by its atmosphere acting as the glass of a greenhouse does, possibly to be increased as pollution adds more and more carbon dioxide to the atmosphere.

greenhouse gas *n.* one of a number of gases found in the atmosphere that contribute to the greenhouse effect.

greenie *n.* *Aust. Informal* a conservationist.

green lung *n.* an area in or near to a city which is covered with vegetation which acts to draw in carbon dioxide and produce oxygen.

greenstick fracture *n.* a partial fracture of a bone of a young person or animal, in which only one side of a bone is broken.

greet *v.* to address with some form of salutation; welcome.

greeting *n.* **1.** the act or words of someone who greets; salutation. **2.** (*usu. pl.*) a friendly message.

gregarious *adj.* **1.** living or growing in groups or clusters. **2.** fond of company.

> For def. 2, the more usual word is **sociable**.

gremlin *n.* something that causes mischief or trouble.

grenade *n.* a small explosive shell thrown by hand or fired from a rifle.

grevillea *n.* one of a large genus of mainly Aust. flowering shrubs and trees.

grew *v.* past tense of **grow**.

grey *adj.* **1.** of a colour between white and black, having no definite hue; ash-coloured. **2.** dark, overcast, dismal, gloomy. **3.** grey-haired. –*n.* **4.** any colour between white and black, having no definite hue. **5.** a grey horse.

greyhound *n.* one of a breed of tall, slender dogs, notable for keen sight and for fleetness.

greywater *n.* untreated domestic or industrial waste water that can be used for watering lawns and gardens, or for other purposes, instead of being drained into the sewerage system.

grid *n.* **1.** a grating of crossed bars. **2.** a network of cables, pipes, etc., for the distribution and supply of electricity, gas, water, etc. **3.** a network of horizontal and vertical reference lines on a map.

griddle *n.* a flat, heated surface on top of a stove.

grief *n.* **1.** keen mental suffering or distress over affliction or loss. –*phr.* **2. come to grief**, to come to a bad end; turn out badly.

grievance *n.* a wrong, real or fancied, considered as grounds for complaint.

grieve *v.* **1.** to feel grief or sorrow. **2.** to cause to feel grief or sorrow: *It grieves me to see you behave so badly.*

For def. 2, the more usual word is **sadden**.

grievous /ˈgriːvəs/ *adj.* **1.** causing grief or sorrow. **2.** flagrant; atrocious.

For def. 1, the more usual word is **dreadful**; for def. 2, **serious**.

grill *n.* **1.** → **griller**. **2.** a meal of grilled meat. –*v.* **3.** to cook by means of a griller. **4.** *Informal* to subject to severe questioning.

grille *n.* a metal lattice screen forming a window or gate or used on the front of a motor car. –**grilled**, *adj.*

griller *n.* a cooking device, or that part of a stove, in which meat, etc., is cooked by exposure to direct radiant heat.

grim *adj.* (**grimmer**, **grimmest**) **1.** stern; unrelenting; uncompromising. **2.** of a fierce or forbidding aspect.

grimace /ˈgrɪməs/ *n.* **1.** a wry face; facial contortion; ugly facial expression. –*v.* (**-maced, -macing**) **2.** to make grimaces.

grime *n.* dirt or foul matter, especially on or ingrained in a surface.

grin *v.* (**grinned, grinning**) **1.** to smile broadly. –*n.* **2.** a broad smile.

grind *v.* (**ground, grinding**) **1.** to wear, smooth, or sharpen by friction; whet. **2.** to reduce to fine particles, as by pounding or crushing. –*n.* **3.** *Informal* laborious or monotonous work or study.

grip *n.* **1.** the act of grasping; a seizing and holding fast; firm grasp. **2.** mental or intellectual hold; competence. **3.** a special mode of clasping hands. –*v.* (**gripped, gripping**) **4.** to grasp or seize firmly; hold fast. **5.** to take hold on; hold the interest of.

gripe *v.* (**griped, griping**) **1.** *Informal* to complain constantly; grumble. –*n.* **2.** an objection; complaint.

grisly /ˈgrɪzli/ *adj.* (**-lier, -liest**) such as to cause a shuddering horror; gruesome.

grist *n.* corn to be ground.

gristle *n.* → **cartilage**.

grit *n.* **1.** fine, stony, or hard particles such as are deposited like dust from the air or occur as impurities in food, etc. **2.** firmness of character; indomitable spirit; pluck. –*v.* (**gritted, gritting**) **3.** to clench or grind.

grizzle *v.* to whimper; whine; complain fretfully.

grizzled *adj.* grey-haired with age.

groan *n.* **1.** a low, inarticulate sound uttered in pain or grief. **2.** a deep murmur uttered in derision, disapproval, etc. –*v.* **3.** to utter a groan.

grocer *n.* a shopkeeper with a small store selling canned and packaged foods and other household goods. **–grocery,** *n.*

This word is not used much in Australia any more, except in the term **green-grocer.** This is probably because different types of shops, such as supermarkets, have become more common.

grog *n. Aust., NZ Informal* alcohol.

groggy *adj.* **(-gier, -giest) 1.** staggering, as from exhaustion or blows. **2.** *Informal* drunk.

groin *n.* the fold or hollow where the thighs join the abdomen.

grommet *n.* **1.** Also, **grummet.** a ring or eyelet of metal, rubber, etc. **2.** *Med.* a small, plastic tube inserted through the eardrum into the middle ear to assist in preventing infection.

groom *n.* **1.** a person in charge of horses or the stable. **2.** a man newly married or about to be married; bridegroom. **–v. 3.** to tend carefully as to person and dress; make neat or tidy. **4.** to prepare for a position, election, etc.

groomsman *n. (pl.* **-men)** a man who attends the bridegroom at a wedding.

groove *n.* **1.** a furrow or channel cut by a tool. **2.** a fixed routine.

groovy *adj.* **(-vier, -viest)** *Informal* **1.** exciting, satisfying, or pleasurable. **2.** fashionable.

grope *v.* **1.** to feel about with the hands; feel one's way. **2.** to search blindly or uncertainly.

groper *n. (pl.* **-per** *or* **-pers)** a large *Aust.* or *NZ* marine fish.

For information about the different plural forms, see the note at **fish.**

gross *adj.* **1.** whole, entire, or total, especially without having had deductions made. **2.** glaring or flagrant. **3.** morally coarse; indelicate or indecent. **4.** large, big, or bulky. **–n. (pl.** **gross) 5.** a unit consisting of 12 dozen, or 144. **–v. 6.** to earn a total of.

grotesque /grou'tɛsk/ *adj.* odd or unnatural; fantastically ugly or absurd; bizarre.

grotto *n. (pl.* **-toes** *or* **-tos)** a cave or cavern.

grotty *adj.* **(-tier, -tiest)** *Informal* **1.** dirty; filthy. **2.** useless; rubbishy.

grouch *Informal –v.* **1.** to be sulky or morose; show discontent; complain. **–n. 2.** a sulky or morose person. **–grouchy,** *adj.*

ground[1] *n.* **1.** the earth's solid surface; firm or dry land. **2.** earth or soil. **3.** *(oft. pl.)* a tract of land given over to a special use. **4.** *(oft. pl.)* a motive; reason. **5.** the underlying or main surface or background, in painting, etc. **–adj. 6.** situated on or at, or adjacent to, the surface of the earth. **–v. 7.** to lay or set on the ground. **8.** to place on a foundation; found; fix firmly; settle or establish. **9.** to prevent (an aircraft or a pilot) from flying. **10.** to restrict, or withdraw privileges from. **–phr. 11. common ground,** matters on which agreement exists. **12. gain ground,** to advance; make progress. **13. hold** *(or* **stand) one's ground,** to maintain one's position. **14. lose ground,** to lose what one has gained; retreat; give way. **15. run to ground,** to hunt down; track down.

ground[2] *v.* past tense and past participle of **grind.**

groundwork *n.* the foundation, base, or basis of anything.

group *n.* **1.** an assemblage; cluster; aggregation. **2.** a number of persons or things ranged or considered together as being related in some way. **–v. 3.** to place in a group, as with others.

Group (defs 1 and 2) is a collective noun and can be used with a singular or plural verb. Look up **collective noun.**

grouse[1] *n. (pl.* **grouse)** a game bird of the Nthn Hemisphere.

grouse[2] *v. Informal* to grumble; complain.

grouse[3] *Aust., NZ Informal –adj.* **1.** very good. **–phr. 2. extra grouse,** excellent.

grout n. a mortar poured into the joints of masonry, brickwork and tilework.

grove n. a small wood or plantation of trees.

grovel v. (-elled or, Chiefly US, -eled, -elling or, Chiefly US, -eling) to humble oneself or act in an abject manner, as in fear or in mean servility.

grow v. (grew, grown, growing) 1. to (cause to) increase by natural development. 2. to increase gradually; become greater. 3. to become by degrees. –phr. 4. grow up, to attain maturity.

growl v. 1. to utter a deep guttural sound of anger or hostility. –n. 2. the act or sound of growling.

growth n. 1. the act, process, or manner of growing; development; gradual increase. 2. a diseased mass of tissue, a tumour.

grub n. 1. the bulky larva of certain insects. 2. Informal food.

grubby adj. (-bier, -biest) 1. dirty; grimy. 2. morally dubious; sleazy: a grubby little film.

grudge n. a feeling of ill will or resentment excited by some special cause, as a personal injury or insult, etc.

gruel n. a light, thin porridge.

gruelling adj. extremely tiring; severe.

The more usual word is **exhausting**.

gruesome adj. inspiring horror.

gruff adj. 1. low and harsh; hoarse. 2. rough; surly.

grumble v. 1. to complain ill-humouredly; murmur. –n. 2. an ill-humoured complaining; murmur.

grummet n. → **grommet** (def. 1).

grumpy adj. (-pier, -piest) Informal surly; ill-tempered. –**grump**, n.

grunge n. 1. a substance of an unpleasant nature, especially a dirty scum or slime. 2. a guitar-based form of heavy rock music. –**grungy**, adj.

grunt v. to utter the deep guttural sound characteristic of a pig.

GST n. → **goods and services tax**.

guarantee n. 1. a warrant, pledge, or promise accepting responsibility for the discharging of another's liabilities, as the payment of a debt. 2. a promise or assurance, usually written, as to the quality of goods, with an undertaking to make good any defects under certain conditions. 3. that which is taken or presented as security. –v. (-teed, -teeing) 4. to secure, as by giving or taking security. 5. to make oneself answerable for on behalf of one primarily responsible. 6. to undertake to secure to another, as rights or possessions. 7. to serve as a warrant or guarantee for. 8. to engage to protect or indemnify (from, against, or in). 9. to promise. Also, **guaranty**.

guarantor n. someone who makes or gives a guarantee.

guard v. 1. to keep safe from harm; protect; watch over. 2. to keep under close watch in order to prevent escape, outbreaks, etc. 3. to take precautions (against). –n. 4. someone who guards, protects, or restrains. 5. something intended or serving to guard or protect; a safeguard. 6. an official in general charge of a railway train.

guardian n. 1. someone who guards, protects, or preserves. 2. someone who is entrusted by law with the care of the person or property, or both, of another. –adj. 3. guarding; protecting.

guava /'gwavə/ n. a tropical tree or shrub with an edible fruit.

guerilla /gə'rɪlə/ n. a member of an irregular, usually politically motivated armed force, which harasses the enemy, usually the regular army, by surprise raids, attacks on communication and supply lines, etc. Also, **guerrilla**.

guernsey n. (pl. **-seys**) 1. a close-fitting knitted jumper. 2. Sport a distinctively coloured or marked top worn by footballers.

guess v. 1. to form an opinion of at random or from evidence admittedly uncertain.

guest *n.* a person entertained at the house or table of another.

guffaw *n.* **1.** a loud, coarse burst of laughter. –*v.* **2.** to laugh loudly.

guide *v.* **1.** to show the way to. **2.** to direct the movement or course of. –*n.* **3.** someone who guides. –**guidance**, *n.*

guide dog *n.* a dog specially trained to lead or guide a vision-impaired person.

guild *n.* an organisation of persons with common professional, cultural or other interests. Also, **gild**.

Nowadays this word is usually seen in the names of associations such as the *Designers Guild*.

guile *n.* cunning or skilful deceit.

guillotine /ˈɡɪlətin/ *n.* **1.** a machine for beheading persons by means of a heavy blade falling in 2 grooved posts. **2.** a device with a long blade for trimming paper. **3.** a time restriction imposed by resolution on a parliamentary debate.

guilt *n.* **1.** the fact or state of having committed an offence or crime. **2.** a feeling of responsibility or remorse for some crime, wrong, etc. –**guilty**, *adj.*

guinea pig *n.* **1.** a short-eared, short-legged rodent. **2.** a person used as the subject of any type of experiment.

guise *n.* **1.** external appearance in general; aspect. **2.** assumed appearance or mere semblance.

guitar *n.* a musical stringed instrument with a long fretted neck and a flat body.

gulf *n.* **1.** a portion of an ocean or sea partly enclosed by land. **2.** a deep hollow; chasm; abyss.

gull *n.* a web-footed, aquatic bird.

gullet *n.* → **oesophagus**.

gullible *adj.* easily deceived or cheated. –**gullibility**, *n.* –**gullibly**, *adv.*

gully *n.* a small valley cut by running water.

gulp *v.* **1.** to swallow eagerly, as when taking large draughts of liquids. **2.** to eat (food) hastily or greedily. –*n.* **3.** the act of gulping.

gum[1] *n.* **1.** any of various viscous, amorphous exudations from plants. **2.** a preparation of such a substance, used as a glue. **3.** Also, **chewing gum**. a sticky flavoured sweet for chewing. **4.** → **gum tree**. –*v.* (**gummed, gumming**) **5.** to smear, stiffen, or stick together with gum. **6.** to clog (*up*) with or as with some gummy substance .

gum[2] *n.* the firm, fleshy tissue enveloping the bases of the teeth.

This is often used in the plural: *I've got sore gums.*

gumboot *n.* a rubber boot reaching to the knee or thigh.

gumption *n. Informal* **1.** initiative or courage; resourcefulness. **2.** shrewd, practical common sense.

gum tree *n.* Also, **gum**. **1.** a tree or shrub used for its timber and strong oil, and which grows mostly in Aust. –*phr.* **2. up a gum tree**, *Informal* **a.** in difficulties; in a predicament. **b.** completely baffled.

gun *n.* **1.** a weapon consisting of a metallic tube from which missiles, ammunition, etc., are thrown by the force of an explosive. **2.** any similar device for projecting something. **3.** *Aust., NZ Informal* a champion, especially in shearing. –*v.* (**gunned, gunning**) **4.** to shoot (*down*) with a gun. –*adj.* **5.** *Aust., NZ Informal* of or relating to someone who is expert, especially in shearing. –**gunnery**, *n.*

gunpowder *n.* an explosive mixture of saltpetre (potassium nitrate), sulphur, and charcoal, used especially in gunnery.

gunwale /ˈɡʌnəl/ *n.* the upper edge of a ship's or boat's side.

gunyah *n.* an Aboriginal person's hut made of boughs and bark; humpy.

gurgle *v.* **1.** to flow in a broken, irregular, noisy current. **2.** to make a sound as of water doing this.

guru *n.* (in Hinduism) a spiritual guide.

gush v. 1. to flow suddenly and copiously. 2. to express oneself extravagantly or emotionally.

gusset n. an angular piece of material inserted in a garment to strengthen, enlarge or give freedom of movement to some part of it.

gust n. a sudden, strong blast, as of wind. –**gusty**, adj.

gusto n. keen relish or hearty enjoyment.

The more usual word is **enthusiasm**.

gut n. 1. → intestine. 2. (pl.) the bowels or entrails. 3. (pl.) Informal courage; stamina; endurance. 4. (pl.) Informal essential information. –v. (**gutted, gutting**) 5. to take out the guts or entrails of; disembowel. 6. to destroy the interior of. –adj. 7. of or relating to feelings, emotion, intuition.

gutter n. 1. a channel at the side of a road for leading off surface water. 2. a channel at the eaves or on the roof of a building, for carrying off rainwater.

guttural adj. 1. relating to the throat. 2. harsh; throaty.

guy¹ n. Informal 1. a man or boy. 2. (pl.) people of either sex, regarded as members of a group: Come on, you guys!

guy² n. a rope, wire, etc., used to guide and steady something being hoisted or lowered, or to secure anything liable to shift its position. Also, **guy rope**.

guzzle v. to eat or drink frequently and greedily.

gym n. 1. a centre providing fitness equipment and classes. 2. → gymnasium.

gymkhana /dʒɪm'kanə/ n. a horseriding event featuring games and novelty contests.

gymnasium n. (pl. -**siums** or -**sia**) a building or room equipped with facilities for gymnastics and sport. Also, **gym**.

gymnast n. someone trained and skilled in, or a teacher of, gymnastics.

gymnastic adj. relating to exercises which develop flexibility, strength, and agility. –**gymnastics**, n.

gynaecology n. that department of medical science which deals with the functions and diseases peculiar to women, especially those affecting the reproductive organs. Also, **gynecology**. –**gynaecologist**, n.

gyp /dʒɪp/ Informal –v. (**gypped, gypping**) 1. to swindle; cheat; defraud or rob by some sharp practice. –n. 2. a swindle.

gyprock /'dʒɪprɒk/ n. Aust. (from trademark) → plasterboard. –**gyprocker**, n.

gypsum /'dʒɪpsəm/ n. a very common mineral, used to make plaster of Paris, as an ornamental material, as a fertiliser, etc.

gypsy n. (pl. -**sies**) someone who has an unconventional or nomadic lifestyle. Also, **gipsy**.

gyrate /dʒaɪ'reɪt/ v. to move in a circle or spiral, or round a fixed point; whirl. –**gyration**, n. –**gyratory**, adj.

The more usual word is **rotate**.

gyre /'dʒaɪə/ n. a ring or circle.

gyroscope /'dʒaɪrəskoʊp/ n. a rotating wheel inside a frame which lets the wheel's axis keep its original direction even though the frame is moved around, used to help make such instruments as stabilisers in ships. –**gyroscopic**, adj.

H, h

H, h *n.* a consonant, the 8th letter of the English alphabet.

haberdashery *n.* (*pl.* **-ries**) a shop which sells (goods such as buttons, needles, etc.). –**haberdasher**, *n.*

habit *n.* **1.** a tendency, constantly shown, to act in a certain way. **2.** garb of a particular religious order, etc. –**habitual**, *adj.*

habitable *adj.* able to be lived in.

habitat *n.* the native environment of an animal or plant.

habitation *n.* a place of abode; dwelling.

habituate *v.* to make used (to); accustom.

háček /ˈhætʃek/ *n.* a mark (ˇ) over a letter used especially in the spelling of Slavic languages to represent particular phonetic qualities.

hack¹ *v.* **1.** to cut irregularly, as with heavy blows. **2.** to damage by cutting harshly. –*n.* **3.** a short, broken cough. –*phr.* **4. hack into**, to gain unauthorised access, as to the information stored on an organisation's computer. –**hacker**, *n.*

hack² *n.* **1.** a horse kept for general work, especially ordinary riding. **2.** a person who for a living undertakes literary or other work of little or no originality. –*v.* **3.** *Informal* to put up with; endure.

hackle *n.* **1.** a neck feather of certain birds, as the domestic cock. **2.** (*pl.*) the hair on a dog's neck.

hackneyed *adj.* overused and trite.

hackwork *n.* the routine aspects of creative or artistic work, considered as of an inferior quality.

had *v.* past tense and past participle of **have**.

Note that this word is often shortened to **'d**: *I'd been there earlier; They'd already told him.*

hadj *n.* → **hajj**.

haemoglobin *n.* a protein responsible for the red colour of blood.

haemophilia /himəˈfiliə, -ˈfil-, -jə/ *n.* a blood disorder of males in which clotting occurs abnormally slowly, resulting in excessive bleeding from even minor injuries. Also, **hemophilia**. –**haemophiliac**, *n.*

haemorrhage /ˈhɛmərɪdʒ/ *n.* a discharge of blood, as from a ruptured blood vessel. Also, **hemorrhage**.

haemorrhoid /ˈhɛmərɔɪd/ *n.* a swelling of a vein of the anus; pile. Also, **hemorrhoid**.

hag *n.* an unpleasant old woman.

haggard *adj.* thin and wild-looking, as from prolonged suffering, anxiety, etc.

haggis *n.* a dish made of the heart, liver, etc., of a sheep, etc.

haggle *v.* to bargain in a petty and tedious manner.

hail¹ *v.* **1.** to salute or greet; welcome. **2.** to acclaim. **3.** to attract the attention of, by calling out, waving the hand, etc. –*phr.* **4. hail from**, to belong to as the place of residence, etc.

hail² *n.* **1.** pellets of ice falling from the clouds in a shower. –*v.* **2.** to pour down hail.

hair *n.* **1.** the natural covering of the human head. **2.** (one of) the mass of the fine, usually cylindrical filaments growing from the skin and forming the coat of most mammals. –**hairy**, *adj.*

Don't confuse **hair** with **hare**, which is a rabbit-like animal.

haircut *n.* **1.** a cutting of the hair. **2.** the style in which the hair is cut and worn. –**haircutting**, *n.*

hairdo *n.* (*pl.* **-dos**) the style in which a person's hair is arranged. Also, **hairstyle**.

hairdresser *n.* someone who arranges or cuts hair.

hairline fracture *n.* a break or fault in a bone, metal casting, etc., which reveals itself as a very thin line on the surface.

hajj /hadʒ/ *n.* the pilgrimage to Mecca, which every Muslim is expected to make at least once in a lifetime. Also, **haj, hadj**.

halal /hæˈlæl/ *adj.* (of meat) from animals slaughtered in accordance with Muslim rites.

halcyon /ˈhælsiən/ *adj.* **1.** calm, tranquil, or peaceful. **2.** carefree; joyous.

hale *adj.* free from disease or infirmity; robust; vigorous.

half *n.* (*pl.* **halves**) **1.** one of the 2 equal parts into which anything may be divided. **2.** *Sport* either of the 2 periods of a game. **3.** one of a pair. *–adj.* **4.** being one of the 2 equal parts into which anything may be divided. **5.** being equal to only about half of the full measure. *–adv.* **6.** to the extent or measure of half. **7.** to some extent.

halfback *n.* *Sport* a player positioned between the centre line and the back line, or next behind the forward line.

half-life *n.* the time required for one half of a sample of unstable material to undergo chemical change, as the disintegration of radioactive material, etc.

halfway *adv.* **1.** to or at half the distance. *–adj.* **2.** midway, as between 2 places or points.

halitosis *n.* bad breath.

hall *n.* **1.** the entrance room of a building. **2.** a corridor or passageway in a building. **3.** a large building or room for public meetings, etc.

Don't confuse this with **haul**, which is to pull something heavy along.

hallelujah /hæləˈluːjə/ *interj.* (a cry expressing pleasure or rejoicing); praise the Lord!

The original meaning of this word was a cry of praise to God, but it is now often used in a humorous way to indicate that something good has happened, especially after a long wait: *You've finally managed to get us tickets to the concert. Hallelujah!*

hallmark *n.* **1.** an official mark or stamp indicating a standard of purity, used in marking gold and silver articles. **2.** any outstanding feature.

hallow *v.* to make holy.

hallucination *n.* a subjective perception for which there is no appropriate external source, as 'hearing voices'. **-hallucinate,** *v.*

halo *n.* (*pl.* **-loes** or **-los**) **1.** a radiance surrounding the head in the representation of a sacred personage. **2.** a circle of light, appearing round the sun or moon.

halt *v.* **1.** to make a temporary or permanent stop. *–n.* **2.** a temporary stop.

halter *n.* a rope or strap with a noose or harness for leading or fastening horses or cattle.

halve *v.* **1.** to divide in halves; share equally. **2.** to reduce to half.

halves *n.* plural of **half**.

halyard *n.* a rope or tackle used to hoist or lower a sail, yard, flag, etc. Also, **halliard**.

ham[1] *n.* meat from one of the rear quarters of a pig.

ham[2] *n.* *Informal* **1.** an actor who overacts. **2.** an amateur.

hamburger *n.* (a bread roll containing) a cooked cake of minced beef.

hamlet *n.* a small village.

hammer *n.* **1.** a tool with a solid metal head set crosswise on a handle, used for beating metals, driving in nails, etc. **2.** any tool or device resembling a hammer. **3.** *Athletics* a metal ball attached to a long, flexible handle, used in certain throwing contests. *–v.* **4.** to beat, drive or impel with or as with a hammer. **5.** to hit with some force; pound. *–phr.* **6. hammer and tongs,** *Informal* with great noise, vigour, or force.

hammerhead *n.* a shark with a head resembling a double-headed hammer.

hammock *n.* a kind of hanging bed made of canvas, etc.

hamper¹ *v.* to impede; hinder.

hamper² *n.* 1. a large basket or receptacle made from cane, wickerwork, etc., usually with a cover. 2. such a basket or other container filled with food or other items, and given as a gift, prize, etc.

hamster *n.* a short-tailed, burrowing rodent.

hamstring *n.* 1. one of the tendons at the back of the knee. –*v.* (**-strung, -stringing**) 2. to cripple; thwart.

hand *n.* 1. the terminal, prehensile part of the arm, consisting of the palm and 5 digits. 2. something resembling a hand. 3. a manual labourer. 4. (*oft. pl.*) power, control or custody: *to have someone's fate in your hands.* 5. a side of a subject, question, etc.: *on the other hand.* 6. style of handwriting. 7. a pledge of marriage. 8. a unit used in measuring the height of horses, etc., equal to approx. 10 cm. 9. *Cards* the cards dealt to or held by each player at one time. 10. a bunch of fruit, leaves, etc. 11. a round of applause. –*v.* 12. to pass with the hand. 13. to pass on: *to hand on an infection.* –*phr.* 14. **at hand,** a. within reach. b. near in time. c. ready for use. 15. **free hand,** freedom to act as desired. 16. **give a hand,** to help. 17. **hand it to,** *Informal* to give due credit to. 18. **in hand,** a. under control. b. in immediate possession. 19. **on hand,** a. in immediate possession. b. before one for attention. c. present.

handbook *n.* a small book serving as a guide to study, etc.

handcuff *n.* one of a pair of ring-shaped shackles for the wrist.

handheld *adj.* 1. held in the hand. 2. of or relating to a device which is designed to be small enough to be held in the hand. –*n.* 3. such a device. Also, **handheld.**

handicap *n.* 1. (a contest involving) disadvantages or advantages of weight, distance, etc., placed upon competitors to equalise their chances of winning. 2. any encumbrance or disadvantage. 3. a physical disability. –*v.* (**-capped, -capping**) 4. to serve as a handicap or disadvantage to.

handicapped *adj.* lacking a physical or mental ability, especially because of an illness or injury.

Note that the use of **handicapped** is considered offensive by many people as it is a very negative term, stressing a lack of some kind.

handicraft *n.* 1. manual skill. 2. a manual art or occupation.

handiwork *n.* work done or a thing or things made by the hands.

handkerchief /ˈhæŋkətʃif/ *n.* a small, usually square piece of fabric for wiping the nose, etc. Also, *Informal,* **hankie, hanky.**

handle *n.* 1. a part of a thing which is intended to be grasped by the hand in using or moving it. –*v.* 2. to touch or feel with the hand. 3. to manage, direct, or control. 4. to deal with or treat in a particular way. 5. to deal or trade in (goods, etc.). 6. to respond to handling.

handsome *adj.* 1. of fine or admirable appearance; good-looking. 2. ample, or liberal in amount.

Note that when you are describing someone's appearance, you would normally only use **handsome** if you were talking about a male. You could use **beautiful** or **pretty** if you were describing a female, or **attractive** or **good-looking,** both of which can refer to either males or females.

handwriting *n.* (a kind or style of) writing done with the hand.

handy *adj.* (**-dier, -diest**) 1. conveniently accessible. 2. ready or skilful with the hands; deft; dexterous. 3. convenient or useful.

hang v. (**hung** or, esp. for capital punishment and suicide, **hanged**, **hanging**) **1.** to fasten (something) so that it is supported only from above. **2.** to be suspended; dangle. **3.** to hang (someone) by the neck until dead. **4.** to (let) droop or bend downwards. **5.** to fasten into position: to hang a painting. **6.** to attach (paper, etc.) to walls. **7.** to cling, or adhere; rest for support (on or upon). **8.** to be dependent (on or upon): His fate hangs on the jury's decision. **9.** to be doubtful; remain unfinished. –n. **10.** the way in which a thing hangs. –phr. **11. hang about** (or **around**), to loiter. **12. hang on, a.** to persevere. **b.** to linger. **c.** to wait. **13. hang out**, Informal (sometimes fol. by at or in) to reside or regularly be found at (a particular place). **14. hang up, a.** to suspend on a hook, etc. **b.** to break off a telephone conversation by putting down the receiver.

Note that, when referring to death by hanging, the usual past form used to be **hanged**, rather than **hung**. However, nowadays, except in legal use, the past form **hung** is often used for this sense.

hangar n. a shed or shelter usually for an aircraft.

Don't confuse this with **hanger**, which is something you hang things on, especially clothes.

hanger n. a shaped support for hanging clothes, etc.

Don't confuse **hanger** with **hangar**, which is a shed where aircraft are kept.

hang-glider n. a simple kite-like glider with a framework from which a person hangs.

hangover n. the after-effects of drinking too much alcohol.

hang-up n. Informal something which causes unease, inhibition, or conflict in an individual.

hank n. a skein.

hanker v. (fol. by after, for, or an infinitive) to have a restless or incessant longing.

hanky-panky n. Informal **1.** trickery; subterfuge. **2.** sexual play.

haphazard adj. dependent on mere chance.

hapless adj. unlucky.

happen v. **1.** to take place, or occur. **2.** to befall, as to a person or thing. **3.** to come by chance (on or upon).

happy adj. (**-pier**, **-piest**) **1.** indicating pleasure, content, or gladness. **2.** delighted, as over a particular thing. **3.** fortunate or lucky.

harangue /həˈræŋ/ n. **1.** a passionate, vehement speech. –v. (**-rangued**, **-ranguing**) **2.** to address in a harangue.

harass /həˈræs, ˈhærəs/ v. to disturb persistently.

harbinger /ˈhɑːbɪndʒə/ n. **1.** someone who goes before and makes known the approach of another. **2.** an omen.

harbour n. **1.** a body of water along the shore deep enough for ships. **2.** any place of shelter or refuge. –v. **3.** to conceal or shelter. **4.** to entertain in the mind: to harbour ill will. Also, **harbor**.

hard adj. **1.** solid and firm to the touch; not soft. **2.** tightly formed. **3.** difficult to do or accomplish; troublesome. **4.** involving or with great exertion or persistence. **5.** violent; harsh. **6.** callous. **7.** confronting to the eye, ear, etc. **8.** severe in terms: a hard bargain. **9.** alcoholic or addictive: hard drink; hard drugs. **10.** (of water) containing mineral salts which interfere with the action of soap. –adv. **11.** with great exertion; with vigour or violence. **12.** harshly or severely; badly. **13.** intently: to look hard at something. –**harden**, v.

hardball phr. **play hardball**, Informal to use tough, uncompromising or ruthless tactics in business, politics, etc.

hard disk n. a disk on which information is stored inside a computer.

Compare this with **floppy disk**.

hardline *adj.* not deviating from a set doctrine, policy, etc.

hardly *adv.* **1.** barely; almost not at all: *There is hardly any milk left.* **2.** with little likelihood; probably not: *She would hardly admit that she broke it herself, would she?*

hardship *n.* something hard to bear, as severe toil, oppression, need, etc.

hardware *n.* **1.** building materials, tools, etc. **2.** the physical components of a computer system.

Compare def. 2 with **software**, which refers to the programs that run on a computer.

hardwired *adj.* **1.** *Computers* **a.** (of a circuit) permanently wired into a computer. **b.** (of a function) determined by the hardware and therefore not programmable. **2.** (of people) inherently equipped to act in a certain way: *humans are hardwired for language.* **3.** not modifiable. Also, **hard-wired.**

hardworking *adj.* willing to expend effort in one's work; diligent.

hardy *adj.* (**-dier, -diest**) capable of enduring fatigue, hardship, exposure, etc.

hare *n.* (*pl.* **hares** *or, especially collectively,* **hare**) a rabbit-like mammal.

Don't confuse this with **hair**, which is what grows on top of your head.

harelip *n.* a congenitally deformed lip.

harem /'hɛərəm, ha'rim/ *n.* (in some Muslim societies) the women of a household.

hark *v.* **1.** (*chiefly imperative*) to listen. –*phr.* **2. hark back**, to return to a previous point.

harlot *n.* a promiscuous woman; prostitute.

harm *n.* **1.** injury; damage; hurt. –*v.* **2.** to injure; damage; hurt.

harmonica *n.* a musical instrument played by the breath; mouth organ.

harmony *n.* (*pl.* **-nies**) **1.** agreement; accord. **2.** a consistent, orderly, or pleasing arrangement of parts. **3.** *Music* any simultaneous combination of notes.

–**harmonise, harmonize,** *v.* –**harmonic,** *adj.* –**harmonious,** *adj.*

harness *n.* **1.** the combination of straps, etc., forming the working gear of a horse, etc. **2.** a similar combination worn by persons for protection, restraint, etc. –*v.* **3.** to put harness on (a horse, etc.). **4.** to bring under conditions for working.

harp *n.* **1.** a triangular stringed instrument, played with the hands. –*v.* **2.** to dwell (*on, upon*) persistently or tediously in speaking or writing.

harpoon *n.* a spear attached to a rope.

harpsichord /'hɑpsɪkɔd/ *n.* a keyboard instrument, with strings being plucked (rather than struck as in a piano).

harridan *n.* (*derog.*) a disreputable violent woman.

harrow *n.* **1.** an implement for levelling soil, etc. –*v.* **2.** to disturb keenly or painfully.

harry *v.* (**-ried, -rying**) **1.** to torment; worry. **2.** to ravage, as in war.

harsh *adj.* **1.** ungentle and unpleasant in action or effect. **2.** rough to the touch, etc.

hart *n.* (*pl.* **harts** *or, especially collectively,* **hart**) a male deer.

harvest *n.* **1.** (the gathering of) a crop, as of grain. **2.** the product of any process. –*v.* **3.** to gather, as a crop. **4.** to gather, as the product of a biological process, experiment, etc.: *to harvest eggs for fertilisation.* **5.** to collect electronically, as in the gathering of email addresses.

has *v.* 3rd person singular present indicative of **have.**

Note that this word is often shortened to **'s**: *She's gone; Nick's already eaten dinner.*

hash *n.* **1.** a mess, jumble, or muddle. **2.** a dish of reheated food.

hashish /hæ'ʃiʃ, 'hæʃiʃ/ *n.* the resin from Indian hemp, smoked, chewed, etc., as a narcotic. Also, **hash.**

hasp *n.* a clasp for a door, lid, etc.

hassle n. 1. a quarrel. 2. a struggle; period of unease. –v. 3. to worry; harass.

hassock n. a thick, firm cushion used for kneeling.

haste n. 1. speed in motion or action. 2. thoughtless or rash speed. –**hasty**, adj.

hasten v. to proceed with haste.

The more usual word is **hurry**.

hat n. a shaped covering for the head, usually worn outdoors.

hatch[1] v. 1. to bring forth (young) from the egg. 2. to contrive; devise.

hatch[2] n. a cover for an opening in a ship's deck, etc.

hatch[3] v. to mark with (usually parallel) lines, as for shading in drawing.

hatchback n. a type of car fitted with a door at the rear which includes the rear window, and which has hinges at the top.

Compare this with **sedan** and **station wagon**.

hatchet n. a small, short-handled axe.

hate v. to regard with a strong dislike; detest. –**hateful**, adj. –**hatred**, n.

hate crime n. criminal violence enacted upon an individual or group perceived as belonging to a social or racial group hated by the attacker.

haughty adj. (**-tier**, **-tiest**) disdainfully proud; arrogant.

haul v. 1. to pull or draw with force. 2. (of the wind) to change direction (round or to). –n. 3. a strong pull or tug. 4. the distance over which anything is hauled. 5. the proceeds of a robbery: the thieves made away with a haul of $25 000. –phr. 6. **in** (or **over**) **the long haul**, in the long term; in a long period of time. 7. **in** (or **over**) **the short haul**, in the short term; in a short period of time.

Don't confuse this with **hall**, which is a corridor or a large room for meetings, etc.

haunch n. the hip.

haunt v. 1. to visit habitually as a ghost. 2. to worry or disturb. 3. to visit frequently. –n. 4. (oft. pl.) a place visited frequently.

have v. 1. to hold or possess. 2. to get, receive, or take. 3. to be required (to). 4. to experience: to have fun. 5. to require or cause: Have it finished by tomorrow. 6. to engage in. 7. to permit or allow. 8. to give birth to. 9. Informal to outwit, or deceive. 10. (a word used as an auxiliary verb with other verbs to form the perfect aspect): He has gone; They have been swimming.

The different forms of the verb **to have** are as follows:

Present tense: I **have**, you **have**, he/she/it **has**, we **have**, they **have**
Past tense: I, you, he/she/it, we, they **had**
Past participle: **had**
Present participle: **having**
Note that **have** is often shortened to **'ve**: I've been here too long.

haven n. 1. a harbour or port. 2. any place of shelter and safety.

haversack n. a backpack.

havoc n. ruinous damage; devastation.

hawk[1] n. a bird of prey.

hawk[2] v. to clear the throat noisily.

hawker n. someone who travels from place to place selling goods.

hawthorn n. a thorny shrub.

hay n. dried grass used as fodder.

hay fever n. inflammation of the eyes, nose and throat, caused by pollen.

haywire adj. 1. in disorder. 2. out of control; crazy.

hazard n. 1. a risk; exposure to danger. –v. 2. to venture to offer (a guess, etc.). 3. to take a risk; expose to risk. –**hazardous**, adj.

haze n. a thin mist, caused by dust, heat, etc. –**hazy**, adj.

hazel n. 1. a small tree which bears edible nuts. 2. light yellowish brown.

he pron. 1. the personal pronoun used to refer to a particular male: He married my *sister yesterday.* **2.** anyone; that person, whether male or female: *If anyone comes to the door, he can just wait.*

He is a third person singular pronoun in the subjective case.
Note that the use of **he** to mean anyone (def. 2) is less common nowadays because it seems to exclude females, and this offends many women. More and more **they** is being used for this sense: *If anyone comes to the door, they can just wait.*

head *n.* **1.** the upper part of the body, joined to the trunk by the neck. **2.** the head as the seat of thought, memory, etc. **3.** the position of leadership. **4.** the top, summit, or upper end of anything. **5.** the foremost part; a projecting part. **6.** (*pl.* **head**) a person or animal considered merely as one of a number. **7.** culmination or crisis; conclusion. **8.** (*pl.*) the side of a coin bearing a head (opposed to *tails*): *Heads or tails?* **11.** the source of a river. **12.** froth, as that formed on beer when poured. **13.** a section of a discourse; topic. *–adj.* **14.** situated at the top or front. **15.** being in the position of leadership or superiority. *–v.* **16.** to go in front of; lead. **17.** to be the head or chief of. *–phr.* **18. head for,** to move towards. **19. head off,** to intercept (something) and force (it) to change course.

headache *n.* **1.** a pain in the head. **2.** *Informal* a worrying problem.

headfirst *adv.* **1.** with the head in front or bent forwards; headlong. **2.** too quickly; rashly; precipitately. Also, **headforemost**.

headhunting *n.* *Informal* **1.** the seeking of a scapegoat for a misfortune or setback. **2.** the search for new executives, usually senior, through personal contacts rather than advertisements.

heading *n.* a title or caption of a page, chapter, etc.

headland *n.* a promontory extending into the sea, etc.

headlight *n.* a light on the front of any vehicle.

headline *n.* a display line over an article, etc., as in a newspaper.

headlong *adv.* **1.** headfirst: *to plunge headlong.* **2.** rashly; without thought. **3.** with great speed; precipitately. *–adj.* **4.** done or going with the head foremost. **5.** marked by haste; precipitate. **6.** rash; impetuous.

headmaster *n.* the male principal of a school.

Note that nowadays the preferred term for this is **principal**.

headmistress *n.* the female principal of a school.

Note that nowadays the preferred term for this is **principal**.

headquarters *pl. n.* any centre of operations.

Although this is a plural noun, it is often treated as singular: *Our headquarters is in Darwin.*

head start *n.* an initial advantage in a race, competition, etc.

headstone *n.* a stone set at the head of a grave.

headstrong *adj.* bent on having one's own way; wilful.

headway *n.* progress.

headwind *n.* a wind that blows directly against the direction of travel.

heady *adj.* (**-dier, -diest**) **1.** rashly impetuous. **2.** intoxicating.

heal *v.* to restore to health.

Don't confuse this with **heel**, which is the back part of your foot.

health *n.* **1.** freedom from disease or ailment. **2.** the general condition of the body or mind.

healthy *adj.* (**-thier, -thiest**) **1.** in a state of good health; free of any sickness or disease. **2.** conducive to good health: *healthy food.* –**healthily**, *adv.*

heap *n.* **1.** an assemblage of things, lying one on another; pile. **2.** (*sometimes pl.*) *Informal* a great quantity or number. –*v.* **3.** to gather in a heap; pile (*up, on, together*, etc.).

hear *v.* (**heard, hearing**) **1.** to perceive (something) by the ear. **2.** to listen (to). **3.** to give a formal hearing to, as a judge does.

Don't confuse **hear** with **here**, which means in this place: *Do you like living here?*

hearing *n.* **1.** the sense by which hearing is perceived. **2.** *Law* the trial of an action. **3.** earshot.

hearing-impaired *adj.* deficient in the ability to hear, ranging from complete to partial hearing loss.

hearsay *n.* gossip; rumour.

hearse /hɜs/ *n.* a funeral vehicle.

heart *n.* **1.** a hollow muscular organ which pumps blood throughout the body. **2.** this organ considered as the seat of life, thought, or emotion. **3.** the seat of emotions (often in contrast to the *head* as the seat of the intellect). **4.** spirit, courage, or enthusiasm. **5.** the innermost part of anything. **6.** a figure with rounded sides meeting in a point at the bottom and curving inwards to a cusp at the top.

A medical word which describes things related to the heart is **cardiac**.

heart attack *n.* a sudden, severe failure of the heart to function normally; myocardial infarct.

heartburn *n.* a burning sensation above the abdomen.

hearten *v.* to give courage to; cheer.

hearth *n.* **1.** that part of the floor on which the fire is made. **2.** the fireside; home.

hearty *adj.* (**-tier, -tiest**) **1.** warm-hearted; affectionate; cordial; friendly. **2.** enthusiastic; vigorous. **3.** substantial or satisfying. –**heartily**, *adv.*

heat *n.* **1.** the quality, condition or sensation of hotness. **2.** hot weather. **3.** warmth or intensity of feeling. **4.** a single division of a race. **5.** *Zool.* sexual excitement in animals, especially females. –*v.* **6.** to make or become hot or warm.

heath *n.* **1.** a tract of open, uncultivated land, especially in European countries. **2.** a low, evergreen shrub.

heathen *n.* an irreligious person.

heather *n.* a heath plant.

heave *v.* (**heaved** *or*, *Chiefly Naut.*, **hove, heaving**) **1.** to lift with effort; hoist. **2.** to rise and fall with a swelling motion. **3.** to vomit; retch.

heaven *n.* **1.** in some religions, the abode of God, the angels, and the spirits of the righteous after death. **2.** (*chiefly pl.*) the sky. **3.** a place or state of supreme bliss. –**heavenly**, *adj.*

A word which describes something related to heaven is **celestial**.

heavy *adj.* (**-vier, -viest**) **1.** of great weight; hard to lift or carry. **2.** burdensome. **3.** concerned with the manufacture of heavy goods. **4.** serious; grave. **5.** exceptionally dense. **6.** (of music, literature, etc.) intellectual or deep. –*n.* (*pl.* **-vies**) *Informal* an influential person.

heavy metal *n.* a style of rock music dominated by electric guitars played very loudly. –**heavy-metal**, *adj.*

heckle *v.* to harass, especially a public speaker, with questions and gibes.

hectare *n.* a unit of land measurement in the metric system, equal to 10 000 square metres (approx. 2.47 acres). *Symbol:* ha

hectic *adj.* characterised by great excitement, activity, confusion, and haste.

hedge *n.* **1.** a row of closely planted bushes as forming a fence or boundary. –*v.* (**hedged, hedging**) **2.** to close (*off, in*, etc) by a hedge. **3.** to protect (a bet, etc.) by taking some offsetting risk. **4.** to avoid taking an open or decisive course.

hedgehog *n.* a small spiny mammal.

hedonism *n.* the doctrine that pleasure or happiness is the highest good. **–hedonist,** *n.*

heed *v.* to give attention to; notice.

heel *n.* **1.** the back part of the foot, below and behind the ankle. **2.** the part of a sock, etc., covering the heel. **3.** *Informal* a despicable person; cad.

Don't confuse this with **heal**, which is to make or become well again.

heeler *n.* a cattle or sheep dog which rounds up stock by following at their heels.

hefty *adj.* (**-tier, -tiest**) *Informal* **1.** heavy. **2.** big and strong; powerful.

hegemony /hə'gɛmənɪ, hə'dʒɛmənɪ, 'hɛgəmənɪ, 'hɛdʒəmənɪ/, *Orig.* US /'hɛdʒəmoʊnɪ, 'hɛdʒəmoʊnɪ/ *n.* leadership; predominance.

heifer *n.* a cow that has not produced a calf and is under 3 years of age.

height *n.* **1.** the state of being high. **2.** extent upwards; altitude; stature. **3.** a high place as a hill, etc. **4.** the highest point; utmost degree.

Height is the noun from the adjective **high**.

Heimlich manoeuvre /'haɪmlɪk/ *n.* a method of helping someone who is choking by applying a sudden squeeze of pressure just below their rib cage, thus forcing air up through the trachea and removing the obstruction.

heinous /'heɪnəs, 'hɪ-/ *adj.* hateful.

heir /ɛə/ *n.* **1.** *Law* someone who inherits the estate (def. 2b) of a deceased person. **2.** someone to whom something falls or is due. **–heiress,** *fem. n.*

heirloom *n.* any family possession transmitted from generation to generation.

heist /haɪst/ *n.* a robbery; burglary.

held *v.* past tense and past participle of **hold**[1].

helicopter *n.* an aircraft which is lifted and sustained in the air by horizontal rotating blades.

helium *n.* an inert gaseous element present in the sun's atmosphere. *Symbol*: He

helix /'hiːlɪks, 'hɛl-/ *n.* (*pl.* **helices** /'hiːləsɪz, 'hɛl-/ *or* **helixes**) a spiral. **–helical,** *adj.*

hell *n.* **1.** in some religions, the abode of evil and spirits of the wicked condemned to punishment after death. **2.** any place or state of torment or misery. *–interj.* **3.** *Informal* (*taboo*) (an exclamation of annoyance, disgust, etc.). **–hellish,** *adj.*

Note that def. 3 may give offence.

he'll contraction of: **1.** he will. **2.** he shall.

hello *interj.* an exclamation used to express greeting, attract attention, etc.

helm *n.* **1.** the tiller or wheel which controls the rudder of a vessel. **2.** the place or post of control.

helmet *n.* a protective covering for the head.

help *v.* **1.** to cooperate effectively with a person; aid; assist. **2.** to rescue. **3.** to relieve (someone) in distress. **4.** to refrain from; avoid: *I could not help laughing.* **5.** to remedy, or prevent: *Nothing will help now.* *–n.* **6.** (a person or thing that gives) aid, assistance or relief. *–phr.* **7. help oneself (to)**, to take or appropriate at will.

Def. 4 is always used in a negative sentence.

helpful *adj.* **1.** willing or eager to help. **2.** useful. **–helpfully,** *adv.* **–helpfulness,** *n.*

helpless *adj.* unable to help oneself; weak or dependent.

helter-skelter *adv.* in disorderly haste.

hem *v.* (**hemmed, hemming**) **1.** to enclose or confine (*in, round,* or *about*). **2.** to fold back and sew down the edge of (cloth, etc.). *–n.* **3.** the folded and sewn border of a garment.

hemisphere *n.* **1.** half of the terrestrial globe or celestial sphere. **2.** the half of a sphere. **–hemispherical,** *adj.*

hemlock n. a poisonous herb.

hemp n. **1.** a tall, Asian herb yielding hashish, etc. **2.** the tough fibre of this plant used for making coarse fabrics, ropes, etc.

hen n. a female bird, especially of the domestic fowl.

The male of this bird is a **cock** or, for domestic chickens, a **rooster**.

hence adv. as an inference from this fact; therefore.

henceforth adv. from now on. Also, **henceforwards**.

henchman n. (pl. **-men**) a trusted attendant or follower.

henna n. (the reddish-orange dye from) a small Asian tree.

hepatitis n. a serious disease marked by inflammation or enlargement of the liver, appearing in various forms caused by different viruses, each form being identified by a letter of the alphabet.

heptathlon n. an athletic contest consisting of 5 different exercises or events. **–heptathlete**, n.

her pron. **1.** the personal pronoun used, usually after a verb or preposition, to refer to a particular female: *I saw her yesterday.*; *Give it to her.* **2.** the possessive form of **she**, used before a noun: *That is her book.*

Her is a third person singular pronoun. Def. 1 is in the objective case. Def. 2 is sometimes called a *determiner* or a *possessive adjective.*

herald n. **1.** a messenger; harbinger. **2.** someone who announces. **–v. 3.** to give tidings of; proclaim. **4.** to usher in.

This word is usually seen nowadays in the names of newspapers, such as the *Newcastle Herald.*

heraldic adj. relating to heralds or heraldry.

heraldry n. the science of tracing and recording coats of arms, family histories, etc.

herb n. a flowering plant whose leaves are used in cooking or in medicine, etc. **–herbal**, adj. **–herbaceous**, adj.

herbivorous adj. feeding on plants. **–herbivore**, n.

Compare this with **carnivorous**, **omnivorous**, and **insectivorous**.

herd n. a number of animals, especially cattle, kept, feeding, or travelling together.

here adv. **1.** in this place (opposed to *there*). **2.** to or towards this place; hither. **3.** at this point.

hereditary adj. **1.** passing naturally from parents to offspring. **2.** *Law* descending by inheritance.

heredity n. the transmission of genetic characteristics from parents to progeny.

heresy n. (the holding of) a doctrine contrary to the orthodox doctrine of a church or religious system. **–heretic**, n. **–heretical**, adj.

heritage n. that which belongs to one by reason of birth; an inheritance.

hermaphrodite /hɜˈmæfrədaɪt/ n. a person or animal with male and female sexual organs and characteristics.

hermetic /hɜˈmɛtɪk/ adj. made airtight by fusion or sealing. **–hermetically**, adv.

hermit n. someone who has retired to a solitary place, especially for religious seclusion. **–hermitage**, n.

hernia n. the protrusion of an organ through an opening in its surrounding tissues, especially in the abdomen.

hero n. (pl. **-roes**) **1.** a person distinguished by their great courage and noble qualities. **2.** the principal male character in a story, etc. **–heroic**, adj.

heroin n. (*from trademark*) an addictive drug derived from morphine.

Don't confuse this with **heroine**.

heroine n. **1.** a woman of heroic character; a female hero. **2.** the principal female character in a story, play, etc.

Don't confuse this with **heroin**.
Note that a woman of heroic character can also be called a **hero**, but this does not work the other way round – a brave man is never called a **heroine**.

heron n. a wading bird with a long neck, bill, and legs.

herpes /'hɜːpiːz/ n. blistering of the skin or mucous membranes caused by a viral infection.

herring n. (pl. **herring** or **herrings**) a food fish.

For information about the different plural forms, see the note at **fish**.

herringbone n. a pattern of parallel lines arranged in the form of a V.

hers pron. **1.** the possessive form of **she**, without a noun following: *That book is hers.* **2.** the person(s) or thing(s) belonging to her: *Hers is the best work I've seen.*

Hers is a third person singular pronoun in the possessive case.

herself pron. **1.** the reflexive form of **she**: *She cut herself.* **2.** an emphatic form of **her** or **she**: *She did it herself; She herself said it.* **3.** her normal state of mind: *She hasn't been herself since her son died.*

hesitate v. **1.** to hold back in doubt or indecision. **2.** to pause. **–hesitation**, n. **–hesitant**, adj.

hessian /'hɛʃən/ n. a strong fabric made from jute, used for sacks, etc.

heterodox adj. not in accordance with established doctrines, especially in theology; unorthodox.

heterogeneous adj. composed of (parts of) different kinds.

heterosexual n. **1.** someone who has sexual feelings for people of the opposite sex. **–adj. 2.** relating to a heterosexual. **–heterosexuality**, n.

Compare this with **homosexual**, which refers to someone who has sexual feelings for people of the same sex.

heuristic /hju'rɪstɪk/ adj. **1.** furthering investigation. **2.** (of a teaching method) encouraging students to discover for themselves.

hew v. (**hewed**, **hewed** or **hewn**, **hewing**) to chop or cut, as with an axe.

Don't confuse **hew** with **hue**, which is a formal or literary word for a colour.

hex n. an evil spell or charm.

hexagon n. a polygon with 6 sides.

hey interj. an exclamation used to call attention, etc.

heyday n. the period of greatest vigour or strength.

hiatus n. (pl. **-tuses** or **-tus**) a break, with a part missing; an interruption.

hibernate v. to spend the winter in a dormant condition, as certain animals. **–hibernation**, n.

hibiscus n. a tree or bush with showy flowers.

hiccup n. an involuntary respiratory spasm producing a characteristic sound. Also, **hiccough**.

hickory n. (pl. **-ries**) a Nth American nut-bearing tree.

hide¹ v. (**hid**, **hidden** or **hid**, **hiding**) **1.** to prevent (oneself) from being seen or discovered. **2.** to keep secret.

hide² n. **1.** the skin of an animal. **2.** Aust. Informal impudence.

hideous adj. very ugly.

hiding n. **1.** a beating. **2.** a defeat.

hierarchy /'haɪəraːki/ n. (pl. **-chies**) any graded order of persons or things.

hieroglyphic /haɪərə'glɪfɪk/ n. **1.** (usu. pl.) writing (especially of Ancient Egypt) using pictures or symbols to represent words or sounds. **–adj. 2.** written in hieroglyphics.

high adj. **1.** having a great extent upwards; lofty; tall. **2.** having a specified extent upwards. **3.** elevated. **4.** of more than average height or depth. **5.** intensified; strong; energetic. **6.** shrill. **7.** of great amount, force, etc. **8.** chief; principal.

9. (of a period of time) at its fullest point of development: *the High Renaissance*. **10.** *Informal* intoxicated with alcohol or drugs. **11.** smelly; bad. *–adv.* **12.** at or to a high point, place, level, rank, amount, price, degree. *–n.* **13.** that which is high; a high level. **14.** *Meteorol.* a pressure system with high pressure at its centre.

high five *n.* a form of salutation in which one slaps the palm of one's right hand against that of another person, often to express solidarity in victory.

high-five *verb –v.* **1.** to give a high five to (someone). **2.** to perform a high five.

high-handed *adj.* overbearing; arbitrary.

highland *n.* an elevated region; plateau.

highlight *v.* **1.** to emphasise or make prominent. **2.** to use a highlighter to emphasise (written or printed text). *–n.* **3.** a conspicuous part. **4.** (*pl.*) gleaming flecks of colour.

highlighter *n.* a pen which puts a translucent colour over parts of a printed or other page to draw the eye to these parts.

highness *n.* **1.** the state of being high; dignity. **2.** (*upper case*) (with *His, Her, Your,* etc.) (a title of honour given to royalty).

high-rise *adj.* → multistorey.

highway *n.* a main road.

highwayman *n.* (*pl.* **-men**) (formerly) a robber on the highway, especially one on horseback.

hijab /haˈdʒab/ *n.* a scarf-like piece of clothing worn by many Muslim women which covers the hair, neck and shoulders, leaving the face uncovered. Also, **hejab**.

hijack *v.* **1.** to seize by (threat of) force (a vehicle, especially an aircraft). **2.** to steal (something) in transit, as a truck and its goods.

hike *v.* **1.** to walk a long distance for pleasure. *–n.* **2.** a long walk, especially in the country. **3.** an increase in wages, prices, etc.

hilarious *adj.* **1.** very funny. **2.** boisterously merry. **–hilarity,** *n.*

hill *n.* a conspicuous natural elevation of the earth's surface, smaller than a mountain.

hillbilly *n.* (*pl.* **-lies**) *Chiefly US* a person living in the backwoods or mountains; yokel.

hilt *n.* the handle of a sword or dagger.

him *pron.* the personal pronoun used, usually after a verb or preposition, to refer to a particular male: *I saw him yesterday; Give it to him.*

Him is a third person singular pronoun in the objective case.

himself *pron.* **1.** the reflexive form of **he**: *He works himself too hard.* **2.** an emphatic form of **him** or **he**: *He did it himself; He himself said it.* **3.** his normal state of mind: *He is now himself again.*

hind[1] *adj.* (**hinder, hindmost** or **hindermost**) situated at the back; posterior.

hind[2] *n.* (*pl.* **hinds** or, especially collectively, **hind**) a female deer.

hinder *v.* to slow down or make difficult. **–hindrance,** *n.*

hindsight *n.* perception of what should have been done after the event.

hinge *n.* **1.** the joint on which a door, gate, etc., turns or moves. *–v.* (**hinged, hinging**) **2.** to depend (*on*).

hint *n.* **1.** an indirect or covert suggestion or implication; an intimation. **2.** a barely perceptible amount. *–v.* **3.** to make indirect suggestion or allusion (*at*).

hinterland *n.* the land lying behind a coastal district.

hip[1] *n.* the projection of the side of the pelvis and the upper part of the femur.

hip[2] *n.* the ripe fruit of a rose.

hip-hop *n.* **1.** an urban, cultural movement, for which rap music, breakdancing and graffiti art are the major expressive forms. **2.** the music associated with hip-hop, usually accompanying rapping. **–hiphopper,** *n.*

hippie n. a person who rejects conventional social values in favour of principles of universal love, union with nature, etc. Also, **hippy**.

hippopotamus n. (pl. **-muses** or **-mi**) a large, hairless, herbivorous, African mammal.

hire v. **1.** to pay money to use or to employ: *to hire a car, to hire a gardener.* **2.** Also, **hire out.** to grant the temporary use of, or the services of, for a payment: *I'll hire my boat to you for $100.* –phr. **3. for hire,** available to be used for a payment: *These canoes are for hire.*

hire purchase n. a purchasing system whereby a person has full use of a commodity being paid for by instalments. Also, **hire-purchase.**

hirsute adj. hairy.

his pron. **1.** the possessive form of **he,** used before a noun: *his book.* **2.** the possessive form of **he,** without a noun following: *That book is his.* **3.** the person(s) or thing(s) belonging to him: *His are the ones on the left.*

> **His** is a third person singular pronoun. Def. 2 is in the possessive case, and def. 1 is sometimes called a *determiner* or a *possessive adjective.*

hiss v. **1.** to make a sharp sound like that of the letter *s* prolonged, especially in disapproval or contempt. –n. **2.** a hissing sound.

hissy fit n. Informal an outburst of bad temper; tantrum.

histamine n. a substance released by the tissues in allergic reactions.

history n. (pl. **-ries**) **1.** the branch of knowledge dealing with past events. **2.** a written record of past events as relating to a particular people, period, etc. –**historian,** n. –**historic,** adj. –**historical,** adj.

histrionics pl. n. melodramatic behaviour, speech, etc., for effect. –**histrionic,** adj.

hit v. (**hit, hitting**) **1.** to come against with an impact or collision. **2.** to strike with a

missile, weapon, blow, etc. **3.** to affect severely. **4.** to reach (a particular level). **6.** a successful stroke, performance, etc. **7.** *Internet* a connection made to a website. **8.** *Informal* a shot of heroin or any drug; fix. –adj. **9.** successful; achieving popularity.

hitch v. **1.** to fasten, especially temporarily, by a hook, rope, etc.; tether. **2.** to raise (up) with jerks. **3.** *Informal* to (seek to) obtain (a ride) from a passing vehicle. –n. **4.** a halt; obstruction.

hitchhike v. to travel by obtaining rides in passing vehicles. Also, **hitch.**

hither adv. to or towards this place; here.

hitherto adv. until now.

HIV /eɪtʃ aɪ 'vi/ n. human immunodeficiency virus; the virus which causes AIDS.

hive n. **1.** Also, **beehive.** a shelter for honey bees. **2.** a place swarming with busy occupants.

hives n. a skin rash.

> Note that this word can be used as either a singular or a plural noun: *Has your hives cleared up yet?; Have your hives cleared up yet?*

hoard n. **1.** something accumulated for preservation or future use. –v. **2.** to accumulate for preservation or future use, especially secretly.

> Don't confuse **hoard** with **horde,** which means a great crowd: *a horde of flies.*

hoarding n. **1.** a temporary fence enclosing a building site. **2.** a large board on which advertisements or notices are displayed; billboard.

hoarse adj. **1.** having a raucous voice. **2.** rough or croaky; husky.

> Don't confuse **hoarse** with **horse,** which is a large animal that you can ride.

hoary adj. (**-rier, -riest**) grey or white with age.

hoax *n.* **1.** a humorous deception. **2.** a deception, especially of the public, and usually for gain.

hobble *v.* **1.** to walk lamely; limp. **2.** to fasten together the legs of (a horse, etc.) so as to prevent free motion.

hobby *n.* (*pl.* **-bies**) a spare-time activity or pastime, etc.

hobgoblin *n.* anything causing superstitious fear.

hobnob *v.* (**-nobbed, -nobbing**) to associate (*with*) on very friendly terms.

hobo *n.* (*pl.* **-bos** *or* **-boes**) a tramp or vagrant.

hock¹ *n.* the joint in the hind leg of the horse, etc., corresponding to the ankle in humans.

hock² *n.* a dry white wine.

hock³ *v. Informal* → **pawn¹**.

hockey *n.* a team game in which curved sticks are used to drive the ball.

hod *n.* a trough for carrying mortar, bricks, etc.

hoe *n.* **1.** a long-handled implement with a thin, flat blade used to break up the soil. *–v.* (**hoed, hoeing**) **2.** to dig, etc., with a hoe.

hog *n.* **1.** a domesticated pig, especially a castrated boar. **2.** *Informal* a selfish, gluttonous, or filthy person. *–v.* (**hogged, hogging**) **3.** *Informal* to take more than one's share of.

hogget *n.* (the meat of) a young sheep, older than a lamb, that has not yet been sheared.

hogwash *n.* meaningless talk; nonsense.

hoist *v.* **1.** to raise or lift, especially mechanically. *–n.* **2.** an apparatus for hoisting, as a lift.

hold¹ *v.* (**held, holding**) **1.** to have or keep in the hand; grasp. **2.** to retain; set aside. **3.** to support with the hand, arms, etc. **4.** to (cause to) remain in a specified state, relation, etc. **5.** to (be able to) contain. **6.** to regard or consider. **7.** to remain valid; be in force. *–n.* **8.** the act of holding

fast by the hand, etc.; grasp; grip. **9.** a controlling force, or dominating influence. *–phr.* **10. hold back, a.** to restrain. **b.** to withhold. **11. hold on, a.** to keep a firm hold on something. **b.** *Informal* (an expression asking someone to stop or wait for a short time.) **12. hold out, a.** to offer or present. **b.** to continue to exist; last. **13. hold to,** to abide by. **14. hold up, a.** to display. **b.** to delay. **c.** to stop in order to rob. *–***holder,** *n.*

hold² *n. Naut.* the space inside a ship for storing cargo.

holding *n.* (*oft. pl.*) property owned, especially stocks and shares, and land.

hold-up *n.* **1.** a forcible stopping and robbing of a person, bank, etc. **2.** a delay; stoppage.

hole *n.* **1.** an opening through anything; an aperture. **2.** a hollow place in a solid body; a cavity. **3.** *Informal* a dirty or unpleasant place: *This town is a hole.* *–***holey,** *adj.*

Don't confuse **holey** with **holy** or **wholly**. **Holey** means full of holes (*holey socks*), **holy** means sacred (*holy books*), and **wholly** means completely (*wholly responsible*).

holiday *n.* **1.** a day on which work or school is suspended in commemoration of some event, person, etc. **2.** (*oft. pl.*) a break from work or school, for recreation; vacation. *–v.* **3.** to take a holiday.

holistic *adj.* of or relating to a medical approach which treats the whole body rather than just dealing with particular manifestations of a disease or symptoms. Also, **wholistic.** *–***holism,** *n.*

hollow *adj.* **1.** having a hole or cavity within; not solid; empty. **2.** sunken, as the cheeks or eyes. *–v.* **3.** to make hollow.

holly *n.* (*pl.* **-lies**) a plant with glossy, spiny-edged leaves and red berries.

holocaust /ˈhɒləkɒst, -kəst/ *n.* great or wholesale destruction of life, especially by fire.

holster *n.* a leather case for a pistol, attached to a belt.

holy *adj.* (**-lier, -liest**) **1.** declared sacred by religious use or observance; consecrated. **2.** dedicated or devoted to the service of a god or religion. –**holiness,** *n.*

Don't confuse this with **holey**, which means full of holes, or with **wholly,** which means completely.

homage *n.* respect or reverence given.

home *n.* **1.** a house, or other shelter that is the fixed residence of a person, etc. **2.** (*oft. upper case*) an institution for the homeless, sick, etc. **3.** the region where something is native or most common. **4.** one's native place or own country. –*adv.* **5.** to, towards, or at home. –*pr.* **6. at home,** familiar and comfortable: *make yourself at home.* **7. bring home to,** to make aware of: *His mother's sadness really brought home to him the effects of his behaviour.* **8. home in on,** to proceed towards; to find or focus on: *Police will home in on drug-related crime.*

homegrown *adj.* **1.** grown at home, as opposed to bought in a shop. **2.** developed in one's own country or region.

homely *adj.* (**-lier, -liest**) **1.** plain and unpretentious. **2.** not good-looking.

homeopathy /houmi'ɒpəθi/ *n.* a method of treating disease by minute doses of drugs, which produce in a healthy person symptoms similar to those of the disease. Also, **homoeopathy.** –**homeopath** /'houmiəpæθ/, *n.* –**homeopathic,** *adj.* –**homeopathically,** *adv.*

home page *n. Internet* the introductory page for a website on the internet, containing information about the site, addresses, menus, etc.

homesick *adj.* longing for home.

homestead *n.* the main residence on a large farm, etc.

home unit *n. Aust., NZ* → **unit** (def. 3).

homework *n.* **1.** work set for a student to do at home, not in class –*phr.* **2. do one's**

homework, *Informal* to prepare for a meeting, interview, discussion, etc., by finding out what one needs to know.

homicide *n.* **1.** the killing of one human being by another. **2.** a murderer. –**homicidal,** *adj.*

homily /'hɒməli/ *n.* (*pl.* **-lies**) a religious address to a congregation; sermon.

hommos /'hɒməs, 'hʊməs/ *n.* → **hummus.**

homoeopathy /houmi'ɒpəθi/ *n.* → **homeopathy.** –**homoeopath** /'houmiəpəθ/, *n.* –**homoeopathic,** *adj.* –**homoeopathically,** *adv.*

homogeneous /houmə'dʒiniəs, hɒmə-/ *adj.* (composed of parts) of the same kind; not heterogeneous. Also, **homogenous.** –**homogeneity,** *n.*

homogenise /hə'mɒdʒənaɪz/ *v.* to make homogeneous. Also, **homogenize.**

homogenous /hə'mɒdʒənəs/ *adj.* **1.** corresponding in structure because of a common origin. **2.** homogeneous.

homologous /hə'mɒləgəs/ *adj.* corresponding in relative position, structure, etc., but not necessarily in use.

homonym *n.* a word like another in sound or spelling, but different in meaning.

If two homonyms are spelt the same, like *bear* (the animal) and *bear* (to carry), they're called **homographs,** but if two homonyms sound the same, like *meet* and *meat,* they're called **homophones.**

homophobia *n.* fear of homosexuals, usually linked with hostility towards them. –**homophobic,** *adj.* –**homophobe,** *n.*

homosexual *n.* **1.** someone who has sexual feelings for people of the same sex as themselves. –*adj.* **2.** relating to a homosexual. –**homosexuality,** *n.*

Compare this with **heterosexual,** which refers to someone who has sexual feelings for people of the opposite sex.

hone *n.* **1.** a stone of fine texture, as for sharpening razors. –*v.* **2.** to sharpen (as on a hone: *to hone a razor; to hone one's skills.*

Don't confuse this with **home** in the phrase **home in on,** as in *We finally homed in on the cause of the problem.*

honest *adj.* **1.** honourable in principles, intentions, and actions; upright. **2.** open; sincere. **3.** genuine or unadulterated. −**honesty,** *n.*

honey *n.* a sweet, viscous fluid produced by bees from the nectar collected from flowers.

honeycomb *n.* **1.** a wax structure of hexagonal cells, formed by bees for keeping honey, pollen and eggs. −*v.* **2.** to pierce with many holes or cavities.

honeydew melon *n.* a sweet-flavoured, white-fleshed melon with a smooth, pale green rind.

honeyeater *n.* a bird which feeds on the nectar from flowers.

honeymoon *n.* a holiday spent by a newly married couple after the wedding.

honeysuckle *n.* a fragrant, climbing plant.

honk *n.* **1.** the cry of the goose. **2.** any similar sound, as a car horn. −*v.* **3.** to emit a honk.

honorarium *n.* (*pl.* **-riums** or **-ria** /-'reəriə/) a fee for professional services.

honorary *adj.* **1.** (holding a position) given for honour only, without the usual duties, etc.: *an honorary degree.* **2.** (of a position, job, etc.) unpaid: *honorary secretary.* **3.** (of an obligation) depending on one's honour for fulfilment. −*n.* **4.** a specialist working in a public hospital.

Don't confuse this with **honourable,** which describes a person of honesty and high morals.

honorific *adj.* doing or conferring honour.

honour *n.* **1.** high public esteem; fame; glory. **2.** reputation for worthy behaviour. **3.** a source of credit: *to be an honour to one's family.* **4.** (*usu. pl.*) a mark or observance of public respect: *full military honours.* **5.** an official award conferred on

someone as a mark of distinction. **6.** a special privilege: *May I have the honour of your company?* **7.** high principles; fine sense of one's obligations. **8.** (*pl.*) (in universities) academic achievement in a degree examination higher than that required for a pass degree. −*v.* **9.** to hold in honour or high respect; revere. **10.** to confer honour upon. **11.** to accept and pay (a cheque, etc.) when due. **12.** to accept the validity of (a document, etc.). Also, **honor.** −**honourable,** *adj.*

Don't confuse **honourable** with **honorary. Honourable** describes a person of honesty and high morals, whereas **honorary** describes a position given as a sign of honour, or one for which you are not paid.

hood[1] *n.* **1.** a part of a jacket, etc., which covers the head and neck. **2.** something resembling this. **3.** a car bonnet.

hood[2] *n. Informal* a hoodlum.

hoodie *n. Informal* a jacket with a hood.

hoodlum *n.* **1.** a petty gangster. **2.** a young person given to street fighting, vandalism, etc.

This word is used in a disapproving way.

hoodwink *v.* to deceive.

hoof *n.* (*pl.* **hoofs** or **hooves**) the horny covering protecting the foot in certain mammals, as the ox, horse, etc.

hook *n.* **1.** a curved or angular piece of metal, etc., for catching or supporting something. **2.** that which catches; a trap. **3.** something resembling a hook. **4.** *Boxing* a curving blow made with the arm bent. −*v.* **5.** to seize, or fasten with a hook. **6.** to become attached by a hook; join on.

hookah *n.* a pipe fitted with water for cooling the smoke of tobacco, marijuana, etc.

hooked *adj.* **1.** bent like a hook. **2.** *Informal* addicted; obsessed (*on*).

hooligan *n.* a rough and noisy young person who causes trouble; hoodlum.

This word is used in a disapproving way.

hoop n. a circular band of wood, metal, etc., or something resembling it.

hooray interj. an exclamation of joy, applause, etc.

hoot v. **1.** to cry out or shout, especially in disapproval. **2.** (of an owl) to utter its cry. **3.** to blow a horn; honk. −n. **4.** the cry of an owl. **5.** any similar sound.

hooves n. a plural of **hoof**.

hop¹ v. (**hopped, hopping**) **1.** to jump on one foot. **2.** Informal to get (in, on or off) a car, train, etc. **3.** Informal to jump off (something elevated), or over (a fence, ditch, etc.). −n. **4.** a leap on one foot.

hop² n. a plant used in brewing.

hope n. **1.** expectation of something desired. **2.** confidence in a future event. −v. **3.** to look forward (to) with desire and confidence. **4.** to trust in the truth of a matter (with a clause). −**hopeless,** adj.

hopeful adj. **1.** full of hope. **2.** promising advantage or success. −n. **3.** a promising young person.

hopefully adv. **1.** in a hopeful way: waiting hopefully for the phone to ring. **2.** it is hoped: Hopefully we will arrive before dark.

Note that, although def. 2 is widely considered to be acceptable, there are some people who regard it as incorrect.

hopscotch n. a children's game in which the player hops from one compartment to another of a diagram traced on the ground, without touching a line.

horde n. (often derog.) a great crowd; a multitude: There was a horde of people at the beach, so we came home early.

Don't confuse this with **hoard**, which is to keep things even if you don't need them anymore.

horizon n. the line forming the apparent boundary between earth and sky.

horizontal adj. **1.** parallel to the horizon; lying down flat. −n. **2.** a horizontal line, plane, or the like.

Compare this with **vertical** and **diagonal**.

hormone n. **1.** a substance, secreted into the body fluids by an endocrine gland, which activates specific receptor organs. **2.** a synthetic substance having the same effect.

horn n. **1.** a hard, often curved, outgrowth (usually one of a pair) on the head of certain mammals. **2.** any hornlike projection. **3.** Music a wind instrument of the brass family. **4.** an instrument for sounding a warning signal, as on a car.

hornet n. a large wasp.

horoscope n. **1.** a forecast of a person's future based on the positions of the constellations and planets at the time of the person's birth. **2.** the diagram of the heavens used for this purpose.

horrendous adj. dreadful; horrible.

horrible adj. **1.** causing horror; dreadful. **2.** extremely unpleasant; deplorable.

horrid adj. **1.** horrible; abominable. **2.** extremely unpleasant or disagreeable.

horrific adj. causing horror.

horrify v. (**-fied, -fying**) to shock or strike with horror.

horror n. **1.** great fear or abhorrence. **2.** Informal something considered atrocious or bad. **3.** intense aversion or repugnance.

hors d'oeuvre /ɔ ˈdɜv/ n. a small piece of food served before a meal.

horse n. **1.** a large, solid-hoofed four-legged animal often used for riding. **2.** a vaulting block, used for gymnastics.

Don't confuse this with **hoarse**, which describes your voice when it is rough and croaky.

horse flu n. → equine influenza.

horseplay n. rough or boisterous play.

horsepower n. a unit for measuring power in the imperial system, defined as 550 foot-pounds per second (equal to 745.7 watts).

horseradish *n.* a plant with a pungent root used as a flavouring.

horseshoe *n.* **1.** a U-shaped iron plate nailed to a horse's hoof to protect it. **2.** a symbol of good luck.

hortatory *adj.* encouraging; exhorting.

horticulture *n.* the science or art of growing plants.

hose *n.* **1.** a flexible tube for conveying water, etc., to a desired point. **2.** → **hosiery.** *–v.* **3.** to apply water, etc., to by means of a hose.

hosiery *n.* socks or stockings of any kind. Also, **hose.**

hospice *n.* **1.** a hospital for terminally ill patients. **2.** (formerly) a refuge for pilgrims, etc., especially one kept by a religious order.

hospital *n.* an institution for the treatment of sick or injured persons. **–hospitalise, hospitalize,** *v.*

hospitality *n.* the kind and generous treatment of guests or strangers. **–hospitable,** *adj.*

host¹ *n.* **1.** someone who entertains guests. **2.** an animal or plant from which a parasite obtains nutrition. **3.** a computer containing data which may be accessed by users at other computer terminals linked to it.

host² *n.* a multitude.

hostage /ˈhɒstɪdʒ/ *n.* a person held as a security for the performance of certain actions as the payment of ransom, etc.

hostel *n.* a supervised place of low-cost accommodation, as for students, travellers, etc.

hostess *n.* a woman who entertains guests.

hostile *adj.* unfriendly; antagonistic. **–hostility,** *n.*

hot *adj.* (**hotter, hottest**) **1.** having or communicating heat; having a high temperature. **2.** having or producing a sensation of great bodily heat. **3.** new; fresh: *hot off the press.* **4.** close: *hot on one's heels.*

5. *Informal* (of motor cars) modified for high speeds. **6.** *Informal* fashionable or popular: *this summer's hottest hits.* **7.** *Informal* recently stolen. **8.** *Informal* sexually attractive; sexually stimulating.

hotchpotch *n.* a heterogeneous mixture; jumble.

hot-desking *n.* the sharing of a desk between a number of employees, especially those whose job takes them out of the office on a regular basis. **–hot-desk,** *v.*

hot dog *n.* a hot frankfurt or sausage, especially as served in a bread roll.

hotel *n.* a building providing accommodation, food, and (alcoholic) drinks.

hotline *n.* **1.** a direct telephone connection open to immediate communication in an emergency. **2.** a telephone line which gives direct access to people who wish to ring up to ask advice, give an opinion, etc.

hotplate *n.* a heated metal plate upon which food may be cooked.

hoummus /ˈhoməs, ˈhɒməs/ *n.* → **hummus.** Also, **hoommos.**

hound *n.* **1.** a (hunting) dog. *–v.* **2.** to hunt with hounds; pursue. **3.** to harass unceasingly.

hour *n.* **1.** a space of time equal to one 24th part of a day; 60 minutes. **2.** a particular time. **3.** distance normally covered in an hour's travelling. **–hourly,** *adv., adj.*

house *n.* /haʊs/ (*pl.* **houses** /ˈhaʊzəz/) **1.** a building for people to live in, usually one which is self-contained and designed for a single family. **2.** a household. **3.** the audience of a theatre, etc. **4.** (the meeting place of) a legislative body. **5.** a commercial establishment. **6.** a subdivision of a school, comprising children of all ages and classes. *–v.* /haʊz/ (**housed, housing**) **7.** to provide with a house. **8.** to put in a safe place.

Compare **house** with **home.** A **house** is a building where people live. Your **home** can also be the building where you live, but it also refers to a place where you feel you belong or were brought up: *I'm going home for the holidays.*

household *n.* **1.** all the people of a house. *—adj.* **2.** relating to a household; domestic. **3.** ordinary or common.

housekeeper *n.* an employee hired to run a house.

house-sit *v.* (**-sat, -sitting**) **1.** to occupy a house, apartment, etc., temporarily and without the payment of rent, for the purpose of providing security or daily maintenance during the absence of the regular occupant. **2.** to occupy (a house, apartment, etc.) under such an arrangement. **–house-sitter,** *n.* **–house-sitting,** *n.*

housewife *n.* (*pl.* **-wives**) a married woman in charge of a household and who does not work outside the home for payment.

housework *n.* the work of cleaning, cooking, etc.

housing *n.* **1.** houses or other dwellings collectively. **2.** the provision of houses for the community. **3.** *Machinery* a frame, plate, etc., that supports a part of a machine, etc.

hove *v.* a past tense and past participle of **heave**.

hovel *n.* a small, shabby dwelling.

hover *v.* **1.** to hang suspended in the air. **2.** to wait near at hand.

hovercraft *n.* a vehicle able to travel above the ground or water, on a cushion of air.

how *adv.* **1.** in what way; by what means: *How did you do it?* **2.** to what extent, etc.: *How much is it?* **3.** in what condition: *How are you?* *—conj.* **4.** concerning the way in which: *I wonder how you managed it.* **5.** concerning the extent to which: *I wonder how far you can go.* **6.** concerning the condition in which: *I wonder how you are.*

however *conj.* **1.** nevertheless; yet. *—adv.* **2.** to whatever extent; no matter how (far, much, etc.). **3.** in whatever condition,

state, or manner. **4.** Also, **how ever.** (interrogatively) how in any circumstances.

howl *v.* **1.** to utter a loud, prolonged, mournful cry, as that of a dog or wolf. *—n.* **2.** the cry of a dog, wolf, etc. **3.** a cry or wail, as of pain or rage.

HR *n.* human resources; the people in an organisation, country, etc.

HTML *n.* hypertext markup language; a computer markup language, similar to SGML, used primarily to create documents for the internet.

hub *n.* **1.** the central part of a wheel supporting the spokes. **2.** the central part around which all else revolves.

huddle *v.* **1.** to gather or crowd together confusedly. *—n.* **2.** a confused heap, mass, or crowd; jumble.

hue¹ *n.* colour: *all hues of the rainbow.* **2.** variety of a colour; tint.

Don't confuse this with **hew**, which is to chop or cut.

hue² *n.* outcry.

huff *n.* **1.** a sudden fit of anger. *—v.* **2.** to puff or blow.

hug *v.* (**hugged, hugging**) **1.** to clasp tightly in the arms, especially with affection; embrace. *—n.* **2.** a tight clasp with the arms; a warm embrace.

huge *adj.* extraordinarily large.

hulk *n.* **1.** the body of an old or dismantled ship. **2.** a bulky or unwieldy person or mass of anything.

hull¹ *n.* the outer covering of a seed or fruit, or the calyx of a strawberry, etc. *—v.* **2.** to remove the hull of.

hull² *n.* the frame or body of a ship.

hullabaloo *n.* a clamorous noise; uproar.

hum *v.* (**hummed, humming**) **1.** to make a low, continuous, droning sound. **2.** to be busy and active.

human *adj.* **1.** of, relating to, or characteristic of people. *—n.* **2.** a human being.

Don't confuse this with **humane**.

human being n. a member of the human race.

humane adj. characterised by compassion for the suffering. –n. 2. a

Don't confuse this with **human**.

humanitarian adj. having regard to the interests of all humankind. –n. 2. a philanthropist.

humanity n. 1. the human race; humankind. 2. the quality of being humane.

humankind n. all human beings. Also, **humanity**.

humble adj. 1. low in rank, importance, etc.; lowly. 2. modest; meek. –v. 3. to lower in dignity; abase.

humbug n. (someone who practises) falseness or deception.

humdrum adj. lacking variety; dull.

humerus n. (pl. **-meri**) Anat. (in humans) the long bone in the arm, from the shoulder to the elbow.

humid adj. moist or damp. **–humidity**, n.

humiliate v. to lower the pride or self-respect of; mortify. **–humiliation**, n. **–humiliating**, adj. **–humiliatingly**, adv.

humility n. the quality of being humble; modesty.

hummingbird n. a small bird whose narrow wings vibrate very rapidly, producing a humming sound.

hummock n. a small hill.

hummus /'hʊməs, 'hɒməs/ n. a Middle Eastern dish made from ground chickpeas and sesame paste. Also, **hommus**, **hom-mos**.

humorous adj. 1. amusing; funny. 2. droll; facetious.

humour n. 1. the quality of being funny. 2. (speech, writing, etc., showing) the ability to perceive what is amusing. 3. frame of mind. –v. 4. indulge: *to humour a child*. Also, **humor**.

hump n. 1. a rounded protuberance, especially on the back. 2. a low, rounded rise of ground; hummock.

humpy n. a temporary bush shelter used by Aboriginal people; gunyah.

humungous adj. Informal of huge size or extent.

humus n. the dark organic material in soils, produced by the decomposition of vegetable or animal matter.

humvee n. Mil. an off-road vehicle designed for military use.

hunch v. 1. to (be) thrust out or up in a hump. –n. 2. a hump. 3. Informal a premonition or suspicion.

hundred n. (pl. **-dreds**, *as after a numeral*, **-dred**) 1. a cardinal number, 10 times 10. –adj. 2. amounting to one hundred in number. **–hundredth**, adj., n.

Numbers used before a noun are sometimes called **determiners**.

hung v. past tense and past participle of **hang**.

hunger n. 1. the painful sensation caused by need of food. 2. strong desire. **–hungry**, adj.

hunk n. a large piece or lump; chunk.

hunt v. 1. to (engage in) chase for the purpose of catching or killing (game etc.). 2. to search or seek (*for*, *after*). –n. 3. the act of hunting game etc.; the chase. 4. pursuit; search.

huntsman n. → **tarantula**.

hurdle n. 1. a barrier in a racetrack, to be leapt by the contestants. 2. a difficult problem to be overcome; obstacle. –v. 3. to leap over (a hurdle, etc.) as in a race. 4. to master (a difficulty, problem etc.).

hurl v. to throw with great force.

hurricane n. a violent tropical cyclonic storm.

hurry v. (**-ried**, **-rying**) 1. to move (someone or something) with (often undue) haste. –n. 2. need or desire for haste.

hurt v. (**hurt**, **hurting**) 1. to cause injury or pain (to). 2. to harm. –n. 3. (a blow that inflicts) injury.

hurtle v. to rush violently and noisily.

husband n. a man joined in marriage to another person.

husbandry n. agriculture; farming.

hush v. 1. to make silent. 2. to suppress mention of; keep concealed.

husk n. the dry external covering of certain fruits or seeds.

husky[1] adj. (**-kier**, **-kiest**) 1. Informal big and strong; burly. 2. spoken in a half-whisper.

husky[2] n. (pl. **-kies**) an Inuit dog used in a team to pull sleds over snow.

hussy n. (pl. **-sies**) 1. an ill-behaved girl. 2. a lewd woman.

hustings pl. n. (a platform for) election proceedings.

hustle v. 1. to proceed energetically. 2. to force roughly or hurriedly. –n. 3. energetic activity.

hut n. a simple, small house.

hutch n. a coop for confining small animals.

hyacinth /ˈhaɪəsənθ/ n. a bulbous plant with spikes of fragrant, bell-shaped flowers.

hybrid n. 1. the offspring of 2 animals or plants of different breeds. 2. anything composed of different or incongruous elements.

hybrid car n. a car which has both an electric and a petrol engine, the latter being required at higher speeds.

hydrangea n. a shrub with large showy flower clusters.

hydrant n. an outlet from a water main.

hydraulic adj. operated by or employing liquid, especially water.

hydrocarbon n. a compound containing only hydrogen and carbon.

hydrofoil n. (a boat fitted with) skis which, at speed, lifts above the surface of the water.

hydrogen n. a colourless, odourless, flammable gas, which combines chemically with oxygen to form water. Symbol: H

hydroplane n. a motorboat, with hydrofoils or a shaped bottom, designed to skim along the surface of the water at high speeds.

hydroponics n. the cultivation of plants by placing the roots in nutrient solutions rather than in soil. **–hydroponic**, adj. **–hydroponically**, adv.

hyena n. a doglike nocturnal carnivore feeding chiefly on carrion.

hygiene n. (the science which deals with) the preservation of health.

hygienic adj. clean and sanitary.

hygrometer n. an instrument for determining the humidity of the atmosphere.

hymen n. a membrane partially closing the external orifice of the vagina.

hymn n. a religious song.

hymnal n. a book of hymns for use in divine worship. Also, **hymnbook**.

hype n. Informal an atmosphere of deliberately stimulated excitement and enthusiasm.

hyperbola /haɪˈpɜːbələ/ n. (pl. **-las**) a curve formed by the intersection of a plane with a cone when the plane makes an angle to the base greater than that of the side of the cone to the base.

hyperbole /haɪˈpɜːbəli/ n. obvious exaggeration, for serious or comic effect.

hyperbolic /haɪpəˈbɒlɪk/ adj. 1. exaggerated. 2. of or relating to the hyperbola.

hyperlink n. Computers an element of a hypertext document which is connected to another document, or to another place in the same document.

hypertension n. elevation of the blood pressure, the chief sign of disease of the arteries. **–hypertensive**, adj.

hypertext n. Computers text created in HTML which has highlighted links to other documents or other areas in the same document.

hyperventilation n. the excessive exposure of the lungs to oxygen resulting in a rapid loss of carbon dioxide from the blood. **–hyperventilate**, v.

hyphen *n.* a short stroke (-) used to connect the parts of a compound or divided word, as in 'part-time', or the parts of a word when it has to be split at the end of a line. –**hyphenate,** *v.* –**hyphenated,** *adj.*

hypnosis *n. Psychol.* a trance-like mental state induced in a cooperative subject by suggestion. –**hypnotise, hypnotize,** *v.* –**hypnotism,** *n.*

hypnotic *adj.* **1.** relating to hypnosis or hypnotism. –*n.* **2.** a drug that produces sleep; sedative.

hypochondria /haipə'kɒndriə/ *n. Psychol.* a condition characterised by depressed spirits and fancies of ill health. –**hypochondriac,** *n.*

hypocrisy /hɪ'pɒkrəsi/ *n.* **1.** the act of pretending to have a character, beliefs, etc., that one does not possess. **2.** pretence of virtue or piety.

hypocrite /'hɪpəkrɪt/ *n.* someone given to hypocrisy. –**hypocritical,** *adj.*

hypodermic *n.* a needle used to introduce liquid medicine, etc., under the skin.

hypotenuse /hai'pɒtənjuz/ *n.* the side of a right-angled triangle opposite the right angle.

hypothalamus /haipə'θæləməs/ *n.* (*pl.* **-thalami**) the part of the middle brain concerned with emotional expression and bodily responses.

hypothermia *n.* the acute condition of having an abnormally low body temperature.

hypothesis /hai'pɒθəsəs/ *n.* (*pl.* **-theses** /-θəsiz/) **1.** a proposed explanation for the occurrence of some specified group of phenomena. **2.** a proposition assumed as a premise in an argument. –**hypothetical,** *adj.*

hysterectomy /histə'rektəmi/ *n.* (*pl.* **-mies**) the surgical excision of the uterus.

hysteria *n.* an uncontrollable emotional state. –**hysterical,** *adj.*

hysterics *pl. n.* wild laughter.

I, i

I, i *n.* the 9th letter of the English alphabet.

I *pron.* the personal pronoun used by a speaker to refer to himself or herself: *I heard that.*

I is a first person singular pronoun in the subjective case.

iamb /ˈaɪæmb, ˈaɪæm/ *n.* a metrical foot of 2 syllables, a short followed by a long. –**iambic**, *adj.*

ibidem *adv.* in the same book, chapter, page, etc.

ibis *n.* (*pl.* **ibis** *or* **ibises**) a wading bird with a long, down-curved bill.

ice *n.* **1.** frozen water. –*v.* **2.** to cover (cakes, etc.) with icing. –**icy**, *adj.*

iceberg *n.* a large mass of ice floating in the sea.

ice-cream *n.* a frozen food made of cream, or milk, sweetened and flavoured.

ice skate *n.* (a shoe fitted with) a thin metal runner for moving along on ice. –**ice-skate**, *v.*

ichthyology /ɪkθiˈɒlədʒi/ *n.* the branch of zoology that deals with fishes.

icicle *n.* a hanging mass of ice formed by the freezing of dripping water.

icing *n.* a preparation of sugar for covering cakes, etc.

icon /ˈaɪkɒn/ *n.* **1.** a representation in painting, enamel, etc., of Christ or a saint, itself venerated as sacred. **2.** a sign or representation, such as a picture on a computer screen representing an instruction or menu option.

iconoclast /aɪˈkɒnəklæst/ *n.* **1.** a destroyer of images, especially those set up for religious veneration. **2.** someone who attacks cherished beliefs as based on error or superstition.

id *n.* (in psychoanalysis) the part of the psyche which is the source of instinctive energy.

ID *n. Informal* **1.** a document providing personal details, such as name, address, date of birth, etc. **2.** an identification of a person: *to get a positive ID.*

idea *n.* any conception or new thought resulting from mental understanding or activity.

ideal *n.* **1.** a conception of something in its highest perfection. **2.** that which exists only in idea. –*adj.* **3.** conceived as a standard of perfection or excellence. **4.** not real or practical.

idealise *v.* to regard or represent as ideal. Also, **idealize**.

idealism *n.* the cherishing or pursuit of ideals. –**idealist**, *n.* –**idealistic**, *adj.*

idem *pron.* the same as previously mentioned.

identical *adj.* **1.** corresponding exactly in nature, appearance, manner, etc. (*to* or *with*): *This leaf is identical to that.* **2.** the very same: *I almost bought the identical dress you are wearing.*

identify *v.* (**-fied**, **-fying**) **1.** to recognise or establish as being a particular person or thing. **2.** to associate in feeling, interest, action, etc. (*with*). –**identification**, *n.*

identity *n.* (*pl.* **-ties**) **1.** the state or fact of being the same. **2.** the condition of being oneself or itself, and not another.

ideology /aɪdiˈɒlədʒi/ *n.* (*pl.* **-gies**) the body of doctrine of a social movement, institution, class, etc. –**ideological**, *adj.* –**ideologist**, *n.*

id est that is.

idiom *n.* **1.** a form of expression peculiar to a language, especially one having a significance other than its literal one. **2.** a distinct style or character, as in music, art, etc. –**idiomatic**, *adj.* –**idiomatically**, *adv.*

idiosyncrasy /ˌɪdɪəʊˈsɪŋkrəsi/ *n.* (*pl.* **-sies**) any behaviour, mode of expression, or the like, peculiar to an individual. **–idiosyncratic,** *adj.* **–idiosyncratically,** *adv.*

idiot *n.* a very foolish person. **–idiotic,** *adj.* **–idiotically,** *adv.* **–idiocy,** *n.*

Note that if you call someone 'an idiot' you are likely meant to insult them.

idle *adj.* (**idler, idlest**) **1.** habitually doing nothing or avoiding work; lazy. **2.** not being used: *idle machinery; idle time.* **–v.** (**idled, idling**) **3.** to pass time in idleness. **4.** *Machinery* to operate, usually at minimum speed, while the transmission is disengaged.

Don't confuse **idle** with **idol**.

idol *n.* **1.** an image or object representing a deity, to which religious worship is addressed. **2.** any person or thing blindly adored or revered. **–idolatry,** *n.* **–idolise, idolize,** *v.*

Don't confuse **idol** with **idle**.

idyll /ˈaɪdəl, ˈɪdəl/ *n.* **1.** a poem or prose composition describing pastoral scenes or events. **2.** an episode or scene of simple or poetic charm. **–idyllic,** *adj.*

if *conj.* **1.** in case that; granting that; on condition that. **2.** whether.

igloo *n.* a dome-shaped Inuit hut, built of blocks of hard snow.

igneous rock *n.* rock formed from magma.

ignite *v.* **1.** to set on fire; kindle. **2.** to begin to burn.

ignition *n.* **1.** the act of igniting. **2.** the state of being ignited. **3.** (in an internal-combustion engine) the process which ignites the fuel in the cylinder.

ignoble *adj.* of low character, aims, etc.; mean; base.

ignominy /ˈɪgnəmɪni/ *n.* disgrace; dishonour. **–ignominious,** *adj.*

ignoramus *n.* (*pl.* **-muses**) an ignorant person.

ignorant *adj.* destitute of knowledge. **–ignorance,** *n.*

ignore *v.* to refrain from noticing or recognising.

iguana /ɪˈgwɑnə/ *n.* a large tropical American lizard.

ilk *n.* family, class, or kind.

ill *adj.* (**worse, worst**) **1.** unwell or sick. **2.** evil, wicked, or bad. **–n.** **3.** evil. **4.** harm or injury. **5.** a disease or ailment. **–adv.** **6.** unsatisfactorily or poorly. **7.** with displeasure or offence. **8.** faultily or improperly. **–illness,** *n.*

illegal *adj.* **1.** not legal. **2.** a person who is an illegal immigrant. **–illegality,** *n.*

illegal immigrant *n.* an immigrant to a country who is deemed to be illegal because they have arrived without prior authority from the government of that country, as in the form of a visa, or because they have stayed beyond the time allowed by their visa.

illegible *adj.* impossible or hard to read or decipher.

illegitimate *adj.* **1.** not legitimate. **2.** born out of wedlock.

Def. 2 is not commonly used nowadays.

ill-gotten *adj.* acquired by dishonest means.

illicit *adj.* not permitted or authorised; unlawful.

illiterate *adj.* **1.** unable to read and write. **–n.** **2.** an illiterate person.

illuminate *v.* **1.** to supply with light; light up. **2.** to enlighten, as with knowledge. **3.** to decorate (a manuscript, etc.) with colour, gold, or the like. **–illumination,** *n.*

illusion *n.* something that deceives by producing a false impression. **–illusory,** *n.*

Don't confuse **illusion** with **allusion** which is a passing mention of something.

illustrate *v.* **1.** to make clear or intelligible, as by examples. **2.** to furnish (a book, etc.) with drawings or pictorial representations. **–illustration,** *n.*

illustrious adj. 1. highly distinguished; famous: an illustrious family. 2. glorious, as deeds, etc.: an illustrious career.

image n. 1. a likeness or representation of a person, animal, or thing. 2. an optical counterpart or appearance of an object. 3. an idea or conception. 4. the public impression made by a politician, etc. 5. Also, **spitting image**. a counterpart or copy. 6. a figure of speech, especially a metaphor or simile. –**imagery**, n.

imaginary adj. existing only in the imagination.

Don't confuse this with **imaginative**, which describes someone who has the ability to form pictures in their mind or to make up interesting stories.

imagination n. the action of forming mental images or concepts of what is not actually present to the senses. –**imaginative**, adj.

Don't confuse **imaginative**, which describes someone with imagination, with **imaginary**, which means not real: A unicorn is an imaginary creature.

imagine v. 1. to form a mental image of (something not actually present to the senses). 2. to think, believe, or suppose.

imam /ʼˈmam/ n. a Muslim religious leader or chief.

imbecile n. a silly person.

Note that if you call someone 'an imbecile' you are intending to insult them.

imbibe v. to drink in, or drink (liquid).

imbroglio /ɪmˈbroʊlioʊ/ n. (pl. **-lios**) a complicated or confused situation, especially involving disagreement.

imbue v. to impregnate or inspire, as with feelings, opinions, etc.

The more usual expression is **fill with**.

imitate v. 1. to follow in action or manner. 2. to mimic or counterfeit. 3. to make a copy of. –**imitation**, n.

immaculate adj. spotlessly clean.

immanent adj. remaining within; indwelling; inherent.

immaterial adj. 1. unimportant. 2. not material; spiritual.

immediate adj. 1. occurring without delay; instant. 2. nearest or next. –**immediacy**, n.

immemorial adj. extending back beyond memory or record.

immense adj. vast; huge; immeasurable.

immerse v. to plunge into or place under a liquid. –**immersion**, n.

immigrate v. to come to live in a country of which one is not a native. –**immigration**, n. –**immigrant**, n., adj.

Don't confuse this with **emigrate**, which is to leave your country to go and live in another. To **migrate** can be to **emigrate** or **immigrate**.

imminent adj. likely to occur at any moment.

Don't confuse this with **eminent**, which means important.

immolate v. to sacrifice.

immoral adj. not conforming to the moral law or accepted patterns of conduct. –**immorality**, n.

Don't confuse this with **amoral**, which describes behaviour which is not based on morals at all.

immortal adj. 1. not liable or subject to death; undying. 2. remembered or celebrated through all time. –**immortality**, n. –**immortalise**, **immortalize**, v.

immune adj. 1. protected from a disease or the like, as by inoculation. 2. exempt. –**immunise**, **immunize**, v. –**immunisation**, **immunization**, n. –**immunity**, n.

immune system n. a complex network of interacting systems within the body which protect it from disease, and which can destroy infected, malignant, or broken-down cells.

immunodeficiency n. Med. an impairment in the autoimmune system caused especially by a lack of white blood cells and resulting in reduced immunity to infection. **–immunodeficient**, *adj.*

immunology *n.* that branch of medical science which deals with immunity from disease.

immure *v.* **1.** to enclose within walls. **2.** to imprison.

immutable *adj.* unchangeable.

The more usual word is **unalterable**.

imp *n.* **1.** a little devil or demon. **2.** a mischievous child.

Def. 2 is usually used affectionately or humorously.

impact *n.* /'ɪmpækt/ **1.** the striking of one body against another. **2.** the effect exerted by a new idea, etc. *–v.* /ɪm'pækt/ **3.** to drive firmly into something; pack in. *–phr.* **4. impact on**, to have an effect on: *This law impacts on all of us.*

impair *v.* to diminish in value, excellence, etc.

impala *n.* (*pl.* **impalas** *or, especially collectively,* **impala**) an African antelope.

impale *v.* to fix upon a sharpened stake or the like.

impart *v.* to give or bestow.

impartial *adj.* unbiased.

impasse /'ɪmpas/ *n.* a position from which there is no escape.

impassive *adj.* without emotion; apathetic.

impatient *adj.* not bearing pain, opposition, etc., with composure. **–impatience**, *n.*

impeach *v. Chiefly US* to accuse (a government official) of a serious crime in connection with their job.

impeccable *adj.* faultless or irreproachable.

The more usual word is **perfect**.

impecunious *adj.* poor; penniless.

impede *v.* to obstruct; hinder.

impediment *n.* **1.** some physical defect, especially a speech disorder. **2.** obstruction or hindrance.

impel *v.* (**-pelled**, **-pelling**) to drive or urge forward.

The more usual word is **force**.

impend *v.* to be imminent.

imperative *adj.* **1.** not to be avoided or evaded. **2.** *Gram.* relating to the verb mood used to express a command, as *stop* in *Stop that at once!*

For def. 2, look up **mood²**.

imperfect *adj.* **1.** having defects. **2.** *Gram.* designating a tense which denotes incomplete past action. Compare **pluperfect**, **perfect** (def. 3).

imperial *adj.* **1.** of or relating to an empire. **2.** of a commanding quality, manner, or aspect. **3.** (of weights and measures) conforming to the former official British standards.

imperial system *n.* a system of nonmetric weights and measures set up in Britain and used in Aust. before the metric system was introduced in 1970.

imperious *adj.* domineering; dictatorial.

impersonal *adj.* **1.** without personal reference or connection. **2.** *Gram.* (of a verb) having only 3rd person singular forms.

impersonate *v.* to mimic or pretend to be. **–impersonation**, *n.*

impertinent *adj.* rude or presumptuous.

impervious *adj.* not penetrable. Also, **imperviable**.

impetigo *n.* a contagious skin disease.

impetuous *adj.* characterised by a sudden or rash energy.

impetus *n.* moving force; impulse; stimulus.

impinge *v.* **1.** to collide. **2.** to encroach (*on* or *upon*).

implacable /ɪm'plækəbəl/ *adj.* not able to be changed in opinion or feelings: *implacable opposition.*

You usually use this word about things that you don't regard as good. For example, you would say *implacable hostility* but not '*implacable happiness*'.

mplant /ɪmˈplænt, -ˈplɑːnt/ v. to instil or inculcate.

mplement n. /ˈɪmpləmənt/ **1.** an instrument, tool, or utensil. –v. /ˈɪmpləmɛnt/ **2.** to put (a plan, etc.) into effect.

mplicate v. **1.** to involve in a matter, affair, condition, etc. **2.** to imply. –**implication**, n.

implicit adj. **1.** (of belief, etc.) unquestioning, unreserved, or absolute. **2.** implied, rather than expressly stated.

implore v. to urgently or piteously beseech.

imply v. (-plied, -plying) **1.** to involve as a necessary circumstance. **2.** to indicate or suggest.

This word is often confused with **infer**, which is to form an opinion based on what you've heard or seen: *I infer from your expression that you know who the thief is, although you're not actually saying so.* If you wanted to use **imply**, you would have to change the sentence so that the subject of the verb becomes your *expression*, rather than *I*: *Your expression implies that you know who the thief is, although you're not actually saying so.*

import v. /ɪmˈpɔːt, ˈɪmpɔːt/ **1.** to bring in from another country, as merchandise or commodities. **2.** to convey as a meaning. –n. /ˈɪmpɔːt/ **3.** that which is imported from abroad. **4.** meaning. **5.** consequence or importance.

Compare defs 1 and 2 with **export**, which is to send to another country to sell.

important adj. **1.** of much significance or consequence. **2.** mattering much (*to*). **3.** of considerable influence or authority. –**importance**, n.

importune /ɪmˈpɔːtʃun, ɪmpɔˈtjuːn/ v. to beg urgently or persistently. –**importunate**, adj.

impose v. **1.** to lay (a burden, charge, penalty, etc.) on. **2.** to obtrude oneself or one's requirements. –**imposition**, n.

imposing adj. making an impression by great size, stately appearance, etc.

impossible adj. **1.** that cannot be, exist, or happen. **2.** that cannot be done. **3.** difficult to deal with: *He's impossible when he hasn't had enough sleep.* –**impossibility**, n.

impostor n. someone who practises deception under an assumed character or name. –**imposture**, n.

impotent /ˈɪmpətənt/ adj. **1.** lacking power or ability. **2.** (of a male) unable to have sexual intercourse because of an inability to have or maintain an erection. –**impotence**, n.

impound v. **1.** to shut up in a pound, as a stray animal. **2.** to seize, take, or appropriate summarily.

impoverish v. to reduce to poverty.

impregnable adj. strong enough to resist attack.

impregnate v. **1.** to make pregnant. **2.** to saturate.

impress v. **1.** to cause a strong response or influence, especially a favourable one, in the mind. **2.** to urge, as something to be remembered or done. **3.** to stamp or imprint (a mark, figure, etc.). –**impressive**, adj.

impression n. **1.** a strong effect produced on the mind, etc. **2.** a notion. **3.** a mark, indentation, etc., produced by pressure. **4.** an imitation of the idiosyncrasies of some well-known person or type. –**impressionable**, adj.

imprint n. /ˈɪmprɪnt/ **1.** a mark, etc., impressed or printed on something. –v. /ɪmˈprɪnt/ **2.** to impress (a quality, character, or distinguishing mark). **3.** to fix firmly on the mind, memory, etc.

imprison v. to confine in a prison.

impromptu /ɪmˈprɒmptjuː/ adj. made or done without previous preparation.

improve v. to (cause to) increase in value, excellence, etc.; make or become better. –**improvement**, n.

improvise v. to provide or perform without previous preparation. –**improvisation**, n.

impudent adj. shamelessly bold.

impugn /ɪmˈpjuːn/ v. to challenge as false.

impulse n. **1.** sudden, involuntary inclination to act. **2.** an impelling action or force. –**impulsive**, adj.

impunity n. exemption from punishment or ill consequences.

impute v. to attribute or ascribe. –**imputation**, n.

in prep. **1.** a particle expressing inclusion within space, limits, a whole, material or immaterial surroundings, etc.: in a box; in the country; in politics. **2.** in or into some place, position, state, relation, etc.: to push a button in. **3.** in one's house or office. **4.** Informal in favour; on friendly terms: he's in with the managing director. **5.** in fashion. **6.** in season.

inability n. lack of the ability, capacity or means required to do something: She apologised for her inability to attend the meeting.

Don't confuse this with **disability**, which is a lack of some physical or mental capacity.

inadvertent /ɪnədˈvɜːtnt/ adj. **1.** not attentive; heedless. **2.** unintentional. –**adv.**

inane adj. lacking sense or ideas; silly. –**inanity**, n.

inanimate adj. **1.** lifeless. **2.** spiritless; dull.

inaugurate v. **1.** to make a formal beginning of. **2.** to install in office with formal ceremonies. –**inaugural**, adj. –**inauguration**, n.

inboard adj. (of the engine of a motorboat) located within the boat. Compare **outboard**.

inborn adj. implanted by nature; innate.

inbreed v. (-**bred**, -**breeding**) to breed (animals) repeatedly within the same strain. –**inbred**, adj.

incalculable adj. that cannot be calculated.

incandescence n. the state of a body caused by approximately white heat, when it may be used as a source of artificial light. –**incandesce**, v. –**incandescent**, adj.

incantation n. the chanting or uttering of words supposed to have magical power.

incapacitate v. to make incapable or unfit

incarcerate /ɪnˈkɑːsəreɪt/ v. to imprison confine.

incarnate adj. /ɪnˈkɑːnət, -neɪt/ **1.** invested with a bodily, especially a human, form. –v. /ɪnˈkɑːneɪt/ **2.** to be the embodiment or type of. –**incarnation**, n.

incendiary /ɪnˈsɛndʒəri/ adj. used or adapted for setting property on fire.

incense¹ /ˈɪnsɛns/ n. an aromatic gum producing a sweet smell when burnt.

incense² /ɪnˈsɛns/ v. to make angry; enrage.

incentive n. that which encourages action, greater effort, etc.

inception n. the beginning or start of something.

incessant adj. continuing without interruption.

incest n. sexual intercourse between persons closely related by blood. –**incestuous**, adj.

inch n. **1.** a unit of length in the imperial system, equal to 25.4 mm. –v. **2.** to move by small degrees.

inchoate /ˈɪnkoʊeɪt/ adj. just begun.

incidence n. the range of occurrence or influence of a thing.

incident n. an occurrence or event.

incidental adj. **1.** happening at the same time as something more important. **2.** incurred casually and in addition to the regular or main amount: incidental expenses. –**incidentally**, adv.

Incidentally is used to introduce something which is not part of the main subject of a conversation, but is connected to it nonetheless: 'Yes, it's very sad that John is so ill. Incidentally, I heard that his daughter has just had a baby.'

incinerate v. to reduce to ashes. –incinerator, n.

incipient adj. in an initial stage.

incise v. to cut into. –incision, n.

incisive adj. penetrating, trenchant, or biting.

incisor n. a tooth in the front part of the jaw.

incite v. to urge on; stimulate or prompt to action.

Don't confuse this with insight, which is an understanding of the inner nature of someone or something.

incline v. /ɪnˈklaɪn/ 1. to (cause to) be disposed in mind, habit, etc. (to). 2. to tend, in a physical sense; approximate. 3. to bow (the head, etc.). 4. to (cause to) lean or bend in a particular direction. –n. /ˈɪnklaɪn, ɪnˈklaɪn/ 5. an inclined surface; a slope. –inclination, n.

include v. 1. to contain, embrace, or comprise, as a whole does parts or any part or element. 2. to place in an aggregate, class, category, or the like. –inclusive, adj.

incognito adv. with the real identity concealed.

income n. the returns that come in from one's work, property, business, etc.; revenue.

incommunicado adj. deprived of communication with others.

incompetent adj. 1. lacking the necessary skill or ability. –n. 2. an incompetent person. –incompetence, n.

incongruous adj. 1. out of keeping or place; inappropriate. 2. lacking harmony of parts, etc. –incongruity, n.

inconsequential adj. 1. of no consequence; trivial. 2. illogical.

incontinence n. the inability to exercise voluntary control over natural functions, especially urination and defecation. Also, incontinency. –incontinent, adj.

incontrovertible adj. not able to be argued against.

inconvenient adj. not convenient; awkward, inopportune, disadvantageous, or troublesome. –inconvenience, n.

incorporate v. 1. to form into a society or corporation. 2. to put into a whole as an integral part or parts.

incorrigible adj. bad beyond correction or reform.

increase v. /ɪnˈkris/ 1. to (cause to) become greater or more numerous. –n. /ˈɪnkris/ 2. growth or augmentation. 3. that by which something is increased.

incredible adj. 1. seeming too extraordinary to be possible. 2. that cannot be believed.

Don't confuse this with incredulous.

incredulous adj. 1. indisposed to believe; sceptical. 2. indicating unbelief.

Don't confuse this with incredible.

increment n. an addition or increase, especially in salary.

incriminate v. 1. to provide evidence of the crime or fault of. 2. to involve in a crime or fault.

incubate v. 1. to sit upon (eggs) for the purpose of hatching. 2. to keep at even temperature, as prematurely born infants. –incubator, n. –incubation, n.

inculcate v. to teach persistently and earnestly; instil (upon or in).

incumbent adj. obligatory.

incur v. (-curred, -curring) to run or fall into (some consequence, usually undesirable or injurious).

incursion n. a sudden hostile entrance into or invasion of a place or territory.

The more usual word is **attack**.

indebted *adj.* being under an obligation for assistance, etc., received.

This comes from the word **debt** meaning something that you owe to someone.

indecent *adj.* offending against recognised standards of propriety or good taste.

indeed *adv.* in fact; truly.

indefatigable /ɪndəˈfætɪgəbəl/ *adj.* incapable of being tired out.

indefensible *adj.* that cannot be justified; inexcusable.

indefinite *adj.* **1.** without a fixed limit. **2.** vague or not clear. **3.** *Gram.* not limiting or making particular, as the indefinite pronoun *some* or the indefinite article *a*. –**indefinitely**, *adv.*

indefinite article *n. Gram.* an article (*a*, *an* or *some*) which implies that the noun is not yet identified.

indelible *adj.* incapable of being deleted or obliterated.

indelicate *adj.* offensive to a sense of propriety, or modesty.

indemnity *n.* (*pl.* -**ties**) **1.** protection or security against damage or loss. **2.** compensation for damage or loss sustained. –**indemnify**, *v.*

indent *v.* /ɪnˈdɛnt/ **1.** to form deep recesses in. **2.** to set in or back from the margin, as the first line of a paragraph. **3.** to order, as commodities. –*n.* /ˈɪndɛnt/ **4.** a tooth-like notch or deep recess. **5.** an order for goods. –**indentation**, *n.*

indenture *n.* a contract by which a person, as an apprentice, is bound to service.

independent *adj.* **1.** not subject to another's authority or influence; autonomous. **2.** not depending on something or someone else for existence, operation, etc. **3.** (of a school) non-government. –*n.* **4.** a politician who is not formally affiliated with a political party. –**independence**, *n.*

indeterminate *adj.* not fixed in extent; indefinite.

index *n.* (*pl.* -**dexes** or -**dices**) **1.** a detailed alphabetical key to names, places and topics in a book with reference to their page number, etc. **2.** a sign, token, or indication. **3.** a number or formula expressing some property, ratio, etc., of a thing indicated. –*v.* **4.** to provide with an index, as a book. **5.** to adjust (wages, taxes, etc.) regularly in accordance with changes in commodity and other prices.

indexation *n.* the adjustment of one variable in the light of changes in another variable, especially the adjustment of wages to compensate for rises in the cost of living.

index finger *n.* → forefinger.

indicate *v.* **1.** to be a sign of; imply. **2.** to point out; direct attention to. –**indication**, *n.*

indicative *adj.* **1.** that indicates; suggestive (*of*). **2.** *Gram.* relating to the verb mood used in ordinary statements, questions, etc., as *rained* in *It rained all day yesterday.*

For def. 2, look up **mood²**.

indicator *n.* **1.** a pointing or directing instrument, as a flashing light on a car. **2.** anything that gives a sign or indication. **3.** a statistic or set of statistics which suggest the state of some aspect of society: *a market indicator.*

indices /ˈɪndəsiz/ *n.* plural of **index**.

indict /ɪnˈdaɪt/ *v.* to charge with an offence or crime. –**indictment**, *n.*

indifferent *adj.* **1.** without interest or concern; apathetic (*to*). **2.** neither good nor bad. **3.** not very good. **4.** immaterial or unimportant.

indigenous /ɪnˈdɪdʒənəs/ *adj.* **1.** originating in and characterising a particular region or country; native (*to*). **2.** (*upper case*) of or relating to Aboriginal and Torres Strait Islander people: *Indigenous issues.*

indigent /ˈɪndədʒənt/ *adj.* poor.

indigestion *n.* difficulty in digesting food; dyspepsia. –**indigestive**, *adj.*

indignation *n.* strong displeasure at something deemed unworthy, unjust, or base. –**indignant**, *adj.*

indignity *n.* (*pl.* **-ties**) injury to dignity.

indigo *n.* (*pl.* **-gos**) **1.** a blue dye. **2.** a deep violet blue.

indiscreet *adj.* not discreet, not wise or carefully judged: *indiscreet praise*.

indiscretion *n.* **1.** lack of discretion; imprudence. **2.** an indiscreet act or step.

indiscriminate *adj.* not discriminating; making no distinction.

indispensable *adj.* absolutely necessary.

indisposed *adj.* **1.** sick, especially slightly. **2.** disinclined or unwilling. –**indisposition**, *n.*

individual *adj.* **1.** single; particular; separate. **2.** relating or peculiar to a single person or thing. **3.** distinguished by unique characteristics. –*n.* **4.** a single human being or thing. –**individuality**, *n.* –**individualise, individualize**, *v.* –**individualist**, *n.*

indoctrinate *v.* to teach or inculcate.

indolent *adj.* avoiding exertion. –**indolence**, *n.*

The more usual word is **lazy**.

indomitable *adj.* that cannot be subdued or overcome.

indoors *adj.* inside a house or building. –**indoor**, *adj.*

indubitable *adj.* that cannot be doubted; unquestionable. –**indubitably**, *adv.*

The more usual word is **certain**.

induce *v.* **1.** to lead or move by persuasion, as to some action, state of mind, etc. **2.** to bring about, produce, or cause. **3.** to initiate (labour) artificially in pregnancy.

induct *v.* to introduce, especially formally, as into a place, office, etc.

induction *n.* **1.** the act of inducting. **2.** a bringing forward, as of facts, evidence, etc. **3.** the act of inducing.

indulge *v.* **1.** to yield to one's own inclinations (*in*). **2.** to yield to (desires, feelings, etc.). **3.** to yield to the wishes or whims of. –**indulgence**, *n.* –**indulgent**, *adj.*

industrial *adj.* **1.** of or relating to, or resulting from industry or productive labour. **2.** having highly developed industries. **3.** relating to the workers in industries. –**industrialise, industrialize**, *v.*

Don't confuse **industrial** with **industrious**.

industrial relations *pl. n.* **1.** the management or study of the relations between employers and employees. **2.** the relationship itself, usually in a particular industry, etc.

industrious *adj.* hardworking; diligent.

Don't confuse **industrious** with **industrial**.

industry *n.* (*pl.* **-ries**) **1.** a particular branch of trade or manufacture. **2.** manufacture or trade as a whole. **3.** assiduous activity at any work or task.

inebriated /ɪnˈiːbrieɪtəd/ *adj.* drunk; intoxicated. Also, **inebriate** /ɪnˈiːbriət/.

ineffable *adj.* that cannot be uttered or expressed.

inept *adj.* **1.** not apt, fitted, or suitable. **2.** absurd or foolish. **3.** clumsy; incompetent.

inert *adj.* having no inherent power of action or motion.

inertia *n.* **1.** inert condition; inactivity; sluggishness. **2.** *Physics* that tendency of matter to retain its state of rest or of uniform motion in a straight line.

inestimable /ɪnˈɛstəməbəl/ *adj.* too great to be estimated. –**inestimably**, *adv.*

inevitable *adj.* that cannot be avoided; certain or necessary.

inexorable /ɪnˈɛksərəbəl, ɪnˈɛgz-/ *adj.* unyielding or unalterable.

infallible *adj.* exempt from liability to error or failure.

infamous /ˈɪnfəməs/ *adj.* having or causing an extremely bad reputation. –**infamy**, *n.*

This word is often used humorously about things that are not seriously bad: *the infamous teacher-dunking incident at last year's swimming carnival.*

infant *n.* **1.** a young child or a baby. –*adj.* **2.** of or relating to infants. **3.** of anything in its initial or developing stages: *an infant industry.* –**infancy**, *n.*

infantile *adj.* **1.** relating to infants: *infantile diseases.* **2.** childish; babyish: *infantile behaviour.*

Def. 2 is usually used in a disapproving way.

infantry *n.* soldiers who fight on foot.

infatuated *adj.* blindly in love (*with*). –**infatuation**, *n.*

infect *v.* **1.** to impregnate with disease-producing germs. **2.** to affect morally or so as to influence feelings or actions. –**infection**, *n.*

infectious *adj.* **1.** (of a disease) transmitted through the air or in a liquid. **2.** tending to spread from one to another: *laughter is infectious.* –**infectiousness**, *n.*

Compare def. 1 with **contagious**, which is similar, except that a contagious disease is one that is caught by touching someone who has the sickness, or by touching something they have used or worn: *Herpes is contagious.* Note that you can use either **contagious** or **infectious** for def. 2: *contagious laughter; infectious laughter.*

infer *v.* (**-ferred**, **-ferring**) to conclude or judge by reasoning. –**inference**, *n.*

The more usual word is **gather**.
Infer is often confused with **imply**, which is to mean something, often without actually stating it: *Your actions imply that you are very nervous.* If you wanted to use **infer**, you would have to change the

subject of the verb: *I infer from your actions that you are very nervous.*

inferior *adj.* **1.** lower in station, rank, or degree (*to*). **2.** lower in place or position (*to*). **3.** poor in quality. –*n.* **4.** someone inferior to another or others, as in rank. –**inferiority**, *n.*

inferno *n.* (*pl.* **-nos**) hell. –**infernal**, *adj.*

infest *v.* to be numerous in, as anything troublesome. –**infestation**, *n.*

infidel /ˈɪnfədl/ *n.* an unbeliever.

This was a word that Christians and Muslims used disapprovingly of each other.

infidelity *n.* (*pl.* **-ties**) **1.** unfaithfulness. **2.** a breach of trust.

infiltrate *v.* **1.** to (cause to) pass in by, or as by, filtering. **2.** to join (an organisation) for the unstated purpose of influencing it. –**infiltration**, *n.*

infinite *adj.* **1.** immeasurably great. **2.** unbounded or unlimited; endless. –**infinity**, *n.*

infinitesimal /ˌɪnfɪnəˈtɛzməl, -ˈtɛsəməl/ *adj.* indefinitely or exceedingly small.

infinitive *n. Gram.* the simple form of the verb (*come, take, eat*) used after certain other verbs (I didn't *eat*), or preceded by *to* (I wanted *to come*).

infirm *adj.* **1.** feeble in body or health. **2.** not steadfast, as persons, the mind, etc. –**infirmity**, *n.*

infirmary *n.* (*pl.* **-ries**) a hospital.

inflame *v.* **1.** to set aflame or afire. **2.** to kindle or excite (passions, anger, etc.). –**inflammatory**, *adj.*

inflammable *adj.* easily set on fire.

Nowadays, the more usual word is **flammable**. This is because many people thought **inflammable** meant *not* easily set on fire because *in-* at the beginning of a word often does mean 'not', as in *inactive* and *insensitive*. This misunderstanding could have placed people in danger, so it was decided to use **flammable** to mean easily set on fire and **nonflammable** as its opposite, meaning not likely to burn easily.

inflammation *n.* a reaction of the body to injurious agents, commonly characterised by heat, redness, swelling, pain, etc.

inflate *v.* **1.** to (cause to) swell or puff out, especially with gas. **2.** to (cause to) puff up with pride, satisfaction, etc. **3.** to expand (currency, prices, etc.) unduly.

inflation *n.* **1.** undue expansion of the currency of a country, especially by the issuing of paper money not redeemable in coin. **2.** a substantial rise of prices. **3.** the act of inflating. **4.** the state of being inflated. –**inflationary**, *adj.*

inflection *n.* **1.** change in pitch or tone of voice. **2.** *Gram.* an added ending or other change made to a word to indicate number, tense, aspect, etc., as the -s in *two cats*, or the -*ing* in *She is running*. **3.** a bend or angle. Also, **inflexion**. –**inflect**, *v.*

inflict *v.* to impose (anything unwelcome). –**infliction**, *n.*

influence *n.* **1.** power of producing effects by invisible or insensible means on another person or thing. **2.** these effects. **3.** a thing or person that affects by invisible or insensible means. –*v.* **4.** to exercise influence on. –**influential**, *adj.*

influencer *n.* a person with a high public profile who is engaged to promote a product, esp. on their social media.

influenza *n.* an acute, contagious, viral disease. Also, **flu.**

influx *n.* the act of flowing in.

infomercial *n.* TV an advertisement of some length, in which the content seems to be instructive.

inform *v.* **1.** to impart knowledge of a fact or circumstance to. **2.** to animate or inspire. –**informant**, *n.*

informal *adj.* **1.** not according to prescribed or customary forms; irregular.

2. without formality; unceremonious. –*phr.* **3. vote informal**, *Aust.* to mark a ballot-paper incorrectly thereby invalidating one's vote. –**informality**, *n.*

information *n.* knowledge communicated concerning some fact or circumstance; news. –**informative**, *adj.*

information report *n.* a written or spoken text type or form which presents facts about an entire class of people, animals or objects.

information technology *n.* the use of computers to produce, store and retrieve information. Also, **IT.**

infra-red *n.* the part of the invisible spectrum contiguous to the red end of the visible spectrum.

infrastructure *n.* **1.** the basic framework (as of an organisation or a system). **2.** the buildings or permanent installations associated with an organisation, operation, etc.

infringe *v.* **1.** to violate or transgress (a law, etc.). –*phr.* **2. infringe on** (or **upon**), to encroach or trespass on: *to infringe on someone's privacy.* –**infringement**, *n.*

For def. 1, the more usual word is **break**.

infuriate *v.* to make furious; enrage.

infuse *v.* **1.** to cause to penetrate; instil (*into*). **2.** to steep in a liquid to extract soluble properties or ingredients. –**infusion**, *n.*

ingenious /ɪn'dʒiniəs/ *adj.* having or showing cleverness in invention or construction. –**ingenuity**, *n.*

ingenuous /ɪn'dʒɛnjuəs/ *adj.* artless; innocent.

ingest *v. Physiol.* to put or take (food, etc.) into the body. –**ingestion**, *n.* –**ingestive**, *adj.*

ingot *n.* an (oblong) cast of metal.

ingrain *v.* to fix deeply and firmly, as in the mind. Also, **engrain.**

ingrate *n.* an ungrateful person.

ingratiate *v.* to establish (oneself) in the favour of others.

ingratitude n. the state of being ungrateful.

ingredient n. an element in a mixture.

inhabit v. to live in (a place). –**inhabitant**, n.

inhale v. to breathe in. –**inhalation**, n.

inherent adj. existing in something as a natural and permanent quality, or attribute. –**inhere**, v.

inherit v. 1. to take or receive (property, a right, a title, etc.) as an heir. 2. to possess as a hereditary characteristic. –**inheritance**, n. –**inheritor**, n.

inhibit v. to restrain or check (an action, impulse, etc.). –**inhibition**, n.

inhibited adj. unable or unwilling to behave or express emotions naturally.

inimical adj. 1. adverse in tendency or effect. 2. unfriendly or hostile. –**inimicality**, n.

inimitable adj. incapable of being imitated.

iniquity n. (pl. **-ties**) gross injustice; wickedness. –**iniquitous**, adj.

initial adj. 1. of or relating to the beginning. –n. 2. the first letter of a word. –v. (**-ialled**, **-ialling**) 3. to mark or sign with initials, especially as an indication of responsibility for or approval of the contents.

initialism n. an abbreviation formed from the initial letters of a sequence of words, as *LPG* (from *liquefied petroleum gas*).

initiate v. 1. to begin, set going, or originate. 2. to introduce into the knowledge of some art or subject. 3. to admit with formal rites into secret knowledge, a society, etc. –**initiation**, n.

initiative n. 1. an introductory act or step. 2. readiness and ability in setting action going; enterprise.

inject v. 1. to force (a fluid) into (a part of the body, etc.). 2. to introduce (something new or different) into (a thing). –**injection**, n.

injunction n. Law a judicial order requiring a person or persons to do or (more commonly) not to do a particular thing.

injure v. 1. to do or cause harm to; damage. 2. to do wrong or injustice to. –**injurious**, adj. –**injury**, n.

injustice n. 1. the quality or fact of being unjust. 2. unjust action or treatment.

ink n. a fluid used for writing or printing.

inkling n. a hint, intimation, or slight suggestion.

inland adj., n. 1. (relating to or situated in) the interior part of a country or region. –adv. 2. in or towards the interior of a country.

in-law n. a relative by marriage.

inlay v. (**-laid**, **-laying**) to decorate (an object) with veneers of fine materials set in its surface.

inlet n. a narrow stretch of water reaching into a shore line or between islands.

inline skate n., v. → **rollerblade**.

inmate n. one of those confined in a hospital, prison, etc.

inn n. a small hotel that provides lodging, food, etc., for travellers.

innards pl. n. the inward parts of the body; entrails.

innate adj. inborn; existing in one from birth. –**inner** adj. 1. interior. 2. mental or spiritual.

inner adj. 1. interior. 2. mental or spiritual.

innings n. 1. Cricket the turn of any one member of the batting team, or of the whole team, to bat. 2. any opportunity for some activity; turn.

Note that this word can be treated as singular or plural: *Australia won by an innings and ten runs*; *He made a century in both innings*.

innocent adj. 1. free from any moral wrong; pure. 2. free from legal or specific wrong; guiltless. 3. harmless. –n. 4. an innocent person. –**innocence**, n.

innocuous adj. causing no harm.

innovate v. to bring in (something new). –**innovation**, n. –**innovator**, n.

innovative adj. new and original. Also, **innovatory**. –**innovativeness**, n. –**innovatively**, adv.

innuendo n. (pl. **-dos** or **-does**) an indirect hint about a person or thing, especially of a derogatory nature.

innumerable adj. **1.** very numerous. **2.** incapable of being definitely counted.

inoculate v. to inject (a person or animal) with a serum, or vaccine in order to secure immunity from a disease. –**inoculation**, n.

inopportune adj. inappropriate; untimely.

inordinate adj. excessive.

inorganic adj. **1.** not having the composition of living bodies. **2.** Chem. denoting or relating to compounds not containing carbon, excepting cyanides and carbonates. Compare **organic** (def. 2).

inpatient n. a patient who is accommodated in a hospital for the duration of their treatment. Also, **in-patient**.

input n. **1.** that which is put in. **2.** Computers information which is fed into a computer before computation.

inquest n. a legal or judicial inquiry.

inquire v. to make investigation (into). Also, **enquire**. –**inquiry**, n.

inquisition n. an investigation, or process of inquiry. –**inquisitor**, n. –**inquisitorial**, adj.

inquisitive adj. **1.** inquiring; eager for knowledge. **2.** unduly curious; prying.

inroad n. (usu. pl.) forcible or serious encroachment.

insane adj. **1.** mentally deranged. **2.** set apart for mentally deranged persons. **3.** utterly senseless. –**insanity**, n. –**insanely**, adv.

insatiable adj. incapable of being satisfied.

inscribe v. **1.** to write or engrave (words, characters, etc.). **2.** to mark (a surface) with words, characters, etc. **3.** to address or dedicate (a book, photograph, etc.) with

writing. **4.** to enrol, as on an official list. –**inscription**, n.

inscrutable adj. not easily understood; mysterious.

insect n. Zool. a small, air-breathing arthropod with a body clearly divided into 3 parts, and with 3 pairs of legs, and usually 2 pairs of wings.

Bees, ants and flies are insects, but spiders and ticks are not, even though some people call them insects.

insecticide n. a substance used for killing insects.

insectivorous adj. feeding on insects. –**insectivore**, n.

Compare this with **carnivorous**, **omnivorous**, and **herbivorous**.

insecure adj. **1.** exposed to danger. **2.** not firm or safe. **3.** not free from fear, doubt, etc. –**insecurity**, n.

inseminate v. to introduce semen into (a female) to cause fertilisation. –**insemination**, n.

insensible adj. incapable of feeling or perceiving; unconscious.

insensitive adj. **1.** not sensitive. **2.** lacking in feeling or sympathy. –**insensitively**, adv. –**insensitivity**, n.

insert v. /ɪn'sɜt/ **1.** to put or set in. –n. /'ɪnsɜt/ **2.** something inserted, or to be inserted. –**insertion**, n.

inset n. something inserted.

inside prep. **1.** on the inner side of; within. **2.** before the elapse of: inside an hour. –adv. **3.** in or into the inner part. **4.** indoors. **5.** by nature; fundamentally: She's very kind inside. –n. **6.** the inner part; interior. –adj. **7.** situated or being on or in the inside; interior.

insider n. someone who belongs to a limited circle of people.

insidious adj. stealthily deceitful.

insight n. **1.** an understanding gained: an insight into country life. **2.** faculty of seeing into inner character or underlying truth.

Don't confuse this with **incite**, which is to urge someone to do something, especially something violent.

insignia /ɪnˈsɪɡnɪə/ n. (pl. **-nia** or **-nias**) a badge or distinguishing mark of office or honour.

insinuate v. **1.** to suggest or hint slyly. **2.** to bring or introduce into a position by indirect or slightly cunning methods. **–insinuation**, n.

insipid adj. without distinctive, interesting, or attractive qualities.

insist v. **1.** to assert or maintain positively. **–phr. 2. insist on**, to be firm, or persistent about (some desire, demand, intention, etc). **–insistent**, adj.

insolent adj. boldly rude or disrespectful. **–insolence**, n.

insolvent adj. unable to pay one's debts. **–insolvency**, n.

insomnia n. inability to sleep, especially when chronic. **–insomniac**, n.

inspect v. **1.** to look carefully at or over. **2.** to examine officially. **–inspection**, n. **–inspector**, n.

inspire v. **1.** to infuse an animating or exalting influence into. **2.** to produce or arouse (a feeling, thought, etc.). **3.** to give rise to, or cause. **4.** to inhale. **–inspiration**, n.

install v. **1.** to place in position for service or use. **2.** to establish in any office, position, or place. **3.** Computers to install a software application onto a hard disk. **–installation**, n.

instalment n. **1.** any of several parts into which a debt is divided for payment. **2.** a single portion of something issued by parts at successive times.

instance n. **1.** a case or example of anything. **–v.** (**-stanced, -stancing**) **2.** to cite as an example.

instant n. **1.** a moment. **2.** a particular moment. **–adj. 3.** immediate. **4.** (of a foodstuff) processed for immediate and simple preparation.

instantaneous adj. occurring, done, or completed in an instant.

instant messaging n. text-based, real-time communication between individuals by means of a network of computers or the internet.

instead adv. **1.** in the place (of): I want a new book instead of this. **2.** in one's (its, their, etc.) stead: She was sick, so her husband came instead.

instep n. the arched upper surface of the human foot between the toes and the ankle.

instigate v. to incite to some action or course. **–instigation**, n.

The more usual word is **start**.

instil v. (**-stilled, -stilling**) to infuse slowly or by degrees into the mind or feelings.

instinct n. **1.** innate impulse or natural inclination. **2.** a natural aptitude for something. **3.** natural intuitive power. **–instinctive**, adj.

institute v. **1.** to set up or establish. **2.** to set in operation. **3.** to establish in an office or position. **–n. 4.** a society or organisation especially of a literary, scientific, or educational character.

institution n. **1.** an organisation or establishment, usually one for some public, educational, charitable, or similar purpose. **2.** a residential establishment for the care of people unable to care for themselves, as the elderly or disabled. **3.** any established law, custom, etc.: the institution of marriage. **4.** the act of instituting or setting up. **–institutional**, adj. **–institutionalise**, institutionalize, v.

Def. 2 often has negative overtones, because in some cases a lot of people live in an institution and don't get individual care.

instruct v. **1.** to direct or command. **2.** to teach; train; educate. **3.** to inform or apprise. **–instructive**, adj. **–instructor**, n.

instruction n. **1.** the act or practice of instructing or teaching; education. **2.** (usu. pl.) an order or direction.

instrument n. **1.** a tool or implement. **2.** a device for producing musical sounds. **3.** a thing with or by which something is effected; a means. **4.** a legal document. –**instrumental**, adj.

insubordinate adj. disobedient; rebellious. –**insubordination**, n.

insufferable adj. not to be endured; unbearable.

insular adj. **1.** of or relating to an island or islands. **2.** narrow or illiberal. –**insularity**, n.

insulate v. **1.** to cover or surround (an electric wire, etc.) with non-conducting material. to place in an isolated situation. **3.** to install a material in the roof of (a house), to retain warmth in winter and keep out heat in summer. –**insulation**, n. –**insulator**, n.

insulin n. a hormone produced in the pancreas, a deficiency of which produces diabetes.

If your body does not make enough insulin, you get the disease **diabetes**.

insult v. /ɪnˈsʌlt/ **1.** to treat with contemptuous rudeness; affront. –n. /ˈɪnsʌlt/ **2.** a contemptuously rude action or speech.

insuperable adj. incapable of being passed over, overcome, or surmounted.

insurance n. the act, system, or business of insuring property, life, the person, etc., against specified loss or harm in consideration of a payment proportionate to the risk involved.

insure v. to guarantee against risk of loss or harm: *The company that insured my house was very helpful when I had to make a claim.*

Don't confuse **insure** with **assure**, which means to tell with certainty, or with **ensure**, which means to make certain.

insurgent n., adj. (someone) rising in forcible opposition to established authority.

insurrection n. the act of rising in arms or open resistance against established authority.

intact adj. remaining uninjured or whole; unimpaired.

intake n. **1.** the act of taking in. **2.** that which is taken in.

integer /ˈɪntɪdʒə/ n. **1.** Also, **positive integer**. a whole number. **2.** a complete entity.

Compare this with **fraction**, which is a part of a whole number.

integral adj. belonging as a part of the whole.

integrate v. **1.** to bring together (parts) into a whole. **2.** to amalgamate (an ethnic, religious, or other minority group) with the rest of the community. –**integration**, n.

integrated circuit n. an array of interconnected circuit elements integrated with or deposited on a single semiconductor base.

integrity n. **1.** uprightness; honesty. **2.** unimpaired condition.

intellect n. the power or faculty of the mind by which one knows, understands, or reasons.

intellectual adj. **1.** of, appealing to or engaging the intellect. **2.** (of a person) possessing and exercising a high degree of mental capacity. –n. **3.** an intellectual person; someone who reads, studies, or thinks a lot.

Compare this with **intelligent** (see **intelligence** def. 1), which means clever. Someone can be intelligent without being intellectual if they are clever but not interested in studying and reading, etc.

intelligence n. **1.** cleverness or aptitude in grasping truths, facts, meaning, etc. **2.** news; information. **3.** the gathering or distribution of secret information which might prove detrimental to an enemy. –**intelligent**, *adj.*

Compare **intelligent** with **intellectual**. **Intelligent** means clever, and **intellectual** describes something which is of interest to the mind (*intellectual games*), or someone who studies and thinks a lot.

intelligentsia *pl. n.* the intellectuals of a society.

intelligible *adj.* capable of being understood.

intemperate *adj.* **1.** indulging excessively in intoxicating drink. **2.** unrestrained or unbridled. –**intemperance**, *n.*

intend *v.* to have in mind as something to be done or thought about.

intense *adj.* **1.** of an extreme kind. **2.** having or showing great strength or vehemence of feeling. –**intensify**, *v.* –**intensity**, *n.*

intensifier /ɪnˈtɛnsəfaɪə/ *n. Gram.* a linguistic element or word which increases the semantic effect of a word or phrase but has itself minimal semantic content, as *very*.

intensive *adj.* **1.** of, relating to, or characterised by intensity. **2.** *Econ.* of or denoting methods designed to increase effectiveness, as, in agriculture.

intent[1] *n.* that which is intended; purpose; aim.

intent[2] *adj.* firmly or steadfastly fixed or directed (upon something).

intention *n.* the act of determining mentally upon some action or result; a purpose or design. –**intentional**, *adj.*

inter /ɪnˈtɜ/ *v.* (**-terred, -terring**) to bury (a dead body), especially with ceremonies.

interact *v.* to act on each other. –**interaction**, *n.* –**interactive**, *adj.*

intercede *v.* to act or speak on behalf of one in difficulty or trouble, as by pleading or petition. –**intercession**, *n.*

intercept *v.* **1.** to take or seize on the way from one place to another. **2.** to stop or check (passage, etc.).

interchange *v.* /ɪntəˈtʃeɪndʒ/ (**-changed, -changing**) **1.** to (cause to) change places, as 2 persons or things. –*n.* /ˈɪntətʃeɪndʒ/ **2.** the act of interchanging; reciprocal exchange. **3.** any major road junction, especially where motorways converge. **4.** a point, in a public transport system, at which passengers can change from one vehicle to another.

intercom *n.* an electronic system for sending spoken messages within an office complex, school, etc.

intercourse *n.* **1.** dealings or communication between individuals. **2.** → **sexual intercourse**.

interdict *n.* /ˈɪntədɪkt, -daɪt/ **1.** *Civil Law* an official prohibitive act or decree. –*v.* /ɪntəˈdɪkt, -ˈdaɪt/ **2.** to forbid; prohibit. –**interdictory**, *adj.* –**interdiction**, *n.*

interest *n.* **1.** the feeling of someone whose attention or curiosity is particularly engaged by something. **2.** the power of exciting such feeling. **3.** a share in the ownership of property, in a commercial or financial undertaking, or the like. **4.** something in which one has an interest, as of ownership, advantage, attention, etc. **5.** benefit or advantage. **6.** *Commerce* **a.** a sum paid for the use of money borrowed. **b.** the rate per cent per unit of time represented by such payments. –*v.* **7.** to engage or excite the attention or curiosity of.

interface *n.* **1.** a surface regarded as the common boundary to 2 bodies or spaces. **2.** *Computers* the point at which an interconnection is made between a computer and a peripheral device or other piece of equipment, or between a computer and the person using it: *trouble lies at the user interface*. **3.** a common boundary or interconnection between 2 groups of people, organisations, etc. **4.** the point or area at which any 2 systems or disciplines interact. –*v.* (**-faced, -facing**) **5.** to bring (a computer, piece of equipment, etc.) into an interface: *to interface the computer* *with the printer.* **6.** (of computer systems, equipment, etc.) to interact.

interfere *v.* **1.** to interpose or intervene in the affairs of others. **2.** to come into opposition, as one thing with another, especially with the effect of hampering action or procedure: *these interruptions interfere with the work.* –**interference**, *n.*

> Note that this is often followed by **with** or **in**: *Don't interfere with my work; I'll try not to interfere in your business.*

interim *adj.* **n.** (belonging to or connected with) an intervening period of time.

interior *adj.* **1.** being within; internal. **2.** relating to the inland. **3.** inner, private, or secret. **–n. 4.** the internal part; the inside. **5.** the inland parts of a region, country, etc.

interject *v.* to throw (a remark) abruptly into a speech or conversation.

> The more usual word is **interrupt**.

interjection *n.* **1.** (the utterance of) an ejaculation or exclamation. **2.** something, as a remark, interjected. **3.** *Gram.* a form of utterance comprising words which stand on their own outside the structure of a sentence, as *Heavens!*, or *Oh my goodness!*

interlace *v.* **1.** to cross (threads, etc.) so that they pass alternately over and under. **2.** to mingle; blend.

interlock *v.* **1.** to (cause to) fit into each other, as parts of machinery, so that all action is simultaneous. **2.** to (cause to) lock one with another. –**interlocker**, *n.*

interlocutor /ɪntəˈlɒkjətə/ *n.* someone who takes part in a conversation. –**interlocutory**, *adj.* –**interlocution**, *n.*

interlope *v.* to intrude into the affairs of others.

interlude *n.* **1.** an intervening episode, period, space, etc. **2.** a period of inactivity; lull.

intermediate¹ /ɪntəˈmidiət, -dʒət/ *adj.* being, situated, or acting between 2 points,

stages, things, persons, etc. –**intermediary**, *n.*

intermediate² /ɪntəˈmidiˌeɪt/ *v.* to act as an intermediary; mediate. –**intermediation**, *n.* –**intermediator**, *n.*

interminable *adj.* unending.

intermission *n.* a break between items in an entertainment, especially in the cinema; interval.

intermittent *adj.* alternately ceasing and beginning again.

intern¹ /ɪnˈtɜn/ *v.* to oblige to reside within prescribed limits.

intern² /ˈɪntɜn/ *n.* a resident doctor at a hospital, usually a recent graduate still in partial training.

internal *adj.* **1.** in, or relating to, the interior of something. **2.** existing or occurring within a country or organisation; domestic.

international *adj.* **1.** between or among nations. **2.** of or relating to different nations or their citizens.

internecine /ɪntəˈnisaɪn/ *adj.* mutually destructive.

internet *n.* **the**, the communications system created by the interconnecting networks of computers around the world. Also, **the Internet**, **the Net**.

internet cafe *n.* an establishment which provides connection to the internet for a fee, sometimes also selling coffee and light refreshments.

internet relay chat *n.* an online discussion forum available through the internet, in which multiple users can communicate in real-time by means of typing text. Compare **newsgroup**. Also, **IRC**.

internet service provider *n.* a company that provides access to the internet, usually for a fee. Also, **ISP**.

interplay *n.* reciprocal play, action, or influence.

interpolate *v.* **1.** to alter (a text, etc.) by the insertion of new matter. **2.** to introduce (something additional or extraneous) between other things or parts. **–interpolation,** *n.*

interpose *v.* **1.** to (cause) to come between other things. **2.** to put in (a remark) by way of interruption.

interpret *v.* **1.** to explain or elucidate. **2.** to explain, construe, or understand in a particular way. **3.** to translate. **–interpretation,** *n.* **–interpreter,** *n.*

interregnum /ɪntəˈrɛgnəm/ *n.* (pl. **-nums** or **-na** /-nə/) **1.** an interval of time between the reigns of 2 successive sovereigns. **2.** any interruption in continuity.

interrogate *v.* to question (a person), especially closely or formally. **–interrogation,** *n.*

interrogative *adj.* Also, **interrogatory.** **1.** relating to or conveying a question. *–n.* **2.** *Gram.* an interrogative word, element, or construction, as 'who?' and 'what?'

interrupt *v.* **1.** to make a break in (something otherwise continuous). **2.** to stop (a person) in the midst of doing or saying something, especially as by an interjected remark. **–interruption,** *n.* **–interruptive,** *adj.*

intersect *v.* to cut or divide by passing through or lying across.

intersection *n.* **1.** the act of intersecting. **2.** a place where 2 or more roads meet.

intersperse *v.* **1.** to scatter among other things. **2.** to diversify with something scattered. **–interspersion,** *n.*

interstate *adj.* **1.** between or jointly involving states. *–adv.* **2.** *Aust.* to, from or in another state. Compare **intrastate.**

interstice /ɪnˈtɜstəs/ *n.* a small or narrow opening between things or parts.

interval *n.* **1.** an intervening period of time; pause. **2.** a space intervening between things, points, limits, qualities, etc. **3.** *Music* the difference in pitch between 2 notes.

intervene *v.* **1.** to come between in action; intercede. **2.** to fall or happen between other events or periods. **–intervention,** *n.*

interview *n.* **1.** a meeting of persons face to face, in which one asks questions of the other. *–v.* **2.** to have an interview with. **–interviewer,** *n.*

intestate *adj.* (of a person) dying without having made a valid will. **–intestacy,** *n.*

intestine *n.* (*oft. pl.*) the lower part of the alimentary canal; gut. **–intestinal,** *adj.*

This word is usually used in the plural: *The butcher removed the animal's intestines.*

intimate[1] /ˈɪntəmət/ *adj.* **1.** associated in close or friendly personal relations. **2.** private; closely personal. **3.** maintaining sexual relations. **4.** involving from close personal connection or familiar experience. **5.** detailed; deep. *–n.* **6.** an intimate friend or associate. **–intimacy,** *n.*

intimate[2] /ˈɪntəmeɪt/ *v.* to make known indirectly; hint. **–intimation,** *n.*

intimidate *v.* **1.** to inspire with fear; overawe. **2.** to force into or deter by inducing fear. **–intimidation,** *n.*

into *prep.* **1.** a word expressing **a.** movement or direction towards the inner part: *to run into the room.* **b.** involvement or placement within: *to be well into a book.* **c.** change to new conditions: *to turn into a frog.* **2.** in mathematics, indicating the number by which something is divided: *2 into 10 equals 5. –phr.* **3. be into something,** *Informal* to be extremely interested in something: *He's really into jazz now.*

Note that **in** and **to** are written as separate words when **to** is part of the following verb, as in *She came in to see me* and *They went in to eat.*

intolerance *n.* **1.** lack of toleration; indisposition to tolerate contrary opinions or beliefs. **2.** incapacity or indisposition to bear or endure: *intolerance of heat.* **3.** an abnormal sensitivity or allergy to a food, drug, etc.: *a lactose intolerance.* **–intolerant,** *adj.*

intonation *n.* the pattern or melody of pitch changes in connected speech.

intone *v.* to speak or recite in a singing voice, especially in monotone.

intoxicate *v.* **1.** to make drunk. **2.** to excite mentally beyond self-control or reason. –**intoxication**, *n.* –**intoxicant**, *n.*

intractable *adj.* not docile; stubborn.

intranet *n. Computers* a website or group of websites belonging to an organisation and accessible only to organisation members, employees, etc.

intransigent *adj.* uncompromising.

The more usual word is **stubborn**.

intransitive verb *n. Gram.* **1.** a verb that is never accompanied by a direct object, as *come*, *sit*, *lie*, etc. **2.** a verb occurring without a direct object, as *drinks* in the sentence *he drinks only when thirsty*.

Compare this with **transitive verb**, such as *put*, which does need an object, as in *I put the book on the table.*

intrastate *adj.* within a state. Compare **interstate**.

intravenous *adj.* within a vein or the veins.

intrepid *adj.* fearless.

The more usual word is **brave**.

intricate *adj.* entangled or involved –**intricacy**, *n.*

intrigue *v.* /ɪnˈtriːɡ/ (**-trigued**, **-triguing**) **1.** to excite the curiosity or interest of by puzzling qualities. **2.** to plot craftily. –*n.* /ɪnˈtriːɡ, ˈɪntriːɡ/ **3.** the use of underhand plots to accomplish designs. **4.** a clandestine or illicit love affair.

intrinsic *adj.* belonging to a thing by its very nature.

introduce *v.* **1.** to bring into notice, knowledge, use, vogue, etc. **2.** to bring forward with preliminary matter. **3.** to bring (a person) (*to*) the knowledge or experience of something. **4.** to bring (a person) into the acquaintance of another.

5. to cause or allow to be established in a new country or geographical region, an animal, a fish, plant, etc., which is native to a different country of origin: *to introduce carp into Australian rivers.* –**introductory**, *adj.*

introduction *n.* **1.** the act of introducing. **2.** something introduced. **3.** a preliminary part, as of a book.

introspection *n.* examination of one's own mental states. –**introspective**, *adj.*

introvert *n.* a person who is often quiet and shy, and does not make friends easily. –**introversion**, *n.* –**introverted**, *adj.*

intrude *v.* **1.** to thrust or bring in without reason, permission, or welcome. **2.** to thrust oneself in; come uninvited. –**intrusion**, *n.* –**intrusive**, *adj.*

intuition *n.* direct perception (of truth, facts, etc.) independent of any reasoning process. –**intuitive**, *adj.*

inundate *v.* to overspread with or as with a flood. –**inundation**, *n.*

inure *v.* to accustom; habituate (*to*).

invade *v.* **1.** to enter as an enemy. **2.** to intrude upon.

invalid[1] /ˈɪnvəlɪd/ *n.* **1.** a chronically ill person. –*adj.* **2.** deficient in health; sick. **3.** of or for invalids. –*v.* **4.** to make or become an invalid.

invalid[2] /ɪnˈvæləd/ *adj.* not valid. –**invalidity**, *n.* –**invalidate**, *v.*

invaluable *adj.* having a value too great to be measured.

Compare this with **valuable**, which also describes something of great worth or value. The difference between the two words is that something **invaluable** is of such huge worth that it can't be measured. It is more precious than something described as **valuable**. **Invaluable** is a confusing word because it appears to be the opposite of **valuable** (*in-* meaning *not*), but in fact it means 'not able to be valued'.

invariable *adj.* unchangeable.

invasion *n.* **1.** the act of invading or entering an enemy. **2.** infringement by intrusion.

invective *n.* an utterance of violent censure or reproach.

The more usual word is **abuse**.

inveigh *v.* to attack vehemently in words; rail (*against*).

inveigle *v.* to draw by beguiling inducements (*into, from, away, etc.*): *We were inveigled into giving a concert.*

The more usual word is **trick**.

invent *v.* to devise (something original); think up. **–inventive**, *adj.* **–inventor**, *n.*

invention *n.* **1.** the act of inventing. **2.** anything invented or devised. **3.** imagination. **4.** falsehood; a lie.

inventory /'mvəntri, m'ventəri/ *n.* a detailed descriptive list of articles.

inverse *adj.* **1.** reversed in position, direction, or tendency. *–n.* **2.** an inverted state or condition. **3.** that which is inverse; the direct opposite.

invert *v.* **1.** to turn upside down, inside out, or inwards. **2.** to reverse in position, direction, order, or tendency. **–inversion**, *n.*

invertebrate *n., adj. Zool.* (an animal) without a backbone.

inverted comma *n.* a quotation mark.

invest *v.* **1.** to put (money) in something offering profitable returns, especially interest or income. **2.** to endow. **3.** to install in an office or position. **–investor**, *n.*

investigate *v.* to search or inquire into the particulars of. **–investigation**, *n.* **–investigative**, *adj.*

investiture *n.* (a ceremony involving) the formal bestowal or presentation of certain rights or powers.

investment *n.* **1.** the investing of money or capital in order to secure profitable returns. **2.** a thing invested in. **3.** that which is invested.

inveterate *adj.* **1.** confirmed in a habit, practice, etc. **2.** firmly established by long continuance.

invidious *adj.* such as to bring hatred or envy.

invigorate *v.* to give vigour to.

invincible *adj.* that cannot be conquered.

Note that **invincible** is sometimes used in the field of sports, giving a rather heroic feeling to whatever is being described: *The Wallabies seem invincible this year.*

inviolable *adj.* that must not be violated, as something sacred.

inviolate *adj.* free from injury, desecration, or outrage.

invisible *adj.* not visible.

invite *v.* **1.** to ask courteously to come or go somewhere or to do something. **2.** to act so as to bring on or render probable. **–invitation**, *n.*

in-vitro fertilisation *n.* → IVF.

invoice *n.* **1.** a written list of merchandise, with prices, or an itemised bill, delivered or sent to a buyer. *–v.* (**-voiced, -voicing**) **2.** to present an invoice to (a customer).

invoke *v.* **1.** to call for with earnest desire. **2.** to call on (a divine being, etc.), as in prayer. **3.** to put (a law, etc.) into use. **–invocation**, *n.*

involve *v.* **1.** to include as a necessary circumstance, condition, or consequence. **2.** to include. **3.** to bring into an intricate or complicated form or condition. **4.** to implicate, as in guilt or crime. **5.** to be highly or excessively interested in.

inward *adj.* **1.** proceeding or directed towards the inside or interior. **2.** situated within; interior, internal. *–adv.* **3.** → **inwards.**

Note that you can use **inward** for both the adjective (*an inward gaze, an inward room, inward peace*) and the adverb (*to look inward*), but **inwards** can only be used for the adverb (*to look inwards*).

inwards *adv.* towards the inside or interior. Also, **inward**.

iodine /'aɪədiːn, 'aɪədaɪn/ *n.* a nonmetallic element, used in medicine as an antiseptic. *Symbol*: I

ion *n. Chem.* an electrically charged atom, radical, or molecule, formed by the loss or gain of one or more electrons.

iota /aɪ'oʊtə/ *n.* a very small quantity: *There's not one iota of truth in what he says.*

Note that this is usually used in a negative sense.

IOU *n.* a written acknowledgment of a debt (I owe you).

IP address *n. Computers* a unique numerical identifier for a computer connected to the internet. Also, **IP number**.

irascible /ɪ'ræsəbəl/ *adj.* easily provoked to anger.

irate *adj.* angry; enraged.

IRC *n.* → **internet relay chat**.

ire *n.* anger; wrath.

iridescent *adj.* displaying colours like those of the rainbow.

iridology *n.* examination of the iris to detect disease in the body. –**iridologist**, *n.*

iris *n.* (*pl.* **irises** *or* **irides** /'aɪrədiːz/) **1.** *Anat.* the coloured portion of the eye around the pupil. **2.** a plant with handsome flowers and sword-shaped leaves.

irk *v.* to weary, annoy, or trouble.

iron *n.* **1.** *Chem.* a ductile, malleable, silver-white metallic element, commonly used for making tools, implements, machinery, etc. *Symbol*: Fe **2.** an iron or steel implement used heated for smoothing or pressing cloth, etc. **3.** a metal-headed golf club. **4.** (*pl.*) an iron shackle or fetter. –*adj.* **5.** made of iron. **6.** resembling iron in colour, firmness, etc. –*v.* **7.** to smooth or press with a heated iron, as clothes, etc.

ironbark *n.* a kind of eucalypt with a characteristic dark deeply-fissured bark.

ironman *n.* (*pl.* **-men**) **1.** a contestant in a sporting event in which male competitors swim, ride bikes and run in succession. –*adj.* **2.** of or relating to such an event.

ironwoman *n.* (*pl.* **-women**) **1.** a contestant in a sporting event in which female competitors swim, ride bikes and run in succession. –*adj.* **2.** of or relating to such an event.

irony *n.* (*pl.* **-nies**) **1.** a figure of speech or literary device in which the literal meaning is the opposite of that intended. **2.** an outcome of events contrary to what was, or might have been, expected. –**ironic**, **ironical**, *adj.*

irradiate *v.* **1.** to shed rays of light or shine (upon). **2.** to illumine intellectually or spiritually. **3.** to radiate (light, heat, etc.). **4.** to expose to radiation. –**irradiation**, *n.* –**irradiant**, *adj.*

irrational *adj.* **1.** without the faculty of reason. **2.** without, or deprived of, sound judgement.

irrespective *adj.* without regard to something else; independent (*of*).

irrevocable /ə'revəkəbəl, ɪrə'voʊkəbəl/ *adj.* not to be revoked, recalled or undone.

irrigate *v.* **1.** to supply (land) with water by means of canals passing through it. **2.** *Med.* to supply (a wound, etc.) with a constant flow of some liquid. –**irrigation**, *n.*

irritable *adj.* easily irritated.

irritate *v.* **1.** to excite to impatience or anger. **2.** *Physiol., Biol.* to excite (a living system) to some characteristic action or function. **3.** to bring (a bodily part, etc.) to a sensitive condition. –**irritating**, *adj.* –**irritation**, *n.* –**irritant**, *n.*, *adj.*

Irukandji jellyfish /ɪrə'kændʒi/ *n.* (*pl.* **-fish** *or* **-fishes**) a small jellyfish, the sting of which is potentially fatal.

For information about the different plural forms, see the note at **fish**.

is *v.* the form of the verb **be** used for the third person singular (*he, she, it*) in the present tense.

Note that this word is often shortened to **'s**: *He's a teacher now*; *Helen's hoping to arrive in the morning.*

island n. **1.** a tract of land completely surrounded by water, and not large enough to be called a continent. **2.** something resembling an island. –**islander**, n.

isle n. a small island.

isobar n. *Meteorol., etc.* a line drawn on a weather map, etc., connecting all points having the same barometric pressure. –**isobaric**, adj.

isolate v. to detach or separate so as to be alone. –**isolation**, n.

isometric adj. Also, **isometrical**. **1.** relating to or having equality of measure. –n. **2.** (pl.) a system of physical exercises in which muscles are pitted against each other or against a fixed object.

isosceles /aɪ'sɒsəliz/ adj. (of a triangle) having 2 sides equal.

isotope n. any of 2 or more forms of a chemical element, having the same atomic number, but different atomic weights. –**isotopic**, adj. –**isotopy**, n.

issue n. **1.** the act of sending, giving out, or promulgation. **2.** that which is issued. **3.** a point in question or dispute. **4.** a point or matter of special or public importance. **5.** offspring or progeny. **6.** a complaint; objection: *do you have an issue with this decision?* –v. (**issued**, **issuing**) **7.** to put out; deliver for use, sale, etc.; put into circulation. **8.** to send out; discharge; emit. **9.** to go, pass, or flow out; come forth; emerge. **10.** to arise as a result or consequence. –phr. **11. have issues**, to have unresolved personal difficulties and conflicts.

isthmus /'ɪsməs, 'ɪsθməs/ n. (pl. -**muses**) a narrow strip of land, bordered on both sides by water, connecting 2 larger pieces of land.

it pron. the personal pronoun used **1.** to refer to a thing, or to a person or animal whose sex is not known: *The desk is ready. You can pick it up today*; *A smile is a wonderful thing. It can really brighten your day*; *The baby is awake. I can hear it crying.* **2.** as the impersonal subject of a sentence whose logical subject is a phrase or clause which usually follows: *It was agreed that she would go*; *It's amazing how often he rings her.* **3.** as the impersonal subject in sentences which refer to such things as the weather (*It is raining*), the time (*It is six o'clock*) and distances (*It is nearly 20 kilometres to his house*).

It is a third person singular pronoun. It can be in the subjective case (*It is crying*) or the objective case (*Pick it up*).

IT n. → **information technology**.

italic adj. **1.** designating or relating to a style of printing types in which the letters usually slope to the right (thus, *italic*), used for emphasis, etc. –n. **2.** (oft. pl.) italic type. –**italicise**, **italicize**, v.

itch v. **1.** to have or feel a peculiar irritation of the skin which causes a desire to scratch. **2.** to have a restless desire to do or get something. –n. **3.** the sensation of itching. –**itchy**, adj.

item n. **1.** a separate article or particular. **2.** a separate piece of information or news.

itemise v. to state by items. Also, **itemize**.

itinerant adj. **1.** travelling from place to place. **2.** moving on a circuit, as a preacher, judge, etc. –**itinerancy**, **itinerary**, n. –**itinerate**, v.

itinerary n. (pl. -**ries**) **1.** a plan of travel. **2.** an account of a journey.

its pron. the possessive form of **it**: *The baby lost its rattle.*

Its is a third person singular pronoun. It is sometimes called a *determiner* or a *possessive adjective*.
Don't confuse this with **it's**, which is the short form of **it is** or **it has**.

it's contraction of *it is* or *it has*.

Don't confuse this with **its**, which is the possessive form of **it**.

itself *pron.* **1.** the reflexive form of **it**: *This kettle turns itself off after boiling.* **2.** an emphatic form of **it**: *The actors were good but the movie itself was not worth watching.* **3.** in its normal state: *Now that the guests have left, the house is itself again.*

IVF *n.* the fertilisation of an egg by a sperm in a test tube, the resulting embryo being placed in a woman's uterus to develop. This is short for **in-vitro fertilisation**.

ivory *n.* (*pl.* **-ries**) the hard white substance composing teeth or tusks.

ivy *n.* (*pl.* **ivies**) an evergreen climbing plant.

J, j

J, j *n.* the tenth letter of the English alphabet.

jab *v.* (**jabbed, jabbing**) **1.** to thrust or poke (something) smartly or sharply. –*n.* **2.** a poke with the end or point of something.

jabber *v.* to utter rapidly, indistinctly, or nonsensically.

jabiru /dʒæbəˈruː/ *n.* a type of white stork found in Aust. that has a green-black head, neck and tail.

jacaranda *n.* a tall tropical tree with lavender-blue flowers.

jack *n.* **1.** a device for raising heavy weights short distances. **2.** any of the 4 knaves in playing cards. **3. a.** a knucklebone or plastic imitation used in a children's game. **b.** (*pl.*) the game itself. **4.** a small bowl used as a mark for the players to aim at, in the game of bowls. –*v.* **5.** to lift or raise with or as with a jack. –*phr.* **6. jack up**, *Aust. Informal* to refuse; be obstinate; resist.

jackal *n.* any of several types of wild dog.

jackaroo *n.* **1.** a young man gaining practical experience on a sheep or cattle station. –*v.* **2.** to work as a trainee on such a station. Also, **jackeroo**.

jackass *n.* **1.** a male donkey. **2.** a very stupid or foolish person.

jacket *n.* **1.** a short coat. **2.** Also, **dust jacket.** a detachable paper cover for protecting the binding of a book.

jackhammer *n.* a handheld drill operated by compressed air, used for drilling rocks.

jack-in-the-box *n.* a toy consisting of a figure, enclosed in a box, which springs out when the lid is unfastened.

jackknife *n.* (*pl.* **-knives**) **1.** a large knife with a blade that folds into the handle. –*v.*

(**-knifed, -knifing**) **2.** to bend or fold up, like a jackknife. **3.** (of a semitrailer or a car pulling a caravan, etc.) to go out of control in such a way that the trailer swings round towards the driver's cab.

jackpot *n.* the chief prize to be won in a lottery, a game or contest.

jade *n.* a mineral, sometimes green, highly esteemed as an ornamental stone.

jaded *adj.* **1.** worn out. **2.** sated.

jaffle *n. Aust.* (*from trademark*) a sealed toasted sandwich with a savoury or sweet filling.

jagged *adj.* having notches, teeth, or ragged edges.

jaguar *n.* a large, ferocious, spotted wild cat.

jail *n.* a prison. Also, **gaol**.

Nowadays **jail** is the main spelling of this word in Australian English, although it used to be **gaol**. This is why you will sometimes see **gaol** in the names of some older prisons, such as *Parramatta Gaol*.

jalopy *n.* (*pl.* **-pies**) *Informal* an old, decrepit, or unprepossessing motor car.

jam¹ *v.* (**jammed, jamming**) **1.** to press or squeeze tightly between bodies or surfaces. **2.** to fill or block up by crowding. **3.** to (cause to) become wedged, caught, or displaced, so that it cannot work. **4.** *Radio* to interfere with (signals, etc.) by sending out others of approximately the same frequency. –*n.* **5.** the act of jamming. **6.** the state of being jammed. **7.** a mass of vehicles, people, or objects jammed together. **8.** *Informal* a difficult or awkward situation; a fix. –*phr.* **9. jam on**, to apply (brakes) forcibly.

Don't confuse this with **jamb**.

jam² *n.* a preserve of boiled and crushed fruit.

jam³ *n.* a meeting of musicians for the spontaneous and improvisatory performance of music. Also, **jam session**.

jamb *n.* a vertical piece forming the side of a doorway or window.

Don't confuse this with **jam**, which means to become stuck (*The door jammed*). It can also be a sweet spread made from fruit, which you put on bread.

jangle v. **1.** to produce a harsh or discordant sound. *–n.* **2.** a harsh or discordant sound.

janitor n. **1.** a caretaker. **2.** a doorkeeper or porter.

jar¹ n. a broad-mouthed earthen or glass vessel.

jar² v. (**jarred, jarring**) **1.** to produce a harsh, grating sound. **2.** to have a harshly unpleasant effect upon the nerves, feelings, etc. **3.** to be at variance; conflict.

jarrah n. a large tree of westn Aust.

jasmine n. a climbing plant with fragrant flowers.

jasper n. a coloured variety of quartz.

jaundice /ˈdʒɔndəs/ n. **1.** a disease characterised by yellowness of the skin, etc. *–v.* (**-diced, -dicing**) **2.** to distort or prejudice, as with pessimism, jealousy, resentment, etc.

jaunt v., n. to (make) a short journey, especially for pleasure.

jaunty adj. (**-tier, -tiest**) easy and sprightly in manner or bearing.

javelin n. a spear to be thrown by hand.

jaw n. one of the 2 bones or structures (upper and lower) which form the framework of the mouth.

jay n. any of a number of noisy birds, as certain currawongs, etc.

jaywalk v. to cross a street otherwise than by a pedestrian crossing.

jazz n. **1.** a type of popular music marked by frequent improvisation and unusually accented rhythms. *–phr.* **2. jazz up**, *Informal* to put vigour and variety into.

jealous adj. **1.** inclined to or troubled by suspicions or fears of rivalry, as in love or aims. **2.** solicitous or vigilant in maintaining or guarding something. **–jealousy**, n.

jeans pl. n. trousers made of denim or other sturdy fabric.

Don't confuse **jeans** with **genes**, which are the biological units responsible for passing on hereditary characteristics.

jeep n. a small military motor vehicle.

jeer v. to speak or shout derisively.

jehad n. → **jihad**.

jelly n. (pl. **-lies**) a food preparation of a soft, elastic consistency.

jellyfish n. (pl. **-fish** or **-fishes**) any of various marine invertebrates of a soft, jelly-like structure.

For information about the different plural forms, see the note at **fish**.

jemmy n. (pl. **-mies**) a short crowbar.

jeopardy n. hazard or risk of loss or harm. **–jeopardise, jeopardize**, v.

jerk n. **1.** a quick, sharp thrust, pull, throw, or the like. **2.** *Informal* a stupid or naive person. *–v.* **3.** to move or throw with a quick, suddenly arrested motion.

jersey n. **1.** a close-fitting, usually woollen, outer garment; jumper. **2.** a machine-knitted fabric.

jest n. **1.** a witticism, joke, or pleasantry. **2.** sport or fun. *–v.* **3.** to speak in a playful or humorous way.

jet¹ n. **1.** a stream of fluid from a nozzle, orifice, etc. **2.** a jet plane. *–v.* (**jetted, jetting**) **3.** to spout. **4.** to fly in a jet plane.

jet² n. a hard black coal, used when polished for making beads, jewellery, buttons, etc.

jet plane n. an aeroplane operated by jet propulsion, where a high velocity jet of gas is discharged from the rear.

jet ski n. (from *trademark*) a small, powered vehicle for one person that skims the water.

jettison v. to throw (cargo, etc.) overboard, especially to lighten a vessel or aircraft in distress.

jetty n. (pl. **-ties**) a wharf or landing pier.

jewel n. a cut and polished precious or semiprecious stone. –**jeweller**, n. –**jewellery**, n.

jewfish n. (pl. **-fish** or **-fishes**) any of several species of large food fishes.

For information about the different plural forms, see the note at **fish**.

jiffy n. (pl. **-fies**) Informal a very short time. Also, **jiff**.

jig[1] n. a device for holding the work in a machine tool.

jig[2] n. **1.** a rapid, lively dance. –v. (**jigged, jigging**) **2.** to move with a jerky or bobbing motion.

jigger[1] n. a measure for alcohol used in cocktails.

jigger[2] v. to break or destroy.

jiggle v. to move up and down or to and fro with short, quick jerks.

jigsaw puzzle n. small, irregularly shaped pieces of cardboard, which, when correctly fitted together, form a picture.

jihad /'dʒihæd, 'dʒɪhad/ n. Islam **1.** the spiritual struggle to be righteous and follow God's path. **2.** a struggle or holy war in support of Islam against unbelievers. Also, **jehad**.

jillaroo n. a young woman gaining practical experience on a sheep or cattle station. Also, **jilleroo**.

jilt v. to cast off (a lover or sweetheart) after encouragement or engagement.

jingle v. **1.** to make clinking or tinkling sounds. –n. **2.** a clinking or tinkling sound. **3.** a simple, repetitious, catchy rhyme set to music.

jingoism n. fervent and excessive patriotism.

jinx Informal –n. **1.** a person, thing, or influence supposed to bring bad luck. –v. **2.** to bring bad luck to someone.

jitters phr. **the jitters,** Informal nervousness; nerves.

jive n. a dance performed to beat music.

job[1] n. **1.** an individual piece of work done in the routine of one's occupation or trade.

2. a post of employment. –v. (**jobbed, jobbing**) **3.** to work at jobs, or odd pieces of work.

job[2] (**jobbed, jobbing**) v. Aust. Informal to jab; hit; punch.

jockey n. someone who professionally rides horses in races.

jockstrap n. Informal a support for the genitals worn by male athletes, dancers, etc.

jocular adj. given to, characterised by, intended for, or suited to joking or jesting.

jocund /'dʒɒkənd/ adj. cheerful; merry.

jodhpurs /'dʒɒdpəz/ pl. n. riding breeches reaching to the ankle, and fitting closely from the knee down.

joey n. (pl. **-eys**) Aust. any young animal, especially a kangaroo.

jog v. (**jogged, jogging**) **1.** to move or shake with a push or jerk. **2.** to stir up by hint or reminder. **3.** to run at a slow, regular pace.

jogger n. **1.** a person who jogs for sport or exercise. **2.** Also, **jogging shoe.** a type of shoe suitable for jogging; runner.

joggle v. to shake slightly; move to and fro as by repeated jerks.

John Dory n. (pl. **-ry** or **-ries**) a thin, deep-bodied food fish.

For information about the different plural forms, see the note at **fish**.

join v. **1.** to come, be, or put together, in contact or connection. **2.** to become a member of. **3.** to come into the company of. **4.** to take part with others (in). –n. **5.** a place or line of joining; a seam.

joiner n. a worker in wood who constructs the fittings of a house, furniture, etc. –**joinery**, n.

joint n. **1.** the place or part in which 2 things, or parts of one thing, are joined. **2.** one of the portions into which a carcass is divided by a butcher, especially one ready for cooking. **3.** Informal someone's house, unit, office, etc. **4.** Informal a marijuana cigarette. –adj. **5.** shared by or common to 2 or more. **6.** sharing or acting in common. –*v.* **7.** to unite by a joint or joints. **8.** to divide at a joint, or separate into pieces.

joist *n.* any of the parallel lengths of timber, steel, etc., used for supporting floors, ceilings, etc.

jojoba /həˈhoʊbə, hoʊˈhoʊbə/ *n.* an evergreen shrub having edible seeds containing an oil with many uses.

joke *n.* **1.** something said or done to excite laughter or amusement. **2.** an amusing or ridiculous circumstance. **3.** *Informal* someone or something that is extremely bad, pathetic, etc.: *The team's performance today was a joke; That new player is a joke.* –*v.* **4.** to speak or act in a playful or merry way. **5.** to say something in mere sport, rather than in earnest.

Note that if you call someone 'a joke', as in def. 3, you are intending to insult them.

joker *n.* an extra playing card in a pack, used in some games.

jolly *adj.* (**-lier, -liest**) **1.** in good spirits. –*adv.* **2.** *Informal* extremely; very.

jolt *v.* **1.** to jar or shake as by a sudden rough thrust. –*n.* **2.** a jolting shock or movement.

jonquil *n.* a plant with white or yellow sweet-smelling flowers.

jostle *v.* **1.** to strike or push roughly or rudely against. **2.** to collide (*with*) or strike or push (*against*) as in passing or in a crowd.

jot *n.* **1.** the least part of something; a little bit. –*v.* (**jotted, jotting**) **2.** to write or mark briefly (*down*).

joule *n.* a measure of work or energy in the metric system. Symbol: J

journal *n.* **1.** a daily record; diary. **2.** a newspaper, especially a daily one. **3.** any periodical or magazine, especially one published by an academic or other society.

journalism *n.* the occupation of writing for, editing, and producing newspapers and other periodicals, and television and radio shows. –**journalist**, *n.*

journey *n.* (*pl.* **-neys**) **1.** a course of travel. –*v.* (**-neyed, -neying**) **2.** to make a journey; travel.

joust *n.* a combat in which 2 armoured knights on horseback opposed each other with lances.

jovial *adj.* having or showing a hearty, joyous humour.

jowl *n.* **1.** a jaw, especially the underjaw. **2.** the cheek. **3.** a fold of flesh hanging from the jaw.

joy *n.* an emotion of keen or lively pleasure; great gladness. –**joyful, joyous**, *adj.*

joystick *n.* **1.** the control stick of an aeroplane. **2.** a stick used to control the movement of the cursor on a computer screen.

jube *n.* a chewy sweet or lolly. Also, **jujube**.

jubilant *adj.* expressing or exciting joy.

jubilation *n.* the act of rejoicing.

jubilee *n.* the celebration of any of certain anniversaries.

judge *n.* **1.** a public officer authorised to hear and determine causes in a court of law. **2.** a person appointed to decide in any competition or contest. –*v.* (**judged, judging**) **3.** to try (a person or a case) as a judge does; pass sentence (on or in). **4.** to form a judgement or opinion (of or upon).

judgement *n.* **1.** the act of judging. **2.** *Law* the judicial decision of a cause in court. **3.** ability to judge justly or wisely. **4.** the forming of an opinion, estimate, notion, or conclusion. Also, **judgment**.

judgemental *adj.* inclined to pass judgement, especially in a dogmatic fashion. Also, **judgmental**.

judicial *adj.* **1.** relating to legal justice. **2.** relating to courts of law or to judges.

judiciary *n.* (*pl.* **-ries**) the system of courts of justice in a country.

judicious *adj.* having, exercising, or showing good judgement.

The more usual word is **wise**.

judo n. a style of self-defence derived from Japanese wrestling.

jug n. a vessel for holding liquids, commonly having a handle.

juggernaut n. **1.** anything requiring blind devotion or extreme sacrifice. **2.** any large, relentless, destructive force.

juggle v. **1.** to keep (several objects) in continuous motion in the air tossing and catching. **2.** to manipulate or alter by artifice or trickery.

jugular adj. **1.** Anat. of or relating to the throat or neck. —n. **2.** one of the large veins in the neck.

juice n. the liquid part of plant or animal substance. —**juicy**, adj.

jukebox n. a coin-operated machine which plays a selected musical item or items.

jumble v. **1.** to put or throw together without order. —n. **2.** a confused mixture.

jumbo n. (pl. **-bos**) **1.** Informal an elephant. **2.** Also, **jumbo jet**, a very large jet. —adj. **3.** very large.

jumbuck n. Aust. Informal a sheep.

jump v. **1.** to spring clear of the ground or over (an obstacle) etc., by a sudden muscular effort; leap. **2.** to move suddenly or abruptly, as from surprise or shock; start. **3.** to pass abruptly, over intervening stages. —n. **4.** the act of jumping; a leap. **5.** a space or obstacle or apparatus cleared in a leap. **6.** a sudden rise in amount, price, etc. **7.** an abrupt transition from one point or thing to another.

jumper n. an outer garment, usually knitted, for the upper part of the body; pullover; sweater.

jumpy adj. (**-pier**, **-piest**) showing nervousness, fear, excitement, etc.

junction n. **1.** the act of joining; combination. **2.** a place of joining or meeting.

juncture n. **1.** a point of time, especially a critical or important one. **2.** the line or point at which 2 bodies are joined.

jungle n. a thick tropical rainforest.

junior adj. **1.** younger. **2.** of lower rank or standing. —n. **3.** a person who is younger than another. **4.** any minor or child, especially a male. **5.** someone employed as the subordinate of another. **6.** Law any barrister who is not a Senior Counsel or Queen's Counsel.

juniper n. any of several coniferous evergreen shrubs or trees.

junk¹ n. **1.** any old or discarded material. **2.** anything regarded as worthless.

junk² n. a kind of seagoing ship used in Chinese and other waters.

junket n. **1.** a sweet custard-like food. **2.** a feast or merrymaking; a picnic.

junkie n. Informal a drug addict.

junk mail n. advertising material sent by post.

junta /ˈdʒʌntə, ˈhʊntə/ n. a small ruling group in a country, especially one which has come to power after a revolution.

jurisdiction n. **1.** the right, power, or authority to administer justice by hearing and determining controversies. **2.** power; authority; control.

jurisprudence n. **1.** the science or philosophy of law. **2.** a body or system of laws. —**jurisprudent**, n., adj. —**jurisprudential**, adj.

jurist n. someone versed in the law.

jury n. (pl. **-ries**) **1.** a body of people selected for a trial and sworn to deliver a verdict on questions of fact presented to them. **2.** a body of persons chosen to adjudge prizes, etc., as in a competition. —**juror**, n.

just adj. **1.** actuated by truth, justice, and lack of bias. **2.** based on right; lawful. **3.** true; correct. **4.** deserved, as a sentence, punishment, reward, etc. —adv. **5.** within a brief preceding time, or but a moment before. **6.** exactly or precisely: just what

I need. **7.** by a narrow margin; barely. **8.** only or merely. **9.** actually; truly; positively: *the view is just spectacular.*

justice *n.* **1.** the quality of being just. **2.** that which is just. **3.** the maintenance or administration of law, as by judicial or other proceedings. **4.** a judicial officer; a judge or magistrate.

justify *v.* (**-fied, -fying**) **1.** to show (an act, claim, etc.) to be just, right, or warranted. **2.** *Typesetting* to adjust exactly; make (lines) of the proper length by spacing. **–justification,** *n.*

jut *v.* (**jutted, jutting**) to extend (*out*) beyond the main body or line.

jute *n.* a strong fibre used for making fabrics, cordage, etc.

juvenile *adj.* **1.** relating to or intended for young people: *juvenile court.* **2.** childish; immature. *–n.* **3.** a young person; a youth.

Def. 2 is used in a disapproving way.

juxtapose to place in close proximity or side by side. **–juxtaposition,** *n.*

K, k

K, k *n.* the 11th letter of the English alphabet.

kaftan *n.* → caftan.

kaleidoscope *n.* an optical instrument in which pieces of coloured glass, etc., in a rotating tube are shown by reflection in continually changing symmetrical forms. –**kaleidoscopic,** *adj.*

Kanaka /kəˈnækə/ *n.* (*sometimes derog.*) a Pacific islander, formerly one brought to Aust. as a labourer.

kangaroo *n.* any of several herbivorous marsupials of the Aust. region, with powerful hind legs developed for leaping. Also, **roo.**

kaput *adj. Informal* **1.** smashed; ruined. **2.** broken; not working.

karaoke /kæriˈoʊki/ *n.* **1.** the entertainment of singing to a karaoke machine: *That restaurant offers karaoke.* –*adj.* **2.** (of bars, restaurants, etc.) equipped with a karaoke machine.

karaoke machine *n.* a music system which plays the backing music of a song with video clip and lyrics so one can sing along with it.

karate *n.* a method of defensive fighting, originating in Japan, in which hands, elbows, feet, and knees are the only weapons used.

karri /ˈkæri/ *n.* (*pl.* -**ris**) a tree valued for its hard, durable timber.

kauri *n.* (*pl.* -**ris**) a tall coniferous tree of NZ, yielding a valuable timber and a resin.

kayak *n.* an Inuit hunting canoe, or similar canoe.

kebab *n.* **1.** → shish kebab. **2.** → doner kebab.

keel *n.* **1.** a long piece of timber, iron plates, or the like supporting the whole frame of a ship. –*phr.* **2. keel over,** *Informal* to collapse suddenly.

keen[1] *adj.* **1.** sharp. **2.** strong and clear, as hearing, eyesight, etc. **3.** having or showing great mental penetration or acumen. **4.** intense, as feeling, desire, etc. **5.** having a fondness or devotion: *keen on rock music.*

keen[2] *v.* to wail in lamentation for the dead.

keep *v.* (**kept, keeping**) **1.** to (cause to) continue in some place, state, or course specified. **2.** to have habitually in stock or for sale. **3.** to withhold from use; reserve. **4.** to maintain or carry on, as an establishment, business, etc.; manage. **5.** to maintain or support (a person, etc.). **6.** to save, or retain in possession. **7.** to continue unimpaired or without change. **8.** to stay (*away, back, off, out,* etc.). –*n.* **9.** subsistence; board and lodging. **10.** the central tower of a medieval castle. –*phr.* **11. for keeps,** *Informal* permanently.

keeping *n.* just conformity in things or elements associated together.

keepsake *n.* anything kept as a token of remembrance, friendship, etc.

keg *n.* a barrel, especially of beer.

kelp *n.* any of the large brown seaweeds.

kelpie *n.* one of a breed of Aust. sheepdogs.

kennel *n.* **1.** a dog house. **2.** (*usu. pl.*) an establishment where dogs are bred or boarded.

kept *v.* past tense and past participle of **keep.**

kerb *n.* a line of joined stones, concrete, or the like at the edge of a street, wall, etc.

kernel *n.* **1.** the softer, usually edible, part contained in the shell of a nut or the stone of a fruit. **2.** the central part of anything; the core.

kero *n. Aust., NZ Informal* kerosene.

kerosene *n.* a mixture of liquid hydrocarbons used for lamps, engines, heaters, etc. Also, **kerosine.**

ketchup *n.* *Chiefly US* tomato sauce. Also, **catsup**.

kettle *n.* a portable container in which to boil water.

kettledrum *n.* a tunable drum with a half-spherical base.

key *n.* (*pl.* **keys**) **1.** an instrument for fastening or opening a lock by moving its bolt. **2.** a means of attaining, understanding, solving, etc. **3.** a systematic explanation of abbreviations, symbols, etc. **4.** one of a set of levers or parts pressed in operating a computer, typewriter, musical instrument, etc. **5.** *Music* the keynote or tonic of a scale. *–adj.* **6.** chief; indispensable. **7.** identifying. *–v.* **8.** Also, **key in**. to enter (information) into a computer using a keyboard. **9.** to bring (*up*) to a particular degree of intensity of feeling. **10.** to adjust (one's speech, actions, etc.) to external factors, as the level of understanding of one's hearers.

keyboard *n.* the row or set of keys on a piano, computer, typewriter, etc. **–keyboarder**, *n.*

keynote *n.* **1.** *Music* the note on which a system of notes is founded; tonic. **2.** the main interest or determining principle of a speech, campaign, etc.

keypad *n.* a panel containing a set of keys for entering data or commands into an electronic machine, system, etc.

keystone *n.* something upon which associated things depend.

keystroke *n.* an instance of pressing down a key on a typewriter or computer keyboard.

khaki /ka'ki, 'kaki/ *n.* (*pl.* **-kis**) **1. a.** a dull yellowish brown. **b.** dull green with a yellowish or brownish tinge. **2.** stout cloth of this colour, worn especially by soldiers.

kibbutz /kɪ'buts/ *n.* (*pl.* **kibbutzim** /kɪ-'butsim, kɪbot'sim/) (in Israel) a communal agricultural settlement.

kick *v.* **1.** to strike (out) with the foot. **2.** to drive, force, make, etc., by or as by kicks.

3. *Football* to score (a goal) by a kick. **4.** *Informal* to resist, object, or complain. **5.** to recoil, as a firearm when fired. *–n.* **6.** the act of kicking; a blow or thrust with the foot. **7.** a recoil, as of a gun. **8.** *Informal* any thrill or excitement that gives pleasure. **9.** *Informal* vigour or energy. *–phr.* **10.** **kick out**, *Informal* to dismiss; get rid of.

kickback *n.* *Informal* **1.** a response, usually vigorous. **2.** any sum paid for favours received or hoped for.

kickboxing *n.* a form of boxing popular in Asian countries, in which the opponent can be kicked with the bare feet. **–kickboxer**, *n.* **–kickbox**, *v.*

kid¹ *n.* **1.** (leather made from the skin of) a young goat. **2.** *Informal* a child or young person. **3.** *Informal* a son or daughter.

Although informal, defs 2 and 3 are used very widely in speech, often in situations that might be considered rather formal. For example, it would be quite usual to use **kids** when talking about your children to a teacher or a doctor.

kid² *v.* (**kidded**, **kidding**) *Informal* to tease; banter; jest with.

kidnap *v.* (**-napped**, **-napping**) to carry off (a person) by unlawful force or by fraud, often with a demand for ransom. **–kidnapper**, *n.*

kidney *n.* (*pl.* **-neys**) either of a pair of bean-shaped glandular organs which excrete urine.

A medical word which describes things related to the kidneys is **renal**.

kidney bean *n.* the dried, somewhat kidney-shaped seed of the French bean.

kikuyu /kaɪ'kuju/ *n.* a lawn grass.

kill *v.* **1.** to deprive of life. **2.** to destroy. **3.** to defeat or veto (a legislative bill, etc.). *–n.* **4.** the act of killing (game, etc.). **5.** an animal or animals killed.

killing *n.* **1.** the act of someone or something that kills. **2.** *Informal* a stroke of extraordinary success.

kiln n. a furnace or oven, especially one for baking bricks.

kilo n. a kilogram.

kilobit n. *Computers* a unit of measurement of computer storage equal to 2^{10} (1024) bits. *Abbrev.*: Kb

kilobyte n. a unit of measurement of computer storage, equal to 1024 bytes. *Symbol*: K

kilogram n. a unit of weight in the metric system, equal to 1000 grams. *Symbol*: kg Also, **kilo**.

kilojoule n. a measure of work or energy in the metric system, equal to 1000 joules or the amount of food needed to produce it. *Symbol*: kJ

kilometre /ˈkɪləmitə, kəˈlɒmətə/ n. a unit of length in the metric system, equal to 1000 metres. *Symbol*: km

kilowatt n. a unit of power equal to 1000 watts. *Symbol*: kW

kilt n. any short, pleated skirt, especially one worn by men in the Scottish Highlands.

kimono /kɪˈmənou, kəˈmounou/ n. (*pl.* **-nos**) a wide-sleeved robe characteristic of Japanese costume.

kin n. relatives collectively.

kind¹ adj. of a good or benevolent nature or disposition. –**kindness**, **kindliness**, n. –**kindly**, adj., adv.

kind² n. **1.** a class or group of individuals of the same nature or character. **2.** nature or character as determining likeness or difference between things. –*phr.* **3. in kind**, in something of the same kind; in the same way. **4. kind of**, *Informal* after a fashion; to some extent.

Note that if you use the plural **kinds of** (as in def. 1), you can follow it with a singular or plural noun: *There are seventy different kinds of orchids on display; There are seventy different kinds of orchid on display.*

kindergarten n. a school or class for young children, usually under the age of 5 or 6.

kindle v. **1.** to set (a fire, flame, etc.) burning or blazing. **2.** to excite (feelings, etc.).

kindling /ˈkɪndlɪŋ/ n. material for starting a fire.

kindred n. **1.** a body of persons related to one another. –adj. **2.** associated by origin, nature, qualities, etc.

kinetic adj. **1.** relating to motion. **2.** caused by motion.

king n. **1.** a male sovereign. **2.** a chess piece.

kingdom n. **1.** a state having a king or queen as its head. **2.** a realm or province of nature.

kingfisher n. any of numerous fish- or insect-eating birds.

King's Counsel n. (in some legal systems) a member of the senior of the two grades of barrister. *Abbrev.*: KC Also, (when the reigning monarch is a woman), **Queen's Counsel**.

kink n. **1.** a twist or curl. **2.** a deviation, especially sexual. –**kinky**, adj.

kinship n. **1.** the state or fact of being of kin. **2.** relationship by nature, qualities, etc.; affinity.

kiosk n. **1.** a small, light structure for the sale of newspapers, cigarettes, etc. **2.** → **canteen** (def. 2).

kipper n. a smoked fish, especially a herring.

kismet n. fate; destiny.

kiss v. **1.** to touch or press (someone or something) with the lips in token of greeting, affection, etc. –n. **2.** the act of kissing.

kit n. **1.** a set or collection of tools, supplies, etc., for a specific purpose. **2.** a set or collection of parts to be assembled.

kitchen n. a room or place for cooking.

kite n. **1.** a light frame covered with some thin material, to be flown in the wind at the

kiteboard n. 1. a small surfboard used in kitesurfing. –v. 2. to engage in the sport of kitesurfing. **–kiteboarder**, n.

kitesurfing n. the sport of riding a kiteboard whilst being pulled by a motorboat and supported by a large controllable kite. Also, **kiteboarding**.

kitsch n. pretentious or worthless art, literature, etc.

kitten n. a young cat.

kitty n. (pl. **-ties**) a jointly held fund or collection.

kiwi n. any of several flightless birds of NZ.

kiwifruit n. a small fruit with hairy, brown skin and green flesh; Chinese gooseberry.

klaxon n. (from trademark) a type of warning hooter, originally used in motor vehicles.

kleptomania n. Psychol. an irresistible desire to steal, without regard to personal needs. **–kleptomaniac**, n.

knack n. a faculty or power of doing something with ease; aptitude.

knacker n. someone who buys old or useless horses for slaughter. **–knackery**, n.

knapsack n. a backpack. Also, **rucksack**.

knave n. 1. an unprincipled or dishonest fellow. 2. Cards a playing card bearing the formalised picture of a prince; jack. **–knavery**, n. **–knavish**, adj.

knead v. to work (dough, etc.) into a uniform mixture by pressing, folding and stretching.

knee n. 1. the joint between the thigh and the lower part of the leg. –v. (**kneed**, **kneeing**) 2. to strike or touch with the knee.

kneecap n. the flat, movable bone at the front of the knee.

kneel v. (**knelt** or **kneeled**, **kneeling**) to fall or rest on the knees or a knee.

knell n. the sound made by a bell rung slowly for a death or a funeral.

knew v. past tense of **know**.

knickerbockers pl. n. loosely fitting breeches gathered in at the knee. Also, **knickers**.

knickers pl. n. 1. women's or girls' underpants. 2. → knickerbockers.

knick-knack n. a pleasing trinket.

knife n. (pl. **knives**) 1. a cutting instrument consisting of a thin blade attached to a handle. –v. (**knifed**, **knifing**) 2. to cut, stab, etc., with a knife.

knight n. 1. Hist. a man, usually of noble birth, bound to chivalrous conduct. 2. a man upon whom the honorific Sir is conferred because of personal merit or for services rendered to the country. 3. a chess piece. –v. 4. to dub or create (a person) a knight.

knit v. (**knitted** or **knit**, **knitting**) 1. to make (a garment, fabric, etc.) by interlacing loops of yarn either with knitting needles or by machine. 2. to join or become joined closely and firmly together, as members or parts. 3. to contract, as the brow does in a frown. –n. 4. fabric produced by interlooping of a yarn or yarns. –phr. 5. **knit together**, to form a closely bound unit.

knob n. 1. a projecting part forming the handle of a door or the like. 2. a rounded lump or protuberance.

knock v. 1. to strike a sounding blow with the fist or anything hard, especially on a door, as in seeking admittance, etc. 2. (of an internal-combustion engine) to make a metallic noise as a result of faulty combustion. 3. to collide (against or into). 4. to drive, force, or render by a blow or blows. 5. Informal to criticise; find fault with. –n. 6. the act or sound of knocking. –phr. 7. **knock off**, Informal to stop an activity, especially work. 8. **knock out**, to render senseless.

knockout n. 1. the act of knocking out. 2. Informal a person or thing that excites admiration. 3. Informal an extremely good-looking person.

knoll n. a small, rounded hill.

knot *n.* **1.** an interlacement of a cord, rope, or the like, drawn tight, as for fastening 2 cords. **2.** the hard mass of wood where a branch joins the trunk of a tree. **3.** a unit of speed, used in marine and aerial navigation, and in meteorology. –*v.* (**knotted, knotting**) **4.** to tie or become tied in a knot or knots.

know *v.* (**knew, known, knowing**) **1.** to perceive or understand as fact or truth. **2.** to have fixed in the mind or memory. **3.** to be acquainted with (a thing, person, etc.), as by experience or report. **4.** to understand from experience or attainment: *to know how to swim.*

knowledge *n.* **1.** acquaintance with facts, truths, or principles, as from study or investigation. **2.** familiarity, as with a particular subject, gained by experience, report, etc.: *knowledge of human nature.* **3.** the fact or state of knowing or being aware of a fact, truth or circumstance: *It happened without my knowledge.* **4.** that which is known, or may be known. –**knowledgeable,** *adj.*

knuckle *n.* **1.** a joint of a finger. –*phr.* **2. knuckle down,** to apply oneself vigorously or earnestly, as to a task. **3. knuckle under,** to yield or submit.

knurl *n.* **1.** a small ridge or the like, especially one of a series. –*v.* **2.** to make knurls or ridges on.

koala *n.* a tailless, grey, furry, small Aust. marsupial, which eats the leaves of certain gum trees.

The term **koala bear** is sometimes used, although the koala is not a bear, so this is regarded by many people as incorrect.

kohl /koʊl/ *n.* a powder, used to darken the eyelids, emphasise eyebrows, etc.

komodo dragon *n.* a giant monitor of the island of Komodo in Indonesia; up to 3.5 m long.

kook *n. Informal* a strange or eccentric person. –**kooky,** *adj.*

kookaburra *n.* either of 2 Aust. kingfishers renowned for their call resembling human laughter.

kosher /ˈkɒʃə, ˈkoʊʃə/ *adj.* fit, lawful, or ritually permitted, according to the Jewish law.

kowtow /kaʊˈtaʊ/ *v.* to act in an obsequious manner.

kudos /ˈkjudɒs/ *n.* glory; renown.

kumquat /ˈkʌmkwɒt/ *n.* → **cumquat.**

kung-fu *n.* an ancient Chinese martial art resembling karate.

kurrajong *n.* a tree valued as fodder.

L, l

, l *n.* the 12th letter of the English alphabet.

label *n.* **1.** a slip of paper, etc., for affixing to something to indicate its nature, ownership, etc. **2.** *Informal* the trade name, especially of a record or clothing company. *–v.* (**-belled, -belling**) **3.** to affix a label to.

laboratory *n.* (*pl.* **-ries**) (a part of) a building fitted with apparatus for conducting scientific investigations or for manufacturing chemicals, medicines, etc.

laborious *adj.* requiring much labour, exertion, or perseverance.

labour *n.* **1.** physical work done for money. **2.** hard or fatiguing work. **3.** the time during which the uterine contractions of childbirth occur. *–v.* **4.** to perform labour; work; toil. Also, **labor**. *–***la-bourer**, *n.*

> Note that a **labourer** is someone who works at a job which requires physical effort rather than special skill or training. Compare this with **worker**, which usually has a more general meaning, referring to someone who works at a particular occupation, whether it requires special skills or not: *office worker; road worker.*

labrador *n.* one of a breed of dogs with black or golden coats.

labyrinth /'læbərɪnθ, 'læbrənθ/ *n.* a complicated arrangement of passages in which it is difficult to find one's way or to reach the exit.

lace *n.* **1.** a net-like ornamental fabric. **2.** a cord for holding or drawing together: *shoe laces*. *–v.* (**laced, lacing**) **3.** to fasten or draw together by a lace: *to lace shoes*. **4.** to intermix, as coffee with spirits.

lacerate *v.* **1.** to tear roughly; mangle. **2.** to hurt. *–***laceration**, *n.*

lack *n.* **1.** the absence of something required, desirable, etc. *–v.* **2.** to be deficient in, or without.

lackadaisical /lækə'deɪzɪkəl/ *adj.* sentimentally or affectedly languishing; weakly sentimental; listless.

lacklustre *adj.* lacking lustre or brightness; dull.

laconic *adj.* using few words.

lacquer *n.* a resinous varnish.

lactate *v.* (of mammals) to produce milk. *–***lactation**, *n.*

lactic acid *n. Chem.* an acid found in sour milk and in muscle tissue after exercise.

lactobacillus /ˌlæktoʊbə'sɪləs/ *n.* (*pl.* **-cilli** /-'sɪlaɪ/) any bacterium which produces large amounts of lactic acid in the fermentation of carbohydrates, especially in milk. See **acidophilus milk**.

lad *n.* a boy or youth.

ladder *n.* **1.** a structure of wood, etc., with 2 sidepieces joined by a series of spaced bars, forming a means of ascent or descent. **2.** a line in a stocking, etc., where a series of stitches have come undone.

laden *adj.* **1.** loaded; burdened. **2.** filled: *a tree laden with fruit.*

ladle *n.* **1.** a long-handled utensil with a cup-shaped bowl for holding liquids. *–v.* **2.** to convey with a ladle.

lady *n.* (*pl.* **-dies**) **1.** a woman of good manners, etc.: *to behave like a lady.* **2.** a polite term for any woman.

> Note that **lady**, def. 2, is a polite way of referring to a woman, as in *Ladies and gentlemen, could I have your attention please* or *There is a lady at the door to see you.* Some older people think that this is the best and most polite way to refer to a woman on all occasions. However, the usual word is **woman** and this is the term now preferred by most women except in situations where it is appropriate to be very polite.

ladybird n. a small beetle usually with an orange back spotted with black.

lady-in-waiting n. (pl. **ladies-in-waiting**) a woman in attendance upon a queen or princess.

lag v. (**lagged, lagging**) to move slowly; fall behind.

lager n. a type of beer.

lagoon n. any small, pond-like body of water.

laid v. past tense and past participle of **lay**[1].

lain v. past participle of **lie**[2].

lair[1] n. the den of a wild beast.

lair[2] n. Aust., NZ Informal a brash, flashily dressed young man.

lairy adj. Informal **1.** exhibitionistic; flashy. **2.** vulgar.

laissez faire /ˌleɪseɪ ˈfɛə/ n. the doctrine of non-interference, especially in the conduct of others. Also, **laisser faire.**

laity /ˈleɪəti/ n. laypeople, as distinguished from the clergy. —**laic,** adj.

lake n. a large body of water surrounded by land.

laksa /ˈlʌksə/ n. a spicy Malay dish consisting of fine rice vermicelli, vegetables, and often meat or tofu, served in a soup.

lama n. a Buddhist priest of some Asian countries.

Don't confuse this with **llama,** which is a type of animal from South America.

lamb n. a young sheep.

lame adj. physically disabled especially in the foot or leg.

Don't confuse this with **lamé.**

lamé /ˈlɑːmeɪ/ n. an ornamental fabric in which metallic threads are woven with silk, etc.

Don't confuse **lamé** with **lame.**

lament v. **1.** to feel or express sorrow or regret (for). —n. **2.** an expression of grief or sorrow. —**lamentable,** adj.

laminate v. **1.** to separate into thin layers. **2.** to construct by placing layer upon layer.

3. to coat (a document, etc.) with a fir layer of clear plastic.

lamington n. a cube of sponge cake co vered in chocolate icing and shredde coconut.

lamp n. a device using gas or electricity etc., to generate heat or light.

lampoon n. a satire upon a person, gov ernment, etc., in either prose or verse.

lamprey n. (pl. **-reys** or **-rey**) an eel-lik fish.

For information about the different plura forms, see the note at **fish.**

lance n. **1.** a long, spear-like weapon wit a metal head. —v. (**lanced, lancing**) t pierce (as) with a lance.

land n. **1.** the solid substance of the earth surface. **2.** agricultural areas as opposed t urban. —v. **3.** to bring to or put on lan or shore. **4.** to alight upon the ground a from an aeroplane, or after a jump. —phr **5. land with,** to give (someone) a tas which they may be unwilling to perform

landcare n. the sustainable management c the environment and natural resources i agriculture. Also, **land care.**

landfill n. **1.** material as garbage, buildin refuse, etc., deposited under layers of eart to raise the level of the site. **2.** the are raised in this fashion.

landing n. **1.** the act of arriving on land, a by a plane, etc. **2.** the floor at the head o foot of a flight of stairs.

landlord n. **1.** someone who owns an leases land, buildings, etc., to another **2.** the proprietor of a hotel. —**landlady,** n.

landlubber n. Naut. someone who live on land.

landmark n. **1.** a conspicuous object o land that serves as a guide, especially t vessels at sea. **2.** a prominent feature event, etc.

landmass n. a body of land, usually ex tensive, as a large island or continent, sur rounded by water. Also, **land mass.**

landscape n. an expanse of rural scenery visible from a single point.

landslide n. **1.** the sliding down of a mass of soil, etc., on a steep slope. **2.** an over-whelming electoral victory.

lane n. a narrow passage, track, etc., as between fences, houses, etc.

language n. **1.** communication by voice using sound symbols in conventional ways with conventional meanings. **2.** any system of such symbols used in such a way as to enable people to communicate intelligibly with one another.

languid adj. **1.** lacking in spirit; indifferent. **2.** lacking in vigour; slack; dull. –**languor**, n.

languish v. **1.** to be or become weak or feeble. **2.** to lose activity and vigour. **3.** to pine with longing for.

lank adj. **1.** lean; gaunt. **2.** (of hair) straight and limp. –**lanky**, adj.

lanky adj. (**-kier, -kiest**) ungracefully tall and thin. –**lankily**, adv. –**lankiness**, n.

lanolin n. a fatty substance, extracted from wool, used in ointments. Also, **lanoline**.

lantana n. a tropical plant, now a trouble-some weed in some areas.

lantern n. a transparent, protective case for enclosing a portable light.

lap¹ n. the front portion of the body from the waist to the knees when one sits.

lap² v. (**lapped, lapping**) **1.** to fold or wrap over or about something. **2.** to get a lap or more ahead of (a competitor) in racing. –n. **3.** a single circuit of the course in racing.

lap³ v. (**lapped, lapping**) **1.** to lick (up) (liquid). –phr. **2. lap up**, to receive avidly.

lapel n. that part of a coat collar folded back on the breast.

lapidary n. (pl. **-ries**) a person who cuts, polishes, etc., precious or semiprecious stones.

lapse n. **1.** a slip or slight error. **2.** a passing away, as of time. **3.** a sinking to a lower condition. –v. (**lapsed, lapsing**)

4. to pass slowly, silently, or by degrees. **5.** to cease to be in force or use.

laptop n. **1.** a portable computer, small enough to be operated while held on one's knees. –adj. **2.** of or relating to the laptop.

larceny n. (pl. **-nies**) Law the theft of the personal goods of another.

lard n. melted pig fat used in cookery.

larder n. a place where food is kept; a pantry.

large adj. being of more than common size, amount, or number.

largesse /lɑˈdʒɛs, -ʒəs/ n. generosity, especially with money. Also, **largess**.

lark¹ n. a small singing bird.

lark² n. a merry adventure; prank.

larrikin n. Aust., NZ Informal **1.** a mischievous young person. **2.** an uncultivated, rowdy, but good-natured person.

larva n. (pl. **-vae** /-viː/ or **-vas**) Entomology the young of any insect which undergoes metamorphosis.

Don't confuse **larva** with **lava**, which is the hot liquid rock that comes out of a volcano.

laryngitis /lærənˈdʒaɪtəs/ n. inflammation of the larynx.

larynx /ˈlærɪŋks/ n. (pl. **larynges** /ləˈrɪndʒiz/ or **larynxes**) the upper part of the throat containing the vocal cords; voice box.

lasagne /ləˈsanjə, ləˈzanjə/ n. **1.** a form of pasta cut into flat sheets. **2.** a dish made with this, especially with minced meat, tomato, and cheese. Also, **lasagna**.

lascivious /ləˈsɪvɪəs/ adj. inclined to lust; lewd.

This is often used in a disapproving way.

laser n. a device for producing a strong, sharply defined, single-colour beam of radiation with waves in phase.

laser disc n. a disc on which digital data, as music, text, or pictures, is stored as tiny pits in the surface, and is read or played by a laser beam which scans the surface of the disc.

lash n. **1.** the flexible, cord-like part of a whip. **2.** a swift stroke with a whip, etc., as a punishment. **3.** an eyelash. –v. **4.** to strike (out) vigorously (at) as with a weapon, whip, etc. **5.** to fasten with a rope, cord, etc.

lass n. a girl or young woman.

lassitude n. weariness.

lasso /læ'suː/ n. (pl. **-sos** or **-soes**) a long rope with a running noose at one end, used for catching horses, etc.

last[1] adj. **1.** coming after all others, as in time, order, or place. **2.** latest; most recent. **3.** being the only remaining. **4.** conclusive: the last word in an argument. –adv. **5.** after all others. **6.** most recently. –n. **7.** that which is last.

last[2] v. to continue in progress or existence; endure.

latch n. a device for holding a door, etc., closed.

late adj. **1.** coming after the usual or proper time. **2.** far advanced in time: a late hour. **3.** having died recently. –adv. **4.** after the usual or proper time, or after delay. **5.** until after the usual time; until late at night.

lately adv. recently.

latent adj. hidden; present, but not apparent. –**latency**, n.

lateral adj. relating to the side: a lateral view.

latex n. Bot. a milky liquid in certain plants, as rubber trees.

lath /lɑːθ/ n. (pl. **laths** /lɑːðz, lɑːθs/) a thin, narrow strip of wood.

lathe n. a machine for use in working metal, wood, etc.

lather n. foam made from soap moistened with water.

latitude /'lætɪtjuːd/ n. **1.** Geog. the angular distance north or south from the equator of a point on the earth's surface, measured on the meridian of the point. **2.** freedom

of action, attitude, etc., from narrow restrictions.

latrine n. a toilet, especially in a camp, etc.

latte /'lɑːteɪ/ n. → **cafe latte**

latter adj. **1.** being the 2nd mentioned of 2 (opposed to former). **2.** later in time. **3.** nearer to the end or close. –**phr. 4. the latter**, the item or person (out of 2) last mentioned.

lattice n. a structure of crossed wooden, etc., strips with open spaces between, used as a screen, fence, etc.

laud /lɔːd/ v. to praise.

laugh v. **1.** to express mirth, joy, contempt, etc., by an explosive, inarticulate sound of the voice, facial expressions, etc. –n. **2.** the act or sound of laughing. **3.** the cry of an animal, as the hyena, or the call of a bird, as the kookaburra, that resembles human laughter. **4.** (often ironic) a cause for laughter: That's a laugh. –phr. **5. have the (last) laugh**, to prove ultimately successful; win after an earlier defeat. –**laughter**, n.

launch[1] n. a heavy, open or half-covered boat.

launch[2] v. **1.** to set (a boat) afloat. **2.** to set going.

launder v. **1.** to wash and iron (clothes, etc.). **2.** to make (money from illegal sources) appear legal.

laundromat n. Orig. US a public laundry with coin-operated washing machines, dryers, etc. Also, **laundrette**.

laundry n. (pl. **-dries**) **1.** articles of clothing, etc., to be washed. **2.** (a room in a house, etc., used for) the washing of clothes.

laurel n. **1.** a small evergreen tree. **2.** (usu. pl.) honour won, as by achievement.

laurel wreath n. a wreath made from the foliage of the laurel or bay tree, seen as an emblem of distinction.

lava n. the molten rock which issues from a volcano.

Don't confuse this with **larva**, which is the young of an insect.

lavatory *n.* (*pl.* **-ries**) (a room with) a toilet.

lavender *n.* a plant with fragrant, pale purple flowers.

lavish *adj.* **1.** (oft. fol. by *in*, *with* or *of*) using or giving generously: *lavish in one's praise.* –*v.* **2.** to use or give generously.

law *n.* **1.** the principles and regulations made by government. **2.** the profession which deals with law and legal procedure. **3.** (in philosophical and scientific use) a statement of a relation between events which is consistent under the same conditions. –**lawful**, *adj.*

lawn[1] *n.* a stretch of grass-covered land, especially one closely mowed.

lawn[2] *n.* a light linen or cotton fabric.

lawn bowls *n.* a game in which the players roll weighted balls along a very smooth lawn, aiming to bring them as near as possible to a stationary ball (the jack). Also, **bowls**.

lawyer *n.* someone whose profession it is to give legal advice and represent people in court.

A lawyer can be a **barrister**, who presents cases in court, or a **solicitor**, who advises clients and prepares cases for barristers to present.

lax *adj.* **1.** not strict; careless or negligent. **2.** loose or slack.

laxative *n.*, *adj. Med.* (a substance) mildly stimulating to the bowels.

lay[1] *v.* (**laid**, **laying**) **1.** to place in a position of rest. **2.** to bring forth and deposit (eggs). **3.** to set (a table). **4.** to present as a claim, charge, etc. **5.** to place on or over a surface, as paint, coverings, etc. –*n.* **6.** the position in which a thing is laid. –*phr.* **7. lay by**, to put away for future use. **8. lay into**, to attack with blows. **9. lay off**, **a.** to dismiss, sometimes temporarily, as an employee. **b.** *Informal* to desist. **10. lay on**, to provide or supply.

Don't confuse **lay** with **lie**[2], which is similar in meaning, but used in a different way. Lie does not normally take an object (*The dog lies on the bed*), while **lay** does take an object (*He's laying the table*). Confusingly, the past tense of **lie** is **lay** (*The dog lay on the bed all day yesterday*). The past form of **lay** is **laid** (*He laid the table earlier*).

lay[2] *v.* past tense of **lie**[2].

lay[3] *adj.* relating to the people or laity, as distinguished from the clergy.

lay-by *n. Aust.*, *NZ* the reserving of an article by payment of a cash deposit. Also, **layby**.

layer *n.* a thickness of some material laid on a surface.

layman *n.* (*pl.* **-men**) **1.** a man who is not a member of the clergy. **2.** a man who is not a member of a particular profession: *He is a layman when it comes to computers.*

Note that you can use **layperson** if you are not particularly talking about a man, or if you don't know the sex of the person you're referring to.

layperson *n.* **1.** a person who is not a member of the clergy. **2.** a person who is not a member of a particular profession: *It is very difficult for the layperson to understand computer jargon.*

lazy *adj.* (**-zier**, **-ziest**) disinclined to exertion or work; idle. –**laze**, *v.*

leach *v.* to cause (water, etc.) to percolate through something.

Don't confuse this with **leech**, which is a small bloodsucking worm.

lead[1] /lid/ *v.* (**led**, **leading**) **1.** to go before or with (someone) to show the way. **2.** to go first. **3.** to guide in direction, opinion, etc.; to influence: *to lead astray.* **4.** to bring (water, wire, etc.) in a particular course. **5.** to command, or direct (an army, organisation, etc.). **6.** to go through or pass (life, etc.): *to lead a life of crime.* **7.** to afford passage (*to*) a place, etc.: *The road leads to the town.* –*n.* **8.** the first or foremost position. **9.** the extent of advance. **10.** a strap for holding a dog or other animal in check. **11.** a clue. **12.** *Elect.* an insulated wire used to connect pieces of electrical apparatus. *–adj.* **13.** solo or dominating: *a lead guitar.*

lead² /led/ *n.* **1.** *Chem.* a heavy, comparatively soft, malleable bluish-grey metal. *Symbol:* Pb **2.** a plummet for measuring the depth of water.

leaden *adj.* **1.** made of lead. **2.** inertly heavy, and hard to move.

leader *n.* **1.** someone or something that leads. **2.** → **editorial**.

leaf *n.* (*pl.* **leaves**) **1.** one of the flat, usually green, organs on the stem of a plant. **2.** any of the sheets of paper, usually printed on both sides, that make up the pages of a book. **3.** a thin sheet of metal, etc. **4.** a detachable flat part, as of a tabletop, etc. *–phr.* **5.** **leaf through**, to turn the pages of quickly.

leaflet *n.* a small sheet of printed matter, as for distribution.

league¹ *n.* **1.** (a group of people, nations, etc., making) an agreement for mutual benefit and promotion of common interests. **2.** a category or class: *They are not in the same league.* **3.** a society or association, especially one with a national or state-wide structure and local branches. **4.** (*upper case*) → **Rugby League**. *–phr.* **5.** **in league**, allied (*with*).

league² *n.* a former unit of measure.

leak *n.* **1.** an unintended hole, etc., allowing fluid, gas, etc., to enter or escape. **2.** an (apparently) accidental disclosure of information. *–v.* **3.** to (let water, etc.) pass in or out through a hole, etc. **4.** to give out (confidential information), especially to the media. *–phr.* **5.** **leak out**, to become known, not by design. **–leakage**, *n.*

Don't confuse **leak** with **leek**, which is a type of vegetable.

lean¹ *v.* (**leaned** *or* **leant** /lent/, **leaning**) **1.** to bend in a particular direction. **2.** to

rest against something for support. **3.** to depend or rely.

lean² *adj.* **1.** (of persons or animals) thin; not plump. **2.** (of meat) containing little fat.

leap *v.* (**leapt** /lept/ *or* **leaped**, **leaping**) **1.** to spring or jump (over). **2.** to pass, come, rise, etc., as if with a bound: *to leap to a conclusion.* *–n.* **3.** a spring, jump, or bound.

leap year *n.* a year containing 366 days, or one day (29 February) more than the ordinary year.

learn *v.* (**learned** /lɜnd/ *or* **learnt**, **learning**) to acquire knowledge of, or skill in, by study, instruction, or experience.

learned /ˈlɜnəd/ *adj.* having much knowledge gained by study; scholarly.

lease *n.* **1.** a contract conveying property to another for a definite period in return for regular rent payments. *–v.* **2.** to grant the temporary possession or use of (lands, etc.) to another for rent; let. **3.** to hold by a lease, as a flat, house, etc.

Note that the verb **lease** can be used in two ways. Someone can lease an apartment *to* you and charge you rent for it, or you can lease an apartment *from* someone and pay them rent for it. The expression *to lease an apartment* is therefore ambiguous, but its context will normally make the meaning clear.

leash *n.* a lead for a dog.

least *adj.* **1.** smallest in size, amount or extent: *the least chance of winning.* *–n.* **2.** the smallest in size, amount or extent: *the least of my problems.* *–adv.* **3.** to the smallest extent, or in the smallest amount: *the least expensive coat.* *–phr.* **4.** **at least**, **a.** at the lowest calculation or judgement: *He must be at least fifty years old.* **b.** at any rate: *I feel very sick, but at least I don't have to go to school.*

Def. 1 is a form of the adjective **little**, meaning 'not much'. It is the *superlative* form. The other form (the *comparative*), meaning 'smaller in size, amount or extent', is **less**: *We have less room in the new school.* **Less** is also the other form of the adverb **least** (def. 3): *Choose the least expensive present.*

leather *n.* the skin of animals prepared for use by tanning.

leave¹ *v.* (**left, leaving**) **1.** to go away, depart (from). **2.** to let stay or use as specified. **3.** to give for use after one's death or departure. **4.** to have as a remainder after subtraction: *2 from 4 leaves 2.* –*phr.* **5. leave out**, to omit or exclude.

leave² *n.* **1.** permission to do something. **2.** permission to be absent, or the period of absence, as from duty. **3.** a farewell.

leaven /'levən/ *n.* a mass of fermenting dough reserved for producing fermentation in a new batch of dough.

lecher *n.* a man constantly making sexual advances. –**lechery,** *n.* –**lecherous,** *adj.*

lectern *n.* a reading desk, especially in a church.

lecture *n.* **1.** a speech delivered before an audience, especially for instruction. –*v.* **2.** to give a lecture (to).

led *v.* past tense and past participle of **lead¹**.

ledge *n.* any relatively narrow, horizontal projecting part.

ledger *n.* *Bookkeeping* an account book with columns for credits and debits.

lee *n.* the side sheltered from the wind.

leech *n.* a bloodsucking worm.

> Don't confuse this with **leach**, which is to cause water, etc., to filter through something.

leek *n.* an onion-like plant.

> Don't confuse this with **leak**, which is a hole or crack that lets liquid or gas in or out accidentally.

leer *n.* a sideways glance, especially a sly or insulting one.

leeway *n.* *Informal* extra space, time, money, etc.

left¹ *adj.* **1.** relating to the side which is turned towards the west when a person or thing is facing north (opposed to *right*). –*n.* **2.** the left side. –*phr.* **3. the Left**, a political party and its supporters favouring socialist or radical policies.

left² *v.* past tense and past participle of **leave¹**.

left-handed *adj.* using the left hand to write and perform other common tasks.

leftover *n.* something remaining.

leg *n.* **1.** one of the limbs which support and move the body. **2.** something resembling a leg in use, position, or appearance. **3.** a portion of a race, journey, etc.

legacy *n.* (*pl.* **-cies**) **1.** *Law* a gift of property, especially money, by will; a bequest. **2.** a consequence.

legal *adj.* **1.** appointed, established, or authorised by law. **2.** of or relating to law. –**legalise, legalize,** *v.*

legate *n.* an official representative of the pope. –**legation,** *n.*

legatee *n.* someone who receives a legacy.

legend *n.* **1.** a story handed down by tradition and popularly accepted as based on historical fact. **2.** an inscription. **3.** *Informal* an admirable person, especially one who excels in a particular field. –**legendary,** *adj.*

> Compare def. 1 with **myth**, which is an ancient story about gods, heroes and supernatural happenings, often made up to explain happenings in nature.

leggings *pl. n.* a covering for the leg.

legible *adj.* able to be read (easily). –**legibility,** *n.*

legion *n.* **1.** an infantry brigade in the army of ancient Rome. **2.** a type of modern military body, as the Foreign Legion. **3.** a multitude of persons or things.

legislation *n.* (the act of making) a law or a body of laws. –**legislate,** *v.* –**legislative,** *adj.*

legislature /'ledʒəsleıtʃə, -lətʃə/ *n.* the legislative body of a country or state.

legitimate adj. **1.** according to law; lawful. **2.** born in wedlock. **3.** genuine; not spurious. –**legitimacy**, n.

Def. 2 is not commonly used nowadays.

legume n. (the edible pod of) a pod-bearing plant.

leisure /ˈlɛʒə/ n. time free from the demands of work; ease.

leisurely adj. unhurried.

lemming n. a small rodent noted for its mass migrations in periods of population increase.

lemon n. **1.** a yellowish acid fruit. **2.** a clear, light yellow colour. **3.** Informal something disappointing or unpleasant.

lemonade n. a lemon-flavoured carbonated soft drink.

lend v. (**lent**, **lending**) **1.** to give the temporary use of (money, etc.) for a fee. **2.** to grant the use of (something) with the understanding that it shall be returned. **3.** to adapt (oneself or itself) to something: The room lends itself to study.

Compare defs 1 and 2 with **borrow**, which is to take something to use for a short time, on the understanding that you will return it.

length n. **1.** the measure of anything from end to end. **2.** extent from beginning to end of a series, book, etc. **3.** a piece of known length: a length of fabric. –**lengthen**, v.

lenient adj. gentle or merciful, as in treatment, spirit, etc.

lens n. (pl. **lenses**) a piece of transparent substance, usually glass, with one or both surfaces curved for converging or dispersing light rays, as in magnifying, or in correcting defective eyesight.

lentil n. an annual plant with flattened, edible seeds.

leonine adj. lion-like.

leopard n. a large, ferocious, spotted carnivore of the cat family.

leotard n. a close-fitting garment worn by acrobats, dancers, etc.

leper n. a person affected with leprosy.

leprechaun /ˈlɛprəkɔn/ n. in Irish folklore, a little sprite, or goblin.

leprosy n. a mildly infectious disease marked by sores, loss of fingers and toes etc.

lesbian n. **1.** a female homosexual. –adj. **2.** relating to female homosexuality.

lesion n. an injury; wound.

less adj. **1.** smaller in size, amount or extent: to use less water. –adv. **2.** to a smaller extent or in a smaller amount: less expensive. –prep. **3.** minus; taking away: It costs $200 less 10 per cent – that's $180.

Def. 1 is a form of the adjective **little**, meaning 'not much'. It is the comparative form. The other form (the superlative) form, meaning 'smallest in size, amount or extent', is **least**: He has least talent of all. **Least** is also the other form of the adverb **less** (def. 2): Choose the least expensive present.
Strictly speaking, it is correct to use **fewer** for things you can count (count nouns) and **less** for things you can't (uncount nouns): You should eat less sugar and fewer biscuits. However, many people do use **less** with count nouns and it is generally regarded as acceptable: The new system means less problems.

lessee n. someone to whom a lease is granted.

If you rent a property from someone else, you are the **lessee**.

lessen v. to become less.

Don't confuse this with **lesson**, which is the time during which you are taught something: Next lesson we'll learn some long division.

lesser adj. being smaller or less important, etc., (than another).

lesson n. 1. something to be learned. 2. a length of time during which a pupil or class studies one subject.

Don't confuse this with **lessen**, which is to make or become less.

lessor n. someone who grants a lease.

If you rent a property from someone else, they are the **lessor**.

lest conj. 1. for fear that. 2. (after words expressing fear, danger, etc.) that.

let v. (**let, letting**) 1. to allow or permit. 2. to grant the use of (property) for rent. 3. to be rented or leased. 4. to cause or make: *to let one know.* 5. (as an auxiliary used to propose or order): *Let me see.*

let[2] n. Tennis, etc. an interference with the course of the ball on account of which the stroke must be replayed.

lethal adj. deadly.

lethargy n. a state of drowsy dullness; apathy; inactivity. **–lethargic,** adj.

letter n. 1. a written communication. 2. one of the signs used in writing and printing to represent speech sounds; an alphabetic character.

letterbox n. 1. a receptacle with a slot for posting mail. 2. a box or other shaped receptacle for incoming mail at the front gate of a house or on the inside of the front door.

lettuce n. a leafy plant, much used in salads.

leukaemia /luˈkimiə/ n. a disease, often fatal, characterised by excessive production of white blood cells. Also, **leukemia.**

leukocyte /ˈlukəsaɪt/ n. one of the white or colourless corpuscles of the blood, concerned in the destruction of disease-producing microorganisms, etc.; white blood cell. Also, **leucocyte.**

levee /ˈlɛvi/ n. a raised riverside.

level adj. 1. having no part higher than another. 2. horizontal. 3. even or uniform. –n. 4. a device used for testing whether something is horizontal. 5. a horizontal position with respect to height: *The water* *level is falling.* –v. (**-elled, -elling**) 6. to make level. 7. to bring (something) to the level of the ground. 8. to make (2 or more things) equal in status, condition, etc. 9. to aim at a mark, as a weapon, criticism, etc. –phr. 10. **level out,** to arrive at a stable level: *Food prices levelled out last year.*

lever n. a rigid bar rotating about a fixed point (fulcrum) which lifts a weight at one end when a force is applied to the other.

leverage /ˈlivərɪdʒ, ˈlevərɪdʒ/ n. 1. the action of a lever. 2. power of action; influence.

levitate v. to rise or float in the air, especially through some allegedly supernatural power. **–levitation,** n

levity n. lack of proper seriousness or earnestness.

levy /ˈlɛvi/ n. (pl. **-vies**) 1. the collecting of money or troops, etc., by authority or force. –v. (**-vied, -vying**) 2. to impose (a tax).

lewd adj. characterised by lust or lechery.

lexicon n. 1. a dictionary, especially of Greek, Latin, or Hebrew. 2. the total stock of words in a given language. **–lexical,** adj.

liability n. (pl. **-ties**) 1. an obligation, especially for payment (opposed to *asset*). 2. something disadvantageous.

liable adj. 1. subject to something possible or likely, especially something undesirable. 2. legally responsible.

liaison /liˈeɪzɒn, -zɒn/ n. 1. a connection or communication. 2. → **affair** (def. 4). **–liaise,** v.

liar n. someone who tells lies.

libel n. Law defamation by written or printed words, pictures, etc., as distinct from spoken words.

Compare **libel** with **slander**, which is a spoken statement which damages someone's reputation.

liberal adj. 1. favourable to progress or reform, as in religious or political affairs. 2. favourable to the policy of freedom of self-expression for the individual.

3. generous. **4.** not strict or rigorous. *–n.* **5.** a person of liberal principles, especially in religion or politics.

liberate *v.* to set free. **–liberation**, *n.* **–liberator**, *n.*

libertine *n.* someone who is free from restraint or control, especially in moral or sexual matters.

liberty *n.* (*pl.* **-ties**) **1.** freedom from control, interference, obligation, restriction, etc. **2.** freedom from captivity. **3.** unwarranted or impertinent freedom in action or speech.

libido /lə'bidoʊ/ *n.* **1.** the instinctive impulses and desires in living beings. **2.** the sexual drive.

library *n.* (*pl.* **-ries**) a place containing books, etc., (which may be borrowed) for reading, study, or reference. **–librarian**, *n.*

lice *n.* plural of **louse**.

licence *n.* **1.** (a certificate giving) formal permission to do something. **2.** excessive or undue freedom: *She allows the children too much licence.*

> Don't confuse the noun **licence** with the verb **license**.
> In America, both the noun and verb are spelt **license**.

license *v.* to grant permission to.

> Don't confuse the verb **license** with the noun **licence**.
> In America, both the noun and verb are spelt **license**.

licentious *adj.* sensually uncontrolled; lewd.

lichen /'laɪkən/ *n.* a plant growing in crust-like patches on rocks, trees, etc.

lick *v.* **1.** to pass the tongue over a surface. **2.** *Informal* to defeat; surpass. *–n.* **3.** a stroke of the tongue over something.

licorice *n.* **1.** (an extract from) the sweet-tasting dried root of a certain plant, used in medicine, confectionery, etc. **2.** any of several types of confectionery made from or flavoured with this. Also, **liquorice**.

lid *n.* a movable cover for closing a vessel, box, etc.

lie¹ *n.* **1.** a false statement made with intent to deceive. *–v.* (**lied**, **lying**) **2.** to speak falsely, intending to deceive.

lie² *v.* (**lay**, **lain**, **lying**) **1.** to be in a recumbent position; recline. **2.** to rest in a horizontal position: *A pen is lying on the table.* **3.** to be situated: *land lying along the coast. –phr.* **4. lie down**, to assume a horizontal position.

> Don't confuse **lie** with **lay¹**, which is similar in meaning, but used in a different way. **Lie** does not normally take an object (*The dog lies on the bed*), while **lay** does take an object (*He's laying the table*). Note that the past tense of **lie** is **lay** (*The dog lay on the bed all day yesterday*), while the past form of **lay** is **laid** (*He laid the table earlier*).

lieu /lu, lju/ *phr.* **in lieu of**, instead of.

lieutenant /lef'tenənt, lu'tenənt/, *Navy* /lə'tenənt/ *n.* **1.** an officer in the army or navy. **2.** a deputy or subordinate officer acting for a superior.

> The pronunciation /lu'tenənt/, still thought of by many as a chiefly American one, is gaining in frequency in Australia.

life *n.* (*pl.* **lives**) **1.** the condition which distinguishes animals and plants from inorganic objects and dead organisms. **2.** (the term of) animate existence of an individual. **3.** the term of effectiveness of something inanimate, as a machine, lease, etc. **4.** a living being. **5.** manner of existence: *married life.* **6.** liveliness. **7.** a prison sentence covering the rest of the convicted person's natural life.

lifeguard *n.* someone employed at a place where people swim to rescue and give first aid to those in distress.

life jacket *n.* an inflatable or buoyant sleeveless jacket for keeping a person afloat in water. Also, **life vest**.

lifeline n. **1.** a line or rope for saving life, as one attached to a lifeboat. **2.** any vital line of communication.

lifesaver n. *Aust.* one of a group of volunteers who patrol surfing beaches, etc., ensuring the safety of swimmers. Also, **lifeguard.** –**lifesaving,** n.

lifestreaming n. the online recording of one's daily life, either by a webcam, or by collecting together personal blogs, micro-blogs, etc.

lifestyle n. one's way or manner of living.

lifetime n. **1.** the time that one's life continues; one's term of life. –*adj.* **2.** lasting a lifetime.

lift v. **1.** to move (something) upwards, as from the ground etc., to some higher position. **2.** to raise in rank, condition, estimation, etc. **3.** to rise and disperse, as clouds, fog, etc. **4.** *Informal* to steal or plagiarise. –n. **5.** the act of lifting, raising, or rising. Also, *Chiefly US,* **elevator.** a moving platform or cage for conveying goods, people, etc., from one level to another, as in a building. **7.** a ride in a vehicle, free of charge. **8.** exaltation or uplift, as in feeling.

lift-off n. Also, **blast-off. 1.** the start of a rocket's flight from its launching pad. –*adj.* **2.** removable by lifting: *a lift-off lid.*

ligament n. *Anat.* a band of fibrous tissue, serving to connect bones, hold organs in place, etc.

ligature n. a tie or bond.

light¹ n. **1.** that which makes things visible, or gives illumination. **2.** an illuminating source, as the sun, a lamp, etc. **3.** the illumination from the sun, or daylight. **4.** the aspect in which a thing appears or is regarded. **5.** a traffic light. –*adj.* **6.** illuminated; not dark. –v. (**lit** *or* **lighted**, **lighting**) **7.** to (cause to) take fire or burn, as a match, candle, etc. **8.** to brighten (*up*) with animation or joy, as the face, eyes, etc.

light² *adj.* **1.** of little weight; not heavy. **2.** gentle; delicate. **3.** easy to endure or perform. **4.** free from care: *a light heart.* **5.** frivolous: *light entertainment.* **6.** having less of a normal standard ingredient: *light beer.*

light³ v. (**lighted** *or* **lit**, **lighting**) **1.** to descend, as from a horse or a vehicle. **2.** to come by chance; happen, or hit (*on* or *upon*).

lighthouse n. a tower displaying a light for the guidance of vessels at sea.

lightning n. a sudden flash of light in the sky, caused by the discharge of atmospheric electricity.

light-year n. the distance traversed by light in one year ($9.460\,55 \times 10^{15}$ metres), used as a unit in measuring stellar distances. *Symbol:* l.y.

ligneous /ˈlɪɡniəs/ *adj.* resembling wood.

like¹ *prep.* **1.** similarly to: *to live like a king.* **2.** bearing resemblance to. **3.** for example; as; such as: *the basic needs, like food and shelter.* **4.** indicating a probability of: *It looks like rain.* **5.** desirous of: *to feel like a drink.* –*phr.* **6. the like,** something of a similar nature: *oranges, lemons and the like.*

like² v. **1.** to find agreeable. **2.** (in social media) to indicate support, enthusiasm, etc., for (a post, image, etc.). –n. **3.** (in social media) an instance of liking (def. 2).

likely *adj.* (**-lier, -liest**) **1.** probably or apparently going to (do, be, etc.). **2.** seeming like truth, fact, or certainty; or reasonably to be believed or expected; probable. –**likelihood,** n.

Note that **likely** is sometimes used in an ironic way. For example, if you say *That's a likely story!* you are implying that you don't really believe it.

liken v. to compare.

likewise *adv.* in like manner.

lilac n. a shrub with large clusters of fragrant purple or white flowers.

lilt n. rhythmic cadence.

lily *n.* (*pl.* **-lies**) a bulbous plant with showy, bell-shaped flowers.

lima bean *n.* a bean with a broad, flat, edible seed.

limb *n.* **1.** a part of an animal body distinct from the head and trunk, as a leg, arm, or wing. **2.** a main branch of a tree.

limber *adj.* **1.** bending readily; flexible; supple. –*phr.* **2. limber up**, to make oneself limber.

limbo *n.* (*oft. upper case*) a supposed region on the border of hell or heaven.

lime¹ *n.* the oxide of calcium, CaO, used in making mortar and cement.

lime² *n.* a small, greenish-yellow, acid fruit allied to the lemon.

limelight *n.* **1.** (formerly) a strong light, made by heating a cylinder of lime. **2.** the glare of public interest or notoriety.

limerick *n.* a type of humorous verse of 5 lines.

limestone *n.* a rock consisting of calcium carbonate.

limit *n.* **1.** the furthest point or boundary. **2.** a boundary that should not be passed: *Two drinks is my limit.* –*v.* **3.** to restrict by fixing limits (*to*): *to limit phone calls to 3 minutes.* **4.** to confine or keep within limits: *to limit expenditures.* –**limitation**, *n.*

A **limited company** is one whose shareholders, if the company goes bankrupt and has to close down, only have to pay the company's debts to the value of their own shares. The abbreviation used in the names of this type of company is **Ltd**, as in *City Business Supplies Ltd.*

limousine *n.* any large, luxurious car.

limp¹ *v.* **1.** to walk with difficulty, as when lame. –*n.* **2.** a lame gait.

limp² *adj.* lacking stiffness or firmness.

limpet *n.* *Zool.* a marine gastropod mollusc found adhering to rocks.

limpid *adj.* clear.

line¹ *n.* **1.** a long, very narrow mark or stroke made with a pen, etc., on a surface. **2.** something like a line, as a band of colour, a seam, etc. **3.** a row of written or printed letters, words, etc. **4.** a verse of poetry. **5.** a course of action, thought, etc.: *to agree with the party line.* **6.** a chronological succession of persons or animals, especially in family descent. **7.** a kind of occupation or business: *What line are you in?* **8.** any transport company or system. **9.** a railway track or system. **10.** *Maths* a continuous extent of length, straight or curved, without thickness; the trace of a moving point. **11.** a supply of commercial goods of the same general class. **12.** the line of arrangement of an army, etc., as drawn up ready for battle. **13.** a thread, string, etc. **14.** a telephonic channel: *The line is busy.* –*v.* (**lined, lining**) **15.** to take a position in a line; queue (*up*). **16.** to bring (*up*) into line with others. **17.** to mark with a line.

line² *v.* to apply a layer of material to the inner side of.

lineage /ˈlɪnɪdʒ/ *n.* lineal descent from an ancestor.

lineal *adj.* being in the direct line, as a descendant, ancestor, etc.

linear *adj.* **1.** extended in a line. **2.** relating to a line or length. **3.** *Maths* of the first degree, as an equation.

linedance *n.* a dance to country music in which dancers perform a repeated sequence of steps while facing the same direction in a line. –**linedancing**, *n.*

linen *n.* (tablecloths, etc., made of) fabric woven from flax.

liner *n.* one of a commercial line of ships or aeroplanes.

linesman *n.* (*pl.* **-men**) *Sport* an official on the sidelines who assists the referee or umpire in determining whether the ball is still in play. Also, **lineman**. –**lineswoman**. –**linesperson**, *n.*

linger *v.* **1.** to remain in a place longer than is usual or expected. **2.** to take more time than usual, especially out of enjoyment: *I lingered over my cup of tea.*

lingerie /ˈlɒnʒəreɪ/ n. women's underwear.

lingo n. (pl. -goes) Informal 1. language. 2. jargon.

linguist n. 1. a person who is skilled in foreign languages. 2. a person who specialises in linguistics.

linguistics n. the science of language. –linguistic, adj.

liniment n. an oily liquid for rubbing on to the skin, as for sprains, bruises, etc.

link n. 1. one of the separate pieces making up a chain. 2. anything connecting one thing with another; a bond or tie. –v. 3. to join (as) by a link.

links pl. n. → golf course.

linoleum n. a type of smooth, hard floor covering. Also, **lino**.

linseed n. the seed of flax.

lint n. 1. a soft material for dressing wounds, etc. 2. bits of thread or fluff.

lintel n. a horizontal supporting member above a window or a door.

lion n. a large member of the cat family, the male of which usually has a mane. –lioness, fem. n.

lip n. 1. either of the 2 fleshy parts or folds forming the margins of the mouth and performing an important function in speech. 2. a lip-like part or structure. 3. any edge or rim.

liposuction /ˈlaɪpoʊsʌkʃən/ n. the removal of fat tissue from the body by means of suction.

lip-service n. insincere profession of devotion or goodwill.

lipstick n. a cosmetic preparation for colouring the lips.

liquefy v. (-fied, -fying) to make or become liquid. Also, **liquify**.

liqueur /lɪˈkjʊə, ləˈkɜ:/ n. a strong, sweet, and highly flavoured alcoholic liquor.

liquid adj. 1. such as to flow like water; fluid. 2. in cash: liquid assets. –n. 3. a liquid substance. –liquidity, n.

liquidate v. 1. to settle or pay (a debt, etc.). 2. (of a company) to pay off debts

and wind up business. 3. to convert into cash. 4. to get rid of, especially by killing or other violent means. –liquidation, n.

liquidator n. a person appointed to conclude the affairs of a company because of bankruptcy, etc.

liquor n. spirits (as brandy or whisky) as distinguished from fermented beverages (as wine or beer).

liquorice n. → licorice.

lisp n. 1. a speech defect consisting in pronouncing s and z like the th sounds of thin and this, respectively. –v. 2. to speak with a lisp.

lissom adj. lithe; limber.

list¹ n. 1. a record consisting of a series of names, words, etc. –v. 2. to set down together in a list.

list² v. (of a ship, etc.,) to incline to one side.

listen v. to give attention with the ear.

listicle n. a type of article in online journalism and blogging which is presented in the form of a list.

listless adj. feeling no interest in anything.

lit v. past tense and past participle of **light**¹ and **light**³.

litany /ˈlɪtəni/ n. (pl. -nies) 1. a form of prayer consisting of a series of invocations with responses from a congregation. 2. a prolonged recitation; monotonous account.

literal adj. 1. following the exact words, of the original, as a translation. 2. true to fact and not exaggerated: a literal account of what happened. 3. using the basic, straightforward sense of a word: the literal meaning. –literally, adv.

> Compare def. 3 with **figurative**, which describes words, phrases, etc., which are not used with their usual meaning.
> Don't confuse **literally** with **literary**.

literary adj. relating to books and writings, especially those classed as literature.

> Don't confuse this with **literally**, which means actually or truthfully: She literally

stopped in the middle of the road and screamed.

literate *adj.* **1.** able to read and write. **2.** educated. –**literacy**, *n.*

literature *n.* **1.** writings in which expression and form, together with ideas of universal interest, are characteristic features, as poetry, biography, essays, etc. **2.** *Informal* printed matter of any kind, as advertising circulars, etc.

lithe /laɪð/ *adj.* pliant; supple.

lithium *n.* a soft silver-white metallic element, the lightest of all metals. *Symbol:* Li

lithography *n.* the process of printing a picture, etc., from a flat surface of aluminium, zinc or stone. –**lithograph**, *n.*

litigant /ˈlɪtɪgənt/ *n.* **1.** someone engaged in a lawsuit. –*adj.* **2.** engaged in a lawsuit.

litigate *v.* **1.** to contest at law. **2.** to dispute (a point, etc). –**litigable**, *adj.* –**litigator**, *n.* –**litigation**, *n.*

litmus *n.* a colouring substance which is turned red by acid solutions and blue by alkaline solutions.

litmus test *n.* **1.** a test of the acid or alkaline levels of a substance. **2.** a decisive test of a person's loyalty, character, etc.

litre *n.* a measure of liquid in the metric system. *Symbol:* L, l

litter *n.* **1.** scattered rubbish. **2.** a condition of disorder or untidiness. **3.** a number of young animals brought forth at one birth. **4.** a couch, often covered and curtained, carried between shafts by people or animals. –*v.* **5.** to strew (a place) with scattered objects.

litterbug *n.* someone who drops rubbish, especially in public places.

little *adj.* **1.** (**littler**, **littlest**) small in size: *a little boy.* **2.** (**less**, **least**) not much; small in amount: *little hope; I have little money.* –*adv.* (**less**, **least**) **3.** not at all (with a verb): *She cares little for such things.* **4.** rarely; infrequently: *I see him very little these days.* –*phr.* **5. a little,** a small amount (of): *I'll just have a little,*

please; I've saved a little money; There's still a little time before we have to leave.

liturgy /ˈlɪtədʒi/ *n.* (*pl.* -**gies**) a form of public worship; a ritual. –**liturgical**, *adj.*

live¹ /lɪv/ *v.* **1.** to be alive, as an animal or plant. **2.** to last: *to live in one's memory.* **3.** to subsist (*on* or *upon*): *to live on potatoes.* **4.** to dwell or reside. **5.** to pass (life): *to live a happy life.*

live² /laɪv/ *adj.* **1.** living, or alive. **2.** characterised by the presence of living creatures. **3.** burning or glowing, as a coal. **4.** unexploded, as a cartridge or shell. **5.** *Elect.* electrically charged. **6.** (of a radio or television program) broadcast or televised at the moment it is being performed.

livelihood *n.* means of maintaining life, as by an occupation or employment.

lively *adj.* (-**lier**, -**liest**) **1.** active, vigorous, or brisk. **2.** vivacious or spirited. **3.** eventful or exciting.

liven *v.* to put life into; cheer (*up*).

liver *n.* an organ secreting bile and performing various metabolic functions.

liver spot *n.* a brownish patch on the skin, usually of an elderly person.

livery /ˈlɪvəri/ *n.* (*pl.* -**ries**) **1.** a kind of uniform worn by servants. **2.** a distinctive dress worn by an official, a member of a company or guild, etc.

livestock *n.* the horses, cattle, sheep, etc., kept or bred on a farm. Also, **stock**.

livid *adj.* **1.** discoloured due to bruising. **2.** angry; enraged.

living *adj.* **1.** alive, or not dead. –*n.* **2.** the act or condition of someone or something which lives. **3.** livelihood.

living room *n.* a room in a house, flat, etc., used both for entertaining and for relaxing, recreation, etc.; lounge room.

lizard *n.* a reptile with a long body and tail and usually short legs, as geckos, monitors, etc.

'll a contraction of *will* or *shall.*

llama *n.* a woolly-haired Sth American ruminant, related to the camel.

Don't confuse this with **lama**, which is a Buddhist priest or monk.

lo *interj. Old-fashioned* look! see! behold!

load *n.* **1.** that which is carried on a cart, etc. **2.** anything borne or sustained: *a load of fruit on a tree.* **3.** something that weighs down: *a load on one's mind.* **4.** the amount of work required of a person, machine, etc. **5.** the weight supported by a structure or part. *–v.* **6.** to put a load on or in. **7.** to supply abundantly with something. **8.** to give emotional or other bias to: *to load a question; to load dice.* **9.** to charge (a firearm, camera, etc.)

loading *n.* **1.** an extra rate paid to employees in recognition of a particular aspect of their employment, as shift work. **2.** *Insurance* an addition to the normal premium for something seen as a risk by the insurance company.

loaf[1] *n.* (*pl.* **loaves**) **1.** a portion of bread, etc., baked in a particular form. **2.** a shaped mass of food, as of sugar, chopped meat, etc.

loaf[2] *v.* to lounge or saunter lazily and idly.

loafer *n. (from trademark)* a casual shoe.

loam *n.* a loose soil composed of clay and sand.

loan *n.* **1.** something lent on condition of being returned, as money lent at interest. *–v.* **2.** to lend; make a loan of.

Don't confuse this with **lone**, which means solitary or alone.

loath /loʊθ/ *adj.* reluctant, or unwilling: *I am loath to lend her anything.*

Don't confuse the adjective **loath** with the verb **loathe**.

loathe /loʊð/ *v.* to feel disgust, or intense hatred for. *–***loathing**, *n. –***loathsome**, *adj.*

Don't confuse the verb **loathe** with the adjective **loath**.

lob *v.* (**lobbed**, **lobbing**) **1.** *Tennis* to strike (a ball) high into the air. **2.** to throw

(something) so that it lands after a high curve.

lobby *n.* (*pl.* **-bies**) **1.** a corridor, or entrance hall. **2.** a group of persons who attempt to influence legislators or other public officials on behalf of some particular cause or interest. *–v.* (**-bied, -bying**) **3.** to frequent the lobby of a legislative chamber to influence the members.

lobe *n.* a roundish projection.

lobotomy /ləˈbɒtəmi/ *n.* (*pl.* **-mies**) the cutting into or across a lobe of the brain.

lobster *n.* a large, edible, marine crustacean.

local *adj.* **1.** relating to or characterised by place, or position in space. **2.** relating to a particular place or part.

local area network *n.* computer networking system which links computers within a limited area to a central computer. Also, **LAN**.

locale /loʊˈkɑl/ *n.* a place or locality.

locality *n.* (*pl.* **-ties**) a place, spot, or district.

locate *v.* to discover the place or location of.

location *n.* **1.** a place of business or residence, etc. **2.** *Film, TV* a place outside the studio where scenes may be shot. *–phr.* **3. on location**, *Film, TV* at a site away from the studio, where filming for a particular scene is taking place.

loch /lɒk/ *n. Scot* a lake.

lock[1] *n.* **1.** a device for securing a door, lid, etc., in position when closed. **2.** an enclosed portion of a canal, river, etc., with gates at each end, for raising or lowering vessels from one level to another. **3.** the number of degrees the steering mechanism of a vehicle is able to turn the front wheels from one extreme to the other. *–v.* **4.** to secure (a door, building, etc.) by the operation of a lock. **5.** to join by interlinking or intertwining. **6.** to become locked. *–phr.* **7. lock up**, **a.** to secure a building, etc., by locking doors, etc.: *Lock up before you leave.* **b.** to restrain by shutting in a place fastened by a lock. **8. lock out,** to exclude by or as by a lock.

lock² *n.* a tress or portion of hair.

lockdown *n.* a state of security alert in which access is cut off and movement of people in and around a location is brought to a halt.

locker *n.* a chest, drawer, etc., that may be locked.

locket *n.* a small case for a miniature portrait, a lock of hair, etc., usually worn on a chain hung round the neck.

lockjaw *n.* → **tetanus.**

locomotion *n.* the act of moving from place to place.

locomotive *n.* a self-propelled vehicle which pulls railway carriages, etc., along a railway track.

locum *n.* a temporary substitute for a doctor, lawyer, etc. Also, **locum tenens.**

locus /'lokəs, 'loukəs/ *n.* (*pl.* **loci** /'loki, 'louki, 'loukai/) a place; a locality.

locust *n.* **1.** a type of grasshopper which swarms in immense numbers and strips plants. **2.** *Informal* → **cicada.**

lode *n.* a veinlike deposit, usually metal bearing.

lodge *n.* **1.** a cabin or hut. **2.** a cottage, as on an estate, occupied by a caretaker, etc. **3.** the meeting place of a branch of a secret society. *–v.* **4.** to have or provide with living quarters, especially temporarily. **5.** to be fixed or implanted. **6.** to lay (information, a complaint, etc.) before a court, etc. **–lodgement, lodgment,** *n.*

loft *n.* the space between the ceiling and the roof.

lofty *adj.* (**-tier, -tiest**) **1.** extending high in the air. **2.** noble or high in character, sentiment or style. **3.** haughty; proud.

log *n.* **1.** an uncut portion of the trunk or a large branch of a felled tree. **2.** the official record of significant data concerning a ship's journey, a machine's operation, etc.

–v. (**logged, logging**) **3.** to cut (trees) into logs. **4.** to cut down trees or timber on (land). **5.** to record in a log. *–phr.* **6. log in** (or **on**), to begin a session on a computer, usually gaining access with a username and password. **7. log off** (or **out**), to end a session on a computer.

logarithm /'lɒgərɪðəm/ *n.* the exponent of that power to which a fixed number (called the *base*) must be raised in order to produce a given number (called the *antilogarithm*).

logic *n.* **1.** the principles of reasoning applicable to any branch of knowledge or study. **2.** reasons or sound sense, as in utterances or actions. **–logical,** *adj.*

login *n.* *Computers* the act of beginning a computer session, usually by gaining access via a username and password. Also, **log-in, logon, log-on.**

logistics *n.* (*oft. construed as pl.*) the branch of military science concerned with the transportation, housing and supply of bodies of troops.

logo *n.* a trademark or symbol designed to identify a company, organisation, etc.

logon *n.* *Computers* → **login.** Also, **log-on.**

logout *n.* *Computers* the act of discontinuing a computer session. Also, **log-out, logoff, log-off.**

loin *n.* (*usu. pl.*) the part of the body of a human or of a quadruped animal on either side of the spine, between the ribs and hipbone.

loiter *v.* to linger idly or aimlessly in or about a place.

loll *v.* to recline in a relaxed or lazy manner; lounge.

lollipop *n.* a kind of boiled sweet, often on the end of a stick.

lollop *v.* to move with bounding, ungainly leaps.

lolly *n.* (*pl.* **-lies**) *Aust., NZ* any sweet, especially a boiled one.

lone *adj.* solitary.

lonely adj. (**-lier**, **-liest**) **1.** lone; solitary. **2.** without sympathetic or friendly companionship.

lonesome adj. depressed by a sense of being alone.

long[1] adj. (**longer**, **longest**) **1.** having considerable or great extent from end to end; not short. **2.** lasting a considerable or great time. **3.** having a specified length in space, duration, etc.: *30 minutes long*. **4.** tall. –adv. **5.** for or through a great extent of space or, especially, time. –phr. **6.** so long, *Informal* goodbye.

long[2] v. to have a very strong or unceasing desire, as for something not immediately (if ever) attainable.

long COVID n. a condition whereby a person who has recovered from COVID-19 continues to experience symptoms such as fatigue, breathlessness, coughing, etc., and sometimes organ damage.

longevity /lɒnˈdʒɛvəti/ n. long life.

longhand n. writing of the ordinary kind, in which the words are written out in full.

Compare this with **shorthand**, which is a system of fast handwriting using lines, curves and dots instead of letters.

longitude /ˈlɒŋɡɪtjud, ˈlɒŋətjud/ n. Geog. angular distance east or west on the earth's surface, measured along the equator. –**longitudinal**, adj.

long-life adj. **1.** → **UHT**. **2.** of or relating to any product which has been treated to extend its utility beyond the normal length of time.

longwinded adj. tediously wordy in speech or writing.

look v. **1.** to fix the eyes upon something or in some direction in order to see. **2.** to glance or gaze, in a manner specified: *to look disapprovingly at someone*. **3.** to use the sight in searching, examining, etc. **4.** to tend, as in bearing or significance: *Conditions look towards war*. **5.** to appear or seem. **6.** to direct the mind or attention. **7.** to afford a view: *The house looks onto* *the park*. **8.** to face or front: *The garden looks north.* –n. **9.** the act of looking. **10.** a visual search or examination. **11.** way of appearing to the eye or mind: *the look of a scoundrel.* **12.** (*pl.*) general appearance. –phr. **13.** look after, to take care of. **14.** look forward to, to anticipate with pleasure. **15.** look in, **a.** to take a look into a place. **b.** to come in for a brief visit. **16.** look into, to investigate. **17.** look like, to seem likely to. **18.** look lively (or sharp), to make haste; be alert. **19.** look on, to be a mere spectator. **20.** look on the bright side, to consider something with optimism. **21.** look out, **a.** to look forth, as from a window, etc. **b.** to be on guard. **c.** to take watchful care (*for*). **22.** look over, to inspect or examine. **23.** look to, to direct the glance or gaze to. **24.** look up, to try to find; seek.

lookout n. **1.** (a person or group stationed to keep) watch, as for something that may happen. **2.** a high place, especially a mountain, from which one can admire the view.

loom[1] n. a machine for weaving yarn into a fabric.

loom[2] v. to come into view in indistinct and enlarged form.

loop n. **1.** a folding of a cord, etc., upon itself, so as to leave an opening between the parts. **2.** anything shaped like a loop. –v. **3.** to form into a loop or loops.

loophole n. an outlet, or means of escape or evasion.

loose adj. **1.** not bound or fettered. **2.** not attached or fastened. **3.** not bound together: *loose papers.* **4.** not put in a package or other container. **5.** characterised by free movement of bodily fluids: *loose bowels.* **6.** not fitting closely, as garments. **7.** not compact in structure or arrangement: *cloth of a loose weave.* **8.** not exact, or precise: *loose thinking.* –v. **9.** to free from bonds or restraint. **10.** to unfasten. **11.** to make less tight; slacken or relax. **12.** to render less firmly fixed, or loosen. **–loosen,** v.

Don't confuse **loose** with **lose.** If you **lose** something you can't find it.

loot n. **1.** spoils or plunder. **2.** *Informal* money. –v. **3.** to plunder or pillage (a city, house, etc.), as in war.

lop v. (**lopped, lopping**) to cut off (protruding parts) of a tree, etc.

lope v. to move or run with a long, easy stride.

lopsided adj. heavier, larger, or more developed on one side than on the other; asymmetrical.

loquacious adj. talkative. **–loquacity,** n.

loquat /'loʊkæt/ n. (a small, evergreen tree bearing) a yellow plum-like fruit.

lord n. **1.** a man who has power over others; a master, chief, or ruler. **2.** a titled nobleman. –phr. **3. lord it over someone,** to behave in a high-handed and dictatorial fashion towards someone.

lore n. the body of knowledge, especially of a traditional, or popular nature, on a particular subject.

lorikeet n. a small, brightly-coloured parrot.

lorry n. → **truck¹** (def. 1).

lose v. (**lost, losing**) **1.** to come to be without, by some chance, and not know the whereabouts of. **2.** to suffer loss (of). **3.** to become separated from and ignorant of (the way, etc.). **4.** to leave far behind in a chase, race, etc. **5.** to fail to win (a prize, etc.). **6.** to engross (oneself) in something.

Don't confuse this with **loose,** which means unfastened (*hair hanging loose*) or not tight (*loose trousers*).

loser n. **1.** someone who has lost a competition or race. **2.** *Informal* a person who is consistently unsuccessful, especially socially: *He's a complete loser.*

Note that if you call someone 'a loser', as in def. 2, you are intending to insult them.

loss n. **1.** disadvantage from failure to keep, have, or get: *to bear the loss of a robbery.* **2.** that which is lost. **3.** amount or number lost. **4.** a being deprived of something that one has had. **5.** a failure to win.

Loss is the noun from the verb **lose.**

lot n. **1.** one of a set of objects drawn from a receptacle, etc., to decide a question by chance. **2.** the decision or choice so made. **3.** one's destiny. **4.** a distinct portion of anything: *Our land is lot no. 49.* **5.** *Informal* a great many or a great deal. –phr. **6. the lot,** the entire amount or quantity.

lotion n. a liquid containing oils or medicines, to be applied externally to the skin for soothing, healing or cleansing.

lottery n. (pl. **-ries**) any scheme for the distribution of prizes by chance.

lotus n. **1.** the fruit of a plant which, according to Greek legend, induced a state of contented forgetfulness in those who ate it. **2.** any of various waterlilies.

loud adj. **1.** striking strongly upon the organs of hearing, as sound, noise, the voice, etc. **2.** offensively showy, as colours, dress or the wearer, etc.; garish.

loudspeaker n. any of various devices by which speech, music, etc., can be made audible throughout a room, etc.

lounge v. (**lounged, lounging**) **1.** to pass time idly. **2.** to lie back lazily; loll. –n. **3.** → **lounge room. 4.** a seat like a wide armchair for two or more people. **5.** a large room in a hotel, airport, etc., used by guests or passengers for relaxation purposes or while waiting for a flight, etc.

lounge room n. *Aust.* the living room of a private residence.

louse n. (pl. **lice** for def. 1, **louses** for def. 2) **1.** a small, wingless, bloodsucking insect. **2.** *Informal* a despicable person. –phr. **3. louse up,** *Informal* to spoil.

lousy adj. (**-sier, -siest**) **1.** infested with lice. **2.** Informal mean, contemptible or unpleasant. **3.** Informal inferior, not good. Also, **lousey.**

lout n. Informal a rough, uncouth and sometimes violent young man.

louvre n. an arrangement of slats covering a window or other opening.

lovable adj. of such a nature as to attract love. Also, **loveable.**

love n. **1.** a passionate affection for another person. **2.** a feeling of warm personal attachment. **3.** strong liking for anything. **4.** Tennis, etc. nothing; no score. –v. (**loved, loving**) **5.** to have love or affection for.

lovebird n. a small parrot; budgerigar.

lovelorn adj. forlorn or pining from love.

lovely adj. (**-lier, -liest**) charmingly or exquisitely beautiful.

lover n. **1.** someone who loves another. **2.** a sexual partner.

low¹ adj. **1.** situated not far above the ground, floor, or base. **2.** below the general level: low ground. **3.** relating to regions near the sea or sea level as opposed to highland or inland regions. **4.** rising only slightly from a surface. **5.** feeble; weak. **6.** small in amount, degree, etc.: a low number. **7.** attributing no great value, or excellence: a low opinion. **8.** depressed or dejected. **9.** far down in the scale of rank or estimation; humble. **10.** lacking in dignity or elevation, as of thought or expression. **11.** Biol. having a relatively simple structure. **12.** produced by relatively slow vibrations, as sounds. **13.** not loud. –adv. **14.** in or to a low position, point, degree, etc. **15.** that which is low. **16.** Meteorol. a pressure system characterised by relatively low pressure at the centre. **17.** a point of least value, amount, etc.

low² v. to utter the sound characteristic of cattle; moo.

lowboy n. a piece of furniture, not as tall as a wardrobe, for holding clothes.

lowdown n. Informal the unadorned facts on some subject.

lower adj. **1.** comparative of **low¹**. –v. **2.** to reduce in amount, price, degree, force, etc. **3.** to cause to descend, or let down.

lower-case letter n. one of the set of smaller letters of the alphabet which are used when a capital letter is not required.

lower class n. the group of people in a society who have the lowest income. –**lower-class**, adj.

Compare this with **upper class** and **middle class.**
Lower class is a collective noun and can be used with a singular or plural verb. Look up **collective noun.**

low-key adj. characterised by restraint; underplayed.

lowly adj. (**-lier, -liest**) humble.

low profile n. a lack of notice or recognition as a result of a deliberate avoidance of publicity or prominence.

loyal adj. **1.** faithful to one's friends, etc. **2.** faithful to one's obligations.

lozenge n. a small flavoured sweet, often medicated.

LSD n. an illegal drug which produces a feeling of heightened sensitivity as well as temporary hallucinations.

The informal term for this is **acid.**
LSD is short for the chemical name lysergic acid diethylamide.

lubricate v. to apply some grease in order to diminish friction. –**lubricant**, n. –**lubrication**, n.

lucerne /ˈlusən/ n. a plant used as feed for animals; alfalfa.

lucid adj. **1.** shining or bright. **2.** clear.

luck n. **1.** that which happens to a person, either good or bad, as if by chance. **2.** good fortune. –**lucky**, adj.

lucrative adj. profitable; remunerative.

lucre /ˈlukə/ n. money as the object of sordid desire.

ludicrous adj. causing laughter or scorn; ridiculous.

lug v. (**lugged**, **lugging**) to pull along or carry with effort.

luggage n. suitcases, etc., used in travelling; baggage.

lugubrious adj. mournful; doleful; dismal.

lukewarm adj. 1. moderately warm; tepid. 2. not enthusiastic; indifferent.

lull v. 1. to soothe or quiet, as into sleep. –n. 2. a temporary quiet or stillness.

lullaby n. a song intended to put a baby to sleep.

lumbar adj. of or relating to the lower back.

lumber[1] n. 1. timber split into planks, boards, etc. –v. 2. to cut timber and prepare it for market. 3. Informal to leave (somebody) with (something or someone unpleasant).

lumber[2] v. to move clumsily or heavily.

lumberjack n. Canada, Chiefly US someone who cuts and prepares timber.

luminary n. (pl. **-ries**) 1. a celestial body, as the sun or moon. 2. a person whose knowledge, etc., enlightens or inspires other people.

luminescence n. an emission of light without the production of heat. –**luminescent**, adj.

luminous adj. 1. radiating or reflecting light; shining. 2. well lighted. 3. clear; readily intelligible. –**luminosity**, n.

lump[1] n. 1. a mass of solid matter without regular shape. –v. 2. to unite into one collection or mass.

lump[2] v. Informal to put up with (a disagreeable necessity).

lunacy n. insanity. –**lunatic**, n., adj.

lunar adj. relating to the moon.

lunch n. 1. a meal taken at around midday. –v. 2. to eat lunch.

luncheon n. (a formal) lunch.

lung n. either of the 2 sac-like respiratory organs in the chest of humans and the higher vertebrates.

A medical word which describes things related to the lungs is **pulmonary**.

lunge n. 1. a sudden thrusting movement forward. –v. (**lunged**, **lunging**) 2. to make a lunge.

lupine adj. relating to or resembling the wolf.

lurch[1] n. 1. a sudden leaning to one side, as of a ship or a staggering person. –v. 2. to make a lurch; stagger.

lurch[2] n. the position of one in a helpless plight.

lure n. 1. anything that attracts or entices. –v. 2. to decoy; entice; allure.

lurid adj. 1. glaringly vivid or sensational. 2. unnatural or ghastly in hue.

lurk v. 1. to remain in a place secretly. –n. 2. Aust. Informal a convenient, often unethical, method of carrying out a task, earning a living, etc.

luscious adj. 1. highly pleasing to the taste or smell. 2. very luxurious; extremely attractive.

lush[1] adj. 1. succulent or luxuriant, as plants. 2. Informal characterised by luxury and comfort.

lush[2] n. Informal someone who drinks too much alcohol.

lust n. 1. passionate or overmastering desire, especially sexual. –v. 2. to have strong or inordinate desire (for or after), especially sexual.

lustre n. glitter, or gloss. –**lustrous**, adj.

lusty adj. (**-tier**, **-tiest**) full of healthy vigour.

lute n. a stringed musical instrument. –**lutenist**, n.

luxuriant adj. abundant in growth, as vegetation.

luxuriate v. 1. to indulge in luxury; revel. 2. to take great delight.

luxury n. (pl. **-ries**) anything conducive to sumptuous, elegant living, which is not a necessity. –**luxurious**, adj.

lychee /ˈlaɪˌtʃi, laɪˈtʃi/ *n.* a fruit with a thin brittle shell, enclosing a sweet jelly-like pulp and a single seed.

lycra *n.* (*from trademark*) a synthetic knitted fabric with great elasticity.

lymph *n.* a clear, yellowish fluid derived from the tissues of the body and conveyed via the lymph glands to the bloodstream. –**lymphatic**, *adj.*

lymph gland *n.* a gland-like body, e.g. the tonsils, where antibodies and white blood cells are produced.

lynch *v.* to put (a person) to death without authority or process of law. –**lynching**, *n.*

lynx *n.* (*pl.* **lynxes** *or, especially collectively,* **lynx**) any of various wildcats having long limbs and short tail.

lyre *n.* a stringed musical instrument of ancient Greece.

lyrebird *n.* either of 2 ground-dwelling birds of sth-east Aust., the males of which have long tails, spread in mating displays.

lyric *adj.* Also, **lyrical**. **1.** (of poetry) having the form and musical quality of a song. **2.** relating to or using singing. –*n.* **3.** a lyric poem. **4.** (*oft. pl.*) the words of a song. –**lyricist**, *n.*

M, m

M, m n. the 13th letter of the English alphabet.

macabre /mə'kab, mə'kabə, -brə/ adj. gruesome; horrible; grim; ghastly.

macadamia n. 1. Also, **macadamia nut**. a hard-shelled, edible nut. 2. a tree, originally from eastn Aust., which bears this nut.

macaroni n. a kind of pasta.

macaroon n. a sweet cake or biscuit, usually with coconut.

macaw n. a large, brightly coloured parrot with a harsh voice.

mace n. 1. Hist. a club-like weapon. 2. a staff borne as a symbol of office.

macerate /'mæsəreɪt/ v. 1. to soften by steeping in a liquid. 2. to cause to grow thin.

mach /mæk/ n. the ratio of the speed of an object to the speed of sound through the same substance, usually air.

machete /mə'ʃeti/ n. a large, heavy knife.

machination /mæʃə'neɪʃən, mækə'neɪʃən/ n. (usu. pl.) a secret plan or scheme, especially aimed at gaining power or doing something bad: political machinations.

machine n. 1. an apparatus consisting of interrelated parts with separate functions, which is used in the performance of some kind of work. 2. a device which transmits and modifies force or motion. –v. 3. to make, prepare, or finish with a machine.

machine gun n. a gun able to fire rapidly and continuously.

machinery n. 1. machines or mechanical apparatus. 2. the parts of a machine, collectively.

machismo /mə'tʃɪzmoʊ, mə'kɪzmoʊ/ n. masculine display emphasising strength.

macho /'mætʃoʊ/ n. 1. a man who displays machismo. –adj. 2. showily virile.

mackerel n. (pl. **-rel** or **-rels**) a common food fish.

For information about the different plural forms, see the note at **fish**.

mackintosh n. a raincoat.

macramé /mə'krami/ n. a kind of lace or ornamental work made by knotting thread or cord in patterns. Also, **macrame**.

macro¹ adj. broad or overarching (opposed to micro): at the macro level.

macro² n. a single computer command which sets in train a number of other commands to perform a specific task.

macrobiotic adj. of or relating to a largely vegetarian dietary system intended to prolong life.

mad adj. (**madder, maddest**) disordered in intellect; insane.

madam /'mædəm/ n. (pl. **mesdames** /meɪ'dæm, meɪ'dam/ or **madams**) a polite term of address to a woman.

made v. 1. past tense and past participle of **make**. –adj. 2. assured of success or fortune.

madeira n. (sometimes upper case) a rich, strong, white wine.

madrigal n. an unaccompanied part-song.

maelstrom n. a restless confusion of affairs, influence, etc.

maestro /'maɪstroʊ/ n. (pl. **-tros** or **-tri** /-tri/) an eminent musical composer, teacher, or conductor.

magazine n. 1. a periodical publication. 2. a place for keeping gunpowder, etc. 3. a metal receptacle for a number of cartridges. 4. a light-proof enclosure containing film.

magenta n., adj. reddish purple.

maggot n. the legless larva of a fly.

magic n. 1. the producing of effects claimed to be beyond the natural. 2. any extraordinary or irresistible influence. **3.** a conjuring. –*adj.* **4.** of, relating to, or due to magic.

magic bullet *n. Informal* **1.** any drug or treatment which acts effectively against a disease and has no harmful or unpleasant side effects. **2.** any remedy which is remarkably effective.

magisterial *adj.* **1.** of or befitting a magistrate or a magistrate's office. **2.** authoritative.

magistrate *n.* a justice of the peace who officiates in a magistrate's court.

maglev *n.* → **magnetic levitation train.**

magma *n.* molten rock under the earth's crust.

magnanimous *adj.* generous in forgiving. –**magnanimity**, *n.*

magnate /ˈmægneɪt, ˈmægnət/ *n.* a person of eminence or distinction in any field.

magnesium *n.* a light, ductile, silver-white metallic element used in lightweight alloys. *Symbol:* Mg

magnet *n.* **1.** a body (as a piece of iron or steel) which possesses the property of attracting certain substances. **2.** a thing or person that attracts. –**magnetic**, *adj.*

magnetic levitation train *n.* a train which, using electromagnetism, travels suspended above the track, moving at very high speed and with little noise or vibration. Also, **maglev.**

magnetic north *n.* the direction in which the needle of a compass points, differing in most places from true north.

magnetic tape *n.* a plastic tape used to record sound, video signals, digital information, etc.

magneto /mægˈnitoʊ/ *n.* (*pl.* **-tos**) a small electric generator, the poles of which are permanent magnets.

magnification *n.* **1.** a magnified copy or reproduction. **2.** (of an optical instrument) the ratio of the linear dimensions of the final image to that of the object.

magnificent *adj.* extraordinarily fine.

magnify *v.* (**-fied, -fying**) **1.** to increase the apparent size of, as a lens does. **2.** to make greater in size; enlarge.

magnitude *n.* **1.** size; extent. **2.** greatness or importance.

magnolia *n.* a shrub or tree with large fragrant flowers.

magnum *n.* (*pl.* **-nums**) a bottle for wine or spirits, holding about 2 normal bottles, or 1.5 litres.

magpie *n.* a common black and white bird.

magpie lark *n.* a common Aust. black-and-white bird which builds its mud nest high in a tree; peewee.

maharajah /mahəˈrɑdʒə/ *n.* the title of certain great ruling princes in India. Also, **maharaja.**

maharani /mahəˈrɑni/ *n.* **1.** the wife of a maharajah. **2.** a female sovereign in her own right. Also, **maharanee.**

mahjong *n.* a game of Chinese origin, with 136 domino-like pieces or tiles.

mahogany /məˈhɒgəni/ *n.* (*pl.* **-nies**) **1.** any of certain tropical American trees yielding a hard, reddish-brown wood. **2.** a reddish-brown colour.

maid *n.* a woman employed for various light domestic duties in houses, hotels, etc. Also, **housemaid.**

maiden *n.* **1.** *Old-fashioned* a young unmarried woman. –*adj.* **2.** made, tried, appearing, etc., for the first time.

maiden name *n.* a woman's surname before marriage.

maiden over *n.* (in cricket) an over in which no runs are made.

mail[1] *n.* **1.** letters, packages, etc., carried by post. **2.** the system of sending letters, etc., by post. –*adj.* **3.** of or relating to mail. –*v.* **4.** to send by mail; place in a post office or post-box for sending.

Don't confuse this with **male,** which is the sex of a man or boy.

mail[2] *n.* flexible armour of interlinked rings.

maim v. **1.** to mutilate; cripple. **2.** to impair; make defective.

main adj. **1.** chief; principal; leading. –n. **2.** a principal water or gas pipe. **3.** the chief or principal part or point. –phr. **4. with might and main,** utmost strength, vigour, force, or effort.

Don't confuse **main** with **mane**, which is the long hair that grows on the neck of a horse or a lion.

mainframe computer n. a large and powerful computer which may be used by several users at the same time. Also, **mainframe**.

mainland n. the principal land mass as distinguished from nearby islands and peninsulas.

mainstream n. the dominant trend; chief tendency.

maintain v. **1.** to keep in existence; preserve. **2.** to affirm; assert.

maintenance n. **1.** the act of maintaining. **2.** Law the money paid for the support of the other spouse or infant children, usually after divorce; alimony.

maize n. → **corn**¹ (def. 1).

majesty n. (pl. **-ties**) **1.** supreme greatness or authority; sovereignty. **2.** (upper case) (preceded by His, Her, Your, etc.) (a title of honour used when speaking of or to a sovereign): Her Majesty, the Queen; Their Majesties, the King and Queen.

major adj. **1.** greater, as in size, amount, extent, importance, rank, etc. **2.** of full legal age. –n. **3.** an officer in the army. **4.** a principal field of study chosen by a student.

majority n. (pl. **-ties**) **1.** the greater part or number; more than half. **2.** in an election or other vote, the difference in the number of votes received by the winner and the person or group coming second.

Note that this word can be used as either a singular or a plural noun, depending on whether you are thinking about the group as a single item or about the individuals that make up the group. For example, in The majority of the population approves of the new law, **majority** is treated as a singular noun because that section of the population is thought of as a single item. However, in The majority of my friends love reading, it is treated as a plural noun because the friends are regarded as a collection of separate individuals.

make v. (**made, making**) **1.** to produce by any action or causative agency. **2.** to cause to be or become; render. **3.** to put into proper condition for use. **4.** to cause, induce, or compel (to do something). **5.** to do; effect. **6.** to become by development; prove to be. **7.** to estimate; reckon. **8.** to arrive at or reach. **9.** to arrive in time for. **10.** to pursue the course: to make for home. –n. **11.** style or manner of being made; form; build. –phr. **12. make a face,** to grimace. **13. make believe,** to pretend. **14. make do,** to operate or carry on using minimal or improvised resources. **15. make love,** Informal to have sexual intercourse. **16. make out, a.** to discern; decipher. **b.** to present as; impute to be. **17. make up, a.** to put together; construct; compile. **b.** to compensate for. **c.** to bring to a definite conclusion, as one's mind. **d.** to apply cosmetics to, as the face. **e.** Also, **make it up.** to become reconciled after a quarrel.

makeover n. cosmetic treatment of the face leading to a very different appearance.

makeshift n. a temporary expedient; substitute.

make-up n. **1.** cosmetics. **2.** → **foundation** (def. 5). **3.** the manner of being made up or put together; composition. **4.** physical or mental constitution.

makings pl. n. material of which something may be made.

malady n. (pl. **-dies**) a bodily disorder or disease.

malapropism *n.* a word ridiculously misused.

malaria *n.* a disease characterised by attacks of chills, fever, and sweating.

malcontent *adj.* **1.** dissatisfied, especially with the existing administration; inclined to rebellion. *–n.* **2.** a malcontent person.

male *adj.* **1.** belonging to the sex capable of fertilising female ova. **2.** relating to or characteristic of this sex; masculine. *–n.* **3.** a male person or animal.

Don't confuse **male** with **mail**, which is the letters and parcels that are sent by post. **Mail** was also a type of armour that knights wore to protect themselves in battle.

malevolent /məˈlevələnt/ *adj.* wishing evil to another or others; showing ill will.

malformation *n.* faulty or anomalous formation or structure, especially in a living body. **–malformed,** *adj.*

malfunction *n.* **1.** a failure to function properly. *–v.* **2.** to fail to function properly.

malice *n.* **1.** desire to inflict injury or suffering on another. **2.** *Law* evil intent on the part of someone who commits a wrongful act injurious to others. **–malicious,** *adj.*

malign *v.* **1.** to speak ill of; slander. **2.** to speak contemptuously to. *–adj.* **3.** malevolent.

malignant *adj.* very dangerous; harmful in influence or effect. **–malignancy,** *n.*

malinger *v.* to feign sickness or injury, especially in order to avoid work, etc.

mall /mɔl, mæl/ *n.* **1.** a street lined with shops and closed off to traffic. **2.** Also, **shopping mall,** a shopping complex.

malleable *adj.* **1.** capable of being extended or shaped by hammering or by pressure with rollers. **2.** adaptable or tractable.

mallee *n.* **1.** eucalypts with a number of almost unbranched stems arising from a large underground tuber. *–phr.* **2. the**

mallee, *Aust. Informal* any remote, isolated or unsettled area.

mallet *n.* a hammer-like tool.

malnutrition *n.* unhealthy condition resulting from lack of nourishing food.

malpractice *n.* improper professional action.

malt *n.* germinated grain (usually barley), used in brewing and distilling.

maltreat *v.* to handle roughly or cruelly; ill-treat.

The more usual word is **abuse**.

mama *n.* mother.

mammal *n.* a member of the class of vertebrates whose young feed upon milk from the mother's breast. **–mammalian,** *adj.*

mammary *adj.* of or relating to the breast.

mammogram *n.* an X-ray taken of the breasts.

mammoth *n.* **1.** a large, extinct elephant. *–adj.* **2.** huge; gigantic.

man *n.* (*pl.* **men**) **1.** an adult male human being. **2.** the human race; humankind. **3.** one of the pieces used in playing certain games, as chess or draughts. *–v.* (**manned, manning**) **4.** to furnish with people, as for service or defence. **5.** to take one's place for service, as at a gun, post, etc.

The use of **man** in the sense of def. 2 which includes women and children is now generally avoided, and **humans** is used instead: *a disease dangerous to humans.* Similarly, **humanity** or **humankind** is preferred to **mankind**.
Note that **man** as in def. 2 is always singular and is used without an article (*the* or *a*): *Man has always hunted.*

manacle *n.* (*usu. pl.*) **1.** a shackle for the hand; handcuff. **2.** a restraint. *–v.* (**-cled, -cling**) **3.** to handcuff.

manage *v.* **1.** to bring about; succeed in accomplishing. **2.** to take charge or care of. **3.** to contrive to get along. **4.** to direct or control affairs.

management n. **1.** the act or manner of managing. **2.** the person or persons managing an institution, business, etc.

manager n. a person charged with the management or direction of an institution, business, or entertainer. –**managerial**, adj.

manchester n. Aust., NZ household linen.

mandarin n. **1.** (formerly) a public official in the Chinese Empire. **2.** Also, **mandarine**. a small, roundish citrus fruit.

mandate n. **1.** a commission given to a nation, by a group such as the League of Nations, to administer a territory. **2.** Politics the instruction as to policy given or supposed to be given by electors to a legislative body.

mandatory adj. obligatory.

mandible n. Anat. the bone of the lower jaw.

mandolin n. a musical instrument with a pear-shaped wooden body and metal strings.

mane n. the long hair growing on the back of or about the neck of some animals.

Don't confuse this with **main**, which means most important: The main thing to remember is to remain calm.

manga /ˈmæŋɡə/ n. the Japanese form of comic book, which has a variety of subject areas for both children and adults.

manga movie n. a Japanese animated movie, made in the style of the Japanese comic books; anime.

manganese n. a hard, brittle, greyish-white metallic element used in alloys. Symbol: Mn

mange n. a skin disease characterised by loss of hair and scabby eruptions. –**mangy**, adj.

manger n. a box or trough from which horses or cattle eat.

mangle¹ v. to cut, slash, or crush so as to disfigure.

mangle² n. a machine for pressing water out of cloth by means of rollers.

mango n. (pl. **-goes** or **-gos**) the oval yellow fruit of a tropical tree.

mangrove n. a tree found in subtropical and tropical countries on salt or brackish mud-flats.

manhandle v. to handle roughly.

manhole n. a hole, usually with a cover, through which a person may enter a sewer, drain, etc.

mania n. **1.** great excitement or enthusiasm; craze. **2.** a form of insanity. –**manic**, adj.

maniac n. a lunatic or mad person.

manic depression n. → **bipolar disorder**. –**manic depressive**, n., adj.

manicure n. (professional) care of the hands and fingernails.

manifest adj. **1.** readily perceived by the eye or the understanding. –v. **2.** to make manifest. –n. **3.** a list of goods or cargo carried by a ship, truck, etc. –**manifestation**, n.

For def. 1, the more usual word is **obvious**; for def. 2, **reveal**.

manifesto n. (pl. **-tos** or **-toes**) a public declaration, making known intentions objects, motives, etc.

manifold adj. **1.** of many kinds; numerous and varied. **2.** having many different parts, elements, features, forms, etc. **3.** a pipe or chamber with a number of inlets or outlets –v. **4.** to make copies of, as with carbon paper.

manipulate v. **1.** to handle, manage, or use. **2.** to adapt or change (accounts, figures, etc.) to suit one's purpose or advantage. –**manipulation**, n.

mankind n. **1.** the human race. **2.** men collectively, as opposed to women.

Because this term, as used in def. 1, includes the word **man**, it is seen by many to exclude women. Other words, such as **humankind** or **humanity**, are preferable.

mannequin *n.* **1.** a model of the human figure for displaying or fitting clothes. **2.** → **model** (def. 4).

manner *n.* **1.** way of doing, being done, or happening. **2.** (*pl.*) ways of behaving. **3.** kind; sort.

> Note that, for def. 2, if you have **good manners** you are polite and if you have **bad manners** you are not polite.
> Don't confuse **manner** with **manor**, which is a large British country house with its land, originally the home of a lord.

mannerism *n.* a habitual peculiarity of manner.

manoeuvre /mə'nuːvə/ *n.* **1.** a planned and regulated movement of troops, war vessels, etc. –*v.* (**-vred, -vring**) **2.** to manipulate with skill or adroitness. **3.** to perform a manoeuvre. **4.** to scheme; intrigue.

manor *n.* a large British country house with its land, originally the home of a lord.

> Don't confuse this with **manner**, which is a way of doing something: *Her manner of speaking is quite peculiar.*

manse *n.* the house and land occupied by a minister or parson.

mansion *n.* an imposing house.

manslaughter *n.* *Law* the killing of a human being unlawfully but without malice (def. 2).

mantelpiece *n.* the structure around a fireplace.

mantelshelf *n.* (*pl.* **-shelves**) the projecting part of a mantelpiece.

mantis *n.* (*pl.* **-tises** or **-tes** /-tiz/) an insect which holds the forelegs doubled up as if in prayer. Also, **praying mantis**.

mantle *n.* **1.** Also, **mantua**. a loose, sleeveless cloak. **2.** something that covers, envelops, or conceals. **3.** the middle layer of the earth.

mantra *n.* a word, phrase or verse intoned, often repetitively, to focus the mind. –**mantric**, *adj.*

manual *adj.* **1.** of or relating to the hand or hands. **2.** using or involving human energy, power, etc. –*n.* **3.** a book, giving information or instructions.

manufacture *n.* **1.** the making of goods or wares by manufacturing. –*v.* **2.** to make or produce by hand or machinery, especially on a large scale. **3.** to invent fictitiously; concoct.

manure *n.* excrement, especially of animals, used as fertiliser.

manuscript *n.* **1.** a book, document, letter, musical score, etc., written by hand. **2.** an author's copy of his or her work, used as the basis for typesetting. **3.** writing, as distinguished from print.

many **1.** constituting or forming a large number. **2.** (preceded by *as, so, too,* or *how*) relatively numerous: *as many as you need; She had never seen so many spiders; too many to count; How many books are there?* **3.** each of a large number (*a* or *an*): *Many a man has failed.* –*n.* **4.** a great number.

map *n.* a representation of the earth's surface, the heavens, etc.

maple *n.* a Nthn Hemisphere tree from which maple syrup is made.

mar *v.* (**marred, marring**) to damage; impair; spoil.

maraca *n.* a gourd filled with pebbles, seeds, etc., and used as a percussion instrument.

marathon *n.* a long-distance race.

maraud *v.* to search for things to steal or destroy. –**marauding**, *adj.*

marble *n.* **1.** a crystalline limestone much used in sculpture and architecture. **2.** something hard, cold or smooth. **3.** *Games* **a.** a little ball of glass, etc., used in a children's game. **b.** (*pl.*) the game itself. –*adj.* **4.** consisting of marble. **5.** like marble, as being hard, cold, unfeeling, etc.

6. of variegated or mottled colour. –v. **7.** to colour or stain like a variegated marble.

Note that def. 3b is used as a singular noun: *Marbles is an easy game to learn.*

march v. **1.** to (cause to) walk with regular tread, as soldiers. **2.** to proceed; advance. –n. **3.** the act or course of marching. **4.** a piece of music with a marching rhythm.

mare n. a female horse.

margarine n. a butter-like product made from refined vegetable or animal oils.

margin n. **1.** a border or edge. **2.** *Commerce* the difference between the cost and the selling price. –**marginal**, adj.

marigold n. a golden-flowered plant.

marijuana /mærə'wanə/ n. the dried leaves and flowers of Indian hemp, used in cigarettes as a narcotic and intoxicant. Also, **marihuana.**

marina /mə'rinə/ n. a facility offering docking and other services for small craft.

marinade n. a liquid, especially wine or vinegar with oil and seasonings, in which meat, fish, vegetables, etc., may be steeped before cooking.

marinate v. to let stand in a liquid before cooking or serving in order to impart flavour.

marine adj. **1.** of or relating to the sea, or to navigation or shipping. –n. **2.** one of a class of naval troops serving both on ship and on land.

Note that Australia does not have **marines** (def. 2).

mariner /'mærənə/ n. a sailor.

marital adj. of or relating to marriage.

Don't confuse this with **martial**, which means related to war or fighting: *martial arts.*

maritime adj. of or relating to the sea.

mark n. **1.** a visible trace or impression upon anything. **2.** a sign, token, or indication. **3.** a symbol used in rating conduct,

proficiency, attainment, etc., as of pupils in a school. **4.** something aimed at, as a target. –v. **5.** to be a distinguishing feature of. **6.** to put a mark or marks on. **7.** to indicate or designate by or as by marks. **8.** to notice, observe, or consider. –phr. **9. mark down**, to reduce the price of. **10. mark up**, to increase the price of.

market n. **1.** a (place for) meeting of people for selling and buying, especially of food. **2.** a body of persons dealing in a specified commodity. **3.** demand for a commodity. –v. **4.** to buy or sell in a market.

marketable adj. readily saleable.

marketplace n. **1.** an open space where a market is held. **2.** the world of business.

market research n. the gathering of information by a firm about the preferences, purchasing powers, etc., of consumers.

markup language n. a computer language in which various elements of a document, database, etc., are marked with tags, making arranging and finding data easy.

marlin n. (pl. **-lin** or **-lins**) a large, powerful game fish.

For information about the different plural forms, see the note at **fish.**

marmalade n. a jelly-like citrus preserve.

marmot n. a bushy-tailed, thickset rodent.

maroon[1] /mə'roon, mə'run/ n. **1.** dark brownish red. –adj. **2.** of a dark brownish red colour.

maroon[2] /mə'run/ v. to put ashore and leave on a desolate island or coast.

marquee n. a large tent or tentlike shelter, sometimes with open sides.

marriage n. **1.** the legal union of two people; wedlock. **2.** the legal or religious ceremony that sanctions or formalises such a union. **3.** any close union.

married adj. united in wedlock; wedded.

marrow *n.* **1.** a soft, fatty, vascular tissue inside bones. **2.** a green-skinned elongated fruit used as a cooked vegetable.

marry *v.* (**-ried, -rying**) **1.** to take in marriage. **2.** to unite in wedlock.

marsala *n.* (*sometimes upper case*) a sweet, dark, fortified wine.

marsh *n.* a tract of low, wet land.

marshal *n.* **1.** someone who organises the activities at a show or other public occasion. –*v.* (**-shalled, -shalling**) **2.** to arrange in an orderly manner.

Don't confuse this with **martial**, which describes something that is related to war or fighting.

marshmallow *n.* a confection with an elastic, spongy texture.

marsupial *n.* any member of the order which includes all of the viviparous but non-placental mammals such as kangaroos, wombats, possums, etc.

mart *n.* market.

martial *adj.* relating to or appropriate for war or fighting.

Don't confuse this with **marshal** or **marital**. A **marshal** is someone who organises the activities at a show or other public occasion, and **marital** is an adjective meaning relating to marriage.

martial art *n.* any of the several methods of unarmed self-defence, as judo, kung-fu, etc.

martinet /matə'net/ *n.* a rigid disciplinarian, especially a military one.

martini *n.* (*from trademark*) a type of cocktail.

martyr /'matə/ *n.* someone who is put to death or endures great suffering for any belief, principle, or cause.

marvel *n.* **1.** something that arouses wonder or admiration. –*v.* (**-velled, -velling**) **2.** to wonder (*at*).

marvellous *adj.* **1.** wonderful; surprising; extraordinary. **2.** excellent; superb. **3.** improbable or incredible.

marzipan *n.* a confection made of almond paste.

mascara *n.* a substance used as a cosmetic to colour the eyelashes.

mascot *n.* a person, animal, or thing supposed to bring good luck.

masculine *adj.* relating to or characteristic of a man.

mash *n.* **1.** a soft, pulpy mass. **2.** mashed potatoes. –*v.* **3.** to reduce to a soft, pulpy mass.

mask *n.* **1.** a disguise or protection for the face. **2.** a disguise; pretence. –*v.* **3.** to disguise or conceal.

masochism /'mæsəkızm/ *n.* a condition in which one compulsively seeks, and sometimes derives pleasure from, suffering. –**masochist**, *n.*

mason *n.* someone who builds or works with stone.

masonry *n.* (*pl.* **-ries**) **1.** the art or occupation of a mason. **2.** work constructed by a mason.

masquerade *n.* **1.** a party at which everyone wears a mask. **2.** disguise, or false outward show. –*v.* **3.** to disguise oneself.

mass[1] *n.* **1.** a body of coherent matter, usually large and of indefinite shape. **2.** an aggregation of particles, parts, or objects regarded as forming one body. –*v.* **3.** to come or gather together; assemble.

mass[2] *n. Roman Catholic Church, etc.* the celebration of the Eucharist.

massacre /'mæsəkə/ *n.* **1.** the unnecessary, indiscriminate slaughter of human beings. –*v.* (**-cred, -cring**) **2.** to kill indiscriminately or in large numbers.

massage *n.* **1.** the act or art of treating the body by rubbing, kneading, etc. –*v.* (**-saged, -saging**) **2.** to treat by massage.

Don't confuse this with **message**, which is a note, etc., sent from one person to another.

masseur *n.* a man who practises massage.

masseuse /mæˈsɜz, məˈsus/ n. a woman who practises massage.

massive adj. consisting of or forming a large mass; bulky and heavy.

mass media n. → media (def. 2).

See the note at **media**.

mass noun n. Gram. a noun referring to something which is thought of as existing as a mass, such as rice and water, rather than one of a series that can be counted. Also, **uncount noun**.

Compare this with **count noun**, which refers to an object which is thought of as existing in numbers so that groups of the objects can be counted.

mass-produce v. to manufacture in large quantities by standardised mechanical processes.

mast n. a tall spar which supports the yards, sails, etc., of a ship.

mastectomy n. (pl. -mies) the operation of removing a breast.

master n. 1. someone who has the power of controlling, using, or disposing of something. 2. the male head of a household. 3. a tradesperson qualified to carry on their trade independently and to teach apprentices. 4. the head teacher in a particular subject department in a secondary school. 5. someone who has been awarded a further degree, usually subsequent to a bachelor's degree, at a university (used only in titles or in certain other expressions relating to such a degree). 6. Music an original recording from which copies, remixes, etc., are made. –adj. 7. being master. 8. chief or principal. –v. 9. to conquer or subdue. 10. to rule or direct as master. 11. to make oneself master of. –**mastery**, n. –**masterly**, adv.

masterpiece n. a consummate example of skill or excellence of any kind.

masterstroke n. a masterly action or achievement.

masticate v. to chew.

masturbation n. sexual stimulation of oneself. –**masturbate**, v.

mat n. 1. a piece of fabric made of plaited or woven fibre, used to cover a floor, to wipe the shoes on, etc. 2. a small piece of material, often ornamental, set under a dish of food, a lamp, vase, etc. 3. a tangled mass. –v. (**matted, matting**) 4. to form into a mat, as by interweaving. 5. to form tangled masses.

matador n. the bullfighter who kills the bull in a bullfight.

match[1] n. a short, slender piece of wood or other material tipped with a chemical substance which produces fire when rubbed on a rough surface.

match[2] n. 1. an equal or likeness. 2. a contest or game. 3. a matrimonial compact or alliance. –v. 4. to equal, or be equal (to). 5. to (make to) correspond; adapt. 6. to fit together, as 2 things.

mate n. 1. one of a pair, especially of mated animals. 2. a. a friend. b. Aust., NZ (a form of address to a friend). 3. an assistant to a tradesperson. –v. (**mated, mating**) 4. to join as a mate or as mates. 5. (of animals) to copulate.

Traditionally, **mate** in def. 2 has been mainly used by men to refer to or address other men. Nowadays, however, many women use **mate** and are addressed as **mate**.

material n. 1. the substance of which a thing is made or composed. 2. information, ideas, or the like on which a report, thesis, etc., is based. 3. a textile fabric. –adj. 4. formed or consisting of matter; physical; corporeal. 5. relating to the physical rather than the spiritual or intellectual aspects of things. 6. pertinent or essential (to).

materialise v. 1. to assume material or bodily form. 2. to come into perceptible existence; appear. Also, **materialize**.

materialist n. someone absorbed in material interests. –**materialistic**, adj.

maternal *adj.* **1.** of or relating to a mother. **2.** related through a mother.

maternity *n.* motherhood.

mathematics *n.* the science that deals with the measurement, properties, and relations of quantities, including arithmetic, geometry, algebra, etc. Also, **maths**. –**mathematician**, *n.* –**mathematical**, *adj.*

maths *n.* → mathematics.

matinee *n.* an entertainment held in the daytime.

matriarch /'meɪtriɑk, 'mæt-/ *n.* a woman holding a position of leadership in a family or tribal society.

matriarchy /'meɪtriɑki, 'mæt-/ *n.* (*pl.* **-chies**) a form of social organisation in which the mother is head of the family, and in which descent is reckoned in the female line, the children belonging to the mother's clan.

matrices *n.* a plural form of **matrix**.

matriculate *v.* to pass matriculation.

matriculation *n.* a secondary-school examination that qualifies for admission to a tertiary education institution.

matrimony *n.* (*pl.* **-nies**) the rite, ceremony, or sacrament of marriage. –**matrimonial**, *adj.*

matrix *n.* (*pl.* **-trices** /-trəsiz/ *or* **-trixes**) **1.** that which gives origin or form to a thing, or which serves to enclose it. **2.** a network of communities, organisations, or people, forming an interconnected whole. **3.** *Maths, Computers* a rectangular array of numbers.

matron *n.* **1.** an older married woman of conservative character. **2.** *Obsolesc.* the most senior nurse in a hospital.

Note that def. 2 is not used much nowadays. The term *Director of Nursing* is usually used instead.

matt *adj.* lustreless and dull in surface.

matter *n.* **1.** the substance of which physical objects consist or are composed.

2. importance or significance. –*v.* **3.** to be of importance; signify. –*phr.* **4. the matter**, the trouble or difficulty.

matter-of-fact *adj.* adhering to actual facts; not imaginative; commonplace. –**matter-of-factly**, *adv.*

mattock *n.* an instrument for loosening soil.

mattress *n.* a case filled with soft material, often reinforced with springs, used as or on a bed.

mature *adj.* **1.** complete in natural growth or development. –*v.* **2.** to make or become mature; ripen. –**maturity**, *n.*

maudlin *adj.* tearfully or weakly emotional or sentimental.

maul *v.* to handle roughly; to injure by rough treatment.

mausoleum *n.* (*pl.* **-leums** *or* **-lea** /-'liə/) **1.** a stately and magnificent tomb. **2.** a large, old, gloomy building.

mauve /moʊv/ *n.* **1.** pale bluish purple. –*adj.* **2.** of the colour of mauve.

mawkish *adj.* sickly or slightly nauseating: *mawkish sentimentality.*

maxim *n.* a saying containing a general truth or rule, especially as to conduct, as *Look before you leap.*

maximise *v.* to increase to the greatest possible amount or degree. Also, **maximize**.

maximum *n.* (*pl.* **-mums** *or* **-ma** /-mə/) the greatest quantity or amount possible, assignable, allowable, etc. (opposed to *minimum*).

may *v.* a verb used **1.** to indicate permission: *You may go now; May I have the last piece of cake?* **2.** to indicate possibility: *They may arrive this afternoon.*

This is a modal verb and is always used with another verb. Look up **modal verb**.

maybe *adv.* perhaps.

mayday *n.* an international radio telephonic signal for help, used by ships or aircraft.

mayhem *n.* **1.** *Law* the crime of violently inflicting a bodily injury. **2.** confusion and chaos.

mayonnaise *n.* a thick dressing used for salads or vegetables.

mayor *n.* the principal officer of a municipality; the chief magistrate of a city or borough. **–mayoress** *fem. n.*

maze *n.* a confusing network of intercommunicating paths or passages; labyrinth.

me *pron.* the personal pronoun used, usually after a verb or preposition, by a speaker to refer to himself or herself: *She passed me in the street, Give it to me.*

Me is a first person singular pronoun in the objective case.

mead *n.* an alcoholic liquor made by fermenting honey and water.

meadow *n. Chiefly Brit* a piece of grassland.

meagre /'miga/ *adj.* deficient in quantity or quality.

meal¹ *n.* food eaten at regular times of the day.

meal² *n.* the edible part of a grain ground to a (coarse) powder.

mealy-mouthed *adj.* avoiding the use of plain language, as from timidity, excessive delicacy, or hypocrisy.

mean¹ *v.* (**meant** /ment/, **meaning**) **1.** to have in the mind as in intention or purpose. **2.** to intend for a particular purpose, destination, etc. **3.** (of words, things, etc.) to signify. **4.** to be minded or disposed; have intentions. **–meaning**, *n.*

mean² *adj.* **1.** inferior in grade, quality or character. **2.** stingy or miserly. **3.** *Informal* powerful, effective.

mean³ *n.* **1.** something intermediate; that which is midway between 2 extremes. **2.** *Maths* a quantity having a value intermediate between the values of other quantities; an average. **–adj.** **3.** occupying a middle position.

meander /mi'ænda/ *v.* to proceed by a winding course.

meaning *n.* something which is intended to be, or is, said or shown; significance; import.

means *pl.* *n.* **1.** a method, etc., used to attain an end. **2.** disposable resources, especially money.

Note that def. 1 is usually used as a singular noun: *The new means of treating the disease has proved very successful.*

means test *n.* an evaluation of the income and resources of a person, in order to determine eligibility for a pension, grant, allowance, etc.

meantime *n.* **1.** the intervening time. **–adv.** **2.** meanwhile.

meanwhile *adv.* in the intervening time; at the same time.

measles *n.* an acute infectious disease occurring mostly in children.

Although this looks like a plural noun, it is actually singular: *Measles is a very dangerous disease.*

measly *adj.* (**-lier, -liest**) *Informal* poor or unsatisfactory; very small.

measure *n.* **1.** size, dimensions, quantity, etc. **2.** a unit or standard of measurement. **3.** a system of measurement. **4.** any standard of comparison, estimation, or judgement. **5.** an action intended as a means to an end. **–v.** **6.** to ascertain the extent, capacity, etc., of, especially by comparison with a standard. **7.** to mark (*off*) or deal (*out*) in a certain quantity. **8.** to take measurements. **9.** to be of a specified size, quantity, etc. **–measurement**, *n.*

meat *n.* **1.** the flesh of animals as used for food. **2.** the edible part of a fruit, nut, etc. **3.** the main substance of something, as an argument.

Don't confuse this with **meet**, which is to come together with someone: *I'll meet you at the theatre.*

mechanic *n.* a skilled worker with tools or machines.

mechanical *adj.* **1.** of or relating to machinery. **2.** relating to, or controlled or effected by, physical forces.

mechanics *n.* **1.** the branch of knowledge concerned with machinery. **2.** the science dealing with the action of forces on bodies and with motion.

mechanise *v.* to introduce machinery into (an industry, etc.). Also, **mechanize**.

mechanism *n.* **1.** the machinery, or the agencies or means, by which a particular effect is produced or a purpose is accomplished. **2.** the way in which a thing works or operates.

medal *n.* a flat piece of inscribed metal, given as a reward for bravery, merit, etc.

Don't confuse **medal** with **meddle**, which is to interfere with something that has nothing to do with you.

medallion *n.* a large medal.

meddle *v.* to concern oneself with or in something without warrant or necessity; interfere.

Don't confuse **meddle** with **medal**, which is a metal disc or cross given as a reward for bravery or as a prize.

medevac /ˈmɛdivæk/ *n.* **1.** evacuation of seriously ill or wounded person, usually by aircraft. *–v.* (**-vaced** /-væk/, **-vacing** /-vækɪŋ/) **2.** to evacuate (such a seriously ill or wounded person). Also, **medivac**.

media *n.* **1.** a plural of **medium**. **2.** Also, **mass media**. the means of communication to large numbers of people, including radio, television, newspapers and magazines.

This word is actually the plural of **medium** but it can be treated as a singular or plural noun: *The media encourages violence; The media are to blame for the loss of the election.* It is mainly used as a plural when a variety of different forms of

media, such as radio, television, newspapers, etc., is being referred to.

medial *adj.* situated in or relating to the middle.

median *adj.* **1.** situated in or relating to the middle. *–n.* **2.** the middle number in a given sequence of numbers.

median strip *n.* a dividing area, often raised or landscaped, between opposing traffic lanes on a highway.

mediate *v.* to act between parties to effect an agreement, compromise, or reconciliation. **–mediator**, *n.* **–mediation**, *n.*

medical *adj.* **1.** of or relating to the science or practice of medicine. *–n.* **2.** a medical examination.

medical imaging *n. Med.* the creation of images of internal organs or parts of the body, as by X-ray, ultrasound or CAT scan, to assist diagnosis and the performance of medical procedures.

medicate *v.* to treat with medicine. **–medication**, *n.*

medicine *n.* **1.** any substance or substances used in treating disease. **2.** the art or science of restoring or preserving health. **3.** the medical profession.

When people use **medicine** as in def. 1, they are usually referring to a liquid medicine rather than tablets. The general term covering both kinds is **medication**.

medieval *adj.* of or relating to the Middle Ages. Also, **mediaeval**.

mediocre /midiˈoʊkə/ *adj.* of middling quality; ordinary.

meditate *v.* to engage in thought or contemplation; reflect. **–meditation**, *n.*

medium *n.* (*pl.* **-dia** or **-diums**) **1.** a middle state or condition. **2.** an intervening substance, as air, etc., through which a force acts or an effect is produced. **3.** the element in which an organism has its natural habitat. **4.** an agency means, or instrument. *–adj.* **5.** intermediate in degree, quality, etc.

medivac /'mɛdivæk/ *n., v.* → **medevac**.

medley *n.* a mixture.

meek *adj.* humbly patient or submissive.

meet *v.* (**met**, **meeting**) **1.** to come into contact, junction, or connection with. **2.** to go to the place of arrival of, as to welcome. **3.** to come into personal acquaintance with. **4.** to cope or deal effectively with. **5.** to come together in opposition or conflict. **–***n.* **6.** a meeting, especially for a sporting event.

Don't confuse **meet** with **meat**, which is animal flesh used as food.

meeting *n.* an assembly or gathering.

mega *Informal* –*adj.* **1.** extremely great in size, importance, etc. **2.** excellent; great. –*adv.* **3.** an intensifier: *She seemed mega unhappy.*

megabit *n.* a unit of measurement of computer memory size equal to one million bits. *Symbol:* Mb

megabyte *n. Computers* a unit of measurement of computer memory size equal to 2^{20} (approximately 10^6) bytes. *Symbol:* MB

megafauna *n.* members of the larger animal species, especially those that are extinct, as the mammoth, and various Aust. marsupials.

megalomania *n.* a form of mental alienation marked by delusions of greatness, wealth, etc.

megaphone *n.* a funnel-shaped device for increasing the volume of a speaker's voice.

megapixel *n. Photography* one million pixels, usually in reference to the resolution of a digital camera.

megaton *n.* **1.** one million tons. **2.** an explosive force equal to that of one million tons of TNT.

megawatt *n. Elect.* a unit of power, equal to one million watts. *Symbol:* MW

meiosis /mar'ousɪs/ *n.* the development process of gametes, consisting of two cell divisions, in the course of which the chromosomes are duplicated only once. –**meiotic**, *adj.*

melaleuca /mɛlə'lukə/ *n.* a type of tree or shrub mainly found in Aust., usually on river banks or in swamps.

melancholy /'mɛlənkɒli/ *n.* **1.** a gloomy state of mind, especially when habitual or prolonged; depression. –*adj.* **2.** affected with melancholy.

melanin *n.* any of various dark pigments in the body of humans and certain animals.

melanoma *n.* a malignant tumour derived from pigment-containing cells, especially in skin.

melatonin *n.* a hormone secreted during the night, which causes lightening of the skin in some animals and the tendency to sleep.

meld *v.* to blend or combine.

melee /'me'leɪ, -'liː/ *n.* **1.** a confused general hand-to-hand fight. **2.** any noisy or confused situation.

mellifluous /mə'lɪfluəs/ *adj.* sweetly or smoothly flowing.

mellow *adj.* **1.** soft and full-flavoured from ripeness, as fruit. **2.** soft and rich, as sound, colour, etc. **3.** genial; jovial. –*v.* **4.** to make or become mellow.

melodic *adj.* **1.** melodious. **2.** relating to melody as distinguished from harmony and rhythm.

melodrama *n.* a play in which the drama is exaggerated.

melody *n.* (*pl.* **-dies**) musical sounds in agreeable succession or arrangement. –**melodious**, *adj.*

melon *n.* a type of large, juicy fruit.

melt *v.* (**melted**, **melted** or **molten**, **melting**) **1.** to liquefy by heat. **2.** to pass, change, or blend gradually (*into*). **3.** to soften in feeling, as a person, the heart, etc.

member *n.* a constituent part of any structural or composite whole.

membrane *n.* **1.** a thin layer of animal or vegetable tissue, as one which lines an organ, etc. **2.** any thin connecting layer.

memento *n.* (*pl.* **-tos** *or* **-toes**) something that serves as a reminder of what is past or gone.

This word is sometimes spelt **momento**, but this spelling is not regarded as correct.

memo *n.* (*pl.* **memos**) **1.** a note, as one sent from one member of an organisation to another. **2.** a note made of something to be remembered.

This is short for **memorandum**.

memoirs /ˈmɛmwaz/ *pl. n.* records of one's own life and experiences. Also, **memoir**.

memorabilia /mɛmərəˈbɪliə/ *pl. n.* **1.** matters or events worthy to be remembered. **2.** things saved or collected as souvenirs.

memorable *adj.* worthy of being remembered.

memorandum *n.* (*pl.* **-dums** *or* **-da**) → **memo**.

memorial *n.* something designed to preserve the memory of a person, event, etc.

memorise *v.* to commit to memory, or learn by heart. Also, **memorize**.

memory *n.* (*pl.* **-ries**) **1.** the mental capacity or faculty of retaining and reviving impressions, or of recalling or recognising previous experiences. **2.** a mental impression retained; a recollection. **3.** the state or fact of being remembered. **4.** *Computers* the part of a digital computer in which data and instructions are held until they are required.

memory stick *n.* → **USB drive**.

men *n.* plural of **man**.

menace *n.* **1.** a threat. **2.** *Informal* a nuisance. –*v.* (**-aced, -acing**) **3.** to threaten.

menagerie *n.* a collection of wild or strange animals, especially for exhibition.

mend *v.* **1.** to make whole or sound by repairing. **2.** to set right; make better.

menial *adj.* **1.** relating or proper to domestic servants. **2.** of lowly status.

meningitis /mɛnənˈdʒaɪtəs/ *n. Pathol.* a disease marked by inflammation of brain tissue.

meningococcal disease /mənɪndʒə-ˈkɒkəl/ *n.* a potentially fatal form of bacterial meningitis marked by the rapid onset of flu-like symptoms.

meningococcus /mənɪndʒəˈkɒkəs/ *n.* a bacterium which can cause meningitis or sepsis. –**meningococcal**, *adj.*

menopause *n.* the cessation of menstruation.

menses /ˈmɛnsiz/ *pl. n.* the monthly discharge of blood and mucous membrane tissue from the uterus.

menstrual cycle *n.* (in most primates) the approximately monthly cycle of ovulation and menstruation.

menstruate *v.* to discharge the menses. –**menstruation**, *n.* –**menstrual**, *adj.*

mensuration *n.* the act, art, or process of measuring.

mental *adj.* **1.** of or relating to the mind. **2.** for or relating to those with disordered minds. **3.** *Informal* foolish or mad.

mentality *n.* (*pl.* **-ties**) mental capacity or endowment.

mention *v.* **1.** to refer to briefly or incidentally. –*n.* **2.** a referring or reference.

mentor *n.* **1.** a wise and trusted counsellor. **2.** (especially in an organisation) a person who is considered to have sufficient experience or expertise to be able to assist others less experienced. –*v.* **3.** to act as a mentor towards: *In our school, the older students mentor the younger ones.* –**mentoring**, *n.*

The more usual word for def. 1 is **adviser**.

menu *n.* **1.** a list of the dishes served at a meal. **2.** *Computers* a range of optional procedures presented to an operator by a computer.

mercantile *adj.* of or relating to merchants or to trade; commercial.

mercenary adj. 1. working or acting merely for gain. –n. (pl. **-ries**) 2. a professional soldier serving in a foreign army.

merchandise n. /ˈmɜːtʃəndaɪs/ 1. the stock of a store. –v. /ˈmɜːtʃəndaɪz/ 2. to trade (in). –**merchandising**, n.

merchant n. 1. someone who buys and sells commodities for profit; a wholesaler. –adj. 2. relating to trade or commerce.

merchant navy n. the vessels of a nation engaged in commerce.

mercury n. Chem. a heavy, silver-white metallic element, remarkable for its fluidity at ordinary temperatures; quicksilver. Symbol: Hg

mercy n. (pl. **-cies**) 1. compassionate or kindly forbearance. –phr. 2. **at the mercy of**, defenceless or unprotected against. –**merciful**, adj. –**merciless**, adj.

mere adj. (**merest**) being nothing more nor better than that stated. –**merely**, adv.

merge v. 1. to unite or combine. 2. to become swallowed up or absorbed (in or into).

merger n. a statutory combination of 2 or more companies.

meridian n. Geog. a line of longitude.

meringue /məˈræŋ/ n. a mixture of sugar and beaten egg whites, baked.

merino n. (pl. **-nos**) one of a variety of sheep valued for its fine wool.

merit n. 1. excellence; worth. 2. (pl.) the essential right and wrong of a matter. –v. 3. to be worthy of; deserve. –**meritorious**, adj.

mermaid n. an imaginary creature with the head and torso of a woman and the tail of a fish.

merry adj. (**-rier**, **-riest**) full of cheer or gaiety.

merry-go-round n. a machine on which children ride for amusement; roundabout; carousel.

mesh n. 1. a network or net. 2. light woven or welded interlocking links or wires. –v. 3. to entangle or become entangled. 4. Machinery to engage, as gear teeth.

mesmerise v. 1. to completely hold the attention of. 2. Obs. to hypnotise. Also, **mesmerize**.

mess n. 1. a dirty or untidy condition. 2. a place used by service personnel, etc., for eating, recreation, etc. 3. excrement, especially of an animal. –phr. 4. **mess around** (or **about**), to waste time. 5. **mess up, a.** to make dirty or untidy. **b.** to throw into confusion.

message n. 1. information, etc. transmitted through a messenger or other agency. 2. the moral or meaning intended to be conveyed by a book, film, play, or the like. –v. (**-aged, -aging**) 3. to communicate with someone by text messaging.

Don't confuse **message** with **massage**, which is the act of rubbing someone's body to relax it or reduce pain.

messaging n. communication by text messages.

messenger n. someone who bears a message or goes on an errand.

met v. past tense and present participle of **meet**.

metabolism n. the sum of the processes in an organism by which food is built up into living protoplasm and protoplasm is broken down into simpler compounds, with the exchange of energy.

metal n. 1. an opaque, ductile, conductive, elementary sub stance, as silver, copper, etc. 2. an alloy or mixture of these. –**metallic**, adj.

Don't confuse **metal** with **mettle**, which is a literary word for the quality of someone's character, especially when spirited or brave.

metallurgy /ˈmetələdʒi, məˈtælədʒi/ n. 1. the science of metals and their structures and properties. 2. the art or science of separating metals from their ores, of compounding alloys or working metals.

metamorphosis /mɛtəˈmɔfəsəs/ *n.* (*pl.* -**phoses** /-fəsiz/) **1.** any complete change in appearance, character, circumstances, etc. **2.** a form resulting from this. –**metamorphic**, *adj.* –**metamorphose**, *v.*

metaphor *n.* a figure of speech in which something is spoken of as if it were actually something else. For example, *Knowledge is a key that opens many doors.* –**metaphorical**, *adj.*

Compare **metaphor** with **simile**, which points out a likeness between two things using the words *like* or *as*, as in *The room was as pretty as a picture.* A metaphor says something *is* something else.

metaphysical *adj.* concerned with abstract thought or subjects.

metaphysics *n.* philosophy, especially in its more abstruse branches. –**metaphysicist**, *n.*

mete *v.* to allot; distribute or measure (*out*).

meteor *n.* a transient fiery streak in the sky produced by a comet, etc., passing through the earth's atmosphere. –**meteoric**, *adj.*

meteorite *n.* a mass of stone or metal that has reached the earth from outer space.

meteorology *n.* the science of weather. –**meteorologist**, *n.*

meter *n.* an instrument that measures.

Don't confuse this with **metre**, which is a unit of length in the metric system. **Metre** is also the rhythm of a piece of poetry.

methadone *n.* a powerful analgesic drug used for the treatment of drug withdrawal symptoms.

methamphetamine /mɛθæmˈfɛtəmin/ *n.* a synthetic drug which acts as a powerful central nervous system stimulant.

methane *n.* a colourless, odourless, flammable gas.

metho *n. Informal* **1.** methylated spirits. **2.** someone addicted to drinking methylated spirits.

method *n.* a way of doing something, especially in accordance with a definite plan.

methodical *adj.* systematic.

methodology *n.* (*pl.* -**gies**) a systematic approach to scientific inquiry, employed in various sciences.

methylated spirits *n.* an alcohol, made unfit for drinking by adding a poisonous substance, used for burning, cleaning, etc.

meticulous *adj.* minutely careful.

metre[1] *n.* a unit of length in the metric system. *Symbol:* m

Don't confuse **metre** with **meter**, which is an instrument that measures something: *a water meter.*

metre[2] *n.* arrangement of words in rhythmic lines or verses.

metric *adj.* relating to the metre or to the system of measures and measures originally based upon it.

metric system *n.* the international standard system of weights and measures based on the number 10. The modern metric system, known as the International System of Units (SI), comprises 7 base units, the metre (m), kilogram (kg), second (s), ampere (A), kelvin (K), mole (mol), and candela (cd).

metronome *n.* a mechanical device for marking time in music.

metropolis *n.* the chief city (not necessarily the capital) of a country, state, or region. –**metropolitan**, *adj.*

mettle *n.* **1.** characteristic disposition or temper. **2.** spirit; courage.

Don't confuse **mettle** with **metal**, which is a shiny element such as iron, copper or gold.

mew *n.* **1.** the sound a cat makes. –*v.* **2.** to make this sound.

mews *pl. n.* a set of stables or garages.

Note that although this word is a plural noun, it is usually treated as a singular: *The mews is at the end of the lane.*

mezzanine *n.* a low storey between 2 other storeys.

mica *n.* any member of a group of minerals that separate readily (by cleavage) into thin, tough, often transparent layers.

mice *n.* plural of **mouse.**

micro *adj.* individual or particular (opposed to *macro*): *at the micro level.*

microbe *n.* a microscopic organism; germ.

microbead *n.* a microscopic sphere of plastic, a quantity of which is used in cosmetics, toothpaste, etc.; can cause pollution of waterways and oceans, creating a hazard to marine life.

microblog *n.* **1.** an internet posting which is extremely short, designed to give a brief but immediate text update. *–v.* (**-blogged, -blogging**) **2.** to issue such an internet posting. **–microblogging**, *n.* **–microblogger,** *n.*

microchip *n.* a very small chip (def. 3).

microcomputer *n.* a small computer which has its central processor functions contained on a single printed circuit board.

microcopy *n.* (*pl.* **-pies**) a greatly reduced photographic copy of a book, page, etc.

microcosm *n.* anything regarded as a world in miniature.

microfiche *n.* a transparency in microfilm about the size and shape of a filing card which may have on it many pages of print.

microfilm *n.* a very small photograph, inspected by optical enlargement.

micron *n.* a millionth part of a metre.

microorganism *n.* a microscopic animal or vegetable organism.

microphone *n.* an instrument which is capable of transforming the air-pressure waves of sound into changes in electric currents or voltages. Also, **mike.**

microprocessor *n.* a small computer, often dedicated to specific functions.

microscope *n.* an optical instrument for inspecting objects too small to be seen clearly by the naked eye.

microscopic *adj.* **1.** so small as to be invisible or indistinct without the use of the microscope. **2.** of or relating to the microscope or its use.

microwave *n.* **1.** an electromagnetic wave of extremely high frequency. **2.** Also, **microwave oven.** an oven which cooks with unusual rapidity, by passing microwaves through food.

mid *adj.* central; at or near the middle point.

midair *n.* any elevated position above the ground.

midday *n.* the middle of the day; noon.

middle *adj.* **1.** equally distant from extremes or limits. **2.** medium. *–n.* **3.** the point, part, etc., equally distant from extremes or limits.

middle-aged *adj.* intermediate in age between youth and old age.

middle class *n.* the group of people of middle income in a society, especially business and professional people and public servants.

Compare this with **upper class** and **lower class**.
Middle class is a collective noun and can be used with a singular or plural verb. Look up **collective noun.**

middleman *n.* (*pl.* **-men**) **1.** a trader who makes a profit by buying from producers and selling to retailers or consumers. **2.** someone who acts as an intermediary between others.

middling *adj.* medium in size, quality, grade, rank, etc.

middy *n.* (*pl.* **-dies**) *Aust.* a medium-sized beer glass; pot.

midge *n.* a small flying insect.

midget *n.* something very small of its kind.

midnight *n.* **1.** 12 o'clock at night. **2.** dark, like midnight. *–phr.* **3. burn the midnight oil,** to study or work far into the night.

midriff *n.* **1.** the middle part of the body, between the chest and the waist. *–adj.* **2.** of a dress, blouse etc., which exposes this part.

midshipman n. (pl. **-men**) a probationary rank held by naval cadets before qualifying as officers.

midst n. the middle point, part, or stage.

midstream n. **1.** the middle of a stream. –phr. **2. in midstream**, Informal in the middle; at a critical point.

midway adv. **1.** halfway. –adj. **2.** in the middle.

midwifery /mɪd'wɪfəri/ n. the art or practice of assisting women in childbirth. –**midwife**, n.

mien /miːn/ n. air, bearing, or aspect, as showing character, feeling, etc.

miffed adj. Informal annoyed; displeased.

might¹ v. **1.** a verb used to indicate possibility: I carried my umbrella because I thought I might need it. –phr. **2. might as well**, an expression used to suggest some course of action in the absence of something better: He won't turn up now – we might as well go home.

This is a modal verb and is always used with another verb. Look up **modal verb**.

might² n. power or force, especially military, political, etc. –**mighty**, adj.

migraine /'maɪgreɪn, 'miːgreɪn/ n. a severe headache, usually associated with nausea.

migrant n. **1.** someone who migrates. **2.** an immigrant, especially a recent immigrant. –adj. **3.** of or relating to migration or migrants.

migrate v. **1.** to pass periodically from one region to another, as certain birds, fishes, and animals. **2.** to go to live in another country. **3.** Computers to transfer (data) from one system to another. –**migration**, n. –**migratory**, adj.

If you want to talk about someone migrating to a country you can say that they are **immigrating**, and if they are migrating from a country you can say they are **emigrating**.

Note that birds and animals **migrate**, but they do not **emigrate** or **immigrate**. Humans do all three.

mike n. Informal → **microphone**.

mild adj. **1.** amiably gentle or temperate in feeling or behaviour towards others. **2.** gentle or moderate in force, effect or intensity.

mildew n. **1.** a plant disease usually characterised by a whitish coating. **2.** a fine coating of fungus appearing on materials exposed to moisture.

mile n. **1.** a unit of measurement of length in the imperial system, equal to about 1.6 kilometres. **2.** (oft. pl.) a large distance or quantity. –**mileage**, n.

milestone n. Also, **milepost**. a stone set up to mark the distance to or from a town, as along a highway. **2.** a significant point in one's life or career.

milieu /'miːljɜ/ n. (pl. **milieus** or **milieux**) the total surrounding area, state or atmosphere in which someone lives or operates: the social milieu.

The more usual word is **environment**.

militant adj. engaged in warfare; warring.

military adj. **1.** of or relating to the army or war. –n. **2.** the armed forces.

militate v. to operate (against or in favour of); have effect or influence.

Don't confuse this with **mitigate**, which means to lessen in severity.

militia /mɪ'lɪʃə/ n. **1.** a body of people enrolled for military service, called out periodically for drill and exercise but for actual service only in emergencies. **2.** a body of citizen soldiers as distinguished from professional soldiers. **3.** a member of a militia.

milk n. **1.** an opaque white liquid food secreted by the mammary glands of female mammals. –v. **2.** to press or draw milk by hand or machine from (a cow, etc.). **3.** to extract (something) as if by milking; draw.

milk bar n. a shop where milk drinks, ice-cream, sandwiches, etc., are sold.

milkshake *n.* a frothy drink made of milk, flavouring, and sometimes ice-cream, shaken together.

milk tooth *n.* a temporary tooth eventually replaced by a permanent tooth. Also, **baby tooth**.

mill *n.* **1.** a building fitted with machinery, in which some mechanical operation or form of manufacture is carried on. **2.** a machine which does its work by rotary motion. *–v.* **3.** to grind, work, treat, or shape in or with a mill. **4.** to move (*about*) confusedly in a circle. *–phr.* **5. run of the mill**, conventional; commonplace.

millennium *n.* (*pl.* **-nia** /-niə/ *or* **-niums**) a period of 1000 years.

This word is often spelt **millenium**, but this is not regarded as correct.

millet *n.* a cereal grass.

millibar *n.* in the metric system, a unit of measurement of air pressure, especially in the atmosphere.

milligram *n.* in the metric system, a unit of weight equal to 0.001 gram. *Symbol:* mg

millilitre *n.* in the metric system, a unit of measurement of liquid equal to 0.001 litre. *Symbol:* mL, ml

millimetre *n.* in the metric system, a unit of length equal to 0.001 metre. *Symbol:* mm

milliner *n.* someone who makes or sells hats for women. **–millinery**, *n.*

million *n.* (*pl.* **-lions**, *as after a numeral,* **-lion**) **1.** a cardinal number, 1000 times 1000, or 10^6. **2.** a very great number. *–adj.* **3.** amounting to one million in number. **–millionth**, *adj.*, *n.*

Numbers used before a noun are sometimes called **determiners**.

millionaire *n.* a person worth a million or millions, as of dollars, pounds, etc.

millipede *n.* an insect with a segmented body and many legs.

millstone *n.* **1.** either of a pair of circular stones used for grinding. **2.** a heavy burden.

mime *n.* **1.** the art of expressing emotion, character, action, etc., by gestures and movements alone. **2.** a performance or performer in mime. *–v.* **3.** to make such gestures.

mimic *v.* (**-icked, -icking**) **1.** to imitate or copy. *–n.* **2.** someone apt at imitating the characteristic voice or gesture of others. **–mimicry**, *n.*

minaret *n.* a tall, thin tower attached to a mosque.

mince *v.* (**minced, mincing**) **1.** to cut or chop into very small pieces. **2.** to act or utter with affected elegance. *–n.* **3.** minced meat.

mincemeat *n.* **1.** a mixture composed of minced apples, suet, candied peel, etc., with raisins, currants, etc., for filling a pie (**mince pie**). **2.** meat chopped fine. **3.** anything cut up very small.

mind *n.* **1.** that part of a person which thinks, feels, and wills, exercises perception, judgement, reflection, etc. **2.** intellectual power or ability. **3.** purpose, intention, or will. *–v.* **4.** to apply oneself or attend to. **5.** to be careful, cautious, or wary concerning. **6.** to perceive or notice. **7.** to object to. *–phr.* **8. make up one's mind**, to come to a decision. **9. out of one's mind**, demented; delirious. **10. to one's mind**, in one's opinion or judgement.

Def. 7 is used in negative sentences (*I don't mind the rain*) or in requests (*Would you mind closing the door?*).

mindful *adj.* attentive; careful (*of*).

The more usual word is **aware**.

mind map *n.* a visual representation of the way in which concepts are related around a central key word or idea.

mine¹ *pron.* **1.** the possessive form of **I**, used without a noun following: *That red* *car is mine.* **2.** the person(s) or thing(s) belonging to me: *Mine is that red car over there.*

Mine is a first person singular pronoun in the possessive case.

mine² *n.* **1.** an excavation made in the earth to get out ores, coal, etc. **2.** an abounding source or store of anything. **3.** an explosive device. –*v.* **4.** to dig (a mine). **5.** to extract (ores, coal, etc.) from a mine. **6.** to dig or lay an explosive device under. –**miner**, *n.*

mineral *n.* **1.** a substance obtained by mining; ore. **2.** any of a class of inorganic substances occurring in nature, having a definite chemical composition and crystal structure.

mineralogy /mɪnəˈrælədʒi, -ˈrɒl-/ *n.* the science of minerals. –**mineralogical**, *adj.* –**mineralogist**, *n.*

mineral water *n.* **1.** water containing dissolved mineral salts or gases. **2.** carbonated water.

minestrone /mɪnəˈstrouni/ *n.* a soup containing vegetables, herbs, pasta, etc., in chicken or meat stock.

mingle *v.* **1.** to become mixed, blended, or united. **2.** to mix, blend or combine. **3.** to associate or mix in company.

mini *n.* something small of its kind, as a skirt or motor vehicle.

miniature /ˈmɪnɪtʃə/ *n.* **1.** a representation or image of anything on a very small scale. –*adj.* **2.** on a very small scale; reduced.

minibus *n.* a motor vehicle for carrying between five and ten passengers.

minigolf *n.* a form of golf played on a very small course with fancifully contrived obstacles and hazards.

minim *n. Music* a note equal in length to one half of a semibreve.

minimise *v.* to reduce to the smallest possible amount or degree. Also, **minimize**.

minimum *n.* (*pl.* **-mums** *or* **-ma**) **1.** the least quantity or amount possible, assignable, allowable, etc. **2.** the lowest amount, value, or degree attained or recorded (opposed to *maximum*). –*adj.* **3.** relating to a minimum. –**minimal**, *adj.*

minion *n.* a subordinate or employee, usually seen as favoured or servile.

minister *n.* **1.** a person authorised to conduct religious worship; member of the clergy; pastor. **2.** a member of the government in charge of a portfolio. –*v.* **3.** to give service, care, or aid. –**ministerial**, *adj.* –**ministry**, *n.*

mink *n.* (*pl.* **minks** *or, especially collectively,* **mink**) **1.** a semi-aquatic weasel-like animal. **2.** its valuable fur.

minnow *n.* **1.** (*pl.* **-nows** *or* **-now**) a small European fish. **2.** an insignificant person or thing.

For information about the different plural forms for def. 1, see the note at **fish**.

minor *adj.* **1.** lesser, as in size, extent, or importance, or being the lesser of 2. **2.** under legal age. –*n.* **3.** a person under legal age.

minority *n.* (*pl.* **-ties**) **1.** the smaller part or number. **2.** a group of people whose ethnic background, religion, political views, etc., differ from those of the majority of people in a country or community. –*adj.* **3.** of or relating to a minority.

Note that this word can be used as a singular or plural noun depending on whether you are thinking about the group as a single item or about all the individuals that make up the group. For example, in *A disruptive minority has spoilt the day for the rest of us,* **minority** is treated as a singular noun because that small group of people is thought of as a single item. However, in *A minority have done well under this system, but most have found it a failure,* it is used as a plural because the group is regarded as a collection of separate individuals.

minstrel *n.* a medieval musician who sang or recited to the accompaniment of instruments.

mint¹ *n.* **1.** an aromatic herb. **2.** a mint-flavoured sweet.

mint² *n.* **1.** a place where money is coined by public authority. *–v.* **2.** to coin (money).

minuet /mɪnju'ɛt/ *n.* a slow stately dance of French origin.

minus *prep.* **1.** less by the subtraction of; decreased by. *–adj.* **2.** algebraically negative. *–n.* **3.** a deficiency or loss.

minuscule /'mɪnəskjul/ *adj.* very small; tiny.

This word is sometimes spelt **miniscule**, but this spelling is not regarded as correct.

minute¹ /'mɪnət/ *n.* **1.** the 60th part of an hour; 60 seconds. **2.** a point of time; an instant or moment. **3.** (*pl.*) the official record of the proceedings at a meeting.

minute² /mar'nju:t/ *adj.* **1.** extremely small. **2.** attentive to or concerned with even very small details or particulars.

minutia /mar'nju:ʃə, -tiə/ *n.* (*pl.* **-tiae** /-ʃii, -tii/) (*usu. pl.*) a small or trivial detail.

minx *n.* a pert, impudent, or flirtatious young woman.

miracle *n.* a wonderful thing; a marvel. *–***miraculous**, *adj.*

mirage *n.* an optical illusion by which reflected images of distant objects are seen, often inverted.

mire *n.* a piece of wet, swampy ground.

The more usual word is **mud**.

mirror *n.* **1.** a reflecting surface, usually glass with a metallic backing; a looking glass. *–v.* **2.** to reflect in or as in a mirror, or as a mirror does.

mirth *n.* amusement or laughter.

misadventure *n.* an accident.

misanthropy /mɪs'zænθrəpi/ *n.* hatred, dislike, or distrust of humankind.

misappropriate *v.* to apply wrongfully or dishonestly to one's own use. *–***misappropriation**, *n.*

The more usual word is **steal**.

miscarriage *n.* **1.** failure to attain the right or desired result. **2.** premature expulsion of a fetus from the uterus, especially before it is viable. *–***miscarry**, *v.*

miscellaneous *adj.* consisting of members or elements of different kinds.

miscellany /mə'sɛləni/ *n.* (*pl.* **-nies**) a miscellaneous collection.

mischief *n.* **1.** teasing or annoying conduct. **2.** an injury due to some cause. *–***mischievous**, *adj.*

misconception *n.* erroneous conception; a mistaken notion.

misdemeanour *n. Law* a less serious crime. Compare **felony**. Also, **misdemeanor**.

miser *n.* a stingy person. *–***miserly**, *adj.*

miserable *adj.* **1.** wretchedly unhappy. **2.** attended with or causing misery.

misery *n.* (*pl.* **-ries**) **1.** great distress of mind. **2.** wretchedness of condition or circumstances.

misfire *v.* **1.** to fail to fire or explode. **2.** to be unsuccessful.

misfit *n.* someone who feels ill at ease or out of place in a given environment.

misgiving *n.* a feeling of doubt, distrust, or apprehension.

mishap /'mɪshæp/ *n.* an unfortunate accident.

mishmash *n.* a hotchpotch; jumble.

mislay *v.* (**-laid**, **-laying**) to put in a place afterwards forgotten.

mislead *v.* (**-led**, **-leading**) to lead or guide wrongly; lead astray.

misnomer *n.* a misapplied name or designation.

misogyny /mə'sɒdʒəni/ *n.* **1.** hatred of women. **2.** entrenched prejudice against women. *–***misogynist**, *n.*

misprint *n.* a mistake in printing.

miss[1] v. **1.** to fail to hit, light upon, meet, catch, receive, obtain, attain, accomplish, see, hear, (something). **2.** to perceive the absence or loss of, often with regret. **3.** to be unsuccessful. –n. **4.** a failure to hit, meet, obtain, or accomplish something. –phr. **5. miss out**, to fail to receive, especially something desired.

miss[2] n. (pl. **misses**) (usu. upper case) the conventional title of respect for an unmarried woman, prefixed to the name.

misshapen adj. badly shaped; deformed.

missile n. an object or weapon that can be thrown, hurled, or shot.

missing adj. lacking; absent; not found.

mission n. **1.** a body of persons sent to a foreign country to conduct negotiations, establish relations, or the like. **2.** the business with which an agent, envoy, etc., is charged. **3.** an establishment for propagating religion.

missionary /ˈmɪʃənri/ n. a person sent to spread their religious faith in another land.

missive n. a written message; a letter.

mist n. a cloudlike aggregation of minute globules of water in the air.

mistake n. **1.** an error in action, opinion or judgement. –v. (**mistook**, **mistaken**, **mistaking**) **2.** to conceive of or understand wrongly.

mister n. (upper case) the conventional title of respect for a man, prefixed to the name, usually written Mr.

mistletoe n. a parasitic plant, traditionally used in Christmas decorations.

mistress n. **1.** a woman who has authority or control. **2.** Aust. a female head teacher in a particular school department in a secondary school. **3.** a woman who has a continuing sexual relationship with a man outside marriage.

mistrust n. **1.** lack of trust or confidence. –v. **2.** to regard with mistrust; distrust.

misunderstanding n. **1.** disagreement or dissension. **2.** failure to understand.

misuse n. /mɪsˈjus/ **1.** wrong or improper use. –v. /mɪsˈjuz/ **2.** to ill-use; maltreat.

mite n. any of various small arachnids, many being parasitic on plants and animals.

mitigate v. **1.** to moderate the severity of (anything distressing). **2.** to become milder. –**mitigation**, n.

> The more usual word is **relieve**.
> Don't confuse **mitigate** with **militate against**, which means to influence against something happening.

mitosis n. an asexual method of cell division in which the chromosomes in the cell nucleus double and then separate to form two identical cells. –**mitotic**, adj.

mitre n. **1.** the ceremonial headdress of a bishop. **2.** a right-angled joint, as of a picture frame.

mitten n. a kind of hand-covering enclosing the 4 fingers together and the thumb separately.

mix v. **1.** to combine (elements) together into one mass or assemblage. **2.** to become mixed. **3.** to associate, as in company. –n. **4.** a mixture.

> Note that **mix** (def. 1) is often used with and or with, as in Mix the flour and the water or Mix the flour with the water.

mixed adj. composed of different constituents or elements.

mixture n. any combination of differing elements.

mix-up n. a confused state of things; muddle; tangle.

mnemonic /nəˈmɒnɪk/ adj. **1.** assisting, or intended to assist, the memory. –n. **2.** a verse or the like intended to assist the memory.

moan n. a prolonged, low, inarticulate sound uttered in suffering. –v. **2.** to utter moans.

moat n. a large water-filled trench surrounding a castle, etc.

mob n. **1.** a large number, especially of people, sometimes disorderly and hostile. **2.** Aust., NZ a group of animals: *a mob of sheep.* –v. **(mobbed, mobbing) 3.** to surround and attack with riotous violence.

mobile adj. **1.** movable; moving readily. –n. **2.** a construction or sculpture of delicately balanced movable parts. **3.** a mobile phone. **–mobility,** n.

mobile home n. **1.** a registrable vehicle such as a motorhome, van, etc., which is used as a dwelling. **2.** freestanding living quarters which can be moved from one site to another.

mobile phone n. a portable cellular telephone.

mobilise v. to put (armed forces) into readiness for active service. Also, **mobilize.**

moccasin /'mɒkəsən/ n. a slip-on shoe made entirely of soft leather.

mocha /'mɒkə/ n. **1.** a choice variety of coffee. **2.** a coffee or coffee and chocolate flavouring.

mock v. **1.** to attack with ridicule. **2.** to scoff; jeer. **3.** to mimic, imitate, or counterfeit. –adj. **4.** being an imitation; pretended.

mockery n. (pl. **-ries**) **1.** ridicule or derision. **2.** a mere travesty, or mocking pretence.

mockingbird n. any of various scrub birds noted for their ability as mimics.

mock-up n. a model, built to scale, of a machine, apparatus, or weapon, used in testing, teaching, etc.

modal verb n. Gram. a type of auxiliary verb which indicates how probable something is (*I might come, The sun will rise, It could rain tomorrow*) or how necessary something is (*He should speak more loudly, The court must decide*).

mod cons pl. n. Informal modern conveniences.

mode¹ n. **1.** manner or way of acting or doing. **2.** the natural disposition or the manner of existence or action of anything; form.

For def. 1, the more usual word is **method**.

mode² n. a prevailing style or fashion.

model n. **1.** a standard or example for imitation or comparison. **2.** a representation in miniature to show the construction of something. **3.** a person who poses for a painter, etc. **4.** someone employed in the fashion industry to wear clothes to display them to customers; mannequin. **5.** a typical or specific form or style. –adj. **6.** worthy to serve as a model; exemplary. –v. (**-elled, -elling**) **7.** to form or plan according to a model. **8.** to display, especially by wearing. **9.** to serve or be employed as a model.

modem n. Computers an electronic device that facilitates the linking of one computer to another via the telephone system.

moderate adj. /'mɒdrət, -ərət/ **1.** not extreme, excessive, or intense. –n. /'mɒdrət, -ərət/ **2.** someone who is moderate in opinion or action, especially in politics or religion. –v. /'mɒdəreɪt/ **3.** to make or become less violent, severe, intense, or rigorous.

moderation n. **1.** the quality of being moderate. **2.** the act of moderating. –phr. **3. in moderation,** without excess; moderately.

moderator n. **1.** someone or something that moderates. **2.** Internet a person who oversees all the messages in a forum, deleting any unregistered messages and assisting members. **–moderatorship,** n.

modern adj. **1.** of or relating to present and recent time; not ancient or remote. –n. **2.** someone whose views and tastes are modern.

modest adj. **1.** moderate or humble about one's merits, importance, etc. **2.** moderate. **3.** decent in behaviour, speech, dress, etc. **–modesty,** n.

modicum n. a moderate or small quantity.

The more usual word is **bit**.

modifier n. Gram. a word which limits or adds to the meaning of another word in some way: 'Desk' is a modifier in 'desk lamp'.

modify v. (-fied, -fying) **1.** to change somewhat the form or qualities of; alter somewhat. **2.** to become changed. **3.** to reduce in degree. **4.** Gram. to limit or add more detail to the meaning of a word: Adverbs modify verbs. –**modification**, n.

modulate v. to regulate by or adjust to a certain measure; soften; tone down. –**modulation**, n.

module n. **1.** a selected unit of measure used as a basis for planning and standardisation of building materials. **2.** a structural component. **3.** Astronautics a detachable section of a space vehicle. –**modular**, adj.

mogul n. an important person.

mohair n. (a fabric made from) the yarn from the hair of the Angora goat.

mohawk adj. (sometimes upper case) of or relating to a hairstyle in which the head is shaved leaving a strip of hair along the centre of the scalp from the forehead to the back of the neck.

moiety n. (pl. **-ties**) a half.

moist adj. moderately or slightly wet; damp.

moisture n. water or other liquid rendering anything moist.

molar n. a tooth adapted for grinding.

molasses n. the thick brown bitter uncrystallised syrup drained from raw sugar.

mole[1] n. a small congenital spot or blemish on the human skin.

mole[2] n. a small insectivorous mammal living chiefly underground.

mole[3] n. the SI base unit of measurement of amount of substance. Symbol: mol

molecule n. Physics, Chem. the smallest physical unit of an element or compound. –**molecular**, adj.

molest v. **1.** to assault sexually. **2.** to interfere with so as to annoy or hurt.

mollify v. (-fied, -fying) to soften in feeling or temper.

mollusc /'mɒləsk/ n. any of a phylum of invertebrates including the snails, bivalves, squids, octopuses, etc.

mollycoddle v. to coddle; pamper.

molt v. → **moult**.

molten adj. liquefied by heat.

moment n. **1.** an indefinitely short space of time; instant. **2.** importance or consequence.

momentary adj. lasting but a moment; very brief.

momentous adj. of great importance or consequence.

momentum n. (pl. **ta** /-tə/) **1.** the quantity of motion of a moving body, equal to the product of its mass and velocity. **2.** impetus, as of a moving body.

monarch n. a hereditary ruler.

monarchy n. (pl. **-chies**) a government or state in which the supreme power is actually or nominally lodged in a monarch.

monastery n. (pl. **-ries**) a place occupied by a community of monks living in seclusion from the world under religious vows. –**monastic**, adj.

monetary adj. of or relating to money.

money n. (pl. **-neys** or **-nies**) **1.** coin or notes generally accepted as payment of goods and debts; cash: Do you have any money with you? **2.** wealth or value viewed in terms of money: to have money in the bank; Is there any money left on this card?

The plural of this word, spelt **moneys** or **monies**, is usually only used in official documents or reports: Upon collection of monies owing, a receipt will be issued.

money laundering n. the illegal practice of transferring funds of illegal origin, usually as cash, into legal enterprises in such a way that they appear to be legitimate. –**money-launderer**, n.

money market n. a market in which large amounts of money are borrowed and lent for short periods of time.

money order n. an order for the payment of money, as one issued by one post office and payable at another.

mongrel n. **1.** any plant or animal resulting from the crossing of different breeds or varieties, especially a dog of mixed or uncertain breed. –adj. **2.** inferior.

monitor n. **1.** a device used to check, observe, or record the operation of a machine or system. **2.** a large lizard. **3.** Computers the component of a desktop computer which houses the screen; visual display unit. –v. **4.** to check, observe, or record the operation of (a machine, etc.).

monk n. **1.** a man living in seclusion under religious vows.

monkey n. (pl. **-keys**) **1.** a long-tailed member of the mammalian order Primates. **2.** any of various mechanical devices. –v. (**-keyed**, **-keying**) **3.** Informal to play or trifle idly.

monkey wrench n. a spanner or wrench with an adjustable jaw.

monochromatic adj. of, producing, or relating to one colour or one wavelength.

monocle n. a glass lens for one eye.

monogamy n. the practice of having only one spouse at a time.

Compare this with **polygamy** and **bigamy**.

monogram n. a design made up of initial letters.

monograph n. a treatise on a particular subject.

monolith n. **1.** a single huge block of stone. **2.** something having a massive, uniform, or unyielding quality or character. –**monolithic**, adj.

monologue /ˈmɒnəlɒg/ n. a prolonged talk by a single speaker.

monoplane n. an aeroplane with only one pair of wings.

monopolise v. **1.** to exercise a monopoly of (a market, commodity, etc.). **2.** to keep (someone) entirely to oneself. Also, **monopolize**.

monopoly n. (pl. **-lies**) exclusive control of a commodity or service.

monorail n. a railway with coaches running on a single rail.

monosodium glutamate n. a sodium salt used in cookery to enhance the natural flavour of a dish. Also, **MSG**.

monosyllabic adj. **1.** having only one syllable, as a word. **2.** having a vocabulary composed exclusively of monosyllables.

monotheism n. the belief that there is only one god.

monotone n. a tone without harmony or variation in pitch.

monotony n. **1.** lack of variety, or wearisome uniformity, as in occupation, scenery, etc. **2.** sameness of tone or pitch, as in utterance. –**monotonous**, adj.

monotreme n. a mammal which lays eggs, as the platypus and echidna.

monounsaturated adj. of or relating to a fat or oil having only one double bond per molecule, as oleic acid in olive oil. Also, **mono-unsaturated**.

monsoon n. seasonal wind, often with rain, in tropical and Indian ocean areas.

monster n. **1.** a huge or monstrous creature. –adj. **2.** huge; enormous; monstrous.

monstrous adj. **1.** huge; extremely great. **2.** revolting; outrageous; shocking. **3.** distorted from the natural form. –**monstrosity**, n.

montage /mɒnˈtɑʒ, ˈmɒntɑʒ/ n. the combination in one picture, etc., of composition elements from several sources.

month n. **1.** a period of 4 weeks or of 30 days. **2.** the period (**lunar month**) of a complete revolution of the moon. –**monthly**, adj., n.

monument *n.* something erected in memory of a person, event, etc.

monumental *adj.* **1.** massive or imposing. **2.** of great importance or significance: *a monumental event in the nation's history.*

mooch *v. Informal* to hang or loiter about.

mood¹ *n.* frame of mind, or state of feeling.

mood² *n. Gram.* A set of verb forms which show the speaker's attitude towards the action expressed by the verb.

For the different verb moods, look up **indicative** (def. 2), **imperative** (def. 2), and **subjunctive**.

moody *adj.* (**-dier, -diest**) **1.** given to gloomy or sullen moods; ill-humoured. **2.** exhibiting sharply varied moods; temperamental.

moon *n.* **1.** the round body that circles the earth every month and can be seen as a light in the sky at night. **2.** this body as it appears at different stages of the month: *the new moon; the full moon.* **3.** any planetary satellite. *–v.* **4.** *Informal* to wander about or gaze idly, dreamily, or listlessly.

A word which describes things related to the moon is **lunar**.

moonlight *n.* **1.** the light of the moon. *–adj.* **2.** relating to or lit by moonlight. *–v.* **3.** to work at an extra job.

moonshine *n.* **1.** the light of the moon. **2.** empty or foolish talk, ideas, etc.; nonsense. **3.** *Informal* smuggled or illicitly distilled liquor.

moonstone *n.* a white translucent stone with a bluish pearly lustre, used as a gem.

moor¹ *n.* a tract of open wasteland; heath.

moor² *v.* to secure (a ship, etc.) in a particular place. *–***moorage**, *n.*

moorings *pl. n.* the place where a ship is moored.

moose *n.* (*pl.* **moose**) a large animal of the deer family.

Note that the plural is the same as the singular: *Three moose were running through the trees.*

moot *adj.* **1.** subject to argument; debatable: *a moot point. –v.* **2.** to bring forward (a subject, etc.) for discussion or debate.

For def. 2, the more usual word is **propose**.

mop *n.* **1.** a bundle of coarse yarn, etc., fastened at the end of a stick or handle, used for washing floors, dishes, etc. **2.** a thick mass, or head of hair. *–v.* (**mopped, mopping**) **3.** to rub, wipe, clean, or remove with a mop.

mope *v.* to be sunk in listless apathy or dull dejection.

moral *adj.* **1.** relating to or concerned with right conduct or the distinction between right or wrong. **2.** conforming to the rules of right conduct. *–n.* **3.** the moral teaching or practical lesson contained in a fable, tale, experience, etc. **4.** (*pl.*) principles or habits with respect to right or wrong conduct; ethics.

Don't confuse **moral** with **morale**.

morale /məˈrɑːl/ *n.* mental condition with respect to cheerfulness, confidence, zeal, etc.

Don't confuse this with **moral**.

moralise *v.* to make moral judgements. Also, **moralize**.

This is often used in a disapproving way: *Stop moralising about the situation and do something helpful!*

morality *n.* (*pl.* **-ties**) conformity to the rules of right conduct.

morass *n.* a tract of low, soft, wet ground.

moratorium *n.* (*pl.* **-ria** /-riə/ or **-riums**) a legal authorisation to delay payment of money due.

morbid *adj.* **1.** showing a strong interest in gruesome things. **2.** affected by, proceeding from, or characteristic of, disease.

mordant *adj.* caustic or sarcastic.

mordent n. a musical embellishment.

more adj. **1.** in greater quantity, amount, measure, degree, or number (as the comparative of *much* and *many*). **2.** additional or further. —n. **3.** an additional quantity, amount, or number. **4.** a greater quantity, amount, or degree. —adv. **5.** in or to a greater extent or degree. —phr. **6. more or less**, to a certain extent; approximately.

Strictly speaking, the opposite of **more** is **less** with things you can't count (*uncount nouns*) and **fewer** with things you can count (*count nouns*). So you would say *less butter* and *less love*, but *fewer children* and *fewer cars*. However, many people do use **less** with count nouns and it is generally regarded as acceptable (*less children, less cars*).

moreover adv. beyond what has been said; further; besides.

mores pl. n. accepted moral customs or conventions.

morgue /mɒg/ n. a place in which the bodies of persons found dead are exposed for identification.

moribund adj. dying.

morning n. **1.** the first part of the day from dawn to noon **2.** the period of the day from midnight until noon: *The intruder broke in at one o'clock in the morning.*

Don't confuse **morning** with **mourning**, which is grief over someone's death.

morning tea n. a short break from work, etc., taken in the late morning, usually with food and drink.

moron n. a stupid person.

Note that if you call someone 'a moron' you are intending to insult them.

morose adj. gloomily or sullenly ill-humoured.

morphine n. a drug used to dull pain, induce sleep, etc. Also, **morphia**.

morphing n. *Computers* the manipulation of digital images to produce a sequence whereby one image changes into another.

morphology n. the study of form, structure, and the like.

Morse code n. a system of dots, dashes, and spaces used to represent the letters of the alphabet, numerals, etc.

morsel n. a small piece or amount of anything; scrap; bit.

mortal adj. **1.** liable or subject to death. **2.** of or relating to human beings as subject to death; human. **3.** causing death. —n. **4.** a human.

mortality n. (pl. **-ties**) **1.** the condition of being mortal. **2.** relative frequency of death in a district or community.

mortar[1] n. **1.** a bowl in which drugs, etc., are reduced to powder or paste with a pestle. **2.** a type of cannon.

mortar[2] n. a cement which binds bricks together.

mortarboard n. a kind of cap with a stiff, square top, worn by university graduates, etc.; trencher.

mortgage /'mɔgɪdʒ/ *Law* —n. **1.** a security by way of conveyance or assignment of property securing the payment of a debt. —v. (**-gaged, -gaging**) **2.** to put (property, especially houses or land) under a mortgage.

mortice n. a rectangular cavity in a piece of wood, etc., for receiving a corresponding projection (tenon) on another piece, so as to form a joint.

mortify v. (**-fied, -fying**) to humiliate. —**mortification**, n.

mortuary n. (pl. **-ries**) a place where dead bodies are temporarily kept.

mosaic n. a picture or decoration made of small pieces of stone, glass, etc.

mosh v. to move as one of a mass of spectators dancing to the music of a live band. —**moshing**, n. —**mosher**, n.

The area in which people mosh is called the **mosh-pit**.

mosque n. a Muslim place of worship.

mosquito *n.* (*pl.* **-toes** *or* **-tos**) a blood-sucking insect.

moss *n.* a small leafy-stemmed plant growing in tufts in moist places.

most *adj.* **1.** in the greatest quantity, amount, measure, degree, or number (as the superlative of *much* and *many*). –*n.* **2.** the greatest quantity, amount, or degree. **3.** the majority of persons. –*adv.* **4.** in or to the greatest extent or degree.

Note that def. 3 is used as a plural noun: *I've spoken to all the employees, and most are willing to try the new system.*

mostly *adv.* for the most part; in the main.

mote *n.* a particle or speck, especially of dust.

motel *n.* a roadside hotel with self-contained units.

moth *n.* an insect similar to the butterfly.

mothball *n.* a small ball of a moth-repellent substance stored with clothes, etc.

mother *n.* **1.** a female parent. **2.** the head or superior of a female religious community. –*adj.* **3.** relating to or characteristic of a mother. –*v.* **4.** to give origin or rise to. **5.** to care for or protect. –**motherly**, *adj.* –**motherhood**, *n.*

motherboard *n.* Computers a printed circuit board plugged into the back of a computer into which other boards (**daughter boards**) can be slotted so that the computer can operate an optional range of peripheral devices. Also, **mother board**.

mother-in-law *n.* (*pl.* **mothers-in-law**) the mother of one's spouse.

mother-of-pearl *n.* a hard, iridescent substance which forms the inner layer of certain shells, as that of the pearl oyster.

motif /mou'tif, 'moutəf/ *n.* a recurring subject or theme as in art, literature, or music.

motion *n.* **1.** the process of moving, or changing place or position. **2.** a bodily movement or gesture. **3.** a proposal formally made to a deliberative assembly.

4. an emptying of the bowel. –*v.* **5.** to direct by a significant motion or gesture, as with the hand.

motivate *v.* to provide with a motive. –**motivation**, *n.*

motivated *adj.* ambitious; determined; energetic.

motive *n.* **1.** something that prompts a person to act in a certain way. –*adj.* **2.** causing, or tending to cause, motion.

motley *adj.* diverse; various.

motor *n.* **1.** a comparatively small and powerful engine. **2.** any self-powered vehicle. –*adj.* **3.** causing or imparting motion.

motorcade *n.* a procession or parade of motor cars.

motor car *n.* a motor-driven vehicle, especially for passengers, for travel on roads.

motorcycle *n.* a large heavy bicycle with an engine. Also, **motorbike**.

motorhome *n.* a small truck-like vehicle with living accommodation in the style of a caravan behind the driver's cabin. Also, **mobile home**.

motorist *n.* someone who drives a motor car.

motor vehicle *n.* a road vehicle driven by a motor.

motorway *n.* a freeway.

mottled *adj.* spotted or blotched in colouring.

motto *n.* (*pl.* **-tos** *or* **-toes**) a maxim adopted as expressing one's guiding principle.

mould¹ *n.* **1.** a hollow form used to shape something in a molten or plastic state. **2.** something formed in or on a mould. –*v.* **3.** to work into a required shape or form; shape.

mould² *n.* a growth of minute fungi forming on vegetable or animal matter.

moulder *v.* to turn to dust by natural decay.

moult v. to cast or shed old feathers or skin. Also, **molt**.

mound n. 1. a hillock or knoll. 2. a heap or raised mass.

mount[1] v. 1. to go up or ascend. 2. to get up on (a platform, horse, etc.) 3. to go or put on (guard). 4. to fix on or in a support, backing, setting, etc. –n. 5. a horse, bicycle, etc., used for riding. 6. a support, backing or setting.

mount[2] n. a mountain or hill.

mountain n. a high natural elevation of the earth's surface. –**mountainous**, adj.

You can also use **mount**, especially in a name, such as *Mount Kosciuszko*.

mountaineer n. 1. a climber of mountains. –v. 2. to climb mountains. –**mountaineering**, n.

mourn v. to feel or express sorrow or grief, especially for (the dead). –**mournful**, adj.

mourning n. 1. the act of someone who mourns. 2. the conventional behaviour expressing sorrow for a person's death, as the wearing of black, the hanging of flags at half-mast, etc. 3. the outward tokens associated with such sorrow, as black garments, etc. –*phr.* 4. **in mourning**, grieving, as after the death of a loved one, etc.

Don't confuse **mourning** with **morning**, which is the first part of the day.

mouse n. (pl. **mice** for defs 1 and 2, **mice** or **mouses** for def. 3) 1. a small rodent. 2. a quiet, shy person. 3. a handheld device for positioning the cursor on a computer screen. –v. (**moused**, **mousing**) 4. to hunt for or catch mice.

moussaka /muˈsakə/ n. a Balkan and Middle Eastern dish based on minced lamb, tomatoes, and eggplant, layered, topped with a thick white sauce and baked.

mousse /mus/ n. any of various preparations of whipped cream, beaten eggs, gelatine, etc., flavoured and usually chilled.

moustache n. the hair growing on the upper lip.

mousy adj. (**mousier**, **mousiest**) 1. drab and colourless. 2. quiet as a mouse. Also, **mousey**.

mouth n. /maʊθ/ (pl. **mouths** /maʊðz/) 1. the opening through which an animal takes in food. 2. utterance or expression. –v. /maʊð/ 3. to utter with unnecessarily noticeable use of the mouth or lips. 4. to form words with the lips, uttering no sound.

mouthful n. (pl. **-fuls**) as much as a mouth can hold.

mouth organ n. → **harmonica**.

mouthpiece n. 1. the part of a musical instrument held in or at the mouth. 2. a person, a newspaper, etc., that voices the opinions, decisions, etc., of another; spokesperson.

move v. 1. to change (the) place or position (of). 2. Also, **move house**. to go and live in a different place. 3. to prompt or impel to some action. 4. to affect with emotion; touch. 5. to make a formal request, application, or proposal. –n. 6. the act of moving; a movement. 7. a change of abode or residence. –**movable**, **moveable**, adj., n.

movement n. 1. the act or process or result of moving. 2. (*chiefly pl.*) a series of actions of a person. 3. the works of a mechanism, as a watch. 4. *Music* a principal division or section of a sonata, symphony, etc.

movie n. → **film** (def. 3).

mow v. (**mowed**, **mown** or **mowed**, **mowing**) 1. to cut down (grass, grain, etc.). 2. to cut down, destroy, or kill indiscriminately.

mozzarella /mɒtsəˈrɛlə/ n. a soft, white, ripened cheese, with a plastic curd, giving it a smooth, close texture.

MP3 n. a digital audio file in which the audio signal is compressed to a size smaller than the original WAV format while still maintaining audio quality. Also, **mp3**.

MP3 player *n.* a device for downloading, storing, and playing MP3s.

MRI *n.* magnetic resonance imaging; a technique which produces an image of internal body organs by means of a magnetic scanner.

MSG *n.* → monosodium glutamate.

much *adj.* (**more**, **most**) **1.** in great quantity, amount, measure, or degree. *–n.* **2.** a great quantity or amount. *–adv.* **3.** to a great extent or degree; greatly; far. *–phr.* **4. make much of**, to treat as being of great importance.

muck *n.* **1.** farmyard dung, decaying vegetable matter, etc.; manure. **2.** filth; dirt. *–v.* **3.** *Informal* to spoil; make a mess of. *–phr.* **4. muck about** (or **around**), *Informal* to idle; potter; fool about. **5. muck out**, to remove muck from. **6. muck up**, *Aust. Informal* to misbehave.

muck-up *n.* *Informal* fiasco; muddle.

mucous *adj.* **1.** relating to, consisting of, or resembling mucus. **2.** containing or secreting mucus.

mucus *n.* a viscous secretion of the mucous membranes.

mud *n.* **1.** wet, soft earth or earthy matter. *–phr. Informal* **2. one's name is mud**, one is in disgrace. **3. throw** (or **sling**) **mud at**, speak ill of; abuse. *–***muddy**, *adj.*

muddle *v.* **1.** to mix up or jumble together in a confused or bungling way. **2.** to make mentally confused. *–n.* **3.** a muddled condition. **4.** a confused mental state.

mudguard *n.* a guard or shield shaped to fit over the wheels of a vehicle to prevent splashing of water, mud etc.

muesli *n.* a breakfast cereal of oats, wheatgerm, chopped fruit and nuts, etc.

muff *n.* **1.** a wrap for the hands. **2.** *Informal* a failure. *–v.* **3.** to bungle (something).

muffin *n.* **1.** a type of small cup-shaped cake. **2.** → **English muffin**.

muffin top *n.* *Informal* the fold of fat around the midriff which, on an overweight woman, spills out over the top of tight-fitting pants or skirts.

muffle *v.* **1.** to wrap or envelop in a cloak, scarf, etc. **2.** to wrap with something to deaden or prevent sound. **3.** to deaden (sound).

muffler *n.* **1.** a heavy neck scarf used for warmth. **2.** any device that reduces noise, especially on an engine.

mufti[1] /'mʌfti, 'mʌfti/ *n.* a Muslim legal adviser in religious law.

mufti[2] /'mʌfti/ *n.* ordinary clothes, as opposed to a uniform.

mug *n.* **1.** a drinking cup. **2.** *Informal* the face. **3.** *Informal* a fool; someone who is easily duped. *–v.* (**mugged**, **mugging**) **4.** *Informal* to assault and rob.

muggy *adj.* (**-gier**, **-giest**) humid and oppressive.

mulberry *n.* (*pl.* **-ries**) **1.** a type of berry. **2.** a dull, dark, reddish-purple colour.

mulch *n.* straw, leaves, loose earth, etc., spread on the ground.

mule *n.* **1.** the sterile offspring of a male donkey and a mare, used especially as a beast of burden. **2.** *Informal* a stupid or stubborn person. **3.** *Informal* a courier of illegal drugs.

mulga *n.* **1.** any of several species of acacia found in drier parts of Aust. **2.** *Aust.* the bush or outback.

mull[1] *v.* to study or ruminate (*over*).

mull[2] *v.* to heat, sweeten, and spice (wine, etc.) for drinking.

mullet *n.* (*pl.* **-let** or **-lets**) a type of freshwater or marine fish.

For information about the different plural forms, see the note at **fish**.

multicoloured *adj.* of many colours. Also, **multicolored**.

multicultural *adj.* of or relating to a society which embraces a number of different cultures.

multidisciplinary *adj.* (of teaching, research, etc.) involving a number of academic disciplines.

multifarious *adj.* of or having many different parts, elements, forms, etc.

multilateral *adj.* **1.** many-sided. **2.** involving many parties; multipartite.

multilingual *adj.* able to speak 3 or more languages.

multinational *adj.* **1.** of, relating to, or spreading across many nations. *–n.* **2.** a large, usually powerful, company with branches, offices or subsidiaries in several nations.

multipartite *adj.* **1.** divided into many parts; having many divisions. **2.** → **multilateral** (def. 2).

multiple *adj.* **1.** consisting of, having, or involving many individuals, parts, elements, relations, etc.; manifold. *–n.* **2.** *Maths* a number which contains another number some number of times without a remainder.

multiple personality disorder *n.* a rare psychotic disorder in which the patient develops several distinct, independent personalities which emerge at different times.

multiple sclerosis *n.* a disease of the nervous system caused by loss of part of the sheath around certain nerve fibres.

The short form of this is **MS**.

multiplicity *n.* (*pl.* **-ties**) a multitude or great number.

multiplier *n. Finance* an indicator of the relative sizes of a given initial increase in investment and the total ultimate increase in income.

multiply *v.* (**-plied**, **-plying**) **1.** to make or become many; increase (in) the number, quantity, etc., of. **2.** *Maths* to take by addition a given number of times. **3.** to produce (animals or plants) by propagation. **–multiplication**, *n.*

multistorey *adj.* (of a building) having a considerable number of storeys.

multi-tasking *n.* **1.** the execution by a computer of several different tasks at the same time, as data processing, printing, etc. *–adj.* **2.** (of computer software) enabling multi-tasking. **3.** (of a computer) performing more than one task at a time.

multitude *n.* a great number or crowd. **–multitudinous**, *adj.*

multi-user *adj.* (of a computer system) allowing more than one user at the same time. Also, **multiuser**.

mum[1] *n. Informal* mother.

mum[2] *adj.* silent; not saying a word.

mumble *v.* **1.** to speak or utter indistinctly or unintelligibly. *–n.* **2.** a low, indistinct utterance or sound.

mummy[1] *n.* (*pl.* **-mies**) the dead body of a human being or animal preserved by embalming.

mummy[2] *n.* (*pl.* **-mies**) *Informal* (with children) mother.

mumps *pl. n.* an infectious viral disease causing swelling of the salivary glands.

Although this is a plural noun, it is used as a singular: *Mumps is not as common as it once was.*

munch *v.* to chew steadily or vigorously, and often audibly.

mundane *adj.* ordinary; boring.

mung bean *n.* a bushy annual herb, a chief source of bean sprouts.

municipality *n.* (*pl.* **-ties**) **1.** an area of land delineated for the purposes of local government; borough. **2.** the governing body of such an area. **–municipal**, *adj.*

munificent *adj.* extremely generous in giving or bestowing.

munitions *pl. n.* materials used in war, especially weapons and ammunition.

mural *adj.* **1.** of or relating to a wall. *–n.* **2.** a painting on a wall.

murder *n.* **1.** *Law* the unlawful killing of another human being deliberately. **2.** *Informal* an uncommonly laborious or difficult task. –v. **3.** *Law* to kill by an act constituting murder. **–murderous,** *adj.*

murky *adj.* (**-kier, -kiest**) cloudy and dirty, as water.

murmur *n.* **1.** any low, continuous sound. **2.** a mumbled or private expression of discontent. –v. **3.** to make a low or indistinct continuous sound. **4.** to speak in a low tone or indistinctly. **5.** to complain quietly, or in private.

muscat *n.* a type of sweet wine. Also, **muscatel.**

muscle /ˈmʌsəl/ *n.* **1.** a bundle of fibres that can contract to produce bodily movement. **2.** muscular strength. **3.** ruthless political or financial strength. –*phr.* **4. muscle in (on),** to force one's way in(to). **–muscular,** *adj.*

> Don't confuse **muscle** with **mussel,** which is a type of shellfish.

muscular dystrophy *n.* a disease causing muscular deterioration and wastage.

muse¹ *v.* to reflect or meditate in silence.

muse² *n.* the goddess thought to inspire a poet.

museum *n.* a building or place for the keeping, exhibition, and study of objects of scientific, artistic, and historical interest.

mush *n.* **1.** any thick, soft mass. **2.** *Informal* weak or maudlin sentiment or sentimental language.

mushroom *n.* **1.** any of various fleshy edible fungi. **2.** anything of similar shape or correspondingly rapid growth. –*adj.* **3.** of or made of mushrooms. **4.** resembling a mushroom in shape. –v. **5.** to spread or grow quickly.

> Compare **mushroom** with **toadstool,** which is like a mushroom, but usually poisonous.

music *n.* **1.** an art of organising sound in significant forms to express ideas and emotions through the elements of rhythm, melody, harmony, and colour. **2.** musical work or compositions. **3.** the score of a

musical composition. –*phr.* **4. face the music,** to face the consequences, usually unpleasant, of one's actions.

musical *adj.* **1.** of, relating to, or producing music. **2.** fond of or skilled in music. –*n.* **3.** a play or film in which singing (and sometimes dancing) features prominently.

musician *n.* someone skilled in playing a musical instrument.

musk *n.* **1.** a substance secreted by certain animals, having a strong smell, and used in perfumery. **2.** a synthetic imitation of this substance.

musket *n.* the predecessor of the modern rifle. **–musketeer,** *n.*

muslin *n.* a fine cotton fabric.

mussel *n.* an edible bivalve marine mollusc.

> Don't confuse this with **muscle,** which is one of the parts of your body which give it the strength and power to move.

must *v.* **1.** a verb used **a.** to indicate that one has to do something: *I must hurry or I won't get this finished.* **b.** to indicate that something is definitely true: *She must be nearly 90 by now.* –*n.* **2.** *Informal* anything necessary or vital: *Safety gear is a must when rollerblading.*

> The verb form is a modal verb and is always used with another verb. Look up **modal verb.**
>
> Note that you can also use **have to** in most cases: *I have to hurry or I won't get this finished; She has to be nearly 90.*

mustard *n.* **1.** a pungent food condiment. –*adj.* **2.** brownish-yellow in colour.

muster *v.* **1.** to gather or summon (*up*). **2.** to come together, collect, or gather. –*n.* **3.** the act of mustering. –*phr.* **4. pass muster,** to measure up to specified standards.

musty *adj.* (**-tier, -tiest**) having a smell or flavour suggestive of mould.

mutant *n.* a new type of organism produced as the result of mutation.

mutate v. to change; undergo mutation.

mutation n. 1. the act or process of changing. 2. a change or alteration, as in form, qualities, or nature.

mute adj. 1. silent; refraining from speech. 2. incapable of speech. –n. 3. someone unable to speak. 4. Also, **mute button.** a button on a television or sound amplifier remote control unit which can be used to switch the sound off and on again. 5. a mechanical device for muffling the tone of a musical instrument. –v. (**muted, muting**) 6. to deaden or muffle the sound of (a musical instrument, etc.).

mutilate v. to remove parts of a body so as to disable or disfigure it. –**mutilation,** n.

mutiny n. (pl. **-nies**) 1. a revolt or rebellion against authority, especially by soldiers or sailors. –v. (**-nied, -nying**) 2. to commit mutiny. –**mutinous,** adj.

mutt n. Informal 1. a dog, especially a mongrel. 2. a simpleton; a stupid person.

mutter v. 1. to utter (words) indistinctly or in a low tone; murmur; grumble. 2. to make a low, rumbling sound.

mutton n. the flesh of sheep, used as food.

mutton-bird n. any of various species of petrel.

mutual adj. possessed, experienced, performed, etc., by each of 2 or more with respect to the other; reciprocal.

muzak /'mjuːzæk/ n. (from trademark) recorded background music.

muzzle n. 1. the mouth of a gun barrel. 2. the jaws, mouth, and nose of an animal. 3. a harness or cage on an animal's jaw. –v. 4. to put a muzzle on. 5. to restrain (by physical, legal, or procedural means) from speech or the expression of opinion; gag.

my pron. 1. the possessive form of I, used before a noun: my shoes. –interj. 2. Informal an exclamation of surprise: My! That's a colourful dress!

My is a first person singular pronoun. Def. 1 is sometimes called a determiner or a possessive adjective.

myna n. 1. a noisy scavenging bird with yellow legs and beak, native to Asia and introduced into Aust. in the 1860s. 2. any of various Asian birds known for their ability to talk. Also, **mynah, mina.**

myocardial infarct /ˌmaɪoʊkardɪəl 'ɪnfakt/ n. → **heart attack.**

myopia n. near-sightedness. –**myopic,** adj.

myriad /'mɪriəd/ n. 1. an indefinitely great number. –adj. 2. innumerable.

myrrh /mɜ/ n. an aromatic resin from certain plants used for incense, perfume, etc.

myrtle n. a type of shrub with fragrant white flowers.

myself pron. 1. the reflexive form of I: I cut myself. 2. an emphatic form of me or I, used for emphasis: I did it myself, I don't like it, myself. –n. 3. one's proper or normal self: I feel myself again today.

mystery n. (pl. **-ries**) 1. anything that is kept secret or remains unexplained or unknown. 2. obscure or puzzling quality. 3. any truth unknowable except by divine revelation. –**mysterious,** adj.

mystic adj. 1. → **mystical.** –n. 2. someone who practises or believes in mysticism.

mystical adj. 1. of or relating to mystics or mysticism. 2. of occult character, power, or significance. 3. spiritually significant or symbolic. Also, **mystic.** –**mystically,** adv. –**mysticalness,** n.

mysticism n. 1. belief in the possibility of attaining an immediate spiritual intuition of truths thought to transcend ordinary understanding, or of a direct, intimate union of the soul with a deity or universal soul through contemplation and love. 2. contemplative practices aimed at achieving such intuition or union.

mystify v. (**-fied, -fying**) 1. to involve (a subject, etc.) in mystery or obscurity. 2. to confuse (someone). –**mystification,** n.

mystique *n.* an air of mystery or mystical power surrounding something.

myth *n.* **1.** a traditional story which attempts to explain natural phenomena. **2.** any invented story. –**mythical**, *adj.* –**mythology**, *n.*

Compare this with **legend**, which is a story that comes from long ago in the past and which is thought by many people to be at least partly true.

myxomatosis /ˌmɪksəmə'toʊsəs/ *n.* a highly infectious viral disease of rabbits.

N, n

N, n *n.* the 14th letter of the English alphabet.

naan /nan/ *n.* a slightly leavened Indian bread, usually round. Also, **nan**.

nab *v.* (**nabbed, nabbing**) *Informal* to catch or seize, especially suddenly.

nachos *pl. n.* a snack consisting of corn chips topped with tomato sauce and melted cheese.

nadir *n.* the lowest point.

nag¹ *v.* (**nagged, nagging**) **1.** to persist in finding fault, complaining, etc. **2.** to cause continual pain, discomfort, or depression.

nag² *n. Informal* a horse.

nail *n.* **1.** a slender pointed piece of metal for driving into or through wood, etc. **2.** a thin, horny plate growing on the upper side of the end of a finger or toe. –*v.* **3.** to fasten with a nail or nails.

naive /naɪˈiv, na-/ *adj.* unsophisticated; ingenuous. Also, **naïve**. –**naivety**, *n.*

naked *adj.* without clothing or covering; nude.

naltrexone *n.* a drug which acts as a blocking agent to the body's opiate receptors, used to treat drug addiction, especially to heroin.

name *n.* **1.** a word or a combination of words by which a person, place, object, etc., is known or described. **2.** a reputation of a particular kind given by common report. –*v.* **3.** to (give a) name (to).

When a child is named (as in def. 3) they can be **named after** someone, which means that they are given the name of another person in the family, a friend of the parents, etc., usually as a sign of respect or affection: *They named him Peter after his grandfather.*

namely *adv.* that is to say.

namesake *n.* **1.** someone having the same name as another. **2.** someone named after another.

naming ceremony *n. (pl. -nies)* **1.** a ceremony at which someone or something is officially named. **2.** an occasion, usually conducted by a civil celebrant, at which a child is named, guardians (or godparents) appointed, etc.

nan /nan/ *n.* → **naan**.

nanna *n. Informal* a grandmother. Also, **nana, nan.**

nanny *n. (pl. -nies)* **1.** a nurse for children. **2.** a grandmother.

nanny goat *n.* a female goat. Also, **nanny-goat.**

nanoscience /ˈnænoʊˌsaɪəns/ *n.* the science concerned with objects of the smallest dimensions.

nanotechnology /ˈnænoʊˌtɛknɒlədʒi/ *n.* technology generated from nanoscience.

nap¹ *v.* (**napped, napping**) **1.** to have a short sleep; doze. –*n.* **2.** a short sleep; doze.

nap² *n.* the short fuzzy ends of fibres on the surface of cloth.

napalm /ˈneɪpɑm, ˈnæpɑm/ *n.* a sticky aluminium gel used in flame throwers and fire bombs.

nape *n.* the back of the neck.

napery *n.* table linen.

naphthalene /ˈnæfθəlin/ *n.* a white crystalline hydrocarbon used in dyes and as a moth-repellent, etc.

napkin *n.* **1.** → **serviette**. **2.** a piece of linen, cotton cloth or paper used as a towel or as a baby's nappy.

nappy *n. (pl. -pies)* a piece of cotton towelling, or some disposable material, fastened round a baby to absorb and contain its excrement.

narcissism /ˈnɑsəsɪzəm/ *n.* an excessive self-love. –**narcissist**, *n.* –**narcissistic**, *adj.*

narcosis *n.* a state of sleep or drowsiness.

narcotic *n.* any of a class of substances that blunt the senses and induce sleep.

nark *n. Informal* **1.** an informer. **2.** a scolding, complaining person.

narrate *v.* to tell the story of (events, experiences, etc.). **–narrator**, *n.* **–narration**, *n.*

narrative *n.* a story, whether true or fictitious.

narrow *adj.* **1.** not broad or wide. **2.** limited in extent or space. **3.** lacking breadth of view or sympathy. *–v.* **4.** to make or become narrower. *–n.* **5.** a narrow part, place or thing.

narrowcast *v.* (**-cast** *or* **-casted, -casting**) **1.** to transmit (data) to a limited number of recipients as in cable television where only subscribers' receivers can take the signal. **2.** an instance of narrowcasting. **–narrowcasting**, *n.* **–narrowcaster**, *n.*

nasal *adj.* of or relating to the nose.

nascent /'neɪsnt, 'næsənt/ *adj.* beginning to exist or develop.

nasturtium *n.* a garden plant with showy flowers.

nasty *adj.* (**-tier, -tiest**) vicious, spiteful, or ugly.

natal *adj.* of or relating to birth.

nation *n.* a body of people associated with a particular territory who possess or seek a government peculiarly their own. **–national**, *adj.*

nationalise *v.* to bring under the control or ownership of a government. Also, **nationalize**.

nationalism *n.* devotion to the interests of one's own nation. **–nationalistic**, *adj.*

nationality *n.* (*pl.* **-ties**) the quality of membership in a particular nation.

native *adj.* **1.** belonging to a person, place or thing by birth or nature. **2.** born or originating in a particular place or country. *–n.* **3.** one of those descended from the original inhabitants of a place or country;

an indigenous person. **4.** someone born in a particular place or country. **5.** an animal or plant indigenous to a particular region.

native title *n.* in Aust., the right to land or water held by Indigenous people who have maintained their connection to the land or water and whose possession under their traditional law or customs is recognised by Aust. law.

nativity *n.* (*pl.* **-ties**) birth.

natural *adj.* **1.** existing in or formed by nature; not artificial. **2.** free from affectation or constraint. **3.** in accordance with the nature of things. **4.** being such by nature; born such. **5.** *Music* without sharps or flats. *–n.* **6.** *Informal* a thing or a person that is by nature satisfactory or successful. **7.** *Music* the sign ♮, placed before a note cancelling the effect of a previous sharp or flat. **–naturally**, *adv.*

naturalise *v.* to confer the rights and privileges of citizenship upon. Also, **naturalize**.

naturalist *n.* a zoologist or botanist.

nature *n.* **1.** the qualities belonging to a person or thing by birth or constitution. **2.** character, kind, or sort. **3.** the material world or its forces. **4.** reality, as distinguished from any effect of art. **5.** an uncultivated state.

naturopathy /næt∫ə'rɒpəθi/ *n.* a system of treating disease in ways considered natural, especially by use of herbs, natural foods, etc. **–naturopath**, *n.*

naught *n.* negation or complete failure.

naughty *adj.* (**-tier, -tiest**) **1.** disobedient; mischievous (especially in speaking to or about children). **2.** improper; obscene.

nausea *n.* sickness in the stomach; a sensation of impending vomiting. **–nauseous**, *adj.* **–nauseate**, *v.*

nautical *adj.* of or relating to sailors, ships, or navigation.

nave *n.* the main body, lengthwise, of a church.

navel n. a pit or depression in the surface of the belly.

Don't confuse this with **naval**, which describes something related to the navy: *naval vessels*.

navigate v. **1.** to traverse (the sea, a river, etc.) in a vessel, or (the air) in an aircraft. **2.** to direct the course of travel, as by map-reading. **3.** *Internet* to find one's way around (a website). **–navigator**, n. **–navigable**, adj. **–navigation**, n.

navigation bar n. *Computers* the bar running along the top, side or bottom of a web page which encloses buttons which take the user to various places on the site.

navy n. (pl. **-vies**) **1.** the whole body of warships and auxiliaries belonging to a country or ruler. **2.** Also, **navy blue**. a dark blue, as of a naval uniform. **–naval**, adj.

Don't confuse the adjective **naval** with **navel**, which is the hollow in your stomach where your umbilical cord was removed when you were born.

nay adv. no (used in dissent, denial, or refusal).

neap adj. designating the lowest tides, those midway between spring tides.

near adv. **1.** close: *Do you live near?* **2.** at, within, or to a short distance; nigh. **3.** close at hand in time. **–adj. 4.** being close by; not distant: *a house in the near distance.* **5.** closely related or connected: *a near relation.* **–prep. 6.** at, within, or to a short distance, or no great distance, from: *We live near the town.* **7.** close to (doing something). **–v. 8.** to approach.

nearby adj., adv. close at hand.

nearly adv. **1.** all but; almost: *nearly there.* **2.** with close approximation: *nearly identical.*

neat adj. **1.** orderly in appearance, condition, etc. **2.** clever, dexterous, or apt. **3.** unadulterated or undiluted, as liquors.

nebula n. (pl. **-las** or **-lae** /-li/) *Astron.* a diffuse, cloudlike patch of gases, particles, etc.

nebuliser /'nɛbjəlaɪzə/ n. *Med.* a device which reduces a liquid medication to a fine mist which is then inhaled into the lungs. Also, **nebulizer**.

nebulous adj. hazy, or confused.

necessary adj. **1.** that cannot be dispensed with. **2.** happening or existing by necessity. **–necessitate**, v.

necessity n. (pl. **-ties**) **1.** something necessary or indispensable. **2.** an imperative requirement or need for something. **3.** a state of being in difficulty or need; poverty. **–necessitous**, adj.

neck n. **1.** the part of an animal's body which connects the head to the trunk. **2.** any narrow, connecting, or projecting part, as of a bottle. **–v. 3.** *Informal* to play amorously.

necklace n. an ornament worn especially by women round the neck.

necromancy n. magic.

nectar n. **1.** *Bot.* the sweet secretion of a plant. **2.** any delicious drink.

nectarine n. a form of the common peach, having a completely smooth skin.

nee /neɪ/ adj. (a word placed after the name of a married woman to introduce her maiden name): *Sally Lee nee Jones.* Also, **née** /neɪ/.

This word comes from French and means born.

need n. **1.** a case or instance in which some necessity or want exists; a requirement. **2.** (a condition marked by) urgent want, as extreme poverty. **–v. 3.** to lack or require. **4.** to be necessary. **5.** to be under a necessity or be obliged (to): *He need only come tomorrow.*

needle n. **1.** a small, slender, pointed instrument with a hole for thread, used in sewing. **2.** a slender, rodlike implement for use in knitting, etc. **3.** *Bot.* a needle-shaped leaf, as of a conifer. —v. **4.** to tease or heckle.

needle exchange n. the exchange of used hypodermic syringes for new ones at no charge, to prevent disease transmission caused by needle sharing among intravenous drug users.

needlework n. the process or the product of working with a needle.

needy adj. (**-dier, -diest**) very poor.

nefarious adj. wicked.

negate v. to deny; nullify. —**negation**, n.

negative adj. **1.** expressing refusal or denial. **2.** lacking positive attributes; undistinguished. **3.** not positive. **4.** Maths denoting a quantity less than zero. **5.** Elect. relating to the kind of electricity present at the pole from which electrons leave an electric generator or battery, having an excess of electrons. See **positive** (def. 6). —n. **6.** something negative. **7.** Photography an image in which the gradations of light and shade are represented in reverse. —**negativity**, n.

negative gearing n. a financial situation in which an investment produces a loss, thus providing taxation benefits.

neglect v. **1.** to pay no attention to. **2.** to be careless about, or not to care for. —n. **3.** the act or fact of neglecting. **4.** the fact or state of being neglected.

negligee /'nɛglʒeɪ/ n. a woman's dressing-gown, especially a very flimsy one.

negligent adj. guilty of or characterised by neglect. —**negligence**, n.

negligible adj. that may be neglected or disregarded.

negotiate v. **1.** to bring about by discussion and settlement of terms. **2.** to clear or pass (an obstacle, etc.). **3.** to dispose of by sale or transfer. —**negotiable**, adj. —**negotiation**, n.

neigh n. the sound a horse makes; whinny.

neighbour n. someone who lives near another. Also, **neighbor**.

neighbourhood n. the region near or about some place or thing, often with reference to its character or inhabitants. Also, **neighborhood**.

neither adj. **1.** not one or the other: *Neither statement is true.* —pron. **2.** not the one or the other: *Neither of the statements is true.* —conj. **3.** not either: *Neither you nor I know the answer.*

Neither takes a singular verb (as in *Neither hat fits*), but sometimes, when you need to use a pronoun after **neither**, there can be a problem if you are not sure about, or if there is a mixture of males and females. It is awkward to have to say *Neither student was happy with his or her result*, so the plural pronoun *their* is often used, as in *Neither student was happy with their result*. Some people say that this is not correct, but it is extremely common and neatly solves a difficult problem.

nemesis /'nɛməsəs/ n. (pl. **-meses** /-məsiːs/) an agent of retribution or punishment.

neologism /niˈɒlədʒɪzəm/ n. a new word or phrase.

neon n. a chemically inert gaseous element chiefly used in lamps. *Symbol:* Ne

neonate n. a newborn child. —**neonatal**, adj.

neophyte n. **1.** a converted heathen, heretic, etc. **2.** a beginner.

nephew n. **1.** a son of one's brother or sister. **2.** a son of one's spouse's brother or sister.

nephritis /nəˈfraɪtəs/ n. inflammation of the kidneys.

nepotism n. patronage bestowed because of family relationship and not of merit.

nerd n. Informal a person who has an awkward personality and dresses in a conservative way; a person who is not cool (def. 4).

Note that if you call someone 'a nerd' you are intending to insult them.

nerve n. 1. one or more bundles of fibres, forming part of a system which conveys impulses of sensation, motion, etc., between the brain or spinal cord and other parts of the body. 2. firmness or courage in trying circumstances. 3. (pl.) nervousness. 4. Informal impertinent assurance.

nervous adj. 1. of or relating to the nerves. 2. characterised by uneasiness or apprehension.

nervy adj. (-vier, -viest) 1. nervous. 2. excitable; irritable.

nest n. 1. a structure used by a bird for incubation and the rearing of its young. 2. an assemblage of things that fit within each other. –v. 3. to build or have a nest.

nest egg n. money saved as the basis of a fund or for emergencies.

nestle v. to lie close and snug.

net[1] n. 1. a mesh of cotton, silk, etc. 2. a piece or bag of net for catching fish, butterflies, etc.

net[2] adj. 1. remaining after deductions, as tax, have been made. 2. final; conclusive. –n. 3. net income, profits, or the like. –v. (netted, netting) 4. to gain or produce as clear profit. Also, **nett**.

Net n. the → internet. Also, **the net**.

netball n. a game played by 2 teams of 7 players, in which players gain points by throwing the ball through a hoop attached to a pole at the opposing team's end of a rectangular court. –**netballer**, n.

nether adj. lower or under.

nettle n. a plant with stinging hairs.

network n. a group of interconnected people, companies, television stations, computer systems, etc.

neural adj. of or relating to a nerve or the nervous system.

neurodiverse adj. of or relating to a person with a condition, such as autism, which is considered to be not neurotypical. Also, **neurodivergent**. –**neurodiversity**, n.

neuron n. any of the cells which make up the nervous tissue; nerve cell. Also, **neurone**.

neurosis n. (pl. **-roses** /-'rousiz/) a relatively mild mental illness in which feelings of anxiety, obsessional thoughts etc., dominate the personality. –**neurotic** adj., n.

neurosurgery n. the branch of surgery relating to the nervous system. –**neurosurgical**, adj. –**neurosurgeon**, n.

neurotransmitter n. a chemical stored in a nerve cell that transmits information across a synapse.

neurotypical adj. conforming to typical norms of neurological functioning.

neuter adj. 1. Gram. of a gender which is neither masculine or feminine. 2. sexless or of indeterminate sex.

neutral adj. 1. (of a person or state) refraining from taking part in a controversy or war between others. 2. indefinite. 3. Chem. neither acid nor alkaline. 4. Elect. neither positive nor negative. –n. 5. a person or a state that remains neutral, as in a war. 6. Machinery the position or state of disengaged gears, etc. –**neutralise**, **neutralize**, v. –**neutrality**, n.

neutron n. a tiny particle present in the nucleus of every atom except normal hydrogen, which has the same mass as a proton but no charge.

Compare this with **electron** and **proton**.

never adv. at no time.

nevertheless adv. notwithstanding; however.

new adj. 1. of recent origin or production. 2. of a kind appearing for the first time. 3. unfamiliar or strange (to). 4. further; additional. 5. fresh or unused. –adv. 6. recently or lately. 7. freshly; anew or afresh.

newbie /'njubi/ n. Informal 1. a newcomer to the internet. 2. a newcomer to any activity.

news pl. n. 1. the report of events as published in a newspaper, journal, radio, television, etc. **2.** information not previously known.

Although this is a plural noun, it is used as a singular: Is the news on yet?; I'm afraid the news is not good.

newsagency *n. (pl.* **-cies**) a shop which sells newspapers, magazines, stationery, etc. **–newsagent,** *n.*

newsflash *n.* an announcement of very recent news on radio or television, usually interrupting a scheduled program.

newsgroup *n. Internet* an online discussion forum for a particular topic, in which users can write and post messages, and read messages posted by others. Compare **internet relay chat.**

newspaper *n.* a printed publication issued at regular intervals, containing news, comment, features, and advertisements.

newsprint *n.* paper to print newspapers on.

newsreel *n.* a short film presenting current news events.

newt *n.* any of various small, semi-aquatic salamanders.

newton *n.* the derived SI unit of force. *Symbol:* N

next *adj.* **1.** immediately following. **2.** nearest. *–adv.* **3.** in the nearest place, time, importance, or order. **4.** on the first subsequent occasion.

There is sometimes confusion about the use of **next** *with days of the week. Some people use* **next** *to mean the very next occurrence of the particular day, so that if today was Tuesday and they said* next Thursday, *they would be referring to the day two days from today. But others use* **next** *to mean the particular day occurring in the next week, so, in the example given,* next Thursday *would be the Thursday in the following week, which is nine days away. It is a good idea to make it absolutely clear which day you mean by saying* this Thursday *(two days away), or* Thursday of next week *(nine days away).*

nexus *n. (pl.* **nexus**) a tie or link.

nib *n.* the point of a pen, especially with a split tip for drawing up ink and for writing.

nibble *v.* **1.** to bite off small bits of (a thing). *–n.* **2.** a small morsel or bit.

nice *adj.* (**-cer, -cest**) **1.** agreeable; pleasant; delightful. **2.** showing great accuracy, delicacy, skill, etc.: *a nice answer.* **3.** minute, fine, or subtle, as a distinction. **–nicety,** *n.*

Nice, as used in def. 1, is a word which has been used too much and so has become slightly boring. You could make your speech or writing more interesting by choosing other words. For example, a meal could be described as delicious, *a person as* friendly, *etc.*

niche *n.* **1.** an ornamental recess in a wall, etc. **2.** a place suitable or appropriate for a person or thing.

nick[1] *n.* **1.** a notch, groove, or the like, cut into something. *–v.* **2.** to notch.

nick[2] *v. Informal* to steal.

nickel *n. Chem.* a hard, silvery-white, ductile and malleable metallic element. *Symbol:* Ni

nickname *n.* a name substituted for the proper name of a person, place, etc.

nicotine *n.* a poisonous substance, the active principle of tobacco.

niece *n.* **1.** a daughter of one's brother or sister. **2.** a daughter of one's spouse's brother or sister.

nifty *adj.* (**-tier, -tiest**) *Informal* smart; stylish; fine.

niggardly *adj. Rare* mean; stingy.

niggle *v.* **1.** to make constant petty criticisms. **2.** to irritate; annoy.

nigh *adv.* **1.** near in space, time, or relation. **2.** nearly or almost: *It is nigh on 12 o'clock.* *–adj.* (**nigher, nighest** *or* **next**) **3.** being near; not distant; near in relationship. **4.** short or direct.

night *n.* the interval of darkness between sunset and sunrise.

nightcap *n.* an alcoholic or other drink taken before going to bed.

nightingale *n.* a small migratory bird of the thrush family, noted for the melodious song of the male.

nightly *adj.* **1.** coming, occurring, etc., at night. **2.** coming or occurring each night. *–adv.* **3.** at or by night. **4.** on every night.

nightmare *n.* a condition during sleep, or a dream, marked by painful emotion.

nihilism /'naɪəlɪzəm, 'nɪ-/ *n.* total disbelief in religion or moral principles or in established laws and institutions.

nil *n.* nothing.

nimble *adj.* quick and light in movement.

nimbus *n.* (*pl.* **-buses** or **-bi** /-baɪ/) a radiance about the head of a divine or sacred personage.

nincompoop *n.* a fool.

nine *n.* **1.** a cardinal number, 8 plus 1. *–adj.* **2.** amounting to 9 in number. **–ninth**, *adj.*, *n.*

Numbers used before a noun are sometimes called **determiners**.

nineteen *n.* **1.** a cardinal number, 10 plus 9. *–adj.* **2.** amounting to 19 in number. **–nineteenth**, *adj.*, *n.*

Numbers used before a noun are sometimes called **determiners**.

ninety *n.* (*pl.* **nineties**) **1.** a cardinal number, 10 times 9. *–adj.* **2.** amounting to 90 in number. **–ninetieth**, *adj.*, *n.*

Numbers used before a noun are sometimes called **determiners**.

ninny *n.* (*pl.* **-nies**) a fool.

nip¹ *v.* (**nipped**, **nipping**) **1.** to pinch or bite. **2.** to check in growth or development. **3.** to affect painfully or injuriously, as cold does. **4.** *Informal* to move or go suddenly or quickly, or slip (*away*, *off*, *up*, etc.).

nip² *n.* **1.** a sip. **2.** a small measure of spirits.

nipple *n.* a protuberance of the breast where, in the female, the milk ducts discharge; teat.

nippy *adj.* (**-pier, -piest**) cold.

niqab /nɪ'kab/ *n.* a veil worn by some Muslim women, covering the face but leaving the area around the eyes uncovered.

nirvana *n.* **1.** *Buddhism* the ultimate state achieved usually after a series of reincarnations, when all passions and self delusions have been shed. **2.** *Hinduism* salvation achieved by absorption into Brahman. **3.** any place or state thought of as characterised by complete freedom from pain, worry and the external world.

nit *n.* the egg of a louse.

nitrogen *n.* a colourless, odourless, gaseous element which forms about four-fifths of the volume of the atmosphere. Symbol: N **–nitrogenous**, *adj.*

nitroglycerine *n.* a colourless, highly explosive oil.

nitty-gritty *n.* *Informal* the hard core of a matter.

nitwit *n.* *Informal* a foolish person.

nix *n.* *Informal* nothing.

no¹ *interj.* **1.** a word used when answering a question to express that a statement is not correct or that you do not agree to a request or offer: *No, you are wrong*; *No you can't leave yet*; *No, thanks, I won't have a coffee.* *–adv.* **2.** not in any degree or at all (used with a comparative): *no better weapon.* *–adj.* **3.** not any: *no money.* **4.** very far from being (something stated): *He is no genius.*

no² *adj.* **1.** not any: *No gold was found.* **2.** not at all: *He's no genius.*

nobble *v.* *Informal* to disable (a horse), as by drugging it.

noble *adj.* **1.** distinguished by birth, rank or title. **2.** of an exalted moral character or excellence. *–n.* **3.** a person of noble birth or rank. **–nobility**, *n.*

nobody *pron.* **1.** no person. *–n.* (*pl.* **-bodies**) **2.** a person of no importance: *She was sick of being treated as a nobody.*

This is sometimes called an *indefinite pronoun.*
Nobody takes a singular verb (as in *Nobody was in the room*), but sometimes, when you need to use a pronoun after **nobody**, there can be a problem because, in most cases, **nobody** begins a general statement that would include both males and females. It is awkward to have to say *Nobody likes it when he or she is ignored,* so the plural pronoun **they** is often used, as in *Nobody likes it when they are ignored.* Some people say that this is not correct, but it is extremely common and neatly solves a difficult problem.

nocturnal *adj.* **1.** of or relating to the night. **2.** active by night.

nod *v.* (**nodded, nodding**) **1.** to make a slight, quick inclination of (the head). *–n.* **2.** a short, quick inclination of the head, as in assent, greeting, command, or drowsiness. *–phr.* **3. nod off,** *Informal* to go to sleep.

node *n.* **1.** a knot, protuberance, or knob. **2.** a centring point of component parts. **–nodal,** *adj.*

nodule *n.* a small rounded mass or lump. **–nodular,** *adj.*

no-fly zone *n.* an area over which all or specified aircraft are forbidden to fly.

noggin *n.* **1.** a small measure of spirits. **2.** *Informal* the head.

noise *n.* sound, especially of a loud, harsh, or confused kind. **–noisy,** *adj.*

noisome *adj.* offensive.

nomad *n.* one of a people or tribe without fixed abode. **–nomadic,** *adj.*

nomenclature /nə'mɛnklətʃə, 'noumən-kleitʃə/ *n.* a set or system of names or terms.

nominal *adj.* **1.** being such in name only. **2.** (of a price, consideration, etc.) trifling in comparison with the actual value. **3.** *Gram.* used as or like a noun.

nominate *v.* to propose as a proper person for appointment or election to an office. **–nomination,** *n.*

nominee *n.* a person nominated as to fill an office or stand for election.

non-action verb *n.* *Gram.* → **stative verb.**

nonagon *n.* a polygon having 9 angles and 9 sides.

nonchalant /'nɒnʃələnt/ *adj.* coolly unconcerned; casual. **–nonchalance,** *n.*

noncommittal *adj.* not committing oneself to a particular view, course, or the like.

nondescript *adj.* of no particular type or kind.

none *pron.* **1.** no one; not one: *None of my friends came; I waited for an answer, but none came.* **2.** not any, as of something indicated: *There is none left.* **3.** no part; nothing: *That is none of your business.* **4.** no, or not any, persons or things: *None was suitable; None were suitable.* *–adv.* **5.** to no extent: *It's none too soon.*

Some people say that **none** should always be used as a singular noun, as in *None of the students has arrived yet.* However, **none** is often treated as a plural and there is no reason to avoid this: *None of the students have arrived yet.*

nonentity *n.* (*pl.* **-ties**) a person or thing of no importance.

nonetheless *adv.* however.

nonflammable *adj.* not likely to burn easily: *Their safety suits are made of non-flammable material.*

The usual opposite of this is **flammable.** The term **inflammable** also has the opposite meaning to **nonflammable,** but it is not used much nowadays. See the note at **flammable.**

nong *n.* *Informal* a fool; idiot.

nonplussed *adj.* confused; perplexed.

non-renewable resource *n.* a natural resource which, once it is depleted, cannot be replaced or restored, such as fossil fuels. Compare **renewable resource.**

nonsense *n.* that which makes no sense or is lacking in sense. **–nonsensical**, *adj.*

non sequitur /non ˈsɛkwɪtə/ *n.* an inference or a conclusion which does not follow from the premises.

noodle *n.* a type of pasta cut into long, narrow, flat strips.

nook *n.* any secluded or obscure corner.

noon *n.* midday.

no-one *pron.* no person.

This is sometimes called an *indefinite pronoun.*
No-one takes a singular verb (as in *No-one was in the room*), but sometimes, when you need to use a pronoun after **no-one**, there can be a problem because, in most cases, **no-one** begins a general statement that would include both males and females. It is awkward to have to say *No-one likes it when he or she is ignored*, so the plural pronoun **they** is often used, as in *No-one likes it when they are ignored*. Some people say that this is not correct, but it is extremely common and neatly solves a difficult problem.

noose *n.* a loop with a running knot which tightens as the rope is pulled.

nor *conj.* a negative conjunction used: **1.** as the correlative to a preceding *neither*: *He could neither read nor write.* **2.** to continue the force of a negative, such as *not, no, never*, etc., occurring in a preceding clause. **3.** after an affirmative clause, or as a continuative, in the sense of *and ... not*: *They are happy; nor need we mourn.*

norm *n.* **1.** a standard, model, or pattern. **2.** a mean or average.

normal *adj.* **1.** conforming to the standard or the common type; regular, usual. *–n.* **2.** the standard or type. **3.** the average or mean. **–normality**, *n.* **–normally**, *adv.*

north *n.* **1.** a cardinal point of the compass lying to the right of a person facing the setting sun or west. *–adj.* **2.** lying towards or situated in the north. **3.** directed or proceeding towards the north. **4.** coming

from the north, as a wind. *–adv.* **5.** towards or in the north. **6.** (of the wind) from the north. Also, *esp. Naut.*, **nor'**. **–northerly**, *adj., adv.* **–northern**, *adj.*

nose *n.* **1.** the part of the face or head which contains the nostrils. **2.** this part as the organ of smell. *–v.* **3.** to perceive as by the nose. **4.** to touch or rub with the nose. **5.** to smell or sniff. **6.** to seek (*after, for*, etc.) as if by smelling or scent; pry (*about, into*, etc.).

A word which describes things related to the nose is **nasal**.

nosedive *n.* a plunge of an aeroplane with the fore part vertically downwards.

nosh *v., n. Informal* (to have) a snack or a meal.

nostalgia *n.* a longing for home, family and friends, or the past. **–nostalgic**, *adj.*

nostril *n.* one of the external openings of the nose.

nostrum *n.* **1.** a patent medicine. **2.** a quack medicine.

nosy *adj.* (**-sier, -siest**) *Informal* prying; inquisitive. Also, **nosey**.

not *adv.* a word expressing negation, denial, refusal, or prohibition.

Note that this word is often shortened to **n't**: *You shouldn't do that; I didn't want to stay.*

notable *adj.* **1.** noteworthy. **2.** prominent or distinguished, as persons.

notation *n.* a system of graphic symbols for a specialised use, other than ordinary writing.

notch *n.* **1.** a more or less angular cut in a narrow surface or an edge. *–v.* **2.** to cut or make a notch or notches in. *–phr.* **3. notch up**, to score, as in a game.

note *n.* **1.** a brief record of something set down, as to assist the memory. **2.** a short informal letter. **3.** a piece of paper money; banknote. **4.** importance or consequence. **5.** notice or heed. **6.** *Music* a sign or character used to represent a sound. **7.** a quality or character. *–v.* **8.** to mark down, as in writing. **9.** to observe carefully; give heed to.

notebook *n.* **1.** a book of or for notes. **2.** Also, **notebook computer**. *Computers* a small, lightweight, portable computer.

noteworthy *adj.* worthy of notice.

nothing *pron.* **1.** not anything: *say nothing; nothing in the cupboard.* **2.** no part, share, or mark: *The place shows nothing of its former beauty.* **3.** something of no importance: *Don't thank me for giving you a lift – it's nothing.* –*phr.* **4. for nothing**, free of charge.

This is sometimes called an *indefinite pronoun.*

notice *n.* **1.** information. **2.** a warning. **3.** a note, placard, or the like. **4.** a notification of the termination of an agreement. **5.** observation or heed. –*v.* (**-ticed, -ticing**) **6.** to pay attention to. **7.** to perceive.

noticeboard *n.* a board, located centrally in a school, office, etc., designed for the display of notices and other information of general interest.

notify *v.* (**-fied, -fying**) to inform of something. –**notification,** *n.*

The more usual word is **tell.**

notion *n.* a more or less general idea of something.

not negotiable *adj.* (of a cheque which is crossed) indicating that the person to whom it is given has no better title to it than the person had from whom it was received.

notorious *adj.* widely but unfavourably known. –**notoriety,** *n.*

Compare **notorious** with **famous,** which means well-known, usually for something good: *a famous actor.*

notwithstanding *prep.* **1.** in spite of. –*adv.* **2.** nevertheless. –*conj.* **3.** although.

nougat /ˈnuːgɑ/ *n.* a hard, paste-like sweet.

nought *n.* a cipher (0); zero.

noun *n.* *Gram.* the part of speech comprising words denoting persons, places, things.

For different types of noun, look up **collective noun, concrete noun, count noun, proper noun** and **uncount noun.**

nourish *v.* **1.** to sustain with food. **2.** to foster or promote. –**nourishment,** *n.*

nous /naʊs/ *n. Informal* common sense.

novel[1] *n.* a fictitious prose narrative of considerable length. –**novelist,** *n.*

novel[2] *adj.* different from anything seen or known before.

novelty *n.* (*pl.* **-ties**) **1.** newness or strangeness. **2.** a novel thing, experience, or proceeding.

novice *n.* someone who is new to the circumstances, work, etc., in which he or she is placed.

novitiate *n.* the state or period of being a novice of a religious order or congregation.

now *adv.* **1.** at the present time or moment. **2.** (more emphatically) immediately or at once. **3.** at the time or moment only just past. **4.** nowadays. –*conj.* **5.** since, or seeing that.

nowadays *adv.* at the present day; in these times.

nowhere *adv.* not anywhere.

noxious /ˈnɒkʃəs/ *adj.* **1.** harmful to health. **2.** (of an animal, insect, plant, etc.) declared harmful by statute.

nozzle *n.* a projecting spout or the like, as of a hose or rocket.

nuance /ˈnjuːəns/ *n.* a shade of meaning, feeling, etc.

nub *n.* **1.** a knob or protuberance. **2.** the point or gist of anything.

nubile *adj.* (of a girl or young woman) marriageable, especially as to age or physical development.

nuclear *adj.* **1.** of or forming a nucleus. **2.** relating to or powered by atomic energy.

nuclear disarmament *n.* the dismantling of nuclear weapons, especially those of major military powers, often coupled with attempts to prevent an increase in the number of nuclear-armed countries.

nuclear fission *n.* the breakdown of an atomic nucleus of an element, with conversion of part of its mass into energy.

nuclear medicine *n.* a branch of medicine in which mildly radioactive material is used for diagnostic or treatment purposes.

nuclear reactor *n.* an apparatus for the production of nuclear energy.

nuclear waste *n.* the radioactive by-products of nuclear fission.

nucleus *n.* (*pl.* **-clei** /-kliar/ *or* **-cleuses**) **1.** a central part or thing about which other parts or things are grouped. **2.** *Biol.* a differentiated mass of protoplasm in the cell, forming an essential element in its growth metabolism and reproduction. **3.** *Physics* the central core of an atom, composed of protons and neutrons.

nude *adj.* **1.** naked or unclothed. **2.** without the usual coverings, furnishings, etc. **–nudity,** *n.*

nudge *v.* (**nudged, nudging**) **1.** to push slightly or jog, especially with the elbow. **–***n.* **2.** a slight push or jog.

nudism *n.* the practice of going nude as a means of healthful living. **–nudist,** *n.*

nugget *n.* a lump of something, especially gold as found in the ground.

nuggety *adj. Informal* short; thickset.

nuisance *n.* **1.** a highly annoying thing or person. **2.** something offensive or annoying to individuals or to the community.

null *adj.* **1.** of no effect or significance. **2.** non-existent. **–nullify,** *v.*

nulla-nulla *n.* an Aboriginal club or heavy weapon. Also, **nulla.**

numb *adj.* deprived of the power of sensation and movement.

numbat *n.* a small, slender, reddish-brown, diurnal Aust. marsupial.

number *n.* **1.** the sum of a collection of units or any generalisation of this concept. **2.** the particular numeral assigned to anything in order to fix its place in a series. **3.** a word or symbol used in counting or to denote a total. **4.** a quantity (large or small) of individuals. **5.** (*pl.*) numerical strength or superiority, as in a political party, organisation, etc. **6.** *Gram.* the number of persons or objects a noun, pronoun or verb refers to. **–***v.* **7.** to number or be numbered. **8.** to mark with or distinguish by a number or numbers. **9.** to amount to in number.

In English grammar, **number** (def. 6) can be *singular* or *plural*.

numeral *n.* a figure or letter denoting a number.

numerate *v.* to number; count.

numerator *n. Maths* that term of a fraction (usually written above the line) which shows how many parts of a unit are taken.

Compare this with **denominator,** which is the number under the line in a fraction.

numerical *adj.* relating to or denoting number.

numerous *adj.* very many.

numismatics *n.* the study and commonly also the collection of coins and medals.

nun *n.* a woman who has joined a religious order and leads a life of religious observance and service.

nunnery *n.* (*pl.* **-ries**) a religious house for nuns; convent.

nuptial *adj.* of or relating to marriage.

nurse *n.* **1.** a person who has the care of the sick or infirm. **–***v.* **2.** to act as a nurse. **3.** to seek to cure (a cold, etc.) by taking care of oneself. **4.** to often carefully so as to promote growth, etc. **5.** to hold in the arms; embrace. **6.** to breastfeed (an infant)

nurse practitioner *n.* a nurse who is legally qualified to take on some of the responsibilities of a doctor, particularly with regard to prescribing medicines.

nursery n. (pl. **-ries**) **1.** a room or place set apart for young children. **2.** a place where young trees or other plants are raised for transplanting or for sale.

nurture v. to feed, nourish, or support during the stages of growth.

nut n. **1.** a dry fruit consisting of an edible kernel enclosed in a woody shell. **2.** *Informal* an enthusiast. **3.** *Informal* an eccentric or insane person. **4.** a perforated block with an internal thread used to screw on the end of a bolt, etc.

nutmeg n. an aromatic spice.

nutrient /'njutriənt/ adj. **1.** nourishing. —n. **2.** a substance that nourishes.

nutriment n. any matter which nourishes.

nutrition n. **1.** the act or process of nourishing or of being nourished. **2.** the process by which the food material taken into an organism is converted into living tissue, etc.

nutritious adj. nourishing, especially in a high degree.

nutritive adj. serving to nourish.

nuzzle v. **1.** to burrow or root with the nose, as an animal does. **2.** to snuggle or cuddle up with someone or something.

nylon n. a synthetic material used for yarn, bristles, etc.

nymph n. **1.** a mythological divinity supposed to inhabit nature as a beautiful maiden. **2.** a beautiful or graceful young woman.

nymphomania n. uncontrollable sexual desire in women. —**nymphomaniac**, adj., n.

O, o

O, o *n.* **1.** the 15th letter of the English alphabet. **2.** the Arabic cipher; zero; nought (0).

o' *prep.* an abbreviated form of **of**.

oaf *n.* a stupid or loutish person.

> Note that if you call someone 'an oaf' you are intending to insult them.

oak *n.* a large deciduous tree.

oar *n.* a long shaft of wood with a blade at one end, used for propelling a boat.

oasis /ouˈeisəs/ *n.* (*pl.* **oases** /ouˈeisiz/) a fertile region in a desert region.

oath *n.* (*pl.* **oaths** /ouðz/) **1.** a solemn promise made, as in a court of law, to tell only the truth, often calling on God as a witness: *to give evidence under oath.* **2.** a curse or saying which uses the name of God or something sacred.

> If you use an oath, as in def. 2, in anger or as a joke, you may give offence, particularly to people who regard holy things with respect.

oats *pl. n.* **1.** a cereal grass cultivated for its edible seed. *–phr.* **2. sow one's wild oats**, to indulge in the excesses or follies of youth.

obdurate *adj.* hardened against persuasions or tender feelings.

> The more usual word is **stubborn**.

obedient *adj.* obeying, or willing to obey. **–obedience**, *n.*

obeisance /ouˈbeisəns/ *n.* deference or homage.

obelisk *n.* a tapering, four-sided shaft of stone.

obese *adj.* excessively fat. **–obesity**, *n.*

obey *v.* **1.** to fulfil the commands or instructions of. **2.** (of things) to respond conformably in action to. **3.** to be obedient.

obituary *n.* (*pl.* **-ries**) a notice of the death of a person, often with a brief biographical sketch.

object *n.* /ˈɒbdʒekt/ **1.** a visible or tangible thing. **2.** the end towards which effort is directed. **3.** *Gram.* the noun or pronoun which receives the action of a verb, as 'ball' in *He hit the ball.* *–v.* /əbˈdʒekt/ **4.** to express or feel disapproval.

objection *n.* something adduced or said in disagreement or disapproval.

objectionable *adj.* unpleasant; offensive.

objective *n.* **1.** an end towards which efforts are directed. *–adj.* **2.** unbiased. **3.** of or relating to objects or something real rather than thoughts or feelings (opposed to *subjective*). **4.** *Gram.* relating to the case of a noun or pronoun which is the object (def. 3) of a verb, as *me* in *She hit me,* or a preposition, as *her* in *He sang for her.* **–objectivity**, *n.*

obligation *n.* **1.** a binding requirement as to action; duty. **2.** a benefit for which gratitude is due. **–obligate**, *v.*

obligatory /əˈblɪɡətəri, -tri/ *adj.* required as a matter of obligation.

oblige *v.* (**obliged**, **obliging**) **1.** to do a favour: *I needed a lift and he obliged.* *–phr.* **2. be obliged**, **a.** to be grateful for someone's kindness: *I am deeply obliged to you for treating me so well.* **b.** to be required to, out of duty or need, or by law: *He was obliged to pay for repairs.*

obliging *adj.* disposed to do favours or services.

oblique *adj.* **1.** neither perpendicular nor parallel to a given line or surface. **2.** not straight or direct.

obliterate *v.* to remove all traces of.

oblivion *n.* the state of being forgotten.

oblivious *adj.* **1.** unmindful or unconscious (*of* or *to*). **2.** forgetful or without remembrance (*of*).

oblong *adj.* in the form of a rectangle of greater length than breadth.

obnoxious *adj.* offensive; odious.

oboe *n.* a woodwind instrument.

obscene *adj.* offensive to modesty or decency. **–obscenity,** *n.*

obscure *adj.* **1.** (of meaning) not clear or plain. **2.** inconspicuous or indistinct. *–v.* **3.** to make obscure, indistinct, etc. **–obscurity,** *n.* **–obscuration,** *n.*

obsequious /əbˈsiːkwiəs/ *adj.* excessively deferential or compliant.

observant *adj.* quick to notice or perceive.

observatory *n.* (*pl.* **-ries**) a place in or from which observations, especially astronomical or meteorological, are made.

observe *v.* **1.** to see or notice. **2.** to regard with attention. **3.** to comment. **4.** to show regard for by some appropriate procedure, ceremonies, etc. **–observation,** *n.*

obsession *n.* a persistent feeling, idea, or the like, which a person cannot escape. **–obsess,** *v.*

obsessive-compulsive disorder *n.* a disorder of the mind in which the sufferer has intrusive irrational thoughts and engages in repetitive rituals to find temporary relief.

obsolescent *adj.* becoming obsolete.

obsolete *adj.* fallen into disuse, or no longer in use.

obstacle *n.* something that stands in the way of progress.

obstetrics *n.* the branch of medicine dealing with childbirth. **–obstetrician,** *n.* **–obstetric,** *adj.*

obstinate *adj.* firmly and often perversely adhering to one's purpose, opinion, etc. **–obstinacy,** *n.*

obstreperous /əbˈstrɛpərəs/ *adj.* resisting control in a noisy manner; unruly.

obstruct *v.* **1.** to block or close up. **2.** to interrupt, make difficult, or oppose the passage, progress, course, etc., of. **–obstruction,** *n.*

obtain *v.* **1.** to get or acquire. **2.** to be prevalent or in vogue.

obtrusive *adj.* undesirably obvious.

obtuse *adj.* **1.** blunt in form. **2.** not sensitive or observant. **3.** *Geom.* (of an angle) more than 90° and less than 180° (opposed to *acute*).

obviate *v.* to meet and dispose of or prevent (difficulties, etc.): *to obviate the necessity of beginning again.*

The more usual word is **remove**.

obvious *adj.* clearly perceptible or evident.

occasion *n.* **1.** a particular time. **2.** the immediate or incidental cause of some action or result. *–v.* **3.** to bring about. *–phr.* **4. on occasion,** now and then.

occasional *adj.* **1.** occurring now and then. **2.** intended for use whenever needed.

occlude *v.* to stop up (a passage, etc.). **–occlusion,** *n.*

occult *adj.* **1.** beyond the bounds of ordinary knowledge. *–n.* **2.** the supernatural.

occupant *n.* a tenant of a house, estate, office, etc. **–occupancy,** *n.*

occupation *n.* **1.** one's habitual employment or calling. **2.** the period during which a country is under the control of foreign military forces.

occupational therapy *n.* a method of therapy which uses self-care, work and play activities to increase development and independent function, and to prevent disability.

occupy *v.* (**-pied, -pying**) **1.** to take up (space, time, etc.). **2.** to engage (the mind, attention, etc.). **3.** to take possession of (a place), as by invasion. **4.** to hold (a position, office, etc.).

occur *v.* (**-curred, -curring**) **1.** to come to pass. **2.** to suggest itself in thought (*to*). **–occurrence,** *n.*

ocean *n.* the vast body of salt water which covers almost $\frac{3}{4}$ of the earth's surface.

ochre *n.* any of a class of natural earths used as pigments, ranging from pale yellow to an orange or reddish yellow.

ocker *Informal –n.* **1.** a supposedly typical Aust. person, speaking with a broad Aust. accent, and affectionately thought of as uncouth and prejudiced but in an amusing way. *–adj.* **2.** distinctively Aust.: *an ocker sense of humour.*

Sometimes this can also be used of a woman: *She's a bit of an ocker.*

o'clock *adv.* of or by the clock: *It's 2 o'clock.*

OCR *n.* optical character recognition; a process which enables an electronic device to recognise letters, numbers, etc.

octagon *n.* a polygon having 8 angles and 8 sides.

octave *n.* a series or group of 8.

octet *n.* any group of 8.

octopus *n.* (pl. **-puses** or **-pi** /-paɪ/) a sea animal with 8 arms.

Some people use **octopi** for the plural of **octopus**, but this is regarded by many people as incorrect. The more accepted plural is **octopuses**.

octopus strap *n.* a stretchable rope with hooks on either end used for securing luggage to roof racks, etc.

OD /oʊ 'diː/ *Informal –n.* **1.** an overdose, especially of an injected addictive drug. *–v.* (**OD'd**, **OD'ing**) **2.** to give oneself an overdose (*on*).

odd *adj.* **1.** differing in character from what is ordinary or usual. **2.** (of a number) leaving a remainder of one when divided by 2 (opposed to *even*). **3.** more or less: *There were 30 odd present.* **4.** (of a pair) not matching. **5.** occasional or casual. **6.** not forming part of any particular group, set, or class: *odd man out.* *–oddity, n.*

oddball *n. Informal* an eccentric.

oddly *adv.* **1.** in an odd manner. **2.** strangely; unexpectedly.

oddment *n.* a remnant, or the like.

odds *pl. n.* **1.** the amount by which the bet of one party to a wager exceeds that of the other. **2.** balance of probability in favour

of something occurring or being the case. *–phr.* **3. at odds**, in disagreement. **4. make no odds**, not to matter. **5. odds and ends**, remnants; fragments.

ode *n.* a lyric poem.

odium *n.* hatred or repulsion. *–odious, adj.*

odometer /ɒ'dɒmətə, oʊ-/ *n.* an instrument for measuring distance.

odour *n.* **1.** that property of a substance which affects the sense of smell. **2.** a fragrance. **3.** a bad smell. Also, **odor**. *–odorous, adj.*

oesophagus /ə'sɒfəgəs/ *n.* (pl. **-gi** /-gaɪ/) a tube connecting the mouth or pharynx with the stomach; gullet. Also, **esophagus**.

oestrogen *n.* any one of a group of female sex hormones. Also, **estrogen**.

of *prep.* a particle indicating: **1.** distance or direction from, separation, deprivation, riddance, etc.: *within a metre of: to cure of.* **2.** derivation or source: *of good family.* **3.** concerning: *and what of your mother?* **4.** occasion or reason: *to die of hunger.* **5.** material or contents: *a packet of sugar.* **6.** a relation of identity: *the city of Sydney.* **7.** reference or respect: *to talk of peace.* **8.** the attribution of a quality to: *good of you to come.*

off *adv.* **1.** away from a position occupied, or from contact. **2.** as a deduction: *5 per cent off.* **3.** distant (in future time). **4.** disconnected: *The electric current is off.* **5.** away from employment or service: *The night nurse is now off.* **6.** into execution or effect: *The games didn't come off.* **7.** on one's way or journey. *–prep.* **8.** away from. **9.** from by subtraction. **10.** away or disengaged from (duty, work, etc.). **11.** *Informal* refraining from: *off the grog.* *–adj.* **12.** no longer in effect or operation. **13.** in bad taste. **14.** (of food) tainted. *–phr.* Also, **on and off. 15. off and on**, intermittently.

offal n. 1. the inedible parts of a meat carcass. 2. the organs of an animal used as food.

offbeat adj. unconventional.

off-chance n. a remote possibility.

off-colour adj. Informal unwell. Also, **off-color**.

offcut n. that which is cut off, as from paper or meat.

offence n. 1. a wrong; sin. 2. a crime which is not indictable, but is punishable summarily (**summary offence**). 3. a feeling of resentful displeasure. 4. attack or assault. –**offensive**, adj.

offend v. 1. to cause resentful displeasure in. 2. to affect (the sense, taste, etc.) disagreeably. 3. to commit a sin, crime, or fault.

offer v. 1. to present for acceptance. 2. to propose or volunteer (to do something). 3. to tender or bid, as a price. 4. to occur. –n. 5. a bid. 6. something offered. –**offering**, n.

offhand adv. 1. without previous thought or preparation. –adj. 2. informal or casual.

office n. 1. a room or place for the transaction of business, or the like. 2. official position.

officer n. someone who holds a position of authority.

official n. 1. someone who is charged with some form of official duty. –adj. 2. of or relating to a position of duty, trust, or authority.

officiate v. to perform the duties of any office or position.

officious adj. pushing one's services upon others.

offing phr. **in the offing**, not very distant.

offline adj. not connected to a computer network. Also, **off-line**.

off-peak adj. of or relating to a period of time of less activity than at the peak time.

off-putting adj. Informal disconcerting; discouraging.

off-season adj. (of a time of year) unpopular for a specific activity.

offset v. (-**set**, -**setting**) 1. to balance by something else as an equivalent. –n. 2. a compensating equivalent.

offshoot n. a shoot from a main stem.

offshore adv. 1. off or away from the shore. 2. at a distance from the shore. 3. in or to another country; abroad: *to study offshore*; *to move operations offshore*. –adj. 4. moving or tending away from the shore: *an offshore wind*. 5. based in an overseas location: *offshore processing of asylum seekers*. 6. (of a business) based in a foreign location where the taxation system is not as burdensome as it is in the country where the business is owned.

offside adj. 1. Sport in an illegal position. 2. Aust., NZ opposed; uncooperative.

offsider n. Aust., NZ a partner; assistant.

offspring n. children or young of a particular parent.

often adv. in many cases; frequently.

ogle v. to eye with amorous or impertinently familiar glances.

ogre n. a hideous giant.

oh interj. an expression denoting surprise, pain, etc., or for attracting attention.

ohm n. the derived SI unit of resistance. Symbol: Ω

oil n. 1. any of a large class of insoluble viscous substances. 2. Painting (a painting done in) oil colour(s). –v. 3. to smear or supply with oil. –adj. 4. concerned with the production or use of oil. 5. using oil, especially as a fuel.

oil colour n. a colour or paint made by grinding a pigment in oil. Also, **oil color**.

oilskin n. a cotton fabric made waterproof by treatment with oil.

ointment n. medicated cream for application to the skin.

okay Informal –adj. 1. all right. –adv. 2. well; acceptably. –v. 3. to endorse; approve; accept. –n. 4. an approval or acceptance. –interj. 5. an exclamation of approval, agreement, delight, etc. Also, **ok, OK**.

old *adj.* (**older** *or* **elder, oldest** *or* **eldest**) **1.** far advanced in years or life. **2.** having reached a specified age. **3.** familiar. **4.** belonging to a past time. **5.** deteriorated through age or long use. *–n.* **6.** (used in combination) a person or animal of a specified age or age-group: *nursery for 2 year olds.* *–phr.* **7. old hat**, *Informal* old-fashioned; out-of-date.

olden *adj.* of old; ancient.

old-fashioned *adj.* out of fashion or use.

old hat *adj.* *Informal* old-fashioned.

old-timer *n.* an old person.

oligarchy /ˈɒləgaki/ *n.* (*pl.* **-chies**) a form of government in which the power is vested in a few.

olive *n.* **1.** (the oily fruit of) an evergreen tree. **2.** a shade of green or yellowish green. *–adj.* **3.** of the colour olive. **4.** (of the complexion or skin) brownish; darker than fair.

olive branch *n.* an emblem of peace.

ombudsman /ˈɒmbədzmən/ *n.* (*pl.* **-men**) an official appointed to investigate complaints by citizens against the government or its agencies.

omelette *n.* a dish consisting of eggs beaten and fried. Also, **omelet.**

omen *n.* a prophetic sign.

ominous *adj.* portending evil; inauspicious.

omit *v.* (**omitted, omitting**) to leave out or fail to do. **–omission,** *n.*

omnibus *n.* (*pl.* **-buses**) **1.** → **bus. 2.** a volume of reprinted works by a single author or ones related in interest or nature.

omnipotent /ɒmˈnɪpətənt/ *adj.* almighty; all-powerful.

omnipresent *adj.* present everywhere at the same time.

omniscient /ɒmˈnɪsiənt, ɒmˈnɪʃənt/ *adj.* knowing all things.

omnivorous *adj.* eating both animal and plant foods. **–omnivore,** *n.*

Compare this with **carnivorous, herbivorous,** and **insectivorous**.

on *prep.* a particle expressing: **1.** position above and in contact with a supporting surface: *on the table.* **2.** contact with any surface: *on the wall.* **3.** support, suspension, dependence, reliance, or means of conveyance: *on foot.* **4.** time or occasion: *on Monday.* **5.** with reference to something else: *on the left.* **6.** membership or association: *on a jury.* *–adv.* **7.** on oneself or itself: *to put clothes on.* **8.** fast to a thing, as for support: *to hold on.* **9.** forwards, onwards or along, as in any course or process: *to go on.* **10.** with continuous procedure: *to work on.* **11.** into or in active operation or performance: *to turn a machine on.* *–adj.* **12.** operating or in use. **13.** taking place. *–phr.* **14. be on about,** to be talking about. **15. not on,** *Informal* not a possibility; not allowable. **16. on and off,** Also, **off and on.** intermittently.

once *adv.* **1.** (at one time) in the past. *–conj.* **2.** if or whenever. *–phr.* **3. all at once,** suddenly. **4. at once,** immediately. **5. once and for all,** finally and decisively. **6. once upon a time,** long ago.

once-over *n.* *Informal* a quick or superficial examination.

oncology *n.* the branch of medical science that deals with tumours. **–oncologist,** *n.*

oncoming *adj.* approaching.

one *adj.* **1.** being a single unit or individual, rather than 2 or more: *one apple.* **2.** being at some time in the future: *We'll meet again one day.* **3.** single through union or agreement: *of one mind; with one voice.* **4.** particular: *one evening last week.* **5.** only: *the one person we can trust.* *–n.* **6.** the first and lowest whole number. **7.** a single person or thing: *There was only one left.* *–pron.* **8.** a person or thing of a particular number or kind: *one of the children.* **9.** anyone: *as good as one would hope.* **10.** a person like oneself: *What* *could one do in that situation?* **11.** a person or thing of the kind just mentioned: *The painting is a fine one.* –*phr.* **12. at one,** in a state of unity and agreement: *We are at one on this question.* **13. one another,** each other: *Mary and John love one another.* **14. one by one,** one after another: *One by one they left.*

The pronoun is sometimes called an *indefinite pronoun.*

Note that the use of **one** as in def. 10 is regarded by some people as a little exaggerated and pompous. Instead of *What could one do in that situation?*, a more natural thing to say would be *What could I do in that situation?* Def. 9 is regarded in a similar way, although to a lesser extent. Many people use *you* for this sense: *as good as you would hope.*

Numbers used before a noun are sometimes called **determiners.**

one-off *adj.* individual; unique.

onerous /'oʊnərəs/ *adj.* burdensome or troublesome.

oneself *pron.* **1.** the reflexive form of the pronoun **one**: *It's hard to make oneself comfortable without a chair to sit on.* **2.** one's proper or normal self.

onion *n.* (a widely cultivated plant with) an edible bulb.

online *Computers* –*adj.* **1.** of or relating to a computer-controlled device which is directly linked to a computer. **2.** having direct access to a computer database: *an online branch of the bank.* **3.** (of information, etc.) able to be accessed directly by connection to a computer database, the internet, etc.: *The newspapers are online.* –*adv.* **4.** while interactively connected to a computer database: *to browse the data online.* Also, **on-line.**

onlooker *n.* a spectator.

only *adv.* **1.** without others or anything further: *Only she remained; She can only play the flute.* **2.** merely or just: *if you would only go away.* **3.** as recently as:

only yesterday. –*adj.* **4.** being the single one or the relatively few of the kind. –*conj.* **5.** but; except that: *I would have gone, only you objected.* –*phr.* **6. only too,** very; extremely: *He is only too willing to help.*

onomatopoeia /ˌɒnəmætə'piə/ *n.* the use of a word or words which sound like the thing or sound they are describing, such as *crunch, splash* or *buzz.* –**onomatopoeic,** *adj.*

onset *n.* **1.** an assault or attack. **2.** a beginning.

onshore *adj.* **1.** towards or located on the shore. –*adv.* **2.** towards the shore.

onside *adj. Aust., NZ* in agreement.

onslaught *n.* an onset, especially a vigorous or furious one.

onto *prep.* to a place or position on: *put the book back onto the shelf.*

Note that **on** and **to** are written as separate words when **to** is part of the following verb, as in *We moved on to discuss other things,* or when **on** is part of the verb coming before, as in *carry on to the end.*

ontology /ɒn'tɒlədʒi/ *n.* **1.** the branch of metaphysics that investigates the nature of being. **2.** *Computers* the structural framework for a database. –**ontological,** *adj.*

onus *n.* a burden; responsibility.

onward *adj.* **1.** directed or moving forwards. –*adv.* **2.** → **onwards.**

Note that you can use **onward** for both the adjective (*onward progress*) and the adverb (*to move onward*), but **onwards** can only be used for the adverb (*to move onwards*).

onwards *adv.* towards a point ahead. Also, **onward.**

oodles *pl. n. Informal* a large quantity.

oomph *n. Informal* vitality; energy.

oops *interj.* an exclamation of surprise or shock.

ooze[1] *v.* (of moisture, etc.) to percolate or exude, as through pores or small openings.

ooze² *n.* soft mud, or slime.

opal *n.* a mineral, some varieties of which are valued as gems.

opaque *adj.* **1.** impenetrable to light. **2.** hard to understand; obscure. **–opacity**, *n.*

Compare this with **transparent**, which describes something that you can see clearly through, and **translucent**, which describes something that you can see through, but not clearly.

open *adj.* **1.** not shut or closed, as a door, house, box, etc. **2.** not enclosed by barriers. **3.** that may be entered, used, etc., by all. **4.** (of shops, etc.) ready to do business. **5.** undecided, as a question. **6.** liable or subject. **7.** unobstructed, as a passage, view, etc. **8.** without prohibition: *open hunting season.* **9.** exposed to general view or knowledge. **10.** expanded or spread out. **11.** generous. *–v.* **12.** to make or become open. **13.** to give or afford access to. **14.** to render accessible to knowledge, etc. **15.** to set in action. **16.** to become receptive to, as the mind. **17.** to disclose or reveal (one's feelings, etc.). **18.** to become less close together. *–n.* **19.** an open competition: *the Australian open.* *–phr.* **20. the open, a.** an open or clear space. **b.** the open air. **c.** a situation in which hitherto restricted knowledge is extended to all parties: *to bring a subject out into the open.*

open-and-shut *adj.* easily decided.

open-ended *adj.* without fixed limits.

opening *n.* **1.** a gap, hole, or aperture. **2.** the initial stage of anything. **3.** a vacancy. **4.** an opportunity. **5.** a formal or official beginning.

opera *n.* an extended dramatic musical composition.

operable *adj.* **1.** capable of being put into practice. **2.** admitting of a surgical operation.

operate *v.* **1.** to (make) work or run, as a machine. **2.** to act effectively. **3.** *Surg.* to

perform surgery on a patient. **4.** to carry on transactions, especially speculatively or on a large scale. **–operation**, *n.*

operating system *n. Computers* the essential program which enables all other programs to be run on a computer, and which establishes an interface between a user and the hardware of the computer.

operational *adj.* ready for use; in working order.

operative *adj.* **1.** exerting force or influence. **2.** relating to work or productive activity.

operator *n.* **1.** someone who deals in shares, currency, etc. **2.** *Informal* someone who successfully manipulates people or situations.

ophthalmic /ɒfˈθælmɪk/ *adj.* of or relating to the eye.

ophthalmology /ɒfθælˈmɒlədʒi/ *n.* the science dealing with the anatomy, functions, and diseases of the eye. **–ophthalmologist**, *n.*

opiate *n.* a medicine that contains opium and induces sleep.

opinion *n.* a personal view, attitude, or estimation.

opinionated *adj.* obstinate or conceited in one's opinions.

opium *n.* a narcotic, used in medicine to induce sleep, relieve pain, etc.

opponent *n.* someone who is on the opposite side.

opportune *adj.* **1.** appropriate or favourable. **2.** occurring at an appropriate time.

For def. 1, the more usual word is **good**; def. 2, **timely**.

opportunism *n.* the practice of adapting actions, etc., to expediency. **–opportunist**, *n.*

opportunistic *adj.* **1.** displaying opportunism. **2.** *Med.* (of an illness) developing as a result of a weakness in the immune system. **–opportunistically**, *adv.*

opportunity *n.* (*pl.* **-ties**) an appropriate occasion.

opportunity shop n. Aust., NZ a shop run by a charity, etc., for the sale of second-hand goods. Also, **op shop**.

oppose v. **1.** to act or contend in opposition to. **2.** to hinder.

opposite adj. **1.** placed over against something else or in a corresponding position. –n. **2.** someone or something that is opposite or contrary. –prep. **3.** in a complementary role or position. –adv. **4.** on opposite sides.

opposition n. **1.** the action of opposing, or combating. **2.** an opposing group.

oppress v. **1.** to lie heavily upon, as care, sorrow, etc. **2.** to burden with cruel or unjust impositions or restraints. –**oppression**, n. –**oppressive**, adj.

opprobrium n. the disgrace incurred by shameful conduct. –**opprobrious**, adj.

opt phr. **1. opt for**, to decide in favour of; choose. **2. opt out**, to decide not to participate.

optical adj. **1.** relating to sight; visual. **2.** acting by means of sight or light, as instruments.

optical scanner n. → **scanner**.

optician n. a maker or seller of optical glasses and instruments.

optimise v. to make the best of; make the most effective use of. Also, **optimize**. –**optimisation**, n.

optimism n. disposition to hope for the best. –**optimist**, n. –**optimistic**, adj.

optimum n. (pl. **-ma** or **-mums**) **1.** the best or most favourable situation, degree, etc. –adj. **2.** best or most favourable.

option n. **1.** power or liberty of choosing. **2.** something which may be or is chosen; choice. **3.** the right to buy within a certain time. –**optional**, adj.

optometry n. the practice or art of testing the eyes for glasses. –**optometrist**, n.

opulent adj. wealthy, as persons or places. –**opulence**, n.

opus /ˈoʊpəs/ n. (pl. **opera** /ˈɒpərə/) a work or composition.

The short form of this word, usually only used in writing, is **op**.

or conj. a particle used: **1.** to connect words, phrases, or clauses representing alternatives: to be or not to be. **2.** often in correlation: either ... or; or ... or; whether ... or.

oracle n. any person or thing serving as an agency of divine communication.

oral adj. **1.** relating to or uttered by the mouth. **2.** employing speech.

orange n. **1.** a common citrus fruit. **2.** a reddish-yellow colour.

orangutan /əˈræŋətæn/ n. a large, long-armed anthropoid ape. Also, **orang-ou-tang**, **orang-utan**.

oration n. a formal speech.

orator /ˈɒrətə/ n. a public speaker, especially one of great eloquence.

oratory n. the art of an orator.

orb n. a sphere or globe.

orbit n. **1.** the curved path described by a planet, satellite, etc., about a body, as the earth or sun. –v. **2.** to travel in such a path around. –**orbital**, adj.

orchard n. a place where fruit trees are grown.

orchestra n. a group of performers on various musical instruments.

Orchestra is a collective noun and can be used with a singular or plural verb. Look up **collective noun**.

orchestrate v. **1.** to compose or arrange (music) for performance by an orchestra. **2.** to put together cohesively. –**orchestration**, n.

orchid n. a tropical plant noted for its beautiful flowers.

ordain v. **1.** (in some religions) to appoint to the church as a priest or minister. **2.** to order, declare or decree.

ordeal n. any severe test or trial.

order n. **1.** an authoritative command. **2.** the disposition of things following one after another. **3.** a condition in which everything is in its proper place. **4.** any class, kind, or sort. **5.** a quantity of goods purchased. **6.** a written direction to pay money or provide or deliver goods. *-v.* **7.** to give an order to or for. **8.** to regulate or manage. *-phr.* **9. in order that,** to the end that. **10. in order to,** as a means to. **11. in short order,** speedily; promptly. **12. on order,** ordered but not yet received.

orderly *adj.* **1.** arranged in order or in a tidy manner. **2.** characterised by order or discipline. *-n.* (*pl.* **-lies**) **3.** a person employed, as in a hospital, for general duties.

ordinal number *n.* any of the numbers *first, second, third,* etc., which indicate the order in which things occur.

Compare this with **cardinal number,** which is a number which tells you how many things are in a given set but not the order in which they appear.

ordinance *n.* **1.** an authoritative command. **2.** a public regulation.

ordinary *adj.* **1.** of the usual kind. **2.** somewhat inferior. *-phr.* **3. out of the ordinary,** unusual or special: *His new car is nothing out of the ordinary.*

ordure *n.* filth; excrement.

ore *n.* a metal-bearing mineral or rock.

oregano *n.* a plant of the mint family, used in cookery.

organ *n.* **1.** a keyboard instrument consisting of one or more sets of pipes sounded by means of compressed air. **2.** (in an animal or a plant) a part or member, as the heart, having some specific function.

organdie *n.* a fine, thin, stiff, cotton fabric.

organic *adj.* **1.** characteristic of, relating to, or derived from living organisms. **2.** *Chem.* relating to a class of compounds consisting of all compounds of carbon except for its oxides, sulphides, and metal carbonates. Compare **inorganic** (def. 2). **3.** of or relating to farming which does not use chemical fertilisers or pesticides. **4.** of

or relating to the organs of an animal or plant. **5.** characterised by the systematic arrangement of parts. **-organically,** *adv.*

organisation *n.* **1.** the process of organising. **2.** the manner of being organised. **3.** any organised whole. **4.** the administrative personnel or apparatus of a business. Also, **organization. -organisational,** *adj.*

organise *v.* **1.** to systematise. **2.** to give organic structure or character to. Also, **organize.**

organism *n.* any form of animal or plant life.

orgasm *n.* a complex series of responses of the genital organs and skin at the culmination of a sexual act.

orgy *n.* (*pl.* **-gies**) **1.** a gathering where people engage in unbridled sexual activity. **2.** wild revelry.

orient *v.* → **orientate.**

oriental *adj.* (*sometimes upper case*) of Asia.

orientate *v.* to adjust with relation to surroundings, etc. Also, **orient. -orientation,** *n.*

orienteering *n.* a race over a course consisting of a number of checkpoints which must be located with the aid of maps, compasses, etc.

orifice *n.* a mouth-like opening or hole.

origami *n.* the art of folding paper into shapes of flowers, birds, etc.

origin *n.* **1.** that from which anything is derived. **2.** derivation from a particular source. **3.** birth; parentage; extraction.

original *adj.* **1.** relating to the origin or beginning of something. **2.** fresh; novel. **3.** arising from a thing itself. **4.** being that from which a copy or the like is made. *-n.* **5.** a primary form or type from which varieties are derived. **-originality,** *n.*

originate *v.* **1.** to arise; spring. **2.** to initiate; invent. **-origination,** *n.*

ornament *n.* **1.** an accessory or detail used to beautify the appearance. *-v.* **2.** to furnish with ornaments. **–ornamental**, *adj.* **–ornamentation**, *n.*

ornate *adj.* elaborately adorned.

ornithology *n.* the branch of zoology that deals with birds.

orphan *n.* **1.** a child bereaved of both parents. *–v.* **2.** to bereave of parents or a parent.

orphanage *n.* an institution for orphans.

orthodontics *n.* the branch of dentistry that is concerned with the straightening of irregular teeth.

orthodox *adj.* (of doctrine, ideas, etc.) accepted or approved. **–orthodoxy**, *n.*

orthopaedics *n.* the correction or cure of deformities and diseases of the skeletal system. Also, **orthopedics**.

orthotic *n.* a remedial device placed in a shoe to correct the position or motion of the foot.

oscillate *v.* **1.** to swing as a pendulum. **2.** to fluctuate or vibrate. **–oscillation**, *n.*

osmium *n.* a hard, heavy, metallic element used for electric-light filaments, etc. *Symbol:* Os

osmosis *n.* the diffusion of fluids through membranes.

ostensible *adj.* outwardly appearing as such; professed; pretended. **–ostensibly**, *adv.*

> The more usual word is **supposed**.

ostentation *n.* pretentious show. **–ostentatious**, *adj.*

osteoarthritis *n.* a degenerative type of chronic arthritis. *Abbrev.*: OA

osteopathy /ɒstiˈɒpəθi/ *n.* the curing of disease by manipulation of parts of the body. **–osteopath**, *n.*

osteoporosis /ɒstioʊpəˈroʊsəs/ *n.* a condition in which bones become thin and brittle.

ostracise *v.* to exclude by general consent from society, privileges, etc. Also, **ostracize**.

ostrich *n.* a large flightless bird.

other *adj.* **1.** additional. **2.** different in kind. **3.** being the remaining one or ones. *–pron.* **4.** the other one. **5.** another person or thing. *–phr.* **6. every other**, every alternate.

otherwise *adv.* **1.** under other circumstances. **2.** differently. **3.** in other respects.

otter *n.* a furred, carnivorous, aquatic mammal with webbed feet.

ottoman *n.* (*pl.* **-mans**) a low cushioned seat or stool.

ouch *interj.* an exclamation expressing sudden pain.

ought *v.* a verb used **1.** to be bound or required, as by duty, moral obligation, necessity, justice, etc.: *You ought to apologise; He ought to be punished; You ought to add more milk.* **2.** to indicate probability: *This glue ought to hold it.*

> **Ought to** acts like a modal verb and is always used with another verb. Look up **modal verb**.

ouija /ˈwidʒə, -dʒi/ *n.* (*from trademark*) a board or table covering marked with words, letters of the alphabet, etc., used during seances.

ounce *n.* a unit of mass in the imperial system, equal to about 29 grams.

our *pron.* the possessive form of **we**, used before a noun: *We took our time.*

> **Our** is a first person plural pronoun. It is sometimes called a *determiner* or a *possessive adjective*.

ours *pron.* **1.** the possessive form of **we** used without a noun following: *Those books are ours.* **2.** the person(s) or thing(s) belonging to us: *Ours are those seats over there.*

> **Ours** is a first person plural pronoun in the possessive case.

ourselves *pron.* **1.** the reflexive form of **we**: *We hurt ourselves.* **2.** an emphatic form of **us** or **we**: *We used it for ourselves; We ourselves did it.*

oust *v.* to expel from a position occupied.

out *adv.* **1.** forth from, away from, or not in a place, position, state, etc. **2.** into the open. **3.** to the end: *The fire burnt itself out. –adj.* **4.** extinguished. **5.** not in vogue or fashion. **6.** into or in public notice or knowledge: *The secret is out.* **7.** on strike. **8.** incorrect or inaccurate. **9.** unconscious. *–prep.* **10.** forth from: *out the door. –n.* **11.** a means of escaping. *–phr.* **12. out of. a.** from a source: *made out of scraps.* **b.** lacking: *out of eggs.* **c.** without: *out of work for at least a month.*

out-and-out *adj.* thoroughgoing.

outback *n. Aust., NZ (sometimes upper case)* remote, sparsely inhabited back country.

outboard *adj.* (of the engine of a motorboat) located on the outside of the boat, at the stern. Compare **inboard**.

outbreak *n.* **1.** an outburst. **2.** a public disturbance.

outbuilding *n.* a detached building subordinate to a main building.

outburst *n.* a sudden and violent outpouring.

outcast *n.* a person who is cast out, as from home or society.

outcome *n.* that which results from something.

outcrop *n.* a protruding mass, as of rock.

outcry *n.* (*pl.* **-cries**) loud or widespread protest or indignation.

outdated *adj.* old-fashioned.

outdoors *adv., n.* (in) the open air.

outer *adj.* **1.** farther out; external; of or relating to the outside. *–n.* **2.** that part of a sportsground which is without shelter. *–phr.* **3. on the outer**, *Aust. Informal* excluded from the group; mildly ostracised.

outfit *n.* **1.** a set of articles, clothes, etc., for any purpose. *–v.* (**-fitted, -fitting**) **2.** to equip.

outgoing *adj.* **1.** departing. **2.** interested in and responsive to others.

outgrowth *n.* **1.** a natural development or result. **2.** an offshoot.

outing *n.* an excursion.

outlandish *adj.* freakish.

outlaw *n.* **1.** a habitual criminal. *–v.* **2.** to prohibit.

outlay *n.* **1.** an amount expended. *–v.* (**-laid, -laying**) **2.** to expend, as money.

For def. 2, the more usual word is **spend**.

outlet *n.* **1.** a vent or exit. **2.** a market for goods.

outline *n.* **1.** the line by which a figure or object is bounded. **2.** a general sketch or report, indicating only the main features. *–v.* **3.** to give or draw an outline of.

outlook *n.* the view from a place.

outpatient *n.* a patient receiving treatment at a hospital but not staying there.

outpost *n.* any remote settlement.

output *n.* **1.** the amount produced, as in a given time. **2.** *Computers* information obtained from a computer on the completion of a calculation. *–v.* (**-put, -putting**) **3.** to supply from a computer database, file, etc.: *we can output the data; I'll output copies for the meeting.*

outrage *n.* **1.** any gross violation of law or decency. *–v.* (**-raged, -raging**) **2.** to shock. **–outrageous**, *adj.* **–outraged**, *adj.*

outright *adj.* **1.** complete or total. *–adv.* **2.** completely; entirely.

outset *n.* the beginning or start.

outside *n.* **1.** the exterior. **2.** the space beyond an enclosure, boundary, etc. *–adj.* **3.** done or originating beyond an enclosure, boundary, etc. **4.** external. **5.** not connected with an institution, society, etc. **6.** extremely unlikely: *an outside chance. –adv., prep.* **7.** on or to the outside (of).

outsider *n.* someone not belonging to a particular group.

outskirts *pl. n.* outer parts or districts.

outsource *v.* (**-sourced, -sourcing**) to send (work) away to be completed by another company or by persons outside one's own staff. **–outsourcing**, *n.*

outspoken *adj.* unreserved in speech.

outstanding *adj.* prominent; striking.

outstrip *v.* (-**stripped**, -**stripping**) to do better than.

outward *adj.* 1. directed towards the outside. 2. of or relating to the outside. –*adv.* 3. → **outwards**

Note that you can use **outward** for both the adjective (*outward signs*, *outward surface*, *outward journey*) and the adverb (*to gaze outward*), but **outwards** can only be used for the adverb (*to gaze outwards*).

outwardly *adv.* as regards appearance or outward manifestation.

outwards *adv.* towards the outside; out. Also, **outward**.

outwit *v.* (-**witted**, -**witting**) to get the better of by superior ingenuity.

ouzo /ˈuːzoʊ/ *n.* an aniseed-flavoured liqueur of Greece.

ova *n.* plural of **ovum**.

oval *adj.* 1. egg-shaped. –*n.* 2. any of various oval things. 3. *Aust.* a flat area on which sporting activities can take place.

ovary *n.* (*pl.* -**ries**) 1. *Anat.*, *Zool.* the female reproductive gland. 2. *Bot.* a container for unfertilised seed. –**ovarian**, *adj.*

ovate *adj.* egg-shaped.

ovation *n.* enthusiastic applause.

oven *n.* a chamber or receptacle for baking or heating.

over *prep.* 1. above in place or position. 2. above and to the other side of. 3. on or upon. 4. here and there on or in: *Debris fell over the town.* 5. more than. 6. in preference to. 7. throughout the duration of: *over the long weekend.* 8. in reference to: *They spoke to him over his drinking.* 9. by the agency of: *The news came over the radio.* 10. besides. –*adv.* 11. over the top or upper portion, or edge of something. 12. so as to cover the surface. 13. through a region, area, etc. 14. all through: *to read a letter over.* 15. so as to bring the upper end or side down or under. 16. in repetition: *10 times over.* –*adj.* 17. higher in authority, station, etc. 18. serving as an

outer covering. 19. in excess or addition. 20. at an end. –*n.* 21. *Cricket* the number of balls delivered between successive changes of bowlers. –*phr.* 22. **all over**, **a.** thoroughly; entirely. **b.** done with; finished.

overall *adj.* 1. covering or including everything. –*adv.* 2. covering or including everything.

overalls *pl. n.* trousers with a bib and shoulder straps.

overarm *adj.* 1. performed with the arm being raised above the shoulder, as bowling or swimming. –*adv.* 2. in an overarm manner.

overawe *v.* to subdue by inspiring awe.

overbalance *v.* to (cause to) lose balance.

overbearing *adj.* domineering; rudely arrogant.

overboard *adv.* over the side of a ship or boat.

overcast *adj.* 1. overspread with clouds. 2. dark; gloomy.

overcharge *v.* (-**charged**, -**charging**) 1. to charge (a person) too high a price. –*n.* 2. a charge in excess of a just price.

overcoat *n.* 1. a coat worn over the ordinary clothing, as in cold weather. 2. an additional coat of paint applied for protection.

overcome *v.* (-**came**, -**come**, -**coming**) to conquer (someone).

overdo *v.* (-**did**, -**done**, -**doing**) 1. to carry to excess. 2. to overcook.

overdose *n.* 1. an excessive dose. –*v.* 2. to take an overdose of a drug.

The abbreviation for this is **OD**.

overdraft *n.* a draft in excess of one's credit balance.

overdraw *v.* (-**drew**, -**drawn**, -**drawing**) to draw upon (an account, allowance, etc.) in excess of the balance at one's disposal.

overdue *adj.* past due, as a late train, or a bill not paid by the assigned date.

overflow *v.* (-**flowed**, -**flown**, -**flowing**) 1. to flow or run over. 2. to be supplied in overflowing measure (*with*). *−n.* **3.** that which flows or runs over.

overhang *v.* (**-hung, -hanging**) **1.** to hang over. **2.** to extend or jut over. *−n.* **3.** an overhanging; projection.

overhaul *v.* **1.** to examine thoroughly. *−n.* **2.** a thorough examination.

overhead *adv.* **1.** over one's head. *−adj.* **2.** situated above. *−n.* **3.** (*pl.*) the general cost of running a business.

overhear *n.* (**-heard, -hearing**) to hear (speech, etc.) without the speaker's intention or knowledge.

overkill *n.* the use of more resources or energy than is necessary to achieve one's aim.

overlap *v.* (**-lapped, -lapping**) **1.** to cover and extend beyond (something else). **2.** to correspond partly with. **3.** to wrap over. *−n.* **4.** the extent or amount of overlapping.

overleaf *adv.* on the other side of the page or sheet.

overlook *v.* **1.** to fail to notice or consider. **2.** to afford a view down over. **3.** to supervise.

overnight *adv.* **1.** during the night. **2.** suddenly: *Everything changed overnight.* *−adj.* **3.** occurring during the night. **4.** staying for one night.

overpass *n.* a bridge over a road or railway.

overpower *v.* to overwhelm.

overreach *v.* **1.** to reach beyond. **2.** to defeat (oneself) by overdoing matters.

overriding *adj.* prevailing over all other considerations.

overrule *v.* to rule against, by higher authority.

overrun *v.* (**-ran, -run, -running**) **1.** to spread over rapidly and occupy. **2.** to exceed. **3.** to overflow.

overseas *adv.* **1.** beyond the sea; abroad: *to travel overseas.* *−adj.* **2.** of, relating to, or situated in countries across the sea: *an overseas holiday.*

oversee *v.* (**-saw, -seen, -seeing**) to direct (work or workers).

overshadow *v.* to tower over.

overshoot *v.* (**-shot, -shooting**) **1.** to go beyond (a point, limit, etc.). **2.** to shoot too far.

oversight *n.* **1.** failure to notice or take into account. **2.** an omission or mistake.

overt *adj.* not concealed or secret: *overt hostility.*

The more usual word is **open**.

overtake *v.* (**-took, -taken, -taking**) to pass (another vehicle).

overthrow *v.* (**-threw, -thrown, -throwing**) **1.** to depose as from a position of power. **2.** to overturn. *−n.* **3.** the act of overthrowing.

overtime *n.* **1.** time during which one works before or after regularly scheduled working hours. **2.** pay for such time.

overtone *n.* (*usu. pl.*) additional meaning or implication: *political overtones*; *an overtone of resentment in his voice.*

overture *n.* **1.** an introductory part. **2.** an opening of negotiations, or offer.

overturn *v.* **1.** to overthrow. **2.** to turn over on its side, face, or back; capsize.

overview *n.* a general survey which avoids getting down to details.

overwhelm *v.* **1.** to overcome completely in mind or feeling. **2.** to defeat, especially by force of numbers.

overwrought *adj.* worked up or excited excessively.

ovine *adj.* relating to, of the nature of, or like sheep.

ovoid *adj.* egg-shaped.

ovulate *v.* to shed eggs from an ovary or ovarian follicle. *−n.* **ovulation,** *n.*

ovum *n.* (*pl.* **ova**) the female reproductive cell; egg.

owe *v.* **1.** to be indebted or beholden for. **2.** to be in debt to.

owing *adj.* **1.** owed or due. *−phr.* **2. owing to, a.** because of. **b.** attributable to.

owl *n.* a nocturnal bird of prey, with broad head and large eyes, and a distinctive cry.

own *adj.* **1.** relating to oneself or itself. *–v.* **2.** to possess. **3.** to admit. *–phr.* **4. get one's own back,** to have revenge. **5. on one's own,** *Informal* responsible for oneself; independent. **6. own up,** to confess.

ox *n.* (*pl.* **oxen**) **1.** → **bullock.** **2.** any member of the cattle family, especially one used for pulling loads in some countries.

oxide *n.* a compound, usually containing 2 elements only, one of which is oxygen.

oxidise *v.* **1.** to combine with oxygen. **2.** to (cover with) rust. Also, **oxidize.**

oxygen *n.* a colourless, odourless gaseous element, constituting about half the volume of the atmosphere. *Symbol:* O

oxymoron /ɒksi'mɔːrɒn/ *n.* (*pl.* **-morons** *or* **-mora** /-'mɔːrə/) a figure of speech which seems to contradict itself, as *cruel kindness* or *make haste slowly.* **–oxymoronic** /ɒksimə'rɒnɪk/, *adj.*

oyster *n.* any of various edible marine bivalve molluscs.

ozone *n. Chem.* a form of oxygen.

ozone hole *n.* a loss in the concentration of ozone in some part of the ozone layer.

ozone layer *n.* a region in the outer part of the stratosphere at a height of about 30 kilometres, where much of the atmospheric ozone (O_3) occurs. Also, **ozonosphere.**

P, p

P, p *n.* the 16th letter of the English alphabet.

pace *n.* **1.** rate of stepping, or of movement in general. **2.** rate or style of doing anything. **3.** the distance covered in a single step. **4.** manner of stepping; gait. *–v.* **(paced, pacing) 5.** to set the pace for, as in racing. **6.** to traverse with paces or steps. **7.** to walk, especially in a state of nervous excitement. *–phr.* **8. off the pace**, *Informal* behind the leader in a race or contest by the specified number of points, length of time, etc.: *two shots off the pace; 25 seconds off the pace.*

pacemaker *n. Med.* an instrument implanted beneath the skin to control the rate of the heartbeat.

pachyderm /ˈpækidɜm/ *n.* a large thick-skinned animal, as the elephant, hippopotamus, and rhinoceros.

pacific *adj.* **1.** peaceable; not warlike. **2.** peaceful; at peace.

pacifism *n.* opposition to war or violence of any kind. *–***pacifist,** *n.*

pacify *v.* **(-fied, -fying)** to bring into a state of peace; calm.

pack¹ *n.* **1.** a quantity of anything wrapped or tied up; a parcel. **2.** a load or burden for carrying. **3.** a company of certain animals of the same kind. **4.** a group of things, usually abstract. **5.** a complete set, as of playing cards. *–v.* **6.** to make into a pack or bundle. **7.** to put (goods, animals, ice, etc.) into a group or compact form. **8.** to press or crowd together (within); cram. **9.** to send summarily (*off, away,* etc.).

pack² *v.* to collect, arrange, or manipulate (cards, persons, facts, etc.) so as to serve one's own purposes: *to pack a jury.*

package *n.* **1.** one or more objects wrapped up or packed; parcel. **2.** a unit, group of parts, or the like, considered as a single entity. *–v.* **(-aged, -aging) 3.** to put into wrappings or a container.

Compare this with **bundler,** which is a group of things tied together in some way, rather than wrapped up in something.

packaging *n.* **1.** the box, wrapper, plastic sleeve, etc., in which an item is presented for sale. **2.** the manner in which a public figure or issue is presented, especially to the media.

packet *n.* a small pack or package.

pact *n.* an agreement; a compact.

pad¹ *n.* **1.** a cushion-like mass of some soft material, for comfort, protection, or stuffing. **2.** Also, **writing pad.** a number of sheets of paper glued together at one edge. **3.** one of the cushion-like protuberances on the underside of the feet of dogs, foxes, etc. *–v.* **(padded, padding) 4.** to cover or stuff with a pad or padding. **5.** Also, **pad out.** to expand (writing or speech) with unnecessary words or matter.

pad² *n.* **1.** a dull sound, as of footsteps on the ground. *–v.* **(padded, padding) 2.** to walk softly.

paddle¹ *n.* **1.** a short oar held in the hands (not resting in the rowlock). *–v.* **2.** to propel (a canoe or the like) by using a paddle.

paddle² *v.* to dabble or play in or as in shallow water.

paddock *n. Aust., NZ* a large fenced area of land, usually used for grazing stock.

paddy *n.* (*pl.* **-dies**) a wet, often flooded field on which rice is grown.

padlock *n.* a portable or detachable lock.

padre /ˈpadreɪ/ *n.* a military or naval chaplain.

paediatrics /pidiˈætnks/ *n.* the study and treatment of the diseases of children. Also, **pediatrics.** *–***paediatric,** *adj.* *–***paediatrician,** *n.*

paedophile /'pedəfaɪl, 'pid-/ n. an adult who engages in sexual activities with children. Also, **pedophile**. –**paedophilia**, n.

pagan n., adj. (a person who is) irreligious or heathenish.

page[1] n. one side of a leaf of a book, manuscript, letter, or the like.

page[2] n. **1.** a boy servant or attendant. –v. (**paged**, **paging**) **2.** to seek (a person) by calling out their name.

pageant n. an elaborate public spectacle. –**pageantry**, n.

pagoda n. (in India, Burma, China, etc.) a temple or sacred building, usually more or less pyramidal.

paid v. past tense and past participle of **pay**.

pail n. a bucket.

> Don't confuse this with **pale**, which means not very bright in colour, or rather whitish.

pain n. **1.** bodily or mental distress. **2.** (pl.) laborious or careful efforts. **3.** Also, **pain in the neck**. Informal an irritating, tedious, or unpleasant person or thing. –v. **4.** to inflict pain on.

> Don't confuse **pain** with **pane**, which is a sheet of glass in a window.

painkiller n. a drug which relieves pain. –**painkilling**, adj.

painstaking adj. assiduously careful.

paint n. **1.** a substance composed of solid colouring matter mixed with a liquid and applied as a coating. –v. **2.** to execute (a picture, design, etc.) in colours or pigment. **3.** to coat, cover, or decorate (something) with colour or pigment. **4.** to apply like paint, as a liquid medicine, etc. –**painting**, n.

painter[1] n. someone who paints.

painter[2] n. a rope for fastening a boat to a ship, stake, etc.

pair n. (pl. **pairs** or **pair**) **1.** 2 things of a kind, used or associated together. –v. **2.** to arrange in pairs. **3.** to join in a pair; mate.

> Note that this word has two plurals. **Pairs** is the more usual, with **pair** being slightly old-fashioned and used mainly with clothing, as in two pair of slippers and four pair of trousers.
> Don't confuse **pair** with **pare** or **pear**. To **pare** something is to peel it, and a **pear** is a fruit.
> Compare **pair** with **couple**. Both words refer to two things, but a **pair** is two things of the same kind that usually go together (a pair of shoes), and a **couple** is two of anything (a couple of drinks, a couple of children).

paisley n. (a soft fabric made from wool and woven with) a colourful and minutely detailed pattern.

pal n. Informal a comrade; friend.

palace n. the official residence of a sovereign, a bishop, etc.

palaeontology /ˌpælɪɒn'tɒlədʒi, ˌpeɪ-/ n. the science of the forms of prehistoric life represented by fossil animals and plants. Also, **paleontology**.

palatable adj. agreeable to the taste.

palate n. **1.** the roof of the mouth. **2.** the sense of taste. –**palatal**, adj.

palatial adj. of the nature of, or befitting a palace.

palaver /pə'lavə/ n. **1.** a discussion or conference, especially a long and tedious one. **2.** any talk or activity regarded as unnecessary or too lengthy.

pale[1] adj. **1.** of a whitish appearance; without intensity of colour. –v. **2.** to become pale.

> Don't confuse **pale** with **pail**, which is an old-fashioned word for a bucket.

pale[2] n. **1.** a stake or picket, as of a fence. **2.** a barrier.

palette /'pælət/ n. a board used by painters to lay and mix colours on.

palindrome /'pæləndroʊm/ n. a word or phrase which reads exactly the same

paling n. a long pointed piece of wood, especially as part of a fence.

palisade n. a fence of pales or stakes, as for enclosure or defence.

pall[1] n. **1.** a cloth for spreading over a coffin, or tomb. **2.** something that covers, especially with darkness or gloom.

pall[2] v. to have a wearying effect (*on* or *upon*).

pallbearer n. one of those who carry or attend the coffin at a funeral.

pallet n. a movable platform on which goods are placed for storage or transportation.

palliate v. **1.** to cause (an offence, etc.) to appear less grave; excuse. **2.** to mitigate or alleviate. **–palliative,** adj.

palliative care n. Med. the care of patients with a terminal illness.

pallid adj. pale. **–pallor,** n.

palm[1] n. **1.** that part of the inner surface of the hand which extends from the wrist to the bases of the fingers. *–v.* **2.** to conceal in the palm, as in cheating at cards.

palm[2] n. **1.** a tropical, tall, unbranched tree surmounted by a crown of large fan-shaped leaves. **2.** a palm leaf as an emblem of victory.

palmistry n. the art or practice of telling fortunes and interpreting character by the lines of the palm of the hand. **–palmist,** n.

palmtop n. a small handheld personal computer.

palomino n. (pl. **-nos**) a tan or cream-coloured horse with a white mane and tail. Also, **palamino.**

palpable adj. **1.** obvious. **2.** that can be touched or felt.

palpate v. to examine by the sense of touch.

palpitate v. to pulsate with unnatural rapidity, as the heart. **–palpitation,** n.

palsy n. paralysis.

paltry adj. (**-trier, -triest**) of small size, importance, etc.

pamper v. to indulge.

pamphlet n. **1.** a very small paper-covered book. **2.** a single sheet of paper with advertisements printed on it, which is handed out to people or put in letterboxes.

pan[1] n. **1.** a metal dish, usually broad and shallow. **2.** a depression in the ground containing salt water, mineral salts etc. *–v.* (**panned, panning**) **3.** to wash gravel, sand, etc., in a pan, to separate the gold, etc. **4.** *Informal* to criticise severely.

pan[2] v. (**panned, panning**) *Film, TV, etc.* (of a camera) to move continuously while filming.

panacea /pænəˈsiə/ n. **1.** a remedy for all diseases. **2.** a solution to all problems: *Technology is not the panacea some thought it would be.*

panache /pəˈnæʃ/ n. a grand or flamboyant manner.

pancake n. a thin flat cake made from batter.

pancreas n. a gland situated near the stomach. **–pancreatic,** adj.

panda n. **1.** a large, black-and-white, bear-like animal found mainly in China. **2.** *Philately* a section of a sheet of postage stamps.

pandemic adj. (of a disease) prevalent throughout an entire country or the whole world.

pandemonium n. (a place of) riotous uproar or lawless confusion.

pander v. to show excessive indulgence (*to*).

pane n. (one of the divisions of a window, etc., consisting of) a single plate of glass.

Don't confuse this with **pain**, which is the suffering or hurt you feel when you are injured or sick.

panegyric /pænəˈdʒɪrɪk/ n. a speech or writing in praise of a person or thing.

panel n. **1.** a distinct portion or division, as of a door, wall, etc. **2.** a broad strip of material set vertically, as for ornament, in or on a woman's dress, etc. **3.** a surface or section of a machine on which controls, dials, etc., are mounted. **4.** the body of persons composing a jury, etc. –v. (**-elled, -elling**) **5.** to arrange in, or furnish with, panels.

pang n. a sharp pain.

panic n. **1.** a sudden demoralising terror. –v. (**-icked, -icking**) **2.** to (cause to) be stricken with panic.

panoply n. (pl. **-lies**) a complete covering or array of something.

panorama n. an unobstructed view or prospect over a wide area. –**panoramic**, adj.

pansy n. a plant with brightly coloured velvety flowers.

pant v. **1.** to breathe hard and quickly, as after exertion. –n. **2.** a short, quick, laboured effort of breathing; a gasp.

pantechnicon n. a large or medium-sized truck or van with an enclosed back section, especially one used for transporting furniture.

panther n. (pl. **-thers** or, especially collectively, **-ther**) the leopard, especially in its black form.

pantihose n. women's tights, usually made of a fine material such as nylon. Also, **pantyhose**.

Note that this word is used as a plural noun: These pantihose have a ladder in them.

pantomime n. a form of theatrical entertainment, especially using stock characters, farce, music, etc.

pantry n. (pl. **-ries**) a room or cupboard in which food and other household items are kept.

pants pl. n. **1.** trousers. **2.** underpants, especially women's.

pap n. books, ideas, etc., lacking intellectual content.

papa n. father

papacy n. (pl. **-cies**) **1.** the office or authority of the pope. **2.** the system of ecclesiastical government in which the pope is the supreme head.

papal adj. of or relating to the pope, the papacy, or the Roman Catholic Church.

paparazzo n. /papə'ratsəu, pæpə-/ n. (pl. **-razzi**) a press photographer who persistently pursues celebrities in order to photograph them.

papaya n. a melon-like tropical fruit, with pinkish flesh.

paper n. **1.** a substance made from rags, straw, wood, etc., usually in thin sheets, for writing or printing on, wrapping things in, etc. **2.** paper money. **3.** a set of questions for an examination. **4.** an essay, article, etc. **5.** a newspaper or journal. **6.** (pl.) documents establishing identity, status, etc. –v. **7.** to decorate with wallpaper.

paperback n. a book bound in a flexible paper cover.

papier-mâché /peɪpə-'mæʃeɪ, pæpieɪ-'mæʃeɪ/ n. a substance made of pulped paper and glue which becomes hard and strong when dry.

pappadum /'pæpədʌm/ n. a thin, crisp Indian wafer bread, made from spiced potato or rice flour. Also, **pappadam**, **poppadum**.

paprika n. the dried fruit of a cultivated form of capsicum, ground as a condiment.

papyrus /pə'paɪrəs/ n. (pl. **-pyri** /-'paɪraɪ/) **1.** a tall aquatic plant of the Nile valley, Egypt, and elsewhere. **2.** a material for writing on, prepared from the pith of this plant.

par n. **1.** an equality in value or standing. **2.** an average or normal amount, degree, quality, condition, or the like. **3.** Commerce the state of shares when they may be purchased at the original price or at their face value. **4.** *Golf* the number of strokes per hole or course, as a target standard.

parable *n.* a short allegorical story, designed to convey some truth or moral lesson.

parabola *n. Geom.* a plane curve formed by the intersection of a cone with a plane parallel to its side.

paracetamol /pærə'sitəmɒl/ *n.* an analgesic, fever-reducing drug.

parachute *n.* an umbrella-shaped apparatus used in descending safely through the air, especially from an aircraft.

parade *n.* **1.** show, display, or ostentation. **2.** the orderly assembly of troops for inspection, display, etc. **3.** a public procession. –*v.* **4.** to display ostentatiously. **5.** to march or proceed with display. **6.** to promenade to show oneself.

paradigm /'pærədaɪm/ *n. Gram.* the set of all inflected forms of a single root, stem, or theme.

paradise *n.* **1.** heaven. **2.** a place of extreme beauty or delight.

paradox *n.* a statement or proposition seemingly self-contradictory or absurd, and yet expressing a truth. –**paradoxicality**, *n.*

paraffin *n.* **1.** *Chem.* any hydrocarbon of the methane series. **2.** Also, **paraffin oil.** a mixture of hydrocarbons obtained from petroleum, used for lighting, etc.

paragon *n.* a model or pattern of excellence.

paragraph *n.* a distinct portion of written or printed matter dealing with a particular point, and usually beginning (sometimes with indentation) on a new line.

parakeet *n.* a small, slender parrot.

parallax *n.* the apparent displacement of an observed object due to a change or difference in position of the observer.

parallel *adj.* **1.** corresponding; similar; analogous. **2.** *Geom.* (of straight lines) lying in the same plane but never meeting. **3.** *Computers, etc.* denoting or relating to

a system in which several activities are carried on concurrently. Compare **serial** (def. 4). –*n.* **4.** anything parallel in direction, course, or tendency. **5.** *Geog.* a line of latitude. **6.** *Elect.* a connection of 2 or more circuits, batteries etc., where positive terminal is connected to positive, and negative to negative. –*v.* (**-lleled**, **-lleling**) **7.** to form a parallel to.

parallelogram *n.* a quadrilateral the opposite sides of which are parallel, as a square, rectangle or rhombus.

parallel verb *n.* a verb which expands the range of actions, processes, states, etc., but which is grammatically identical to the preceding verb.

paralysis /pə'ræləsəs/ *n.* (*pl.* **-lyses** /-ləsiz/) **1. a.** loss of power of a voluntary muscular contraction. **b.** a disease characterised by this; palsy. **2.** a more or less complete crippling, as of powers or activities. –**paralyse**, *v.* –**paralytic**, *n.*, *adj.*

paramedical *adj.* related to the medical profession in a supplementary capacity, as an ambulance officer, etc.

parameter *n.* any constituent variable quality.

Don't confuse this with **perimeter**, which is the outside edge of a shape or area.

paramount *adj.* chief in importance.

paramour *n.* an illicit lover.

paranoia *n.* a psychotic disorder characterised by systematised delusions. –**paranoiac**, *n.*, *adj.*

parapet *n.* any protective wall on a balcony, roof, bridge, or the like.

paraphernalia /pærəfə'neɪliə/ *pl. n.* miscellaneous articles.

Although this is a plural noun, it is usually treated as singular: *All your paraphernalia is in my way!*

paraphrase *n.* **1.** a restatement of the sense of a text or passage, as for clearness, –*v.* **2.** to restate in a paraphrase.

paraplegia *n.* paralysis of both lower or upper limbs. **–paraplegic**, *adj.*, *n.*

parasite *n.* an animal or plant which lives on or in another organism from the body of which it obtains nutriment. **–parasitic**, *adj.*

parasol *n.* a woman's small or light sun umbrella.

parboil *v.* to boil partially, or for a short time.

parcel *n.* **1.** a quantity of something wrapped or packaged together. **2.** a part or portion of anything. *–v.* (**-celled, -celling**) **3.** to make up into a parcel. *–phr.* **4. parcel out** (or **up**), to distribute in parcels or portions.

parch *v.* to make dry or thirsty.

parchment *n.* the skin of sheep, goats, etc., prepared for use as a writing material, etc.

pardon *n.* **1.** courteous excusing of fault or seeming rudeness. **2.** *Law* a remission of penalty. *–v.* **3.** to remit the penalty of (an offence). **4.** to release (a person) from liability for an offence. **5.** to excuse (an action or circumstance, or a person).

pare *v.* to cut off the outer part of.

Don't confuse this with **pair** or **pear**. A **pair** is a set of two things that go together, and a **pear** is a fruit.

parent *n.* **1.** a father or a mother. **2.** an author or source. **–parental**, *adj.* **–parentage**, *n.*

parenthesis /pəˈrɛnθəsəs/ *n.* (*pl.* **-theses** /-əsiz/) **1. a.** a set of the upright brackets ( ), used to mark off an interjected explanatory or qualifying remark, indicate groupings in mathematics, etc. **b.** either of these brackets individually; round bracket. **2.** *Gram.* a qualifying or explanatory word, phrase, clause, sentence, or other sequence of forms, shown in writing by commas, parentheses, or dashes. *–phr.* **3. in parenthesis**, as an aside: *She told me the son would be here today, and*

added in parenthesis that he was married now. **–parenthetic, parenthetical**, *adj.*

pariah *n.* an outcast.

parietal /pəˈraɪətl/ *adj. Anat.* referring to the side of the skull, or to any wall or wall-like structure.

parish *n.* an ecclesiastical district having its own church and member of the clergy. **–parishioner**, *n.*

parity *n.* **1.** equality, as in amount, status, or character. **2.** equivalence; similarity or analogy. **3.** *Finance* equivalence in value in the currency of another country.

park *n.* **1.** an area of land within a town, set aside for public use, often landscaped with trees and gardens, and with recreational and other facilities. *–v.* **2.** to put or leave (a car, etc.) for a time in a particular place.

parka *n.* a strong waterproof jacket with a hood; anorak.

Parkinson's disease *n.* a form of paralysis.

parlance *n.* way of speaking, or language; idiom.

parley *n.* a discussion.

parliament *n.* (*usu. upper case*) an assembly of elected representatives, often comprising an upper and lower house, which forms the legislature of a nation or constituent state. **–parliamentary**, *adj.* **–parliamentarian**, *n.*

Parliament is a collective noun and can be used with a singular or plural verb. Look up **collective noun**.

parlour *n.* a room for the entertainment of visitors. Also, **parlor**.

parmesan /ˈpɑməzən/ *n.* a hard, dry, strong-tasting cheese.

parochial /pəˈroʊkiəl/ *adj.* **1.** of or relating to a parish or parishes. **2.** narrow in range or interest.

parody *n.* (*pl.* **-dies**) **1.** a humorous or satirical imitation of a serious piece of literature or writing. **2.** a poor imitation;

a travesty. –v. (-died, -dying) 3. to imitate in such a way as to ridicule.

parole n. the liberation of a person from prison, conditional upon good behaviour, prior to the end of sentence.

paroxysm /'pærəksɪzəm/ n. a fit of violent action or emotion.

parquetry n. mosaic work of wood used for floors, wainscoting, etc.

parrot n. a hook-billed, gaily coloured bird.

parry v. (-ried, -rying) to ward off (a thrust, stroke, weapon, etc.).

parse v. Gram. to describe a sentence, etc., by giving the parts of speech of all the words.

parsimony /'pɑsəməni/ n. extreme or excessive economy or frugality. –**parsimonious**, adj.

parsley n. a garden herb used to garnish or season food.

parsnip n. (a plant with) a large, whitish, edible root.

parson n. a member of the clergy.

part n. 1. a portion or division of a whole. 2. (usu. pl.) a region, quarter, or district. 3. one of the sides to a contest, question, agreement, etc. 4. a character sustained in a play or in real life; a role. 5. a parting in the hair. –v. 6. to divide (a thing) into parts; divide. 7. to comb (the hair) away from a dividing line. 8. to put or keep asunder; separate. 9. to go apart from each other, as persons. –adj. 10. in part; partial.

partake v. (-took, -taken, -taking) 1. to participate or take part (in): to partake in the festivities. 2. to receive or have a share (of): to partake of some wine.

For def. 1, the more usual expression is **take part** in; for def. 2, **have some of**. Note that def. 2 is usually used to talk about food or drink, and is often used in a humorous way.

partial adj. 1. being such in part only; incomplete. 2. biased or prejudiced in

favour of a person, group, side, etc. –**partiality**, n.

participate v. to take or have a part or share (in). –**participant**, n., adj. –**participation**, n.

participle n. Gram. an adjective form derived from a verb, as burning in a burning candle, and devoted in a devoted friend. –**participial**, adj.

particle n. 1. a minute portion, piece, or amount. 2. a small word of functional or relational use, such as an article, preposition, or conjunction.

particular adj. 1. relating to some one person, thing, group, class, occasion, etc.; special, not general. 2. attentive to or exacting about details or small points.

particulate adj. existing as, composed of, or relating to particles.

partisan n. an adherent or supporter of a person, party, or cause.

partition n. 1. division into or distribution in portions or shares. 2. something that separates. –v. 3. to divide into parts or portions.

partner n. 1. a sharer or partaker; an associate. 2. Commerce someone associated with another or others in a business or a joint venture. 3. a person in a romantic relationship. –v. 4. to be, or act as, the partner of. –**partnership**, n.

part of speech n. Gram. any of the main types of words in a language, such as noun, verb, pronoun, adjective, adverb, preposition, conjunction, or interjection.

partridge n. (pl. -tridges or, especially collectively, -tridge) a game bird.

part-time adj. 1. done for a shorter period than normal working hours: a part-time job. –adv. 2. during less than normal working hours: to work part-time.

Compare this with **full-time**.

parturition n. the act of bringing forth young; childbirth.

party n. (pl. **-ties**) **1.** a group gathered together for some purpose, as for amusement or entertainment. **2.** (oft. upper case) a number or body of persons united in purpose or opinion, in opposition to others, as in politics, etc. **3.** someone who participates in some action or affair. **4.** a person in general. –v. (**-tied, -tying**) **5.** to take part in festivities at or as at a party. –phr. **6. be (a) party to**, to help, take part in, or be involved in.

pashmina n. **1.** a fine woollen fabric made from the underbelly fur of Himalayan goats, sometimes blended with silk. **2.** a shawl made from this fabric.

paspalum n. a grass widespread in Aust.

pass v. **1.** to go by (something) or move onwards. **2.** to go by without acting upon or noticing; leave unmentioned. **3.** to go or get through. **4.** to undergo successfully (an examination, etc.). **5.** to exist through; spend. **6.** to convey, transfer, or transmit. **7.** to discharge or void, as excrement. **8.** to sanction or approve. **9.** to express or pronounce, as an opinion or judgement. **10.** to elapse, as time. **11.** to happen; occur. **12.** to be interchanged, as between 2 persons. **13.** to go unheeded, uncensured, or unchallenged. –n. **14.** a narrow route across a depression in a mountain barrier. **15.** a permission or licence to pass, go, come, or enter. **16.** the passing of an examination. **17.** the transference of a ball, etc., from one player to another, as in football. –phr. **18. pass away**, (euphemistic) to die.

passage n. **1.** an indefinite portion of a writing, speech, or the like. **2.** the act of passing. **3.** liberty, leave, or right to pass. **4.** a means of passing; a way, route, avenue, channel, etc. **5.** a voyage across the sea from one port to another.

passenger n. someone who travels by some form of conveyance.

passer-by n. (pl. **passers-by**) someone who passes by.

passion n. **1.** any kind of feeling or emotion, especially when of compelling force. **2.** a strong enthusiasm, or desire for anything. **3.** the object of this. –**passionate**, adj.

passionfruit n. (the edible fruit of) a type of climbing vine.

passive adj. **1.** not acting. **2.** submitting without resistance. **3.** Gram. denoting a verb form or voice, in which the subject is represented as being acted on. For example, in the sentence He was hit, was hit is in the passive voice.

Compare def. 3 with **active** (def. 5).

passive aggressive adj. **1.** deliberately uncooperative; employing methods that frustrate the objectives of others without confronting them with outright refusal. –n. **2.** a person who behaves in such a manner.

passive smoking n. the inhaling by a non-smoker of the smoke produced by cigarette, cigar and pipe smokers, seen as detrimental to health. –**passive smoker,** n.

passport n. an official document authenticating the identity and citizenship of a person visiting foreign countries.

password n. **1.** a secret word or expression used to gain access to a restricted area or to distinguish a friend from an enemy. **2.** Computers a private code, usually a word or expression, used to gain access to a computer system.

past adj. **1.** gone by in time. **2.** belonging to, or having existed or having occurred in a previous time. –n. **3.** (the events of) the time gone by. –adv. **4.** so as to pass by or beyond. –prep. **5.** beyond in time, position or amount.

pasta n. a preparation made from a dough, such as spaghetti, macaroni, etc.

paste n. **1.** a mixture of flour and water, used for causing paper, etc., to adhere. **2.** any material or preparation in a soft or plastic mass. **3.** a brilliant, heavy glass, used for making artificial gems. –v.

4. to fasten or stick with paste or the like.

pastel *n.* **1.** a soft, subdued shade. **2.** a crayon. **3.** a drawing done with crayons.

pasteurise *v.* to expose (milk, etc.) to a high temperature in order to destroy certain micro-organisms. Also, **pasteurize**.

pastie /'pæsti, 'pasti/ *n.* a circular piece of pastry folded around a filling of vegetables, meat, etc., and baked. Also, **Cornish pastie, pasty.**

pastille /'pæstil, 'pæstl/ *n.* a lozenge.

pastime *n.* that which serves to make time pass agreeably.

pastor *n.* a minister or member of the clergy with reference to his or her congregation.

pastoral *adj.* **1.** used for pasture, as land. **2.** relating to the country or life in the country. **3.** relating to a minister or member of the clergy, or to his or her duties, etc. **4.** (especially in a school) of or relating to guidance provided to students regarding personal wellbeing and moral and ethical concerns. –*n.* **5.** a poem, play, or the like, dealing with the life of shepherds, or with simple rural life generally.

pastoralism *n.* the process of developing land for pasture for the grazing of domesticated or partially domesticated animals. –**pastoralist**, *n.*

pastry *n.* (*pl.* **-tries**) food made of a biscuit-like dough.

past tense *n. Gram.* the form of the verb which indicates that the action happened at some time in the past, as *came* in *She came to our house.*

pasture *n.* ground used or suitable for the grazing of cattle, etc.; grassland.

pasty /'pæsti, 'pasti/ *n.* → **pastie**.

PA system *n.* → **public-address system**.

pat[1] *v.* (**patted, patting**) **1.** to strike lightly with something flat. –*n.* **2.** a light stroke or blow with something flat. **3.** a small mass of something, as butter.

pat[2] *adj.* **1.** exactly to the point or purpose. **2.** apt; opportune. –*adv.* **3.** exactly or perfectly.

patch *n.* **1.** a piece of material used to mend a hole or break. **2.** a small piece or scrap of anything. **3.** *Informal* an area of responsibility. **4.** *Computers* a correction (usually temporary) made by the user to a computer program supplied by a software publisher, allowing the program to be customised for special uses. **5.** Also, **skin patch.** *Med.* an adhesive dressing which slowly dispenses medicine or other needed chemicals which are absorbed through the skin of the body. –*v.* **6.** to mend as with a patch or patches. **7.** *Telecommunications* to connect (a telephone or radio caller) to another caller or location: *patch me through to head office.* –*phr.* **8. patch up, a.** to repair or restore, often in a hasty way. **b.** to settle or smooth over: *They patched up their quarrel.*

patchwork *n.* work made of pieces of cloth or leather of various colours or shapes sewn together.

pate *n.* the head.

pâté /'pæteɪ, 'pa-/ *n.* a paste or spread made of finely minced liver, meat, fish, etc.

patella *n.* (*pl.* **-las** *or* **-lae** /-li/) *Anat.* the kneecap.

patent *n.* **1.** a government grant for a stated period of time, conferring the exclusive right to make, use, and vend an invention or discovery. –*adj.* **2.** of a kind specially protected by a patent. **3.** open to view or knowledge; evident. –*v.* **4.** to take out a patent on (an invention).

patent leather *n.* leather lacquered to produce a hard, glossy, smooth finish.

paternal *adj.* **1.** fatherly. **2.** related on the father's side.

paternity *n.* fatherhood.

path *n.* **1.** a way beaten or trodden by the feet of people or beasts. **2.** a course of action, conduct, or procedure.

pathetic *adj.* exciting pity or sympathetic sadness.

pathogen *n.* a disease-producing organism. −**pathogenic**, *adj.*

pathology *n.* 1. the science that deals with the origin, nature, and course of diseases. 2. also, **clinical pathology**. the study of diseased body organs, tissues, or cells, using laboratory tests. −**pathologist**, *n.* −**pathological**, *adj.*

pathos *n.* the quality or power, as in speech, music, etc., of evoking a feeling of pity or sympathetic sadness.

patient *n.* 1. someone who is under medical or surgical treatment. −*adj.* 2. quietly persevering or diligent. 3. quietly enduring strain, annoyance, etc. −**patience**, *n.*

patina *n.* 1. an attractive film of green on old bronze. 2. the shiny quality of well polished old timber.

patio *n.* (*pl.* **-tios**) an area adjoining a house, used for outdoor living.

patriarch /ˈpeɪtriak, ˈpæt-/ *n.* 1. the male head of a family or tribal line. 2. a high-ranking bishop in some Eastn Christian churches.

patriarchy /ˈpeɪtriaki, ˈpæt-/ *n.* (*pl.* **-archies**) a form of social organisation in which the father is head of the family, and in which descent is reckoned in the male line.

patrician *n.* 1. a member of the aristocracy in ancient Rome. 2. any noble or aristocrat.

patricide *n.* 1. someone who kills their father. 2. the act of killing one's father. −**patricidal**, *adj.*

patriot *n.* a person who loves and defends their country zealously. −**patriotic**, *adj.* −**patriotism**, *n.*

patrol *v.* (**-trolled, -trolling**) 1. to walk or march round as a guard. −*n.* 2. a person or a body of persons charged with patrolling. 3. the act of patrolling.

patron *n.* 1. someone who spends money at a shop, hotel, or the like. 2. a protector or supporter, as of a person, cause, institution, art, or enterprise. −**patronage**, *n.*

patronise *v.* 1. to be a customer of (a shop, restaurant, etc.). 2. to treat in a condescending way. Also, **patronize**.

patter[1] *v.* 1. to strike or move with a succession of slight tapping sounds. −*n.* 2. the act of pattering.

patter[2] *n.* the glib and rapid speech used by a salesperson, etc.

pattern *n.* 1. a decorative design. 2. style or type in general. 3. anything serving as a model or guide for something to be made. −*v.* 4. to make after a pattern.

patty *n.* (*pl.* **-ties**) a savoury mixture formed into a flattened ball, usually fried.

paucity *n.* smallness of quantity.

paunch *n.* the belly, especially if large.

pauper *n.* a very poor person.

pause *n.* 1. a temporary stop or rest. −*v.* 2. to make a pause; stop; hesitate.

pave *v.* 1. to cover or lay (a road, walk, etc.) with stones, concrete, etc. 2. to prepare (the way) for.

pavement *n.* a paved footway at the side of a street or road.

pavilion *n.* a light structure for purposes of shelter, shade, etc., as in a park.

pavlova *n.* a dessert made with a large soft-centred meringue.

paw *n.* 1. the foot of an animal with nails or claws. −*v.* 2. to touch with, or as if with, the paws.

> Don't confuse this with **pour**, **poor** or **pore**. To **pour** a liquid is to make it flow, **poor** describes someone with not much money, and **pore** can be a tiny opening in your skin or it can be to read something very carefully.

pawl *n.* a pivoted bar adapted to engage with the teeth of a ratchet or the like.

pawn[1] *v.* to deposit as security, as for money borrowed; hock.

pawn² n. a chess piece, of the lowest value.

pawnbroker n. someone who lends money at interest on pledged personal property. –**pawnbroking**, n.

pawpaw n. a large melon-like fruit with orange flesh.

pay v. (**paid, paying**) **1.** to discharge (a debt, obligation, etc.), as by giving or doing something. **2.** to give compensation for. **3.** to yield a return profit to. **4.** to give or render (attention, regard, court, compliments, etc.) **5.** to make (a call, visit, etc.). **6.** to suffer, or be punished, as for something. –n. **7.** payment, as of wages, salary, or stipend. **8.** paid employ. –**payable**, adj. –**payment**, n.

payroll n. **1.** a roll or list of persons to be paid, with the amounts due. **2.** the aggregate of these amounts.

pay TV n. a television service available to viewers who pay a subscription fee. Also, **pay television**.

PC **1.** personal computer. **2.** politically correct.

pea n. a small, round, highly nutritious seed, widely used as a vegetable.

peace n. **1.** freedom from war, hostilities, strife or dissension. **2.** a state of being tranquil or serene. –**peaceful**, adj. –**peaceable**, adj.

Don't confuse this with **piece**, which is a part of something.

peach n. a juicy, yellow-orange, stone fruit.

peacock n. the male of the peafowl distinguished by its long, colourful tail.

peafowl n. a kind of pheasant.

peahen n. the female peafowl.

peak n. **1.** the pointed top of a mountain. **2.** the highest point or degree of anything. **3.** a projecting front piece, or visor, of a cap.

Don't confuse this with **peek** or **pique**. To **peek** is to take a quick or secret look, and **pique** is a feeling of anger or resentment.

peak body n. an organisation which represents a group of enterprises engaged in similar activities: *the peak body of the advertising industry.*

peak hour n. the time when there is most traffic on the road because people are going to or leaving work. Also, **rush hour**.

peal n. **1.** a loud, prolonged sound of bells, thunder, laughter, etc. –v. **2.** to sound forth in a peal; resound.

Don't confuse this with **peel**, which is to take the skin off something: *to peel an orange.*

peanut n. the fruit (pod) or the edible seed of a plant native to Brazil. Also, **groundnut**.

peanut butter n. a paste or spread made from ground peanuts. Also, **peanut paste, peanut spread**.

pear n. an edible fruit, typically rounded but growing smaller towards the stem.

Don't confuse **pear** with **pair** or **pare**. A **pair** is a set of two things that go together, and to **pare** something is to peel it.

pearl n. **1.** a hard, smooth concretion, white or variously coloured, secreted within the shell of various molluscs, and often valuable as a gem. **2.** something precious or choice.

peasant n. a person living in the country and engaged usually in agricultural labour. –**peasantry**, n.

Nowadays, this word is usually only used about people who lived in the past or about people in developing countries.

peat n. a highly organic soil of partially decomposed vegetable matter, in marshy or damp regions, used as fuel.

pebble n. a small, rounded stone.

pecan /'pikæn, pi'kæn/ *n.* (the oval, smooth-skinned nut of) a type of hickory tree.

peccadillo *n.* (*pl.* **-loes** *or* **-los**) a petty sin or offence.

peck[1] *n.* a dry measure in the imperial system, equal to 8 quarts or $9.092\,18 \times 10^{-3}\ m^3$.

peck[2] *v.* **1.** to strike or indent with the beak, as a bird does, or with some pointed instrument. **2.** to kiss in a hasty dabbing manner. –*n.* **3.** a pecking stroke. **4.** a hasty kiss.

peckish *adj. Informal* mildly hungry.

pectin *n.* a substance in ripe fruits which helps form a gel in jam-making.

pectoral *adj.* of or relating to the breast or chest.

peculiar *adj.* **1.** strange, odd, or queer. **2.** belonging characteristically (*to*). –**peculiarly,** *adv.* –**peculiarity,** *n.*

pecuniary *adj.* consisting of or relating to money.

The more usual word is **financial**.

pedagogue /'pɛdəgɒg/ *n.* a teacher of children.

pedal *n.* **1.** a lever worked by the foot. –*v.* (**-alled, -alling**) **2.** to work or use the pedals, as of a bicycle, organ, etc.

Don't confuse this with **peddle**, which is to take something around from place to place in order to sell it.

pedant *n.* someone who makes an excessive or tedious show of learning. –**pedantic,** *adj.*

peddle *v.* to carry about for sale. –**peddler,** *n.*

Don't confuse this with **pedal**, which is a lever worked by the foot, as on a bicycle. Note that you can also use **pedlar** for someone who peddles their goods. In British English the usual spelling is **pedlar**, with **peddler** being used for someone who deals in illegal drugs. Either spelling is used in Australia. Note

that in America **peddler** is the only spelling.

pederasty *n.* sexual relations between an adult male and a boy. Also, **paederasty**. –**pederast,** *n.*

pedestal *n.* **1.** a supporting structure or piece; a base. –*phr.* **2. put** (or **place**) (or **set**) **someone on a pedestal,** to hold someone in high esteem; idealise someone: *he put her on a pedestal until he discovered her true nature.*

pedestrian *n.* **1.** someone who goes on foot. –*adj.* **2.** prosaic; dull.

pediatrics *n.* → **paediatrics**. –**pediatrician,** *n.*

pedicure *n.* professional care or treatment of the feet.

pedigree *n.* an ancestral line.

pediment *n. Archit.* a low triangular gable.

pedlar *n.* someone who travels around selling things. Also, **peddler**.

In British English the usual spelling is **pedlar**, with **peddler** being used for someone who deals in illegal drugs. Either spelling is used in Australia. Note that in America **peddler** is the only spelling.

pedophile /'pɛdəfaɪl, 'pid-/ *n.* → **paedophile**. –**pedophilia,** *n.*

peek *v.* to peep; peer.

Don't confuse this with **peak** or **pique**. A **peak** is the pointed top of a mountain, and **pique** is a feeling of anger or resentment.

peel *v.* to strip off the skin, rind, bark, etc.

Don't confuse this with **peal**, which is to ring: *The bells pealed.*

peep[1] *v.* **1.** to peer through a small aperture or from a hiding place. –*n.* **2.** a peeping look.

peep[2] *v.* **1.** to utter a shrill little cry; cheep. **2.** to speak in a thin, weak voice. –*n.* **3.** a peeping cry or sound.

peer[1] *n.* **1.** someone who ranks with another in respect to endowments, status, etc.; an equal. **2.** a nobleman. **–peerless**, *adj.*

Don't confuse **peer** with **pier**, which is a jetty that you can tie a boat to.

peer² *v.* to look narrowly, as in the effort to discern clearly.

peevish *adj.* cross, querulous, or fretful.

peewee *n.* → **magpie lark**.

peg *n.* **1.** a pin of wood or other material used to fasten parts together, to hang things on, or to mark some point etc. *–v.* (**pegged, pegging**) **2.** to fasten with or as with pegs. **3.** *Informal* to identify as a particular type, having certain abilities, etc.: *I pegged him as a cricketer.* **4. have someone pegged**, *Informal* to have summed up the character or nature of someone.

pejorative *adj.* expressing disapproval; deprecatory.

pelican *n.* a bird with a large fish-catching bill.

pellet *n.* a small round or spherical body.

pellucid *adj.* **1.** allowing the passage of light; translucent. **2.** clear in meaning.

pelmet *n.* a drapery or board, placed across the top of a window in order to hide the curtain rail.

pelt¹ *v.* **1.** to assail with repeated blows or with missiles. **2.** (of rain) to fall very heavily. *–n.* **3.** the act of pelting. *–phr.* **4. full pelt**, the utmost energy or speed.

pelt² *n.* the skin of an animal.

pelvis *n.* the basin-like cavity in the lower part of the trunk of many vertebrates.

pen¹ *n.* **1.** any instrument for writing with ink. *–v.* (**penned, penning**) **2.** to write with a pen.

pen² *n.* an enclosure for domestic animals.

penal *adj.* of or relating to punishment.

penalty *n.* (*pl.* **-ties**) **1.** a punishment for a violation of law or rule. **2.** any disadvantageous consequence. **–penalise, penalize,** *v.*

penance *n.* punishment undergone in token of penitence for sin.

pence *n.* a plural of **penny**.

penchant *n.* a taste or liking (for something).

pencil *n.* **1.** a thin tube of wood, etc., with a core of graphite, chalk, or the like, for drawing or writing. *–v.* (**-cilled, -cilling**) **2.** to execute, draw, colour, or write with or as with a pencil.

pendant *n.* a hanging ornament, as of a necklace or earring.

pendent *adj.* **1.** hanging or suspended. **2.** overhanging.

pending *prep.* **1.** until: *pending a decision.* **2.** during: *All should be in attendance pending his visit.* *–adj.* **3.** remaining undecided.

pendulous *adj.* hanging freely.

pendulum *n.* a body so suspended from a fixed point as to move to and fro.

penetrate *v.* **1.** to pierce into or through. **2.** to reach (a wide number of buyers, customers, etc): *to penetrate a market.* **–penetrable,** *adj.* **–penetration,** *n.*

penfriend *n.* a person, usually in another country, whom one has not met but with whom one corresponds by mail. Also, **penpal.**

penguin *n.* a flightless aquatic bird of the Sthn Hemisphere, with webbed feet, and wings reduced to flippers.

penicillin *n.* a powerful antibacterial substance.

peninsula *n.* a piece of land almost surrounded by water. **–peninsular,** *adj.*

Note the difference between **peninsula** and **peninsular**. Peninsula is the noun (*We drove along the peninsula*), and **peninsular** is the adjective (*The peninsular vegetation is very sparse*).

penis *n.* the male organ of copulation and urination.

penitent *adj.* sorry for sin or fault and disposed to atonement and amendment. –**penitence**, *n.* –**penitential**, *adj.*

penitentiary *n.* (*pl.* **-ries**) *US* a prison.

pennant *n.* **1.** Also, **pendant, pennon.** a long triangular flag. **2.** any flag serving as an emblem, as of success in an athletic contest.

penne /'penei/ *n.* a type of tube-shaped pasta.

penny *n.* (*pl.* **pennies** *or, especially collectively,* **pence**) a bronze or copper coin worth only a small amount, that was once used in Aust. and still is in Britain and some other countries.

penpal *n.* → **penfriend.**

pension *n.* a fixed periodical payment made in consideration of past services, injury, poverty, etc. –**pensioner**, *n.*

pensive *adj.* deeply or sadly thoughtful.

pentagon *n.* a polygon having 5 angles and 5 sides.

pentathlon *n.* an athletic contest consisting of 5 different exercises or events. –**pentathlete**, *n.*

penthouse *n.* a separate flat on the top floor or floors of a tall building.

pent-up *adj.* confined; restrained: *pent-up emotions.*

penultimate *adj.* next to the last.

penumbra /pə'nʌmbrə/ *n.* (*pl.* **-brae** /-bri/ *or* **-bras**) the partial or imperfect shadow outside the complete shadow (umbra) of an opaque body.

penury *n.* extreme poverty. –**penurious**, *adj.*

peony /'piəni/ *n.* (*pl.* **-nies**) a garden plant with large showy flowers.

people *pl. n.* **1.** human beings. **2.** (*construed as sing., with pl.* **peoples**) the whole body of persons constituting a tribe, race, or nation: *a nomadic people*; *the peoples of the world.* **3.** the members of a particular group or community: *the people of Hobart*; *working people.* –*v.* **4.** to furnish with people; populate.

Note that **people** is generally used as a plural noun (*People are strange*). However, when it is used to refer to a particular national, racial or tribal group (as in def. 2), it is often regarded as a singular word (*a peace-loving people*) with the plural **peoples** (*the peoples of Africa*).

pep *n. Informal* vigour.

pepper *n.* **1.** a pungent condiment obtained from the dried berries of certain plants. **2.** any species of capsicum. –*v.* **3.** to season with or as with pepper. **4.** to shower with shot, etc.

peppermint *n.* **1.** a herb cultivated for its aromatic pungent oil. **2.** a lozenge or confection flavoured with peppermint.

pepperoni /ˌpepə'rouni/ *n.* a type of salami, much used on pizzas. Also, **peperoni.**

pepper spray *n.* an aerosol spray derived from capsicum, which irritates the face, especially the eyes; used by police to subdue offenders. Also, **capsicum spray.**

peptic *adj.* relating to or concerned in digestion.

per *prep.* for each: *take two tablets per day.*

perambulator *n.* → **pram.**

per annum *adv.* by the year; yearly.

per capita *adv.* by the individual person.

perceive *v.* **1.** to gain knowledge of through one of the senses. **2.** to apprehend with the mind; understand. –**perception**, *n.* –**perceptive**, *adj.*

per cent *adv.* by the hundred; for or in every hundred (used in expressing proportions, rates of interest, etc.). *Symbol:* %

percentage *n.* **1.** a rate or proportion per 100. **2.** a proportion in general.

percentile *n.* one of the values of a variable which divides the variable into 100 groups having equal frequencies.

perceptible *adj.* capable of being perceived.

perch¹ *n.* **1.** a pole or rod as a roost for birds. **2.** a rod, or linear measurement in the imperial system of 5½ yards or 16½ feet, equal to 5.0292 m. –*v.* **3.** to alight or rest upon; to sit upon, as upon, a perch.

perch² *n.* (*pl.* **perch** *or* **perches**) an Aust. fish, mainly freshwater.

For information about the different plural forms, see the note at **fish**.

percolate *v.* **1.** to pass through a porous substance; filter. **2.** to become known gradually.

percolator *n.* a kind of coffeepot in which boiling water is forced up a hollow stem and filters back through ground coffee.

percussion *n.* **1.** the striking of one body against another with some violence. **2.** *Music* the instruments in an orchestra which are played by striking.

perdition *n.* final spiritual ruin or damnation.

peremptory *adj.* leaving no opportunity for denial or refusal; imperious; dictatorial: *a peremptory command.*

perennial *adj.* **1.** lasting for an indefinitely long time; enduring. **2.** *Bot.* having a life cycle lasting more than 2 years. –*n.* **3.** a perennial plant.

perfect *adj.* /'pɜfəkt/ **1.** having all essential elements, characteristics, etc.; lacking in no respect; complete. **2.** in a state of complete excellence. **3.** *Gram.* relating to the form of a verb (its *aspect*) which shows that the action referred to by the verb is now completed (*I have run*), was completed in the past (*I had run*), or will be completed in the future (*I will have run*). Compare **pluperfect, imperfect** (def. 2). –*v.* /pə'fɛkt/ **4.** to bring to completion. **5.** to make perfect or faultless. –**perfection**, *n.* –**perfected**, *adj.*

Note that, because **perfect** describes something which is as good as it is possible to be, some people think that you shouldn't say 'more perfect', as this

doesn't make logical sense – something is either perfect or it is not.

perfidy *n.* (*pl.* **-dies**) a deliberate breach of faith or trust; treachery. –**perfidious**, *adj.*

perforate *v.* to make a hole or holes through. –**perforation**, *n.*

perform *v.* **1.** to carry out (a command, promise, undertaking, etc.); execute. **2.** to act (a play, a part, etc.), as on the stage. **3.** to render (music), as by playing or singing. **4.** to display anger.

performance *n.* **1.** a musical, dramatic or other entertainment. **2.** the act of performing. **3.** the way in which something fulfils the purpose for which it was intended.

perfume *n.* a substance imparting a fragrant or agreeable smell; scent.

perfunctory *adj.* performed merely as an uninteresting or routine duty.

perhaps *adv.* maybe; possibly.

peril *n.* risk; danger. –**perilous**, *adj.*

This word is slightly formal or literary, so that you would usually use *danger* or *risk* in normal conversation or writing (*the risks of driving too fast* rather than *the perils of driving too fast*).

perimeter *n.* the outer boundary of a two-dimensional figure.

Don't confuse this with **parameter**, which is a factor which can vary.

period *n.* **1.** an indefinite portion of time, characterised by certain features or conditions. **2.** any specified division or portion of time. **3.** an episode of menstruation. **4.** → **full stop**. –*adj.* **5.** relating to, denoting, characteristic of, imitating, or representing a specific period of history.

periodic *adj.* **1.** occurring or appearing at regular intervals. **2.** intermittent.

periodical *n.* a magazine, journal, etc., issued at regularly recurring intervals.

peripheral *adj.* **1.** relating to, situated in, or constituting the periphery. **2.** of minor

importance; not essential; superficial. –*n.*
3. → peripheral device. –**peripherally**,
adv.

periphery *n.* (*pl.* **-ries**) the external
boundary of any surface or area.

periphrastic *adj.* circumlocutory; roundabout.

periscope *n.* an optical instrument by
which a view at the surface of water,
etc., may be seen from below or behind.
–**periscopic**, *adj.*

perish *v.* **1.** to die or be destroyed. **2.** to
decay and disappear. **3.** to rot.

perishable *adj.* **1.** subject to decay or
destruction. –*n.* **2.** (*usu. pl.*) a perishable
thing, as food.

perjure *v.* to render (oneself) guilty of
wilfully making a false statement under
oath. –**perjury**, *n.*

perk¹ *n. Informal* any fringe benefit, bonus
or other advantage received by an employee in addition to his or her normal
salary: *One of the perks of the job is that I
get to use the company car.*

This word is often used in the phrase **lurks
and perks**.

perk² *phr.* **perk up**, to regain liveliness or
vigour.

perky *adj.* (**-kier**, **-kiest**) jaunty; brisk;
pert.

permanent *adj.* lasting or intended to last
indefinitely; enduring; abiding. –**perma-
nence**, *n.*

permeate *v.* **1.** to penetrate through the
pores, interstices, etc., of. **2.** to be diffused
through; pervade. –**permeable**, *adj.*
–**permeability**, *n.*

permission *n.* formal or express allowance or consent.

permissive *adj.* sexually or morally tolerant.

permit *v.* /pə'mɪt/ (**-mitted**, **-mitting**) **1.** to
allow (a person, etc.) to do something.
2. to let (something) be done or occur. –*n.*

/'pɜmɪt/ **3.** a written order granting leave to
do something, as a licence.

permutation *n.* **1.** *Maths* **a.** the act of
changing the order of elements arranged in
a particular order (as, *abc* into *acb*, *bac*,
etc.). **b.** any of the resulting arrangements
or groups. **2.** any rearrangement.

The more usual word is **variation**.

pernicious *adj.* ruinous; highly hurtful.

peroxide *n. Chem.* that oxide of an element or radical which contains an unusually large amount of oxygen.

perpendicular *adj.* **1.** vertical; upright.
2. *Geom.* meeting a given line or surface
at right angles.

perpetrate *v.* to perform, execute, or
commit (a crime, deception, etc.). –**per-
petration**, *n.* –**perpetrator**, *n.*

Don't confuse **perpetrate** with **perpetuate**, which is to make something last for a
long time: *The policies of this government
have perpetuated the problems of rural
communities.*

perpetual *adj.* continuing or enduring
for ever or indefinitely. –**perpetuate**, *v.*
–**perpetuity**, *n.*

Don't confuse **perpetuate** with **perpetrate**, which is a formal word meaning to
carry out: *to perpetrate a crime.*

perplex *v.* to cause to be puzzled; bewilder;
confuse mentally.

perquisite *n.* an incidental benefit over
and above fixed income, salary, or wages.

per se *adv.* by or in itself; intrinsically.

The more usual expression is **in itself**.

persecute *v.* **1.** to harass persistently.
2. to oppress with injury or punishment
for adherence to principles or religious
faith. –**persecution**, *n.*

Don't confuse **persecute** with **prosecute**, which is to take legal action
against someone.

persevere v. (-vered, -vering) to persist in anything undertaken in spite of difficulty or obstacles. –**perseverance**, n.

persimmon /'pɜːsəmən, pəˈsɪmən/ n. (a tree bearing) an astringent plumlike fruit.

persist v. to continue steadily or firmly, especially in spite of opposition. –**persistent**, adj.

person n. **1.** a human being. **2.** the living body of a human being. **3.** Gram. (in some languages) a category of verb inflection and of pronoun classification, distinguishing between the speaker (**first person**), the one addressed (**second person**), and anyone or anything else (**third person**). –phr. **4. in person**, in one's own bodily presence.

personable adj. of pleasing personality or appearance.

personage n. **1.** a person of importance. **2.** any person.

This is often used humorously.

personal adj. **1.** of, relating to, or directed to a particular person; individual; private. **2. a.** relating to the physical presence or involvement of a person: a personal appearance at the concert; a personal interest in the shop. **b.** relating to what serves the advantage of a particular person: personal gain. **3.** relating to the person, body, or bodily aspect: personal hygiene. **4.** Gram. relating to one of the pronouns, such as I, you, it, them, etc., which refer to a person or thing

Don't confuse **personal** with **personnel**, which is the group of people working for an organisation.

personal best n. **1.** Sport (in timed or measured events) an athlete's best performance. **2.** one's greatest achievement in any field of activity. Abbrev.: PB

personal computer n. a microcomputer designed for individual use, as in the office, at home, etc., for such applications as word processing, accounting, etc. Also, **PC**.

personality n. (pl. -ties) **1.** distinctive or notable personal character. **2.** a well known or prominent person.

personify v. (-fied, -fying) **1.** to attribute human nature or character to (an inanimate object or an abstraction). **2.** to be an embodiment of; typify. –**personification**, n.

personnel /pɜːsəˈnel/ n. the body of persons employed in any work, undertaking, or service.

Don't confuse this with **personal**, which means private, or relating to a particular person.

perspective n. **1.** the art of depicting on a flat surface, various objects in such a way as to express dimensions and spatial relations. **2.** a mental view or prospect.

Don't confuse this with **prospective**, which describes something that is likely to happen: The prospective profits are enormous.

perspex n. (from trademark) a plastic substitute for glass.

perspicacious adj. having keen mental perception; discerning.

perspire v. to excrete watery fluid through the pores; sweat. –**perspiration**, n.

persuade v. to prevail on (a person, etc.), by reasons, inducements, etc., to do or believe something. –**persuasion**, n. –**persuasive**, adj.

pert adj. bold; cheeky.

pertain v. to have reference or relation; relate.

pertinacious adj. extremely persistent.

pertinent adj. relating or relating to the matter in hand; relevant.

perturb v. to disturb or disquiet greatly in mind; agitate.

peruse v. **1.** to read through, as with thoroughness or care: to peruse a document. **2.** to read in a leisurely way, with little attention to detail. –**perusal**, n.

pervade v. to go, pass, or spread throughout. –**pervasive**, adj.

perverse *adj.* disposed to go counter to what is expected or desired; contrary.

perversion *n.* **1.** the act of perverting. **2.** a perverted form of something. **3.** a type of behaviour, usually sexual, which is not generally considered normal or acceptable.

pervert *v.* /pə'vɜt/ **1.** to turn away from what is considered right. **2.** to distort. –*n.* /'pɜvɜt/ **3.** someone who has sexual habits which are generally unacceptable.

pessary *n.* (*pl.* **-ries**) *Med.* **1.** an instrument worn in the vagina to remedy uterine displacement. **2.** a vaginal suppository.

pessimism *n.* disposition to take the gloomiest possible view. –**pessimist**, *n.* –**pessimistic**, *adj.*

pest *n.* a noxious, destructive, or troublesome thing or person; nuisance.

pester *v.* to harass with petty annoyances; torment.

pesticide *n.* a chemical substance for destroying insect pests.

pestilence *n.* a deadly epidemic disease. –**pestilential**, *adj.*

pestilent *adj.* destructive to life; deadly.

pestle *n.* an instrument for grinding substances in a mortar.

pesto *n.* a thick green sauce made of basil, pine nuts, garlic, parmesan cheese and oil, used in Italian cooking.

pet *n.* **1.** any domesticated or tamed animal that is cared for affectionately. –*adj.* **2.** treated as a pet, as an animal. **3.** favourite. –*v.* (**petted, petting**) **4.** to treat as a pet; fondle; indulge.

petal *n.* one of the coloured, leaf-like parts of a flower.

peter *phr.* **peter out,** to diminish gradually and then disappear or cease.

petite *adj.* (of women) small.

petition *n.* **1.** a formally drawn-up request addressed to a person or a body of persons in authority or power. –*v.* **2.** to address a formal petition to.

petrel *n.* a seabird.

petrify *v.* (**-fied, -fying**) **1.** to convert into stone or a stony substance. **2.** to stupefy or paralyse with fear, or other strong emotion.

petrol *n.* a mixture of volatile liquid hydrocarbons used as a solvent and extensively as a fuel in internal-combustion engines; gasoline.

petroleum *n.* an oily, usually dark-coloured liquid (a form of bitumen or mixture of various hydrocarbons). Also, **rock-oil**.

petrol station *n.* → **service station**.

petticoat *n.* an underskirt, worn by women and girls; a slip.

petty *adj.* (**-tier, -tiest**) **1.** of small importance; trifling. **2.** having or showing narrow ideas, interests, etc.

petty cash *n.* a small cash fund set aside to meet incidental expenses.

petulant *adj.* showing sudden, impatient irritation, especially over some trifling annoyance.

petunia *n.* a plant with funnel-shaped flowers of various colours.

pew *n.* (in a church) a fixed bench-like seat with a back.

pewter *n.* any of various alloys in which tin is the chief constituent.

phallus *n.* an image of the erect male reproductive organ. –**phallic**, *adj.*

phantom *n.* **1.** an image appearing in a dream or formed in the mind. **2.** an apparition or spectre.

pharmaceutical *adj.* relating to pharmacy. Also, **pharmaceutic**.

pharmacology *n.* the science of drugs, their preparation, uses, and effects.

pharmacy *n.* (*pl.* **-cies**) **1.** the art or practice of preparing and dispensing drugs and medicines. **2.** a dispensary; chemist's shop. –**pharmacist**, *n.*

pharyngitis /ˌfærən'dʒaɪtəs/ *n.* inflammation of the mucous membrane of the pharynx.

pharynx /'færɪŋks/ *n.* (*pl.* **pharynxes** or **pharynges** /fə'rɪndʒiz/) the tube or cavity which connects the mouth with the oesophagus.

phase n. 1. a stage of change or development. –*phr.* 2. **phase in**, to introduce gradually into a system, or the like. 3. **phase out**, to withdraw gradually from a system.

pheasant n. a large, long-tailed bird.

phenomenon n. (pl. **-na**) 1. a fact, occurrence, or circumstance observed or observable. 2. a remarkable thing or person. –**phenomenal**, adj.

> There is some evidence to show that the plural form, **phenomena**, is being used in the singular (as in *This phenomena has been widely noted*), and so is following the path that *data* and *media* have already travelled. However, note that many people regard this use as incorrect.

phial n. a small vessel, usually of glass, for liquids. Also, **vial**.

philander v. (of a man) to be promiscuous.

philanthropy n. love of humankind, especially as manifested in deeds of practical beneficence. –**philanthropist**, n. –**philanthropic**, adj.

philately /fə'lætəli/ n. the collecting and study of postage stamps. –**philatelic**, adj. –**philatelist**, n.

philistine n. (*sometimes upper case*) someone lacking in and indifferent to culture, aesthetic refinement, etc.

philology n. the study of written records, their authenticity, etc.

philosophy n. (pl. **-phies**) 1. the study or science of the truths or principles underlying all knowledge and being (or reality). 2. a system of principles for guidance in practical affairs. 3. wise composure throughout the vicissitudes of life. –**philosopher**, n. –**philosophical**, adj.

phishing n. a form of internet fraud in which an email purporting to be from a legitimate sender, such as a bank, government institution, etc., encourages the recipient to provide personal information, passwords, etc. –**phisher**, n.

phlegm /flɛm/ n. *Physiol.* the thick mucus secreted in the respiratory passages and discharged by coughing, etc.

phlegmatic /flɛg'mætɪk/ adj. not easily excited to action or feeling.

phobia n. any extreme or irrational fear or dread.

> This word is often joined with another word part to refer to a fear of a particular thing, as in *claustrophobia* which is fear of being shut in a small space, or *agoraphobia* which is fear of open areas.

phoenix n. a mythical bird.

phone n., v. → **telephone**.

phonetics n. the science of speech sounds and their production. –**phonetician**, n. –**phonetic**, adj.

phoney adj. (**-nier**, **-niest**) *Informal* not genuine; counterfeit; fraudulent. –**phoniness**, n.

phosphorescence n. the property of being luminous at temperatures below incandescence. –**phosphorescent**, adj.

phosphorus n. *Chem.* a solid nonmetallic element used in matches and fertilisers. *Symbol:* P –**phosphoric**, adj.

photo n. (pl. **-tos**) → **photograph**.

photochemical adj. of, relating to, or produced by the action of light triggering a chemical process: *photochemical smog.*

photocopy n. (pl. **-copies**) 1. a photographic reproduction of written or printed material. –v. (**-copied**, **-copying**) 2. to make a photocopy of.

photoelectric cell n. a device used for the detection of light.

photogenic adj. (of a person) looking attractive when photographed.

photograph n. 1. a picture produced by photography. –v. 2. to take a photograph of.

> The short form of def. 1 is **photo**.

photography *n.* the process or art of producing images of objects on sensitised surfaces by the chemical action of light or of other forms of radiant energy. –**photographer**, *n.* –**photographic**, *adj.*

photon *n.* a quantum of light energy, proportional to the frequency of the radiation.

photo shoot *n.* a session during which a professional photographer takes shots of fashion models, a location, etc., as for a magazine, advertisement, website, etc. Also, **photoshoot**.

photoshop *v.* (**-shopped, -shopping**) (*from trademark*) to alter a digital image on a computer.

photostat (*from trademark*) –*n.* **1.** a special camera for making facsimile copies of documents, etc., which photographs directly as a positive on sensitised paper. **2.** a copy so made. –*v.* (**-statted, -statting**) **3.** to make such a copy or copies of.

photosynthesis *n.* the synthesis of complex organic materials by plants from carbon dioxide, water, and inorganic salts using sunlight as the source of energy and a catalyst such as chlorophyll.

phrase *n.* **1.** *Gram.* a sequence of words acting as a unit in the sentence. **2.** a characteristic, current, or proverbial expression. **3.** *Music* a group of notes making up a recognisable entity. –*v.* **4.** to express or word in a particular way. –**phrasal**, *adj.*

phraseology *n.* manner or style of verbal expression.

phrenology *n.* the theory that one's mental powers are indicated by the shape of the skull.

phylum *n.* (*pl.* **-la**) *Biol.* a primary division of the animal or vegetable kingdom.

physical *adj.* **1.** relating to the body. **2.** of or relating to material nature. **3.** of or relating to physics.

physician *n.* a person legally qualified to practise medicine.

physics *n.* the science dealing with natural laws and processes, and the states and properties of matter and energy. –**physicist**, *n.*

physiognomy *n.* (*pl.* **-mies**) the face or countenance, especially as considered as an index to the character.

physiology *n.* **1.** the science dealing with the functioning of living organisms or their parts. **2.** the processes and functions of a particular organism or part of an organism. –**physiologist**, *n.* –**physiological**, *adj.*

physiotherapy *n.* a type of treatment using physical remedies such as massage, exercise, etc. Also, *Informal*, **physio**. –**physiotherapist**, *n.*

physique *n.* human bodily structure or type.

pi *n.* (*pl.* **pis**) *Maths* the ratio (3.141 592) of the circumference of a circle to its diameter.

piano *n.* (*pl.* **-nos**) a musical instrument in which hammers, operated from a keyboard, strike upon metal strings. –**pianist**, *n.*

This word comes from Italian and is short for **pianoforte**.

piano accordion *n.* an accordion having a piano-like keyboard for the right hand.

pianoforte /piænou'fɔteɪ, pianoʊ-/ *n.* → **piano**.

pianola *n.* a mechanical piano operated by pedals.

picador *n.* a mounted bullfighter who pricks the bull with lances.

piccolo *n.* (*pl.* **-los**) a small flute, sounding an octave higher than the ordinary flute.

pick[1] *v.* **1.** to choose or select carefully. **2.** to choose (one's way or steps), as over rough ground or through a crowd. **3.** to steal the contents of (a person's pocket, purse, etc.). **4.** to open (a lock) as for robbery. **5.** to pierce, indent, dig into, or break up (something) with a pointed instrument. **6.** to pluck or gather. **7.** *Music*

pick to pluck (the strings of an instrument). **8.** to eat with dainty bites. –*n.* **9.** the choicest or most desirable part or example. **10.** → **plectrum.** –*phr.* **11. pick on,** *Informal* **a.** to annoy; tease; bully. **b.** to single out (a person), often indiscriminately, for something unpleasant, as punishment or criticism. **12. pick out, a.** to choose. **b.** to distinguish (a thing) from surrounding or accompanying things. **c.** to make out (sense or meaning). **13. pick someone's brains**, to find out as much as one can, from someone else's knowledge of a subject. **14. pick to pieces**, to criticise. **15. pick up, a.** to take up; lift and hold. **b.** to learn without special teaching. **c.** to get casually. **d.** to take (a person or thing) into a car, ship, etc., or along with one. **e.** to have within the range of reception, observation, etc. **f.** to get faster. **g.** *Informal* to improve. **h.** *Informal* to arrest.

pick² *n.* a hand tool for loosening and breaking up soil, etc. Also, **pickaxe.**

picket *n.* **1.** a pointed bar or stake. **2.** anyone stationed by a trade union in front of a place of work and attempting to dissuade or prevent workers from entering the building during a strike. –*v.* **3.** to stand or march by a place of employment as a picket.

pickle *n.* **1.** (*oft. pl.*) vegetables preserved in vinegar, etc., and eaten as a relish. **2.** a liquid or marinade prepared with salt or vinegar for the preservation of food or for the hardening of wood, leather, etc. **3.** *Informal* a predicament. –*v.* **4.** to preserve or steep in pickle.

pickpocket *n.* **1.** someone who steals from the pockets, handbags, etc., of people in public places. –*v.* **2.** to steal from a pocket, handbag, etc., in a public place.

picnic *n.* **1.** an outing or excursion with a meal in the open air. **2.** *Informal* an enjoyable experience or time. **3.** *Informal* an easy undertaking. –*v.* (**-nicked, -nicking**) **4.** to hold, or take part in, a picnic.

pictorial *adj.* relating to, expressed in, or of the nature of, a picture or pictures.

picture *n.* **1.** a representation, upon a surface, as a painting, photograph, etc. **2.** any visible image, however produced. **3.** → **film** (def. 3). –*v.* **4.** to form a mental image of (something). –*phr.* **5. in the picture**, informed; kept up-to-date. **6. the big picture**, a view of a situation, plan, etc., which gives principal attention to its major aspects.

picturesque /ˌpɪktʃəˈrɛsk/ *adj.* visually charming or quaint.

pide /ˈpiːdeɪ/ *n.* **1.** a Turkish flatbread. **2.** a dish consisting of this bread wrapped around various fillings, as meat, spinach, cheese, etc., and baked; Turkish pizza.

pidgin *n.* a language used for communication between groups having different first languages, as between European traders or colonisers and indigenous peoples, and which typically has features deriving from each of those languages. Compare **creole.** Also, **pigeon.**

pie *n.* a baked dish consisting of a sweet or savoury filling in pastry.

piebald *adj.* having patches of black and white or of other colours; particoloured.

piece *n.* **1.** a limited portion or quantity, of something. **2.** one of the parts into which something may be divided or broken. **3.** an individual article of a set. **4.** a disc, block or other small shape used in a board game. **5.** a short musical composition. **6.** a firearm. –*v.* (**pieced, piecing**) **7.** to put together, as parts or pieces: *to piece together a jigsaw*; *to piece together a broken plate.* –*phr.* **8. a piece of the action,** *Informal* a share in an enterprise or activity, especially a profitable one.

Don't confuse this with **peace,** which is calm, quiet or stillness. It is also freedom from war.

piecemeal *adv.* piece by piece; gradually.

pier n. 1. a structure built out into the water to serve as a landing place for ships. 2. one of the supports of a span of a bridge.

Don't confuse **pier** with **peer**, which is someone of your age or of the same rank as you. To **peer** at something is to look long and hard at it.

pierce v. 1. to penetrate or run into or through (something); puncture. 2. to penetrate with the eye or mind. 3. to sound sharply through (the air, stillness, etc.) as a cry.

piety n. reverence for God, or regard for religious obligations.

pig n. 1. an omnivorous non-ruminant mammal; a sow, hog, or boar; swine. 2. Informal a greedy, dirty person. 3. Informal (derog.) a police officer.

pigeon n. a bird with a compact body and short legs, often bred for racing, etc.

pigeonhole n. 1. one of a series of small compartments in a desk, cabinet, etc. –v. 2. to put away for future reference. 3. to assign a definite place in some orderly system.

piggyback adv. sitting on the back or shoulders of another.

pig-headed adj. stupidly obstinate.

piglet n. a little pig.

pigment n. a colouring matter or substance used as paint, ink, etc.

pigmy n. (pl. -mies) → pygmy.

pigtail n. a braid of hair hanging down the back of the head.

pike¹ n. (pl. pike or pikes) a large, thin, long-nosed, fierce fish of the Nthn Hemisphere.

For information about the different plural forms, see the note at **fish**.

pike² n. a sharp point; spike.

pikelet n. a small thick, sweet pancake.

piker n. Aust. Informal someone who opts out of a commitment or who does not do their fair share.

Pilates /pə'latiz/ n. a fitness regimen that introduces comprehensive stretching and strengthening movements into an exercise routine. Also, **Pilates method**.

pilchard n. (pl. **pilchards** or **pilchard**) a small abundant fish.

For information about the different plural forms, see the note at **fish**.

pile¹ n. 1. an assemblage of things laid or lying one upon another. –v. 2. to load or stack. –phr. 3. **pile up**, to heap up or accumulate.

pile² n. a heavy timber stake driven vertically into the ground or the bed of a river, etc., to support some structure.

pile³ n. 1. hair, especially soft, fine hair or down. 2. a raised surface on cloth.

pile⁴ n. (usu. pl.) → haemorrhoid.

pilfer v. to steal (a small amount or object). –**pilferage**, n.

pilgrim n. someone who journeys to some sacred place as an act of devotion. –**pilgrimage**, n.

pill n. a small rounded mass of medicinal substance, to be swallowed whole; tablet.

pillage v. (-laged, -laging) 1. to strip of money or goods by open violence, as in war; plunder. –n. 2. the act of plundering.

pillar n. a tall, relatively narrow, upright supporting part.

pillion n. an extra seat behind the driver's seat on a bicycle, etc.

pillory n. (pl. -ries) 1. a wooden structure into which an offender is locked to be exposed to public scorn or abuse. –v. (-ried, -rying) 2. to expose to public scorn or abuse.

For def. 2, the more usual word is **attack**.

pillow n. a bag filled with some soft material, commonly used as a support for the head during sleep.

pilot n. 1. someone who steers ships through difficult waters. 2. someone who controls an aircraft. 3. a guide or leader.

4. a sample episode for a television series. –*v.* **5.** to steer. **6.** to guide or conduct.

pimp *n.* someone who solicits for a prostitute, or brothel; a procurer; ponce.

pimple *n.* a small, usually inflammatory swelling on the skin.

pin *n.* **1.** a small, slender, sometimes tapered or pointed piece of wood, metal, etc., used to fasten, or hold things together, etc. –*v.* (**pinned**, **pinning**) **2.** to fasten or attach with a pin. **3.** to hold (a person, etc.) fast in a spot or position.

PIN *n.* personal identification number; a sequence of numbers and/or letters used as part of an identification procedure in electronic banking, etc. Also, **PIN number**.

Note that **PIN** stands for *personal identification number*, so when you say **PIN number** you are really repeating 'number'. However, despite this, many people do say **PIN number**, and it is not generally regarded as incorrect.

pinafore *n.* an apron. Also, **pinny**.

pinball *n.* a game played on a sloping board, in which a ball, driven by a spring, hits pins or bumpers which electrically record the score.

pince-nez /ˈpæns-neɪ, ˈpɪns-neɪ/ *n.* a pair of spectacles kept in place by a spring which pinches the nose.

pincers *pl. n.* **1.** a gripping tool consisting of 2 pivoted limbs forming a pair of jaws and a pair of handles. **2.** *Zool.* a grasping organ or pair of organs resembling this.

pinch *v.* **1.** to compress between the finger and thumb, the jaws of an instrument, or any 2 opposed surfaces. **2.** to cramp or stint. **3.** *Informal* to steal. **4.** *Informal* to arrest. **5.** to cause sharp discomfort or distress. –*n.* **6.** the act of pinching; nip; squeeze. **7.** a very small quantity of anything. **8.** sharp or painful stress.

pine¹ *n.* an evergreen coniferous tree with long needle-shaped leaves.

pine² *v.* to suffer with longing, or long painfully (*for*).

pineapple *n.* a large juicy tropical fruit.

pine nut *n.* the edible nut found in the pine cone of any of several pine trees.

ping-pong *n.* (*from trademark*) → **table tennis**.

pinion¹ *n. Machinery* a small cogwheel engaging with a larger cogwheel or with a rack.

pinion² *n.* **1.** (the end joint of) a bird's wing. –*v.* **2.** to cut off a bird's pinions or bind its wings, to prevent it flying. **3.** to bind (a person's arms or hands) so as to deprive them of their use.

pink¹ *n.* **1.** a light tint of crimson. **2.** the highest form or degree: *in the pink of condition*. –*adj.* **3.** of the colour pink. –*phr.* **4. in the pink**, *Informal* in good health and spirits.

pink² *v.* **1.** to pierce with a rapier or the like; stab. **2.** to finish (cloth) at the edge with a notched pattern.

pinnacle *n.* **1.** a lofty peak. **2.** the highest or culminating point.

PIN number *n.* → **PIN**.

pint *n.* a measure of liquid in the imperial system, equal to almost 600 millilitres.

pin-up *n. Informal* **1.** a picture, usually pinned to the wall, of an attractive person. **2.** the person depicted.

pioneer *n.* **1.** one of those who first enter or settle a region. **2.** one of those who are first or earliest in any field of inquiry, enterprise, or progress. –*v.* **3.** to open or prepare (a way, etc.), as a pioneer does. **4.** to open a way for. **5.** to be a pioneer in.

pious *adj.* **1.** fervently religious or dutiful in religious observance. **2.** sanctimonious.

pip¹ *n.* **1.** one of the spots on dice, playing cards, or dominoes. **2.** *Mil. Informal* a badge of rank worn on the shoulders of certain commissioned officers.

pip² *n.* a small fruit seed.

pip³ *n.* **1.** a brief high-pitched sound made by a radio receiver, echo-sounder, etc. **2.** the signal on the screen of a radar set.

pipe n. 1. a hollow cylinder for carrying water, gas, steam, etc.; tube. 2. a tube of wood, clay, etc., with a small bowl at one end, used for smoking tobacco, etc. 3. a musical wind instrument. –v. 4. to play on a pipe. 5. to convey by means of pipes. 6. to utter in a shrill tone. –phr. 7. **put that in your pipe and smoke it!**, Informal an exclamation indicating that an unpleasant ultimatum has been given.

pipedream n. a futile hope, far-fetched fancy, or fantastic story.

pipeline n. 1. pipe(s) used for the transmission of petroleum, etc. –phr. 2. **in the pipeline**, on the way; in preparation.

pipette n. a slender graduated tube for measuring and transferring liquids from one vessel to another. Also, **pipet**.

pipi n. an edible, smooth-shelled burrowing, bivalve mollusc; surf clam. Also, SA, **Goolwa cockle**.

piping n. 1. a cordlike ornamentation made of icing, used on cakes, pastry, etc. 2. a tubular band of material, sometimes containing a cord, for trimming garments, chair covers, etc.

pipsqueak n. Informal a small or insignificant person or thing.

piquant /ˈpikənt, piˈkɒnt/ adj. 1. agreeably pungent or sharp in taste. 2. agreeably stimulating, interesting, or attractive. –**piquancy**, n.

pique /pik/ v. (**piqued**, **piquing**) 1. to affect with sharp irritation and resentment, especially by some wound to pride. 2. to excite (interest, curiosity, etc.). –n. 3. ill feeling from wounded pride; offence taken.

Don't confuse this with **peek** or **peak**. To **peek** is to take a quick or secret look, and a **peak** is the pointed top of a mountain.

piranha /pəˈranə/ n. (pl. **piranha** or **piranhas**) a small fish noted for its voracious habits.

For information about the different plural forms, see the note at **fish**.

pirate n. 1. someone who robs or commits illegal violence at sea or on the shores of the sea. 2. any plunderer. 3. someone who uses the literary or other work of another as their own. 4. Also, **pirate radio**, a radio station broadcasting on an unauthorised wavelength so as to avoid legal restrictions. –v. 5. to act as a pirate. –**piracy**, n.

pirouette n. a whirling about on one foot or on the points of the toes, as in dancing.

piscatorial adj. of or relating to fishing.

piss Informal (taboo) –v. 1. to urinate. –n. 2. urine. 3. urination. –phr. 4. **piss off**, (oft. used imperatively in dismissal) to go away: I'm sick of your complaining – just piss off!; The party was boring so we pissed off.

Note that this word is taboo and may give offence.

pistachio /pəˈstaʃiəʊ, pəˈstæʃiəʊ/ n. (pl. **-chios**) a hard-shelled nut with an edible greenish kernel.

pistil n. Bot. the organ of a flower bearing the rudimentary or unfertilised seed.

pistol n. a short firearm intended to be held and fired with one hand.

piston n. a movable disc or cylinder fitting closely within a tube and capable of being driven alternately forwards and backwards in the tube by pressure, as in an internal-combustion engine.

pit¹ n. 1. a hole or cavity, especially in the ground. 2. an excavation made in digging for some mineral deposit. 3. an enclosure for combats, as of dogs or cocks. 4. an area beside the motor-racing track in which competing cars undergo running repairs, are refuelled, etc., during a race. –v. (**pitted**, **pitting**) 5. to mark with pits or depressions. 6. to set in active opposition, as one against another.

pit² n. the stone of a fruit.

pita *n.* a small, flat, round, slightly leavened bread forming a pocket. Also, **pita bread**, **pitta**.

pitch¹ *v.* **1.** to set up or erect (a tent, camp, etc.). **2.** *Cricket* **a.** to bowl (a ball) so that it bounces on a certain part of the wicket: *to pitch the ball up.* **b.** (of a ball) to bounce on a certain part of the wicket: *to pitch short.* **3.** *Music* to set at a particular pitch (def. 8). **4.** to throw, fling or toss. **5.** to plunge or fall forward or headlong. **6.** to plunge with alternate fall and rise of bow and stern, as a ship, aeroplane, etc. –*n.* **7.** relative point, position, or degree. **8.** *Acoustics, Music* the apparent predominant frequency of a sound from an acoustical source, musical instrument, etc. **9.** inclination or slope. **10. a.** *Sport* the playing area. **b.** *Cricket* the area between the wickets. **11.** a sales talk. –*phr. Informal* **12. cruel** (or **queer**) **someone's pitch**, to spoil someone's opportunity or plan. **13. pitch in**, to contribute or join in.

pitch² *n.* a dark viscous substance used for covering the seams of vessels after caulking, for making pavements, etc.

pitchblende *n.* a mineral, the principal ore of uranium and radium.

pitcher *n.* a container for holding and pouring liquids.

pitchfork *n.* a fork for lifting and pitching hay, etc.

piteous *adj.* such as to excite or deserve pity.

pitfall *n.* any trap or danger for the unwary.

pith *n.* **1.** the soft, spongy lining of the rind of oranges and other citrus fruits. **2.** *Bot.* the central cylinder of soft tissue in the stems of certain plants. **3.** the important or essential part; essence.

pithy *adj.* **(-thier, -thiest)** full of vigour, substance, or meaning; terse.

pitiable *adj.* **1.** piteous; lamentable; deplorable. **2.** such as to excite a contemptuous pity; miserable; contemptible.

pitiful *adj.* **1.** piteous. **2.** contemptibly small or mean.

pittance *n.* **1.** a small allowance or sum for living expenses. **2.** a scanty income or remuneration.

pituitary gland *n.* a small, oval gland attached to the base of the brain.

pity *n.* (*pl.* **pities**) **1.** sympathetic or kindly sorrow excited by the suffering or misfortune of another. –*v.* (**pitied**, **pitying**) **2.** to feel pity or compassion for.

pivot *n.* **1.** a pin or short shaft on the end of which something rests and turns, or upon and about which something rotates or oscillates. **2.** that on which something turns, hinges, or depends. –*v.* **3.** to turn on or as on a pivot.

pixel *n.* the smallest element of an image on a computer or television screen.

pixie *n.* a fairy or sprite. Also, **pixy**.

pixilation *n.* an animation technique in which the animator photographs real objects and people frame by frame to achieve unusual effects of motion.

pizza *n.* an Italian dish made from yeast dough formed into a flat, round shape, covered with any of a variety of foods and baked in an oven.

placard *n.* a written or printed notice to be posted in a public place or carried, as in a demonstration.

placate *v.* to appease; pacify. –**placatory**, *adj.*

place *n.* **1.** a particular portion of space: *to look out over a wide place.* **2.** space in general: *time and place.* **3.** any part or spot: *the wrong place to look.* **4.** a space or seat in a theatre, train, etc. **5.** position, situation, or circumstances: *I wouldn't like to be in your place.* **6.** a short street. **7.** a job, post, or office. **8.** stead or lieu: *to use gas in place of coal.* **9.** *Arithmetic* the position of a figure in a series. **10.** *Sport* a position among the leading competitors. *—v.* **(placed, placing) 11.** to put in a particular place; set. **12.** to fix (confidence, esteem, etc.) in a person or thing. **13.** to appoint (a person) to a post or office. **14.** to put or set in a particular situation, or relation. **15.** to identify: *His face is familiar but I can't place him.*

placebo *n.* (*pl.* **-bos** *or* **-boes**) *Med.* a medicine which performs no physiological function but may benefit the patient psychologically.

placenta *n.* (*pl.* **-tas** *or* **-tae** /-ti/) the organ providing for the nourishment of the fetus and the elimination of its waste products.

placid *adj.* pleasantly calm.

plagiarism /ˈpleɪdʒərɪzəm/ *n.* the appropriation or imitation of another's ideas and manner of expressing them, as in art, literature, etc., to be passed off as one's own. **—plagiarist,** *n.* **—plagiaristic,** *adj.* **—plagiarise, plagiarize,** *v.*

plague *n.* **1.** an epidemic disease of high mortality; pestilence. **2.** any cause of trouble or vexation. *—v.* **(plagued, plaguing) 3.** to trouble or torment in any manner.

plaid /plæd/ *n.* any fabric woven of different coloured yarns in a cross-barred pattern.

plain *adj.* **1.** clear or distinct to the eye or ear. **2.** clear to the mind; evident, manifest, or obvious. **3.** easily understood. **4.** ordinary. **5.** not beautiful; unattractive. **6.** without pattern, device, or colouring. **7.** flat or level. *—adv.* **8.** simply; absolutely. **9.** clearly or intelligibly. *—n.* **10.** a large (fairly) flat area of land.

Don't confuse this with **plane**, which can be a flat surface, an aeroplane or a tool for smoothing wood.

plaintiff *n.* *Law* someone who brings an action in a civil case.

plaintive *adj.* expressing sorrow or melancholy discontent; mournful.

plait /plæt/ *n.* **1.** a braid, as of hair or straw. *—v.* **2.** to braid (hair, etc.).

plan *n.* **1.** a scheme of action or procedure. **2.** a design or scheme of arrangement. **3.** a representation, as a map or diagram. *—v.* **(planned, planning) 4.** to arrange a plan or scheme for (any work, enterprise, or proceeding). **5.** to form a plan, project, or purpose of. *—phr.* **6. off (the) plan,** from the architect's plan of a proposed building before it is built: *to buy a unit off plan.*

plane[1] *n.* **1.** a flat or level surface. **2.** *Maths* a surface such that the straight line joining any 2 distinct points in it lies entirely within it. **3.** an aeroplane. **4.** flat or level, as a surface. **5.** *Maths* on one plane only, not multi-dimensional: *a plane figure.*

Don't confuse **plane** with **plain**. If something is **plain** it is clear and simple. A **plain** is also a large flat area of land.

plane[2] *n.* **1.** a tool with an adjustable blade for smoothing or finishing the surface of wood, etc. *—v.* **2.** to smooth or dress with or as with a plane.

planet *n.* a solid body revolving around a star. **—planetary,** *adj.*

plank *n.* a long, flat piece of timber thicker than a board.

plankton *n.* the mass of very small animal and plant organisms that float or drift in the water, especially at or near the surface.

plant *n.* **1.** any member of the vegetable group of living organisms. **2.** the equipment, including the fixtures, machinery, tools, etc., and often the buildings, necessary to carry on any industrial business. **3.** *Informal* a. something or someone intended to trap, decoy, or lure, as criminals. **b.** a spy. *—v.* **4.** to put or set in the ground for growth, as seeds, young trees, etc. **5.** to introduce and establish (principles, doctrines, etc.) **6.** to insert or set firmly in or on the ground or some other body or surface. **7.** to put or place. **8.** *Informal* to hide or conceal, as stolen goods. **9.** to place (evidence) so that it will be discovered and incriminate an innocent person.

plantation n. a farm or estate, especially in a (semi)tropical country, on which cotton, tobacco, coffee, sugar, etc., is cultivated.

plaque n. 1. a plate or tablet of metal, porcelain, etc., as on a wall or set in a piece of furniture, for ornamentation or, if inscribed, commemoration. 2. a film on teeth harbouring bacteria.

plasma n. 1. the liquid part of blood or lymph, as distinguished from the corpuscles. 2. Physics a highly ionised gas which, because it contains an approximately equal number of electrons and positive ions, is electrically neutral and highly conducting. 3. Astrophysics a. a system of charged particles large enough to behave collectively, as in the sun. b. the ionised region of the earth's upper atmosphere.

plasma display n. a system for illuminating tiny coloured fluorescent lights in a plasma display panel, each set of three having one red, one green and one blue, to produce a sharp and from many pixels to form an image; used for television screens, computer screens, etc.

plasma display panel n. a panel with numerous cells filled with plasma (def. 2) which is activated by passing an electronic current through it to produce light photons which are then amplified by the phosphorus material on the inside wall of the cell. See **plasma display**.

plasma screen n. a screen for a television set, computer, etc., which uses plasma display.

plaster n. 1. a pasty composition, as of lime, sand and water, used for covering walls, ceilings, etc., where it hardens in drying. 2. an adhesive covering for a wound. –v. 3. to cover (walls, etc.) with plaster. 4. to overspread with anything, especially too thickly.

plasterboard n. plaster in paper-covered sheets, used for walls; gyprock.

plastic adj. 1. capable of being moulded or of receiving form. 2. produced by moulding. –n. 3. any of a group of synthetic or natural organic materials which may be shaped when soft and then hardened.

plasticine n. (from trademark) a plastic modelling compound, in various colours.

plastic surgery n. the reconstruction or repair by surgery of part of the body for restorative or cosmetic purposes. –**plastic surgeon**, n.

plate n. 1. a shallow, usually circular dish, now usually of earthenware or porcelain, from which food is eaten. 2. Aust., NZ a plate of sandwiches, cakes, etc., brought to a social occasion. 3. a thin, flat sheet or piece of metal or other material. 4. plated metallic ware. 5. Dentistry a piece of metal or plastic with artificial teeth attached. –v. 6. to coat (metal) with a thin film of gold, silver, nickel, etc. –phr. 7. plate up, to arrange food on an individual plate or plates for serving.

plateau n. (pl. -teaus or -teaux /-touz/) 1. a tabular surface of high elevation, often of considerable extent. 2. any period of minimal growth or decline.

platelet n. one of many small, cell-like fragments formed from special white blood cells, which help blood to clot in wounds.

platform n. 1. a raised floor or structure. 2. a plan or set of principles. 3. a. Computers an operating system. b. a telecommunications system: an SMS platform.

platinum n. Chem. a heavy, greyish white, highly malleable and ductile metallic element. Symbol: Pt

platitude n. a flat, dull, or trite remark.

platonic adj. purely spiritual; free from sensual desire.

platoon n. a group of soldiers forming a unit.

platter n. a large, shallow dish.

platypus n. (pl. -puses or -pi /-pai/ or, especially collectively, -pus) an amphibious, egg-laying monotreme with webbed feet and a muzzle like the bill of a duck.

Some people use **platypi** for the plural of **platypus**, but this is regarded by many people as incorrect. The more accepted plural is **platypuses**.

plaudit n. (usu. pl.) a demonstration or round of applause.

plausible adj. having an appearance of truth or reason.

play n. **1.** a dramatic composition or piece; a drama. **2.** exercise or action by way of amusement or recreation. **3.** fun, jest, or trifling, as opposed to earnest. **4.** a set manoeuvre in the playing of a game: *a set play*. **5.** action, activity, or operation. **6.** freedom of movement, as within a space, as of a part of a mechanism. –v. **7.** to act or sustain (a part) in a dramatic performance or in real life. **8.** to engage in (a game, pastime, etc.). **9.** to contend against in a game. **10.** to perform on (a musical instrument): *to play the piano*. **11.** to perform (music) on an instrument or instruments: *to play a song from a record*. **12.** to cause (a CD, record, etc.) to produce the sound recorded on it. **13.** to cause (music or other sound) to be produced by a compact disc player, record-player, etc. **14.** to do, perform, bring about, or execute. **15.** to amuse oneself or toy (*with*). **16.** to work on (the feelings, weaknesses, etc., of another) for one's own purposes: *He's playing on your emotions*. –phr. **17. play around**, **a.** to behave in a lighthearted or irresponsible manner. **b.** (oft. fol. by *with*) to experiment with something in order to solve a problem, familiarise oneself, or produce a different result. **18. play it safe**, to act cautiously. –**player**, n.

playground n. **1.** an outside area with equipment like swings, slides, etc., for children to play on. **2.** an outside area at a school, where students can play at recess and lunch.

playhouse n. **1.** a theatre. **2.** a one-room imitation house built for children to play in.

plaything n. a thing to play with; toy.

playwright n. a writer of plays.

plaza n. a public square.

plea n. **1.** an excuse; pretext. **2.** *Law* an allegation made by, or on behalf of, a party to a legal suit, in support of his or her claim or defence. **3.** an appeal or entreaty.

plea bargaining n. the negotiation for an agreement between the prosecution and the defence in a law suit that the accused will face only specified charges or reduced penalties if a plea of guilty is entered.

plead v. (**pleaded** or **plead** /pled/ or, *Chiefly US*, **pled**, **pleading**) **1.** to make earnest appeal or entreaty. **2.** *Law* **a.** to make any allegation or plea in an action at law. **b.** to address a court as an advocate. **3.** to allege or urge in defence, justification, or excuse.

pleasant adj. pleasing, agreeable; giving enjoyment.

pleasantry n. (pl. **-ries**) pleasant humour in conversation.

please **1.** to act to the pleasure or satisfaction of. **2.** to be the pleasure or will of; seem good to. **3.** to find something agreeable; like, wish or choose: *Go where you please*. –interj. **4.** (as a polite addition to requests, etc.) if you are willing: *Please come here*.

pleasurable adj. such as to give pleasure; agreeable; pleasant.

pleasure n. **1.** the state or feeling of being pleased. **2.** enjoyment or satisfaction derived from what is to one's liking; gratification; delight.

pleat n. **1.** a fold made by doubling cloth upon itself. –v. **2.** to fold or arrange in pleats.

plebeian /pləˈbiən/ *adj.* **1.** belonging or relating to the common people. *–n.* **2.** a plebeian person.

plebiscite /ˈplebəsaɪt, -sət/ *n.* a direct vote of all the qualified electors in regard to some important issue.

plectrum *n.* (*pl.* **-trums** or **-tra** /-trə/) a piece of metal, plastic, etc., for plucking the strings of a guitar, etc.; pick.

pledge *n.* **1.** a solemn promise. **2.** anything given or regarded as a security of something. **3.** a toast. *–v.* (**pledged, pledging**) **4.** to bind by or as by a pledge. **5.** to promise solemnly. **6.** to give or deposit as a pledge; pawn.

plenary *adj.* **1.** complete; entire; absolute. **2.** attended by all qualified members, as a council.

plenipotentiary *n.* (*pl.* **-ries**) **1.** a person, especially a diplomatic agent, invested with full power or authority to transact business. *–adj.* **2.** invested with full power or authority.

plenitude *n.* abundance.

plenty *n.* **1.** a full or abundant supply. **2.** abundance. **–plentiful, plenteous,** *adj.*

plethora /ˈpleθərə/ *n.* overfullness.

pleurisy *n.* an inflammation of the membrane surrounding the lungs.

pliable *adj.* **1.** easily bent; flexible; supple. **2.** easily influenced; yielding; adaptable.

pliant *adj.* pliable.

pliers *pl. n.* small pincers with long jaws, for bending wire, etc.

plight *n.* condition, state, or situation (usually bad).

plinth *n. Archit.* the lower square part of the base of a column.

plod *v.* (**plodded, plodding**) **1.** to walk heavily; trudge; move laboriously. **2.** to work with dull perseverance; drudge.

plonk[1] *v.* to place or drop heavily or suddenly (*down*).

plonk[2] *n. Informal* cheap wine.

plop *v.* (**plopped, plopping**) to make a sound like that of a flat object striking water without a splash.

plot[1] *n.* **1.** a secret plan to accomplish some purpose, especially a hostile, unlawful, or evil purpose. **2.** the plan, scheme, or main story of a play, novel, poem, or the like. *–v.* (**plotted, plotting**) **3.** to plan secretly (something hostile or evil). **4.** to determine and mark (points), as on graph paper, by means of measurements or coordinates.

plot[2] *n.* a small piece or area of ground.

plough *n.* **1.** an agricultural implement for cutting and turning over the soil. *–v.* **2.** to furrow, remove, etc., or make (a furrow, groove, etc.) with or as with a plough. **3.** to till (the soil) with a plough. *–phr.* **4. plough into,** to attack energetically. **5. plough through,** to work at something persistently and laboriously.

ploy *n.* a manoeuvre or stratagem.

pluck *v.* **1.** to pull off or out from the place of growth. **2.** to pull with a jerk. **3.** to sound (the strings of a musical instrument) by pulling at them. *–n.* **4.** the act of plucking; a pull, tug, or jerk. **5.** courage or resolution in the face of difficulties.

plucky *adj.* (**-kier, -kiest**) having or showing pluck or courage; brave. **–pluckily,** *adv.* **–pluckiness,** *n.*

plug *n.* **1.** a piece of rubber or plastic for stopping the flow of water from a basin, etc. **2.** a pronged device for establishing contact between an electrical appliance and a power supply. *–v.* (**plugged, plugging**) **3.** to stop or fill with or as with a plug. **4.** *Informal* to mention (a product, etc.) favourably. *–phr.* **5. plug in,** to connect (an electrical device) with a power supply.

plum *n.* **1.** a purplish-coloured stone fruit. *–adj.* **2.** good or choice: *a plum job.*

Don't confuse this with **plumb** which means exactly upright.

plumage *n.* feathers collectively.

plumb /plʌm/ *n.* **1.** a small mass of lead or heavy material, used for various purposes. *–adj.* **2.** true according to a plumbline; perpendicular. *–adv.* **3.** in a vertical direction. **4.** exactly, precisely, or directly. *–v.* **5.** to sound (the sea, etc.) with or as with a plumbline. **6.** to make vertical. *–phr.* **7. out of plumb, a.** not perpendicular. **b.** not functioning properly.

Don't confuse this with **plum** which is a fruit.

plumbing /'plʌmɪŋ/ *n.* the system of pipes and drains for carrying water, liquid wastes, etc., into or out of a building. **–plumber,** *n.*

plumbline *n.* a string to one end of which is attached a metal weight, used to determine perpendicularity, find the depth of water, etc.

plume *n.* **1.** a feather. **2.** a flow of matter, especially a waste material or other pollutant, spreading from a source.

plummet *n.* **1.** a plumbline. *–v.* **2.** to plunge.

plump¹ *adj.* well filled out or rounded in form; somewhat fat.

plump² *v.* **1.** to fall heavily or suddenly and directly: *to plump into a chair.* **2.** to vote exclusively for or choose one out of a number: *Which team are you plumping for?*

plunder *v.* **1.** to rob of goods or valuables by open force. *–n.* **2.** the act of plundering; pillage. **3.** loot.

plunge *v.* **(plunged, plunging) 1.** to cast or thrust (oneself) forcibly or suddenly into a liquid, etc. **2.** to rush or dash with headlong haste. **3.** to throw oneself impetuously or abruptly into some condition, situation, matter, etc. **4.** to descend abruptly or precipitously, as a cliff, a road, etc. *–n.* **5.** the act of plunging.

pluperfect *adj. Gram.* perfect with respect to a temporal point of reference in the past. Compare **perfect** (def. 3), **imperfect** (def. 2).

plural *adj.* **1.** consisting of, containing, or relating to more than one, such as the words 'children' and 'hear' in *The children hear the bell.* *–n.* **2.** a word in the plural form: 'Cats' is the plural of 'cat'.

plus *prep.* **1.** with the addition of; with. *–adj.* **2.** involving or denoting addition. **3.** positive. *–n.* (*pl.* **-ses** *or* **-sses**) **4.** a plus quantity. **5.** an advantage, asset, or gain.

plush *n.* **1.** a fabric of silk, cotton, wool, etc., having a longer pile than that of velvet, often used to make soft toys. *–adj.* **2.** luxurious and costly, especially a room or furnishings.

plutocracy *n.* (*pl.* **-cies**) the rule or power of wealth or of the wealthy.

plutonium *n. Chem.* a radioactive element. *Symbol:* Pu

pluvial *adj.* **1.** of or relating to rain; rainy. **2.** *Geol.* due to rain.

ply¹ *v.* **(plied, plying) 1.** to use; employ busily, or work with or at. **2.** to carry on, practise, or pursue. **3.** to supply pressingly with. **4.** to address persistently or importunately; importune. **5.** to travel or run regularly over a fixed course or between certain places, as a vessel or vehicle.

ply² *n.* (*pl.* **plies**) **1.** a fold; a thickness. **2.** a strand of yarn.

plywood *n.* a material consisting of an odd number of thin sheets or strips of wood glued together.

pneumatic *adj.* **1.** of or relating to air, or gases in general. **2.** operated by air. **3.** containing air.

pneumonia *n.* inflammation of the lungs.

poach¹ *v.* **1.** to take game or fish illegally. **2.** to encroach on another's rights.

poach² *v.* to simmer in liquid in a shallow pan.

pock *n.* a pustule on the body in an eruptive disease, as smallpox.

pocket *n.* **1.** a small bag inserted in a garment, for carrying a purse, etc. **2.** money, means, or financial resources. **3.** a small isolated area. –*adj.* **4.** small enough to go in the pocket; diminutive.: *a pocket edition of a novel.* –*v.* **5.** to put into one's pocket. **6.** to take possession of as one's own, often dishonestly.

pocket-dial *v.* to make an unintended call from a mobile phone by accidentally activating the phone's speed dial while it is in one's pocket.

pod *n.* a long, hinged seed vessel.

podcast (*from trademark*) –*v.* **(-cast** *or* **-casted, -casting) 1.** to deliver a (radio) program) over the internet as a file to be stored and played as required on a computer or MP3 player. –*n.* **2.** such a program. –**podcasting**, *n.*, *adj.*

poddy *n.* (*pl.* **-dies**) a handfed calf.

podiatry /pə'daɪətri/ *n.* the investigation and treatment of foot disorders. –**podiatrist**, *n.*

podium *n.* (*pl.* **-diums** *or* **-dia**) a small platform for the conductor of an orchestra, for a public speaker, for the recipients of awards, medals, etc.

poem *n.* a composition in verse, especially one characterised by artistic construction and imaginative or elevated thought.

poet *n.* **1.** someone who composes poetry. **2.** someone having the gift of poetic imagination and creation, together with eloquence of expression. –**poetic**, *adj.*

poetry *n.* the art of rhythmical composition, written or spoken, for exciting pleasure by beautiful, imaginative, or elevated thoughts.

poignant /'pɔɪnjənt/ *adj.* keenly affecting the feelings, especially of sorrow. –**poignancy**, *n.*

poinciana *n.* a tree or shrub with showy orange or scarlet flowers.

poinsettia *n.* a perennial with brilliant usually scarlet bracts.

point *n.* **1.** a sharp or tapering end. **2.** a mark made (as) with a sharp end of something; dot. **3.** something that has position but not extension, as the intersection

of 2 lines. **4.** any definite position, as in a scale, course, etc. **5.** a degree or stage. **6.** a particular instant of time. **7.** the important or essential thing. **8.** a particular aim, end, or purpose. **9.** a single unit, as in counting, scoring a game, etc. –*v.* **10.** to direct (the finger, a weapon, the attention, etc.) at, to or upon something. **11.** to direct attention to: *Point him out to me; to point out a problem.* **12.** to have a tendency, as towards something. **13.** to face in a particular direction, as a building.

point-blank *adj.* **1.** aimed or fired at close range; direct. **2.** straight-forward, plain, or explicit.

pointy *adj.* **(-tier, -tiest) 1.** being pointed at the end: *pointy shoes; a pointy nose.* –*phr.* **2. at the pointy end**, at the moment of engagement or crisis.

poise *n.* **1.** a state of balance or equilibrium. **2.** composure; self-possession. –*v.* **(poised, poising) 3.** to balance evenly; adjust, hold, or carry in equilibrium. **4.** to hold supported or raised, as in position for casting, using, etc.

poison *n.* **1.** a substance with the inherent property of being harmful to life or health. –*v.* **2.** to administer poison to (a person or animal). –**poisonous**, *adj.*

poke *v.* **1.** to thrust against or into (something) with the finger, a stick, etc.; prod. **2.** to thrust obtrusively. **3.** to pry; search curiously (*about* or *around*). –*n.* **4.** a thrust or push. –*phr.* **5. better than a poke in the eye with a blunt stick** (or **a dead mullet**), an interjection, said grudgingly of some small benefit received, or humorously of a great one.

poker[1] *n.* a metal rod for poking or stirring a fire.

poker[2] *n.* a card game, usually involving gambling.

poker machine *n.* a gambling machine which can be operated by inserting coins, credit cards, etc.

You can also use **pokies** if you are talking about poker machines in general. It is an informal word: *We were playing the pokies in the pub last night.*

poky *adj.* (**-kier**, **-kiest**) (of a place) small and cramped. Also, **pokey**.

polarise *v.* **1.** to send in different, especially opposite, directions. **2.** to cause (a community, organisation, etc.) to divide on an issue. **3.** to bring about sharp division in: *to polarise the tax debate.* Also, **polarize**. **–polarisation**, *n.*

polarity *n.* (*pl.* **-ties**) **1.** in physics, the possession of a positive or negative pole, or both poles, by magnets, batteries, etc. **2.** the possession of two directly opposite ideas, principles or qualities.

polaroid (*from trademark*) *n.* **1.** a type of camera which produces individual photographs instantly. **2.** a photograph taken with such a camera.

pole[1] *n.* **1.** a long, rounded, usually slender piece of wood, metal, etc. *–v.* (**poled**, **poling**) **2.** to push, strike, propel, etc., with a pole.

pole[2] *n.* **1.** each of the extremities of the axis of the earth or of any more or less spherical body. **2.** *Physics* each of the 2 regions or parts of a magnet, electric battery, etc., at which certain opposite forces are manifested or appear to be concentrated. **3.** one of 2 opposites. **–polar**, *adj.*

poleaxe *n.* an axe, usually with a hammer opposite the cutting edge, used in felling or stunning animals.

polecat *n.* a mammal of the weasel family.

polemic *n.* **1.** a controversial argument; argumentation against some opinion, doctrine, etc. *–adj.* Also, **polemical**. **2.** of or relating to disputation; controversial.

police *n.* **1.** (the members of) an organised civil force for maintaining order, preventing and detecting crime, and enforcing the laws. *–v.* (**-liced**, **-licing**) **2.** to regulate, control, or keep in order (as) by police.

policy[1] *n.* (*pl.* **-cies**) **1.** a definite course of action adopted as expedient. **2.** prudence, practical wisdom, or expediency.

policy[2] *n.* (*pl.* **-cies**) a document embodying a contract of insurance.

poliomyelitis *n.* an acute viral disease resulting in paralysis. Also, **polio**.

polish *v.* **1.** to make smooth and glossy, especially by friction. **2.** to render finished, refined or elegant. *–n.* **3.** the act of polishing. **4.** (a substance used to give) smoothness or gloss. **5.** superior or elegant finish; refinement; elegance. *–phr.* **6. polish off**, *Informal* to finish, or dispose of quickly.

polite *adj.* showing good manners towards others, as in behaviour, speech, etc.; courteous; civil.

politic *adj.* **1.** sagacious; prudent; judicious. **2.** shrewd; expedient.

political *adj.* **1.** relating to the science or art of politics. **2.** relating to a political party. **3.** relating to the state or its government.

politically correct *adj.* conforming to current beliefs about correctness in language and behaviour with regard to sexism, racism, etc. **–political correctness**, *n.*

politics *n.* **1.** the science, practice or profession of governing a nation, state, etc. **2.** the interplay of relationships within an organisation. **–politician**, *n.*

Note that def. 1 is used as a singular noun, as in *Politics is a difficult career*, but def. 2 is used as a plural noun, is in *The politics in this office are hard to avoid.*

polka *n.* a lively dance.

poll *n.* **1.** the registering of votes, as at an election. **2.** the number of votes cast. **3.** an analysis of public opinion on a subject, usually by selective sampling. **4.** the head, especially the part of it on which the hair grows. *–v.* **5.** to receive at the polls, as votes. **6.** to take or register the votes of, as persons. **7.** to cut off or cut short.

pollen n. the fertilising cells of flowering plants.

pollinate v. to convey pollen for fertilisation to. –**pollination**, n.

pollute v. to make foul or unclean. –**pollutant**, n.

pollution n. 1. the act of polluting. 2. the results of this polluting, as city smog, etc.

polo n. a game resembling hockey, played on horseback.

poltergeist /ˈpɒltəgaɪst/ n. a ghost or spirit which manifests its presence by noises, knockings, etc.

polyandry /pɒliˈændri/ n. the practice or the condition of having more than one husband at one time.

polyester n. a synthetic polymer used in fabrics, etc.

polygamy /pəˈlɪgəmi/ n. the practice or condition of having more than one spouse at one time. –**polygamous**, adj.

Compare this with **monogamy** and **bigamy**.

polygon n. a figure, especially a closed plane figure, having many (more than 4) angles and sides.

polygyny /pəˈlɪdʒəni/ n. the practice of having more than one wife at one time.

polyhedron n. (pl. **-drons** or **-dra** /-drə/) a solid figure having many faces.

polymer n. a compound of high molecular weight derived by the combination of many smaller molecules. –**polymerise**, **polymerize**, v.

polyp /ˈpɒləp/ n. 1. Zool. an animal form with a more or less fixed base and free end with mouth and tentacles. 2. a projecting growth from a mucous surface.

polyphonic ringtone /pɒliˈfɒnɪk/ n. a ringtone for a mobile phone which can play multiple notes at the same time.

polystyrene n. a clear plastic easily coloured and moulded and used as an insulating material.

polytheism n. the doctrine of, or belief in, many gods.

polythene n. a plastic used for containers, electrical insulation, packaging, etc.

polyunsaturated adj. Chem. 1. of or relating to, a fat or oil with bonds not saturated with hydrogen. 2. of or relating to foodstuffs based on polyunsaturated oils, mainly of vegetable origin.

Pom n. Aust., NZ Informal (sometimes derog.) (also lower case) an English person. Also, **Pommy**.

Historically a mildly insulting term for a newly arrived British immigrant, this word became merely a colloquialism, used in contexts that might be affectionate, disparaging or neutral. However, the use of **Pom** has come to be seen by some as a form of stereotyping, and therefore derogatory.

pomegranate n. a several-chambered, many-seeded fruit.

pommel n. 1. a terminating knob. 2. the protuberant part at the front and top of a saddle. Also, **pummel**.

pomp n. stately or splendid display.

pompom n. an ornamental tuft or ball of feathers, wool, or the like.

pompous adj. 1. characterised by an ostentatious parade of dignity or importance. 2. (of language, style, etc.) ostentatiously lofty.

ponce Informal –n. 1. → **pimp**. –v. (**ponced**, **poncing**) 2. to flounce (about); behave in a foolishly effeminate fashion. –**poncy**, adj.

poncho n. (pl. **-chos**) a blanket-like cloak.

pond n. a body of water smaller than a lake, often made artificially.

ponder v. to consider deeply; weigh in the mind; meditate.

ponderous adj. 1. heavy; massive. 2. serious and dull.

pontiff n. 1. a bishop. 2. the bishop of Rome (the pope). –**pontifical**, adj.

pontificate v. to speak in a pompous manner. –**pontification**, n.

The more usual word is **lecture**.

pontoon[1] n. a boat, or some other floating structure, used as one of the supports for a temporary bridge over a river.

pontoon[2] n. a gambling card game, the object being to try to score 21 points; twenty-one; blackjack.

pony n. (pl. **-nies**) a small horse.

ponytail n. a bunch of hair tied at the back of the head.

poo n. Informal (euphemistic) faeces.

pooch n. Informal a dog.

poodle n. one of a breed of intelligent dogs with thick curly hair.

poofter n. Informal (often derog.) a male homosexual.

This word is generally derogatory but can be used within the gay community without being offensive.

pooh interj. **1.** an exclamation of disdain or contempt. **2.** an exclamation indicating revulsion, especially from an unpleasant smell.

pool[1] n. **1.** a small body of standing water; pond. **2.** a swimming pool.

pool[2] n. **1.** a combination of interests, funds, etc., for common advantage, especially in business. **2.** a facility or service that is shared by a number of people. **3.** any of various games played on a billiard table in which the object is to drive all the balls into the pockets with the cue ball. –v. **4.** to put (interests, money, etc.) into a pool.

poop[1] n. the enclosed space at the stern of a ship.

poop[2] v. Informal to tire or exhaust.

poor adj. **1.** having little or nothing in the way of wealth, goods, or means of subsistence. **2.** of an inferior, inadequate, or unsatisfactory kind. **3.** humble. **4.** unfortunate.

Don't confuse **poor** with **paw**, **pour** or **pore**. A **paw** is an animal's foot, to **pour**

a liquid is to make it flow, and **pore** can be a tiny opening in your skin or it can be to read something very carefully.

poorly adv. **1.** in a poor manner or way. adj. **2.** in poor health.

pop[1] v. (**popped**, **popping**) **1.** to (cause to) make a short, quick, explosive sound or report. **2.** to burst open with such a sound. **3.** to come or go quickly, suddenly or unexpectedly (in, into, out, etc.). **4.** (of the ears) to adjust to a sudden change in air pressure. **5.** Informal to take (a pill or recreational drug) orally. **6.** to force air into the Eustachian tubes so as to adjust the pressure on the ear drums. –n. **7.** a short, quick, explosive sound. **8.** Informal each: $5 a pop.

pop[2] adj. **1.** denoting or relating to a type of commercial modern music with wide popular appeal, especially among the young, and usually being tuneful, repetitive and having an insistent rhythmic beat. **2.** denoting or relating to a singer or player of such music.

pop[3] n. Informal father, or grandfather.

popcorn n. any of several varieties of maize whose kernels burst open and puff out when subjected to dry heat.

pope n. (oft. upper case) the bishop of Rome as head of the Roman Catholic Church.

poplar n. a tall, spire-shaped tree.

poplin n. a strong, finely ribbed, cotton material.

poppadum /ˈpɒpədʌm/ n. → **pappadum**. Also, **poppadom**.

poppet n. (a term of endearment for a girl or child).

poppy n. (pl. **-pies**) a plant with showy flowers of various colours.

populace n. the inhabitants of an area; population.

The more usual word is **people**.
Note that **populace** may be used as a singular or plural noun: The populace

were angry about the new law; The populace has always adored the princess.

popular *adj.* **1.** regarded with general favour or approval. **2.** relating to the (common) people. –**popularity,** *n.*

populate *v.* **1.** to inhabit. **2.** to furnish with inhabitants, as by colonisation; people.

population *n.* **1.** the total number of persons inhabiting a country, town, or any area. **2.** the body of inhabitants of a place.

populous *adj.* full of people or inhabitants, as a region.

porcelain *n.* a vitreous, more or less translucent, ceramic material; china.

porch *n.* an exterior appendage to a building, forming a covered approach to a doorway.

porcine /ˈpɔsaɪn/ *adj.* of or resembling pigs.

porcupine *n.* a rodent covered with stout, stiff spines or quills.

pore¹ *v.* to meditate or ponder intently: *to pore over a document.*

> Don't confuse this with **paw, poor** or **pour**. A **paw** is an animal's foot, **poor** describes someone with not much money, and to **pour** a liquid is to make it flow.

pore² *n.* a minute opening, as in the skin or a leaf, a rock, etc. –**porous,** *adj.*

pork *n.* the flesh of pigs used as food.

pornography *n.* obscene literature, art, or photography, designed to excite sexual desire. –**pornographic,** *adj.*

porpoise *n.* (*pl.* **-poises** *or, especially collectively,* **-poise**) any of various cetaceans, some of which are commonly called dolphins.

porridge *n.* an oatmeal breakfast dish.

port¹ *n.* **1.** a town or place where ships load or unload. **2.** a place along the coast where ships may take refuge from storms.

port² *n.* the left-hand side of a ship or aircraft facing forward (opposed to *starboard*).

port³ *n.* a sweet fortified wine, usually dark red.

port⁴ *n.* **1.** *Naut.* a porthole. **2.** a steel door in the side of a ship for loading and unloading cargo. **3.** *Computers* an interface to which a peripheral device can be connected.

port⁵ *n. Aust.* a suitcase.

portable *adj.* capable of being carried.

portal *n.* **1.** a door, gate, or entrance. **2.** → **web portal**.

portend *v.* to indicate beforehand.

porter¹ *n.* someone employed to carry luggage.

porter² *n.* someone who has charge of a door or gate; janitor.

portfolio *n.* (*pl.* **-lios**) **1.** a portable case for loose papers. **2. a.** the office or post of a minister of state or member of a cabinet. **b.** the public service department for which a minister is responsible. **3.** a list of financial assets. **4.** a collection of an artist's drawings, photographs, etc., to be shown to prospective employers, etc.

porthole *n.* a round window in the side of a ship.

portion *n.* **1.** a part of any whole, whether actually separated from it or not. **2.** the part of a whole allotted to or belonging to a person; share.

portly *adj.* (**-lier, -liest**) stout.

> This is rather literary and can sometimes be used in a humorous way to describe a man who is overweight.

portmanteau *n.* (*pl.* **-teaus** *or* **-teaux**) a suitcase.

portrait *n.* a painting or drawing of a person, especially of the face.

portray *v.* **1.** to represent by a drawing, painting, etc. **2.** to represent dramatically, as on the stage. **3.** to describe in words. –**portrayal,** *n.*

pose *v.* **1.** to affect a particular character in order to impress others. **2.** to assume or hold a position for some artistic purpose.

3. to present: *the fire poses a threat to nearby residents.* –*n.* **4.** posture of body. **5.** a studied attitude or mere affectation.

posh *adj. Informal* elegant; luxurious.

This word is sometimes used in a disapproving way.

position *n.* **1.** condition with reference to place; location. **2.** proper or appropriate place. **3.** a post of employment. **4.** mental attitude; way of viewing a matter; stand. **5.** condition (of affairs, etc.). –*v.* **6.** to put in a particular or appropriate position; place.

positive *adj.* **1.** explicitly laid down or expressed. **2.** admitting of no question. **3.** confident in opinion or assertion, as a person. **4.** absolute. **5.** characterised by optimism. **6.** *Elect.* having a deficiency of electrons. See **negative** (def. 5). **7.** *Maths* denoting a quantity greater than zero.

posse /'posi/ *n.* (formerly, in the US) the body of citizens that a sheriff was empowered to call to assist in preserving the peace, making arrests, and serving writs.

possess *v.* **1.** to have as property; to have belonging to one. **2.** to have as a faculty, quality, or the like. **3.** (of a spirit, especially an evil one) to occupy and control.

possession *n.* **1.** the act or fact of possessing. **2.** ownership. **3.** a thing possessed. **4.** control over oneself, one's mind, etc.

possessive *adj.* **1.** exerting or seeking to exert excessive influence on the affections, behaviour, etc., of others. **2.** *Gram.* relating to the case of a pronoun, noun form or adjective which indicates ownership, as *his* or *Jane's.*

possible *adj.* capable of existing, happening, being done, being used, etc. –**possibility,** *n.*

Don't confuse **possible** with **probable**, which means *likely* to happen rather than simply *able* to happen. There is a stronger

chance of something happening if it's **probable**.

possum *n.* a herbivorous, largely arboreal, Aust. marsupial.

post¹ *n.* **1.** a strong piece of timber, metal, or the like, set upright as a support. –*v.* **2.** to affix (a notice, etc.) to a post, wall, or the like.

post² *n.* a position of duty, employment, or trust to which one is appointed.

post³ *n.* **1.** a single collection or delivery of letters, packages, etc. **2.** the letters, packages, etc., themselves; mail. –*v.* **3.** to place (a letter, etc.) in a post-box, etc., for transmission. **4.** to supply with up-to-date information; inform. **5.** *Internet* **a.** to send (a message) electronically to a mailing list or newsgroup on the internet. **b.** to send such a message to all the members of (a mailing list or newsgroup). –**postage,** *n.*

post⁴ *n.* an examination held after the main examination.

postbox *n.* a letterbox (def. 1), especially one on a public thoroughfare.

postcode *n.* a group of numbers or letters added as part of the address.

postdate *v.* **1.** to date (a document, cheque, invoice, etc.) with a date later than the current date. **2.** to follow in time.

poster *n.* a large placard or bill.

posterior *adj.* **1.** situated behind, or hinder (opposed to *anterior*). –*n.* **2.** the hinder parts of the body; the buttocks.

posterity *n.* succeeding generations collectively.

postgraduate *n.* someone studying at a university for a higher degree.

posthaste *adv.* with all possible speed or promptness.

posthumous /'pɒstʃəməs/ *adj.* **1.** (of books, music, medals, etc.) published or awarded after a person's death. **2.** arising, existing, or continuing after one's death.

postmark *n.* an official mark stamped on letters or other mail, to indicate the place and date of sending.

postmodernism n. a style of literature, art, architecture, etc., developed in the 1970s and characterised by references to earlier styles. –**postmodern**, adj., n. –**postmodernist**, adj., n.

post-mortem adj. **1.** after death. –n. **2.** an examination of the body after death; autopsy.

post office n. **1.** the authority responsible for a country's postal and telecommunications services. **2.** a local office of this authority for receiving, distributing, and transmitting mail, selling postage stamps, providing telecommunications services, etc. –**post-office**, adj.

postpone v. to put off to a later time; defer.

postscript n. a paragraph, sentence, etc., added to a letter which has already been concluded and signed by the writer.

The short form of this is **PS**.

postulate v. to claim or assume the existence or truth of, especially as a basis for reasoning. –**postulation**, n.

The more usual words are **suggest** or **propose**.

posture n. **1.** the relative disposition of the various parts of anything, especially of the body and limbs. –v. **2.** to pose or assume a particular posture or attitude.

posy n. (pl. **-sies**) a bouquet (def. 1).

pot n. **1.** a container, usually round and deep, and usually for domestic purposes. **2.** a wicker vessel for trapping fish or crustaceans. **3.** Informal marijuana. –v. (**potted**, **potting**) **4.** to put into a pot. **5.** to preserve or cook (food) in a pot. **6.** to plant in a pot of soil. **7.** Informal to capture, secure, or win. –phr. **8. pot out**, to replant a (potted plant) into a garden bed. **9. pot up**, to replant (a potted plant) into a bigger pot.

potash n. **1.** potassium carbonate, especially the crude impure form obtained from wood ashes. **2.** potassium.

potassium n. a silvery-white metallic element whose compounds are used as fertiliser and in special hard glasses. Symbol: K –**potassic**, adj.

potato n. (pl. **-toes**) the round and white edible tuber of a cultivated plant.

potato scallop n. → **scallop** (def. 3). Also, **potato cake**.

potato wedge n. → **wedge** (def. 4).

potch n. an inferior opal or opal matrix.

potent adj. powerful. –**potency**, n.

potentate n. someone who possesses great power.

potential adj. **1.** possible as opposed to actual. **2.** capable of being or becoming; latent. –n. **3.** possibility; latent skill or capability.

pothole n. a hole in the surface of a road.

potion n. a drink or draught, especially one of a medicinal, poisonous, or magical kind.

potoroo n. a small, long-nosed, Aust. animal with a pointed head like a bandicoot, found in low thick scrub and grassland.

potpourri /pɒt'puəri, poupu'ri/ n. a mixture of dried petals, spices, etc., kept in a jar for the fragrance.

potter[1] n. someone who makes earthen pots or other vessels. –**pottery**, n.

potter[2] v. to busy or occupy oneself in an ineffective manner.

potty adj. Informal foolish; crazy.

pouch n. **1.** a small bag or sack. **2.** Zool. a bag-like or pocket-like part, as the sac beneath the bill of pelicans, or the receptacle for the young of marsupials.

pouf n. a stuffed cushion of thick material forming a low seat.

poultice n. a soft, moist mass of some substance, as bread, meal, linseed, etc., applied as a medicament to the body.

poultry n. domestic fowls collectively, as chickens, turkeys, etc.

pounce v. (**pounced**, **pouncing**) **1.** to leap or swoop down suddenly and lay hold (as a bird does of its prey). *–n.* **2.** a sudden leap or swoop.

pound¹ *v.* **1.** to strike (heavy blows) repeatedly and with great force. **2.** to beat or throb violently, as the heart. *–n.* **3.** the act of pounding.

pound² *n.* **1.** a unit of weight in the imperial system, equal to just under half a kilogram. *Symbol:* lb **2.** a unit of money used in Aust. until 1966 and still used in Britain and some other countries. *Symbol:* £

pound³ *n.* **1.** an enclosure maintained by public authorities for confining stray or homeless animals. **2.** a place of confinement or imprisonment.

pour *v.* **1.** to send (a fluid, or anything in loose particles) flowing or falling, as from a container, or into, over, or on something. **2.** to issue, move, or proceed in great quantity or number. **3.** to rain heavily. *–n.* **4.** the act or process of pouring molten metal, concrete, etc., into a mould.

> Don't confuse **pour** with **paw**, **poor** or **pore**. A **paw** is an animal's foot, **poor** describes someone with not much money, and **pore** can be a tiny opening in your skin or it can be to read something very carefully.

pout *v.* to thrust out the lips in displeasure or sullenness.

poverty *n.* the condition of being poor with respect to money, goods, or means of subsistence.

poverty line *n.* officially, the level of income below which one cannot afford to obtain the necessities of life.

powder *n.* **1.** any solid substance in the state of fine, loose particles; dust. *–v.* **2.** to reduce to powder; pulverise. **3.** to sprinkle or cover (as) with powder.

power *n.* **1.** ability to do or act. **2.** great or marked ability to do or act; strength; might; force. **3.** the possession of control or command over others; dominion; authority. **4.** a state or nation having international

authority or influence. **5.** mechanical energy as distinguished from human labour. **6.** *Maths* the product obtained by multiplying a quantity by itself one or more times. *–***powerful**, *adj.*

power board *n.* a single moulded plastic unit comprising a number of power points. Also, **powerboard**.

powerful owl *n.* a large endemic owl of sth-eastn Aust.

power nap *n.* a short sleep taken during the day in order to restore one's energy.

pox *n.* **1.** a disease characterised by multiple skin pustules, as smallpox. **2.** *Informal* any venereal disease.

PR *n.* → **public relations**.

practicable *adj.* capable of being put into practice, done, or effected, especially with prudence; feasible.

practical *adj.* **1.** relating to practice or action. **2.** relating to or connected with the ordinary activities, business, or work of the world. **3.** adapted for actual use. **4.** mindful of the results, usefulness, disadvantages, etc., of action or procedure. **5.** matter-of-fact; prosaic. **6.** being such in practice or effect; virtual. *–***practicality**, *n.*

practical joke *n.* a trick played upon a person, often involving physical action.

practice *n.* **1.** habitual or customary performance. **2.** repeated performance or systematic exercise for the purpose of acquiring skill. **3.** the action or process of performing or doing something (opposed to *theory*). **4.** the exercise of a profession or occupation, especially law or medicine.

> Don't confuse this with **practise**, which is the verb related to this noun: *I need to practise more.*
> In America, both the noun and verb are spelt **practice**.

practise *v.* **1.** to carry out, perform, or do habitually or usually. **2.** to perform or do repeatedly in order to acquire skill or proficiency. **3.** to pursue (a profession).

Don't confuse this with **practice**, which is the noun related to this verb: *I'll try and get in a bit more practice before the concert tonight.*
In America, both the noun and verb are spelt **practice**.

practising *adj.* **1.** actively pursuing a particular profession in which one is qualified to work. **2.** actively observing or following a particular religion, philosophy, way of life, etc.

practitioner *n.* someone engaged in the practice of a profession or the like.

pragmatic *adj.* concerned with practical consequences or values.

prairie *n.* an extensive or slightly undulating treeless tract of land.

praise *n.* **1.** the expression of approval or admiration. *–v.* **2.** to express approval or admiration of. *–***praiseworthy**, *adj.*

pram *n.* a small, four-wheeled vehicle used for carrying a baby.

This is short for **perambulator**.

prance *v.* **1.** to spring, or move by springing, from the hind legs, as a horse. **2.** to move or go in an elated manner; swagger.

prang *v.* **1.** *Informal* to crash (a car or the like). *–n.* **2.** a crash in a motor vehicle or the like.

prank *n.* a playful or malicious trick.

prattle *v.* to talk or chatter in a simple-minded or foolish way; babble.

prawn *n.* a shrimp-like crustacean, often used as food.

pray *v.* to make earnest or devout petition to (God, etc.).

Don't confuse this with **prey**, which is an animal hunted by another for food.

prayer *n.* **1.** a devout petition to, or any form of spiritual communion with, God or an object of worship. **2.** a petition or entreaty.

praying mantis *n.* → **mantis**.

preach *v.* **1.** to proclaim or make known by sermon (the gospel, good tidings, etc.). **2.** to deliver a sermon. *–***preacher**, *n.*

preamble *n.* an introductory statement; preface.

precarious *adj.* **1.** uncertain; unstable; insecure. **2.** dangerous; perilous.

precaution *n.* a measure taken beforehand to ward off possible evil or secure good results.

precede *v.* to go before.

Don't confuse this with **proceed**, which is to move forwards, especially after stopping for a while.

precedence *n.* **1.** the act or fact of preceding. **2.** priority in order, rank, importance, etc.

precedent *n.* a preceding instance or case which may serve as an example or justification in subsequent cases.

precept *n.* a commandment or direction given as a rule of action or conduct.

precinct *n.* a place or space of definite limits.

precious *adj.* **1.** of great price or value; valuable; costly. **2.** dear or beloved.

precipice *n.* a steep cliff.

precipitate *v.* /prɪˈsɪpɪteɪt/ **1.** to hasten the occurrence of; bring about in haste or suddenly. **2.** *Chem.* to separate (a substance) in solid form from a solution. **3.** to cast down headlong; fling or hurl down. *–adj.* /prɪˈsɪpɪtət/ **4.** proceeding rapidly or with great haste. **5.** exceedingly sudden or abrupt.: *a precipitate exit. –n.* /prɪˈsɪpɪtət/ **6.** *Chem.* a substance precipitated from a solution. *–***precipitately**, *adv.*

precipitation *n.* **1.** the act of precipitating. **2.** falling products of condensation in the atmosphere, as rain, snow, hail.

precipitous *adj.* extremely or impassably steep.

precis /ˈpreɪsiː/ *n.* (*pl.* **-cis** /-siːz/) an abstract or summary.

precise *adj.* **1.** definite or exact. **2.** carefully distinct, as the voice. **3.** excessively or rigidly particular. –**precision**, *n.*

preclude *v.* to shut out or exclude.

precocious *adj.* **1.** unusually highly developed in mind. **2.** (of a child) cheeky; forward; impertinent.

preconceive *v.* to form an idea of in advance. –**preconception**, *n.*

precursor *n.* someone or something that precedes; predecessor.

precycle *v.* to anticipate the causes of waste and take action to prevent it. –**precycling**, *v.* –**precycler**, *n.*

predatory *adj.* **1.** relating to plundering, pillaging, or robbery. **2.** *Zool.* habitually preying upon other animals. –**predator**, *n.*

predecessor *n.* someone who precedes another in an office, position, etc.

predestine *v.* to destine beforehand; predetermine.

predicament *n.* an unpleasant, trying, or dangerous situation.

predicate *v.* /ˈprɛdɪkeɪt/ **1.** to proclaim; declare; affirm or assert. –*n.* /ˈprɛdɪkət/ **2.** *Gram.* the active verb in a sentence or clause together with all the words it governs and those which modify it, as *is here* in *Jack is here.* –**predicative**, *adj.*

predict *v.* to foretell (the future); prophesy. –**prediction**, *n.*

predilection *n.* a tendency to like or favour something; preference.

The more usual word is **liking**.

predispose *v.* **1.** to give a previous inclination or tendency to. **2.** to render subject, susceptible, or liable.

predominate *v.* **1.** to be the stronger or leading element. **2.** to have or exert controlling power (*over*). –**predominant**, *adj.*

pre-eminent *adj.* superior to or surpassing others; distinguished beyond others. –**pre-eminence**, *n.*

pre-empt *v.* to acquire or appropriate beforehand. –**pre-emptive**, *adj.*

preen *v.* **1.** to trim or dress with the beak, as a bird does its feathers. **2.** to prepare, dress, or array (oneself) carefully.

preface *n.* **1.** a preliminary statement by the author or editor of a book. **2.** something preliminary or introductory. –*v.* (**-faced, -facing**) **3.** to provide with or introduce by a preface. **4.** to serve as a preface to.

prefect *n.* a person appointed to any of various positions of command, authority, or superintendence. –**prefecture**, *n.*

prefer *v.* (**-ferred, -ferring**) **1.** to like better; choose rather. **2.** to put forward (a statement, suit, charge, etc.) for consideration or sanction. **3.** to put forward or advance, as in rank or office. **4.** to favour: *to prefer kicking with your right foot.* –**preferable**, *adj.* –**preference**, *n.* –**preferential**, *adj.*

Note that you don't use *more* with **preferable**. For example, you would not say 'Rice is more preferable to potatoes'. You would say 'Rice is preferable to potatoes.'

prefix *n.* *Gram.* a meaningful word part added to the beginning of a word, as *un-* in *unkind.*

pregnant *adj.* **1.** being with child or young; having a fetus in the womb. **2.** full of meaning; highly significant. –**pregnancy**, *n.*

prehensile *adj.* adapted for seizing, grasping, or laying hold of anything.

prehistory *n.* the history of humanity in the period before recorded events. –**prehistoric**, *adj.*

prejudice *n.* **1.** any preconceived opinion or feeling, favourable or unfavourable. **2.** disadvantage resulting from some judgement or action of another. –*v.* **3.** to affect with a prejudice, favourable or unfavourable. **4.** to affect disadvantageously. –**prejudicial**, *adj.*

prelate /'prɛlət/ n. an ecclesiastic of a high order, as an archbishop, bishop, etc.

preliminary n. (pl. **-ries**) **1.** something introductory or preparatory. –adj. **2.** introductory or preparatory.

prelude n. **1.** a preliminary to an action, event, condition, or work of broader scope and higher importance. **2.** Music a piece which precedes a more important movement. –v. **3.** to serve as a prelude or introduction to.

premarital adj. before marriage.

premature /'prɛmətʃə, prɛmə'tjuə/ adj. coming into existence or occurring too soon.

premeditate v. to plan beforehand. –premeditation, n.

premier /'prɛmiə/ n. **1.** the leader of a state government. –adj. **2.** first in rank; chief; leading. **3.** earliest.

> In Australia, this is the title given to the head of a state government. The head of the federal government is called the **prime minister**.
> Don't confuse **premier** with **premiere**.

premiere /'prɛmiˌɛə/ n. a first public performance of a play, etc.

> Don't confuse this with **premier**.

premise n. **1.** (pl.) a house or building with the grounds, etc., belonging to it. **2.** Also, **premiss**. Logic a proposition (or one of several) from which a conclusion is drawn. –v. **3.** to set forth beforehand, as by way of introduction or explanation.

premium n. **1.** a bonus, prize, or the like. **2.** the amount paid or agreed to be paid, in one sum or periodically, for a contract of insurance. –adj. **3.** of highest quality; best. –phr. **4. at a premium**, in high esteem; in demand.

premonition n. **1.** a forewarning. **2.** → presentiment.

prenatal adj. before birth; during pregnancy: a prenatal clinic. Also, **antenatal**.

preoccupy v. (**-pied, -pying**) to absorb or engross to the exclusion of other things.

preparation n. **1.** a proceeding, measure, or provision by which one prepares for something. **2.** homework. **3.** the act of preparing. **4.** something prepared, manufactured, or compounded.

prepare v. **1.** to make ready, or put in due condition, for something. **2.** to get ready for eating. **3.** to manufacture, or compose. –preparatory, adj.

preponderate v. to be superior in power, force, influence, number, amount, etc.; predominate. –preponderance, n.

preposition n. Gram. a word placed before a noun to indicate its relation to other words or their function in the sentence. By, to, in, from are prepositions in English.

> Don't confuse this with **proposition**, which is a rather formal word for a suggestion: I have a proposition for this year's concert.

prepossessing adj. impressing favourably beforehand.

> This is usually used in negative sentences, such as The house was not very prepossessing on the outside, but inside it was beautiful.

preposterous adj. directly contrary to nature, reason, or common sense; absurd, senseless.

> The more usual word is **ridiculous**.

prepuce n. the fold of skin covering the head of the penis or clitoris.

prerogative n. an exclusive right or privilege.

presage n. /'prɛsɪdʒ/ **1.** an omen. –v. /'prɛsɪdʒ, prə'seɪdʒ/ (**-saged, -saging**) **2.** to forecast; predict.

prescribe v. **1.** to lay down as a rule or a course to be followed; appoint, ordain, or enjoin. **2.** Med. to designate or order for use, as a remedy or treatment. –prescriptive, adj.

Don't confuse this with **proscribe**, which is a formal word meaning to forbid.

prescription *n. Med.* a direction (usually written) by the doctor to the pharmacist for the preparation and use of a medicine.

presence *n.* **1.** the state or fact of being present, as with others or in a place. **2.** personal appearance or bearing, especially of a dignified or imposing kind. **3.** a divine or spiritual being.

present[1] /'prezənt/ *adj.* **1.** being, existing, or occurring at this time or now. **2.** being here or there, rather than elsewhere. *–n.* **3.** the present time.

present[2] *v.* /prə'zent/ **1.** to furnish or endow with a gift. **2.** afford or furnish (an opportunity, possibility, etc.). **3.** to hand or send in, as a bill or a cheque for payment. **4.** to introduce (a person) to another. **5.** to show or exhibit. **6.** to level or aim (a weapon, especially a firearm). *–n.* /'prezənt/ **7.** (a thing presented as) a gift. **–presentation**, *n.* **–presenter**, *n.*

presentable *adj.* fit to be seen.

presentiment *n.* a feeling or impression of something about to happen, especially something evil; premonition; foreboding.

presently *adv.* **1.** in a little while or soon. **2.** at this time, currently.

present tense *n. Gram.* the form of the verb which indicates that the action is happening at the moment of speaking.

preservative *n.* a chemical substance used to preserve foods, etc.

preserve *v.* **1.** to keep safe from harm or injury; save. **2.** to keep up; maintain. **3.** to prepare (food or any perishable substance) so as to resist decomposition or fermentation. **4.** to keep (accrued superannuation benefits) in a superannuation or roll-over fund until retirement age has been reached. *–n.* **5.** something preserved, as food. **6.** something reserved exclusively for someone's use.

preset *v.* /,pri'set/ (**-set, -setting**) **1.** to set in advance. *–adj.* /'priset/ **2.** determined in

advance to follow a certain course or the like: *a preset missile*.

preside *v.* to occupy the place of authority or control.

president *n.* **1.** (*oft. upper case*) the highest official in a republic. **2.** an officer appointed or elected to preside over a society, etc. **–presidency**, *n.* **–presidential**, *adj.*

press[1] *v.* **1.** to act upon with weight or force. **2.** to compress or squeeze, as to alter in shape or size. **3.** to make flat by subjecting to weight. **4.** to iron (clothes, etc.). **5.** to urge (a person, etc.). **6.** to compel haste. **7.** to crowd or throng. *–n.* **8.** printed publications collectively, especially newspapers and periodicals. **9.** a machine used for printing. **10.** an establishment for printing books, etc. **11.** an instrument or machine for exerting pressure. **12.** a crowd or throng. **13.** pressure or urgency, as of affairs or business. **14.** a piece of furniture, for holding clothes, books, etc.

press[2] *v.* to force into service, especially naval or military service.

pressure *n.* **1.** the exertion of force upon a body by another body in contact with it; compression. **2.** harassment; oppression. **3.** a constraining or compelling force or influence.

pressure system *n. Meteorol.* an atmospheric circulation system which may be a low pressure system such as a cyclone, or a high pressure system.

pressurise *v.* to maintain normal air pressure in an aeroplane designed to fly at high altitudes. Also, **pressurize**.

prestige *n.* reputation or influence arising from success, achievement, rank, etc. **–prestigious**, *adj.*

presume *v.* **1.** to take for granted, assume, or suppose. **2.** to act or proceed with impertinent boldness. **–presumption**, *n.*

presumptuous *adj.* impertinently bold; forward.

pretence n. 1. pretending or feigning; make-believe. 2. a false show of something. 3. an alleged or pretended reason or excuse, or a pretext. 4. insincere or false profession.

pretend v. 1. to put forward a false appearance; feign. 2. to allege or profess, especially insincerely or falsely. 3. to make believe. 4. to lay claim (to).

pretension n. the assumption of or a claim to dignity or importance. –**pretentious**, adj. –**pretentiousness**, n.

preterite adj. Gram. designating a tense usually denoting an action or state which was completed in the past.

preterm adj. 1. (of a baby) born before a pregnancy has reached its full term. 2. (of an election) held before the parliament or other body for which members are elected has reached its full term. Also, **pre-term**.

pretext n. that which is put forward to conceal a true purpose or object; an ostensible reason.

pretty adj. (**-tier, -tiest**) 1. pleasing, fair or attractive to the eye. –adv. 2. moderately: *Her work was pretty good.* 3. quite; rather: *The wind blew pretty hard.* –v. (**-tied, -tying**) 4. to make pretty.

Note that when you are describing someone's appearance, you would normally only use **pretty** if you were talking about a female or a baby of either sex. You could use **handsome** if you were describing a man, or **attractive** or **good-looking**, both of which can refer to either males or females.

pretzel n. 1. a crisp, dry biscuit. 2. a soft bun, sweet or savoury, in a tie shape.

prevail v. 1. to be widespread or current; to exist everywhere or generally. 2. to be or prove superior in strength, power, or influence. –phr. 3. **prevail upon**, to persuade successfully.

prevalent adj. widespread.

prevaricate v. to act or speak evasively; equivocate; quibble. –**prevarication**, n.

prevent v. to keep from doing or occurring; hinder. –**prevention**, n.

preventive adj. 1. Med. warding off disease. 2. serving to prevent or hinder. Also, **preventative**.

preview n. a view in advance, as of a film.

previous adj. coming or occurring before something else; prior.

prey n. 1. an animal hunted or seized for food. 2. a person or thing that falls a victim to an enemy, a disease, etc. –v. 3. to seek for and seize prey. –phr. 4. **easy prey**, someone who will easily fall victim to a deception or imposition.

Don't confuse this with **pray**, which is to communicate with a god or other spiritual being.

price n. 1. the amount of money for which anything is bought or sold. 2. that which must be given, done, or undergone in order to obtain a thing. –v. (**priced, pricing**) 3. to fix the price of.

priceless adj. valuable.

prick n. 1. a puncture made by a needle, thorn, or the like. 2. Informal (taboo) **a.** the penis. **b.** an unpleasant or despicable person. –v. 3. to pierce with a sharp point; puncture. 4. to (cause to) stand erect or point upwards.

Note that defs 2a and 2b are taboo uses and may give offence. If you call someone 'a prick', you are intending to insult them.

prickle n. 1. a sharp point. 2. a small, pointed process growing from the bark of a plant. –v. 3. to prick. 4. to cause a pricking sensation in.

pride n. 1. high or inordinate opinion of one's own dignity, importance, merit, or superiority. 2. self respect. 3. the best or most admired part of anything. 4. a company of lions. –phr. 5. **pride oneself on** (or **upon**), to indulge (oneself) in a feeling of pride.

priest n. someone whose office it is to perform religious rites.

prig n. someone who is precise to an extreme in attention to principle or duty, especially in a self-righteous way.

prim adj. (**primmer, primmest**) affectedly precise or proper.

primacy n. (pl. **-cies**) **1.** the state of being first in order, rank, importance, etc. **2.** the office, rank, or dignity of an archbishop.

primal adj. first; original; primeval.

primary adj. **1.** first or highest in rank or importance; chief; principal. **2.** constituting, or belonging to, the first stage in any process. **3.** original, not derived or subordinate; fundamental; basic. **4.** of or relating to the first stage of child education, from the age of about 6 to about 11 years. **–primarily,** adv.

primate n. **1.** Eccles. an archbishop. **2.** any mammal of the order that includes humans, the apes, the monkeys, the lemurs, etc.

prime adj. **1.** first in importance, excellence, or value. **2.** original; fundamental. **3.** typical: a prime example. –n. **4.** the most flourishing stage or state. **5.** the choicest or best part of anything. –v. **6.** to prepare or make ready for a particular purpose or operation. **7.** to supply (a firearm) with powder for communicating fire to a charge. **8.** to supply or equip with information, words, etc., for use.

prime minister n. (oft. upper case) the first or principal minister of certain governments; the chief of the cabinet or ministry. **–prime ministry,** n.

In Australia, this is the title given to the head of the federal government. The head of a state government is called the **premier**.

primer n. **1.** an elementary book for teaching children to read. **2.** any, often small, book of elementary principles.

primeval adj. of or relating to the first age or ages, especially of the world. Also, **primaeval**. **–primevally,** adv.

primitive adj. **1.** early in the history of the world or of humankind. **2.** characteristic of early ages or of an early state of human development. **3.** unaffected or little affected by civilising influences.

primrose n. a garden plant usually with yellow flowers.

prince n. **1.** a non-reigning male member of a royal family. **2.** a sovereign or monarch; king. **3.** the ruler of a small state.

princess n. **1.** a non-reigning female member of a royal family. **2.** a female sovereign. **3.** the consort of a prince.

principal adj. **1.** first or highest in rank, importance, value, etc.; chief; foremost. –n. **2.** a chief or head. **3.** something of principal or chief importance. **4.** Law a person authorising another (an agent) to represent him or her. **5.** a person primarily liable for an expenditure. **6.** Commerce a capital sum, as distinguished from interest or profit.

Don't confuse this with **principle**.

principality n. (pl. **-ties**) a state ruled by a prince.

principle n. **1.** an accepted or professed rule of action or conduct. **2.** a fundamental, primary, or general truth, on which other truths depend. **3.** guiding sense of the requirements and obligations of right conduct. **4.** a rule or law exemplified in natural phenomena, in the construction or operation of a machine, the working of a system, or the like.

Don't confuse this with **principal**.

print v. **1.** to produce (a text, a picture, etc.) by applying inked types, plates or blocks, or the like, with direct pressure to paper or other material. **2.** to write in letters like those commonly used in print. **3.** to produce or fix (an indentation, mark, etc.) by pressure. **4.** Photography to produce a positive picture from (a negative) by the transmission of light. **5.** Also, **print out.** Computers to produce (a result, data, etc.) in a legible form on paper. –n. **6.** the state of being printed: *in print*. **7.** printed lettering. **8.** printed matter. **9.** (cotton cloth with) a printed design. **10.** *Photography* a picture made from a negative.

printer *n*. **1.** someone engaged in the printing industry. **2.** a device, linked to a computer, which prints data onto paper.

printout *n*. printed material produced by a printer linked to a computer.

prior[1] *adj.* **1.** preceding in time, or in order; earlier or former; anterior or antecedent. –*adv.* **2.** previously (*to*).

prior[2] *n*. the superior of certain monastic orders and houses.

priority *n*. (*pl.* **-ties**) **1.** the state of being earlier in time, or of preceding something else. **2.** precedence in order, rank, etc.

prise *v*. to raise, move, or force with or as with a lever. Also, **prize**.

Don't confuse this with **prize**, which is a reward for winning something or doing well. Note that **prise** can also be spelt **prize**.

prism *n*. **1.** *Optics.* a transparent, usually triangular body used for decomposing light into its spectrum or for reflecting light beams. **2.** *Geom.* a solid whose bases or ends are any congruent and parallel polygons, and whose sides are parallelograms. –**prismatic**, *adj.*

prison *n*. a public building for the confinement or safe custody of criminals and others committed by law.

prisoner *n*. someone who is confined in prison or kept in custody, especially as the result of legal process.

prison officer *n*. an official having charge of prisoners in a jail; warder.

prissy *adj.* (**-sier, -siest**) *Informal* precise; prim; affectedly nice.

pristine *adj.* **1.** so clean as to appear new: *The house was in pristine condition.* **2.** of or relating to the earliest period or state; original; primitive. **3.** having its original purity.

private *adj.* **1.** belonging to some particular person; being one's own. **2.** confidential: *a private meeting.* **3.** not holding public office or employment, as a person. **4.** removed from or out of public view or knowledge; secret. **5.** alone; secluded. –*n.* **6.** a soldier of the lowest military rank. –**privacy**, *n.*

privation *n*. lack of the usual comforts or necessaries of life.

The more usual word is **hardship**.

privatise *v*. to change the status of (land, industries, etc.) from that of state to private ownership. Also, **privatize**. –**privatisation**, *n.*

privet *n*. a shrub with evergreen leaves and small, white, heavily perfumed flowers now considered noxious.

privilege *n*. **1.** a right or immunity enjoyed by a person or persons beyond the common advantages of others: *parliamentary privilege.* **2.** an advantage, or opportunity enjoyed by anyone in a favoured position (as distinct from a right). –*v.* (**-leged, -leging**) **3.** to grant a privilege to.

privy *n*. (*pl.* **-vies**) **1.** an outside building containing a toilet. –*phr.* **2. privy to** participating in the knowledge of something private or secret. –**privily**, *adv.*

prize[1] *n*. **1.** a reward of victory or superiority, as in a contest or competition. **2.** that which is won in a lottery or the like.

Don't confuse **prize** with **prise**, which is to separate two things using a lever. **Prise** can also be spelt **prize**.

prize[2] *v*. to value or esteem highly.

prize[3] *v.* → **prise**.

pro *adv.* **1.** in favour of a proposition, opinion, etc. (opposed to *con*). –*n*. (*pl.* **pros**) **2.** an argument, consideration, vote, etc., for something (opposed to *con*).

proactive *adj.* taking the initiative, rather than waiting until things happen and then reacting. –**proactively**, *adv.*

probability n. (pl. **-ties**) **1.** the quality or fact of being probable. **2.** a likelihood or chance of something. **3.** a probable event, circumstance, etc.

probable adj. **1.** likely to occur or prove true. **2.** affording ground for belief.

Don't confuse **probable** with **possible**, which simply means *able* to happen rather than *likely* to happen. There is a greater chance of something happening if it is **probable**.

probate n. Law the official proving of a will as authentic or valid.

probation n. **1.** the act of testing. **2.** Law a method of dealing with offenders, especially young persons guilty of minor crimes or first offences, by allowing them to go free conditionally and under supervision.

probe v. **1.** to search into or examine thoroughly; question closely. –n. **2.** the act of probing. **3.** a slender surgical instrument for exploring a wound, sinus, etc.

probiotic adj. **1.** of or relating to a food containing live bacteria which have health-promoting properties: *probiotic yoghurt.* –n. **2.** such a food.

probity n. integrity; uprightness; honesty.

problem n. **1.** any question or matter involving doubt, uncertainty, or difficulty. **2.** a question proposed for solution or discussion. –**problematic**, **problematical**, adj.

pro bono /prou 'bounou/ adj. **1.** (especially of legal work) performed without charge. –adv. **2.** without charging a fee.

proboscis /prə'bɒskɪs, prə'bɒsəs/ n. (pl. **-boscises** /-'bɒskəsəz, -'bɒsəsəz/ or **-boscides** /-'bɒskədiz, -'bɒsədiz/) n. **1.** an elephant's trunk. **2.** any long flexible snout.

procedural adj. **1.** of or relating to procedure. **2.** of or relating to a text type or form which shows how something can be done, as a recipe.

procedure n. the act or manner of proceeding in any action or process; conduct.

proceed v. /prə'sid/ **1.** to go on with or carry on any action or process. **2.** to take legal proceedings (*against*). **3.** to be carried on, as an action, process, etc. **4.** to go or come forth; issue. –pl. n. **5. proceeds,** the sum derived from a sale or other transaction.

Don't confuse this with **precede**, which is a formal word meaning to go before someone or something: *Bill Clinton preceded George W Bush as American president.*

proceeding n. **1.** action, course of action, or conduct. **2.** (pl.) records of the doings of a society. **3.** Law **a.** the instituting or carrying on of an action at law. **b.** a legal step or measure.

process n. **1.** a systematic series of actions directed to some end. **2.** the whole course of the proceedings in an action at law. **3.** a protuberance or appendage. **4.** the action of going forward or on. **5.** the condition of being carried on. **6.** course or lapse, as of time. –v. **7.** to treat or prepare by some particular process, as in manufacturing. **8.** *Computers* (of data) to manipulate in order to abstract the required information.

procession n. a line of persons, vehicles, etc., moving along in an orderly or ceremonious manner.

proclaim v. to announce or declare, publicly and officially. –**proclamation**, n.

proclivity n. (pl. **-ties**) natural or habitual inclination or tendency.

procrastinate v. to defer action; delay. –**procrastinator**, n. –**procrastination**, n.

procreate v. to produce offspring. –**procreation**, n.

The more usual word is **breed**.

procure v. to obtain, especially after much effort.

prod v. (**prodded**, **prodding**) **1.** to poke or jab with something pointed. –n.

2. a poke or jab. **3.** a pointed instrument, as a goad.

prodigal *adj.* **1.** wastefully or recklessly extravagant. –*n.* **2.** a spendthrift.

prodigious *adj.* **1.** extraordinary in size, amount, extent, degree, force, etc. **2.** wonderful or marvellous.

The more usual word is **great**.

prodigy /ˈprɒdədʒi/ *n.* (*pl.* **-gies**) a person, especially a child, endowed with extraordinary gifts or powers.

produce *v.* /prəˈdjus/ **1.** to bring into existence. **2.** to make; create. **3.** *Econ.* to create (something having an exchangeable value). **4.** to yield. **5.** to bring forward. **6.** to bring (a play, film, etc.) before the public. –*n.* /ˈprɒdus/ **7.** that which is produced; yield; product. **8.** agricultural or natural products collectively. –**production**, *n.* –**productive**, *adj.* –**productivity**, *n.*

producer *n.* someone who supervises the production of a film, play, television or radio show, etc.

product *n.* **1.** a thing produced by any action or operation, or by labour; an effect or result. **2.** a thing produced by nature or by a natural process. **3.** *Maths* the result obtained by multiplying 2 or more quantities together. –**production**, *n.* –**productive**, *adj.* –**productivity**, *n.*

profane *adj.* characterised by irreverence or contempt for God or sacred things. –**profanity**, *n.*

profess *v.* **1.** to lay claim to (a feeling, etc.), often insincerely; pretend to. **2.** to declare openly; announce or affirm; avow or acknowledge.

profession *n.* a vocation requiring knowledge of some department of learning or science.

professional *adj.* **1.** following an occupation as a means of livelihood or for gain. **2.** relating or appropriate to a profession. **3.** earning a living by an occupation ordinarily engaged in as a pastime. –*n.*

4. someone belonging to one of the learned or skilled professions. **5.** someone who earns a living by a skill, sport, etc.: *a golfing professional.*

Someone who follows an occupation or plays a sport for enjoyment rather than being paid is called an **amateur**.

professor *n.* a teacher of the highest rank, usually holding a chair in a particular branch of learning, in a university or college.

proffer *v.* to put before a person for acceptance.

The more usual word is **offer**.

proficient *adj.* well advanced or expert in any art, science, or subject; skilled. –**proficiency**, *n.*

profile *n.* **1.** the outline or contour of the human face, especially as seen from the side. **2.** the outline of something seen against a background. **3.** a vivid and concise sketch of the biography or personality of an individual.

profit *n.* **1.** (*oft. pl.*) monetary gain resulting from any transaction. **2.** *Econ.* the surplus left to the producer or employer after deducting wages, rent, cost of raw materials, etc. **3.** advantage; benefit; gain. –*v.* **4.** to gain advantage or benefit. **5.** to make profit. –**profitable**, *adj.*

Don't confuse this with **prophet** which is someone who speaks on behalf of a god or someone who predicts the future.

profiteer *n.* someone who makes exorbitant profits out of public need.

profiterole /prəˈfɪtərəʊl/ *n.* a small ball of pastry cooked, then filled with cream, jam, cheese, or the like.

profligate *adj.* carelessly wasteful.

The more usual word is **extravagant**.

profound *adj.* **1.** penetrating or entering deeply into subjects of thought or knowledge. **2.** deep. –**profundity**, *n.*

profuse *adj.* **1.** extravagant. **2.** abundant; in great amount. –**profusion**, *n.*

progeny /ˈprɒdʒəni/ n. offspring; issue; descendants. –**progenitor**, n.

Note that **progeny** may be used as a singular or plural noun: *The dying duke's progeny were all gathered at his bedside; The progeny of a horse and a donkey is a mule.*

progesterone /prəˈdʒɛstərəʊn/ n. a female hormone.

prognosis n. (pl. **-noses** /-ˈnəʊsiz/) a forecasting of the probable course and termination of a disease. –**prognostic**, adj.

prognosticate v. to prophesy.

program n. **1.** a plan or policy to be followed. **2.** a list of items in an entertainment. **3.** an entertainment with reference to its items. **4.** a prospectus or syllabus. **5.** *Computers* a series of instructions which will cause a computer to perform a desired operation. –v. (**-grammed, -gramming**) **6.** to insert instructions into (a device) in order to make it perform a certain task: *to program the video.* **7.** to plan a program. **8.** to write a computer program. Also, **programme**. –**programmer**, n.

In Australia until fairly recently, this word was spelt **programme**, and **program** was considered the American spelling. Nowadays, however, most Australians use **program**, and even those people who have kept the **programme** spelling always use **program** for the computing sense.

programming language /ˈprəʊgræs/ n. → **computer language**.

progress n. /ˈprəʊgrɛs/ **1.** advancement, growth or development. **2.** course of action, of events, of time, etc. –v. /prəˈgrɛs/ **3.** to advance. –**progression**, n.

progressive adj. **1.** favouring progress or reform, especially in political matters. **2.** progressing or advancing.

prohibit v. to forbid by authority. –**prohibition**, n.

prohibitive adj. **1.** that prohibits or forbids something. **2.** serving to prevent the use, purchase, etc., of something. Also, **prohibitory**.

project n. /ˈprəʊdʒɛkt, ˈprɒ-/ **1.** a plan; scheme; undertaking. –v. /prəˈdʒɛkt/ **2.** to propose, contemplate, or plan. **3.** to throw, cast, or impel forwards or onwards. **4.** to communicate; make known (an idea, impression, etc.). **5.** to (cause to) extend or protrude. –**projection**, n.

projectile n. an object set in motion by an exterior force which then continues to move by its own inertia.

The more usual word is **missile**.

projector n. an apparatus for throwing an image on a screen.

prolapse n. a falling down of an organ or part, as the uterus, from its normal position.

proletariat /prəʊləˈtɛəriət/ n. **1.** the unpropertied class; that class which is dependent for support on the sale of its labour. **2.** the working class, or wage-earners in general. –**proletarian**, adj., n.

The more usual expression is **working class**.

proliferate v. to grow or produce by multiplication of parts, as in budding or cell division. –**proliferation**, n.

prolific adj. producing offspring, fruit, work, etc., especially abundantly; fruitful.

prolix adj. tediously long.

prologue n. an introduction or introductory speech to a discourse, play, etc.

prolong v. to make longer.

promenade /prɒməˈnɑːd, prɒməˈneɪd, ˈprɒmənad, ˈprɒməneɪd/ n. **1.** a leisurely walk, especially in a public place for pleasure or display. **2.** an area suited to leisurely walking, especially one along a beachfront. –v. **3.** to take a promenade.

For defs 1 and 3, the more usual word is **stroll**.

prominent adj. **1.** standing out so as to be easily seen; conspicuous. **2.** important; leading; well-known. –**prominence**, n.

promiscuous adj. having many casual sexual partners. –**promiscuity**, n.

This word is usually used in a disapproving way.

promise n. **1.** an express assurance on which expectation is to be based. **2.** indication of future excellence or achievement. –v. **3.** to engage or undertake by promise (with an infinitive or clause). **4.** to make a promise of. –phr. **5.** promise well (or **fair**), to afford ground for expectation.

promissory note n. a written promise to pay a specified sum of money to a person designated.

promontory n. (pl. **-ries**) a high point of land or rock projecting into the sea; headland.

promote v. **1.** to advance in rank, dignity, position, etc. **2.** to further the growth, development, progress, etc., of; encourage. –**promotion**, n.

prompt adj. **1.** done at once or without delay. **2.** quick to act as occasion demands. –v. **3.** to move or incite to action. **4.** to assist (a person speaking) by suggesting something to be said. –n. **5.** something that prompts. **6.** a message from a computer, appearing as words or symbols on the screen, which indicate to the user that the computer is ready for further instructions.

promulgate v. **1.** to make known by open declaration. **2.** to set forth or teach publicly (a creed, doctrine, etc.).

The more usual word is **announce**.

prone adj. **1.** having a natural inclination or tendency to something; disposed; liable. **2.** lying face downwards. **3.** lying flat; prostrate.

prong n. one of the pointed divisions or tines of a fork.

pronoun n. Gram. a word used as a substitute for a noun, especially to avoid having to repeat the noun, as she and it in the sentence Helen's bag was broken, so she threw it away. –**pronominal**, adj.

pronounce v. **1.** to enunciate or articulate (words, etc.). **2.** to utter or sound in a particular manner in speaking. **3.** to declare (a person or thing) to be as specified. **4.** to utter or deliver formally or solemnly. **5.** to give an opinion or decision (on). –**pronunciation**, n. –**pronouncement**, n.

pronounced adj. **1.** strongly marked. **2.** clearly indicated.

pronumeral n. a letter used in a mathematical expression to stand for a number.

proof n. **1.** evidence sufficient to establish a thing as true. **2.** the establishment of the truth of anything; demonstration. **3.** an arithmetical operation serving to check the correctness of a calculation. **4.** Photography a trial print from a negative. **5.** Printing a trial impression as of composed type, taken to correct errors and make alterations. –adj. **6.** impenetrable, impervious, or invulnerable. **7.** of tested or proved strength or quality.

proofread v. (**-read** /-rɛd/, **-reading**) to read (printers' proofs, etc.) in order to detect and mark errors.

prop v. (**propped**, **propping**) **1.** to rest against a support: to prop a ladder against a wall. –n. **2.** a stick, rod, pole, beam, or other rigid support. **3.** a person or thing serving as a support or stay. –phr. **4.** prop up, to support or sustain.

propaganda n. dissemination of ideas, information or rumour for the purpose of injuring or helping an institution, a cause or a person.

propagate v. **1.** to cause (plants, animals, etc.) to multiply by natural reproduction. **2.** to transmit (traits, etc.) in reproduction or through offspring. **3.** to spread (a report, doctrine, practice, etc.) from person; disseminate. **4.** to cause to extend to a greater distance, or transmit through space or a medium. **–propagation**, *n.*

propane *n.* a gaseous hydrocarbon found in petroleum.

propel *v.* (**-pelled, -pelling**) to drive, or cause to move, forwards.

propellant *n.* **1.** a propelling agent. **2.** *Aeronautics* one or more substances used in rocket motors for the chemical generation of gas at the controlled rates required to provide thrust. Also, **propellent**.

propeller *n.* a device having a revolving hub with radiating blades, for propelling a ship, aircraft, etc. Also, **propellor**.

propensity *n.* (*pl.* **-ties**) natural or habitual inclination or tendency.

proper *adj.* **1.** adapted or appropriate to the purpose or circumstances; fit; suitable. **2.** conforming to established standards of behaviour; correct or decorous. **3.** belonging exclusively or distinctly to a person or thing. **4.** strict; accurate.

proper noun *n. Gram.* a noun that is not usually preceded by an article, and is the name of a single person or thing, or a unique class of persons or things. Also, **proper name**.

Note that proper nouns are spelt with a capital letter.
Compare this with **common noun**, which refers to any of a class of things, such as *boy* as opposed to *Peter*.

property *n.* (*pl.* **-ties**) **1.** the possession or possessions of a particular owner. **2.** a piece of land owned. **3.** *Aust., NZ* a farm, station, orchard, etc. **4.** an essential or distinctive attribute or quality of a thing. **5.** Also, **prop**. *Theatre* an object, item of furniture, ornament, or decoration in a stage setting.

prophecy /ˈprɒfəsi/ *n.* (*pl.* **-cies**) prediction.

Don't confuse the noun **prophecy** with the verb **prophesy**.

prophesy /ˈprɒfəsaɪ/ *v.* (**-sied, -sying**) to foretell or predict. **–prophesier**, *n.*

Don't confuse the verb **prophesy** with the noun **prophecy**.

prophet *n.* **1.** someone who speaks for God or a deity, or by divine inspiration. **2.** someone who predicts what is to come.

Don't confuse this with **profit** which is the money made from selling something at a higher price than you paid for it.

prophylactic *adj.* **1.** defending or protecting from disease, as a drug. *–n.* **2.** a contraceptive, especially a condom. **–prophylaxis**, *n.*

propitiate *v.* to make favourably inclined; appease.

propitious *adj.* favourable.

proponent *n.* **1.** someone who puts forward a proposal. **2.** someone who supports a cause or doctrine.

proportion *n.* **1.** comparative relation between things; ratio. **2.** proper relation between things or parts. **3.** (*pl.*) dimensions. **4.** a portion or part, especially in its relation to the whole. **5.** symmetry; harmony; balanced relationship. **–proportional**, *adj.* **–proportionate**, *adj.*

propose *v.* **1.** to put forward (a matter, idea, etc.) for consideration, acceptance, or action. **2.** to plan or intend. **3.** to suggest marriage. **–proposal**, *n.* **–proposer**, *n.*

For def. 1, the more usual word is **suggest**.
Don't confuse **proposition** (something that is proposed) with **preposition**, which is a word placed before another word to show its relationship to other words in the sentence, such as *to* in We drove to the city.

propound *v.* to put forward for consideration, acceptance, or approval.

proprietary *adj.* **1.** manufactured and sold only by the owner of the patent, formula, brand name, or trademark associated with the product: *a proprietary medicine.*

2. insistent on one's ownership of something: *She is very proprietary about her car.*

A **proprietary limited company** is one that is not listed on the stock exchange and has a maximum of 50 shareholders. They have limited liability, which means that, if the company goes bankrupt and has to close down, they only have to pay the company's debts up to the value of their own shares. The abbreviation used in the names of this type of company is **Pty Ltd**, as in *Western Heights Pool Supplies Pty Ltd.*

proprietor *n.* the owner of a business establishment, a hotel, newspaper, etc. –**proprietorship**, *n.*

propriety *n.* (*pl.* **-ties**) **1.** conformity to established standards of behaviour or manners. **2.** appropriateness to the purpose or circumstances; suitability.

propulsion *n.* the act of propelling or driving forward or onward.

pro rata *adv.* /prou 'rata/ **1.** in proportion; according to a certain rate. –*adj.* /'prou rata/ **2.** proportionate.

prorogue *v.* to discontinue meetings of (parliament) until the next session.

prosaic *adj.* commonplace or dull; matter-of-fact.

proscenium *n.* (*pl.* **-nia** /-niə/) (in the modern theatre) the decorative arch or opening between the stage and the auditorium.

proscribe *v.* **1.** to denounce or condemn (a thing) as dangerous; to prohibit. **2.** to banish, exile or outlaw.

Don't confuse this with **prescribe**. A doctor **prescribes** medicine to make you better.

prose *n.* the ordinary form of spoken or written language, without metrical structure (as distinguished from poetry or verse).

prosecute *v. Law* **1.** to institute legal proceedings against (a person, etc.). **2.** to

seek to enforce or obtain by legal process. **3.** to conduct criminal proceedings in court against. –**prosecution**, *n.* –**prosecutor**, *n.*

Don't confuse **prosecute** with **persecute**, which is to constantly treat unfairly or cruelly.

proselyte *n.* a convert.

proselytise /'prosələtaɪz/ *v.* to try to change another's opinion, religious belief etc., to one's own. Also, **proselytize**. –**proselytism**, *n.*

prosody /'prosədi, 'proz-/ *n.* the science or study of poetic metres.

prospect *n.* **1.** (*usu. pl.*) an apparent probability of advancement, success, profit, etc. **2.** the outlook for the future. **3.** a view or scene. –*v.* **4.** to search or explore (a region), as for gold. –**prospector**, *n.*

prospective *adj.* **1.** of or in the future. **2.** potential; likely; expected.

Don't confuse this with **perspective**, which is the appearance of distance as well as height and width, produced on a flat surface, such as in a painting.

prospectus *n.* **1.** an advertisement inviting applications from the public to subscribe for securities of a (proposed) corporation. **2.** a pamphlet issued by an institution giving details about itself.

prosperous *adj.* **1.** having or characterised by continued good fortune; flourishing; successful. **2.** well-to-do or well-off. –**prosper**, *v.* –**prosperity**, *n.*

prostate gland the gland which surrounds the urethra of males at the base of the bladder.

prosthesis /prɒs'θiːsəs, prəs-/ *n.* (*pl.* **-theses** /-'θiːsiːz/) the use of an artificial part to replace a damaged or missing part of the body.

prostitute *n.* a person, especially a woman, who engages in sexual intercourse for money as a livelihood. –**prostitution**, *n.*

prostrate v. /pros'treit/ **1.** to throw (oneself) down in humility, worship, etc. –adj. /'prostreit/ **2.** lying flat or at full length on the ground, esp. as sign of humility, worship, etc. **3.** Bot. (of a plant or stem) lying flat on the ground.

protagonist n. the leading character in a play, novel, etc.

protea /'proutiə/ n. any of various sthn African shrubs or trees with large showy flowers.

protean adj. readily assuming different forms or characters.

protect v. to defend or guard or shield from attack, injury or danger. –**protective**, adj. –**protection**, n.

protectorate n. **1.** the relation of a strong state towards a weaker state or territory which it protects and partly controls. **2.** a state or territory so protected.

protégé /'prouteʒei/ n. someone who is under the protection or friendly patronage of another.

protein n. Biochem. any of the polymers formed from amino acids, which are found in all cells and which include enzymes and plasma proteins.

protest n. /'proutest/ **1.** an expression or declaration of objection or disapproval. **2.** a demonstration or meeting of people protesting against something. –v. /prə'test, 'prou-/ **3.** to give formal expression to objection or disapproval; remonstrate. **4.** to declare solemnly or formally; affirm; assert. –**protestation**, n.

protist n. Biol. one of a variety of eukaryotic organisms, including some algae, protozoans, and moulds. Also, **protistan**.

protistan n. **1.** → protist. –adj. **2.** of or relating to a protist.

protocol n. **1.** the customs and regulations dealing with the etiquette of the diplomatic corps and others at a court or capital. **2.** Computers a set of rules governing the format in which messages are sent from one computer to another, as in a network.

proton n. a tiny particle present in the nucleus of every atom, which has a positive electric charge that balances the negative charge of the electron.

Compare this with **electron** and **neutron**.

prototype n. the original or model after which anything is formed. –**prototypical**, adj.

protract v. **1.** to prolong. **2.** Surveying, etc. to plot; to draw by means of a scale and protractor.

protractor n. a flat instrument, graduated around the semicircular edge, used to measure angles.

protrude v. to jut out. –**protrusion**, n.

protuberant adj. bulging.

The more usual word is **swollen**.

proud adj. **1.** feeling or showing pleasure or satisfaction over something conceived as highly creditable to oneself. **2.** having too high an opinion of one's own abilities, importance, etc. **3.** (of things) stately, majestic, or magnificent.

Note that it is good to be proud in the sense of def. 1, but not good to be proud in the sense of def. 2.

prove v. **1.** to establish the truth or genuineness of, as by evidence or argument. **2.** to put to the test; try or test. **3.** to determine the characteristics of by scientific analysis.

provenance n. the place of origin, as of a work of art, etc.

provender n. dry food for livestock, as hay; fodder.

proverb n. a short popular saying, in use for a long time, expressing some familiar truth or useful thought. –**proverbial**, adj.

provide v. **1.** to furnish or supply. **2.** to supply means of support, etc. (for).

provided conj. on the condition or supposition (that).

providence n. **1.** in Christianity, the foreseeing care and guardianship of God over his creatures. **2.** provident or prudent management of resources; economy.

provident *adj.* **1.** having or showing foresight; careful in providing for the future. **2.** careful in the management of money.

For def. 2, the more usual word is **economical**.

provider *n.* **1.** a person who supplies a means of support; breadwinner. **2.** a company which provides access to a service: *mobile phone provider.* **3.** → **internet service provider.**

providing *conj.* provided.

province *n.* **1.** an administrative division or unit of a country. **2.** the sphere or field of action of a person, etc.

provincial *adj.* **1.** local. **2.** countrified; rustic. **3.** unsophisticated or narrow.

provision *n.* **1.** a clause in a legal instrument, a law, etc., providing for a particular matter; stipulation; proviso. **2.** arrangement or preparation beforehand. **3.** (*pl.*) supplies of food.

provisional *adj.* temporary; conditional.

proviso *n.* (*pl.* **-sos** *or* **-soes**) a stipulation or condition.

provoke *v.* **1.** to anger, enrage, exasperate, or vex. **2.** to stir up, arouse, or call forth. **3.** to give rise to, induce, or bring about. **–provocation,** *n.* **–provocative,** *adj.*

provost /ˈprɒvəst/ *n.* a person appointed to superintend or preside. **–provostship,** *n.*

prow *n.* the front part of a ship or boat above the waterline; the bow.

prowess *n.* outstanding ability.

The more usual word is **skill**.

prowl *v.* to rove or go about stealthily in search of prey, plunder, etc.

proximity *n.* nearness.

proxy *n.* (*pl.* **-xies**) someone who stands in or acts for another, in either an official or an informal capacity.

proxy server *n. Internet* a server which acts as a buffer between the user and the

internet, performing a range of functions such as storing frequently used data in a cache to speed access, imposing restrictions on access to some users, or hiding IP addresses to ensure anonymity. Also, **proxy.**

prude *n.* a person who affects extreme modesty or propriety. **–prudery,** *n.*

prudence *n.* **1.** cautious practical wisdom; good judgement; discretion. **2.** prudent care in management; economy or frugality. **–prudential,** *adj.* **–prudent,** *adj.*

prune[1] *n.* a purplish black dried plum.

prune[2] *v.* to cut superfluous twigs, branches, or roots from; trim.

prurient *adj.* inclined to or characterised by lascivious thought.

pry *v.* (**pried, prying**) **1.** to look closely or curiously; peer, or peep. **2.** to search or inquire curiously or inquisitively into something.

psalm /sam/ *n.* a sacred or solemn song, or hymn.

pseudonym /ˈsjudənɪm/ *n.* an assumed name adopted by an author to conceal their identity; pen-name.

psyche /ˈsaɪki/ *n.* the human soul, spirit, or mind.

psychedelic /saɪkəˈdelɪk/ *adj.* **1.** relating to a mental state of enlarged consciousness, especially as experienced through drugs. **2.** *Informal* having bright colours and imaginative patterns.

psychiatry /saɪˈkaɪətri/ *n.* the practice or the science of treating mental diseases. **–psychiatric,** *adj.* **–psychiatrist,** *n.*

psychic /ˈsaɪkɪk/ *adj.* Also, **psychical.** **1.** of or relating to the human soul or mind; mental. **2.** *Psychol.* relating to super- or extra-sensory mental functioning, such as clairvoyance, telepathy, etc. **–n.** **3.** a person specially susceptible to psychic influences.

psychoanalysis *n.* a technical procedure for investigating unconscious mental processes, and for treating neuroses. **–psychoanalyse,** *v.*

psychology /saɪˈkɒlədʒi/ n. **1.** the science of mind, or of mental states. **2.** the science of human and animal behaviour. –**psychologist**, n. –**psychological**, adj.

psychopath n. someone affected with a mental disorder. –**psychopathic**, adj. –**psychopathy**, n.

psychosis /saɪˈkoʊsəs/ n. (pl. **-choses** /-koʊsiz/) a severe mental disorder. –**psychotic**, adj., n.

psychosomatic /ˌsaɪkoʊsəˈmætɪk/ adj. denoting a physical disorder which is caused by or notably influenced by the emotional state of the patient.

ptomaine /təˈmeɪn/ n. any of a class of basic nitrogenous substances, some of them very poisonous, produced during putrefaction of animal or plant proteins.

pub n. Informal a hotel, especially one that is primarily a provider of alcoholic drinks rather than accommodation.

Note that you would not usually use **pub** to refer to a big international hotel or the sort of hotel you might stay in on a holiday. A pub is usually a place where you would go for a drink, a meal and possibly to listen to music.

puberty n. sexual maturity.

pubic adj. relating to the lower part of the abdomen.

public adj. **1.** relating to the people as a whole or the community, state, or nation. **2.** open to all the people. **3.** relating to or engaged in the affairs or service of the community or nation. –n. Also, **the general public**. **4.** the people of a community, state, or nation.

public-address system n. an electronic system consisting of microphone, amplifier, and a loudspeaker, which serves to amplify sound. Also, **PA system, PA**.

publican n. the owner or manager of a pub or hotel.

A **publican**'s hotel is usually a small one that mainly serves drinks, meals and sometimes provides entertainment such as a band. You would not normally refer to the owner or manager of an international hotel as a publican.

publication n. **1.** the publishing of a book, piece of music, etc. **2.** that which is published.

publicity n. **1.** the measures, process, or business of securing public notice. **2.** advertisement matter intended to attract public notice. –**publicise**, **publicize**, v. –**publicist**, n.

public relations n. (functioning as sing. or pl.) the practice of establishing and maintaining the favourable reputation of a particular organisation, public person, etc. Also, **PR**.

publish v. **1.** to issue in printed copies for sale or distribution to the public. **2.** to make publicly or generally known.

puce n. dark or purplish brown.

pucker v. to draw or gather into wrinkles or irregular folds.

pudding n. **1.** a sweet or savoury dish made in many forms and of various ingredients. **2.** a course in a meal following the main or meat course.

puddle n. **1.** a small pool of water left on a road, etc., after rain. **2.** a small pool of any liquid.

puerile /ˈpjʊəraɪl, ˈpjʊrail/ adj. **1.** of or relating to a child or boy. **2.** childishly foolish, irrational, or trivial.

Puerile is usually used in a disapproving way.

puff n. **1.** a short, quick blast, as of wind or breath. **2.** a swelling; protuberance. **3.** inflated or exaggerated praise. –v. **4.** to blow with short, quick blasts, as the wind. **5.** to send forth (air, vapour, etc.) in short quick blasts. **6.** to inflate or distend, especially with air. –phr. **7. out of puff**, Informal out of breath. **8. puff up**, to become inflated or distended.

puffin n. a seabird with a brightly coloured bill.

puff pastry n. a rich, flaky pastry used for pies, tarts, etc.

puffy adj. (**-fier, -fiest**) inflated or distended.

pug n. a breed of dog.

pugilist /ˈpjuːdʒəlɪst/ n. a boxer.

pugnacious adj. given to fighting; quarrelsome.

The more usual word is **aggressive**.

pull v. **1.** to draw or haul towards oneself or itself. **2.** to exert a drawing, tugging, or hauling force. **3.** to draw, or tear (*apart, to pieces*, etc.). **4.** to pluck away from a place of growth, attachment, etc. **5.** to cause to form: *to pull a face.* **6.** to strain, as a ligament. –n. **7.** the act of pulling or drawing. **8.** force used in pulling; pulling power. **9.** *Informal* influence, as with persons able to grant favours. –phr. **10. pull out, a.** to leave; depart. **b.** *Informal* to withdraw, as from an agreement or enterprise. **11. pull through,** *Informal* to recover or survive. **12. pull up, a.** to stop. **b.** to correct or rebuke.

pull-down menu n. *Computers* a computer menu which is instantly accessible and which leaves the screen exactly as it was once an option has been chosen. Also, **drop-down menu**.

pullet n. a young hen.

pulley n. a wheel with a grooved rim for carrying a line, especially as part of a block (def. 4a).

pullover n. → **jumper**.

pulmonary /ˈpʌlmənri, ˈpol-/ adj. of or relating to the lungs.

pulp n. **1.** the succulent part of a fruit. **2.** any soft, moist, slightly cohering mass.

pulpit n. a platform or raised structure in a church, from which the priest or minister, etc., delivers a sermon, etc.

pulsate v. **1.** to expand and contract rhythmically, as the heart; beat; throb. **2.** to vibrate; quiver.

pulse n. **1.** the regular throbbing of the arteries caused by the successive contractions of the heart, especially as felt in an artery at the wrist. **2.** a single stroke, vibration, or undulation. **3.** a throb of life, emotion, etc. –v. **4.** to beat or throb; pulsate.

pulverise v. to reduce to dust or powder, as by pounding, grinding, etc. Also, **pulverize**.

puma n. a large tawny wild cat; cougar.

pumice n. a porous or spongy form of volcanic glass, used especially when powdered, as an abrasive, etc.

pummel v. (**-melled** or, *Chiefly US*, **-meled, -melling** or, *Chiefly US*, **-meling**) to beat or thrash with rapid blows, as with the fists.

pump¹ n. **1.** an apparatus for raising, driving, exhausting, or compressing fluids, as by means of a piston, etc. –v. **2.** to raise or drive (water) with a pump. **3.** to free from water, etc., by means of a pump. **4.** to try to get information from. **5.** to operate as a pump does.

pump² n. a type of shoe.

pumpkin n. a large, melon-like vegetable.

pun n. a play on words.

punch¹ n. **1.** a thrusting blow, especially with the fist. –v. **2.** to give a sharp thrust or blow to, especially with the fist.

punch² n. a tool for perforating tickets, leather, etc.

punch³ n. a beverage consisting of wine or spirits mixed with water, fruit juice, etc.

punchline n. the culminating sentence, line, phrase, or the like of a joke, especially that on which the whole joke depends.

punctilious adj. strict in the observance of forms in conduct or actions.

The more usual word is **careful**.

punctual *adj.* strictly observant of an appointed or regular time; not late. **–punctuality,** *n.*

punctuation *n.* (the inserting of) marks or points in writing or printing in order to make the meaning clear.

puncture *n.* **1.** a perforation. *–v.* **2.** to prick, pierce or perforate.

pundit *n.* a self-important expert.

pungent *adj.* sharply affecting the taste; biting; acrid.

punish *v.* to subject to a penalty, or to pain, loss, confinement, death, etc., for some offence, transgression, or fault. **–punishment,** *n.* **–punitive,** *adj.*

punk *n.* **1.** *Chiefly US Informal* something or someone regarded as worthless, degraded, or bad. *–adj.* **2.** relating to a style of dress, rock music, etc., characterised by rebelliousness and aggression.

punnet *n.* a small, shallow container, as for strawberries.

punt¹ *n.* **1.** a shallow, flat-bottomed, square-ended boat. **2.** a ferry for carrying vehicles across rivers, etc.

punt² *v.* to gamble; wager.

puny *adj.* **(-nier, -niest)** small and weak.

pup *n.* **1.** Also, **puppy.** a young dog. **2.** a young seal.

pupa /ˈpjupə/ *n.* **(pl. -pae** /-piː/ *or* **-pas)** an insect in the cocoon between the larva and mature adult stages. **–pupal,** *adj.*

pupil¹ *n.* someone learning from an instructor or teacher; student.

pupil² *n.* the expanding and contracting opening in the iris of the eye, through which light passes to the retina.

puppet *n.* **1.** a doll. **2.** *Theatre* an artificial figure of a person, animal or object, usually in miniature and capable of articulated movement, controlled by a puppeteer. **–puppeteer,** *n.* **–puppetry,** *n.*

puppy *n.* **(pl. -pies) 1.** a young dog. **2.** the young of certain other animals, as the shark. **3.** a presuming, conceited, or empty-headed young man.

purchase *v.* **1.** to acquire by the payment of money or its equivalent; buy. *–n.* **2.** something which is purchased or bought.

purdah /ˈpɜːdə/ *n.* (in some Muslim and Hindu communities) the custom of women remaining secluded, especially from men who are not relatives, remaining in a particular part of their home and wearing clothing that completely covers them when they are in public.

pure *adj.* **1.** free from extraneous matter, or from mixture with anything of a different, inferior, or contaminating kind. **2.** being that and nothing else; mere. **3.** spotless, or unsullied **4.** untainted with evil; innocent. **–purify,** *v.* **–purity,** *n.*

puree *n.* a cooked and sieved vegetable or fruit.

purgative *n.* purging; cleansing; specifically, causing evacuation of the bowels.

purgatory *n.* **(pl. -ries)** any condition, situation, or place of temporary suffering, expiation, or the like.

purge *v.* **(purged, purging) 1.** to cleanse; rid of whatever is impure or undesirable. *–n.* **2.** the elimination, especially by killing, of political opponents and others.

purism *n.* scrupulous or excessive observance of or insistence on purity in language, style, etc. **–purist,** *n.*

puritan *n.* someone who aspires to great purity or strictness of life in moral and religious matters. **–puritanical,** *adj.*

purl *n.* a stitch used in hand knitting to make a rib effect.

purloin *v.* to steal.

purple *n.* **1.** any colour having components of both red and blue, especially a dark shade of such a colour. *–adj.* **2.** of the colour of purple.

purport *v.* /pɜːˈpɔːt, ˈpɜːpɔːt/ **1.** to profess or claim. **2.** to convey to the mind as the meaning or thing intended; express; imply. *–n.* /ˈpɜːpɔːt, -pət/ **3.** tenor, import, or meaning. **4.** purpose or object.

purpose n. **1.** the object for which anything exists or is done, made, used, etc. **2.** an intended or desired result; end or aim. **3.** intention or determination. –**purposeful**, adj.

purr v. to utter a low, continuous murmuring sound.

purse n. **1.** a small bag for carrying money on the person. **2.** a sum of money offered as a prize.

purser n. an officer, especially on board a ship, charged with keeping accounts, etc.

pursuant adv. according (to).

pursue v. **1.** to follow with the view of overtaking, capturing, killing, etc.; chase. **2.** to seek to attain or accomplish. **3.** to carry on (action, thoughts, etc.). **4.** to continue to discuss (a subject). –**pursuit**, n.

purvey v. to provide, furnish, or supply (especially food or provisions). –**purveyor**, n. –**purveyance**, n.

purview n. range of operation, activity, concern, etc.

pus n. a yellow-white substance produced by suppuration and found in abscesses, sores, etc.

push v. **1.** to exert force upon or against (a thing) in order to move it away; shove. **2.** to press or urge (a person, etc.) to some action or course. **3.** to peddle (narcotics). –n. **4.** the act of pushing; a shove or thrust. **5.** a determined pushing forward or advance. **6.** the pressure of circumstances.

pushover n. Informal anything done easily.

pusillanimous adj. faint-hearted; cowardly.

pussy[1] /ˈpʊsi/ n. (pl. **-sies**) a cat. Also, **puss**.

pussy[2] /ˈpʌsi/ adj. containing pus. Also, **pusy**.

pustule n. a small elevation of the skin containing pus.

put v. (**put**, **putting**) **1.** to move or place (anything) so as to get it into or out of some place or position. **2.** to bring into some relation, state, etc.: to put everything in order. **3.** to estimate: He puts the distance at 2 metres. **4.** to express or state: to put it in writing. **5.** to set, give, or make: to put an end to a practice. **6.** to throw or cast, especially with a forward motion of the hand when raised close to the shoulder: to put the shot. **7.** Naut. to go out to sea. –phr. **8. put across**, to communicate; cause to be understood. **9. put down**, **a.** to write down. **b.** to repress or suppress. **c.** to attribute (to). **d.** to pay as a lump sum. **e.** to destroy an animal, for reasons of disease, etc. **f.** to nominate. **10. put in**, **a.** Naut. to enter a port or harbour. **b.** to apply (for). **c.** to devote, as time, work, etc. **11. put off**, **a.** to postpone. **b.** to disgust or cause to dislike. **12. put on**, **a.** to assume: to put on airs. **b.** to dress in (clothing). **c.** to produce; stage. **d.** to cause to speak on the telephone. **13. put out**, **a.** to extinguish (fire, etc.). **b.** to confuse or embarrass. **c.** to disturb or interrupt. **d.** to irritate. **14. put up**, **a.** to erect. **b.** to provide (money, etc.). **c.** to give lodging to. **15. put up to**, to persuade to do. **16. put up with**, to tolerate or endure.

putative /ˈpjuːtətɪv/ adj. commonly regarded as such; reputed; supposed.

putrefy v. (**-fied**, **-fying**) to become putrid; rot.

putrid adj. **1.** in a state of foul decay or decomposition. **2.** disgustingly objectionable or bad.

putt v. Golf to strike (the ball) gently and carefully.

putty n. (pl. **-ties**) a cement, of dough-like consistency, used for securing panes of glass, stopping up holes in woodwork, etc.

puzzle n. **1.** a toy or game that presents difficulties to be solved by ingenuity or patient effort. **2.** something puzzling; a puzzling matter or person. –v. **3.** to cause to be at a loss; bewilder; confuse. –phr.

4. puzzle out, to come to understand by careful study or effort.

pygmy *n.* *(pl.* **-mies)** *Informal (chiefly derog.)* a small or dwarfish person. Also, **pigmy.**

pyjamas *pl. n.* nightclothes consisting of loose trousers and jacket.

pylon *n.* **1.** a steel tower or mast carrying high-tension, telephonic or other cables and lines. **2.** a structure at either side of a gate, bridge, or avenue, marking an entrance or approach.

pyramid *n.* **1.** *Archit.* a massive stone structure with usually square base and sloping sides meeting at an apex, such as those built by the ancient Egyptians. **2.** anything of such form. **3.** *Geom.* a solid having a triangular, square, or polygonal base, and triangular sides which meet in a point.

pyre *n.* a pile or heap of wood or other combustible material, especially one for burning a dead body.

pyromania *n.* a mania for setting things on fire. **-pyromaniac,** *n.*

pyrotechnics *n.* **1.** the making and use of fireworks for display, military purposes, etc. **2.** a brilliant or sensational display.

python *n.* a large non-venomous snake which kills by squeezing its prey to death.

Q, q

Q, q *n.* the 17th letter of the English alphabet.

QR code *n.* quick response code; a code which, when scanned by a mobile phone, connects to a website for the downloading of information, as for example, a QR code at a transport terminal which connects the user to a timetable.

quack[1] *v.* to utter the cry of a duck, or a sound resembling it.

quack[2] *n.* someone who pretends to have skills or qualifications which they do not actually possess, especially in the medical field. **–quackery,** *n.*

quad *n. Informal* **1.** → quadruplet (def. 2). **2.** → quadrangle (def. 2).

quad bike *n.* a four-wheeled motorcycle designed to travel over rough terrain.

quadrangle *n.* **1.** a plane figure having 4 angles and 4 sides, as a square. **2.** Also, **quad.** a quadrangular space or court. **–quadrangular,** *adj.*

quadrant *n.* the quarter of a circle; an arc of 90°.

quadratic *adj.* **1.** square. **2.** *Algebra* involving the square and no higher power of the unknown quantity.

quadriceps /ˈkwɒdrəsɛps/ *n.* the great muscle of the front of the thigh, which extends the leg and is considered as having four points of connection. Also, **quads.**

quadrilateral *adj.* **1.** having 4 sides. *–n.* **2.** a plane figure having 4 sides and 4 angles.

quadrille *n.* a square dance for 4 couples.

quadriplegia *n.* a condition in which the arms and legs are paralysed. **–quadriplegic,** *n., adj.*

quadruped /ˈkwɒdrəpɛd/ *adj.* **1.** four-footed. *–n.* **2.** an animal having 4 feet.

quadruple *adj.* **1.** consisting of 4 parts. *–v.* **2.** to make or become 4 times as great.

quadruplet *n.* **1.** any group or combination of 4. **2.** Also, **quad.** one of 4 children born at one birth.

quaff *v.* to drink (a beverage, etc.), copiously and heartily.

quagmire *n.* a piece of boggy ground.

quail[1] *n.* (*pl.* **quails** or, *especially collectively,* **quail**) a small ground-dwelling bird.

quail[2] *v.* to lose heart or courage in difficulty or danger.

quaint *adj.* strange or odd in an interesting, pleasing, or amusing way.

quake *v.* **1.** to shake from cold, weakness, fear, anger, or the like. *–n.* **2.** an earthquake.

qualify *v.* (**-fied, -fying**) **1.** to invest with or possess proper or necessary skills etc.; make or become competent. **2.** to attribute some quality or qualities to; characterise, call, or name. **3.** to modify in some way. **–qualification,** *n.*

qualitative *adj.* relating to or concerned with quality or qualities.

quality *n.* (*pl.* **-ties**) **1.** a characteristic, property, or attribute. **2.** grade or worth: *poor quality; good quality.* **3.** high grade; superior excellence: *clothes of quality. –adj.* **4.** of fine or good quality: *quality goods.*

Defs 2 and 3 are similar, but there is an important difference in meaning depending on what comes before **quality**. Compare these three phrases: *clothes of poor quality, clothes of good quality* and *clothes of quality*. The first two are examples of def. 2, and have adjectives (*poor* and *good*) describing **quality**. Def. 2 must be used with an adjective to say what kind or level of quality it is. Without it, we get the third example above (*clothes of quality*). This is an example of def. 3 which is *not* used with an adjective and *always* means good or high quality.

qualm *n.* an uneasy feeling as to conduct.

quandary *n.* (**-ries**) a state of uncertainty, especially as to what to do; dilemma.

quandong /'kwɒndɒŋ/ *n.* an Aust. tree with fruit which can be eaten raw or made into jams and jellies.

quantify *v.* (**-fied, -fying**) to determine the quantity of; measure.

quantitative *adj.* of or relating to the measuring of quantity.

quantity *n.* (*pl.* **-ties**) **1.** a particular, indefinite, or considerable amount of anything. **2.** amount or measure.

quantum physics *n.* the branch of physics that uses quantum theory.

quantum theory *n.* a theory concerning the behaviour of physical systems which states that a system has certain properties, such as energy and momentum in discrete amounts (quanta).

quarantine *n.* **1.** a strict isolation designed to prevent the spread of disease. *–v.* **2.** to put in or subject to quarantine.

quarrel *n.* **1.** an angry dispute or altercation. *–v.* (**-relled, -relling**) **2.** to disagree angrily; squabble. –**quarrelsome**, *adj.*

quarry¹ *n.* (*pl.* **-ries**) **1.** an open excavation or pit from which building stone, slate, or the like is obtained. *–v.* (**-ried, -rying**) **2.** to obtain (stone, etc.) from, or as from, a quarry.

quarry² *n.* (*pl.* **-ries**) an animal or bird hunted or pursued.

quart *n.* a liquid measure in the imperial system, equal to ¼ of a gallon, or approximately 1.137 litres.

quarter *n.* **1.** one of the 4 equal parts into which anything is or may be divided. **2.** *Astron.* a 4th of the moon's period or monthly revolution. **3.** a region, district, or place. **4.** (*usu. pl.*) a place of stay; lodgings. **5.** a part or member of a community,

government, etc., which is not specified. *–v.* **6.** to divide into 4 equal parts. **7.** to provide with lodgings in a particular place.

quarterback *n.* **1.** *American Football* a back (**back¹** def. 4) who lines up immediately behind the centre and directs the offensive play of the team. *–v.* **2.** to play in this position.

quarterdeck *n.* the upper deck between the mainmast and the stern.

quarterly *adj.* **1.** occurring, done, etc., at the end of every 3 months. *–n.* (*pl.* **-lies**) **2.** a periodical issued every 3 months.

quartermaster *n. Mil.* a regimental officer in charge of quarters, rations, clothing, equipment, and transport.

quartet *n.* a group of 4 singers or players.

quarto *n.* a size of paper.

This is an old paper size. A4 is mainly used nowadays.

quartz *n.* one of the commonest minerals, having many varieties which differ in colour, lustre, etc.

quartzite *n.* a granular rock consisting essentially of quartz in interlocking grains. –**quartzitic**, *adj.*

quasar *n. Astron.* one of many extremely luminous objects lying close to the edge of the known universe.

quash *v.* **1.** to put down or suppress completely; subdue. **2.** to make void; annul, or set aside (a law, indictment, decision, etc.).

quaternary *adj.* **1.** consisting of 4. **2.** arranged in fours.

quaver *v.* **1.** to quiver, or tremble (now said usually of the voice). *–n.* **2.** a quavering or tremulous shake, especially in the voice. **3.** *Music* a note equal in length to half a crotchet.

quay /ki/ *n.* an artificial landing place for vessels.

queasy *adj.* (**-sier, -siest**) inclined to nausea.

queen n. 1. the wife or consort of a king. 2. a female sovereign or monarch. 3. a fertile female of ants, bees, etc. 4. a chess piece. 5. *Informal* a male homosexual.

Queen's Counsel n. (in some legal systems) a senior barrister who has received a commission to act as adviser to the crown, as a form of recognition of his or her eminence. *Abbrev.*: QC Also, (*when the reigning monarch is a man*), **King's Counsel**.

queer adj. 1. strange from a conventional point of view; odd. 2. slightly unwell. 3. *Informal* homosexual. –n. 4. *Informal* a homosexual.

This word used to be used disapprovingly about homosexuals, but nowadays is quite a positive term used by many homosexual people themselves.

quell v. 1. to suppress (disorder, mutiny, etc.). 2. to quiet or allay (feelings, etc.).

quench v. 1. to slake, as thirst; allay; satisfy. 2. to suppress; stifle; subdue.

querulous adj. full of complaints; complaining.

query n. (pl. **-ries**) 1. a question; inquiry. 2. a doubt; uncertainty. –v. (**-ried, -rying**) 3. to ask or inquire about. 4. to question (a statement, etc.) as doubtful or obscure. 5. to ask questions of.

quest n. a search or pursuit made in order to find or obtain something.

question n. 1. a sentence in an interrogative form, addressed to someone in order to elicit information. 2. a matter for investigation. 3. a matter or point of uncertainty or difficulty: *a question of etiquette*. –v. 4. to ask a question or questions of. 5. to make a question of; doubt. 6. to challenge; dispute. –**questionable**, adj.

question mark n. a mark (?) indicating a question.

questionnaire /kwɛstʃən'ɛə, kɛs-/ n. a list of questions, usually printed on a form, to obtain opinions on some subject.

queue n. 1. a file or line of people, vehicles, etc., waiting. –v. (**queued, queuing** or **queueing**) Also, **queue up**. 2. to form in a line while waiting.

quibble n. 1. trivial or carping criticism. –v. 2. to make trivial criticisms.

quiche /kiʃ/ n. a savoury tart with a filling of eggs, milk, etc.

quick adj. 1. done or proceeding with promptness or rapidity. 2. hasty; impatient. 3. lively or keen, as feelings. 4. of ready intelligence. –n. 5. the sensitive flesh under the nails of the human hand: *nails bitten down to the quick.* –**quickly**, adv.

quicksand n. an area of soft or loose wet sand of considerable depth, dangerous to persons, animals, etc.

quicksilver n. mercury.

quid n. (pl. **quid** or **quids**) *Informal* 1. (formerly) a pound in money. 2. (pl.) money, especially a large amount.

quiescent /kwi'esənt/ adj. being at rest, inactive or motionless.

quiet n. 1. freedom from disturbance or tumult. –adj. 2. making no disturbance or trouble. 3. free from disturbing emotions, etc. 4. refraining or free from activity. 5. motionless or moving gently. 6. making no noise or sound. 7. restrained in speech, manner, etc. –v. 8. to make or become quiet.

quill n. 1. one of the large feathers of a bird. 2. a feather, as of a goose, formed into a pen for writing. 3. one of the hollow spines on a porcupine or hedgehog.

quilt n. 1. a cover for a bed. –v. 2. to stitch together (2 pieces of cloth with a soft interlining).

quince n. a hard, yellowish, acid fruit.

quinine n. a bitter colourless substance, used in medicine as a stimulant and to treat malaria.

quinoa /'kinwa, kwɑ'noʊə/ n. a plant cultivated for its seeds which are ground and eaten as a cereal.

quintessence *n.* **1.** the pure and concentrated essence of a substance. **2.** the most perfect embodiment of something.

quintessential /kwɪntəˈsɛnʃəl/ *adj.* of, relating to, or embodying a quintessence. **–quintessentially,** *adv.*

quintet *n.* a set of 5 singers or players.

quintuple *adj.* **1.** fivefold; consisting of 5 parts. *–v.* **2.** to make or become 5 times as great.

quintuplet *n.* **1.** any group or combination of 5. **2.** one of 5 children born at one birth.

quip *n.* **1.** a clever or witty saying. *–v.* (**quipped, quipping**) **2.** to utter quips.

quirk *n.* **1.** a trick or peculiarity. **2.** a sudden twist, turn, or curve.

quisling *n.* a person who betrays their own country.

quit *v.* (**quit** or **quitted, quitting**) **1.** to cease from doing (something); discontinue. **2.** to depart (from); leave. **3.** to give up (one's job or position); let go.

quite *adv.* **1.** completely, wholly. **2.** actually, really, or truly. **3.** *Informal* to a considerable extent.

quiver[1] *v.* to shake with a slight but rapid motion; tremble.

quiver[2] *n.* a case for holding arrows.

quixotic /kwɪkˈsɒtɪk/ *adj.* extravagantly chivalrous or romantic. **–quixotically,** *adv.*

quiz *v.* (**quizzed, quizzing**) **1.** to question closely. **2.** to examine or test informally by questions. *–n.* (*pl.* **quizzes**) **3.** a general knowledge test.

quizzical *adj.* odd or comical.

quoin /kɔɪn/ *n.* an external solid angle of a wall or the like.

quoit *n.* **1.** Also, **deck quoit.** a flattish ring thrown in play to encircle a peg. **2.** (*pl.*) the game so played.

Note that def. 2 is used as a singular noun: *Quoits is a game that many children enjoy.*

quokka /ˈkwɒkə/ *n.* a species of small wallaby.

quoll *n.* a marsupial with a long tail and spots, about the size of a cat.

quorum *n.* the number of members of a body required to be present to transact business legally.

quota *n.* **1.** a proportional share of a fixed total quantity. **2.** the number of persons allowed to immigrate to a country, join an institution, etc.

quotation *n.* **1.** that which is quoted, from a book, speech, etc. **2.** a price nominated for services, goods, etc.

quotation mark *n.* one of the punctuation marks (" ") or (' ') used before and after a quotation, as in He said, "Stop right there."; "What does the word 'honesty' mean to you?" she asked. Also, **quote mark, inverted comma, speech mark.**

quote *v.* **1.** to repeat (a passage, etc.) from a book, speech, etc. **2.** to bring forward, refer to, or cite. **3.** to state the current price of. *–n.* **4.** a quotation.

quotient *n. Maths* the result of division: *In the sum* 15 ÷ 3, *the quotient is* 5.

Compare this with **divisor,** which is the number you divide another number by, and with **dividend,** which is the number to be divided by another number.

R, r

R, r *n.* the 18th letter of the English alphabet.

rabbi /ˈræbaɪ/ *n.* (*pl.* **-bis**) the spiritual leader of a Jewish community.

rabbit *n.* **1.** a small, long-eared, burrowing mammal. *–v.* (**-bited, -biting**) **2.** to hunt rabbits.

rabble *n.* a disorderly crowd.

rabid *adj.* **1.** irrationally extreme in opinion or practice. **2.** furious or raging. **3.** affected with or relating to rabies; mad.

rabies *n.* a fatal, infectious disease of the brain, transmitted by the bite of an afflicted animal, generally the dog; hydrophobia.

raccoon *n.* any of several small nocturnal carnivores with a bushy ringed tail.

race¹ *n.* **1.** a contest of speed, as in running, riding, etc. **2.** (*pl.*) a series of races, especially horseraces or greyhound races. **3.** any contest or competition. **4.** a narrow passageway. *–v.* (**raced, racing**) **5.** to compete (against) in a contest of speed; run a race (with). **6.** to (cause to) run in a race or races. **7.** to engage in horseracing. **8.** to run or go swiftly.

race² *n.* a group of persons connected by common descent.

racial *adj.* **1.** relating to or characteristic of race or races. **2.** relating to the relations between people of different races.

racism *n.* the belief that human races have distinctive characteristics which determine their respective cultures. **–racist,** *n., adj.*

rack¹ *n.* **1.** a framework of bars, wires, or pegs on which articles are arranged. **2.** an apparatus formerly in use for torturing persons by stretching the body. **3.** violent strain. *–v.* **4.** to strain in mental effort.

rack² *phr.* **rack off,** *Aust. Informal* to leave; go.

racket¹ *n.* **1.** a loud noise. **2.** *Informal* an organised illegal activity.

racket² *n.* → **racquet**.

raconteur *n.* a person skilled in relating stories.

racquet *n.* a light bat having a network of nylon cord or similar stretched in a frame, used in tennis, etc. Also, **racket**.

racy *adj.* (**-cier, -ciest**) **1.** vigorous; lively; spirited. **2.** suggestive; risqué.

radar *n.* a device using radio waves to determine the presence and location of an object.

radial *adj.* of, or relating to a radius or a ray.

radian /ˈreɪdiən/ *n.* the supplementary SI unit of measurement of plane angle. *Symbol:* rad

radiant *adj.* emitting rays of light; shining; bright.

radiate *v.* **1.** to spread or move like rays or radii from a centre. **2.** to emit rays, as of light or heat. **3.** (of persons) to exhibit abundantly (good humour, benevolence, etc.).

radiation *n.* *Physics* the emission and spreading of particles or waves such as by a radioactive substance.

radiator *n.* a device which radiates heat.

radical *adj.* **1.** going to the root or origin; fundamental. **2.** thoroughgoing or extreme. **3.** favouring drastic political, social or other reforms. **4.** *Maths* relating to or forming a root. *–n.* **5.** someone who holds or follows extreme principles, especially left-wing political principles. **6.** *Chem.* a group of atoms which behaves as an unchangeable unit in many reactions.

radio *n.* (*pl.* **-dios**) **1.** the sending of electrical signals through the air to a set which receives them. **2.** an apparatus for receiving radio broadcasts. *–v.* (**-dioed, -dioing**) **3.** to transmit a message by radio.

An old-fashioned word for def. 2 is **wireless**.

radioactivity n. the property of spontaneous disintegration possessed by certain elements due to changes in their atomic nuclei. –**radioactive**, adj.

radiography n. the production of images by the action of X-rays on a photographic plate. –**radiographer**, n.

radiology n. the science dealing with X-rays or rays from radioactive substances, especially for medical uses. –**radiologist**, n.

radiotherapy n. Med. treatment of disease by means of X-rays or of radioactive substances. –**radiotherapist**, n.

radish n. the crisp, pungent, edible root of a plant.

radium n. a naturally occurring radioactive metallic element. Symbol: Ra

radius n. (pl. -**dii** /-diə/ or -**diuses**) 1. a straight line extending from the centre of a circle or sphere to the circumference or surface. 2. that one of the 2 bones of the forearm which is on the thumb side.

raffia n. a fibre from certain palms used for making matting, baskets, etc.

raffle n. 1. a lottery in which the prizes are usually goods rather than money. –v. Also, **raffle off**. 2. to dispose of by a raffle.

raft n. a floating platform used for the conveyance of people, goods, etc., over water.

rafter n. one of the sloping timbers that form the framework of a roof.

rag¹ n. 1. a worthless piece of cloth, etc. especially an old or worn one. 2. Informal a newspaper or magazine, especially one considered as being of little value.

rag² v. (**ragged, ragging**) to tease.

ragamuffin n. a ragged child.

rage n. 1. angry fury. 2. the object of widespread enthusiasm. –v. (**raged, raging**) 3. to show or feel violent anger.

ragged adj. 1. torn or worn to rags. 2. full of rough or sharp projections; jagged.

raglan adj. relating to sleeves which are cut so as to continue up to the collar.

raid n. 1. a sudden attack, as upon something to be seized. –v. 2. to make a raid on.

rail¹ n. 1. a horizontal bar of wood or metal used as a barrier or support. 2. one of a pair of steel bars that provide a running surface for the wheels of vehicles. 3. the railway, as a means of transportation.

rail² v. to utter bitter complaint or vehement denunciation (at or against).

raillery n. (pl. -**ries**) good-humoured ridicule.

railway n. 1. a permanent road or way, laid with rails on which trains run. 2. the company owning or operating it.

raiment n. Old-fashioned clothing; apparel; attire.

rain n. 1. water in drops falling from the sky to the earth. 2. (pl.) the seasonal rainfalls in tropical regions. –v. 3. (of rain) to fall. 4. to fall like rain. 5. to offer or give abundantly. –phr. 6. **rain cats and dogs**, to rain heavily.

Don't confuse **rain** with **rein** or **reign**. A **rein** is a strap which a rider uses to direct a horse. The **reign** of a king or queen is how long they rule.

rainbow n. 1. a bow or arc of colours appearing in the sky opposite the sun, due to the refraction and reflection of the sun's rays in drops of rain. 2. the spectrum. –adj. 3. multicoloured.

rainfall n. 1. a shower of rain. 2. the amount of water falling as rain, snow, etc., within a given time and area.

rainforest n. dense forest found in tropical and temperate areas.

raise v. (**raised, raising**) 1. to move to a higher position. 2. to cause to rise or stand up. 3. to build; erect. 4. to cause to be or appear. 5. to cultivate, produce, breed (crops, plants, animals, etc.). 6. to bring up; rear (children, etc.). 7. to give rise to; bring up or about. 8. to give vigour to; animate (the mind, spirits, hopes). 9. to gather together. 10. to increase in degree, intensity, pitch, or force. **11.** to increase in amount, as rent, prices, wages, etc. –*n.* **12.** a rise (in wages). **13.** a raising, lifting, etc.

Don't confuse **raise** with **rise**, which is to get up (*We rise early on Mondays*), or to go upwards (*The bubbles rise to the surface*). Note that **raise** takes an object but **rise** does not.

raisin *n.* a dried grape.

rake¹ *n.* **1.** a long-handled tool with teeth, used for various purposes. –*v.* **2.** to gather together, draw, or remove (leaves, grass, etc.) with or as with a rake. **3.** to search as with a rake. –*phr.* **4. rake in,** to gather or collect abundantly. **5. rake up, a.** to collect, especially with difficulty. **b.** to reveal, as to discredit someone.

rake² *n.* a profligate or dissolute man.

rally *v.* (**-lied, -lying**) **1.** to bring together or into order again. **2.** to draw or call (persons) together for common action. **3.** to come to the assistance of a person, party, or cause. **4.** to acquire fresh strength or vigour. –*n.* (*pl.* **-lies**) **5.** a recovery from dispersion or disorder, as of troops. **6.** a renewal or recovery of strength, etc. **7.** a drawing or coming together of persons, as for common action. **8.** *Tennis, etc.* a relatively long exchange of strokes.

ram *n.* **1.** an uncastrated male sheep. **2.** a device for battering, crushing, driving, or forcing something. –*v.* (**rammed, ramming**) **3.** to drive or force by heavy blows. **4.** to push firmly.

RAM *n.* random-access memory; computer memory designed so that each stored item can be accessed equally quickly.

ramble *v.* **1.** to wander about in a leisurely manner. –*n.* **2.** a leisurely walk.

ramification *n.* **1.** a division or subdivision derived from a main stem or source. **2.** an implied result or complication.

ramp *n.* **1.** a sloping surface connecting 2 different levels. –*v.* **2.** to act violently; rage; storm.

rampage *n.* **1.** violent or furious behaviour. –*v.* (**-paged, -paging**) **2.** to rush, move, or act furiously or violently.

rampant *adj.* in full sway; unchecked.

rampart *n.* a mound of earth used as a fortification or defence.

ram raid *n.* a robbery involving gaining access to a property, such as a shop, service station, etc., by driving a vehicle into the front window. –**ramraid,** *v.*

ramrod *n.* **1.** a rod for ramming down the charge of a muzzle-loading firearm. **2.** any person or thing considered as exemplifying or exercising stiffness.

ramshackle *adj.* loosely made or held together; rickety.

ran *v.* past tense of **run.**

ranch *n.* (especially in the US) any farm, especially for cattle, horses, etc.

rancid *adj.* having a rank, stale smell or taste.

rancour *n.* a continuing bitter resentment or ill will. Also, **rancor.** –**rancorous,** *adj.*

random *adj.* **1.** without aim, pattern or method; haphazard. –*phr.* **2. at random,** in a haphazard way. –**randomness,** *n.*

randy *adj.* sexually aroused.

rang *v.* past tense of **ring²**.

range *n.* **1.** the extent of the operation or efficacy of something. **2.** an area in which shooting at targets is practised. **3.** a row or line, as of persons or things. **4.** the region over which something is distributed, is found, or occurs. **5.** a chain of mountains. **6.** a cooking stove. –*v.* (**ranged, ranging**) **7.** to set in order; arrange. **8.** to make straight or level as lines of type. **9.** to pass over or extend through (an area or region) in all directions, as in exploring or searching. **10.** to vary within certain limits. **11.** to have range of operation. **12.** to extend in a certain direction.

ranger *n.* a person employed to patrol a public reserve, wildlife park, etc.

rank¹ n. **1.** position or standing in the social scale or in any graded body. **2.** a row or series of things or persons. –v. **3.** to assign to or take up or occupy a particular position, station, class, etc.

rank² adj. **1.** growing with excessive luxuriance. **2.** having an offensively strong smell or taste. **3.** utter; unmistakable. **4.** grossly coarse or indecent.

rankle v. to produce within the mind keen irritation or bitter resentment.

ransack v. to search thoroughly through.

ransom n. **1.** the redemption of a prisoner, slave, kidnapped person, captured goods, etc., for a price. **2.** the sum or price paid or demanded. –v. **3.** to redeem from captivity, bondage, etc., by paying a price demanded.

rant v. to talk in a wild or vehement way.

rap¹ v. (**rapped, rapping**) **1.** to strike, especially with a quick, smart, or light blow. **2.** to knock smartly or lightly. –n. **3.** a quick, smart, or light blow.

rap² n. a form of pop music in which the words are rhythmically spoken rather than sung.

rapacious adj. extraordinarily greedy.

rape n. **1.** the crime of having sexual intercourse with a person against their will. –v. (**raped, raping**) **2.** to commit the crime or act of rape on.

rapid adj. **1.** moving or acting with great speed. –n. **2.** (usu. pl.) a part of a river where the current runs very swiftly. –**rapidity**, n.

rapier n. a slender sword used only for thrusting.

rap music n. a type of pop music in which the lyrics are rhythmically spoken rather than sung.

rapport /ræˈpɔ/ n. relation; connection, especially of a harmonious or sympathetic kind.

rapt adj. **1.** deeply engrossed or absorbed. **2.** transported with emotion; enraptured.

rapture n. ecstatic joy or delight.

rare¹ adj. **1.** few in number. **2.** of low density or pressure. **3.** remarkable or unusual, especially in excellence or greatness.

rare² adj. (of meat) not thoroughly cooked; underdone.

rarefied adj. **1.** of air, having little oxygen: *The air is very rarefied at this high mountain altitude.* **2.** limited or refined: *the rarefied atmosphere of the ancient university.*

rarity n. (pl. **-ties**) something rare or uncommon.

rascal n. a base, dishonest person.

rash¹ adj. acting too hastily or without due consideration.

rash² n. **1.** an eruption on the skin. **2.** a proliferation.

rasher n. a thin slice of bacon.

rasp v. **1.** to scrape or grate with a rough instrument. **2.** to utter with, or make, a grating sound. –n. **3.** a coarse form of file, having separate point-like teeth. –**raspy**, adj.

raspberry¹ n. (pl. **-ries**) a small reddish-coloured edible berry.

raspberry² n. (pl. **-ries**) Informal a sound expressing contempt, made with the tongue and lips.

rat n. **1.** any of certain long-tailed rodents. **2.** Informal someone who abandons friends or associates, especially in time of trouble. –v. (**ratted, ratting**) Informal **3.** to desert one's party or associates, especially in time of trouble. **4.** to inform (on). –phr. **5. smell a rat**, to be suspicious.

Note that if you call someone 'a rat' you are intending to insult them.

ratchet n. a toothed bar with which a pawl engages.

rate n. **1.** a certain quantity or amount of one thing considered in relation to a unit of another thing and used as a standard or measure: *a rate of 5 cents in the dollar.* **2.** a fixed charge per unit of quantity. **3.** degree of speed, of travelling, working, etc. **4.** (*usu. pl.*) a tax on property, imposed by a local authority. –*v.* (**rated, rating**) **5.** to estimate the value or worth of; appraise. **6.** to fix at a certain rate, as of charge or payment. **7.** to have value, standing, etc.

rather *adv.* **1.** more so than not; to a certain extent: *rather good.* **2.** in preference; as a preferred or accepted alternative: *I would rather go today.* –*phr.* **3. rather than,** instead of: *a hindrance rather than a help.*

ratify *v.* (**-fied, -fying**) to confirm by expressing consent or formal sanction: *The full meeting ratified the committee's decision.*

The more usual word is **approve**.

rating *n.* **1.** classification according to grade or rank. **2.** a person's or firm's credit standing.

ratio *n.* (*pl.* **-tios**) proportional relation; rate; quotient of 2 numbers.

ration *n.* **1.** a fixed allowance of provisions or food. –*v.* **2.** to put on, or restrict to, rations.

rational *adj.* **1.** agreeable to reason; sensible. **2.** endowed with the faculty of reason. **3.** proceeding or derived from reason. **4.** *Maths* expressible as the quotient of 2 integers. –**rationality,** *n.*

rationale *n.* a reasoned exposition of principles.

rationalise *v.* **1.** *Psychol.* to justify (behaviour) by inventing a rational, acceptable explanation. **2.** to employ reason; think in a rational manner. **3.** to reorganise and integrate (an industry), especially when this results in job losses. Also, **rationalize.**

rat-race *n.* **1.** the fiercely competitive struggle for success, especially in career. **2.** the frantic pace of city life.

rat run *n. Informal* a circuitous route through suburban streets, usually taken by a driver wishing to avoid major thoroughfares. –**rat-running,** *n.*

rattan *n.* the tough stems of certain palms, used for wickerwork etc.

rattle *v.* **1.** to (cause to) give out a rapid succession of short sharp sounds. **2.** to utter or perform in a rapid or lively manner. **3.** *Informal* to disconcert or confuse (a person). –*n.* **4.** a rapid succession of short, sharp sounds. **5.** an instrument contrived to make a rattling sound, as a child's toy.

rattlesnake *n.* any of various venomous American snakes with a rattling appendage at the end of the tail.

raucous *adj.* hoarse; harsh-sounding, as a voice.

raunchy *adj.* (**-chier, -chiest**) coarse; earthy; lusty. –**raunchiness,** *n.*

ravage *n.* **1.** havoc; ruinous damage. –*v.* (**-aged, -aging**) **2.** to damage or work havoc upon.

rave *v.* (**raved, raving**) **1.** to talk wildly, as in delirium. –*n.* **2.** extravagantly enthusiastic praise. –*adj.* **3.** praising with extravagant enthusiasm.

ravel *v.* (**-elled** *or, Chiefly US,* **-eled, -elling** *or, Chiefly US,* **-eling**) **1.** to tangle or become tangled. **2.** to become separated thread by thread; fray.

raven *n.* **1.** a large, glossy black bird with a loud harsh call. –*adj.* **2.** lustrous black.

ravenous *adj.* extremely hungry.

Don't confuse **ravenous** with **ravishing**, which means extremely beautiful.

ravine *n.* a long, deep, narrow valley, especially one eroded by water.

ravioli *n.* small pieces of filled pasta.

ravish *v.* **1.** to fill with strong emotion, especially joy. **2.** to seize and carry off by force.

ravishing *adj.* very beautiful; entrancing; enchanting.

Don't confuse **ravishing** with **ravenous**, which means extremely hungry.

raw *adj.* **1.** not having undergone processes of preparing, refining, or manufacture.

ray *n.* **1.** a narrow beam of light. **2.** *Maths* one of a system of straight lines emanating from a point.

ray[2] *n.* a flat fish living on the sea bottom.

rayon *n.* a synthetic textile.

raze *v.* to tear down, demolish.

Don't confuse **raze** with **raise** (def. 3), which sounds the same but means the opposite.

razor *n.* a sharp-edged instrument used especially for shaving hair from the skin.

razor wire *n.* coiled stainless-steel wire having pieces of protruding metal with razor-sharp points attached at intervals along the wire.

re /ri, reɪ/ *prep.* in the case of; with reference to: *re my memorandum.*

Re is usually used in business contexts, particularly in letters.

reach *v.* **1.** to get to, or get as far as, in moving, travelling, etc. **2.** to stretch or extend so as to touch or meet. **3.** to stretch in space; extend in length, distance, etc. **4.** to establish communication with. **5.** to make a stretching movement, as with the hand or arm. *–n.* **6.** the act of reaching. **7.** the extent of reaching. **8.** a continuous stretch of something, as a river. *–***reachable**, *adj.*

react *v.* **1.** to act in return on an agent or influence. **2.** to act in opposition, as against some force. *–***reactor**, *n.* *–***reactive**, *adj.*

reaction *n.* the act or an instance of reacting.

reactionary *n.* (*pl.* **-ries**) **1.** a person opposed to progress or reform. *–adj.* **2.** opposing progressive policies; conservative.

read[1] /riːd/ *v.* (**read** /red/, **reading**) **1.** to peruse and understand (something written, etc.). **2.** to render in speech (something written, etc.). **3.** to understand (something read or observed) in a particular way: *to read a look as a sign of disapproval.* **4.** to introduce (something not expressed or directly indicated) into what is read or considered. **5.** to register or indicate, as a thermometer or other instrument. **6.** to obtain by reading. **7.** to be able to be read or interpreted (as stated). *–n.* **8.** the act or process of reading.

Don't confuse **read** with **reed**, which is a tall grass growing in a marsh or swamp.

read[2] /red/ *adj.* having knowledge gained by reading.

ready *adj.* (**-dier**, **-diest**) **1.** completely prepared for immediate action or use. **2.** willing. **3.** prompt or quick in perceiving, speaking, writing, etc. **4.** present or convenient. *–v.* (**-died**, **-dying**) **5.** to make ready; prepare.

reagent *n.* a substance which, on account of the reactions it causes, is used in chemical analysis.

real *adj.* **1.** true. **2.** genuine; not counterfeit, artificial, or imitation. *–adv.* **3.** *Informal* very.

Don't confuse this with **reel**, which is a cylinder for winding something on, such as thread. A **reel** is also a type of dance, and to **reel** is to sway.

real estate *n.* property in the form of land, buildings, etc.; realty: *a valuable piece of real estate.*

real estate agent *n.* a person who acts as an intermediary between the buyer and the vendor of real estate; real estate broker; realtor.

realise *v.* **1.** to understand clearly. **2.** to give reality to (a hope, fear, plan, etc.). **3.** to convert (property or goods) into cash or money. **4.** to obtain (as) a profit by trade, labour, or investment. Also, **realize**.

---

2. denoting figures, etc., before adjustments have been made. **3.** painfully open, as a sore, wound, etc. **4.** *Informal* harsh or unfair.

Don't confuse **raw** with **roar**, which is to make a loud sound like a lion.

realism n. 1. the taking of a practical rather than a moral view in human problems, etc. 2. the tendency to view or represent things as they really are. –**realist**, n.

realistic adj. 1. accepting situations as they really are and not hoping for things that are unlikely to happen: *We should be realistic and accept the fact that we can't afford a new car.* 2. based on facts or a realistic way of thinking: *a realistic estimate of costs.* 3. of a film, book, etc., having characters and events that are like real people and events. –**realistically**, adv.

reality n. 1. the state of being real. 2. a real thing or fact.

reality check n. *Informal* 1. an appraisal of the facts of a situation, often providing a contrast with expectations. 2. any event which triggers such an appraisal of one's expectations, beliefs, etc.

reality TV n. a television program format which uses actual footage of events as they occur, often in a contrived situation and with some competitive element providing the motivation for people to interact. Also, **reality television**.

really adv. 1. in reality; actually: *to see things as they really are.* 2. truly; genuinely: *a really honest man.* 3. indeed: *Really, this is too much.* 4. extremely: *really hot.*

realm n. the region, sphere, or domain within which anything rules or prevails.

real-time adj. *Computers* happening immediately, without delay: *real-time processing.* Also, **realtime**.

realtor n. *Chiefly US* → **real estate agent**.

realty n. → **real estate**.

ream n. a standard quantity of paper equal to 500 sheets (formerly 480 sheets).

reap v. to gather or cut (a crop, harvest, etc.) with a sickle, machine etc.

rear¹ n. 1. the back of anything, as opposed to the front. 2. the space or position behind anything. –adj. 3. situated at or relating to the rear.

rear² v. 1. to care for and support up to maturity. 2. to raise to an upright position. 3. to rise on the hind legs, as a horse or other animal.

reason n. 1. a cause, as for a belief, action, fact, event, etc. 2. the mental powers concerned with drawing conclusions or inferences. 3. sound judgement or good sense. –v. 4. to think (*out*) (a problem, etc.) logically. 5. to conclude or infer (*that*). 6. to bring, persuade, etc., by reasoning.

Reason (def. 1) is usually followed by *that, for* or *why*: *the reason that we are late; the reason for our lateness; the reason why we are late.* Note that you don't follow any of these with *because*. You would not say 'The reason that we are late is because of the bad weather'. Instead, you would say 'The reason that we are late is the bad weather'.

reasonable adj. 1. endowed with reason. 2. agreeable to reason or sound judgement. 3. moderate, as in price etc.

reassure v. to restore (a person, etc.) to assurance or confidence.

rebate n. 1. a return of part of an original amount paid for some service or merchandise. –v. 2. to allow as a discount. –**rebatable**, **rebateable**, adj.

rebel n. /ˈrɛbəl/ 1. someone who resists, or rises in arms against, the established government or ruler. –adj. /ˈrɛbəl/ 2. of or relating to rebels. –v. /rəˈbɛl/ (**-belled, -belling**) 3. to rise in arms or active resistance against one's government or ruler. –**rebellious**, adj.

rebellion n. the act of rebelling.

rebound v. 1. to bound or spring back from impact. –n. 2. the act of rebounding; recoil.

rebuff *n.* **1.** a peremptory refusal of a request, offer, etc.; a snub. **2.** a check to action or progress. –*v.* **3.** to give a rebuff to.

rebuke *v.* (**-buked, -buking**) **1.** to reprove or reprimand. –*n.* **2.** a reproof; a reprimand.

rebut *v.* (**-butted, -butting**) to refute by evidence or argument. –**rebuttal,** *n.*

recalcitrant *adj.* **1.** resisting authority or control. –*n.* **2.** a recalcitrant person. –**recalcitrance, recalcitrancy,** *n.*

recall *v.* /rə'kɔl/ **1.** to recollect or remember. **2.** to call back; summon to return. –*n.* /'rikɔl/ **3.** the act of recalling. **4.** memory; recollection.

recant *v.* to withdraw or disavow (a statement, etc.), especially formally.

The more usual expression is **take back**.

recap *v.* (**-capped, -capping**) to repeat the main points of a discussion, lesson, etc.: *To recap, the most important thing is to look after our customers.*

This is short for **recapitulate**.

recapitulate *v.* to review (statements or matters) by way of an orderly summary.

recede *v.* **1.** to go or move back, to or towards a more distant point. **2.** to slope backwards.

receipt /rə'sit/ *n.* **1.** a written acknowledgement of having received money, goods, etc. **2.** (*pl.*) the amount or quantity received. **3.** the state of being received.

receive *v.* **1.** to take (something) into one's possession. **2.** to take into the mind. **3.** to meet with; experience. **4.** to greet (guests, etc.) upon arriving. **5.** to accept as authoritative, valid, true, or approved. **6.** *Radio* to convert incoming electromagnetic waves into the original signal. –**receival,** *n.*

receiver *n.* **1.** a device or apparatus which receives electrical signals, and renders them perceptible to the senses. **2.** *Commerce* a person appointed to receive money due. **3.** someone who receives stolen goods.

recent *adj.* lately happening, done, made, etc.

receptacle *n.* that which serves to receive or hold something.

reception *n.* **1.** the act of receiving. **2.** a manner of being received. **3.** a function where people are formally received. **4.** a place, office, desk, or the like where callers are received.

receptionist *n.* a person employed to receive and direct callers, as in an office or hotel.

receptive *adj.* able or quick to receive ideas, etc.

recess *n.* /rə'sɛs, 'risɛs/ **1.** a part or space that is set back or recedes. **2.** withdrawal or cessation for a time from the usual occupation, work, or activity. –*v.* /rə'sɛs/ **3.** to place or set in a recess. **4.** to make a recess or recesses in. **5.** to take a recess.

recession *n.* **1.** a receding part of a wall, etc. **2.** a period of adverse economic circumstances.

recessive *adj.* tending to recede; receding.

recipe *n.* any formula, especially one for preparing a dish in cookery.

recipient *n.* someone or something that receives something given or offered; a favour, etc.

reciprocate *v.* **1.** to give, feel, etc., (something) in return. **2.** to give and receive reciprocally; interchange. –**reciprocity,** *n.* –**reciprocal,** *adj.*

recite *v.* **1.** to repeat the words of, (a poem, etc.) as from memory, especially in a formal manner. –**recital,** *n.*

reckless *adj.* utterly careless of the consequences of action.

reckon *v.* **1.** to count, compute, or make a calculation (as to number or amount). **2.** to esteem or consider (as stated). **3.** *Informal* to think or suppose. **4.** to settle accounts. **5.** to count or rely (*on*), as in expectation.

reclaim v. to bring (waste, or marshy land) into a usable condition. **–reclamation,** n.

recline v. to (cause to) lean or lie back (on something).

recluse n. a person who lives in seclusion. **–reclusiveness,** n.

recognise v. **1.** to identify from knowledge of appearance or character. **2.** to perceive as existing or true. **3.** to acknowledge or treat as valid. Also, **recognize.** **–recognition,** n.

recoil v. /rə'kɔɪl/ **1.** to draw back, as in alarm, disgust, etc. **2.** to spring or fly back, as from force of impact, as a firearm. *–n.* /rə'kɔɪl, 'rikɔɪl/ **3.** the act of recoiling.

recollect v. to recall to mind; remember.

recommend v. to present as worthy of confidence, acceptance, use, etc. **–recommendation,** n.

recompense v. **(-pensed, -pensing)** **1.** to make compensation to or reward or repay (a person, etc.). *–n.* **2.** compensation made, as for loss, injury, or wrong.

> For def. 1, the more usual words are **compensate** or **reward**.

reconcile v. to bring into agreement; make compatible or consistent. **–reconciliation,** n.

reconnoitre /rɛkə'nɔɪtə/ v. to examine (a region, etc.) for engineering, geological, or other purposes. **–reconnaissance,** n.

record v. /rə'kɔd/ **1.** to set down or register (something) in some permanent form. *–n.* /'rɛkɔd/ **2.** an account, especially written, preserving the memory or knowledge of facts or events. **3.** information or knowledge so preserved. **4.** a black vinyl disc on which music has been recorded. **5.** the highest or best recorded rate, amount, degree, etc. attained. *–adj.* /'rɛkɔd/ **6.** best in performance in a sport or any other activity: *in record time. –phr.* **7. off the record,** unofficially; without intending to be quoted.

recorder n. **1.** a recording or registering apparatus or device. **2.** a soft-toned flute played in vertical position.

recording n. a record of music, speech, or the like made on magnetic tape or a suitable medium for reproduction; a compact disc, record or tape.

recount v. **1.** to relate or narrate. *–n.* **2.** a written or spoken text type or form which typically records events in the order in which they happened.

recoup /rə'kup/ v. **1.** to obtain an equivalent for (money lost, time spent, etc.): *to recoup one's losses.* **2.** to regain or recover: *to recoup one's dignity.*

recourse n. **1.** application to a person or thing for help or protection. **2.** *Commerce* the right to apply to a person for compensation in money.

recover v. **1.** to get again, or regain (something lost or taken away). **2.** to make up for or make good (loss, damage, etc., to oneself). **3.** to regain the strength, composure, balance, etc., of (oneself). **4.** to regain a former (and better) state or condition. **–recovery,** n.

recreation n. (an agreeable pastime, exercise, etc., affording) refreshment and relaxation. **–recreational,** adj.

recriminate v. to accuse in return. **–recrimination,** n.

recruit n. **1.** a newly secured member of any body or class. *–v.* **2.** to enlist (people) for service in the armed forces.

rectangle n. a parallelogram with all its angles right angles. **–rectangular,** adj.

> Note that, when a shape is described as a **rectangle**, it is usually longer than it is wide. However, strictly speaking, a square is also a rectangle.

rectify v. **(-fied, -fying)** to set right; remedy; correct.

> The more usual expression is **put right**.

rectitude n. rightness of principle or practice.

rector n. *Anglican Church* a cleric who has the charge of a parish.

rectum n. (*pl.* **-tums** *or* **-ta**) the comparatively straight terminal section of the intestine, ending in the anus.

recumbent adj. lying down; reclining; leaning.

recuperate v. 1. to recover from sickness, exhaustion, etc. 2. to recover from financial loss. –**recuperation**, n.

For def. 1, the more usual expression is **get better**.

recur v. (**-curred**, **-curring**) to occur again, as an event, experience, etc. –**recurrent**, adj.

recycle v. 1. to treat (waste materials) so that new products can be manufactured from them. 2. to prepare (something) for a second use. –**recyclable**, adj.

red adj. (**redder**, **reddest**) 1. of a hue beyond orange in the spectrum. 2. (of wines) darkish red in colour (opposed to *white*). 3. *Informal* having radical left-wing political views. –n. 4. any of the hues adjacent to orange in the spectrum, such as scarlet, vermilion, cherry. –*phr.* 5. **the red**, loss or deficit, as recorded in red ink in accounting practice.

red-back n. a small, venomous, Aust. spider.

red blood cell n. → erythrocyte.

red-blooded adj. vigorous; virile.

redeem v. 1. to buy or pay off. 2. to recover (something pledged or mortgaged) by payment etc. 3. to make amends for. 4. to obtain the release or restoration of, as from captivity, by paying a ransom. –**redemption**, n.

red-handed adj. in the very act of a crime or other deed: *to catch the thief red-handed.*

Note that this adjective always follows the noun it describes.

red herring n. something to divert attention; a false clue.

redolent adj. 1. having a pleasant smell; fragrant. 2. odorous or smelling (*of*). 3. suggestive; reminiscent (*of*).

redoubtable adj. that is to be feared; formidable.

redound v. to come back or recoil, as upon a person.

redress n. 1. the setting right of what is wrong. 2. compensation for wrong or injury. –v. 3. to set right; remedy (wrongs, injuries, etc.). 4. to adjust evenly again, as a balance.

reduce v. 1. to bring down to a smaller extent, size, amount, etc. 2. to lower in degree, intensity, etc. 3. to lower in price. 4. to bring to a certain state, condition, etc. 5. to bring under control or authority; subdue. 6. to thin (paints, etc.) with oil or turpentine. 7. to become reduced. –**reduction**, n.

redundant adj. 1. being in excess. 2. relating to an employee who is no longer needed by the employer.

reed n. 1. the straight stalk of any of various tall grasses. 2. a small piece of reed, fitted into the mouthpiece of some instruments, such as clarinets, etc.

Don't confuse this with **read**, which is to look at writing and understand it.

reef n. a narrow ridge of rocks, sand, coral, etc., at or near the surface of water.

reefer n. *Informal* a marijuana cigarette.

reef knot n. a kind of flat knot.

reek n. 1. a strong, unpleasant smell. –v. 2. to smell strongly of something.

reel[1] n. 1. a cylinder, frame, etc., turning on an axis, on which to wind something. –v. 2. to draw with a reel, or by winding. –*phr.* 3. **reel off**, to say, write, or produce in an easy, continuous way.

Don't confuse this with **real**, which means true or actual.

reel[2] v. to sway or rock from dizziness, intoxication, or under a blow, shock, etc.; stagger.

reel[3] n. a lively dance popular in Scotland.

refectory n. (pl. **-ries**) a dining hall in an institution.

refer v. (**-ferred, -ferring**) **1.** to direct for information or requirements. **2.** to hand over or submit for information, consideration, decision, etc. **3.** to have relation; relate; apply. **4.** to direct a remark or mention. –**referral**, n.

referee n. **1.** someone to whom something is referred, especially for decision or settlement; arbitrator; umpire. –v. (**-reed, -reeing**) **2.** to preside over as referee; act as referee in.

reference n. **1.** the act or fact of referring. **2.** a mention; allusion. **3.** a direction, as to some source of information. **4.** use or recourse for purposes of information. **5.** (a person to whom one refers for) testimony as to one's character, abilities, etc. **6.** relation, regard, or respect.

referendum n. (pl. **-dums** or **-da**) the procedure of referring measures proposed or passed by a legislative body to the vote of the electorate for approval or rejection.

refine v. **1.** to bring to a fine or a pure state; free from impurities. **2.** to make or become more elegant or cultured.

reflect v. **1.** to cast back (light, heat, sound, etc.). **2.** to give back or show: *The results reflect her hard work.* **3.** to be turned, reflected, or cast back. **4.** to serve or tend to bring reproach or discredit. **5.** to think, ponder, or meditate. –**reflection**, n. –**reflective**, adj.

reflector n. a body, surface, or device which reflects light, heat, sound, etc.

reflex adj. **1.** occurring in reaction; responsive. **2.** bent or turned back. –n. **3.** Physiol. a reflex action or movement.

reflexive adj. Gram. **1.** (of a verb) having identical subject and object, as *shave* in He shaved himself. **2.** (of a pronoun) indicating identity of object with subject, as *himself* in the example above.

reform n. **1.** the improvement or amendment of what is wrong, corrupt, etc. –v. **2.** to improve by alteration, substitution, abolition, etc. **3.** to (cause a person to) abandon wrong or evil ways.

reformatory n. (pl. **-ries**) a penal institution for the reformation of young offenders. Also, **reform school**.

refraction n. Physics the change of direction of a ray of light, heat, or the like, in passing obliquely from one medium into another.

refractory adj. stubborn; unmanageable.

refrain[1] v. to keep oneself back (from).

refrain[2] n. a phrase or verse recurring at intervals in a song or poem; chorus.

refresh v. **1.** to reinvigorate or be revived by rest, food, etc. **2.** to stimulate (the memory). **3.** Computers to update the image on (a computer screen).

refreshment n. that which refreshes, especially food or drink.

refrigerate v. to make or keep cold or cool. –**refrigeration**, n.

refrigerator n. a cabinet, compartment or room in which food, drink, etc., is kept cool, now usually by means of mechanical refrigeration. Also, **fridge**.

refuge n. shelter or protection from danger, trouble, etc.

refugee n. someone who flees for refuge or safety, especially to a foreign country.

refund v. /rəˈfʌnd/ **1.** to give back or restore (especially money); repay. **2.** to make repayment to; reimburse. –n. /ˈriːfʌnd/ **3.** a repayment.

refurbish v. to renovate.

refuse[1] /rəˈfjuːz/ v. **1.** to decline to accept (something offered). **2.** to deny (a request, demand, etc.). **3.** to express a determination not (to do something). –**refusal**, n.

refuse[2] /ˈrɛfjuːs/ n. something discarded as worthless; rubbish.

refute v. to prove to be false.

Some people use this word to mean reject or deny, rather than *prove* to be wrong. This can cause confusion – if someone says that they **refute** an argument, it may not be clear whether they have proven that the argument is false or that they are merely denying it.

regal *adj.* **1.** of or relating to a king; royal. **2.** stately; splendid. **3.** tall, dignified, and elegant.

regale *v.* to entertain agreeably; delight.

regard *v.* **1.** to look upon or think of with a particular feeling. **2.** to have or show respect or concern for. **3.** to take into account; consider. **4.** to look at; pay attention (to). **5.** to relate to; concern. *–n.* **6.** reference; relation. **7.** a point or particular: *satisfactory in this regard.* **8.** thought; attention; concern. **9.** look; gaze. **10.** respect; deference. **11.** kindly feeling; liking. **12.** (*pl.*) sentiments of esteem or affection.

regatta *n.* a boat race.

regenerate *v.* **1.** to re-create or make over or reform especially in a better form or condition. **2.** to come into existence or be formed again. *–***regeneration**, *n.*

regent *n.* someone who exercises the ruling power in a kingdom during the minority, absence, or disability of the sovereign. *–***regency**, *n.*

reggae /'regei/ *n.* a type of modern music, originating in the West Indies, with a strong bass part and guitar chords played on the unaccented beat.

regime /rei'ʒiːm/ *n.* a mode or system of rule or government.

regimen *n.* any prevailing system, as a regulated course of diet, exercise, etc.

regiment *n.* /'redʒəmənt/ **1.** *Mil.* a unit of ground forces. *–v.* /'redʒəment/ **2.** to form into an organised body or group. *–***regimentation**, *n.* *–***regimental**, *adj.*

region *n.* **1.** any more or less extensive, continuous portion of a surface or space. **2.** a district without respect to boundaries or extent.

register *n.* **1.** a record of acts, occurrences, attendances, etc. **2.** a mechanical device by which certain data are automatically recorded, as a cash register. *–v.* **3.** to enter or have entered formally in a register. **4.** to indicate or show, as on a scale. **5.** to show (surprise, joy, anger, etc.). **6.** to enter one's name in an electoral or other register; enrol. **7.** *Informal* to make an impression. *–***registrant**, *n.* *–***registration**, *n.*

registered nurse *n.* a nurse who holds a degree in nursing from a university, or who qualified under the former system of intensive hospital training. *Abbrev.*: RN Compare **enrolled nurse**.

registrar *n.* someone who keeps official records.

registry *n.* (*pl.* **-ries**) a place where a register is kept.

regress *v.* to move backwards, especially to an earlier (undesirable) state. *–***regression**, *n.* *–***regressive**, *adj.*

regret *v.* (**-gretted**, **-gretting**) **1.** to feel sorry about (anything disappointing, unpleasant, etc.). **2.** to think of with a sense of loss. *–n.* **3.** a sense of loss, disappointment, etc. **4.** the feeling of being sorry for some fault, act, omission, etc., of one's own.

regrowth *n.* **1.** a growing again: *this forest is undergoing regrowth.* **2.** new hair growth, especially that which contrasts in colour with previously dyed hair.

regular *adj.* **1.** usual; normal; customary. **2.** conforming in form or arrangement; symmetrical. **3.** adhering to rule or procedure. **4.** orderly. **5.** *Informal* complete; thorough. *–n.* **6.** *Informal* a regular customer.

regulate *v.* **1.** to control or direct by rule, principle, method, etc. **2.** to adjust to some standard or requirement. *–***regulation**, *n.*

regurgitate *v.* **1.** to bring (swallowed food) back up; vomit. **2.** to repeat (information read or heard), especially without understanding it.

For def. 1, the more usual expression is **bring up**.

rehabilitate v. to restore to a good condition. –**rehabilitation**, n.

rehearse v. to perform in private by way of practice (a play, part, etc.). –**rehearsal**, n.

rehydrate v. **1.** to replenish the fluid in dehydrated plants. **2.** to replenish the bodily fluids. **3.** to reconstitute dried food, etc., by adding or soaking in water.

reign /reɪn/ n. **1.** the period or term of ruling, as of a sovereign. –v. **2.** to possess or exercise sovereign power or authority.

Don't confuse this with **rain** or **rein**. **Rain** is water that falls from the sky in drops. A **rein** is a strap which a rider uses to direct a horse.

reimburse v. to make repayment to for expense or loss incurred.

The more usual expression is **pay back**.

rein /reɪn/ n. **1.** a long, narrow strap for guiding a horse. **2.** any means of curbing, controlling, or directing; a check; restraint. –v. **3.** to curb; restrain; control.

Don't confuse this with **rain** or **reign**. **Rain** is water that falls from the sky in drops. The **reign** of a king or queen is how long they rule.

reincarnation n. rebirth of the soul in a new body after death.

reindeer n. (pl. **-deer** or **-deers**) a large deer.

reinforce v. **1.** to strengthen; make more forcible or effective. **2.** to augment; increase.

reinstate v. to put back or establish again, as in a former position or state.

reinvent v. **1.** to produce (a device, solution, etc.), believing it to be original, when it has in fact been invented before. –phr. **2. reinvent oneself**, to create a new character, appearance, role, etc., for oneself. **3. reinvent the wheel**, to attempt to work out again a method, solution,

procedure, etc., which is already known and widely adopted.

reiterate v. to repeat; say or do again.

reject v. /rəˈdʒɛkt/ **1.** to refuse to have, take, recognise, etc. **2.** to refuse to accept (someone) as a friend, member of a group, etc. **3.** to cast out or off. –n. /ˈrɪdʒɛkt/ **4.** something rejected, as an imperfect article. **5.** Informal (derog.) a person despised by a particular group.

rejoice v. to be glad; take delight (in).

rejoinder n. an answer to a reply; response.

rejuvenate v. to make young again.

relapse v. (**-lapsed, -lapsing**) **1.** to fall or slip back into a former state, practice, etc. –n. **2.** the act of relapsing.

relate v. **1.** to tell. **2.** to bring into association, connection, or have some relation (to). **3.** to have reference (to).

relation n. **1.** an existing connection; a particular way of being related. **2.** connection between persons by blood or marriage. **3.** a relative. **4.** reference; regard; respect.

relationship n. **1.** a particular connection. **2.** a connection between people by blood or marriage. **3.** an emotional connection between people, sometimes involving sexual relations.

relative n. **1.** someone who is connected with another or others by blood or marriage. **2.** something having, or standing in, some relation to something else (as opposed to absolute). –adj. **3.** considered in relation to something else. **4.** having relation or connection. **5.** correspondent; proportionate. **6.** Gram. **a.** relating to a clause which performs the function of an adjective, such as 'who was old' in the following sentence The woman, who was old, struggled up the hill. **b.** relating to one of the pronouns who, whom, whose, which or that, when they are used at the start of a relative clause. –**relativity**, n.

relax v. **1.** to make or become lax, or less tense, rigid, or firm. **2.** to diminish the force of. **3.** to become less strict or severe. **4.** to slacken in effort, application, etc.

relay n. /ˈriːleɪ/ **1.** a set of persons relieving others or taking turns; a shift. **2.** Also, **relay race** a race between 2 or more teams, each member running, swimming, etc., one of the lengths of the distance. **3.** an electrical device for operating the controls of a larger piece of equipment. –v. /rəˈleɪ, ˈriːleɪ/ **4.** to carry forward by or as by relays: *to relay a message.*

release v. **1.** to free from restraint as confinement, bondage, obligation, pain, etc. **2.** to allow to become known, be issued or exhibited. –n. **3.** (a device for effecting) liberation from anything that restrains or fastens. **4.** the releasing of something for public exhibition or sale. **5.** the article so released.

relegate v. to send or consign to some obscure position, place, or condition. –**relegation**, n.

relent v. to soften in feeling, temper, or determination.

relevant adj. bearing upon the matter in hand; to the purpose; pertinent.

reliable adj. that may be relied on; trustworthy.

reliant adj. confident; trustful; dependent. –**reliance**, n.

relic n. **1.** a surviving memorial of something of historical interest. **2.** a surviving trace of something.

relief n. **1.** (something affording) deliverance or ease through the removal of pain, distress, oppression, monotony, etc. **2.** the person or persons relieving another or others. **3.** prominence, distinctness, or vividness due to contrast. **4.** projection of a figure from its background.

relieve v. **1.** to ease or free from (pain, distress, anxiety, need, etc.). **2.** to make less tedious, unpleasant, or monotonous. **3.** to bring into relief or prominence. **4.** to release (one on duty) by providing a substitute. **5.** to take the place of (an absent

worker). –phr. **6. relieve oneself**, to empty the bowels or bladder.

religion n. belief in a controlling superhuman power entitled to obedience, reverence, and worship. –**religious**, adj.

relinquish v. to renounce or surrender (a possession, right, etc.).

The more usual expression is **let go of**.

relish n. **1.** pleasurable appreciation or enjoyment. **2.** something appetising or savoury added to a meal, as chutney. **3.** a taste or flavour. –v. **4.** to take pleasure in; like; enjoy.

reluctant adj. unwilling; disinclined.

rely v. (**-lied, -lying**) to put trust in; depend confidently (on or upon).

remain v. **1.** to continue in the same state or place; continue to be (as specified). **2.** to be left after the removal, departure, loss, etc., of another or others. –n. (pl.) **3.** that which remains or is left; a remnant. **4.** what remains of a person after death; dead body.

remainder n. **1.** that which remains or is left. –v. **2.** to dispose of or sell at reduced price, as unsold copies of a book.

remand v. **1.** to send back, remit, or consign again. –n. **2.** the state of being remanded.

remark v. **1.** to say (something) casually, as in making a comment (on or upon). **2.** to note; perceive. –n. **3.** a casual or brief expression of thought or opinion.

remarkable adj. worthy of remark or notice.

remediate /rəˈmidiət/ v. (**-mediated, -mediating**) to correct (a fault or impairment). –**remediation**, n.

remedy n. (pl. **-dies**) **1.** something that corrects or removes an evil or illness of any kind. –v. (**-died, -dying**) **2.** to cure or heal. **3.** to put right, or restore to the natural or proper condition. –**remedial**, adj.

remember v. **1.** to recall to the mind by an act or effort of memory. **2.** to retain in the memory; bear in mind. **3.** to mention to another as sending kindly greetings. **4.** to possess or exercise the faculty of memory. –**remembrance**, n.

remind v. to cause to remember. –**re-minder**, n.

reminiscence n. the act or process of remembering one's past. –**reminiscent**, adj. –**reminisce**, v.

remiss adj. characterised by negligence or carelessness.

remit v. (-mitted, -mitting) **1.** to send (money, etc.) to a person or place. **2.** to refrain from exacting, as a payment or service. **3.** to slacken; abate. **4.** to put back into a previous position or condition. **5.** to slacken; abate. –**remission**, n.

remittance n. the remitting of money, etc., to a recipient at a distance. n. money etc., so sent.

remnant n. a part, quantity, or number (usually small) remaining.

remonstrance n. a protest. –**remon-strate**, v.

remorse n. deep and painful regret for wrongdoing; compunction.

The more usual word is **sorrow**.

remote adj. **1.** distant in time or space. **2.** out-of-the-way; secluded. **3.** slight or faint. **4.** abstracted; cold and aloof.

remote control n. **1.** the control of a system by means of electrical, radio, or other signals from a point at a distance from the system. **2.** a usually handheld device for the control of domestic appliances such as televisions, VCRs, air conditioners, etc.

remove v. (-moved, -moving) **1.** to move from a place or position; take away; take off. **2.** to take, withdraw, or separate (from). **3.** to move from one place to another, especially to another locality or residence. n. **4.** the act of removing. **5.** a step or degree, as in a graded scale. –**removal**, n.

removed adj. remote; separate; distinct from.

remunerate v. to pay, recompense, or reward for work, trouble, etc. –**remunera-tion**, n. –**remunerative**, adj.

renal adj. of or relating to the kidneys.

rend v. (**rent**, **rending**) to tear apart, split, or divide.

render v. **1.** to make, or cause, to be or become. **2.** to do; perform. **3.** to present for consideration, approval, payment, action, etc., as an account. **4.** to give in return, as reward or retaliation. **5.** to cover (brickwork, stone etc.), with plaster. –**rendition**, n.

rendezvous /ˈrɒndɪvuː, rɒndeˈvuː/ n. an appointment to meet at a fixed place and time.

renegade n. someone who deserts a party or cause for another.

renege /rəˈneɡ, -ˈnɪɡ/ v. Informal to go back on one's word.

The more usual expression is **go back on**.

renew v. **1.** to begin or take up again (an acquaintance, conversation etc.). **2.** to make effective for an additional period, as a lease etc. **3.** to restore or replenish. –**renewal**, n.

renewable resource n. a natural resource which is not finite but can be renewed, such as the sun, wind, or biomass. Compare **non-renewable resource**.

renounce v. **1.** to give up voluntarily. **2.** to repudiate; disown.

renovate v. **1.** to make new or as if new again; restore to good condition; repair. **2.** to reinvigorate; refresh; revive. –**reno-vation**, n. –**renovator**, n.

renown n. widespread and high repute; fame. –**renowned**, adj.

rent[1] n. **1.** a payment made periodically by a tenant to an owner or landlord for the use of land or building. –v. **2.** Also, **rent out**. to grant the possession and use of (property) in return for regular payments. **3.** to take and hold (property) in return for regular payments.

Note that the verb **rent** can be used in two ways. Someone can rent an apartment *to* you and charge you money for it, or you can rent an apartment *from* someone and pay them for it. The expression *to rent an apartment* is therefore ambiguous, but its context will normally make the meaning clear.

rent² *n.* **1.** an opening made by rending or tearing; slit. *–v.* **2.** past tense and past participle of **rend.**

rental *n.* **1.** an amount received or paid as rent. *–adj.* **2.** available for rent.

renunciation *n.* the formal abandoning of a right, title, etc.

rep *n. Informal* **1.** a travelling salesperson. **2.** someone who is selected to represent their area in sport. **3.** a union representative.

repair¹ *v.* **1.** to restore to a good or sound condition; mend. *–n.* **2.** the act, process, or work of repairing. **3.** the good condition resulting from repairing. *–***reparable,** *adj.*

repair² *v.* to take oneself off or go, as to a place.

reparation *n.* the making of amends for wrong or injury done.

repartee *n.* skill in making witty replies.

repast *n.* a meal.

repatriate *v.* to bring or send back (a person) to their own country. *–***repatriation,** *n.*

repay *v.* **(-paid, -paying) 1.** to pay back or refund (money, etc.). **2.** to make return for.

repeal *v.* **1.** to revoke or withdraw formally or officially. *–n.* **2.** the act of repealing; revocation; abrogation.

repeat *v.* **1.** to do, make or say again (something already done, made or said by oneself or another). *–n.* **2.** something repeated. **3.** a duplicate or reproduction of something.

repel *v.* **(-pelled, -pelling) 1.** to drive or force back (an assailant, invader, etc.).

2. to keep off or out; fail to mix with. **3.** to excite feelings of distaste or aversion in. *–***repellent,** *adj., n.*

repent *v.* to regret or feel sorry. *–***repentance,** *n.*

repercussion *n.* an after-effect, often an indirect result, of some event or action.

repertoire /ˈrɛpətwɑː/ *n.* a list of plays, operas, parts, pieces, etc., which a company, actor, singer, etc., is prepared to perform.

repertory *n.* **(pl. -ries)** a theatrical company.

repetition *n.* **1.** the act of repeating. **2.** a repeated action, performance, etc. *–***repetitious, repetitive,** *adj.*

replace *v.* **1.** to take the place of: *she replaced him as manager.* **2.** to renew or exchange, especially something damaged: *to replace worn tyres.* **3.** to restore to a former or the proper place: *to replace the toys in the cupboard.* *–***replacement,** *n.*

Compare **replace** with **substitute.** Both words involve putting something or someone in a position which was previously occupied by another. However, the people or things involved need to be placed in a different order for each of these words. The following sentences mean the same thing: *They replaced Nick with Helen as captain of the team; They substituted Helen for Nick as captain of the team.* Note also that **replace** is used with *with* and **substitute** is used with *for.*

replay *n.* **1.** (in sport) a match, contest, etc. which is played again because of some difficulty or disagreement. **2.** (in television coverage of sport) the playing again of some highlight of a game, often immediately after it has happened. *–v.* **3.** to repeat (a sporting event, match, etc. or a sequence from it) on radio or television.

replenish *v.* to bring back to a state of fullness or completeness.

replete *adj.* gorged with food and drink.

replica n. an exact copy or reproduction.

reply v. (**-plied, -plying**) **1.** to make answer in words or writing. **2.** to respond by some action, performance, etc. **3.** to return as an answer: *He replied that he would come today.* –n. (pl. **-plies**) **4.** an answer or response.

report n. **1.** an account brought back or presented. **2.** a statement generally circulated; rumour. **3.** repute; reputation. **4.** a loud noise, as from an explosion. –v. **5.** to relate or tell (what has been learned by observation or investigation). **6.** to give or render a formal account or statement (of). **7.** to lay a charge against (a person), as to a superior. **8.** to present oneself duly, as at a place.

reporter n. **1.** someone employed to gather and report news. **2.** someone who prepares official reports, as of legal or legislative proceedings.

repose n. **1.** the state of resting; sleep. **2.** dignified calmness, as of manner or demeanour. –v. (**-posed, -posing**) **3.** to lie at rest; take rest.

repository n. (pl. **-ries**) a place where things are deposited, stored, or offered for sale.

repossess v. **1.** to possess again; regain possession of. **2.** to put again in possession of something: *They repossessed him of his property.*

reprehensible adj. deserving to be censured or reproved.

The more usual words are **terrible** and **shocking**.

represent v. **1.** to serve to express, designate, stand for, or denote, as a word or symbol. **2.** to speak and act for by delegated authority. **3.** to present in words; set forth; describe. **4.** to serve as an example or specimen of; exemplify. **5.** to be the equivalent of.

representative adj. **1.** serving to represent; typical. **2.** representing a constituency or community or the people generally in legislation or government. **3.** characterised by, founded on, or relating to representation of the people in government. –n **4.** someone who represents another or others; an agent or deputy. **2.** a commercial traveller; a travelling salesperson.

repress v. to keep under control or suppress.

reprieve v. **1.** to relieve temporarily from any punishment or evil. –n. **2.** respite from impending punishment, especially from execution of a sentence of death.

reprimand n. **1.** a severe reproof, especially a formal one by a person in authority. –v. **2.** to reprove severely, especially in a formal way.

reprisal n. (an act of) retaliation.

reproach v. **1.** to reprove severely. –n. **2.** censure or reproof: *beyond reproach full of reproach.*

reprobate n. **1.** an unprincipled, or reprehensible person. –adj. **2.** morally depraved; unprincipled; bad.

reproduce v. **1.** to make a copy, representation, or close imitation of. **2.** to produce (its kind), as an animal or plant; propagate. **3.** to produce, form, make, again or anew in any manner. **4.** to turn out (well, etc.) when copied. –**reproducible**, adj. –**reproducer**, n. –**reproduction**, n. –**reproductive**, adj. –**reproductively**, adv.

reproof n. an expression of censure or rebuke.

The more usual word is **criticism**.

reprove v. to address words of disapproval to (a person, etc.). –**reproval**, n.

The more usual word is **scold**.

reptile n. any of various cold-blooded creeping or crawling animals, as lizards, snakes, etc.

republic n. a nation in which the head of the state is a president, usually either elected or nominated, not a hereditary monarch. –**republican**, n., adj.

repudiate v. **1.** to reject as having no authority or binding force: *to repudiate a claim.* **2.** to refuse to acknowledge and pay, as a debt.

repugnant adj. distasteful or objectionable. –**repugnance**, n.

The more usual word is **disgusting**.

repulse v. **1.** to drive back or repel (an attack, assailant, etc.). **2.** to reject or refuse, especially rudely (an offer, etc.). **3.** to disgust: *the thought of it repulsed him.*

For def. 1, the more usual expression is **drive back**; for def. 2, **reject**. Note that some people think that def. 3 is wrong and that only the word **repel** can have this meaning. However, it is quite common to use **repulse** in this way, and most people consider it perfectly acceptable.

repulsive adj. causing strong dislike. –**repulsion**, n.

reputable /'rɛpjətəbəl/ adj. held in good repute; honourable.

reputation n. the estimation in which a person or thing is held.

repute n. estimation in the view of others.

The more usual word is **reputation**.

request n. **1.** the act of asking for something. –v. **2.** to ask for, especially politely or formally. **3.** to make request to, (a person, etc.) to do something.

requiem n. any musical service, or funeral hymn, for the repose of the dead.

require v. **1.** to have need of; need. **2.** to ask for authoritatively or imperatively; demand. **3.** to place under an obligation or necessity.

requisition n. **1.** an authoritative or official demand. **2.** the state of being required for use or called into service. –v. **3.** to require or take for use; press into service.

rescind /rə'sɪnd/ v. to invalidate or repeal (an act, measure, etc.) by a later action or a higher authority. –**rescission**, n.

rescue v. (**-cued, -cuing**) **1.** to free or deliver from confinement, violence, danger, or evil. –n. **2.** the act of rescuing.

research n. **1.** diligent and systematic inquiry or investigation into a subject. –v. **2.** to make researches; investigate carefully. –adj. **3.** of or relating to research.

resemble v. to be like or similar to. –**resemblance**, n.

resent v. to feel or show a sense of injury or insult.

reservation n. **1.** the making of some exception or qualification. **2.** → **reserve** (def. 6). **3.** the allotting or the securing of accommodation at a hotel, on a train or boat, etc.

reserve v. **1.** to keep back or save for future use, disposal, etc. **2.** to secure or book in advance, as accommodation, theatre seats, etc. **3.** *Law* to delay handing down (a judgement or decision). –n. **4.** something reserved, as for some purpose or contingency. **5.** a tract of public land set apart for a special purpose, as a nature reserve. **6.** Also, **reservation**. an area of land set aside by a government for indigenous people, to allow them to pursue a traditional lifestyle or to concentrate them under supervision and control. **7.** → **army reserve**. –adj. **8.** kept in reserve; forming a reserve.

Don't confuse this with **reverse**, which is to make something go backwards.

reserve bank n. the national banking organisation of a country.

reserved adj. **1.** kept in reserve. **2.** reticent or silent in disposition, manner, etc.

reserve price n. the lowest price at which a person is willing that their property shall be sold at auction. Also, **reserve**.

reservoir /ˈrɛzəvwa, ˈrɛzəvɔ/ n. a natural or artificial place where water is collected and stored.

reshuffle v. to make a new allocation of jobs, especially within a government or cabinet.

reside v. **1.** to dwell, especially for a considerable time: *We reside in Australia.* **2.** to rest or be vested, as powers, rights, etc. –**resident**, adj., n.

For def. 1, the more usual word is **live**.

residence n. **1.** the place, especially the house, in which one resides. **2.** a large house. **3.** the time during which one resides in a place. –**residential**, adj.

residue n. that which remains after a part is removed; remainder. –**residual**, adj.

resign v. **1.** to give up formally (an office, position, etc.). **2.** to submit (oneself, one's mind, etc.); yield. –**resignation** /rɛzɪɡˈneɪʃən/, n.

resilient adj. **1.** returning to the original form after being bent, compressed, or stretched. **2.** readily recovering, as from sickness, reverses, etc.

resin n. any of a class of organic substances used especially in the making of varnishes and plastics.

resist v. to act in opposition; oppose; withstand.

resistance n. **1.** the opposition offered by one thing, force, etc., to another. **2.** *Elect.* the property of a device which opposes the flow of an electric current.

resolute adj. firmly resolved or determined.

resolution n. **1.** a resolve or determination. **2.** the mental state or quality of being resolute. **3.** the act or process of resolving or separating into constituent parts.

resolve v. **1.** to fix or settle on by deliberate choice and will; determine (to do something). **2.** to separate into constituent or elementary parts. **3.** to deal with (a question, etc.) conclusively. **4.** to come to

a determination; make up one's mind. **5.** to break up or disintegrate. –n. **6.** a resolution or determination made. **7.** determination; firmness of purpose.

resonance n. the state or quality of resounding or re-echoing; reverberation. –**resonate**, v. –**resonant**, adj.

resort v. **1.** to have recourse for use, service, or help. –n. **2.** a place frequented by the public. **3.** a resorting to some person or thing for aid, service, etc. **4.** a person or thing resorted to for aid, service, etc.

resound v. **1.** to re-echo (a sound) or ring with sound. **2.** to be echoed, or ring, as sounds. **3.** to proclaim loudly (praises, etc.).

resource n. **1.** a source of supply, support, or aid. **2.** (pl.) monetary or other wealth, especially of a country.

resourceful adj. skilful in dealing with situations, meeting difficulties, etc.

respect n. **1.** esteem or deferential regard felt or shown. **2.** (pl.) deferential or friendly compliments. **3.** a particular, detail, or point: *in some respect; in many respects.* –v. **4.** to hold in esteem or honour. **5.** to treat with consideration; refrain from interfering with. –phr. **6.** in respect of (or to) or with respect to, in relation or reference to.

Note that def. 1 is often followed by *for*: *I have enormous respect for volunteer firefighters.*

respectable adj. **1.** worthy of respect or esteem. **2.** having socially accepted standards of moral behaviour. **3.** of presentable appearance.

Don't confuse this with **respectful**.

respectful adj. having or showing respect for someone or something. –**respectfully**, adv.

Don't confuse this with **respectable**.

respective adj. relating individually or severally to each of a number of persons, things, etc. –**respectively**, adv.

respiration *n.* the inhalation and exhalation of air; breathing.

respite /'respɒt, 'respaɪt/ *n.* a cessation for a time, especially of anything distressing.

The more usual word is **relief**.

resplendent *adj.* shining brilliantly; gleaming; splendid.

respond *v.* to answer; give a reply.

respondent *n. Law* a defendant, especially in divorce cases.

response *n.* an answer or reply in words, action, etc.

responsible *adj.* **1.** answerable or accountable (*to* or *for*) as for something within one's power. **2.** able to discharge obligations or pay debts. **3.** reliable in business or other dealings. **–responsibility,** *n.*

responsive *adj.* responding readily to influences, appeals, etc.

rest[1] *n.* **1.** refreshing ease or inactivity after exertion or labour. **2.** relief or freedom, especially from anything that wearies or disturbs. **3.** cessation or absence of motion. **4.** a pause or interval. **5.** a support, or supporting device. *–v.* **6.** to refresh oneself, as by sleeping or relaxing. **7.** to be quiet or still. **8.** to bring or come to rest, or stop. **9.** to remain without further action or notice. **10.** to lie, sit or lean (*in*, *on*, *against*, etc.). **11.** to base or be based or founded (*on* or *upon*). **12.** to be a responsibility, as something to be done: *This duty rests with you.*

rest[2] *n.* that which is left or remains.

restaurant *n.* an establishment where meals are served to customers.

restitution *n.* the restoration of property or rights previously surrendered or removed.

restive *adj.* impatient of control, restraint, or delay.

restless *adj.* **1.** characterised by or showing inability to remain at rest: *a restless mood.* **2.** unquiet or uneasy, as a person, the mind, heart, etc. never at rest, motionless, or still; never ceasing.

4. without rest; without restful sleep: *a restless night.* **5.** characterised by unceasing activity; averse to quiet or inaction, as persons. **–restlessly,** *adv.* **–restlessness,** *n.*

restore *v.* **1.** to bring back to a former, original, or normal condition. **2.** to put back to a former place, position, rank, etc. **3.** to give back. **–restoration,** *n.*

restrain *v.* to hold back from action; keep in check. **–restraint,** *n.*

restrict *v.* to confine or keep within limits, as of space, action, choice, quantity, etc. **–restriction,** *n.* **–restrictive,** *adj.*

result *n.* **1.** that which results; the outcome. *–v.* **2.** to arise, or proceed as a consequence. **3.** to end in a specified manner or thing.

resume /rə'zjum/ *v.* to take up or go on with (something) again after interruption.

Don't confuse **resume** with **résumé**.

résumé /'rezjəmeɪ/ *n.* a short written summary of one's education and previous employment; CV. **2.** a summary.

Don't confuse this with **resume**.

resurrect *v.* to raise from the dead; bring to life again.

resuscitate /rə'sʌsəteɪt/ *v.* to revive, especially from apparent death or from unconsciousness. **–resuscitation,** *n.*

retail *n.* **1.** the sale of (small quantities of) goods directly to the consumers. *–adj.* **2.** relating to or engaged in sale at retail. *–adv.* **3.** at a retail price or quantity. *–v.* **4.** to sell directly to the consumer; be sold at retail.

Compare this with **wholesale**, which is the sale of goods to shop owners rather than directly to the public.

retain *v.* **1.** to continue to use, practise, etc. **2.** to continue to hold or have. **3.** to keep in mind; remember. **–retention,** *n.*

retainer *n.* **1.** a fee paid to secure services, as of a barrister. **2.** a reduced rent paid during absence as an indication of future requirement.

retaliate v. 1. to return like for like, especially evil for evil. **–retaliation,** n.

retard v. 1. to delay or hinder the progress of. 2. to delay or limit (a person's intellectual or emotional development).

retch v. 1. to make the sound and spasmodic movement of being about to vomit. –n. 2. the act or an instance of retching.

retentive adj. 1. tending or serving to retain something. 2. having power or capacity to retain.

reticent adj. inclined to be silent **–reticence,** n.

reticulate v. to form a network. **–reticulation,** n.

retina n. (pl. **-nas** or **-nae** /-ni/) the innermost coat of the back part of the eyeball, serving to receive the image.

retinue n. a body of people in attendance upon an important personage.

retire v. 1. to withdraw, or go away to a place of abode, shelter, or seclusion. 2. to go to bed. 3. to withdraw from office, business, or active life. **–retirement,** n.

retort v. 1. to reply in retaliation. –n. 2. a severe, incisive, or witty reply.

retrace v. to trace back; go back over.

retract v. 1. to draw back or in. 2. to withdraw or revoke (a decree, promise, etc.). **–retractable,** adj.

retread v. (**-treaded, -treading**) 1. to recondition (a worn motor-vehicle tyre) by moulding a fresh tread on to it. –n. 2. a retreaded tyre.

retreat n. 1. the act of withdrawing, as into safety or privacy. 2. a place of refuge or seclusion. –v. 3. to withdraw or retire, especially for shelter or seclusion.

retrench v. 1. to dismiss, as part of an effort to economise. 2. to economise; reduce expenses.

retribution n. repayment according to merits or deserts, especially for evil.

The more usual word is **punishment**.

retrieve v. 1. to recover or regain. 2. to bring back to a former and better state. **–retrieval,** n.

retro adj. of or relating to fashion or popular music of previous times which has become fashionable again.

retroactive adj. operative with respect to past occurrences, as a statute; retrospective.

retrograde adj. returning to an earlier and inferior state.

The more usual word is **backward**.

retrospect n. contemplation of the past. **–retrospection,** n.

retrospective adj. 1. looking or directed backwards. 2. retroactive, as a statute. **–retrospectivity,** n.

retrovirus n. any of a family of viruses including HIV and a number of viruses suspected of causing cancer.

return v. 1. to go or come back, as to a former place, position, state, etc. 2. to put, bring, take, give, or send back. 3. to make reply; retort. 4. to yield (a profit, revenue, etc.). 5. to elect, as to a legislative body. 6. to turn back or in the reverse direction. –n. 7. the act or fact of returning. 8. response or reply. 9. (oft. pl.) a yield or profit. 10. the report or statement of financial condition. –adj. 11. sent, given, or done in return. 12. done or occurring again. –phr. 13. **by return,** by the next post.

reunion n. a gathering of relatives, friends, etc. after separation.

rev n. a revolution (in an engine or the like). –v. (**revved, revving**) Also, **rev up.** 2. to change, especially to increase the speed of.

revamp v. to renovate.

reveal v. 1. to make known; disclose; divulge. 2. to lay open to view; display. **–revelation,** n. **–revelatory,** adj.

reveille /rə'væli/ n. a signal to waken soldiers or sailors.

revel v. (-elled, -elling) 1. to take great pleasure or delight (in). -n. 2. (oft. pl.) an occasion of noisy festivity with dancing, etc. -revelry, n.

revenge n. 1. retaliation for injuries or wrongs; vengeance. -v. (-venged, -venging) 2. to take vengeance on behalf of (a person) or for (a wrong).

revenue n. 1. the income of a government from taxation, excise duties, customs, etc. 2. a regular income, as the return or yield from any kind of property.

reverberate v. to re-echo or resound.

revere v. to regard with respect and awe; venerate. -reverence, n. -reverent, adj.

reverend adj. 1. (oft. upper case) (a title of respect for a member of the clergy). -n. 2. Informal a member of the clergy.

reverie n. a state of dreamy meditation.

reverse adj. 1. opposite or contrary in position, direction, order, or character. 2. producing a backward motion. -n. 3. the opposite or contrary of something. 4. the back or rear of anything. 5. an adverse change of fortune. 6. Motor Vehicles reverse gear. -v. 7. to turn (something) inside out or upside down. 8. to turn or move (something) in the opposite direction. 9. to revoke or annul (a decree, judgement, etc.). 10. to drive (a motor vehicle) backwards.

Don't confuse **reverse** with **reserve**, which is to keep or save something for later.

reverse-engineer v. to analyse the construction of (a product), especially as a preliminary to designing a similar product.

revert v. 1. to return to a former habit, practice, etc. 2. Law to go back to the former owner or his or her heirs. -reversion, n.

review n. 1. a critical article or report on some literary work, film, play, etc. 2. a periodical publication containing articles on current events, books, art, etc.

3. consideration of past events, circumstances, or facts. 4. a general survey of something, especially in words. -v. 5. to view or look over again. 6. to look back upon; view retrospectively. 7. to present a survey of in speech or writing. 8. to discuss (a book, etc.) in a critical review.

Don't confuse **review** with **revue**, which is a humorous musical show.

revile v. to address, or speak of, abusively or contemptuously.

The more usual word is **abuse**.

revise v. 1. to amend or alter. 2. to go over or study (a subject, book, etc.) again. -revision, n.

revive v. 1. to bring back into notice, use, or currency. 2. to restore to life or consciousness. -revival, n.

revoke v. to take back or withdraw; annul. -revocation, n.

revolt v. 1. to break away from or rise against constituted authority. 2. to turn away in mental rebellion or abhorrence. 3. to affect with disgust or abhorrence. -n. 4. an insurrection or rebellion.

revolution n. 1. a complete overthrow of an established government. 2. procedure or course as if in a circuit. 3. a single turn of this kind.

revolutionary adj. 1. relating to a revolution. -n. (pl. -ries) 2. someone who advocates or takes part in a revolution.

revolutionise v. to bring about a revolution in. Also, **revolutionize**.

revolve v. 1. to rotate, as on an axis. 2. to move in a circular or curving course, or orbit.

revolver n. a pistol which can be fired repeatedly without reloading.

revue n. a form of theatrical entertainment in which recent events, popular fads, etc., are parodied.

Don't confuse this with **review**, which is an article in a newspaper or magazine which describes and comments on a film, book, etc.

revulsion *n.* a violent dislike or aversion for something or someone.

reward *n.* **1.** something given or received in return for service, merit, hardship, etc. –*v.* **2.** to give something (to someone) in return for service, etc.

rewarding *adj.* giving satisfaction that the effort made was worthwhile.

rhapsody /'ræpsədi/ *n.* (*pl.* **-dies**) **1.** an exaggerated expression of enthusiasm. **2.** *Music* an instrumental composition suggestive of improvisation.

Rhesus factor /'risəs/ *n.* → **Rh factor**.

rhesus monkey *n.* a monkey, common in India, much used in medical research.

rhetoric /'rɛtərık/ *n.* **1.** the art of literary uses of language. **2.** (in prose or verse) the use of exaggeration in an unfavourable sense.

rhetorical question /rə'tɒrıkəl/ *n.* a question designed to produce an effect and not to draw an answer.

rheumatism *n.* any of various painful ailments with stiffness and inflammation of the joints or muscles. –**rheumatic**, *adj.*

Rh factor *n.* a substance often present in human blood. Mixing of Rh positive blood (containing this substance) with Rh negative blood (lacking it) may cause the formation of antibodies and the destruction of red blood cells, as during pregnancy.

rhinestone *n.* an artificial gem made of glass.

rhinoceros *n.* (*pl.* **-ceroses** *or, especially collectively,* **-ceros**) any of various large mammals with one or two upright horns on the snout. Also, **rhino**.

rhizome *n.* a root-like horizontal underground stem.

rhododendron *n.* any of several ornamental, flowering shrubs and trees.

rhombus *n.* (*pl.* **-buses** *or* **-bi** /-baɪ/) an oblique-angled parallelogram with all sides equal.

rhubarb *n.* a garden plant with edible leafstalks.

rhyme *n.* **1.** agreement in the terminal sounds of lines of verse, or of words. –*v.* (**rhymed, rhyming**) **2.** to form a rhyme, as one word or line with another. –*phr.* **3. rhyme or reason**, logic; explanation; meaning.

rhythm *n.* any movement or procedure marked by the regular recurrence of particular elements or phases, as the recurring beat, accent, etc. in music. –**rhythmic**, **rhythmical**, *adj.*

rhythm and blues *n.* a style of music which first became popular in the early 1960s, using both vocal and instrumental elements based on the guitar, and derived ultimately from the African-American blues style and but with a quicker tempo and more complex rhythms. *Abbrev.*: R & B

rib¹ *n.* **1.** one of a series of long, slender, curved bones, more or less enclosing the chest. **2.** something resembling a rib in form, position, or use, as a supporting or strengthening part. –*v.* (**ribbed, ribbing**) **3.** to furnish or strengthen with ribs.

rib² *v.* (**ribbed, ribbing**) *Informal* to tease; ridicule; make fun of. –**ribbing**, *n.*

ribald /'rɪbəld, 'raɪ-, 'raɪbɒld/ *adj.* coarsely mocking or abusive. –**ribaldry**, *n.*

ribbon *n.* **1.** a band of fine material, used for ornament, tying, etc. **2.** anything resembling a ribbon or woven band. **3.** a band of material supplying ink, as in a typewriter. **4.** *Sport* an award for success in a competition.

riboflavin /raɪbou'fleɪvən/ *n.* vitamin B₂, one of the vitamins in the vitamin B complex.

rice *n.* the starchy grain of a species of grass, used for food.

rich *adj.* **1.** abundantly supplied with resources, means, or funds. **2.** abounding (*in* or *with*). **3.** of great value or worth; valuable. **4.** (of wine, gravy, etc.) strong and full flavoured. **5.** (of colour) deep, strong, or vivid. **6.** (of sound, the voice, etc.) full and mellow in tone. **7.** *Informal* ridiculous or absurd.

riches *pl. n.* wealth.

rickets *n.* a childhood disease, caused by malnutrition and often resulting in bone deformities.

rickety *adj.* liable to fall or collapse; shaky.

rickshaw *n.* a small two-wheeled vehicle drawn by one or more people.

ricochet /ˈrɪkəʃeɪ/ *n.* the motion of an object or projectile which rebounds one or more times from the surface or surfaces it strikes.

ricotta *n.* a soft unripened cheese with a fresh bland flavour.

rid *v.* (**rid** or **ridded**, **ridding**) **1.** to clear or free of something unwanted: *to rid the house of mice.* –*phr.* **2. get rid of,** to get free, or relieved of.

riddle[1] *n.* **1.** a question or statement so framed as to exercise one's ingenuity in answering it. **2.** a puzzling question, problem, or matter.

riddle[2] *v.* to pierce with many holes.

ride *v.* (**rode**, **ridden**, **riding**) **1.** to sit on and control (a horse, bicycle, etc.) in motion. **2.** to be carried on something as if on horseback or in a vehicle. **3.** to ride over, along or through (a road, boundary, region, etc.). **4.** to be based or rely on something. **5.** to work or move (*up*) from the proper position, as a skirt, or the like. –*n.* **6.** a journey or excursion on a horse, etc., or on or in a vehicle. –*phr.* **7. ride out,** to sustain or endure successfully.

rider *n.* **1.** someone who rides. **2.** an addition or amendment to a document, etc. –**riderless,** *adj.*

ridge *n.* **1.** a long, narrow elevation of land. **2.** any raised narrow strip. –*v.* (**ridged**, **ridging**) **3.** to provide with or form into a ridge or ridges.

ridicule *n.* **1.** words or actions intended to excite contemptuous laughter at a person

or thing. –*v.* (**-culed**, **-culing**) **2.** to deride; make fun of.

ridiculous *adj.* absurd, preposterous, or laughable.

rife *adj.* of common occurrence; prevalent.

riffraff *n.* worthless or low persons.

rifle[1] *n.* a shoulder firearm.

rifle[2] *v.* to ransack and rob (a place, receptacle, etc.).

rift *n.* **1.** an opening made by splitting. **2.** a break in friendly relations as between people or countries etc.

rig *v.* (**rigged**, **rigging**) **1.** to equip with the necessary ropes and lines: *to rig a yacht.* **2.** to control dishonestly: *to rig an election.* –*n.* **3.** the structure and equipment used in drilling an oil or gas well. –*phr.* **4. rig up,** to put together or in proper working order: *to rig up a dance floor; to rig up a tent.*

rigging *n.* the ropes, chains, etc., which operate the masts, yards, sails, etc., on a ship.

right *adj.* **1.** in accordance with what is just or good. **2.** in conformity with fact, reason, or some standard or principle; correct. **3.** in good health or spirits, as persons. **4.** in good order. **5.** most convenient, desirable, or favourable. **6.** belonging or relating to the side which is turned towards the east when a person or thing is facing north (opposed to *left*). **7.** socially and politically conservative. **8.** *Geom.* having the axis perpendicular to the base. **9.** *Informal* unquestionable; unmistakable; true. –*n.* **10.** a just claim or title to anything. **11.** that which is due to anyone by just claim. **12.** that which is ethically good and proper and in conformity with the moral law. **13.** that which accords with fact, reason, or propriety. **14.** the right side or what is on the right side. –*adv.* **15.** quite or completely. **16.** immediately. **17.** exactly, precisely, or just. **18.** correctly or accurately. **19.** properly or fittingly. **20.** advantageously, favourably, or well. **21.** towards the right hand; to the right. **22.** very (used in certain titles). –v. **23.** to bring or restore to, or resume an upright or the proper position. **24.** to set in order or put right. **25.** to redress (wrong, etc.). –phr. **26. the Right**, a political party and its supporters holding conservative views.

right angle n. an angle of 90°.

righteous adj. **1.** characterised by up-rightness or morality; virtuous. –phr. **2. the righteous**, righteous people collectively.

rigid adj. stiff or unyielding; not pliant or flexible; hard.

rigmarole n. a long and complicated process.

rigour /'rɪgə/ n. **1.** strictness or harshness, as in dealing with persons. **2.** severity of life; hardship. Also, **rigor. –rigorous,** adj.

rile v. to irritate.

rim n. **1.** the outer edge, border, or margin, esp. of a circular object. –v. **(rimmed, rimming) 2.** to furnish with a rim, border, or margin. **–rimless,** adj.

rind n. a thick and firm coat or covering, as of fruits, cheeses, etc.

ring[1] n. **1.** a circular band of metal etc., especially one for wearing on the finger. **2.** anything having the form of a circular band. **3.** a circular course. **4.** an enclosed circular or other area, as one in which some sport or exhibition takes place. **5.** a group of persons cooperating for selfish or illegal purposes. –v. **(ringed, ringing) 6.** to surround with a ring; encircle. **7.** to form (into) a ring. **8.** to move in a ring or a constantly curving course.

ring[2] v. **(rang, rung, ringing) 1.** to (cause to) give forth a clear, resonant sound when set in sudden vibration by a blow or otherwise, as a bell. **2.** to be filled with sound; re-echo with sound, as a place. **3.** to proclaim, summon, signal, etc., by or as by the sound of a bell. **4.** to telephone. **5.** to seem (true, false, etc.) in the effect produced on the mind. –n. **6.** a resonant sound or noise. **7.** a telephone call. **8.** a characteristic or inherent quality. –phr. **9. ring a bell**, to arouse a memory; sound familiar. **10. ring off**, to end a telephone conversation. **11. ring the changes**, to vary the manner of performing an action, especially one that is often repeated; execute a number of manoeuvres or variations. **12. ring up, a.** to telephone. **b.** to record (the cost of an item) on a cash register.

ringbark v. to cut away the bark in a ring around a tree trunk or branch, in order to kill the tree or the affected part.

ringer[1] n. Aust. a station hand, especially a stockworker or drover.

ringer[2] n. Informal **1.** an athlete, horse, etc., entered in a competition under false representations as to identity or ability. **2.** a person or thing that closely resembles another.

ringer[3] n. Aust., NZ the fastest shearer of a group.

ring-in n. Aust., NZ Informal **1.** someone or something that does not belong in a group or set. **2.** a person substituted for another at the last minute. **3.** a thing substituted for another at the last minute, as a horse fraudulently substituted for another in a race.

ringlet n. a curled lock of hair.

ringtone n. Telecommunications **1.** a tone returned by receiving equipment that tells a caller that the called telephone is ringing. **2.** the sound produced by a mobile phone to indicate that a call is being received, originally a ringing sound, but now any of various recorded sounds, fragments of music, etc. Also, **ring tone, ringing tone.**

ringworm n. → tinea.

rink n. **1.** an area of ice for skating. **2.** a smooth floor for rollerskating.

rinse v. **(rinsed, rinsing) 1.** to put through clean water, as a final stage in cleansing. –n. **2.** an act or instance of rinsing. **3.** any liquid preparation used for impermanently tinting the hair.

riot *n.* **1.** any disturbance of the peace by an assembly of persons. **2.** a violent outbreak, as of emotions, passions, etc. **3.** a brilliant display. **4.** *Informal* someone or something that causes great amusement, enthusiasm, etc. *–v.* **5.** to take part in a riot or disorderly public outbreak. *–phr.* **6. run riot**, to act without control or restraint. *–***riotous**, *adj.*

rip[1] *v.* **(ripped, ripping) 1.** to cut or tear apart roughly or vigorously. **2.** *Informal* to move along with violence or great speed. *–n.* a rent made by ripping; a tear.

rip[2] *n.* a fast current, especially one at a beach.

ripcord *n.* a cord or ring which opens a parachute during a descent.

ripe *adj.* complete in natural growth or development.

ripen *v.* to make or become ripe.

rip-off *n.* an excessive charge or exorbitant price; swindle. *–***rip off**, *v.*

riposte /rə'post/ *n.* a quick, sharp return in speech or action. Also, **ripost**.

ripper *n.* *Informal* something or someone exciting extreme admiration.

ripple *v.* to form small waves on the surface, as water.

rise *v.* **(rose, risen, rising) 1.** to get up from a reclining, sitting, kneeling position. **2.** to get up from bed. **3.** to become active in opposition or resistance; rebel. **4.** to spring up or grow. **5.** to move upwards or ascend. **6.** to come above the horizon, as a heavenly body. **7.** to extend directly upwards. **8.** to attain higher rank, importance, etc. **9.** to prove oneself equal (*to*) a demand, emergency, etc. **10.** to become animated or cheerful, as the spirits. **11.** to swell or puff up, as dough from the action of yeast. **12.** to increase in amount, as prices, etc. **13.** to increase in degree, intensity, or force, as colour, fever, etc. **14.** to become louder or of higher pitch, as

the voice. **15.** to adjourn, or close a session, as a parliament or court. *–v.* **16.** the act of rising; upward movement or ascent. **17.** appearance above the horizon: *sunrise.* **18.** elevation or advance in rank, fortune, etc. **19.** an increase in amount, as of wages, etc. **20.** an increase in degree or intensity, as of temperature. **21.** origin, source, or beginning. **22.** extension upwards. **23.** upward slope, as of ground or a road. **24.** a piece of rising or high ground. *–phr.* **25. get** (or **take**) **a rise out of**, to provoke to anger, annoyance, etc., by banter, mockery, deception, etc.

> Don't confuse **rise** with **raise**, which is to lift something up (*They tried to raise the ship from the bottom of the ocean*), or to bring up (*She raised seven children*), or to increase (*They have raised the price of petrol again*). The meaning of **rise** is similar but you never rise *something* – it does not take an object.

risk *n.* **1.** a hazard or dangerous chance. *–v.* **2.** to expose to the chance of injury or loss, or hazard. **3.** to venture upon; take or run the risk of.

risotto /rə'zɒtoʊ, rə'sɒtoʊ/ *n.* (*pl.* **-tos**) an Italian dish of rice fried in butter with onion, flavoured with parmesan, and other flavourings.

risqué /'riskeɪ, rɪs'keɪ/ *adj.* daringly close to indelicacy or impropriety.

rissole *n.* a small fried ball of minced meat or fish.

rite *n.* a ceremonial act or procedure customary in religious or other solemn use.

ritual *n.* **1.** (the act of following) an established procedure, form, etc., for a religious or other rite. **2.** any solemn or customary action, code of behaviour, etc., regulating social conduct.

rival *n.* **1.** someone who strives to equal or outdo another; a competitor. *–adj.* **2.** being a rival. *–v.* **(-valled, -valling) 3.** to strive to equal or outdo.

river n. 1. a defined watercourse of considerable size and length, whether flowing or dry according to the seasons, and whether a single channel or a number of diverging or converging channels. 2. any abundant stream or copious flow.

rivet n. 1. a metal pin or bolt. –v. 2. to fasten or fix firmly.

rivulet n. a small stream.

road n. 1. a way, usually open to the public for the passage of vehicles, persons, and animals. 2. a way or course.

roadhouse n. an inn, hotel, restaurant, etc., on a main road.

roadkill n. the remains of any animal or animals struck and killed by a motor vehicle and lying on or beside a road.

road rage n. violent behaviour by a motorist towards other motorists.

roadway n. a way used as a road.

roam v. to walk, go, or travel about without fixed purpose or direction.

roan adj. (chiefly of horses) brown in colour with splashes of grey or white.

roar v. 1. to utter or express (in) a loud, deep sound, especially of excitement, distress, or anger. 2. to laugh loudly or boisterously. 3. to make a loud noise or din, as thunder, cannon, waves, wind, etc. –n. 4. the sound of roaring.

Don't confuse this with **raw**, which means not cooked: *raw carrot*.

roast v. 1. to bake and brown (meat, coffee etc.) by dry heat, as in an oven. 2. *Informal* to criticise, rebuke or ridicule severely. –n. 3. a piece of roasted meat.

rob v. (**robbed**, **robbing**) to steal something from by unlawful force or threat of violence. –**robber**, n. –**robbery**, n.

robe n. any long, loose garment, especially one worn on official occasions.

This word is sometimes used in the plural, as in *coronation robes*.

robin n. any of various small brightly coloured Aust. birds.

robot n. 1. a manufactured device capable of performing some human-like functions. 2. *Computers* → **web crawler**.

robust adj. 1. strong and healthy, hardy, or vigorous. 2. suited to or requiring bodily strength or endurance.

rock¹ n. 1. *Geol.* mineral matter assembled in masses or considerable quantities in nature. 2. stone in the mass. 3. something resembling or suggesting a rock. 4. a firm foundation or support. 5. a stone of any size. –phr. 6. **on the rocks**, **a.** *Informal* into or in a state of disaster or ruin. **b.** (of drinks) with ice-cubes.

rock² v. 1. to (cause to) move or sway to and fro or from side to side. –n. 2. → **rock music**. 3. → **rock'n'roll**.

rock-and-roll n. → **rock'n'roll**.

rock climbing n. the sport of climbing on steep rock faces, both sheer and uneven, using specialised ropes and equipment. Also, **rockclimbing**. –**rock climber**, n.

rocker n. 1. one of the curved pieces on which a cradle or a rocking chair rocks. 2. any of various devices that operate with a rocking motion. –phr. 3. **off one's rocker**, *Informal* crazy; mad; demented.

rockery n. (pl. **-ries**) a garden, or part of a garden, featuring plants grown among rocks.

rocket n. 1. *Aeronautics* a structure propelled by an emission of heated gas from the rear. –v. (**-eted**, **-eting**) 2. to move like a rocket.

You may see the forms of the verb spelt **rocketted** and **rocketting**, although this is not very common. Usually, verbs ending in *t* do not double the *t* if the last part of the word is not said with a strong stress.

rockmelon n. *Aust.*, *NZ* a type of melon with orange-coloured flesh; cantaloupe.

rock music n. contemporary music which has developed from 1950s rock'n'roll. Also, **rock**.

rock'n'roll *n.* a form of popular music of the 1950s. Also, **rock**, **rock-and-roll**, **rock-'n'-roll**.

rock pool *n.* a swimming pool beside the sea which may be either artificially constructed or naturally occurring but which is made entirely or almost entirely of rocks in the locality, and which is filled and freshened by the recurring tides. Also, **rockpool**.

rococo *n.* **1.** an ornate style of art, architecture and decoration of the 18th century. –*adj.* **2.** decorated in exaggeratedly elaborate style.

rod *n.* **1.** a stick, shaft, etc., of wood, metal, or other material. **2.** a pole used in fishing. **3.** a stick used as an instrument of punishment. **4.** a wand or staff carried as a symbol of office, authority, power, etc.

rode *v.* past tense of **ride**.

rodent *n.* one of the order of gnawing or nibbling mammals, that includes the mice, squirrels, beavers, etc.

rodeo /rou'deɪou, 'roudiou/ *n.* (*pl.* **-deos**) a public exhibition, sometimes competitive, showing the skills of riding horses or steers bareback, roping calves, etc.

roe *n.* the mass of eggs of the female fish.

roger *interj.* message received and understood (used in telecommunications).

role *n.* **1.** the character which an actor presents in a play. **2.** proper or customary function.

Don't confuse **role** with **roll**.

roll *v.* **1.** to (cause to) move along a surface by turning over and over, as a ball or a wheel. **2.** to move or be moved on wheels, as a vehicle or its occupants: *The truck rolled down the hill.* **3.** to extend in undulations, as land. **4.** to continue with or have a deep, prolonged sound, as thunder, etc. **5.** to turn over, or over and over, as a person or animal lying down. **6.** to sway or rock from side to side, as a ship. **7.** to

form into a roll, or curl up from itself. **8.** to spread out from being rolled up; unroll: *Roll out the carpet.* **9.** to spread out as under a roller. **10.** to cause to turn round in different directions, as the eyes. **11.** to make by forming a roll. **12.** to wrap, enfold, or envelop, as in some covering. **13.** to operate upon so as to spread out, level, compact or the like, as with a roller, rolling pin, etc. –*n.* **14.** a list, register, or catalogue. **15.** anything rolled up in cylindrical form. **16.** Also, **bread roll**. a small cake of bread. **17.** a deep, prolonged sound, as of thunder, etc. **18.** the continuous sound of a drum rapidly beaten. **19.** a single throw of dice. **20.** *Informal* a wad of paper currency.

Don't confuse **roll** with **role**.

rolled gold *n.* metal covered with a thin coating of gold.

roller *n.* **1.** a cylinder, wheel, or the like, upon which something is rolled along. **2.** a cylinder of plastic, wire, etc., around which hair is rolled to set it. **3.** a cylindrical body, as one for rolling over something to be spread out, levelled, crushed, etc.

rollerblade (*from trademark*) –*n.* **1.** one of a pair of rollerskates designed in imitation of an ice-skating shoe with a single row of rollers instead of a skate; inline skate. –*v.* **2.** to move on rollerblades. Also, **blade**.

roller-coaster *n.* **1.** an amusement park ride, on a steep twisting track. –*adj.* **2.** experiencing severe fluctuations in direction or momentum, and apparently proceeding without control: *a roller-coaster economy.*

rollerskate *n.* **1.** a form of skate running on small wheels or rollers. –*v.* **2.** to move along on rollerskates. –**rollerskater**, *n.* –**rollerskating**, *n.*

rollicking *adj.* swaggering and jolly.

rollout *n.* the launch of a new product, service, etc.

roly-poly adj. **1.** plump. –n. (pl. **-lies**) **2.** a type of pudding.

ROM n. read-only memory; computer memory whose contents can be read but not changed.

romance n. **1.** a tale depicting heroic or marvellous achievements. **2.** a made-up story; fanciful or extravagant invention. **3.** romantic character or quality. **4.** a romantic affair or experience. –v. (**-manced, -mancing**) **5.** to think or talk romantically.

Roman numerals pl. n. the numerals used by the ancient Romans still used for certain purposes. The common basic symbols are I(= 1), V(= 5), X(= 10), L(= 50), C(= 100), D(= 500), and M(= 1000).

romantic adj. **1.** of, relating to, or of the nature of romance. **2.** proper to romance rather than to real life. **3.** displaying or expressing love, emotion, etc. **4.** imaginary or fictitious. –n. **5.** a romantic person. –**romanticise, romanticize,** v.

romp v. **1.** to play or frolic in a lively or boisterous manner. –phr. **2.** romp home (or **in**) to win easily.

roo n. Aust. Informal a kangaroo.

roof n. (pl. **roofs** /rufs, ruvz/) **1.** the external upper covering of any building. **2.** something which resembles this in form or position.

rook[1] n. **1.** a large black European bird like a crow. –v. **2.** to cheat; fleece; swindle.

rook[2] n. a chess piece; castle.

rookery n. (pl. **-ries**) **1.** a breeding place or colony. **2.** any instance of cheating, sharp practice, exorbitant prices, etc.

rookie n. Informal a raw recruit.

room n. **1.** a portion of space within a building, separated by walls from other parts. **2.** space, or extent of space, occupied by or available for something. **3.** opportunity or scope for or to do something. –v. **4.** to occupy a room or rooms; to share a room; lodge.

roomy adj. (**-mier, -miest**) affording ample room; spacious; large.

roost n. a perch upon which domestic fowls rest at night. –v. **2.** to settle or stay, especially for the night.

rooster n. a domestic cock.

root[1] n. **1.** a part of the plant which grows downwards into the soil, fixing the plant and absorbing nutriment and moisture. **2.** the embedded part of a hair, tooth, nail, etc. **3.** the fundamental or essential part. **4.** the base or point of origin of something. **5.** (pl.) a person's real home and environment. **6.** Maths a quantity which, when multiplied by itself a certain number of times, produces a given quantity. –v. **7.** to send out roots and begin to grow. **8.** to become fixed or established. **9.** to fix by, or as if by, roots. **10.** to pull, tear, or dig (up, out, etc.) by the roots.

> Don't confuse **root** with **route**, which is a way or road from one place to another.

root[2] phr. **1.** root around, to poke or search, as if to find something. **2.** root out (or **up**), to unearth; bring to light.

rope n. **1.** a strong, thick line or cord. **2.** death by hanging as a punishment. **3.** (pl.) methods of operation of a business, etc. –v. (**roped, roping**) **4.** to tie, bind, or fasten with a rope. –phr. **5.** rope in, Informal to draw or entice into something.

ropeable adj. Informal extremely angry or bad-tempered. Also, **ropable**.

rort Aust., NZ Informal –n. **1.** an incident or series of incidents involving reprehensible or suspect behaviour, especially by officials or politicians. **2.** a wild party. –v. **3.** to take wrongful advantage of; abuse: to rort the system.

rosary n. (pl. **-ries**) **1.** a string of beads used for counting prayers in reciting them. **2.** the series of prayers recited.

rose[1] n. **1.** (the flower of) any of various showy-flowered shrubs. **2.** an ornament shaped like or suggesting a rose. **3.** the traditional reddish colour of the rose. **4.** a perforated cap, as at the end of the spout of a watering-can, etc., to break a flow of water into a spray.

rose² v. past tense of **rise**.

rosé n. a light, pale red wine.

rosella n. any of a number of brilliantly coloured parrots.

rosemary n. (pl. **-ries**) an aromatic herb used in cookery.

rosette n. any arrangement, part, object, or formation more or less resembling a rose.

rosin n. a hard, brittle resin used in making varnish, or for rubbing on violin bows, etc.

roster n. a list of persons or groups showing their periods of duty. **-rostered**, adj.

rosti /ˈrɒsti/ n. in Swiss cooking, grated potato mixed with other ingredients, as cheese, bacon, egg, tomato, vegetables, and then fried on both sides. Also, **rösti, roesti** /ˈrɜːsti/.

rostrum n. (pl. **-trums** or **-tra**) any platform, stage, etc., for public speaking.

rosy adj. (**-sier, -siest**) **1.** pink or pinkish red. **2.** (of persons, the cheeks, lips, etc.) having a fresh, healthy redness. **3.** bright or promising. **4.** cheerful or optimistic.

rot v. (**rotted, rotting**) **1.** to (cause to) undergo decomposition; decay. *-n.* **2.** rotting or rotten matter. **3.** any of various diseases characterised by decomposition. **4.** Informal nonsense.

rotary adj. **1.** turning round as on an axis, as an object. **2.** having a part or parts that rotate, as a machine.

rotate v. **1.** to (cause to) turn round like a wheel on its axis. **2.** to proceed in a fixed routine of succession: *The seasons rotate.* **-rotation,** n.

rote phr. **by rote,** in a mechanical way without thought of the meaning.

rotisserie n. a mechanical rotating spit on which food can be cooked.

rotten adj. **1.** in a state of decay; putrid. **2.** Informal wretchedly bad, unsatisfactory, or unpleasant. **3.** contemptible. **4.** Informal extremely drunk.

rotund adj. rounded; plump.

rotunda n. a round building, especially one with a dome.

rouge /ruːʒ/ n. **1.** a red cosmetic for colouring the cheeks or lips. *-v.* (**rouged, rouging**) **2.** to colour with rouge.

rough adj. **1.** uneven of surface; not smooth. **2.** shaggy. **3.** acting with or characterised by violence. **4.** unmannerly or rude. **5.** Informal severe, hard, or unpleasant. **6.** without ordinary comforts or conveniences. **7.** requiring exertion or strength rather than intelligence or skill, as work. **8.** unpolished, as language, verse, style, etc. **9.** made or done without any attempt at exactness, completeness, or thoroughness. *-n.* **10.** that which is rough. **11.** the rough, hard, or unpleasant side or part of anything. *-adv.* **12.** in a rough manner; roughly. *-phr.* **13. rough up,** to treat roughly or harshly. **14. rough in** (or **out**), to cut, shape, or sketch roughly. **15. rough it,** Informal to live without the usually expected comforts or conveniences. **16. rough on,** a. severe towards. **b.** unfortunate for (someone). **-roughness,** n.

roughage n. the coarser parts of food, of little nutritive value, but aiding digestion.

roughly adv. **1.** in a crude, harsh or violent manner. **2.** approximately; about.

roulette n. **1.** a gambling game. **2.** a small toothed wheel, mounted in a handle, for making lines of marks, dots, or perforations.

round adj. **1.** circular, as a disc. **2.** ring-shaped, as a hoop. **3.** curved like part of a circle, as an outline. **4.** spherical or globular, as a ball. **5.** free from angularity; curved, as parts of the body. **6.** full, complete, or entire. **7.** roughly correct. **8.** (of a literary character) described in depth. *-n.* **9.** something round. **10.** any complete course, series, or succession. **11.** (*sometimes pl.*) a circuit of any place, series of places, etc., covered in a customary way. **12.** a distribution of drink, etc., to all the members of a company. **13.** a standard cut of beef from the lower part of the butt. **14. a.** (of bread) a slice. **b.** a sandwich. *–adv.* **15.** in a circle, ring, etc., or so as to surround something. **16.** on all sides or about. **17.** in a circular or rounded course. **18.** throughout a period of time: *all year round.* **19.** by a roundabout course. **20.** with change to another direction, course, opinion, etc.: *to look round.* *–prep.* **21.** so as to encircle, surround, or envelop. **22.** around; about. **23.** in the vicinity of. **24.** so as to make a turn or partial circuit about or to the other side of. *–v.* **25.** to free or become free from angularity or flatness; become plump. **26.** to encircle or surround. **27.** to develop to completeness or perfection. *–phr.* **28. a round of applause**, a single outburst of cheering, clapping, etc. **29. round on** (or **upon**), to attack, usually verbally, with sudden and often unexpected vigour. **30. round the bend** (or **twist**), *Informal* insane. **31. round up**, to collect (cattle, people, etc.) in a particular place.

roundabout n. **1.** → **merry-go-round**. **2.** a road junction at which the traffic moves in one direction only round a circular arrangement. *–adj.* **3.** circuitous or indirect.

rounders pl. n. a game played with bat and ball.

Note that this word is usually used as a singular noun: *Rounders is similar to softball.*

roundly adv. vigorously or briskly.

rouse¹ /raʊz/ v. to bring or come out of a state of sleep, inactivity, depression, etc.

rouse² /raʊs/ phr. **rouse on** (or **at**), *Aust., NZ* to scold or upbraid.

rouseabout n. *Aust., NZ* a general hand on a station, in a hotel, etc. Also, **roustabout**.

rout¹ /raʊt/ n. **1.** a defeat attended with disorderly flight. **2.** a clamour or fuss. *–v.* **3.** to defeat utterly.

rout² /raʊt/ v. to turn over or dig up with the snout, as swine.

route /rut/, *Chiefly US and Computers* /raʊt/ n. **1.** a way or road taken or planned for passage or travel. **2.** *Computers* any path, such as that between hosts in a computer network. *–v.* (**routed, routeing** or **routing**) **3.** to send by a particular route: *The parcel was routed via the city; The data is routed through the university's main computer.*

Don't confuse this with **root**, which is the part of a plant which is under the ground. This word is pronounced /raʊt/ in America, and nowadays the verb is sometimes pronounced this way in Australia as well, especially when used in the context of computers.

router /ˈraʊtə/ n. *Computers* a device used in connecting networks which configures the best route between hosts; gateway.

routine n. **1.** a customary or regular course of procedure. *–adj.* **2.** of the nature of, proceeding by, or adhering to routine. *–***routinely**, adv.

rove v. to wander about without definite destination.

row¹ /roʊ/ n. a number of persons or things arranged in a straight line.

row² /roʊ/ v. **1.** to propel (a boat, etc.) by or as by the use of oars. *–n.* **2.** an act of rowing.

row³ /raʊ/ n. **1.** a noisy dispute or quarrel; commotion. **2.** *Informal* noise or clamour.

rowdy adj. (**-dier, -diest**) rough and disorderly.

rowlock /ˈrɒlək/ n. a device on which an oar rests and swings.

royal *adj.* of, relating to, established by, or existing under the patronage of, a sovereign.

royalist *n.* a supporter or adherent of a monarch or monarchy.

royalty *n.* (*pl.* **-ties**) **1.** royal persons collectively. **2.** royal status, dignity, or power; sovereignty. **3.** a payment received by an author, composer, etc., usually a percentage of the sales of their work.

rub *v.* (**rubbed, rubbing**) **1.** to subject (an object) to pressure and friction, especially in order to clean, smooth, polish, etc. **2.** to move, spread, or apply (something) with pressure and friction against something else. **3.** to remove or erase by rubbing: *to rub a mark off a wall; to rub out writing*. **4.** to chafe or abrade. –*n.* **5.** the act of rubbing. –*phr.* **6. rub it in**, to remind someone repeatedly of their mistakes, failures or shortcomings. **7. rub off on**, to be transferred to, especially as a result of repeated close contact.

rubber¹ *n.* **1.** an elastic material, derived from the latex of certain plants. **2.** a synthetic material resembling rubber. **3.** a piece of such material as used for erasing pencil marks, etc.

rubber² *n.* *Bridge, Whist, etc.* a set of games.

rubbish *n.* **1.** waste or refuse material; debris; litter. **2.** nonsense. –*v.* **3.** *Informal* to speak of scornfully; criticise; denigrate.

rubble *n.* rough fragments of broken stone.

rubella *n.* → **German measles**.

rubric *n.* a title, heading, direction, etc., in a manuscript, book, etc.

ruby *n.* (*pl.* **-bies**) **1.** a red gemstone. **2.** deep red; carmine. –*adj.* **3.** ruby-coloured. **4.** made from or containing a ruby.

ruck *n.* **1.** *Aust. Rules* a group of 3 players who do not have fixed positions. **2.** *Rugby Football* a group of players struggling for the ball in no set pattern of play.

rucksack *n.* → **knapsack**.

ruction *n.* *Informal* a disturbance, quarrel or row.

rudder *n.* a board of wood or metal at the stern of a boat used as a means of steering. –**rudderless**, *adj.*

ruddy *adj.* (**-dier, -diest**) **1.** reddish in colour, as from good health. –*adv.* **2.** *Informal* extremely.

rude *adj.* **1.** discourteous or impolite. **2.** without culture, learning, or refinement.

rudiments *pl. n.* the elements or first principles of a subject. –**rudimentary**, *adj.*

rue *v.* (**rued, ruing**) to feel sorrow over; repent of.

ruff *n.* a collar of lace, etc., gathered into deep folds.

ruffian *n.* a violent, lawless man; a rough brute.

ruffle *v.* **1.** to destroy the smoothness or evenness of. **2.** to annoy or disturb. **3.** to draw up (cloth, lace, etc.) into a ruffle. **4.** to be or become ruffled. –*n.* **5.** a break in the smoothness or evenness of some surface. **6.** a strip of cloth, lace, etc., drawn up by gathering along one edge.

rug *n.* **1.** a small, often thick, carpet. **2.** a thick, warm blanket. –*phr.* **3. rug (oneself) up**, to make or keep oneself warm by covering oneself in thick clothing, etc.

Rugby football *n.* either of 2 forms of football, **Rugby League** and **Rugby Union**, played by teams of 13 and 15 players respectively.

rugged *adj.* **1.** roughly broken, rocky, hilly, or otherwise difficult of passage. **2.** severe, hard, or trying.

ruin *n.* **1.** (*pl.*) the remains of a fallen building, town, etc. **2.** a ruined building, town, etc. **3.** fallen and wrecked or decayed state. **4.** the complete loss of means, position, or the like. –*v.* **5.** to reduce to ruin. –**ruinous**, *adj.*

rule *n.* **1.** a principle or regulation governing conduct, action, procedure, etc. **2.** that which customarily occurs or holds good. **3.** control, government, or dominion. –*v.* (**ruled, ruling**) **4.** to control or direct. **5.** to declare judicially; decree. **6.** to mark with lines, especially parallel straight lines, with the aid of a ruler or the like. **7.** to prevail or be current. –*phr.* **8. rule out**, to exclude; refuse to admit.

ruler *n.* **1.** someone or something that rules or governs. **2.** a strip of wood, metal, or other material with a graduated straight edge, used in drawing lines, measuring, etc.

rum *n.* an alcoholic spirit.

rumble *v.* **1.** to make a deep, continuous, resonant sound, as thunder, etc. –*n.* **2.** *Informal* a fight, especially between teenage gangs.

ruminant *n.* any of the cloven-hoofed, cud-chewing quadrupeds, as cattle, sheep, goats, etc.

ruminate *v.* **1.** to chew the cud, as a cow. **2.** to muse or meditate (*on*); ponder.

For def. 2, the more usual word is **consider**.

rummage *v.* (**-maged, -maging**) to search by moving things around: *to rummage through boxes*; *to rummage around*.

rummy *n.* a card game.

rumour *n.* **1.** a story or statement in general circulation without confirmation or certainty as to facts. –*v.* **2.** circulate, report, or assert by a rumour. Also, **rumor.**

rump *n.* the hind part of the body of an animal.

rumple *v.* **1.** to draw or crush into wrinkles. **2.** to become wrinkled or crumpled.

rumpus *n.* *Informal* disturbing noise; uproar.

run *v.* (**ran, run, running**) **1.** to move quickly on foot, so as to go more rapidly than in walking. **2.** to (cause to) move easily or swiftly. **3.** to make a short, journey, as for a visit, etc. **4.** to stand as a

candidate for election. **5.** to traverse a route, as a public conveyance. **6.** to melt, flow, or stream, as a liquid. **7.** to recur or be inherent. **8.** to come undone, as knitted fabric; ladder. **9.** to be or keep in operation, as a machine. **10.** to exist or occur within a specified range of variation. **11.** to pass into a certain state or condition; become: *to run wild.* **12.** to cause (an animal, etc.) to move quickly on foot. **13.** to cause (a vehicle, etc.) to move. **14.** to traverse (a distance or course) in running. **15.** to perform by or as by running. **16.** to run or get past or through: *to run a blockade.* **17.** to keep (livestock), as on pasture. **18.** to convey or transport, as in a vessel or vehicle. **19.** to expose oneself to or be exposed to (a risk, etc.). **20.** to bring, lead, or force into some state, action, etc.: *to run oneself into debt.* **21.** to conduct, as a business, experiment, etc. –*n.* **22.** an act, instance, or spell of running. **23.** a running pace. **24.** an act or instance of escaping, running away, etc. **25.** a quick, short trip. **26.** the amount of something produced in any uninterrupted period of operation. **27.** a place in knitted or sewn work where a series of stitches have slipped or come undone; a ladder. **28.** freedom to range over, go through, or use. **29.** any rapid or easy course or progress. **30.** a continuous course of some condition of affairs, etc. **31.** a continuous series of something. **32.** any continued or extensive demand, call, or the like. **33.** a series of sudden and urgent demands for payment, as on a bank. **34.** the ordinary or average kind. **35.** an enclosure within which domestic animals may range about. **36.** the area and habitual route covered by a vendor who delivers goods to houses, etc. **37.** *Aust., NZ* a large area of grazing land. –*phr.* **38. in the long run**, ultimately. **39. run down**, **a.** to slow up before stopping, as a clock or other mechanism. **b.** to knock down and injure, as a vehicle or driver; run over. **c.** to denigrate. **d.** to find, especially after extensive searching. **40. run in, a.** to operate (new machinery, especially a motor vehicle) carefully for an initial period. **b.** *Informal* to arrest (def. 1). **41. run off, a.** to depart quickly. **b.** to produce by a printing process. **c.** to write or otherwise create quickly. **42. run over, a.** to knock down and injure. **b.** to exceed (a time-limit or the like). **c.** to review, rehearse, or recapitulate. **43. run up, a.** to amass or incur, as a bill. **b.** to make, especially quickly, as something sewn. **44. the runs,** *Informal* diarrhoea.

run-down *adj.* **1.** in a poor or deteriorated state of health; depressed, sick, or tired. **2.** fallen into disrepair. *−n.* **3.** a cursory review or summary of points of information.

rung¹ *v.* past tense and past participle of **ring²**.

rung² *n.* **1.** one of the rounded crosspieces forming the steps of a ladder. **2.** a horizontal supporting rod, as between the legs of a chair.

run-in *n. Informal* disagreement; argument; quarrel.

runner *n.* **1.** someone whose business it is to solicit patronage or trade. **2.** something in or on which something else runs or moves, as the strips of wood that guide a drawer, etc. **3.** a long, narrow strip, as of material. **4.** → **jogger** (def. 2).

runner-up *n.* (*pl.* **runners-up**) the competitor or team finishing in 2nd place.

running *n.* **1.** the managing or directing, as of a business, etc. *−adj.* **2.** moving or passing rapidly or smoothly. **3.** creeping or climbing, as plants. **4.** sliding easily, as a knot or a noose. **5.** operating, as a machine. **6.** cursive, as handwriting. **7.** going or carried on continuously. **8.** following in succession (placed after the noun): *2 days running. −phr.* **9. in the running,** having a chance of success.

runny *adj.* **1.** (of matter) fluid or tending to flow. **2.** tending to flow with or discharge liquid.

run-off *n.* **1.** a deciding final contest held after a principal one. **2.** something which runs off, as rain which flows off from the land in streams.

run-of-the-mill *adj.* ordinary; mediocre; commonplace.

runt *n.* the smallest in a litter.

runway *n.* **1.** a paved or cleared strip on which aeroplanes land and take off; airstrip.

rupture *n.* **1.** the state of being broken or burst. *−v.* **2.** to break or burst (a blood vessel, etc.). **3.** to cause a breach of (relations, etc.).

rural *adj.* **1.** of, relating to, or characteristic of the country (as distinguished from towns or cities). **2.** relating to agriculture.

ruse *n.* a trick, stratagem, or artifice.

rush¹ *v.* **1.** to (cause to) move or go with speed or violence. **2.** to perform, complete, or organise (some process or activity) with special haste. **3.** to attack with a rush. *−n.* **4.** the act of rushing; a rapid, impetuous, or headlong onward movement. **5.** a hurried state, as from pressure of affairs: *in a rush.* **6.** a period of intense activity. **7.** a great demand for a commodity, etc. *−adj.* **8.** requiring or performed with haste: *a rush job.*

rush² *n.* **1.** hollow-stemmed grass-like herbs found in marshy places. **2.** a stem of such a plant, used for making chair seats, mats, baskets, etc.

rush hour *n.* → **peak hour.**

rusk *n.* a crisp cake, given especially to babies when teething, and invalids.

russet *n., adj.* light reddish or yellowish brown.

rust *n.* **1.** the red or orange coating which forms on the surface of iron when exposed to air and moisture. **2.** rust colour; reddish brown or orange. *−v.* **3.** to become covered with rust. **4.** to deteriorate as through inaction or disuse. **5.** to impair as if with rust. **–rusty,** *adj.*

rustic *adj.* **1.** rural. **2.** made of rough timber, as garden seats, etc. *–n.* **3.** an unsophisticated country person.

rustle *v.* **1.** to (cause to) make a succession of slight, soft sounds, as of parts rubbing gently one on another, as leaves, silks, papers, etc. **2.** to steal (cattle, etc.). *–n.* **3.** the sound made by anything that rustles. *–phr.* **4. rustle up,** *Informal* to seek out from what is to hand; provide: *rustle up breakfast.*

rut[1] *n.* **1.** any furrow, groove, etc. **2.** a fixed or established way of life; a dull routine.

rut[2] *n.* the periodically recurring sexual excitement of the deer, goat, sheep, etc.

ruthless *adj.* without pity or compassion; pitiless; merciless.

rye *n.* **1.** (the seed of) a widely cultivated cereal grass. **2.** an American whisky distilled from rye.

S, s

S, s *n.* the 19th letter of the English alphabet.

Sabbath *n.* the day of the week reserved for rest and religious observance.

sabbatical *n.* a year, term, or other period of freedom from duties, granted to a university teacher or someone in one of certain other professional areas, often after seven years of service, as for study or travel. Also, **sabbatical leave**.

sable *n.* **1.** a small mammal of the weasel family, valued for its dark brown fur. –*adj.* **2.** made of the dark brown fur of the sable.

sabotage /ˈsæbətaʒ/ *n.* **1.** malicious injury to work, tools, machinery, etc. **2.** any malicious attack on or undermining of a cause. –*v.* **3.** to attack by sabotage. –**saboteur**, *n.*

sabre /ˈseɪbə/ *n.* **1.** a heavy one-edged sword. **2.** a light sword for fencing.

sac *n.* a bag-like structure in an animal or plant.

saccharin *n.* a very sweet crystalline compound. Also, **saccharine**.

sachet /ˈsæʃeɪ/ *n.* a small sealed bag used for packaging.

sack¹ *n.* **1.** a large bag of stout woven material. **2.** *Informal* dismissal from employment. –*v.* **3.** *Informal* to dismiss from employment.

sack² *v.* **1.** to pillage or loot after capture. –*n.* **2.** the plundering of a captured place.

sacrament *n.* an outward sign signifying something spiritual or religious.

sacred *adj.* **1.** relating to or connected with religion. **2.** immune from violence, interference, etc.

sacrifice *n.* **1.** the offering of life or some material possession to a deity, as in propitiation or homage. **2.** the surrender or destruction of something prized for the sake of a benefit expected. **3.** the thing so surrendered or offered. –*v.* **4.** to make a sacrifice or offering of. –**sacrificial**, *adj.*

sacrilege /ˈsækrəlɪdʒ/ *n.* the violation or profanation of anything held sacred. –**sacrilegious**, *adj.*

sacrosanct *adj.* especially sacred or inviolable.

sad *adj.* (**sadder, saddest**) **1.** sorrowful or mournful. **2.** causing sorrow. –**sadly**, *adv.* –**sadness**, *n.*

saddle *n.* **1.** a seat for a rider on the back of a horse, bicycle, etc. **2.** something resembling a saddle. –*v.* **3.** to put a saddle upon (a horse, etc.). **4.** to load or charge, as with a burden.

sadism *n.* **1.** sexual gratification gained through causing physical pain and humiliation. **2.** any enjoyment in inflicting mental or physical pain. –**sadist**, *n.* –**sadistic**, *adj.*

safari *n.* (*pl.* **-ris**) a journey; an expedition, especially for hunting.

safe *adj.* **1.** secure from harm, injury, danger, or risk. **2.** involving no risk. –*n.* **3.** a receptacle for the storage or preservation of articles.

safeguard *n.* **1.** something ensuring safety. –*v.* **2.** to guard; protect.

safety *n.* the state of being safe; freedom from danger.

safety belt *n.* → **seatbelt**.

safflower *n.* a herb cultivated for its oil which is used in cookery, etc.

saffron *n.* an orange-coloured plant product used to colour food and as a spice.

sag *v.* (**sagged, sagging**) **1.** to bend downwards by weight or pressure, especially in the middle. –*n.* **2.** the degree of sagging. **3.** a place where anything sags.

saga *n.* any narrative or legend of heroic exploits.

sagacious *adj.* having acute mental discernment and keen practical sense; shrewd. –**sagacity**, *n.*

The more usual word is **wise**.

sage¹ *n.* **1.** a profoundly wise man. –*adj.* (**sager, sagest**) **2.** wise, judicious, or prudent.

sage² *n.* a herb used in cookery.

sago *n.* a starchy foodstuff used in making puddings, etc.

said *v.* **1.** past tense and past participle of **say**. –*adj.* **2.** named or mentioned before.

sail *n.* **1.** an expanse of canvas or similar material spread to the wind to make a vessel move through the water. **2.** some similar piece or apparatus. **3.** a voyage or excursion, especially in a sailing vessel. –*v.* **4.** to travel in a ship. **5.** to move along like a sailing vessel. **6.** to sail upon, over, or through. **7.** to navigate (a ship, etc.). –**sailor**, *n.*

Don't confuse this with **sale**, which is when something is sold (*the sale of a house*).

sailboard *n.* **1.** a light surfboard with a mast and sail which you stand on and ride by moving the sail; windsurfer. –*v.* **2.** to ride a sailboard; windsurf. –**sailboarding**, *n.* –**sailboarder**, *n.*

saint *n.* **1.** someone who has been formally recognised by the Christian Church as being exceptionally holy. **2.** a person who is exceptionally good, virtuous, etc.

When def. 1 is written as part of a saint's name, it is usually shortened to **St**, as in **St John**.

sake¹ /setk/ *n.* **1.** cause, account, or interest. **2.** purpose or end.

sake² /'saki/ *n.* a Japanese alcoholic drink made from rice.

salacious *adj.* lustful or lecherous.

salad *n.* a dish of uncooked vegetables.

salamander *n.* **1.** any of various tailed amphibians, most of which have an aquatic larval stage but are terrestrial as adults. **2.** a mythical lizard or other reptile, or a being supposedly able to live in fire.

salami *n.* a kind of sausage, often flavoured with garlic.

salary *n.* (*pl.* **-ries**) a fixed periodical payment, usually monthly, paid to a person for regular work or services, especially office work. –**salaried**, *adj.*

Compare this with **wage**, which is also regular pay, but sometimes **salary** is used for the yearly amount you earn, and is usually paid monthly, whereas **wage** is used for pay that you get weekly. **Wage** is used especially for work in a factory or as a labourer.

sale *n.* **1.** the act of selling. **2.** the quantity sold. **3.** a special disposal of goods at reduced prices.

Don't confuse this with **sail**, which is a sheet of canvas or nylon attached to a boat, which catches the wind and makes the boat move through the water.

salesperson *n.* (*pl.* **-people** or **-persons**) someone employed to sell goods, as in a shop, etc.

sales tax *n.* a tax imposed on sales of goods.

salient *adj.* prominent or conspicuous.

The more usual word is **noticeable**.

saline *adj.* **1.** containing or tasting of common table salt. –*n.* **2.** a health drink or medicine.

salinity *n.* **1.** the degree of salt present in a substance. **2.** a level of salt rising from the substratum to the surface of the earth which turns surface freshwater into brackish water and reduces the value of the soil for agriculture.

saliva *n.* the fluid secretions produced by glands in the mouth.

sallow *adj.* of a yellowish, sickly hue or complexion.

sally *v.* (**-lied, -lying**) to set out briskly or energetically.

salmon *n.* (*pl.* **-mon** *or* **-mons**) **1.** a marine and freshwater food fish with pink flesh. **2.** a light yellowish pink.

For information about the different plural forms, see the note at **fish**.

salon *n.* **1.** a drawing room or reception room in a large house. **2.** a fashionable business establishment or shop.

saloon *n.* a room or place for public use for a specific purpose.

salsa *n.* **1.** a type of popular dance music originating in Latin America. **2.** a Mexican sauce usually based on tomatoes and chilli.

salt *n.* **1.** a crystalline compound, sodium chloride, NaCl, used for seasoning food, as a preservative, etc. **2.** *Chem.* a compound formed when an inorganic acid and a base react with each other. **3.** wit; pungency. *–v.* **4.** to season with salt. **5.** to cure, preserve, or treat with salt. *–adj.* **6.** containing salt.

saltbush *n.* any of various drought-resistant plants used as grazing plants in arid areas.

saltcellar *n.* a shaker or vessel for salt.

saltpetre *n.* a white salt used in making gunpowder, etc.

salubrious *adj.* (especially of air, climate, etc.) favourable to health.

salutary *adj.* promoting some beneficial purpose.

The more usual word is **beneficial**.

salutation *n.* something uttered, written, or done as a greeting.

salute *v.* **1.** to address with expressions of goodwill, respect, etc.; greet. **2.** *Mil., Navy* to pay respect to or honour by some formal act, etc. *–n.* **3.** an act of saluting. **4.** → **Australian salute**.

salvage *n.* **1.** the saving of anything from fire, danger, etc., or the property so saved. *–v.* (**-vaged, -vaging**) **2.** to save from shipwreck, fire, etc.

salvation *n.* **1.** the state of being saved or delivered. **2.** a source or means of deliverance.

salve *n.* **1.** a healing ointment. *–v.* **2.** to soothe as if with salve. *–pron.* **4.** the same person or thing. *–phr.* **5. the same**, with the

salvo *n.* (*pl.* **-vos** *or* **-voes**) a discharge of artillery or other firearms.

same *adj.* **1.** identical. **2.** agreeing in kind, amount, etc. **3.** unchanged in character, condition, etc. *–pron.* **4.** the same person or thing. *–phr.* **5. the same**, with the same manner (used adverbially).

sample *n.* **1.** a small part of anything or one of a number, intended to show the quality, style, etc., of the whole. *–adj.* **2.** serving as a specimen. *–v.* **3.** to take or test a sample or samples of.

sanatorium *n.* (*pl.* **-toriums** *or* **-toria**) an establishment for the treatment of invalids, convalescents, etc.

sanctimonious *adj.* making a show of holiness.

sanction *n.* **1.** support given to an action, etc. **2.** (*usu. pl.*) action taken by one or more countries towards another to force it to comply with legal obligations: *trade sanctions. –v.* **3.** to authorise or allow. **4.** to ratify or confirm.

For def. 3, the more usual word is **approve**.

sanctity *n.* (*pl.* **-ties**) **1.** holiness. **2.** sacred or hallowed character.

sanctuary *n.* (*pl.* **-ries**) **1.** a sacred or holy place. **2.** (a place of) protection from something.

sand *n.* **1.** the fine debris of rocks, consisting of small, loose grains. **2.** a dull reddish-yellow colour. *–v.* **3.** to smooth or polish with sand or sandpaper.

sandal *n.* any of various kinds of low open shoes.

sandalwood *n.* the fragrant inner wood of certain Asian and Aust. trees.

sandbar *n.* a bar of sand formed in a river or sea.

sandpaper *n.* a strong paper coated with a layer of sand, used for smoothing or polishing.

sandshoe *n.* Aust., NZ a rubber-soled canvas shoe, worn especially for sports, etc., and as part of casual wear.

sandstone *n.* a rock formed by the consolidation of sand.

sandwich *n.* **1.** two slices of bread, plain or buttered, with a layer of meat, cheese, etc., between. –*v.* **2.** to insert or hem in between 2 other things.

sane *adj.* **1.** free from mental derangement. **2.** having or showing reason, sound judgement, or good sense. –**sanity**, *n.*

sanguine /ˈsæŋgwən/ *adj.* hopeful or confident.

sanitary *adj.* **1.** of or relating to health. **2.** free from dirt, germs, etc.

sanitation *n.* (the protection of public health, especially by) drainage systems.

sank *v.* past tense of **sink**.

sap¹ *n.* **1.** the vital circulating fluid of a woody plant. **2.** *Informal* a fool or weak person.

sap² *v.* (**sapped, sapping**) to undermine; weaken or destroy insidiously.

sapling *n.* a young tree.

sapphire *n.* **1.** a transparent blue gemstone. **2.** a deep blue. –*adj.* **3.** deep blue.

sarcasm *n.* harsh or bitter derision or irony. –**sarcastic**, *adj.*

sarcoma *n.* (*pl.* **-mas** *or* **-mata**) a malignant tumour attacking especially the bones.

sarcophagus /saˈkɒfəgəs/ *n.* (*pl.* **-phagi** /-fəgaɪ/ *or* **-phaguses**) a stone coffin.

sardine *n.* (*pl.* **-dines** *or* **-dine**) the young of the common pilchard, often preserved in oil and canned for food.

sardonic *adj.* bitterly ironical; sneering.

sari *n.* (*pl.* **-ris**) a long piece of cotton or silk, the principal outer garment of Hindu women. Also, **saree**.

sarong *n.* the piece of cloth worn like a skirt as the main garment by both sexes in the Malay Archipelago.

SARS /saz/ *n.* severe acute respiratory syndrome; an acute form of pneumonia caused by a virus.

SARS-CoV-2 /saz-koʊ viˈtu/ *n.* the coronavirus which causes COVID-19. Also, **SARS-2**.

sarsaparilla /saspəˈrɪlə/ *n.* **1.** a climbing plant having a root used medicinally. **2.** an extract made of it.

sartorial *adj.* of or relating to clothes or dress, generally men's.

sash¹ *n.* a long band or scarf of silk, etc.

sash² *n.* a movable framework in which panes of glass are set, as in a window.

sashimi /ˈsæʃimi/ *n.* a Japanese dish of fresh seafood fillets cut into bite-sized, oblong strips, and eaten raw with soy sauce and Japanese horseradish.

sassafras *n.* any of several Aust. trees with fragrant bark.

satanic *adj.* characteristic of Satan; extremely wicked. Also, **satanical**.

satay *n.* **1.** Also, **satay sauce**. a spicy peanut-based sauce used in South-East Asian cookery. **2.** a dish consisting of pieces of marinated meat, chicken or seafood grilled on a skewer and served with satay sauce or a similar hot, spicy sauce.

satchel *n.* a bag with a shoulder strap, used for carrying schoolbooks.

sate *v.* to satisfy (any appetite or desire) to the full.

satellite *n.* **1.** a small body which revolves round a planet. **2.** a device for launching into orbit round the earth, another planet, or the sun, for purposes of communication, research, etc.

satiate /'seɪʃieɪt/ v. to supply with anything to excess.

The more usual word is **satisfy**.

satin n. **1.** a very smooth, glossy fabric. –*adj*. **2.** smooth; glossy.

satire n. irony, sarcasm, ridicule, etc., used in exposing, vice, folly, etc. –**satirical**, *satiric*, *adj*.

satirise v. to make the object of satire. Also, **satirize**.

satisfaction n. **1.** the state of being satisfied. **2.** payment, as for debt. –**satisfactory**, *adj*.

satisfy v. (**-fied, -fying**) **1.** to fulfil (the desires, expectations, etc.) of. **2.** to discharge fully (a debt, etc.). –**satisfied**, *adj*.

saturate v. to soak, or imbue thoroughly. –**saturation**, *n*.

saturnine *adj*. gloomy; taciturn.

satyr /'seɪtə, 'sætə/ n. **1.** in classical mythology, a god, part human and part goat. **2.** a lascivious man.

sauce n. any preparation, usually liquid or soft, eaten as an accompaniment to food.

Don't confuse this with **source**, which is the place or thing that something comes from (*a source of information*).

saucepan n. a container for boiling, stewing, etc.

saucer n. a small, round, shallow dish to hold a cup.

saucy *adj*. (**-cier, -ciest**) *Informal* **1.** impertinent. **2.** pert.

sauerkraut /'saʊəkraʊt/ n. cabbage cut fine, salted, and allowed to ferment.

sauna n. (a room or device for taking) a type of steam bath.

saunter v. **1.** to walk with a leisurely gait. –*n*. **2.** a leisurely walk or ramble.

sausage n. minced meats packed into a special skin.

sauté /'souteɪ/ v. (**sautéed, sautéing**) to cook in a small amount of fat.

sauterne /sou'tɜn, sə-/ n. (*sometimes upper case*) a rich, sweet, white, table wine.

savage *adj*. **1.** uncivilised; barbarous. **2.** fierce or cruel. –*n*. **3.** an uncivilised human being. –*v*. **4.** to assail violently; maul. –**savagery**, *n*.

Def. 3 was once commonly used to refer to someone belonging to any society that wasn't part of Western civilisation, but now this usage is old-fashioned and is regarded as offensive.

save[1] v. **1.** to rescue from danger. **2.** to avoid the spending, consumption, or waste of. **3.** to set apart or reserve. **4.** to prevent the occurrence, use, or necessity of. **5.** to accumulate or put aside (money, etc.) as the result of economy. –*n*. **6.** the act or instance of saving, especially preventing a goal being scored in soccer, etc.

save[2] *prep., conj.* except; but: *nothing save her good sense could help her now.*

saveloy n. → **frankfurt**.

saving *adj*. **1.** that saves; rescuing; preserving. **2.** redeeming. –*n*. **3.** a reduction or lessening of expenditure. **4.** (*pl.*) sums of money saved by economy. –*prep*. **5.** except.

saviour n. someone who saves, rescues, or delivers. Also, **savior**.

savour n. **1.** a particular taste or smell. **2.** distinctive quality or property. –*v*. **3.** to perceive by taste or smell, especially with relish. **4.** to give oneself to the enjoyment of. Also, **savor**.

savoury *adj*. **1.** piquant, pungent, or salty to the taste. –*n*. (*pl.* **-ries**) **2.** a usually salty, bite-sized morsel on a small biscuit. Also, **savory**.

savvy *adj*. (**-vier, -viest**) well-informed or experienced.

saw[1] n. **1.** a tool or device for cutting, typically a thin serrated metal blade. –*v*. (**sawed, sawn** or **sawed, sawing**) **2.** to cut with a saw.

Don't confuse this with **sore** or **soar**. **Sore** describes something which is painful, and to **soar** is to fly upwards.

saw² v. past tense of **see¹**.

saxophone n. a musical wind instrument.

say v. (**said, saying**) **1.** to utter or pronounce. **2.** to express in words. **3.** to assume as a hypothesis or an estimate. **4.** to declare; express an opinion. –n. **5.** *Informal* the right or opportunity to say, speak or decide.

saying n. something said, especially a proverb.

scab n. **1.** the crust which forms over a sore during healing. **2.** someone who continues to work during a strike; blackleg. –v. (**scabbed, scabbing**) **3.** to act or work as a scab.

Note that defs 2 and 3 are used in a disapproving way.

scabbard n. a sheath or cover for the blade of a sword, dagger, etc.

scabies n. an infectious skin disease occurring in animals or humans, caused by parasitic mites.

scaffold n. a raised framework or platform. Also, **scaffolding**.

scald v. **1.** to burn or affect painfully with hot liquid or steam. –n. **2.** a burn caused by hot liquid or steam.

scale¹ n. **1.** one of the thin, flat, horny or hard plates that form the covering of certain animals, as fishes. **2.** any thin piece such as peels off from a surface. –v. **3.** to remove the scale(s) from.

scale² n. (*usu. pl.*) a device for weighing; balance.

scale³ n. **1.** a succession of steps or degrees. **2.** a graduated line, as on a map, representing proportionate size. **3.** an instrument with graduated spaces, for measuring, etc. **4.** the proportion which the representation of an object bears to the object. **5.** *Music* a succession of notes ascending or descending according to fixed intervals. –v. **6.** to climb (as) by a ladder; climb up or over. –phr. **7. scale down**, to decrease, especially according to a fixed proportion. **8. scale up**, to

increase, especially according to a fixed proportion.

scallop n. **1.** a bivalve mollusc with fluted shells. **2.** one of a series of rounded projections along the edge of pastry, a garment, etc. **3.** Also, **potato scallop, potato scallop potato cake**. a thin slice of potato dipped in batter and deep-fried. –v. **4.** to finish (an edge) with scallops.

scallywag n. a mischievous child; scamp.

This word is used affectionately.

scalp n. **1.** the skin of the upper part of the head. –v. **2.** to cut or tear the scalp from.

scalpel n. a light knife used in surgery.

scam *Informal* –n. **1.** a ruse or confidence trick. –v. (**scammed, scamming**) **2.** to practise a confidence trick on (someone) **3.** to get (something) from someone by plausible deceit rather than paying: *he scammed some cakes from the tuckshop.* –**scammer**, n.

scamp n. a mischievous child.

scamper v. to run or go quickly and playfully.

scan v. (**scanned, scanning**) **1.** to glance at or run through hastily. **2.** *Radar* to sweep a region with a beam from a radar transmitter. **3.** (of verse) to conform to the rules of metre. –n. **4.** close examination or scrutiny. **5.** *Med.* an image of a part of the body gained by passing a moving detector or beam of radiation over it.

scandal n. **1.** a disgraceful or discreditable action, circumstance, etc. **2.** damage to reputation. **3.** malicious gossip. –**scandalous**, adj.

scandalise v. to shock or horrify by something considered immoral or improper. Also, **scandalize**.

scanner n. a device, linked to a computer, which converts printed material into digital form.

scant adj. **1.** barely sufficient. **2.** barely amounting to as much as indicated.

scapegoat *n.* someone who is made to bear the blame for others.

scapula *n.* (*pl.* **-las** *or* **-lae** /-liː/) → **shoulderblade**.

scar *n.* **1.** the mark left by a healed wound. *–v.* (**scarred, scarring**) **2.** to mark with a scar.

scarab *n.* a type of beetle. Also, **scarab beetle**.

scarce *adj.* seldom met with; not plentiful.

scarcely *adv.* barely; hardly: *I could scarcely move.*

Note that you can say **scarcely any**, as in *There's scarcely any butter in the fridge*, but not **scarcely no**, as in *There's scarcely no butter in the fridge*.

scare *v.* (**scared, scaring**) **1.** to strike with sudden fear. **2.** to become frightened. *–n.* **3.** a sudden fright or alarm.

scarecrow *n.* an object, usually a figure of a man, set up to frighten birds away from crops.

scarf *n.* (*pl.* **scarfs** *or* **scarves**) a long, broad strip of fabric worn about the neck, shoulders, or head for ornament or protection.

scarify /'skærəfaɪ/ *v.* (**-fied, -fying**) to make scratches or superficial incisions in.

scarlet *adj., n.* (of) a bright red colour inclining towards orange.

scarlet fever *n.* a contagious disease, now chiefly of children.

scat *v.* (**scatted, scatting**) *Informal* to go off hastily (usually in the imperative).

scathing *adj.* intended to hurt the feelings.

The more usual word is **scornful**.

scatter *v.* **1.** to throw loosely about. **2.** to separate and drive off in various directions. **3.** to go in different directions. *–n.* **4.** the act of scattering. **5.** something scattered.

scavenge *v.* to search for, and take (anything usable) from discarded material.

scenario *n.* (*pl.* **-rios**) an outline of the plot of a dramatic work.

scene *n.* **1.** the place where any action, real or fictional, occurs. **2.** any view or picture. **3.** an exhibition or outbreak of excited or violent feeling before others. **4.** a unit of dramatic action within a play. **5.** an episode or situation as described in writing.

scenery *n.* (*pl.* **-ries**) **1.** the general appearance of a place. **2.** the setting on a stage to represent some place.

scenic *adj.* of or relating to natural scenery; having fine scenery.

scent *n.* **1.** distinctive smell, especially when agreeable. **2.** a track or trail as indicated by such a smell. **3.** → **perfume**. *–v.* **4.** to perceive or recognise by the sense of smell. **5.** to sprinkle with perfume.

Don't confuse this with **sent** or **cent**. **Sent** is the past form of the verb **send** (*I sent the letter yesterday*). A **cent** is a coin worth a hundredth of a dollar.

sceptic *n.* someone who has a doubting, pessimistic attitude towards people, plans, ideas, etc.

sceptre *n.* a rod or wand carried as an emblem of royal power.

schedule *n.* **1.** a plan of procedure. **2.** a list of items to be dealt with during a specified time. **3.** a timetable. *–v.* **4.** to enter in a schedule. **5.** to plan for a certain date.

scheme *n.* **1.** a plan or design. **2.** a policy or plan officially adopted by a company, business, etc. **3.** an underhand plot; intrigue. **4.** any system of correlated things, parts, etc., or the manner of its arrangement. *–v.* **5.** to plan. **6.** to plot; intrigue.

schism /'skɪzəm, 'ʃɪzəm/ *n.* division into mutually opposed parties.

The more usual word is **split**.

schizophrenia *n.* any of various psychotic disorders characterised by breakdown of integrated personality functioning, withdrawal from reality, emotional dullness and distortion, and disturbances in thought and behaviour. –**schizophrenic**, *n.*, *adj.*

schlep /ʃlɛp/ *Chiefly US Informal* –*v.* (**schlepped**, **schlepping**) **1.** to carry; cart or lug. –*phr.* **2. schlep around**, to traipse or trudge around. Also, **shlep**.

schmaltz /ʃmɒlts, ʃmælts/ *n. Informal* excessive sentimentality, especially in the arts. Also, **schmalz**. –**schmaltzy**, *adj.*

schnapps *n.* a type of gin.

scholar *n.* **1.** a learned or erudite person. **2.** a student; pupil. –**scholarly**, *adj.*

scholarship *n.* **1.** knowledge acquired by study. **2.** the sum of money or other aid granted to a scholar.

scholastic *adj.* of or relating to schools, scholars, or education.

school[1] *n.* **1.** a place or establishment where instruction is given, especially one for children. **2.** a department or faculty in a university, etc. **3.** a body of scholars, artists, writers, etc., united by a similarity of method, style, principles, etc. –*v.* **4.** to educate in or as in a school.

school[2] *n.* a large number of fish, porpoises, whales, etc., swimming together.

schooner *n.* **1.** a sailing vessel. **2.** *Aust., NZ* a large glass of beer.

sciatica /saɪˈætɪkə/ *n.* any painful disorder extending from the hip down the back of the thigh and surrounding area.

science *n.* **1.** systematised knowledge in general. **2.** the systematic study of humans and the physical world.

science fiction *n.* a form of fiction which draws imaginatively on scientific speculation.

The short form of this is **sci-fi**.

scientific *adj.* **1.** of or relating to science or the sciences. **2.** systematic or accurate. –**scientifically**, *adv.*

scientific method *n.* a method of research in which you identify a problem, collect relevant data, formulate a hypothesis on the basis of this data, and, finally, test the hypothesis to prove if it is valid.

scientist *n.* someone versed in or devoted to science.

scintillate /ˈsɪntəleɪt/ *v.* **1.** to twinkle, as the stars. **2.** to be witty, brilliant in conversation.

scion /ˈsaɪən/ *n.* a descendant.

scissors *pl. n.* a cutting instrument with 2 blades whose edges work against each other.

sclerophyll /ˈsklɛrəfɪl, ˈsklɪə-/ *Bot.* –*n.* **1.** any of various plants, typically found in low rainfall areas, having tough leaves which help to reduce water loss. –*adj.* **2.** of or relating to such plants.

scoff[1] *v.* to jeer (*at*).

scoff[2] *v. Informal* to eat greedily and quickly.

scold *v.* **1.** to find fault (with). –*n.* **2.** a person, especially a woman, who is habitually verbally abusive.

scoliosis /skɒliˈoʊsəs/ *n.* abnormal lateral curvature of the spine.

scone *n.* **1.** a small light plain cake. **2.** *Aust., NZ Informal* the head.

scoop *n.* **1.** a ladle or similar utensil. **2.** an item of news, etc., published or broadcast in advance of, or to the exclusion of, rivals. –*v.* **3.** to take up or out with, or as with a scoop.

scoot *v. Informal* to go swiftly or hastily.

scooter *n.* a child's vehicle with 2 wheels.

scope *n.* **1.** extent or range of view, operation, etc. **2.** space for movement or activity.

scorch *v.* **1.** to affect in colour, taste, etc., by burning slightly. **2.** to parch or shrivel with heat.

score *n.* **1.** the record of points made by the competitors in a game or match. **2.** a notch or scratch. **3.** (*pl.* **score**) a group or set of 20. **4.** account, reason, or ground. **5.** *Music* a written or printed piece of music. –*v.* **6.** to make a score of. **7.** to make notches, cuts, or lines in or on. **8.** to make a point or points in a game or contest. **9.** to keep score, as of a game.

scorn n. 1. open or unqualified contempt. –v. 2. to treat or regard with scorn.

scorpion n. any of numerous arachnids having a long narrow abdomen with a venomous sting.

scotch v. to injure so as to make harmless.

scot-free adj. free from penalty.

scoundrel n. an unprincipled, dishonourable man.

scour¹ v. to cleanse or polish by hard rubbing.

scour² v. to range over, as in search.

scourge n. 1. a cause of affliction or calamity. –v. (**scourged, scourging**) 2. to punish or chastise severely; afflict.

scout n. 1. a person sent out to obtain information. –v. 2. to examine or watch in order to find something or to get information: *to scout the area for a new house; to scout out some help; to scout around for a new sax player.*

scowl v. 1. to have a gloomy or threatening look. –n. 2. a scowling expression.

scrabble v. 1. to scratch or scrape, as with the claws or hands. –n. 2. a scrabbling or scramble.

scraggly adj. (**-lier, -liest**) irregular; ragged; straggling.

scraggy adj. (**-gier, -giest**) 1. lean or thin. 2. meagre.

scram v. (**scrammed, scramming**) *Informal* to get away quickly.

scramble v. 1. to make one's way hurriedly (*over*) by use of the hands and feet. 2. to struggle with others for possession. 3. to mix together confusedly. –n. 4. a climb or progression over rough, irregular ground, etc. 5. any disorderly struggle or proceeding.

scrap¹ n. 1. a small piece. –adj. 2. consisting of scraps. 3. discarded or left over. –v. (**scrapped, scrapping**) 4. to discard as useless.

scrap² n. *Informal* a fight or quarrel.

scrape v. (**scraped, scraping**) 1. to free from an outer layer by rubbing with a sharp instrument. 2. to remove (an outer layer, adhering matter, etc.) in this way. 3. to rub harshly on or across (something). 4. to practise laborious economy. –n. 5. a scraped place. 6. an embarrassing situation. –phr. 7. **scrape by** (or **through**), to manage with difficulty. 8. **scrape together** (or **up**), to collect by or as by scraping, or laboriously.

scratch v. 1. to dig, scrape, or to tear (*out*, *off*, etc.) with the claws, the nails, etc. 2. to rub or scrape lightly with the fingernails, etc. 3. to erase or strike (*out*). 4. to use the nails, claws, etc., for tearing, digging, etc. 5. to relieve itching by scratching. 6. to make a slight grating noise. –n. 7. a mark produced by scratching. 8. an act of scratching. –phr. 9. **from scratch**, from the beginning. 10. **up to scratch**, satisfactory.

scrawl v. 1. to write or draw in a sprawling awkward manner. –n. 2. awkward or careless handwriting.

scrawny adj. (**-nier, -niest**) lean; thin; scraggy.

scream v. 1. to utter a loud, sharp, piercing cry. –n. 2. a loud, sharp, piercing cry or sound. 3. *Informal* someone or something very funny.

screech v., n. (to utter) a harsh, shrill cry.

screed n. a long speech or piece of writing.

screen n. 1. a covered frame serving as a shelter, partition, etc. 2. a surface for displaying slides, slides, etc. 3. films collectively. 4. the component of a television, computer monitor, etc., on which the visible image is displayed. 5. anything that shelters, protects, or conceals. –v. 6. to shelter, protect, or conceal with a screen. 7. to project (pictures, etc.) on a screen.

screen grab n. an image taken from a computer screen and saved as a pdf file.

screenplay n. the script of a film.

screensaver *n. Computers* a program which is activated when the mouse or keyboard has not been used for a specified length of time, replacing the screen's contents with either a blank screen or graphics, designed to save power and to entertain. Also, **screen saver.**

screw *n.* **1.** a metal nail-like device with a slotted head and a spiral ridge. –*v.* **2.** to force, press, etc., by or as by means of a screw. **3.** to twist; contort. **4.** to turn as or like a screw: *Screw the lid on.*

screwdriver *n.* a tool for driving in or withdrawing screws.

scribble *v.* **1.** to write hastily or carelessly. **2.** to make meaningless marks. –*n.* **3.** a hasty or careless piece of writing or drawing.

scribe *n.* someone who used to make copies of books before the invention of printing.

scrimp *v.* to be sparing or in; stint.

scrip *n.* **1.** a writing, especially a receipt or certificate. **2.** *Finance* shares or stock issued to shareholders.

script *n.* **1.** the working text of a play, film, etc. **2.** handwriting.

scripture *n.* any writing or book, of a sacred nature, especially the Bible.

scroll *n.* **1.** a roll of parchment or paper. **2.** an ornament with a spiral or coiled form. –*v.* **3.** *Computers* to move (text, images, etc.) up, down, left or right on a computer screen in order to view material which is outside the limits of the screen.

scrooge *n.* a miserly, ill-tempered person.

scrotum *n.* (*pl.* **-ta** or **-tums**) the pouch of skin that contains the testicles.

scrounge *v.* to obtain by borrowing, foraging, or pilfering.

scrub[1] *v.* (**scrubbed, scrubbing**) **1.** to wash by rubbing hard with a brush, cloth, etc. **2.** *Informal* to cancel; get rid of. –*n.* **3.** the act of scrubbing.

scrub[2] *n.* **1.** low trees or shrubs, collectively. **2.** a tract of land covered with such vegetation. –**scrubby,** *adj.*

scruff *n.* the nape or back of the neck.

scruffy *adj.* (**-fier, -fiest**) *Informal* unkempt or dirty. –**scruffily,** *adv.* –**scruffiness,** *n.*

scrumptious *adj. Informal* deliciously tasty.

scrupulous *adj.* **1.** minutely careful, precise, or exact. **2.** having or showing a strict regard for what is right.

scrutineer *n.* someone who is authorised to inspect the counting of votes.

scrutinise *v.* to examine closely or critically. Also, **scrutinize.** –**scrutiny,** *n.*

The more usual word is **inspect**.

SCSI /ˈskʌzi/ *n.* small computer system interface; an interface standard for connecting peripheral devices to a computer system.

scuba *n.* a portable breathing device for divers.

scud *v.* (**scudded, scudding**) to run or move quickly or hurriedly.

scuff *v.* **1.** to mar by scraping or hard use. –*n.* **2.** a type of slipper or sandal without a back.

scuffle *v.* **1.** to struggle or fight in a confused manner. –*n.* **2.** a confused struggle or fight.

scullery *n.* (*pl.* **-ries**) (formerly) a small room where the rough, dirty work of a kitchen was done.

sculpture *n.* **1.** the fine art of making three-dimensional figures or designs. **2.** a piece of such work. –*v.* **3.** to carve or make by sculpture. –**sculptor,** *n.*

scum *n.* a film of foul or extraneous matter on a liquid.

scurrilous *adj.* grossly or indecently abusive.

scurry *v.* (**-ried, -rying**) **1.** to go or move quickly. –*n.* (*pl.* **-ries**) **2.** a quick movement.

scurvy *n.* **1.** a disease caused by lack of vitamin C. *–adj.* (**-vier, -viest**) **2.** low, mean, or contemptible.

scuttle *v.* **1.** to run (*off, away,* etc.) with quick, hasty steps. *–n.* **2.** an act of scuttling.

scythe *n.* an agricultural implement for mowing grass, etc., by hand.

sea *n.* **1.** the salt waters that cover the greater part of the earth's surface. **2.** a division of these waters. **3.** a large lake. **4.** a huge quantity or expanse. *–phr.* Also, **all at sea. 5. at sea,** a. sailing or on the ocean. **b.** bewildered; confused.

sea anemone *n.* any of several marine coelenterates having a column-shaped body topped by a disc bearing one or more circles of tentacles.

seabird *n.* a bird frequenting the sea or coast.

seafood *n.* any saltwater fish or shellfish used for food.

seagull *n.* a web-footed marine bird.

seahorse *n.* a type of small fish with a prehensile tail and a head at right angles to the body.

seal¹ *n.* **1.** a device affixed to a document as evidence of authenticity or attestation. **2.** anything that effectively closes a thing. **3.** a road surface of hard material. *–v.* **4.** to approve, authorise, or confirm. **5.** to close by any form of fastening that must be broken to open it. **6.** to surface a road with tar, bitumen, etc.

seal² *n.* (*pl.* **seals** *or, especially collectively,* **seal**) any of several furred, amphibious mammals with flippers for limbs.

seam *n.* **1.** the line formed by sewing together pieces of cloth. **2.** any line between abutting edges; a crack or fissure. *–v.* **3.** to join with a seam. **4.** to furrow; mark with wrinkles. **5.** to become cracked, fissured, or furrowed.

Don't confuse this with **seem**, which is to appear to be (*She seemed happy*).

seamstress /'simstrəs, 'sɛm-/ *n.* a woman whose occupation is sewing.

seamy *adj.* (**-mier, -miest**) vulgar; sordid.

seance /'seɪɒns/ *n.* a meeting of people seeking to communicate with spirits of the dead with the help of a medium. Also, **séance**.

sear *v.* to burn or char the surface of.

search *v.* **1.** to go or look carefully to find something. **2.** to examine (a person) for concealed objects. **3.** to bring or find (*out*) by a search. **4.** to seek. *–n.* **5.** the act of searching.

search engine *n. Computers* software which enables a user to find items on a database on the internet.

seasickness *n.* nausea caused by the motion of a vessel at sea.

season *n.* **1.** a period of the year characterised by particular conditions of weather, etc. **2.** the period of the year when something is best or available. **3.** any period or time. **4.** *Agric.* the time for mating in female stock. *–v.* **5.** to heighten or improve the flavour of (food) with condiments, etc. **6.** to dry and harden (timber). **7.** to become seasoned, matured, hardened.

seasonable *adj.* **1.** suitable to the season. **2.** timely; opportune.

seasonal *adj.* periodical. **–seasonally,** *adv.*

seasoning *n.* **1.** something that seasons, especially salt, spices, herbs, or other condiments. **2.** *Aust., NZ* a savoury filling for poultry, etc.; stuffing.

seat *n.* **1.** something for sitting on, as a chair or bench. **2.** the buttocks, or the part of a garment which covers the buttocks. **3.** a place or centre of some activity: *a seat of learning.* **4.** a parliamentary constituency. *–v.* **5.** to place on a seat or seats. **6.** to find seats for.

seatbelt *n.* a belt attached to the frame of a motor vehicle, aircraft, etc., for holding a person safely in place against sudden turns, stops, collision, etc. Also, **safety belt**.

sea urchin *n.* a small globe-shaped sea creature with a spiny shell.

seaweed n. any plant or plants growing in the ocean.

secant n. Maths a straight line which cuts a circle or other curve.

secateurs /ˈsɛkətəz, ˈsɛkətɜz, sɛkəˈtɜz/ pl. n. a scissor-like cutting instrument for pruning shrubs, etc.

secede v. to withdraw formally from an alliance or association. **–secession,** n.

seclude v. to shut off or keep apart; withdraw into solitude. **–seclusion,** n.

second¹ /ˈsɛkənd/ adj. **1.** an ordinal number, next after the first in order, quality, etc. **2.** alternate: every second day. **3.** additional: a second chance. –n. **4.** that which comes after the first, in order, etc. **5.** (sometimes pl.) Commerce a product that is below the normal or required standard. –v. **6.** to support, back up, or assist. –adv. **7.** in the second place, group, etc.

second² /ˈsɛkənd/ n. **1.** a 60th part of a minute of time. **2.** a moment or instant. **3.** Geom., etc. the 60th part of a minute of a degree.

Note in informal language def. 2 can be shortened to **sec:** Hang on a sec.

second³ /səˈkɒnd/ v. to transfer (someone) temporarily to another post or organisation.

secondary adj. **1.** next after the first in order, place, time, importance, etc. **2.** derived; not primary or original. **3.** of or relating to the processing of primary products. **4.** of minor importance; subordinate.

second-hand adv., adj. (after having been) previously used or owned.

second person n. See person (def. 3).

seconds pl. n. **1.** the plural of **second¹**. **2.** the plural of **second²**. **3.** (at a meal) **a.** a second helping. **b.** a second course.

secret adj. **1.** done or made without the knowledge of others. –n. **2.** something secret or hidden.

secretariat n. the officials or office entrusted with maintaining records, etc., especially for an international organisation.

secretary n. (pl. **-ries**) a person who conducts correspondence, keeps records etc., for an individual or an organisation.

secrete v. **1.** Biol. to separate off or convert from the blood, as in the physiological process of secretion. **2.** to hide or conceal. **–secretion,** n.

secret service n. **1.** a government department concerned with security. **2.** espionage.

sect n. a body of persons adhering to a particular religious faith.

section n. **1.** one of a number of parts that fit together to make a whole. **2.** the act of cutting; separation by cutting. **3.** a representation of an object as it would appear if cut across. **4.** NZ → **block** (def. 4).

sector n. **1.** Geom. a plane figure bounded by 2 radii and the included arc of a circle, ellipse, or the like. **2.** any field or division of a field of activity.

Compare def. 1 with **segment** (def. 1).

secular adj. of or relating to the world, or to things not religious; temporal.

secure adj. **1.** free from or not exposed to danger. **2.** not liable to fall, yield, become displaced, etc. **3.** free from care or anxiety **4.** sure. –v. **5.** to get hold or possession of **6.** to make secure or certain. **7.** to assure a creditor of (payment) by a pledge on mortgage.

security n. (pl. **-ties**) **1.** freedom from danger, risk, etc.; safety. **2.** freedom from worry or doubt; confidence. **3.** something that secures or makes safe; a protection a defence. **4.** an assurance; guarantee **5.** Law something given or deposited as a guarantee for the fulfilment of a promise or an obligation, the payment of a debt etc. **6.** (usu. pl.) stocks and shares, etc.

sedan n. a four-door passenger car with two rows of seats and a separate boot.

Compare this with **station wagon** and **hatchback**.

sedate *adj.* **1.** calm, quiet, or composed. –*v.* **2.** to calm or put to sleep by means of sedatives. –**sedation**, *n.*

sedative *adj.* **1.** tending to calm or soothe. –*n.* **2.** a sedative agent or remedy.

sedentary /ˈsɛdəntri/ *adj.* characterised by or requiring a sitting posture.

sediment *n.* matter which settles to the bottom of a liquid.

sedition *n.* incitement of rebellion against the government.

seduce *v.* **1.** to induce to have sexual intercourse. **2.** to win over; entice. –**seduction**, *n.* –**seductive**, *adj.*

see¹ *v.* (**saw**, **seen**, **seeing**) **1.** to observe or be aware of. **2.** to perceive or be aware of with any or all of the senses. **3.** to view, or visit or attend as a spectator. **4.** to discern with the intelligence. **5.** to find out, or learn, as by inquiry. **6.** to visit. **7.** to accompany or escort. **8.** to ensure. **9.** to have or use the power of sight. **10.** to inquire or find out. **11.** to give attention or care.

Don't confuse **see** with **sea**, which is a large area of water.

see² *n.* the centre of jurisdiction of a bishop.

seed *n.* (*pl.* **seeds** or **seed**) **1.** the part of a plant that propagates, including ovules, tubers, bulbs, etc. **2.** (*usu. pl.*) the germ or beginning of anything. **3.** *Sport* a player who has been seeded. –*v.* **4.** to sow (land) with seed. **5.** *Sport* to distribute certain outstanding players so that they will not meet in the early rounds of play: *Jones is number 3 seed this year.* **6.** to produce or shed seed.

seed bank *n.* a store of seeds as a source for their future planting should they become extinct in the natural world.

seedling *n.* a young plant developed after germination of a seed.

seedy *adj.* (**-dier**, **-diest**) rather disreputable or shabby.

seek *v.* (**sought**, **seeking**) **1.** to go in search of. **2.** to try or attempt (followed by

an infinitive): *He seeks to please.* **3.** to ask for.

seem *v.* to appear or look to be; appear (to be, feel, do, etc.).

Don't confuse this with **seam**, which is the line where two pieces of fabric have been joined.

seemly *adj.* fitting or becoming with respect to propriety or good taste.

seep *v.* to pass gradually, as liquid, through a porous substance.

seer *n.* someone who foretells future events; prophet.

seesaw *n.* **1.** a plank or beam balanced at the middle so that its ends may rise and fall alternately. –*v.* **2.** to move up and down or back and forth.

seethe *v.* to surge or foam, as a boiling liquid.

segment *n.* /ˈsɛgmənt/ **1.** *Geom.* a part cut off from a figure (especially a circular or spherical one) by a line or a plane. **2.** one of the parts into which anything naturally separates or is naturally divided. –*v.* /sɛgˈmɛnt/ **3.** to separate or divide into segments.

Compare def. 1 with **sector** (def. 1).

segregate *v.* to separate, or set or go apart from the others or from the main body. –**segregation**, *n.*

segue /ˈsɛgweɪ/ *n.* any smooth transition, as from one topic of discussion to another.

seismic /ˈsaɪzmɪk/ *adj.* relating to an earthquake. Also, **seismal**, **seismical**. –**seismically**, *adv.*

seize *v.* **1.** to lay hold of suddenly or forcibly. **2.** to take possession of by legal authority. **3.** to take advantage of promptly. **4.** Also, **seize up.** to become jammed, as an engine through excessive heat.

seizure *n.* **1.** the act of seizing. **2.** a sudden attack, as of disease.

seldom *adv.* not often; rarely.

select v. **1.** to choose in preference to another or others. –adj. **2.** specially chosen; excellent. –**selectively**, adv.

selection n. **1.** the act of selecting or the fact of being selected. **2.** a thing or a number of things selected. **3.** a range of things from which selection may be made.

selective adj. **1.** making selection. **2.** choosing the best in anything; discriminating. **3.** marked by selection. **4.** Educ. of or relating to a school to which entry is restricted to those applicants who successfully complete a prescribed test or series of tests. –**selectivity**, n.

self n. (pl. **selves**) **1.** a person or thing referred to with respect to individuality; one's own person. –pron. (pl. **selves**) **2.** myself, himself, etc.

self-conscious adj. excessively conscious of oneself as observed by others.

self-evident adj. evident in itself without proof.

self-government n. political independence of a country, people, region, etc.

self-interest n. excessive regard for one's own interest or advantage.

selfish adj. devoted to or caring only for oneself.

self-opinionated adj. obstinate in one's own opinion.

self-possessed adj. having or showing control of one's feelings, behaviour, etc. –**self-possession**, n.

self-raising flour n. wheat flour with baking powder already added.

selfsame adj. (the) very same; identical.

self-seeking adj. selfish.

self-service adj. (of a service station, restaurant, shop, etc.) operating on the principle that the customers perform part or all of the service themselves. Also, **self-serve**.

sell v. (**sold**, **selling**) **1.** to dispose of to a purchaser for a price. **2.** to deal in. **3.** to be on sale; find purchasers. –n. **4.** Informal an act of selling or salesmanship. –phr.

5. sell out, **a.** to sell all of. **b.** Informal to betray. **6. sell up**, to liquidate by selling the assets (of).

sellout n. Informal **1.** a betrayal. **2.** a play, show, etc., for which all seats are sold.

selvage n. the edge of woven fabric finished to prevent fraying. Also, **selvedge**.

semantic adj. relating to meaning.

semaphore n. a system of signalling by handheld flags.

semblance n. an outward aspect or appearance.

semen n. the impregnating fluid produced by male reproductive organs.

semester n. (in educational institutions) one of 2 divisions of the academic year.

Compare this with **term**, which is also a division of the teaching year, but a term is usually shorter, with three or four in a year. **Term** is also more often used in relation to schools rather than universities and colleges, where **semester** is more common.

semibreve /ˈsemibriv/ n. Music a note half the length of a breve, and worth four crotchets.

semicolon n. a mark of punctuation (;) used to indicate a more distinct separation between parts of a sentence than that indicated by a comma.

semiconductor n. **1.** a substance which conducts electricity to a limited degree. **2.** a device based on the electronic properties of such substances, as a transistor. –**semiconducting**, adj.

semidetached adj. of or relating to a pair of houses joined by a common wall but detached from other buildings.

A semidetached house is often called a **semi**.

seminal adj. **1.** highly original and influential: *a seminal work*. **2.** relating to semen: *seminal fluid*.

seminar n. a meeting organised to discuss a specific topic.

seminary n. (pl. **-ries**) Roman Catholic Church a college for the training of priests.

semitone n. Music the smallest interval in the chromatic scale of Western music.

semitrailer n. an articulated goods vehicle. Also, **semi**.

semolina n. the large, hard parts of wheat grains used for making puddings, etc.

senate n. (sometimes upper case) **1.** a legislative assembly. **2.** a governing or disciplinary body, as in certain universities. **–senator**, n.

send v. (**sent, sending**) **1.** to cause to go. **2.** to cause (a message, messenger) to be conveyed or transmitted to a destination. **3.** to give (forth, out, etc.), as light, smell, or sound. –phr. **4. send up**, Informal to mock or ridicule.

senile adj. mentally or physically infirm due to old age.

senior adj. **1.** older or elder. **2.** of higher rank or standing. –n. **3.** a person who is older than another. **–seniority**, n.

Senior Counsel (in some legal systems) a member of the senior of the two ranks of barrister. Abbrev.: SC Compare **junior** (def. 6).

sensation n. **1.** the operation or function of the senses; perception through the senses. **2.** a (cause of a) state of excited feeling or interest.

sensational adj. **1.** able to produce a sensation. **2.** (of a book, film, etc.) sensationalised. **3.** Informal very pleasing, exciting or excellent.

sensationalism n. the exploitation of cheap emotional excitement by popular newspapers, novels, etc. **–sensationalise, sensationalize,** v.

sense n. **1.** each of the special faculties connected with bodily organs, commonly reckoned as sight, hearing, smell, taste, and touch. **2.** a feeling or perception produced through these organs. **3.** any more or less vague perception or impression. **4.** sound practical intelligence. **5.** what is

sensible or reasonable. **6.** the meaning of a word, statement, etc. –v. **7.** to perceive by or as by the senses. –phr. **8. in a sense**, according to one interpretation.

sensibility n. (pl. **-ties**) **1.** mental susceptibility or responsiveness. **2.** (pl.) emotional capacities.

sensible adj. **1.** having, using, or showing good sense. **2.** keenly aware (of).

Don't confuse **sensible** with **sensitive**.

sensitive adj. **1.** readily affected by external agencies or influences. **2.** easily affected, pained, annoyed, etc. **3.** (of an issue, topic, etc.) arousing strong feelings.

Don't confuse **sensitive** with **sensible**.

sensory adj. relating to sensation.

sensual adj. relating to or given to the gratification of the senses or the indulgence of appetite.

sensuous adj. readily affected through the senses.

sent v. past tense and past participle of **send**.

Don't confuse this with **cent** or **scent**. A **cent** is a coin worth a hundredth of a dollar. A **scent** is a pleasant smell.

sentence n. **1.** a word or a sequence of words expressing an independent statement, inquiry, command, as Fire! or Summer is here or Who's there? **2.** Law **a.** the judicial determination of the punishment to be inflicted on a convicted criminal. **b.** the punishment itself. –v. (**-tenced, -tencing**) **3.** to pronounce sentence upon.

sententious adj. moralising; self-righteous.

sentient adj. having the power of sense perception.

sentiment n. **1.** mental attitude with regard to something; opinion. **2.** refined or tender emotion. **3.** the thought or feeling intended to be conveyed by words.

The more usual word is **feeling**.

sentimental *adj.* **1.** relating to or dependent on sentiment. **2.** weakly emotional.

sentinel *n.* a person on watch.

sentry *n.* (*pl.* **-ries**) a soldier stationed at a place to keep guard.

separate *v.* /'sepəreɪt/ **1.** to keep apart or divide. **2.** to part or divide (an assemblage, mass, compound, etc.) into individuals, components, or elements. **3.** to take (*from* or *out*) by such parting or dividing. **4.** to part company (*from*). **5.** to become disconnected or disengaged. **6.** to become parted from a mass or compound. –*adj.* /'seprət/ **7.** separated, disconnected, or disjoined. **8.** unconnected or distinct. –**separation**, *n.*

sepia *n.* **1.** a brown pigment. **2.** *Photography* a brown-coloured image. –*adj.* **3.** brown.

sepsis *n.* bacterial invasion of the body.

septic *adj.* infected.

septicaemia /septɪ'simiə/ *n.* a bacterial invasion of the bloodstream; blood poisoning. Also, **septicemia.**

septic tank *n.* a tank in which solid organic sewage is decomposed and purified by anaerobic bacteria.

septum *n.* (*pl.* **septa**) *Biol.* a dividing wall, membrane, or the like in a plant or animal structure.

sepulchre /'sepəlkə/ *n.* a tomb, grave, or burial place.

sequel *n.* **1.** a literary work, film, etc., continuing a preceding work. **2.** an event or circumstance following something.

sequence *n.* **1.** the following of one thing after another. **2.** order of succession. **3.** a continuous or connected series.

sequester /sə'kwestə, sɪ-/ *v.* to remove or withdraw into solitude or retirement. –**sequestration**, *n.*

sequin *n.* a small shining disc or spangle used to ornament a dress, etc.

serenade *n.* **1.** a song sung in the open air at night, as by a man to his lover. –*v.* **2.** to entertain with a serenade.

serene *adj.* calm; peaceful; tranquil –**serenity**, *n.*

serf *n. Hist.* a person required to render services to their lord.

serge *n.* cotton, rayon, wool, or silk in twill weave.

sergeant /'sadʒənt/ *n.* **1.** an officer in the army. **2.** a police officer ranking above constable.

serial *n.* **1.** anything published, broadcast etc., in regular instalments. –*adj.* **2.** published in instalments. **3.** of, relating to or arranged in a series. **4.** *Computers* etc. of or relating to a system in which information is transmitted along a path digit by digit. Compare **parallel** (def. 3).

> Don't confuse this with **cereal**, which is a grain plant such as wheat or corn. It can also be a breakfast food made from such grain.

serial killer *n.* someone who murders several people over a period of time.

serial number *n.* an individual number given for identification.

series *n.* (*pl.* **-ries**) a number of things, events, etc., ranged or occurring in succession; sequence.

serious *adj.* **1.** of thoughtful or solemn disposition or character. **2.** being in earnest. **3.** weighty or important. –**seriously**, *adv.*

sermon *n.* **1.** a talk for the purpose of religious instruction, usually delivered from a pulpit. **2.** a long, tedious speech.

serotonin /serə'toʊnən/ *n.* a hormone found in the brain, intestines, and platelets, deficiencies linked to mood disorders, anxiety, etc.

serpent *n.* a snake. –**serpentine**, *adj.*

serrated *adj.* having a notched or grooved edge.

serum *n.* (*pl.* **-ra** /-rə/ or **-rums**) the clear, pale yellow liquid forming the basis of blood.

servant n. a person in the paid service of another.

serve v. **1.** to act as a servant. **2.** to hand food to (guests). **3.** to render assistance (to). **4.** Tennis, etc. to put the ball in play. **5.** to work for. **6.** to go through (a term of service, imprisonment, etc.). **7.** to answer the requirements of; suffice. **8.** to wait upon. **9.** (of a male animal) to mate with. **10.** Law to make legal delivery of (a process or writ). —n. **11.** the act, manner, or right of serving, as in tennis.

server n. **1.** something used for serving food: cake server. **2.** Tennis, etc. the player who puts the ball in play. **3.** Computers **a.** a program which provides services to another computer via a network. **b.** the computer on which the program operates.

servery n. an area in which food is set out on plates.

service n. **1.** an act of helpful activity. **2.** the supplying or supplier of any articles, commodities, activities, etc. **3.** occupation or employment as a servant. **4.** (pl.) Mil. the armed forces. **5.** the act of keeping a piece of machinery, especially a motor vehicle, in operation. **6.** public religious worship. **7.** Tennis, etc. the act or manner of putting the ball in play. —adj. **8.** of, relating to, or used by, servants, tradespeople, etc. **9.** of or relating to the armed forces. —v. (**-viced, -vicing**) **10.** to make fit for use. **11.** (of a male animal) to inseminate (a female animal). **12.** to meet interest and other payments on, as a debt.

serviceable adj. capable of doing good service.

service station n. a commercial premises selling fuel, oil, etc., and for repairing cars; garage. Also, **petrol station**.

serviette n. a piece of cloth or paper used to protect the clothes, etc., while eating; table napkin; napkin.

servile adj. obsequious.

serving n. a portion of food or drink.

servitude n. slavery; bondage.

sesame n. the small edible seeds of a tropical plant.

session n. a period of time during which an activity is performed.

> Don't confuse this with **cession**, which is the giving up of rights or property by treaty or agreement.

set v. (**set, setting**) **1.** to put in a particular place, position, condition or relation. **2.** to apply. **3.** to incite to attack. **4.** to fix or appoint. **5.** to prescribe or assign, as a task. **6.** to adjust or arrange. **7.** to cause to sit. **8.** to put into a fixed, rigid, or settled state: to set the jaw. **9.** to cause (something, as mortar) to become firm or hard. **10.** to cause (hair, etc.) to assume a desired shape. **11.** Surg. to put (a broken or dislocated bone) back in position. **12.** Music to fit, as words to music. **13.** (of the sun or moon) to pass below the horizon. **14.** to become set. —n. **15.** the act or state of setting. **16.** a number of things customarily used together or forming a complete collection or series. **17.** a group of persons associating or classed together. **18.** fixed direction, as of the mind, etc. **19.** a radio or television receiving apparatus. **20.** a construction representing a place in which a play takes place in a play, etc. —adj. **21.** fixed beforehand. **22.** fixed; rigid. **23.** resolved or determined; habitually or stubbornly fixed. **24.** ready. —phr. **25. dead set**, Informal true; certain. **26. set about**, to begin. **27. set off, a.** to explode. **b.** to begin, as on a journey. **c.** to intensify or improve by contrast. **28. set out, a.** to arrange. **b.** to state or explain methodically. **c.** to start, as on a journey. **29. set to. a.** to apply oneself. **b.** to start to fight.

set square n. a flat piece of plastic, etc., in the shape of a right-angled triangle.

settee n. a seat for 2 or more persons.

setter n. a long-haired hunting dog.

setting *n.* **1.** the surroundings or environment of anything. **2.** the articles required for setting a single place at a table.

settle *v.* **1.** to agree upon (a time, price, conditions, etc.). **2.** to pay (a bill, account due, etc.). **3.** to (cause to) take up residence in a country, etc. **4.** to establish in a way of life, a business, etc. **5.** to bring to rest. **6.** to (cause to) sink down gradually. **7.** to arrange or decide (*on* or *upon*). **8.** to come to rest in a particular place.

settlement *n.* **1.** the act of settling. **2.** a colony, especially in its early stages.

settler *n.* a person who settles in a new country or region, especially one who takes up portions of the land for agriculture.

set-top box *n.* a device, connected to a conventional television set, which receives and decodes digital television broadcasts.

seven *n.* **1.** a cardinal number, 6 plus 1. –*adj.* **2.** amounting to 7 in number.

Numbers used before a noun are sometimes called **determiners**.

seventeen *n.* **1.** a cardinal number, 10 plus 7. –*adj.* **2.** amounting to 17 in number. –**seventeenth**, *adj.*, *n.*

Numbers used before a noun are sometimes called **determiners**.

seventy *n.* **1.** a cardinal number, 10 times 7. –*adj.* **2.** amounting to 70 in number. –**seventieth**, *adj.*, *n.*

Numbers used before a noun are sometimes called **determiners**.

sever *v.* **1.** to divide into parts, especially forcibly. **2.** to break off or dissolve (ties, relations, etc.). –**severance**, *n.*

The more usual expression is **cut** or **cut off**.

several *adj.* **1.** being more than 2 or 3, but not many. **2.** respective; individual. **3.** separate; different.

severe *adj.* **1.** harsh; harshly extreme. **2.** serious; stern. **3.** rigidly restrained in style or taste. **4.** rigidly exact. –**severity**, *n.*

sew /sou/ *v.* (**sewed**, **sewn** or **sewed**, **sewing**) **1.** to join or attach by stitching. **2.** to make (a garment) by such means. **3.** to work with a needle and thread, or with a sewing machine.

Don't confuse this with **so**, which has several meanings, such as therefore (*I missed the bus, so I was late*) or to such a degree (*Don't run so fast*). Another word which is pronounced the same way is **sow**, which is to plant seeds. The other **sow**, which is a female pig, is pronounced /sau/.

sewage *n.* the waste matter that passes through sewers.

Don't confuse this with **sewerage**, which is the process of removing this waste matter.

sewer *n.* an artificial conduit, usually underground, for carrying off waste water and refuse, as from a town or city.

sewerage *n.* **1.** the removal of waste water and refuse by means of sewers. **2.** the pipes and fittings conveying sewage.

Don't confuse this with **sewage**, which is the actual waste matter removed.

sex *n.* **1.** the sum of the physical differences which distinguish the male and the female: *What sex is their new baby?* **2.** the characteristic or condition of being either male or female: *You can't discriminate between people on the basis of sex.* **3.** the activity by which people give each other or themselves pleasure centred on their penis or vagina, especially when a man's penis enters a woman's vagina. –*v.* **4.** to ascertain the sex of.

sexist *adj.* **1.** of an attitude which stereotypes a person according to gender. –*n.* **2.** a person who displays sexist attitudes.

sexual *adj.* **1.** of or relating to sex. **2.** occurring between or involving the 2 sexes.

sexual harassment *n.* unwanted behaviour of a sexual nature towards another person.

sexual intercourse n. a sexual act between two people, usually one in which a man's penis enters a woman's vagina. Also, **intercourse**.

The more usual word is **sex**.

sexualise v. 1. to make sexual in nature: *to sexualise a relationship.* 2. to imbue with sexual character: *to sexualise a marketing campaign.* Also, **sexualize.** –**sexualisation,** n. –**sexualised,** adj.

sexuality n. sexual character.

sexually transmitted disease n. → STD[1].

sexy adj. (**-xier, -xiest**) 1. sexually interesting or exciting. 2. involving a predominant concern with sex: *a sexy novel.*

shabby adj. (**-bier, -biest**) 1. having the appearance impaired by wear, use, etc. 2. meanly ungenerous or unfair.

shack n. a rough cabin. –phr. 2. **shack up,** *Informal* to live (*with*).

shackle n. 1. a metal ring or fastening for securing the wrist, ankle, etc.; fetter. 2. something that prevents freedom of procedure, thought, etc. –v. 3. to confine or restrain.

shade n. 1. the comparative darkness caused by the blocking of light. 2. anything used for protection against excessive light, heat, etc. 3. degree of darkening of a colour. 4. a slight variation, amount, or degree. –v. 5. to produce shade in or on. 6. to screen. 7. to pass or change by slight graduations.

shadow n. 1. a dark shape cast by a body intercepting light. 2. an area of comparative darkness. 3. a slight suggestion; trace. –v. 4. to follow (a person) about secretly. –adj. 5. *Govt* of or relating to members of the chief opposition party, as *shadow cabinet.*

shaft n. 1. a long pole or rod forming the body of a spear, lance, etc. 2. something directed in attack. 3. a ray or beam. 4. the handle of a long implement. 5. either of the parallel bars of wood between which

the animal drawing a vehicle is placed. 6. any vertical enclosed space.

shag[1] n. rough, matted hair, wool, or the like. –**shaggy,** adj.

shag[2] n. any of various marine cormorants.

shake v. (**shook, shaken, shaking**) 1. to move or sway with short, quick, irregular vibratory movements. 2. to tremble. 3. to become unsteady. 4. to brandish or flourish (something). 5. to bring, throw, force, rouse, etc., by shaking. 6. to agitate or disturb profoundly. –n. 7. the act of shaking. 8. tremulous motion. 9. → **milkshake.** 10. (pl.) *Informal* a state of trembling.

shale n. a layered, easily split rock formed by the consolidation of clay.

shall v. a verb used 1. (with *I* and *we*) to show simple future time: *I shall go tomorrow.* 2. to indicate that someone has to do something: *You shall do as I say.*

This is a modal verb and is always used with another verb. Its past tense is **should**. Look up **modal verb.**

shallot n. a plant of the lily family whose small bulbs are used in cookery.

shallow adj. 1. of little depth. –n. 2. (usu. pl.) a shallow part of a body of water.

sham n. 1. something that is not what it purports to be. –adj. 2. pretended. –v. (**shammed, shamming**) 3. to assume the appearance of.

shamble v. to walk or go awkwardly; shuffle.

shambles pl. n. any place or thing in confusion or disorder.

Note that this word is usually used as a singular noun: *Your room is a shambles!*

shame n. 1. the painful feeling arising from the consciousness of something dishonourable, improper, ridiculous, etc., done by oneself or another. 2. disgrace. –v. 3. to cause to feel shame.

shampoo v. (**-pooed, -pooing**) 1. to wash (the hair, carpets, etc.) with a cleaning preparation. *—n.* **2.** a preparation used for shampooing.

shamrock *n.* a three-leafed plant.

shandy *n.* a mixed drink of beer with ginger beer or lemonade.

shanghai[1] *v.* (**-haied, -haiing**) *Naut.* to obtain (a person) for the crew of a ship by kidnapping.

shanghai[2] *n. Aust., NZ* a child's catapult.

shank *n.* **1.** that part of the leg in humans between the knee and the ankle. **2.** the corresponding part in an animal.

shanty *n.* (*pl.* **-ties**) a roughly built hut.

shape *n.* **1.** the quality of a thing depending on its outline or external surface. **2.** a particular or definite form. **3.** something used to give form, as a mould. *—v.* **4.** to give definite form, shape, or character to. *—phr.* **5.** shape up, to develop; assume a definite form or character.

shard *n.* a fragment, especially of broken earthenware.

share *n.* **1.** the portion belonging to, or contributed or owed by, someone. **2.** one of the equal parts into which the capital stock of a limited company is divided, generally classed as either **ordinary shares** or **preference shares.** *—v.* (**shared, sharing**) **3.** to use, participate in, enjoy, etc., jointly.

sharebroker *n.* → stockbroker.

sharia /ʃəˈriːə/ /ʃəˈriːɑ/ *n.* Islamic law. Also, **shariah.**

shark *n.* a type of fish, certain species of which are large and ferocious.

sharp *adj.* **1.** having a thin cutting edge or a fine point. **2.** not blunt or rounded. **3.** clearly outlined; distinct. **4.** keen or acute: *sharp eyesight.* **5.** shrewd to the point of dishonesty. *—adv.* **6.** keenly or acutely. **7.** abruptly or suddenly. **8.** punctually. *—n.* **9.** *Music* **a.** a note that is one semitone above a given note. **b.** the music sign '♯' which raises a note by a semitone when it is placed before it.

shatter *v.* to break suddenly into fragments.

shave *v.* (**shaved, shaved** or **shaven, shaving**) **1.** to remove hair from (the face, legs, etc.) **2.** to cut or scrape away the surface of with a sharp-edged tool. *—n.* **3.** the act or process of shaving. **4.** a narrow miss or escape.

shaving *n.* (*oft. pl.*) a very thin piece or slice, especially of wood.

shawl *n.* a piece of material, worn as a covering for the shoulders, head, etc.

she *pron.* the personal pronoun used to refer to a particular female: *She walked towards me.*

She is a third person singular pronoun in the subjective case.

sheaf *n.* (*pl.* **sheaves**) a bundle into which wheat, etc., is tied after being cut.

shear *v.* (**sheared** or **shore, shorn** or **sheared, shearing**) **1.** to remove by or as by cutting with a sharp instrument. **2.** to cut the hair, fleece, wool, etc., from. *—n.* **3. shears,** scissors of large size.

You can also use **a pair of shears** for def. 3, but note that this is always used as a singular, as opposed to **shears** by itself, which is always plural. Compare the following: *This pair of shears is blunt; These shears are blunt.*

Don't confuse this with **sheer,** which describes something which is so thin you can see through it. **Sheer** also means very steep, and if you **sheer** away from something you change direction to avoid hitting it.

sheath *n.* **1.** a case for the blade of a sword, dagger, etc. **2.** any similar covering.

shed[1] *n.* a structure, sometimes open at the sides or end, built for shelter, storage, etc.

shed[2] *v.* (**shed, shedding**) **1.** to emit and let fall (tears). **2.** to cast off or let fall by natural process.

she'd contraction of: **1.** she had. **2.** she would.

sheen *n.* lustre; brightness; radiance.

sheep n. (pl. **sheep**) **1.** a ruminant mammal, valuable for its flesh, fleece, etc. **2.** a meek, timid, or stupid person.

sheepdog n. a dog trained to guard and round up sheep.

sheepish adj. awkwardly bashful or embarrassed.

sheer¹ adj. **1.** transparently thin. **2.** unmixed with anything else. **3.** very steep.

Don't confuse this with **shear**, which is to clip the wool from a sheep.

sheer² v. to deviate from a course, as a ship.

This is a slightly uncommon word. The word more commonly used is **swerve**.

sheet n. **1.** a large rectangular piece of linen, cotton, etc., used as an article of bedding. **2.** a broad, thin mass, layer, or covering. **3.** a rectangular or square piece of paper.

sheikh /ʃeɪk, ʃiːk/ n. (oft. upper case) (in Arab and other Muslim use) **1.** a chief or head; the head person of a village or tribe. **2.** the head of a Muslim religious body. Also, **sheik**.

shelf n. (pl. **shelves**) **1.** a thin slab of wood or other material fixed horizontally to a wall, or in a frame, for supporting objects. **2.** a shelf-like surface or projection; ledge.

shelf life n. the period for which a product may remain on a shop shelf, and still be saleable.

shell n. **1.** a hard outer covering of an animal, as a mollusc, turtle, etc. **2.** an object resembling a shell. **3.** the exterior surface of an egg. **4.** an enclosing case or cover. **5.** a cartridge (def. 1). –v. **6.** to take out of the shell, pod, etc. **7.** to remove the shell of.

she'll contraction of: **1.** she will. **2.** she shall.

shellfish n. (pl. **-fish** or **-fishes**) an aquatic animal having a shell, as the oyster, lobster, etc.

For information about the different plural forms, see the note at **fish**.

shelter n. **1.** a place of refuge or safety. **2.** protection. –v. **3.** to be a shelter for. **4.** to take shelter.

shelve v. to put aside from consideration.

she-oak n. → **casuarina**.

shepherd n. **1.** a person who minds sheep. **2.** someone who watches over or protects a group of people. –v. **3.** to tend or guard as a shepherd.

sherbet n. **1.** a powdered confection. **2.** Also, **sorbet**. a frozen fruit-flavoured mixture.

sheriff n. **1.** in Aust., an officer in some courts of law who has duties such as organising juries. **2.** in the US, the chief law-enforcement officer in a county.

sherry n. (pl. **-ries**) a fortified and blended wine.

shield n. **1.** anything used or serving to protect, especially a piece of armour carried on the left arm. **2.** a shield-shaped escutcheon on which a coat of arms is displayed. –v. **3.** to protect (as) with a shield.

shift v. **1.** to move or transfer from one place, position, etc., to another. –n. **2.** a transfer. **3.** the portion of the day scheduled as a day's work when a factory, etc., operates day and night. **4.** an expedient. **5.** a woman's loose-fitting dress. **6.** → **gearstick**.

shiftless adj. lacking in resource or ambition; lazy.

shiftwork n. a system of work in which different employees work different hours over a 24 hour period. –**shiftworker**, n.

shifty adj. (**-tier**, **-tiest**) furtive.

shilling n. (in Aust. until 1966) a coin equal to $^1/_{20}$ of a pound.

shimmer n. **1.** a subdued, tremulous light or gleam. –v. **2.** to shine with a shimmer.

shin n. **1.** the front part of the leg from the knee to the ankle. –v. (**shinned**, **shinning**) **2.** to climb by holding fast with the hands or arms and legs and drawing oneself up.

shine v. (**shone** or **shined**, **shining**) 1. to give forth, or glow with, light. 2. to be bright with reflected light. 3. to excel. 4. to cause to shine. *−n.* 5. radiance. 6. lustre; polish. 7. sunshine. 8. *Informal* a liking; fancy. **−shiny**, *adj.*

shiner n. *Informal* a black eye.

shingle[1] n. a thin piece of wood, slate, etc., used to cover the roofs and sides of houses.

shingle[2] n. small, water-worn stones or pebbles such as on the seashore.

shingles n. (construed as *sing.* or *pl.*) a viral disease of the skin.

ship n. 1. a large vessel for navigating deep water, propelled by sail, steam, etc. 2. an airship or aeroplane. *−v.* (**shipped**, **shipping**) 3. to send or transport by ship, rail, etc. 4. to bring (an object) into a ship or boat.

Note that some people do not think a **ship** should be referred to as a boat. They say that ships are big and boats are small.

shipment n. 1. the act of shipping goods, etc. 2. that which is shipped.

shipshape adj. in good order.

shiralee n. *Aust.* → **swag**.

shire n. an area of land administered by local government.

shirk v. to evade (work, duty, etc.).

shirt n. a garment for the upper part of the body.

shirty adj. (**-tier**, **-tiest**) *Informal* bad-tempered.

shish kebab n. small pieces of meat cooked on a skewer, usually with vegetables.

shit *Informal* (taboo) *−v.* (**shitted** or **shat** or **shit**, **shitting**) 1. to defecate. *−n.* 2. faeces; dung. 3. the act of defecating. *−interj.* 4. an exclamation expressing anger, disgust, surprise, etc.

Note that this word is taboo and may give offence.

shiver v. 1. to shake or tremble with cold, fear, excitement, etc. *−n.* 2. a trembling movement.

shlep v. (**shlepped**, **shlepping**) → **schlep**.

shoal[1] n. a sandbank or sandbar in the bed of a body of water.

shoal[2] n. a massed group of fish.

shock[1] n. 1. a sudden and violent blow or impact. 2. something that shocks mentally, emotionally, etc. 3. a sudden collapse of the nervous mechanism caused by trauma. 4. the physiological effect produced by the passage of an electric current through the body. *−v.* 5. to strike with intense surprise, horror, disgust, etc. 6. to cause a shock in. *−adj.* 7. causing intense surprise, horror, etc.

shock[2] n. a thick, bushy mass, as of hair.

shockumentary n. (*pl.* **-ries**) 1. a documentary film or television show featuring footage of accidents or violence. 2. a documentary film or television show which gives damaging information about government bodies, industries, etc.

shoddy adj. (**-dier**, **-diest**) of poor quality or badly made.

shoe n. (*pl.* **shoes**) 1. a covering, usually of leather, for the foot. 2. some thing or part resembling a shoe in form, position, or use. *−v.* (**shod**, **shoeing**) 3. to provide or fit with a shoe or shoes.

shoehorn n. a shaped device held at the heel of a shoe to make it slip on more easily.

shoosh interj. hush (a command to be quiet or silent). Also, **shush**.

shoot v. (**shot**, **shooting**) 1. to hit, wound, or kill with a missile discharged from a weapon. 2. to send forth (arrows, bullets, etc.). 3. to discharge (a weapon). 4. to send forth like an arrow or bullet. 5. to pass rapidly along with. 6. *Photography* to photograph or film. 7. to move suddenly or swiftly; dart; be propelled (*ahead*, *away*, *into*, *off*, etc.). **8.** to grow (*up*), especially rapidly. *–n.* **9.** an expedition for shooting animals. **10.** a young branch, stem, twig, or the like.

shop *n.* **1.** a building where goods are sold retail. **2.** a place for doing certain work; workshop. *–v.* (**shopped**, **shopping**) **3.** to visit shops to buy goods. *–phr.* **4. talk shop**, to discuss one's trade, profession, or business.

shopfront *n.* that part of an organisation which deals directly with the public.

shoplift *v.* to steal (goods) from a shop while appearing to be a legitimate shopper.

shoplifting *n.* the crime of stealing goods from a shop while appearing to be a legitimate customer. Also, **shop stealing**.

shopping mall *n.* → **mall** (def. 2).

shop steward *n.* a trade-union official representing workers in a factory, workshop, etc.

shore¹ *n.* land along the edge of a sea, lake, large river, etc.

Don't confuse this with **sure**, which means certain (*I'm sure I saw him yesterday*).

shore² *v.* to support or prop (*up*).

short *adj.* **1.** having little length. **2.** having little height. **3.** brief. **4.** rudely brief; curt. **5.** below the standard in extent, quantity, duration, etc. *–adv.* **6.** on the nearer side of an intended or particular point. *–n.* **7.** something that is short. *–phr.* **8. for short**, by way of abbreviation. **9. in short**, briefly. **10. short on**, deficient in. *–shorten*, *v.*

shortage *n.* deficiency in quantity.

shortbread *n.* a thick, crisp biscuit, rich in butter.

short-change *v. Informal* to give less than proper change to.

short circuit *n.* an accidental connection between 2 points of different potential in an electrical circuit, thus enabling excess current to bypass the normal path. *–short-circuit*, *v.*

shortcoming *n.* a failure or defect in conduct, condition, etc.

short cut *n.* a shorter or quicker way.

shortening *n.* any fat used to make pastry, etc.

shorthand *n.* a method of rapid handwriting using simple strokes in place of letters.

Compare this with **longhand**, which is writing in which the words are written out in full.

shortly *adv.* in a short time.

shorts *pl. n.* short trousers, usually not extending beyond the knee.

short-sighted *adj.* unable to see far.

short-tempered *adj.* having a hasty temper.

short-winded *adj.* short of breath; liable to difficulty in breathing.

shot¹ *n.* **1.** the act of shooting. **2.** small pellets of lead as used in a shotgun. **3.** a person who shoots. **4.** a heavy metal ball which competitors cast as far as possible in shot-putting contests. **5.** an aimed stroke, throw, the like, as in games, etc. **6.** an attempt or try. **7.** *Informal* an injection of a drug, vaccine, etc. **8.** a small measure of alcoholic liquor. **9.** *Photography* a photograph.

shot² *v.* **1.** past tense and past participle of **shoot**. *–adj.* **2.** woven so as to present a play of colours, as silk.

shotgun *n.* a gun for firing small shot.

shot-put *n.* **1.** the athletic exercise of casting a heavy metal ball (the **shot**) as far as possible. **2.** the ball itself.

should *v.* **1.** past tense of **shall**. **2.** (a verb used) **a.** to indicate that it is important to do something out of duty, kindness, etc: *You should ring her.* **b.** to express probability: *He should be here soon.* **c.** to express uncertainty: *Should he mention it, pretend you don't know.*

This is a modal verb and is always used with another verb. Look up **modal verb.**

shoulder n. **1.** either of 2 corresponding parts of the human body extending on either side of the neck to the upper joint of the arm. **2.** a corresponding part in animals. **3.** a shoulder-like part or projection. **4.** either of 2 strips of land bordering a road. –v. **5.** to push, as with the shoulder, especially roughly. **6.** to take upon or support with the shoulder. **7.** to assume as a burden, or responsibility.

shoulderblade n. either of the two flat, triangular bones, each forming the back part of a shoulder.

The scientific name for this is **scapula.**

shout¹ v. **1.** to call or cry out loudly and vigorously. –n. **2.** a loud call or cry.

shout² Aust., NZ Informal –v. **1.** to pay for something for (another person). –n. **2.** one's turn to pay.

shove v. **1.** to move along by force from behind. **2.** to push roughly or rudely. –n. **3.** an act of shoving.

shovel n. **1.** an implement similar to a spade but with a scooped blade. –v. **(-elled, -elling) 2.** to take up and remove with a shovel.

show v. **(showed, shown** or **showed, showing) 1.** to cause or allow to be seen. **2.** to point out. **3.** to guide. **4.** to indicate. **5.** to make evident by appearance, behaviour, etc. **6.** to be or become visible. –n. **7.** a display. **8.** ostentatious display. **9.** an indication. **10.** any undertaking, organisation, etc. –phr. **11. show off,** to exhibit for approval or admiration, or ostentatiously.

showdown n. a final confrontation.

shower n. **1.** a brief fall, as of rain, etc. **2. a.** an apparatus for spraying water for bathing. **b.** a washing of the body under such an apparatus. –v. **3.** to pour (something) down in a shower. **4.** to rain in a shower. **5.** (of a person) to take a shower. (def. 2b).

shower tea n. Aust. → **bridal shower.**

show-off n. Informal someone given to pretentious display.

showroom n. a room used for the display of goods or merchandise.

shrapnel n. fragments of an exploded bullet, bomb, etc.

shred n. **1.** a narrow strip cut or torn off. –v. **(shredded** or **shred, shredding) 2.** to cut or tear into small strips.

shrew n. **1.** a small, insectivorous mouse-like mammal. **2.** a woman of violent temper and speech.

shrewd adj. astute or sharp.

shriek n. **1.** a loud, sharp, shrill cry. –v. **2.** to cry out sharply in a high voice.

shrift phr. **short shrift,** little consideration in dealing with someone or something.

shrill adj. **1.** high-pitched and piercing. –v. **2.** to cry shrilly.

shrimp n. **1.** any of various small, long-tailed, edible shellfish. **2.** Informal a diminutive person.

shrine n. any structure or place consecrated or devoted to some deity or revered person(s).

shrink v. **(shrank** or **shrunk, shrunk** or **shrunken, shrinking) 1.** to draw back, as in retreat or avoidance. **2.** to become reduced in extent. **3.** to cause to shrink or contract. –**shrinkage,** n.

shrink-wrap v. **(-wrapped, -wrapping)** to enclose (an object) in a flexible plastic wrapping which shrinks to the shape of the object, sealing it in. –**shrink-wrapped,** adj.

shrivel v. **(-elled** or, Chiefly US, **-eled, -elling** or, Chiefly US, **-eling)** to contract and wrinkle, as from great heat or cold.

shroud n. **1.** a cloth in which a corpse is wrapped for burial. **2.** something which covers or conceals. –v. **3.** to cover; hide from view.

shrub *n.* a woody perennial plant smaller than a tree, usually branching from or near the ground.

shrug *v.* (**shrugged, shrugging**) **1.** to raise and lower (the shoulders), expressing indifference, disdain, etc. *−n.* **2.** this movement.

shudder *v.,* *n.* (to tremble with) a sudden convulsive movement.

shuffle *v.* **1.** to walk without lifting the feet. **2.** to mix (cards in a pack). *−n.* **3.** the act of shuffling.

shun *v.* (**shunned, shunning**) to keep away from.

shunt *v.* to move or turn aside or out of the way.

shush *interj.* → **shoosh**.

shut *v.* (**shut, shutting**) **1.** to put (a door, cover, etc.) in position to close or obstruct. **2.** Also, **shut up.** to close the doors of. **3.** to close by folding or bringing together the parts. **4.** to become shut or closed. *−phr.* **5. shut in,** to confine; enclose. **6. shut out,** to bar; exclude. **7. shut up,** *Informal* to stop talking.

shutter *n.* a hinged or otherwise movable cover for a window or other opening.

shuttle *n.* **1.** the sliding container that carries the lower thread in a sewing machine. *−v.* **2.** to move quickly and to and fro like a shuttle.

shuttlecock *n.* a piece of cork with feathers stuck in one end, used in badminton.

shy *adj.* (**shyer** or **shier, shyest** or **shiest**) **1.** bashful; retiring. **2.** easily frightened away. *−v.* (**shied, shying**) **3.** to draw back.

SI *n.* the International System of Units, an internationally recognised system of metric units now adopted as the basis of Australia's metric system.

Siamese twins *pl. n.* → **conjoined twins.**

sibilant *adj.* hissing.

sibling *n.* a brother or sister.

sic *adv.* so; thus (often used parenthetically to show that something, especially an error, has been copied exactly from the original).

sick *adj.* **1.** affected with nausea. **2.** affected with any disorder of health. **3.** of or appropriate to sick persons. **4.** macabre: *a sick joke.* *−n.* **5.** vomit.

sick bay *n.* a place in a school where students go if the are ill or injured.

sickie *n. Aust., NZ Informal* A day taken off work with pay, because of genuine or feigned illness.

sickle *n.* a short-handled implement with a curved blade for cutting grain, etc.

sick leave *n.* leave of absence granted because of illness.

side *n.* **1.** one of the surfaces or lines bounding a thing. **2.** one of the 2 surfaces of an object other than the front, back, top, and bottom. **3.** either of the 2 lateral (right and left) parts of a thing. **4.** the space immediately beside someone or something. **5.** one of 2 or more parties concerned in a case, contest, etc. *−adj.* **6.** being at or on one side. **7.** coming from or directed towards one side. **8.** subordinate. *−phr.* **9. side with / against,** to place oneself with / against (a side or party).

sideboard *n.* a piece of furniture for holding articles of table service.

sideburns *pl. n.* short whiskers worn with an unbearded chin. Also, **sidelevers, sideboards.**

sidecar *n.* a small car attached on one side to a motorcycle and supported on the other by a wheel of its own.

side effect *n.* any effect produced other than those originally intended.

sidelong *adj.* **1.** directed to one side. *−adv.* **2.** towards the side; obliquely.

sideways *adv.* **1.** with the side foremost. **2.** towards or from one side. *−adj.* **3.** towards or from one side. Also, **sidewise.**

sidle *v.* to edge along furtively.

SIDS *n.* sudden infant death syndrome; a syndrome leading to sudden death in babies as they sleep.

siege *n.* the attacking, surrounding of, and cutting off of supplies to a fortified place in order to capture it.

siemens *n.* (*pl.* **-mens**) the SI unit of electrical conductance. *Symbol:* S

siesta *n.* a midday or afternoon rest or nap.

sieve *n.* an instrument, with a meshed or perforated bottom which holds back coarse or solid matter while allowing fine matter or liquid to pass through.

sievert /'siːvət/ *n.* the SI derived unit of radiation dose. *Symbol:* Sv

sift *v.* 1. to separate the coarse parts of (flour, ashes, etc.) with a sieve. 2. to scatter by means of a sieve. 3. to examine closely.

sigh *v.* 1. to let out one's breath audibly, as from sorrow, etc. 2. to yearn or long. 3. to express with a sigh. –*n.* 4. the act or sound of sighing.

sight *n.* 1. the power or faculty of seeing. 2. the act or fact of seeing. 3. range of vision. 4. a view; glimpse. 5. something seen or to be seen. –*v.* 6. to get sight of.

> Don't confuse this with **site**, which is a piece of land where something is built, or with **cite**, which is to mention (*He cited two examples*).

sign *n.* 1. a token; indication. 2. a sign used instead of words in science, trade, etc. 3. an inscribed board, space, etc., serving for information, advertisement, warning, etc. –*v.* 4. to affix a signature to. 5. to communicate by a sign or signal. 6. to write one's signature.

signal *n.* 1. a gesture, act, light, etc., serving to warn, direct, command, or the like. 2. an act, event, or the like, which precipitates an action. 3. a token; indication. 4. *Radio, etc.* the impulses, waves, sounds, etc., transmitted or received. –*adj.* 5. serving as a sign. –*v.* (**-nalled, -nalling**) 6. to make a signal to. 7. to make

known by a signal. 8. to make communication by a signal or signals.

signatory *adj.* 1. that has signed a document. –*n.* (*pl.* **-ries**) 2. someone who has signed a document.

signature *n.* 1. a person's name written by himself or herself. 2. the act of signing a document.

signet *n.* a small official seal.

significance *n.* 1. importance. 2. meaning. –**significant**, *adj.*

signify *v.* (**-fied, -fying**) 1. to make known by signs, speech, or action. 2. to be a sign of; mean. 3. to be of importance.

sign language *n.* a communication system using gestures rather than speech or writing.

silence *n.* 1. absence of any sound or noise. –*v.* 2. to cause to be silent. –*interj.* 3. be silent! –**silent**, *adj.*

silhouette *n.* a dark image outlined against a lighter background.

silica *n.* a silicon dioxide, appearing as quartz, sand, flint, and agate.

silicon *n.* a nonmetallic element used in steelmaking, etc. *Symbol:* Si

silk *n.* 1. (the thread or cloth made from) the fine, soft, lustrous fibre obtained from the cocoon of a caterpillar. 2. any fibre resembling silk. –*adj.* 3. made of silk. 4. of or relating to silk. –*phr.* 5. **take silk**, to become a Queen's or King's Counsel. –**silken**, *adj.*

silk-screen *v.* to produce by silk-screen printing.

silk-screen printing *n.* a process of printing from stencils, which may be photographically made or cut by hand, through a fine mesh of silk, metal or other material. –**silk-screen print**, *n.*

sill *n.* the horizontal piece beneath a window or door.

silly *adj.* (**-lier, -liest**) 1. lacking good sense; foolish. 2. absurd or ridiculous. –*n.* (*pl.* **-lies**) 3. *Informal* a silly person.

silo n. (pl. **-los**) a tower-like structure for storing grain.

silt n. earthy matter deposited as a sediment by moving water. –**siltation**, n.

silver n. **1.** Chem. a white ductile metallic element. Symbol: Ag **2.** coin made of silver or of a metal resembling silver; money. **3.** table articles made of or plated with silver. **4.** a lustrous greyish white or whitish grey. –adj. **5.** made of or plated with silver. **6.** of or relating to silver. **7.** (of coins) made of a metal or alloy resembling silver. **8.** having the colour silver. **9.** indicating the 25th event of a series, as a wedding anniversary.

silverbeet n. a form of beet with large leaves and a long fleshy stalk, used as a vegetable; spinach.

silverfish n. (pl. **-fish** or **-fishes**) any of certain small, wingless insects damaging to books, wallpaper, etc.

silverside n. a cut of beef from the outside portion of a full butt.

SIM card n. a circuit-bearing card inserted into a mobile phone which contains the subscriber's authorisation to use a certain mobile phone network.

similar adj. having a general likeness or resemblance.

simile /'smali/ n. a figure of speech which points out a likeness between two generally unlike things, usually using the word 'like' or 'as', as to *sing like a bird, as strong as an ox*.

Compare this with **metaphor**, which describes something as if it actually *were* something else, as in *Knowledge is a key that opens many doors.*

similitude n. **1.** likeness; resemblance. **2.** a likening or comparison.

simmer v. **1.** to cook in a liquid just below the boiling point. –n. **2.** state or process of simmering. –phr. **3. simmer down**, *Informal* to become calm or calmer.

simper v. to smile in a silly, self-conscious way.

simple adj. **1.** easy to understand, deal with, use, etc. **2.** not complex. **3.** sincere. **4.** unlearned. **5.** Gram. relating to the most basic one-word form of a verb such as 'ran' in *I ran* (the simple past tense of 'run'). –**simplicity**, n.

Don't confuse this with **simplistic**, which actually means *too* simple. Something is **simplistic** if it is put so simply that it is not accurate. It is used disapprovingly.

simpleton n. a fool.

simplistic adj. oversimplified.

This is used disapprovingly and should not be confused with **simple**. Something is **simple** if it is straightforward and easy to understand.

simply adv. **1.** in a simple manner. **2.** plainly; unaffectedly. **3.** not deceitfully or craftily. **4.** merely; only. **5.** unwisely; foolishly. **6.** absolutely: *simply irresistible.*

simulation n. **1.** assumption of a particular appearance or form. **2.** the practice of constructing a model of a machine in order to test behaviour. –**simulate**, v.

simulcast n. simultaneous broadcast, as by a radio and a television station.

simultaneous adj. existing, occurring, or operating at the same time.

sin n. **1.** (an act of) transgression of divine law. –v. (**sinned**, **sinning**) **2.** to do such an act.

since adv. **1.** (oft. preceded by *ever*) from then till now. **2.** between a particular past time and the present; subsequently. **3.** ago. –prep. **4.** continuously from or counting from: *since noon.* **5.** between a (past time or event) and the present: *since the war.* –conj. **6.** in the period following the time when: *he has written only once since he left.* **7.** because.

sincere adj. free from any element of deceit or hypocrisy. –**sincerity**, n.

sine n. Maths a trigonometric function defined for an acute angle in a right-angled triangle as the ratio of the side opposite the angle to the hypotenuse.

sinecure n. a well-paid office requiring little or no work.

sinew n. 1. a tendon. 2. strength; vigour.

sing v. (**sang** or **sung**, **sung**, **singing**) 1. to utter (words or sounds) in succession with musical modulations of the voice. 2. to produce melodious sounds, as certain birds, insects, etc. 3. to make a short ringing, whistling, or whizzing sound. 4. to bring, send, put, etc., with or by singing.

singe v. (**singed**, **singeing**) 1. to burn superficially. –n. 2. a superficial burn.

single adj. 1. one only; separate. 2. of or relating to one person, family, etc. 3. alone; solitary. 4. without a spouse or permanent partner. 5. consisting of one part, element, or member. –v. 6. to pick or choose (out) from others. –n. 7. something single or separate.

single-handed adj. acting or working alone or unaided.

single-minded adj. having or showing undivided purpose.

singlet n. a short garment, with or without sleeves, usually worn next to the skin.

singsong n. 1. an informal gathering at which the company sing. –adj. 2. characterised by a regular rising and falling intonation.

singular adj. 1. being the only one of the kind. 2. out of the ordinary; unusual. 3. Gram. indicating one person or thing, as the words 'she', 'hears' and 'bell', in the sentence She hears the bell. –n. 4. Gram. the singular form of a word: 'Child' is the singular of 'children'.

For def. 2, the more usual word is **odd**.

sinister adj. threatening or portending evil.

sink v. (**sank** or, Chiefly US, **sunk**, **sunk** or **sunken**, **sinking**) 1. to descend gradually to a lower level. 2. to become submerged. 3. to pass or fall into some lower state. 4. to fall in, as the cheeks. 5. to cause to sink. 6. to make (a hole, shaft, well, etc.) by excavating or boring

downwards. –n. 7. a basin with a water supply and outlet. 8. a low-lying area where waters collect. –phr. 9. **sink in**, to enter or permeate the mind. 10. **sink into**, to be or become deeply absorbed in (a mental state).

sinker n. a weight of lead, etc., on a fishing line, net, etc.

sinuous adj. having many curves, bends, or turns; winding.

The more usual word is **twisting**.

sinus n. one of the hollow cavities in the skull connecting with the nasal cavities.

sip v. (**sipped**, **sipping**) 1. to drink a little at a time. –n. 2. an act of sipping. 3. a small quantity taken by sipping.

siphon n. 1. a tube through which liquid flows over the side of a container to a lower level by atmospheric pressure. –v. 2. to convey or pass through a siphon. Also, **syphon**.

sir n. a respectful or formal term of address used to a man.

sire n. 1. the male parent of an animal. –v. 2. to beget.

siren n. 1. Classical Myth. a sea nymph, part woman and part bird, supposed to lure mariners to destruction with seductive singing. 2. a device used as a warning sound.

sirloin n. the portion of the loin of beef in front of the rump.

sissy n. (pl. **-sies**) Informal a timid or cowardly person. Also, **cissy**.

sister n. 1. a daughter of the same parents. 2. a female associate. 3. a female member of a religious community. –adj. 4. being a sister; related by, or as by, sisterhood.

If you want to use one word to refer to a brother and a sister, or to talk about brothers and sisters in general, you have to use the word **sibling**. This is more formal than **brother** or **sister**.

sister-in-law n. (pl. **sisters-in-law**) 1. the sister of one's spouse. 2. the wife of one's sibling. **3.** the wife of one's spouse's sibling

sit *v.* (**sat**, **sitting**) **1.** to rest on the lower part of the body. **2.** to be situated. **3.** to fit or be adjusted, as a garment. **4.** to occupy a seat in an official capacity, as a judge or bishop. **5.** to be convened or in session, as an assembly. **6.** to cause to sit; seat (*down*). **7.** to sit upon (a horse, etc.). **8.** to provide seating room for.

sitar *n.* a guitar-like instrument of India, having a long neck and usually three strings.

sitcom *n.* a comedy based on the situations of ordinary life.

site *n.* **1.** the area on which anything, as a building, is, has been or is to be situated. –*v.* **2.** to locate; place.

Don't confuse this with **sight**, which is the ability to see, or with **cite**, which is to mention (*He cited two examples*).

situate *v.* to give a site to; locate.

situation *n.* **1.** a location or position with reference to environment. **2.** a place or locality. **3.** the state of affairs. **4.** a position or post of employment.

six *n.* **1.** a cardinal number, 5 plus 1. –*adj.* **2.** amounting to 6 in number.

Numbers used before a noun are sometimes called **determiners**.

sixteen *n.* **1.** a cardinal number, 10 plus 6. –*adj.* **2.** amounting to 16 in number. –**sixteenth**, *adj.*, *n.*

Numbers used before a noun are sometimes called **determiners**.

sixth sense *n.* a power of perception beyond the 5 senses; intuition.

sixty *n.* **1.** a cardinal number, 10 times 6. –*adj.* **2.** amounting to 60 in number. –**sixtieth**, *adj.*, *n.*

Numbers used before a noun are sometimes called **determiners**.

size[1] *n.* **1.** the dimensions or magnitude of anything. –*v.* **2.** to separate or sort according to size. **3.** to make of a certain

size. –*phr.* **4. size up**, to form an estimate of.

size[2] *n.* **1.** any of various gelatinous or glutinous preparations used for glazing or coating paper, cloth, etc. –*v.* **2.** to treat with size.

sizzle *v.* **1.** to make a hissing sound, as in frying or burning. –*n.* **2.** a sizzling sound.

skate *n.* **1.** a steel blade attached to the bottom of a shoe, enabling a person to glide on ice. **2.** → **rollerskate**. –*v.* **3.** to glide over ice, the ground, etc., on skates.

skateboard *n.* a short plank on rollerskate wheels, ridden standing up.

skein *n.* a length of thread or yarn wound in a coil.

skeleton *n.* **1.** the bones of a human or other animal body considered together. **2.** *Informal* a very lean person or animal. **3.** a supporting framework. –*adj.* **4.** of or relating to a skeleton. –**skeletal**, *adj.*

skeleton key *n.* a key which may open various locks. Also, **pass key**.

skerrick *n.* *Aust.*, *NZ* a very small quantity; scrap.

sketch *n.* **1.** a simply or hastily executed drawing. **2.** a rough plan or draft, as of a literary work. **3.** a brief or hasty outline of facts, occurrences, etc. –*v.* **4.** to make a sketch (of).

skew *v.* **1.** to turn aside or swerve. **2.** to give an oblique direction to; shape or form obliquely.

skewer *n.* **1.** a long pin of wood or metal for holding meat together while being cooked. –*v.* **2.** to fasten (as) with skewers.

ski *n.* (*pl.* **skis**) **1.** one of a pair of long, slender pieces of hard wood, metal, or plastic, one fastened to each shoe, used for travelling or gliding over snow. –*v.* (**ski'd** or **skied**, **skiing**) **2.** to travel on or use skis.

skid *n.* **1.** a plank or log on which something heavy may be slid or rolled along.

2. an act of skidding. *–v.* (**skidded, skidding**) **3.** to slide along without rotating, as a wheel to which a brake has been applied. **4.** to slide forward under its own momentum, usually out of control, as a car.

skill *n.* the ability to do something well that comes from knowledge, practice, etc. –**skilful,** *adj.*

skilled *adj.* **1.** showing, involving, or requiring skill, as work. **2.** of or relating to workers specially trained in their trade.

skillet *n.* a small frying pan.

skillshare *v.* **1.** to share one's acquired skills with other people, as between students. *–n.* **2.** the process of such sharing.

skim *v.* (**skimmed, skimming**) **1.** to take up or remove (floating matter) from a liquid. **2.** to clear (liquid) thus. **3.** to move or glide lightly over or along the surface of. *–n.* **4.** the act of skimming.

skim milk *n.* milk which has had the cream skimmed off and has a low fat content. Also, **skimmed milk.**

skimming *n. Informal* the practice of taking the details of (a plastic card) so as to steal money from the account of the owner.

skimp *v.* **1.** to be sparing with; scrimp. *–phr.* **2. skimp on,** to be extremely thrifty.

skimpy *adj.* (**-pier, -piest**) hardly enough in quantity, size, etc.: *a skimpy meal; a skimpy jumper.* –**skimpily,** *adv.* –**skimpiness,** *n.*

skin *n.* **1.** the external covering of an animal body, especially when soft and flexible. **2.** any outer coating, or surface layer, as the rind or peel of fruit, or a film on liquid. *–v.* (**skinned, skinning**) **3.** to strip or deprive of skin.

skindiving *n.* underwater swimming with an aqualung or snorkel, and foot fins.

skinflint *n.* a mean person.

skink *n.* any of various harmless, generally smooth-scaled lizards.

skinny *adj.* (**-nier, -niest**) lean; emaciated.

skip *v.* (**skipped, skipping**) **1.** to spring, jump, or leap lightly (over). **2.** to pass from one point, thing, subject, etc., to another, disregarding or omitting what intervenes. **3.** to miss out part of. **4.** *Informal* to leave hastily, or flee from. *–n.* **5.** a skipping movement.

skipper *n.* the leader of a team or crew.

skirmish *n.* **1.** any brisk encounter, as for fighting or argument. *–v.* **2.** to engage in a skirmish.

skirt *n.* **1.** (the lower part of) a garment, hanging from the waist. **2.** some part resembling or suggesting the skirt of a garment. *–v.* **3.** to pass along or around the border or edge of. **4.** to be, lie, live, etc., on or along the edge of something.

skirting board *n.* a line of boarding on an interior wall next to the floor.

skit *n.* a slight parody or satire, especially dramatic or literary.

skite *Aust., NZ Informal –v.* **1.** to boast. *–n.* **2.** a boast. **3.** Also, **skiter.** a boaster; braggart.

skittish *adj.* restlessly or excessively lively.

skittle *n.* **1.** (*pl.*) ninepins. *–v.* **2.** to knock over.

skivvy *n.* (*pl.* **-vies**) *Aust., NZ* a close-fitting stretch garment with long sleeves.

skulduggery *n.* dishonourable proceedings. Also, **skullduggery.**

skulk *v.* to lie or keep in hiding, as for some evil or cowardly reason.

skull *n.* the bony framework of the head, enclosing the brain, etc.

skunk *n.* **1.** a small Nth American mammal which ejects a stinking fluid when attacked. **2.** *Informal* a thoroughly contemptible person.

sky *n.* (*oft. pl.*) the region of the clouds or the upper air.

skydiving *n.* the sport of free-falling from an aeroplane for a great distance before releasing one's parachute.

skylight *n.* an opening in a roof or ceiling, fitted with glass or other translucent material.

sky marshal *n.* a guard placed on an aeroplane to maintain security.

skyscraper *n.* a tall building of many storeys.

slab *n.* a broad, flat, somewhat thick piece of some solid material.

slack *adj.* **1.** not tense or taut. **2.** indolent, negligent or inactive. *–n.* **3.** a slack condition, interval, or part. *–v.* **4.** to neglect or shirk (some matter, duty, etc.).

slacks *pl. n.* long trousers, worn by either men or women as informal wear.

slag *n.* matter separated during the reduction of a metal from its ore.

slake *v.* to satisfy (thirst, desire, wrath, etc.).

slalom /ˈslɑːləm, ˈslæləm/ *n.* a downhill skiing race with a winding course.

slam *v.* (**slammed**, **slamming**) **1.** to shut with force and noise. **2.** to dash, strike, etc., with noisy impact. *–n.* **3.** a violent and noisy closing, dashing, or impact.

slander *n.* **1.** defamation by spoken words, as distinct from written or printed words, pictures, etc. *–v.* **2.** to utter slander concerning.

> Compare **slander** with **libel**, which is defamation by written or printed words.

slang *n.* language differing from and more informal than standard or written language, and sometimes regarded as being inferior.

slant *v.* **1.** to slope; be oblique. **2.** to direct or turn so as to make (something) oblique. **3.** to distort or give partisan emphasis to (a newspaper story, article, etc.). *–n.* **4.** slanting or oblique direction. **5.** a mental leaning or tendency, especially unusual or unfair; bias.

slap *v.* (**slapped**, **slapping**) **1.** to strike with a smart blow, especially with the open hand. *–n.* **2.** such a blow.

slapdash *adv.*, *adj.* carelessly hasty or offhand.

slapstick *n.* comedy featuring rough play and clowning.

slap-up *adj. Informal* first-rate; excellent.

slash *v.* **1.** to cut with a violent or random sweep. **2.** to cut, reduce, or alter, especially drastically. *–n.* **3.** (a cut or wound made with) a sweeping stroke.

slat *n.* **1.** a long, thin, narrow strip of wood, metal, etc. *–v.* (**slatted**, **slatting**) **2.** to furnish or make with slats.

slate¹ *n.* **1.** a fine-grained rock that tends to split along parallel cleavage planes. **2.** a thin piece or plate of this rock or a similar material, used especially for roofing, or for writing on. **3.** a dull, dark bluish grey. *–v.* **4.** to cover with slate.

slate² *v.* to censure or reprimand severely.

slather *v.* to use in large quantities. *–phr.* **2. open slather**, *Aust., NZ Informal* complete freedom.

slaughter *n.* **1.** the killing or butchering of cattle, sheep, etc., for food. **2.** the killing by violence of great numbers of people *–v.* **3.** to kill (people or animals).

slave *n.* **1.** someone who is the property of and wholly subject to, another. *–v.* **2.** to work like a slave; drudge. *–***slavery**, *n.* *–***slavish**, *adj.*

slaver *v.* to let saliva run from the mouth.

slay *v.* to kill by violence.

sleazy *adj.* (**-zier**, **-ziest**) **1.** relating to behaviour which is not regarded as morally acceptable, especially in relation to sexual matters. **2.** shabby, shoddy, untidy, or dirty.

sled *n.* a vehicle mounted on runners for travelling over snow, etc. Also, **sledge**.

sledge *n.* → **sled**.

sledgehammer *n.* a very large heavy hammer.

sleek *adj.* **1.** smooth; glossy, as hair, an animal, etc. **2.** well-fed or well-groomed. **3.** suave.

sleep v. (**slept**, **sleeping**) **1.** to take the repose or rest afforded by the natural suspension of consciousness. **2.** to be dormant or inactive. **3.** to have beds or sleeping accommodation for. –n. **4.** the state of one that sleeps. **5.** a period of sleeping.

sleep apnoea /'æpniə/ n. a temporary cessation of breathing during sleep, often caused by obstruction of the air passages, as by enlarged tonsils, etc. Also, **sleep apnea**.

sleeper n. **1.** someone who sleeps. **2.** a cross beam (usually heavy) serving as a foundation for the rails of a railway track. **3.** a bed or sleeping compartment in a carriage on a passenger train. **4.** a small ring, bar, etc., worn in the ear lobe after piercing.

Def. 1 is usually used in a phrase describing how someone sleeps, as in *She is a light sleeper* (meaning she wakes up easily) or *He is a heavy sleeper* (meaning he sleeps soundly and isn't easily woken up).

sleeper cell n. a small group of people, committed to a cause, who infiltrate a community waiting for an instruction to carry out sabotage, undertake a specific terrorist activity, etc.

sleepwalk v. to walk or perform other activities while asleep. –**sleepwalking**, n. –**sleepwalker**, n.

sleet n. snow or hail and rain falling together.

sleeve n. **1.** the part of a garment that covers the arm. **2.** something resembling this.

sleigh n. a sledge.

sleight /slaɪt/ n. skill; dexterity.

slender adj. **1.** small in circumference in proportion to height or length. **2.** small in size, amount, extent, etc.

sleuth n. Informal a detective.

slew[1] v. past tense of **slay**.

slew[2] v. **1.** to turn or twist (something), especially upon its own axis or without moving it from its place. **2.** to (cause to) swing round. **3.** to swerve awkwardly. –n. **4.** such a movement.

slew[3] n. Informal a large number: *a whole slew of DVDs.*

slice n. **1.** a thin, broad, flat piece cut from something. **2.** any of various implements with a thin, broad blade. –v. (**sliced**, **slicing**) **3.** to cut into slices. **4.** to cut (*off, away, from*, etc.) as or like a slice.

slick adj. **1.** smooth of manners, speech, etc. **2.** ingenious or adroit. –n. **3.** a patch or film of oil, as on the sea.

slide v. (**slid**, **slid** or **slidden**, **sliding**) **1.** to (cause to) move along in continuous contact with a smooth or slippery surface. **2.** to slip, as one losing foothold or as a vehicle skidding. **3.** to go easily, quietly, or unobtrusively (*in, out, away*, etc.). –n. **4.** the act of sliding. **5.** a single image for projection in a projector; transparency.

slide rule n. a device for rapid arithmetic calculation, marked with logarithmic scales.

slight adj. **1.** small in amount, degree, etc. **2.** frail; flimsy. –v. **3.** to treat with indifference; ignore or snub. –n. **4.** an affront.

For def. 4, the more usual word is **insult**.

slim adj. (**slimmer**, **slimmest**) **1.** slender, as in girth or form. –v. (**slimmed**, **slimming**) Also, **slim down**. **2.** to make oneself slim, as by dieting, exercise, etc.

slime n. **1.** thin, glutinous mud. **2.** viscous secretion of animal or vegetable origin. –**slimy**, **slimey**, adj.

sling n. **1.** an instrument for hurling stones, etc., by hand. **2.** a strap, band, or the like forming a loop by which something is suspended or carried. –v. (**slung**, **slinging**) **3.** to throw, cast or hurl. **4.** to suspend. **5.** Aust. Informal to give money as a bribe.

slingshot n. a catapult.

slink v. (**slunk**, **slinking**) to move stealthily, as to evade notice.

slip[1] v. (**slipped**, **slipping**) **1.** to pass or go smoothly or easily; glide; slide. **2.** to lose one's foothold. **3.** to move or slide from place, a fastening, etc. **4.** to go, come, get, etc., easily or quickly. **5.** to go quietly. **6.** to cause to slip. **7.** to untie or undo (a knot). **8.** to escape (one's memory, notice, knowledge, etc.). −n. **9.** the act of slipping. **10.** a mistake, as in speaking or writing. **11.** the eluding of a pursuer, etc. **12.** a woman's sleeveless undergarment. **13.** a pillowcase. −phr. **14. slip up**, to make a mistake.

slip[2] n. **1.** any long, narrow piece or strip, as of wood, paper, land, etc. −phr. **2. a slip of a ...**, a young person, especially one of slender form: *a slip of a girl; a slip of a thing*.

slipper n. a light shoe for indoor wear.

slippery adj. (**-rier**, **-riest**) **1.** tending to cause slipping or sliding, as ground, surfaces, etc. **2.** likely to slip away or escape.

slippery dip n. Aust. a structure with a smooth slope for children to slide down. Also, **slippery slide**.

slipshod adj. untidy, or slovenly; careless.

slip-stitch n. one of a series of stitches used for dress hems, etc.

slipstream n. an air current behind any moving object.

slit v. (**slit**, **slitting**) **1.** to cut apart or open along a line. −n. **2.** a straight, narrow cut or opening.

slither v. to slide down or along a surface, especially unsteadily or noisily. −**slithery**, adj.

sliver n. a slender piece, as of wood, split, broken, or cut off.

slob n. Informal a lazy, uncouth or slovenly person.

slobber v. **1.** to let saliva, etc., run from the mouth. **2.** to indulge in mawkish sentimentality. −n. **3.** saliva or liquid dribbling from the mouth.

slog Informal −v. (**slogged**, **slogging**) **1.** to hit hard, as in boxing, cricket, etc. **2.** to toil. −n. **3.** a strong crude blow. **4.** a spell of hard work or walking.

slogan n. a distinctive cry or phrase of any party, class, body, or person.

slop v. (**slopped**, **slopping**) **1.** to spill or splash. −n. **2.** (*oft. pl.*) the dirty water, liquid refuse, etc., of a household, etc.

slope v. **1.** to take or have an inclined direction from the horizontal. **2.** to direct at a slope or inclination. −n. **3.** inclination or slant. **4.** an inclined surface.

sloppy adj. (**-pier**, **-piest**) **1.** muddy, slushy, or very wet. **2.** Informal weak, silly, or maudlin. **3.** Informal loose, careless, or slovenly.

sloppy joe n. a loose, thick sweater.

slosh v. to pour or splash sloppily.

slot n. **1.** a narrow, elongated depression or aperture, especially one to receive or admit something. **2.** a position within a system. −v. (**slotted**, **slotting**) **3.** to provide with a slot or slots. −phr. **4. slot in, a.** to insert into a slot. **b.** to settle in; adapt.

slothful adj. indolent; lazy.

slouch v. **1.** to sit, stand, or walk in an awkward, drooping posture. **2.** to cause to droop or bend down. −n. **3.** a drooping of the head and shoulders.

slouch hat n. an army hat of soft felt.

slough /slʌf/ v. to cast (*off*).

slovenly /'slʌvənli/ adj. dirty and untidy. −**sloven**, n.

slow adj. **1.** taking or requiring a comparatively long time. **2.** sluggish. **3.** dull of perception or understanding. **4.** slack, as trade. **5.** showing a time earlier than the correct time. −adv. **6.** in a slow manner. −v. **7.** to make or become slow or slower.

slowmo n. Informal (in film or television) slow motion. Also, **slow-mo**, **slo-mo**.

slow motion n. the process or technique used in film or television production in which images are made to move more slowly than their originals, as a result of having been photographed at a greater number of frames per second than normal, or being projected more slowly than normal.

sludge n. mud, mire.

slug¹ n. **1.** any of various small, slimy, gastropods related to the snails, but having no shell. **2.** a piece of lead or other metal for firing from a gun.

slug² v. (**slugged**, **slugging**) **1.** to strike heavily. –n. **2.** a heavy blow, especially with the fist.

sluggard n. someone who is habitually lazy.

sluggish adj. inactive, slow, or of little energy or vigour.

sluice n. **1.** any device for regulating a flow of water. **2.** a channel or a drain. –v. (**sluiced**, **sluicing**) **3.** to flush or cleanse with a rush of water.

slum n. (oft. pl.) an overpopulated, squalid part of a city.

slumber v. **1.** to sleep, especially deeply. –n. **2.** (oft. pl.) sleep, especially deep sleep.

slump v. **1.** to drop heavily and limply. **2.** to fall suddenly and markedly, as prices. –n. **3.** a decline in prices or sales.

slur v. (**slurred**, **slurring**) **1.** to pronounce (a syllable, word, etc.) indistinctly. –n. **2.** a disparaging remark. **3.** a blot or stain, as upon reputation.

slurp v. **1.** to eat or drink noisily. –n. **2.** the noise produced in this way.

slush n. **1.** snow in a partly melted state. **2.** Informal silly, sentimental, or weakly emotional writing, talk, etc. Also, **slosh**.

slushy adj. (**-shier**, **-shiest**) **1.** of or relating to slush. –n. Also, **slushie**. **2.** a semifrozen drink consisting of flavoured liquid to which finely crushed ice is added.

slut n. (derog.) a promiscuous woman.

It is offensive to refer to a woman as 'a slut'.

sly adj. (**slyer** or **slier**, **slyest** or **sliest**) cunning or wily.

smack¹ n. **1.** a slight taste or flavour, suggestive of something. –v. **2.** to have a taste, flavour, trace, or suggestion (of).

smack² v. **1.** to strike smartly, especially with the open hand. **2.** to bring, put or throw with a sharp, resounding blow. **3.** to come or strike smartly or forcibly, as against something. –n. **4.** a smart, re-sounding blow. **5.** a resounding or loud kiss. **6.** Informal heroin. –adv. **7.** Informal directly; straight.

small adj. **1.** of limited size; little. **2.** not great in amount, degree, extent, duration, value, etc. **3.** of minor importance. –adv. **4.** in a small manner. **5.** into small pieces. –n. **6.** the lower central part of the back.

small fry n. young or unimportant persons or objects.

smallgoods pl. n. Aust., NZ processed meats, as salami, frankfurts, etc.

smallpox n. an acute, highly contagious disease caused by a virus and characterised by pustular sores.

smarmy n. flattering; unctuous.

smart v. **1.** to be a source of sharp local and usually superficial pain, as a wound. **2.** to suffer keenly from wounded feelings. –adj. **3.** sharp or keen, as pain. **4.** sharply severe, as blows. **5.** sharply brisk, vigorous, or active. **6.** clever. **7.** dashingly or effectively neat or trim in appearance. **8.** socially elegant, or fashionable. **9.** (of a device or set of devices) controlled with computer software so that it performs some functions without the human input usually required. –n. **10.** sharp local pain, usually superficial.

smart card n. a plastic card containing integrated circuits capable of storing digital information, used for performing financial transactions, etc. Also, **smart-card**.

smartphone n. a mobile phone with access to the internet and the functionality of a personal computer.

smash v. **1.** to break to pieces, often with a crashing sound. **2.** to break to pieces from a violent blow or collision. −n. **3.** a smashing or shattering, or the sound of it. **4.** a destructive collision. **5.** Also, **smash-hit**, a film, play, recording, etc., that is a great success.

smashing adj. Informal excellent or extremely good; first-rate.

smattering n. a slight or superficial knowledge of something.

smear v. **1.** to rub or spread with oil, dirt, etc. −n. **2.** a mark or stain made by, or as by, smearing.

smell v. (**smelt** or **smelled**, **smelling**) **1.** to perceive through the nose. **2.** to test by the sense of smell. **3.** to search or pieces (out) as if by smell. **4.** to search or investigate (around). **5.** to give out an odour (of), especially as specified. **6.** to seem or be unpleasant or bad. −n. **7.** the faculty or sense of smelling. **8.** that quality of a thing which is or may be smelled. **9.** the act of smelling.

smidgen n. a very small quantity. Also, **smidgin**, **smidgeon**.

smile v. **1.** to widen the mouth, turn up the lips, etc., in pleasure, amusement, scorn, etc. **2.** to assume or give (a smile). **3.** to express by a smile. **4.** to look with favour or support (on or upon). −n. **5.** the act of smiling; a smiling expression of the face.

smirk v. **1.** to smile in a condescending or knowing way. −n. **2.** such a smile.

smite v. (**smote**, **smitten** or **smit**, **smiting**) **1.** to strike or hit hard. **2.** to affect suddenly and strongly with a specified feeling.

smith n. a worker in metal.

Note that this word is often joined to the name of a particular metal, as **goldsmith**, **silversmith** and **tinsmith**. A **black-smith** works with iron.

smithereens pl. n. Informal small fragments.

smock n. any loose overgarment.

smog n. a mixture of smoke and fog.

smoke n. **1.** the visible exhalation given off by a burning or smouldering substance. **2.** something resembling this, as vapour or mist. **3.** an act or spell of smoking tobacco, or the like. **4.** that which is smoked, as a cigar or cigarette. −v. **5.** to give off or emit smoke. **6.** to draw into the mouth and puff the smoke of (tobacco or the like). **7.** to expose to smoke.

smoked adj. (of food items) treated with smoke to preserve them or to add flavour: smoked ham; smoked almonds

smoking ceremony n. an Aboriginal cleansing ritual in which green leaves from local plants are burnt creating smoke which is said to cleanse and heal the area; often used to prepare a site for a new purpose, or after a death to remove spirits.

smoking gun n. **1.** a gun that has just been fired. **2.** a piece of incontrovertible evidence which points to the perpetrator of a crime, the cause of a disaster, etc.

smooch v. Informal to kiss; cuddle.

smoodge v. (**smoodged**, **smoodging**) Informal **1.** to kiss; caress. **2.** to flatter.

smooth adj. **1.** free from irregularities of surface. **2.** of uniform consistency. **3.** pleasant, agreeable, or ingratiatingly polite. −v. **4.** to make smooth of surface, as by scraping, pressing, etc. (down). **5.** to remove (projections, etc.) (away or out). −n. **6.** a smooth part or place.

smorgasbord n. a buffet meal of various dishes.

smother v. **1.** to stifle or suffocate, especially by smoke or by depriving of air. **2.** to extinguish or deaden (fire, etc.) by excluding air. **3.** to oppress by giving too much, as of love, kindness. *—n.* **4.** an overspreading profusion of anything.

smoulder *v.* **1.** to burn or smoke without flame. **2.** to exist or continue in a suppressed state or without outward demonstration.

SMS *n.* (*pl.* **SMSs** *or* **SMSes** *or* **SMS's**) **1.** short message service; a service which enables a user to key in the text of a message on a mobile phone and send it to another mobile phone where it can be read on the screen. **2.** a text message. (**SMS'ed** *or* **SMSed**, **SMS'ing** *or* **SMSing**) **3.** to send someone a text message using this system.

SMS code *n.* a code designed to reduce the length of words when sending SMS messages, such as *u* for *you*, *b4* for *before*, etc.

smudge *v.* (**smudged**, **smudging**) **1.** to mark with a dirty mark or smear. *—n.* **2.** such a mark or smear.

smug *adj.* (**smugger**, **smuggest**) complacently proper, righteous, clever, etc.

smuggle *v.* to import or export (goods) secretly, and illegally.

smut *n.* **1.** a black or dirty mark. **2.** indecent talk or writing.

snack *n.* **1.** a small portion of food or drink; a light meal. **2.** *Informal* anything easily done.

snag¹ *n.* **1.** any sharp or rough projection. **2.** any obstacle or impediment. **3.** a small hole caused by a snag. *—v.* (**snagged**, **snagging**) **4.** to catch upon, or damage by, a snag.

snag² *n.* *Aust.*, *NZ Informal* a sausage.

snail *n.* **1.** a land gastropod having a single, usually spirally coiled shell. **2.** a slow or lazy person.

snail mail *n.* (*humorous*) the ordinary post (as opposed to email).

snake *n.* **1.** a scaly, limbless, usually slender reptile, sometimes venomous. **2.** a treacherous person. **3.** something resembling a snake in form or manner. *—v.* **4.** to

move, twist, or wind in the manner of a snake.

snap *v.* (**snapped**, **snapping**) **1.** to move, strike, shut, catch, etc. with a sharp sound. **2.** to break suddenly. **3.** to make a quick or sudden bite or snatch. **4.** to utter a quick, sharp speech, reproof, retort, etc. **5.** to seize (*up* or *off*) with, or as with, a quick bite or snatch. **6.** *Photography* to take a snapshot of. *—n.* **7.** (an action causing) a sharp, crackling or clicking sound. **8.** a quick or sudden bite or snatch. **9.** a short spell, as of cold weather. **10.** → **snapshot**. *—adj.* **11.** denoting devices closing by pressure on a spring catch. **12.** made, done, taken, etc., suddenly.

snapper *n.* (*pl.* **-per** *or* **-pers**) a marine food fish widely distributed in Aust. and NZ coastal waters. Also, **schnapper**.

> For information about the different plural forms, see the note at **fish**.

snapshot *n.* an informal photograph. Also, **snap**.

snare *n.* anything serving to entrap, entangle, or catch unawares.

snarl¹ *v.* **1.** to growl angrily or viciously. *—n.* **2.** the act of snarling. **-snarling**, *adj.*

snarl² *n.* **1.** a tangle, as of thread or hair. *—v.* **2.** to bring into a tangled condition, as thread, hair, etc.

snatch *v.* **1.** to make a sudden effort to seize something (*at*). **2.** to seize (*up*, *from*, *out of*, *away*, etc.) by a sudden or hasty grasp. *—n.* **3.** the act of snatching. **4.** a bit, scrap, or fragment of something.

snazzy *adj.* (**-zier**, **-ziest**) *Informal* very smart; strikingly fashionable.

sneak *v.* (**sneaked** *or*, *Informal*, **snuck**, **sneaking**) **1.** to go in a stealthy or furtive manner (*about*, *along*, *in*, *off*, *out*, etc.). **2.** to act in a furtive, underhand, or mean way. **3.** to move, put, pass, etc., in a stealthy or furtive manner. *—n.* **4.** a contemptible person; telltale.

sneaker *n.* a shoe with a rubber or other soft sole, worn for sport or as part of casual fashion.

sneer *v.* **1.** to smile or curl the lip in a manner that shows scorn, contempt, etc. *–n.* **2.** an act of sneering.

sneeze *v.* **1.** to emit air or breath suddenly, forcibly, and audibly through the nose and mouth by involuntary, spasmodic action. *–n.* **2.** an act or sound of sneezing.

snick *v.* to cut, snip, or nick.

snide *adj.* derogatory in a nasty, insinuating manner.

sniff *v.* **1.** to draw air through the nose in short, audible inhalation. **2.** to draw in or up through the nose by sniffing, as air, smells, liquid, powder, etc. *–n.* **3.** an act of sniffing.

sniffle *v.* **1.** to sniff repeatedly, as from a cold, etc. *–n.* **2. the sniffles**, *Informal* a cold with a runny nose. Also, **snuffle**. **–sniffling**, *n., adj.*

snigger *v.* to laugh in a half-suppressed, disrespectful, manner.

snip *v.* (**snipped, snipping**) **1.** to cut with a small, quick stroke. *–n.* **2.** the act of snipping. **3.** a small cut, notch, slit, etc., made by snipping.

snipe *n.* **1.** a type of small bird which frequents seashores, estuaries, etc. *–v.* **2.** to shoot at individual soldiers, etc., as opportunity offers from a concealed or long-range position. *–phr.* **3. snipe at**, to make critical or damaging comments about (someone) without entering into open conflict. **–sniper**, *n.*

snippet *n.* a small piece snipped off.

snivel *v.* (**-elled** *or, Chiefly US,* **-eled, -elling** *or, Chiefly US,* **-eling**) **1.** to weep or cry with sniffing. **2.** to draw up mucus audibly through the nose.

snob *n.* someone who affects social importance and exclusiveness. **–snobbish, snobby**, *adj.*

This word is used in a disapproving way.

snooker *n.* a game played on a billiard table.

snoop *Informal* *–v.* **1.** to prowl or pry; go about in a sneaking, prying way. *–n.* **2.** an act or instance of snooping. **3.** someone who snoops.

snooze *Informal* *–v.* **1.** to sleep; doze. *–n.* **2.** a rest; short sleep.

snore *v.* **1.** to breathe during sleep with hoarse or harsh sounds. *–n.* **2.** the sound made.

snorkel *n.* a tube enabling an underwater swimmer to breathe.

snort *v.* **1.** to force the breath violently and noisily through the nostrils, as a horse, etc. **2.** to express contempt, indignation, etc., by such a sound. *–n.* **3.** the act or sound of snorting.

snot *n.* *Informal* mucus from the nose.

snout *n.* the part of an animal's head projecting forward and containing the nose and jaws.

snow *n.* **1.** the aqueous vapour of the atmosphere, partially frozen, and falling to the earth in white flakes. **2.** something resembling snow. *–v.* **3.** (of snow) to fall: *it snowed last night.* *–phr.* **4. be snowed under**, to be overcome by something: *I'm snowed under with work at the moment.*

snowboard *n.* **1.** a board for gliding over snow, on which a rider stands. *–v.* **2.** to glide over the snow on a snowboard. **–snowboarder**, *n.* **–snowboarding**, *n.*

snub *v.* (**snubbed, snubbing**) **1.** to treat with disdain or contempt. **2.** to check or rebuke sharply. *–n.* **3.** an act of snubbing. *–adj.* **4.** (of the nose) short, and turned up at the tip.

snuff[1] *n.* a preparation of powdered tobacco inhaled into the nostrils.

snuff[2] *v.* **1.** to extinguish: *to snuff out a candle.* *–phr.* **2. snuff it**, *Informal* to die.

snuffle *v.* **1.** to speak through the nose or with a nasal twang. **2.** → **sniffle**. *–n.* **3.** an act of snuffling.

snug *adj.* (**snugger, snuggest**) **1.** comfortable or cosy, as a place. **2.** fitting closely, but comfortably, as a garment.

snuggle *phr.* **1. snuggle up**, to lie closely together, as for comfort or from affection. *–n.* **2.** a cuddle.

so *adv.* **1.** in the way or manner indicated, described, or implied. **2.** as stated or reported. **3.** to that extent; in that degree. **4.** for a given reason; hence; therefore. **5.** in the way that follows; in this way. *–conj.* **6.** *Informal* consequently; with the result that. *–pron.* **7.** such as has been stated: *to be good and stay so. –phr.* **8. and so on**, et cetera. **9. or so**, about thus: *a day or so ago.* **10. so that**, **a.** with the effect or result that. **b.** in order that: *You'll have to move so that you can see.*

Don't confuse this with **sew**, which is to join with stitches, using a needle and thread, or with **sow**, which is to plant seeds. The other **sow**, which is a female pig, is pronounced /sau/.

soak *v.* **1.** to lie in and become saturated or permeated with a liquid. **2.** to pass, as a liquid, through pores or openings: *The rain soaked through our clothes.* **3.** to place and keep in liquid in order to saturate thoroughly. **4.** to permeate thoroughly, as liquid or moisture. **5.** to absorb: *The sponge soaked up the water. –n.* **6.** the act of soaking.

soap *n.* **1.** a substance used for washing and cleansing. *–v.* **2.** to rub, cover or treat with soap.

soapbox *n.* (formerly) a wooden box used as a temporary platform by street speakers.

soap opera *n. Informal* a television series, usually dealing with domestic problems, especially in a highly emotional manner. Also, **soapie, soapy.**

soar *v.* **1.** to fly upwards: *the balloon soared into the sky.* **2.** (of a bird) to fly at a great height hardly moving the wings: *the eagle soared over the valley.* **3.** to rise to a great height: *prices are soaring.*

Don't confuse this with **saw** or **sore**. A **saw** is a cutting tool with teeth. **Saw** is also the past tense of the verb **to see**. **Sore** describes something which is painful.

sob *v.* (**sobbed, sobbing**) **1.** to weep with a sound caused by a convulsive catching of the breath. *–n.* **2.** a convulsive catching of the breath in weeping.

sober *adj.* **1.** not intoxicated or drunk. **2.** (of a person) quiet or sedate in demeanour. **3.** free from excess, extravagance, or exaggeration. *–v.* **4.** to make or become sober. *–***sobriety**, *n.*

For def. 2, the more usual word is **serious.**

soccer *n.* a form of football in which the use of the hands and arms is prohibited except to the goalkeeper.

sociable *adj.* enjoying the company of others.

social *adj.* **1.** relating to friendly companionship or relations. **2.** of or relating to the life and relation of human beings in a community. *–n.* **3.** a social gathering or party.

socialise *v.* **1.** to educate to conform to society. **2.** to go into society. Also, **socialize.**

socialism *n.* a political, economic and social system in which all industry, wealth and property in a society is meant to be owned and controlled by the people as a whole.

Compare this with **capitalism** and **communism.**

socialite *n.* a member of the social elite.

social media *n.* online social networks used to disseminate information through online social interaction.

social network *n.* **1.** a supportive group of friends, relatives, acquaintances, etc. **2.** such a group whose point of contact is an online website. *–***social networker**, *n.* *–***social networking**, *n.*

social sciences *pl. n.* a broad group of subjects, as anthropology, sociology, etc., relating to the study of human societies.

social security *n.* a system of payments and other benefits provided by the government to assist people who are poor, sick, unemployed, etc.

social welfare *n.* a system of services set up by a government or other organisation for the benefit of the community in areas such as health, housing, etc.

social work *n.* organised work directed towards the betterment of social conditions, especially among the disadvantaged in the community.

society *n.* (*pl.* **-ties**) **1.** a body of individuals living as members of a community. **2.** people regarded as a body divided into classes according to worldly status. **3.** an association for religious, benevolent, literary, scientific, etc., purposes. *–adj.* **4.** of or relating to polite society.

sociology *n.* the systematic study of the development, organisation, and functioning of human society. **–sociologist,** *n.*

sock[1] *n.* (*pl.* **socks** *or* **sox**) a garment that is worn under a shoe, covering the foot and the ankle and sometimes reaching up to the knee.

sock[2] *v.* *Informal* to strike or hit hard.

socket *n.* a hollow part or piece for receiving and holding some part or thing.

soda *n.* **1.** sodium (in phrases). **2.** soda water. **3.** a drink made with soda water, served with fruit or other syrups, ice-cream, etc.

soda water *n.* an effervescent drink consisting of water charged with carbon dioxide.

sodden *adj.* soaked with liquid or moisture.

sodium *n.* a soft, silver-white metallic element which oxidises rapidly in moist air. *Symbol:* Na

sodium chloride *n.* common salt, NaCl.

sodomy *n.* any sexual practice regarded as unnatural or perverted.

sofa *n.* a long upholstered seat, or couch.

soft *adj.* **1.** yielding readily to touch, cutting or pressure; not hard or stiff. **2.** smooth and agreeable to the touch. **3.** producing agreeable sensations. **4.** gentle, mild. **5.** not strong or robust. **6.** *Informal* involving little effort. **7.** (of water) relatively free from mineral salts that interfere with the action of soap. **8.** (of drugs) non-addictive, as marijuana and LSD. **–softness,** *n.*

softball *n.* a form of baseball played with a larger and softer ball.

soft drink *n.* a drink which is not alcoholic or intoxicating.

soft-serve *adj.* of or relating to a type of soft ice-cream made largely from beaten gelatine.

soft target *n.* an enemy target without military protection.

software *n.* programs which enable a computer to perform a desired operation or series of operations.

Compare this with **hardware** (def. 2), which refers to the physical components of a computer.

soggy *adj.* (**-gier, -giest**) **1.** soaked; thoroughly wet. **2.** damp and heavy, as ill-baked bread.

soil[1] *n.* **1.** the ground or earth in which plants grow. **2.** a particular kind of earth.

soil[2] *v.* to make or become dirty or foul, especially on the surface.

sojourn *v.* **1.** to dwell for a time in a place. *–n.* **2.** a temporary remaining in a place.

solace *n.* **1.** comfort in sorrow or trouble. **2.** something that gives comfort. *–v.* (**-aced, -acing**) **3.** to comfort, console, or cheer (someone).

solar *adj.* **1.** of, relating to, or determined by the sun. **2.** proceeding from the sun, as light or heat. **3.** operating by the light or heat of the sun.

solar heating n. the use of solar energy to provide heating for air or water in a building. –**solar-heated**, adj.

solar panel n. a panel which is part of a solar heating system.

solar plexus n. a network of nerves situated at the upper part of the abdomen.

solar system n. the sun together with all the planets, satellites, asteroids, etc., revolving around it.

sold v. past tense and past participle of **sell**.

solder n. 1. melted alloys applied to metal surfaces, joints, etc., to unite them. –v. 2. to unite with solder.

soldier n. 1. someone who serves in an army for pay. –v. 2. to act or serve as a soldier.

sole¹ adj. 1. being the only one or ones: *the sole survivor*. 2. belonging or relating to one individual or group to the exclusion of all others: *to take sole charge of the children*.

> Don't confuse **sole** with **soul**, which is the spiritual part of a person.

sole² n. 1. the bottom or under surface of the foot. 2. the corresponding under part of a shoe, boot, or the like.

sole³ n. (pl. **sole** or **soles**) a flatfish with a hooklike snout.

> For information about the different plural forms, see the note at **fish**.

solecism /ˈsɒləsɪzəm/ n. 1. a use of language regarded as non-standard. 2. any error, impropriety, or inconsistency.

solemn adj. 1. grave, sober, or mirthless: *solemn music*. 2. serious or earnest: *a solemn promise*. 3. formal or ceremonious. –**solemnity**, n.

solenoid n. *Elect.* a coiled electrical conductor which, when a current passes through, establishes a magnetic field.

solicit v. 1. to seek for by entreaty, earnest or respectful request, etc. 2. to accost another with immoral intention. 3. to endeavour to obtain orders or trade. –**solicitation**, n.

solicitor n. a lawyer who advises clients and prepares cases for a barrister to present in court.

solicitous adj. anxious or concerned.

> The more usual word is *caring*.

solid adj. 1. having 3 dimensions (length, breadth, and thickness). 2. having the interior completely filled up. 3. without openings or breaks. 4. firm, hard, or compact in substance. 5. dense, thick, or heavy in nature or appearance. 6. whole or entire. 7. financially sound. –n. 8. a body or magnitude having length, breadth, and thickness. 9. a solid substance or body.

solidarity n. union or fellowship arising from common responsibilities and interests.

> The more usual word is *unity*.

solid-state adj. of or relating to electronic devices which are composed of components in the solid state, as transistors, integrated circuits, etc.

solidus /ˈsɒlədəs/ n. (pl. **-di** /-daɪ/) a short, sloping line (/) representing the old long form of the letter 's' (abbreviation of solidus) generally used as a dividing line, as in dates, fractions, etc.; forward slash; slash.

soliloquy n. (pl. **-quies**) a speech made when alone or as if alone, as by an actor in a play.

solitaire n. 1. a game played by one person alone. 2. a precious stone set by itself.

solitary adj. 1. without companions. 2. done without assistance or accompaniment. 3. secluded, or lonely.

solitude n. the state of being or living alone.

solo n. (pl. **-los** or **-li**) 1. any performance by one person. –adj. 2. performed alone. –adv. 3. alone.

solstice n. *Astron.* the shortest (winter) or longest (summer) day of the year.

soluble adj. 1. capable of being dissolved. 2. capable of being solved or explained.

solution *n.* **1.** an explanation or answer. **2.** the fact of being dissolved. **3.** a homogeneous molecular mixture of 2 or more substances.

solve *v.* **1.** to clear up or explain. **2.** to work out the answer or solution to.

solvent *adj.* **1.** able to pay all just debts. **2.** having the power of dissolving. *–n.* **3.** the component of a solution which dissolves the other component. *–***solvency**, *n.*

somatic *adj.* of the body; physical.

sombre /ˈsɒmbə/ *adj.* gloomily dark, shadowy, or dimly lit.

sombrero *n.* (*pl.* **-ros**) a broad-brimmed hat, as worn in Mexico.

some *adj.* **1.** of a certain number or amount that is not specified: *I bought some apples.* **2.** of time or distance, of an unspecified large amount: *he stayed with us some weeks.* **3.** being one thing or person not named: *some type of small car.* **4.** *Informal* of considerable account or consequence; notable of the kind: *that was some storm we had last night!* **5.** *Informal* (used ironically to express displeasure): *some friend you turned out to be! –pron.* **6.** certain people, or instances, etc., that are not named: *some think he is dead.* **7.** a number, amount, etc., that is marked off from the rest: *some of this work is good.*

The adjective is sometimes called a *determiner* and the pronoun is sometimes called an *indefinite pronoun.*
Don't confuse this with **sum**, which can mean an amount of money, the total of different amounts, or a maths exercise.

somebody *pron.* **1.** some person. *–n.* (*pl.* **-bodies**) **2.** a person of some note or importance.

This is sometimes called an *indefinite pronoun.*

somehow *adv.* in some way not specified, apparent, or known.

someone *pron.* somebody.

This is sometimes called an *indefinite pronoun.*

somersault *n.* an acrobatic movement of the body in which it describes a complete revolution, heels over head.

something *pron.* some thing; a certain thing which is not named.

This is sometimes called an *indefinite pronoun.*

sometimes *adv.* on some occasions; now and then.

somewhat *adv.* in some measure or degree; to some extent.

somewhere *adv.* in, at or to some place not specified, determined, or known.

somnambulism *n.* sleepwalking.

son *n.* **1.** a male child or person in relation to his parents. **2.** any male descendant. **3.** someone related as if by ties of sonship.

sonar *n.* a device or method for determining depth using echoes of sound.

sonata *n. Music* an extended instrumental composition.

song *n.* **1.** a short metrical composition combining words and music. **2.** poetical composition. **3.** the tuneful sounds produced by certain birds, insects, etc.

sonic *adj.* **1.** of or relating to sound. **2.** denoting a speed approximating that at which sound travels.

son-in-law *n.* (*pl.* **sons-in-law**) the husband of one's daughter or son.

sonnet *n.* a poem of 14 lines.

sonorous *adj.* loud, deep, or resonant, as a sound.

sook *n. Aust., NZ Informal* (usually of children) a timid, shy, cowardly person.

soon *adv.* **1.** within a short period after this (or that) time, event, etc. **2.** promptly or quickly.

soot *n.* a black carbonaceous substance produced during the imperfect combustion of coal, wood, oil, etc.

soothe v. **1.** to tranquillise or calm. **2.** to mitigate or allay, as pain, sorrow, doubt, etc.

sop n. **1.** something given to pacify or quiet, or as a bribe. –v. (**sopped, sopping**) **2.** to drench or become drenched. **3.** to take (water, etc.) (up) by absorption.

sophisticated adj. **1.** (of a person, ideas, tastes, manners, etc.) altered by education, experience, etc., to be worldly-wise. **2.** of intellectual complexity; reflecting a high degree of skill, intelligence, etc.; subtle. –**sophistication**, n.

soporific adj. causing or tending to cause sleep.

soppy adj. (**-pier, -piest**) Informal excessively sentimental.

soprano Music –n. (pl. **-nos** or **-ni**) **1.** the range of notes which can be sung by a woman or boy with a high voice. **2.** a woman or boy who sings in this range. –adj. **3.** having a soprano voice or range of notes: a soprano saxophone.

sorbet /'sɔbeɪ/ n. an iced dessert made with fruit and egg whites and sometimes liqueur or wine.

sorcery n. magic, especially black magic. –**sorcerer**, n.

sordid adj. **1.** filthy; squalid. **2.** morally mean or ignoble.

sore adj. **1.** physically painful or sensitive, as a wound. **2.** suffering bodily pain. **3.** causing very great suffering, misery, hardship, etc. –n. **4.** a sore spot or place on the body, especially an ulceration.

Don't confuse this with **saw** or **soar**. A **saw** is a cutting tool with teeth. **Saw** is also the past tense of the verb **to see**. To **soar** is to fly upwards.

sorrow n. **1.** distress caused by loss, affliction, disappointment, etc. **2.** a cause or occasion of grief or regret. –v. **3.** to feel sorrow.

sorry adj. (**-rier, -riest**) **1.** feeling regret, compunction, sympathy, pity, etc. **2.** of a deplorable, pitiable, or miserable kind.

sort n. **1.** a particular kind, species, variety, class, or group. –v. **2.** to arrange according to sort, kind, or class. –phr. **3. of sorts**, of a mediocre or poor kind. **4. out of sorts**, not in a normal condition of good health, spirits, or temper. **5. sort of**, to a certain extent; in some way. **6. sort out, a.** to separate or take out from other sorts, or from others. **b.** to find a solution for: to sort out a problem.

sorted adj. Informal effectively dealt with; resolved: There was a problem with the bill but it's sorted now.

so-so adj. neither very good nor very bad.

sotto voce /sɒtoʊ 'voʊtʃeɪ/ adv. in a low tone intended not to be overheard.

soufflé /'sufleɪ/ n. a light savoury or sweet (baked or unbaked) dish made fluffy with beaten eggwhites.

sought v. past tense and past participle of **seek**.

soul n. **1.** the spiritual part of humans; spirit (opposed to body). **2.** the seat of the feelings or sentiments. **3.** the embodiment of some quality. **4.** a human being.

Don't confuse **soul** with **sole**, which has several meanings. It can refer to the underneath part of a shoe or a particular type of fish. It can also mean only (a sole parent).

soul music n. commercial African American blues music which combines gospel music with a blues style.

sound¹ n. **1.** the sensation produced in the organs of hearing by certain vibrations in the surrounding air. **2.** a noise, vocal utterance, musical note, or the like. **3.** mere noise, without meaning. –v. **4.** to (cause to) make or emit a sound. **5.** to be heard, as a sound. **6.** to convey a certain impression when heard or read. **7.** to give forth (a sound).

sound² *adj.* **1.** free from injury, defect, etc. **2.** financially strong, secure, or reliable.

sound³ *v.* **1.** to measure or try the depth of (water, a deep hole, etc.) by letting down a lead or plummet at the end of a line. −*phr.* **2. sound out**, to seek to elicit the views or sentiments of (a person) by indirect inquiries, etc.

sound⁴ *n.* an inlet (usually narrow) of the sea.

soundtrack *n.* **1.** a strip at the side of a cinema film which carries the sound recording. **2.** such a recording, especially when transferred on to a CD or cassette.

soup *n.* a liquid food made of various ingredients boiled together.

sour *adj.* **1.** having an acid taste, such as that of vinegar, lemon juice, etc. **2.** acidified or affected by fermentation; fermented. **3.** distasteful or disagreeable.

source *n.* **1.** any thing or place from which something comes, arises, or is obtained. −*v.* (**sourced, sourcing**) **2.** to establish the source of. **3.** to obtain (a product) from a particular producer.

Don't confuse this with **sauce**, which is a liquid used to flavour food.

souse *v.* to plunge into water or other liquid.

south *n.* **1.** a cardinal point of the compass directly opposite to the north. **2.** the direction in which this point lies. −*adj.* **3.** lying towards or situated in the south. **4.** directed or proceeding towards the south. **5.** coming from the south, as a wind. −*adv.* **6.** towards or in the south. **7.** from the south. Also, *esp. Naut.*, **sou'**. −**southerly**, *adj., n.* −**southern**, *adj.*

souvenir *n.* something given or kept for remembrance.

souvlaki /suv'laki/ *pl. n.* a Greek dish of diced lamb and vegetables cooked on skewers.

sovereign *n.* **1.** a monarch. **2.** a former British gold coin. −*adj.* **3.** belonging to or characteristic of a sovereign or sovereignty.

sow¹ /sou/ *v.* (**sowed, sown** or **sowed, sowing**) **1.** to scatter (seed) for growth. **2.** to scatter seed over (land, earth, etc.).

Don't confuse this with **so**, which has several meanings, such as therefore (*I missed the bus, so I was late*) or to such a degree (*Don't run so fast*). Another word which is pronounced the same way is **sew**, which is to join with stitches, using a needle and thread. The other **sow**, which is a female pig, is pronounced /sao/.

sow² /sao/ *n.* an adult female pig.

soybean *n.* a leguminous plant with an oil-yielding seed used as food. Also, **soy, soya bean**.

soy sauce *n.* a salty dark brown sauce, made by fermenting soybeans in brine. Also, **soya sauce**.

spa *n.* **1.** a small pool or an enclosed section of a swimming pool in which heated water is agitated and aerated. **2.** Also, **spa bath**. a bath equipped with submerged water jets which create water turbulence. **3.** a mineral spring, or a locality in which such springs exist.

space *n.* **1.** the unlimited expanse extending in all directions in which the universe is placed. **2.** Also, **outer space**. that part of the universe which lies outside the earth's atmosphere. **3.** (a particular) extent or area. **4.** extent, or a particular extent, of time. −*v.* (**spaced, spacing**) **5.** to set some distance apart.

spacecraft *n.* a vehicle capable of travelling in space.

space shuttle *n.* a spacecraft designed to transport equipment and personnel between earth and a satellite.

spacious *adj.* containing much space, as a house, street, etc.

spade¹ *n.* **1.** a tool for digging. **2.** some implement, piece, or part resembling this.

spade[2] *n.* a black figure shaped like an inverted heart with a short stem used on playing cards.

spadework *n.* laborious or tedious preliminary work.

spaghetti *n.* a kind of pasta.

spam *(from trademark)* –*n.* **1.** a type of cooked tinned meat. **2.** *Informal* unsolicited email, especially advertising material. –*v.* (**spammed, spamming**) **3.** *Informal* to send (someone) spam (def. 2). –**spammer,** *n.* –**spamming,** *n.*

span *n.* **1.** the distance between the tip of the thumb and the tip of the little finger when the hand is fully extended. **2.** the distance or space between 2 supports of a bridge, beam, or similar structure. **3.** the full extent, stretch, or reach of anything. –*v.* (**spanned, spanning**) **4.** to encircle with the hand or hands. **5.** to extend over or across.

spangle *n.* **1.** a small, thin piece of sparkling material, usually metal, for decorating clothes, etc. –*v.* **2.** to decorate with spangles.

spaniel *n.* a small dog usually with a long, silky coat and drooping ears.

spank *v.* **1.** to strike (a person, usually a child) with the open hand, a slipper, etc., especially on the buttocks. –*n.* **2.** a blow given in spanking.

spanner *n.* a tool for gripping and turning the head of a bolt, a nut, a pipe, etc.

spar[1] *n. Naut.* a stout pole such as those used for masts, etc.; a mast, yard, boom, or the like.

spar[2] *v.* (**sparred, sparring**) to box with light blows, especially while seeking an opening in an opponent's defence.

spare *v.* (**spared, sparing**) **1.** to refrain from harming or destroying. **2.** to save from strain, discomfort, annoyance, or the like. **3.** to part with or let go, as from a supply, especially without inconvenience. **4.** to use economically or frugally. **5.** to use economy; be frugal. –*adj.* (**sparer,**

sparest) **6.** kept in reserve. **7.** being in excess of present need. **8.** being thin or lean, as a person. –*n.* **9.** an extra thing, part, etc.

spark *n.* **1.** a fiery particle thrown off by burning wood, etc., or produced by one hard body striking against another. **2.** *Elect.* the light produced by a sudden discontinuous discharge of electricity. –*v.* **3.** to emit or produce sparks.

sparkle *v.* **1.** to emit little sparks, as burning matter. **2.** to shine with little gleams of light. **3.** to effervesce, as wine. –*n.* **4.** a little spark.

spark plug *n.* a device inserted in the cylinder of an internal-combustion engine, containing 2 terminals between which passes the electric spark for igniting the explosive gases. Also, **sparking plug.**

sparrow *n.* a small, hardy, brown bird, common in many parts of the world.

sparse *adj.* thinly scattered or distributed.

The more usual word is **scattered**.

spasm *n.* a sudden, involuntary muscular contraction.

spasmodic *adj.* like a spasm; intermittent.

spastic *n.* a person who has had an injury to the brain causing difficulty in controlling some voluntary muscles.

The name of the condition suffered by these people is **cerebral palsy**. Because some people use **spastic** to refer informally to someone they think is foolish, the term has taken on negative and offensive overtones. For that reason, it is avoided by many people when referring to sufferers of cerebral palsy.

spat[1] *n.* a petty quarrel.

spat[2] *v.* past tense and past participle of **spit**[1].

spate *n.* a sudden, almost overwhelming, outpouring.

The more usual word is **flood**.

spatial *adj.* of or relating to space.

spatter v. 1. to scatter or dash in small particles or drops. 2. to splash with small particles.

spatula n. a broad, flexible blade, used for mixing and spreading.

spawn v. 1. to shed the sex cells, especially as applied to animals that shed eggs and sperm directly into water. 2. to give birth to; give rise to.

spay v. to remove the ovaries of (a female animal).

speak v. (**spoke**, **spoken**, **speaking**) 1. to utter words or articulate sounds. 2. to deliver an address. 3. to make communication by any means: *Her music speaks to me.* 4. to use; or be able to use, in oral utterance, as a language.

speaker n. 1. someone who speaks, especially before an audience. 2. part of a sound system that produces the sound. 3. (*usu. upper case*) the presiding officer of the lower house of a parliament.

spear n. 1. a weapon for thrusting or throwing, being a long staff with a sharp head, of iron or steel. –v. 2. to pierce with or as with a spear.

spearmint n. an aromatic herb.

special adj. 1. of a distinct or particular character. 2. being a particular one. 3. relating or peculiar to a particular person, thing, instance, etc. 4. extraordinary. –*phr.* 5. **on special**, *Informal* available at a bargain price.

specialise v. 1. to pursue some special line of study, work, etc. 2. to invest with a special character, function, etc. 3. to adapt to special conditions. Also, **specialize**. –**specialisation**, n.

specialist n. someone who is devoted to one subject, or to one particular branch of a subject or pursuit.

speciality n. (*pl.* **-ties**) an article of unusual or superior design or quality.

specialty n. (*pl.* **-ties**) 1. a special study, line of work, etc. 2. an article particularly dealt in, manufactured, etc.

species n. (*pl.* **-cies**) a group of individuals having some common characteristics or qualities; distinct sort or kind.

specific adj. 1. specified, precise, or particular. 2. peculiar or proper to something, as qualities, characteristics, effects, etc. 3. of a special or particular kind. 4. something specific, as a statement, quality, etc. –**specificity**, n.

specification n. 1. the act of specifying. 2. a statement of particulars.

specify v. (**-fied**, **-fying**) 1. to mention or name specifically or definitely. 2. to name or state as a condition.

The more usual word is **say**.

specimen n. something taken as an example or sample.

specious adj. apparently good or right but without real merit.

speck n. 1. a small spot differing in colour or substance from its background. 2. a small particle. –v. 3. to mark with, or as with, a speck or specks.

speckle n. 1. a small speck, spot, or mark, as on skin. –v. 2. to mark with speckles.

spectacle n. 1. something striking presented to the sight or view. 2. (*pl.*) → **glass** (def. 2). –**spectacular**, adj.

spectator n. someone who looks on; an onlooker.

spectre n. a ghost; phantom.

spectrum n. 1. *Physics* the band of colours (red, orange, yellow, green, blue, indigo, violet) revealed when white light passes through a prism. 2. a range of interrelated images, objects, opinions, etc.

speculate v. 1. to engage in thought or reflection (*on* or *upon*). 2. to indulge in conjectural thought. 3. *Commerce* to buy and sell commodities, shares, etc., in the expectation of profit. –**speculation**, n. –**speculative**, adj. –**speculator**, n.

For def. 1, the more usual word is **think**.

sped v. past tense and past participle of **speed**.

speech *n.* **1.** the faculty or power of speaking. **2.** that which is spoken. **3.** a communication made by a speaker before an audience for a given purpose. **4.** a characteristic form of language or dialect. **5.** manner of speaking, as of a person.

speed *n.* **1.** rapidity in moving. **2.** *Physics* the ratio of the distance covered to the time taken. **3.** *Informal* amphetamines. –*v.* (**sped** *or* **speeded, speeding**) **4.** to move or proceed with rapidity. **5.** to drive a vehicle faster than the maximum permitted. –*phr.* **6. speed up,** to increase the speed or progress (of).

speed dial *n.* a feature of a phone in which telephone numbers are entered into the memory to be accessed by pressing one button.

speedometer *n.* a device attached to a motor vehicle or the like to indicate the rate of travel. Also, **speedo.**

speleology *n.* the exploration and study of caves. Also, **spelaeology.**

spell¹ *v.* (**spelt** *or* **spelled, spelling**) **1.** to name or write in order, the letters of (a word, syllable, etc.). **2.** (of letters) to form (a word, syllable, etc.). **3.** to name, write, or give the letters of words, etc.

spell² *n.* a combination of words supposed to possess magic power.

spell³ *n.* **1.** a continuous course or period of work or other activity. **2.** *Informal* an interval or space of time, usually indefinite or short. **3.** an interval or period of rest. –*v.* (**spelled, spelling**) **4.** to give an interval of rest to.

spellchecker *n.* a computer program which checks the spelling of words.

spelling *n.* the manner in which words are spelt.

spencer *n. Aust., NZ* a woman's undergarment, worn for extra warmth.

spend *v.* (**spent, spending**) **1.** to pay out, disburse, or expend; dispose of (money, wealth, resources, etc.). **2.** to spend money, etc.

spendthrift *n.* someone who spends the possessions or money extravagantly.

sperm *n.* a male reproductive cell.

spermatozoon /ˌspɜːmətəʊˈzəʊən/ *n.* (*pl.* **-zoa**) a mature male reproductive cell.

spew *v.* to vomit.

SPF *n.* sun protection factor; the effectiveness of a sunscreen preparation in protecting the skin from ultraviolet radiation indicated on a scale, usually from 2 to 30.

sphere *n.* **1.** a round body whose surface is at all points equidistant from the centre. **2.** a field of activity. –**spherical,** *adj.*

sphincter *n. Anat.* a circular band of voluntary or involuntary muscle which encircles an orifice of the body or one of its hollow organs.

spice *n.* **1.** any of a class of pungent or aromatic substances of vegetable origin used as seasoning or preservatives. **2.** something that adds interest. –*v.* **3.** to prepare or season with a spice or spices. –**spicy,** *adj.*

spick-and-span *adj.* **1.** neat and clean. **2.** perfectly new; fresh.

spider *n.* any of the eight-legged wingless, predatory, insect-like arachnids, most of which spin webs.

spiel /spiːl, ʃpiːl/ *n.* a salesperson's, conjurer's or swindler's patter.

spigot *n.* a small peg or plug for stopping the vent of a cask, etc.

spike *n.* **1.** a stiff, sharp-pointed piece or part. –*v.* **2.** to fasten or secure with a spike or spikes. **3.** to pierce with a spike. **4.** set with something suggesting spikes. **5.** to make ineffective, or frustrate the action or purpose of. **6.** *Informal* to add alcoholic liquor to a drink.

spill *v.* (**spilt** *or* **spilled, spilling**) **1.** to cause or allow (liquid, or any matter in grains or loose pieces) to run or fall from a container, especially accidentally. **2.** (of a liquid, loose particles, etc.) to run or escape from a container. –*n.* **3.** a spilling

4. a quantity spilt. **5.** a throw or fall from a horse, vehicle, or the like.

spin *v.* (**spun, spinning**) **1.** to make (yarn) from fibres. **2.** to form (any material) into thread. **3.** to cause to turn round rapidly, as on an axis. **4.** to make up or tell (a story): *He spins a good tale.* **5.** to turn round rapidly, as on an axis, the earth, a top, etc. **6.** to produce a thread from the body, as spiders, silkworms, etc. *–n.* **7.** a spinning motion given to a ball or the like when thrown or struck. **8.** *Informal* the particular slant deliberately given to a media story so as to achieve the desired outcome in terms of public awareness and acceptance.

spinach *n.* **1.** Also, **English spinach.** an annual herb cultivated for its succulent leaves. **2.** a form of beet with large, firm, strongly veined green leaves and a long fleshy stalk, used as a vegetable; silverbeet.

spin control *n.* a method of controlling the point of view presented in the media, especially in relation to politics.

spindle *n.* **1.** the rod on a spinning wheel by which the thread is twisted and on which it is wound. **2.** any similar rod or pin.

spindly *adj.* (**-lier, -liest**) long or tall and slender.

spine *n.* **1.** the vertebral or spinal column; backbone. **2.** any backbone-like part. **3.** a stiff, pointed process or appendage. **4.** the part of a book's cover that holds the front and back together. *–spinal, adj.*

spinechilling *adj.* terrifying.

spinifex *n.* spiny-leaved, tussock-forming grasses of coastal or inland Aust.

spinnaker *n.* a large triangular sail with a light boom (**spinnaker boom**).

spinning top *n.* a child's toy, with a point on which it is made to spin.

spinning wheel *n.* a device for spinning wool, flax, etc., into yarn or thread.

spin-off *n.* an object, product or enterprise derived as an incidental or secondary development of a larger enterprise.

spinster *n.* a woman who has not been married.

Note this word is rather old-fashioned now, especially because it implies that the woman should have got married.

spiny *adj.* (**-nier, -niest**) **1.** having many spines; thorny, as a plant. **2.** covered with spines, as an animal.

spiny anteater *n.* → **echidna**.

spiral *n.* **1.** a plane curve running continuously round a fixed point or centre while constantly receding from it. **2.** a spiral object, formation, or form. **3.** *Econ.* a reciprocal interaction of price and cost changes forming an overall economic change. *–adj.* **4.** resembling or arranged in a spiral or spirals. *–v.* (**-ralled, -ralling**) **5.** to (cause to) take a spiral form or course.

spiralise *v.* to shred (vegetables) into ribbon or noodle-like lengths which form loose curls. Also, **spiralize.** *–spiraliser, n.*

spire *n.* a tall, tapering structure erected on a tower, roof, etc.

spirit *n.* **1.** the vital principle in humans, animating the body or mediating between body and soul. **2.** a supernatural, incorporeal being. **3.** (*pl.*) feelings with respect to exaltation or depression. **4.** fine or brave vigour or liveliness. **5.** the true intent of a statement, etc. **6.** (*oft. pl.*) a strong distilled alcoholic liquor. *–adj.* **7.** relating to something which works by burning alcoholic spirits. *–v.* **8.** to carry (*away, off,* etc.) mysteriously or secretly.

spiritual *adj.* **1.** of, relating to, or consisting of spirit or incorporeal being. *–n.* **2.** a traditional religious song, especially of African Americans.

spirulina /spɪrə'liːnə/ *n.* a human and animal food supplement made from organisms which contain unusually high amounts of protein.

spit[1] v. (**spat** or **spit**, **spitting**) **1.** to eject saliva from the mouth. **2.** to sputter. **3.** to fall in scattered drops or flakes, as rain or snow. **4.** to eject (saliva, etc.) from the mouth. **5.** to throw out or emit, especially violently. —n. **6.** saliva, especially when ejected. **7.** the act of spitting. —phr. **8. dead spit**, *Informal* the image, likeness, or counterpart of a person, etc.

spit[2] n. **1.** any of various rods, pins, or the like used for particular purposes. **2.** a narrow point of land projecting into the water. —v. (**spitted** or **spitting**) **3.** to thrust a spit through, as roasting meat.

spite n. **1.** an ill-natured desire to humiliate or injure another. —v. **2.** to annoy or thwart, out of spite. —phr. **3. in spite of**, in disregard or defiance of.

spittle n. saliva; spit.

spittoon n. a bowl, etc., for spitting into.

splash v. **1.** to wet or soil by dashing masses or particles of water, mud, etc., against. **2.** to dash (water, etc.) about in scattered masses or particles. **3.** *Informal* to display or print very noticeably, as in a newspaper. **4.** to fall or move in scattered masses or particles. —n. **5.** the act or sound of splashing. **6.** a striking show, or an ostentatious display.

splatter v. to splash.

splay v. **1.** to spread out, expand, or extend. **2.** to spread or flare.

spleen n. **1.** *Anat.* a glandlike organ, in the upper left of the abdomen, which modifies the blood. **2.** ill humour, peevish temper, or spite.

splendid adj. **1.** gorgeous; magnificent. **2.** strikingly admirable or fine.

splendour n. brilliant or gorgeous appearance, colouring, etc. Also, **splendor**.

splice v. to join together or unite, especially by the interweaving of strands.

splint n. **1.** a thin piece of wood or other rigid material used to immobilize a fractured or dislocated bone. —v. **2.** to support with splints.

splinter n. **1.** a thin, sharp piece of wood, bone, etc., split or broken off from a main body. —v. **2.** to split or break into splinters.

split v. (**split**, **splitting**) **1.** to divide into distinct parts or portions. **2.** to separate (a part) by such division. **3.** to break or part lengthways. **4.** to part, divide, or separate in any way. **5.** to become separated off as a piece or part from a whole. **6.** *Informal* to leave hurriedly. —n. **7.** the act of splitting. **8.** a crack, rent, or fissure caused by splitting. **9.** (*usu. pl.*) the feat of separating the legs at right angles to the body while sinking to the floor. —adj. **10.** that has undergone splitting.

split personality n. **1.** (in popular use) → **schizophrenia**. **2.** (in popular use) → **multiple personality disorder**. **3.** *Informal* an unpredictable or extremely changeable personality.

splurge v. *Informal* to be extravagant.

splutter v. **1.** to talk hastily and confusedly. **2.** to spatter, as a liquid.

spoil v. (**spoiled** or **spoilt**, **spoiling**) **1.** to damage or impair (a thing) irreparably. **2.** to impair in character or disposition. **3.** to become spoiled, bad, or unfit for use. —n. **4.** (*oft. pl.*) booty, loot, or plunder taken in war or robbery.

spoilsport n. someone who interferes with the pleasure of others.

spoilt v. **1.** a past form of **spoil**. —adj. **2.** selfish; indulged too much.

spoke[1] v. past tense of **speak**.

spoke[2] n. one of the rungs radiating from the hub of a wheel.

spoken v. **1.** past participle of **speak**. **2.** (in compounds) speaking, or using speech, as specified.

spokesperson n. someone who speaks for another or others.

sponge n. **1.** the light, porous, fibrous skeleton of certain marine animals which absorbs water readily, becoming soft but retaining toughness. **2.** someone or something that absorbs something freely, as a sponge does water. **3.** a light, sweet cake. –*v.* (**sponged, sponging**) **4.** to wipe or rub with a wet sponge. **5.** *Informal* to live at the expense of others. –**spongy**, *adj.* –**sponger**, *n.*

sponsor *n.* **1.** someone who vouches or is responsible for a person or thing. **2.** a person, firm, etc., that finances a radio or television program in return for advertisement. –*v.* **3.** to act as sponsor for.

spontaneous *adj.* **1.** natural and unconstrained. **2.** independent of external agencies.

spoof *n. Informal* a parody.

spook *n.* **1.** *Informal* a ghost; spectre. –*v.* **2.** to frighten. –**spooky**, *adj.* –**spookily**, *adv.*

Note that def. 1 is generally used in children's stories.

spooky *adj.* (**-kier, -kiest**) *Informal* like or suggesting a ghost; eerie: *a spooky noise.* –**spookily**, *adv.* –**spookiness**, *n.*

spool *n.* any cylindrical piece on which something is wound.

spoon *n.* **1.** a utensil consisting of a bowl or concave part and a handle, for taking up or stirring liquid or other food. –*v.* **2.** to take up or transfer in or as in a spoon. **3.** *Informal* to show affection, especially in an openly sentimental manner.

spoonerism *n.* the transposition of initial sounds of words, as in 'our queer old dean' for 'our dear old queen'.

spoor *n.* a track or trail of a wild animal.

sporadic *adj.* appearing or happening at intervals. –**sporadically**, *adv.*

The more usual word is **occasional**.

spore *n.* a germ, germ cell, seed, or the like.

sporran *n.* (in Scottish Highland costume) a large pouch hanging from the belt over the front of the kilt.

sport *n.* **1.** an energetic activity pursued for exercise or pleasure. **2.** a pleasant pastime. **3.** something sported with or tossed about like a plaything. **4.** *Aust., NZ Informal* (a term of address, usually between males).

–*v.* **5.** to amuse oneself with some pleasant pastime. **6.** to have or wear, especially ostentatiously.

sporting *adj.* **1.** sportsmanlike. **2.** willing to take a chance. **3.** even or fair.

sports *adj.* **1.** of, relating to, or devoted to a sport or sports. **2.** (of garments, etc.) suitable for outdoor or informal use.

sports car *n.* a high-powered car, usually a two-seater with a low body, built for speed and manoeuvrability.

sports drink *n.* a drink which contains sugars, salts and water; designed to rehydrate the body during or after periods of intense physical exertion. Also, **sport drink**.

sportsman *n.* **1.** a man who engages in sport, usually with a degree of expertise. **2.** someone who shows qualities highly valued in those who play sport, such as fairness, courage, etc. –**sportsmanlike**, *adj.* –**sportsmanship**, *n.*

Note that def. 2 can be used about women, along with **sportsmanlike** and **sportsmanship**. However, because these terms include the word *man*, they can be seen as excluding women.

Another expression you could use for **sportsman** is **a good sport**, and for **sportsmanlike** you could use **sporting** or **fair**. **Sportsmanship** has two senses: you can use **skill** for one (ability in playing a sport) and **fairness** for the other (qualities such as are admired in sport).

sportsperson *n.* (*pl.* **-people**) a person who engages in sport, usually with a degree of expertise.

sportswoman *n.* a woman who plays sport with some skill.

spot *n.* **1.** a mark made by foreign matter. **2.** a blemish of the skin, as a pimple. **3.** a relatively small, usually roundish, part of a surface differing from the rest in appearance or character. **4.** a moral blemish. **5.** a place or locality. **6.** *Informal* a small quantity of something. **7.** *Informal* a predicament. *–v.* (**spotted**, **spotting**) **8.** to stain with spots. **9.** to see or perceive, especially suddenly, by chance, or when it is difficult to do so. **10.** to make a spot.

spotlight *n. Theatre* a strong light thrown upon a particular spot on the stage.

spot-on *adj. Informal* absolutely right or accurate.

spouse *n.* one's husband or wife.

spout *v.* **1.** to discharge or emit (a liquid, etc.) in a stream with some force. **2.** to issue with force, as vines, buildings, etc. **3.** a tube by which a liquid is discharged or poured.

sprain *v.* to overstrain or wrench (a joint), as an ankle, etc.

sprat *n.* (*pl.* **sprats** *or* **sprat**) a small, herring-like marine fish.

For information about the different plural forms, see the note at **fish**.

sprawl *v.* **1.** to lie or sit with the limbs stretched out in a careless or ungraceful posture. **2.** to spread out in a straggling or irregular manner, as vines, buildings, handwriting, etc. **3.** to stretch out (the limbs) as in sprawling.

spray[1] *n.* **1.** fine particles of water or other liquid blown or falling through the air. *–v.* **2.** to scatter (as) in fine particles. **3.** to direct a spray of particles, missiles, etc., upon. **4.** to issue as spray.

spray[2] *n.* a single flower or small bouquet of flowers designed to be pinned to one's clothes.

spray can *n.* → aerosol.

spread *v.* (**spread**, **spreading**) **1.** to draw or stretch out to the full width. **2.** to distribute in a sheet or layer. **3.** to overlay or coat with something. **4.** to diffuse or disseminate, as knowledge, news, disease, etc. **5.** to become stretched out or extended. **6.** to admit of being applied in a thin layer. **7.** to become diffused abroad, or disseminated. *–n.* **8.** expansion; extension; diffusion. **9.** a stretch, expanse, or extent of something. **10.** a cloth covering for a

bed, table, etc. **11.** any food preparation for spreading on bread, etc.

spread-eagle *v.* to stretch out with arms and legs wide apart. *–***spread-eagled**, *adj.*

spreadsheet *n.* a computer program especially useful for organising numerical data.

spree *n.* a session or period of excessive indulgence: *a spending spree.*

sprig *n.* a shoot, twig, or small branch.

sprightly *adj.* (**-lier**, **-liest**) animated or vivacious; lively.

spring *v.* (**sprang** *or* **sprung**, **sprung**, **springing**) **1.** to rise or move suddenly and lightly. **2.** to go or come suddenly as if with a leap. **3.** to come into being; rise or arise (*up*). **4.** to cause to spring. **5.** to bring out, disclose, produce, make, etc., suddenly. **6.** to equip or fit with springs. **7.** to make a surprise attack on (someone). *–n.* **8.** a leap, jump, or bound. **9.** elasticity or springiness. **10.** an issue of water from the earth. **11.** a beginning or cause of origin. **12.** the season of the year between winter and summer. **13.** the first and freshest period. **14.** an elastic device which recovers its shape after being compressed, bent, etc. *–adj.* **15.** of or relating to the season of spring. **16.** resting on or containing springs. *–***springy**, *adj.*

springboard *n.* **1.** a projecting, semi-flexible board used for diving. **2.** a flexible board used as a take-off in vaulting, tumbling, etc.

sprinkle *v.* **1.** to scatter, as a liquid or a powder, in drops or particles. **2.** to disperse or distribute here and there. **3.** to overspread with drops or particles. *–n.* **4.** a sprinkling.

sprint *v.* **1.** to race at full speed, especially for a short distance, as in running, rowing, etc. *–n.* **2.** a short race at full speed.

sprite *n.* **1.** an elf, fairy, or goblin. **2.** an icon which moves around a screen in computer graphics.

sprocket n. *Machinery* one of a set of projections on the rim of a wheel which engage the links of a chain.

sprout v. 1. to begin to grow. 2. (of a seed, plant, the earth, etc.) to put forth buds or shoots. –n. 3. a shoot of a plant.

spruce[1] n. an evergreen tree with short angular needle-shaped leaves.

spruce[2] adj. (**sprucer, sprucest**) 1. smart in dress or appearance. –phr. (**spruced, sprucing**) 2. **spruce up**, to make oneself smart.

spry adj. (**spryer, spryest, sprier, spriest**) active; nimble.

spud n. *Informal* a potato.

spume n. foam; froth; scum.

spun v. past tense and past participle of **spin**.

spunk n. 1. *Informal* pluck; spirit; mettle. 2. *Aust. Informal* a good-looking person. –**spunky**, adj.

spur n. 1. a pointed device attached to a rider's boot heel, for goading a horse onwards, etc. –v. (**spurred, spurring**) 2. to prick with, or as with, spurs or a spur. –phr. 3. **on the spur of the moment**, suddenly; without premeditation.

spurious adj. not genuine or true.

spurn v. to reject with disdain.

spurt v. 1. to gush or issue suddenly in a stream or jet. 2. to show marked activity or energy for a short period. –n. 3. a forcible gush of water, etc., as from a confined place. 4. a sudden outburst, as of feeling.

sputter v. 1. to emit particles of anything in an explosive manner, as a candle does in burning. 2. to emit (anything) in small particles, as if by spitting.

spy n. (pl. **spies**) 1. someone who keeps secret watch on the actions of others. 2. someone employed by a government to obtain secret information or intelligence. –v. (**spied, spying**) 3. to make secret observations. 4. to find (out) by observation. 5. to catch sight of; see.

spyware n. software which, once installed on a computer, secretly collects information as the user goes about their normal computer tasks, as tracking internet viewing for advertising purposes, copying files from the hard disk, or copying logins and passwords.

squabble v. 1. to engage in a petty quarrel. –n. 2. a petty quarrel.

squad n. any small group or party of persons engaged in a common enterprise, etc.

> Squad is a collective noun and can be used with a singular or plural verb. Look up **collective noun**.

squadron n. an air force unit.

> Squadron is a collective noun and can be used with a singular or plural verb. Look up **collective noun**.

squalid adj. foul and repulsive.

squall[1] n. a sudden strong wind which dies away rapidly.

squall[2] v. to cry out loudly.

squalor n. filth and misery.

squander v. to spend or use wastefully.

square n. 1. a right-angled, four-sided plane having all its sides equal. 2. anything having this form or a form approximating it. 3. *Maths* the 2nd power of a number or quantity. 4. *Informal* someone who is ignorant of or uninterested in the latest fads. –v. (**squared, squaring**) 5. to reduce to square, rectangular, or cubic form. 6. *Maths* to multiply (a number or quantity) by itself. 7. Also, **square off**. to make straight, level, or even. 8. to accord or agree (*with*). –adj. (**squarer, squarest**) 9. of the form of a right angle. 10. at right angles, or perpendicular. 11. designating a unit representing an area in the form of a square. 12. of a specified length on each side of a square. 13. having all accounts settled. 14. just, fair, or honest. 15. conservative. –adv. 16. in square or rectangular form. –phr.

17. square up, to pay or settle a bill, debt, etc.

square dance n. a dance by couples arranged in a square or in some set form.

square root n. *Maths* the quantity of which a given quantity is the square (def. 3).

squash[1] v. **1.** to press into a flat mass or pulp. –n. **2.** the act or sound of squashing. **3.** the fact of being squashed. **4.** something squashed or crushed. **5.** a game for 2 players, played in a small walled court with light racquets and a small rubber ball.

squash[2] n. a vegetable similar to the pumpkin.

squat v. (**squatted** or **squat**, **squatting**) **1.** to crouch close to the ground with the knees bent and the back more or less straight. **2.** to occupy a building without title or right. –adj. **3.** low and thick or broad. –n. **4.** a squatting position or posture.

squatter n. **1.** *Aust., NZ Hist.* someone who settled on crown land to run stock. **2.** someone who occupies a building without right or title.

squawk v. **1.** to utter a loud, harsh cry, as a duck. –n. **2.** a loud, harsh cry or sound.

squeak n. **1.** a short, sharp, shrill cry. –v. **2.** to utter or emit a sound of this kind.

squeal n. **1.** a more or less prolonged, sharp, shrill cry, as of pain, fear, etc. –v. **2.** to utter or emit a sound of this kind.

squeamish adj. easily nauseated or sickened.

squeeze v. **1.** to press forcibly together. **2.** to apply pressure to extract something. **3.** to thrust forcibly; force by pressure. **4.** to exert a compressing force. **5.** to force a way through some narrow or crowded place: *They could just squeeze through the crack.* –n. **6.** the act of squeezing. **7.** a restriction, demand, or pressure, as imposed by a government. **8.** a small quantity obtained by squeezing. **9.** Also,

main squeeze. *Informal* a girlfriend or boyfriend.

squelch v. **1.** to strike or press with crushing force. **2.** to make a splashing sound.

squid n. (pl. **squids** or, especially collectively, **squid**) any of various slender marine creatures with 10 tentacles.

When squid is used for food, it is called **calamari**.

squint v. **1.** to look with the eyes partly closed. **2.** to look or glance obliquely or sideways. **3.** to close (the eyes) partly. –n. **4.** a disorder of the eye. **5.** a looking obliquely. –adj. **6.** looking obliquely.

squire n. **1.** a personal attendant of a person of rank. –v. **2.** to attend as or in the manner of a squire.

squirm v. to wriggle or writhe.

squirrel n. **1.** any of various arboreal, bushy-tailed rodents. **2.** *Informal* a person who hoards objects of little value.

squirt v. **1.** to eject (liquid) in a jet from a narrow orifice. **2.** to wet or bespatter with a liquid so ejected. **3.** to issue in a jet-like stream. –n. **4.** a jet, as of water.

stab v. (**stabbed**, **stabbing**) **1.** to pierce or wound with a pointed weapon. **2.** to thrust or plunge (a knife, etc.) into something. **3.** to thrust with a knife or other pointed weapon. –n. **4.** the act of stabbing. **5.** a sudden, usually painful sensation.

stable[1] n. **1.** a building for the lodging and feeding of horses. **2.** a collection of horses belonging in such a building. **3.** a group of people associated in some way with a centre of creative production. –v. **4.** to put or lodge (as) in a stable.

stable[2] adj. not likely to fall or give way, as a structure, support, etc. –**stability**, n. –**stabilise**, **stabilize**, v.

Note that the opposite of **stable** is **unstable**, but the opposite of **stability** is **instability** (not 'unstability').

staccato /stəˈkɑːtoʊ/ adj. *Music* detached, disconnected, or abrupt.

stack n. **1.** an orderly pile or heap. **2.** *Informal* a great quantity or number. **3.** that part of a library in which the main holdings of a library are kept. –v. **4.** to pile in a stack. **5.** to cover or load something in stacks. **6.** to bring a large number of one's own supporters to (a meeting) in order to outvote those of opposing views. –phr. **7. stack up**, to accumulate.

stadium n. a sporting facility, often enclosed, comprising an arena, tiers or seats for spectators.

staff n. (pl. **staffs** or **staves** for defs 1, 2 and 4, **staffs** for def. 3) **1.** a pole or rod to aid in walking. **2.** something which serves to support or sustain. **3.** a body of persons charged with carrying out the work of an establishment. **4.** *Music* → **stave** (def. 1). –v. **5.** to provide with a staff.

Def. 3 is a collective noun and can be used with a singular or plural verb. Look up **collective noun**.

stag n. **1.** an adult male deer. –adj. **2.** *Informal* for or of men only.

stage n. **1.** a single step or degree in a process; a particular period in a process of development. **2.** a raised platform. **3.** the theatre, the drama, or the dramatic profession. **4.** the scene of any action. –v. (**staged**, **staging**) **5.** to put or represent on or as on a stage. **6.** to arrange; set up, as for a particular event.

stagecoach n. a coach that runs regularly over a fixed route.

stagger v. **1.** to walk, move, or stand unsteadily. **2.** to cause to reel, as with shock. **3.** to arrange in some order in which there is a continuous overlapping. –n. **4.** the act of staggering.

stagnant adj. not running or flowing, as water, air, etc.

stagnate v. **1.** to become foul from standing, as a pool of water. **2.** to become inactive, sluggish, or dull. **3.** to make no progress; stop developing. –**stagnation**, n.

staid adj. of settled or sedate character.

The more usual word is **conservative**.

stain n. **1.** a semipermanent discolouration produced by foreign matter. **2.** a cause of reproach. **3.** a solution or suspension of colouring matter in water, spirit, or oil. –v. **4.** to discolour with spots or streaks of foreign matter. **5.** to become stained.

stair n. a series or flight of steps.

Don't confuse this with **stare**, which is to look at something for a long time, usually with your eyes wide open.

staircase n. a flight of stairs.

stairwell n. the vertical opening containing a stairway.

stake¹ n. **1.** a stick or post pointed at one end for driving into the ground. **2.** a post to which a person is bound for execution. –v. **3.** to mark (in or out) or separate with stakes. **4.** to protect or separate by a barrier of stakes. **5.** to support with a stake or stakes, as a plant. **6.** to surround (a building, etc.) for the purposes of a raid or keeping watch (out).

Don't confuse this with **steak**, which is a thick slice of meat. It is pronounced the same as **stake**.

stake² n. **1.** that which is wagered. **2.** an interest held in something. –v. **3.** to put at risk upon the result of a game, venture, etc. –phr. **4. at stake**, involved; in a state of being at hazard.

stalactite n. a calcium deposit shaped like an icicle, hanging from the roof of a cave.

stalagmite n. a calcium deposit shaped like an inverted stalactite, formed on the floor of a cave.

stale adj. having lost freshness or interest.

stalemate n. any position in which no action can be taken.

stalk¹ n. the stem or main axis of a plant.

Don't confuse this with **stork**, which is a long-legged water bird.

stalk² v. **1.** to pursue or approach game, etc., stealthily. **2.** to walk with slow, stiff, or haughty strides. **3.** to pursue (game, a person, etc.) stealthily. **–stalker,** n.

stall n. **1.** a compartment in a stable or shed to accommodate one animal. **2.** a booth or stand on which goods are displayed for sale. –v. **3.** to come or bring to a standstill, especially unintentionally: *The car stalled at the lights; She stalled the car; The building work has stalled because of wet weather.* **4.** to put off, avoid, or deceive: *Stall the visitors until next week.*

stallion n. a male horse not castrated.

stalwart /'stɔːlwət/ adj. **1.** strong and brave. **2.** firm; steadfast.

stamen /'steɪmən/ n. (pl. **stamens** or **stamina** /'stæmənə/) Bot. the pollen-bearing organ of a flower.

stamina n. strength of physical constitution.

stammer v. **1.** to speak with spasmodic repetitions of syllables or sounds. –n. **2.** a stammering mode of utterance.

stamp v. **1.** to strike or beat with a forcible downward thrust of the foot. **2.** to bring (the foot) down forcibly or smartly on the ground, etc. **3.** to impress with a particular mark or device. **4.** to impress (a design, figure, words, etc.) on something; imprint deeply or permanently on anything. **5.** to affix an adhesive paper stamp to (a letter, etc.). –n. **6.** the act or an instance of stamping. **7.** a die, engraved block, etc., for impressing a design, etc. **8.** an official mark indicating genuineness, validity, etc., or payment of a duty or charge. **9.** a small adhesive piece of paper for attaching to documents, goods subject to duty, letters, etc., to show that a charge has been paid.

stampede n. **1.** a sudden scattering or headlong flight. –v. **2.** to (cause) scatter or flee in a stampede.

stance n. the position or bearing of the body while standing.

stand v. (**stood, standing**) **1.** to (cause to) take or keep an upright position on the feet. **2.** (of things) to be in an upright position. **3.** to cease moving. **4.** to take a position or attitude. **5.** to have a specified height: *He stands almost 2 metres tall.* **6.** to be or remain in a specified position or condition. **7.** to resist change, decay, or destruction. **8.** to become or be a candidate, as for parliament. **9.** to tolerate: *I will stand no nonsense.* –n. **10.** the act of standing. **11.** a coming to a position of rest. **12.** a determined opposition to or support for some cause, etc. **13.** a raised platform. **14.** a framework on or in which articles are placed for support, exhibition, etc. –phr. **15. stand by, a.** to wait in a state of readiness. **b.** to aid, uphold, or sustain. **16. stand down, a.** to withdraw, as from a contest. **b.** to dismiss (employees) who are not involved in direct strike action but who are not able to carry out their normal duties. **17. stand in,** to act as a substitute or representative.

standard n. **1.** an approved model. **2.** a certain commodity in which the basic monetary unit is stated, historically usually either gold or silver. **3.** a level of excellence, achievement, etc. **4.** a level of quality which is regarded as normal or acceptable. **5.** Mil. a flag. **6.** an upright support or supporting part. –adj. **7.** serving as a basis of weight, measure, value, comparison, or judgement. **8.** normal, adequate, acceptable, or average.

standardise v. **1.** to bring to or make of an established standard size, weight, quality, etc. **2.** to compare with or test by a standard. Also, **standardize.**

stand-by n. **1.** something or someone upon which one can rely. **2.** something kept in a state of readiness for use.

stand-in n. a substitute.

standing n. **1.** position or status. **2.** good position, financial viability, or credit. **3.** length of existence, continuance, residence, membership, experience, etc. –adj.

4. performed in or from a stationary or an erect position. **5.** continuing in operation, force, use, etc.

stand-out *n. Informal* a person in a team, competition, etc., who obviously has abilities greater than all the others. Also, **standout**.

standpoint *n.* the mental position from which one views something.

stanza *n.* a group of lines of verse, forming a regularly repeated metrical division of a poem.

staphylococcus /stæfələ'kɒkəs/ *n.* (*pl.* **-cocci** /-'kɒkaɪ, -'kɒki/) any of certain species of bacteria.

staple[1] *n.* **1.** a bent piece of wire used to bind papers, sections of a book, etc., together. *–v.* **2.** to secure or fasten by a staple.

staple[2] *n.* **1.** a principal item, thing, feature, element, or part. *–adj.* **2.** principally used.

stapler *n.* a stapling machine.

star *n.* **1.** any of the heavenly bodies appearing as apparently fixed luminous points in the sky at night. **2.** (*pl.*) a horoscope. **3.** a conventional five-pointed figure considered as representing a star of the sky. **4.** a prominent actor, singer, or the like. *–adj.* **5.** brilliant, prominent, or distinguished. *–v.* (**starred**, **starring**) **6.** to set with, or as with, stars. **7.** to present or feature (an actor, etc.) as a star. **8.** to mark with a star or asterisk. **9.** (of an actor, etc.) to appear as a star.

starboard /'stabəd/ *n. Naut.* the side of a ship to the right of a person looking towards the bow (opposed to *port*).

starch *n.* **1.** a white, tasteless, solid, carbohydrate, occurring in plants. **2.** a commercial preparation of this substance. **3.** stiffness or formality, as of manner. *–v.* **4.** to stiffen or treat with starch.

stare *v.* (**stared**, **staring**) **1.** to gaze fixedly, especially with the eyes wide open.

2. to stand out boldly or obtrusively to view. *–n.* **3.** a staring gaze.

> Don't confuse **stare** with **stair**, which is one of a series of steps.

starfish *n.* (*pl.* **-fish** or **-fishes**) a marine animal in the form of a star.

> For information about the different plural forms, see the note at **fish**.

stark *adj.* **1.** sheer, utter, downright, or arrant. **2.** harsh, grim, or desolate to the view. *–adv.* **3.** utterly or absolutely.

starling *n.* a small bird, introduced and now widespread in eastn Aust.

start *v.* **1.** to begin to move, go, or act. **2.** to begin (any course of action). **3.** (of a process or performance) to begin. **4.** to move with a sudden, involuntary jerk or twitch, as from a shock. **5.** to set in operation. *–n.* **6.** the beginning or outset of anything. **7.** the first part of anything. **8.** a sudden, involuntary movement. **9.** a lead or advance over competitors or pursuers. **10.** a spurt of activity.

startle *v.* to cause to start involuntarily, as under a sudden shock.

starve *v.* **1.** to die or cause to die or perish from hunger. **2.** to cause to suffer for lack of something desired: *The strike starved the city of petrol.* *–starvation, n.*

stash *v.* **1.** to put away, as for safekeeping or in a prepared place. *–n.* **2.** a hoard.

state *n.* **1.** the condition of a person or thing, as to circumstances or attributes. **2.** condition as to constitution, structure, etc. **3.** a particular condition of mind or feeling. **4.** a particularly tense, nervous, or excited condition. **5.** a body of people occupying a definite territory and organised under one government. **6.** of or relating to the supreme civil government. **7.** characterised by, attended with, or involving ceremony. *–v.* **8.** to declare definitely. **9.** to set forth formally in speech or writing.

stately *adj.* (**-lier**, **-liest**) dignified or majestic.

statement *n.* **1.** something stated. **2.** a public or formal expression of fact, intention, etc. **3.** the act of expressing facts, ideas, etc. **4.** a non-verbal expression of one's beliefs, opinions, personality, etc.: *her clothes really made a statement.* **5.** *Commerce* an account rendered to show the balance due. **6.** *Gram.* an expression of fact, etc., as *My new shoes are red.*, as opposed to a question, exclamation or command.

statesman *n.* (*pl.* **-men**) a man who is versed in the management of affairs of state.

Note that the more usual word is **politician** or **diplomat**, depending on the position of the person. The use of the formal word **statesman** suggests that the person is highly respected or is worthy of respect. Note also that because **statesman** includes the word *man*, it is seen by many to exclude women. This is another reason for choosing a term such as **politician**, unless you specifically want to refer to a widely respected man.

static *adj.* **1.** relating to or characterised by a fixed or stationary condition. *—n.* **2.** a crackling noise or interference with sound waves such as that caused by electrical activity in the air.

static electricity *n.* **1.** electricity at rest, as that produced by friction. **2.** electricity in the atmosphere which interferes with the sending and receiving of radio messages, etc.

station *n.* **1.** the place in which anything stands. **2.** the place at which trains stop. **3.** a place equipped for some particular kind of work, service, or the like. **4.** *Aust., NZ* a property on which sheep or cattle are raised. **5.** standing, as of persons in a social scale. **6.** the wavelength on which a radio or television program is broadcast. *—v.* **7.** to place or post in a station or position.

stationary *adj.* standing still; not moving.

Don't confuse the adjective **stationary** with the noun **stationery**.

stationery *n.* writing materials, as pens, pencils, paper, etc. **—stationer**, *n.*

Don't confuse the noun **stationery** with the adjective **stationary**.

station hand *n.* an employee who does routine work on a rural property.

station wagon *n.* a car with an extended interior behind the rear seat, and a door at the back.

Compare this with **sedan** and **hatchback**.

statistic *n.* a numerical fact.

statistics *n.* **1.** the science which deals with the collection, classification and use of numerical facts or data relating to a particular subject or matter. **2.** the numerical facts or data themselves. **—statistician**, *n.* **—statistical**, *adj.*

Note that def. 1 is used as a singular noun, as in *Statistics is quite an interesting subject*, but def. 2 is used as a plural noun, as in *These statistics on drug use are very worrying.*

stative verb /ˈsteɪtɪv/ *n. Gram.* a verb which indicates a state or condition which is not changing, as in *I own a house*, or *I hate vegetables.* Compare **dynamic verb**. Also, **non-action verb**.

statue *n.* a solid representation of a person or an animal, usually made out of stone, wood or bronze.

Don't confuse this with **stature**, which is how tall someone is, or with **statute**, which is a law.

stature *n.* **1.** the height of an animal body, especially of a human. **2.** degree of development or achievement attained.

Don't confuse **stature** with **statute**, which is a law, and with **statue**, which is an image of someone made out of stone, wood or metal.

status /'steɪtəs, 'stætəs/ n. **1.** condition, position, or standing socially, professionally, or otherwise. **2.** the relative standing, position, or condition of anything.

status quo n. the existing state or condition.

statute n. a permanent rule established by an institution, corporation, etc., for the conduct of its internal affairs. –**statutory**, adj.

Don't confuse this with **stature**, which is how tall someone is, or with **statue**, which is an image of someone made out of stone, wood or metal.

staunch¹ v. to stop the flow of (a liquid, especially blood).

staunch² adj. firm or steadfast.

The more usual word is **loyal**.

stave n. Also, **staff. 1.** Music a set of horizontal lines on which music is written. –phr. (**staved** or **stove, staving**) **2. stave in**, to break a hole in; crush inwards. **3. stave off**, to put, ward, or keep off.

stay¹ v. **1.** to remain in a place, situation, company, etc. **2.** to pause or wait. **3.** to hold back, detain, or restrain. **4.** to remain through or during (a period of time, etc.). **5.** to remain to the end of. –n. **6.** a sojourn or temporary residence.

stay² n. **1.** a prop; brace. **2.** (pl.) a corset.

STD¹ n. any disease such as syphilis, gonorrhoea, AIDS, etc., which is transmitted through sexual contact between people.

This is short for **sexually transmitted disease**.

STD² n. **1.** a system for making direct long-distance telephone calls without going through an operator. –adj. **2.** of or relating to this system: an STD call.

This is short for **subscriber trunk dialling**.

stead /stɛd/ n. the place of a person or thing as occupied by a successor or substitute.

steadfast adj. **1.** firmly fixed; constant or unchanging. **2.** firm and unchanging in one's beliefs, friendships, etc.

The more usual word is **unwavering**; also for def. 2, **loyal**.

steady adj. (**-dier, -diest**) **1.** firmly placed or fixed; stable. **2.** uniform; continuous. **3.** settled, staid, or sober. –v. (**-died, -dying**) **4.** to make or become steady, as in position, etc. –adv. **5.** in a firm or steady manner.

steak /steɪk/ n. a thick slice of meat or fish.

Don't confuse this with **stake**, which is a pointed stick. It can also be the amount of money you bet on something.

steal v. (**stole, stolen, stealing**) **1.** to take or take away dishonestly or wrongfully, especially secretly. **2.** to get, take or do secretly: to steal a glance; to steal a nap. **3.** to move, go, or come secretly, quietly, or unobserved. –n. **4.** Informal something acquired at a cost well below its true value.

Don't confuse **steal** with **steel**, which is a type of metal.

stealth n. secret, clandestine, or surreptitious procedure. –**stealthy**, adj.

steam n. **1.** water in the form of gas or vapour. **2.** water changed to this form by boiling, and extensively used for the generation of mechanical power, for heating purposes, etc. –v. **3.** to emit or give off steam or vapour. **4.** to become covered with condensed steam, as a surface. **5.** to expose to or treat with steam, as in order to heat, cook, soften, renovate, etc. –adj. **6.** heated by or heating with steam. **7.** operated by steam.

steamroller n. a heavy locomotive, originally steam-powered, having a roller or rollers, for crushing or levelling materials in road-making.

steed n. a horse, especially one for riding.

steel n. **1.** iron in a modified form, artificially produced, and possessing hardness, elasticity and strength. —adj. **2.** relating to or made of steel. **3.** like steel in colour, hardness, or strength. —v. **4.** to make (oneself) unfeeling, determined, etc.

Don't confuse this with **steal**, which is to take something that doesn't belong to you.

steep[1] adj. **1.** having a relatively high gradient, as a hill, stairs, etc. **2.** Informal unduly high, or exorbitant, as a price or amount.

steep[2] v. to soak or lie soaking in water or other liquid.

steeple n. a lofty tower, especially one with a spire, attached to a church, etc.

steeplechase n. a horserace over a course furnished with artificial ditches, hedges, and other obstacles.

steer[1] v. to guide the course of (anything in motion) by a rudder, helm, wheel, etc.

steer[2] n. a castrated bull, especially one raised for beef; ox; bullock.

steerage n. (in a passenger ship) the part allotted to the passengers who travel at the cheapest rate.

stellar adj. **1.** of or relating to the stars; consisting of stars. **2.** starlike.

stem[1] n. **1.** the ascending axis of a plant growing above the ground. **2.** something resembling or suggesting this. —v. (**stemmed**, **stemming**) **3.** to originate (from).

stem[2] v. to stop, hold back or plug.

stem cell n. an unspecialised form of cell, capable of dividing and giving rise to various specialised cells.

stench n. an offensive smell.

stencil n. **1.** a thin sheet of stiff material cut through so as to reproduce a design, letters, etc., when colour is rubbed through it. **2.** the letters, designs, etc., produced. —v. (**-cilled**, **-cilling**) **3.** to produce (letters, etc.) by means of a stencil.

stenographer n. someone who is skilled in taking dictation in shorthand.

stentorian adj. very loud or powerful in sound.

step n. **1.** a movement made by lifting the foot and setting it down again in a new position, as in walking, etc. **2.** the space passed over or measured in making a step. **3.** pace uniform with that of another or others, or in time with music. **4.** a move or proceeding, as towards some end. **5.** a degree or stage in ascending or descending. **6.** a support for the foot in ascending or descending. —v. (**stepped**, **stepping**) **7.** to move by a step or steps. **8.** to tread (on or upon). **9.** to move or set (the foot) in taking a step. **10.** to measure (off or out) (a distance, ground, etc.) by steps. **11.** to make or arrange in the manner of a series of steps. —phr. **12. step down, a.** to decrease. **b.** to resign; relinquish a position.

stepladder n. a ladder having flat steps or treads in place of rungs and a hinged support to keep it upright.

steppe n. an extensive grassland plain, especially one without trees.

stereo n. (pl. **-reos**) **1.** stereophonic sound reproduction. **2.** any system, equipment, etc., for reproducing stereophonic sound. —adj. **3.** relating to stereophonic sound, stereoscopic photography, etc.

stereophonic adj. **1.** of or relating to a three-dimensional auditory perspective. **2.** of or relating to the multi-channel reproduction or broadcasting of sound which simulates three-dimensional auditory perspective.

stereotype n. **1.** an oversimplified and conventional image, used to label or define people. —v. **2.** to make a stereotype of. —**stereotypical**, adj.

sterile adj. **1.** free from living germs or micro-organisms. **2.** incapable of producing offspring. —**sterility**, n. —**sterilise**, **sterilize**, v.

sterling adj. **1.** consisting of or relating to British money. **2.** (of silver) being of standard quality, 92½ per cent pure silver.

stern[1] adj. firm, strict, or uncompromising.

stern[2] n. the hinder part of anything.

sternum n. (pl. **-nums** or **-na**) Anat. the breastbone.

steroid n. **1.** a chemical substance with a specific action on the body. **2.** a hormone, used by some athletes for body building.

sterol n. any of a group of steroid alcohols derived from plants or animals, as cholesterol.

stethoscope n. an instrument placed on the body, used to convey sounds within the body to the ear of the examiner.

stevedore n. a firm or individual engaged in the loading or unloading of a vessel.

stew v. **1.** to cook (food) by simmering or slow boiling. **2.** to undergo cooking by simmering or slow boiling. –n. **3.** a preparation of food cooked by stewing.

steward n. **1.** any attendant on a ship or aircraft who waits on passengers. **2.** someone who arranges the details and conduct of a public meeting, race meeting, public entertainment, etc.

stick[1] n. **1.** a relatively long and slender piece of wood or similar material. –phr. **2. the sticks**, remote and little developed areas.

stick[2] v. (**stuck**, **sticking**) **1.** to pierce or puncture with a pointed instrument. **2.** to thrust (something pointed) in, into, through, etc., as for fastening. **3.** to place in a specified position. **4.** to (cause to) cling together more or less permanently. **5.** to endure. **6.** to remain firm in resolution, etc. **7.** to be at a standstill. –phr. **8. stick at** (or **to**), to keep steadily at a task or undertaking. **9. stick out**, to project or protrude. **10. stick up**, Informal to rob, especially at gunpoint. **11. stick up for**, to speak or act in favour of.

sticker n. an adhesive label, usually with a message printed on it.

stickler n. a person who insists on something unyieldingly.

stickybeak n. Aust., NZ someone who pries.

sticky tape n. an adhesive tape, made of cellulose and usually transparent.

stiff adj. **1.** rigid or firm in substance. **2.** not moving or working easily. **3.** rigidly formal. **4.** severe, as a penalty. –n. **5.** Informal a dead body. –adv. **6.** in a rigid state.

stifle v. **1.** to smother or suffocate. **2.** to suppress. **3.** to become stifled or suffocated.

stigma n. (pl. **-mas** or **-mata** /-mətə/) a mark of disgrace. **–stigmatic**, adj. **–stigmatise**, **stigmatize**, v.

The more usual word is **blot**.

stile n. a series of steps for getting over a fence, etc.

stiletto n. **1.** a dagger with a narrow blade. **2.** a high, thin heel on a woman's shoe, or the shoe itself.

still[1] adj. **1.** remaining at rest. **2.** tranquil or quiet. **3.** not effervescent, as wine. –n. **4.** a single photographic picture. –adv. **5.** up to this or that time: *It's still cold.* **6.** even or yet (with comparatives or the like): *The blue one is better still.* **7.** even then: *She was wealthy and still worried about money.* –conj. **8.** and yet: *He's old, still he goes out.* –v. **9.** to calm or allay.

still[2] n. a distilling apparatus.

stillbirth n. the birth of a dead child or organism.

still life n. (pl. **still lifes**) a picture representing inanimate objects, such as fruit, flowers, etc.

stilt n. **1.** one of 2 poles, each with a support for the foot at some distance above the ground. **2.** a post underneath any structure built above land or over water.

stilted adj. stiffly dignified or formal.

The more usual word is **unnatural**.

stimulant *n.* any beverage or food that stimulates.

stimulate *v.* 1. to rouse to action or effort. 2. to invigorate as by an alcoholic or other stimulant. –**stimulation**, *n.*

stimulus *n.* (*pl.* **-li** /-laɪ, -li/ *or* **-luses**) something that incites to action, etc.

sting *v.* (**stung, stinging**) 1. to use or have a sting, as bees. 2. to (cause to) feel a smarting pain. –*n.* 3. any sharp pain (physical or mental). 4. anything that wounds, pains, or irritates.

stingray *n.* any of the rays having a long flexible tail armed near the base with a strong, serrated bony spine with which they can inflict severe and very painful wounds.

stingy /ˈstɪndʒi/ *adj.* (**-gier, -giest**) reluctant to give or spend.

stink *v.* (**stank** *or* **stunk** *or* **stunk, stinking**) 1. to emit a strong offensive smell. –*n.* 2. such a smell.

stint *v.* 1. to limit, often unduly. 2. to be frugal. –*n.* 3. a period of time allotted to a particular activity.

stipend *n.* fixed or regular pay.

stipulate *v.* 1. to make an express demand (*for*), as a condition of agreement. 2. to require as an essential condition. –**stipulation**, *n.*

The more usual word is **state**.

stir *v.* (**stirred, stirring**) 1. to move or agitate (a liquid, etc.). 2. to (cause to) move, especially in some slight way. 3. to rouse from inactivity. 4. to excite. 5. to incite a heated discussion deliberately. –*n.* 6. the act of stirring or moving, or the sound made. 7. a state or occasion of general excitement.

stir-fry *v.* (**-fried, -frying**) to fry lightly in a little hot fat or oil, stirring continually.

stirrup *n.* a loop suspended from the saddle of a horse to support the rider's foot.

stitch *n.* 1. a loop made by one movement in sewing, knitting, etc. 2. a sudden, sharp pain in the side, brought on by physical exertion. –*v.* 3. to work upon or fasten with stitches.

stoat *n.* the ermine in its brown summer phase.

stock *n.* 1. an aggregate of goods kept on hand by a merchant, etc. 2. a quantity of something accumulated, as for future use. 3. a breed, variety, or other related group of animals or plants. 4. the handle of a whip, etc. 5. a pole used in skiing. 6. *Finance* a. the capital of a company converted from fully paid shares. b. the shares of a particular company. –*adj.* 7. of common type or use. 8. relating to livestock raising. –*v.* 9. to furnish with stock. –*phr.* 10. **take stock**, to make an appraisal of resources, prospects, etc.

stockade *n.* *Fortifications* a defensive barrier consisting of strong posts or timbers fixed upright in the ground.

stockbroker *n.* a broker who buys and sells stocks and shares for customers for a commission; sharebroker.

stock exchange *n.* 1. (*oft. upper case*) a building or place where stocks and shares are bought and sold. 2. an association of brokers in stocks and bonds.

Stockholm syndrome /ˈstɒkhoʊm/ *n.* the tendency of hostages to form a sympathetic bond with their captors.

stocking *n.* a close-fitting covering for the foot and leg.

stockman *n.* (*pl.* **-men**) a man employed to tend livestock, especially cattle.

Because this term includes the word *man*, it is seen by many to exclude women. If you are not referring specifically to a man, it is best to use **stockworker**, a term which is becoming more common nowadays.

stock market *n.* a stock exchange. Also, **stockmarket**.

stockpile *n.* 1. a large supply of essential materials, held in reserve. –*v.* 2. to accumulate for future use.

stockworker n. a person employed to tend livestock, especially cattle.

stocky adj. (**-kier, -kiest**) of solid and sturdy form or build.

stoic /ˈstoʊɪk/ adj. noted for calm or silent strength and courage; impassive. Also, **stoical**. **–stoically**, adv.

stoke v. to poke, stir up, and feed (a fire). **–stoker**, n.

stole[1] v. past tense of **steal**.

stole[2] n. a type of long scarf.

stolen v. past participle of **steal**.

stolid adj. not easily moved or stirred mentally; impassive; unemotional.

stomach n. **1.** (in humans and other vertebrates) an organ of storage and digestion. **2.** the part of the body containing the stomach. –v. **3.** to endure or tolerate.

stomp v. Informal to stamp.

stone n. **1.** the hard substance of which rocks consist. **2.** a piece of rock of small or moderate size. **3.** (pl. **stone**) a unit of mass in the imperial system, equal to a little more than 6 kilograms. **4.** something resembling a small stone, as the central seed of certain fruits. –adj. **5.** made of stone. –v. **6.** to throw stones at. **7.** to free from stones, as fruit. **–stony**, adj.

stoned adj. Informal completely drunk or under the influence of drugs.

stood v. past tense and past participle of **stand**.

stooge n. someone who acts on behalf of another.

stool n. **1.** a seat without arms or a back. **2.** faeces.

stoop v. **1.** to bend (the head and shoulders, or the body generally) forwards and downwards. **2.** to condescend; deign. –n. **3.** a stooping position or carriage of body.

stop v. (**stopped, stopping**) **1.** to (cause to) cease. **2.** to cut off, intercept, or withhold. **3.** to prevent from continuing, etc. **4.** Also, **stop up.** to block (a passageway, duct, etc.). **5.** to stay. –n. **6.** the act of stopping. **7.** a stay or sojourn. **8.** a place

where buses or other vehicles halt. **9.** any piece or device that serves to check or control movement or action in a mechanism. **10. → full stop. 11. stop by,** to call somewhere briefly on the way to another destination.

stopover n. any brief stop in the course of a journey.

stopper n. a plug or piece for closing a bottle, tube, or the like.

stop press n. news inserted in a newspaper after printing has begun.

stopwatch n. a watch in which the timing mechanism can be stopped or started at any instant.

storage n. **1.** the state or fact of being stored. **2.** a place where something is stored.

store n. **1.** a supply or stock of (something). **2.** a shop, usually large. **3.** measure of esteem or regard. –v. **4.** to lay (up) or put (away), for future use.

storey n. (pl. **-reys** or **-ries**) one complete level or floor of a building.

> Don't confuse this with **story**, which is the telling of something, either true or made up.

stork n. a long-legged, long-necked, long-billed wading bird.

> Don't confuse this with **stalk**, which is to follow someone secretly. It is also the stem of a plant.

storm n. **1.** a heavy fall of rain, snow, or hail or a violent outbreak of thunder and lightning, often with strong winds. **2.** a violent outburst or outbreak. –v. **3.** to rage or complain with violence or fury. **4.** to assault or attack.

story n. (pl. **-ries**) **1.** a narrative designed to interest or amuse the hearer or reader. **2.** the plot of a novel, poem, drama, etc. **3.** Informal a lie; fib.

> Don't confuse this with **storey**, which is a level of a building (three storeys high).

stout adj. **1.** bulky or thickset. **2.** bold or hardy. –n. **3.** any of various beers darker and heavier than ales.

stove[1] n. an apparatus for supplying heat.

stove[2] v. a past tense and past participle of **stave**.

stow v. to put in a place or receptacle; pack.

stowaway n. someone who hides aboard a ship or other conveyance, as to get a free trip.

straddle v. to walk, stand, or sit with one leg on each side of.

strafe v. to bombard heavily.

straggle v. to go, come, or spread in a scattered, irregular fashion.

straight adj. **1.** without a bend. **2.** honest or upright. **3.** right or correct. **4.** undiluted, as an alcoholic beverage. –adv. **5.** in a straight line. **6.** honestly or virtuously. **7.** in the proper order or condition, as a room. –**straighten**, v.

Don't confuse this with **strait**, which is a narrow channel of water between two large bodies of water.

straightaway adv. immediately.

straightforward adj. **1.** free from deceit. **2.** uncomplicated.

strain[1] v. **1.** to exert to the utmost. **2.** to impair by stretching or overexertion. **3.** to make excessive demands upon. **4.** to pass (liquid matter) through a filter, sieve, or the like, in order to hold back the denser or solid constituents. **5.** to stretch one's muscles, nerves, etc., to the utmost. –n. **6.** an injury due to excessive tension or use. **7.** damaging or wearing pressure or effect. **8.** (usu. pl.) a passage of music or song as rendered or heard: the sweet strains of a violin.

strain[2] n. **1.** any of the different lines of ancestry united in a family or an individual. **2.** a variety, especially of micro-organisms.

strainer n. a filter, sieve, or the like for straining liquids.

strait n. **1.** (oft. pl.) a narrow passage of water connecting 2 large bodies of water. –phr. **2.** in dire straits, in great difficulty or danger.

Note that the plural form of def. 1 may be used to refer to a single passage of water: The straits were calm as we sailed between the two islands.

Don't confuse this word with **straight**, which describes something which is not bent or curved. It also means directly or immediately (Come straight home).

straitjacket n. a kind of coat for confining the arms of violently insane persons, etc. Also, **straightjacket**.

straitlaced adj. excessively strict in conduct or morality.

strand[1] v. **1.** (usu. in the passive) to bring into a helpless position. **2.** to be driven or run ashore.

strand[2] n. **1.** each of a number of strings twisted together to form a rope, cord, etc. **2.** a thread of the texture of anything.

strange adj. **1.** unusual or extraordinary. **2.** coming from outside one's own or a particular locality.

stranger n. **1.** a person with whom one has (hitherto) had no personal acquaintance. –phr. **2.** no stranger to ..., a person accustomed to (something specified): he is no stranger to poverty.

strangle v. to kill by stopping the breath.

strap n. **1.** a long, narrow piece or object. –v. (**strapped**, **strapping**) **2.** to secure with a strap.

strapping adj. Informal tall, robust, and strongly built: a strapping young athlete.

The more usual word is **healthy**.

stratagem n. **1.** a plan or trick for deceiving the enemy. **2.** any trick.

strategy n. (pl. **-gies**) **1.** the planning and tactics used in war. **2.** a cleverly devised scheme. –**strategic**, adj.

For def. 2, the more usual word is **plan**.

stratify v. (**-fied**, **-fying**) to form in strata or layers. **–stratification**, n.

stratosphere n. the region of the atmosphere at an altitude of about 20 to 50 km above the earth. **–stratospheric**, adj.

stratum n. (pl. **-ta** or **-tums**) a layer of material, often one of a number of parallel layers.

straw n. 1. a single stalk or stem, especially in certain species of grain. 2. a mass of such stalks used as fodder, etc. 3. a hollow tube used in drinking. –adj. 4. made of straw.

strawberry n. (pl. **-ries**) a small, red, fleshy fruit.

stray v. 1. to wander (away, off, from, into, to, etc.). 2. to go astray. –n. 3. a domestic animal found wandering at large or without an owner. –adj. 4. wandering or lost. 5. found or occurring as an isolated or casual instance.

streak n. 1. a long, narrow mark, smear, band of colour, or the like. 2. an admixture of anything. –v. 3. to make or become streaked. 4. to flash or go rapidly.

stream n. 1. any flow of water or other liquid. 2. prevailing direction; drift. –v. 3. to (cause to) flow in a stream. 4. to run or flow (with). 5. to transmit digital data in a continuous, steady flow, so that it may be processed and displayed as it is being received, rather than being stored and only received and processed. **–streaming**, n.

streamer n. a long, narrow strip of paper, usually brightly coloured, thrown in festivities, or used for decorating.

streamline v. 1. to make streamlined. 2. to simplify, especially to improve efficiency.

streamlined adj. 1. having a shape designed to offer the least possible resistance in passing through the air, etc. 2. simplified, especially to improve efficiency.

street n. a public way or road in a town or city.

street smart adj. skilled at living in an urban environment, especially under sordid or dangerous conditions.

strength n. 1. the quality or state of being strong. 2. something that makes strong.

strenuous adj. characterised by vigorous exertion.

> The more usual word, particularly if you are talking about work, is **hard**.

streptococcus /ˌstrɛptəˈkɒkəs/ n. (pl. **-cocci** /-ˈkɒkaɪ, -ˈkɒki/) any of certain species of bacteria. **–streptococcic** /-ˈkɒksɪk/, **streptococcal** /-ˈkɒkəl/, adj.

stress v. 1. to emphasise. –n. 2. importance or significance attached to a thing. 3. emphasis in music, rhythm, etc. 4. the physical force exerted on one thing by another. 5. (a disturbing influence which produces) a state of severe tension in an individual.

stressful adj. causing anxiety and tension.

stretch v. 1. to draw out or extend. 2. to lengthen or enlarge by tension. 3. to force beyond the natural or proper limits. 4. to reach, as for something. 5. to extend over a distance, area, period of time, etc. 6. to stretch oneself by extending the limbs, straining the muscles, etc. 7. to become stretched, as any elastic material. –n. 8. capacity for being stretched. 9. a continuous length or expanse. 10. an extent in time or duration. –adj. 11. made to stretch, as clothing. –phr. 12. **stretch out**, to recline at full length.

stretcher n. 1. a light, folding bed. 2. a bed-like device designed for transporting an ill or injured person.

strew v. (**strewed**, **strewed** or **strewn**, **strewing**) to scatter or sprinkle.

stricken adj. struck down or afflicted, as with disease, sorrow, etc.: *stricken with the flu*; *stricken with remorse*.

> When talking about emotions, the more usual word is **overcome**.

strict *adj.* **1.** in close conformity to requirements or principles. **2.** rigorously enforced. **3.** precise.

stricture *n.* **1.** strong criticism. **2.** the narrowing of any passage of the body as a result of disease.

For def. 1, the more usual word is **censure.**

stride *v.* (**strode**, **stridden**, **striding**) **1.** to take a long step. **2.** to walk with long steps (*along, on, through, over,* etc.). *–n.* **3.** a long step in walking. **4.** (*pl.*) *Informal* trousers.

strident *adj.* making or having a harsh sound.

strife *n.* conflict or discord.

strike *v.* (**struck**, **striking**) **1.** to deal a blow or stroke (to). **2.** to inflict (a blow, stroke, etc.). **3.** to drive or thrust forcibly. **4.** to produce (fire, sparks, light, etc.). **5.** to come into forcible contact (with). **6.** to fall upon (something), as light or sound. **7.** to enter the mind of. **8.** to impress strongly. **9.** to come upon or find (ore, oil, etc.). **10.** to indicate (the hour of day), as a clock. **11.** to assume (an attitude or posture). **12.** to reach by agreement, as a compromise. **13.** to take root. **14.** (of an employee or employees) to engage in a strike. *–n.* **15.** the act of striking. **16.** a concerted stopping of work to compel an employer to accede to demands. *–phr.* **17. strike off,** to exclude (someone) from a profession because of unprofessional conduct, etc. **18. strike out, a.** to direct one's course boldly. **b.** to efface or cancel with or as with a pen. **19. strike up, a.** to begin (a friendship, conversation, etc.) **b.** (of an orchestra or band) to begin to play.

string *n.* **1.** a cord used for tying parcels, etc. **2.** a number of objects arranged on a cord. **3.** any series of things following closely one after another. **4.** (in musical instruments) a tightly stretched cord or wire which produces a note when caused to vibrate. *–v.* (**strung**, **stringing**) **5.** to furnish with strings. **6.** to extend or stretch (a cord, etc.) from one point to another. **7.** to thread on a string. **8.** to arrange in a series. *–phr.* **9. string along,** *Informal* to deceive (someone) repeatedly.

stringent *adj.* narrowly binding.

strip¹ *v.* (**stripped**, **stripping**) **1.** to make bare or naked. **2.** to take away or remove. **3.** to take off one's clothes.

strip² *n.* a long, narrow piece.

stripe *n.* **1.** a relatively long, narrow, contrasting band. *–v.* **2.** to mark with stripes.

striptease *n.* an act in which someone strips before an audience.

strive *v.* (**strove** or **strived**, **striven** /'strɪvən/ or **strived**, **striving**) to make strenuous efforts towards any end.

The more usual word is **try.**

stroganoff /'strɒgənɒf/ *n.* a Russian dish of meat cooked in a sauce of sour cream and mushrooms.

stroke¹ *n.* **1.** a blow. **2.** something likened to a blow, as an attack of paralysis. **3.** a repeated or characteristic movement, as in a machine, or in swimming, tennis, etc. **4.** a mark traced by a pen, etc.

stroke² *v.* **1.** to pass the hand or an instrument over (something) lightly or with little pressure. *–n.* **2.** the act or an instance of stroking.

stroll *n.* **1.** a leisurely walk. *–v.* **2.** to take a leisurely walk.

stroller *n.* a light collapsible chair on wheels, used for carrying small children. Also, **pushchair, pusher.**

strong *adj.* **1.** physically vigorous or robust. **2.** mentally or morally powerful. **3.** powerful in influence, authority, resources. **4.** of great force, effectiveness, potency, or cogency. **5.** containing alcohol, or much alcohol. **6.** intense, as light or colour. **7.** of an unpleasant or offensive flavour or smell. *–adv.* **8.** in a strong manner. **9.** in number: *The team was 15 strong.*

stronghold *n.* a strong or well-fortified place; a fortress.

strop *n.* **1.** material used for sharpening razors. *–v.* (**stropped, stropping**) **2.** to sharpen on a strop.

stroppy *adj. Informal* rebellious or complaining.

strove *v.* past tense of **strive**.

struck *v.* past tense and a past participle of **strike**.

structure *n.* **1.** arrangement of parts, elements or constituents. **2.** something built or constructed. **3.** anything composed of parts arranged together. *–v.* **4.** to give form or organisation to. **–structural**, *adj.*

struggle *v.* **1.** to contend with an opposing force. *–n.* **2.** the act or process of struggling.

strum *v.* (**strummed, strumming**) **1.** to play on a (stringed musical instrument) unskilfully or carelessly. **2.** to play (chords, etc., especially on a guitar) by sweeping across the strings with the fingers or with a plectrum.

strung *v.* past tense and past participle of **string**.

strut¹ *v.* (**strutted, strutting**) to walk with a vain, pompous bearing, as with head erect and chest thrown out.

strut² *n.* a structural part designed to take pressure.

strychnine /ˈstrɪknin, -nən/ *n.* a colourless crystalline poison.

stub *n.* **1.** a short remaining piece. *–v.* (**stubbed, stubbing**) **2.** to strike, as one's toe, against something. *–phr.* **3. stub out**, to extinguish (a cigarette) by pressing the lighted end against a hard surface.

stubble *n.* any short, rough growth, as of beard.

stubborn *adj.* unreasonably obstinate.

stubby *adj.* (**-bier, -biest**) **1.** short and thick; thickset. *–n.* (*pl.* **-bies**) **2.** *Aust., NZ* a small squat beer bottle.

stuck *v.* past tense and past participle of **stick²**.

stud¹ *n.* **1.** a small protuberance projecting from a surface or part, especially as an ornament. **2.** a kind of small button or fastener. *–v.* (**studded, studding**) **3.** to set with or as with studs. **4.** to set or scatter (objects) at intervals over a surface.

stud² *n.* **1.** an establishment in which horses cattle, etc., are kept for breeding. *–adj.* **2.** retained for breeding purposes.

student *n.* someone who studies.

studio *n.* (*pl.* **-dios**) **1.** a room or place in which some form of art is pursued. **2.** a room or set of rooms for broadcasting radio or television programs or making recordings.

study *n.* (*pl.* **-dies**) **1.** application of the mind to the acquisition of knowledge, as by reading, investigation, or reflection. **2.** a thorough examination and analysis of a particular subject. **3.** a room set apart for private study, reading or writing. **4.** something produced as an educational exercise. *–v.* (**-died, -dying**) **5.** to apply oneself to acquiring knowledge (of). **6.** to examine or investigate carefully and in detail. **–studious**, *adj.*

stuff *n.* **1.** the material of which anything is made. **2.** matter or material indefinitely: *cushions filled with some soft stuff.* *–v.* **3.** to fill (a receptacle), especially by close packing. **4.** to fill (poultry, meat, etc.) with seasoned breadcrumbs or other savoury matter. **5.** to thrust or cram (something) tightly into a receptacle, etc. **6.** *Informal* to cause to fail; render useless. **7.** to cram (oneself) with food. *–phr.* **8. stuff up**, *Informal* to cause to fail; render useless.

stuffing *n.* that with which anything is or may be filled.

stuffy *adj.* (**-fier, -fiest**) **1.** close or ill-ventilated, as a room. **2.** old-fashioned; immune to new ideas.

stumble *v.* **1.** to strike the foot against something so as to stagger or fall; trip. **2.** to walk or go unsteadily. *–n.* **3.** the act of stumbling. *–phr.* **4. stumble on**

(or **across**), to find accidentally or un-expectedly.

stump n. **1.** something left after a part has been cut off or used up, as of a tree, leg, pencil, etc. **2.** *Cricket* each of the 3 upright sticks which form a wicket. –v. **3.** to embarrass or render completely at a loss. **4.** to walk heavily or clumsily.

stun v. (**stunned, stunning**) **1.** to deprive of consciousness or strength by a blow, fall, etc. **2.** to strike with astonishment.

stung v. past tense and past participle of **sting**.

stunt¹ v. to check the growth or development of.

stunt² n. a performance serving as a display of skill, or the like; feat.

stunt double n. someone whose job is to perform hazardous or acrobatic feats, especially one who replaces a film actor in scenes requiring such feats.

stuntman n. a male stunt double.

stuntwoman n. a female stunt double.

stupefy v. (-**fied,** -**fying**) to put into a state of stupor. –**stupefaction,** n.

stupendous adj. such as to cause amazement.

stupid adj. lacking ordinary activity and keenness of mind; dull.

stupor n. a state of suspended or deadened sensibility.

sturdy adj. (-**dier,** -**diest**) strongly built, stalwart, or robust.

sturgeon n. (pl. -**geon** or -**geons**) a large fish of the Nthn Hemisphere, valued as a source of caviar.

For information about the different plural forms, see the note at **fish.**

stutter v. **1.** to utter (sounds) in which the rhythm is interrupted by blocks or spasms, repetitions, or prolongation. –n. **2.** unrhythmical and distorted speech. Also, **stammer.**

sty n. (pl. **sties**) a pen or enclosure for pigs.

stye n. a small inflammation on the eyelid. Also, **sty.**

style n. **1.** a particular kind, sort, or type. **2.** a particular, distinctive, or characteristic mode of action, speech, literary expression, etc. **3.** a mode of fashion; elegance; smartness. **4.** a descriptive or distinguishing title. –v. **5.** to call by a particular title. **6.** to design in accordance with a given or new style. –**stylistic,** adj.

stylise v. to bring into conformity with a particular (especially simplistic) style. Also, **stylize.**

stylish adj. smart; elegant.

stylus n. **1.** a needle tipped with diamond, sapphire, etc., for reproducing the sound of a gramophone record. **2.** *Computers* a pen-shaped instrument used to write, draw, etc., directly onto a touch-sensitive computer screen, the resultant text or image being digitised by the computer's software. **3.** any instrument used in drawing, etc.

suave /swav/ adj. (of persons or their manner, speech, etc.) smoothly agreeable or polite.

sub n. **1.** subeditor. **2.** submarine. **3.** subscription.

subconscious adj. **1.** existing or operating beneath or beyond consciousness. –n. **2.** the totality of mental processes of which the individual is not aware.

subcontract *Law* –n. **1.** a contract by which one agrees to render services necessary for the performance of another contract. –v. **2.** to make a subcontract (for). –**subcontractor,** n.

subcutaneous adj. situated or lying under the skin, as tissue.

subdivide v. to divide anew after a first division. –**subdivision,** n.

subdue v. **1.** to overpower by superior force. **2.** to bring into mental subjection. **3.** to reduce the intensity, force, or vividness of.

subeditor n. *Journalism* someone who edits and prepares copy for printing; an assistant or subordinate editor.

subheading n. a title or heading of a section in an essay, newspaper article, etc.

subject n. /ˈsʌbdʒɛkt/ **1.** something that forms a matter of thought, discourse, investigation, etc. **2.** a branch of knowledge forming a course of study. **3.** someone who is under the dominion or rule of a sovereign, state, etc. **4.** Gram. the word or words of a sentence which represent the person or object performing the action, as he in He raised his hat. **5.** someone or something that undergoes some action. –adj. /ˈsʌbdʒɛkt/ **6.** being under domination, control, or influence: subject to the law. **7.** open or exposed: subject to ridicule. **8.** being dependent or conditional upon something: subject to government approval. –v. /səbˈdʒɛkt/ **9.** to cause to undergo: he was subjected to cruel treatment. –**subjection**, n.

subjective adj. **1.** belonging to the thinking person rather than to the object of thought (opposed to objective). **2.** Gram. relating to the case of a noun or pronoun which is the subject (def. 4) of a verb, as she in She ate the apple.

subjugate v. to bring under complete control; subdue; conquer.

subjunctive adj. Gram. relating to the verb mood used to express hypothetical action, as were in If I were you, I'd tell her.

Look up **mood²**.

sublimate v. Psychol. to deflect (sexual or other biological energies) into socially constructive or creative channels.

sublime adj. supreme or perfect.

subliminal adj. Psychol. (of stimuli, etc.) being or operating below the threshold of consciousness or perception.

submarine n. **1.** a type of vessel that can operate under water. –adj. **2.** operating or living under the surface of the sea or any large body of water.

submerge v. to sink or plunge under water.

submit v. (-mitted, -mitting) **1.** to yield in surrender, compliance, or obedience. **2.** to state or urge with deference (usually followed by a clause). **3.** to refer to the decision or judgement of another or others. –**submission**, n. –**submissive**, adj.

For def. 1, the more usual expression is **give in**.

subordinate /səˈbɔdənət/ adj. **1.** of lesser importance; secondary. **2.** subject to the authority of a superior. –n. **3.** a subordinate person or thing.

subpoena /səˈpinə/ Law –v. (-naed, -naing) **1.** to serve with a writ for the summoning of witnesses. –n. **2.** a writ for the summoning of witnesses.

subscribe v. **1.** to sign (one's name) to a document, etc., especially as a sign of assent. **2.** to obtain a subscription to a magazine, newspaper, etc. **3.** to give or pay money as a contribution, payment, etc.

subscription n. **1.** a monetary contribution towards some object or a payment for shares, a book, a periodical, etc. **2.** the dues paid by a member of a club, society, etc.

subsequent adj. occurring or coming later or after.

subservient adj. excessively submissive; obsequious.

subside v. to sink to a low or lower level.

subsidiary adj. **1.** serving to assist or supplement. **2.** subordinate or secondary. –n. **3.** a company whose controlling interest is held by another company.

subsidy n. (pl. -dies) a supporting payment made by a government or other organisation. –**subsidise, subsidize**, v.

subsist v. to live, as on food, resources, etc., especially when these are limited: to subsist on $100 a week. –**subsistence**, n.

substance n. **1.** that of which a thing consists; matter. **2.** a matter of definite chemical composition. **3.** substantial or solid character or quality. **4.** the meaning or gist, as of speech or writing.

substantial *adj.* **1.** real or actual. **2.** of considerable amount, importance, value, etc. **3.** of solid character or quality. **4.** wealthy or influential.

substantiate *v.* to establish by evidence.

The more usual word is **prove**.

substantive *n.* **1.** *Gram.* a word or phrase functioning as a noun. –*adj.* **2.** *Gram.* of or relating to substantives. **3.** real or actual. **4.** of considerable amount or quantity.

substitute *n.* **1.** a person or thing acting or serving in place of another. –*v.* **2.** to put or act in the place of another.

Compare **substitute** with **replace**. Both words involve putting something or someone in a position which has been occupied by another. However, they are used differently – the people or things involved need to be placed in a different order for each of these words. The following sentences mean the same thing: *They replaced Nick with Helen as captain of the team*; *They substituted Helen for Nick as captain of the team*. Note also that **substitute** is followed by *for* and **replace** is followed by *with*.

subsume *v.* **1.** to consider (an idea, etc.) as part of a more comprehensive one. **2.** to bring (a case, instance, etc.) under a rule.

subterfuge *n.* an artifice or expedient employed to evade or hide something etc.

The more usual word is **trick**.

subterranean *adj.* underground.

subtitle *n.* **1.** a secondary title of a literary work, usually explanatory. **2.** *Film* a caption on the screen translating the dialogue of foreign language films.

subtle /ˈsʌtl/ *adj.* **1.** fine or delicate, often when likely to elude perception: *subtle differences.* **2.** requiring mental acuteness; skilful: *subtle humour.* **3.** insidious in operation, as poison, etc. –**subtlety**, *n.*

For def. 1, the more usual word is **slight**; for def. 2, **clever**.

subtract *v.* to take away (something or a part) from a whole.

suburb *n.* a more or less self-contained district of a town or city. –**suburban**, *adj.*

subvert *v.* to cause the downfall, ruin, or destruction of.

subway *n.* a pedestrian passage or tunnel beneath a street, railway line, etc.

Note that the American use of **subway** to mean an underground railway system is not used in Australia. There is no common short term for an underground railway in Australia.

succeed *v.* **1.** to turn out or terminate according to desire. **2.** to accomplish what is attempted or intended. **3.** to follow or replace (another) by descent, election, appointment, etc. **4.** to come next after (something else) in an order or series. –**succession**, *n.* –**successive**, *adj.*

For def. 3, the more usual expression is **take over from**.

success *n.* **1.** the favourable termination of attempts or endeavours. **2.** the gaining of wealth, position, or the like. **3.** a thing or a person that is successful. –**successful**, *adj.*

successor *n.* someone or something that succeeds or follows.

succinct *adj.* concisely expressed.

succour *n.* help; relief; aid. Also, **succor**.

succulent *adj.* full of juice.

succumb *v.* to give way to superior force; yield.

The more usual expressions are **give in** and **give way**.

such *adj.* **1.** of the kind, character, degree, extent, etc., indicated or implied: *You won't meet another such as her*; *oranges, apples and such fruit.* **2.** of so extreme a kind: *He is such a liar.* **3.** being as indicated: *The true facts are such.* **4.** **such and such.** particular, but not named or specified: *Ring me at such time as he arrives.* –*adv.* **5.** so, or in such a manner

or degree: *such dreadful events.* –*pron.*
6. the person or thing, or the persons or
things, indicated. –*phr.* **7. as such, a.** as
being what is indicated; in that capacity.
b. in itself or themselves.

suck *v.* **1.** to draw into the mouth by action
of the lips and tongue. **2.** to draw (water,
moisture, air, etc.) by any process resembling this. **3.** to apply the lips or mouth to,
and draw upon for extracting fluid contents. **4.** to hold in the mouth and dissolve
in the saliva, assisted by the action of the
tongue, etc. –*n.* **5.** the act or instance of
sucking.

sucker *n. Informal* a person easily deceived
or imposed upon.

suckle *v.* **1.** to nurse (a child) at the breast.
2. to suck milk at the breast.

sucrose *n.* the sugar obtained from the
sugar cane, the sugar beet, etc.

suction *n.* **1.** the act, process, or condition
of sucking. **2.** the process by which a
substance is sucked into an interior space
when the atmospheric pressure is reduced
in the space.

sudden *adj.* happening, coming, made, or
done quickly or unexpectedly.

sudoku /sə'dəuku/ *n.* a logic puzzle in
which the solution depends on correctly
inserting digits from 1 to 9 in a grid so that
each row and each column and each
marked subset within the grid has only one
occurrence of each digit.

suds *pl. n.* soapy water; lather.

sue *v.* (**sued, suing**) to take legal action
against (someone), as to obtain reparation,
divorce, etc.

suede /sweɪd/ *n.* kid or other leather finished on the flesh side with a soft, napped
surface.

suet *n.* hard animal fat used in cookery, etc.

suffer *v.* **1.** to undergo or feel (pain or
distress). **2.** to endure patiently or bravely.
3. to tolerate or allow.

sufferance *phr.* **on sufferance,** reluc-
tantly tolerated.

suffice *v.* (**-ficed, -ficing**) **1.** to be enough
or adequate. –*phr.* **2. suffice (it) to say,**
let it be enough to say.

The more usual expression is **be enough**.

sufficient *adj.* that suffices. –**sufficiency,**
n.

suffix *n. Gram.* a meaningful word part
added to the end of a word, as *-ness* in
kindness.

suffocate *v.* **1.** to kill by preventing
the access of air to the blood through the
lungs. **2.** to become suffocated; stifle;
smother. –**suffocation,** *n.*

suffrage *n.* the right of voting, especially
in political elections.

suffuse *v.* to overspread with or as with a
liquid, colour, etc.

Note that this verb is usually in the passive: *Her face was suffused with pink.*

sugar *n.* **1.** a sweet crystalline substance
used as food. **2.** a member of the same
class of carbohydrates. –*v.* **3.** to cover or
sweeten with sugar.

sugar beet *n.* a variety of beet cultivated
for the sugar it yields.

sugar cane *n.* a tall grass of tropical and
warm regions, constituting the chief source
of sugar.

suggest *v.* **1.** to put forward (an idea, etc.)
consideration or possible action: *he suggested a new plan to us.* **2.** to propose (a
person or thing) as suitable or possible:
*may I suggest that you take the tram into
the city?* –**suggestion,** *n.*

Note that you **suggest** something *to*
someone, and you **suggest** *that* somebody does something.

suggestible *adj.* open to influence by
suggestion.

suggestive *adj.* **1.** tending to suggest
thoughts, ideas, etc. **2.** such as to suggest
something improper or indecent.

suicide *n.* **1.** someone who intentionally
takes their own life. **2.** the intentional
taking of one's own life. –*v.* (**-cided,**

-ciding) **3.** to commit suicide. **–suicidal**, *adj.*

suit /sut/ *n.* **1.** a set of garments intended to be worn together. **2.** the act or process of suing in a court of law. **3.** a number of things forming a series or set, as of cards. *–v.* **4.** to make or be appropriate. **5.** to be satisfactory, agreeable, or acceptable. **–suitable**, *adj.*

Don't confuse this with **suite** (pronounced /swit/), which is a set of things such as rooms (*a hotel suite*) or furniture (*a dining suite*).

suitcase *n.* a travelling bag, usually with stiffened frame, for carrying clothes, etc.

suite /swit/ *n.* a number of things forming a series or set: *a suite of rooms; a lounge suite.*

Don't confuse this with **suit**, which has a similar spelling but is pronounced /sut/. A **suit** is a set of clothes. Don't confuse **suite** with **sweet** either, as they are pronounced the same way (/swit/). **Sweet** describes something with a pleasant taste like sugar or honey.

sulfur /'sʌlfə/ *n.* → **sulphur**.

sulk *v.* to hold aloof in a sullen, morose, or offended mood. **–sulky**, *adj.*

sullen *adj.* showing ill humour by a gloomy silence or reserve.

sully *v.* (**-lied**, **-lying**) to soil, stain, or tarnish.

The more usual word is **spoil**.

sulphur *n. Chem.* a nonmetallic element which exists in several forms. Symbol: S Also, **sulfur**. **–sulphurous**, *adj.*

sultan *n.* the sovereign of a Muslim country.

sultana *n.* a small, green, seedless grape, often dried.

sultry *adj.* (**-rier**, **-riest**) oppressively hot and close or moist.

sum *n.* **1.** the total of 2 or more numbers as determined by mathematical process. **2.** a series of numbers or quantities to be added

up. **3.** any mathematical problem or exercise. **4.** a quantity or amount, especially of money. **5.** the total amount, or the whole. *–adj.* **6.** denoting or relating to a sum. *–phr.* (**summed**, **summing**) **7. sum up. a.** to combine into a total. **b.** to express in a shortened form. **c.** to form an opinion about: *She summed him up at once.*

Don't confuse this with **some**, which means a few (*some people*) or a little (*some butter*).

summary *n.* (*pl.* **-ries**) **1.** a brief and comprehensive presentation of facts or statements. *–adj.* **2.** brief and comprehensive; concise. **3.** direct and prompt; unceremoniously fast. **–summarise, summarize**, *v.*

summer *n.* the warmest season of the year between spring and autumn.

summit *n.* **1.** the highest point or part. *–adj.* **2.** (in diplomacy) between heads of state.

summon *v.* **1.** to call, as with authority. *–phr.* **2. summon up**, to call into action; rouse: *to summon up one's courage.*

summons *n.* (*pl.* **-monses**) an authoritative command, message, or signal by which one is summoned.

sump *n.* a pit or receptacle in which water or other liquid is collected.

sumptuous *adj.* luxuriously fine.

sun *n.* **1.** the star which is the central body of the solar system. **2.** sunshine. *–v.* (**sunned**, **sunning**) **3.** to warm, dry, etc., in the sunshine. **–sunny**, *adj.*

A word which describes things related to the sun is **solar**.

sunbake *v. Aust.* to expose one's body to the sun.

sunblock *n.* → **sunscreen** (def. 1).

sunburn *n.* superficial inflammation of the skin, caused by excessive exposure to the sun's rays.

suncream *n.* → **sunscreen** (def. 1).

sundae *n.* a portion of ice-cream with syrup poured over it.

sundial n. an instrument for indicating the time of day by the position of a shadow cast by the sun.

sundries pl. n. sundry things or items.

sundry adj. **1.** various. –phr. **2. all and sundry**, everyone.

sunflower n. a tall plant grown for its showy flowers, and for its seeds, valuable as a source of oil.

sunglasses pl. n. spectacles with tinted lenses to protect the eyes from glare.

sunk v. a past tense and past participle of **sink**.

sunlight n. the light of the sun.

sunrise n. the rise of the sun above the horizon in the morning.

sunscreen n. **1.** Also, **sunblock**, **suncream**, **blockout**. a lotion or cream which protects the skin against damage from the rays of the sun. **2.** an awning, etc., which provides a screen against the sun.

sunset n. the setting of the sun below the horizon in the evening.

sunshine n. **1.** the direct light of the sun. **2.** cheerfulness, happiness, or prosperity.

sunspot n. **1.** one of the relatively dark patches which appear periodically on the sun. **2.** a discolouration and roughening of part of the skin, usually as a result of exposure to the sun.

sunstroke n. a condition of physical weakness caused by excessive exposure to the sun.

super adj. **1.** of a superior quality, grade, size, etc. –n. **2.** Aust., NZ Informal superannuation.

superannuation n. Aust., NZ **1.** a pension or allowance to a retired person. **2.** a sum paid periodically as contribution to a pension fund. Also, **super**.

superb adj. admirably fine or excellent.

supercilious adj. haughtily disdainful or contemptuous.

supercontinent n. any great landmass that existed in the geological past and split into smaller landmasses.

superficial adj. **1.** being at, on, or near the surface. **2.** concerned with or comprehending only what is on the surface or obvious; shallow. **3.** apparent, rather than real.

superfluous adj. being over and above what is sufficient or required.

superfood n. a nutrient-dense food.

superintendent n. someone in charge of work, a business or a building. –**superintend**, v.

superior adj. **1.** higher in station, rank, degree, or grade. **2.** of higher quality. **3.** greater in quantity or amount. **4.** showing a feeling of being better than others. –n. **5.** one superior to another or others. –**superiority**, n.

superlative adj. **1.** surpassing all others. **2.** Gram. relating to the form of an adjective or adverb which expresses the greatest degree of comparison: 'Smoothest' is the superlative form of 'smooth' and 'most easily' is the superlative form of 'easily'.

Compare def. 2 with **comparative** (def. 3), which describes an adjective or adverb which expresses a greater degree than something else. For example, smoother is the comparative form of smooth, and more easily is the comparative form of easily.

supermarket n. a large, usually self-service, retail store or market.

supernatural adj. **1.** not explicable in terms of natural laws or phenomena. **2.** of or relating to supernatural beings, as ghosts, spirits, etc. –n. **3.** supernatural forces, effects, and beings collectively.

supernova n. (pl. **-vas** or **-vae** /-viː/) Astron. the sudden gravitational collapse of a giant star resulting in an explosion of stellar matter and energy into space and leaving a black hole or neutron star as a remnant.

superphosphate n. an artificial fertiliser.

superpower n. an extremely powerful and influential nation.

supersede v. to replace (something which has become obsolete or outdated): *electric lighting has superseded gas lighting.*

supersize v. 1. to increase in magnitude to an unusual degree: *to supersize one's income.* –adj. 2. unusually large: *supersize ice-creams.*

supersonic adj. (of velocities) above the velocity of sound.

superstar n. a show business personality who is very famous.

superstition n. 1. a belief or notion entertained, regardless of reason or knowledge, of the ominous significance of a particular thing, circumstance, etc. 2. any blindly accepted belief or notion.

superstructure n. all of an edifice above the basement or foundation.

supervise v. to oversee (a process, work, workers, etc.). –**supervision**, n.

supper n. 1. a light meal taken late at night. 2. *Chiefly Brit, US* the evening meal.

supplant v. to take the place of (another). The more usual word is **replace**.

supple adj. bending readily or easily.

supplement n. 1. something added to complete or extend a thing. –v. 2. to complete or extend by a supplement; form a supplement to.

supplicate v. to make humble and earnest entreaty.

supply v. (-**plied**, -**plying**) 1. to furnish (a person, establishment, place, etc.) with what is lacking or required. 2. to furnish or provide (something wanting or requisite). –n. (pl. -**plies**) 3. the act of supplying. 4. a quantity of something provided or available, as for use or sale.

support v. 1. to sustain or withstand (weight, etc.) without giving way. 2. to undergo or endure; tolerate. 3. to sustain (a person, the mind, etc.) under trial or affliction. 4. to maintain (a person, institution, etc.) by supplying with things necessary to existence; provide for. 5. to uphold (a person, cause, policy, etc.). –n. 6. the act of supporting. 7. the state of being supported. 8. a thing or a person that supports.

suppose v. 1. to assume (something), without reference to its being true or false, for the sake of argument, etc. 2. to assume as true, or believe, in the absence of positive knowledge. 3. (of facts, circumstances, etc.) to require logically; presuppose. –**supposition**, n.

suppository n. (pl. -**ries**) a medicinal substance inserted into the rectum or vagina to be dissolved therein.

suppress v. 1. to keep in or repress. 2. to vanquish or subdue.

suppressant n. something, especially a medication, which acts to suppress or reduce the intensity of a specific symptom: *a cough suppressant.*

suppurate v. to produce or discharge pus.

supreme adj. 1. highest in rank or authority. 2. greatest, utmost, or extreme. –**supremacy**, n.

surcharge n. 1. an additional sum added to the usual cost, in restaurants, etc. –v. (-**charged**, -**charging**) 2. to subject to an additional sum added to the usual cost.

sure adj. (**surer**, **surest**) 1. free from a pprehension or doubt; confident. 2. worthy of confidence; reliable. 3. firm or stable. 4. never missing, slipping, etc. 5. inevitable. –adv. 6. *Informal* surely, undoubtedly, or certainly.

Don't confuse **sure** with **shore**, which is the land along the edge of the sea, a lake, etc. Another sense of **shore** is in the expression **shore up**. If you **shore** something up you strengthen it by supporting it.

surely /ˈʃɔːli/ adv. 1. in a sure manner: *she spoke surely.* 2. (in emphatic utterances that are not necessarily sustained by fact) it is unlikely to be otherwise (that): *surely he*

surety *n.* (*pl.* **-ties**) security against loss or damage, non-payment of a debt, etc.

surf *n.* **1.** the swell of the sea which breaks upon a shore. *–v.* **2.** to engage in surfing. **3.** *Computers* to explore (an information network).

surface *n.* **1.** the outer face, or outside, of a thing. *–adj.* **2.** of, on, or relating to the surface. **3.** superficial; apparent, rather than real. **4.** of, on, or relating to land and/or sea. *–v.* (**-faced, -facing**) **5.** to give a particular kind of surface to. **6.** to rise to the surface.

surfboard *n.* a long, narrow board used in riding waves towards the shore.

surfeit /ˈsɜːfət/ *n.* an excessive amount or number.

The more usual expressions are **too much** or **too many**.

surfing *n.* **1.** the sport in which one attempts to ride on or with a wave towards the shore standing on a surfboard. **2.** Also, **body-surfing**, the sport of riding waves without a surfboard.

surf lifesaving *n. Aust., NZ* lifesaving which is appropriate for emergency situations occurring on surf beaches.

surge *n.* **1.** a strong forward or upward movement, as or like that of swelling or rolling waves. *–v.* (**surged, surging**) **2.** to rise or roll in waves, or like waves.

surgeon *n.* a doctor qualified to practise surgery.

surgery *n.* (*pl.* **-ries**) **1.** the treating of diseases, injuries, or deformities by manual operation or instrumental appliances. **2.** the consulting room of a medical practitioner, dentist, or the like. *–surgical, adj.*

surly /ˈsɜːli/ *adj.* (**-lier, -liest**) churlishly rude or ill-humoured.

is mistaken! **3.** inevitably or without fail: *prices will surely rise.*

Don't confuse **surely** with **surly**, which is pronounced /ˈsɜːli/ and means unfriendly and bad-tempered.

Don't confuse this with **surely**, which is pronounced /ˈʃʊəli/ and means almost certainly: *Surely it will rain tonight.*

surmise *v.* /sɜˈmaɪz/ **1.** to think or infer without certain or strong evidence. *–n.* /sɜˈmaɪz, ˈsɜːmaɪz/ **2.** a matter of conjecture.

The more usual word is **guess**.

surmount *v.* to get over or across (barriers, obstacles, etc.).

The more usual word is **overcome**.

surname *n.* a family name, as distinguished from a first or given name.

surpass *v.* to go beyond in amount, extent, or degree.

The more usual word is **outdo**.

surplus *n.* that which remains above what is used or needed.

surprise *v.* **1.** to catch (a person, etc.) in the act of doing something. **2.** to assail without warning. **3.** to strike with a sudden feeling of wonder. *–n.* **4.** a sudden and unexpected event, action, or the like. **5.** the state or feeling of wonder or alarm at something unexpected. *–adj.* **6.** sudden and unexpected.

surreal /səˈriːl/ *adj.* of dreamlike experience, especially in art.

surrender *v.* **1.** to give (something) up to the possession or power of another. **2.** to give oneself up to an emotion, course of action, etc. *–n.* **3.** the act of surrendering.

surreptitious *adj.* obtained, done, made, etc., by stealth.

The more usual word is **secret**.

surrogate *n.* **1.** a person appointed to act for another. **2.** a substitute.

For def. 1, the more usual word is **deputy**.

surround *v.* **1.** to enclose on all sides, or encompass. *–n.* **2.** a border which surrounds.

surroundings *pl. n.* all that is around or near someone or something.

surveillance *n.* watch kept over a person, etc.

survey *v.* /sɜ'veɪ, 'sɜveɪ/ **1.** to take a general or comprehensive view of. **2.** to inspect in detail, especially officially. **3.** to collect sample opinions, or the like in order to estimate the overall situation. **4.** to determine the form, boundaries, etc., of (land). *–n.* /'sɜveɪ/ (*pl.* **-veys**) **5.** a comprehensive view. **6.** a formal or official examination. **7.** a gathering of sample opinions, etc., in order to estimate the overall situation. **8.** the act of surveying land, or plans resulting from this.

survive *v.* to remain alive or in existence after the death of (someone) or after the cessation of (something). **–survivor**, *n.* **–survival**, *n.*

susceptible /sə'septəbəl/ *adj.* **1.** impressionable. *–phr.* **2. susceptible to**, easily affected by: *susceptible to colds; susceptible to praise.* **–susceptibility**, *n.*

sushi /'suʃi, 'suʃi/ *n.* (in Japanese cuisine) any of various preparations of boiled Japanese rice flavoured with a sweetened rice vinegar and combined with toppings or fillings of raw seafood, vegetables, nori, etc.

suspect *v.* /sə'spekt/ **1.** to imagine to be guilty, defective, bad, etc., with insufficient or no proof. **2.** to imagine (something, especially something evil, wrong, or undesirable) to be the case. *–n.* /'sʌspekt/ **3.** a person suspected of a crime, offence, or the like. *–adj.* /'sʌspekt/ **4.** suspected; open to suspicion.

suspend *v.* **1.** to hang by attachment to something above. **2.** to defer or postpone. **3.** to (cause to) stop or stay, usually for a time, as payment. **4.** to debar, usually for a time, from the exercise of an office or privilege.

suspender *n.* a strap with fastenings to support women's stockings.

suspense *n.* a state of mental uncertainty, as in awaiting a decision or outcome, usually with anxiety.

Don't confuse **suspense** with **suspension**.

suspension *n.* **1.** the act of suspending. **2.** the state of being suspended. **3.** something on or by which something else is hung. **4.** the arrangement of springs, shock absorbers, hangers, etc., in a motor vehicle.

Don't confuse this with **suspense**.

suspicion *n.* **1.** the act of suspecting. **2.** a vague notion of something. **3.** a slight trace. **–suspicious**, *adj.*

sustain *v.* **1.** to hold or bear up from below. **2.** to bear (a burden, charge, etc.). **3.** to suffer (injury, loss, etc.). **4.** to keep going, as an action or process. **5.** to supply with food and drink, or the necessities of life. **–sustainable**, *adj.*

sustenance *n.* means of sustaining life; nourishment.

suture *n.* **1.** a sewing together, or a joining as by sewing. *–v.* **2.** to unite by or as by a suture.

svelte /svɛlt, sfɛlt/ *adj.* slender, especially gracefully slender in figure; lithe.

swab *n.* **1.** absorbent material for cleaning wounds, etc. **2.** matter collected with such material for medical testing, etc. *–v.* (**swabbed**, **swabbing**) **3.** to wipe or clean. **4.** to take a swab (def. 2).

swag *n.* *Aust., NZ* a bundle or roll containing the bedding and personal belongings of a traveller through the bush, etc.; shiralee.

swagger *v.* to walk or strut with a defiant or insolent air.

swagman *n.* *Aust.* (formerly) a man who travelled the country on foot, living on occasional jobs or gifts.

swallow¹ *v.* **1.** to take (food, etc.) into the stomach through the throat. **2.** to take in so as to envelop. **3.** *Informal* to accept without question or suspicion. *–n.* **4.** the act of swallowing.

swallow² *n.* a small, long-winged, migratory bird.

swamp *n.* **1.** a piece or tract of wet, spongy land. *–v.* **2.** to flood or drench with water or the like.

swan *n.* a large, stately swimming bird with a long, slender neck.

swank *n. Informal* dashing smartness; ostentation or style.

swap *v.* (**swapped, swapping**) **1.** to exchange, barter, or trade, as one thing for another. *–n.* **2.** an exchange. Also, **swop**.

swarm *n.* **1.** a body of bees moving together. **2.** a great number of things or persons, especially in motion. *–v.* **3.** to move in great numbers, as things or persons. **4.** (of a place) to be thronged or overrun (*with*).

swarthy *adj.* (**-thier, -thiest**) dark in complexion.

swat *v.* (**swatted, swatting**) *Informal* to hit with a smart or violent blow.

swathe *v.* to wrap, bind, or swaddle with bands of some material.

sway *v.* **1.** to (cause to) move to and fro. **2.** to fluctuate or vacillate, as in opinion. **3.** to cause to think or act in a particular way. *–n.* **4.** rule; dominion. **5.** dominating power or influence.

> For def. 3, the more usual word is **persuade**.

swear *v.* (**swore, sworn, swearing**) **1.** to make a solemn declaration with an appeal to God or some sacred being. **2.** to engage or promise on oath or in a solemn manner. **3.** to use profane or taboo language. **4.** to affirm or say with solemn earnestness or great emphasis. *–phr.* **5. swear in**, to admit to office or service by administering an oath.

sweat *v.* (**sweat** *or* **sweated, sweating**) **1.** to excrete (watery fluid through the pores of the skin), as from heat, exertion, etc. **2.** *Informal* to exert oneself strenuously. *–n.* **3.** the process of sweating. **4.** the secretions of sweat glands; perspiration. *–phr.* **5. sweat it out**, *Informal* to endure until the end.

sweated *adj.* underpaid and overworked.

sweater *n.* → **jumper**.

sweatshirt *n.* a loose pullover.

sweep *v.* (**swept, sweeping**) **1.** to move, drive, or bring, by or as if by, passing a broom, brush, or the like over the surface occupied. **2.** to pass or draw (something) over a surface, or about, along, etc., with a steady, continuous stroke. **3.** to clear or clean (a floor, room, etc.) by means of a broom. **4.** to move steadily and strongly or swiftly (*down, over,* etc.). **5.** to walk in long, trailing garments. **6.** to extend in a continuous or curving stretch, as a road, etc. *–n.* **7.** the act of sweeping. **8.** a swinging or curving movement or stroke. **9.** a continuous extent or stretch.

sweepstake *n.* a method of gambling, as on the outcome of a horserace, in which each participant contributes a stake, the winnings being provided from the stake money. Also, **sweepstakes, sweep**.

sweet *adj.* **1.** having the pleasant taste or flavour characteristic of sugar, honey, etc. **2.** pleasing or agreeable. **3.** pleasant in disposition or manners. **4.** dear; beloved. *–adv.* **5.** in a sweet manner; sweetly. *–n.* **6.** that which is sweet. **7.** Also, **sweetie**. any of various small confections made from sugar. **8.** (*oft. pl.*) any sweet dish served at the end of a meal. **9.** a beloved person; sweetheart.

> Don't confuse **sweet** with **suite**, which is pronounced the same as **sweet**. A **suite** is a set of things such as rooms (*a hotel suite*) or furniture (*a dining suite*).

sweetbread *n.* the pancreas or thymus gland of an animal, especially a calf or a lamb, used for food.

sweet corn *n.* the unripe and tender ears of maize, especially when used as a table vegetable.

sweetheart *n.* (a term of address for a beloved person).

sweetmeat *n.* a sweet delicacy.

sweet potato n. a plant cultivated for its edible root.

swell v. (**swelled**, **swollen** or **swelled**, **swelling**) 1. to grow in bulk, as by absorption of moisture, by distension, addition, or the like. 2. to rise in waves, as the sea. 3. to grow in amount, degree, force, or the like. 4. to puff up with pride. –n. 5. increase in bulk. 6. a part that bulges out. 7. a wave, especially when long and unbroken, or such waves collectively. 8. an elevation of the land. 9. increase in amount, degree, force, etc. a person of high social standing. –adj. Informal 10. (of things) stylish; elegant. 11. first-rate; excellent.

swelling n. a swollen part.

swelter v. to suffer or languish with oppressive heat.

swerve v. to turn aside abruptly in movement or direction.

swift adj. 1. moving with great speed; rapid. –n. 2. any of several rapidly flying birds.

swill n. 1. any liquid matter, especially kitchen waste given to pigs. –v. 2. to wash or cleanse by flooding with water.

swim v. (**swam**, **swum**, **swimming**) 1. to move on or in water or other liquid in any way. 2. to be immersed or flooded with a liquid. 3. to be dizzy or giddy. –n. 4. an act of swimming. –phr. 5. **in the swim**, actively engaged in current affairs, social activities, etc.

swimmers pl. n. → **swimming costume**.

swimming costume n. a garment or garments worn for swimming. Also, **bathers**, **cossie**, **cozzie**, **swimmers**, **swimsuit**, **togs**.

swimsuit n. → **swimming costume**.

swindle v. 1. to cheat (a person) out of money, etc. –n. 2. a fraudulent transaction or scheme.

swine n. (pl. **swine**) 1. the domestic pig. 2. a contemptible person.

Note that if you call someone 'a swine' you are intending to insult them.

swing v. (**swung**, **swinging**) 1. to (cause to) move to and fro, as something suspended from above. 2. to (cause to) move in alternate directions about a fixed point, as a door on its hinges. 3. to sway, influence, or manage as desired. 4. to move to and fro on a swinging seat. 5. to move in a curve, as around a corner. 6. to change or shift one's attention, opinion, interest, etc. 7. to aim at or hit something with a sweeping movement of the arm. 8. Informal to be lively or modern. –n. 9. the act or the manner of swinging. 10. the amount of such movement. 11. active operation. 12. a seat suspended from above by ropes, etc., in which one may sit and swing to and fro for amusement. 13. Also, **swing music**, a smooth, orchestral type of jazz popular in the 1930s.

swipe n. 1. Informal a sweeping stroke. –v. 2. Informal to strike with a sweeping blow. 3. Informal to steal. 4. to move (a card with a magnetic strip) through the slot of an electronic device.

swirl v. to move with a whirling motion.

swish v. 1. to move with or make a hissing sound. –n. 2. a swishing movement or sound. –adj. Also, **swishy**. 3. Informal smart; stylish.

switch n. 1. a slender, flexible rod used especially in whipping, beating, etc. 2. Elect. a device for turning on or off or directing an electric current. 3. Aust. → **switchboard**. –v. 4. to swing, or whisk (a cane, a fishing line, etc.) with a swift, lashing stroke. 5. to exchange; shift. 6. to change direction or course. –phr. 7. **switch off**, to cause (an electric current or appliance) to stop. 8. **switch on**, to cause (an electric current) to flow or (an electric appliance) to operate.

switchblade n. → **flick-knife**.

switchboard n. an arrangement of switches, plugs, and jacks mounted on a board or frame enabling an operator to make temporary connections between telephone users. Also, **switch**.

swivel v. (-elled, -elling) to turn around: *He swivelled around to have a better look.*

swoon v. to faint; lose consciousness.

swoop v. 1. to sweep through the air, as a bird upon prey. –n. 2. the act of swooping. –phr. 3. at (or in) one fell swoop, in a single action or coordinated series of actions. 4. swoop down, to come down in a sudden swift attack (on or upon). 5. swoop up, to take, lift or remove, with, or as with, a sweeping motion.

sword n. a weapon with a long, straight or slightly curved blade fixed in a hilt or handle.

swordfish n. (pl. -fish or -fishes) a large marine game fish with the upper jaw elongated into a swordlike weapon.

> For information about the different plural forms, see the note at **fish**.

swot Informal –v. (**swotted, swotting**) 1. to study hard. –n. 2. someone who studies hard. Also, **swat**.

sycophant /ˈsɪkəfænt/ n. a self-seeking flatterer.

syllable n. Phonetics a segment of speech uttered with a single impulse of air pressure from the lungs. –**syllabic**, adj.

syllabus n. (pl. -buses or -bi /-baɪ/) an outline or summary of a course of studies, lectures, etc.

symbiosis /sɪmbaɪˈoʊsəs, -bi-/ n. Biol. the living together of two species of organisms. –**symbiotic**, adj.

symbol n. something used or regarded as representing something else. –**symbolic**, adj.

symbolise v. 1. to be a symbol of. 2. to represent by a symbol or symbols. Also, **symbolize**.

symmetry n. (pl. -ries) the correspondence, in size, form, and arrangement, of opposite parts. –**symmetrical**, adj.

sympathetic adj. 1. characterised by, proceeding from, exhibiting, or feeling sympathy. –phr. 2. sympathetic to (or towards), looking with favour or liking upon.

sympathise v. 1. (oft. fol. by with) to feel a compassionate sympathy. 2. to agree, correspond, or accord. Also, **sympathize**.

sympathy n. (pl. -thies) 1. the fact or the power of entering into the feelings of another. 2. agreement in feeling, opinion, etc. 3. agreement, consonance, or accord.

> Note that if **sympathy** is followed by for it has the meaning of def. 1, and if it is followed by with it has the meaning of def. 2.
> **Empathy** is an even stronger sense of sympathy where you can actually imagine yourself experiencing the same things as someone else.

symphony n. (pl. -nies) Music an elaborate instrumental composition written for an orchestra.

symposium n. (pl. -siums or -sia /-ziə/) a meeting or conference for discussion of some subject.

symptom n. a sign or indication of something. –**symptomatic**, adj.

synagogue /ˈsɪnəgɒg/ n. a Jewish house of worship.

synapse /ˈsaɪnæps/ n. Biol. the region of contact between the processes of two or more nerve cells, across which an impulse passes. –**synaptic**, adj.

synchronise v. to (cause to) occur at the same time, or coincide or agree in time. Also, **synchronize**. –**synchronisation**, n.

syncopate /ˈsɪŋkəpeɪt/ v. to place accents on musical beats which are normally unaccented. –**syncopation**, n.

syndicate n. /'sɪndɪkət, 'sɪndəkət/ **1.** a combination of business associates, commercial firms, etc., formed for the purpose of carrying out some project. −v. /'sɪndəkeɪt/ **2.** to combine into a syndicate. **3.** *Journalism* to publish simultaneously in a number of newspapers or other periodicals in different places. −**syndication**, n.

syndrome n. a number of characteristic symptoms occurring together, as in a disease.

synonym n. a word having the same, or nearly the same, meaning as another, as *happy* and *glad*.

synopsis n. (pl. **-nopses** /-'nɒpsiz/) a brief or condensed statement giving a general view of some subject.

The more usual word is **summary**.

syntax n. *Gram.* the patterns of formation of sentences and phrases from words in a particular language.

synthesis n. (pl. **-theses** /-θəsiz/) the combination of parts or elements into a complex whole (opposed to *analysis*).

synthesise v. to make up by combining parts or elements. Also, **synthesize**.

synthesiser n. a machine which creates speech or music by combining the controlled outputs of a number of electronic circuits. Also, **synthesizer**.

synthetic adj. **1.** of, relating to, or involving synthesis (opposed to *analytic*). **2.** (of materials, etc.) made by chemical process, as opposed to being of natural origin.

syphilis n. a chronic, infectious venereal disease.

syphon n., v. → **siphon**.

syringe n. *Med.* a small tube used for injecting fluids into the body, etc.

syrup n. any of various sweet, viscous liquids.

system n. **1.** an assemblage or combination of things or parts forming a complex or unitary whole. **2.** a coordinated body of methods, or a complex scheme or plan of procedure. **3.** the entire human or animal body. **4.** a method or scheme of classification. −**systematise**, **systematize**, v.

systematic adj. having, showing, or involving a system, method, or plan.

systemic adj. relating to or affecting the whole bodily system.

T, t

T, t *n.* the 20th letter of the English alphabet.

tab[1] *n.* **1.** a small strap, loop, etc. as on a garment, etc. **2.** a protruding label for ready identification.

tab[2] *n.* a key on a typewriter or computer keyboard which is depressed to set the point at which the line or section of the line of type begins.

tabby *n.* (*pl.* **-bies**) a cat with a striped or brindled coat.

tabernacle *n.* **1.** the tent used by the Jews as a portable sanctuary before their final settlement in Palestine. **2.** any (large) place of worship.

table *n.* **1.** an article of furniture consisting of a flat top resting on legs or on a pillar. **2.** a flat surface. **3.** an arrangement of words, numbers, or signs to exhibit a set of facts in a compact form: *multiplication tables.* **5.** to place on a table. **4.** to form into a table or list.

tableau /'tæbloʊ/ *n.* (*pl.* **-leaux** /-loʊz, -loʊ/ *or* **-leaus**) a picturesque grouping of persons or objects.

tableland *n.* an elevated, usually level region.

tablespoon *n.* a large spoon.

tablet *n.* **1.** a pad of writing paper. **2.** a small, flat slab, especially one bearing an inscription, carving, etc. **3.** a small, flat piece of some solid substance, as a drug, chemical, etc. **4.** Also, **tablet computer**. a small portable computer consisting of a single panel with a touch screen and an onscreen virtual keyboard.

table tennis *n.* a game similar to tennis but played indoors on a table, with small bats and a hollow plastic ball; ping-pong.

tabloid *n.* a newspaper, about ½ the ordinary page size, emphasising pictures and concise writing.

taboo *adj.* **1.** forbidden to general use; prohibited or banned. **2.** generally unacceptable for religious or social reasons: *a taboo word.* –*n.* **3.** a prohibition or exclusion from use or practice.

tabouli /tə'buli/ *n.* a salad of cracked wheat, chopped parsley, mint, tomato, oil, lemon juice, etc. Also, **tabouleh, tabbouli**.

tabular *adj.* relating to or arranged as a table (def. 3).

tabulate *v.* to put or form into a table, scheme, or synopsis. –**tabulator,** *n.*

tacit *adj.* **1.** silent. **2.** not openly expressed, but implied.

For def. 2, the more usual word is **unspoken**.

taciturn *adj.* inclined to silence, or reserved in speech.

The more usual word is **quiet**.

tack *n.* **1.** a short, sharp-pointed nail or pin. **2.** a long stitch used before permanent sewing. **3.** *Naut.* the direction or course of a ship in relation to the position of her sails, a course obliquely against the wind. **4.** a course of action, especially one differing from some preceding course. **5.** all the equipment relating to the saddling and harnessing of horses. –*v.* **6.** to fasten by a tack. **7.** *Naut.* to change the course of a ship.

tackle *n.* **1.** equipment, especially for fishing. **2.** apparatus, as a rope and block or a combination of these, for hoisting, lowering, etc. materials. **3.** an act of tackling, as in football. –*v.* **4.** to undertake to deal with, master, solve, etc. **5.** *Rugby Football, etc.* to seize and pull down (an opponent having the ball).

tacky *adj.* (**-kier, -kiest**) *Informal* **1.** shabby. **2.** superficially attractive but lacking quality or craftsmanship. –**tackiness,** *n.*

taco *n.* a Mexican dish consisting of a flat piece of crisp corn bread folded around a spicy savoury filling.

tact *n.* a keen sense of what to say or do to avoid giving offence. –**tactful**, *adj.*

tactic *n.* a plan for achieving a desired end.

tactile *adj.* of or relating to the organs or sense of touch.

tad *n.* a small amount.

tadpole *n.* the aquatic larva of frogs, toads, etc.

tae bo /taɪ ˈboʊ/ *n.* an aerobic exercise regime using martial arts sequences at a rapid pace.

taekwondo /taɪkwɒnˈdoʊ/ *n.* a Korean martial art, similar to karate. Also, **tae kwon do**.

tag¹ *n.* **1.** a piece of strong paper, leather, etc., attached to something as a label. **2.** any small loosely-attached part or piece; tatter. –*v.* (**tagged**, **tagging**) **3.** to attach as a tag to something else. **4.** *Informal* to follow (*along*) closely.

tag² *n.* a game in which one child chases others so as to touch another who then becomes the pursuer.

tai chi /taɪ ˈtʃi/ *n.* a form of exercises based on Chinese martial arts.

tail *n.* **1.** the rear end of an animal especially when forming a distinct flexible appendage to the trunk. **2.** something resembling this in shape or position. **3.** the bottom or concluding part of anything. **4.** (*pl.*) the side of a coin opposite the side bearing a head (opposed to *heads*): *Heads or tails?* **5.** *Informal* the buttocks. **6.** *Informal* a person who follows another, especially in order to observe or hinder escape. –*v.* **7.** *Informal* to follow in order to hinder escape or to observe. –*phr.* **8. tail off**, to decrease gradually.

Don't confuse **tail** with **tale**, which is a story.

tailor *n.* **1.** someone whose business it is to make or mend clothing, especially

men's suits. **2.** (*pl.* **-lor** *or* **-lors**) Also **tailer**, **taylor**, an Aust. sport and food fish.

For information about the different plural forms for def. 2, see the note at **fish**.

taint *n.* **1.** a trace of infection, contamination, etc. –*v.* **2.** to infect, contaminate, or corrupt. **3.** to sully or tarnish.

taipan /ˈtaɪpæn/ *n.* a long-fanged, highly venomous snake.

take *v.* (**took**, **taken**, **taking**) **1.** to get into one's hands, possession, control, etc. **2.** to seize: *to take prisoners.* **3.** to select: *Take which one you like.* **4.** to obtain by making payment: *take a holiday house.* **5.** to carry off or remove (*away*, etc.). **6.** to subtract or deduct: *take 2 from 4.* **7.** to carry or convey. **8.** to use (a vehicle, etc.) as a means of travel. **9.** to conduct or lead: *This road will take you to the town.* **10.** to absorb or be absorbed, as ink, etc. **11.** to proceed to deal with: *to take a matter under consideration.* **12.** to proceed to occupy: *to take a seat.* **13.** to occupy or use up (space, material, time, etc.). **14.** to attract and hold: *a display which takes one's eye.* **15.** to write down (notes, a copy, etc.). **16.** to make (a photograph, etc., of something). **17.** to make (a measurement, observation, etc.). **18.** to assume the obligation of (a vow, pledge, etc.). **19.** to assume or adopt as one's own: *to take the credit for something.* **20.** to comply with (advice, etc.). **21.** *Gram.* to have by usage (a particular form, case, etc.). **22.** to engage, as a mechanical device. **23.** to begin to grow, as a plant. **24.** to have the intended effect, as a medicine, inoculation, etc. **25.** to become (sick or ill). –*n.* **26.** an act or instance of taking. **27.** that which is taken. **28.** *Film, etc.* (a portion of) a scene photographed without any interruption. **29.** *Informal* a cheat; swindle. –*phr.* **30. take off, a.** to remove (clothing, etc.). **b.** to leave the ground, as an aeroplane. **c.** *Informal* to imitate or mimic. **31. take place**, to happen; occur.

takeover *n.* acquisition of control, especially of a business company, by the purchase of the majority of its shares.

takings *pl. n.* money received, as from sales in a shop.

talc *n.* a soft greenish-grey mineral used in making lubricants, powder, etc. Also, **talcum**.

tale *n.* a story about some real or imaginary event.

Don't confuse this with **tail**, which is what some animals have growing from the end of their backs.
Note that if you **tell tales** about someone, you are telling stories about them that are not very pleasant or are designed to get them into trouble.

talent *n.* a special natural ability.

talisman *n.* (*pl.* **-mans**) any charm, especially worn for magical effect.

talk *v.* **1.** to perform the act of speaking. **2.** to make known by means of spoken words. **3.** to express in words: *to talk nonsense.* **4.** to discuss: *to talk politics.* –*n.* **5.** speech; conversation, especially of a familiar or informal kind. **6.** a lecture or informal speech. **7.** report or rumour; gossip.

talkative *adj.* liking to talk a lot.

tall *adj.* of more than average height.

tallow *n.* the fatty tissue of animals, used in making candles, soap etc.

tally *n.* (*pl.* **-lies**) **1.** an account or record of a score. –*v.* (**-lied**, **-lying**) **2.** to count or reckon up.

talon *n.* a claw, especially of a bird of prey.

tambourine *n.* a small handheld drum with pairs of metal discs inserted into the frame.

tame *adj.* **1.** changed from the wild state; domesticated. **2.** tractable, docile, or submissive. **3.** spiritless. **4.** only mildly risqué; weak or relatively inoffensive: *a tame joke.* –*v.* **5.** to make tame; subdue. **6.** to soften; tone down.

tamp *v.* to force in or down by repeated, somewhat light strokes.

tamper *v.* to meddle (*with*), especially for the purpose of altering, damaging, etc.

tampon *n.* **1.** a plug of cotton put into an opening, wound, etc., as to stop haemorrhage. **2.** a similar device used internally to absorb menstrual flow.

tan *v.* (**tanned, tanning**) **1.** to convert (a hide) into a leather. **2.** to make brown by exposure to the sun. **3.** *Informal* to beat or thrash. –*n.* **4.** the brown colour of skin exposed to the sun.

tandem *adv.* **1.** one behind another. –*n.* **2.** a bicycle for 2 riders.

tandoori /æn'dʊəri/ *adj.* in Indian cookery, relating to dishes traditionally cooked in a cylindrical clay oven (**tandoor oven**).

tang *n.* **1.** a strong taste or flavour. **2.** a pungent or distinctive smell.

tangent *adj.* **1.** touching. –*n.* **2.** a sudden divergence from one course, thought, etc., to another.

tangerine *n.* a type of mandarin.

tangible *adj.* **1.** discernible by the touch; material or substantial. **2.** real rather than imaginary.

tangle *v.* **1.** to bring or be brought together into a mass of twisted threads, etc. –*n.* **2.** a tangled condition.

tango *n.* (*pl.* **-gos**) **1.** a dance of Spanish-American origin. –*v.* (**-goed, -going**) **2.** to dance the tango.

tank *n.* **1.** a large container for holding liquid or a gas. **2.** *Mil.* an armoured combat vehicle, armed with cannon and machine-guns and moving on continuous tracks.

tankard *n.* a large drinking cup, now usually with a handle and (sometimes) a hinged cover.

tanker *n.* a ship or vehicle designed to carry liquid in bulk.

tannin *n.* a substance used in tanning.

tantalise *v.* to torment or tease (as) with the sight of something desired but out of reach. Also, **tantalize**.

tantamount adj. equivalent, as in value, effect, etc. (to).

tantrum n. a fit of ill temper or passion.

tap¹ v. (**tapped, tapping**) **1.** to strike with slight, audible blows. –n. **2.** a light blow.

tap² n. **1.** any device for controlling the flow of liquid from a pipe, etc., by opening or closing an orifice; cock. –v. (**tapped, tapping**) **2.** to draw off (liquid) by opening a tap, or by piercing the container. **3.** to gain secret access to. **4.** to open outlets from (power lines, roads, pipes, etc.).

tapas /'tæpəs/ pl. n. traditional Spanish snacks or appetisers.

tape n. **1.** a long narrow strip of fabric used for tying garments, etc. **2.** a long narrow strip of paper, metal, etc. –v. **3.** to furnish with a tape. **4.** to record on a tape recorder.

tape measure n. a long strip of flexible material, used for measuring. Also, **tape**.

taper v. **1.** to make or become gradually thinner towards one end. **2.** to reduce gradually. –n. **3.** gradual decrease of width, thickness, force, capacity, etc. **4.** a long, narrow candle.

tape recorder n. a device for recording sound on magnetic tape.

tapestry n. (pl. **-ries**) an open weave fabric upon which coloured threads are woven by hand to produce a decorative design.

tapeworm n. a parasitic flat or tapelike worm.

tapioca n. a granular, starchy food used for making puddings, etc.

taproot n. Bot. a main root descending downwards and branching into small lateral roots.

tar n. **1.** any of various dark, sticky products obtained by processing substances, such as coal, wood, etc. –v. (**tarred, tarring**) **2.** to smear (as) with tar.

tarantula /tə'ræntʃələ/ n. a large, furry, Aust. spider which often shelters indoors when it is raining; huntsman.

tardy adj. (**-dier, -diest**) **1.** slow; sluggish. **2.** late.

tare n. **1.** the weight of the container holding goods. **2.** the weight of a vehicle without cargo, passengers, etc.

target n. **1.** a device, usually marked with concentric circles, to be aimed at in shooting practice or contests. **2.** a goal to be reached. –v. (**-eted, -eting**) **3.** to have as a target or goal.

> You may see the forms of the verb spelt **targetted** and **targetting**, although this is not very common. Usually, verbs ending in *t* don't double the *t* if the last part of the word is not said with a strong stress.

tariff n. a duty imposed by a government on imports or, less commonly exports.

tarmac n. (a road or airport runway surfaced with) a mixture of gravel and tar.

tarnish v. **1.** to (cause to) become dull or discoloured, as metals. **2.** to destroy the purity of; stain; sully. –n. **3.** tarnished or discoloured condition. **4.** stain or blemish.

tarot /'tærou/ n. a pack of cards, usually used in fortune-telling.

tarpaulin n. a protective waterproof covering of canvas or other material.

tarragon n. a herb with aromatic leaves.

tarry v. (**-ried, -rying**) **1.** to remain or stay, as in a place. **2.** to delay in acting, starting, coming, etc. **3.** to wait.

tart¹ adj. sour or acid.

tart² n. a shell of pastry with a sweet or savoury filling and no top crust.

tart³ Informal –n. **1.** a female prostitute or promiscuous woman. –phr. **2. tart up**, to adorn; make attractive, especially with cheap ornaments and cosmetics.

> It is offensive to refer to a woman as 'a tart', as in def. 1.

tartan *n.* a woollen or worsted cloth woven with stripes crossing at right angles, worn chiefly by the Scottish Highlanders.

tartar *n.* **1.** a hard substance deposited on the teeth. **2.** the deposit from wines.

task *n.* **1.** a definite piece of work assigned to a person; duty. **2.** a demanding or difficult matter. *–v.* **3.** to subject to severe exertion; make great demands on.

tassel *n.* **1.** a clasp consisting commonly of a bunch of threads, etc., hanging from a knob. **2.** something resembling this.

taste *v.* **1.** to try or perceive the flavour or quality of (something) by taking some into the mouth. **2.** to eat or drink a little of. **3.** to have or get a (slight) experience of. **4.** to smack or savour (*of*). *–n.* **5.** the act of tasting. **6.** the sense by which the flavour of things is perceived when they are brought into contact with special organs of the tongue. **7.** a small quantity tasted. **8.** a liking or predilection for something. **9.** the sense of what is appropriate, harmonious, or beautiful; the perception and enjoyment of excellence in the fine arts, literature, etc. **10.** a slight experience of something.

tastebud *n.* any of a number of small, flask-shaped bodies on the tongue, etc., the special organs of taste.

tasteless *adj.* **1.** (of food) not having much taste or flavour. **2.** unsuitable for the situation or likely to give offence.

tasty *adj.* (**-tier, -tiest**) pleasing to the taste; savoury.

tatter *n.* a torn piece hanging loose (or being separate) from the main part, as of a garment, etc.

tatting *n.* (the making of) a kind of hand-made knotted lace.

tattle *v.* to tell secrets.

tattoo[1] *n.* an outdoor military pageant or display.

tattoo[2] *n.* an indelible pattern made on the skin.

taught *v.* past tense and past participle of **teach**.

taunt *v.* to reproach or provoke in a sarcastic or insulting manner.

taut *adj.* tightly drawn; tense.

tautology *n.* (*pl.* **-gies**) needless repetition of an idea. **–tautological,** *adj.*

tavern *n.* premises where food and alcoholic drink are served.

tawdry *adj.* (**-drier, -driest**) (of finery, etc.) gaudy; showy and cheap.

tawny *adj.* (**-nier, -niest**) of a dark yellowish-brown colour.

tawny frogmouth *n.* a medium-sized Aust. night-bird, with differently coloured mottled plumage, and a low but penetrating call.

tax *n.* **1.** a compulsory monetary contribution demanded by a government for its support, and levied on incomes, property, goods purchased, etc. *–v.* **2.** to impose tax on. **3.** to lay a burden on; make serious demands on. **–taxable,** *adj.*

taxation *n.* **1.** the act of taxing. **2.** the revenue raised by taxes.

taxi *n.* (*pl.* **taxis**) Also, **taxicab, cab. 1.** a motor car for public hire, with a driver and a meter which calculates the fare. *–v.* (**taxied, taxiing** *or* **taxying**) **2.** (of an aeroplane) to move over the surface of the ground or water under its own power.

taxidermy *n.* the art of preserving the skins of animals, and stuffing and mounting them in lifelike form. **–taxidermist,** *n.*

taxonomy *n.* scientific classification, especially in relation to its laws.

T cell *n.* a white blood cell derived from or processed by the thymus, responsible for cellular immune reactions.

tea *n.* **1.** the dried and prepared leaves of an oriental shrub, from which a somewhat bitter, aromatic beverage is made by infusion in boiling water. **2.** a drink or medicine made from tea or other plants. **3.** a light meal taken in the late afternoon. **4.** the main evening meal.

teach v. (**taught**, **teaching**) **1.** to impart knowledge of or skill in; give instruction in (a subject). **2.** to give instruction to (someone). –**teacher**, n.

teak n. a large tree with a hard, yellowish-brown, resinous wood.

teal **1.** a small freshwater duck. –n. **2.** a deep greenish-blue colour. –adj. **3.** of the colour of teal.

team n. **1.** a number of persons associated in some joint action, especially one of the sides in a match. **2.** two or more horses, oxen, etc., harnessed together to draw a vehicle, plough etc. –v. **3.** to join together in a team.

Don't confuse this with **teem**, which is a word used in the expression **teem with**, which means to be full of. **Teem** can also mean to rain very hard.

Team is a collective noun and can be used with a singular or plural verb. Look up **collective noun**.

team spirit n. the camaraderie and loyalty which members of a team display towards each other.

tear[1] /tɪə/ n. a drop of fluid flowing from the eye, chiefly as the result of sadness, pain, etc.

Don't confuse **tear** with **tier**, which is a row or layer (*three tiers of seats*).

tear[2] /tɛə/ v. (**tore**, **torn**, **tearing**) **1.** to pull apart especially so as to leave ragged edges. **2.** to pull violently or with force. **3.** to divide. **4.** to become torn. **5.** *Informal* to move with violence or great haste. –n. **6.** the act of tearing. **7.** a crack or split.

tease v. **1.** to irritate by persistent petty requests, or other annoyances, often in jest. **2.** to pull apart the fibres of. **3.** to flirt with, especially insincerely. –n. **4.** the act of teasing. **5.** someone or something which teases.

teat n. **1.** the protuberance on the breast or udder in female mammals where the milk ducts discharge; a nipple. **2.** something

resembling a teat, especially for feeding a baby from a bottle.

techie /ˈtɛki/ n. *Informal* someone with a professional or passionate interest in technology, especially computing. Also, **tech**.

technical adj. **1.** relating to an art, science, etc. **2.** having practical skills in a particular art, trade, etc., as a person. **3.** relating to the mechanical or industrial arts and the applied sciences.

technicality n. (pl. **-ties**) a literal, often narrow-minded interpretation of a rule, etc.

technician n. someone skilled in the technique of an art or science.

technique n. method of performance.

technology n. **1.** the branch of knowledge that deals with (the practice and application of) science and engineering. **2.** equipment of a technologically sophisticated nature, such as computers, internet connections, audiovisual equipment, etc. –**technological**, adj. –**technologist**, n.

tectonic adj. of or relating to building or construction.

tectonic plate n. a section of the earth's crust and uppermost part of the mantle, which moves in relation to the other plates causing earthquakes, volcanoes, mountain-building and the formation of oceanic trenches.

teddy bear n. a stuffed toy bear.

tedium n. the state of being dull and tiresome. –**tedious**, adj.

tee *Golf* –n. **1.** (the wooden, etc, holder at) the beginning of each fairway from which the ball is driven. –phr. (**teed**, **teeing**) **2. tee off**, to strike the ball from a tee.

teem[1] phr. **teem with**, to be full of large numbers of: *streets teeming with people*.

Don't confuse this with **team**, which is a group of people doing something together: *a soccer team*.

teem[2] v. to rain very hard.

teenager n. a person aged between 12 and 20. –**teenage**, adj.

teeter v. to move unsteadily.

teeth n. plural of **tooth**.

teethe v. to have one's teeth grow and emerge through the gums.

teetotal adj. pledged to total abstinence from alcohol. –**teetotaller**, n.

telco n. a telecommunications company.

telecast v. (**-cast** or **-casted**, **-casting**) **1.** to broadcast by television. –n. **2.** a television broadcast.

telecommunications pl. n. the science of sending information by line or radio transmission.

teleconference n. a conference in which the people at locations remote from each other can take part using an audio and video telecommunications system. –**teleconferencing**, n.

telegram n. a message sent by telegraph.

telegraph n. a system or device for sending messages by electric signals along wire. –**telegraphic**, adj.

telemarketing n. the selling of goods or services by contacting potential customers on the telephone. –**telemarketer**, n.

telepathy n. communication of one mind with another by some means other than the normal use of the senses. –**telepathic**, adj.

telephone n. **1.** an (electrical) apparatus or system for sending sound or speech to a distant point. –v. **2.** to contact or try to contact a person by telephone: *I'll telephone him later*; *She telephoned last night*. –**telephonist**, n. –**telephony**, n.

The short form of this is **phone**.

teleprinter n. an instrument with a typewriter keyboard which sends and receives messages by changing typed information into electrical signals. Also, **teletype**.

telescope n. **1.** an optical instrument for making distant objects appear nearer and larger. –v. **2.** to force or slide together, one into another, or into something else, in the manner of the sliding tubes of a jointed telescope. **3.** to condense; shorten. –**telescopic**, adj.

teletype n. (*from trademark*) → **teleprinter**.

television n. **1.** the broadcasting of images via radio waves to receivers which project them electronically on a screen for viewing. **2.** a television receiver. –**televise**, v.

A short form of this is **TV**. Another informal short form is **telly** (or **tellie**).

telex n. an international two-way communications system which uses the public telecommunications network to link teleprinters at remote locations.

tell v. (**told**, **telling**) **1.** to give an account or report (of); relate (a story, etc.). **2.** to make known by speech or writing (information, etc.); communicate. **3.** to utter (the truth, a lie, etc.). **4.** to recognise or distinguish: *You can't tell the difference between them.* **5.** to give evidence (*of*): *Her handbag tells of her arrival.* **6.** to play the informer (*on*). **7.** to produce a marked effect: *The strain was telling on his face.*

teller n. someone employed in a bank to receive or pay out money over the counter.

temerity n. reckless boldness.

temper n. **1.** a particular state of mind or feelings. **2.** passion, shown in outbursts of anger, resentment, etc. **3.** *Metallurgy* the particular degree of hardness and elasticity imparted to steel, etc., by tempering. –v. **4.** to moderate or mitigate. **5.** to bring to a desirable state (as) by blending. **6.** to heat and cool or quench (metal) to bring to the proper degree of hardness, elasticity, etc.

tempera n. paint made from pigment ground in water and mixed with egg yolk or some similar substance.

temperament n. the individual character of a person, as shown by the manner of thinking, feeling, and acting.

temperamental adj. **1.** moody, irritable, or sensitive. **2.** unstable; unreliable.

temperance n. 1. habitual moderation. 2. total abstinence from alcohol.

temperate adj. 1. moderate or self-restrained. 2. not excessive.

temperate rainforest n. a coniferous or broadleaf forest occurring in coastal mountains with high rainfall. Compare **tropical rainforest**.

temperature n. 1. a measure of the degree of hotness or coldness of a body or substance. 2. Physiol. **a.** the degree of heat of a living body, especially the human body. **b.** the excess of this above the normal (37°C or about 98.4°F in adult humans).

tempest n. a violent storm.

tempestuous adj. tumultuous; turbulent.

template n. 1. a formula. 2. a pattern, mould, or the like, usually consisting of a thin plate of wood, etc., used as a guide in transferring designs, etc.

temple[1] n. a place of worship, especially a large or imposing one.

temple[2] n. the flattened region on either side of the human forehead.

tempo n. (pl. **-pos** or **-pi** /-pi/) Music relative rate of movement.

temporal adj. 1. of or relating to time. 2. relating to the present life or this world; worldly.

temporary adj. 1. lasting for a short time only; not permanent. 2. lasting or in use for a limited time: a temporary job.

temporise v. 1. to act indecisively to gain time or delay matters. 2. to (appear to) yield temporarily to the demands of the occasion. Also, **temporize**.

tempt v. 1. to persuade by enticement or allurement. 2. to cause to be strongly disposed (to do something). –**temptation**, n.

tempura /'tem'pura/ n. a Japanese food made from seafood or vegetables coated in a light batter and deep-fried in oil.

ten n. a cardinal number, 9 plus 1. –adj. 2. amounting to 10 in number. –**tenth**, adj., n.

Numbers used before a noun are sometimes called **determiners**.

tenable adj. capable of being held, maintained, or defended, as against attack or objection.

tenacious adj. 1. holding on firmly: a tenacious grip. 2. highly retentive, as memory. 3. persistent or obstinate. –**tenacity**, n.

tenant n. someone who leases a house, etc., from the owner. –**tenancy**, n.

tend[1] v. to be inclined (to do something). –**tendency**, n.

tend[2] v. 1. to attend to by work or services, etc. 2. to care for.

tendentious adj. presenting a particular bias or point of view.

tender[1] adj. 1. soft or delicate. 2. weak or fragile in constitution. 3. warm and affectionate. 4. gentle. 5. painfully sensitive.

tender[2] v. 1. to offer formally for acceptance. –n. 2. an offer of something for acceptance. 3. Commerce an offer made in writing by one party to another to carry out work, supply certain commodities, etc., at a given cost.

tendon n. Anat. a cord of dense, white fibrous tissue, connecting a muscle with a bone or part; sinew. –**tendinous**, adj.

tendonitis /tendən'aitəs/ n. inflammation of a tendon. Also, **tendinitis**.

tendril n. Bot. a leafless curly organ of climbing plants.

tenement house /'tenəmənt/ n. a house divided into flats, especially one in the poorer, crowded parts of a large city.

tenet n. any opinion, doctrine, etc., held as true.

The more usual word is **belief**.

tennis n. a game in which players with racquets hit a ball to each other over a net.

tenon n. an end of a piece of wood, etc., shaped for insertion in a corresponding cavity (mortice) in another piece.

tenor *n.* **1.** the meaning which runs through something written or spoken; purport; drift. **2.** *Music* **a.** the highest natural male voice. **b.** a singer with such a voice. –*adj.* **3.** *Music* of, relating to, or having range of a tenor: *a tenor saxophone.*

For def. 1, the more usual word is **gist**.

tenpin bowling *n.* a form of bowling played with ten wooden pins at which a ball is bowled to knock them down.

tense¹ *adj.* **1.** stretched tight; rigid. **2.** in a state of nervous strain, as a person. –*v.* **3.** to make or become tense.

tense² *n. Gram.* a form of a verb which specifies the time and length of the action or state expressed by the verb.

Look up **present tense**, **past tense**, **future tense**.

tensile *adj.* **1.** relating to tension. **2.** capable of being stretched. –**tensility**, *n.*

tension *n.* **1.** the act of stretching or straining. **2.** mental or emotional strain, as anxiety, suspense, or excitement. **3.** *Elect.* electromotive force; potential.

tent *n.* a portable shelter of strong cloth, formerly usually of canvas.

tentacle *n. Zool.* any of various slender, flexible appendages in animals, especially invertebrates, used for grasping, touching, etc.

tentative *adj.* **1.** experimental. **2.** hesitant; diffident.

tenterhooks *phr.* **on tenterhooks**, in a state of painful suspense or anxiety.

tenuous *adj.* weak or vague: *a tenuous connection.*

tenure *n.* (the period or terms of) the possessing of anything.

tepid *adj.* moderately warm.

term *n.* **1.** any word or expression naming something, especially as used in some particular field of knowledge. **2.** the time through which something lasts or is fixed to last. **3.** (in schools, etc.) a period of the year during which instruction is regularly organised. **4.** (*pl.*) conditions with regard to payment, price, etc. **5.** (*pl.*) footing or standing: *to be on good terms with someone.* –*v.* **6.** to name; call; designate. –*phr.* **7. a contradiction in terms**, a statement which is self-contradictory.

terminal *adj.* **1.** situated at or forming the end of something. **2.** occurring at or causing the end of life. –*n.* **3.** an end or extremity. **4.** the end of a railway line, shipping route, air route, etc., at which loading and unloading of passengers, goods, etc., takes place. **5.** *Elect.* the point of connection in an electrical circuit. **6.** a computer input or output device.

terminally *adv.* incurably: *terminally ill.*

terminate *v.* **1.** to end, conclude, or cease (something). **2.** to end (a pregnancy) by causing the fetus to be expelled before it is viable. –**terminable**, *adj.* –**termination**, *n.*

terminology *n.* (*pl.* **-gies**) the system of terms belonging to a subject; nomenclature.

terminus *n.* (*pl.* **-ni** /-naɪ/ *or* **-nuses**) the station or town at the end of a railway line, bus route, etc.

termite *n.* a social insect, sometimes very destructive to buildings, etc.

A termite is often called a **white ant**, although it is not really an ant.

tern *n.* a seabird.

ternary *adj.* threefold; triple.

terrace *n.* **1.** one of a series of raised level areas formed across a mountain side, etc., usually for the purposes of cultivation. **2.** an open (usually paved) outdoor living area adjoining a house. **3. a.** a row of adjoining, identical houses, often of 19th-century construction, often with two storeys and iron lace. **b.** one such house.

terracotta *n.* a hard, usually unglazed earthenware of fine quality.

terrain n. an area of land, especially as considered with reference to its natural features, military advantages, etc.

terrestrial adj. **1.** relating to, consisting of, or representing the earth. **2.** of or relating to the land as distinct from the water.

terrible adj. **1.** exciting terror or great fear; dreadful; awful. **2.** very bad.

terrier n. a small dog, originally bred for hunting.

terrific adj. **1.** extraordinarily great, intense, etc. **2.** Informal very good.

terrify v. (**-fied, -fying**) to fill with terror.

territory n. (pl. **-ries**) **1.** any area of land; region or district. **2.** the land and waters belonging to or under the jurisdiction of a state, sovereign, etc. **3.** the field of action, thought, etc. **-territorial**, adj.

terror n. **1.** intense, sharp, overpowering fear. **2.** Informal a person or thing that is a particular nuisance.

terrorise v. to fill with terror. Also, **terrorize**.

terrorism n. deliberate acts of armed violence to further political aims. **-terrorist**, n., adj. **-terroristic**, adj.

terry towelling n. cotton fabric with loops on one or both sides.

terse adj. **1.** concise or brief, as language. **2.** abrupt or bad-tempered, especially in one's speech.

tertiary adj. of the 3rd order, rank, etc.

tessellated adj. arranged in a chequered pattern.

test n. **1.** a trial by which the presence, quality, or genuineness of anything is determined. **2.** Educ. a form of examination for evaluating the abilities of a student or class. **-v. 3.** to subject to a test; try.

testament n. **1.** Law a formal declaration, usually in writing, of a person's wishes as to the distribution of his or her property after his or her death. **2.** something which serves as proof or evidence of some quality: *Her behaviour was a testament to*

her maturity. **3.** (*upper case*) either of the 2 main divisions of the Bible.

> Def. 1 is used mainly in the expression **last will and testament**, which is a rather old-fashioned legal term for a will.

testator n. someone who makes a will.

testes n. plural of **testis**.

testicle n. one of the paired male sex glands situated in the scrotum. Also, **testis**.

testify v. (**-fied, -fying**) **1.** to bear witness (to); give evidence (of). **2.** to make solemn declaration.

testimonial n. **1.** written evidence as to a person's character, conduct, or qualifications. **2.** something given or done as an expression of esteem, or gratitude.

testimony n. (pl. **-nies**) **1.** Law the statement of a witness under oath or affirmation, usually in court. **2.** evidence.

testis n. (pl. **testes**) → **testicle**.

testosterone /tɛsˈtɒstərɒn/ n. a male sex hormone, secreted by the testes, which stimulates development of masculine characteristics.

test tube n. a thin glass tube with one end closed, used in chemical tests.

testy adj. (**-tier, -tiest**) touchy.

tetanus /ˈtɛtnəs/ n. an infectious, often fatal disease, marked by spasms and muscle rigidity; lockjaw.

tether n. **1.** a rope, chain, etc., tied to an animal to limit its movement. **-v. 2.** to fasten (as) with a tether. **-phr. 3. the end of one's tether**, the limit of one's patience or resources.

text n. **1.** the main body of matter in a book, etc. **2.** the actual wording of anything written or printed. **-v. 3.** to send (someone) a text message. **-textual**, adj. **-texter**, n.

texta n. (*from trademark*) → **felt pen**.

textbook n. a book used by students for a particular branch of study. Also, **text**.

textile n. a woven material.

text message *n.* a message sent by mobile phone using SMS. –**text messaging**, *n.*

texture *n.* the characteristic appearance or structure of something, especially as conveyed to the touch.

than *conj.* **1.** a particle used after comparative adjectives and adverbs and certain other words, such as *other*, *otherwise*, *else*, etc., to introduce the second member of a comparison: *He is taller than I am.* –*prep.* **2.** in comparison with: *taller than me.*

thank *v.* to give thanks to. –*n.* **2. thanks**, **a.** feelings of being grateful or words showing one is grateful: *filled with thanks*. **b.** thank you.

thankful *adj.* feeling or showing thanks. –**thankfully**, *adv.* –**thankfulness**, *n.*

thank you *phr.* an expression used to tell someone that you are grateful to them: *Thank you for coming; Thank you, I would really like to come.*

that *pron.* **1.** a demonstrative pronoun used to indicate: **a.** a person, thing, idea, etc., as pointed out, mentioned, etc.: *That is my husband.* **b.** of 2 or more persons, things, etc., already mentioned, the one more remote in place, time, or thought: *That is the one I want, not this.* **2.** a relative pronoun used as the subject or object of a relative clause: *How old was the car that was stolen?* –*adj.* **3.** a demonstrative adjective used to indicate: **a.** a person, thing, idea, etc., as pointed out, mentioned, etc.: *That man is my husband.* **b.** of 2 or more persons, things, etc., already mentioned, the one more remote in place, time, or thought: *It was that one, not this one.* –*adv.* **4.** an adverb used with adjectives and adverbs of quality or extent to indicate precise degree or extent: *that much; that far.* –*conj.* **5.** a conjunction used to introduce a noun clause: *That he will come is certain; I know that you will do it.*

The plural of **that** (defs 1 and 3) is **those**: *Those are riper than these; It was those books I wanted.*
Demonstrative adjectives (see def. 3) are sometimes called **determiners**.

thatch *n.* **1.** a material, as straw, rushes, etc. used to cover roofs, haystacks, etc. –*v.* **2.** to cover (as) with thatch.

thaw *v.* to pass from a frozen to a liquid or semiliquid state; melt.

the *definite article* a word used especially before nouns: **1.** with a specifying or limiting effect. **2.** denoting an individual, a class or an abstract notion: *to help the poor.*

Articles are sometimes called **determiners**.

theatre *n.* **1.** a building or room designed to stage dramatic presentations, screen films, etc. **2.** drama as a branch of art. **3.** Also, **lecture theatre**. a hall fitted with tiers of seats, as used for lectures, etc. **4.** Also, **operating theatre**. a room in a hospital in which surgical operations are performed. **5.** a place of action: *theatre of war.*

theatrical *adj.* **1.** of or relating to the theatre. **2.** suggestive of the theatre or of acting. Also, **theatric**.

thee *pron.* Old-fashioned the objective case of the pronoun **thou**.

theft *n.* the act of stealing.

Note that someone who commits a theft is called a **thief**.

their *pron.* the possessive form of **they** used before a noun: *Those are their bags.*

Their is a third person plural pronoun. It is sometimes called a *determiner* or a *possessive adjective*.
See the note at **they** regarding the use of **their** as a singular pronoun, as in *If anyone has lost their form, please come to the information desk.*

theirs *pron.* **1.** the possessive form of **they**, used without a noun following:

Those books are theirs. **2.** the person(s) or thing(s) belonging to them: *Theirs is the red car parked around the back.*

Theirs is a third person plural pronoun in the possessive case.
See the note at **they** regarding the use of **theirs** as a singular pronoun, as in *If anyone thinks this watch is theirs, please see me after class.*

theism /'θiːɪzəm/ *n.* the belief in a god as the creator and ruler of the universe.

them *pron.* **1.** (the personal pronoun used, usually after a verb or preposition, to refer to a number of people or things): *put them away; give it to them.* **2.** (a personal pronoun used, usually after a verb or preposition, to refer to a single person when the sex of the person is unknown): *If anyone calls, tell them I'm busy.*

Them is a third person plural pronoun in the objective case.
See the note at **they** regarding the use of **them** as a singular pronoun, as in def. 2.

theme *n.* a subject of discussion, a composition, etc. –**thematic**, *adj.*

themself *pron.* a reflexive form of **they** used as a singular pronoun when the sex of the person being referred to is unknown.

This is regarded as incorrect by many people. See the note at **themselves**.

themselves *pron.* **1.** the reflexive form of **they**: *they hurt themselves.* **2.** a form of **them** or **they** used for emphasis: *They did it themselves.*

Like **they** and **them**, **themselves** can be used as a singular pronoun when the sex of the person being referred to is unknown (*If anyone comes to the door they can let themselves in*). Sometimes, the form **themself** is used in this situation (*A child might hurt themself on this equipment*). Note, however, that some people still regard **themself** as an incorrect use.

then *adv.* **1.** at that time. **2.** next in order of time. **3.** in that case.

thence *adv.* **1.** from that place or time. **2.** for that reason; therefore.

theodolite /θi'ɒdəlaɪt/ *n.* Surveying an instrument for measuring horizontal or vertical angles.

theology *n.* the study of divine things or religious truth. –**theologian**, *n.* –**theological**, *adj.*

theorem *n.* a rule or law, especially one expressed by an equation or formula.

theoretical *adj.* **1.** of, relating to, or consisting in theory; not practical. **2.** hypothetical.

theorise *v.* **1.** to form a theory. **2.** to speculate or conjecture. Also, **theorize**.

theory *n.* (*pl.* -**ries**) **1.** a coherent group of propositions used to explain something. **2.** the part of a science or art which deals with its principles or methods (opposed to *practice*). **3.** conjecture or opinion.

therapeutic *adj.* relating to the treating or curing of disease.

therapy *n.* (*pl.* -**pies**) the treatment of disease, etc., as by some remedy. –**therapist**, *n.*

there *adv.* in, at, to, or into that place (opposed to *here*).

thereby *adv.* by means of that.

therefore *adv.* as a result; consequently.

thereupon *adv.* immediately following that.

thermal *adj.* of or relating to heat or temperature. Also, **thermic**.

thermodynamics *n.* the science concerned with the relations between heat and mechanical energy and the conversion of one into the other.

thermometer *n.* an instrument for measuring temperature.

thermonuclear *adj.* capable of producing extremely high temperatures resulting from nuclear fusion.

thermostat *n.* a device which establishes and maintains a desired temperature automatically.

thesaurus /θə'sɔːrəs, -'zɔː-/ n. (pl. **-ruses** or **-ri** /-raɪ/) a dictionary of synonyms.

these pron., adj. plural of **this**: These are my favourite paintings; These plates are dirty.

thesis /'θiːsɪs/ n. (pl. **theses** /'θiːsiːz/) **1.** a proposition laid down or stated, especially one to be discussed and proved. **2.** a subject for a composition or essay. **3.** a dissertation, as one presented by a candidate for a postgraduate degree.

they pron. **1.** the personal pronoun used to refer to a number of people or things, not including the speaker or the person spoken to. It is the plural of **he**, **she** and **it**: Will they be coming? **2.** a personal pronoun used to refer to a single person when the sex of the person is unknown: If anyone wants it, they are welcome to it.

They (def. 1) is a third person plural pronoun in the subjective case. Def. 2 is used as a singular pronoun.
The use of **they** as a singular pronoun (def. 2) is becoming more widespread when the sex of the person being referred to is unknown. Nowadays, speakers try to avoid using he because it can be considered sexist, and he or she because it is clumsy. Instead of saying If anyone knows the answer, he should speak up or If anyone knows the answer, he or she should speak up, it is neater to say If anyone knows the answer, they should speak up. The other forms of the pronoun (**them**, **their** and **theirs**) are used in the same way. Also look up **themselves**.

thiamine /'θaɪəmɪn/ n. a vitamin (B$_1$) required by the nervous system.

thick adj. **1.** having relatively great extent from one surface or side to its opposite; not thin. **2.** measuring as specified between opposite surfaces. **3.** set close together; dense. **4.** viscous. **5.** (of an accent) very pronounced.

thicket n. a thick or dense growth of small trees, etc.

thief n. (pl. **thieves**) someone who steals.

thieve v. to take by theft; steal. –**thievery**, n.

thigh n. that part of the leg between the hip and the knee in humans.

thimble n. a metal cap, worn on the finger to push the needle in sewing.

thin adj. (**thinner**, **thinnest**) **1.** having relatively little extent from one surface or side to its opposite; not thick. **2.** of small cross-section in comparison with the length; slender. **3.** having little flesh; lean. **4.** not dense; sparse. **5.** without solidity; unsubstantial. **6.** transparent, or flimsy: a thin excuse. –phr. (**thinned**, **thinning**) **7. thin down** (or **out**), to make or become thin or thinner.

thine pron., adj. Old-fashioned the possessive form corresponding to **thou** used with or without a noun following, or before a noun beginning with a vowel or h. Compare **thy**.

thing n. **1.** a material object without life or consciousness. **2.** that which is or may become an object of thought.

think v. (**thought**, **thinking**) **1.** to have in the mind as an idea, conception, or the like. **2.** to form or have an idea or conception of (a thing, fact, circumstance, etc.). **3.** to hold as an opinion; believe; suppose. **4.** to consider (something) to be (as specified). **5.** to use the mind, especially the intellect, actively; cogitate or meditate. **6.** to reflect upon the matter in question.

third adj. **1.** next after the 2nd in order, quality, etc. –n. **2.** someone or something which comes next after the 2nd. **3.** a third part, especially of one.

third party n. any person other than those directly involved in some transaction, etc.

third-party insurance n. an insurance policy which protects against damaging another's person or property.

third person n. See **person** (def. 3).

thirst n. **1.** a sensation of dryness in the mouth and throat caused by need of drink.

2. strong or eager desire; craving. –**thirsty**, *adj.*

thirteen *n.* **1.** a cardinal number, 10 plus 3. –*adj.* **2.** amounting to 13 in number. –**thirteenth**, *adj.*, *n.*

Numbers used before a noun are sometimes called **determiners**.

thirty *n.* **1.** a cardinal number, 10 times 3. –*adj.* **2.** amounting to 30 in number. –**thirtieth**, *adj.*, *n.*

Numbers used before a noun are sometimes called **determiners**.

this *pron.* **1.** a demonstrative pronoun used to indicate: **a.** a person, thing, idea, etc., as pointed out, present, or near, as before mentioned etc.: *This is my husband.* **b.** one of 2 or more persons, things, etc., already mentioned, referring to the one nearer in place, time, or thought: *This is the one I want, not that.* –*adj.* **2.** a demonstrative adjective used to indicate: **a.** a person, place, thing, idea, etc., as pointed out, present, or near, before mentioned, etc.: *This man is my husband.* **b.** one of 2 or more persons, things, etc., already mentioned, referring to one nearer in place, time, or thought: *I want this one, not that one.* –*adv.* **3.** an adverb used with adjectives and adverbs of quality or extent to indicate precise degree or extent: *this much; this far.*

The plural of **this** (defs 1 and 2) is **these**: *These are your seats; These books are very boring.*
Demonstrative adjectives (see def. 2) are sometimes called **determiners**.

thistle *n.* a prickly plant.

thither *adv.* to or towards that place.

thong *n.* **1.** a narrow strip of leather, used as a fastening, as the lash of a whip, etc. **2.** *Aust.* a sandal held loosely on the foot by 2 strips of leather, rubber, etc.; flip-flop.

thorax *n.* (pl. **thoraces** /ˈθɔrəsiz, θɔˈreisiz/ or **thoraxes**) *Anat.* (in humans and the higher vertebrates) the part of the trunk between the neck and the abdomen; the chest. –**thoracic**, *adj.*

thorn *n.* a sharp-pointed outgrowth on a plant; a prickle.

thorough *adj.* **1.** carried out through the whole of something; complete or perfect. **2.** leaving nothing undone.

thoroughfare *n.* a road, street, etc., open at both ends, especially a main road.

those *pron.*, *adj.* plural of **that**: *Those are my shoes; Do you like those colours?*

thou *pron. Old-fashioned* the personal pronoun used to denote the person spoken to; formerly in general use, but now little used, having been replaced by *you.*

though *conj.* **1.** in spite of the fact that. **2.** even if. **3.** if (usually in *as though*). –*adv.* **4.** for all that; however. Also, *Poetic,* **tho'**.

thought *v.* **1.** past tense and past participle of **think**. –*n.* **2.** that which one thinks. **3.** the capacity or faculty of thinking. **4.** meditation.

thoughtful *adj.* **1.** occupied with or given to thought; contemplative. **2.** characterised by or manifesting thought: *a thoughtful essay.* **3.** careful, heedful, or mindful. **4.** showing consideration for others; considerate. –**thoughtfully**, *adv.* –**thoughtfulness**, *n.*

thoughtless *adj.* **1.** not taking thought; unthinking, careless, or heedless. **2.** lacking in consideration for others; inconsiderate. –**thoughtlessly**, *adv.* –**thoughtlessness**, *n.*

thousand *n.* (pl. **-sands**, as after a numeral, **-sand**) **1.** a cardinal number, 10 times 100. –*adj.* **2.** amounting to one thousand in number. –**thousandth**, *adj.*, *n.*

Numbers used before a noun are sometimes called **determiners**.

thrash *v.* **1.** to beat soundly by way of punishment. **2.** to toss, or plunge violently about.

thread n. **1.** a fine cord, especially that used for sewing. **2.** the spiral ridge of a screw. **3.** that which runs through the whole course of something, as the sequence of events in a narrative. –v. **4.** to pass the end of a thread through (a needle, beads, etc.).

threadbare adj. **1.** (of fabric, etc.) worn thin; shabby. **2.** meagre, scanty, or poor.

threat n. **1.** a declaration of an intention to inflict punishment, pain or loss on someone. **2.** an indication of probable evil to come. –**threaten**, v.

three n. **1.** a cardinal number, 2 plus 1. –adj. **2.** amounting to 3 in number.

Numbers used before a noun are sometimes called **determiners**.

3D adj. **1.** three-dimensional. –n. **2.** a three-dimensional form or appearance. Also, **3-D.**

three-dimensional adj. **1.** having depth as well as height and breadth. **2.** realistic; lifelike.

thresh v. to separate the grain or seeds from (a cereal plant, etc.).

threshold n. **1.** the entrance to a house or building. **2.** any place of entering or beginning. **3.** Psychol., Physiol. the point at which a stimulus becomes perceptible or strong enough to produce an effect.

threw v. past tense of **throw**.

thrice adv. 3 times.

thrift n. economical management; frugality. –**thrifty**, adj.

thrill v. **1.** to affect or be affected by a sudden wave of keen emotion, so as to produce a tingling sensation through the body. –n. **2.** a tingling sensation passing through the body as the result of sudden keen emotion or excitement. **3.** thrilling quality, as of a story. –**thrilling**, adj.

thriller n. a book, etc., dealing with crime, mystery, etc., in an exciting manner.

thrive v. to grow strongly or flourish.

throat n. **1.** the passage from the mouth to the stomach or to the lungs. **2.** the front of the neck below the chin and above the collarbones.

throb v. (**throbbed, throbbing**) **1.** to beat with increased force or rapidity, as the heart. –n. **2.** the act of throbbing. **3.** any pulsation.

throes pl. n. **1.** any violent disturbance or struggle. –phr. **2. in the throes of**, engaged in.

thrombosis n. coagulation of the blood in the heart or blood vessels.

throne n. the seat occupied by a sovereign, or other important person on ceremonial occasions.

throng n. many people crowded together.

throttle n. **1.** a device to control the amount of fuel being fed to an engine. –v. **2.** to strangle.

through prep. **1.** in at one end, side, or surface, and out at the other, of. **2.** by the means of. **3.** because of: He lost his job through no fault of his own. –adv. **4.** in at one end, side, or surface and out at the other. **5.** from the beginning to the end. **6.** to the end. –adj. **7.** that goes through the whole of a long distance with little or no interruption. Also, **thro, thro', thru.**

throughout prep. **1.** in or to every part of. –adv. **2.** in every part.

throw v. (**threw, thrown, throwing**) **1.** to propel forcibly through the air. **2.** to put hastily. **3.** to shape on a potter's wheel. **4.** to deliver (a blow or punch). **5.** to cast (dice). **6.** (of a horse, etc.) to cause to fall off. **7.** Informal to astonish; confuse. **8.** to arrange: to throw a party. –n. **9.** an act of throwing.

throwback n. reversion to an ancestral type.

thrush¹ n. a migratory songbird.

thrush² n. a disease, especially of the vagina, caused by a parasitic fungus; monilia.

thrust v. (**thrust, thrusting**) **1.** to push forcibly (against something). **2.** to make a lunge, or stab at something. –n. **3.** the act of thrusting; a lunge or stab.

thud n. **1.** a dull sound, as of a heavy blow. –v. (**thudded, thudding**) **2.** to strike with a dull sound.

thug n. a brutal or murderous ruffian.

thumb n. **1.** the short, thick inner digit of the human hand, next to the forefinger. –v. **2.** to run (*through*) (the pages of a book, etc.) quickly.

thumbnail n. **1.** the nail of the thumb. **2.** Also, **thumbnail sketch. a.** a concise or rudimentary drawing. **b.** a brief description of a person or account of an event. **3.** a small computer graphics image which offers a preview of a full-size image.

thump n. **1.** a heavy blow producing a dull sound. –v. **2.** to strike or beat with something thick and heavy, so as to produce a dull sound. **3.** Informal to punch; thrash severely.

thunder n. **1.** the loud noise which accompanies a flash of lightning. –v. **2.** to speak in a very loud tone. –**thunderous**, adj.

thus adv. **1.** in this way. **2.** consequently.

For def. 2, the more usual word is **therefore**.

thwack v. to strike with something flat; whack.

thwart v. to oppose successfully or frustrate (a purpose, etc.).

The more usual word is **block**.

thy pron., adj. Old-fashioned the possessive form corresponding to **thou** and **thee**, used before a noun. Compare **thine**.

thyme /taɪm/ n. a plant of the mint family, with aromatic leaves.

thymus n. Anat. a ductless gland lying near the base of the neck.

thyroid gland n. Anat. a two-lobed gland lying on either side of the trachea which secretes a hormone stimulating bodily and mental activity.

tiara n. a small jewelled ornamental crown worn by women.

tibia n. (pl. **-bias** or **-biae** /-bii/) Anat. the inner of the 2 bones which extend from the knee to the ankle.

tic n. a sudden, involuntary muscular contraction in the face or extremities.

Don't confuse this with **tick**.

tick¹ n. **1.** a slight, sharp click or beat, as of a clock. **2.** a small mark as a hooked, sloping dash (✓), indicating that something has been done or is correct. –v. **3.** to produce a tick, as a clock. **4.** to mark (an item, etc.) with a tick. –phr. **5. tick off**, Informal to rebuke; scold.

Don't confuse this with **tic**.

tick² n. a bloodsucking animal like a mite.

ticket n. **1.** a small piece of paper serving as evidence of the holder's right to some service. **2.** a label or tag. **3.** a list of candidates nominated by a political party, etc. **4.** a summons issued for a traffic or parking offence. **5.** Informal the right or proper thing: *That's the ticket*.

tickle v. **1.** to touch lightly so as to excite a tingling or itching sensation in. **2.** to poke in some sensitive part of the body so as to excite spasmodic laughter.

ticklish adj. **1.** sensitive to tickling. **2.** requiring careful handling; risky.

tidal wave n. (in non-technical use) a tsunami.

tiddler n. a very small fish.

tiddly adj. (**-lier, -liest**) Informal slightly drunk.

tide n. **1.** the periodic rise and fall of the waters of the ocean due to the attraction of the moon and sun. **2.** a tendency or trend: *the tide of public opinion*. –phr. **3. tide someone over**, to help someone to get over a period of difficulty, distress, etc. –**tidal**, adj.

tidings pl. n. news or information.

tidy adj. (**-dier, -diest**) **1.** neat; trim; orderly. **2.** Informal considerable: *a tidy* *sum of money.* –v. (**-died, -dying**) Also, **tidy up. 2.** to make tidy or neat.

tie v. (**tied, tying**) **1.** to bind or draw together (the parts of) with a knotted string or the like. **2.** to draw together into a knot, as a cord. **3.** to join, or connect in any way. **4.** to confine, restrict, or limit. **5.** to bind or oblige, as to do something. **6.** to make the same score in a contest. –n. **7.** a narrow strip of material worn round the neck and tied in front. **8.** anything that fastens, secures, or unites. **9.** something that restricts one's freedom of action. **10.** a state of equality in points, votes, etc., as among competitors.

tier n. a row or rank.

Don't confuse this with **tear**, which is one of the drops of salty water that fall from your eyes when you are very sad. Note that the other word **tear**, meaning to rip, is pronounced /trə/.

tiff n. a petty quarrel.

tiger n. a large tawny, black-striped animal of the cat family.

tight adj. **1.** firmly fixed in place; secure. **2.** stretched so as to be taut. **3.** fitting closely, especially too closely. **4.** impervious to water, air, etc. **5.** strict. **6.** Informal mean with money; stingy; parsimonious. **7.** Informal intoxicated; drunk. **8.** Finance (of credit) not easily obtained. –**tighten,** v.

tightrope n. a rope or wire stretched tight, on which acrobats perform feats of balancing. Also, **tightwire**.

tights pl. n. a close-fitting, finely woven garment covering the body from the waist to the feet.

tilde /'tɪldə/ n. a mark (~) placed over a letter, as over the letter 'n' in Spanish to indicate a palatal nasal sound, as in *señor*.

tile n. **1.** a thin slab of baked clay used for covering roofs, floors, etc. –v. (**tiled, tiling**) **2.** to cover with tiles.

till¹ prep. **1.** up to the time of; until. **2.** (with a negative) before: *He cannot come till*

Thursday. –conj. **3.** to the time that or when; until. **4.** (with a negative) before.

till² v. to cultivate (land).

till³ n. (in a shop, etc.) a box, drawer, etc. in which cash is kept.

tilt v. **1.** to (cause to) lean, incline, slope or slant. –n. **2.** a slope.

timber n. wood, especially for use in carpentry, joinery, etc.

Don't confuse this with **timbre**.

timbre /'tɪmbə, 'tæmbə/ n. the characteristic quality of a sound.

Don't confuse this with **timber**.

time n. **1.** the system of those relations which any event has to any other as past, present, or future. **2.** a limited extent of time, as between 2 events: *a short time.* **3.** (oft. pl.) the era now (or then) present. **4.** an allotted period, as of one's life, for payment of a debt, etc.: *Your time is up.* **5.** a particular point in time. **6.** a particular part of a year, day, etc. **7.** the period in which an action is completed: *The winner's time was 2 minutes.* **8.** each occasion of a recurring event: *He climbed the mountain 5 times.* **9.** (pl.) used in multiplication. **10.** Music, etc. tempo. –adj. **11.** relating to the passage of time. –v. **12.** to ascertain the duration, or rate of. **13.** to choose the moment or occasion for.

time line n. **1.** a representation of historical events in the form of a line with date divisions and important events marked on it. **2.** a schedule with deadlines indicated. Also, **timeline.**

timely adj. (**-lier, -liest**) occurring at a suitable time; opportune.

timepiece n. a clock or a watch.

timetable n. any plan listing the times at which certain things are due to take place, as the departure of buses, trains, etc.

time trial n. a race in which participants race against the clock, the race being decided on who completes the course in the fastest time.

timid adj. subject to fear; shy.

timing n. **1.** the controlling of the speed of an action, event, etc. **2.** the mechanism which ensures that the valves in an internal-combustion engine open and close at the correct time.

timorous adj. fearful; timid.

timpani /'timpəni/ pl. n. a set of kettle-drums.

tin n. **1.** a low-melting, metallic element. Symbol: Sn **2.** any shallow metal pan, especially one used in baking. **3.** a sealed container for food. –v. (**tinned, tinning**) **4.** to coat with a thin layer of tin. **5.** to preserve in tins, as foodstuffs.

Note that, in the past, tin was commonly used to make pots, pans, cans and many other things. Nowadays iron coated with another metal, such as zinc, is more commonly used and so terms like *tin roof*, *tin shed* and *tin can* actually refer to iron objects.

tincture n. Pharmaceutical a solution of a medicinal substance in alcohol.

tinder n. any dry substance that readily takes fire from a spark.

tine n. a sharp prong, as of a fork. Also, **tyne**.

tinea n. a contagious skin disease caused by fungi.

tinge v. (**tinged, tingeing** or **tinging**) **1.** to impart a trace of colour to; tint. –n. **2.** a trace of colour.

tingle v. **1.** to have a prickling or stinging sensation. –n. **2.** such a sensation.

tinker n. **1.** a (travelling) mender of pots, kettles, pans, etc. –v. **2.** to busy oneself with something, especially an appliance, usually without useful results.

tinkle v. **1.** to make a succession of short, light, ringing sounds. –n. **2.** a tinkling sound.

tinny adj. (**-nier, -niest**) **1.** lacking resonance. **2.** not strong or durable.

tinsel n. a (strip of) cheap, glittering, metallic material.

tint n. **1.** (a variety of) a colour; hue. **2.** a colour diluted with white. –v. **3.** to colour slightly or delicately; tinge.

tiny adj. (**-nier, -niest**) very small.

tip¹ n. **1.** a slender, pointed end of anything long or tapered. **2.** the top, summit, or apex.

tip² v. (**tipped, tipping**) **1.** to incline; tilt. –n. **2.** a place where waste material is deposited. –phr. **3.** to **tip over** (or **up**), to tumble or topple.

Note that def. 2 can also be called a **garbage tip, rubbish tip, rubbish dump,** or **dump**.

tip³ n. **1.** a small sum of money given to a waiter, porter, etc., for performing a service. **2.** a useful hint or idea. –v. (**tipped, tipping**) **3.** to give a small sum of money to.

tipple v. to drink (wine, spirits, etc.). especially to excess.

tipsy adj. (**-sier, -siest**) slightly intoxicated.

tiptoe v. (**-toed, -toeing**) to go on the tips of the toes, as with caution or stealth.

tirade n. a prolonged outburst of denunciation.

tire v. **1.** to (cause to) become exhausted or wearied by exertion. –phr. **2. tire of,** to have one's interest, patience, etc., exhausted.

Don't confuse **tire** with **tyre**, which is the band of rubber fitted around a wheel.

tired adj. **1.** weakened by effort, work, etc., and needing to sleep. –phr. **2. tired of,** bored with. –**tiredness,** n.

tiresome adj. **1.** such as to tire one; wearisome. **2.** annoying or exasperating.

tissue n. **1.** Biol. the substance of an organism. **2.** a soft gauzelike paper. **3.** a paper handkerchief.

tit¹ n. a small bird.

tit² n. Informal a female breast.

Note that this word is mildly taboo and may give offence.

titanic *adj.* of enormous size.

titanium *n.* a metallic element. *Symbol*: Ti

titbit *n.* a choice or delicate bit, especially of food.

tithe *n.* (*oft. pl.*) the tenth part of the annual produce of agriculture, etc., due or paid as a tax.

titian /ˈtɪʃən, ti-/ *n.* a reddish-brown colour.

titillate *v.* **1.** to tickle. **2.** to excite agreeably.

title *n.* **1.** the distinguishing name of a book, piece of music, etc. **2.** a name given to a person by right of rank, office, attainment, etc. **3.** *Sport* the championship. **4.** established or recognised right to something. **5.** *Law* (legal document giving the) right to the possession of property.

titter *v.* to laugh in a low, half-restrained way, as from nervousness or in ill-suppressed amusement.

tittle-tattle *n.* gossip.

titular *adj.* **1.** relating to a title. **2.** existing in title only.

tix *pl. n. Informal* tickets.

tizz *n. Informal* a state of somewhat hysterical confusion and anxiety, often expressed in frantic but ineffectual activity.

tizzy *adj.* (**-zier, -ziest**) *Informal* excessively decorated; gaudy: *a tizzy hat.*

to *prep.* **1.** expressing motion or direction towards something. **2.** expressing limit of movement or extent: *rotten to the core.* **3.** expressing a point in time: *to this day.* **4.** expressing aim, or intention: *going to the rescue.* **5.** expressing limit in degree or amount: *goods to the value of $50.* **6.** indicating addition or amount: *adding insult to injury.* **7.** expressing comparison: *The score was 9 to 5.* **8.** expressing reference or relation: *What will he say to this?* **9.** expressing relative position: *next to the wall.* **10.** indicating proportion or ratio: *one teacher to every 30 students.* **11.** used as the ordinary sign or accompaniment of the infinitive. *–adv.* **12.** towards a person, thing, or point implied or

understood. **13.** to consciousness; to one's senses: *after he came to.*

Don't confuse this with **two**, which is the number after one, or with **too**, which means also (*Can I come too?*) or more than is needed (*There are too many people to count*).

toad *n.* an amphibian similar to a frog.

toadstool *n.* a usually poisonous fungus, similar to a mushroom.

toast¹ *n.* bread in slices browned on both surfaces by heat.

toast² *n.* **1.** words of congratulation, loyalty, etc., spoken before drinking. *–v.* **2.** to drink to the health of, or in honour of.

tobacco *n.* a plant whose leaves are prepared for smoking or chewing or as snuff.

toboggan *n.* a light sledge with low runners.

today *n.* **1.** this present day. *–adv.* **2.** on this present day.

toddle *v.* to go with short, unsteady steps, as a child. **–toddler** *n.*

toddy *n.* (*pl.* **-dies**) a warm, sweet, alcoholic drink.

to-do *n.* (*pl.* **to-dos**) bustle; fuss.

toe *n.* **1.** (in humans) one of the digits of the foot. **2.** an analogous part in other animals. **3.** something like a toe in shape or position.

toff *n. Informal* (*usually derog.*) a rich, upper-class, usually well-dressed person.

toffee *n.* a sweet made of boiled sugar or treacle, often with butter, nuts, etc.

tofu *n.* a curd made from white soybeans; bean curd.

toga *n.* the loose outer garment of the citizens of ancient Rome.

together *adv.* **1.** in(to) one gathering, place, or body. **2.** at the same time. **3.** in cooperation. *–adj.* **4.** capable and calm.

toggle *n.* a transverse pin, etc., placed through an eye of a rope, etc., for various purposes.

togs *pl. n. Informal* **1.** clothes. **2.** → **swimming costume.**

toil *n.* **1.** hard and continuous work. *–v.* **2.** to engage in exhausting and continuous work.

toilet *n.* **1. a.** an apparatus for the disposal of urine and faeces, usually consisting of a bowl connected to a drainage system and with a device for flushing water. **b.** a room containing such an apparatus. **2.** the process of dressing, including bathing, arranging the hair, etc.

toiletry *n.* (*pl.* **-ries**) an article or substance used in dressing or hygiene.

token *n.* **1.** something serving to represent or indicate some fact, event, feeling, etc.; sign. **2.** a characteristic mark or indication; symbol. **3.** a ticket, metal disc, etc. used instead of money for ferry fares, etc.

told *v.* **1.** past tense and past participle of **tell.** *–phr.* **2. all told,** in all.

tolerant *adj.* **1.** willing to put up with behaviour or conditions which doesn't like or agree with. **2.** willing to accept other people's beliefs and customs. **–tolerance,** *n.*

tolerate *v.* **1.** to allow; permit. **2.** to put up with. **3.** *Med.* to endure or resist the action of (a drug, poison, etc.). **–tolerable,** *adj.* **–toleration,** *n.*

toll¹ *v.* (of a bell) to (cause to) sound with slow, regular, single strokes.

toll² *n.* **1.** Also, **tollage.** a payment exacted by the government for the right to travel along a road. **2.** cost etc., especially in terms of death or loss.

tomahawk *n.* a small, short-handled axe.

tomato *n.* (*pl.* **-toes**) a widely cultivated plant bearing a slightly acid, pulpy, red, edible fruit.

tomb *n.* an excavation in earth or rock to receive a corpse.

tomboy *n.* an adventurous, athletic girl.

tombstone *n.* a stone, usually bearing an inscription, set to mark a tomb or grave.

tome *n.* a book, especially a large or scholarly one.

tomfoolery *n.* foolish or silly behaviour.

tomorrow *n.* **1.** the day after this day. *–adv.* **2.** on the day after this day.

tom-tom *n.* a type of drum.

ton /tʌn/ *n.* a unit of mass in the imperial system equal to about 1016 kg.

The imperial measure **ton** is commonly confused with the metric measure **tonne** (pronounced /tɒn/).

tone *n.* **1.** any sound considered with reference to its quality, pitch, strength, source, etc. **2.** quality or character of sound. **3.** intonation of the voice. **4.** *Music* an interval equivalent to 2 semitones. **5.** a tint or shade of colour. **6.** *Physiol.* the state of firmness proper to the organs or tissues of the body. **7.** style, distinction, or elegance. *–v.* **8.** to sound with a particular tone. **9.** to give the proper tone to. **10.** to modify the tone or character of. *–phr.* **11. tone (in) with,** to harmonise in tone or colour. **–tonal,** *adj.*

tongs *pl. n.* an implement with 2 arms fastened together, for holding something.

tongue *n.* **1.** an organ situated in the mouth of humans and most vertebrates, responsible for taste, and, in humans, articulate speech. **2.** the power of speech. **3.** the language of a particular people, country, or locality. **4.** something like an animal's tongue in shape, position, or function.

tonic *n.* **1.** a strengthening medicine. **2.** anything invigorating physically, mentally, or morally. **3.** *Music* the first note of the scale; keynote. *–adj.* **4.** restoring the tone or healthy condition of the body, as a medicine. **5.** invigorating physically, mentally, or morally.

tonight *n.* **1.** this present or coming night. *–adv.* **2.** on this present night.

tonne /tɒn/ *n.* a measure of mass in the metric system, equal to 1000 kilograms. *Symbol:* t

The metric measure **tonne** is commonly confused with the imperial measure **ton** (pronounced /tʌn/).

tonsil n. Anat. either of 2 masses of lymphoid tissue at the back of the throat.

tonsillitis /tonsə'laɪtəs/ n. inflammation of the tonsils.

tonsure n. the shaving of the head as a religious rite.

too adv. **1.** in addition; also: *young, clever, and rich too.* **2.** to an excessive degree: *too long.*

Don't confuse this with **two**, which is the number after one, or with **to**, which is a common word often used to indicate movement in some direction (*I went to the shops*).

took v. past tense of **take**.

tool n. **1.** a (handheld) instrument for performing mechanical operations, as a hammer, saw, etc. **2.** a person used by another for that person's own ends. **3.** *Informal* a stupid person. –v. **4.** to work with a tool.

toolbar n. *Computers* a rectangular bar, usually at the top of a computer screen, containing buttons marked with icons or words which enable specific computer functions.

toot v. to (cause to) sound, as a horn.

tooth n. (pl. **teeth** /tiːθ/) **1.** (in most vertebrates) one of the hard bodies set in a row to each jaw, used for chewing, etc. **2.** any projection like a tooth.

toothpaste n. a preparation for cleaning teeth in the form of paste.

top[1] n. **1.** the highest point or part of anything; summit. **2.** the highest position, rank, etc.: *the top of the class.* **3.** the highest pitch, or degree: *the top of one's voice.* **4.** a covering or lid. **5.** a garment which covers the torso. –adj. **6.** highest; uppermost; upper. **7.** greatest. **8.** foremost or principal. **9.** *Informal* the best; excellent. –v. (**topped, topping**) **10.** to put a top on. **11.** to be at the top of. **12.** to reach the top of. **13.** to surpass. **14.** to remove the top of; prune.

top[2] n. → **spinning top**.

topaz n. a gem stone occurring in crystals of various colours.

topiary adj. (of hedges, trees, etc.) clipped into shapes.

topic n. a subject of conversation or discussion.

topical adj. **1.** relating to current or local interest. **2.** relating to the subject of a discourse, etc.

topography n. the geographical features of an area. –**topographic**, adj.

topple v. to fall forwards from having too heavy a top.

topsoil n. the upper layer of the soil.

topsy-turvy adj. upside down; inverted; reversed.

top-up n. a further supply of something, usually a liquid, to replenish a container.

torch n. **1.** a small portable electric lamp powered by dry batteries. **2.** a flame carried in the hand to give light. **3.** a device which burns gas to produce a hot flame used for soldering, etc.

tore v. past tense of **tear**[2].

toreador /'toriədɔ/ n. a bullfighter.

torment v. **1.** to afflict with great bodily or mental suffering. –n. **2.** a state or source of great bodily or mental suffering; agony; misery.

torn v. past participle of **tear**[2].

tornado n. (pl. **-does** or **-dos**) a violent whirlwind.

torpedo n. (pl. **-does** or **-dos**) **1.** a self-propelled cigar-shaped missile containing explosives. –v. (**-doed, -doing**) **2.** to damage, or destroy with a torpedo.

torpid adj. slow or lethargic.

torpor n. lethargy; apathy.

torque n. *Mechanics* that which produces torsion or rotation.

torrent n. a stream of water flowing with great rapidity and violence. –**torrential**, adj.

torrid *adj.* **1.** (of regions) oppressively hot or burning. **2.** ardent; passionate.

torsion *n.* the act or result of twisting.

torso *n.* (*pl.* **-sos**) the trunk of the human body.

tort *n.* *Law* **1.** any wrong other than a criminal wrong, as negligence, defamation, etc. **2.** (*pl.*) the field of study of torts.

tortoise *n.* a slow-moving, land-dwelling reptile, with a hard shell covering its body and with toed feet rather than flippers. —**tortoiseshell**, *adj.*, *n.*

Compare this with **turtle**. Turtles have flippers and live in the sea.

tortuous *adj.* **1.** full of twists, turns, or bends. **2.** not straightforward.

The more usual word is **winding**.

torture *n.* **1.** the act of inflicting excruciating pain. **2.** agony of body or mind. —*v.* **3.** to subject to torture. —**torturous**, *adj.*

toss *v.* **1.** to throw, especially lightly or carelessly. **2.** to pitch, rock, sway: *to toss on rough seas.* **3.** to move restlessly about. **4.** to throw a coin to decide something according to which side falls face up. —*n.* **5.** the act of tossing.

tosser *n.* someone or something that tosses. **2.** *Informal* a stupid person.

total *adj.* **1.** entire; whole. **2.** complete; absolute. —*n.* **3.** the total amount; sum. —*v.* (**-talled, -talling**) **4.** to add up (to).

totalisator *n.* a form of betting, as on horseraces, in which those who bet on the winners divide the bets or stakes, less a percentage for the management, taxes, etc.

totalitarian *adj.* of or relating to a centralised government in which those in control grant neither recognition nor tolerance to parties of differing opinion.

totality *n.* (*pl.* **-ties**) **1.** the entirety. **2.** total amount; whole.

tote *v.* *Informal* to carry.

totem *n.* an object or natural phenomenon, often an animal, assumed as the emblem of a clan, family, etc. —**totemic**, *adj.*

totter *v.* **1.** to walk falteringly or weakly. **2.** to sway or rock, as if about to fall.

toucan *n.* a strikingly coloured bird with a huge beak.

touch *v.* **1.** to put the hand, etc., on (something) to feel it. **2.** to come into or be in contact with (something). **3.** to give rise to some emotion in (someone). **4.** *Informal* to apply to for money. **5.** to speak or write (*on* or *upon*) briefly or casually. —*n.* **6.** the act of touching. **7.** that sense by which anything is perceived by means of the contact with the body. **8.** the sensation caused by touching something, regarded as a quality of the thing. **9.** a slight stroke or blow. **10.** a slight attack, as of illness or disease. **11.** manner of execution in artistic work. **12.** a slight amount.

touchpad *n.* **1.** a control panel used to operate an appliance. **2.** *Computers* a small, pressure-sensitive pad on some computers, used to control the cursor.

touchy *adj.* (**-chier, -chiest**) **1.** easily annoyed or offended. **2.** likely to give rise to strong emotions: *a touchy subject; a touchy situation.*

tough *adj.* **1.** not easily broken or cut. **2.** (of food) difficult to cut or chew. **3.** capable of great endurance. **4.** difficult to perform, accomplish, or deal with. **5.** vigorous; severe; violent.

Note that **hard** and **tough** are close in meaning. The difference is that **hard** usually refers to the surface of a thing or how it feels to the touch, while **tough** usually refers to the strength of something or how hard it is to break.

toupee *n.* a wig worn to cover a bald spot.

tour *v.* **1.** to travel from place to place. —*n.* **2.** a journey to a place or places. **3.** *Chiefly Mil.* a period of duty at one place.

tourism *n.* the provision of local services, as entertainment, lodging, food, etc., for tourists.

tourist *n.* someone who tours, especially for pleasure.

tournament *n.* a meeting for contests in athletic or other sports.

tourniquet /ˈtɔːnəkeɪ, ˈtʊə-/ *n.* any device for stopping bleeding by forcibly compressing a blood vessel.

tousle *v.* to disorder or dishevel.

tout *v.* **1.** to solicit business, votes, etc., persistently. **2.** *Racing* to sell betting information, take bets, etc. −*n.* **3.** someone who touts.

tow *v.* **1.** to pull (a boat, car, etc.) with a rope or chain. −*n.* **2.** the act of towing.

towards *prep.* **1.** in the direction of. **2.** with respect to. **3.** as a help or contribution to. Also, **toward**.

towel *n.* a cloth for wiping and drying something wet.

towelling *n.* any absorbent fabric used for towels, beachwear, etc.

tower *n.* **1.** a tall, narrow structure. **2.** any tower-like objects. −*v.* **3.** to extend far upwards. −*phr.* **4. tower over** (or **above**), **a.** to be higher and taller than. **b.** to surpass, as in ability, etc.

town *n.* **1.** a distinct densely populated area, usually smaller than a city. **2.** urban life, opposed to rural. **3.** the main shopping, business, or entertainment centre of a large town, contrasted with the suburbs. **4.** the people of a town.

town hall *n.* a building used for the transaction of a town's business, etc.

township *n.* a small town or settlement.

toxic *adj.* **1.** of, relating to, affected with, or caused by a toxin or poison. **2.** poisonous. **3.** detrimental to a good outcome; extremely disadvantageous. −**toxicity** /tɒkˈsɪsəti/, *n.* −**toxically**, *adv.*

toxic debt *n.* debt which, although initially acquired as a legitimate business transaction, proves subsequently to be financially worthless.

toxin *n.* **1.** a poison produced by a disease-producing microorganism. **2.** any of various organic poisons.

toy *n.* **1.** a (children's) plaything. −*v.* **2.** of or like a toy, especially in size. −*v.* **3.** to act idly or absent-mindedly. **4.** to trifle (*with*).

trace¹ *n.* **1.** a mark or evidence of the former existence, or action of something; a vestige. **2.** a very small amount. **3.** a record traced by a self-registering instrument. −*v.* (**traced**, **tracing**) **4.** to follow the footprints, track, or traces of. **5.** to follow the course or development of. **6.** to copy (a drawing, plan, etc.) by following the lines of the original on a superimposed transparent sheet. **7.** to make a plan, diagram, or map of.

trace² *n.* each of the 2 straps by which a carriage, etc. is drawn by a horse, etc.

tracery *n.* any delicate interlacing work of lines, threads, etc.

trachea /trəˈkiə/ *n.* (*pl.* **-cheas** or **-cheae** /-ˈkiiː/) the main tube which conveys air to and from the lungs; windpipe.

track *n.* **1.** a rough path, or trail. **2.** a railway line. **3.** the mark, or series of marks, left by anything that has passed along. **4.** an endless jointed metal band around the wheels of some heavy vehicles. **5.** a course of action or conduct. **6.** a course laid out for racing. **7.** one of the distinct sections of compact disc, gramophone record, etc., having one song or division of a piece of music. −*v.* **8.** to hunt by following the tracks of. **9.** to follow (a track, course, etc.). −*phr.* **10. track down**, to catch or find, after pursuit or searching.

track record *n.* an account of successes or failures in a specific field.

tracksuit *n.* a loose, two-piece overgarment worn by athletes.

tract¹ *n.* a stretch or extent, as of land, water, etc.

tract² *n.* a brief treatise, especially one dealing with religion.

tractable adj. easily managed, or docile.

traction n. 1. the act of drawing or pulling. 2. the adhesive friction which stops a body from slipping, as a tyre on the road.

tractor n. a motor vehicle, usually having tyres with deep treads, used to draw farm implements.

trade n. 1. the buying and selling, or exchanging, of goods within a country or between countries. 2. market: *the tourist trade*. 3. commercial occupation (as against professional). 4. a skilled occupation, especially one requiring manual labour. –v. 5. to carry on trade. 6. to exchange; barter. –phr. 7. **trade in**, to give in part exchange: *to trade in an old car on a new one*.

trademark n. the exclusive symbol, mark, etc. used by a manufacturer to distinguish their own goods from those manufactured by others.

trade name n. 1. the name under which a firm does business. 2. a word or phrase used to designate a business or a particular class of goods but which is not technically a trademark. 3. Also, **brand name**. the name by which an article is known to the trade.

trade-off n. a concession made in a negotiation in return for one given.

trade union n. an organisation of employees for mutual aid and protection, and for dealing collectively with employers. Also, **trades union**. –**trade unionism**, n. –**trade unionist**, n.

Trade union is a collective noun and can be used with a singular or plural verb. Look up **collective noun**.

tradition n. the handing down of beliefs, legends, customs, etc., from generation to generation, especially by word of mouth or by practice. –**traditional**, adj. –**traditionally**, adv.

traditional custodian n. a person who is entitled, by Indigenous tradition, to have certain cultural knowledge.

traffic n. 1. the coming and going of persons, vehicles, ships, etc., along a way of passage or travel. 2. (commercial) dealings between parties, people etc. –v. (**-ficked, -ficking**) 3. to carry on dealings, especially of an illicit or improper kind.

tragedy n. (pl. **-dies**) 1. a serious dramatic composition with an unhappy ending. 2. a disaster or calamity.

tragic adj. 1. characteristic or suggestive of tragedy. 2. dreadful, calamitous, or fatal. –n. 3. *Informal* someone who is excessively devoted to a particular celebrity, sport, hobby, etc.: *a cricket tragic*. –**tragically**, adv.

trail v. 1. to draw or be drawn along the ground or behind. 2. to hang down loosely from something. 3. to follow, especially slowly. –n. 4. a track made over rough country, by the passage of people or animals. 5. the track or scent left by an animal, person, or thing, especially as followed in pursuit.

Don't confuse this with **trial**, which is a testing of someone's guilt or innocence in a law court.

trail bike n. → dirt bike.

trailblazer n. 1. a person who blazes a trail. 2. a leader or innovator in a particular field. –**trailblazing**, adj., n. –**trailblaze**, v.

trailer n. 1. a vehicle designed to be towed by a motor vehicle, and used in transporting loads. 2. *Film* an advertisement for a forthcoming film, usually consisting of extracts from it.

train n. 1. *Railways* a series of carriages or wagons, whether self-propelled or connected to a locomotive. 2. a procession of persons, vehicles, etc. 3. a long, trailing part of a skirt or dress. 4. a succession of circumstances, etc. 5. a succession of connected ideas. –v. 6. to educate (a person) or become educated in some art, profession, or work. 7. to make or become fit by proper exercise, diet, etc., as for some athletic feat or contest. 8. to discipline and instruct (an animal) to perform specified actions.

rainee n. **1.** a person receiving training. *–adj.* **2.** receiving training.

rainer n. **1.** someone who trains others in a particular skill or activity. **2.** someone who prepares racehorses for racing. **3.** someone who trains athletes in a sport. **4.** equipment used in training, especially that which simulates the conditions of a sport. **5.** a shoe which is designed for use in sport.

train wreck n. **1.** the wreck of a train. **2.** *Informal* a complete disaster: *Her life is a train wreck.*

traipse v. to walk (about) aimlessly.

trait /treɪt, treɪ/ n. a distinguishing feature.

> Don't confuse this with **tray**, which is a flat piece of wood, plastic or metal used for carrying things.

traitor n. **1.** someone who betrays a person, a cause, or any trust. **2.** someone who betrays their country. *–traitorous, adj.*

trajectory n. (pl. **-ries**) the curved flight path of a projectile.

tram n. a passenger vehicle moving on tracks laid in urban streets. Also, **tramcar.**

trammel n. (usu. pl.) a restraint.

tramp v. **1.** to walk with a firm, heavy, resounding step. **2.** to go about as a vagrant. *–n.* **3.** the act of tramping. **4.** a person who travels about on foot from place to place, especially a vagrant living on occasional jobs or gifts of money or food.

trample v. to tread heavily, roughly, or carelessly on or over.

trampoline n. a canvas springboard attached to a horizontal frame used when performing acrobatics.

trance n. **1.** a dazed or bewildered condition. **2.** a state of complete mental absorption. **3.** an unconscious hypnotic condition.

tranquil adj. **1.** peaceful; quiet; calm. **2.** unaffected by disturbing emotions.

–tranquillity, n. –tranquillise, tranquillize, v.

transact v. to carry through (affairs, business, negotiations, etc.) to settlement. *–transaction, n.*

transcend v. to go or be above or beyond; surpass or exceed. *–transcendent, adj.*

transcendental adj. transcending ordinary experience, thought, or belief.

transcribe v. **1.** to reproduce in writing or print (as from speech, etc.). **2.** to write out in other characters. *–transcript, n. –transcription, n.*

trans fat n. fat composed of trans fatty acid.

trans fatty acid n. a type of unsaturated fat occurring naturally in meat and dairy products but also created in the production of margarine; thought to increase the risk of coronary heart disease.

transfer v. **1.** to convey or remove from one place, person, etc., to another. *–n.* **2.** the means, system or act of transferring. **3.** a drawing, pattern, etc., which may be transferred to a surface, especially by direct contact. **4.** *Law* a conveyance, by sale, gift, or otherwise, of real or personal property, to another. *–transferable, adj. –transference, n. –transferral, n.*

transfigure v. to change in outward form or appearance.

transfix v. **1.** to pierce through, (as) with a pointed weapon. **2.** to make motionless with amazement, terror, etc.

transform v. to change in appearance, condition, nature, or character, especially completely or extensively. *–transformation, n. –transformative, adj.*

transformer n. a device which transforms electric energy from circuit to circuit, usually also changing voltage and current.

transfuse v. **1.** to pour from one container into another. **2.** *Med.* to transfer (blood) from the veins or arteries of one person or animal into those of another. *–transfusion, n.*

transgender *adj.* of or relating to a person whose gender identity is different from their physiological gender as designated at birth.

transgress *v.* to go beyond the limits imposed by (a law, command, etc.). –**transgression**, *n.*

transient *adj.* **1.** not lasting or enduring. **2.** temporary. –*n.* **3.** someone or something that is transient. –**transience**, *n.*

For def. 1, the more usual word is **passing**.

transistor *n.* **1.** *Electronics* a miniature solid-state device for amplifying or switching. **2.** a radio equipped with transistors.

transit *n.* passage or conveyance from one place to another. –**transitional**, *adj.*

transition *n.* passage from one position, state, stage, etc., to another. –**transitional**, *adj.*

The more usual word is **change**.

transitive verb *n.* **1.** a verb which can only be used with a direct object. **2.** a verb used with a direct object, as *drink* in the sentence *he drinks water* where *water* is the direct object.

Compare this with **intransitive verb**, such as *come*, which does not need an object.

transitory *adj.* passing away; not lasting or permanent.

translate *v.* **1.** to turn (something written or spoken) from one language into another. **2.** to interpret; explain. –**translation**, *n.*

translucent *adj.* transmitting light imperfectly, as frosted glass.

Compare this with **opaque**, which describes something that you cannot see through at all, and **transparent**, which describes something that you can see clearly through.

transmission *n.* **1.** the act of transmitting. **2.** that which is transmitted. **3.** *Machinery* a device for transmitting power from the engine to the wheels of a motor vehicle.

transmit *v.* (-mitted, -mitting) **1.** to send over or along, as to a person or place. **2.** to communicate, as information, news, etc. **3.** to broadcast (a radio or television program). **4.** to allow (heat, light, etc.) to pass through.

transom *n.* a lintel.

transparency *n.* (*pl.* **-cies**) **1.** Also, **transparence**. the property or quality of being transparent. **2.** a transparent positive photographic image used for projection onto a screen.

transparent *adj.* **1.** transmitting light perfectly so that bodies situated beyond can be distinctly seen. **2.** open, frank, or candid. **3.** easily seen through or understood.

Compare def. 1 with **opaque**, which describes something that you cannot see through at all, and **translucent**, which describes something that you can see through, but not clearly.

transpire *v.* **1.** to occur or happen. **2.** to emit waste matter, etc., through the surface, as of the body, of leaves, etc.

transplant *v.* **1.** to remove (a plant) from one place and plant it in another. **2.** *Surg.* to transfer (an organ or a portion of tissue) from one part of the body to another or from one person or animal to another. –*n.* **3.** a transplanting. **4.** something transplanted.

transport *v.* **1.** to carry from one place to another. **2.** to carry away by strong emotion. –*n.* **3.** the act, method, or system of transporting or conveying. **4.** a means of transporting, as a ship, large truck, aeroplane, etc. **5.** strong emotion, as ecstatic joy, bliss, etc. –**transportation**, *n.*

transpose *v.* **1.** to alter the relative position or order of: *to transpose the letters in a word*. **2.** to cause (2 or more things) to change places. **3.** *Music* to reproduce in a different key.

ranssexual n. someone who has undergone a sex change operation. Also, **transsexual**.

ransverse adj. lying or being in a crosswise direction.

ransvestism n. the desire to wear clothing typical of the opposite sex. –**transvestite**, n., adj.

trap n. 1. a device used for catching game or other animals. 2. any stratagem for catching someone unawares. 3. a device for preventing the passage of steam, water, etc. 4. a light two-wheeled carriage. –v. (**trapped, trapping**) 5. to catch in a trap.

trapdoor n. a door, etc., cut into the surface of a floor, ceiling, etc.

trapeze n. an apparatus for gymnastics, consisting of a short horizontal bar attached to the ends of 2 suspended ropes.

trapezium n. (pl. **-ziums** or **-zia** /-ziǝ/) a four-sided plane figure in which only one pair of opposite sides is parallel.

trapezoid n. Geom. 1. (especially in the UK) a quadrilateral plane figure of which no two sides are parallel. 2. (especially in the US) a quadrilateral plane figure of which two sides are parallel.

trappings pl. n. (ornamental) articles of equipment or dress.

trash n. 1. anything worthless or useless; rubbish. –v. Informal 2. to destroy utterly, especially as an act of vandalism. 3. to subject to scathing criticism.

trauma n. (pl. **-mas** or **-mata** /-mǝtǝ/) 1. a bodily injury. 2. Psychol. a shock which has a lasting effect on mental life. –**traumatic**, adj.

travail n. (painful) physical or mental exertion.

travel v. (**-elled, -elling**) 1. to move or go from one place to another. –n. 2. journeying, especially in distant or foreign places. 3. (pl.) journeys. 4. Machinery the complete movement of a moving part in one direction, or the distance traversed. –**traveller**, n.

traverse v. 1. to pass across, over, or through. 2. to go to and fro over or along. 3. Law to deny formally, in pleading at law. –n. 4. the act of traversing. 5. something that obstructs or thwarts. 6. a place where one may cross. –adj. 7. transverse.

travesty n. (pl. **-ties**) any grotesque or debased imitation.

trawl n. Also, **trawl net**. 1. a strong net dragged along the sea bottom to catch fish. –v. 2. to fish with a trawl 3. to troll.

tray n. a flat piece of wood, metal, etc., with slightly raised edges used for carrying things.

> Don't confuse this with **trait**, which can be pronounced the same as **tray**. A trait is a particular characteristic or quality.

treachery n. (pl. **-ries**) betrayal of trust; treason. –**treacherous**, adj.

treacle n. the dark, sticky syrup obtained in refining sugar.

tread v. (**trod, trodden** or **trod, treading**) 1. to step or walk on, about, in, or along. 2. to trample underfoot. 3. to domineer harshly; crush. –n. 4. (the sound of) treading, stepping, or walking. 5. manner of treading or walking. 6. a single step as in walking. 7. the horizontal upper surface of a step. 8. that part of a tyre, etc., which touches the road, etc.

treadle n. a lever or the like worked by the foot to set a machine in motion.

treadmill n. 1. a machine with a continuous, rotating track for walking or running on. 2. a monotonous or wearisome round, as of work or life.

treason n. violation by a subject of allegiance to his or her sovereign or to the state; high treason.

treasure n. 1. accumulated riches, especially precious metals or money. 2. any thing or person greatly valued. –v. 3. to regard as precious; cherish.

treasurer n. 1. someone who has charge of the funds of a company, private society, or the like. **2.** (*upper case*) government minister responsible for the Treasury.

treasury *n.* (*pl.* **-ries**) **1.** a place where public money, or the funds of a company, etc., are kept. **2.** (*upper case*) the department of government which has control over public revenue.

treat *v.* **1.** to act towards in some specified way: *to treat someone kindly.* **2.** to deal with: *to treat a matter as unimportant.* **3.** to subject to some, usually chemical, agent in order to bring about a particular result. **4.** to discuss terms of settlement, or negotiate. *–n.* **5.** anything that gives particular pleasure. **6.** one's turn to pay, as for a joint outing, etc. *–***treatment***, n.*

treatise /'tritəs/ *n.* a book or writing on some particular subject.

treaty *n.* (*pl.* **-ties**) a formal agreement between 2 or more independent states in reference to peace, alliance, commerce, etc.

treble *adj.* **1.** *Music* of the highest pitch or range. **2.** three times as much as; triple. *–n.* **3.** *Music* a high-pitched voice or sound. *–v.* (**-bled, -bling**) **4.** to become 3 times as great; triple.

tree *n.* a perennial plant having a woody, self-supporting main stem or trunk, usually growing to a considerable height, and usually developing branches at some distance from the ground.

trek *n.* a journey, especially a difficult one on foot.

trellis *n.* a lattice.

tremble *v.* **1.** (of persons, the body, etc.) to shake with quick, short, involuntary movements, as from fear, excitement, weakness, cold, etc. **2.** to be tremulous, as light, sound, etc.

tremendous *adj.* **1.** extraordinarily great in size, amount, degree, etc. **2.** extraordinary; unusual; remarkable.

tremor *n.* **1.** involuntary shaking of the body or limbs, as from fear, weakness, etc. **2.** a vibration. **3.** a trembling or quivering

effect, as of light, etc. **4.** a tremulou[s] sound or note.

tremulous *adj.* **1.** (of persons, the body etc.) characterised by trembling. **2.** (c[] things) vibratory or quivering.

trench *n.* a deep furrow, ditch, or cut.

trenchant *adj.* incisive or cutting, as lan[] guage or a person.

trencher *n.* → **mortarboard**

trend *n.* **1.** the general course, drift, o[r] tendency. **2.** style; fashion. *–v.* **3.** (of topic on a social network) to appear at an increasingly high level of frequency[] *–***trendy***, adj.*

trepidation *n.* tremulous alarm or agitation[]

The more usual word is **fear**.

trespass *n.* **1.** *Law* **a.** an unlawful ac[t] causing injury to the person, property, o[] rights of another, committed with force or violence. **b.** a wrongful entry upon the lands of another. **2.** an encroachment o[] intrusion. *–v.* **3.** to commit trespass.

tress *n.* (*usu. pl.*) any long lock of hair.

trestle *n.* a supporting frame, usually con[] sisting of a horizontal beam or bar fixed a[] each end to a pair of spreading legs.

trevally *n.* (*pl.* **-ly** or **-lies**) a sport and food fish.

For information about the different plural forms, see the note at **fish**.

triad *n.* **1.** a group of 3. **2.** a Chinese secret[] criminal organisation.

triage /'triaʒ/ *n.* the sorting of casualties according to the urgency of treatmen[t] required.

trial *n.* **1.** *Law* **a.** the examination in a cour[t] of law of the facts of a case. **b.** the determination of a person's guilt or innocenc[e] by a court. **2.** the act of trying or testing **3.** a contest. **4.** an attempt to do something. **5.** an experiment. **6.** an affliction or trouble. *–v.* (**trialled, trialling**) **7.** to put ([] plan, procedure, etc.) into operation, often on a small scale, to test its feasibility.

Don't confuse this with **trail**, which is a path made through rough country.

triangle n. **1.** a three-sided plane figure. **2.** Music a triangular percussion instrument. –**triangular**, adj.

triathlon n. an athletic contest comprising 3 events, usually swimming, cycling, and running, one immediately after the other. –**triathlete**, n.

tribe n. a group of people united by such features as descent, language or land ownership. –**tribal**, adj.

Tribe is a collective noun and can be used with a singular or plural verb. Look up **collective noun**. Because this word has been associated with negative attitudes to traditional societies, in some cases, other words such as *people(s)* or *community* are preferable.

tribulation n. grievous trouble.

tribunal n. **1.** a body set up to investigate and resolve disputes. **2.** a court of justice. **3.** a place or seat of judgement.

tributary n. (pl. **-ries**) **1.** a stream flowing into a larger stream or other body of water. –adj. **2.** contributory; auxiliary. **3.** paying or required to pay tribute.

tribute n. **1.** a personal offering given as if due, in acknowledgement of gratitude or esteem etc. **2.** an enforced payment made by one sovereign or state to another as the price of peace, security, etc.

triceps /ˈtraɪsɛps/ n. Anat. a muscle at the back of the upper arm.

trick n. **1.** a crafty or fraudulent expedient. **2.** the knack of doing something. **3.** a clever or dexterous feat, as for exhibition or entertainment. **4.** Cards the cards which are played and won in one round. –v. **5.** to deceive by trickery. –**trickery**, n.

trickle v. **1.** to flow or fall by drops, or in a small, gentle stream. **2.** to come, go, pass, or proceed by bit, slowly, irregularly, etc. –n. **3.** a trickling flow or stream.

tricky adj. (**-kier**, **-kiest**) **1.** given to or characterised by deceitful or clever tricks; clever; wily. **2.** deceptive, requiring careful handling or action. –**trickily**, adv. –**trickiness**, n.

tricycle n. a cycle with 3 wheels.

trident n. a three-pronged instrument or weapon.

tried v. past tense and past participle of **try**.

trifle n. **1.** something of small value, amount or importance. **2.** a dessert of sponge, jelly, cream, etc. –v. **3.** to deal lightly or without due seriousness or respect (with). –**trifling**, adj.

trigger n. **1.** (in firearms) a small projecting piece which, when pressed by the finger, discharges the weapon. –v. **2.** to start (off) (something), as a chain of events.

trigonometry n. the branch of mathematics that deals with the relation between the sides and angles of triangles and the calculations, etc., based on these.

trill v. **1.** to resound vibrantly, or with a rapid succession of sounds, as the voice, song, laughter, etc. **2.** to perform a trill with the voice or on a musical instrument. –n. **3.** the act or sound of trilling.

trilogy n. (pl. **-gies**) a group of 3 related dramas, operas, novels, etc.

trim v. (**trimmed**, **trimming**) **1.** to reduce to an orderly state by clipping, paring, pruning, etc. **2.** to modify (opinions, actions) according to expediency. **3.** to decorate with ornaments, garnish, etc. **4.** proper condition or order. **5.** dress, array, or equipment. **6.** material used for decoration. **7.** a trimming by cutting, clipping, or the like. **8. a.** the upholstery, knobs, handles, etc., inside a motor car. **b.** ornamentation on the exterior of a motor car. –adj. (**trimmer**, **trimmest**) **9.** pleasingly neat or smart in appearance. **10.** in good condition or order. **11.** healthily slim.

trimaran /ˈtraɪməræn/ n. a boat with a main middle hull and 2 outer hulls.

trinity n. (pl. **-ties**) a group of 3; a triad.

trinket n. **1.** any small fancy article, bit of jewellery, etc., usually of little value. **2.** anything trifling.

trio n. (pl. **trios**) any group of 3 persons or things.

trip n. **1.** a journey. **2.** Informal a period under the influence of a hallucinatory drug. **3.** a stumble. –v. (**tripped**, **tripping**) **4.** to (cause to) stumble. **5.** to step lightly or nimbly. –phr. **6. trip up**, to (cause to) make a slip or error.

tripartite adj. consisting of 3 parts.

tripe n. **1.** part of the stomach of a ruminant, especially the ox, prepared for use as food. **2.** Informal anything poor or worthless, especially written work.

triple v. (**-pled, -pling**) **1.** to multiply by 3. –adj. **2.** having 3 parts. **3.** three times as great.

triplet n. **1.** one of 3 children born at one birth. **2.** any group or combination of 3. **3.** a thin bar of opal set between 2 layers of plastic, or one layer of potch and one of crystal.

triplicate adj. threefold; triple.

tripod n. a stool, stand, etc., with 3 legs, especially as for a camera.

triptych /ˈtrɪptɪk/ n. Art a set of 3 panels side by side, bearing pictures, carvings, or the like.

trite adj. made commonplace by constant use.

triumph n. **1.** victory; conquest. **2.** a notable achievement; striking success. –v. **3.** to achieve success. –**triumphal**, adj. –**triumphant**, adj.

trivia pl. n. **1.** unimportant, or inconsequential things; trivialities. **2.** inconsequential and often arcane items of information. –**trivial**, adj.

trochee /ˈtroʊki/ n. (in poetry) a group of 2 syllables, a long followed by a short, or an accented followed by an unaccented. –**trochaic** /troʊˈkeɪɪk/, adj.

trod v. past tense and past participle of **tread**.

trodden v. past participle of **tread**.

troll[1] v. **1.** to fish with a moving line, as one trailed behind a boat. **2.** Internet to behave in the manner of a troll (def. 3). –n. **3.** Internet someone who posts messages in an internet discussion forum, chat room etc., that are designed to be upsetting.

troll[2] n. an imaginary being in fairytales either a dwarf or giant, who lives under ground.

trolley n. a kind of low cart.

trollop n. **1.** an untidy or slovenly woman. **2.** a prostitute.

trombone n. a brass wind instrument consisting of a cylindrical metal tube expanding into a bell and bent twice in U shape, usually equipped with a slide. –**trombonist**, n.

troop n. **1.** a company or band of persons or things. **2.** (pl.) a body of soldiers, marines, etc. –v. **3.** to walk as if on a march.

trophy n. (pl. **-phies**) anything taken in war, hunting, etc., especially when preserved as a memento; a spoil or prize.

tropic n. **1.** Geog. either of 2 corresponding parallels of latitude on the terrestrial globe, one (**tropic of Cancer**) about 23½° north, and the other (**tropic of Capricorn**) about 23½° south of the equator, being the boundaries of the Torrid Zone. –phr. **2. the tropics**, the regions lying between and near these parallels of latitude. –**tropical**, adj.

tropical rainforest n. rainforest occurring in tropical areas. Compare **temperate rainforest**.

trot v. (**trotted, trotting**) **1.** (of a horse etc.) to go at a gait between a walk and a run. **2.** to move briskly, bustle, or hurry. –n. **3.** a jogging gait between a walk and a run. –phr. **4. the trots, a.** races for trotting or pacing horses; a trotting meeting. **b.** Informal diarrhoea.

troth /troʊθ/ n. one's word or promise.

trotter n. **1.** a horse bred and trained for harness racing. **2.** the foot of an animal, especially of a sheep or pig, used as food.

troubadour n. a minstrel.

trouble v. **1.** to distress; worry. **2.** to put to inconvenience. –n. **3.** molestation, harassment, annoyance, or difficulty. **4.** misfortunes. **5.** disturbance; disorder; unrest. **6.** disturbance of mind, distress, or worry. –**troublesome**, adj.

trough n. **1.** an open, boxlike receptacle, usually long and narrow, as for holding water or food for animals. **2.** Meteorol. an elongated area of relatively low pressure.

trounce v. **1.** to beat or thrash severely. **2.** to defeat thoroughly.

troupe n. a company or band, especially of actors or singers.

trousers pl. n. an outer garment covering the lower part of the trunk and each leg separately, extending to the ankles.

trout n. (pl. **trout** or **trouts**) a game and food fish.

For information about the different plural forms, see the note at **fish**.

trowel n. **1.** a tool with a metal plate fitted into a short handle, used for spreading, shaping, or smoothing plaster, etc. **2.** a small garden spade.

truant n. a pupil who stays away from school without permission. –**truancy**, n.

truce n. (an agreement calling for) an end to fighting between armies for a period; an armistice.

truck¹ n. **1.** a motor vehicle with a back section for carrying goods, etc.; lorry. –v. **2.** to transport by truck.

truck² n. dealings.

truculent /ˈtrʌkjələnt/ adj. aggressive; belligerent.

trudge v. (**trudged**, **trudging**) to walk, especially laboriously or wearily.

true adj. (**truer**, **truest**) **1.** being in accordance with the actual state of things; not false. **2.** real or genuine. **3.** loyal; faithful; trusty. **4.** exact. **5.** legitimate.

6. accurately shaped or placed, as a surface, instrument, or part of a mechanism. **7.** Navig. (of a bearing) fixed in relation to the earth's axis rather than the magnetic poles. –adv. **8.** in a true manner; truly or truthfully. **9.** exactly or accurately. –**truly**, adv.

truffle n. **1.** a subterranean edible fungus. **2.** a type of confection.

truism n. a self-evident, obvious truth. –**truistic**, adj.

trump Cards –n. **1.** any playing card of a suit that ranks above the other suits. –v. **2.** to take with a trump.

trumpet n. **1.** a brass wind instrument consisting of a tube, once or twice curved round upon itself, with a cup-shaped mouthpiece at one end and a flaring bell at the other. –v. **2.** to sound on a trumpet.

truncate v. to shorten by cutting off a part.

truncheon n. a short club carried by a police officer.

trundle v. **1.** to roll (a ball, hoop, etc.). **2.** Informal to walk in a leisurely fashion.

trunk n. **1.** the main stem of a tree, as distinct from the branches and roots. **2.** a chest for holding clothes etc. as for use on a journey. **3.** the body of a human being or of an animal, excluding the head and limbs. **4.** (pl.) Obs. men's shorts, either tight-fitting or loose, worn by athletes, swimmers, etc. **5.** the long, flexible nose of the elephant.

trunk line n. a telephone line between 2 exchanges, which is used for long-distance calls.

truss v. **1.** to tie, bind, or fasten. –n. **2.** Building Trades, etc. a combination of beams, bars, ties, etc., so arranged as to form a rigid framework. **3.** Med. an apparatus for maintaining a hernia in a reduced state.

trust n. **1.** reliance on the integrity, justice, etc., of a person, or on some attribute of a thing; confidence. **2.** hope. **3.** the state of being relied on. **4.** the obligation imposed on one in whom confidence or authority is placed. **5.** *Law* **a.** a relationship in which one person (the trustee) holds the title to property for the benefit of another (the beneficiary). **b.** a fund of securities, cash or other assets, held by trustees on behalf of a number of investors. –*v.* **6.** to have trust or confidence (in); rely on. **7.** to expect confidently, hope (usually followed by a clause or an infinitive).

trustee *n. Law* **1.** a person appointed to administer the affairs of a company, institution, etc. **2.** a person who holds the title to property for the benefit of another.

trustworthy *adj.* reliable.

truth *n.* **1.** the true or actual facts of a case. **2.** a verified or indisputable fact, proposition, etc.

try *v.* (**tried, trying**) **1.** to attempt to do. **2.** to test the quality, accuracy, etc, of. **3.** *Law* to examine and determine in a court of law, the guilt or innocence of (a person). **4.** to put to a severe test; strain the endurance, etc., of. –*n.* (*pl.* **tries**) **5.** an attempt or effort. **6.** *Rugby Football* a score of 4 points (in Rugby League) or 5 points (in Rugby Union) earned by putting the ball down behind the opposing team's goal line.

When **try** is followed by another verb, you can sometimes use *to* or *and* between the two verbs: *I will try to come tomorrow; I will try and come tomorrow.* Some people think that *to* is more correct, but both are widely used and most people consider them both to be acceptable.

trying *adj.* annoying; distressing.

tryst /trɪst/ *n.* an appointment, especially between lovers.

tsar /zɑː/ *n.* **1.** an emperor or king. **2.** (*usu. upper case*) (formerly) the emperor of Russia. Also, **tzar, czar.**

T-shirt *n.* a lightweight, close-fitting top, usually short-sleeved and collarless. Also, **t-shirt, tee-shirt.**

tsunami /suˈnɑːmi, sə-, tsu-, tsə-/ *n.* a large, often destructive sea wave or series of waves caused by an underwater earthquake, etc.

tuan /ˈtjuən/ *n.* a small mouse-like marsupial, mostly tree-dwelling, with a hairy-tipped tail.

tub *n.* **1.** a large, open, flat-bottomed vessel used for bathing, washing clothes, etc. **2.** a vessel resembling a tub.

tuba *n.* a brass wind instrument of low pitch.

tubby *adj.* (**-bier, -biest**) short and fat.

tube *n.* **1.** a hollow, usually cylindrical body of metal, glass, rubber, etc., used for conveying or containing fluids, etc. **2.** a small, soft metal or plastic cylinder closed at one end and capped at the other, for holding paint, toothpaste, etc., to be squeezed out by pressure. –**tubular**, *adj.*

tuber *n. Bot.* a fleshy, long or rounded outgrowth (as the potato) of a subterranean stem.

tuberculosis *n.* an infectious disease, especially of the lungs.

The short form of this is **TB**.

tuck *v.* **1.** to thrust into some narrow or concealed space. **2.** to draw up in folds. –*n.* **3.** a tucked piece or part. **4.** *Sewing* a fold made by doubling cloth upon itself, and stitching along the edge of the fold.

tucker¹ *n. Aust., NZ Informal* food.

tucker² *v. Informal* to weary; tire (*out*).

tuckshop *n.* → **canteen** (def. 2).

tuft *n.* a bunch of grass, feathers, hairs, etc., fixed at the base while the upper part loose.

tug *v.* (**tugged, tugging**) to pull at forcefully.

tuition *n.* teaching or instruction.

tulip *n.* a plant with large, showy, cup-shaped or bell-shaped flowers.

tumble *v.* **1.** to roll or fall down as by losing footing. **2.** to fall rapidly, as stock market prices. –*n.* **3.** a fall. **4.** disorder or confusion.

tummy n. (pl. **-mies**) Informal (usually with children) stomach.

tumour n. an abnormal swelling in any part of the body. Also, **tumor**.

tumult n. **1.** the noisy disturbance of a multitude; an uproar. **2.** a mental or emotional disturbance. –**tumultuous**, adj.

tuna n. (pl. **tuna** or **tunas**) a large, fast-swimming, marine food fish.

For information about the different plural forms, see the note at **fish**.

tundra n. one of the vast, treeless plains of the arctic regions of Europe, Asia, and Nth America.

tune n. **1.** a succession of musical sounds forming a melody. **2.** the state of being in the proper pitch. **3.** accord; agreement. –v. (**tuned**, **tuning**) **4.** Also, **tune up**. to adjust (a musical instrument) to a given standard of pitch. **5.** to bring into harmony. **6.** Also, **tune up**. to adjust (an engine, etc.) for proper running. **7.** Radio to adjust a receiving apparatus so as to receive (the signals of a sending station).

tuner n. the part of a radio receiver which produces an output suitable for feeding into an amplifier.

tungsten n. a rare metallic element Symbol: W

tunic n. **1.** a coat worn as part of a military or other uniform. **2.** a loose, sleeveless dress, especially as worn by girls as part of a school uniform.

tunnel n. **1.** an underground passage. –v. (**-nelled**, **-nelling**) **2.** to make a tunnel through or under.

turban n. a form of headdress consisting of a scarf wound around the head.

turbid adj. **1.** (of liquids) muddy with suspended particles. **2.** disturbed; confused.

turbine n. a hydraulic motor in which a vaned wheel is made to revolve by the pressure of liquid, gas, steam or air.

turbulent adj. disturbed; agitated; troubled; stormy. –**turbulence**, n.

turd n. Informal (taboo) **1.** a piece of excrement. **2.** an unpleasant person.

Note that this word is taboo and may give offence.

tureen n. a large, deep, covered dish, for holding soup, etc.

turf n. (pl. **turfs** or **turves**) **1.** a surface of grass, etc., with its matted roots. **2.** a piece cut from this; a sod. –v. **3.** to cover with turf or sod. –phr. **4. turf out**, Informal to throw out.

turgid /ˈtɜdʒəd/ adj. **1.** pompous or bombastic, as language, style, etc. **2.** swollen; distended.

turkey n. a large, domesticated fowl.

Turkish bread n. → pide.

Turkish pizza n. → pide (def. 2).

turmeric /ˈtɜmərik, ˈtjuːmərik/ n. (a yellow powder prepared from) the aromatic rhizome of a tropical Asian plant, used as a seasoning, dye etc.

turmoil n. a state of commotion, tumult or agitation.

turn v. **1.** to (cause to) move round on an axis or about a centre; rotate. **2.** to reverse the position of: to turn a page. **3.** to alter the course of; to divert. **4.** to alter the nature, character, or appearance (of). **5.** to change or be changed (into or to): to turn water into ice. **6.** to put to some use. **7.** to pass (a certain age, time, amount, etc.). **8.** to bring into or assume a rounded or curved form. **9.** to express gracefully: to turn a phrase. **10.** to cause to go; send; drive: to turn someone from one's door. **11.** to curve, bend, or twist. **12.** to direct the gaze in a particular direction. **13.** to direct one's course in a particular direction. **14.** to devote oneself to something: to turn to crime. **15.** to shift the body about as if on an axis. **16.** to be affected with nausea, as the stomach. –n. **17.** a movement of rotation, whether total or partial. **18.** the time for action which comes in order to each of a number of persons, etc. **19.** a place where a road, river, etc., turns. **20.** a single revolution, as of a wheel. **21.** a change in nature, circumstances, etc. **22.** a twisting of one thing round another as of a rope around a mast. **23.** a distinctive form or style imparted: *a happy turn of expression.* **24.** a short walk, ride, etc. **25.** natural inclination or aptitude. **26.** a spell of action. **27.** an attack of illness or the like. **28.** (preceded by *good, bad, kind,* etc.) an act of service or disservice. **29.** *Informal* a nervous shock, as from fright or astonishment. *–phr.* **30. turn down, a.** to fold. **b.** to lessen the intensity of. **c.** to refuse or reject (a person, request, etc.). **31. turn off, a.** to stop the flow of (water, gas, etc.) as by closing a valve, etc. **b.** to switch off (a radio, light, etc.). **c.** to branch off; diverge. **d.** to arouse antipathy in. **32. turn on, a.** to cause (water, gas, etc.) to flow as by opening a valve, etc. **b.** to switch on (a radio, light, etc.). **c.** *Informal* to attack without warning. **d.** *Informal* to excite or interest (a person). **33. turn out, a.** to extinguish or put out (a light, etc.). **b.** to become ultimately. **34. turn over, a.** to move or be moved from one side to another. **b.** to ponder. **c.** *Commerce* to purchase and then sell (goods or commodities).

turnaround *n.* **1.** a reversal in circumstances. **2.** the total time taken to perform a task.

turnip *n.* a plant with a thick, fleshy, edible root.

turnover *n.* **1.** the total amount of business done in a given time. **2.** (the rate of) replacement of goods, personnel, etc.

turnstile *n.* a horizontally revolving gate which allows people to pass one at a time.

turpentine *n.* an oil used for dissolving paint, etc., originally from the resin of various trees, now usually made from petroleum.

The short form of this is **turps**. It is a more informal word.

turpitude *n.* shameful wickedness.

turquoise *n.* **1.** a sky blue or greenish-blue mineral, used in jewellery. **2.** a greenish blue or bluish green.

turret *n.* a small tower, especially one at an angle of a building.

turtle *n.* a reptile having the body enclosed in a shell from which the head, tail, and 4 flipper-like legs protrude; most live in the sea.

Compare this with **tortoise**. Tortoises have feet and live on land.

tusk *n.* a tooth developed to great length usually as one of a pair, as in the elephant, walrus, wild boar, etc.

tussle *v.* **1.** to struggle or fight roughly; scuffle. *–n.* **2.** a rough struggle.

tussock *n.* a tuft or clump of growing grass, etc.

tutelage *n.* **1.** the office or function of a guardian. **2.** instruction. **–tutelary,** *adj.*

tutor *n.* **1.** someone employed to educate another, especially a private instructor. **2.** a university teacher who supervises the studies of certain undergraduates. *–v.* **3.** to act as a tutor to.

tutorial *n.* a period of instruction given by a university tutor to an individual student or a small group of students.

tutu *n.* a short, full, ballet skirt.

tuxedo *n.* (*pl.* **-dos**) a man's black jacket for formal occasions.

TV *n.* → **television.**

twain *adj., n. Old-fashioned* two.

twang *v.* **1.** to give out a sharp, ringing sound. *–n.* **2.** the sharp, ringing sound produced by plucking a tense string. **3.** a sharp, nasal tone, as of the human voice.

tweak *v.* **1.** to seize and pull with a sharp jerk and twist. **2.** to make minor adjustments.

twee *adj. Informal* affected; excessively dainty.

tweed *n.* a coarse wool cloth in a variety of weaves and colours.

tweeny (pl. **-nies**) n. a child, especially a girl, between the ages of 8 or 9 and 13 or 14. Also, **tween, tweener, tweenie**.

tweet¹ n. **1.** the weak chirp of a young or small bird. –v. **2.** to utter a tweet or tweets.

tweet² v. **1.** to post a message on the social network site formerly known as Twitter (now X). **2.** to post such a message to (someone). –n. **3.** such a message.

tweezers pl. n. small pincers for plucking out hairs, taking up small objects, etc.

twelve n. **1.** a cardinal number, 10 plus 2. –adj. **2.** amounting to 12 in number. –**twelfth**, adj., n.

Numbers used before a noun are sometimes called **determiners**.

twenty n. **1.** a cardinal number, 10 times 2. –adj. **2.** amounting to 20 in number. –**twentieth**, adj., n.

Numbers used before a noun are sometimes called **determiners**.

24/7 Informal –adv. **1.** continuously; uninterruptedly: *this channel broadcasts news 24/7.* –adj. **2.** uninterrupted; constant: *24/7 broadcasting of tennis.*

twenty-one n. → **pontoon²**.

twice adv. **2** times.

twiddle v. to turn round and round, especially with the fingers.

twig¹ n. **1.** a slender shoot of a plant. **2.** a small, dry, woody piece fallen from a branch.

twig² v. (**twigged, twigging**) Informal to understand.

twilight n. the light when the sun is just below the horizon, especially in the evening.

twill n. a fabric woven so as to produce an effect of parallel diagonal lines.

twin n. **1.** one of 2 children or animals born at a single birth. –adj. **2.** being 2, or one of 2, such children or animals. **3.** forming a pair or couple.

twine n. **1.** a strong string composed of 2 or more strands twisted together. –v.

(**twined, twining**) **2.** to twist together. **3.** to wind in a sinuous course.

twinge n. a sudden, sharp pain.

twinkle v. **1.** to shine with quick, flickering, gleams of light, as stars, etc. **2.** to sparkle in the light. **3.** (of the eyes) to be bright with amusement, etc. –n. **4.** a twinkling with light. **5.** a twinkling brightness in the eyes.

twirl v. to (cause to) rotate rapidly; spin; whirl.

twist v. **1.** to combine or be combined by winding together, as threads. **2.** to wind or twine (something) about a thing. **3.** to (cause to) take a spiral form or course; wind, curve, or bend. **4.** to turn or rotate, as on an axis. **5.** to change the proper form or meaning; pervert. –n. **6.** a curve, bend, or turn. **7.** a peculiar bent, bias, etc., as in the mind or nature. **8.** an unexpected alteration to the course of events, as in a play. **9.** a vigorous dance of the 1960s.

twit n. Informal a fool.

Note that if you call someone 'a twit' you are intending to insult them, but often not in a serious way.

twitch v. **1.** to give a short, sudden pull or tug at; jerk. –n. **2.** a quick, jerky movement of (some part of) the body.

twitter v. to utter a succession of small, tremulous sounds, as a bird.

two n. **1.** a cardinal number, 1 plus 1. –adj. **2.** amounting to 2 in number.

Don't confuse this with **too**, which means also (*Can I come too?*) or more than is needed (*There are too many people to count*), or with **to**, a common word often used to indicate movement in some direction (*I went to the shops*).

Numbers used before a noun are sometimes called **determiners**.

two-dimensional adj. having 2 dimensions, as height and width.

$2 shop n. a shop which sells a wide range of inexpensive goods. Also, **two-dollar shop**.

two-up n. a gambling game in which 2 coins are spun in the air and bets are laid on whether they will fall heads or tails.

tycoon n. a businessperson having great wealth and power.

tyke n. *Informal* a mischievous child.

tyne n. → tine.

type n. **1.** a kind, class, or group as distinguished by a particular characteristic. **2.** the general style distinguishing a particular kind, class or group. **3.** the model from which something is made. **4.** *Printing* **a.** a rectangular metal piece, having on its upper surface a letter or character in relief. **b.** a printed character or printed characters. −v. **5.** to write (a letter, etc.) by means of a computer keyboard or typewriter. **6.** to be a type or symbol of.

typecast v. to cast (an actor, etc.) continually in the same kind of role.

typeface n. → face (def. 7).

typescript n. typewritten material, as distinct from handwriting or print.

typeset v. (-set, -setting) *Printing* to set in type.

typewriter n. a machine for writing mechanically in letters and characters.

typhoid fever n. an infectious, often fatal, fever. Also, **typhoid**.

typhoon n. a tropical cyclone or hurricane.

typhus n. an acute infectious disease, transmitted by lice and fleas, characterised by exhaustion, severe nervous symptoms, and the eruption of reddish spots on the body. Also, **typhus fever**. −**typhous**, adj.

typical adj. **1.** relating to type or emblem; symbolic. **2.** serving as a type or representative specimen. **3.** conforming to the type. −**typically**, adv.

typify v. (-fied, -fying) to serve as the typical specimen of.

typist n. someone who types by means of a computer keyboard or typewriter, especially as an occupation.

Note that someone employed to type in text on a word processor is often called a **keyer**. If they are entering data onto a database they are called a **data-entry operator**.

typo n. (pl. **typos**) *Informal* a typographical or keying error.

typography n. **1.** the work or process of printing with types. **2.** the general character of printed matter. −**typographical**, adj.

tyranny n. (pl. **-nies**) **1.** despotic abuse of authority. **2.** the government or rule of a tyrant. **3.** undue severity or harshness. −**tyrannical**, adj. −**tyrannise**, **tyrannize**, v.

tyrant n. **1.** a ruler who uses power oppressively or unjustly. **2.** any person who exercises power despotically.

tyre n. a band of metal or (usually inflated) rubber, fitted round the rim of a wheel as a running surface.

Don't confuse **tyre** with **tire**, which is to make sleepy or weak.

tzar /zɑ/ n. → tsar.

U, u

U, u *n.* the 21st letter of the English alphabet.

ubiquity /juˈbɪkwəti/ *n.* the state or capacity of being everywhere at the same time. **–ubiquitous,** *adj.*

udder *n.* a mammary gland, especially with more than one teat, as in cows.

UFO *n.* (*pl.* **UFOs** or **UFO's**) unidentified flying object.

ugg boot *n. Aust.* a comfortable shoe made from sheepskin with the soft fleece being on the inside of the boot and the leather on the outside. Also, **ug boot, ugh boot**.

ugly *adj.* (**-lier, -liest**) **1.** offensive to the sense of beauty. **2.** troublesome or dangerous.

UHT *adj.* ultra heat treated; (of milk products) treated by heating briefly to a high temperature and then packaged in hermetically sealed containers; long-life.

ukulele *n.* a small, four-stringed, guitar-like musical instrument. Also, **ukelele.**

ulcer *n.* a pus-filled sore open either to the surface of the body or to a natural cavity. **–ulcerous,** *adj.* **–ulcerate,** *v.*

ulna /ˈʌlnə/ *n.* (*pl.* **-nae** /-niː/ *or* **-nas**) *Anat.* that one of the 2 bones of the forearm which is on the side opposite to the thumb.

ulterior *adj.* intentionally kept concealed: *ulterior motives.*

ultimate *adj.* **1.** forming the final aim or object. **2.** coming at the end, as of a course of action, a process, etc. **–n. 3.** the final point or result. **4.** a fundamental fact or principle.

ultimatum *n.* (*pl.* **-tums** *or* **-ta** /-tə/) a final proposal or statement of conditions.

ultramarine *n.* a deep blue colour.

ultrasound *n.* sound vibrations above the audible range, used in medicine for creating images of internal organs of the body.

ultraviolet *adj.* of the invisible rays of the spectrum lying outside the violet end of the visible spectrum.

ululate /ˈjuljəleɪt/ *v.* to howl, as a dog or wolf.

umami /uˈmami/ *n.* a taste category, distinguished from sweet, sour, salt, and bitter, which is described as being the taste of freshness common to savoury food such as meat, cheese, mushrooms, etc.; associated with Japanese cuisine.

umber *n.* a brown pigment.

umbilical cord /ʌmˈbɪləkəl, ʌmbəˈlaɪkəl/ *n.* a cord connecting the embryo or fetus with the placenta of the mother, and transmitting nourishment from the mother.

umbrage *n.* offence; resentful displeasure: *He took umbrage at her rude remarks.*

umbrella *n.* a portable shade or screen for protection from sunlight, rain, etc.

umpire *n.* **1.** a person selected to see that a game is played in accordance with the rules. **2.** a person to whose decision a controversy between parties is referred; an arbiter or referee.

unanimous *adj.* in complete accord.

unassuming *adj.* unpretending; modest.

unbelievable *adj.* **1.** not believable; not able to be accepted as true. **2.** *Informal* wonderful; excellent. **–unbelievably,** *adv.*

uncanny *adj.* **1.** such as to arouse superstitious uneasiness. **2.** abnormally good.

uncle *n.* **1.** a brother of one's father or mother. **2.** the husband of one's aunt or uncle.

unconscionable /ʌnˈkɒnʃənəbəl/ *adj.* **1.** not just or reasonable. **2.** not guided by conscience; unscrupulous.

unconscious *adj.* **1.** not conscious; unaware. **2.** temporarily devoid of consciousness. **3.** occurring below the level of conscious thought. **4.** unintentional.

uncount noun *n.* → **mass noun.**

uncouth adj. clumsy or rude.

unction n. the act of anointing, especially for medical purposes or as a religious rite.

unctuous adj. oily; greasy.

under prep. **1.** beneath and covered by. **2.** at a point or position lower than or farther down than. **3.** subject to. **4.** below in degree, amount, price, etc. **5.** below in rank, dignity, or the like. **6.** authorised, warranted, or attested by: *under licence*. **7.** in accordance with: *under the rules*. –adv. **8.** under or beneath something. **9.** in a lower place. **10.** in a lower degree, amount, etc. **11.** in a subordinate position or condition. –phr. **12. go under**, *Informal* **a.** to sink (as) in water. **b.** to fail, especially of a business.

underarm adj. *Cricket, Tennis, etc.* executed with the hand below the shoulder as in bowling, service, etc.

undercarriage n. the portions of an aeroplane beneath the body.

undercut v. (**-cut**, **-cutting**) to sell or work at a lower price than.

underdog n. **1.** a victim of oppression. **2.** the loser or expected loser in a competitive situation, fight, etc.

undergo v. (**-went**, **-gone**, **-going**) **1.** to be subjected to; experience. **2.** to endure; sustain; suffer.

undergraduate n. a student in a university or college who has not completed a first degree.

underground adj. **1.** existing, situated, operating, or taking place beneath the surface of the ground. **2.** hidden or secret; not open. –n. **3.** the place or region beneath the surface of the ground. **4.** a secret organisation, etc.

undergrowth n. shrubs or small trees growing beneath or among large trees.

underhand adj. secret and crafty or dishonourable.

underline v. to mark with a line or lines underneath, especially for emphasis in writing, etc.

underling n. (*usually derog.*) a subordinate.

undermine v. to weaken insidiously; destroy gradually.

underneath prep. **1.** under; beneath. –adv. **2.** beneath; below. –adj. **3.** lower.

underpants pl. n. a garment worn under the clothes covering the lower part of the body from the waist or hips to the top of the thighs.

understand v. (**-stood**, **-standing**) **1.** to perceive the meaning of; grasp the idea of; comprehend. **2.** to be thoroughly familiar with; apprehend clearly the character or nature of. **3.** to regard or take as a fact, or as settled. **4.** to perceive what is meant.

understanding n. **1.** the act of someone who understands; comprehension; personal interpretation. **2.** superior intelligence; power of recognising the truth. **3.** a mutual private agreement. –adj. **4.** sympathetic and tolerant.

understate v. to state or represent less strongly than is desirable or necessary. –**understatement**, n.

understudy n. (pl. **-dies**) an actor or actress who stands by to replace a (sick) performer.

undertake v. (**-took**, **-taken**, **-taking**) to take on oneself (some task, performance, etc.); attempt.

undertaker n. someone whose business it is to prepare the dead for burial or cremation and to take charge of funerals.

undertaking n. a task, enterprise, etc., undertaken.

undertone n. **1.** a low or subdued tone, as of utterance. **2.** an underlying quality, element, or tendency.

undertow n. the backward flow or pull of the water, below the surface, from waves breaking on a beach.

underwear n. clothes worn under outer clothes, especially those next to the skin.

underworld n. **1.** the lower or criminal part of human society. **2.** *Myth.* the lower world of the dead.

underwrite v. (**-wrote**, **-written**, **-writing**) **1.** to agree to meet the expense of. **2.** to guarantee the sale of (shares or bonds to be offered to the public for subscription). **3.** to accept liability in case of certain losses specified in (an insurance policy).

undo v. (**-did**, **-done**, **-doing**) **1.** to unfasten and open (something closed, tied, locked, barred, etc.). **2.** to cause to be as if never done. **3.** to bring to ruin or disaster.

undue adj. **1.** excessive: *undue haste*. **2.** not proper, fitting, or right: *undue influence*. **–unduly**, adv.

For def. 1, the more usual word is **unwarranted**; for def. 2, **unjustified**.

undulate v. to have a wavy motion.

unearth v. to uncover or bring to light by digging, searching, or discovery.

uneasy adj. (**-sier**, **-siest**) not at ease in body or mind; disturbed.

unemployed adj. without work or employment.

unerring adj. **1.** without error or mistake. **2.** unfailingly right, exact, or sure.

unfeeling adj. unsympathetic; callous.

unforeseen adj. not predicted; unexpected.

unfortunate adj. **1.** tending to suffer mishaps or misfortune: *an unfortunate child*. **2.** constituting a misfortune: *an unfortunate accident*. **3.** likely to have undesirable results: *an unfortunate decision*. **4.** unsuitable: *an unfortunate choice of words*. –n. **5.** an unfortunate person. **–unfortunately,** adv.

unfriend v. to delete (someone) as a friend from a site on a social network. Also, **de-friend**.

ungainly adj. not graceful.

unguent n. any soft preparation or ointment.

unhinged adj. *Informal* mentally or emotionally disturbed.

uni n. *Informal* a university.

unicameral adj. having a single parliamentary chamber. Compare **bicameral**.

unicorn n. a mythological animal with a single long horn.

uniform adj. **1.** having always the same form or character; unvarying. **2.** regular; even. **3.** agreeing with one another in form, character, appearance, etc.; alike. –n. **4.** a distinctive dress of uniform style, materials, and colour, worn by all the members of a group or organisation. **–uniformity,** n.

unify v. (**-fied**, **-fying**) to form into one; reduce to unity. **–unification,** n.

unilateral adj. **1.** relating to, occurring on, or affecting one side only. **2.** considering only one side of a matter or question.

uninstall v. **1.** to remove from any office, position, place, etc. **2.** *Computers* to remove (a software application).

uninterested adj. having or showing no feeling of interest; indifferent. **–uninterestedly,** adv. **–uninterestedness,** n.

Don't confuse this with **disinterested**, which means not directly or personally involved in a situation.

union n. **1.** the act of uniting 2 or more things into one. **2.** the state of being so united; conjunction. **3.** something formed by uniting 2 or more things; combination. **4.** a number of persons, societies, states, or the like, joined together or associated for some common purpose. **5.** → **trade union**. **6.** (*upper case*) → **Rugby Union**.

Union (defs 4 and 5) is a collective noun and can be used with a singular or plural verb. Look up **collective noun**.

unionise v. to organise into a trade union. Also, **unionize**.

unique adj. **1.** having no like or equal; different from all others: *Each fingerprint is unique*. **2.** remarkable, rare, or unusual: *a unique opportunity*.

Some people say that def. 1 is the only correct meaning for **unique**. Therefore, they say, phrases like *very unique* and *more unique* do not make sense because something can't be 'very different from all others' or 'more different from all others' – it is either different or not. However, many people use **unique** to mean remarkable (def. 2), and so *do* use phrases like *very unique* and *more unique*, and most people find this perfectly acceptable.

unisex *adj.* without the traditional differentiations between the sexes.

unison *n.* **1.** *Music* coincidence in pitch of 2 or more notes, voices, etc. *–phr.* **2. in unison, a.** together; simultaneously: *the children shouted in unison.* **b.** in accord or in agreement.

unit *n.* **1.** a single thing or person; any group of things or persons regarded as an individual. **2.** any specified amount of a quantity by comparison with which any other quantity of the same kind is measured: *The metre is a unit of length.* **3.** Also, **home unit** *Aust., NZ* one of a number of dwelling apartments in the same building, each owned under separate title.

unite *v.* **1.** to join, combine, or incorporate in one; cause to be one. **2.** to associate (persons, etc.) by some bond or tie; join in action, interest, opinion, feeling, etc.

unity *n.* **1.** the state or fact of being one. **2.** the oneness of a complex or ordered whole. **3.** freedom from diversity or variety. **4.** oneness of mind, feeling, etc.

universal *adj.* **1.** without exception. **2.** applicable to many individuals or single cases. **3.** affecting, concerning, or involving all. **4.** of or relating to the universe, all nature, or all existing things. **5.** adapted or adaptable for all or various uses, angles, sizes, etc. *–n.* **6.** that which may be applied throughout the universe to many things.

universe *n.* **1.** all of space, and all the matter and energy which it contains; the cosmos. **2.** a world or sphere in which something exists or prevails.

university *n.* (*pl.* **-ties**) an institution of higher learning, conducting teaching and research at the undergraduate and postgraduate level.

unkempt *adj.* in a neglected, or untidy state.

unless *conj.* except on condition that; except when.

unload *v.* to remove the burden, cargo, or freight from.

unnerve *v.* to deprive of nerve, strength, or physical or mental firmness; upset.

unravel *v.* (**-elled** *or, Chiefly US,* **-eled, -elling** *or, Chiefly US,* **-eling**) to disentangle; disengage the threads or fibres of.

unreal *adj.* **1.** not real; imaginary; artificial; unpractical or visionary. **2.** *Informal* **a.** unbelievably awful. **b.** unbelievably wonderful.

unremitting *adj.* not stopping or slackening.

unrequited *adj.* (used especially of affection) not returned or reciprocated.

unrest *n.* strong, almost rebellious, dissatisfaction and agitation.

unruly *adj.* not submissive or conforming to rule.

unsavoury *adj.* unpleasant or offensive. Also, **unsavory**.

unscathed *adj.* not harmed in any way.

unscrupulous *adj.* untroubled by conscience; lacking sound moral principles.

unsettle *v.* to shake or weaken (beliefs, feelings, etc.); disturb.

unsightly *adj.* not pleasing to the sight.

until *conj.* **1.** up to the time that or when: *He kept trying until he succeeded.* **2.** before: *not until she is finished. –prep.* **3.** onward to (a specified time); up to the time of (some occurrence): *until midnight.* **4.** before: *not until evening.* Also, **till**.

Defs 2 and 4 are always used in negative sentences, that is those that use words such as *not* and *never*: *He never leaves work until 7 p.m.*

unto *prep. Old-fashioned* to (in its various uses, except as the accompaniment of the infinitive).

untoward *adj.* **1.** unfavourable or unfortunate. **2.** unseemly.

unwieldy *adj.* **1.** not easily handled or used, due to size, shape, or weight. **2.** ungainly; awkward.

unwitting *adj.* unaware; unconscious.

unzip *v.* (**-zipped, -zipping**) **1.** to open the zip of (a garment). **2.** *Computers* → **decompress** (def. 2).

up *adv.* **1.** to, towards, or in a more elevated position. **2.** into the air. **3.** to or in an erect position. **4.** out of bed: *Get up.* **5.** to or at any point that is considered higher, as the north, a capital city, etc. **6.** to or at a higher point or degree in a scale, as of rank, size, value, pitch, etc. **7.** to or at a point of equal advance, extent, etc. **8.** well advanced or versed, as in a subject. **9.** to a state of maturity: *Grow up.* **10.** to a state of completion. *–prep.* **11.** to, towards, or at a higher place on or in. **12.** to, towards, near, or at a higher condition or rank in. *–adj.* **13.** going or directed upwards. **14.** travelling towards a terminus or centre. **15.** standing and speaking. **16.** out of bed: *He is up.* **17.** well informed or advanced, as in a subject. **18.** appearing before a court on some charge. **19.** in a leading position. *–v.* (**upped, upping**) **20.** to raise or increase: *We need to up the pace a bit.*

upbraid *v.* to reproach for some fault or offence.

The more usual word is **scold**.

upbringing *n.* the bringing up or rearing of a person from childhood.

update 1. to bring up to date. *–n.* **2.** the process of updating. **3.** an updated version; revision.

up-end *v.* **1.** to set on end. **2.** to upset.

up-front *adj.* **1.** open; straightforward. **2.** (of money) payable in advance: *an up-front fee.*

upgrade 1. to improve. **2.** to allocate to (someone) a seat on a plane, etc., in a class higher than the one ticketed. *–n.* **3.** such a seat reallocation: *to give someone an upgrade.* **4.** *Computers* a new version of a product, usually software, designed to replace a previous version of the product.

upheave *v.* **1.** to heave or lift up. **2.** to disturb or change violently or radically. *–upheaval, n.*

uphold *v.* (**-held, -holding**) to support or maintain, as by advocacy or agreement.

upholstery *n.* the cushions, fabric and other material used to cover furniture.

upkeep *n.* (the cost of) the maintenance of an establishment, machine, etc.

uplift *v.* **1.** to lift up. **2.** to exalt emotionally or spiritually.

upload *v. Computers* to transfer or copy data from a computer to a larger system, such as a network.

up-market *adj.* of or relating to commercial services and goods of superior status, quality and price.

upon *prep.* **1.** upwards so as to get or be on. **2.** on, in any of various senses.

upper *adj.* **1.** higher (than something implied) or highest, as in place, or position, or in a scale. **2.** forming the higher of a pair. **3.** (of a surface) facing upwards. *–n.* **4.** anything which is higher or highest. **5.** the part of a shoe or boot above the sole.

upper-case letter *n.* → **capital letter**.

upper class *n.* the wealthiest group of people in a society. *–upper-class, adj.*

Compare this with **lower class** and **middle class**.
Upper class is a collective noun and can be used with a singular or plural verb. Look up **collective noun**.

upright *adj.* **1.** erect or vertical. **2.** righteous, honest, or just. *–n.* **3.** something standing erect or vertical, as a piece of timber.

uprising n. an insurrection or revolt.

uproar n. violent and noisy disturbance.

uproarious adj. **1.** characterised by or in a state of uproar. **2.** extremely funny.

upscale adj. Informal **1.** of high quality; superior. **2.** affluent.

upset v. (**-set, -setting**) **1.** to overturn; knock or tip over. **2.** to disturb (someone) mentally or emotionally; distress. **3.** to put out of order. **4.** to make feel sick in the stomach. **5.** to defeat (a competitor or opponent), especially contrary to expectation. –n. **6.** a physical upsetting. **7.** an emotional disturbance. **8.** a defeat, especially unexpected. –adj. **9.** emotionally disturbed; distressed.

upshot n. the final issue, the conclusion, or the result.

upstage adv. **1.** on or to the back of the stage. –v. (**-staged, -staging**) **2.** to steal attention (from another).

upstairs adv. **1.** to or on an upper floor. **2.** Informal to or in a higher rank or office. –adj. **3.** on or relating to an upper floor.

upstanding adj. **1.** standing upright. **2.** straightforward, open, or honourable.

upstart n. a person who has risen suddenly in wealth or power, especially one who is self-important and unpleasant.

This word is usually used in a disapproving way.

uptake n. the action of understanding.

uptight adj. Informal tense, nervous, or irritable.

up-to-date adj. extending to the present time; modern.

upturn n. an upward turn, as in prices, business, etc.

upward adj. **1.** directed, tending, or moving towards a higher point or level. –adv. **2.** → **upwards**.

Note that you can use **upward** for both the adjective (*upward movement*) and the

adverb (*to look upward*), but **upwards** can only be used for the adverb (*to look upwards*).

upwards adv. towards a higher place, position, level or degree. Also, **upward**.

uranium n. a white, lustrous, radioactive, metallic element. *Symbol:* U

urban adj. of, relating to, or comprising a city or town.

urbane adj. having the refinement and manners of city-dwellers.

urchin n. a mischievous or shabbily dressed youngster.

urethra /juˈriːθrə/ n. (pl. **-thrae** /-θriː/ or **-thras**) *Anat.* the membranous tube which extends from the bladder to the exterior. In the male it conveys semen as well as urine.

urge v. (**urged, urging**) **1.** to endeavour to induce or persuade. **2.** to press, push, or hasten (the course, activities, etc.). –n. **3.** the fact of urging or being urged. **4.** an involuntary, natural, or instinctive impulse.

urgent adj. **1.** requiring immediate action or attention. **2.** insistent or earnest in solicitation. –**urgency**, n.

urinal /ˈjʊərənəl, jʊˈraɪnəl/ n. a fixture, room, or building for discharging urine in.

urinate v. (**-ated, -ating**) to discharge urine. –**urination**, n.

urine n. the secretion of the kidneys (in mammals, a fluid). –**urinary**, adj.

URL n. *Internet* the address of a resource on the internet.

urn n. **1.** a kind of vase. **2.** a vessel with a tap, used for heating liquids in quantity.

ursine adj. of or relating to bears.

us pron. the personal pronoun used, usually after a verb or preposition, by a speaker to refer to himself or herself along with at least one other person: *Could you please take us home?*

Us is a first person plural pronoun in the objective case.

usage *n.* **1.** customary way of doing; a custom or practice. **2.** customary manner of using a language or any of its forms. **3.** usual conduct or behaviour. **4.** the act or fact of using or employing; use. Also, **useage**.

The spelling **useage** is gaining in frequency, especially in contexts which are not to do with language usage.

USB *n. Computers* universal serial bus; a standard for connection sockets.

USB drive *n.* a small portable data storage device that plugs into the USB port of a computer; memory stick. Also, **USB, USB stick, flash drive**.

USB stick *n. Computers* a memory stick for a USB port.

use *v.* /juz/ (**used, using**) **1.** to employ for some purpose. **2.** to operate or put into effect. **3.** to act or behave towards (a person). **4.** to exploit (a person) for one's own ends. *–n.* /jus/ **5.** the act of employing or using; or putting into service. **6.** the state of being employed or used. **7.** a purpose for which something is used. **8.** the power, right, or privilege of using something. **9.** help; profit; resulting good. **10.** custom; practice. **11.** way of using or treating. **–useful,** *adj.* **–useless,** *adj.*

use-by date *n.* the date by which the manufacturer of a product recommends that it should be used.

used[1] /juzd/ *adj.* **1.** worn; showing signs of wear. **2.** second-hand.

used[2] /just/ *phr.* **used to, 1.** accustomed or inured to: *used to hard work*. **2.** (sometimes fol. by infinitive or infinitive implied) an auxiliary expressing habitual past action: *I used to sing; she plays now but she used not to*.

user *n.* **1.** someone who uses something: *a road user; a computer user*. **2.** *Informal* a drug user, especially someone who takes heroin. **3.** *Informal* a person who selfishly exploits others.

user-friendly *adj.* (of computer equipment) designed to provide little difficulty to the inexperienced operator.

userid /ˈjuzərɑːˈdiː/ *n.* a personal identification code entered into a computer when signing on. Also, **username**.

username *n.* → **userid**.

usher *n.* **1.** someone who escorts persons to seats in a church, theatre, etc. **2.** an attendant who keeps order in a law court. *–v.* **3.** to conduct or escort, as an attendant does.

usual *adj.* **1.** habitual or customary: *his usual good humour*. **2.** such as is commonly met with or observed in experience; ordinary: *the usual January weather*. **3.** in common use; common: *to say the usual things*. *–n.* **4.** that which is usual or habitual. **–usually,** *adv.*

usurp *v.* to seize and hold (an office or position, power, etc.) by force or without right.

The more usual word is **take**.

usury *n.* the practice of lending money at an exorbitant rate of interest.

ute *n. Aust., NZ* → **utility** (def. 4).

utensil *n.* any instrument, vessel, or implement.

uterus *n.* (*pl.* **uteri** /ˈjuːtərɑɪ/ *or* **-ses**) that portion of the female reproductive system in which the fertilised ovum implants itself and develops until birth; womb. **–uterine,** *adj.*

utilise *v.* to put to use. Also, **utilize**.

utilitarian *adj.* **1.** concerning practical or material things. **2.** having regard to usefulness rather than beauty.

utility *n.* (*pl.* **-ties**) **1.** the state or character of being useful. **2.** something useful; a useful thing. **3.** a public service, as a railway, gas supply, etc. **4.** Also, **utility truck, ute** *Aust., NZ* a small truck with an enclosed cabin and a rectangular tray with sides.

utmost *adj.* **1.** of the greatest degree, quantity, etc. **2.** being at the farthest point or extremity; farthest. –n. **3.** the greatest degree or amount. **4.** the best of one's power. Also, **uttermost**.

utopia n. (*sometimes upper case*) a place or state of ideal perfection. –**utopian**, adj.

utter¹ v. **1.** to give audible expression to (words, etc.). **2.** to express in any manner. **3.** to make publicly known; publish. **4.** to put into circulation, especially counterfeit money, forged cheques, etc. –**utterance**, n.

utter² adj. complete; total; absolute: *utter madness*; *utter joy*. –**utterly**, adv.

U-turn n. **1.** a turn made by a car or other motor vehicle so that it faces the direction from which it was coming **2.** any complete change of direction: *The government made a U-turn in its policy on defence.*

The short form of this is **U-ey** /ˈju-i/. It is more informal.

uvula /ˈjuvjələ/ n. (pl. **-las** or **-lae** /-li/) the small, fleshy, conical body projecting downwards above the back of the tongue. –**uvular**, adj.

V, v

V, v *n.* the 22nd letter of the English alphabet.

vacant *adj.* **1.** having no contents; empty. **2.** having no occupant. **–vacancy,** *n.*

vacate *v.* **1.** to make vacant; to empty. **2.** to give up the occupancy of.

vacation *n.* **1.** a part of the year when schools, etc., are suspended or closed. **2.** an extended period of exemption from work, for recreation.

vaccinate *v.* to inoculate with a vaccine. **–vaccination,** *n.*

vaccine *n.* the (modified) virus of any of various diseases, used for preventive inoculation.

vacillate *v.* **1.** to sway unsteadily. **2.** to fluctuate. **–vacillation,** *n.*

vacuous *adj.* **1.** empty. **2.** empty of ideas or intelligence. **–vacuity,** *n.*

vacuum *n.* (*pl.* **vacuums** *or* **vacua**) **1.** a space entirely void of matter. **2.** → **vacuum cleaner.**

vacuum cleaner *n.* a machine for cleaning floors, carpets, etc., which functions by sucking up dirt and dust.

vagabond *n.* a vagrant.

vagary *n.* (*pl.* **-ries**) **1.** an extravagant idea or notion. **2.** a wild, capricious, or fantastic action. **3.** uncertainty: *the vagaries of life.*

vagina *n.* the passage leading from the uterus to the vulva in a female mammal. **–vaginal,** *adj.*

vagrant *n.* **1.** someone who wanders with no settled home or means of support. *–adj.* **2.** wandering or roaming. **–vagrancy,** *n.*

vague *adj.* **1.** not definite in statement or meaning. **2.** indistinct to the sight or other sense. **3.** (of persons, etc.) not clear in thought or understanding.

Don't confuse **vague** with **vogue,** meaning fashion.

vain *adj.* **1.** without real value or importance. **2.** futile; useless. **3.** having excessive pride in oneself; conceited.

Don't confuse **vain** with **vein,** which is a blood vessel in your body.

valance *n.* a short piece of gathered material, especially around the base of a bed.

valedictory /vælə'dɪktəri/ *adj.* **1.** bidding farewell. **2.** of or relating to an occasion of leave-taking. *–n.* (*pl.* **-ries**) **3.** a valedictory speech. **–valediction,** *n.*

valency *n.* (*pl.* **-cies**) *Chem.* the combining capacity of an atom.

valet /'vælet, 'vælər/ *n.* **1.** a male servant who is his employer's personal attendant. **2.** someone who performs similar services for the patrons of a hotel, etc.

valet parking /'vælei/ *n.* a service provided in a hotel, etc., in which patrons drive to the door and leave their cars with an attendant to park.

valiant *adj.* brave; courageous.

valid *adj.* **1.** sound, just, or well-founded. **2.** having force, weight, or cogency; authoritative. **3.** legally sound, effective, or binding. **–validity,** *n.* **–validate,** *v.*

valley *n.* an elongated depression between uplands, hills, or mountains, especially one following the course of a stream.

valour *n.* bravery or heroic courage, especially in battle. Also, **valor.**

valuable *adj.* **1.** of monetary worth. **2.** of considerable use, service, or importance.

Compare this with **invaluable,** which describes something which is of such huge worth that it can't be measured. You cannot put a 'value' on its worth. It is more precious than something described as **valuable.**

valuation n. an estimating or fixing of the value of a thing.

value n. 1. (measure of) that quality which makes something esteemed, desirable, or useful; merit; worth. 2. the worth of a thing as measured by the amount of other things, especially money, for which it can be exchanged. –v. (**-ued, -uing**) 3. to estimate the value of; appraise. 4. to regard or esteem highly.

value-add v. to add to the value of a product or service at any stage of production. –**value-added**, adj. –**value-adding**, n.

valve n. 1. any device for controlling the flow of liquids, gases, etc. 2. Anat. a structure which permits blood to flow in one direction only.

vamp[1] n. 1. the front part of the upper of a shoe or boot. 2. anything patched up or pieced together. –v. 3. to patch (up); renovate.

vamp[2] n. a woman who uses her charms to seduce and exploit men.

vampire n. 1. a preternatural being, supposed to suck blood of sleeping persons at night. 2. Also, **vampire bat**. a bat which feeds on the blood of animals including humans.

van n. a covered vehicle for moving furniture, goods, etc.

vandal n. someone who wilfully destroys or damages anything. –**vandalism**, n. –**vandalise, vandalize**, v.

vane n. a flat piece of metal, etc., especially one which moves with the wind and indicates its direction.

vanguard n. the leading position in any field.

vanilla n. a tropical orchid whose pod-like fruit is used in flavourings, perfumery, etc.

vanish v. to become invisible, especially by magic or quickly.

vanity n. (pl. **-ties**) 1. the quality of being personally vain. 2. Also, **vanity unit**. an item of bathroom furniture consisting of a

cabinet with a bench top and an inset basin.

vanquish v. to conquer or defeat.

vantage point n. a position affording a clear view.

vapid adj. having lost life, sharpness, or flavour.

vaporise v. to make gaseous. Also, **vaporize**.

vapour n. 1. a visible exhalation, as fog, mist, condensed steam. 2. a gas. Also, **vapor**.

variable adj. 1. apt or liable to vary or change. 2. inconsistent or fickle. –n. 3. something variable. 4. Maths a representation of a quantity or any one of a given set of numbers. –**variability**, n.

variance n. the state or fact of varying; divergence or discrepancy.

variant adj., n. (being) an altered or different form.

variation n. 1. change in condition, character, degree, etc. 2. amount or rate of change. 3. a different form; a variant.

varicose adj. abnormally enlarged or swollen.

variegate v. to mark with different colours.

variety n. (pl. **-ties**) 1. the state or character of being various or varied. 2. a number of things of different kinds. 3. a kind or sort. 4. a different form, condition, or phase of something.

various adj. 1. differing one from another. 2. several or many.

varnish n. 1. a liquid which dries as a hard, glossy, usually transparent, coating for wood, metal, etc. –v. 2. to apply varnish to.

vary v. (**-ried, -rying**) 1. to change or alter, as in form, appearance, character, substance, degree, etc. 2. to (cause to) be different, one from another. 3. to relieve from uniformity or monotony. 4. to alternate. 5. to diverge; deviate (from).

vascular *adj.* relating to, composed of, or provided with vessels or ducts which convey fluids, as blood, lymph, or sap.

vase *n.* a container for cut flowers.

vasectomy *n.* (*pl.* **-mies**) the surgical excision of the duct from testicle to penis, as a contraceptive measure.

vassal *n.* (in the feudal system) a person holding lands by the obligation to render (military) service to his lord.

vast *adj.* **1.** of very great extent or area; immense. **2.** of very great size or proportions; huge; enormous. **3.** very great in number: *a vast army.* **4.** very great in intensity: *of vast importance.*

vat *n.* a large container for liquids.

vaudeville *n.* a light or amusing theatrical piece, interspersed with songs and dances.

vault[1] *n.* **1.** an arched space, chamber, or passage. **2.** a strongroom for storing and safeguarding valuables.

vault[2] *v.* to leap or spring, especially over (something).

vaunt *v.* **1.** to speak boastfully of. *–n.* **2.** boastful utterance.

VDU *n.* visual display unit; a computer terminal which displays information on a screen.

veal *n.* the flesh of the calf as used for food.

vector *n.* **1.** a quantity which possesses both magnitude and direction. **2.** *Biol.* a transmitter of germs or disease.

veer *v.* to change direction or course.

vegan *n.* a strict vegetarian who does not eat or use any products of animal origin, including milk, eggs, leather, etc.

vegetable *n.* **1.** any herbaceous plant whose fruits, seeds, roots, bulbs, leaves, etc., are used as food. **2.** any member of the plant kingdom. **3.** *Informal* a person who is entirely dependent on others for subsistence, usually due to severe brain damage.

vegetarian *n.* someone who does not eat the flesh of animals or fish.

Compare this with **vegan**.

vegetate *v.* to live in a passive or unthinking way.

vegetation *n.* the plant life of a particular region considered as a whole.

vehement /'viəmənt/ *adj.* **1.** eager, impetuous, or impassioned. **2.** (of actions) marked by great energy or exertion.

vehicle *n.* **1.** any receptacle, or means of transport, in which something is carried or conveyed, or travels. **2.** a medium by which ideas or effects are communicated. *–***vehicular,** *adj.*

veil *n.* **1.** a piece of material worn over the head and face, as that worn by some Muslim women, to conceal the face. **2.** a piece of material worn over the head and sometimes the face as an adornment, or to protect the face. **3.** something that covers, screens, or conceals. *–v.* **4.** to cover or conceal (as) with a veil.

vein *n.* **1.** one of the branching vessels or tubes conveying blood to the heart. **2.** one of the strands or bundles of vascular tissue forming the principal framework of a leaf. **3.** any body or stratum of ore, coal, etc., clearly separated or defined. **4.** a quality traceable in character or conduct, writing, etc.

Don't confuse this with **vain**, which describes someone who is conceited.

velcro *n.* (*from trademark*) a type of fastening comprising 2 strips of fabric which hook onto each other when pressed together.

velocity *n.* (*pl.* **-ties**) **1.** rapidity of motion or operation. **2.** *Physics* rate of motion, especially when the direction of motion is also specified.

velodrome *n.* an arena with a suitably banked track for cycle races.

velour *n.* any of various fabrics with a fine raised finish.

velvet *n.* **1.** a fabric with a thick, soft pile. **2.** something likened to the fabric velvet in softness, etc. *–***velvety,** *adj.*

venal adj. accessible to bribery; corruptly mercenary.

vend v. to sell. –**vendor**, n.

vendetta n. 1. a private feud. 2. any prolonged or persistent quarrel, rivalry, etc.

veneer n. 1. a thin layer of wood or other material used for facing or overlaying wood. 2. a superficially pleasing appearance or show.

venerable adj. worthy of veneration or reverence, as on account of high character or office.

venerate v. to regard with reverence. –**veneration**, n.

venereal disease n. any sexually transmitted disease, especially syphilis and gonorrhoea.

The short form of this is **VD**.

vengeance n. the avenging of wrong, injury, or the like. –**vengeful**, adj.

venial adj. eligible for forgiveness or pardon.

venison n. the flesh of a deer or similar animal.

venom n. the poisonous fluid which some animals, as certain snakes, spiders, etc., secrete and inject into the bodies of their victims. –**venomous**, adj.

vent¹ n. an opening serving as an outlet for air, smoke, fumes, etc.

vent² v. to give free course or expression to (an emotion, passion, etc.).

ventilate v. 1. to provide (a room, mine, etc.) with fresh air. 2. to air or discuss (a problem, etc.). –**ventilation**, n.

ventricle n. Anat. 1. any of various hollow organs or parts in an animal body. 2. one of the 2 main cavities of the heart.

ventriloquism n. the art or practice of speaking in such a manner that the voice appears to come from some other source, such as a dummy. Also, **ventriloquy**. –**ventriloquist**, n.

venture n. 1. any undertaking or proceeding involving uncertainty as to the outcome. 2. a business enterprise or proceeding in which loss is risked in the hope of profit. –v. 3. to make a venture. 4. (oft. fol. by on or upon or an infinitive) to take a risk; dare or presume.

venturous adj. 1. disposed to venture; bold; daring. 2. hazardous; risky.

venue n. the scene of any action or event.

veracious adj. truthful. –**veracity**, n.

verandah n. an open or partly open portion of a building, roofed usually by the main structure. Also, **veranda**.

verb n. Gram. one of the major parts of speech, comprising words which express the occurrence of any action, existence of a state, and the like.

verbal adj. 1. of or relating to words. 2. spoken, rather than written. 3. Gram. of, relating to, or derived from a verb.

Defs 1 and 2 may appear to create ambiguity. Someone who requests a verbal assurance may be asking for spoken assurance, or for assurance in words, whether spoken or written. The word **oral** is more reliable than *verbal* when def. 2 is intended.

verbalise v. to express (ideas, emotions, etc.) in words. Also, **verbalize**.

verbatim /vɜ'beitəm/ adv. in exactly the same words.

verbiage n. abundance of useless words; wordiness.

verbose adj. expressed in or using many or too many words; wordy.

verdant adj. green with vegetation.

verdict n. 1. Law the finding or answer of a jury. 2. a judgement or decision.

verdure n. greenness, especially of fresh, flourishing vegetation.

verge n. 1. the edge, rim, or margin of something. 2. the limit or point beyond which something begins or occurs. –v. (**verged**, **verging**) 3. to be on the verge or border, or touch at the border. 4. to come close to, approach, or border (on or upon) some state or condition.

verger *n.* an official who takes care of the interior of a church and acts as attendant.

verify *v.* (**-fied**, **-fying**) **1.** to prove (something) to be true; confirm or substantiate. **2.** to ascertain the truth or correctness of, especially by examination or comparison. **–verification,** *n.*

veritable *adj.* being truly such; genuine or real.

verity *n.* the quality of being true.

verjuice /ˈvɜːdʒuːs/ *n.* an acidic liquid made from the sour juice of unripe grapes, etc., used especially in cooking.

vermiform *adj.* like a worm in form; long and slender.

vermiform appendix *n.* → **appendix** (def. 2).

vermilion *n.* brilliant scarlet red.

vermin *n.* (*pl.* **vermin**) (*construed as pl.*) troublesome, destructive, or disease-carrying animals collectively.

vermouth *n.* a white wine in which herbs, roots, and other flavourings have been steeped.

vernacular *adj.* **1.** native or originating in the place of its occurrence or use, as language or words (often as opposed to *literary* or *learned* language). *–n.* **2.** the native speech or language of a place.

vernal *adj.* of or appropriate to spring.

versatile *adj.* capable of or adapted for a variety of tasks, subjects, etc. **–versatility,** *n.*

verse[1] *n.* **1.** a stanza or other subdivision of a metrical composition. **2.** one of the lines of a poem. **3.** a short division of a chapter in the Bible.

verse[2] *v. Sport* (*esp. in children's language*) to play against in a game or competition: *Who are we versing this week?*

versed *adj.* experienced or skilled (*in*).

version *n.* **1.** a particular account of some matter, as contrasted with another. **2.** a translation.

versus *prep.* against; in opposition to.

This word is used especially in sport with reference to the two opposing teams or players, and in law with reference to the opposing sides in a case.
The short form of this is **v** or **vs**.

vertebra *n.* (*pl.* **-brae** /-briː/ *or* **-bras**) *Anat.* any of the bones or segments composing the spinal column.

vertebrate *n.* **1.** a vertebrate animal. *–adj.* **2.** having vertebrae; having a backbone or spinal column.

vertex *n.* the highest point of something; apex.

vertical *adj.* **1.** perpendicular to the horizon; upright. *–n.* **2.** a vertical line, plane, or the like.

Compare this with **horizontal** and **diagonal**.

vertigo *n.* a feeling of dizziness.

verve *n.* enthusiasm or energy, as in literary or artistic work.

very *adv.* **1.** in a high degree, extremely, or exceedingly. **2.** precise or identical: *the very amount.* **3.** mere: *the very idea.* **4.** actual: *the very gun.*

vesicle *n.* a little sac or cyst.

vessel *n.* **1.** a craft for travelling on water. **2.** a container for holding liquid or other contents. **3.** a tube or duct, as an artery, vein, or the like, containing or conveying blood or some other body fluid.

vest *n.* **1.** a short, warm undergarment; singlet. **2.** a waistcoat. *–v.* **3.** to clothe, dress, or robe. **4.** to place or settle (something, especially property, rights, powers, etc.) (*in*) in the possession or control of a person or persons.

vestal *adj.* virginal; chaste.

vestibule *n.* an entrance passage, hall, or room.

vestige *n.* a mark, trace, or visible evidence of something which is no longer present or in existence. **–vestigial,** *adj.*

vestment *n.* an official or ceremonial robe.

vestry n. (pl. **-tries**) a room in or a building attached to a church.

vet n. **1.** a veterinary surgeon. –v. (**vetted, vetting**) **2.** to examine with a view to acceptance, rejection, or correction.

veteran n. **1.** someone who has seen long service in any occupation or office. –adj. **2.** experienced through long service or practice.

veterinary science n. that branch of medicine that concerns itself with animal diseases.

veterinary surgeon n. someone who practises veterinary science or surgery. Also, **veterinarian**.

veto n. (pl. **-tos** or **-toes**) **1.** the power or right of preventing action by an authority. –v. (**-toed, -toing**) **2.** to prevent (a proposal, legislative bill, etc.) being put into action by exercising the right of veto. **3.** to refuse to consent to.

vex v. to irritate; annoy; provoke. –**vexatious**, adj.

via /'vaɪə/ prep. **1.** by way of; by a route that passes through. **2.** by means of.

viable adj. **1.** capable of living. **2.** practicable; workable.

viaduct n. a bridge for carrying a road, railway, etc., over a valley, etc.

vial n. → **phial**.

vibes pl. n. Informal quality or atmosphere.

vibrant adj. **1.** moving to and fro rapidly; vibrating. **2.** full of vigour; powerful.

vibrate v. **1.** to move to and fro, as a pendulum; oscillate. **2.** to move to and fro or up and down quickly and repeatedly; quiver; tremble. –**vibration**, n. –**vibrator**, n.

vibrato n. (pl. **-tos**) Music a pulsating effect produced by rapid small oscillations in pitch about the given note.

vicar n. a member of the clergy acting as priest of a parish.

vicarious adj. performed, exercised, received, or suffered in place of another.

vice[1] n. **1.** an immoral or evil habit or practice. **2.** immoral conduct or life.

vice[2] n. a device used to hold an object firmly while work is being done upon it.

vice[3] prep. a word used as part of someone's title to show that they are a deputy or substitute: vice-president.

Note that this is usually part of a hyphenated word.

vice versa adv. conversely; the order being changed (from that of a preceding statement).

vicinity n. (pl. **-ties**) the region near or about a place.

vicious adj. **1.** addicted to or characterised by vice or immorality; depraved; profligate. **2.** spiteful or malignant. **3.** unpleasantly severe.

vicissitude /və'sɪsətjud/ n. a change or variation occurring in the course of something.

victim n. a sufferer from any destructive, injurious, or adverse action or agency.

victimise v. **1.** to make a victim of. **2.** to discipline or punish selectively. Also, **victimize**.

victory n. (pl. **-ries**) **1.** the ultimate and decisive superiority in a battle or any contest. **2.** any success or successful performance achieved over an adversary or opponent, opposition, difficulties, etc. –**victor**, n. –**victorious**, adj.

video adj. **1.** relating to recording pictures, or both sound and pictures: video image. **2.** of or relating to a video recording. –n. **3.** a recording of a film, television program, event, etc., on videotape. **4.** a video cassette. **5.** a video cassette recorder. –v. (**-oed, -oing**) **6.** to make a video recording of.

video cassette n. a cassette enclosing a length of videotape for video recording or playing. Also, **videocassette**.

video cassette recorder n. a videotape recorder which allows for playing on or recording from a television set, the videotape being held in a video cassette. *Abbrev.:* VCR

videotape *n.* magnetic tape upon which a video signal is recorded, used for storing a television program or film.

vie *v.* to compete with another; to contend for superiority.

view *n.* **1.** a seeing or beholding; an examination by the eye. **2.** range of sight or vision. **3.** a sight or prospect of some landscape, scene, etc. **4.** aim, intention, or purpose. **5.** a conception, notion, or idea of a thing; an opinion or theory. *–v.* **6.** to see or behold. **7.** to look at, survey, or inspect. **8.** to contemplate mentally; consider.

viewpoint *n.* a point of view; an attitude of mind.

vigil *n.* a keeping awake for any purpose during the normal hours of sleep.

vigilant *adj.* keenly attentive to detect danger; wary. **–vigilance**, *n.*

vigilante /vɪdʒə'lænti/ *n. Chiefly US* a member of an unauthorised body organised for the maintenance of order.

vigour *n.* **1.** active strength, energy or force, as of body or mind. **2.** active or effective force. Also, **vigor. –vigorous**, *adj.*

vile *adj.* **1.** wretchedly bad. **2.** repulsive or disgusting. **3.** of mean or low condition, as a person.

vilify *v.* (**-fied, -fying**) to speak evil of; defame. **–vilification**, *n.*

villa *n.* **1.** a large country residence, especially in a Mediterranean country. **2.** *Aust.* a small house, often one of a set of connected dwellings.

village *n.* a small community in a country district.

villain *n.* a wicked person; scoundrel. **–villainous**, *adj.* **–villainy**, *n.*

vim *n.* force; energy; vigour in action.

vindicate *v.* **1.** to clear, as from a charge, imputation, suspicion, or the like. **2.** to uphold or justify by argument or evidence. **–vindicatory**, *adj.* **–vindication**, *n.*

vindictive *adj.* disposed or inclined to revenge; revengeful.

vine *n.* **1.** a long, slender stem that trails or creeps on the ground or climbs by winding itself about a support. **2.** a plant bearing such stems.

vinegar *n.* a sour acidic liquid used as a condiment, preservative, etc.

vineyard *n.* a plantation of grapevines for winemaking, etc.

vintage *n.* **1.** the wine from a particular harvest or crop. **2.** an exceptionally fine wine from the crop of a good year. *–adj.* **3.** of or relating to wine or winemaking. **4.** (of wines) designated and sold as the produce of a specified year. **5.** of high quality; exceptionally fine. **6.** old-fashioned; out of date.

vintner *n.* a wine merchant.

vinyl *n.* a type of plastic made from a particular chemical compound, used formerly in the making of gramophone records.

viol *n.* a musical instrument similar to the violin.

viola *n.* a four-stringed musical instrument slightly larger than the violin.

violate *v.* **1.** to break, infringe, or transgress (a law, promise, instructions, etc.). **2.** to deal with or treat in a violent or irreverent way. **–violation**, *n.*

violent *adj.* **1.** acting with or characterised by uncontrolled, strong, rough force. **2.** intense in force, effect, etc.; severe; extreme. **–violently**, *adv.* **–violence**, *n.*

violet *n.* **1.** a small plant with purple, blue, yellow, white, or variegated flowers. **2.** a bluish-purple colour.

violin *n.* a bowed four-stringed instrument held nearly horizontal by the player's arm, with the lower part supported against the shoulder.

violoncello /vaɪələn'tʃɛloʊ/ *n.* (*pl.* **-los** or **-li**) → **cello.**

VIP *n. Informal* someone who is treated specially because they are important or famous.

This is short for **very important person**.

viper n. a venomous snake.

virago /vəˈrɑːgoʊ/ n. (pl. **-goes** or **-gos**) a violent or ill-tempered scolding woman.

viral adj. relating to or caused by a virus.

virgin n. 1. a person, especially a young woman, who has had no sexual intercourse. –adj. 2. being a virgin. 3. pure; unsullied. 4. untouched or unused: virgin bush.

virginal[1] adj. of, relating to, characteristic of, or befitting a virgin.

virginal[2] n. a small harpsichord of rectangular shape.

virile adj. 1. of, relating to, or characteristic of a man. 2. having masculine vigour, especially sexually. –**virility**, n.

virology n. the study of viruses and the diseases caused by them.

virtual adj. 1. being such in power, force, or effect, although not actually or expressly such: a virtual prisoner in her own home. 2. Computers existing only as a computer representation, as opposed to physically: a virtual bookshop. –**virtually**, adv.

Note that if someone is **virtually** a prisoner in their own home, they are not actually or **literally** a prisoner.

virtualise v. to create in virtual reality rather than in the material world: to virtualise a museum. Also, **virtualize**.

virtual reality n. an artificial environment represented by a computer and intended to appear real to the user, with the use of devices such as goggles and earphones connected to the computer.

virtue n. 1. moral excellence or goodness. 2. a particular moral excellence, as justice, prudence, etc. 3. an excellence, merit, or good quality. –phr. 4. **by** (or **in**) **virtue of**, by reason of; because of.

virtuoso n. (pl. **-sos** or **-si** /-si, -zi/) someone who has special knowledge

or skill in any field, as in music. –**virtuosity**, n.

virtuous adj. morally excellent or good.

virulent adj. 1. actively poisonous, malignant, or deadly. 2. Med. highly infective.

virus n. 1. an infective agent smaller than a common microorganism, inert outside a cell but able to reproduce within the host cell. 2. any disease caused by a virus. 3. a rogue program introduced into a computer network.

visa /ˈviːzə/ n. an authority to enter a foreign country, issued by the government of that country and usually stamped in a passport.

visage n. the face.

viscount /ˈvaɪkaʊnt/ n. a nobleman next below an earl or count and next above a baron.

viscous adj. sticky, adhesive, thick, or glutinous. –**viscosity**, n.

visibility n. 1. the state or fact of being visible. 2. Meteorol. visual range.

visible adj. capable of being seen; perceptible by the eye.

vision n. 1. the power, faculty, or sense of sight. 2. the act or power of perceiving what is not actually present to the eye. 3. a mental view or image of what is not actually present or commonly accepted to exist in place or time. 4. something seen; an object of sight.

visionary adj. 1. given to or characterised by radical, often unpractical ideas, views, or schemes. 2. given to or concerned with seeing visions. –n. (pl. **-ries**) 3. someone who sees visions. 4. someone who is given to visionary ideas.

vision-impaired adj. 1. Med. deficient in sight, ranging from complete blindness to partial vision. 2. of or relating to a person with partial vision (opposed to blind). –**visually-impaired**, adj.

visit v. 1. to go to see (a person, place, etc.) in the way of friendship, ceremony, duty, business, curiosity, or the like. 2. (in general) to come or go to. 3. to come upon or assail. **4.** *Internet* to access (a website). *–n.* **5.** an act of visiting. **–visitor,** *n.*

visitation *n.* **1.** a visit, especially for an official inspection or examination. **2.** a punishment or reward from a divinity.

visor *n.* **1.** the movable front parts of a helmet, especially the uppermost part which protects the eyes. **2.** a small shield in a car which may be swung down to protect a driver's eyes from glare.

vista *n.* a view or prospect.

visual *adj.* **1.** of or relating to sight. **2.** perceptible by the sight; visible.

visualise *v.* to form a mental image of. Also, **visualize.**

vital *adj.* **1.** of or relating to life. **2.** having remarkable energy, enthusiasm, vivacity. **3.** necessary to life, existence, continuance, or wellbeing; indispensable. **4.** of critical importance.

vitality *n.* exuberant physical vigour; energy; enthusiastic vivacity.

vitamin *n.* any of a group of food factors essential in small quantities to maintain life.

vitiate /ˈvɪʃieɪt/ *v.* **1.** to impair the quality of; mar. **2.** to contaminate; spoil. **3.** to make legally defective or invalid.

viticulture *n.* cultivation of grapevines. **–viticulturist,** *n.*

vitreous *adj.* of the nature of glass; resembling glass.

vitrify *v.* (**-fied, -fying**) to make or become vitreous.

vitriol *n.* something highly caustic, or severe in its effects, as criticism. **–vitriolic,** *adj.*

vituperate *v.* **1.** to criticise abusively. **2.** to address abusive language to.

vivacious *adj.* lively, animated, or sprightly. **–vivacity,** *n.*

vivid *adj.* **1.** strikingly bright, as colour, light, objects, etc. **2.** lively or intense, as feelings, etc. **3.** clearly perceptible to the eye or mind.

vivify *v.* (**-fied, -fying**) to enliven; render lively or animated; brighten.

viviparous *adj. Zool.* bringing forth living young (rather than eggs), as most mammals and some reptiles and fishes.

vivisect *v.* to dissect the living body of. **–vivisection,** *n.*

vixen *n.* a female fox.

vlog /vlɒg/ *n.* a blog with video streaming. **–vlogging,** *n.* **–vlogger,** *n.*

vocabulary *n.* (*pl.* **-ries**) **1.** the stock of words used by a people, or by a particular class or person. **2.** a glossary, dictionary, or lexicon.

vocal *adj.* **1.** of or relating to the voice; uttered with the voice; oral. **2.** rendered by or intended for singing; as music.

vocal cords *pl. n. Anat.* folds of mucous membrane projecting into the cavity of the larynx, vibration of which produces vocal sound.

vocalise *v.* to make vocal; utter or articulate; sing. Also, **vocalize.**

vocalist *n.* a singer.

vocation *n.* a particular occupation, business, profession; calling. **–vocational,** *adj.*

vociferous *adj.* crying out noisily; clamorous.

vodcasting *n.* the online delivery of video on demand.

vodka *n.* an alcoholic drink of Russian origin.

vogue *n.* the fashion, as at a particular time.

Don't confuse this with **vague,** which means unsure or uncertain.

voice *n.* **1.** the sound or sounds uttered through the mouth of living creatures, especially of human beings. **2.** such sounds considered with reference to their character or quality. **3.** expressed opinion or choice. **4.** the right to express an opinion or choice; vote. **5.** *Phonetics* the sound produced by vibration of the vocal cords. **6.** *Gram.* a verb form showing the relationship between the action expressed by the verb and the subject, as the passive and active voices. *–v.* (**voiced, voicing**) **7.** to give voice, utterance, or expression to; express; declare.

voice box *n.* → larynx.

voicemail *n.* **1.** a system for recording messages over the telephone to be played back later. **2.** a message received on such a system.

void *adj.* **1.** *Law* without legal force or effect. **2.** useless; ineffectual; vain. **3.** completely empty; devoid; destitute (*of*). –*n.* **4.** an empty space. **5.** a place without the usual or desired occupant. **6.** emptiness; vacancy. –*v.* **7.** to make void or of no effect; invalidate; nullify. **8.** to empty or discharge the contents of.

volatile *adj.* **1.** evaporating rapidly. **2.** light and changeable of mind; frivolous; flighty. –**volatility**, *n.*

volcano *n.* (*pl.* **-noes** or **-nos**) an opening in the earth's crust through which molten rock (lava), steam, ashes, etc., are expelled. –**volcanic**, *adj.*

volcanology *n.* the study of volcanoes and volcanic phenomena. Also, **vulcanology**.

vole *n.* a type of rodent.

volition *n.* the act of willing; exercise of choice to determine action.

volley *n.* (*pl.* **-leys**) **1.** the discharge of a number of missiles or firearms simultaneously. **2.** a burst or outpouring of many things at once or in quick succession. **3.** *Tennis, etc.* **a.** a return of the ball before it touches the ground. **b.** a succession of such returns. –*v.* (**-leyed**, **-leying**) **4.** to discharge in or as in a volley. **5.** *Tennis, Soccer, etc.* to return, kick, etc., (the ball) before it strikes the ground.

volleyball *n.* a game in which a large ball is struck from side to side over a high net with the hands or arms.

volt *n.* the derived SI unit of electric potential. *Symbol:* V

voltage *n.* electromotive force or potential expressed in volts.

voluble *adj.* characterised by a ready and continuous flow of words: *a voluble child; a voluble explanation.*

When referring to a person, the more usual word is **talkative**.

volume *n.* **1.** a collection of written or printed sheets bound together and constituting a book. **2.** the size, measure, or amount of anything in 3 dimensions; the SI unit of volume is the cubic metre (m³). **3.** a mass or quantity, especially a large quantity, of anything. **4.** loudness or softness.

volumetric *adj.* denoting, relating to, or depending upon measurement by volume. Also, **volumetrical**.

voluminous /vəˈluːmənəs, -ˈljuː-/ *adj.* of ample size, extent, or fullness.

voluntary *adj.* **1.** done, made, brought about, undertaken, etc., of one's own accord or by free choice. **2.** *Physiol.* subject to or controlled by the will.

volunteer *n.* **1.** someone who enters into any service of their own free will and for no financial gain. –*v.* **2.** to offer oneself for some service or undertaking.

voluptuous *adj.* **1.** full of, characterised by, directed towards, or ministering to pleasure or luxurious or sensual enjoyment. **2.** sensually pleasing. **3.** (of the female figure) curvaceous.

vomit *v.* **1.** to bring up (the contents of the stomach) by the mouth; spew. **2.** to eject or be ejected with force or violence.

voodoo *n.* a class of mysterious rites or practices, of the nature of sorcery or witchcraft.

voracious *adj.* devouring or craving food in large quantities.

vortex *n.* (*pl.* **-texes** or **-tices** /-təsiz/) a whirling movement or mass of water, as a whirlpool.

vote *n.* **1.** a formal expression of will, wish, or choice in some matter, signified by voice, by ballot, etc. **2.** the right to such expression; suffrage. **3.** an expression of feeling, as approval, or the like. –v. **4.** to express or signify choice in a matter undergoing decision, as by a voice, ballot, or otherwise. **5.** to enact, establish, or determine by vote; bring or put (*in*, *out*, *down*, etc.) by vote.

votive *adj.* offered, given, dedicated, etc., in accordance with a vow.

vouch *v.* **1.** to answer (*for*) as being true, certain, reliable, justly asserted, etc. **2.** to give one's own assurance, as surety or sponsor (*for*).

voucher *n.* **1.** a document, receipt, stamp, or the like, which proves the truth of a claimed expenditure. **2.** a ticket used as a substitute for cash.

vouchsafe *v.* to grant or give, by favour or graciousness.

vow *n.* **1.** a solemn promise, pledge, or personal engagement. –v. **2.** to promise by a vow, as to God or a saint. **3.** to pledge oneself to do, make, give, observe, etc.

vowel *n.* **1.** *Phonetics* a speech sound made by allowing air to pass through the middle of the mouth without obstruction by the tongue or lips. **2.** a letter which usually represents a vowel, as in English *a*, *e*, *i*, *o* and *u*, and sometimes *y*.

Compare this with **consonant**, which is a speech sound made by blocking the flow of your breath by the tongue or lips, or any letter of the alphabet except *a*, *e*, *i*, *o* or *u*.

voyage *v.* (**-aged**, **-aging**) **1.** to make or take a passage, or course of travel, by sea or water. –n. **2.** such a passage.

voyeur *n.* someone who attains sexual gratification by looking at sexual objects or situations. –**voyeurism**, *n.* –**voyeuristic**, *adj.*

vulgar *adj.* **1.** marked by ignorance of or lack of good breeding or taste. **2.** crude; coarse; unrefined. **3.** ostentatious; unsubtle. **4.** common or ordinary. –**vulgarity**, *n.*

vulnerable *adj.* susceptible to being hurt physically or emotionally. –**vulnerability**, *n.*

vulture *n.* any of various large, carrion-eating birds, some related to eagles, hawks, etc., and others related to storks.

vulva *n.* (*pl.* **-vae** /-vi/ *or* **-vas**) the external female genitalia.

vuvuzela *n.* a plastic horn, up to one metre in length, which emits a loud buzzing sound.

W, w

W, w n. the 23rd letter of the English alphabet.

wad n. **1.** a small mass or lump of anything soft. **2.** a roll or bundle, especially of banknotes.

wadding n. any fibrous or soft material for padding, etc.

waddle v. to walk with short steps and swaying or rocking from side to side, as a duck.

waddy n. (pl. **-dies**) an Aboriginal heavy wooden war club.

wade v. to walk through any substance, as water, snow, sand, etc., that impedes free motion.

wafer n. **1.** a thin, crisp cake or biscuit. **2.** any of various other thin, flat cakes, sheets, or the like.

waffle¹ n. a kind of batter cake.

waffle² *Informal* –v. **1.** to speak or write vaguely, pointlessly, and at considerable length. –n. **2.** verbose nonsense.

waft v. **1.** to bear or carry through the air or over water. **2.** to bear or convey lightly as if in flight. **3.** to float or be carried, especially through the air.

wag¹ v. (**wagged, wagging**) **1.** to move in different directions, rapidly and repeatedly. **2.** *Informal* to be absent from (school, etc.) without permission. –n. **3.** the act of wagging.

wag² n. a humorous person; joker.

wage n. **1.** (*oft. pl.*) that which is paid, usually weekly, for work or services; hire; pay. –v. (**waged, waging**) **2.** to carry on (a battle, war, conflict, etc.).

Compare this with **salary**, which is also regular pay, but sometimes **salary** is used for the yearly amount you earn, and is usually paid monthly, whereas **wage** is used for pay that you get weekly. **Salary** is used especially for office work.

wager n. **1.** something staked or hazarded on an uncertain event; bet. –v. **2.** to hazard (something) on the issue of a contest or any uncertain event or matter; stake; bet.

waggle v. **1.** to wag with short, quick movements. –n. **2.** a waggling motion.

wagon n. any of various kinds of four-wheeled vehicles, especially one designed for the transport of heavy loads, delivery, etc.

wagtail n. a small bird with a long, narrow tail.

waif n. a person without home or friends, especially a child.

wail v. **1.** to utter a prolonged, inarticulate, mournful cry. –n. **2.** a wailing cry, as of grief, pain, etc.

Don't confuse this with **whale**, which is a very large sea mammal.

wainscot n. wooden panels serving to line the walls of a room, etc. –**wainscoting,** n.

waist n. the part of the human body between the ribs and the hips.

Don't confuse this with **waste**, which is to use something up without much result.

waistcoat n. a close-fitting, sleeveless garment which reaches to the waist.

wait v. **1.** to stay or rest in expectation (*for, till,* or *until*). **2.** to continue stationary or inactive in expectation of; await. –n. **3.** an act, period or interval of waiting; delay. –*phr.* **4. wait on,** to serve someone, especially while they are eating a meal.

Don't confuse **wait** with **weight**, which is how heavy something is.

waiter *n.* someone who serves customers at table, as in a restaurant, etc. **–waitress**, *fem. n.*

waive *v.* to forbear to insist on; relinquish.

The more usual word is **forgo**.

Don't confuse **waive** with **wave**, which is to move something up and down: *to wave a flag.*

waiver *n.* an intentional relinquishment of some right, interest, or the like.

wake¹ *v.* (**woke**, **woken**, **waking**) **1.** to stop being asleep: *I woke at seven.* **2.** to rouse from sleep: *My alarm woke me at seven.* *–n.* **3.** a watch, especially at night, near the body of a dead person before burial, often accompanied by drinking and feasting.

You can also use **wake up** for defs 1 and 2. It is more usual to say **wake up** than **wake**: *She wakes up early every morning; Wake me up before you go.* You can use **awaken** as well for both defs, and for def. 1 you can also use **awake**: *She awakes early every morning.* **Awaken** and **awake** are rather formal words.

wake² *n.* the track left by a ship or other object moving in the water.

walk *v.* **1.** to go or travel by steps, or by advancing the feet in turn. **2.** to proceed through, over, or upon by walking. **3.** to lead, drive, or ride at a walk, as an animal. *–n.* **4.** the act or course of going on foot. **5.** a spell of walking for exercise or pleasure. **6.** a gait or pace. **7.** a department or branch of activity.

walkabout *n.* a period of wandering as a nomad, especially by Aboriginal people.

walkie-talkie *n.* a lightweight combined radio transmitter and receiver.

walkman *n. (from trademark)* a small portable transistor radio, cassette player, etc., with earphones.

walkover *n. Informal* an unopposed or easy victory.

wall *n.* **1.** an upright structure of stone, brick, etc., serving for enclosure, division,

support, protection, etc. **2.** anything which resembles or suggests a wall.

wallaby *n. (pl.* **-bies** *or, especially collectively,* **-by)** any of several types of plant-eating marsupial found throughout Aust.

wallaroo *n.* a stocky, coarse-haired kangaroo; euro.

wallet *n.* a small, book-like folding case for carrying papers, paper money, etc., in the pocket.

wall-eyed *adj.* having eyes with little or no colour or with an abnormal amount of white showing.

wallop *v. Informal* to beat soundly; thrash.

wallow *v.* **1.** to roll the body about, or lie, in water, snow, mud, dust, or the like. **2.** to indulge oneself (*in*).

wallpaper *n.* **1.** coloured or patterned paper for covering the walls or ceilings of rooms, etc. **2.** *Computers* a picture or design forming the background image on a computer screen.

walnut *n.* (a tree bearing) an edible nut.

walrus *n. (pl.* **-ruses** *or, especially collectively,* **-rus)** either of 2 large marine mammals having flippers, a pair of large tusks, and a thick, tough skin.

waltz /wɒls, wɒls/ *n.* **1.** a ballroom dance. *–v.* **2.** to dance a waltz.

wan *adj.* (**wanner**, **wannest**) of an unnatural or sickly pallor; pallid.

wand *n.* a slender stick or rod, especially one supposedly used for working magic.

wander *v.* **1.** to ramble without any certain course or object in view; roam. **2.** to stray from a path, companions, etc.

Don't confuse **wander** with **wonder**, which is to think about something with curiosity or surprise.

wane *v.* (**waned**, **waning**) **1.** (of the moon) to decrease periodically in the extent of its illuminated portion after the full moon (opposed to *wax*). **2.** to decline in power, importance, prosperity, etc. —*n.* **3.** gradual decline.

wangle *v. Informal* to bring about or obtain by indirect or insidious methods.

wank *Informal (taboo)* —*v.* **1.** to masturbate. —*n.* **2.** an act or instance of masturbation. **3.** self-indulgent or egotistical behaviour.

wanker *n. Informal (taboo)* an annoying person, especially one who thinks they are very important.

Note that this is a taboo word and may give offence. If you call someone 'a wanker', you are intending to insult them.

wannabe /'wɒnəbi/ *n. Informal* someone who aspires to be something or someone specified, but who is unlikely to be successful: *a wannabe poet; a Lady Gaga wannabe.*

want *v.* **1.** to feel a need or a desire for; wish for. **2.** to be without or be deficient in. **3.** to wish; like; feel inclined (*to*). **4.** to be deficient by the absence of some part or thing: *to want for money.* **5.** to be in a state of destitution or poverty. **6.** to be lacking or absent, as a part or thing necessary to completeness. —*n.* **7.** something wanted or needed; a necessity. —*phr.* **8. in want,** poor or destitute.

wanton *adj.* **1.** done maliciously or unjustifiably. **2.** reckless or disregardful of right, justice, humanity, etc. **3.** sexually unrestrained; lascivious.

war *n.* **1.** a conflict carried on by force of arms, as between nations or between parties within a nation. **2.** active hostility or contention; conflict; contest. —*v.* (**warred, warring**) **3.** to make or carry on war; fight.

waratah *n.* a shrub or small tree with a dense globular head of red flowers.

warble *v.* to sing with trills, quavers, or melodic embellishments.

ward *n.* **1.** an administrative division or district of a municipality, city or town. **2.** a division of a hospital or prison. **3.** *Law* a

person, especially a minor, who has been legally placed under the care or control of a legal guardian. —*phr.* **4. ward off,** to avert, repel, or turn aside, as danger, an attack, assailant, etc.

warden *n.* **1.** someone charged with the care or custody of something; keeper. **2.** the head of certain colleges, hospitals, youth hostels, etc.

warder *n.* → **prison officer**.

wardrobe *n.* **1.** a stock of clothes or costumes. **2.** a piece of furniture for holding clothes.

ware *n.* (*usu. pl.*) goods for sale: *the shopkeeper displayed her wares.*

Note that this word can also be used in combination with another word to mean a particular type or class of goods for sale, as in *kitchenware, silverware,* etc. Don't confuse this with **wear,** which can also be used in combinations but means a particular type of clothing, as in *menswear, sleepwear,* etc.

warehouse *n.* a storehouse for wares or goods.

warfare *n.* **1.** the act of waging war. **2.** armed conflict.

warlock *n.* someone who practises magic arts by the aid of the devil; a sorcerer or wizard.

warm *adj.* **1.** having or communicating a moderate degree of heat. **2.** (of colour) suggesting warmth; inclining towards red or orange, as yellow (rather than towards green or blue). **3.** having or showing lively feelings, passions, sympathies, etc. —*v.* **4.** to make warm; heat: *warm the milk.* **5.** to excite ardour, enthusiasm, or animation in. **6.** to inspire with kindly feeling. —*phr.* **7. warm up, a.** to prepare for a sporting event, musical or theatrical performance, etc. **b.** to make or become warm: *warm your feet up by the fire;* the weather has warmed up. —**warmth,** *n.*

warm-blooded *adj.* designating or relating to animals whose body temperature stays more or less the same regardless of the temperature of the surrounding medium.

warn v. **1.** to give notice to (a person, etc.) of danger, possible harm, etc. **2.** to admonish or exhort as to action or conduct. **3.** to give notice to (a person, etc.) to go, stay, or keep (away, off, etc.). **–warning,** n.

warp v. **1.** to bend or become bent out of shape, especially from a straight or flat form. **2.** to distort from the truth, fact, true meaning, etc.; bias or pervert. **3.** to turn or change from the natural or proper course, state, etc. –n. **4.** a bend or twist in something, as in wood that has dried unevenly. **5.** a mental twist or bias. **6.** yarns placed lengthwise in the loom, across the weft or woof, and interlaced.

warrant n. **1.** authorisation, sanction, or justification. **2.** that which serves to give reliable or formal assurance of something; guarantee. **3.** a writing or document certifying or authorising something. –v. **4.** to give authority to; authorise. **5.** to afford warrant or sanction for, or justify. **6.** to give a formal assurance, or a guarantee or promise, to or for; guarantee.

warranty n. (pl. **-ties**) **1.** the act of warranting; warrant; assurance. **2.** Law an engagement, express or implied, in assurance of some particular in connection with a contract, as of sale.

warren n. a place where rabbits breed or abound.

warrior n. a person engaged or experienced in warfare; soldier.

wart n. **1.** a small, usually hard, abnormal elevation on the skin, caused by a virus. **2.** a small protuberance.

wary adj. (**-rier, -riest**) watchful, or on the alert; cautious; careful.

was v. first and 3rd person singular past tense indicative of **be**: I was happy; She was there.

The form of the verb **be** you use for the first person (I) and the third person (he, she, it) in the past tense.

wasabi /wə'sabi/ n. a green paste with a hot, spicy taste, eaten with Japanese food.

wash v. **1.** to apply water or some other liquid to for the purpose of cleansing. **2.** to flow over or against. **3.** to carry or bring, (as) with water or any liquid: The tide washed up seaweed. **4.** Informal to stand being put to the proof; bear investigation. –n. **5.** the act of washing with water or other liquid. **6.** a quantity of clothes, etc., washed, or to be washed, at one time. **7.** a liquid with which something is washed, wetted, coloured, etc. **8.** the flow, sweep, dash, or breaking of water. **9.** a broad, thin layer of colour, as in watercolour painting.

washer n. **1.** a flat ring used to give tightness to a joint, to prevent leakage, and to distribute pressure. **2.** → face washer.

wasp n. a stinging insect.

waspish adj. quick to resent a trifling affront or injury; snappish.

waste v. **1.** to consume, spend, or employ uselessly or without adequate return; squander. **2.** to fail to use. **3.** to wear down or reduce, especially in health or strength. **4.** to destroy or devastate. **5.** Also, **waste away.** to become physically deteriorated. **6.** Also, **waste away.** to diminish gradually, as wealth, power, etc. –n. **7.** useless consumption or expenditure, or use without adequate return. **8.** neglect, instead of use. **9.** gradual destruction or decay. **10.** a desolate stretch of land. **11.** anything left over, as excess materials, etc. –adj. **12.** not used or in use. **13.** (of land, etc.) uninhabited and waste; desolate. **14.** left over or superfluous. **–wastage,** n.

Don't confuse **waste** with **waist**, which is the part of your body between the ribs and the hips.

wastrel n. a wasteful person; spendthrift.

watch v. **1.** to be on the lookout, look attentively, or be closely observant. **2.** to look or wait attentively and expectantly (for). **3.** to view attentively or with interest. **4.** to guard for protection or safekeeping. —n. **5.** close, constant observation for the purpose of seeking or discovering something. **6.** a lookout, as for something expected. **7.** vigilant guard, as for protection, restraint, etc. **8.** a small, portable timepiece, usually worn on the wrist.

watchful adj. vigilant or alert; closely observant.

water n. **1.** the liquid which in a more or less impure state constitutes rain, oceans, lakes, rivers, etc., and which in a pure state is a transparent, odourless, tasteless compound of hydrogen and oxygen, H_2O. **2.** (pl.) a body of water. **3.** any liquid or aqueous organic secretion. —v. **4.** to sprinkle, moisten, or drench with water. **5.** to supply (animals) with water for drinking. **6.** to dilute or adulterate (as) with water. **7.** to produce a wavy lustrous pattern, marking, or finish on (fabrics, metals, etc.). **8.** to fill with or secrete water or liquid, as the eyes, or as the mouth at the sight or thought of tempting food. —**watery**, adj.

waterbed n. a heavy, durable, plastic bag filled with water, used as a mattress.

water bomb n. a balloon filled with water, used as a missile in play. Also, **waterbomb**.

water-bomb v. **1.** to fight (a bushfire) by means of water bombing. **2.** to throw a balloon filled with water at (someone) as in play. —n. **3.** → **water bomb**. Also, **waterbomb**.

water buffalo n. the largest buffalo, originally from India but now widely used as a draught animal; feral in nthn Aust. Also, **water ox**.

water closet n. a receptacle in which human excrement is flushed down a drain by water from a cistern.

watercolour n. (a painting executed in) pigments dispersed in water-soluble gum. Also, **watercolor**.

watercourse n. (the bed of) a stream of water, as a river or brook.

watercress n. a plant, usually growing in clear, running water, and bearing pungent leaves used in salads, etc.

waterfall n. a steep fall or flow of water from a height; cascade.

waterfront n. **1.** land abutting on a body of water. **2.** workers in industries using wharf facilities.

waterhole n. a natural hole or hollow in which water collects, as a spring in a desert, a cavity in the dried-out course of a river, etc.

waterlog v. (**-logged**, **-logging**) to soak or saturate with water.

watermark n. **1.** a mark indicating the height to which water rises or has risen, as in a river, etc. **2.** a figure or design impressed in the fabric in the manufacture of paper and visible when the paper is held to the light.

watermelon n. a large melon with pink, juicy flesh.

water police n. a civil force whose function is to police waterways.

water polo n. a water game played by 2 teams of swimmers.

watershed n. the ridge or crest line dividing 2 drainage areas.

waterski n. **1.** a type of ski used for gliding over water. —v. (**-ski'd** or **-skied**, **-skiing**) **2.** to glide over water on waterskis by grasping a rope towed by a speedboat.

watertable n. the upper limit of underground water-saturated layers of rock.

waterway n. a river, canal, or other body of water as a route or way of travel or transport.

watt n. the derived SI unit of power, defined as one joule per second. Symbol: W

wattle n. **1.** any of the very numerous Aust. acacias, with spikes or globular heads of yellow or cream flowers. **2.** (pl. or sing.) rods or stakes interwoven with twigs or branches of trees, used for making fences, walls, roofs, etc. **3.** a fleshy lobe hanging down from the throat or chin, as of certain birds.

wattle and daub n. wattles (interwoven rods) plastered with mud or clay and used as a building material.

WAV /wæv/ n. a sound file format for computers, widely used to distribute sound over the internet.

wave n. **1.** liquid rising as a ridge or swell, as water in the sea. **2.** a swell, surge, or rush, as of feeling, excitement, prosperity, etc. **3.** a widespread movement, feeling, opinion, tendency, etc. **4.** Physics a progressive vibrational disturbance propagated through a medium, as air, without corresponding progress or advance of the parts or particles themselves, as in the transmission of sound or electromagnetic energy. –v. **5.** to (cause to) move loosely to and fro or up and down. **6.** to undulate. –**wavy**, adj.

> Don't confuse **wave** with **waive**, which is a rather formal word meaning to decide not to insist on something: They are waiving the usual entrance fee.

wavelength n. Physics the length of each cycle of a wave (def. 4).

waver v. **1.** to sway to and fro; flutter. **2.** to become unsteady or begin to fail or give way. **3.** to feel or show doubt or indecision; vacillate.

wax¹ n. **1.** a solid, non-greasy, insoluble substance which has a low melting or softening point. **2.** a substance secreted by certain insects and plants. **3.** something suggesting wax as being readily moulded, worked upon, handled, managed, etc. –v. **4.** to rub, smear, stiffen, polish, etc., with wax.

wax² v. (**waxed, waxed** or, Poetic, **waxen, waxing**) **1.** to increase in extent, quantity, intensity, power, etc. **2.** (of the moon) to increase in the extent of its illuminated portion before the full moon (opposed to wane). **3.** to grow or become (as stated): to wax pale at the thought.

waxwork n. figures, ornaments, etc., made of wax.

way n. **1.** manner, mode, or fashion. **2.** a course, plan, or means for attaining an end. **3.** respect or particular: defective in several ways. **4.** direction: Look this way. **5.** passage or progress on a course. **6.** a path or course leading from one place to another. **7.** (oft. pl.) a habit or custom: his funny little ways. **8.** course of life, action, or experience. **9.** Informal extremely: she's way cool; open till way late. –adv. **10.** by the way, in the course of one's remarks. **11.** give way to, **a.** to yield to. **b.** to lose control of (one's emotions, etc.). **12.** in the way, forming an obstruction or hindrance. **13.** make way for, **a.** to allow to pass. **b.** to give up or retire in favour of. **14.** under way, in motion or moving along.

> Don't confuse **way** with **weigh**, which is to measure how heavy something is, or with **whey**, which is a liquid produced in cheese-making.

wayfarer n. a traveller.

waylay v. (**-laid, -laying**) to fall upon or assail from ambush, as in order to rob, seize, or slay.

wayside n. the border or edge of the road or highway.

wayward adj. turned or turning away from what is right or proper; perverse.

we pron. the personal pronoun used by a speaker to refer to himself or herself along with at least one other person: I'm ready. You're ready. We can go; We need to elect a new mayor.

> **We** is a first person plural pronoun in the subjective case.

weak *adj.* **1.** liable to yield, break, or collapse under pressure; fragile; frail. **2.** deficient in bodily strength; feeble; infirm. **3.** lacking in force, potency, or efficacy. **4.** deficient in amount, volume, loudness, intensity, etc.; faint; slight. –**weaken**, *v.* –**weakly**, *adv.*

Don't confuse **weak** with **week**, which is a period of seven days.

weakling *n.* a weak or feeble creature (physically or morally).

weal *n.* → **welt**.

wealth *n.* **1.** a great store of valuable possessions, property, or riches. **2.** a rich abundance or profusion of anything. –**wealthy**, *adj.*

wean *v.* to accustom (a child or animal) to food other than its mother's milk.

weapon *n.* any instrument for use in attack or defence in fighting.

weapon of mass destruction *n.* a biological, chemical or nuclear weapon capable of killing a great number of people. Also, **WMD**.

wear *v.* (**wore**, **worn**, **wearing**) **1.** to carry or have on the body or about the person as a covering, equipment, ornament, or the like. **2.** to bear or have in the aspect or appearance. **3.** to cause or undergo gradual impairment, reduction, etc., by or from wear, use or attrition: *The rock has worn away*; *The pattern has worn off this plate*; *Your shoes have worn out*. **4.** to make (a hole, channel, way, etc.) by such action. **5.** to hold out or last under wear, use, or any continued strain. –*n.* **6.** gradual impairment, wasting, diminution, etc., as from use.

Note that this word can also be used in combination with another word to mean a particular type of clothing, as in *menswear, sleepwear*, etc. Don't confuse this with **ware**, which can also be used in combinations but means a particular type of goods for sale, as in *kitchenware, silver-ware*, etc.

wearisome *adj.* tedious.

weary *adj.* (**-rier, -riest**) **1.** exhauste physically or mentally by labour, exertio strain, etc.; fatigued. **2.** impatient or dis satisfied at excess or overlong continuanc (*of*). –*v.* (**-ried, -rying**) **3.** to make o become weary; fatigue. **4.** to make o grow impatient or dissatisfied at havin too much (*of*) something. –**weariness, *

For defs 1 and 2, the more usual word i **tired**; for defs 3 and 4, the more usua word is **tire**.

weasel *n.* a small carnivore having a lon slender body, short legs and rounded ear and feeding largely on small rodents.

weather *n.* **1.** the state of the atmospher with respect to wind, temperature, cloudi ness, moisture, pressure, etc. –*v.* **2.** to bea up against and come safely through (storm, danger, trouble, etc.). **3.** to underg change, as discolouration or disintegratio as the result of exposure to atmospheri conditions.

Don't confuse this with **whether** o **wether**. **Whether** is a word which intro duces the first of two choices: *I need t know whether you want to come with m or not*. A **wether** is a castrated ram.

weatherboard *n.* one of a series of thi boards nailed on an outside wall or a roo to form a protective covering.

weathervane *n.* a vane for indicating th direction of the wind.

weave[1] *v.* (**wove** or **weaved**, **wove** or **weaved**, **weaving**) **1.** to interlac (threads, cloth) so as to form a fabric o texture. –*n.* **2.** a manner of interlacin yarns.

weave[2] *v.* (**weaved** or **wove**, **weaving**) t follow in a winding course; to move fron side to side.

web[1] *n.* **1.** something formed as by weav ing or interweaving. **2.** a thin silken fabri spun by spiders, and also by the larva of some insects. **3.** a tangled intricate stat of circumstances, events, etc. **4.** *Zool.*

membrane which connects the digits of some animals and birds.

web² n. the, (also upper case) a large-scale, networked, hypertext information system available over the internet. Also, **World Wide Web.**

webbed adj. having the digits connected by a web, as the foot of a duck or a beaver.

web browser n. → **browser.**

webcam n. Informal a web camera. Also, **web cam.**

web camera n. a digital video camera linked to a computer for transmission of images over the internet. Also, Informal, **webcam.**

webcast v. (-cast or -casted, -casting) 1. to broadcast information on the internet to multiple recipients simultaneously. –n. 2. such a broadcast on the internet. –**webcaster**, n. –**webcasting**, n.

web crawler n. an internet search engine, originally designed to search keywords specified at URLs to locate required websites, but now capable of searching for other kinds of information, such as email addresses; robot.

webliography n. (pl. **-phies**) a list of resources on a particular subject available on the internet.

web log n. → **blog.** Also, **weblog.**

webmaster n. a person responsible for the development and maintenance of a web server or website.

web page n. Internet a document with a unique URL on the World Wide Web. Also, **webpage.**

web portal n. a website which offers information and sometimes direct links to other websites along with a range of services such as email, online shopping, etc. Also, **portal, portal site.**

web server n. Internet 1. the software running at a website which sends out web pages in response to remote browsers. 2. a computer which connects a user's computer to the World Wide Web on request. Also, **webserver.**

website n. Internet a location on the World Wide Web where there is a set of resources, as text files, images, etc. Also, **web site.**

wed v. (**wedded** or **wed, wedding**) 1. to bind oneself to (a person) in marriage; take for husband or wife. 2. to unite (a couple) or join (one person to another) in marriage or wedlock; marry.

The more usual word is **marry.**

wedding n. the act or ceremony of marrying; marriage.

wedge n. 1. a device consisting of a piece of hard material with 2 principal faces meeting in a sharply acute angle. 2. a piece of anything of like shape. 3. Also, **potato wedge.** a thick wedge of potato, usually seasoned, and deep-fried. 4. something that serves to part, divide, etc. –v. (**wedged, wedging**) 5. to pack or fix tightly by driving in a wedge or wedges. 6. to thrust, drive, or fix (in, between, etc.) like a wedge.

wedgie n. Informal the experience of having one's pants pulled up so sharply as to cause discomfort, usually done as a prank.

wedlock n. the state of marriage; matrimony.

wee Informal –n. 1. urine. –v. (**wee'd, wee'ing**) 2. to urinate.

weed n. 1. a plant growing wild, especially where unwanted. 2. a thin or weakly person, especially one regarded as stupid or infantile. –v. 3. to free from weeds. –phr. 4. **weed out,** to rid of what is undesirable or superfluous.

week n. 1. a period of 7 successive days. 2. the working portion of this period. 3. 7 days after a specified day: Tuesday week.

Note that a **week** is normally thought to begin on Sunday and last until Saturday. However, the usual **working week** starts on Monday and lasts until Friday, leaving Saturday and Sunday as the **weekend.**

Don't confuse **week** with **weak**, which means not strong.

weekend n. the end of the working week, from Friday evening to Sunday evening, as a time for recreation for most people.

weekly adj. **1.** relating to a week, or to each week. **2.** done, happening, appearing, etc., once a week, or every week. –adv. **3.** once a week. **4.** by the week. – n. (pl. **-lies**) **5.** a periodical appearing once a week.

weep v. (**wept**, **weeping**) **1.** to shed (tears) as from sorrow or any overpowering emotion; cry. **2.** to exude water or liquid, as a plant stem, a sore, etc.

For def. 1, the more usual word is **cry**.

weevil n. a type of beetle destructive to nuts, grain, fruit, etc.

weft n. **1.** Textiles yarns which run from selvage to selvage in a loom, interlacing with the warp; woof. **2.** a woven piece.

weigh v. **1.** to find the weight of by means of a balance, etc. **2.** to bear (down) by weight, heaviness, oppression, etc. **3.** Also, **weigh up**. to consider carefully in order to reach an opinion, decision, or choice. **4.** to raise or lift (now chiefly in the phrase to weigh anchor). **5.** to have weight or heaviness, often as specified.

Don't confuse **weigh** with **way**, which is a method of doing something, or with **whey**, which is a liquid produced in cheese-making.

weight n. **1.** amount of heaviness. **2.** a piece of metal of a certain mass, for using on a balance or scale. **3.** any heavy mass or object, especially an object used because of its heaviness. **4.** importance, moment, consequence, or effective influence. **5.** something oppressive. –v. **6.** to add weight to; load with additional weight. –**weightless**, adj.

Don't confuse **weight** with **wait**, which is to stay until something happens.

weightlifting n. the sport of lifting steel bars with disc-shaped weights attached in competition with or for exercise.

weighty adj. (**-tier, -tiest**) **1.** having considerable weight; heavy. **2.** of considerable importance; serious. –**weightily**, adv.

weir n. a dam in a river or stream to stop and raise the water.

weird adj. **1.** involving or suggesting the supernatural; unearthly or uncanny. **2.** Informal startlingly or extraordinarily singular, odd, or queer.

welcome n. **1.** a kindly greeting or reception. –v. (**-comed, -coming**) **2.** to greet the coming of (a person, etc.) with pleasure or kindly courtesy. –adj. **3.** gladly received.

welcome to country n. a welcoming speech, performance, etc., given by a representative or representatives of the traditional Indigenous custodians of the land on which a public event, meeting, etc., is taking place.

weld v. to unite or fuse (pieces of metal, etc.), especially with the use of heat.

welfare n. wellbeing.

well adv. (**better, best**) **1.** in a satisfactory, favourable, or advantageous manner; fortunately or happily. **2.** in a good or proper manner. **3.** thoroughly or soundly. **4.** easily; clearly. **5.** to a considerable extent or degree. –adj. (**better, best**) **6.** in good health. **7.** satisfactory or good. –phr. **8. as well**, in addition. **9. as well as**, in addition to; no less than. **10. very well**, **a.** with certainty; undeniably. **b.** (a phrase used to indicate consent, often with reluctance). **c.** (ironic) satisfactory; pleasing.

Note that the other forms of **well** are **better** and **best**. Better is the comparative form and **best** is the superlative. Compare the adverb **well** with **good**, which is an adjective. You use **well** with verbs, so you would say 'She sings well', not 'She sings good'.

well² n. **1.** a hole drilled into the earth for the production of water, petroleum, natural gas, etc. **2.** a spring or natural source of water. –v. **3.** to rise, spring, or gush (up, out, or forth), as water, from the earth.

wellbeing n. good or satisfactory condition of existence; welfare.

well-done adj. (of meat) cooked thoroughly.

well-heeled adj. Informal wealthy; prosperous.

wellington boot n. a waterproof knee-high boot; gumboot.

well-known adj. **1.** clearly or fully known. **2.** familiarly known, or familiar. **3.** generally or widely known. Also, (especially in predicative use), **well known**.

well-off adj. in good or easy circumstances as to money or means; moderately rich. Also, **well-to-do**.

well-to-do adj. having a sufficiency of means for comfortable living; well-off or prosperous.

welsh v. Informal to cheat (on) by evading payment, especially of a gambling debt.

welt n. a ridge made on the surface of the body, as from the stroke of a stick or whip; weal.

welter n. **1.** a rolling or tumbling about. **2.** commotion, turmoil, or chaos.

wend v. to direct or pursue (one's way, etc.).

wept v. past tense and past participle of weep.

were v. the form of the verb **be** used with the first person plural (we), the second person singular and plural (you) and the third person plural (they) in the past tense.

werewolf /ˈweəwʊlf/ n. (pl. **-wolves** /-wʊlvz/) (in old superstition) a human being turned into a wolf.

west n. **1.** a cardinal point of the compass corresponding to the point where the sun is seen to set. –adj. **2.** directed or proceeding towards the west. **3.** coming from the west. –adv. **4.** in the direction of the

sunset; towards or in the west. **5.** from the west (as of wind). –**westerly**, adj., adv.

western adj. **1.** lying towards or situated in the west. **2.** directed or proceeding towards the west. **3.** coming from the west, as a wind. **4.** (also upper case) of or relating to countries with a Western European background, including Aust., especially as contrasted politically and culturally with other parts of the world. –n. **5.** (usu. upper case) a story or film about frontier life in the American west.

wet adj. (**wetter**, **wettest**) **1.** covered or soaked, wholly or in part, with water or some other liquid. **2.** not yet dry; moist; damp. **3.** rainy; having a rainy climate. –n. **4.** that which makes wet, as water or other liquid; moisture. **5.** rain. –v. (**wet** or **wetted**, **wetting**) **6.** to make wet.

wet blanket n. a person or thing that has a discouraging or depressing effect.

wether n. a ram castrated when young.

> Don't confuse this with **weather** or **whether**. **Weather** refers to the condition of the atmosphere as far as heat, rain, etc., are concerned. **Whether** is a word which introduces the first of two choices: *I need to know whether you want to come with me or not.*

wetland n. an area in which the soil is mostly wet or under water, as a swamp.

wet nurse n. a woman hired to breastfeed another's infant.

wet season n. the period of an annual cycle in the tropics when rainfall and humidity increases markedly. Compare **dry season**.

wetsuit n. a tight-fitting rubber suit worn by divers, surfers, etc.

whack v. Informal to strike with a smart, resounding blow or blows.

whale n. Zool. a large cetacean with a fishlike body, flippers, and a horizontally flattened tail.

> Don't confuse **whale** with **wail**, which is to give a long sad cry.

whalebone *n.* an elastic horny substance found in certain whales, used especially in earlier times in corsets.

wham *v.* (**whammed, whamming**) to hit forcefully.

wharf *n.* (*pl.* **wharves** *or* **wharfs**) a structure built on the shore of, or projecting out into, a harbour, stream, etc., so that vessels may be moored alongside to load or unload or to lie at rest; quay.

what *pron.* **1.** an interrogative pronoun used when **a.** asking for something to be named or stated: *What is your name?*; *What did he do?* **b.** asking about the nature, character, class, origin, etc., of a thing or person: *What is that animal?* **c.** asking about the importance of something: *What is wealth without health?* **2.** a relative pronoun used to mean 'the thing that', or 'that which': *This is what he said*; *She didn't say what she wanted*; *I don't know what he meant*; *It doesn't matter what I do, I always seem to get it wrong*; *Say what you please.* *–adv.* **3.** to what extent or degree: *What does it matter?* *–adj.* **4.** which one: *What book are you reading?*

It is quite common for people to say *What?* when they have not heard something someone has said to them. However, many people think this is rude. Polite expressions to use in this situation include *I beg your pardon?* and *Pardon?*

whatever *pron.* **1.** anything that: *do whatever you like*; *do whatever they tell you.* **2.** any amount or measure (of something) that: *Throw out whatever is left over.* **3.** no matter what: *Do it, whatever happens*; *Whatever you do, don't press the red button.* **4.** (used to show that the thing under discussion is not important): *Big, small, whatever – I like them all*; 'Should I come over at 5 or 6 o'clock?' 'Whatever – I'll be here all evening.' **5.** a stronger form of the word *what* used when asking about something that has surprised you: *Whatever do you mean?*; *Whatever could that*

noise be? *–adj.* **6.** any: *Whatever time you can spare.* **7.** no matter what or which: *Whatever the problem, just ignore it and keep going*; *For whatever reason, he's not coming.* *–adv.* **8.** used to add strength to a negative comment; at all: *It's no use whatever asking her.*

For def. 8 you can also use **whatsoever**: *There is no point whatsoever in asking her.*

wheat *n.* the grain of a cereal grass used for food.

wheedle *v.* to endeavour to influence (a person) by smooth or flattering words.

wheel *n.* **1.** a circular frame or solid disc arranged to turn on an axis, as in vehicles, machinery, etc. **2.** anything resembling or suggesting a wheel. **3.** (*pl.*) moving, propelling, or animating agencies. **4.** (*pl.*) *Informal* a motor vehicle. **5.** a wheeling or circular movement. **6.** *Informal* a person of considerable importance or influence. *–v.* **7.** to cause to rotate, as on an axis. **8.** to move, roll, or convey on wheels, castors, etc. **9.** to revolve. **10.** to move in a circular or curving course. **11.** to turn or change in procedure or opinion (*about* or *round*).

wheelbarrow *n.* a small cart supported at one end by a wheel on which it is pushed along.

wheelchair *n.* a chair mounted on large wheels, and used by invalids or disabled people.

wheeze *v.* to breathe with difficulty and with a whistling sound.

whelk *n.* a large spiral-shelled marine gastropod.

whelp *n.* the young of the dog, or of the wolf, bear, lion, tiger, seal, etc.

when *adv.* **1.** at what time: *When are you coming?* *–conj.* **2.** at what time: *to know when to be silent.* **3.** at the time that: *We will leave when it gets dark.* **4.** at any time; whenever: *He gets impatient when he is kept waiting.* **5.** whereas: *You say you*

didn't do it, when I know you did. –pron.
6. what time: *since when?* **7.** which time:
*They left on Monday, since when we have
heard nothing.*

whenever *conj.* **1.** at any time when:
Come whenever you like. –*adv.* **2.** when:
Whenever did she say that?

Def. 2 is used to give more force to a
question.

where *adv.* **1.** a word used to ask **a.** in or
at what place?: *Where is he?* **b.** in what
position?: *Where do you want to stand?*
c. to what place?: *Where are you going?*
d. from what source?: *Where did you get
this information? –conj.* **2.** in or at what
place, part, point, etc.: *Find where he is.*
3. in or at the place, part, point, etc., in or
at which: *It's where you left it.* **4.** in or
at which place; and there: *They came to the
town, where they stayed overnight. –pron.*
5. what place: *From where?*

whereabouts *adv.* **1.** about where?
where? –*conj.* **2.** near or in what place.
–*pl. n.* **3.** the place where a person or thing
is; the locality of a person or thing.

whereas *conj.* **1.** while on the contrary.
2. it being the case that, or considering
that.

whereby *adv., conj.* by what or by which.

whereupon *conj.* at or after which.

wherever *conj.* **1.** in, at, or to whatever
place: *wherever she goes.* –*adv.* **2.** where:
Wherever did you find that?

Def. 2 is used to give more force to a
question.

wherewithal *n.* means or supplies for the
purpose or need, especially money.

whet *v.* (**whetted, whetting**) **1.** to sharpen
(a knife, tool, etc.) by grinding or friction.
2. to make keen or eager.

whether *conj.* **1.** a word used to introduce
the first of 2 or more alternatives, in
correlation with **or**: *I can't remember
whether she said two or three.* **2.** a word
used to introduce a single alternative, the

other being implied or understood: *I don't
know whether he has finished yet.*

Def. 1 is used with **or**: *I don't know
whether to go or stay.*
Don't confuse **whether** with **weather** or
wether. **Weather** refers to the condition
of the atmosphere as far as heat, rain,
etc., are concerned. A **wether** is a castrated ram.

whey *n.* a watery liquid separating from the
thickened mass of milk curd, formed in
cheese-making.

Don't confuse this with **way**, which is a
method of doing something, or with
weigh, which is to measure how heavy
something is.

which *pron.* **1.** an interrogative pronoun
used to ask what one (of a certain number): *Which of these do you want?* **2.** a
relative pronoun used **a.** as the subject or
object of a relative clause: *The house,
which was deep in the bush, burnt down;
What colour was the car which they stole?*
b. to indicate what particular one or any
one that: *She knows which she wants;
Choose which you like.* **c.** to mean 'a thing
that': *And, which is worse, they didn't pay.*
–*adj.* **3.** what one (of a certain number of
things): *Which book do you want?*

Don't confuse this with **witch**, which is a
woman who practises magic.

whichever *pron.* **1.** any one (of those in
question) that: *Take whichever you like.*
2. no matter which: *Whichever you
choose, someone will be offended.* –*adj.*
3. no matter which: *whichever book you
like.*

whiff *n.* **1.** a slight blast or puff of wind or
air. **2.** a waft of scent or smell.

while *n.* **1.** a space of time. –*conj.* Also,
whilst. 2. during or in the time that.
3. throughout the time that, or as long
as. **4.** at the same time that (implying
opposition or contrast). –*phr.* (**whiled,
whiling**) **5.** while away, to cause (time)

to pass, especially in some easy or pleasant manner.

whim *n.* an odd or fanciful notion.

whimper *v.* 1. to cry with low, plaintive, broken sounds, as a child, a dog, etc. *–n.* 2. a whimpering cry or sound.

whimsical *adj.* of an odd, quaint, or comical kind.

whimsy *n.* (*pl.* **-sies**) an odd or fanciful notion.

whine *v.* (**whined, whining**) 1. to utter a nasal, complaining cry or sound, as from uneasiness, discontent, peevishness, etc. *–n.* 2. a whining utterance, sound, or tone.

Don't confuse this with **wine**, which is an alcoholic drink made from grapes.

whinge *v.* to complain; whine.

whinny *v.* (**-nied, -nying**) (of a horse) to utter its characteristic cry; neigh.

whip *v.* 1. to strike with quick, repeated strokes of something slender and flexible; lash. 2. to beat with a whip or the like, especially as punishment; flog; thrash. 3. to move quickly: *to whip down to the shop.* 4. to beat (eggs, cream, etc.) to a froth with a whisk, fork, etc. 5. to beat or lash about, as a pennant in the wind. *–n.* 6. an instrument for striking or punishing, typically consisting of a flexible part with a more rigid handle. 7. *Parliament* a party manager who supplies information to members about the government business, secures their attendance for voting, etc. *–phr.* 8. **whip out**, to bring out with a sudden movement: *He whipped out a gun.* 9. **whip up**, **a.** to create quickly. **b.** to arouse to fury, intense excitement, etc.

whiplash *n.* an injury to the spine caused by sudden movement forwards or backwards, as in a motor accident.

whippet *n.* a dog similar to a small greyhound.

whirl *v.* 1. to turn round, spin, or rotate rapidly. 2. to move rapidly along on wheels or otherwise. 3. to cause to turn or rotate rapidly. *–n.* 4. rapid rotation or gyration. 5. a short drive, run, walk, or the like; spin. 6. a rapid round of events, feelings, thoughts, etc.

whirlpool *n.* a whirling eddy or current, as in a river or the sea.

whirlwind *n.* a mass of rapidly rotating air.

whirr *v.* (**whirred, whirring**) to go, fly, dart, revolve, or otherwise move quickly with a vibratory or buzzing sound.

whisk[1] *v.* 1. to sweep (dust, crumbs, etc., or a surface) with a brush, or the like. 2. to move with a rapid, sweeping stroke.

whisk[2] *v.* 1. to whip (eggs, cream, etc.) to a froth with a whisk or beating implement. *–n.* 2. a small bunch of grass, straw, hair, or the like, especially for use in brushing. 3. an implement, in one form a bunch of loops of wire held together in a handle, for beating or whipping eggs, cream, etc.

whisker *n.* 1. (*pl.*) a beard. 2. a single hair of a beard.

whisky *n.* a distilled spirit made from grain.

whisper *v.* 1. to speak or utter with soft, low sounds, using the breath, lips, etc., without vibration of the vocal cords. 2. (of trees, water, breezes, etc.) to make a soft, rustling sound. *–n.* 3. the mode of utterance, or the voice, of someone who whispers. 4. a whispering sound. 5. confidential information; rumour.

whist *n.* a card game.

whistle *v.* 1. to make a musical sound by forcing the breath through a small opening of the lips, helped by the tongue. 2. to make such a sound by blowing on a particular device. *–n.* 3. an instrument for producing such sounds. 4. a sound produced by or as by whistling.

white *adj.* 1. of the colour of pure snow, reflecting all or nearly all the rays of sunlight. 2. having a pale, colourless skin. 3. pallid or pale, as from fear or other strong emotion, or pain or illness. 4. (of wines) light-coloured or yellowish (opposed to *red*). **5.** (of coffee) with milk or cream. *–n.* **6.** an achromatic visual sensation of relatively high luminosity. A white surface reflects light of all hues completely and diffusely. **7.** lightness of skin pigment. **8.** something white, or a white part of something. **9.** a pellucid viscous fluid which surrounds the yolk of an egg; albumen. **10.** the white part of the eyeball.

white ant *n.* any of various species of wood-eating insects.

This insect is not really an ant. It is a **termite**.

white blood cell *n.* → **leukocyte**.

white-collar *adj.* belonging or relating to non-manual workers, as those in professional and clerical work.

This term comes from the clothing traditionally worn by men in these positions: suit, white shirt and tie.
Compare this with **blue-collar**, which refers mainly to factory or production workers.

white flag *n.* an all-white flag, used as a symbol of surrender, etc.

white gold *n.* any of several gold alloys possessing a white colour due to the presence of nickel or platinum.

whitegoods *pl. n.* electrical goods as refrigerators, washing machines, etc., which have a white enamel surface.

white heat *n.* an intense heat at which a substance glows with white light.

white lie *n.* a lie uttered from polite, amiable, or pardonable motives.

white-out *n.* a thin white paint that is used to cover written mistakes on paper.

whitewash *n.* **1.** a composition, as of lime and water, used for painting walls, woodwork, etc., white. **2.** anything used to cover up faults, gloss over faults or errors, or give a specious semblance of respectability, honesty, etc., especially a dishonest official investigation.

white water *n.* any stretch of water in which the surface is broken, as in rapids or breaking waves, due to movement over a shallow bottom. *–whitewater, adj.*

whither *adv. Old-fashioned* to what place? where?

whiting *n.* (*pl.* **-ting** *or* **-tings**) an Aust. fish valued for eating and for sport fishing.

For information about the different plural forms, see the note at **fish**.

whittle *v.* **1.** to cut, trim, or shape (a stick, piece of wood, etc.) by taking off bits with a knife. *–phr.* **2. whittle down,** to cut in order to reduce. *–whittler, n.*

whiz[1] *v.* (**whizzed, whizzing**) to make a humming or hissing sound, as an object passing rapidly through the air.

whiz[2] *n. Informal* a person who shows outstanding ability in a particular field or who is notable in some way; expert.

who *pron.* **1.** an interrogative pronoun used when **a.** asking the question 'what person?': *Who told you that?* **b.** asking 'what?', as to the character, origin, position, importance, etc., of a person: *Who is the man in uniform?* **2.** a relative pronoun introducing an adjectival clause describing a person: *I know who did it; The woman who sold it to me. –phr.* **3. who's who,** the people who carry influence or importance in society

Who is used as the subject of a verb (*Who gave it to you?*), while, strictly speaking, **whom** is used as the object (*Whom did you see?*). However, many people use **who** instead of **whom** (*Who did you see?*), and it is generally regarded as acceptable. In fact, many people would regard the use of **whom** as overly formal.

whoever *pron.* **1.** a relative pronoun meaning 'whatever person' or 'anyone that'. **2.** an interrogative pronoun used emphatically when asking the question 'who?'.

whole *adj.* **1.** comprising the full quantity, amount, extent, number, etc., without diminution or exception; entire, full, or total. **2.** undivided, or in one piece. **3.** uninjured, undamaged, or unbroken; sound; intact. *–n.* **4.** the whole assemblage of parts or elements belonging to a thing; the entire quantity, account, extent, or number. **5.** a thing complete in itself, or comprising all its parts or elements. *–wholly, adv.*

Don't confuse **wholly** with **holey** or **holy**. **Wholly** means completely (*wholly responsible*), **holey** means full of holes (*holey socks*), and **holy** means sacred (*holy books*).

wholehearted *adj.* hearty; earnest; sincere.

wholemeal *adj.* prepared with the complete wheat kernel, as flour or the bread baked with it.

whole number *n.* Maths an integer as 0, 1, 2, 3, 4, 5, etc.

wholesale *n.* **1.** the sale of commodities in large quantities, as to retailers, rather than to consumers. *–adj.* **2.** extensive and indiscriminate: *wholesale destruction of rainforests. –adv.* **3.** in a wholesale way. *–v.* **4.** to sell by wholesale.

Compare this with **retail**, which is the sale of goods to the public rather than to shops.

wholesome *adj.* **1.** conducive to or suggestive of moral or general wellbeing. **2.** conducive to bodily health; healthful; salubrious.

wholistic /houl'ıstık/ *adj.* → **holistic**. *–wholism, n.*

whom *pron.* **1.** the objective case of the interrogative pronoun **who**: *To whom did you speak?; Whom did you see?* **2.** the objective case of the relative pronoun **who**: *the woman whom I saw; the man to whom I gave the cheque.*

Strictly speaking, **whom** is used as the object of a verb instead of **who** (*Whom*

did you see?). However, many people use **who** instead of **whom** (*Who did you see?*), and it is generally regarded as acceptable. In fact, many people would regard the use of **whom** in everyday speech as slightly pompous.

whoop *n.* **1.** a loud cry or shout, as one uttered by children or warriors. *–v.* **2.** to utter a loud cry or shout, as a call, or in enthusiasm, excitement, frenzy, etc.

whooping cough /'hupıŋ/ *n.* an infectious disease of the respiratory mucous membrane, especially of children.

whoops *interj.* an exclamation of mild surprise, dismay, etc. Also, **whoops-a-daisy**.

whoosh *n.* a loud rushing noise, as of water or air.

whopper *n. Informal* **1.** something uncommonly large of its kind. **2.** a big lie.

whore *n.* a female prostitute.

whorl *n.* **1.** a circular arrangement of like parts, as leaves, flowers, etc., round a point on an axis. **2.** anything shaped like a coil.

whose *pron.* **1.** the possessive case of the interrogative pronoun **who**: *Whose is this jacket?* **2.** the possessive case of the relative pronoun **who**: *the man whose dog I bought.* **3.** the possessive case of the relative pronoun **which**: *the book whose cover is red. –adj.* **4.** of, belonging or relating to whom: *Whose dog is this?*

Note that some people think that **whose** should only refer to people, so feel that def. 3 is incorrect. It is, however, extremely common and accepted by most people. As an adjective (def. 4), it refers only to people.

why *adv.* **1.** (a word used to ask 'for what cause, reason, or purpose?': *Why did you go? –conj.* **2.** for what cause or reason: *Tell me why you did it.* **3.** for which: *the reason why she refused.* **4.** the reason for which: *That is why I raised this question* *again.* *–interj.* **5.** an expression of surprise, hesitation, etc.: *Why, it's all gone!*

wick *n.* a twist of soft threads, which draws up the melted tallow of a candle to the flame, or some similar device.

wicked *adj.* **1.** evil or morally bad; iniquitous; sinful. **2.** *Informal* excellent.

wickerwork *n.* work consisting of plaited or woven willow twigs.

wicket *n.* **1.** a small door or gate, especially one beside, or forming part of, a larger one. **2.** *Cricket* **a.** either of the 2 frameworks, each consisting of 3 stumps with 2 bails in grooves across their tops, at which the bowler aims the ball. **b.** the area between the wickets, especially with reference to the state of the ground. **c.** the achievement of a player's dismissal by the fielding side.

wide *adj.* **1.** having considerable or great extent from side to side; broad; not narrow. **2.** of great range or scope. **3.** open to the full or a great extent; expanded; distended. *–adv.* **4.** to a great, or relatively great, extent from side to side. **5.** to the full extent of opening. **6.** away from or to one side of a point, mark, purpose, or the like; aside; astray. **–width**, *n.*

wide area network *n.* a computer network which connects computers over a wide area. *Abbrev.:* WAN

widespread *adj.* **1.** spread over or occupying a wide space. **2.** distributed over a wide region, or occurring in many places or among many persons or individuals.

widget *n.* **1.** *Informal* (*humorous*) a mechanical device or gadget, the name of which you do not know or cannot think of: *Where's that widget to clean the barbecue?* **2.** *Computers* a component of a graphical user interface that displays information that a user can interact with to change the information, such as a window or a text box.

widow *n.* a woman whose spouse has died and who has not married again. **–widower**, *masc. n.*

wield *v.* **1.** to exercise (power, authority, influence, etc.), as in ruling or dominating. **2.** to manage (a weapon, instrument, etc.) in use; handle or employ in action.

wife *n.* (*pl.* **wives**) a woman joined in marriage to another person.

wig *n.* an artificial covering of hair for the head.

wiggle *v.* **1.** to (cause to) move or go with short, quick, irregular movements from side to side; wriggle. *–n.* **2.** a wavy line.

wigwam *n.* a Native American hut made of poles with bark, mats or skins laid over them.

wiki /'wɪki/ *n. Internet* a website in which the contents are contributed and edited by visitors to the site.

wild *adj.* **1.** living in a state of nature, as animals that have not been tamed or domesticated. **2.** growing or produced without cultivation or the care of humans, as plants, flowers, fruit, honey, etc. **3.** of unrestrained violence, fury, intensity, etc.; violent; furious. **4.** extravagant or fantastic. **5.** disorderly or dishevelled. **6.** *Informal* intensely eager or enthusiastic. *–adv.* **7.** in a wild manner; wildly. *–n.* **8.** (*oft. pl.*) an uncultivated, uninhabited, or desolate region or tract; waste; wilderness; desert.

wildcard *n.* **1.** *Computers* a symbol used when searching for a word, phrase, etc., to represent an unspecified character or characters. **2.** *Sport* a player or team allowed into a competition without having to compete in qualifying matches.

wildebeest /'wɪldəbist/ *n.* a large African antelope with an oxlike head; gnu.

wilderness *n.* a wild region, as of forest or desert.

wildlife *n.* animals living in their natural habitat.

wile n. a trick, artifice, or stratagem.

wilful adj. **1.** willed, voluntary, or intentional. **2.** self-willed; perversely obstinate.

will¹ v. a verb used to indicate **1.** simple future time: *I will do that tomorrow; He will probably like that.* **2.** willingness: *I will help you.* **3.** likelihood or habitual behaviour: *He will sit for hours watching birds.*

Note that this word is often shortened to '**ll**: *I'll see you tomorrow; That'll be the day!; What'll I do if you're late?* * This is a modal verb and is always used with another verb. Its past tense is **would**. Look up **modal verb**.

will² n. **1.** the faculty of conscious and especially of deliberate action. **2.** the power of choosing one's own actions. **3.** wish or desire. **4.** purpose or determination. **5.** disposition (good or ill) towards another. **6.** *Law* a legal declaration of a person's wishes as to the disposition of his or her (real) property, etc., after his or her death, usually in writing. –v. (**willed**, **willing**) **7.** to give by will or testament; bequeath or devise. **8.** to influence by exerting willpower. **9.** to purpose, determine on, or elect, by act of will.

willing adj. **1.** disposed or consenting (without being particularly desirous). **2.** cheerfully consenting or ready.

willow n. a tree or shrub with tough, pliable twigs or branches which are used for wickerwork, etc.

willpower n. control over one's impulses and actions.

willy-willy n. *Aust.* a strong wind that moves around in circles, often collecting dust, waste matter, etc.

wilt v. to become limp and drooping, as a fading flower; wither.

wily adj. (**-lier**, **-liest**) crafty.

wimp n. *Informal* a weak, cowardly person. –**wimpish**, adj. –**wimpy**, adj.

If you call someone 'a wimp', you are intending to insult them.

wimple n. a woman's headcloth drawn in folds about the chin, as worn by some nuns.

win v. (**won**, **winning**) **1.** to succeed by striving or effort. **2.** to gain the victory. **3.** to be placed first in a race or the like. **4.** to get by effort, as through labour, competition, or conquest. **5.** to be successful in (a game, battle, etc.). –n. **6.** an act of winning; success; victory.

wince v. to shrink, as in pain or from a blow; start; flinch.

winch n. the crank or handle of a revolving machine.

wind¹ /wɪnd/ n. **1.** air in natural motion, as along the earth's surface. **2.** any stream of air, as that produced by a fan, etc. **3.** a hint or intimation. **4.** gas generated in the stomach and bowels. –v. (**winded**, **winding**) **5.** to expose to wind or air. **6.** to deprive momentarily of breath, as by a blow. –**windy**, adj.

Note that def. 1 can be used as an uncount noun (*Is there enough wind to go sailing?*) and a count noun (*Strong winds destroyed the village*).

wind² /waɪnd/ v. (**wound**, **winding**) **1.** to change direction; bend; turn; meander. **2.** to have a circular or spiral course or direction. **3.** to proceed indirectly. **4.** to encircle, as with something twined, wrapped, or placed about. **5.** Also, **wind up**. to roll or coil (thread, etc.) into a ball or on a spool or the like. **6.** Also, **wind up**. to adjust (a mechanism, etc.) for operation by some turning or coiling process.

windbreak n. a growth of trees, a structure of boards, or the like, serving as a shelter from the wind.

windcheater n. (*from trademark*) a fleecy-lined garment for the upper part of the body designed to give protection against the wind.

windfall n. an unexpected piece of good fortune.

wind farm n. an array of wind turbines set up in a windy location to produce electricity.

wind generator n. → wind turbine.

windlass n. a device for raising weights, etc.

windmill n. a mill or machine, as for grinding or pumping, operated by the wind.

window n. **1.** an opening in a wall or roof for the admission of air or light. **2.** anything likened to a window in appearance or function, such as a boxed-off section of a computer screen in which secondary text or information is shown.

windpipe n. → trachea.

windscreen n. the sheet of glass which forms the front window of a motor vehicle.

windsock n. a wind-direction indicator, installed at airports and elsewhere, consisting of an elongated truncated cone of textile material, flown from a mast.

windsurfer (from trademark) n. **1.** → sailboard (def. 1). **2.** a person who rides a sailboard. **–windsurf**, v. **–windsurfing**, n.

wind turbine n. a modern windmill, usually with blades designed like aeroplane wings, which drives a generator to produce electricity when wind turns the blades. Also, **wind generator**, **aerogenerator**.

wine n. the fermented juice of the grape.

Don't confuse this with **whine**, which is a complaining cry.

wing n. **1.** either of the 2 appendages, of most birds and bats, which are adapted for flight. **2.** either of 2 corresponding parts in certain flightless birds, such as emus and penguins. **3.** (in insects) one of the thin, flat, movable extensions from the back of the thorax by means of which the insects fly. **4.** any similar structure with which gods, angels, demons, etc., are thought to fly. **5.** that portion of a main supporting surface confined to one side of an aeroplane. **6.** a part of a building projecting on one side of, or subordinate to, a central or main part. **7.** (pl.) the insignia or emblem worn by a qualified pilot. **8.** Sport a player to one side of a centre player or position. **9.** Theatre the platform or space on the right or left of the stage proper. –v. **10.** to equip with wings. **11.** to wound or disable (a bird, etc.) in the wing. **12.** to travel on or as on wings; fly.

wink v. **1.** to close and open (the eyes) quickly. **2.** to close and open one eye quickly as a hint or signal or with some sly meaning: She smiled and winked at me. **3.** to shine with little flashes of light, or twinkle. –n. **4.** the act of winking. **5.** the time required for winking once; an instant or twinkling.

winning adj. **1.** being the one that won: the winning runner. **2.** causing a win: the winning goal. **3.** attractive or charming: a winning smile.

winnow v. **1.** to free (grain, etc.) from chaff, refuse particles, etc., by means of wind or driven air; fan. **2.** to subject to some process of separating or distinguishing; analyse critically; sift.

winsome adj. engaging or charming; winning.

winter n. **1.** the coldest season of the year. **2.** a period like winter, as the last or final period of life; a period of decline, decay, inertia, dreariness, or adversity. –adj. **3.** of, relating to, or characteristic of winter. **4.** suitable for wear or use in winter.

wipe v. **1.** to rub lightly in order to clean or dry. **2.** to remove by rubbing (away, off, out, etc.) with or on something. **3.** to destroy or eradicate, as from existence or memory. –n. **4.** the action of wiping. –phr. **5.** wipe out, to destroy completely.

wire n. **1.** a long piece of slender, flexible metal. **2.** a length of such material used as a conductor of electricity, usually included in a flex. –v. **3.** to install an electric system of wiring, as for lighting, etc.

wired *adj. Informal* **1.** equipped with a (sometimes hidden) recording device, as a person or a room. **2.** (of a person) stimulated or excited.

wireless *adj.* **1.** having no wire. **2.** of or relating to any of various devices which are operated with or set in action by electromagnetic waves. **3.** of or relating to telecommunications technology which is independent of telephone lines, cables, etc. *–n.* **4.** a radio.

wiry *adj.* (**-rier, -riest**) lean and sinewy.

wisdom *n.* knowledge of what is true or right coupled with just judgement as to action; sagacity, prudence, or common sense.

wise *adj.* **1.** having the power of discerning and judging properly as to what is true or right. **2.** possessed of or characterised by scholarly knowledge or learning; learned; erudite. **3.** having knowledge or information as to facts, circumstances, etc.

wish *v.* **1.** to want; desire. *–n.* **2.** a distinct mental inclination towards something; a desire, felt or expressed. **3.** that which is wished.

wishbone *n.* the forked bone in front of the breastbone in most birds.

wishy-washy *adj.* lacking in substantial qualities; weak, feeble, or poor.

wisp *n.* **1.** a handful or small bundle of straw, hay, or the like. **2.** anything small or thin, as a shred, bundle, or slip of something: *a wisp of cloud.*

wisteria /wɪsˈtɪəriə, wəs-/ *n.* a climbing shrub with handsome purple or white flowers.

wistful *adj.* **1.** pensive or melancholy. **2.** showing longing tinged with melancholy; regretful; sad.

wit *n.* **1.** keen perception and cleverly apt expression of connections between ideas which may arouse pleasure and especially amusement. **2.** a person endowed with or noted for such wit. **3.** (*pl.*) mental faculties, or senses.

witch *n.* a person, especially a woman, who professes or is supposed to practise magic. *–***witchery***, n.*

> Don't confuse **witch** with **which**: *Which book would you like? The book which has the blue cover.*

witchetty grub *n.* any of various large, white, edible, wood-boring grubs which are the larvae of certain Aust moths and beetles.

with *prep.* **1.** in the company of: *I will go with you.* **2.** in some particular relation to: *to mix water with milk.* **3.** showing agreement or similarity: *in harmony with him.* **4.** *Informal* understanding the thinking of: *Are you with me?* **5.** in the same direction as: *with the flow of traffic.* **6.** by the use or means of: *Cut it with a knife.* **7.** at the same time as: *I rise with the dawn.* **8.** against: *fighting with each other for years.* **9.** in the care or keeping of: *Leave it with me.*

withdraw *v.* **1.** to draw back or away; take back; remove. **2.** to retire; retreat; go apart or away. **3.** to retract (a statement). *–***withdrawal***, n.*

wither *v.* **1.** to shrivel; fade; decay. **2.** to make flaccid, shrunken, or dry, as from loss of moisture; cause to lose freshness, bloom, vigour, etc.

withers *pl. n.* the highest part of a horse's or other animal's back, behind the neck.

withhold *v.* (**-held, -holding**) **1.** to hold back; restrain or check. **2.** to refrain from giving or granting.

within *adv.* **1.** in or into the interior or inner part, or inside. *–prep.* **2.** in or into the interior of or the parts or space enclosed by. **3.** at or to some amount or degree not exceeding.

without *prep.* **1.** not with; with no; with absence, omission, or avoidance of; lacking. **2.** beyond the compass, limits, range, or scope of (now used chiefly in opposition to *within*).

withstand v. (**-stood**, **-standing**) to stand or hold out against; resist or oppose, especially successfully.

The more usual word is **resist**.

witness v. **1.** to see or know by personal presence and perception. **2.** to be present at (an occurrence) as a formal witness or otherwise. –n. **3.** someone who, being present, personally sees or perceives a thing; eyewitness. **4.** someone who gives testimony, as in a court of law. **5.** someone who signs a document in attestation of the genuineness of its execution.

witticism /'wɪtəsɪzəm/ n. a witty remark.

witty adj. (**-tier**, **-tiest**) possessing wit in speech or writing; amusingly clever in perception and expression.

wizard n. someone who professes to practise magic; a magician or sorcerer.

wizened adj. dried-up; withered; shrivelled.

WMD n. → **weapon of mass destruction**.

wobbegong /'wɒbɪgɒŋ/ n. a shark with a flattened body and mottled skin.

wobble v. **1.** to incline to one side and to the other alternately, as a wheel, top, or other rotating body, when not properly balanced. **2.** to move unsteadily from side to side.

woe n. grievous distress, affliction, or trouble. –**woeful**, adj.

woebegone /'woʊbəgɒn/ adj. beset with woe; mournful or miserable.

wog[1] n. *Informal* (*derog.*) a person of Mediterranean extraction, or of similar complexion and appearance.

The use of this word may give offence. Note, however, that **wog** is one of a small number of words which are offensive if used by people outside the group being referred to, but which are often used *within* the group without causing any offence. That is, people with a Mediterranean

background sometimes refer to *each other* as **wogs** with no negative feeling, but if a non-Mediterranean person used the term it would be offensive.

wog[2] n. *Aust. Informal* **1.** a germ, especially one leading to a minor disease. **2.** a cold, stomach upset, etc. **3.** a small insect.

wok n. a large, shallow, metal pan used especially in Chinese cookery.

woke v. a past tense of **wake**.

woken v. past participle of **wake**.

wolf n. (*pl.* **wolves**) **1.** a large, wild carnivore belonging to the dog family. **2.** *Informal* a man who is boldly flirtatious or amorous towards many women. –v. **3.** *Informal* to eat ravenously.

woman v. (*pl.* **women**) an adult female person.

womb n. the uterus of the human female and some of the higher mammalian quadrupeds.

wombat n. a large, heavily-built burrowing marsupial with short legs and a rudimentary tail, found throughout Aust.

women n. plural of **woman**.

won v. past tense and past participle of **win**.

wonder v. **1.** to think or speculate curiously. **2.** to be affected with wonder; marvel (*at*). **3.** to be curious about; be curious to know (followed by a clause). **4.** to feel wonder at (now only followed by a clause as object). –n. **5.** something strange and surprising; a cause of surprise, astonishment, or admiration. **6.** a feeling of surprised or puzzled interest, sometimes tinged with admiration.

Don't confuse this with **wander**, which is to go about with no definite aim.

wonderful adj. excellent; delightful; extremely good or fine.

wondrous adj. wonderful.

wonky adj. (**-kier**, **-kiest**) *Informal* **1.** shaky; unsound. **2.** unwell; upset.

wont /woʊnt, wɒnt/ adj. **1.** accustomed; used: *he is wont to talk too much.* –n. **2.** custom; habit; practice.

won ton /ˈwɒn tɒn/ n. a small ball of spicy pork wrapped in thin dough, usually boiled and served in soup in Chinese cooking. Also, **wonton**.

woo v. **1.** to seek the favour, affection, or love of, especially with a view to marriage. **2.** to seek to win.

wood n. **1.** the hard, fibrous substance composing most of the stem and branches of a tree or shrub, and covered by the bark. **2.** the trunks of trees as suitable for architectural and other purposes; timber or lumber. **3.** (*oft. pl.*) a large and thick collection of growing trees, smaller than a forest. –adj. **4.** made of wood; wooden. **5.** used to cut, carve, or otherwise shape wood. –v. **6.** to cover or plant with trees. –**woody**, adj.

Note that when wood is sawn or shaped into pieces for building it is called **timber**.

woodchip n. **1.** (*pl.*) small pieces of wood, made by mechanically reducing trees to fragments for later industrial use. –adj. **2.** of or relating to an industry, company, etc., which deals in woodchips. –**woodchipping**, n.

wooden adj. **1.** consisting or made of wood. **2.** stiff, ungainly, or awkward. **3.** without spirit or animation.

woodpecker n. a bird with a hard, chisel-like bill for boring into wood after insects.

woodwind n. the group of wind instruments which comprises the flutes, clarinets, oboes, and bassoons.

woodwork n. **1.** the interior wooden fittings of a house or the like. **2.** the art or craft of working in wood; carpentry.

woof[1] n. → **weft**.

woof[2] n. the sound of a dog barking, especially deeply and loudly.

wool n. **1.** a fibre produced from sheep's fleece. **2.** any finely fibrous or filamentous matter suggesting the wool of sheep.

wool clip n. the amount of wool yielded from the annual shearing season (by a station, district, etc.). Also, **clip**.

woollen adj. made or consisting of wool.

woolly adj. (**-lier**, **-liest**) **1.** consisting of wool. **2.** resembling wool. **3.** blurred, confused or indistinct, as thinking, expression, depiction.

woolshed n. a large shed for shearing and baling of wool.

woomera n. a type of throwing stick with a notch at one end for holding a dart or spear. Also, **womera**.

woozy adj. *Informal* **1.** muddled, or stupidly confused. **2.** dizzy, nauseous, etc.

word n. **1.** a sound or a combination of sounds, or its written or printed representation, used in any language as the sign of a concept. **2.** (*pl.*) angry speech; a quarrel. **3.** warrant, assurance, or promise. **4.** news. –v. **5.** to express in words, or phrase.

wordbreak n. the point of division in a word which runs over from one line to the next.

word processor n. a computer program designed for storing, editing and basic typesetting of text. –**word processing**, n.

word wrap n. *Computers* the automatic formatting of lines of text to fit into a computer screen, column, etc.

wordy adj. (**-dier**, **-diest**) characterised by or given to the use of many, or too many, words; verbose.

wore v. past tense of **wear**.

work n. **1.** exertion directed to produce or accomplish something; labour; toil. **2.** something to be made or done; a task or undertaking. **3.** *Physics* the product of the force acting upon a body and the distance through which the point of application of force moves. The derived SI unit of work is the joule. **4.** employment; a job, especially that by which one earns a living. **5.** (pl.) a place or establishment for carrying on some form of labour or industry: *steel works.* –v. (**worked** or, Old-fashioned except for def. 12, **wrought**, **working**) **6.** to exert oneself. **7.** to be employed. **8.** to be in operation, as a machine. **9.** to act or operate effectively: *That trick never works.* **10.** to use or manage (an apparatus, machine, etc.) in operation. **11.** to operate (a mine, farm, etc.). **12.** to effect, accomplish, cause, or do. **13.** to expend work on; manipulate or treat by labour. **14.** to move, stir, or excite in feeling, etc. (*up*). –*phr.* **15. work out, a.** to solve, find out or calculate by thinking. **b.** to turn out: *to work out well.* **c.** to train or practise a sport or exercise: *He works out every morning.*

> Note that def. 5 is usually used as a singular noun: *The steel works is at the end of the street.*

workable *adj.* practicable or feasible.

workaday *n.* humdrum.

worker *n.* **1.** someone or something that works: *He's a good steady worker.* **2.** someone who has a particular job: *an office worker; a road worker.* **3.** someone employed in manual or industrial labour: *The workers here get on well with the management.*

workflow *n.* the chain of events in a work process.

workforce *n.* the total of all those engaged in employment.

working class *n.* the group of people in a society who do manual work for a living –**working-class**, *adj.*

> Working class is a collective noun and can be used with a singular or plural verb. Look up **collective noun**.

workload *n.* the amount of work done or to be done in a specified time.

workmanship *n.* **1.** skill in working or execution. **2.** quality or mode of execution.

work-out *n.* **1.** a trial match, race, etc. **2.** energetic physical exercise.

workplace *n.* a place of employment.

workshop *n.* **1.** a room or building in which work, especially mechanical work, is carried on (considered as smaller than a factory). **2.** a group meeting to exchange ideas and study techniques, skills, etc.: *a theatre workshop.* –v. (**-shopped**, **-shopping**) **3.** to revise (a theatre piece, television show, etc.) in collaboration with others, while reading or performing a provisional script.

workstation *n.* an area in an office, etc., assigned to a particular worker, especially one containing a computer or other equipment.

world *n.* **1.** the earth or globe. **2.** a particular section of the world's inhabitants. **3.** humanity. **4.** a particular class of humankind, with common interests, aims, etc. **5.** any sphere, realm, or domain: *the world of surfing.* **6.** the entire system of created things; the universe; macrocosm.

worldling *n.* someone devoted to the interests and pleasures of this world; a worldly person.

worldly *adj.* (**-lier, -liest**) **1.** earthly or mundane (as opposed to *heavenly, spiritual,* etc.). **2.** devoted to, directed towards, or connected with the affairs, interests, or pleasures of this world. **3.** secular (as opposed to *ecclesiastical, religious,* etc.). –*adv.* in a worldly manner. –**worldliness**, *n.*

world music *n.* the popular or folk music of different cultures and nationalities from around the world, outside the tradition of Western rock or pop music.

World Wide Web *n.* → **web**². *Abbrev.:* WWW

worm *n.* **1.** *Zool.* a long, slender, soft-bodied invertebrate. **2.** (in particular language) any of numerous small creeping animals. **3.** something resembling or suggesting a worm in appearance, movement, etc. **4.** a grovelling, abject, or contemptible person. **5.** (*pl.*) any disease or disorder arising from the presence of parasitic worms in the intestines or other tissues. **6.** *Computers* a rogue program which, once it is loaded on a computer, replicates itself until it takes up all the available memory. –*v.* **7.** to creep, crawl, or advance slowly or stealthily. **8.** to make, cause, bring, etc., along by creeping or crawling, or by stealthy or devious advances.

worn *v.* **1.** past participle of **wear**. –*adj.* **2.** impaired by wear or use. **3.** Also, **worn out**. wearied or exhausted.

worry *v.* (**-ried, -rying**) **1.** to feel uneasy or anxious; fret; torment oneself with or suffer from disturbing thoughts. **2.** to cause to feel uneasy or anxious; plague, pester, or bother. **3.** to harass by repeated biting, snapping, etc. –*n.* (*pl.* **-ries**) **4.** uneasiness or anxiety. **5.** a cause of uneasiness or anxiety; a trouble. –**worrisome,** *adj.*

worse *adj.* **1.** bad or ill in a greater or higher degree; inferior. –*n.* **2.** that which is worse. –*adv.* **3.** in a more disagreeable, evil, wicked, severe, or disadvantageous manner. **4.** with more severity, intensity, etc. **5.** in a less effective manner. –**worsen,** *v.*

worship *n.* **1.** reverent honour and homage paid to God, or to any object regarded as sacred. **2.** adoring reverence or regard. **3.** (*upper case*) (with *Your, His, Her,* etc.) (a title of honour, particularly for magistrates in court). –*v.* (**-shipped, -shipping**) **4.** to render religious reverence and homage to.

worst *adj.* **1.** bad or ill in the greatest or highest degree. **2.** most faulty, unsatisfactory, or objectionable. –*n.* **3.** that which is worst or the worst part. –*adv.* **4.** in the most evil, wicked, or disadvantageous manner. **5.** with the most severity, intensity, etc. **6.** in the least satisfactory, complete or effective manner.

worsted /'wustəd/ *n.* (cloth woven from) a type of woollen yarn.

worth *adj.* **1.** good or important enough to justify (what is specified). **2.** having a value of, or equal in value to, as in money. –*n.* **3.** excellence of character or quality as commanding esteem. **4.** usefulness or importance, as to the world, to a person, or for a purpose. **5.** value, as in money.

worthwhile *adj.* such as to repay one's time, attention, interest, work, trouble, etc.

worthy *adj.* (**-thier, -thiest**) **1.** of adequate merit or character. **2.** deserving: *worthy of merit.*

would *v.* **1.** past tense of **will**[1]. **2.** a verb used **a.** to indicate future time from a past point of view: *He said that he would do it the next day.* **b.** to express habitual behaviour from a past point of view: *They would talk to each other on the phone for hours every day.* **c.** in expressing condition: *I would have come if you had asked me.* **d.** to make a statement or question less direct or blunt: *That would scarcely be fair; Would you like to come with us?*

Note that this word is often shortened to '**d**: *She asked if I'd like to come to the movies; You can come too if you'd like.* This is a modal verb and is always used with another verb. Look up **modal verb**.

would-be *adj.* **1.** wishing or pretending to be. **2.** intended to be.

wound[1] /wund/ *n.* **1.** an injury to an organism due to external violence rather than disease. –*v.* **2.** to inflict a wound upon; injure; hurt.

wound[2] /waʊnd/ *v.* past tense and past participle of **wind**[2].

wove *v.* past tense and occasional past participle of **weave**[1].

woven *v.* past participle of **weave**[1].

wow *interj.* *Informal* (an exclamation of surprise, wonder, pleasure, dismay, etc.).

wowser *n.* *Aust., NZ Informal* a prudish teetotaller; killjoy.

wraith *n.* a visible spirit.

wrangle v. to argue or dispute, especially in a noisy or angry manner.

wrap v. (**wrapped**, **wrapping**) **1.** Also, **wrap up**. to enclose, envelop, or muffle in something wound or folded about. **2.** to wind, fold, or bind (something) about as a covering. **3.** to surround, envelop, shroud, or enfold. *–n.* **4.** something to be wrapped about the person, as a shawl, scarf, or mantle. *–phr.* **5. wrap up,** *Informal* to conclude or settle.

wrapped *adj. Aust. Informal* enthused.

wrath /roθ/, *Originally US* /ræθ/ *n.* strong, stern, or fierce anger; deeply resentful indignation; ire.

wreak v. to inflict or execute (vengeance, etc.).

wreath /riθ/ *n.* (*pl.* **wreaths** /riðz/) something twisted or bent into a circular form, especially a circular band of flowers, foliage, etc.

wreathe /rið/ v. **1.** to encircle or adorn with or as with a wreath or wreaths. **2.** to surround in curving or curling masses or form.

wreck *n.* **1.** a vessel in a state of ruin from disaster at sea, on rocks, etc. **2.** the ruin or destruction of anything. *–v.* **3.** to cause the wreck of (a vessel). **4.** to cause the ruin or destruction of; spoil.

wren *n.* a small bird with long legs and a long, almost upright tail.

wrench v. **1.** to pull, jerk, or force by a violent twist. *–n.* **2.** a sudden, violent twist. **3.** a sharp, distressing strain, as to the feelings. **4.** a spanner.

wrest v. **1.** to twist or turn; pull, jerk, or force by a violent twist. **2.** to take away by force.

wrestle v. **1.** to engage in wrestling. **2.** to contend, as in a struggle for mastery; grapple.

wrestling *n.* a sport in which 2 persons struggle hand to hand, each striving to throw or force the other to the ground.

wretch *n.* a deplorably unfortunate or unhappy person.

wretched *adj.* very unfortunate in condition or circumstances; miserable; pitiable.

wrick v. to wrench or strain.

wriggle v. to twist to and fro, writhe, or squirm.

wring v. (**wrung**, **wringing**) **1.** to twist forcibly. **2.** Also, **wring out**. to twist and compress in order to force out moisture. **3.** to clasp (one's hands) together, as in grief, etc.

wrinkle *n.* **1.** a ridge or furrow on a surface, due to contraction, folding, rumpling, or the like; crease. *–v.* **2.** to form wrinkles in; crease.

wrist *n.* the part of the arm between the forearm and the hand.

writ *n. Law* a formal order under seal, issued in the name of a sovereign, government, court, etc., directing the person to whom it is addressed to do or refrain from doing some specified act.

write v. (**wrote**, **written**, **writing**) **1.** to express in writing; give a written account of. **2.** to produce as author or composer. **3.** to trace or form (characters, words, etc.) with a pen, etc. **4.** to be a writer, journalist, or author for one's living. **5.** to write a letter. *–phr.* **6. write off, a.** to cancel, as an entry in an account, as by an offsetting entry. **b.** to damage irreparably. **c.** to consider as dead.

Note that **write** can be followed by many prepositions, including *on* (*to write on a piece of paper, to write on a topic*), *about* (*to write about someone, to write about a topic*), *in* (*to write in a book*), *to* (*to write to someone*) and *for* (*to write for information*).

write-off *n.* **1.** *Accounting* something written off from the books. **2.** *Informal* something irreparably damaged.

write-up *n.* a written description or account, as in a newspaper or magazine.

writhe v. to twist the body about, or squirm, as in pain, violent effort, etc.

wrong *adj.* **1.** not in accordance with what is morally right or good. **2.** deviating from truth or fact; erroneous. **3.** not correct; in error. **4.** not suitable or appropriate. *–n.* **5.** that which is not in accordance with morality, goodness, justice, truth, or the like; evil. **6.** an unjust act; injury. *–adv.* **7.** in a wrong manner; not rightly; awry or amiss. *–v.* **8.** to do wrong to; treat unfairly or unjustly; injure or harm. **9.** impute evil to unjustly.

wrongdoing *n.* blameworthy action; evil behaviour.

wrought *v.* **1.** *Old-fashioned* a past tense and past participle of **work**. *–adj.* **2.** fashioned or formed by manufacture. **3.** produced or shaped by beating with a hammer, etc., as iron or silver articles. **4.** ornamented or elaborated.

wry *adj.* (**wryer** *or* **wrier**, **wryest** *or* **wriest**) **1.** distorted to show dislike, etc., as the features. **2.** ironically or bitterly amusing. **3.** twisted or crooked.

wuss /wʊs/ *n. Informal* an overly timid or ineffectual person, especially a male; wimp. Also, **wus**, **wooz** /wʊz/.

If you call someone 'a wuss', you are intending to insult them.

WYSIWYG /ˈwɪziwɪɡ/ *n.* what you see is what you get; a computer system which displays text and images on screen exactly as it will appear in printed output.

X, x

X, x *n.* **1.** the 24th letter of the English alphabet. **2.** a term often used to designate a person, thing, or the like, whose true name is unknown or withheld.

xenon /'zinɒn/ *n.* a heavy, colourless, chemically unreactive gaseous element. *Symbol*: Xe

xenophobia *n.* fear or hatred of foreigners.

X-ray *n.* **1.** (*oft. pl.*) *Physics* electromagnetic radiation of shorter wavelength than light, which is able to penetrate solids, expose photographic plates, etc. **2.** a picture produced by the action of X-rays. –*v.* **3.** to examine by means of X-rays.

xylophone *n.* *Music* a percussion instrument consisting of a graduated series of wooden bars, usually sounded by striking.

Y, y

Y, y n. the 25th letter of the English alphabet.

yabber Informal −v. **1.** to talk. −n. **2.** talk; conversation.

yabby n. (pl. **-bies**) an Aust. freshwater crayfish.

yacht /jɒt/ n. a sailing vessel mostly used for non-commercial purposes.

yahoo n. an uncouth person.

yak n. a long-haired, hollow-horned, wild ruminant.

yakka n. Aust., NZ Informal work. Also, **yacker**, **yacka**, **yakker**.

yam n. the starchy, tuberous root of certain climbing vines.

yank v., n. Informal (to pull or move with) a sudden jerking motion.

yap v. (**yapped**, **yapping**) **1.** to yelp. **2.** Informal to talk snappishly, noisily, or foolishly.

yard¹ n. **1.** a unit of length in the imperial system, equal to about 91 centimetres. **2.** Naut. a long cylindrical spar suspending a sail.

yard² n. **1.** a piece of enclosed ground next to a house, etc. **2.** an enclosure within which any work or business is carried on.

yardarm n. either end of a yard of a square sail.

yardstick n. any standard of measurement.

yarn n. **1.** thread made by twisting fibres, as nylon, cotton or wool, and used for knitting and weaving. **2.** Informal a story, especially a long one about incredible events. **3.** a talk, chat. −v. **4.** Informal to tell stories. **5.** to talk, chat.

yaw v. to deviate temporarily from the straight course.

yawn v. **1.** to open the mouth involuntarily with a prolonged, deep intake of breath, as from drowsiness or weariness. **2.** to open wide like a mouth. −n. **3.** the act of yawning.

ye pron. Old-fashioned you.

yea /jeɪ/ interj. yes.

yeah interj. Informal yes.

year n. **1.** a period of 365 or 366 days, now reckoned as beginning 1 January and ending 31 December (**calendar year**). **2.** such a period reckoned from any point. **3.** the true period of the earth's revolution round the sun. **4.** a level or grade in an academic program. **5.** (pl.) age, especially of a person. **6.** (pl.) time, especially a long time.

yearling n. an animal one year old or in the 2nd year of its age.

yearly adj. **1.** done, made, happening, appearing, coming, etc., once a year, or every year. −adv. **2.** once a year; annually. −n. (pl. **-lies**) **3.** a publication appearing once a year.

yearn v. to have an earnest or strong desire.

yeast n. a substance consisting of the cells of certain fungi, used to induce fermentation in the manufacture of beer, etc., to leaven bread, and in medicine.

yell v., n. (to call out with) a strong, loud, clear cry.

yellow adj. **1.** of a bright colour like that of butter, lemons, etc.; between green and orange in the spectrum. **2.** Informal cowardly. −n. **3.** a hue between green and orange in the spectrum.

yellowcake n. uranium oxide in an unprocessed form.

yellow fever n. a dangerous, infectious febrile disease.

yelp v., n. (to give) a quick, sharp bark or cry.

yen n. desire; longing.

yes interj. a word used **a.** when answering a question to express that a statement is correct, or to agree to a request or offer.

Yes, that's right; *Yes, you may go*; *Yes, I'd love a coffee.* **b.** to emphasise that you know a statement is true: *Yes, I know she said that, but I don't think it's true.* **c.** to tell someone you are ready to listen to them: *Yes? Can I help you?* **d.** to disagree with a negative statement: *'I can't do that.' 'Yes, you can.'*

yesterday *adv., n.* (on) the day preceding this day.

yet *adv.* **1.** at the present time: *Don't leave me yet.* **2.** up to a particular time: *He had not gone yet.* **3.** now or then as previously; still: *There is hope yet.* **4.** in addition: *Yet once more.* **5.** even or still: *He could not run, nor yet walk.* **6.** nevertheless: *strange yet true.* —*conj.* **7.** nevertheless: *It was raining yet he came.*

yew *n.* an evergreen coniferous tree.

yield *v.* **1.** to give forth or produce by a natural process or in return for cultivation. **2.** to produce or furnish as payment, profit, or interest. **3.** to give up, as to superior power or authority. **4.** to give way to influence, entreaty, argument, or the like. —*n.* **5.** the action of yielding or producing. **6.** that which is yielded. **7.** the quantity or amount yielded.

yobbo *n. Informal* **1.** an unrefined, uncultured, slovenly young man. **2.** a hooligan or lout: *football yobbos.* Also, **yob.**

yodel *v.* (**-delled** *or, Chiefly US,* **-deled, -delling** *or, Chiefly US,* **-deling**) to sing with frequent changes from the natural voice to falsetto.

yoga *n.* any of various systems of discipline in the Hindu philosophical system concerned with achieving the union of the mind and body with the Universal Spirit, employing practices such as physical control of the body through the use of special movements or postures, etc.

yoghurt *n.* a prepared food made from milk that has been curdled by the action of enzymes or other cultures. Also, **yogurt, yoghourt.**

yogi *n.* (*pl.* **-gis** /-giz/) someone who practises yoga.

yoke *n.* **1.** a device for joining a pair of draught animals. **2.** something resembling a yoke in form or use. **3.** a shaped piece in a garment from which the rest of the garment hangs. —*v.* **4.** to put a yoke on.

yokel *n.* a country person who is thought of as uneducated and awkward.

yolk *n.* the yellow and principal substance of an egg.

yonder *adj.* **1.** being the more distant. **2.** being in that place or over there. —*adv.* **3.** at, in, or to that place; over there.

yore *phr.* **of yore,** time long past.

you *pron.* **1.** the personal pronoun used to refer to the person or people spoken to. **2.** one; anyone; people in general: *It really makes you mad when you hear that kind of thing.*

You is a second person pronoun. It is used for one person (singular) or more than one (plural). It is also used in both the subjective and objective case. The following are some examples. *You need to be alone for a while* (singular subject). *You can come in one at a time, children* (plural subject). *I'll call you later, Mum* (singular object). *I'll see you tomorrow, everyone.* (plural object).

You is sometimes used together with the noun to which it is referring: *You children on my left go to the hall, and you on my right go to the library.* This can be quite informal: *Will you kids stop making such a racket?*

young *adj.* **1.** being in the first or early stage of life, or growth. **2.** of or relating to youth. **3.** comparatively not far advanced in years. —*n.* **4.** young offspring. **5.** young people collectively.

youngster *n.* a young person.

your *pron.* the possessive form of **you,** used before a noun.

Your is a second person pronoun. It can be singular or plural. It is sometimes called a *determiner* or a *possessive adjective*.

yours *pron.* **1.** the possessive form of **you** used without a noun following: *That book is yours.* **2.** the person(s) or thing(s) belonging to you: *Yours is the plate on the left.*

Yours is a second person pronoun in the possessive case. It can be singular or plural.

yourself *pron.* **1.** the reflexive form of **you** (singular): *You've cut yourself.* **2.** a form of **you** (singular) used for emphasis: *You did it yourself.* **3.** your proper or normal self: *you'll soon be yourself again.*

yourselves *pron.* **1.** the reflexive form of **you** (plural): *Have you washed yourselves?* **2.** a form of **you** (plural) used for emphasis: *You've done it all yourselves.*

youth *n.* **1.** (*pl.* **youths**) a young man: *There were a couple of youths leaning on the fence.* **2.** young people collectively: *The youth of this town need more support.*

3. the condition of being young: *Youth would be an advantage in this job.* **4.** the time of being young: *He was a boxer in his youth.* **5.** the first or early period of anything. –**youthful**, *adj.*

Note that def. 2 is used to refer to both males and females, and is used as a plural noun: *Our youth are our future.*

yowl *v.* to utter a long distressed cry.

yo-yo *n.* (*pl.* **yo-yos**) (*from trademark*) a round toy with a groove round the edge, in which a string is wound by which it can be spun up and down.

This is from a trademark.

yuck *interj.* (an expression of disgust). Also, **yuk**. –**yucky**, **yukky**, *adj.*

yum cha /jʌm 'tʃa/ *n.* a form of Chinese meal in which diners choose individual serves from many offered.

yuppie *n.* a young urban professional person, typified as having a good income and luxurious lifestyle.

Note this word is used in a mildly disapproving way.

Z, z

Z, z n. the 26th letter of the English alphabet.

zany adj. **1.** extremely comical; clownish. **2.** slightly crazy.

zeal /ziːl/ n. ardour for a person, cause, or object; enthusiastic diligence. –**zealous** /ˈzɛləs/, adj.

zealot /ˈzɛlət/ n. **1.** someone who displays zeal, especially excessively. **2.** Informal a religious fanatic. –**zealotry** n.

zebra n. a wild, horse-like animal, with regular black and white stripes.

zenith n. **1.** Astron. the point in the heavens vertically above any place or observer. **2.** any highest point or state.

zephyr /ˈzɛfə/ n. a soft, mild breeze.

zeppelin n. a large dirigible.

zero n. (pl. **-ros** or **-roes**) **1.** the figure or symbol 0, which stands for the absence of quantity. **2.** the line or point from which anything is measured. **3.** naught or nothing. **4.** the lowest point or state. –phr. (**-roed**, **-roing**) **5. zero in on**, **a.** to focus attention on. **b.** to adjust a rifle, etc., so as to come to bear directly at.

zest n. **1.** (anything added to impart) agreeable or piquant flavour. **2.** piquancy, interest, or charm.

zigzag n. a line, course, or progression characterised by sharp turns first to one side and then to the other.

zillion n. Informal a very great number. –**zillionth**, adj., n.

zinc n. Chem. a metallic element used in making alloys, and as a protective covering for roofs, etc. Symbol: Zn

zine n. Informal a magazine, especially one about an alternative subculture, or one in electronic form published on the internet. Also, **zeen**, **'zine**.

zinnia n. an annual plant with colourful flowers.

zip n. **1.** Also, **zipper**, **zip-fastener**. a fastener consisting of an interlocking device set along 2 edges, which unites (or separates) them when an attached piece sliding between them is pulled. **2.** Informal energy or vim. –v. (**zipped**, **zipping**) **3.** to proceed with energy. **4.** Also, **zip up**. to fasten with a zip. **5.** Computers → **compress** (def. 2).

zip file n. Computers a compressed version of a file. Also, (in filenames), **.zip**.

zircon n. a common mineral used as a gem.

zit n. Informal a pimple.

zither n. a stringed musical instrument.

zodiac n. Astron. an imaginary belt of the heavens, containing 12 constellations and hence 12 divisions (called signs). –**zodiacal**, adj.

zombie n. **1.** a corpse supposedly brought to life by a supernatural force. **2.** (derog.) a person having no independent judgement, intelligence, etc. Also, **zombi**.

zone n. **1.** any continuous distinguishable tract or area. **2.** an area or district where certain conditions or circumstances prevail. –v. **3.** to divide into zones, according to existing characteristics, or for some purpose, use, etc. –**zonal**, adj.

zoning n. the marking out of an area of land with respect to its use.

zoo n. a park or other large enclosure in which live animals are kept for public exhibition.

zoology n. the science that deals with animals or the animal kingdom. –**zoological**, adj.

zoom v. **1.** to make, or move with, a continuous humming sound. **2.** (of prices) to rise rapidly. **3.** Film, TV, etc. to use a lens which makes an object appear to approach or recede from the viewer.

zounds *interj. Old-fashioned* (an exclamation of surprise, anger, etc.).

zucchini *n.* (*pl.* **-ni** *or* **-nis**) a small vegetable marrow; courgette.

zygote *n. Biol.* the cell produced by the union of 2 gametes. **–zygotic**, *adj.*

common prefixes

PREFIX	MEANING	EXAMPLE
andro-	male	androgynous
anthropo-	human	anthropology
ante-	before	antedate
anti-	against	antibiotic
astro-	star	astronomy
audio-	hearing	audiology
auto-	self	autobiography
bi-	twice, two	bifocal
biblio-	book	bibliography
bio-	life, living things	biography, biology
cardio-	heart	cardiovascular
centi-	hundredth	centimetre
chrom-	colour	chromatic
chron-	time	chronology
co-	together, associated	coordinate
contra-	against	contraception
counter-	opposite, contrary	counteract
cyber-	internet, computers	cyberthreat
de-	separation, negation, down, reversal	debug, demerit, descend, decode
dec(a)-	ten	decathlon
deci-	tenth	decibel

PREFIX	MEANING	EXAMPLE
dermato-	skin	dermatology
dis-	negation	disability
dys-	poor, bad	dysfunctional
e-	internet	email
	electronic	e-tag
eco-	ecology, ecological	ecosystem
equi-	equal	equivalent
ex-	out of	exhale
	former	ex-wife
extra-	outside	extraordinary
fore-	front	forehead
geo-	earth	geology
gyn(o)-	female	gynaecology
haemo-	blood	haemophilia
hetero-	different	heterogeneous
homo-	same	homonym
hydro-	water	hydrofoil
hyper-	over	hyperactive
hypo-	under	hypodermic
in-	in or into	inland
	not	infallible
infra-	below, beneath	infrastructure
inter-	between	international
intra-	within	intravenous
iso-	equal	isobar
kilo-	thousand	kilometre
mal-	bad, wrong	malformation
mega-	million	megawatt
	huge	megafauna
micro-	very small	microfilm
milli-	thousandth	millimetre

PREFIX	MEANING	EXAMPLE
mis-	fault, not	misfit
mono-	single	monochromatic
multi-	many	multitude
neo-	new	neonate
neuro-	nerve	neurosurgery
non-	not	nonfiction
omni-	all	omniscient
paed-	child	paediatrics
pan-	all	pandemic
photo-	light	photosynthesis
poly-	many	polygon
post-	after, behind	postdate
pre-	before	predict
pro-	in favour of	pro-British
pseudo-	false	pseudonym
psycho-	the mind	psychology
proto-	earliest form	prototype
re-	again	reassure
	back	recall
retro-	backwards	retrospective
semi-	half	semitone
sub-	under	submarine
super-	over, above	supernatural
syn-	together	synthesis
therm-	heat, temperature	thermometer
trans-	across	transport
ultra-	beyond	ultraviolet
un-	not	uncertain
uni-	one	unilateral

common suffixes

NOUN-FORMING

SUFFIX	MEANING	EXAMPLE
-age	collection	baggage
	condition or state	bondage
-ance, -ancy	action, state, quality	assistance
-ant	someone who or something that	assistant
-cide	killer, act of killing	homicide
-cracy	government	democracy
-crat	ruler	autocrat
-ee	object of an action	trainee
-eer	someone connected with something	engineer
-ence	action, state, quality	consequence
-ent	someone who or something that	president
-er	someone who or something that	teacher
	something connected with something	officer
	action or process	reminder
-ery	type or place of work	bakery

	character	misery
	activity	sorcery
-ess	feminine form	actress
-ette	diminutive form	cigarette
-hood	state, character, etc.	childhood
-ian	someone connected with someone or something	electrician
-ing	action, result	building
-ion	process, state, result	rebellion
-sion		compulsion
-tion		affection
-ation		administration
-ution		evolution
-ition		nutrition
-ism	action, principles, etc.	capitalism
-ity	condition, qualities, etc.	activity
-logy	science, knowledge	biology
-ment	action, state, result	agreement
-ness	quality, state	happiness
-oma	tumour	melanoma
-or	someone who or something that	actor
-scope	viewing instrument	microscope
-ship	condition	friendship
	office, skill, etc.	leadership

ADJECTIVE-FORMING

SUFFIX	MEANING	EXAMPLE
-able	ability, likelihood, etc.	favourable
-al	connected with, like	natural

-ant	having quality of	buoyant
-ent	having quality of	dependent
-er	comparative degree	smaller
-est	superlative degree	smallest
-ful	full of, marked by	beautiful
-ic, -ical	having to do with	poetic
-ish	characteristic of	childish
	somewhat, rather	yellowish
-ive	serving to, able to	corrective
-less	without	careless
-ous	full of	joyous

ADVERB-FORMING

SUFFIX	MEANING	EXAMPLE
-er	comparative degree	faster
-est	superlative degree	fastest
-ly	manner	gladly
-ward(s)	direction	upward(s)

VERB-FORMING

SUFFIX	MEANING	EXAMPLE
-ate	cause or do	activate
-en	make or do	lengthen
-ise	make or do	legalise